PSALMS VOLUME 1

THE NIV APPLICATION COMMENTARY

From biblical text . . . to contemporary life

GERALD H. WILSON

GRAND RAPIDS, MICHIGAN 49530 USA

We want to hear from you. Please send your comments about this book to us in care of the address below. Thank you.

GRAND RAPIDS, MICHIGAN 49530 USA

WWW.ZONDERVAN.COM

ZONDERVAN™

The NIV Application Commentary: Psalms—Volume 1

Requests for information should be addressed to:
Zondervan, *Grand Rapids, Michigan 49530*

Library of Congress Cataloging-in-Publication Data

Wilson, Gerald Henry.
Psalms: from biblical text—to contemporary life / Gerald H. Wilson.
p. cm.—(NIV application commentary)
Includes bibliographical references and indexes.
ISBN: 0-310-20635-9
1. Bible. O.T. Psalms—Criticism, interpretation, etc. I. Title. II. Series.
BS1430.52 .W55 2002
223'.2077—dc21 2002007545
CIP

This edition printed on acid-free paper.

Printed in the United States of America

04 05 06 07 08 /❖ DC/ 10 9 8 7 6 5 4

Contents

7
Series Introduction

11
General Editor's Preface

13
Author's Preface

17
Abbreviations

19
Introduction

82
Outline

85
Select Bibliography

89
Text and Commentary on Psalms 1–72

996
Scripture Index

1014
Subject Index

The NIV Application Commentary Series

When complete, the NIV Application Commentary
will include the following volumes:

Old Testament Volumes

Genesis, John H. Walton
Exodus, Peter Enns
Leviticus/Numbers, Roy Gane
Deuteronomy, Daniel I. Block
Joshua, L. Daniel Hawk
Judges/Ruth, K. Lawson Younger
1-2 Samuel, Bill T. Arnold
1-2 Kings, Gus Konkel
1-2 Chronicles, Andrew E. Hill
Ezra/Nehemiah, Douglas J. Green
Esther, Karen H. Jobes
Job, Dennis R. Magary
Psalms Volume 1, Gerald H. Wilson
Psalms Volume 2, Gerald H. Wilson
Proverbs, Paul Koptak
Ecclesiastes/Song of Songs, Iain Provan
Isaiah, John N. Oswalt
Jeremiah/Lamentations, J. Andrew Dearman
Ezekiel, Iain M. Duguid
Daniel, Tremper Longman III
Hosea/Amos/Micah, Gary V. Smith
Jonah/Nahum/Habakkuk/Zephaniah, James Bruckner
Joel/Obadiah/Malachi, David W. Baker
Haggai/Zechariah, Mark J. Boda

New Testament Volumes

Matthew, Michael J. Wilkins
Mark, David E. Garland
Luke, Darrell L. Bock
John, Gary M. Burge
Acts, Ajith Fernando
Romans, Douglas J. Moo
1 Corinthians, Craig Blomberg
2 Corinthians, Scott Hafemann
Galatians, Scot McKnight
Ephesians, Klyne Snodgrass
Philippians, Frank Thielman
Colossians/Philemon, David E. Garland
1-2 Thessalonians, Michael W. Holmes
1-2 Timothy/Titus, Walter L. Liefeld
Hebrews, George H. Guthrie
James, David P. Nystrom
1 Peter, Scot McKnight
2 Peter/Jude, Douglas J. Moo
Letters of John, Gary M. Burge
Revelation, Craig S. Keener

To see which titles are available,
visit our web site at www.zondervan.com

11/00

NIV Application Commentary
Series Introduction

THE NIV APPLICATION COMMENTARY SERIES is unique. Most commentaries help us make the journey from our world back to the world of the Bible. They enable us to cross the barriers of time, culture, language, and geography that separate us from the biblical world. Yet they only offer a one-way ticket to the past and assume that we can somehow make the return journey on our own. Once they have explained the *original meaning* of a book or passage, these commentaries give us little or no help in exploring its *contemporary significance*. The information they offer is valuable, but the job is only half done.

Recently, a few commentaries have included some contemporary application as *one* of their goals. Yet that application is often sketchy or moralistic, and some volumes sound more like printed sermons than commentaries.

The primary goal of the NIV Application Commentary Series is to help you with the difficult but vital task of bringing an ancient message into a modern context. The series not only focuses on application as a finished product but also helps you think through the *process* of moving from the original meaning of a passage to its contemporary significance. These are commentaries, not popular expositions. They are works of reference, not devotional literature.

The format of the series is designed to achieve the goals of the series. Each passage is treated in three sections: *Original Meaning*, *Bridging Contexts*, and *Contemporary Significance*.

THIS SECTION HELPS you understand the meaning of the biblical text in its original context. All of the elements of traditional exegesis—in concise form—are discussed here. These include the historical, literary, and cultural context of the passage. The authors discuss matters related to grammar and syntax and the meaning of biblical words.[1] They

1. Please note that in general, when the authors discuss words in the original biblical languages, the series uses a general rather than a scholarly method of transliteration.

also seek to explore the main ideas of the passage and how the biblical author develops those ideas.

After reading this section, you will understand the problems, questions, and concerns of the *original audience* and how the biblical author addressed those issues. This understanding is foundational to any legitimate application of the text today.

THIS SECTION BUILDS a bridge between the world of the Bible and the world of today, between the original context and the contemporary context, by focusing on both the timely and timeless aspects of the text.

God's Word is *timely*. The authors of Scripture spoke to specific situations, problems, and questions. The author of Joshua encouraged the faith of his original readers by narrating the destruction of Jericho, a seemingly impregnable city, at the hands of an angry warrior God (Josh. 6). Paul warned the Galatians about the consequences of circumcision and the dangers of trying to be justified by law (Gal. 5:2–5). The author of Hebrews tried to convince his readers that Christ is superior to Moses, the Aaronic priests, and the Old Testament sacrifices. John urged his readers to "test the spirits" of those who taught a form of incipient Gnosticism (1 John 4:1–6). In each of these cases, the timely nature of Scripture enables us to hear God's Word in situations that were *concrete* rather than abstract.

Yet the timely nature of Scripture also creates problems. Our situations, difficulties, and questions are not always directly related to those faced by the people in the Bible. Therefore, God's word to them does not always seem relevant to us. For example, when was the last time someone urged you to be circumcised, claiming that it was a necessary part of justification? How many people today care whether Christ is superior to the Aaronic priests? And how can a "test" designed to expose incipient Gnosticism be of any value in a modern culture?

Fortunately, Scripture is not only timely but *timeless*. Just as God spoke to the original audience, so he still speaks to us through the pages of Scripture. Because we share a common humanity with the people of the Bible, we discover a *universal dimension* in the problems they faced and the solutions God gave them. The timeless nature of Scripture enables it to speak with power in every time and in every culture.

Those who fail to recognize that Scripture is both timely and timeless run into a host of problems. For example, those who are intimidated by timely books such as Hebrews, Galatians, or Deuteronomy might avoid reading them because they seem meaningless today. At the other extreme, those who are convinced of the timeless nature of Scripture, but who fail to discern its timely element, may "wax eloquent" about the Melchizedekian priesthood to a sleeping congregation, or worse still, try to apply the holy wars of the Old Testament in a physical way to God's enemies today.

The purpose of this section, therefore, is to help you discern what is timeless in the timely pages of the Bible—and what is not. For example, how do the holy wars of the Old Testament relate to the spiritual warfare of the New? If Paul's primary concern is not circumcision (as he tells us in Gal. 5:6), what *is* he concerned about? If discussions about the Aaronic priesthood or Melchizedek seem irrelevant today, what is of abiding value in these passages? If people try to "test the spirits" today with a test designed for a specific first-century heresy, what other biblical test might be more appropriate?

Yet this section does not merely uncover that which is timeless in a passage but also helps you to see *how* it is uncovered. The authors of the commentaries seek to take what is implicit in the text and make it explicit, to take a process that normally is intuitive and explain it in a logical, orderly fashion. How do we know that circumcision is not Paul's primary concern? What clues in the text or its context help us realize that Paul's real concern is at a deeper level?

Of course, those passages in which the historical distance between us and the original readers is greatest require a longer treatment. Conversely, those passages in which the historical distance is smaller or seemingly nonexistent require less attention.

One final clarification. Because this section prepares the way for discussing the contemporary significance of the passage, there is not always a sharp distinction or a clear break between this section and the one that follows. Yet when both sections are read together, you should have a strong sense of moving from the world of the Bible to the world of today.

THIS SECTION ALLOWS the biblical message to speak with as much power today as it did when it was first written. How can you apply what you learned about Jerusalem, Ephesus, or Corinth to our present-day needs in Chicago, Los Angeles, or London? How can you take a message originally spoken in Greek, Hebrew, and Aramaic and communicate it clearly in our own language? How can you take the eternal truths originally spoken in a different time and culture and apply them to the similar-yet-different needs of our culture?

In order to achieve these goals, this section gives you help in several key areas.

(1) It helps you identify contemporary situations, problems, or questions that are truly comparable to those faced by the original audience. Because contemporary situations are seldom identical to those faced by the original audience, you must seek situations that are analogous if your applications are to be relevant.

(2) This section explores a variety of contexts in which the passage might be applied today. You will look at personal applications, but you will also be encouraged to think beyond private concerns to the society and culture at large.

(3) This section will alert you to any problems or difficulties you might encounter in seeking to apply the passage. And if there are several legitimate ways to apply a passage (areas in which Christians disagree), the author will bring these to your attention and help you think through the issues involved.

In seeking to achieve these goals, the contributors to this series attempt to avoid two extremes. They avoid making such specific applications that the commentary might quickly become dated. They also avoid discussing the significance of the passage in such a general way that it fails to engage contemporary life and culture.

Above all, contributors to this series have made a diligent effort not to sound moralistic or preachy. The NIV Application Commentary Series does not seek to provide ready-made sermon materials but rather tools, ideas, and insights that will help you communicate God's Word with power. If we help you to achieve that goal, then we have fulfilled the purpose for this series.

The Editors

General Editor's Preface

THE TASK OF APPLYING the Scriptures to modern life means more than just "translating of words" from ancient to modern languages and "transposing of meanings" from Bible times to the twenty-first century cultures. The task also means finding the appropriate ways to use the biblical text, ways that may be different from the way these texts were used in their original settings—call it "transfer of use."

Gerald Wilson, in this insightful commentary on the first half of the book of Psalms, shows how our use of Psalms illustrates this principle. He argues that the Psalms were originally used in public Jewish worship. Only centuries after they were first composed and sung did they begin to be used in private devotional settings, one of the most common uses of the Psalms today.

Is this "transfer of use" legitimate? Wilson, along with many other biblical scholars, argues that it can be. Perhaps it will be helpful to illustrate from history the many ways the Psalms have been used. As just noted, they were probably used in public worship—though many scholars feel that Mowinckel, the scholar who proposed this thesis, overemphasized the cultus use of the Psalms. The Psalms were also used as private cries of lament of individual sick people (Seybold). The early Qumran community on the edge of the Dead Sea used the Psalms as a hymnbook. Early Jewish leaders used the Psalms in mishnaic argument and in temple liturgies. Early Christian monastics memorized the Psalms for personal devotion and used them in community recitation. Clearly, the Psalms have been used in many different ways throughout their history.

Those same scholars, however, caution that not all such uses are legitimate. Many of us cringe, for example, when we see the way Old Testament texts are used in Masonic rites, or when the words of Scripture are used for demonic ends by Satanists. Satan himself uses Scripture with the best of them.

Thus, as we consider the proper use of the Psalms today, what are we to think of all these possibilities? Are some more correct than others? Can we say that one or another of these early uses should guide us in their use today? Do we need to know the earliest, original use of the Psalms in order to know how to properly use them today? Are there rules of guidance when we find our application of Scripture is leading us toward possible "transfer of use" territory?

Perhaps two rules of thumb, one negative and one positive, can guide us. (1) The negative rule: We should ask the question whether or not the use we make of the Psalms contradicts the message of the Psalms themselves. Although the Psalms contain many "messages" of a historical, theological, and practical nature, their primary message is that God is great and God is good. A corollary of this primary message is that we should begin all of our thinking, feeling, and acting with an acknowledgement of God's primacy.

More than anything else the Psalms tell us that God is great. Psalm 29 starts with the words, "Ascribe to the LORD, O mighty ones, ascribe to the LORD glory and strength. Ascribe to the LORD the glory due his name; worship the LORD in the splendor of his holiness" (vv. 1–2). But the Psalms also emphasize over and over that God is good. Psalm 135 says, "Praise the LORD, for the LORD is good; sing praises to his name, for that is pleasant" (v. 3).

The psalmist knew to put God first in all things. Psalm 86 shows the proper sequence of God's greatness first, our needs second: "You are forgiving and good, O Lord, abounding in love to all who call to you. Hear my prayer, O LORD; listen to my cry for mercy" (vv. 5–6).

(2) The other rule of thumb is more positive: Are we using the Psalms in ways that will glorify God, not just glorify us? A popular use of the Psalms is as personal devotionals. Although this use, on the face of it, is legitimate, it can become self-centered. The Psalms are not mantras designed to transport us into alternate states of consciousness. They are not psychological recipes for healthier living. They are opportunities for us to get right, one more time, the proper relationship between us, God's created beings, and God, the creator and ruler of the universe.

Contrast these therapeutic uses of Psalms with Eugene Peterson's brilliant translation of the Psalms in *Praying With the Psalms* (San Francisco: HarperCollins, 1993). Peterson's craft insists that we see in the Psalms the ultimate textual guide to acknowledging our maker and the proper way for us to make requests to God.

One of the reasons we properly understand Scripture to be God's final and complete revelation to us is because of the extraordinary versatility of the texts. They do indeed address all the needs of life, and do so in ways that more than keep pace with the developments of modern culture. But the biblical texts are not infinitely elastic in either their definition or use. The easiest way to keep a rein on the boundaries is to fully absorb the main lesson of the Psalms: God reigns. God is great. God is good.

Terry C. Muck

Author's Preface

PICTURE YOURSELF AS ONE OF A CROWD, packed together with thousands of others—shoulder to shoulder, elbow to elbow—to experience as one a common event. Depending on your interest, it might be a sporting event or a packed opera house, a massive political rally or an evangelistic crusade. There is in the air a sense of excitement and anticipation. A sense of common purpose and experience draws the whole crowd together as you respond to the events of the moment. In this setting you discover that your individual response becomes part of something larger than just yourself as you react in community to the joys and sorrows, victories and defeats that are acted out before you.

If you can imagine such a setting or recall one from your own past, then you have some sense of what reading the book of Psalms ought to be like. For whenever we crack open this biblical book and read from its collection of 150 songs, whenever we allow ourselves to become truly immersed in the world they bring to life, we are taking our stand within a huge crowd of the faithful who have sung the psalms throughout the generations of the people of God.

The psalms in their origins span a period of almost eight hundred years. If we accept the names preserved in the headings of the individual psalms as designations of authorship, then one psalm (Ps. 90) is attributed to Moses, who in the second millennium B.C. led Israel out of Egypt and into covenant relationship with their God, Yahweh, on Mount Sinai. Almost half of the 150 psalms (73, to be exact) are attributed to the great king, David, who around 1000 B.C. welded the disparate tribes of Israel into a single, cohesive nation. Other authors followed: Solomon (2 psalms), Heman (1), Ethan (1), Asaph (12), and the Sons of Korah (11) enriched the prayer and worship of the people of God with their compositions. At the other end of this period of composition, the very latest psalms are dated by many to the third or second century B.C. That means that within the compass of this one book we have some of the oldest and some of the newest compositions in the entire Old Testament.

Up to now I have been talking just about the period of the psalms' composition. That in itself constitutes quite a cloud of witnesses—authors and faithful worshipers spanning more than eight hundred years. But that time span, as amazing as it is, represents only the starting point for this book. For since their origin, the psalms have constantly been on the lips of the faithful from that time to this. The psalms have constituted the core repertory of believers, Jewish and Christian, Catholic and Protestant, Eastern and Western Christian, from their origin to the present day. That means, if we take even the most conservative estimate, that the psalms represent a common religious heritage for practically three millennia—three thousand years!

Thus, whenever you read the psalms, when you sing them or pray them, you are praying, singing, and reading alongside a huge crowd of faithful witnesses throughout the ages. The words you speak have been spoken thousands—even millions—of times before: in Hebrew, Greek, Latin, English, and a myriad of other languages. As you read or sing or pray, off to your right stand Moses and Miriam, in front of you David and Solomon kneel down, to your left are Jesus, Peter and Paul, Priscilla and Aquila, while from behind come the voices of Jerome, St. Augustine, Theresa of Avila, Luther, Calvin, and more—so many more!

If you can catch but a glimpse of this far-flung spiritual community of believers and take your place within it, then you can begin to understand why we still read, sing, and pray the psalms after all these years. These 150 compositions, probably only a fraction of the psalms composed and used in centuries of Israelite temple worship, have been preserved and transmitted to us through the ages because they were recognized in each generation as powerful songs that are more than models of appropriate human response to God (which they are) and more than a source of God's divine word of guidance to humans (which they certainly are). The book of Psalms and the psalms within it were preserved because they offer those who read, sing, and pray them the opportunity to take their stand within that worldwide, historical, and eschatological community of faith who seek to live out their lives with all its pain and joy, love and hate, fear and hope, before the God who is the source of all life, joy, love, and hope.

My personal prayer for you is that as you use this commentary on the book of Psalms you will find many reasons to affirm the words and sentiments of these ancient songs as your own and that you will find yourself taking your place within this chorus of the faithful—taking a stand with all those believers past, present, and future who together sing songs celebrating the steadfast love of our God.

By the end of a project such as this, an author has amassed such a list of debts that it is impossible to acknowledge them all or ever hope to repay them. But there are those who must and should be mentioned. I am grateful for the support of trusted and caring colleagues who have sustained me with their personal, spiritual, and academic interest over the many years in which this volume was being written. In particular I wish to thank Dr. Bill Yarchin, chair of the department of religion and philosophy of Azusa Pacific University, for his friendship, support, and encouragement over the last three years. I am also deeply appreciative to Azusa Pacific University, the provost, Dr. Patricia Anderson, and the Dean's Council for a series of Accomplished Scholar Awards that facilitated the completion of this work over the last several years.

A teacher rises to the challenges of his students. Thus, many of the insights expressed in this book would never have developed without the creative interaction and earnest questioning of a multitude of students at a variety of institutions. Their love of the Psalms and their struggles with the dark and painful issues of life have driven me to reflect more deeply and broadly on the power of the Psalms to encourage, confront, challenge, and heal than I ever could have had on my own. Without them this commentary (and my life) would have been much impoverished.

The process of publication has brought home to me the great skill, vision, and, above all, patience of Zondervan and their editorial staff. A number of persons have added their insights and skills to make this volume better. I must mention the theological and editorial acumen of Tremper Longman III, who commented extensively on the manuscript from beginning to end. And the tireless editorial work of Verlyn Verbrugge has often brought light to darkness and clarity to confusion.

Finally, the top award for patience must certainly go to my wife, who has been with me in this project from the beginning. Yes, Diane, it did *finally* become a book!

Azusa, California
May, 2002

Abbreviations

AB	Anchor Bible
ANETP	*The Ancient Near East: An Anthology of Texts and Pictures*
BA	*Biblical Archaeologist*
BASORSup	Bulletin of the American Schools of Oriental Research Supplement Series
BHS	*Biblia Hebraica Stuttgartensia*
Bib	*Biblica*
BTB	*Biblical Theology Bulletin*
CHALOT	*Concise Hebrew and Aramaic Lexicon of the Old Testament*
EDB	*Eerdman's Dictionary of the Bible*
HBT	*Horizons in Biblical Theology*
HUCA	*Hebrew Union College Annual*
ICC	International Critical Commentary
IDB	*Interpreter's Dictionary of the Bible*
Int	*Interpretation*
ISBE[2]	*International Standard Bible Encyclopedia* (2d ed.)
JBL	*Journal of Biblical Literature*
JSS	*Journal of Semitic Studies*
JSOT	*Journal for the Study of the Old Testament*
JSOTSup	Journal for the Study of Old Testament Supplement Series
LXX	Septuagint
MT	Masoretic Text
NIBC	New International Biblical Commentary
NIDOTTE	*New International Dictionary of Old Testament Theology and Exegesis*
NAB	New American Bible
NASB	New American Standard Bible
NIV	New International Version
NIVSB	NIV Study Bible
NJB	New Jerusalem Bible
NRSV	New Revised Standard Version
OTT[2]	*Old Testament Theology* by G. von Rad (2d ed.)
OTL	Old Testament Library
REB	Revised English Bible
SBLDS	Society of Biblical Literature Dissertation Series
TOTC	Tyndale Old Testament Commentaries

TZ	*Theologische Zeitschrift*
UT	*Ugaritic Textbook*, by Cyrus Gordon
VT	*Vetus Testamentum*
VTSup	Supplements to Vetus Testamentum
WBC	Word Biblical Commentary
WTJ	*Westminister Theological Journal*
ZAW	*Zeitschrift für die alttestamentliche Wissenschaft*

Introduction

Some General Observations

A FEW GENERAL observations about the psalms are in order before beginning our study. Some of these observations have been alluded to in the preface but need to be developed more clearly. Others provide important groundwork for understanding the context of the biblical psalms. All can provide us depth and nuance in interpreting specific psalms as well as the whole collection and in understanding the lives of faith that both produced and continue to employ these ancient compositions.

Collection and Authorship

AS MENTIONED IN the preface, the composition of the individual psalms covers a period of more than eight hundred years. Add to this the time involved in gathering and shaping the Psalter collection and you have almost a millennium. This in itself is remarkable. Consider the differences that have occurred in English language and culture since the time of Geoffrey Chaucer (600 years) and you have only two-thirds of the time span involved in the creation of the psalms! One has only to read the prologue to Chaucer's *Canterbury Tales* to discover a clear example of how much language and culture can change in six centuries.

> Whan that Aprille with his shoures soote
> The droote of Marche hath perced to the roote
> And bathed every veyne in swich licour
> Of which vertu engendred is the flour
> Whan Zephyrus eke with his swete breeth
> Inspired hath in evry holt and heath
> The tendre croppes and the younge sunne
> Hath in the Ram his halfe course eronne
> And smalle foules maken melodie
> That slepen all the nicht with open eye
> So priketh him nature in her courages
> Than longen folkes to goon pilgrimages
> And palmeres for to seken stranges strandes
> To ferne halwes couth in sondry landes
> And specially from evry shires end

> Of England to Canterbury they wende
> The hooly blissful martyr for to seke
> That them hath holpen whan that they were sick.

The book of Psalms then represents the end result of a long history of composition, transmission, collection, and arrangement. It contains some of the earliest and some of the latest texts in the Old Testament and is in a sense a microcosm of the whole Old Testament corpus. This is not a book that trickled off the tip of the pen of a single author. It is, like so many of the Old Testament books, a collection of compositions by many different authors in many different times and settings. It even bears within itself evidence of earlier psalms collections. Psalms 3–42 surely represent an earlier collection of Davidic psalms, as their headings attest. Psalms 120–134 all share the common heading "Psalm of Ascent," probably a much later collection of psalms sung by pilgrims on their way to Jerusalem. The Asaph psalms (50; 73–83) and the psalms of the Sons of Korah (42; 44–49; 84–85; 87–88) probably represent the remains of collections of songs written by these two guilds of temple singers.

At a later date, toward the end of the B.C. period, more and more psalms were assumed to have been written by David. The Greek translation of the Old Testament (the Septuagint, abbreviated LXX) expands Davidic authorship by supplying a number of additional psalm headings in which David is explicitly mentioned. The Qumran *Psalms Scroll*, treasured and preserved by the sectarian community who lived at a desert commune on the northwest edge of the Dead Sea from the second century B.C. until A.D. 70, "davidizes" the Psalter even further by adding more Davidic headings, new psalms attributed to him, and a prose statement celebrating David as prophet and author of 4,050 psalms and songs. It is little wonder that by the time of the New Testament writings, this growing collection, despite clear reference to other authors throughout, could be referred to as David (Heb. 4:7). Indeed, the Jewish rabbis came ultimately to affirm the Davidic authorship of all the 150 canonical psalms.

This assumption that David composed all the psalms in the book of Psalms remains with us today despite clear evidence for other authors in the psalm headings themselves and the lack of certainty whether these references (where they exist) always indicate authorship. The easy and exhaustive assumption of Davidic authorship can obscure references in some psalms to events or settings long after the death of David and inhibit rather than aid our interpretation of them. Also at risk is our appreciation of the long history of psalm composition that parallels the life of the nation Israel from beginning to end, from monarchy to Exile and beyond.

The Title of the Book

A VARIETY OF names has been applied to this book, each of which reflects a distinct way of viewing the collection over the ages. One of the earliest titles took its departure from the Davidic character of nearly half of the psalms. As early as the New Testament period, then, it was possible to refer to this collection as "David," in deference to its primary author. This is not surprising in light of the growing tendency (at Qumran and among the rabbis) to attribute more and more psalms to David. It is, however, not a completely apt title for such a diverse collection, and it is not unexpected that this form of reference did not last, despite the continuing assumption, up to the present, of the Davidic authorship of the psalms.

What this early designation may indicate is the existence of a precanonical form of the book of Psalms that was made up almost entirely of Davidic psalms. The first two books of the Psalter (Pss. 3–72) may well embody this early Davidic collection, the conclusion of which is marked out by a postscript (the only such postscript in the whole Psalter) in 72:20: "This concludes the prayers of David son of Jesse." While it is true that even these two books are not exclusively Davidic (Book 2 contains one psalm ascribed to Asaph and a series attributed to the Sons of Korah), the collection both begins and ends with Davidic psalms, and the concluding postscript emphasizes the Davidic character of the whole.[1]

Almost equally contemporary to the Davidic title is the practice of referring to the individual compositions with the general designation "psalms." This form of designation is also known in the New Testament (Acts 13:33). The term *psalm* is derived from the Greek *psalmos*, which was the regular LXX translation for the Hebrew genre term *mizmor*, which appears frequently in the psalm headings. *Mizmor* means "a composition/song performed to musical accompaniment"; *psalmos* is similar in meaning, designating a "song sung to the accompaniment of the harp." The Hebrew is not as specific as the Greek in describing the nature of the accompanying instrument, nor does it claim to describe all the compositions included in the book of Psalms.

It is from the Greek reference to the individual psalms that the more current title for the collection as the book of Psalms is taken. Despite its longevity, however, this title remains somewhat inadequate as a designation for all the diverse compositions included in the book. It is certainly not clear that all the canonical psalms were originally intended to be accompanied by the harp. The psalm headings offer a large variety of types of compositions

1. This, of course, assumes that the attribution *lišlomoh* ("to Solomon") in the heading of Ps. 72 does not mean that Solomon is the *author* of the psalm but that the psalm is written in his behalf ("for/to Solomon").

and indicate a number of instruments to be employed in accompaniment. Regardless of these deficiencies, the title book of Psalms does have the advantage of being a more inclusive general designation with the weight of extensive historical and traditional usage.

Within the Hebrew Bible, from the earliest period, the common designation for the collection of canonical psalms was *tehillim* ("praises"). The term is taken from the same root *hll*, from which the frequent call to praise Yahweh (*hallelujah*) that punctuates the final third of the Psalter is derived. Once again, however, the term seems inadequate to describe the full range of the contents of the Psalter, since the book is replete with laments, wisdom psalms, historical poems, and other compositions that defy this designation.

It is interesting in light of this Hebrew title that the final third of the book of Psalms is dominated by the appearance of praise and thanksgiving psalms, in strong contrast to the first two-thirds of the book, where lament psalms strongly predominate.[2] The decision to characterize the whole collection as "praises" may be influenced by this decisive movement from lament to praise, so clearly illustrated by the final grouping of the Hallelujah Psalms (146–150). While the title does not adequately indicate the nature of all the compositions in the book, it does capture the effect of the theological arrangement of the psalms in the book, which in the final analysis does become a book of praise in full awareness of and in spite of the experience of lament and sorrow in life. This is an important point to which I will return at a later point in a discussion of the shape of the Psalter and its theological import.

So, these different ways of titling the book of Psalms offer us competing ways of understanding the contents of this book. For the Christian Scriptures, the attempt was and is to employ the title "Psalms" in order to provide a more general description of the nature of the psalms that emphasizes their character as songs to be sung. This is hardly surprising in light of the early use of musical versions of the psalms for singing as an important part of Christian worship (cf. Eph. 5:19; Col. 3:16) and the continuation of that practice through the use of metrical psalms throughout the centuries since. In contrast, the Hebrew title (*tehillim*) highlights the overall effect of the collection with its movement from lament to praise, establishing the confidence and hope that despite the suffering realized in life, Yahweh's final word is always deliverance and benefit worthy of our most extravagant praise.

As for the use of the title "David" to characterize the whole Psalter, it is true that David assumes an important role in relation to the collection of

---

2. It is true that many lament psalms conclude with an expression of confidence or praise for anticipated deliverance. That may be the result of a later reworking of an earlier lament after deliverance was experienced.

the psalms. From the significant number of psalms attributed to him (whether in the canonical collection, the LXX, or the Qumran *Psalms Scroll*), to the editorial shaping of the first two books as the prayers of David (cf. 72:20), to the distribution of Davidic psalms through the whole canonical collection, to the influence of the Davidic covenant on the editorial shaping of the final Psalter, the book of Psalms is in a real sense (without assuming the Davidic authorship of all 150 psalms) the Book of David.

As to the exact referent of the allusion in Hebrews 4:7, my study of the shaping of the final canonical collection (see the essays on "The Shape of the First Three Books" and "The Shape of the Psalter as a Whole" in vol. 2 of this commentary) suggests that the author of Hebrews may have had in mind an earlier form of the book of Psalms complete only through Book 2 (Ps. 72) or Book 3 (Ps. 89), where the Davidic motif is most strongly maintained. The subsequent addition of Books 4 and 5 (perhaps as late as the end of the first century A.D.) would have changed the character of the whole and opened the door to new titles, reflecting alternative ways of understanding the Psalter.

The Historical Use of the Psalms

MOST OFTEN TODAY, when we think of the psalms, we understand them as ancient models of private prayer spoken by individuals to God. The fact that we can still consider all 150 psalms the products of David, regardless of evidence to the contrary, is proof that belief in the private, personal nature of the psalms is still alive today. As the prayers of ancient individuals, the psalms can either be inspiring models that we adapt profitably for our own personal life of prayer, or they can be puzzling or even offensive proclamations from an alien land—difficult if not impossible for us to relate to.

It is true that over the centuries of their use the psalms have been viewed this way and have come to serve fruitfully as models for our own prayer life, and our tendency is to think of the psalms in this way—as if they were simply written by private individuals for use in their personal prayer closets, so to speak. But such a view misunderstands the very public nature of most of these compositions and misses out on a wealth of interpretive detail that can be drawn from their original function and setting.

Origin in Temple Worship

SCHOLARS GENERALLY AGREE today that most of the psalms (some even say all) were composed, not for private prayer, but for public performance in the temple worship of ancient Israel. If this is so, then even the individual psalms were not composed simply for private use but were intended to be presented—performed, if you will—within community worship. Many of the notices in the psalm headings lend support to this view. Some appear to be instructions to the music director (*lamnaṣṣeaḥ*, "to the director"), describing the type of composition (*mizmor, maśkil, tehillah, šir hammaᶜalot*, etc.), appropriate instrumentation (*binginot*, "for the strings"; *haggittit*, "the Gittite harp"), the tune (*ᶜal ᵓayyelet haššahar*, "according to the Gazelle of the Dawn"; *ᶜal yonat-ᵓelem-reḥoqim*, "according to the Dove of the Distant Terebinth"), and even the musical tuning to be followed (*ᶜal haššeminit*, "according to the eighth"). It is clear from these notices that many of the psalms were traditionally used as performance pieces during the worship services of ancient Israel.

Some of the psalm headings even include mention of specific worship settings. For instance, the heading of Psalm 100 contains the phrase "For the *todah* [thanksgiving offering]." The best explanation seems to be that this psalm was composed to accompany the presentation of the *todah* or thanksgiving offering celebrating divine deliverance from some distress. A similar reference is found in Psalms 38 and 70: "For the *hazkir* [memorial offering]." Following the same pattern, Psalm 30 was performed "At the Dedication of the House," possibly a reference to the dedication of the temple of Solomon or some later restoration of that edifice after the Exile. Psalm 92 declares itself "A psalm. A song. For the Sabbath day."

Another support for this idea of public use of the psalms in worship is the mention in the headings of twenty-four psalms of several guilds of temple singers (Asaph: 50; 73–83; the Sons of Korah: 42; 44–49; 84–85; 87–88; Heman: 88; and Ethan: 89), who are described in the accounts of 1 and 2 Chronicles as part of the official worship structure of the temple from the time of David and Solomon on. The name of another singer known from Chronicles, Jeduthun (cf. 1 Chron. 16:41–42; 2 Chron. 5:12), also appears several times in the psalm headings, but always in connection with another author name (Pss. 39 and 62: "a psalm of David"; 77: "a psalm of Asaph"), so that the significance of the word *yedutun* in these circumstances must be questioned. The appearance of so many names so clearly associated with the official organization of the musical worship of the Jerusalem temple adds weight to the view that many of the psalms originated as public performance pieces produced by groups of singers with official oversight of the temple service.

Other psalms open windows into Israel's worship practices within the body of the psalm itself. In Psalm 42, for example, the speaker recalls "how I used to go with the multitude, leading the procession to the house of God, with shouts of joy and thanksgiving among the festive throng" (42:4). A similar procession is described in 68:24–27:

Your procession has come into view, O God,
  the procession of my God and King into the sanctuary.

In front are the singers, after them the musicians;
with them are the maidens playing tambourines.
Praise God in the great congregation;
praise the LORD in the assembly of Israel.
There is the little tribe of Benjamin, leading them,
there the great throng of Judah's princes,
and there the princes of Zebulun and of Naphtali.

Elsewhere the psalmists mention moments of worship as the context of praise, lament, and thanksgiving.

With my mouth I will greatly extol the LORD;
in the great throng I will praise him. (109:30)

I wash my hands in innocence,
and go about your altar, O LORD,
proclaiming aloud your praise
and telling all your wonderful deeds. (26:6–7)

How can I repay the LORD
for all his goodness to me?
I will lift up the cup of salvation
and call on the name of the LORD.
I will fulfill my vows to the LORD
in the presence of all his people. . . .
I will sacrifice a thank offering to you
and call on the name of the LORD.
I will fulfill my vows to the LORD
in the presence of all his people. (116:12–14, 17–18)

Add to these explicit references the abundant indications of worship performance within the text of the psalms themselves and you have clear evidence of the use of the psalms in the temple worship system. The antiphonal structure of Psalm 136 is best explained by the liturgical demands of worship, where two choirs respond to each other, or leader and congregation answer back and forth. Similarly, in 24:7–10, we hear the voices of worshipers inside the temple compound query the approaching throng that demands entrance:

Lift up your heads, O you gates;
be lifted up, you ancient doors,
that the King of glory may come in.
Who is this King of glory?
The LORD strong and mighty,
the LORD mighty in battle.

Lift up your heads, O you gates;
lift them up, you ancient doors,
that the King of glory may come in.
Who is he, this King of glory?
The LORD Almighty—
he is the King of glory.

All these indications of the liturgical use of the psalms make it difficult to deny that many (if not all) of the psalms originated and enjoyed a long history in the temple worship of ancient Israel. Despite our present tendency to regard the psalms of the canonical collection as private prayers written by individuals in response to personal circumstances, the singing of the psalms through the centuries has continued to reflect the more communal nature of these songs as worship hymns.

From Public Performance to Private Piety

HOW IS IT, then, that these performance pieces intended for presentation in communal worship came to be regarded as private prayers and were used instead as models for the personal prayers of the faithful? Some particularly significant national event would seem to be required to account for such a distinctive shift in use of the psalms—some crucial experience that created a change of national perspective so strong that the original connection of the psalms with temple worship might be forgotten, or at least obscured.

Two such events come readily to mind and have been frequently offered as the occasion behind this change in the understanding and use of the psalms. Both events involve the destruction of the Jerusalem temple and the loss of the temple worship system in which the psalms figured so prominently. Both required a process of national reidentification in response to extreme cultural dislocation. The two events are separated by some 650 years and herald the two major transitional periods in the development of Judaism out of ancient Israelite faith and practice.

The end of the first temple. The first of these two events is the destruction of the first temple (known as the temple of Solomon) at the hands of the invading Babylonian army in 586 B.C. and the subsequent national dislocation of the nation of Israel in the Exile. The temple was razed to the ground, temple worship no longer existed, and the vast majority of Israelite population was transported out of their native land to live out their days in the alien environment of the far reaches of the Babylonian Empire. The kingdom to which they had claimed citizenship no longer existed.

Their passports cancelled, standing on unfamiliar and hostile ground, forced to take stock of their rather naive earlier faith in Yahweh's unconditional protective care for his covenant people, exilic Israel underwent a painful reidentification process in order to develop a new understanding of what it meant to be a faithful follower of Yahweh. The devastating pain of the Exile and its effect on the Israelites and their use of the psalms can be heard clearly in the harsh and grating language of Psalm 137.

> By the rivers of Babylon we sat and wept
>   when we remembered Zion.
> There on the poplars
>   we hung our harps,
> for there our captors asked us for songs,
>   our tormentors demanded songs of joy;
>   they said, "Sing us one of the songs of Zion!"
> How can we sing the songs of the LORD
>   while in a foreign land? (137:1–4)

Unfortunately, we have little historical material that describes the life of exilic Israelites during this time. Ezra, Nehemiah, Daniel, and Esther offer but tantalizing glimpses of Israel in captivity, practicing their faith in a hostile environment. We do know that most of the Old Testament as we now have it was written or shaped during this period. We can discover traces of the reidentification process that led the exilic Israelites into Judaism in the way the historical books Samuel through Kings interpret the monarchical experience and explain why it came to ruin. We can learn about the issues that concerned the exilic community when we read the prophets, especially their hopes for the future.

We even know that it was during the Exile that the synagogue arose as a local center for Jewish political, social, and religious cohesion. Isolated in the midst of a foreign nation, far from everything familiar and comforting, exilic Jews faced the siren's call of assimilation to the majority culture and founded the synagogue as a hedge against the loss of their identity—their very soul. It is true that by the time of Jesus in the first century A.D., the synagogue was a well-established institution with regular Sabbath services. But exactly when it began is still something of a mystery, and what its services were like remains a matter of conjecture and debate.

What we do know is that the synagogue became the site for the collection, interpretation, preservation, application, and transmission of the growing biblical corpus. In light of the exilic experience, the Jewish community, gathered around synagogues throughout the world, selected and shaped the holy writings of Hebrew Scripture to help their dispersed nation understand what it meant to be faithful followers of their ancestral God, Yahweh, in their new circumstances.

Among the materials collected, sifted, and preserved as part of this incipient collection of Scripture were most certainly the psalms. When the Jerusalem temple was destroyed in 586 B.C., temple worship—and, by extension, the performance of the psalms—ceased as well. It is in this setting that the first step in the remarkable shift in the way the psalms were perceived and used was taken. It became important to record them, preserve them, and transmit them safe until their use would be restored. If you could no longer sing them in communal worship, you could study them for what Yahweh wished to teach you, and their laments, praises, and thanksgivings served as models of personal piety that remained at the same time poignant reminders of what had been lost and hopeful imagining of what would one day be restored. The early collections in the Psalter (David, Asaph, Sons of Korah) may reflect this initiative to collect and preserve. The notations in the psalm headings reflect similar concern to pass on details of performance to future generations of the faithful.

In other words, in response to the loss of the temple and temple worship the perception of the psalms began to shift from public performance pieces to written Scripture, to be studied for insight into the ongoing life of the exilic Jewish community. While it is likely that the exilic experience *began* the process of understanding the temple worship psalms as written Scripture, it is less likely that the seventy-year period between the destruction of the first temple by the Babylonians and the restoration of worship in the second temple during the time of Ezra and Nehemiah was sufficient to obliterate completely the memory of the psalms as temple worship songs. It is clear that new, postexilic psalms were added to the preexilic collections, since some have found their way into the canonical Psalter (e.g., Ps. 137). The Ascent Psalms (120–134) are most certainly psalms sung by exilic Jews on pilgrimage to the restored Jerusalem temple. Thus, with the resumption of temple worship, the psalms resumed their place as an important part of the communal worship experience.

So, if the exilic period does not represent the final impetus for the psalms becoming Scripture rather than performance pieces, when did sufficient time exist to allow for the transition? When would the psalms be so removed from communal worship performance that the musical notations and instructions in the psalm headings could become vague and obscure terminology, as they clearly have in the LXX? This leads us to the discussion of the second cataclysmic event that forced a further reidentification process on worldwide Judaism.

The demise of the second temple. As the first event described involves the destruction of the first temple by the Babylonians, so the second event, some 650 years later, was precipitated by the destruction of the second temple (also known as Herod's temple), this time by the Romans in A.D. 70. As in the first instance, the destruction of the second temple also meant the cessation of temple worship and the use of the psalms in this context. The effects of this second disruption were much more far-reaching than the first. The second temple was built only seventy years after the destruction of the first. From the time of the Roman destruction until the present day, however, there has been no restoration of the temple or temple worship—almost two thousand years later!

The destruction of the second temple and the long-term cessation of the temple worship system confronted worldwide Judaism with another reidentification problem equivalent to that faced in the Exile. Prior to A.D. 70, the Jewish community had retained hopes of reestablishing the national identity they had lost in the sixth century B.C. This dream was fostered by the success of the Maccabees and Hasmoneans in the second and first centuries B.C. and encouraged numerous rebellions against foreign rule by Zealot groups in the first century A.D. It was one such rebellion, beginning about A.D. 67, that occasioned the Roman suppression that resulted in the destruction of the second temple.

Not all parts of the Jewish community agreed that violent overthrow of foreign overlords was the appropriate response. At least one influential member of first century A.D. Judaism, Yoḥanan ben Zakkai, argued forcefully that dedicated piety and pacifistic waiting for divine intervention ought to replace the Zealots' violent attempts to overthrow Roman rule and to force Yahweh's hand by their bold action. Yoḥanan refused to participate in the rebellion and withdrew to the Roman occupied coastal town Yavneh. From there he was highly influential in the restructuring of Judaism in the aftermath of the destruction of the second temple. It was also here that the final debates regarding the contents of the last section of the Hebrew Bible, the Writings (of which the Psalms are a part), were carried out in the concluding decades of the first century.

Yoḥanan's program was simple, but it has provided the defining structure of orthodox Judaism ever since. According to Yoḥanan, faithful followers of Yahweh, wherever they live, are to demonstrate their faith through regular prayer, good deeds, and study of Scripture, while waiting for God to intervene in their behalf, in his own time. These "sacrifices" of pious living form an adequate replacement for the lacking temple worship system until God sees fit to restore the temple. Yoḥanan discouraged active rebellion against Rome but encouraged the Jewish community to maintain their distinct identity as a religious minority set apart from majority culture by their dress, customs, and religious practices.

Yoḥanan's encouragement to pacifist submission to Roman rule was not easy for any of the Jewish community to accept—especially the Zealots. But when the Bar Kokhba rebellion between A.D. 132 and 135 met equally swift retribution from Rome and was mercilessly crushed, the wisdom of Yoḥanan's teaching sank home at last. Through this change in focus from communal worship to personal piety and public performance in the temple to study and meditation on Scripture, the authority for everyday Jewish life shifted from the priestly celebrants involved in temple worship to the rabbis, learned scholars who immersed themselves in Scripture and thus were best able to interpret its application to the ongoing needs of life.

It is in this environment that the final impetus to reunderstand the psalms as written texts of Scripture to be studied and meditated upon, both as models for personal prayer and as sources of divine guidance for daily living, took place. What had begun in response to the devastations of the Exile was now brought to completion in response to the lasting destruction and reorientation of A.D. 70. From this point on, the psalms, while retaining in their headings memories of their liturgical usage in temple worship, were firmly established and even emphasized as texts to be read and studied as the Word of God to humans.

In my opinion, the canonical arrangement of the book of Psalms preserves clues of these two formative historical events in its shaping. The core of the first three books (Pss. 1–89), with their shared focus on authorship collections, reflects the response to the first cataclysmic event of the Exile. The final two books (Pss. 90–150) and the final shaping of the whole Psalter are a later response to the events occurring toward the end of the first century A.D.

Christian Adoption of the Psalms

UP TO THIS point I have been speaking of the use of the psalms within the Jewish community. With the advent of Christianity in the last half of the first century A.D., Christian use of the psalms shares some similarities with Jewish usage while at the same time exhibiting some distinctives. I have already mentioned that the early Christians were known to sing the psalms as part of their worship (Eph. 5:19; Col. 3:16). This is hardly surprising, given the origin of early Christianity within Judaism and the common practice of Jewish Christians to worship regularly in the synagogue and temple.

Christians also shared with their non-Christian Jewish contemporaries a desire to employ Scripture as a means to understand God's will for their present circumstances. For Jew and Christian alike ancient Scripture continued to speak a guiding message into each new time and circumstance. Both communities searched the prophets to understand present history. This is particularly illustrated by the scriptural interpretation of the Qumran community, who explained details of their own sectarian history by recourse to a pastiche of biblical passages distinctively interpreted in their *pesherim* (commentaries), including the Qumran *Psalms Scroll* and the fragmentary commentaries on the psalms discovered among the Dead Sea Scrolls.

In the Christian New Testament, no book is cited more often as a warrant for understanding the life of Jesus than the book of Psalms. Particularly influential are Psalms 2 and 22, which mirror the two sides of Jesus that the church came to regard as key to understanding his work: his messianic sonship (Ps. 2) and his vicarious, sacrificial death (Ps. 22). But pride of place certainly goes to the messianic interpretations of Psalm 110, the most frequently cited psalm in the entire New Testament. Thus, in the end, while Jews and Christians shared a reverence for the psalms as Scripture and a method of engaging them for contemporary guidance, the Christian use of the psalms to buttress their claims about Jesus must have represented a major point of separation.

Through the past nineteen centuries, Christian use of the psalms has continued to recognize the three distinctive elements of their character that we have mentioned above. (1) The psalms serve as guides to personal, private prayer. (2) They continue to find their way into Christian worship through liturgy and through metrical versions for singing. When the psalms themselves are not sung directly, they often form the basis of many hymns and praise choruses. (3) Finally, the psalms still serve as a scriptural resource for the divine Word of God speaking to our present circumstances.

The Poetry of the Psalms

Understanding Poetic Conventions

I DON'T KNOW what you think about poetry. Many people either love it or hate it. Some find it moving and compelling, while others simply do not understand it. Some respond to poetry emotionally, while others appreciate the technical skill by which poets choose and arrange their words to create alternative worlds of powerful vision.

Regardless of your evaluation of the poetic form, if you are like most people, you have some sense of it—some idea of what makes it poetry and not prose. Your experience may be limited to childhood nursery rhymes and juvenile doggerel. Or you may have studied poetry broadly and deeply, in school or privately. You may even be a poet yourself.

A poem is not a laundry list or a legal document. Nor is it a novel or a letter, although these latter may have "poetic" moments—when they share some of the distinctive qualities of poetry. Part of this distinctive character of poetry we recognize intuitively. To this I will return directly. But mostly we recognize poetry because it corresponds to a body of conventions that sets it apart—that distinguishes poetry from other forms of written (and spoken) communication. Most of these conventions we have learned, either picking them up casually through exposure to poetry or formally through a direct process of instruction.

In the Western world, dominated by Eurocentric ways of thinking, three primary conventions have characterized classic poetic composition: rhyme, rhythm, and meter. *Rhyme*, the use of similar or identical sounds to conclude multiple lines of poetry, is perhaps the more obvious poetic technique:

I never saw a purple *cow*.
I never hope to *see one*,
But, I can tell you any*how*,
I'd rather see than *be one*![3]

The arrangement of rhymes within a poem—whether on successive or more distant lines, or even within a line—enables the poet to introduce variety into the composition, to establish controlled, regular movement, or in some instances to define the nature of the poetic form and distinguish it from other similar ones. All sonnets, for example, are made up of fourteen lines of poetry of identical meter. How the lines are grouped and how the rhymes are distributed among the lines reflect formal patterns that clearly distinguish English (Shakespearean) sonnets from their Italian (Petrarchan) counterparts.

A second obvious (though less obvious than rhyme!) poetic convention that characterizes classic Western poetry is *rhythm*—the attempt to regularize various combinations of stressed and unstressed syllables in poetic lines. Such concerns are actually reflective of the originally *oral* character of poetry, since this kind of stress and lack of stress is only operative in spoken language. All spoken language naturally employs a variety of combinations of stressed and unstressed syllables (to avoid any stress in speech is to be *monotone* and is considered peculiar or unnatural). Classical Western poetry differs from normal speech by limiting the appearance of stress and unstress to a controlled and regular pattern.

Two frequently employed forms of poetic rhythm can serve to illustrate the point. In the first example the rhythm is made up of a series of single unstressed syllables [x], each of which is followed immediately by a single stressed syllable [/]. The result, if exaggerated slightly, produces a rather *rocking* rhythm and is formally described as *iambic* rhythm. (Notice also the use of rhyme in alternating lines.)

x / x / x / x / x /
My true love hath my heart and I have his,

3. A poem by Gelett Burgess.

x / x / x / x / x /
By just exchange one for the other given.
x / x / x / x / x /
I hold his dear, and mine he cannot miss,
x / x / x / x / x /
There never was a better bargain driven.[4]

Dactylic rhythm provides a suitable contrast to the previous example. In this second form of rhythm, a single stressed syllable is followed immediately by two unstressed syllables.

/ x x / x x / x
This is the forest primeval
x / x x / x x / x
the murmuring pines and the hemlocks[5]

Other common types of poetic rhythm include *trochaic* (a single stressed syllable followed by a single unstressed syllable [/ x]) and *anapestic* (two unstressed syllables followed by a single stressed syllable [x x /].

Along with rhythm, *meter* provides the basis for a formal analysis of poetic rhythm in combination with line length. In metrical description, each occurrence of the regular rhythmic pattern is considered a *foot*. The name of the pattern (iambic, anapestic, dactylic, etc.) combined with the number of feet in a given line is considered the *meter* of that line. Our first example above is composed of single unstressed syllables followed by single stressed syllables. This is the *iambic* pattern. Lines 1 and 3 each contain four repetitions (*feet*) of this pattern and are therefore described as *iambic tetrameter.* Lines 2 and 4 have only three feet and represent what is called *iambic trimeter.*

Shakespeare's favorite meter was *iambic pentameter*—five repetitions of the *iambic* pattern described above in each line. Most of his plays employ this convention, subtly spreading the lines with their characteristic meter across the dialogue. Other poets have employed a variety of metrical combinations to achieve creative effects. Witness the opening passage of Longfellow's *The Highwayman*, which uses varied meter to mimic the galloping gait of the highwayman's steed.

The wind was a torrent of darkness among the gusty trees
The moon was a ghostly galleon, tossed upon cloudy seas,
The road was a ribbon of moonlight over the purple moor
When the highwayman came riding, riding, riding,
The highwayman came riding, up to the old inn door.

---

4. From a sonnet by Sir Philip Sidney.
5. From *Evangeline* by W. W. Longfellow.

We might think of these conventions as "rules" that must be followed to create poetry. As children we often follow them slavishly to create youthful celebrations of fancy, fantasy, and love. Only later do we come to a more mature understanding that these "rules" of poetry are in reality only our after-the-fact attempts to describe what poets do and so to bring order to our understanding of poetry. Poets are wont to rebel against too much convention as stultifying to their artistic creativity. One important "rule" of poetic convention is that rules may be stretched and even broken to achieve a desired effect.

Modern poetry frequently departs from all these poetic conventions. Blank verse, for example, retains both rhythm and meter (iambic pentameter) but avoids rhyme altogether. Free verse, on the other hand, demonstrates no regular rhythm, rhyme, or meter, preferring to conform the poetic structure of a poem only to the expressive needs of the poet. Obvious poetic conventions are left behind along with the most recognizable landmarks of poetry. The distinction between poetry and prose becomes more difficult to observe and to articulate.

It may be *difficult*, but for the most part it remains *possible* to recognize poetry. A poem is still a poem and not a grocery list. Even without signposts it may be possible to tell what part of the country you are in. So, even without obvious rhyme, rhythm, and meter, one can distinguish a poetic composition from its more prosaic counterpart. It is at this point that those more intuitive characteristics I mentioned before become important. Let me mention just two of these that I have found helpful: *imagery* and *compression*.

Because poetry is essentially an oral medium, relying on a memorable word and a receptive ear, it is filled with vivid *imagery* to tease the ear and engage the visual and emotional receptors of the brain rather than the merely rational. While it is true that prose can and does employ imagery, poetry far exceeds prose in the amount of imagery it exhibits. For prose, imagery is a subsidiary tool trotted out in support of the author's primary object. With poetry, however, imagery is the dominant stock in trade to cement the poet's ideas securely in the mind and heart of the hearers.

Together with imagery *compression* offers a second intuitive way we distinguish poetry. I know of no better illustration of compression than to observe carefully how most modern translations of the Bible present poetry and prose on the printed page. If you turn in your Bible to, say, Genesis 6 (the beginning of the Flood narrative), you will find the page covered with type from margin to margin—perhaps in columns, but still consistently filled with type.

Now turn to Psalm 119, Proverbs 14, or Isaiah 60. You will immediately notice considerably more white space on these pages—less type. The difference is that, while the Genesis text is prose, these last three are set in poetic lines. The lines of poetry are relatively equal in length and considerably shorter than the sentences found in the prose section. That begins to give a sense of what I mean by *compression*. Poets choose their words carefully. They seek just the right words to communicate their meanings with power and punch. Not just any word will do.

Prose is more expansive, achieving clarity of meaning by adding words and sentences to define and refine meaning. But poetry tends to be more concise, relying on the power of words rightly chosen and arranged to communicate the desired effect. The result is compression—tightly constructed lines of similar length, with an economy of carefully selected words.

Because of compression, poetry often seems condensed and powerful. Reading a poem can be a little like eating a spoonful of honey directly from the jar. The experience can be overpowering and unsettling. Each word is important and contributes to the whole. None can be lightly exchanged without altering the effect of the whole. That is part of the purpose of poetry. The careful selection and arrangement of words can have a powerful effect on the reader—recreating a spiritual, emotional, and intellectual world in which one is challenged to see, feel, and understand differently.

But because of compression, poetry is also less able to explain and refine its meaning than is prose. Poetry must rely on the effect of its words and images to carry meaning. Thus, poetry can sometimes be more ambiguous and difficult to follow. Because of the compression of meaning into few words, things are not "spelled out," and the concentrated words may offer more than one possibility for interpretation. That is the beauty (and sometimes the frustration) of poetry. Often, it can take as much care to *understand* good poetry as it does to *construct* it!

The Art of Hebrew Poetry

FROM THE PREVIOUS discussion it is clear that poetry operates within a set of conventions that shape it, provide boundaries for it, and ultimately distinguish it from other forms of oral and written speech—in particular, *prose*. These conventions, whether overt and obvious (e.g., rhyme, rhythm, and meter) or more subtle (e.g., use of imagery or compression), provide the artistic structures that challenge the poet's task. Ultimately these conventions, along with a poet's acceptance, implementation, and even resistance to them, conspire together to define the borders of the poetic act that allows us, the readers, to recognize a poem for what it is.

It would be simpler, I suppose, if all cultures adopted the same set of poetic conventions. (Simpler, but not so creatively rich and exciting!) We would then be able to transfer our poetic understanding and appreciation (or lack thereof!) across cultural and linguistic boundaries. But different cultures and different peoples—separated by place and time—step to distinctively different poetic rhythms and conventions. In each society, poetry operates by canons of conventions distinct from prose, but those conventions are not necessarily shared from society to society, culture to culture.

The Hebrew poetry of the Bible, of which the book of Psalms is an important part, is no exception. It conforms to a group of poetic conventions that give it shape and character, and these conventions distinguish it from Hebrew prose. In some of its more subtle characteristics (e.g., use of imagery, compression), Hebrew poetry has much in common with universal poetic expression. Even some of its more specific stylistic features (to be discussed below) find counterparts in the poetry of other cultures. But by and large, most of the explicit conventions of Western poetry discussed above are missing in Hebrew poetry.

Rhyme. For example, Hebrew poetry shows no clear evidence of a purposeful use of rhyme. Occasional occurrences of apparent rhyme are normally the result of parallel structures employing similar verbal forms with the same inflected endings. Such rhymes are the result of grammar and happenstance, not the choice of the author to produce rhyme combinations. Moreover, such occurrences are infrequent.

Meter. While certainly rhythmical, Hebrew poetry has no generally recognized or persuasively demonstrated system of meter. It is generally agreed that Hebrew poetry did exercise certain limitations on the length of lines. Thus it is possible to observe a relative balance between poetic lines. The use of *ballast* components to compensate for *ellipses* in parallel lines is another indication that poetic lines conformed to similar expectations of length. Having admitted this, however, it remains unclear precisely what factors were at work in determining line length.

Of the numerous attempts made to describe and delineate such a metrical system for Hebrew poetry, two deserve particular notice.

Stressed syllables. The earlier of the two systems remains as the more persuasive. Here meter is related to the number of *stressed syllables* in each poetic line. In spoken communication, almost every word bears some stress in pronunciation. The stressed-syllable system makes a distinction between *word stress* (the stress placed on individual words when spoken singly) and *tone stress* (the stress placed on groups of words combined together in rapid speech or especially in phrases encountered in singing). Ancient oral poetry was akin to song, and probably much psalmic poetry was intended to be performed with music. Note the combination of words and syllables into phrases in the following examples. In each, phrases are produced composed of two or more independent words that share a single stress in rapid speech. In Psalm 1:1, for example, *lo᾽-ha-lak*, *lo᾽-ʿa-mad*, and *lo᾽-ya-šab* are all combinations of the negative *lo᾽* and a perfect verb form.

᾽aš-re	*ha-᾽iš*	*᾽a-šer*
lo᾽-ha-lak	*ba-ʿa-ṣat*	*re-ša-ʿim*
u-be-de-rek	*haṭ-ṭa-᾽im*	*lo᾽-ʿa-mad*
u-be-mo-šab	*le-ṣim*	*lo᾽-ya-šab*

The phrases grouped together with hyphens (-) represent units that would receive a single stress in singing or rapid speech. Such stress on phrases is called *tone stress*.

This first theory of Hebrew meter suggests that lines of poetry demonstrate regular patterns of *tone stress* in their lines. In Psalm 1:1, the number of words in each line, and therefore the number of *word stresses*, vary from line to line, but the tone stress remains fixed (three per line).

The system is somewhat akin to our own concept of musical "time" with a number of beats per musical passage. A 3/4 time is distinctively different from 4/4 time, as you can tell from singing "Away in a Manger" (3/4) and then "Jingle Bells" (4/4). Clearly the beats accord with musical phrasing, not with individual word stress.

This discussion makes the system sound clear and convincing. I wish it were only so simple. In the real world of Hebrew poetry, it is often difficult, if not impossible, to determine a continuing pattern of meter. Some attribute this to textual corruption in transmission and seek to restore the pattern by textual emendation. It is, however, problematic in my opinion to prove a theory by emending the text when it does not correspond to one's expectations. It has too often happened that difficult texts are changed "because of the meter," as the critical notes in *BHS* frequently demonstrate. Elsewhere it may be that certain elements were intended to stand outside the meter of a poem or that we simply have got the lines or word combinations wrong.

The description of meter based on *tone stress* does seem to work *sometimes*, but it cannot be consistently demonstrated in all cases. Thus it remains a tantalizing possibility. Perhaps the most persuasive assessment of the findings is that Hebrew poetry does seem to preserve *relative balance* in stressed meaning units grouped as phrases. This might reduce the need for perfection in poetic description—perfection that probably exceeds our ability to grasp it, given the long history of transmission of the biblical text and the ancient silence on Hebrew poetic technique.

Having said this, it is clear that relative similarity of line length is present in most Hebrew poetry. It is also clear that intentional patterns involving different line length can be observed and are in some instances significant. One of the clearest of these is the "limping meter" associated with the biblical laments. This form is composed of a three- or four-stress line followed immediately by a line with only two stresses, as in Lamentations 1:1:

ya-še-bah	*ba-dad*	*ha-ʿir-rab-ba-ti-ʿam*
ha-ye-tah	*ke-ʾal-ma-nah*	
rab-ba-ti	*ba-go-yim*	*śa-ra-ti-bam-me-di-not*
ha-ye-tah	*la-mas*	

Some scholars think this rather hobbling rhythm mimicked or even accompanied a limping dance that visibly demonstrated the grieving and suffering of the lamenters.

Syllable counting. The second theory of meter in Hebrew poetry revolves around counting the number of syllables in poetic lines. The idea is that poets created lines containing identical numbers of syllables or at least some regular and recognizable pattern of syllables. This system developed as an alternative to the earlier theory of word stress and in response to that system's failure to explain consistently all features of biblical poetry.

It is obvious that syllable counting is related to relative balance of line length, but it seeks to bring greater precision to its description. Several significant difficulties face the proponents of this view. (1) Since Hebrew was originally written without indications of vowels, the syllabic structure of this ancient language has always had a certain degree of ambiguity. Add to this the fact that the consonantal text reflects several different dialects of Hebrew across a period of a thousand years or more, and the complexity of the issue becomes immense.

(2) The vocalic system represented in our current Hebrew text was not fully developed until the sixth or seventh century A.D. There are three competing systems of vocalization known (the Tiberian system that is generally employed, the Babylonian system, and the Palestinian system). These alternate attempts to fix pronunciation demonstrate some significant differences in their interpretation of specific texts.

These vocalic systems represent the way these biblical texts were pronounced in the sixth century A.D., and it is clear that pronunciation only imperfectly fits the consonantal text at many points. As a result, attempts to describe the original syllabic structure of poetic texts almost always involves hypothetical reconstruction based on some theory as to how Hebrew was pronounced at the date when the text in question was assumed to have been produced.

Such hypothetical reconstruction is exceedingly complex and offers too much opportunity for manipulation of the text to support one's theory of syllable counting. This can lead to circular reasoning where the system is "proved" by the emendation of texts because of the demands of the system.

For this reason there has been much disagreement, even among proponents of the method, and the theory lacks consistent ability to persuade.

Conclusions. What these two attempts to describe the nature of Hebrew poetic meter *do* demonstrate is the existence of relative balance in poetic line length. Both systems are able to find supportive examples because there does appear to be some limitation to the length of lines. Lines do not simply run on forever but stay within relative bounds. Beyond this, neither system has yet to provide consistent explanation of all existing texts. While the system based on *tone stress* seems more persuasive in my opinion, we may have to accept the fact that, because of the historical distance and theoretical ambiguity that stand between us and the text, a full understanding of the ins and outs of Hebrew meter will probably continue to elude our grasp.

Techniques of Hebrew Poetry

OBVIOUSLY, THE HEBREW poets had at their disposal the broad range of literary and stylistic techniques known to poets throughout the ages. Metaphor, simile, personification, onomatopoeia, and more offered each biblical poet ample opportunity to shape and texture individual compositions personally. But without such familiar poetic features as rhyme and meter, Hebrew poetry can often strike us as strange and uncomfortable. As we enter the world of the psalms, therefore, we may feel we have taken a wrong turn and are moving through alien terrain. So, to understand and appreciate the poetry of the biblical psalms, we will need to construct a new map of the land; we will need to become familiar with a new set of conventions that reflect the world of Hebrew poetry in general and of the psalms in particular.

Parallelism. It has long been recognized that the most distinctive characteristic of Hebrew poetry is to be found in the frequent linking of successive lines of poetry in a manner that emphasizes grammatical, structural, and thematic similarities between them. This relationship between lines has been traditionally called *parallelism*. The sense of this description is that after the statement of an initial line, a second (and sometimes a third) line is generated that shares some obvious grammatical-structural similarities with the first and yet redirects the focus of the first through alternate words and expressions. The close grammatical-structural similarity between lines provides continuity that emphasizes the *parallel* character of the two lines, while the distinctive phraseology of each phrase lifts the phenomenon beyond *mere repetition* and offers the opportunity for expansion or advancement on the original line's meaning.

At least from the time of Robert Lowth's *De sacra poesi Hebraeorum* ... (1753), a relatively standard terminology has been used to describe the variations of parallelism within Hebrew poetry. It is generally agreed today that these terms only inadequately describe the categories under consideration, and in some cases they are even misleading. Although they are well entrenched in the discipline, I will presume to replace them with more accurately descriptive terms here while noting the traditional terms at the first appearance of each.

Affirming parallelism.[6] This first of the traditional forms of parallelism comes closest to repetition or restatement. In this case, the second line restates the first in a similar or positive fashion while employing distinctive phraseology. This can approach almost exact repetition in some instances.[7]

So God created the *ʾadam* in his image;
in the image of God he created him.
—Genesis 1:27

In this example, except for the rearrangement of parallel elements, the second line restates the first with little advance or addition. Perhaps the phrase "in the image of God" clarifies the more ambiguous "in his image" of the first line, but the overall effect here is repetition for emphasis rather than advancement or refinement of thought.

In other cases the positive parallel of elements between lines is preserved, but the terminology employed in each is more distinctive.

Wash away all my iniquity
and cleanse me from my sin.
—Psalm 51:2

There is close and positive structural parallel between these two lines: similar imperative verbs ("wash away" vs. "cleanse me") and similar noun constructions ("my iniquity" vs. "my sin"). There is also positive parallel in the meaning of these two lines; washing away my iniquity is much the same as cleansing me from my sin. However, the second line does not simply restate the meaning of the first but advances or expands it by adding new nuances to the thought world created.

Sometimes the advancement offered by the second (or third) line can be quite unexpected and significant. If we return to Genesis 1:27, we will discover that a third line adds another affirming parallelism to the first two.

6. Traditionally, this form of parallelism has been called *synonymous parallelism*. That description is not very apt, and confusion arises especially with the addition of the other terms to be introduced later, *antithetical* and *synthetical parallelism*—terms that are often associated with a particular form of philosophical reasoning. For this reason I prefer the more accurately descriptive terms employed here.

7. The contrasting discussions of Alter and Kugel are helpful in this case, especially to highlight the fact that *affirming parallelism* is *not* mere repetition but actually "seconds" or heightens the force of the initial sentence. Kugel expresses the relationship between two affirming lines as "A, and what's more, B." Note that in all the following examples, I will be using my own translation of the biblical text to bring out the points under discussion.

So God created the *ʾadam* in his image;
in the image of God he created him;
male and female he created them.

By comparing the related structural elements in these lines ("God created/he created/he created"; "the *ʾadam*/him/them"; "in his image/in the image of God/male and female"), we conclude that the new phrase in the third line ("male and female") is intended to expand (in an unexpected way) our understanding of what it means to be created in God's image. This is clearly *not* simple repetition but an important advancement in the thinking of the poet!

Thus, in *affirming parallelism*, a second or third line of poetry restates a preceding line in a positive fashion that maintains continuity with the structure and meaning of the first, while in subtle (or not so subtle) ways expanding and advancing the thought begun there through the introduction of alternate expressions into the growing thought world created by the combination. Recognition and appreciation of the art and subtlety of this form of poetic expression will require additional study and exposure. A few examples are provided below to illustrate the variety of synonymous constructions encountered in the Hebrew Bible.

Their mischief returns upon their own heads,
and on their own heads their violence descends.
—Psalm 7:16

My hand shall always remain with him;
my arm also shall strengthen him.
—Psalm 89:21

Like those forsaken among the dead,
like the slain that lie in the grave.
—Psalm 88:5

Opposing parallelism.[8] A second form of parallelism in Hebrew poetry is clearly distinguished from the first. In this construction, the second line maintains clear continuity with the structure and meaning of the first but relates to it in a *negative* rather than a positive fashion. A few examples should bring clarity to this description.

A wise son causes a father to rejoice;
a foolish son is a pain to his mother.
—Proverbs 10:1

8. The traditional terminology is in this case *antithetical parallelism*. The confusion that arises with the Hegelian philosophical method of "thesis-antithesis-synthesis" renders this term less than useful or helpful.

The similarity of structure and meaning is obvious: A certain type of son has a particular effect on a parent. At this level, the parallel between lines is almost exact. But rather than the positive restatement characteristic of *affirming parallelism*, these lines demonstrate a decidedly negative or contrasting relationship. The "wise son" and resultant "joy" of relationship in line 1 is contrasted with the "foolish son" and the consequent "pain" in line 2.

The contrasting character of *opposing parallelism* has great potential for instruction because it presents in brief compass both a positive example and a negative caution that point the student to the more prosperous of two paths (wisdom and folly; righteousness and wickedness) that the biblical sages recognize as the basic opportunities of life. As a result of this didactic potential, *opposing parallelism* is frequently found throughout the biblical wisdom literature—especially in Proverbs, where it appears as the most common feature of chapters 10–29.

He who keeps the commandment keeps his life;
he who despises the word will die.
—Proverbs 19:16

The heart of the sage is in the house of mourning,
but the heart of fools is in the house of mirth.
—Ecclesiastes 7:4

If he withholds the waters, they dry up;
if he sends them out, they overwhelm the land.
—Job 12:15

This form is not limited to the wisdom literature, however, but appears regularly in the psalms and other Hebrew poetry. Here are a few more examples to illustrate the varied nature of *opposing parallelism*.

Yahweh watches over the sojourners,
he upholds the widow and the fatherless;
but the way of the wicked he brings to ruin.
—Psalm 146:9

The first two lines represent *affirming parallelism* and expand on the theme of God's care for and protection of the helpless in society ("watches/upholds"; "sojourners/widow and fatherless"). In a parallel but *opposing* manner the third line ("brings to ruin") introduces the contrasting fate of the wicked at the hand of a God concerned with justice.

The wicked borrows and cannot pay back,
but the righteous is generous and gives;

for those blessed by Yahweh shall possess the land,
but those cursed by him shall be cut off.
—Psalm 37:21–22

Two sets of *opposing parallel* lines appear within this single verse. In the first set the wicked and righteous clearly oppose each other, as do their respective relationship to finances (borrowing without repayment vs. generous giving). In the second set, the poet contrasts the futures of those who are blessed or cursed by Yahweh. The rather harsh contrast introduced by the use of the parallel phrase "cut off" (normally implying death!) adds a new dimension to the blessing of the land that Israel experienced and ultimately lost in the Exile. Loss of the land is here understood to represent not merely geographical dislocation but physical and, even more importantly, spiritual death!

Advancing parallelism. The third form of parallelism traditionally recognized is really not *parallel* at all. In this type, the second line has lost all semblance of similarity of structure, syntax, or meaning with the preceding line and unabashedly charges ahead, advancing and furthering the poet's thought. The name traditionally applied (*synthetical parallelism*) is, therefore, doubly misleading. There is no more *parallel* here than there is *synthesis*. The philosophical term *synthesis* that is pressed into thankless service here assumes a preceding *thesis* statement with a countering *antithesis*, which then interact to create a new and better response or *synthesis*.

It has long been recognized that this terminology in relation to Hebrew poetry is confusing at best and misleading at worst. Although the term is entrenched in usage, I prefer in the discussion that follows to use the more accurately descriptive term *advancing parallelism*, fully realizing that in this case *parallelism* is an inadequate descriptor.

In *advancing parallelism*, then, after an initial line, a second (or third or, in some cases, even more!) line continues the thought, theme, or narrative of the poem without any obvious concern to maintain grammatical, structural, or thematic similarity to the initial line. The poem simply continues to develop its theme, while parallelism fades from view. This lack of parallel structure may be limited to a single set of poetic lines or may be more extensive in nature, affecting several verses or even whole compositions.

Again, let's consider several examples to get a sense of the varied appearance of *advancing parallelism*.

Our God is in the heavens;
he does whatever he pleases.
Their idols are silver and gold,
the work of men's hands.
—Psalm 115:3–4

In each of these couplets, the second line builds on the preceding line without being parallel to it grammatically, structurally, or thematically. The first couplet goes on to describe the exalted freedom of the God who resides in the heavens—a freedom that is certainly related to his exalted position and perhaps even derived from it, but it is not expressed in any sense of parallelism. The second couplet begins by describing the inanimate stuff (albeit rich) from which idols are constructed, but it continues in the second line to drive home their inferiority to the free God of the heavens by emphasizing the idols' creation by human hands. Again, there is relationship, connection, and continuity between line 1 and line 2, but no clear, or even subtle, parallelism.

> You have put more joy in my heart
> than they have when their grain and wine abound.
> In peace I will both lie down and sleep;
> for you alone, Yahweh, make me dwell in safety.
> —Psalm 4:7–8

Once again the second line of the first couplet simply carries the thought begun in the first on to its proper conclusion, emphasizing the great joy the psalmist experiences in relation to Yahweh in contrast to those who find their joy in the abundant grain and wine he provides. The next couplet employs the second line to describe the basis of the psalmist's security in Yahweh that makes it possible to lie down and sleep peacefully, even in the face of personal attack and distress described earlier in this psalm.

Advancing parallelism clearly offers a poet maximum flexibility in the creation of lines that develop, direct, and advance the movement of a poem. Freed from the relative constraints of the demands of parallel structure, the poet can introduce more complex and extended argumentation that goes beyond the more restrictive, two-line format characteristic of parallelism. As a consequence of this freedom, compositions can become more flowing, less fragmented, and more unified (and in some instances *longer*!). For this reason alone, *advancing parallelism* is a frequent player in Hebrew poetry. Some psalms are even primarily composed of synthetical lines with little or no attention to parallelism at all. Take a look at Psalms 110 and 111 in this regard. Neither makes much use of parallel forms. The interior dialogue sections of the book of Job and parts of Ecclesiastes owe much of their subtly and complexity to their ability to advance, expand, and sustain the discussion through frequent use of *advancing parallelism*.

So, in *advancing parallelism*, Hebrew poets broke with the strictures of similarity with the preceding line and experienced their greatest freedom to advance, direct, redirect, and structure the thought of a poem. How differently poets can proceed from the same starting line is illustrated in the examples below.

O sing to Yahweh a new song;
sing to Yahweh, all the earth.
—Psalm 96:1

O sing to Yahweh a new song,
for he has done marvelous things!
—Psalm 98:1

O sing to Yahweh a new song,
his praises in the assembly of the faithful.
—Psalm 149:1

Here, the same initial line gives rise to three distinctively different treatments. The first (96:1) offers a variation on the *synonymous* form by expanding the second line ("all the earth") to compensate for the omission of an element ("a new song") from the first. This expansion to replace an ellipsis is sometimes referred to as a *ballast* line or element.

The third set of couplets is another example of ellipsis with compensation in the second line. Here, however, it is the lead phrase ("Sing to Yahweh") that is omitted in the second line. It is perhaps more correct to say that this phrase is understood (by both poet and reader) to govern both lines. As a result of this ellipsis, the remaining phrase ("his praises in the assembly of the faithful") is greatly expanded over its parallel ("a new song") while the lines together remain *synonymous* in relationship.[9]

In the middle example (98:1), the initial line is continued *synthetically* in the second. The poet goes beyond the opening invocation to praise Yahweh with a justification of Yahweh's praiseworthiness ("for he has done marvelous things!"). These very different directions from the same starting point demonstrate just how much flexibility the Hebrew poetic system afforded creative poets seeking new and unique forms of expression.

Here is another group of similar examples.

Turn to me and be gracious to me;
give your strength to your servant,
and save the son of your handmaid.
—Psalm 86:16

---

9. The expansion preserves the relative balance in length between the two lines of the couplet—an indication that, while we know no universally accepted system of meter in Hebrew poetry, relative line length was still a matter of sufficient significance as to require some compensation in this circumstance.

Turn to me and be gracious to me,
for I am lonely and afflicted.
—Psalm 25:16

Turn to me and be gracious to me,
as is your wont to those who love your name.
—Psalm 119:132

Once again, the same opening line generates three distinctive responses. In the first (86:16), the poet continues with two lines that are *synonymously* related to each other but not to the first line. The *synonymous* couplet explores *how* the psalmist desires God to turn and be gracious (by strengthening and saving). In the second example (25:16), the successive line explains *why* the psalmist needs God to return ("for I am lonely and afflicted"), while the focus of the third passage (119:132) is the divine character that undergirds the poet's hope for a gracious divine response.

Climactic parallelism. There is one additional Hebrew poetic form that has received attention of late under the rubric of parallel structure. Again, there is some discussion whether *climactic parallelism*, as this feature has been called, is an altogether happy designation. As will be clear from the examples that follow, there is continuity of thought and syntax between the related lines. In fact, at least part of the initial line is repeated verbatim in successive ones. The question in my mind, however, is whether the few examples we have of this form constitute an independent type of parallelism or whether they rather illustrate an expansion and adaptation of the more recognized forms. Let's look at two examples.

Ascribe to Yahweh, O heavenly beings,
Ascribe to Yahweh glory and strength,
Ascribe to Yahweh the glory of his name;
Worship Yahweh in holy array.
—Psalm 29:1–2

The interrelation of the lines in this example is obvious. The threefold repetition of the opening imperative phrase ("Ascribe to Yahweh") binds the first three lines together, while the fourth and final line offers a summation of the whole complex. Lines 2 and 3 form together a clear example of *affirming parallelism*, with "glory of his name" in line 3 providing expansion and subtle redirection of the theme introduced by "glory and strength" in line 2. It is not simply glory and strength that is at issue here, but the glory and strength that proceed from the divine name (and thus the character and essence) of Yahweh.

It is only the placement of line 1 with its identical phrase that lifts this composition to a new level of poetic intensity. The completion of the initial phrase is postponed by the intrusion of the "heavenly beings" called to acknowledge and exalt the name of Yahweh. This delay intensifies the interest of the hearer/reader, who must wait for the resolution until the end of the next line. The intensity is heightened even further by the thrice repeated command, "Ascribe to Yahweh. . . ."

A similar use of triple repetition to intensify the effect of poetic lines is found in our next example.

> The floods have lifted up, O Yahweh,
> The floods have lifted up their voice,
> The floods lift up their roaring.
>
> —Psalm 93:3

Here the floods most likely represent the chaotic waters subdued by Yahweh at creation (associated in more general ancient Near Eastern mythology with precreation deities). These powerful waters, which represent a potent threat to the very human poet and reader, rise up in tumult and appear to endanger the very fabric of the orderly creation established by God—the creation on which the very existence of humans depends. Perhaps the scene is intended to reflect the Flood narrative of Genesis 6–9, where the chaotic waters restricted by Yahweh at creation are unleashed once more and threaten to dissolve creation once and for all.

As in the previous example, lines 2 and 3 are synonymously parallel, with line 3 intensifying the growing effect of line 2 by substituting the powerfully descriptive "roaring" for the more pallid "voice." Line 1 provides additional intensification—delaying the completion of the initial phrase ("The floods lift up") by inserting the vocative address to Yahweh. The result is a poetic depiction of the gradual ascent of the powerful clamor made by the tumultuous waters in their opposition to God.

You may now understand why I questioned at the outset whether these examples illustrate an independent form of parallelism. There are so few examples of this type offered, and those examples exhibit strong characteristics of *affirming parallelism* (lines 2 and 3 in the examples above) and *advancing parallelism* (the relation of line 1 to lines 2 and 3). It seems best, in my estimation, to view *climactic parallelism* as a particularly artful adaptation of traditional forms of parallelism for purposes of intensification.

Summary. For the purposes of our general discussion, then, the three traditionally recognized forms of parallelism (affirming, opposing, and advancing) constitute the basic literary arsenal of the ancient Hebrew poet and provide the peculiar flavor that makes this poetry distinctive. Our discussion has for the most part remained rudimentary, and there remains much for the student of Hebrew poetry to learn through direct experience and observation.

Only through such personal exploration can one gain a more complete sense of the subtle, nuanced variations of form that demonstrate biblical poets' skill and mastery in pursuing their craft.

Before we leave the discussion of Hebrew poetry, however, I will discuss five other conventions or techniques. While these stylistic features are not unique to the Bible, their use adds dimension and breadth to our understanding of the psalms and biblical poetry.

Word pairs. The phenomenon of parallelism in Hebrew poetry highlights the close relationship that can exist between parallel words and phrases in the related lines. As we have seen, a significant word in one line can be augmented or expanded by its parallel in the next. In some instances this expansion may represent mere stylistic variation. But on most occasions the second word adds a significant semantic or theological dimension to the first. This is particularly clear in the first example I used of *affirming parallelism* (Gen. 1:27). The phrase in line 1 ("in his image") is only slightly varied in line 2 ("in the image of God"), but it is significantly expanded both semantically and theologically in line 3 by the parallel phrase "male and female."

The important theological advancement accomplished in these three lines is illustrative of the kind of use that can be made of parallelism. James Kugel is certainly right when he stresses the "seconding" effect of parallel lines: "A, *and what's more,* B." The sum of the two parts is always more, in his opinion, than mere repetition.[10] One must always take into consideration this expansive nature of parallelism in interpreting couplets. In most instances the poet is building a semantic context in which the subtle nuances of two or more words brought together in parallelism expand the possibilities for understanding.

The same expansion can also be subtly understood in *opposing parallelism.* Here the negative parallel can once again add nuances to our understanding of the original word. Take, for example, the concluding verse of Psalm 1:

> For God *knows* the way of the righteous,
> but the way of the wicked *will perish.*
>
> —Psalm 1:6

The initial line leaves open what it might mean for the path of the righteous to be *known* by God. But the negative parallel in the following line makes it clear that God's *knowing* is a source of protection and preservation not experienced by the wicked. Thus, the semantic world in which the ideas of the

10. James Kugel, *The Idea of Biblical Poetry: Parallelism and Its History* (New Haven, Conn.: Yale Univ. Press, 1981).

poet operate are significantly expanded by juxtaposing these two phrases and their nuances. Thus, it is important for an interpreter to recognize that more than repetition is at work behind the words chosen to be in parallelism. Through the chosen words the biblical writer creates an expanded semantic thought world.

Traditional word pairs. The choice of word pairs for parallelism can sometimes become a matter of fixed, traditional association. Through long usage, certain words become connected as expected parallels balancing their respective lines. "Wisdom" is normally balanced by "folly." The "wicked" are most often paralleled by the "righteous." "Heaven" is most often linked with "earth." "Man" (*ʾadam*) finds its reflex in many instances in "son of man" (*ben ʾadam*). Many other commonly employed word pairs have been recognized as operative in Hebrew poetry.[11]

Traditional word pairs such as these can even play a role in textual criticism, as attempts to restore the fragmentary Canaanite religious texts from Ugarit (Ras Shamra) demonstrate. These texts, written in an alphabetic cuneiform script on clay tablets, were discovered in the late 1920s in excavations at a site on the coast of northern Syria. Among other documents, these texts include poetic religious documents from the third millennium B.C. in a language closely resembling ancient Hebrew. The poetry used in these ancient texts also employs parallel lines and exhibits extensive use of traditional word pairs.

When a clay tablet has been damaged so that parts of lines are no longer legible, it is often possible to make a confident reconstruction based on the plausible anticipation of fixed word pairs. Occasionally such a scholarly conjecture has been proven correct by the discovery of additional copies of the text where the lines in question are still extant or by comparing repeated passages elsewhere in the same tablet. It has now become common practice for biblical textual critics to suggest emendation of incoherent or difficult poetic passages on the basis of expected completion of fixed pairs.

The frequent appearance of so many fixed pairs in parallel lines ought perhaps to caution us against making too much of the possibilities for theological expansion in such cases. Is the poet's choice of terms driven by a desire to nuance the literary context? Or is it determined by the expectations of the

11. See Robert Alter, *The Art of Biblical Poetry* (New York: Basic Books, 1985), 12–14, 28. James Kugel also offers an extended discussion of the phenomenon in *The Idea of Biblical Poetry*, 27–40. P. B. Yoder, in his "A-B Pairs and Oral Composition in Hebrew Poetry," in *Poetry in the Hebrew Bible*, ed. David E. Orton (Leiden: Brill, 2000), 90–109, understands the presence of such fixed word pairs in Hebrew poetry as indicating an extended period of oral transmission and composition. See also Wilfred G. E. Watson, *Traditional Techniques in Classical Hebrew Verse* (JSOTSup 170; Sheffield: Sheffield Academic Press, 1994), 28–30.

fixed word pair? Such caution is probably appropriate. However, the use of words as fixed pairs does not prohibit their use singly in other contexts or even in connection to other words in parallel lines. "Man" (*ʾadam*) is not always paralleled by "son of man" (*ben ʾadam*), nor is "wicked" inexorably connected to "righteous." Fixed pairs represent only one possible word choice that Hebrew poets could use to good effect.

Merism. Sometimes psalmists use word pairs describing opposites or extremes to refer inclusively to all that lies between. This is known technically as *merism* or *merismus*. Some obvious examples include *great* and *small*, *rich* and *poor*, *far* and *near*. Such merisms often appear as fixed word pairs in parallel lines of Hebrew poetry. It can be helpful to understand the more inclusive intent that lies behind a *merism*.

> You will not fear the terror of the *night*,
> nor the arrow that flies by *day*,
> nor the pestilence that stalks in the *darkness*,
> nor the destruction that wastes at *noonday*.
>
> —Psalm 91:5–6

The intent of these verses and their obvious merisms is not to note those times of the day when those who trust in Yahweh should be unafraid—suggesting by implication that there are other times when fear is entirely appropriate. The clear affirmation of the psalmist is rather that there is *never a time* that Yahweh fails to protect those who fear him. The use of merismus brings this point home in a particularly artistic and forceful manner.

Merismus also plays a significant role in Psalm 103:11–12.

> For as the *heavens* are high above the *earth*,
> so great is his steadfast love toward those who fear him;
> as far as the *east* is from the *west*,
> so far does he remove our transgressions from us.

The tension produced and maintained by "heaven" and "earth," "east" and "west," magnify the absolute character of God's redemptive forgiveness. Heaven and earth mark the boundaries of God's creative work; elsewhere together they represent all that God has made. Coupled with east and west, they suggest that God in his mercy has removed our transgressions and their consequences to the furthest distances of the creation.

Chiasm. Closely related to parallelism and drawing often on the connecting links between word pairs is the frequent use of *chiastic structure* in Hebrew poetry. For our purposes, *chiasm* is a poetic technique in which a set of sentence elements are introduced in a particular order in one line, while the parallel elements are stated in reverse order in the succeeding line. Consequently, if beginning and ending elements in line 1 were to be connected by straight lines to their parallel elements in line 2, a large X would result.

So—God—created—the—*ʾadam* in—his—image
in—the—image—of—God he—created—him

Since in the Greek language the letter *Chi* has the form of an X, this poetic technique is called *chiasm*.

Because *chiasm* is dependent on word order in the *original language* (in this case Hebrew), discovering this kind of structure in successive lines of *translated* poetry is sometimes problematic since the order and arrangement of words and phrases can often be modified in the translation process. One must exercise care, therefore, to make certain that a chiasm apparent in the translated text actually reflects a chiasm present in the original language. In the case above, the chiasm is original as the transliterated Hebrew of the passage demonstrates.

wayyibraʾ ʾelohim ʾet haʾadam beṣalmo
beṣelem ʾelohim baraʾ ʾoto

A particularly impressive chiasm stretching across *three* lines is found in Psalm 90:1–2.

-0- O my Lord,
A a refuge you have been for us
B in each and every age
C before mountains were birthed;
C′ and [before] you formed earth and heaven,
B′ from everlasting to everlasting,
A′ you are God.

Here the complexity and length of the form make it difficult to exhibit the chiastic schema in the traditional parallel format. An alternate style used to demonstrate chiasm extending over several lines is to indicate parallel elements by means of balanced indentation and by labeling related elements A and A′, B and B′, and so on.

In this particular instance, the opening vocative "O my Lord" stands outside the chiastic structure and is thus labeled -0- since it has no balancing reflex. The rest of the chiasm appears as a gradual indentation to the right (A, B, C) and then a return to the left (C′, B′, A′). The *chiastic* nature of this construction is obscured by the presentation but becomes more apparent when the labels are arranged in the traditional format.

A B C
C′ B′ A′

Chiasm was used not only to structure individual elements within successive lines of poetry, but it can also be extended to larger segments and even to whole compositions, including longer narratives. For example, consider Genesis 3, where the initial order in which important characters are introduced (serpent—woman—man) are reversed when God confronts their disobedience (man—woman—serpent), and are reversed again in God's pronouncement of consequences (serpent—woman—man).

Where a whole composition (and not just parallel lines) is considered chiastically arranged, parallels are most often deduced not at the level of balanced words or phrases, but often on the basis of balanced *meanings* expressed by related lines. This can sometimes lead to strained and forced connections that ultimately fail to convince. The interpreter is on surer ground when it can be demonstrated that related meaning is paralleled by related words/phrases and sentence structure. For numerous serious explications of the structure of individual psalms including extensive chiasms, see the stimulating and insightful works of Pierre Auffret.[12] Chiasm has also been the object of intensive investigation by Wilfred G. E. Watson.[13]

Inclusio. Repetition is a particularly common feature of oral poetry. It aids the memory, recalls previous detail, enhances anticipation where the composition is familiar, and can serve to drive home the essential point of the composition. I have alluded previously to the appearance of repeated passages in Ugaritic poetry and how these repetitions can offer opportunity to emend broken passages. One particularly clear case of triple repetition occurs in the Krt Epic, when messengers are described as they are being instructed in the communication they are to deliver to a distant king, then again as they carry out their embassy verbatim, and finally when they return to report the successful completion of their task.[14]

Among the various forms of repetition employed in Hebrew poetry, one of the most artful and striking is the *inclusio*, where identical or nearly identical phrases frame the beginning and ending of a composition. The effect is to create a sort of literary envelope marking the extreme boundaries of a poem. Perhaps the most beautiful example of the form from the biblical Psalter is found in Psalm 8:1, 9:

---

12. For just a few examples of Auffret's extensive work on the psalms, see P. Auffret, *The Literary Structure of Psalm 2* (JSOTSup 3; Sheffield: Sheffield Academic Press, 1977), 1–41, and "Note sur la structure littéraire di Psaumes CXXXVI," *VT* 27 (1977): 1–13.

13. Watson, *Traditional Techniques in Classical Hebrew Verse*, 262–312.

14. Translations of the Krt Epic can be found in: H. L. Ginsberg, *The Legend of King Keret: A Canaanite Epic of the Bronze Age* (BASORSup 2–3; New Haven, Conn.: American Schools of Oriental Research, 1946), and J. C. L. Gibson, *Canaanite Myths and Legends*, 2d ed. (Edinburgh: T. & T. Clark, 1977).

O Yahweh, our Lord, how majestic is your name in all the earth!

. . . .

O Yahweh, our Lord, how majestic is your name in all the earth!

The inclusio sets the context within which the thrust of the poem is played out. The awesome power and majesty of Yahweh provides the framework against which human insignificance is scrutinized. The stark contrast between divine magnificence and human poverty provides an almost dumbfounded recognition of the exalted honor received by the gracious election of God. But everywhere the focus is on the God who gives, not the human who receives. And the inclusio clarifies this theme both before and behind.

Other inclusios are found in Psalms 103 and 104, where the phrase "Bless Yahweh, O my soul!" both begins and ends each psalm, and in Psalm 118, where the operative phrase is "O give thanks to Yahweh, for he is good; his steadfast love endures forever!" In addition, several of the Hallelujah Psalms begin and end with this characteristic call to praise (Pss. 106; 113; 135; 146–150).

In other words, inclusios encapsulate a psalm, emphasizing the dominant theme that is expected to remain. The reader (or hearer) is led back to the beginning at the end, and all encountered between must be understood in the light of this twin witness.

Repeated refrains. A second form of repetition that appears prominently in some psalms is the use of a *repeated refrain*. In this technique, a line or series of lines is repeated almost verbatim at intervals throughout the poem. The result is somewhat akin to a chorus alternating with the verses of a hymn or ballad. A straightforward example of the repeated refrain is found in Psalm 49, where the verbatim refrain "Man cannot abide in his pomp; he is like the beasts that perish" appears at the midpoint (v. 12) and conclusion (v. 20) of this psalm.

Refrains punctuate their compositions and break the flow of the poetry. Thus, they provide an obvious means of structuring compositions into smaller components. In Psalm 49, after an introductory preface (vv. 1–4), the remainder of the psalm is divided into two equally weighted components of eight verses each (vv. 5–12, 13–20). The repeated refrain serves to drive home the poet's pessimistic evaluation of human self-reliance, since humans and animals alike perish regardless of their wealth or status. As a result, the wise will rely wholly on Yahweh, who can ransom their souls from Sheol. Like the inclusio, therefore, refrains can serve to emphasize (repeatedly) the key point or focus of a psalm.

A more complicated refrain is featured in Psalm 107. Once again this refrain serves to structure the psalm into smaller components. The introductory verses (vv. 1–3) call those whom Yahweh has redeemed and gathered in from where they have been scattered throughout the world to sing praises for Yahweh's enduring goodness and steadfast love. The body of the poem is then structured into a series of vignettes illustrating how groups of these scattered peoples met trouble on their way, cried out to Yahweh, and experienced redemption.

The refrains that conclude these sections (vv. 6+8, 13+15, 19+21, 28+31) contain sections that are verbatim repetitions. Each is subtly adapted to its particular section by the addition of phrases reflecting the characteristic experience of that group of witnesses.

> Then they cried to Yahweh in their trouble,
> and he delivered them from their distress;
> *he brought them out of the darkness and gloom*
> *and broke their bonds asunder.*
> Let them thank Yahweh for his steadfast love,
> for his wonderful works to the sons of men!
> *For he shatters the doors of bronze*
> *and cuts in two the bars of iron.*
>
> —Psalm 107:13–16

The italicized portions mark the variations directed to the experience of the first group of witnesses. Compare now the second refrain:

> Then they cried to Yahweh in their trouble,
> and he delivered them from their distress;
> *he sent forth his word and healed them*
> *and delivered them from destruction.*
> Let them thank Yahweh for his steadfast love,
> for his wonderful works to the sons of men!
> *And let them offer sacrifices of thanksgiving*
> *and tell of his deeds in songs of joy!*
>
> —Psalm 107:19–22

Another example of a refrain is found in Psalms 42 and 43, where the appearance of the repeated phrases "Why are you cast down, O my soul, and why are you disquieted within me? Hope in God; for I shall again praise him, my help and my God" (42:5, 11; 43:5) has led to the recognition that these two psalms probably represent an originally unified composition.

The most extreme demonstration of repetition in the Psalter occurs in Psalm 136, where each half verse is followed by the fixed response "for his steadfast love endures forever." Without these repeated refrains, the psalm presents a straightforward narrative of God's history with his people Israel, including his creative acts (v. 1–9) and his powerful protection against the enemies of his people (vv. 10–26). The constant refrain confirms the liturgical use of this composition in antiphonal performance in worship and may suggest that other repeated refrains likewise provided opportunities for the congregation (or choir) to add their affirmation to the poet's declarations in the body of these psalms.

In the Psalter, psalms with repeated refrains are found concentrated in the second book (Pss. 42+43; 46; 49; 56; 57; 59; 62; 67), with only a single example each in the third (80) and fourth (99) books. The fifth and final book offers two examples (107; 136).

Acrostic psalms. The last important stylistic feature of Hebrew poetry we will consider is the use of the acrostic arrangement in a number of psalms. In general, an acrostic poem is one in which lines are so arranged or created that the initial letters of successive lines produce a recognizable pattern. As children, many of us have indulged our romantic and poetic bent by creating acrostics out of the names of our current romantic interests. In one instance, the LXX records in Greek such an acrostic composition highlighting the name of the Hasmonean ruler Alexander Janneus.[15]

As far as Hebrew acrostics go, however, the pattern exhibited is much less free and variable. The initial letters of successive lines consistently follow the order of the Hebrew alphabet's twenty-two characters, beginning with *aleph, bet, gimel, dalet,* . . . and continuing in order to completion with *sin* and *taw*. Thus, Hebrew acrostics will usually demonstrate twenty-two lines or (in the case of more than one line for each letter) multiples of twenty-two lines. In some cases a twenty-third line beginning with the letter *pe* is added at the end of an acrostic psalm (see Pss. 25; 34), so that the first line begins with *aleph*, the middle with *lamed*, and the final line with *pe*. As a result, the combination of these letters—*ʾlp*—spells out the name of the initial alphabetic character as well as the Hebrew verb "to train," since one purpose of an alphabetic acrostic might be as a mnemonic aid to learning.[16] Alphabetic acrostics have especially enjoyed association with the wisdom tradition in ancient Israel.

There are in the Hebrew Psalter eight acrostic psalms (9–10; 25; 34; 37; 111; 112; 119; 145). The first of these involves the recognition that Psalms 9 and 10 represent an originally unified composition that has at some point

---

15. See the discussion of this and other acrostics in P. Skehan and A. Di Lella, *The Wisdom of Ben Sira* (AB 39; New York: Doubleday, 1987), 74.

16. It may be that in the case of acrostic psalms adding a final verse, the *waw* line is also omitted. See the comments of Peter C. Craigie, *Psalms 1–50* (WBC; Waco, Tex..: Word, 1983), 128–31, 216–17 (on Ps. 25:5a and Excursus III).

in its history been divided in two.[17] The acrostic pattern is clear in the lines of Psalm 9 and in the concluding verses of Psalm 10 (vv. 7–18) but is somewhat disturbed and imperfect at the beginning of Psalm 10 (vv. 1–6), where the original unity of these two psalms has been obscured by separation. The remainder of these eight psalms exhibit the alphabetic pattern clearly.

Seven of the acrostics found in the Psalter offer but a single occurrence of each alphabetic character. The number of poetic lines introduced by each letter may vary (compare Pss. 111 and 112 with Ps. 37), but there is only one line beginning with *aleph*, one beginning with *bet*, and so on. The single exception to this norm is the massive Psalm 119, in which each of the twenty-two letters is represented by no fewer than eight lines beginning with the same letter. The effect is visually impressive, and the similar beginning of lines, once pointed out, can even be observed by those unfamiliar with the Hebrew language.

Why the Hebrew poets chose this particular form of acrostic composition as their traditional pattern is unknown. Unfortunately, no contemporary discussion of biblical poetic technique has been preserved for us. The pattern does, however, set the poet an additional challenge for mastery. To arrange one's thoughts in such a way as to ensure that each successive line begins with the appropriate letter of the alphabetic sequence is no mean task. To do so with artistic skill and power is remarkable. The skill required, however, is probably no more exacting than that involved in composing a sonnet in which fourteen lines of poetry concluding in a final couplet must conform to a particular pattern of rhyme, meter, and arrangement (depending on which sonnet style the poet is following). Either task could be daunting for anyone less than a skilled poet. Some critics, in fact, find the artistry of Psalm 119 less than satisfactory. It is in their view overlong, stultifying, repetitious, and dull.

Outside the Psalter, acrostic compositions occur in Lamentations. Of the five chapters of the book, all but the last are acrostic psalms of lament. Chapters 1, 2, and 4 exhibit single occurrences of each letter, while chapter 3 offers three-lined stanzas in which each line begins with the same letter. Another particularly effective biblical acrostic appears in Proverbs 31:10–31 (the "noble wife" passage).

Hebrew alphabetic acrostics are also known to us from the Dead Sea Scrolls discovered near Qumran. The important Qumran *Psalms Scroll* (11QPs[a]) contains three such alphabetic acrostic psalms, two previously known to us in Greek form (Ps. 155 and Sir. 51:13–30) and the other ("Apostrophe to Zion") entirely new to us.

---

17. The LXX actually combines these two psalms into a single composition.

Acrostic compositions are particularly difficult to observe in translation. However, most translations indicate the acrostic nature of a psalm in some external way. In some cases a note is attached at the bottom of the page. Elsewhere the convention is to mark each line with the appropriate Hebrew character in the margin or between stanzas. Otherwise, without knowledge of the Hebrew language, it is practically impossible for an interpreter to identify alphabetic compositions.

Summary

THE ARTISTIC TOOLBOX available to Hebrew poets is as varied and nuanced as that of any other nation. While a few of the techniques used may seem unfamiliar to us and therefore awkward, an appreciation of the skill and style of Hebrew poetry can only increase with continued exposure and acquaintance with those conventions that provide challenge and shape to their literary enterprise.

The Hebrew poets and psalmists were products of their day and culture. There is much sentiment abroad today in our own postmodern environment that views convention with suspicion and disrespects those who choose to express themselves within a set of defining structures, such as Hebrew poetry represents. There is a tendency to exalt those who resist—even seek to annihilate—conventional structures as heroes (or antiheroes). As a result, too often the consummate skill and artistry of the biblical poets is underappreciated and even denigrated.

The amazing fact for me is that these ancient poetic compositions, with all their alien form and content, continue to attract and repulse, inspire, confront, and challenge their readers across all the intervening centuries. To those who learn a little and listen with ears even moderately open, the poetry of the psalms will crack open a window to the soul of a people who lived in honest recognition of personal and communal pain, joy, and the contradictions of life these both illuminate. It is a window that, once opened and peered through, can never be slammed fully shut again, and the vision gained, willingly or not, will make us different people. For this we can give credit and thanks, at least in some small part, to the unique and traditional style of Hebrew poetic expression.

Types of Psalms

HAVING CONSIDERED THAT the psalms are poetic compositions created according to a recognizable set of poetic conventions, we are left to ask, "What kinds of compositions did these ancient Hebrew poets write?" In the Western world we find sonnets, and odes, the humorous limerick, as well as other poetic forms. What types of poems are characteristic of Hebrew poetry?

Ancient Psalm Types

IF YOU WILL look closely at the psalm headings (especially in the original Hebrew), you will discover a number of terms (such as *mizmor, higgayon, miktam, tepillah, maśkil, šir, šir hammaᶜalot, tehillah,* perhaps *yedidot*, and the even more obscure *ᶜedut*) that seem to describe types of psalms. It seems probable, then, that the ancient Hebrew poets who wrote and transmitted the psalms had some sense of the category of composition each psalm represented and were able to designate them appropriately.

It is unfortunate that we nowhere possess a contemporary Hebrew discussion of poetic technique and psalm types. While the psalmists must have known how to compose psalms of various types, they clearly felt no need to leave us any description of what constitutes the characteristics of a particular type of psalm—a *higgayon*, for example—and what distinguishes it from a *miktam* or a *maśkil*. As a result, we are mostly left in the dark, having to rely on our own surmises from literary analyses of the psalms themselves and by comparison of psalms that bear the same designations in their headings. Scholarly investigation into this subject has been done with somewhat mixed results.

By and large, psalms with the same ancient designations fail to manifest any constellation of formal similarities except in the most general sense. While it may be true (as many suggest) that the fifteen Songs of Ascent (Pss. 120–134) are a collection of pilgrim songs, the literary character of these psalms ranges from prayers for deliverance (120; 123; 125; 126; 129; 130) through worship liturgies (121; 132; 134) to a thanksgiving hymn (124), praises of Zion (122), acts of submission (131), and descriptions of the blessings of the faithful (127; 128; 133). While the whole collection bears a stamp of similar themes and language, there is no clear way to distinguish the prayers of deliverance found here from others outside the collection.

Other of these ancient terms apparently do mark out psalms of more consistent character. The term *miktam*, for example, is found in the heading of six psalms (16; 56; 57; 58; 59; 60). Of these six, the five contiguous psalms (56–60) fall within the modern category of laments or prayers for deliverance from trouble. The sixth (the more isolated Ps. 16) disrupts this apparent consistency, however, because it is a decidedly different expression of confidence in Yahweh. Even if one were to assume that the true nature of the *miktam* is exhibited by the five grouped psalms, one must admit there is no certain way to distinguish the prayers for deliverance *they* represent from other such prayers found throughout the rest of the Psalter.

The same is true of the *tepillah* psalms (17; 86; 90; 102; 142?), all of which appear also to be prayers for deliverance or healing but are indistinguishable from similar psalms found elsewhere in the Psalter. Thus, the comparison of psalms bearing the same ancient designation in their headings has offered no convincing evidence of distinctive structure or content that sets each of these types of psalms apart from other psalms designated differently.

Some have attempted to illuminate these ancient designations of poetic form by relating them to similar terms in the broader ancient Near East. The enigmatic *biggayon* (Ps. 7) is sometimes connected to the Akkadian *šegu* ("lament"), while others have derived the meaning "psalm of expiation" for *miktam* from the Akkadian *katamu* ("cover"). In all instances, these connections are tenuous at best, far from compelling, and provide little help in determining the formal distinctives that characterize these compositions.

The upshot of all this investigation is that, while we are almost certain that the ancient poets composed psalms in a variety of forms and knew the distinctive characteristics of each type (it would seem utterly ridiculous if they did not!), we are no longer able to recover with any assurance what those ancient categories were or how they differed from one another. For this reason, modern attempts to categorize the psalms have most often proceeded in a different direction, using literary analysis and comparison to develop a new taxonomy of the psalms—from the inside out, so to speak.

Modern Attempts to Categorize the Psalms

ONE OF THE most fruitful attempts to understand the psalms in the modern period began in the early 1900s and sought to describe various categories into which the biblical psalms could be sorted, based on literary analysis of the structure and contents of the psalms rather than any prior knowledge of the ancient terminology employed in the psalm headings or any assumption of authorship and provenance of the psalms. The methodology grew in response to several centuries of *historical criticism* on the biblical texts, which tended to disregard or certainly to question the widely held assumption of the Davidic authorship of most of the psalms. These historical critics had concluded (with a great deal of truth and insight, I believe) that it is difficult and practically impossible to place each psalm in a precise historical setting that explains its origin and illumines its references. More skeptically (and with less insight, in my opinion) many critics concluded that most of the psalms are late products of the Second Temple period and tell little about the period of the united or divided monarchy with which they have always been associated.

By way of contrast and correction, *form criticism*, as the newer method of inquiry came to be called, drew on increasing evidence of centuries-long periods of *oral* transmission of fundamental traditions and socially significant narratives in tribal societies. The form critics held that behind the written literary form of the biblical literature (which may have been fixed at a later date) stood a long history of oral transmission of Israelite narratives and traditions that originated far earlier and much closer to the events described than historical critics had assumed. In regards to the biblical psalms, this suggested that many of the psalms might well date from the divided and even the united monarchy and reflect accurately the social, political, and religious setting of those periods.

Hermann Gunkel and psalm types. Early form criticism on the psalms is traced to the fundamental work of the German scholar Hermann Gunkel (1862–1932). Gunkel was strongly influenced by the earlier work of the Brothers Grimm to collect, analyze, and categorize German folk tales that had circulated for centuries in mostly oral form. The Grimm brothers had discovered that centuries of oral repetition of these tales shaped the way they were presented.

Often these stories began and ended with formulaic phrases. We may recognize this from our own exposure to childhood fairy tales (many of which are derived from the collections of the Brothers Grimm!). Just ask any child how a fairy tale begins, and she will reply knowingly, "Once upon a time. . . ." How do they end? "And they lived happily ever after!" The Grimms concluded such stock phrases were the result of oral presentation, making the stories easier to remember for the teller, to communicate to the audience from the beginning the nature of the tale to come, and to heighten everyone's anticipatory participation.

The literary shape that structured the fairy tales (and other kinds of literary units derived from oral tradition) was called a *form* (German *Gattung*), which explains why the kind of literary analysis and investigation that led to the discovery of more and more new forms was termed *form criticism* (German *Gattungsforschung*). Form critics hold that each form develops from a particular setting in life (German *Sitz im Leben*) and serves a distinct purpose and that both setting and purpose can be perceived by paying close attention to the formulaic phrases, literary structure, and content of the various examples of the type.

Compare, for example, two distinct types of musical composition known as the *march* and the *waltz*. The former is derived from a military context and is intended to move masses of soldiers forward in unison, enlivening their loyalty, and encouraging and emboldening them for the attack. Marches employ a regular rhythm matching the stride of marching soldiers (hence the name). Some marches are accompanied by lyrics that make their purpose plain. By contrast, waltzes hardly ever have lyrics. Their rhythm is lyrical and romantic, with a certain syncopation. Their distinctives are the result of their purpose: whirling dances, intended to heighten joy and romantic excitement. They allow individual movement of couples in concert with others on the dance floor. Setting and purpose dictate form.

A literary example might be various types of letters. In our contemporary world, most letters conform to a standardized structure or "form." Usually the name and address of the recipient is given, followed by an opening greeting. The latter almost always begins with the descriptive adjective "Dear," regardless of whether one is greeting one's lawyer, accountant, grandmother, lover, or an unknown person ("Dear Occupant"). This standardized form has essentially lost its original function. We no longer intend to communicate endearment with this greeting, as can be realized by its frequent use to address obviously "un-dear" recipients (like creditors or the IRS). Following the salutation comes the body of the letter, and then the whole communication is concluded with a description of the writer's sincerity ("Sincerely yours") or affection ("Cordially," "Affectionately"), and the signature.

Almost all letters share these common elements of form: address, greeting, body, conclusion, signature. These formal elements distinguish a letter from, let's say, a will or a short story. It is possible, however, to distinguish further categories within the general classification of letters. These are usually marked out by the content of the body of the letter or how the formal elements described above are varied for different purposes. In informal letters between friends, the opening address is often omitted, relegated to the outside of the envelope. The greeting can also vary considerably, depending on whether you are addressing someone unknown ("To Whom It May Concern") or an intimate associate or romantic partner ("My Dearest Darling").

When Hermann Gunkel began to apply the method of form criticism to the biblical psalms, he opened up what led to almost a century of exciting and fruitful investigation of these texts. Prior to Gunkel's work, most of the psalms had been considered the products of individuals in response to specific moments of personal history. Often, where no author was mentioned, David was assumed to have written a psalm, and numerous speculations were made to place the psalms within specific historical circumstances of his life. Such a move was obviously encouraged by the historical notices in thirteen psalm headings that describe some specific circumstances in David's life thought to have provided occasion for that psalm (cf. Pss. 3; 18; 34; 51; 52;

54; 56; 57; 59; 60; 63; 142). But when no such setting is suggested in the heading of the psalm itself, any attempt to provide such a connection is always speculative, subject to considerable debate, and is, as a result, usually less than fully persuasive. Form criticism, despite its support for the early origin of many psalms, has proven little better in achieving consensus in describing the actual, specific historical circumstances of individual psalms.

The genius of Gunkel's approach, however, is that form-critical analysis offers a means of discovering a more general *Sitz im Leben* that stands behind all psalms of a similar type, while stopping short of claiming to have found the specific historical occasion of the psalm. Even if the author and the specific historical setting of a psalm remain cloaked from view, the more general *Sitz im Leben* can be divined through clues in the text, language, and form of the psalm itself. All laments share an experience of a time of "trouble" from which the psalmist seeks deliverance, regardless of whether that trouble is disease, oppression, personal sin, military threat, poverty, injustice, or slander. It is the common response to "trouble" that influences the form or shape of the laments and makes them together into a form-critical *Gattung*.

It is in fact the *lack* of extreme specificity about historical setting and its details that frees the psalms to continue to speak powerfully to a variety of settings and circumstances throughout history. It is this adaptability that makes the psalms such an important source of spiritual insight and application even today, and this fact may well explain why a particular selection of 150 psalms came to be chosen out of several centuries worth of psalmic compositions to form the authoritative collection of canonical Scripture. The more closely a psalm is tied to a specific historical setting and its attendant details, the more difficult it becomes to use it insightfully in my own present circumstances.[18]

Sigmund Mowinckel and liturgical setting. As a result of his form-critical analysis, Hermann Gunkel began to isolate a variety of distinctive psalm types and to define their characteristics. I will return to a discussion of these individual types a bit later. Gunkel further categorized each type of psalm depending on the dominant voice he found displayed in the text. If the voice is first person and singular ("I"), the psalm is an *individual* psalm. When the speaker is first- or second-person plural ("we" or "you"), the psalm regardless

18. A brief introduction in English to the essentials of Gunkel's approach is available in: Hermann Gunkel, *The Psalms*, trans. Thomas M. Horner (Philadelphia: Fortress, 1967). A recent translation of Gunkel's original *Einleitung in den Psalmen* is now available in Hermann Gunkel and Joachim Begrich, *An Introduction to the Psalms: The Genres of the Religious Lyric of Israel*, trans. James D. Nogalski (Macon, Ga.: Mercer Univ. Press, 1998).

of its type is considered a *communal* composition, expressing the insights and circumstances of the community as a whole.

Gunkel held that some individual psalms were just that: private declarations of individual persons to their God. Other psalms, while marked by the voice of an individual, nevertheless exhibited clear evidence of having been part of communal worship. Gunkel recognized the liturgy of the temple worship system could represent one important setting behind many psalms, whether individual or communal.

Other form critics, however, claimed a much more extensive role for temple liturgy in understanding the psalms. Scandanavian scholar Sigmund Mowinckel (1884–1965) went so far as to deny the private nature of *any* of the 150 canonical psalms. He was influenced by the Scandanavian *myth and ritual* school of interpretation, which held that all religious texts were shaped within the religious worship system of a people. According to this viewpoint, religious texts were used in worship to reenact significant recurring experiences (proponents called them "myths") of religious faith.

Mowinckel sought to relate all 150 psalms to what he described as a yearly reenactment within temple worship of the enthronement of Yahweh as king of Israel and of the cosmos. The major stumbling block for such a view is that there is no clear indication in Scripture (or outside it, for that matter) that such a reenactment ever took place in Israel, nor is there any description of the nature, contents, and structure of such a festival. Consequently, Mowinckel had to draw on the yearly Mesopotamian Akitu Festival celebrating the marriage of the Mesopotamian king (representing the god Tammuz) and the high priestess of Ishtar (representing the goddess herself) as a model for the kind of celebration he assumed occurred with each new year in Israel.

According to Mowinckel, Psalms 93–99, with their prevailing theme of the kingship of Yahweh, formed the core liturgy of this enthronement festival. The Israelite king was assumed to play the role of Yahweh in the festivities, and most (if not all) of the 150 psalms were assigned a role in Mowinckel's hypothetically reconstructed festival liturgy.

Although Mowinckel's theory won a number of supporters, it seems problematic in my opinion. First, there is no mention or description of any such fall enthronement festival anywhere in the biblical corpus, which seems an amazing omission if an event of such proportions and significance truly existed. The Old Testament describes many other annual festivals in considerable detail, but Mowinckel's festival remains hidden. As a result, this theory must be reconstructed according to nonbiblical parallels from Mesopotamia. Attempts to place all 150 psalms within the hypothetical framework of the festival are frequently forced and have achieved little consensus.

Second, the claim that a full understanding of the psalms can be gained only by rearranging them to fit within a hypothetical liturgical structure has several additional negative results. Such a move erodes our ability to read the psalms separately as models of individual prayer. This flies in the face of the long history of interpretation of the psalms and runs counter to the strong textual tradition maintaining the distinct identity of the 150 psalms within a particular canonical arrangement. This is a matter to which I will return in my discussion of "The Shape of the Psalter" in the second volume of this commentary.

Moreover, connecting the psalms to a specific historical festival in the life and worship of ancient Israel heightens the alien *otherness* of these compositions and increases to an extreme the historical and cultural distance between them and our own contemporary circumstance. This tends to make it much more difficult to interpret the psalms for application to our own lives.

As a result of these difficulties, Mowinckel's theory and the later developments introduced by those who followed his lead have not gained universal acceptance. However, they have had the positive effect of opening our eyes to the strong rooting that many psalms have within the temple worship system of Israel and have encouraged us to notice and highlight evidence of such usage whenever it is present.[19]

Other scholars, including Artur Weiser, have adopted more modest modifications of Mowinckel's festival claims. Weiser proposes a yearly covenant-renewal festival taking place at the Israelite New Year and during which the kingly authority of Yahweh over Israel was reaffirmed, employing the core Psalms 93–99. He did not try to fit all of the psalms into such a framework, admitting many psalms were independent from such concerns. Weiser's claims are less radical and less objectionable than Mowinckel's in my mind, especially since he relies primarily on categories derived from Israelite religious tradition and thought. The covenant motif is well established throughout the Hebrew Bible, and we do have evidence of covenant renewal ceremonies in several Old Testament passages (although never on an annual basis). His model, however, still suffers from some of the same criticisms as Mowinckel's, including the silence on such a yearly covenant-renewal festival in biblical literature and the largely hypothetical nature of his reconstruction and the requisite rearrangement of the psalms.[20]

19. A good introduction to Mowinckel's thought in relation to the psalms can be found in Sigmund Mowinckel, *The Psalms in Israel's Worship*, 2 vols., trans. D. R. Ap-Thomas (Nashville, Tenn.: Abingdon, 1962).

20. For an English version of Weiser's own discussion of his views on the covenant-renewal festival, see Artur Weiser, *The Psalms: A Commentary*, trans. Herbert Hartwell (OTL; Philadelphia: Westminster, 1962), esp. 23–51.

Three Primary Categories

WHILE GUNKEL'S ANALYSIS of the biblical psalms uncovered a number of distinct psalms types, three categories emerged as primary forms: praise, lament, and thanksgiving. When viewed together, these three primary psalm types exhibit a similar structure. While there are a variety of exceptions to the rule, most psalms of these types begin with an introduction, continue with a body, and draw to a conclusion. What provide the distinguishing characteristics of each category of psalm are the specific contents of these structural sections. I will make a few general remarks about these distinctions here. For a more complete discussion with examples, see the extended essays on specific types later in the commentary.

Praise. Praise psalms contain an appeal (to self or others) to praise God, coupled with numerous descriptions of his praiseworthy name, deeds, attributes, and character. The focus is on God's role as creator, sustainer, and stabilizer of the universe—humanity's sole assurance of continued stability and reliability in a chaotic world. For the most part praise psalms admit no hint of suffering or disorder; rather, they express an awe-filled sense of confidence in God's power, authority, and everlasting character displayed both in the world of nature and of human affairs. Examples of the type include Psalms 8; 29; 33; and 146–150.[21]

Lament. By contrast, the lament psalms direct their appeal to God himself, seeking deliverance from trouble and distress. The world of the lamenting psalmist is fully aware of the possibilities and realities of suffering, disorder, sin, and oppression that are a part of living in the world. Indeed, the laments find their focus in recounting how life has run amok despite the power and grace of Yahweh. Experience of pain often drives the psalmists to question the sure foundation represented by God's creative power and sustaining authority. They experience God as distant (or even hostile, as in Ps. 88), and like Job muster arguments to motivate him to act in their behalf. Examples of laments include Psalms 22; 74; 88; and 130.[22]

Thanksgiving. Thanksgiving psalms occupy a territory that lies somewhere between praise and lament. Like the laments, thanksgiving songs are only too well aware of the reality of pain in all its forms. The heart of most thanksgiving psalms is a narrative of sin, treachery, oppression, suffering, or threat that characterizes the disordered world of the psalmist. The distinction that sets these narratives apart from those present in lament psalms is one

21. See the section "Praise and Thanksgiving" in the materials preceding the commentary to Pss. 90–106.

22. For further discussion, see "The Laments" at the end of the comments on Ps. 3.

of time. For the lament, suffering describes the *present and continuing* experience of the psalmist, while in thanksgiving psalms the suffering and pain described lie *in the past.*

Alongside this very real awareness of pain and suffering in life, the thanksgiving psalms reaffirm a confidence in the saving power and grace of a God who has entered the life of the psalmist (and readers) to redeem and transform. Their grateful response to the experience of deliverance draws the thanksgiving psalms more closely to the language and spirit of the praise songs. As a result, thanksgiving and praise often become difficult to distinguish since they employ a similar vocabulary and explore a similar terrain. Ultimately, however, it is thanksgiving's deep roots in the pain and disorder of a sinful world at odds with its creator that draws the line between thanksgiving and praise. Examples of thanksgiving psalms include Psalms 104; 107; 116; and 136.[23]

Other psalm types. Alongside these three primary types of psalms, Gunkel and subsequent form critics have isolated a number of distinctive psalm types present in the Psalter. There is less agreement about some of these categories than in the case of praise, lament, and thanksgiving, but several significant types of psalms ought to be included in our discussion. Some will receive fuller treatment at appropriate points within the commentary.

Royal psalms. The earlier discussion of Mowinckel's enthronement festival has already noted the important role envisioned for the Israelite king in the festal liturgy. While Mowinckel's specific festival of enthronement remains doubtful, a number of psalms suggest the king could exercise an important function in temple worship. These psalms, which clearly focus their concern on matters relating to the king and his political, social, and religious duties, are considered a form-critical category and are usually referred to as royal psalms.

It is generally accepted that this group of psalms was used in "ceremonies whose central figure was the king" (von Rad). There is fairly close agreement on the contents of this category, with most scholars listing nine to eleven compositions (Pss. 2; 18; 20; 21; 45; 72; 89; 101; 110; 132; 144:1–11). While these eleven psalms do share a common concern with the king that sets them apart as a category, they reflect a variety of psalm types, some of which can be fruitfully compared with other psalms of similar type. These psalms include kingly laments (Pss. 89; 144) and thanksgiving (Ps. 18), quite comparable to those included in the broader contents of these primary categories.

23. See "Praise and Thanksgiving" in the materials preceding the commentary on Pss. 90–106.

Other royal psalms reflect circumstances and concerns more narrowly related to the role of the king. In Psalms 2 and 132, for example, the psalmists celebrate the divine selection of the Davidic dynasty for rulership. By contrast, Psalm 89 laments the apparent demise of the Davidic kingdom in the Exile. Psalm 45 was likely written on the occasion of a royal wedding, while Psalms 20–21 and 110 are concerned to secure divine support for the king's military endeavors. In Psalm 101, the king pledges to rule justly, while Psalm 72 seeks to pass on divine blessing to the king's descendants and successors.

The number and variety of these royal psalms point up the important role the Israelite kings played in religious life in general and temple worship in particular. A number of Old Testament passages describe the king's acting in priestly ways—such as offering sacrifices, leading processions—and David and Solomon in particular are revered for their roles in establishing the Jerusalem temple and temple worship system.

Liturgical psalms. While it appears unreasonable to claim that *all* of the 150 canonical psalms were created for use in the temple worship of Israel, it is certainly true that many psalms show clear evidence of having been shaped in this context. These psalms exhibit clear awareness of the ritual activities of Israelite worship, including sacrifice, ritual processions, pilgrimage, antiphonal singing, and physical movements of the worshipers and celebrants (prostration, bowing, movement of the hands, etc.).

Particularly clear in their liturgical character are certain of the thanksgiving psalms (Heb. *todah*) that offer evidence of having been recited in the temple as testimony to the deliverance from trouble provided by Yahweh. Most likely thanksgiving psalms were recited along with the presentation of the thanksgiving sacrifice (*todah*), which publicly testified to the offerer's experience of deliverance. In Psalm 66:13–15 for example, the psalmist, who has thus far been calling others to praise and bless Yahweh for his terrible deeds and mighty acts, repeats the vow made earlier during the time of distress to offer sacrifice in the temple when deliverance came:

> I will come to your temple with burnt offerings
>   and fulfill my vows to you—
> vows my lips promised and my mouth spoke
>   when I was in trouble.
> I will sacrifice fat animals to you
>   and an offering of rams;
>   I will offer bulls and goats.

Such passages illustrate how recitation of the psalms (and thanksgiving psalms in particular) could be at once individual acts of worship enacted corporately within the communal setting of temple worship.

Psalm 118 offers a further, yet more enigmatic example of liturgical activity in temple worship when, in the midst of thanksgiving, the psalmist calls out in verse 19:

Open for me the gates of righteousness;
I will enter and give thanks to the LORD.

This seems to describe a moment in liturgical action at which the psalmist approaches the temple gates and requests admittance. In the following verse (v. 20), the requirement for entry is set forth—as if from the gatekeeper:

This is the gate of the LORD
through which [only] the righteous may enter.

A number of psalms speak of entering God's gates or courts (e.g., 100:4) or of coming into the divine presence (cf. 95:1–2; 109:30).

Even more enigmatic is the apparent liturgical instruction inserted in the midst of Psalm 118:27:

With boughs in hand, join in the festal procession
up to the horns of the altar.

While the verse is notoriously difficult and obscure, it still reflects the kind of liturgical activity in temple worship that stands behind many of the psalms.

Other psalms, rather than describing ritual liturgical activity and ceremony in temple worship, reflect the influence of such activity on their form and structure. The appearance of repeated phrases and refrains, for example, probably reflects the antiphonal singing of the temple choir guilds or perhaps moments of congregational response to choral singing. See especially the artfully varied repeated refrain that punctuates Psalm 107 after each segment describing the plight of various groups of faithful exiles, or perhaps pilgrims winding their dangerous way to the holy city (cf. 107:6–9, 13–16, 19–22, 28–32).

An even more exhaustive example of antiphonal response is to be found in Psalm 136, where every half verse is followed by an identical refrain.

Give thanks to the LORD, for he is good.
His love endures forever.
Give thanks to the God of gods.
His love endures forever.
Give thanks to the Lord of lords:
His love endures forever.
to him who alone does great wonders,
His love endures forever.

who by his understanding made the heavens,
His love endures forever. . . .

What might otherwise seem overly repetitious in a written text achieves great energy when recited orally in antiphonal form, drawing the participants into the ethos of thanksgiving and driving home the major theme of the psalm in a powerful way.

One subcategory of liturgical psalms derives from the moment at which the worshiper prepares for entry to the holy space of the Temple Mount. Before entering the steps leading up to the holy place, worshipers underwent a ritual cleansing by bathing themselves in the ceremonial *mikwaʾot* carved out of the limestone rock near the base of the steps. This ritual washing was a sign of the worshiper's repentance in preparation for entering the presence of Yahweh at the temple. Psalm 15 captures this moment in a challenging recitation of the qualifications expected of those who would presume to approach the holy place.

LORD, who may dwell in your sanctuary?
Who may live on your holy hill?
He whose walk is blameless
and who does what is righteous,
who speaks the truth from his heart
and has no slander on his tongue,
who does his neighbor no wrong
and casts no slur on his fellowman,
who despises a vile man
but honors those who fear the LORD,
who keeps his oath
even when it hurts,
who lends his money without usury
and does not accept a bribe against the innocent.
He who does these things
will never be shaken.

It is possible—evenly likely—that these words were spoken by a priest challenging worshipers to prepare themselves within and without, ritually and spiritually, to come to the house of God.

Psalm 24 envisions a similar challenge to a group of worshipers approaching the temple precincts. In verses 3–5 they ask:

Who may ascend the hill of the LORD?
Who may stand in his holy place?
He who has clean hands and a pure heart,
who does not lift up his soul to an idol

> or swear by what is false.
> He will receive blessing from the LORD
> and vindication from God his Savior.

The crowd then calls out twice (vv. 7, 9) as they approach the temple gates:

> Lift up your heads, O you gates;
> be lifted up, you ancient doors,
> that the King of glory may come in.

Those within the temple twice challenge those outside (vv. 8, 10):

> Who is this King of glory?

The psalm concludes in verse 10 with the worshiping throng's shouted profession of faith:

> The LORD Almighty—
> he is the King of glory.

Yahweh malak psalms. Related to the royal psalms by their emphasis on kingship, the *Yahweh malak* psalms are, however, distinguished by their concern with the kingly reign of Yahweh. Rather than the earthly kingship of the Israelite monarchs, this group of compositions celebrate the kingdom and rule of God.

The psalms that make up this category are for the most part found grouped together in the middle of the fourth book of the Psalter and include Psalms 93 and 95–99. The group takes its name from the exclamation "The LORD reigns!" (Heb. *yhwh malak*), which is repeated at the beginning of Psalms 93; 97; and 99.[24] Besides this distinctive phrase, these psalms refer in other contexts to Yahweh as king or mention his kingship or kingdom (cf. 95:3; 98:6; 99:4).

Yahweh's sovereign kingship is grounded in his creative power and authority. In 93:1–4, he establishes the world and overpowers the chaotic floods (cf. 96:10). Psalm 98:7–8 describes Yahweh's control of the depths and heights of the earth as well as the sea and dry land.[25] Yahweh is rightful king because the creation is his work. The whole earth breaks forth in joyful song in praise of the creator king (98:4, 7–8).

The theme of divine judgment is another repeated characteristic of the *Yahweh malak* psalms, a logical step from Yahweh's creative sovereignty and kingship is his right to judge the earth and all that lives in it. In 96:13, the whole creation rejoices because Yahweh arrives to "judge the world in righteousness and the peoples in his truth." There is such joy in the face of judg-

---

24. This phrase (or its near surrogate *malak ʾelohim*) is also found in Pss. 47:8; 96:10.
25. This is, of course, a double *merism*, indicating Yahweh's authority over the whole earth.

ment because the creation, distorted by sin and evil, anticipates being set right by the king who establishes order and justice (cf. also 98:9; 99:4).

These themes and characteristic language allow us to extend the number of *Yahweh malak* psalms beyond the core collection in Book 4. At least four such psalms share some of this distinctive phraseology. Three of these seem closely bound to the group, while the other appears more tangential in its relationship.

The first category (Pss. 33; 47; 149), despite being far removed from the core group, seem to deserve inclusion in the *Yahweh malak* collection. In Psalm 33, we encounter the instruction "Sing to him [Yahweh] a new song," a characteristic of this group. The psalm is a praise directed to Yahweh and makes references to his justice (v. 5) and creative power (vv. 6–7), counseling readers to respond in dependence and trust (vv. 12–22). While Yahweh acts in kingly ways throughout this psalm, however, he is never referred to using the term *melek* ("king").

Psalm 47 shares with the core group distinctive reference to Yahweh as king (47:2, 6, 7), his exercise of kingly authority (vv. 3–5), as well as a slight variation on the characteristic exclamation "*God* reigns" (v. 8), employing the more generic term *ʾelohim*.[26] The psalm further shares with the core group the emphasis on praise. Psalm 149 agrees with Psalm 47 and the core psalms by naming Yahweh as king and creator (v. 2), describing the exercise of justice (vv. 4, 6–9), and enjoining the reader to join in praising him (vv. 1–4, 6, 9).

The more tangential psalm (Ps. 144) shares certain phrases and concerns with the *Yahweh malak* collection but is clearly set off by its being a lament rather than a praise psalm. This psalm employs the characteristic term "new song" (144:9; cf. 33:3) in a narrative description of the psalmist's intent to praise Yahweh ("I will sing a new song to you, O God") rather than the more characteristic call to praise. But there is no mention of Yahweh as creator or connection to justice and righteousness. Instead, the psalmist calls on Yahweh to deliver Israel from her enemies (144:5–8, 11) and to bless her agriculturally (vv. 12–14).

The *Yahweh malak* psalms are an important collection in the theological emphases of the Psalter. They play a significant role in the shaping of the whole Psalter collection by providing a refocusing of emphasis from limited human kingship to enduring divine sovereignty of Yahweh.

Wisdom and Torah psalms. While a number of biblical psalms have traditionally been considered "wisdom psalms," considerable debate has raged—especially in the last twenty years or so—regarding what in fact constitutes

26. Ps. 47 is part of a Psalter subcollection known as the Elohistic Psalter. The chief characteristic of this subunit is that it employs more frequently the more generic term for God (*ʾelohim*), often in place of the more particular *Yahweh*.

a wisdom text and how one might go about identifying one. It seems appropriate, therefore, to begin with a brief description of wisdom and those characteristics that are generally agreed to set it apart from other types of literary approaches.

Wisdom is first and foremost a way of looking at life—similar to what we might call a "philosophy of life." The sages [Heb. *ḥakam/ḥakamim*] based their understanding of life on personal and transmitted observation and experience of life. Their concern was to enable themselves and others to understand how to relate to life appropriately so that they would achieve benefit rather than hurt. Out of this desire to observe, analyze, and teach are derived several of the most characteristic features of wisdom and its extant literature.[27]

(1) Perhaps most clearly wisdom literature is intended to teach. That is, it is didactic in form, tone, and contact. It often employs brief, memorable proverbs in order to communicate its findings and conclusions to those who would learn and benefit. The sages' writings are full of admonitions and exhortations (didactic tools), encouraging conformity to the way of wisdom and righteousness.

(2) Wisdom literature also often uses comparison and contrast to illustrate the respective consequences of wisdom and folly, obedience and rebellion, righteousness and wickedness. The proverbs are perfect examples of studied contrasts in their most condensed form, but the longer excursions of the sages—Proverbs 1–9, Job, and Ecclesiastes—are also shaped by contrast. The sages saw only two options in life—two ways that characterized human response to their teaching: The way of wisdom ended in life and blessing, while the way of folly followed rebellion to its ultimate end of judgment and death.[28]

(3) Traditional wisdom thinking reflected in the biblical wisdom literature also believed in retribution, that is, in an observable connection between human conduct and divine judgment or blessing. Most simply stated, the view concludes that "the wise prosper while the foolish perish." While some proverbial literature may give the impression that wisdom rather naively anticipated an immediate and consistent operation of retribution in all cases, the biblical wisdom literature, taken as a whole, recognizes and discusses at

---

27. The wisdom books of the Hebrew Bible are Proverbs, Ecclesiastes, and Job. The Apocrypha contains additional wisdom books, including the Wisdom of Ben Sira (Sirach) and the Wisdom of Solomon. Outside the Bible, wisdom was an international phenomenon known in Egypt and Mesopotamia, producing its own literature that is similar but not identical to biblical wisdom literature.

28. See esp. Proverbs, but also the discussions in Job and Ecclesiastes. Jesus' conclusion to the Sermon on the Mount follows in the wisdom tradition with his illustration of the contrasting fates of those who enter the wide or narrow gates and the two houses built on rock and sand.

length the complexity of the issue. Ecclesiastes, Job, and some of Proverbs recognize the reality of pain, suffering, and injustice for the righteous, debating at length how a good God of order can allow this to be so. But in the end the sages did not throw out retribution entirely but allowed the debate to stand enshrined in their literature, marking the tensions of a faith that could acknowledge the firm good intent of God toward those who fear him in the face of the clear vagaries of human pain and suffering.

(4) Wisdom vocabulary, while not always a conclusive proof of wisdom origin of a text, is nevertheless a helpful indicator of wisdom interests. One frequently finds the righteous opposed to the wicked or the wise contrasted with the fool. Explicit or implicit description of two ways—one ending in blessing and life, the other in judgment and death—are strong indicators of wisdom themes. The use of the Hebrew term *ʾašre* ("blessed") to describe the anticipated reward of the righteous/wise is common, as well as the phrase "fear Yahweh" to describe the appropriate relation of the wise to God.

(5) A final indicator of wisdom influence is the occasional use of the alphabetic acrostic form (see comments on acrostics in the section on "Types of Psalms," above).

In the Psalter, one can note wisdom interests and vocabulary to various degrees in a number of psalms. Psalm 1 shows clear contrast between the behavior and destiny of the righteous and the wicked. Psalm 37 also reflects interest in the two ways and the operation of retribution. It even contains clearly proverbial segments (cf. vv. 16–17, 35–36). Psalm 49 is didactic in tone and purpose, reflecting on the folly of pursuing wealth (similar to Eccl. 3:18–21) while concluding that righteousness and wisdom will prevail.

Psalm 34, like several other psalms,[29] is an alphabetic acrostic that also employs traditional wisdom terminology in phrases such as "blessed" (v. 8) and "fear the LORD" (v. 9). Since acrostic poems are employed on several occasions outside the Psalter to conclude compositions (Prov. 31:10–31; Sir. 51), it is particularly interesting to speculate on the placement of the acrostic wisdom Psalm 145, which appears toward the end of Book 5 and just before the concluding Hallel (Pss. 146–150).

Wisdom in its origins appears to have been founded primarily on what might today be called a "natural theology"—in others words, what can be known by observation and experience of the world rather than through special divine revelation. For that reason, wisdom texts often seem to ignore important elements of Israel's traditional religious worldview. There is little discussion of the covenant with Yahweh and necessary obedience to it, nor is much attention paid to worship, sacrifice, or the temple.

---

29. Pss. 9–10; 25; 37; 111; 112; 119; 145.

It does appear, however, that at a later point (some would pinpoint the Exile) Israel's sages came to equate the demands of wisdom with the covenant commandments of Yahweh. This is most clearly seen in the Apocrypha, where the identification of wisdom and the Torah (the revealed law and commandments) of Yahweh is complete.[30] As a result, some psalms that are focused on the praise of Torah and exhortation to obedience should be included among the wisdom psalms.

These Torah psalms certainly include Psalm 1, with its encouragement to delight in the Torah of Yahweh day and night, the continuous contrast between the righteous and wicked, and the acknowledgment of the two ways of life and death. Psalm 19:7–11 also celebrates the perfection of Torah, which, like the creation in the earlier verses of the same psalm, reveals the nature of Yahweh and offers the righteous blessing and reward. Finally, one should not forget the expansive Torah Psalm 119, which in each of its 176 verses of its alphabetic acrostic form offers some reflection on the excellence of the divine Torah.

Like the royal psalms, wisdom and Torah psalms frequently overlap other psalms types. Some wisdom psalms take the form of praise psalms, while others are akin to the laments (e.g., Ps. 34) or thanksgivings (e.g., Ps. 73). With the exception of the acrostics, it is ultimately the content, vocabulary, and thematic concerns that mark these compositions off as wisdom psalms.

In an additional similarity to the royal psalms, psalms reflecting wisdom concerns, themes, and vocabulary appear in significant locations within the Psalter, giving rise to the idea that they were purposefully placed to provide a structuring framework to the whole Psalter.[31] It is probably no accident that Psalm 1 stands at the beginning of the Psalter as an introduction. Neither is it coincidental, in my view, that wisdom concerns appear in Psalm 73, at the beginning of Book 3 of the Psalter, in Psalm 90 at the beginning of Book 4, and in Psalms 107 (vv. 41–43) and 145 (an alphabetic acrostic) at the beginning of Book 5.[32]

Miscellaneous types. Other terms are sometimes used to describe categories of psalms less common than those discussed above. I will discuss these types in conjunction with the commentary on specific psalms. Let me give a brief listing and examples of some of the more significant of these:

---

30. See esp. Sir. 24 and 39 for this complete identification. The process of identification may already be seen in its earlier stages in Prov. 1–9, where the commandments of the sages and wisdom are spoken of in terms similar to those normally reserved for the commandments of Yahweh. See Gerald H. Wilson, "The Words of the Wise: The Intent and Significance of Qohelet 12:9–14," *JBL* 103 (1984): 175–92.

31. See Wilson, *The Shape and Shaping of the Psalter*, 72–82.

32. For further discussion of this *wisdom* shaping of the whole Psalter, see "The Shape of the Psalter" in volume 2 of this commentary.

- psalms of confidence (trust): e.g., the familiar Pss. 23 and 91, along with 11; 62; and 131
- historical psalms: e.g., Pss. 78; 105; and 106
- entrance liturgies: e.g., Pss. 15 and 24 (esp. vv. 7–10)
- minor categories such as oracles, psalms of integrity, vows, and instructions

The Psalm Headings: Superscripts and Postscripts

SUPERSCRIPTS AND POSTSCRIPTS are well known in ancient writings, from Mesopotamian clay tablets, to Egyptian papyrus scrolls, to the literary scrolls and codex texts of the Greeks and Romans. These editorial comments appended to the beginning (*super*scripts) or the end (*post*scripts) of a literary composition provide information or instructions about the composition (or, in some cases, its assumed author or circumstances); they are not an integral literary part of it. In general one can say that in biblical literature and in related Canaanite literature from Ugarit, superscripts provide comments or instructions regarding the particular composition to which the superscript is attached, while postscripts are directed to larger organizational concerns.[33]

A Single Postscript

A SURVEY OF the biblical psalms turns up a large number of widely varied superscripts attached to individual compositions, but only a single clearly distinguished postscript. This lonely postscript is attached to the end of Psalm 72, in verse 20:

> This concludes the prayers of David son of Jesse.

This verse apparently marks the conclusion of a preceding collection of Davidic prayers; as a result it tells us little about the particular psalm to which it is attached.

There is some discussion and debate, however, about what comprises the collection to which this verse refers. Some suggest it has been misplaced

---

33. Haim M. I. Gevaryahu thinks that the psalm headings were originally colophons appended to the end of their psalm. He notes the psalm in Hab. 3, which has material normally included in psalm headings both at the beginning and the end (Hab. 3:1, 19) as evidence in this regard. For an English version of Gevaryahu's theory see H. M. I. Gevaryahu, "Biblical Colophons: A Source for the 'Biography' of Authors, Texts, Books," in *Congress Volume: Edinburgh 1974* (VTSup 28; Leiden: Brill, 1975), 42–59. For a more complete discussion of the function of superscripts and postscripts in Israel and the ancient Near East, see Gerald H. Wilson *The Editing of the Hebrew Psalter* (SBLDS; Chico, Calif.: Scholars Press, 1985), 139–55.

from an original position at the conclusion of Book 1 (Pss. 1–41), since all the psalms in the first book are Davidic, excepting the introductory Psalms 1 and 2, as well as Psalms 10 and 33, which have a tradition of being combined with the psalm that immediately precedes them (Pss. 9 and 32 respectively). Others limit the reference of the postscript to the immediately preceding Davidic psalms (Pss. 51–65; 68–70). Still others take it as referring to the combined collection of Psalms 1–72, which are dominated by the earlier Davidic collection in Book 1 and a significant contingent of Davidic psalms toward the end of Book 2 (51–65; 68–70).[34]

Perhaps the decisive factor in the discussion is the fact that this postscript appears directly *after* the expansive doxology (blessing pronounced on God) in 72:18–19. This doxology, as will be discussed below, is one of several similar doxologies that apparently were employed to mark the conclusions of the five books of the Psalter collection. If the postscript was intended to mark the final group of Davidic psalms in Book 2, it should have *preceded* the doxology. Whether the postscript ever graced the end of the first Davidic collection is a matter of pure speculation. Even if that were the case, its present placement at the end of Book 2 and after the doxology is not simply an accident but seems intended to mark the conclusion of the combined Psalter collection to that point.

The fact that Davidic psalms dominate Book 1 and bracket the combined two books at beginning and end, along with the Davidic emphasis provided by the thirteen psalms with historical notices connected to David's life, would seem sufficient warrant for the postscript's message. It is clear that this postscript makes no exclusive claim of Davidic authorship for the psalms contained in the combined first two books, since groupings of Davidic psalms appear throughout the three books of the Psalter that follow.[35]

Concluding Doxologies

AS BRIEFLY MENTIONED above, four somewhat similarly structured and worded doxologies appear at the conclusion of Psalms 41; 72; 89; and 106, which

34. It is of note that these Davidic psalms in Book 2 exhibit the greatest concentration of historical notices linking psalms to specific events in the life of David found anywhere in the Psalter. This certainly has the effect of heightening the Davidic character of the collection they conclude. Note also that Ps. 71, which separates the last Davidic psalm in Book 2 from Ps. 72 and its superscript, has considerable manuscript evidence of having been combined with Ps. 70.

35. It is interesting to speculate that the strong reference to the conclusion of the prayers of "David *son of Jesse*" that ties this collection closely to the specific human king David may suggest that later attributions of psalms to David in the succeeding books are increasingly intended to be taken as eschatologically focused references to the *messianic* David.

have long been thought to mark the segmentation of the Psalter into five "books." While it is not entirely correct to describe these doxologies with the term *postscript* since they contain no explicit instruction or explanation regarding the texts or collection to which they are appended, closer observation reveals that the doxologies do *function* similarly to the one true postscript mentioned above. Like 72:20, the doxologies are concerned with more than the composition to which they seem attached, and their concern is to mark the conclusion of the segment that precedes.

These doxologies appear in the earliest Hebrew manuscripts of the Psalter and are included in the Greek translation of the LXX as well. At an early date some of the rabbis and other interpreters of Scripture related the five Psalter divisions thus delineated to the five books of Moses in the Torah.[36] Some scholars have suggested that the fivefold division came about to order the psalms so they could be read in the synagogue along with the Torah selection. Attempts to show how psalms and Torah readings were intended to fit have been forced and less than persuasive, in my opinion.[37]

Regardless of *why* five divisions were created in the Psalter, it seems unquestionable now that the doxologies *were* employed for this purpose. In Mesopotamia, doxology was employed similarly to structure hymn collections.[38] Thus, it appears that structural elements attached at the end of a psalm should be understood as marking the conclusion of a series of psalms rather than just the composition to which they are attached.[39]

You may have noticed in the above discussion that no mention was made of a fifth doxology concluding the final book of the Psalter. The solution to this seeming omission is the generally accepted observation that the final Hallel (Pss. 146–150) stands at the conclusion of the whole Psalter collection and admirably fulfills the role of concluding praise of Yahweh.

---

36. "As Moses gave five books of laws to Israel, so David gave five Books of Psalms to Israel," in William G. Braude, *The Midrash on Psalms* (New Haven, Conn.: Yale Univ. Press, 1954), line 5.

37. For further discussion of the relationship of the Psalter books and the synagogal lectionary cycle see: Anton Arens, "Hat die Psalter seine 'Sitz im Leben' in der Synagogalen Leseordnung des Pentateuch?" in *Le Psautier, ses origines, ses problemes litteraires, son influence*, ed. Robert de Langhe (Orientalia et Biblica Lovaniensia 4; Louvain: Louvain Univ. Press, 1962); idem, *Die Psalmen in Gottesdienst des Altes Bundes* (Trier: Paulinus-Verlag, 1968); N. H. Snaith, "The Triennial Cycle and the Psalter," *ZAW* 10 (1933): 302–7; Wilson, *The Editing of the Hebrew Psalter*, 199–203.

38. See Åke Sjöberg, *The Collection of Sumerian Temple Hymns* (Texts from Cuneiform Sources 3; Locust Valley, N.Y.: J. J. Augustin, 1960). My own comments on the Sumerian Temple Hymn Collection are included in Wilson, *The Editing of the Hebrew Psalter*, 13–24.

39. For a more detailed discussion of why the doxologies in the Psalter ought to be considered purposeful indicators of division, see Wilson, *The Editing of the Hebrew Psalter*, 182–86.

Superscripts

UNLIKE THE POSTSCRIPTS that are concerned to organize, arrange, and ultimately to conclude what precedes, superscripts introduce the single composition to which they are attached and provide information about it. Most of the psalm headings contain a variety of terms that explain the presumed "author" of the psalm and the ancient category or type of psalm it represents; in many instances they go further to give instructions about the manner of performance (melody to be employed, instruments for accompaniment, tuning of the instruments, and setting in worship).

Twenty-four of the 150 canonical psalms have no heading.[40] An additional ten psalms are introduced only by the cultic shout "Hallelujah," which also concludes a few of these "untitled" psalms.[41] That leaves the vast majority of psalms (126) bearing some sort of psalm heading. These headings may be as brief as a single word—e.g., *ledawid* ("to/for/of/by/concerning David"; cf. Pss. 25–28; 138; 144) or *mizmor* ("psalm"; cf. Ps. 98)—or may be quite complex and extended (e.g., the headings to Pss. 60 and 88).

Authorship. Of the psalms, 101 bear in their headings the name of some specific person or group of persons. Those mentioned are: David (73 psalms), Asaph (12), the Korahites (11), Solomon (2), Moses (1), Ethan (1), and Heman (1). The exact nature of these references to persons continues to be debated. It has traditionally been assumed they are attributions of the author of specific psalms. The debate centers on the significance of the Hebrew preposition *le-* attached to each of these names. This preposition has a variety of nuances, including "of, by, for, to, concerning, about." This ambiguity has led others to suggest these names might represent the style of composition (as "in the style of David"), the one providing authorization for a composition ("by the authority of David"), the person to whom the composition was dedicated ("[dedicated] to/for David"), or in some instances the person(s) responsible for performing the psalm in temple worship ("for the Korahites").[42]

---

40. Pss. 1; 2; 10; 32; 42; 71; 91; 93; 94; 95; 96; 97; 99; 104; 105; 107; 114; 115; 116; 117; 118; 119; 136; 137.

41. Hallelujah introduces Pss. 106; 111; 112; 113; 135; 146; 147; 148; 149; 150. Hallelujah concludes Pss. 104; 105; 106; 115; 116; 117; 135; 146; 147; 148; 149; 150. This distinctive phrase functions like neither superscript or postscript. It is rather a liturgical shout within worship.

42. The debate has found its way into the modern translations of the psalm headings. Compare, e.g., the NIV translation of the heading of Ps. 50 ("A psalm of Asaph") with that of the REB ("A psalm: for Asaph"). The NIV's use of the translation "of" allows more ambiguity, since it can be understood both in the sense "psalm *written by* David" or "psalm written *in the style of* the Davidic psalm type." The REB, however, has eliminated the possibility of a reference to authorship by its use of "for." The ancient Greek translation of the LXX has chosen to render the Heb. preposition *le-* with the dative case (*tō* rather than *tou*).

It is impossible to resolve this issue decisively. Even the appearance in a significant number of psalms of historical notices connecting each psalm to a specific context in David's life does not necessarily presume Davidic authorship, since they may just as well be "*about* David . . . when he was in the Desert of Judah" (Ps. 63).

Ancient types of psalms. Also included in many psalm headings are terms describing ancient categories of psalms. These include: *mizmor* (57 psalms), *šir* (30), *maśkil* (13), *miktam* (6), *tepillah* (5), *tehillah* (Ps. 145), *šiggayon* (Ps. 7). Some would include *halleluyah*[43] (16) in this list, although it is not clear that this phrase represents a psalm heading, since it often appears at the conclusion of psalms and may represent a liturgical shout within worship and would thus be an integral part of the literary composition. (For further discussion of these ancient psalm types, see "Types of Psalms," above.)

Musical instructions. Other terms within the psalm headings seem clearly to reflect instructions concerning the musical presentation of these psalms in temple worship.[44] These can be divided into the following:

(1) reference to the director: the frequently occurring phrase *lamnaṣṣeaḥ* ("To the director. . .")

(2) instructions regarding melody or tuning of the harp: usually introduced by the Hebrew preposition *ʿal*, as in Psalm 6: *ʿal haššeminit* (". . . according to *sheminith*"—a tuning of the harp); Psalm 9: *ʿalmut labben* ("To the tune of *To the Death of the Son*")

(3) instrumentation: introduced by the Hebrew preposition *be-*, as in Psalm 6: *binginot* ("with stringed instruments . . .")

(4) context within worship: introduced by the Hebrew preposition *le*, as in Psalm 92: *leyom haššabbat* ("for the Sabbath day"); Psalms 38 and 70: *lehazkir* ("for the memorial offering)"; Psalm 100: *letodah* ("for the thank offering").

---

43. *BHS* suggests the *halleluyah* postscript at the end of Ps. 113 should instead be taken as the superscript of the following Ps. 114—the only psalm in the sequence of Pss. 111–117 not to bear either a *halleluyah* superscript or postscript. If this shift were made alone, the total number of *halleluyah* psalms would be 16. However, *BHS* (following the Greek and Syriac versions) also recommends that Ps. 115 should be read together with 114 as a single psalm and that the postscripts of Pss. 115–117 should all be shifted to superscripts of the following psalms (Pss. 116–118). In this reconstruction the number of *halleluyah* psalms would remain 15, but would be expanded to include Ps. 118.

44. One of the better and more consistent discussions of the terminology of the psalm headings is found in J. F. A. Sawyer, "An Analysis of the Context and Meaning of the Psalm-Headings," in *Transactions of the Glasgow University Oriental Society 1967/1968* (Leiden: Brill, 1970), 26–38. Also useful and insightful is the extended treatment of the psalm titles in the commentary by H.-J. Kraus, *Psalms 1–59: A Commentary* (Minneapolis: Augsburg, 1988), 21–23.

Historical notations. Thirteen psalms[45] include with their headings reference to some event in the life of David presumed to be the context for the psalm's composition. While most of the events mentioned can be found in the narratives of Samuel–Kings, others are more ambiguous or obscure.

Origin of the Psalm Headings

SCHOLARS HAVE ATTEMPTED to describe the historical development of the psalm headings.[46] There has been a general willingness to distinguish temporally between the origin of the liturgically oriented references of the headings and the more narrative historical notices relating to David's life. Normally the historical notices are understood to be later than the liturgical elements. Some have suggested that attributions of authorship may have been added independently of the liturgical notices—and probably at a later date. Others go so far as to view the different elements of the liturgical instructions as representing several distinct layers of additions built up over a longer period of time—a view that has yet to win general acceptance.[47]

The most usual scenario suggested sees three layers of accretion. (1) The liturgical elements were added—perhaps while the psalms were still in use in temple worship (thus the references to the director), but perhaps representing notes appended when the psalms were gathered into more literary collections before inclusion in the Psalter. (2) Traditions of "authorship" were added, with collections developing around specific authors. (3) The historical notices were appended—possibly as the result of exegetical interpretation of the texts in light of the presumed author's life setting.

Several features of the psalm headings in the LXX add some weight to this suggestion. The Greek translation of the liturgical terms and notices evidence a degree of uncertainty and confusion. The rather standard instruction "To the director" is translated *eis to telos* ("To the end [of time]"). This and other equally awkward renderings suggest the translators had only an imperfect understanding of these liturgical terms. This likely means that the liturgical elements were early enough for their meaning to have been partially

---

45. The thirteen psalms with historical notices are: Pss. 3; 7; 18; 34; 51; 52; 54; 56; 57; 59; 60; 63; and 142.

46. See Gevaryahu, "Biblical Colophons," 42–59; idem, "Notes on Authors and Books in the Bible," *Beth Mikra* 43 (1970): 368; Jesús Encisco Viana, "¿Como se formo la primera Parte del libro de los Saomos?" *Bib* 44 (1963): 129–58; idem, "Los titulos de los Salmos Y la historia de la formacion del Salterio," *Estudios Biblicos* 13 (1954): 135–66; Brevard S. Childs, "Psalm Titles and Midrashic Exegesis" *JSS* 16 (1971): 137–50; Shemaryahu Talmon, "*Pisqah beᶜemṣaᵓ pasuq* and 11 Q Ps^{a}," *Textus* 5 (1966): 11–21.

47. Viana, "Los titulos de los Salmos," 135–66.

obscured by the time of the Greek translation—at least those terms specifically related to temple worship.

By contrast, the LXX not only acknowledges the author designations in the Hebrew psalm headings but adds to them considerably, increasing the number of Davidic psalms and including attributions to persons and historical contexts that do not appear in the Hebrew versions.[48] This suggests that the author attributions and historical references were later than the liturgical elements and were still in a state of some fluidity. The appearance among the Qumran psalms scrolls and fragments of additional psalms, Davidic attributions, and historical notices not included in the canonical Psalter supports this developing view.

Consequently, it appears that the psalm headings developed over a considerable period of time. Certain elements—probably the liturgical instructions—were appended quite early, while others (designation of authors and historical notices) continued to be added over time. If the evidence of the Qumran scrolls suggests continued fluidity in psalm collection and the addition of psalm headings, then this process does not seem to have been completed before the mid-first century A.D.[49]

48. The LXX includes references to Jeremiah and Ezekiel in the heading of Ps. 65 (LXX 64) and mentions Haggai and Zechariah in the headings of four psalms (LXX 145 = MT 146; LXX 146 = MT 147:1–11; LXX 147 = MT 147:12–20; LXX 148 = MT 148). The LXX includes Davidic references in LXX 70 = MT 71 and LXX 90 = MT 91, which the Heb. text leaves completely untitled. A historical reference to the "Assyrian" appears in the heading to LXX 79 = MT 80. Pss. 93–95, which are untitled in the Heb., receive liturgical headings in the LXX (92–94). A historical reference in LXX 143 = MT 144 mentions Goliath.

49. For an interesting consideration of how the psalm headings can bring light to the arrangement of psalms and the shaping of the whole Psalter, see "The Shape of the Psalter" in the second volume of this commentary.

Outline

I. Book 1 (Pss. 1–41)
  A. Introduction to the Psalter
    Psalm 1 The Way God Knows
  B. Establishment of Davidic Covenant
    1. Introduction: Great Expectations
      Psalm 2 Promise of Eternal Rule of the King
    2. Facing Contradictions of the Real World
      Psalm 3 The Attack of Many Foes
      Psalm 4 Distorted Worship
      Psalm 5 Deceitful Enemies
      Psalm 6 Personal Weakness
      Psalm 7 Protestation of Innocence
      Psalm 8 Humility in the Presence of God
      Psalms 9/10 God Is King and Refuge
      Psalm 11 God Is Judge and Refuge
      Psalm 12 The Arrogance of the Wicked
      Psalm 13 Trust in the Face of Divine Absence
      Psalm 14 Corruption of the Fools
      Psalm 15 The Standard of Divine Support
      Psalm 16 God Is Support and Refuge
      Psalm 17 Commitment to Righteousness
      Psalm 18 God Is Strength and Refuge
      Psalm 19 Divine Revelation and Guidance
      Psalm 20 Prayer for Divine Deliverance of the King
      Psalm 21 The King Trusts in God's Strength
      Psalm 22 The Agony of Divine Absence
    3. Hope for Dwelling in the House of Yahweh
      Psalm 23 Protection in the Presence of Enemies
      Psalm 24 Who Can Dwell in the House of God?
      Psalm 25 Trusting in God
      Psalm 26 Protestation of Righteousness
      Psalm 27 Desiring to Dwell in Yahweh's House
      Psalm 28 Relying on God's Mercy
      Psalm 29 Meeting in the House of Yahweh
      Psalm 30 Thanksgiving for Deliverance

4. God as Refuge and Hiding Place
   - Psalm 31 God Is Deliverer and Refuge
   - Psalm 32 Hiding Place for Those Who Confess
   - Psalm 33 Joy and Reliance in God the Almighty
5. Hope for the Destruction of the Wicked
   - Psalm 34 God Will Cut off the Wicked
   - Psalm 35 God Will Vindicate the Righteous
   - Psalm 36 Evildoers Lie Fallen, Never to Rise
   - Psalm 37 The Evil Will Be No More
6. Confession and Waiting for God
   - Psalm 38 Confession as Foundation of Deliverance
   - Psalm 39 Humility as Foundation of Deliverance
   - Psalm 40 Endurance as Foundation of Deliverance
   - Psalm 41 The King Waits for Yahweh

II. Book 2 (Pss. 42–72)

A. Davidic Covenant Continues

1. Communal Longing for Restoration
   - Psalms 42/43 Longing and Hope for Restoration
   - Psalm 44 Historical Contradictions
2. God as King and Hope for the Future
   - Psalm 45 The Glory of God and King
   - Psalm 46 God Is Fortress and Refuge
   - Psalm 47 God Rules as King over the Earth
   - Psalm 48 God Rules from Zion
   - Psalm 49 World Called to Understand Redemption of God
3. Call to Repentance and Confession
   - Psalm 50 God Calls Israel to Repentance
   - Psalm 51 The King as Model Confessor
   - Psalm 52 The Evil Destroyed, the Righteous Flourish
   - Psalm 53 Foolish Resistance to Repentance
4. Communal Plea for Restoration
   - Psalm 54 Desire for Vindication
   - Psalm 55 Attack from Within and Without
   - Psalm 56 Trust in the Face of Attack
   - Psalm 57 God Is Faithful and Refuge
   - Psalm 58 God Condemns Rulers of the Earth
   - Psalm 59 God Judges the Nations of the Earth
5. The Agony of Divine Rejection
   - Psalm 60 Trust in the Face of Divine Delay

6. Reliance and Universal Restoration
   - Psalm 61 — Commitment from the Ends of the Earth
   - Psalm 62 — God Is Salvation and Refuge
   - Psalm 63 — Trust in God Is Better Than Life
   - Psalm 64 — All Humanity Will Fear God
   - Psalm 65 — The World Comes to God in Hope
   - Psalm 66 — The World Bows Down to God
   - Psalm 67 — All the Peoples of the Earth Praise God
   - Psalm 68 — God Establishes His Kingship over All the Earth
7. Deliverance and Praise
   - Psalm 69 — Continued Need for Forgiveness and Deliverance
   - Psalms 70/71 — Praising God for Deliverance and Refuge

B. The Hope of the Davidic Kings
   - Psalm 72 — The King's Son Rules the World

Select Bibliography

Commentaries

Allen, Leslie C. *Psalms 101–150*. WBC 21. Waco, Tex.: Word, 1983.

Broyles, Craig C. *Psalms*. NIBC. Peabody, Mass.: Hendrickson, 1999.

Cheyne, T. K. *The Book of Psalms*. New York: Thomas Whittaker, 1895.

Craigie, Peter C. *Psalms 1–50*. WBC 19. Waco, Tex.: Word, 1983.

Dahood, Mitchell. *Psalms I (1–50)*. AB. Garden City, N.Y.: Doubleday, 1965.

_____. *Psalms II (51–100)*. AB. Garden City, N.Y.: Doubleday, 1968.

_____. *Psalms III (101–150)*. AB. Garden City, N.Y.: Doubleday, 1970.

Delitzsch, Franz. *Biblical Commentary on the Psalms*. 3 vols. Grand Rapids: Eerdmans, repr. 1970.

Hossfeld, F.-L., and E. Zenger. *Die Psalmen. Psalm 1–50*. Die Neue Echter Bibel. Wurzburg: Echter Verlag, 1993.

Kidner, Derek. *Psalms 1–72*. TOTC. Downers Grove, Ill.: InterVarsity, 1973.

_____. *Psalms 73–150*. TOTC. Downers Grove, Ill.: InterVarsity, 1975.

Kirkpatrick, A. F. *The Book of Psalms*. Cambridge: Cambridge Univ. Press, 1957.

Kraus, H.-J. *Psalms 1–59:. A Commentary*. Minneapolis: Augsburg, 1988.

_____. *Psalms 60–150: A Commentary*. Minneapolis, Augsburg, 1989.

Mays, James L. *Psalms*. Interpretation. Louisville, Ky.: John Knox, 1994.

Rogerson, J. W., and J. W. McKay. *Psalms 1–50*. The Cambridge Bible Commentary. Cambridge: Cambridge Univ. Press, 1977.

_____. *Psalms 51–100*. The Cambridge Bible Commentary. Cambridge: Cambridge Univ. Press, 1977.

_____. *Psalms 101–150*. The Cambridge Bible Commentary. Cambridge: Cambridge Univ. Press, 1977.

Schaefer, Konrad. *Psalms*. Berit Olam. Collegeville, Minn.: Liturgical, 2001.

Tate, Marvin E. *Psalms 51–100*. WBC 20. Dallas, Tex.: Word, 1990.

Weiser, Artur. *The Psalms*. OTL. Philadelphia: Westminster, 1962.

Introductions

Anderson, Bernhard W. *Out of the Depths: The Psalms Speak for Us Today*. 3d ed. Louisville: Westminster John Knox, 2000.

Bonhoeffer, Dietrich. *Psalms: The Prayer Book of the Bible*. Trans. James H. Burtness. Minneapolis: Augsburg, 1970.

Bullock, C. Hassell. *Encountering the Book of Psalms: A Literary and Theological Introduction.* Grand Rapids: Baker, 2001.

Crenshaw, James L. *The Psalms: An Introduction.* Grand Rapids: Eerdmans, 2001.

Drijvers, Pius. *The Psalms: Their Structure and Meaning.* New York: Herder & Herder, 1965.

Gerstenberger, Erhard S. *Psalms. Part I.* Forms of the Old Testament Literature. Grand Rapids: Eerdmans, 1988.

Gunkel, Hermann. *The Psalms.* Trans. Thomas M. Horner. Minneapolis: Augsburg Fortress, 1967.

Gunkel, Hermann, and Joachim Begrich. *An Introduction to the Psalms: The Genres of the Religious Lyric of Israel.* Trans. James D. Nogalski. Macon, Ga.: Mercer Univ. Press, 1998.

Lewis, C. S. *Reflections on the Psalms.* New York: Harcourt Brace, 1958.

Longman, Tremper III. *How to Read the Psalms.* Downers Grove, Ill.: InterVarsity, 1988.

McCann, J. Clinton, Jr. *A Theological Introduction to the Book of Psalms: The Psalms as Torah.* Nashville, Tenn.: Abingdon, 1993.

Miller, Patrick D., Jr. *Interpreting the Psalms.* Philadelphia: Fortress, 1986.

Murphy, Roland E. *The Gift of the Psalms.* Peabody, Mass.: Hendrickson, 2000.

Seybold, Klaus. *Introducing the Psalms.* Trans. Graeme Dunphy. Edinburgh: T. & T. Clark, 1990.

Other Studies

Allen, Leslie C. *Psalms.* Word Biblical Themes. Waco, Tex.: Word, 1987.

Alter, Robert. *The Art of Biblical Poetry.* New York: Basic Books, 1985.

Bellinger, W. H. *Psalms: Reading and Studying the Book of Praises.* Peabody, Mass.: Hendrickson, 1990.

Braude, William G. *The Midrash on Psalms.* New Haven, Conn.: Yale Univ. Press, 1954.

Brueggemann, Walter. *The Message of the Psalms.* Minneapolis: Augsburg, 1984.

_____. *Israel's Praise: Doxology Against Idolatry and Ideology.* Philadelphia: Fortress, 1988.

_____. *Abiding Astonishment: Psalms, Modernity, and the Making of History.* Louisville, Ky.: Westminster John Knox, 1991.

Childs, Brevard S. "Psalm Titles and Midrashic Exegesis," *JSS* 16 (1971): 137–50.

Creach, Jerome. *Yahweh as Refuge and the Editing of the Hebrew Psalter.* JSOTSup 217. Sheffield: JSOT Press, 1996.

Crim, Keith R. *The Royal Psalms.* Richmond, Va.: John Knox, 1962.

Eaton, John. *Psalms of the Way and the Kingdom: A Conference with the Commentators.* JSOTSup 199. Sheffield: Sheffield Academic, 1995.

Gerstenberger, Erhard S. "Enemies and Evildoers in the Psalms: A Challenge for Christian Preaching." *HBT* 4 (1982–1983): 61–77.

Gevaryahu, H. M. I. "Biblical Colophons: A Source for the 'Biography' of Authors, Texts and Books." Pp. 42–59 in *Congress Volume: Edinburgh 1974*. VTSup 28. Leiden: Brill, 1975.

Hobbs, T. R., and P. K. Jackson. "The Enemy in the Psalms." *BTB* 21 (1991): 22–29.

Holladay, William L. *The Psalms Through Three Thousand Years*. Minneapolis: Fortress, 1993.

Köhler, Ludwig H. "Psalm 23." *ZAW* 68 (1956): 227–34.

Kraus, Hans-Joachim. *Theology of the Psalms*. Trans. Keith Crim. Minneapolis: Augsburg, 1986.

Kugel, James. *The Idea of Biblical Poetry: Parallelism and Its History*. New Haven, Conn.: Yale Univ. Press, 1981.

Lewis, C. S. "Meditation in a Toolshed." Pp. 212–15 in *God in the Dock*. Grand Rapids: Eerdmans, 1970.

Longman, Tremper III. *How to Read the Psalms*. Downers Grove, Ill.: InterVarsity, 1988.

Mays, James L. *The Lord Reigns*. Louisville: Westminster John Knox, 1994.

_____. "The Place of the Torah Psalms in the Psalter." *JBL* 106 (1987): 3–12.

Miller, Patrick D., ed. *The Psalms and the Life of Faith*. Minneapolis: Augsburg Fortress, 1995.

_____. *They Cried to the Lord: The Form and Theology of Biblical Prayer*. Minneapolis: Fortress, 1994.

Mowinckel, Sigmund. *The Psalms in Israel's Worship*. 2 vols. Trans. D. R. Ap-Thomas. Nashville, Tenn.: Abingdon, 1962.

McCann, J.Clinton Jr., ed. *The Shape and Shaping of the Psalter*. Sheffield: JSOT Press, 1993.

Reid, Stephen Breck, ed. *The Psalms and Practice: Worship, Virtue, and Authority*. Collegeville, Minn.: Liturgical, 2001.

Rösel, Christoph. *Die messianische Redaktion des Psalters: Studien zu Enstehung und Theologie der Sammlung Ps. 2–89**. Stuttgart: Calwer Verlag, 1999.

Rowley, H. H. *The Servant of the Lord and Other Essays on the Old Testament*. London: Lutterworth, 1952.

Sanders, James A. *The Dead Sea Psalms Scroll*. Ithaca, N.Y.: Cornell Univ. Press, 1967.

Sawyer, J. F. A. "An Analysis of the Context and Meaning of the Psalm-Headings." *Transactions of the Glasgow University Oriental Society* 22 (1967/1968): 26–38.

Watson, Wilfred G. E. *Traditional Techniques in Classical Hebrew Verse*. JSOTSup 170. Sheffield: Sheffield Academic, 1994.

Westermann, Claus. *Praise and Lament in the Psalms*. Trans. Keith R. Crim and Richard N. Soulen. Atlanta, Ga.: John Knox, 1981.

_____. *The Psalms: Structure, Content and Message*. Trans. Ralph D. Gehrke. Minneapolis: Augsburg, 1980.

Whybray, Norman. *Reading the Psalms as a Book*. JSOTSup 222. Sheffield: Sheffield Academic, 1996.

Willis, John T. "Psalm 1—An Entity." *ZAW* 9 (1979): 381–401.

Wilson, Gerald H. *The Editing of the Hebrew Psalter*. Chico, Calif.: Scholars, 1985.

_____. "The Use of Royal Psalms at the 'Seams' of the Hebrew Psalter." *JSOT* 35 (1986): 85–94.

_____. "The Shape of the Book of Psalms." *Int* 46 (1992): 129–42.

_____. "Songs for the City: Interpreting Biblical Psalms in an Urban Context." Pp. 231–43 in *Psalms and Practice*. Collegeville, Minn.: Liturgical, 2000.

_____. "A First Century C.E. Date for the Closing of the Hebrew Psalter?" *Jewish Bible Quarterly* 28 (2000): 102–10.

_____. "Psalms and Psalter: Paradigm for a Biblical Theology." In *Biblical Theology: Retrospect and Prospect*. Ed. Scott Hafemann. Downers Grove, Ill.: InterVarsity, forthcoming.

Yoder, P. B. "A-B Pairs and Oral Composition in Hebrew Poetry." Pp. 90–109 in *Poetry in the Hebrew Bible*. Ed. David E. Orton. Leiden: Brill, 2000.

Zenger, Erich. *A God of Vengeance? Understanding the Psalms of Divine Wrath*. Louisville, Ky.: Westminster, 1994.

Psalm 1

The Shape of Book 1 (Psalms 1–41)

THE MOST IMMEDIATELY obvious characteristic of Book 1 of the Psalter is its dominant Davidic character. Assuming the special character of the untitled Psalms 1 and 2 as introductory, we are left in this initial section with thirty-nine psalms, of which all but two bear attribution to David in their headings—employing the simple although somewhat ambiguous[1] construction *ledawid*, meaning "to/for/by/concerning/under the authority of/in the style of David." The two anomalous psalms (Pss. 10 and 33) have no headings, but each preserves a textual tradition of having been combined with the psalm that immediately precedes (Pss. 9 and 32 respectively). If we accept the tradition for the combination of these aberrant psalms with their immediate predecessors, Book 1 of the Psalter is a uniformly Davidic collection bounded at the beginning by Psalms 1 and 2 and concluded by the doxology in 41:13: "Praise be to the LORD, the God of Israel, from everlasting to everlasting. Amen and Amen."[2]

Between these two boundary posts, Book 1 is characterized largely by individual psalms and pleas for deliverance. Of the compositions in the book, twenty-seven are *clearly* individual psalms,[3] of which eighteen are pleas for deliverance.[4] An additional seven psalms (9; 10; 18; 21; 30; 32; 34) offer thanksgiving for deliverance from trouble, and five more (14; 15; 35; 36; 37) provide instruction regarding the experience of evil in the world. By contrast, unambiguous praise of Yahweh is encountered in only five psalms (8; 16; 19; 29; 33), and confident reliance on Yahweh is expressed in only three (11; 23; 27). A single psalm (24) represents an entrance liturgy.

---

1. For further discussion of the ambiguity of the Heb. construction (preposition *le-* + personal name) that is generally assumed to indicate authorship, see the section "Psalm Headings" in the Introduction.

2. The references in the English Psalter are often one verse different from the Hebrew Psalter, since the latter often considers the title as verse 1. This commentary will follow English versification.

3. To say a psalm is "individual" is not to say that it could not have been performed as part of the communal worship of Israel. This may often have been the case, esp. when the individual was the king, who exercised a representative role within temple worship.

4. Pss. 3; 4; 5; 6; 7; 12; 13; 17; 20; 22; 25; 26; 28; 31; 38; 39; 40; 41.

Following the elevated hopes for kingship expressed in Psalm 2, Book 1 shifts decisively into a block of pleas for deliverance at its opening (3–7) and concludes with an extended block of psalms focused on instruction concerning continuing evil in the world (35–37) and additional pleas for deliverance (38–41). Between these two extremes, psalms with an awareness of evil and trouble (thanksgiving, instruction, pleas) outnumber psalms of praise and reliance two to one.[5] The effect of this arrangement is to focus the collection on the experience of pain and suffering rather than on praise of God for a well-ordered and firmly established world.

Despite the appearance of reliance and praise scattered through the middle of this first book, the overriding sense expressed is of attack, suffering, and the need for divine deliverance. Even though the central expression of the collection (Ps. 21) is a thanksgiving psalm celebrating the victory granted the king against his enemies, this joyous psalm is preceded by a prayer for deliverance (20) and followed by agonized prayer of suffering and abandonment (22). This leaves the reader with the impression that any sense of victory is fleeting while suffering and distress are constant in life.

Elsewhere I have suggested that the first three books of the Psalter (Pss. 1–89) are arranged in a sort of rough commentary on the Davidic kingship by the strategic placement of royal psalms.[6] Book 1 announces the institution of the kingship with the promises of universal dominion (Ps. 2), but quickly slides into mourning and pleas for divine deliverance in Psalm 3 and following. A real sense is established here of the frailty of human power,[7] the secure refuge God affords, and the need for divine deliverance and protection. The last four psalms (38–41) are bounded before and after with prayers for deliverance from sickness—a circumstance that accords well with David at the conclusion of his own life and reign. While some may question whether these psalms were actually written by David, they do reflect the uncertainty, confusion, and plotting that characterize the transition between kings, even within the Davidic dynasty.

---

5. From Ps. 8 to Ps. 34, there are eighteen psalms categorized as plea, thanksgiving, or instruction, as compared to only nine psalms in the categories of praise, reliance, or entrance liturgy.

6. Gerald H. Wilson, "The Use of Royal Psalms at the 'Seams' of the Hebrew Psalter," *JSOT* 35 (1986): 85–94; idem, "The Shape of the Book of Psalms," *Int* 46 (1992): 129–42.

7. Ps. 8: "What is man that you are mindful of him, the son of man that you care for him?" (8:4). Ps. 19: "Who can discern his errors? Forgive my hidden faults. Keep your servant also from willful sins; may they not rule over me. Then will I be blameless, innocent of great transgression" (19:12–13). Ps. 33: "No king is saved by the size of his army; no warrior escapes by his great strength. A horse is a vain hope for deliverance; despite all its great strength it cannot save" (33:16–17).

If this were the end of the Davidic collection, then the situation would seem dismal indeed. But the combination of this first book with the second, as the postscript in 72:20 suggests, expands the Davidic collection by the addition of Psalms 42–72. This provides the first Davidic collection with a different terminus ("This concludes the prayers of David son of Jesse"), and, as we will consider in "The Shape of Book 2," with a different character. As it stands, Book 1 does not represent the end of the Davidic dynasty but mirrors at its conclusion (38–41) the difficulty of transition from one king to subsequent generations.

The uncertainty reflected in these concluding psalms is also consonant with that experienced by the Diaspora community, who had known not just the death of a king but of the monarchy altogether. The grouping of Psalms 38–41 here provides counsel and hope that would have resonated deeply with the needs of those struggling to survive in exile. These psalms affirm that despite the suffering of attack, Yahweh is the only source of salvation; he *is* salvation! (38:22). The appropriate response to the continuing suffering is to acknowledge it is a just, divine rebuke for sin (38:1; 39:10) and to wait silently for divine redemption (38:13–16; 39:1–3, 8–9). Psalm 40 mirrors this same kind of enduring patience in the face of suffering and adds an attitude of expectant anticipation (see the Bridging Contexts section of Ps. 40).

The whole grouping and Book 1 conclude with Psalm 41 and its description of the suffering weakness of one facing death from disease. Remarkably this psalm begins with the by-now familiar cry "Blessed" (*ʾašre*), which links this final psalm back to 2:8 and its triumphant celebration of the election of the Davidic dynasty for powerful rule over the nations. Although the situation reflected at the conclusion of Book 1 is radically different (as was the circumstance of the exilic community), the call for blessing remains unchanged. Those who took refuge in the conquering king in 2:8 have now become those who cast their lot with the "weak" (41:1), but both remain "blessed" in their enduring patience to wait for the coming one.

1 Blessed is the man
who does not walk in the counsel of the wicked
or stand in the way of sinners
or sit in the seat of mockers.
2 But his delight is in the law of the LORD,
and on his law he meditates day and night.
3 He is like a tree planted by streams of water,
which yields its fruit in season
and whose leaf does not wither.
Whatever he does prospers.

[4]Not so the wicked!
They are like chaff
that the wind blows away.
[5]Therefore the wicked will not stand in the judgment,
nor sinners in the assembly of the righteous.
[6]For the LORD watches over the way of the righteous,
but the way of the wicked will perish.

IF YOU WERE to open a handwritten medieval manuscript of the Psalms at its beginning, chances are that you would discover this psalm—the first in the canonical collection—written in red ink and without any evidence of a number.[8] That is because at an early date the psalm we now know as Psalm 1 was understood to be an introduction to the *whole Psalter* rather than just another psalm. It is likely that the final editors of the Psalter chose Psalm 1 as the gateway to the psalms because it encourages the readers/hearers[9] to consider the songs that follow to have the effect of divine guidance or *torah*. This psalm also exhorts the readers both to read the psalms and to meditate deeply on the message God is communicating through them. It strongly affirms that how one responds to the revelation of God unleashed by reading the psalms determines one's ultimate destiny.

The use of Psalm 1 as an unnumbered preface to the whole Psalter may also explain the description in Acts 13:33 (in some Western manuscripts of the Greek New Testament) of a quotation from what we now consider Psalm 2:7 as having been taken from the "first psalm." Apparently in that manuscript tradition what we now call Psalm 1 was either unnumbered or had not yet been appended to the beginning of the collection.[10] In either case, the special character of this psalm as introductory is affirmed.

---

8. The two great collators of manuscripts of the Heb. Old Testament and their numerous variations, Benjamin Kennicott and Johannes Bernhardus de Rossi—both of whom did their work in the mid to late eighteenth century—each list a number of manuscripts in which Ps. 1 is left unnumbered as a *preface* to the whole Psalter. Cf. Wilson, *The Editing of the Hebrew Psalter*, 204–5.

9. We must always remember that while the psalms are now part of Scripture and accessed primarily through the act of reading and meditation, in their origin they were performance pieces, spoken out loud and thus available to the ear. It is important to consider how *hearing* the psalms in the context of public, corporate worship is a decidedly different experience from *reading* them in the course of private study and devotion.

10. The final fixation of the Psalter arrangement may have taken place as late as the end of the first century A.D. (cf. Gerald H. Wilson, "A First Century C.E. Date for the Closing for

Psalm 1 is described both as a *wisdom* psalm and as a *Torah* psalm.[11] The former designation recognizes the standard wisdom motif of the "two ways" (1:6) of righteousness and wickedness (1:1, 4–6) as well as the characteristic wisdom exhortation "Blessed!" (*ʾašre*) at the beginning of the psalm. The designation as a Torah psalm is a response to the centrality accorded the *torah* (NIV "law") in verse 2. Other such Torah psalms (19; 119) appear in significant locations within the Psalter and provide a thematic focus for the final form of the whole collection.[12]

Structurally Psalm 1 is arranged into a series of two-verse comparisons between the lifestyle, consequences, and divine evaluation of the alternative "ways" taken by the righteous and wicked. Three such comparisons are offered: (1) guilt by association (1:1–2); (2) identifying fruits (2:3–4); (3) ultimate consequences (1:5–6). In addition, the first and fifth verses intentionally employ similar terms and motifs of standing in the public assembly to drive home the contrast between the ultimate destiny of the righteous and the wicked.

The psalm is, then, an exhortation—through positive and negative examples—to adopt the fruitful and satisfying life characterized by immersion in God. Then and only then will the faithful find themselves on the "way" that is blazed and watched over by God himself.

Guilt by Association (1:1–2)

THE OPENING BLESSING of the psalm (*ʾašre*) is common enough in the wisdom teaching of the Old Testament to recognize it as a characteristic method of the sages to exhort hearers to right action.[13] The word "blessed" conveys the

---

the Hebrew Psalter," *Jewish Bible Quarterly* 28 [2000]: 102–10). An alternative solution is that Pss. 1 and 2 were read *together* as a single psalm and introduction to the Psalter. Kennicott also mentions seven Hebrew manuscripts of the Old Testament that do not separate between Pss. 1 and 2. The joining of untitled psalms with adjacent compositions that *do* have titles is relatively common in ancient manuscripts of the Psalter (cf. the chart in Wilson, *The Editing of the Hebrew Psalter*, 134–35). Others suggest that these originally independent compositions have been purposefully placed together at the beginning of the Psalter to introduce the whole collection (cf. Craig C. Broyles, *Psalms* [NIBC; Peabody, Mass.: Hendrickson, 1999], 41–42).

11. See the discussion of the Torah psalms in James L. Mays, *The Lord Reigns* (Louisville, Ky.: Westminster John Knox, 1994), 128–35.

12. Cf. James L. Mays, "The Question of Context in Psalm Interpretation," in *The Shape and Shaping of the Psalter*, ed. J. C. McCann (Sheffield: JSOT Press, 1993), 14–20; idem, "The Place of the Torah-Psalms in the Psalter," *JBL* 106 (1987): 3–12.

13. Outside the Psalms, the term *ʾašre* is found at Deut. 33:29; 1 Kings 10:8; 2 Chron. 9:7; Job 5:17; Prov. 3:13; 8:32, 34; 14:21; 16:20; 20:7; 28:14; 29:18; Eccl. 10:17; Isa. 30:18; 32:20; 56:2; Dan. 12:12. Within the Psalms *ʾašre* is found at Pss. 1:1; 2:12; 32:1, 2; 33:12; 34:8; 40:4; 41:1; 65:4; 84:4, 5, 16; 89:15; 94:12; 106:3; 112:1; 119:1, 2; 127:5; 128:1, 2; 137:8, 9; 144:15; 146:5.

idea of happiness that flows from a sense of well-being and rightness. The same term probably originally underlies the "blessed" of the Beatitudes in Matthew 5.[14]

Who does not walk . . . stand . . . sit. The positive exhortation leads to a negative example. This is a lifestyle to be avoided, not emulated. The sequence of verbs employed describe a life immersed and focused on association with all that is opposed to God. The order of these verbs may indicate a gradual descent into evil, in which one first walks alongside, then stops,[15] and ultimately takes up permanent residence[16] in the company of the wicked.

The passage has interesting similarities with the important command following the Shema (Deut. 6:4: "Hear, O Israel: The LORD our God, the LORD is one") that faithful Israelites were to share Yahweh's commandments with their children "when you sit at home and when you walk along the road, when you lie down and when you get up" (Deut. 6:7).[17] While the parallels are not exact, both passages illustrate a totality of experience in which one is immersed, focused, and committed to a culture of association that dominates and shapes a worldview. In light of the move in Psalm 1:2 to direct the hearer's attention to constant meditation on and delight in Yahweh's *torah*, the contrasting profession and command from Deuteronomy may well have been in the back of the psalmist's mind.

Wicked . . . sinners . . . mockers. The categories of persons mentioned can be instructive as well, and these groups of opponents of God return often in the remainder of the psalms. The "wicked" (*rešaᶜim*) are those who have been judged "guilty" in a court of law or would be if brought to trial. In a legal contest between two parties, a judge would hear the testimony of the parties and make a determination (*mišpaṭ*) of the facts of the case and what the individual parties *should* have done in response. What actually happened is then compared with this *mišpaṭ*, and judgment is pronounced on each party. Those who appropriately fulfilled the expectations of the *mišpaṭ* were proclaimed *ṣaddiq* ("righteous"), while those who failed to live up to this standard were pronounced *rašaᶜ* ("guilty"). These pronouncements were

14. "Blessed" in the Beatitudes is a translation of the Greek *makarios*. This same Greek word is used to translate *ʾašre* in the LXX version of Ps. 1.

15. The verb *ᶜmd* has more the sense of "take a stand" than simply "stand still." There is volition (and therefore responsibility) assumed in this action.

16. The verb *yšb* can mean "sit down" or often "dwell, take up permanent residence" in a place.

17. This exhortation to Israel also occurs at Deut. 11:19 in almost exactly the same language—an indication that this idea of the need to keep God's guiding instruction constantly present and in mind was an important and formative part of Israel's religious identity.

made publicly, and so the *rešaʿim* (plural of *rašaʿ*) bore the approbation of their community.

The second term, *ḥaṭṭaʾim* ("sinners"), emphasized the fallibility of individuals who have an inclination to sin. Such persons have not just committed an isolated act of evil but live lives dominated and shaped by their inclinations. The difference of nuance between *rešaʿim* and *ḥaṭṭaʾim* is perhaps similar to that of the person convicted of a single theft compared with a career criminal. In the psalms, however, these two terms are often synonyms.

The final term, *leṣim* ("mockers"), describes those who have gone beyond a few sinful acts and even a personal life marked by an inclination to wrongdoing. They actively seek through their mockery to express disdain for right living and seek to belittle and undermine those who want to be righteous.[18] Mockers act out of overweening pride (Prov. 21:24) and refuse to seek or accept instruction or correction (9:7, 8; 13:1; 15:12). Through their disdain they stir up anger and strife (20:1; 22:10; 29:8). There is solidarity in numbers, and those who associate with such mockers often adopt their mocking ways and their ridicule of the path of righteousness.

Delight . . . in the law of the LORD. The psalmist now turns to describe an alternative lifestyle and association that lead to the blessing with which Psalm 1 begins. The transition is marked by a significant "but" (*ki ʾim*). This phrase is often used (as here) to introduce an exception after a negative statement and has the effect of "but rather," expressing an appropriate alternative to what has preceded. Rather than associating with the proponents of evil, the readers/hearers are encouraged to immerse themselves in daily delight in Yahweh's Torah.

Often the Hebrew word *torah* is identified with *the* Law—the primary identifying document of Israelite (and later Jewish) faith. The Torah in this sense refers to the first five books of our Old Testament—Genesis through Deuteronomy—which as a unified collection came to a final form as authoritative Scripture only in the exilic period (ca. 450–400 B.C.).[19] While this is an appropriate understanding of *torah* in many contexts, the word often has

18. This is the only occurrence of *leṣ/leṣim* (a Qal participle of *lyṣ*) in the psalms. Outside the Psalter the term occurs only once in Isa. 29:20 and fourteen times in Proverbs (1:22; 3:34; 9:7, 8; 13:1; 14:6; 15:12; 19:25, 29; 20:1; 21:11, 24; 22:10; 24:9).

19. This is not to suggest that these books were simply created wholesale during the Exile, but that the ancient traditions about Israel's formative circumstances were given their final shaping at that time and in response to the needs of the exilic community. This final shaping is most often associated with the work of the scribe Ezra, who returned from Babylonian exile (ca. 450 B.C.) with a copy of the "Book of the Law" with which to guide the life of the fledgling religious community of returnees in Jerusalem. This Torah became the primary understanding of Jewish faith and practice.

a much more general sense of "guidelines, instruction." This sense is by far the more common use in wisdom contexts, and since our psalm clearly moves in the wisdom environment, many have suggested it is this more general meaning that is appropriate here.

It may be possible to affirm both levels of meaning in this instance. As James L. Mays has shown us,[20] Psalm 1 is the first of several Torah psalms strategically placed within the book of Psalms (1; 19; 119). These psalms exhort the hearers/readers to pay close attention to God's commandments and to be faithful in their response to them. At the same time, however, the wisdom understanding of *torah* prevents easy limitation to the five books of *the* Torah. Biblical wisdom literature had already begun to identify *torah* (the life-giving commandments of Yahweh) with the life-giving insights given by Yahweh through the wisdom tradition.[21] Thus, most likely *torah* here implies the traditional commandments of God in *the* Torah—commandments Israel is expected to obey—as well as the life-giving guidance God gives elsewhere in Scripture. Brevard Childs is undoubtedly right when he observes that the function of this exhortation in the introductory psalm of the Psalter is to encourage the readers to meditate on the book of Psalms as Scripture and to seek there God's message that guides and establishes the life of faith.[22]

Meditates day and night. The verb *hgh* ("meditates") is onomatopoeic in that it imitates the sound of low voices murmuring or muttering as one reads Scripture in a low undertone. It appears to have been normal practice at the time to read out loud in a low voice rather than silently. The term can also mean "ponder/reflect" by talking to oneself. In Psalm 2:1, the same verb may be rendered "hatch a plot" in low conversations with one's coconspirators. Psalm 1, however, stresses careful, diligent attention to Scripture seeking God's guidance for life.

The seriousness of the investigation is indicated by its duration during both "day and night." This is, of course, a merism, in which the two extremes are mentioned to include all in between as well. The sectarian community of

---

20. James L. Mays, "The Place of the Torah Psalms in the Psalter," *JBL* 106 (1987): 3–12.

21. This identification of wisdom and *torah* is seen in subtle ways within the canonical literature, such as when Prov. 1–9 subtly speaks of wisdom in terms normally reserved for *the* Torah or when Deuteronomy speaks of Israel's obedience to *the* Torah as her *wisdom* (Deut. 4:1–6; cf. Gerald H. Wilson, "The Words of the Wise: The Intent and Significance of Qohelet 12:9–14," *JBL* 103 [1984]: 175–92.) The identification of *torah* and wisdom is more completely and explicitly mentioned in the later apocryphal wisdom books (cf. Sir. 24; 39).

22. Brevard S. Childs, *Introduction to the Old Testament as Scripture* (Philadelphia: Fortress, 1985), 513–14.

Essenes, who withdrew from general society to a commune near the shore of the Dead Sea from approximately 160 B.C. to A.D. 70, took seriously such enjoinders to constant study. Their community rule explicitly mandated that at every hour of day or night someone should be studying and interpreting God's *torah*.[23] The psalmist clearly sees such purposeful immersion in the *torah* as an effective antidote to the inappropriate association with evil described in verse 1. Not only are students of *torah* occupied, but *torah* so feeds and shapes the mind and heart of those who give themselves to it that their feet are kept firmly on the path of life.

Fruitful Living (1:3–4)

THE SECOND COMPARISON flows out of the first: Diligent study of *torah* is not only delightful occupation but yields fruitful results as well. The image of the tree planted by a source of abundant water is known to us also from the similar passage in Jeremiah 17:7–8. There as here the description of the fruitful tree is part of a balanced comparison between those who trust in humans and those who place their trust in Yahweh. In both passages, the tree is part of a blessing on the faithful—although in the Jeremiah passage the term "blessing" is *baruk* rather than Psalm 1's *ʾasre*. The opening phrases of these descriptions are almost identical:

Jeremiah 17:8	"He will be like a tree planted by the water. . . ."
Psalm 1:3	"He is like a tree planted by streams of water. . . ."

Both passages go on to comment on the enduring quality of the tree's leaves as well as its consistent fruitfulness, although not in terms as identical as the opening phrase. Thus, in both passages a fruitful tree planted near abundant water describes the effective future of the faithful who cast their lot with God rather than on human strength and evil.

Planted. The faithful tree is not simply a wild oak that takes its position by happenstance. Those who delight in Yahweh's *torah* are "planted" (a passive participle)—as by a master gardener—in the place where they can receive the nourishment they need to flourish. Like a tree planted in a conservatory, well watered and provided with a protective climate, the leaves of this tree never wither, and it is able to remain consistently fruitful.

Whatever he does prospers. At the end the description shifts over to express more directly the consequence of faithfulness for the human being who delights in Yahweh's *torah*. Like the well-watered tree, such a one rooted

23. The reference in found in the sixth column of the *Community Rule* (1QSerek), lines 7–8.

in the life-giving water of God's *torah* will know fruitfulness. The term translated "prospers" here has more the sense of "be successful, bring to a successful conclusion." Like the tree, the work of one who is rooted and grounded in God's guiding Word is also fruitful.

Chaff that the wind blows away. By studied contrast, those who have rooted themselves in evil and have drawn their nourishment and delight from their association with the wicked will dry up and blow away. While the rooted and watered tree exudes an aura of endurance and stability, the unnourished wicked have no permanence. In the process of winnowing, the lightweight and useless chaff—the husk of grain that has been loosened from the kernel by beating—is swept away when the prepared grain is tossed into a strong wind, allowing the heavier seed to fall to the ground to be gathered. The contrast is acute: between fruitful tree and useless chaff; between well-watered stability and dry, dusty, windblown impermanence.

Ultimate Consequences (1:5–6)

HOW ONE LIVES and where one takes a stand has life-shaping consequences. The final set of comparisons sets out the contrasting ways and consequent result of the lives of the righteous and the wicked. The use of "two ways"—of righteousness and wickedness, wisdom and folly—is a characteristic teaching tool of biblical wisdom. Such a contrast provides readers with both positive and negative examples for life. This is the reason that so much of the proverbial literature (esp. that in Prov. 10–31) employs the poetic form of *opposing parallelism*.[24]

The appearance in these verses of words and ideas from the opening verse suggests the psalmist is intentionally balancing the beginning admonition with this concluding one. Verse 1 cautions the reader to beware of seeking and accepting the influence of three categories of persons—the "wicked," the "sinners," and the "mockers"—or of taking up residence there. Here the two most general of these categories—the "wicked" and "sinners"—return as examples of those who will be unable to "stand" in the final judgment. Nor will these guilty ones be able to associate with the assembly of those who are declared "righteous" (1:5b *baᶜadat ṣaddiqim*; cf. 1:1b *baᶜaṣat rešaᶜim*) in that same judgment. The similar wording is intended to drive home the fact that the one who enjoys the "counsel of the wicked" will ultimately be cut off from any association with the "assembly of the righteous."

The way of the righteous. The "way" (*derek*) of a person is a chosen life path that, if left unchanged, determines one's ultimate goal. Biblical wisdom

24. See the discussion of parallelism in the introduction, "The Art of Hebrew Poetry."

literature often contrasts the way of the righteous and the wicked (wise and fool) as a way of demonstrating the consequences of evil and encouraging righteousness (cf., e.g., Prov. 10:9, 16, 24; 15:19, 24, 26, 29; 16:4, 7, 17, 25). Here at the end of Psalm 1, the reader is presented with a choice: the way of righteousness that God oversees or the way of wickedness that will ultimately perish. The verb that the NIV translates "watches over" is *yd*ᶜ ("know"). Knowing in Hebrew understanding is not simply intellectual knowledge of information about something or someone. Rather, knowledge is the end result of experience and relationship. Thus, the "way of the righteous" is one that God knows well from experience because he has traveled it before and knows all its twists and turns. He is the great pathfinder who has blazed the safe and secure trail for those who come behind. By contrast, the way of the wicked seeks to explore territory in which God is absent and consequently will lead to separation from God and destruction.

IT GOES WITHOUT saying that in these explanatory sections of the commentary, we cannot expound exhaustively every facet of each psalm. This is both the frustration and the beauty of the psalms and of Scripture as a whole: One never reaches the bottom of the well from which God's life-giving water flows. There are always new insights to be gained, new moments of understanding to be experienced every time you read the psalms with an open heart and mind. Thus, in these sections of the commentary I will be dealing with certain insights and issues that seem to me most important for understanding how these ancient works make contact with our contemporary lives—how we can gain access to the guidance for life that God has chosen to reveal to us through these originally Hebrew words from a distant and now-extinct culture.

Psalm 1 introduces the Psalter. In the case of Psalm 1, perhaps the most important insight is for us to understand the role of this composition as an introduction to the whole Psalter. This function is the least understood among most general and even advanced students of the psalms. The *fact* of Psalm 1 as an individual composition is fairly straightforwardly apparent, but what does it *mean* to read this psalm as introduction to the book that follows? How might this understanding transform the way we read, understand, and appropriate the Psalms as a whole?

Meditation. A true approach to the psalms involves continual, long-term meditation on and study of these compositions. The wisdom nature of Psalm 1 encourages us to read the term *torah* ("law") in the more general sense of "guidelines, instruction"—a meaning that incorporates the psalms (and indeed the whole of Scripture) as God's revelation of his will and purpose for our lives. The psalms are no longer *just* songs to be sung in worship or even heartfelt prayers with which we resonate emotionally in our own heart. Even more, they are a source of God's word to us—a word that must be considered carefully and incorporated daily into the very fabric of our lives. Beyond being models for our own prayers to God, the psalms, when meditated upon, become texts in which God speaks to us in all parts of our being: body, soul, mind, and spirit.

Close and enduring association. Kathleen Norris recounts how during a month-long retreat among Trappist monastics the daily recitation of the psalms began to reshape and restructure her spiritual understanding and priorities for life.[25] Such an extended encounter with the depths of praise, lament, thanksgiving, and a myriad of other moments of life poured out before God can have the (intended) effect of challenging our often simplistic understanding of life and faith, tearing us down and rebuilding us from the ground up to be more in the image of the God who made us. There is something about reading the psalms from the beginning of the Psalter to the end, day after day, that does not allow us to master them—picking and choosing what suits us, shaping them to *our* will, fitting them to *our* perceived needs and moods. Instead, such daily and continuing familiarity with these texts—more than any other, I believe—ultimately *masters us and shapes us to the will of God* in ways we can hardly anticipate. That is the fearsome challenge of the psalms: In exposing ourselves to them for the long term, we discover that God knows us and our "way" far better than we know ourselves.

A matter of life and death. The "way" of the psalms is a path to life that is "known" by God himself (1:6). When we immerse ourselves in the world of the psalms and make it our own, we are following the path that God himself took, the path he took in Jesus—a path of suffering and hurt; rejection and abandonment; deliverance, salvation, exaltation, and great joy. Together the psalms lead us on the path of *real life*—not the pallid substitutes for life we sometimes construct for ourselves where everything is hermetically sealed, sterile, and safe.

The life of the psalms is messy life where pain and joy, self-knowledge and self-doubt, love and hatred, trust and suspicion break in upon one another, overlapping and competing for our attention. It is a life in which we have real choices on a daily basis between life and death. It is the life that still lives both outside and inside our windows—if we allow ourselves to admit it—and the psalms will never allow us to forget it.

---

25. Kathleen Norris, *The Cloister Walk* (New York: Macmillan, 1997), esp. the chapter on "The Paradox of the Psalms."

And in these psalms this messy life—this real life—is constantly brought before God as our own messiness ought to be, *before* it is cleaned up and sanitized. God wants us to bring *all* of life before him as the psalmists do rather than just the parts we consider acceptable. How else can God's healing, revealing, confronting, forgiving love penetrate to the darkest corners of our secret places unless we open the door to let in the light?

On avoiding association with evil. Psalm 1 makes it clear that the "way" God knows is not discovered by following the footsteps or taking up residence in the company of sinners. Just who are these wicked ones we are encouraged to avoid? A variety of studies have been made of the "enemies" who appear in the psalms.[26] Most often the enemies confronted there fall into one of three broad categories: (1) pagan unbelievers hostile to the faith and Yahweh, (2) members of the faith community who nevertheless live contrary lives, and (3) those within the faith community who misguidedly attack what they see as the faithless living of the psalmists.

As Christians whose community of faith cuts across boundaries of nationality and ethnicity, we must find new ways of understanding those references to the national enemies of Israel. Our kingdom—the kingdom of God that Jesus says is not of this world—can never be equated with any particular nation of the world, regardless how tempted we are to do so. Perhaps the best response to these national enemies is to relate them in our experience to the enemies of the kingdom of God—those who stand outside the faith and seek to tear it down, or those who in all they say and do stand directly opposed to the world-shaping principles of love, forgiveness, and the absolute dependence on God that Jesus calls citizens of God's kingdom to display.[27]

The wicked in the psalms are more than just national enemies. Many are clearly influential members of the psalmist's society who use their influence and power for evil, oppressing those who are less powerful and exploiting them for personal gain. The collective voice of the psalmists calls the readers/hearers to take their stand with the oppressed, afflicted, and poor—and over against those who abuse power and pervert justice.

The psalmists' treatment of the enemies is often harsh. Frequently they envision (and even desire) for the wicked complete rejection by God and total destruction. Such attitudes can leave us troubled when we remember Jesus' encouragement to love our enemies and pray for rather than against them.

---

26. Cf. T. R. Hobbs and P. K. Jackson, "The Enemy in the Psalms," *BTB* 21 (1991): 22–29; Erhard S. Gerstenberger, "Enemies and Evildoers in the Psalms: A Challenge for Christian Preaching," *HBT* 4 (1982–1983): 61–77.

27. Cf. Matt. 5–7; John 13–17.

Jesus himself was condemned for associating with sinners.[28] How then can we justify the kind of separation Psalm 1 seems to enjoin? Two responses may help to set this question in its proper perspective.

(1) The psalmists are only too aware how narrow a line separates them from the wicked. While they may at points come across as very sure of their righteousness (e.g., Pss. 17; 26), they are also fully aware of their own sinfulness and how easy it would be to adopt the callous attitude and lifestyle of the wicked (cf. Pss. 32; 38; esp. 73). When Jesus' association with sinners is questioned, he responds to his critics somewhat cryptically: "It is not the healthy who need a doctor, but the sick. . . . For I have not come to call the righteous, but sinners" (Matt. 9:12–13). The less than immediately obvious point of this retort is that the Pharisees themselves were sinners in need of the saving grace extended by Jesus to all those who acknowledged their sin. He was not implying that the Pharisees had no need of him, but rather that they needed to recognize their essential identity with the sinners they so strongly condemned. The psalmists are deeply aware of their need of God's grace and the redeeming power of his forgiveness (cf. Pss. 32; 103).

(2) It is important to note that what Psalm 1 cautions against is adopting the *attitude* and *lifestyle* of the wicked, not some casual contact with them or especially not the kind of redemptive association that Jesus modeled. The warning is against taking the "way" or path of the wicked, standing with them, and ultimately taking up residence in their territory. The kind of association with unbelievers Jesus models is an essential part of our redemptive role as bearers of good news and witnesses to the transforming power of Jesus Christ in our own lives.

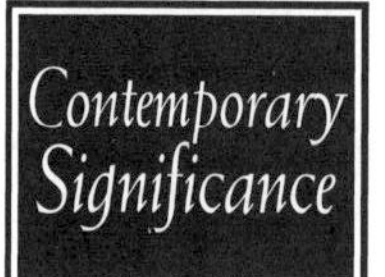

DELIGHTING IN THE TORAH OF YAHWEH. If we truly wish to follow the "way" that God knows rather than a path that leads to destruction, how do we set about finding it? In the New Testament, toward the end of the Sermon on the Mount, Jesus warns his hearers, in words similar to the conclusion of Psalm 1, that entering the kingdom of heaven is like choosing between a broad, well-trodden roadway and a barely distinguishable footpath. The incentive to find and take the narrow path is that it leads ultimately to life, while the broad and easy road ends in destruction (Matt. 7:13–14). But how does one find this path of life in order to enter it? And once on the road, what map ensures we won't get lost?

28. Matt. 9:11; Mark 2:16; Luke 5:30.

Jesus' response to such questions comes at the end of his sermon when he introduces the story of the wise and foolish house builders. The wise builder built on a rock-solid foundation so that his house continued to stand in the face of the storms and floods of life. The fool, by contrast, took the easy way and built on the shifting sands. His house suffered complete collapse when the storms blew and the floods rose (Matt. 7:24–27). The only difference between the two, Jesus says, is their attention and response to his teaching. The former both heard and put into practice what Jesus taught. The latter failed to listen deeply or else refused to act altogether.

Psalm 1 offers the same warning: Hear and do. Delight in the *torah*, meditate on it, and act. Let what you hear, read, and study so permeate your being that your life takes up residence on the path that God knows and exudes a character that sets it clearly apart from the wicked, sinners, and mockers of verse 1. Such a person is truly "blessed." Jesus describes the characteristics of the "blessed" in the Beatitudes at the beginning of the Sermon on the Mount (Matt. 5:3–10). Taken together, these blessings set the citizen of God's kingdom clearly apart from those who refuse to follow Christ along that path. The Beatitudes are not rules to be followed but characteristics growing in those who have bound their lives to Jesus Christ and have planted their roots deep in the stream of life that flows out from his words, life, and person.

In Psalm 1, the blessed one will send down roots deeply into the stream of life that flows out of God's *torah*—his teaching and guidelines. These teachings cannot be confined to the laws of the Pentateuch but refer to the picture anywhere in Scripture of faithful living, miraculously lived by persons of little faith empowered by God when they heard and obeyed what he said. The psalmists are just such people who have their roots planted deep in the streams of God's Word. They listen carefully, and they act out of what they hear. That is why their words of faith—sometimes anguished, often angry, deeply questioning, but always honest and coupled with an abiding sense of confidence and even joy—can be God's words to us, guiding us, challenging us, shaping us, leading us. If only we will listen and obey.

Meditating day and night. How do we meditate "day and night" on God's *torah*? Most of us have enough difficulty just establishing a daily routine of Bible study that marks our day. Who can give over the whole of each day to such study? Even the Essenes of Qumran, who took this responsibility seriously, established a rotation of interpreters to study and expound *torah* twenty-four hours a day, realizing that no one person could hope to accomplish the task.

Surely this is metaphorical language, but is it *only* hyperbole? Or is there some important truth behind it? Brother Lawrence, in his powerful little book *Practicing the Presence of God*, maintains that it is possible to call God and his guiding word to mind constantly throughout the hours of the day and even in the midst of the most mundane and distracting labors of life. By consciously dedicating each task to the service of God and our fellows, it is possible to make even the most unpleasant job a meditation on the grace and purpose of our God.

Some have encouraged the use of breath prayers—brief prayers repeated throughout the day whenever the person becomes aware of his or her breathing. Others have set their watch alarms to sound at regular intervals to remind them to be aware of God and his will and purpose in their lives. On television recently I heard the commentators at a golf tournament remarking on the WWJD (What Would Jesus Do?) bracelet one of the top contenders was wearing.

These and other simple mechanisms can serve to remind us that there is—as Psalm 139 so beautifully affirms—no place in life where God is not already present before us and with us. Knowing this, we need only remind ourselves (as in the previous examples) to be aware of God, or, in the words of the step 11 of Alcoholics Anonymous, to seek "through prayer and meditation to improve our conscious contact with God. . . ."

The psalms can and should be a part of the constant practice of the presence of God. Regularly read from beginning to end, they lead us again and again to consider aspects of life and of God's will that we might not otherwise choose to remember or confront—let alone to embody in our living. Memorized in chunks the psalms can provide ready response to the pressing realities of our days. When I have wakened in a panic in the darkness of the early morning hours—submerged in fear, self-pity, or self-doubt—the psalms have often provided the assurance that my anxieties are known by God, who enlightens my dark places. So, I encourage you to make the psalms your constant companion. Keep a copy at hand, and keep their words in your mind and heart and on your lips as you meet the challenges of your days and nights.

Planted by streams of water. When we meditate on and memorize the psalms, we are planting our roots deeply into the life-giving water of God's Word. This is the same "living water" that Jesus offers to the Samaritan woman at the well (John 4). As the woman learned when she accepted that gift, the water of God's Word reveals our innermost contradictions and points up our need for restoration (4:15–18). Also, the living water is not easily distracted by theological quibbling but cuts immediately to the quick (the "life") of every matter.

The power of the psalms is not that they present us with a neat, theologically consistent package we can assent to (or reject!) intellectually. Instead, they confront us with the messiness and conflict of the life of faith lived out in the real word of body, mind, and spirit. In so doing they allow God's Word to penetrate deeply to "dividing soul and spirit, joints and marrow," laying bare our inward contradictions, yet at the same time encouraging us to "approach the throne of grace with confidence, so that we may receive mercy and find grace to help us in our time of need" (Heb. 4:12–16).

Psalm 2

1 Why do the nations conspire
    and the peoples plot in vain?
2 The kings of the earth take their stand
    and the rulers gather together
against the LORD
    and against his Anointed One.
3 "Let us break their chains," they say,
    "and throw off their fetters."

4 The One enthroned in heaven laughs;
    the Lord scoffs at them.
5 Then he rebukes them in his anger
    and terrifies them in his wrath, saying,
6 "I have installed my King
    on Zion, my holy hill."

7 I will proclaim the decree of the LORD:

He said to me, "You are my Son;
    today I have become your Father.
8 Ask of me,
    and I will make the nations your inheritance,
    the ends of the earth your possession.
9 You will rule them with an iron scepter;
    you will dash them to pieces like pottery."

10 Therefore, you kings, be wise;
    be warned, you rulers of the earth.
11 Serve the LORD with fear
    and rejoice with trembling.
12 Kiss the Son, lest he be angry
    and you be destroyed in your way,
for his wrath can flare up in a moment.
    Blessed are all who take refuge in him.

DIVINE SONSHIP (2:7) is a characteristic we as Christians most often associate with Jesus, and through him we can claim it for ourselves (John 1:12–13). Yet almost a thousand years before Christ (e.g., 2 Sam. 7:14; Ps. 2:7), the Davidic kings of Israel were already claiming to be sons of Yahweh. When the Gospel writers reported that at Jesus' baptism the heavenly voice combined parts of Psalm 2 ("my Son") with a citation from the servant song in Isaiah 42:1–4 ("in whom I delight"), they were indicating that Jesus knew from the beginning of his public ministry that his special nature of sonship involved an unexpected coincidence of messianic authority and suffering servanthood—a combination that made his role difficult to understand, if not entirely mystifying, for many of those who experienced him.

Psalm 2 is the first example in the Psalter of the category of psalms known as "royal psalms"—compositions primarily concerned with the human kings of Judah who understood themselves to be uniquely authorized and empowered as Yahweh's adopted sons. Along with the other psalms in this category (see the unit at the end of this chapter entitled "Royal Psalms"), Psalm 2 offers us insight into the ideology of Jerusalem kingship—how the kings understood themselves, their authority, their roles, and their hopes.[1]

In another vein, however, Psalm 2—and the rest of the royal psalms—have taken on a continuing significance that exceeded their original concern with the human kings of the Davidic dynasty. In the aftermath of the Exile, with the destruction of the national identity and hopes of Judah, many of these psalms took on a new life of *messianic* hope and expectation. What the human kings of Israel and Judah had been unable to do, God would accomplish through his "Anointed One," the Messiah (cf. 2:2).[2] This "Anointed One" would come in the future, empowered by God to usher in the kingdom of God over all the earth.[3]

Because of its association with the ideology of Davidic kingship *and* the later messianic hopes of the exilic community, the position of Psalm 2 at the beginning of the first book of the Psalter has a significant effect on how we read the psalms that follow. Like Psalm 1, this one has no heading or any indication of authorship, as do the rest of the psalms in the first three books of

---

1. For a discussion of the interpretation of royal psalms, see the Bridging Contexts section of the commentary on Ps. 20.

2. The word "Messiah" is taken from the Hebrew root *mšḥ* ("anoint") and means the "anointed one."

3. See the section on "The Messianic Reading of the Psalms" in "Theology of the Psalms," in the second volume of this commentary.

the Psalter.[4] This suggests that Psalm 2 (like Ps. 1) functions in an introductory capacity, shaping how we read and understand what follows.[5] The reference in Acts 13:33 (in some Western manuscripts of the New Testament) to a passage from the canonical Psalm 2 as being taken from "the *first* psalm" may indicate that at some early point in the history of the Psalter, Psalm 2 provided the only introduction.[6]

Others claim that Psalms 1 and 2 ought to be read as a single, combined introduction to the whole Psalter.[7] Together these two psalms emphasize the centrality of *torah* in the *present* life of the faithful (Ps. 1) while stimulating enduring hope in the *future* messianic deliverance and rule of Yahweh (Ps. 2). While ultimately this assessment is persuasive, it also has the unfortunate effect (in my opinion) of obscuring Psalm 2's concurrent function to assist in the shaping of the first three books of the Psalter (Pss. 2–89).[8] In the latter capacity, Psalm 2 has the effect of introducing the covenant relationship between Yahweh and the Davidic kings who ruled from Jerusalem. This psalm establishes the authority of the Davidic king and cautions worldwide submission to him as part of Yahweh's plan for the whole earth. In this capacity the psalm's gaze is firmly fixed on the *past*.

Perhaps we can have our "cake" and eat it too! In what follows, I will first treat Psalm 2 in its original setting and intent as a psalm regarding the powers and blessing of the human Davidic kings. Then, in the Bridging Contexts section, I will explore how messianic hopes have provided the psalm with a new understanding and a new purpose.

As far as literary structure goes, this psalm should be divided into four stanzas of three verses each: (1) international conspiracy (2:1–3); (2) divine response (2:4–6); (3) covenant of kingship (2:7–9); and (4) warning to the nations (2:10–12).

---

4. While it is true that four additional psalms in this segment of the Psalter evidence no headings (Pss. 10; 33; 43; 71), there is strong evidence of a tradition of combining each of these psalms with its predecessor (Pss. 9; 32; 42; 70). See Gerald H. Wilson, "The Use of 'Untitled' Psalms in the Hebrew Psalter," *ZAW* 97 (1985): 405–13.

5. See comments on Ps. 1.

6. See the discussion in Gerald H. Wilson, *The Editing of the Hebrew Psalter*, 204–6. An alternative explanation for the reading in Acts would be that Pss. 1 and 2 were in that tradition being read as a single introductory psalm.

7. Broyles, *Psalms*, 41–42; but cf. John T. Willis, "Psalm 1—An Entity," *ZAW* 9 (1979): 381–401.

8. See the essays on "The Shape of Book 1" and "The Shape of Book 2" in this volume, as well as the sections on "The Shape of Book 3" and "The Shape of the Psalter," in vol. 2 of this commentary.

International Conspiracy (2:1–3)

PICTURE IF YOU will an international gathering of the chief leaders of the world's mighty nations. At this august meeting one leader, because of the political, economic, technological, and military power of his nation, is poised to impose his will on all those present. In the restless murmur of voices of the assembled company, a few dissatisfied representatives are seen with their heads together cautiously and earnestly discussing how to end once and for all the domination of this arrogant opponent and how to assume once more their roles as free and independent nations of the world. A contemporary scene, is it not?—one replayed frequently in gatherings of powers and superpowers and other nations around our world.

The opening section of Psalm 2 describes just such an international conspiracy against the authority of Yahweh and his "anointed" representative (2:2c). The conspirators in this case are the non-Israelite "nations" (*goyim*) and the "peoples" (*leʾummim*)[9] of the world. What may seem to us as rather arrogant and inflated pretensions to world domination and rule certainly never described historical *reality* for the Jerusalem-based kingdom of the Davidic dynasty. These claims were part of the *ideology* of kingship and brought together Israel's understanding of Yahweh as creator of all the earth, humanity's intended role as God's regent to extend Yahweh's authority to the world,[10] and Yahweh's covenant with David and his descendants to provide leadership for God's people. What God is doing with Israel and Judah in the Davidic dynasty mirrors God's purposes for the whole world, and thus God's ultimate purpose (from this ideological view point) is for the "nations" and "peoples" of the world to acknowledge his power and authority as mediated through the Davidic kings.

Since the "kings" and "rulers" of the earth do not acknowledge Yahweh, they have no allegiance to him and are depicted here as fomenting rebellion to cast off his overlordship. The scenario as described assumes the nations and peoples have been subjected to God's rule and are now seeking to cast off the strictures ("their chains ... their fetters") of that rule. It is futile to seek a historical setting when Israel and Judah could claim such world domination, for as just noted, such pretensions must be traced to the Jerusalem ideology and its assumptions of divine authorization to power by Yahweh.

---

9. The *goyim* are "nations"—political entities with recognizable boundaries, while *leʾummim* ("peoples") is a reference to ethnically related people groups within these national boundaries. See the discussion of these and other terms for "peoples" and "nations" in the commentary and notes to Ps. 47.

10. The role of world dominion described for the Davidic kings (cf. Pss. 2; 72; etc.) is essentially the role given to all humanity in the creation (cf. Gen. 1:26–28; Ps. 8). The Davidic kings seem to have adapted this creation command as part of their ideological raison d'être.

The conspiracy is one of restless motion (*rgš* ["conspire"; NIV "rage"])[11] and empty murmuring (*hgh* ["plot in vain"]).[12] Ostensibly gathered to acknowledge their loyalty to Yahweh, the dissidents gravitate to one another ("gather together") in the crowd and ultimately present a consolidated front ("take their stand")[13] against the purposes of "the LORD and against his Anointed One." Their rallying cry is "Freedom!": "Let us break their chains . . . and throw off their fetters."[14]

Divine Response (2:4–6)

YAHWEH IS NOT unaware of the squabbling and dissatisfaction inhabiting the fringes of his courtroom. The coalescing plots are transparent to him, but he is unafraid. The description of God as "enthroned in heaven" is not an attempt to stress his distance and removal from the fray. It is a sign of his exaltation and power that is "out of this world." How can these puny, earthbound "kings of the earth" (2:2) presume to reject and resist the rightful authority of the creator God who sits enthroned in heaven over all the earth?[15]

The enthroned God sees these human beings, knows their plots and pretensions, and is unconcerned. Like an earthly monarch facing down his opponents, God "laughs" (*śḥq*) and "scoffs" (*lᶜg*).[16] Although we may not find the psalmist's chosen imagery of a laughing, scoffing God appealing, the intended message remains clear: God's power is so great and his position so secure that he need not take any coalition of human powers as serious threats to his rule. Such power and security never characterized the reigns of the human kings of Israel and Judah. Thus, this passage is a hopeful part of the Jerusalem ideology based on confidence in the God who undergirds the Davidic kings.

11. In Ps. 55:14, the noun from this same root describes the "restless throng" of pilgrims and other worshipers who approach the house of God.

12. This same verb that describes the murmuring plots of the nations here is used in Ps. 1:2 for the faithful student of *torah* murmuring meditatively over the words and meaning of God's guiding words. The common element is the low murmuring of voices as the one reads aloud and the others hatch their plots.

13. The verb *yṣb* has connotations of "taking a stand *against*" someone in resistance.

14. The images of bondage here seem to assume binding by rope or chain to a stake that can be "pulled up" and then "thrown down" to the ground when removed from the body.

15. I am reminded in this connection of the song from Bob Dylan's Christian period in the early 1980s—"When He Returns." Faced by the turmoil of human existence and the violent pretensions to independent power of human nations and individuals, "he is unconcerned."

16. The verb *śḥq* (cf. *ṣḥq*), "laugh; make sport," is used in Judg. 16:25 to describe Samson providing "entertainment" for the gathered Philistines who saw their blinded and bound enemy as representing no threat. The root sense of *lᶜg* is to "stammer" in someone's face as if ridiculing their speech. Here the terms mock the murmuring plots of the nations and points up the futility of their united speech in 2:3.

He rebukes them. Divine laughter turns to "anger" and scoffing to "rebuke" as Yahweh himself pronounces judgment on the assembled conspirators. The pronouncement is surprising, however, since it does not describe, as we might expect, some act of divine punishment on the rebellious kings. Instead, Yahweh declares his establishment of "my King on Zion, my holy hill" (2:6).[17] This reference to a single king clearly alludes to the Jerusalem dynasty of Davidic kings, who are understood here as uniquely Yahweh's kings and as such are a force the rest of the earth's rulers must reckon with.

This special relationship with Yahweh sets the Davidic dynasty apart from those other human kings who rebel against God's authority and power. The whole psalm shifts at this point to an exposition of the grounds of enduring world rule for the kings of Judah based on the covenant between Yahweh and David.

Covenant of Kingship (2:7–9)

THE NARRATOR RECEDES and the king himself takes center stage to testify in his own voice to the authorizing covenant established between Yahweh and the king. The background of this relationship is clearly the Davidic covenant described in 2 Samuel 7:4–16. There, as here, Yahweh describes his relationship to the Davidic kings in terms of sonship (2 Sam. 7:14). Such sonship with God would have imparted to the kings special power and privilege as well as the responsibility to mediate justice and equity to all God's people and to lead them in the way of true faith.[18]

I will make the nations your inheritance. The idea of world domination expressed in 2:8 is not derived directly from 2 Samuel 7, which focuses primarily on an enduring, just rule over God's people of Israel and Judah. The submission of the kings of the earth to the Davidic monarch also appears in Psalm 72:8–11—another royal psalm that reflects the official ideology of

---

17. The verb "installed" (*nsk*), in the Qal stem as here, normally means "to pour out" as with wine in a libation offering or molten metal into a mold. The sense here is unclear, and commentators resolve the issue by assuming a Niphal perfect form with the conjectural meaning "be consecrated, exalted" by a drink offering (cf. Holladay, *CHALOT*, 239). Use of the passive form would place this statement in the mouth of the king who would be reporting God's exaltation of the human king ("I have been installed as his king..."). This would require further emendation of the pronominal suffixes accompanying "king" and "holy hill" from first person ("my") to third person ("his"). Support for this emendation is found in the LXX as noted in the *BHS* apparatus. Regardless of the difficulty with the meaning of *nsk*, the traditional rendering seems preferable to me. (Cf. the comments of Craigie, *Psalms 1-150*, 63-64).

18. Because the New Testament narratives of Jesus' birth connect his sonship with his possessing the same essence and being as God himself—God made flesh—we often forget how this title must have been understood by his contemporaries. The "son of God" was the *king*, and by the time of Jesus the *Messiah*.

the Jerusalem monarchy. No matter how unlikely it may seem to us, the "official line" of these Davidic kings was their right to rule all the earth by Yahweh's authorization and support—a presumption that must have affected their dealings with foreign nations.

The nations are to become the king's "inheritance" (*naḥalah*). Most often this word describes the tribal allotments of the Promised Land or the whole land as the inheritance of the combined nation. Here, however, the vision of the Davidic monarchs expands to include as their divinely given inheritance the "ends of the earth" (*ʾapse ʾareṣ*).[19] Obviously, this ideology of the divine gift of the lands of the nations would have legitimated territorial expansion during the monarchical period, although Israel and Judah never experienced complete fulfillment.

You will rule them with an iron scepter. The rule over the rebellious nations will be no gentle thing but, as a warning, is described in harsh terms. The king will "rule them" (*rʿʿ*)[20] with an "iron scepter" (or "iron rod") and will "smash them" (*npṣ*) as a potter breaks up defective pottery.[21] The image is one of divine judgment but also emphasizes the fragility of the seemingly great and powerful nations of the world.

Warning to the Nations (2:10–12)

THE NARRATOR RETURNS in the final section of the psalm to issue a stern warning to the rebellious kings—a warning founded on the preceding description of the covenant that exists between Yahweh and his anointed king. The kings are told to "wise [up]" (*śkl* ["be perceptive, gain understanding"]) and

19. The Hebrew behind the phrase "your possession" (*ʾaḥuzzatka*) is derived from the verb *ʾḥz* "lay hold of; seize; hold fast" (Holladay, *CHALOT*, 8). Although it has assumed the meaning "property," the origins of the word still reflect a context of taking by force that is consistent with the kind of conquest of territory associated with expanding kingdoms.

20. The NIV's translation emends the text on the basis of the LXX and other versions to *tirʿem* (from *rʿh* ["shepherd; lead"]). The metaphor of shepherding seems inconsistent with the harsh smashing in the second half of the verse and would necessitate taking the "iron scepter" as some sort of iron-tipped shepherd's staff. The Hebrew of the text (*teroʿem*) understands the verb as derived from the root *rʿʿ* ("break")—a translation that seems to me more balanced with the second half of the verse. The resultant translation is offered in NIV's note as an alternate.

21. The image of broken pottery is employed elsewhere for divine judgment on a rebellious people (cf., e.g., Isa. 30:12–14; Jer. 19:1–13; 25:34). Broken pottery was (and still is) endemic in the ancient Near East—the surfaces of ancient city mounds are littered with fragments, and the presence of pottery throughout the strata of archaeological excavations is one of the most reliable means of dating occupation layers. Fragments of broken pottery were put to secondary use as scrapers (Job 2:8), coal shuttles (Isa. 30:14), and for message writing (e.g., the Lachish Ostraca). Such fragments were so common that their presence eventually receded from awareness (cf. Ps. 31:12)—it was so ubiquitous than no one even noticed it.

to accept the reality of their situation (*ysr* ["take advice, listen to reason"]). Resistance to Yahweh is futile, and they must submit with appropriate indications of respect and "fear."

The exact nature of these acts of submission continue to be debated because of the difficult text of the verse. The opening phrase is most clear ("serve the LORD with fear"), although at least one important manuscript reads "rejoicing" instead of "fear." The literal rendering of the following phrases is something like: "shriek joyously with trembling, kiss the son." In the first instance trembling and joyous shrieking seem awkward companions, while the rather murky meaning of the second phrase is made even more difficult by the appearance of the Aramaic word for "son" (*bar*)[22] rather than the traditional Hebrew *ben* (as in 2:7). This has led to a number of attempts at resolution through rearranging the text. The most common suggestion is to transpose *naššequ bar* ("kiss the son") before *gilu birʿadah* ("shriek joyously with trembling"), combining the central words into *beraglayw* ("on his feet") and render the whole passage as "kiss his [Yahweh's] feet" as a sign of submission and respect.[23] The NIV's translation "kiss the Son" assumes a show of respect to the king rather than Yahweh and emphasizes a messianic reading of the psalm by capitalizing "Son."

In other words, depending on which translation and tack you take, the final verse of the psalm describes the action of God, the kingly son, or the messianic Anointed One. While later interpretation clearly shifted toward the last possibility, the original meaning of the text must have been one of the first two. The final phrase of the psalm ("Blessed are all who take refuge in him") seems more compatible with reference to Yahweh, suggesting *he* is the active party in these lines. However, it is possible that this final admonition to trust was appended to the psalm at a later date when the messianic interpretation was already well established.[24]

---

22. This would be the only occurrence of this Aramaic word outside those portions of Daniel and Ezra that are composed in the Aramaic language. While other Aramaisms are found in a predominantly Hebrew context, *bar* is never found in such contexts, and the contrast with the previous term *ben* in 2:7 militates against its appearance here.

23. Since Jesus is the fulfillment of *the* messianic Son anticipated in this passage, the account in Luke 7:45 of the sinful woman who kisses Jesus' feet while the Pharisees disdain his contact with a sinner has particular poignancy. The woman sees what the Pharisees resist—that Jesus is *the anticipated messianic Son* who must nevertheless suffer and die. With their rejection of Jesus' messianic role, the Pharisees side with the rebellious nations.

24. Those who suggest that Ps. 1 functions together with Ps. 1 as an introduction to the whole Psalter note the appearance of the term *ʾašre* ("Blessed") at the beginning of Ps. 1 and the end of Ps. 2 as evidence that these originally separate psalms were intended to be read together. In that case, this final line may easily have been attached to the end of Ps. 2 for the purpose of binding the two psalms together.

As they currently stand, these final lines provide a concluding contrast to the appeal of the psalm to submit to God and his anointed representative. On the one hand, the rebellious are admonished to submit to avoid the angry outpouring of divine wrath and destruction. On the other hand, those who acknowledge Yahweh's rightful authority and power over their lives find refuge in him and are considered "blessed" (*ʾašre*).[25]

From King to Messiah. A close reading of Psalm 2 will uncover at least three levels of meaning: (1) its original use for ideological authorization of the Davidic kings of Jerusalem (see the above exposition of the psalm); (2) its later reuse as part of the originally independent early segment of the Psalter (including Pss. 2–89);[26] and (3) the enduring function of the psalm in its present connection with Psalm 1 as a joint introduction to the complete and final form of the canonical Psalter.

Each of these levels involves an interpretation or reinterpretation of the role of Yahweh's "anointed"—the Messiah. (1) At the earliest level during the monarchal period, these references designated the human king of Israel and Judah as the one chosen and authorized by Yahweh for special leadership and responsibility. In these instances there was an existing human leader who could be pointed to as fulfilling these expectations and hopes.

(2) With the demise of the monarchy in the Babylonian Exile the situation changed. Since there was no longer a presiding king, these psalms with their exalted view of anointed human leadership became the source of hope for future restoration of Yahweh's purposes for Israel and Judah. The "Anointed One"—Messiah—was the rightful descendant of David, who would in God's own timing restore the monarchy, defeat the nation's enemies, and accomplish the worldwide dominion envisioned in Psalms 2 and 72.

These hopes for restoration are most closely associated with the early collection and shaping of Psalms 2–89, where royal psalms play such an important role in setting the interpretive agenda. Psalm 2 introduces the extended collection of three books with an expectation of divine authorization and world dominion. Psalm 72—at the conclusion of the combined collection of Books 1 and 2—describes the continuing hopes of the Davidic

---

25. The theme of finding refuge in Yahweh is a dominant one—esp. in the first two books of the Psalter (Pss. 2–72), where nouns and verbs of the root *ḥsh* employed in 2:12 occur no less than twenty-five times. These same terms appear only once in Book 3 (73:28) and five additional times in each of the last two books. Cf. Jerome Creach, *Yahweh as Refuge and the Editing of the Hebrew Psalter* (JSOTSup 217; Sheffield: JSOT Press, 1996).

26. See the discussion in "The Shape of the Psalter" in volume 2 of the commentary.

kings for enduring rule "from sea to sea and from the River to the ends of the earth." In contrast, the concluding psalm of this segment laments the failure of Yahweh's promises to David (89:38–45) and practically demands its restoration (89:49–51).

This early segment of the Psalter, then, responds in its arrangement to the exilic experience of the failure of the Davidic kingdom and the consequent loss of national identity and self-determination. It is little wonder that this part of the Psalter is dominated by lament psalms. The agonized question of 89:46, "How long, O LORD? Will you hide yourself forever?" hangs like a pall over the landscape of the first three books. This early collection arranged the psalms in such away as to capture this agony and to entreat God for the restoration of the Davidic dynasty and kingdom. Those who read this group of psalms from beginning to end could not help but be caught up in the painful memory of the glorious kingdom lost and the ardent plea for its return.

(3) The third and final stage in the reinterpretation of Psalm 2 (and indeed the rest of the royal psalms in the Psalter) comes with the addition of the final two books (Pss. 90–150) and the placement of Psalm 1 as introduction to the whole. Exactly when this final shift took place is not clear. The two strongest possibilities are (a) a time in the later postexilic period, when the gradual pressure toward cultural assimilation of the Diaspora community began to erode expectation for the reestablishment of a national political Judahite entity; or (b) late in the first century A.D., when the failure of the first Jewish rebellion against Rome (67–70) and the destruction of the Jerusalem temple led many to modify their militaristic messianic expectations for restoration.[27]

While it remains difficult to decide with absolute certainty which of these quite separated time periods provides the historical context for the final stage of the canonical Psalter, it is nevertheless possible to see how the addition of the last two books of the Psalter to the earlier three subtly alters the way in which the royal psalms (like Ps. 2) scattered throughout the canonical collection were read. One primary indicator of change is the distribution of the normal Hebrew word for political-military ruler—*melek* ("king"). In the first three books this word is used in four ways: (1) to refer in the most general sense to "kings" or "kingship (e.g., 33:16); (2) to describe foreign human kings of other nations (e.g., 2:2, 10; 45:9; 76:12); (3) to refer to the human kings of Israel and Judah (e.g., 2:6; 21:1, 7; 45:11; 89:18); and (4) to describe the divine kingship of Yahweh (5:2; 10:16; 24:7, 8, 9, 10; 29:10; 44:4; 47:2, 6, 7; 48:2?; 68:24; 74:12; 84:3).

When, however, we cross the boundary between the earlier segment of the Psalter (2–89) and enter the final two books (90–150), we discover an

27. See the discussion of this latter option in Wilson, "A First Century C.E. Date," 102–10.

interesting change. While *melek* is still used to describe kings in general (e.g., 140:10), the human kings of the foreign nations (102:15; 105:14, 20, 30; 110:5; 119:46; etc.), and Yahweh as king (95:3; 98:6; 99:4; 145:1; 149:2), references to the kings of Israel and Judah using this term are entirely lacking! The effect of this change highlights the growing emphasis on the kingship of Yahweh established early in the fourth book through the introduction of the *Yahweh malak* ("Yahweh reigns/has become king") psalms,[28] while deflecting attention away from human kingship in Israel.

By way of contrast, two other important words applied in the earlier segment of the Psalter to describe the kings of Israel and Judah in general and David in particular—"servant" (*ʿebed*) and "Anointed One" (*mešiaḥ*)—continue unabated into the second segment as well.[29] The effect of this shift is to focus attention on the roles of the Davidic kings as "anointed servants" while distancing them from the "rulership" normally associated with the term *melek*.

This change implies a shift in the way these royal psalms and references to the Davidic kings were interpreted. While the anointed servants of Israel continue to play an important role in the future plans of Yahweh for his people, that role is increasingly distanced from the kind of "kingship" associated with *melek*. Yahweh is the eternal king (*melek*), who rules over his people. Even with the decidedly militaristic picture of David in Psalm 132 and the reference there to the promise of an enduring throne for David and his descendants based on the Davidic covenant (cf. 132:10–12), it is also clear that it is *Yahweh who sits enthroned in Zion for ever and ever* (132:13–14) as king. While it must have been immensely difficult among the Diaspora community to entirely disassociate David and his descendants from kingship, nevertheless the role of *melek* recedes in the final form of the Psalter while David's role as eschatological Messiah and Servant who ushers in the kingdom and reign of Yahweh is emphasized.

That final form of the Psalter affects the way the royal psalms and references to Davidic kingship were likely interpreted. In light of the distancing that takes place in the later books, the earlier references would be increasingly understood eschatologically as a hopeful anticipation of the Davidic descendant who would—as Yahweh's anointed servant—establish God's

---

28. On these psalms see the discussion in "Types of Psalms" in the introduction.

29. After appearing seven times in six psalms in the first three books (2:2; 18:50; 20:6; 28:8; 84:9; 89:38, 51), the term *mešiaḥ* occurs only three times in two psalms in the last two books (105:15; 132:10, 17), a slight reduction in emphasis. The term "servant" (*ʿebed*) also occurs in reference to kings seven times in four psalms in the earlier segment (18:0; 36:0; 78:70; 89:3, 20, 39, 50) and only two times in two psalms (132:10; 144:10) in the latter.

direct rule over all humanity in the kingdom of God.[30] Ultimately, of course, this shift prepared the way for Jesus' own understanding of his role as the suffering, dying kind of Messiah, who inaugurates an eternal kingdom of God that is "not of this world" but of the spirit.

SERVE YAHWEH WITH FEAR. The rather astonished "why?" at the beginning of Psalm 2 reflects Israel's amazement over the nations' inability to recognize the rightness of God's purposes for the world. On the one hand, can't the nations see that resistance is futile? That God is firmly in control? Why can't they simply accept the inevitable? On the other hand, can't they see that God's rule is gracious and beneficent, providing all they could ever want or need? For the nations, however, the benevolent rule of Yahweh is seen as bondage ("chains") and restriction ("fetters"), limits to their freedom that must be cast off.

In an age that glorifies independence and freedom of will, we often find ourselves on the side of the nations. We thrill to the moment in the movie *Braveheart*—a Hollywoodized version of the life of Scottish nationalist William Wallace—when Wallace, under the torturer's knife, musters his last breath, not to submit but to scream out the rallying cry of "freedom!" Our own national history recalls the rallying cry attributed to Patrick Henry: "Give me liberty, or give me death!"

These are stirring moments and stirring words! And often freedom from oppression and repression *is* worth dying for. Jesus taught that clearly when he went to the cross in our place. But more often than not we take the determination of these historical persons to win freedom for whole nations—for others—and we twist it into a banner for personal freedom from all restraint. In the words of a recent song:

> I need me to be for me,
> To be free and to discover.
> I need me to be for me,
> And then we both can be for each other.[31]

Our society would have us believe that true happiness comes through personal freedom, that in sexual abandon, unbridled material acquisition, and self-focused relational "flexibility" we can achieve personal satisfaction.

---

30. This may even offer a partial solution for the apparent confusion between king and Yahweh in such passages as 45:2–7, where the king appears in verse 5 to be called "God."

31. Sung by Mary Travers, written by Peter Yarrow and Larry Weiss, "I Need Me to Be for Me" (Silver Dawn/Ram's Head/ASCAP, 1979).

They are, however, mistaken—and so are we if we take their lead. Remember that at the time this text was written, we "Johnny-come-lately" Christians were the nations—outside the people of God, seeking to make our own way in the world. Before the death of Jesus brought down the dividing wall, we were part of the non-Israelite world, seeking by self-will and the worship of other gods to carve out a place of security and satisfaction in an often hostile world.

We must still count ourselves on the side of the nations when we take up their banner of "freedom" from God's rule. Even Israel—*the* people of God—could think of God's bonds as restrictive chains and seek to throw them off. Jeremiah makes this clear when he accuses the people of Israel: "Long ago you broke off your yoke and tore off your bonds; you said, 'I will not serve you!'" (Jer. 2:20).[32] Whenever we buy into the world's way of placing self and satisfaction before all else, we become the nations once again. We essentially negate the work of Christ to bring us into the family of God.

The nations in this passage want to throw off the "fetters" and "chains" of God, thinking of them as heavy shackles that weigh them down and prevent them from becoming what *they want to be*. In reality, however, those who submit their lives to God discover instead the "bonds" of relationship—family "ties" that bind one closely into a relationship of loyal love. As in marriage, the bonds of commitment may represent for one a "ball and chain" of restriction, but for another the boundless freedom of love.

So whenever we read this psalm, we must be careful not to reduce it to a mere messianic prediction of the ultimate submission of the unbelieving nations to the authority of God's rule and kingdom. It is that, but it remains much more than that. It is also not just a threat of judgment to scare our unbelieving friends into the kingdom of God. Although it should encourage us to witness to them of the boundless love poured out in Christ *for them*, it should remain *for us* who name the name of Jesus a powerful caution to lay down daily our own banners of personal freedom and self-satisfaction in order to "kiss the Son." When we do so, we avoid the path of destruction that Psalm 1 warns against, and we also discover that the imagined fetters and chains are instead the "cords of human kindness" and the "ties of love" with which God leads us into "the glorious freedom of the children of God" (Rom. 8:21).[33]

---

32. See also Jer. 5:5, where the leaders are taken to task as well: "'So I will go to the leaders and speak to them; surely they know the way of the LORD, the requirements of their God.' But with one accord they too had broken off the yoke and torn off the bonds."

33. Cf. also Hos. 11:3–4, where Yahweh heals rebellious Israel, taking the yoke of oppression from off their neck and leading them with "cords of human kindness, with ties of love" while bending down "to feed them"—a beautiful picture of his satisfying their deepest wants and needs.

THE ROYAL PSALMS

I have mentioned in the section on "Types of Psalms" in the Introduction the existence of a group of related psalms that represent diverse categories of psalms and yet share a common concern with the Israelite monarch. A broad consensus includes eleven psalms in this category of royal psalms (2; 18; 20; 21; 45; 72; 89; 101; 110; 132; 144), and it is generally accepted that these psalms originally functioned to provide liturgy to accompany the king's participation in the rituals of temple worship, either on a regular basis or for special occasions.

Among these royal psalms we find the following:

- compositions concerned with the divine authorization of the Davidic dynasty by Yahweh (Ps. 2)
- the enthronement of the king (Pss. 101, 110)
- celebration of the divine election of Zion or Jerusalem (Ps. 132)
- thanksgiving for victory (Ps. 18—almost identical with the song sung by David in 2 Sam. 22:1–51)
- a plea for divine favor and protection in behalf of the king (Ps. 20)
- a song of thanksgiving for the victories granted the king (Ps. 21)
- a song of praise on the wedding day of the king (Ps. 45)
- a song transmitting the blessings and responsibilities of kingship from the king to his descendants (Ps. 72)
- a confused plea for the restoration of the failed Davidic covenant (Ps. 89)
- a vow to walk blamelessly and to establish right rule (Ps. 101—following almost immediately the *Yahweh malak* psalms celebrating the kingship of Yahweh)

Elements of Form

This list of psalm types demonstrates that the category of royal psalms cuts across a variety of literary types, combining the traditional literary structures of thanksgiving, plea for deliverance, and blessing with the distinguishing concerns of the king and the activities of kingship. Within the varied psalm types represented here one often hears the voice of the king raised—usually within the context of the corporate worship of Israel—celebrating or despairing, vowing or pleading in response to the changing experience of kingship.

We hear the king celebrate the divine promise of kingly victory and rule over Israel's enemies, as in the first-person singular section in 2:7–9:

I will proclaim the decree of the LORD:
He said to me, "You are my Son;
today I have become your Father.
Ask of me,
and I will make the nations your inheritance,
the ends of the earth your possession.
You will rule them with an iron scepter;
you will dash them to pieces like pottery."

Elsewhere the king recalls in dramatic imagery the divine deliverance that led to victory and security:

The LORD lives! Praise be to my Rock!
Exalted be God my Savior!
He is the God who avenges me,
who subdues nations under me,
who saves me from my enemies.
You exalted me above my foes;
from violent men you rescued me.
Therefore I will praise you among the nations, O LORD;
I will sing praises to your name.
—Psalm 18:46–49

The king also vows that loyalty to Yahweh will issue forth in right rule:

I will be careful to lead a blameless life—
when will you come to me?
I will walk in my house
with blameless heart.
I will set before my eyes
no vile thing.
The deeds of faithless men I hate;
they will not cling to me.
Men of perverse heart shall be far from me;
I will have nothing to do with evil. . . .
My eyes will be on the faithful in the land,
that they may dwell with me;
he whose walk is blameless
will minister to me. . . .
Every morning I will put to silence
all the wicked in the land;
I will cut off every evildoer
from the city of the LORD.
—Psalm 101:2–4, 6, 8

In some of the royal psalms we hear other voices lifted in behalf of the king (second-person singular). These may indicate moments of worship when the priest steps forward to seek intercession for the king in distress:[34]

May the LORD answer you when you are in distress;
may the name of the God of Jacob protect you.
May he send you help from the sanctuary
and grant you support from Zion.
May he remember all your sacrifices
and accept your burnt offerings.
—Psalm 20:1–3

The voices of prophets can also be heard delivering public oracles of victory or divine establishment of security:[35]

Your hand will lay hold on all your enemies;
your right hand will seize your foes.
At the time of your appearing
you will make them like a fiery furnace.
In his wrath the LORD will swallow them up,
and his fire will consume them.
You will destroy their descendants from the earth,
their posterity from mankind.
—Psalm 21:8–10

The Context

Psalms like these seem clearly to suggest a liturgical setting within the public worship of Israel. The kings are described in texts outside the psalms as participating in significant roles within worship. David led the procession bringing the ark of the covenant into Jerusalem (2 Sam. 6:12–15). Many kings—including Saul, David, and Solomon—are portrayed as offering sacrifices and presiding over corporate worship.[36] It is not surprising or difficult, then, to imagine the king assuming such a leadership role—especially on important national occasions of celebration, commemoration, or intercession.

To bring a greater specificity to the occasions behind the individual royal psalms (more than a time of distress, a victory, or a wedding) has been a difficult challenge. A certain line of scholarship has developed around the

34. In addition to the priestly intercessor in Ps. 20, we hear the voice of the king himself in Ps. 72, offering intercession for his successor.

35. Cf. Pss. 21; 110; 132.

36. Cf. 1 Sam. 13:7–14; 2 Sam. 6:17–19; 24:24–25; 1 Kings 3:4, 15; 8:62.

speculations of Mowinckel regarding an annual New Year Festival celebrating and renewing the enthronement of Yahweh as king of Israel and the cosmos. Those who follow this position understand these royal psalms as elements of the liturgy of that celebration, in which the king participated as the earthly representative of the heavenly king, Yahweh. The royal psalms are each assigned a particular place in the imaginatively reconstructed ritual of this hypothetical festival.[37] This extreme speculation has failed to establish any consensus among the broader constituency of Psalms scholarship.

Somewhat more modest, although equally speculative, are the suggestions that these royal psalms reflect a yearly festival in which the divine authorization of the king by Yahweh and the election of Zion/Jerusalem as the locus of his reign were renewed. Rather than a mythological celebration of Yahweh's establishing cosmic order reflected in the national order established by the monarchy, this proposed event is a yearly reminder to the king and the people that Yahweh is king and that any human power is authorized and derived from him.[38]

Even less radical are proposals that the royal psalms are part of the liturgy employed in the *initial* enthronement of a new king.[39] We know from Scripture that such enthronement ceremonies did take place (cf. David in 2 Sam. 5; Solomon in 1 Kings 2) and were accompanied with much pomp and circumstance, including religious rituals and temple worship. Nevertheless, any reconstruction of a liturgical structure through which to order and understand the royal psalms remains hypothetical and vulnerable to the theorist's understanding of what such a festival might have been like and what it was intended to accomplish.

In the end, there is no unambiguous external evidence of an annual enthronement festival in Israel. If such a festival ever existed, its nature, purpose, and related liturgical structures have been lost (or perhaps even purged?) from the transmitted traditions of Israel. The use and function of the royal psalms in their present context do not appear to be dependent on recovering such a festival.

Finally, it is certainly possible, and indeed probable, that in their present context these royal psalms are intended to function not as a retrospective or nostalgic look backward at the golden era of Israelite monarchy but messianically and eschatologically as offering future security and hope. Read

37. For further discussion of Mowinckel's theories, see Mowinckel, *The Psalms in Israel's Worship*, 1:106–92; also see the section on "Types of Psalms" in the Introduction to this commentary.

38. Artur Weiser, *The Psalms* (OTL; Philadelphia: Westminster, 1962), is one of the most articulate proponents of the yearly covenant-renewal festival as the context for the psalms.

39. This could, of course, be *every* new king or *one specific* king.

along with the central theme of the kingship of Yahweh in Psalms 93–99 and other significant admonitions to beware of the limits and failures of human kingship (cf. 146:3–5), these royal psalms are employed within the shaping of the Psalter to draw on past royal themes in order to offer a new hope for the future. The king introduced in Psalm 2, to whom the kings of the nations are warned to bow, the "horn of David" in Psalm 132, who is the fulfillment of the renewed promise of an eternal Davidic throne, is the David of Psalm 144, who acknowledges the frailty of humanity (144:3–4), exalts Yahweh as king in 145:1, and admits that when even princes fail (146:3–4), "Blessed is he whose help is the God of Jacob, whose hope is in the LORD his God" (146:5; cf. 144:15).

Strategic Placement

In light of the messianic reinterpretation of the royal psalms in the Psalter, the placement of these psalms (at least some of them) within the structure and arrangement of the whole Psalter indicates the importance of these poems in the minds of the editors and readers of the Psalter. At least four of the eleven psalms usually identified as royal psalms stand at particularly significant structural positions within the Psalter. Together these four psalms (2; 72; 89; 144) lend a royal covenantal concern and focus to the shape of the Psalter.

The first three of these psalms stand at the seams that mark the transitions between the early books of the Psalter. Psalm 2 stands at the beginning of Book 1 of Psalms (1–41), while Psalms 72 and 89 mark the end of Book 2 (42–72) and Book 3 (73–89). Although one might expect a similar royal conclusion to Book 1, no royal composition stands at that position. This apparent omission can be explained by the evidence of the unique postscript in 72:20 ("This concludes the prayers of David son of Jesse"), which suggests the first two books of psalms have been combined into a single cohesive collection bound together at beginning and end by psalms attributed to David.[40]

The placement of these royal compositions at the boundaries of the first three books of the Psalter provides a sort of extended theological reflection

---

40. The presence in the psalm headings of this combined collection of names of persons other than David may well be explained by the Chronicler's affirmation that indeed it was David who established and organized the temple worship system, including the Levitical servants and singers who had responsibility for all aspects of temple ritual and practice (see esp. 1 Chron. 25:1–26:1, where the names of Asaph and the Sons of Korah are mentioned prominently among those set apart for temple service by David). It is tempting in this light to consider the postscript in 72:20 to refer not to a group of private personal prayers composed by David but to a collection of pieces authorized for use in temple worship.

on the Davidic covenant that shapes the way the psalms within this collection are read. Briefly stated, Psalm 2 describes the inauguration of the Davidic covenant, whereby the Israelite king is chosen as the "son" of Yahweh and embued with authority and stature to rule over the nations in Yahweh's behalf. Psalm 72—a prayer for the king—reflects the passing on of the blessings and responsibilities of the Davidic covenant to successive generations of Israelite kings. Psalm 89 agonizes bitterly over Yahweh's apparent rejection of the Davidic covenant and the consequent destruction of the nation in the Exile. Within this framework the psalms of the first three books are to be read as a tense dialogue between promise and responsibility, blessing and failure—all in the light of the exilic experience of loss and destruction.

The placement of Psalm 144 near the end of the final book of the Psalter is again no accident. Insofar as the final Hallel (Pss. 146–150) is an expanded conclusion to the whole Psalter, the actual conclusion of the fifth book occurs in Psalm 145, with its call to praise expressed in verse 21 providing the trigger for the following five psalms. In this important position, Psalm 144 recalls again the important themes inherent in all the royal psalms: backward reflection on Israel's great monarchical experiment, painful acknowledgment of the apparent failure of kingship (144:3–4), and enduring hope for the restoration of a purified kingship of Yahweh through the agency of the coming Davidic Messiah (144:14–15).

The words found in the mouth of David in Psalm 144, coupled with those in the final Psalm 145 and the initial Hallel Psalm 146,[41] mirror the appropriate attitude of humility and dependence on Yahweh that must mark human leaders, who trust in the deliverance provided by Yahweh and anticipate (together with the rest of the exilic community) the divine action that will rescue both king and people "from the hands of foreigners" (144:7), so that the pain and dislocation of the Exile may end (144:14–15; 146:7–9) and the blessings of God's kingly rule be restored (144:12–14; 145:1, 13; 146:10).[42]

David in the Psalms

The use, placement, and reinterpretation of the royal psalms within the literary context of the whole Psalter shifts the figure of the Davidic king into a new interpretive role. As I have already stated, these psalms are not included here (in an exilic Psalter) as nostalgic reflections on the "good old days" or as historical record of how the kings functioned in temple worship.

---

41. Ps. 146 is surely intended to represent the praise of David invoked in the first half of 145:21: "My mouth will speak in praise of the LORD. . . ."

42. For further comments of the significance of this structure for the shape of the first book and the whole Psalter, see "The Shape of the Psalter" in the second volume of this commentary as well as the essays on the individual books (consult index).

On several levels the depiction of "David" in the psalm headings and in the royal psalms provides a new paradigm for appropriate response to Yahweh and to the vagaries of human existence that inevitably overwhelm us.

On one level, the David of the psalms is a model for anyone—a paradigm of how one is to sustain a faithful and enduring conversation with God in the midst of the pain and pressures of life. This David responds to significant events in his life by turning to Yahweh in confession, trust, confidence, complaint, anger, thanksgiving, and praise. By so doing David authorizes all who would faithfully follow Yahweh to do the same, opening the interior realities of their own personal beings to the divine scrutiny that at once judges, threatens, comforts, and heals. What better way for me to open myself to God than to follow the example of the "man after God's own heart"—perhaps even adopting or adapting his words as my own?

On another level, however, the David of the psalms is more than a paradigm for all faithful worshipers to follow. By the use and placement of the royal psalms, the editors of the Psalter intended to suggest a corrective interpretation of human kings and kingship. In this regard David provides a critique of the abuses of power inherent in Israel's monarchical experience. This David acknowledges the limits of human kingship, confesses its failings and shortcomings, eschews all confidence in the trappings of kingly power, acknowledges and accepts the sovereign kingship of Yahweh, and admits the total dependency of all human kings on the gracious empowering of Yahweh. Through this reinterpretation and reorientation of the traditional understanding of kingship, the readers of the Psalter are led to question old assumptions of kingship, including permanent unconditional covenants and divinely authorized human rule, and to arrive at an understanding of the sovereign kingship of Yahweh to which even earthly rulers must bow the knee.

The third and final level on which David of the headings and royal psalms comes to function is to provide a radical messianic hope for Israel's future. Even as the Davidic critique of the psalms succeeds in undermining absolute confidence in human kingship, the Davidic model of piety, humility, confession, and reliance on Yahweh catapult the old traditions of kingship into a new role. As Israel sought to understand how Yahweh would direct divine rule over Israel, several barriers stood in the way. The old way of monarchy had not succeeded because of the weakness of human kings (they abused their power and they died!). In addition, Israel now found herself in exile, suffering under the overwhelming oppression of the foreign nations. Thus, the divine promises enshrined in the Davidic covenant for eternal security within the kingdom had seemingly come to an end without fulfillment.

The solution to these barriers is to be found in the messianic king epitomized by the David of the Psalms. This messianic David, as depicted in the royal psalms scattered throughout the Psalter, acknowledges the failing and shortcomings of human kingship and yet is still empowered by God to establish the rule of Yahweh with all its blessings on earth.[43] This David, rather than seeking self-power, points away from himself to the kingship of Yahweh.

A rather complex portrait emerges as one explores the multifaceted David revealed through the royal psalms preserved in the Psalter. David is at once the great historical king of Israel, a fitting model for individual piety in his response to the difficult circumstances of life, a critique of traditional hopes for human kingship, an explanation of the failure of those hopes in the exilic collapse of a nation, and finally a still-potent hope for the messianic restoration of the blessed promises of the kingdom of God through the agency of the coming Messiah.

It is important to recognize this multilevel understanding of David and its impact on the interpretation of the psalms. To limit our understanding of David to any one of these levels is to greatly impoverish our ability to interpret these psalms and to gain access to their rich insights for our own lives. While the prayers of David may truly be "concluded"[44] in terms of the personal voice of the historical king, they live on without end in the psalms and find voice throughout the ages in the mouths of those who read, sing, and pray the psalms as their own.

43. See esp. Ps. 144, in its reference to the empowerment of Yahweh (vv.1, 10), the frailty of humans (vv. 3–4), the "new song" theme of the *Yahweh malak* psalms (v. 9), and its dramatic depiction of the blessings of Yahweh (vv. 12–14).

44. As in the postscript in 72:20. Might it be that the inclusion of numerous Davidic psalms *after* this conclusion marks a shift in the interpretation of David away from a strictly historical personage toward the king as spiritual model and guide anticipated in the Messiah?

Psalm 3

A PSALM OF DAVID. When he fled from his son Absalom.

¹ O LORD, how many are my foes!
How many rise up against me!
² Many are saying of me,
"God will not deliver him." *Selah*
³ But you are a shield around me, O LORD;
you bestow glory on me and lift up my head.
⁴ To the LORD I cry aloud,
and he answers me from his holy hill. *Selah*
⁵ I lie down and sleep;
I wake again, because the LORD sustains me.
⁶ I will not fear the tens of thousands
drawn up against me on every side.
⁷ Arise, O LORD!
Deliver me, O my God!
Strike all my enemies on the jaw;
break the teeth of the wicked.
⁸ From the LORD comes deliverance.
May your blessing be on your people. *Selah*

THIS PSALM PRESENTS us with a number of "firsts" in the Psalter. It is the first psalm to exhibit a psalm heading, and that heading contains the first genre designation attached to a psalm (*mizmor*),[1] the first attribution to David (*ledawid*),[2] and the first description of the historical setting in David's life thought to have occasioned the writing of a psalm.[3] In the body of the psalm is the first occurrence of the rather enigmatic

1. The term *mizmor* is one of two more general designations employed in the psalm headings (the other being *šir* ["song"]). Taken from the Hebrew verbal root *zmr*, the term describes "a song sung to the accompaniment of stringed instruments."

2. Of the forty-one psalms (Pss. 1–41) that compose the first book of the Psalter, all but four (1; 2; 10; 33) are attributed to David by the presence of this phrase in their heading.

3. Of the seventy-three psalms in the Psalter bearing *ledawid* ("to, for, of, by David") in their headings, thirteen (3; 7; 18; 34; 51; 52; 54; 56; 57; 59; 60; 63; 142) also have historical notices highlighting specific circumstances in David's life as the precipitating influence behind the psalm.

term *selah* to structure the composition (vv. 2, 4, 8). Finally, Psalm 3 is by type the first lament to appear in the Psalter (see the discussion of this type of psalm in the section on "Types of Psalms" in the Introduction; also see the discussion on "The Laments" at the end of this chapter).

The Heading (3:0)

WHILE THE HISTORICAL notice in the psalm heading relates this lament to the occasion of David's nocturnal flight from Jerusalem to escape the attacking forces of his rebellious son Absalom (2 Sam. 15–16), there is no specific reference to that event in the text of the psalm. It is a rather general plea for deliverance from enemies, who are here described as "many" (v. 1) and "ten of thousands" (v. 6), but never identified. This has led some to doubt whether the psalm was created in response to that specific event, while others go so far as to deny Davidic authorship altogether.

Our interpretation and application of this psalm is not severely affected, regardless of how one resolves that issue. While linking the psalm with the event in 2 Samuel 15–16 may offer some insight into the internal mindset of David at the time, that is more helpful for understanding the Absalom narrative than for interpreting the psalm. The psalm stands up on its own strength, and indeed, the attempt to spell out the specifics of the setting behind the distress of the psalmist and to identify the enemy precisely as Absalom often has the unfortunate effect of so fixing the historical reference that the reader is distanced even further from the psalm and hindered from appropriating its insights for personal application. If this is merely a psalm describing David's response to a personal circumstance centuries—even millennia—ago, why ought I to assume that this psalm can influence the way I respond today to my own situations of distress? It may well be that the 150 psalms included in the canonical collection were chosen (for the most part) precisely *because* they were not so tied to specific historical situations as to inhibit their appropriation and application in any day and age.

The psalm is divided into three sections by the appearance of the Hebrew word *selah* at the close of each section. This word is generally thought to indicate a pause in the musical presentation of the psalm, or perhaps an instrumental interlude. In any case, the appearance of *selah* seems most often to correspond with structural divisions within a text and can be helpful in understanding the various components of a poem. For Psalm 3, exclusive of the heading, the three divisions thus concluded by *selah* are (1) verses 1–2; (2) verses 3–4; and (3) verses 5–8. Each section exhibits a cohesive theme, and together the three sections offer coherent movement in the psalm.

Surrounded by the Enemy (3:1–2)

THE PSALMIST IS surrounded, hemmed in by many foes. There are a number of Hebrew words used to describe enemies. The most common (*ʾoyeb*) means "one who hates [me]." That is not, however, the term used here. Instead, the psalmist describes the enemy with the word *ṣar* ("oppressor"), from a root that emphasizes narrowness or constriction. The reference may be to hand-to-hand military struggle in the heat of battle. One can almost sense the panic as the psalmist, turning this way and that, seeking a way out, sees only the multitude of enemies pressing ever closer, about to overwhelm. Perhaps the image is of being tightly bound and unable to escape—something like what the victim of the boa constrictor experiences as the relentless coils draw ever tighter, cutting off escape and crushing life.

The enemy is not only numerous but is constantly multiplying. The word translated "many" in verse 1a is a verb meaning "have become many, have multiplied." Again, the psalmist is not recounting a static circumstance of oppression but a dangerously escalating situation that threatens imminently to consume the psalmist. This sense of threat is increased by the realization in verse 1b that the multiplying horde of encompassing enemies is rising en masse to confront the psalmist. As they do so to strike down their foe, the "many" spew forth invectives calculated both to embolden themselves and to demoralize the psalmist at the very core of his being.

The Hebrew *nepeš*, translated in the NIV as "[of] me," has often been translated "soul" and was sometimes confused with that distinct, separate, and eternal spiritual part of the human being that survives the body after death.[4] This word, however, portrays much more accurately the essential being of humans, animated by God at creation (Gen. 2:7); in the Hebrew way of thinking, the *nepeš* cannot be separated from the physical body. To speak to one's own *nepeš* is to consider the most deeply held beliefs, needs, desires, and hopes that characterize a being physically, emotionally, or spiritually. To speak to another's *nepeš* is to seek to exercise influence and control over that person at the deepest level (cf. Pss. 11:1; 35:3). Thus, as the many enemies of the psalmist rush together to snuff out his life, their cry is intended to shake him to the very roots—to leave him naked and vulnerable to their attack: "God will not deliver him."[5]

---

4. This is a Greek way of thinking. The Greeks used the term *psyche* to designate this ephemeral though eternal spiritual substance in humans.

5. The LXX casts this phrase in the second person ("no deliverance for *you*"), making the enemies' intent to undermine and demoralize the psalmist even more clear.

The deliverance to which the enemies refer here in their arrogant denial of its possibility is that associated with the Hebrew word *yešuaᶜ*,[6] the most common term employed in the Old Testament to express the general idea of salvation or deliverance. The core meaning of the term denotes removing restriction and providing room—a most appropriate connotation in the context of this psalm.[7] What the psalmist desires most as the enemies close in for the kill is room, space to breathe, maneuver, perhaps even escape. This is what the opponents intend to deny.

It is also notable that in their denying deliverance to the narrator of the psalm, the enemies cannot bring themselves to name the name of the psalmist's God—Yahweh. Instead, they substitute the more generic designation *ʾelohim* ("God"). Might this suggest that the enemies here are unbelievers or pagans rather than opponents from within the believing community? There is a tendency in the psalms to resist putting the divine name Yahweh in the mouth of pagans or severe unbelievers.[8]

The enemies' cry as they close in on the psalmist brings the first section of this psalm to a conclusion dominated by threat. Their taunt dramatically poses the question the psalmist must resolve in the face of this threat and to which he will return directly at the end of the psalm: "Does Yahweh deliver?"

A Shield Around Me (3:3–4)

THE PSALMIST IS undefeated by the attempt to undermine and demoralize him. Faced with the real and immediate threat the enemies represent, confronted with their contention that Yahweh can provide no escape from their relentless pursuit, the psalmist does not flee, nor does he capitulate in silence. Instead, he responds with a cry of his own—directed not to the enemies but to God himself. The cry of confidence that issues from his lips has the distinct appearance of hindsight gained after the fact of actual deliverance. In recalling the event, the psalmist remarks what he could not have known in the midst of the conflict: that Yahweh would hear and respond. The psalmist's cry is introduced by the adversative phrase "But you ... O LORD" and begins to counter the enemies' confident assumption that they control the outcome of the situation.

---

6. In this case using the more ancient form *yešuᶜatah*.

7. H.-J. Kraus (*Psalms 1–59*, 139) suggests this meaning for *yešuaᶜ*. I like this nuance much better in this particular context since there seems to be little indication of "victory" as this passage is often translated. See also the article on "Salvation" in *ISBE*², 4:287–95.

8. Cf. the ignorant pronouncement of the fool in 14:1 or the arrogant dismissal of the wicked in 10:4.

Shield. The opening phrase of the psalmist's cry is entirely appropriate to the rather military context I have sketched out above. "But you are a shield around me, O LORD." Confronted by impending destruction, the psalmist calls on his God as a protective barrier to inhibit and frustrate those who plan to do him harm. The term *magen* used here normally refers to a smaller round shield held in the hand and designed to protect the arm and upper torso of the soldier in battle[9] while permitting freedom of movement to maneuver and counterattack. Yahweh, however, is complete protection—a *magen* that surrounds the psalmist before and behind.

Glory. The second phrase of the psalmist's cry for help is somewhat less expected. While the need for protection is clear, the description of Yahweh as the psalmist's "glory"[10] and the one who "lifts up my head" is more obscure in this context. The Hebrew term *kabod* ("glory") is used most often of God, though it can also on occasion refer to humans. Human glory is that recognizable dignity or honor a person can lay claim to in public circles. Some humans receive glory by virtue of their status (e.g., the king) or wealth and sartorial splendor; others are recognized because of their wisdom or righteousness. But for all humans there is a basic human dignity conferred by God (cf. Ps. 8:3–8, esp. v. 5). Any kind of human glory or dignity, whether basic or elevated, divinely given or conferred by public opinion, is at risk when the enemies seek to destroy the psalmist's very *nepeš*. So in our context, when the psalmist's own glory is under attack, he recognizes that his only hope is in the unimpeachable honor and dignity supplied and guaranteed by Yahweh alone.

Lift up my head. Yahweh is the giver of dignity and also the one who lifts up the head of the psalmist. Lifting the head is a public indication of dignity and honor. For the king to lift one's head is a sign of acceptance and approval (cf. Gen. 40:13)—in studied contrast to the common symbolic act of publicly subjugating enemies by putting one's foot on their necks as they lie prostrate. To lift one's own head, by contrast, is to be guilty of pride and arrogance. Confronted by the threat of the enemies, the psalmist acknowledges the vulnerability of his own honor and dignity in these circumstances and turns in confidence to the true source of glory and the establisher of human dignity: Yahweh.

What the beleaguered psalmist is looking for is a public demonstration of support from Yahweh in the presence of the enemies' onslaught—something akin to the anointing of the head in the presence of one's enemies

---

9. At least one scholar reads *magan* instead of *magen* and translates the whole phrase as "You are my suzerain. . . ." This seems overly speculative and unnecessary, since the normal understanding of *magen* as "shield" is entirely appropriate to the context.

10. See the NIV text note on 3:3.

mentioned in Psalm 23 (a participle from the Hebrew root *srr*, related to the noun used in our text), or to a present-day ruler speaking out in behalf of a cabinet appointee under attack by a political opponent. Such a request seems more appropriate in a setting of political conflict than an actual military engagement and suggests the hand-to-hand combat imagery is just that: a figurative description rather than depiction of a military conflict.

I cry aloud. Having established the foundation of Yahweh's good intent to maintain the dignity and honor of the faithful, the psalmist continues with a statement of confidence. "To the LORD I cry aloud, and he answers me from his holy hill." The passage is perhaps better rendered as a conditional sentence: "Whenever I cry aloud ... he answers me...." This implies that the psalmist's confidence is grounded in previous experience of divine deliverance. As Yahweh has protected in the past, so he can be trusted to save in the present—no matter how hopeless the circumstances.

Despite the sense of confidence exuded in these verses, the psalmist is not naively unrealistic about the dangers encountered in the present. The threat is real and about to have drastic consequences. The Hebrew construction emphasizes that the psalmist's plea for divine help is an audible shout, as one might expect in the heat of battle or if one were attacked on the street. Yahweh's answer comes immediately "from his holy hill"—a probable reference to the Temple Mount in Jerusalem on which the Israelite temple stood. The whole hill was considered holy ground, not just the temple itself. Before approaching the Temple Mount, worshipers took care to consider their moral preparedness (cf. Ps. 24) and to undergo ceremonial washing to symbolize their repentance and cleansing of sin.

Just what form Yahweh's answer took is not clear in this psalm. Some suggest a ritual background in which a priest or prophet utters God's promise of deliverance to the supplicant. Once again, this may suggest the psalmist is using descriptive imagery of the battle to dramatize the real conflict he is experiencing. The *selah* in verse 4 marks the end of the second section of Psalm 3.

The Realization of Deliverance (3:5–8)

THE FINAL SEGMENT of the psalm exudes an almost eerie sense of confidence and security. As a result of the perception gained in the preceding verses that Yahweh is the unshakable source of human dignity and honor, the psalmist is able to "lie down and sleep" without fear of the multitude of enemies arrayed against him. Although his opponents are "drawn up ... on every side," the psalmist can rely on the God who is "a shield around me" (v. 3) to protect his honor and establish his dignity.

Lie down and sleep. Some suggest this reference to lying down, sleeping, and awaking indicates the psalmist's participation in a ritual known as *incubation*, a form of supplication in which supplicants spent the night in the temple before God seeking his mercy and deliverance. Alternatively, the psalmist, unable to stay awake to protect himself from the looming enemies, is nevertheless sustained by God so that he rises again in the morning unharmed.

I will not fear. The psalmist now interprets to the hearer the picture of confident rest in the midst of insecurity hinted at in the preceding verse. In a situation calculated by the enemy to invoke fear, the psalmist is unshaken. In the face of unimaginable odds ("tens of thousands") the psalmist, who has recognized Yahweh's protective strength and good intent to maintain human dignity and honor, is unafraid.

Arise, O LORD! From the depiction of confident rest, earnest supplication, and divine protection of the exhausted psalmist in verses 5–6, the psalmist turns at last to the plea for deliverance anticipated from the opening verses. Unlike the earlier reflection of his hindsight reported in verse 4, this later plea shows no awareness that God has already answered the psalmist's cry. Here the psalmist, still desperate for deliverance, adjures Yahweh in imperative terms to come to his aid and frustrate the plans of the enemy. "Arise, O LORD!"

The phrase used here (*qumah yhwh*) employs an unusual form of the second-person imperative of the verb *qum* with an ending added that is often described as intensifying the force of the imperative. This particular form occurs only sixteen times in the Old Testament. Of these sixteen, thirteen are pleas directed to God for deliverance (with ten of these thirteen found in the Psalter).[11] The imperative denotes a command to "get up" from a sedentary position in preparation for action. One might call others to prepare to depart on a journey, participate in an attack, or ask God to act in judgment or deliverance. The emphasis is that the anticipated action will follow the rising *immediately*. The use of the phrase here underscores the psalmist's desire to have Yahweh act in his behalf—now!

Strike all my enemies on the jaw. The psalmist envisions Yahweh as intervening like a champion warrior in the battle fray, striking out right and left with a battle mace or club. While striking the jaw seems like an appropriate action

11. The sixteen passages where *qumah* occurs are Judg. 18:9; 1 Sam. 9:26; and Jer. 46:16—these three do not address God—and Num. 10:35; Ps. 3:8; 7:6; 9:19; 10:12; 17:13; 35:2; 44:26; 74:22; 82:8; 132:8; Jer. 2:27; 2 Chron. 6:41 (which is identical with Ps. 132:8). Three of these psalms appear in the *Elohistic Psalter* and therefore refer to God (*ʾelohim*) rather than Yahweh.

in hand-to-hand combat, a further nuance is involved. Striking someone on the jaw (or cheek)[12] was a means of public disgrace and humiliation. In 1 Kings 22:24, the arrogant court prophet Zedekiah slapped Micaiah on the cheek after Micaiah had prophesied disaster for the king's military campaign against Ramoth Gilead. In Micah 5:1, the prophet declares how besieging enemies will "strike Israel's ruler on the cheek." Elsewhere (Job 16:10; Lam. 3:30) striking the cheek is considered a form of public disgrace. Once again it seems as if the psalmist is seeking public vindication—this time by turning the humiliation and disgrace the enemies intended for the psalmist back against them.

Additionally, to "break the teeth" is sometimes associated with ending the almost inhumane treatment by the wicked of those who call out to God for deliverance. The wicked can be described as ravenous lions mauling the righteous (cf. Joel 1:6), and breaking the teeth is a way to disarm them and to make them drop their innocent prey (Job 29:17; Ps. 58:6).

Deliverance . . . blessing. The final verse of this psalm encapsulates and drives home the essential message of the whole: Deliverance and blessing come only from Yahweh. At the end the psalmist confronts what the enemies claimed in verse 2: "God will not deliver him." This assertion is effectively countered throughout the psalm and especially here by the psalmist's dogged refusal to be swayed from the recognition that "deliverance belongs to the LORD."[13] Regardless of the multitude of enemies surrounding and closing in, despite their arrogant rejection of the possibility of deliverance, the psalmist remains confident in the good intent of Yahweh to deliver and even to bless the faithful.

The final verse of the psalm reflects how an essentially individual psalm was expanded to the broader concern of the community. In these final phrases, it is not just the psalmist but the whole people of God who declare what the psalmist has affirmed and exhibited in his own experience: "Deliverance belongs to the LORD!" Together they affirm through their concluding petition that he also is the only source and hope of "blessing" for those who are called his people.

---

12. The Heb. word *leḥi* is translated both "jaw" and "cheek," depending on the verse translated or the modern translation being used.

13. The NIV translation of the Heb. phrase *leyhwh hayšuʿah* as "From the LORD comes deliverance," while idiomatically correct, obscures the almost exact rebuttal made in this verse to the enemies' denial in verse 2, where they declare *ʾen yešuʿatah . . . beʾlohim*: "There is no deliverance . . . with God." The construction used in verse 8 is the common Hebrew way to express possession, and the most straightforward translation of the phrase is: "To the LORD deliverance belongs."

MILITARY LANGUAGE. MANY of us may have difficulty with the militant and military language in much of this psalm. Some may never have served in a military setting or experienced battle or hand-to-hand combat. We may never have experieniced an enemy attack on our land. We may be ardently opposed to war and violence in all its forms. As a result, much of the experience of the psalmist may seem alien to us and the warlike language offensive to those who affirm the Christian faith in the words of Jesus, "Love your enemies and pray for those who persecute you" (Matt. 5:44).

But war, violence, and the consequences of both were not unfamiliar to the ancient Israelites. A glance through the pages of their recollected history from Genesis through Esther illustrates how greatly their communal memory was affected by centuries of war, oppression, and violence. Abraham had to gird on his sword and gather his militia to rescue his nephew Lot from the clutches of the four kings who carried him off (Gen. 14). Moses led the Israelites to flee the oppression of the Egyptian pharaohs (Exodus). Joshua directed the conquest campaign against the armies and peoples of Canaan (Joshua). The book of Judges records the constant cycle of oppression of Israel by foreign powers punctuated by periods of peace brought on by the military success of such leaders as Deborah and Barak, Gideon, and even Samson. The official national history of Israel written down in the books of Samuel, Kings, and Chronicles is replete with descriptions of how the Israelites' struggles against foreign oppression—both victory and defeat—defined their experience with Yahweh and their faithfulness to him.

Thus, we must remember that regardless of how foreign and unfamiliar these words and images seem to us, they were not alien to the Israelites who recorded this history and who sang these psalms. Political and military maneuvering and struggle were almost a commonplace in Israel's experience and certainly provided a defining understanding of their relationship to God.

Those who have experienced the violence of military conflict, the threat of invasion, or the tightening noose of siege will have less difficulty empathizing with the experience of the psalmist, if not fully with his sentiments. But even those of us who do not share such experiences need not be unduly distanced from the words and meaning of this psalm. There are indications within the psalm itself that the psalmist may be drawing on military language as dramatic images to speak to a circumstance that is less military and more political or social in nature.

The fact that the psalmist's chief concern in verse 3 seems to be with the preservation of honor and dignity rather than life seems to suggest a more metaphorical or figurative understanding of the military imagery. Rather than deliverance from actual life-threatening military combat, the psalmist is seeking public affirmation of his dignity and honor and the concomitant discrediting of his opponents. This is perhaps a situation that more of us recognize: our sense of personal dignity and honor questioned or attacked, the fear (or reality) of public ridicule, and anger at those who accuse us falsely or undermine us maliciously. These are experiences that most of us can acknowledge as our own or at least understand. In these instances it is not difficult for us to leap over the centuries and to find ways to apply the psalmist's *experience* of threat, oppression, and violation to our own time and place.

Understanding invectives. But when it comes to the *sentiments* the psalmist expresses, we may continue to have difficulty. True, we can understand his fear and panic, we can relate to his ardent plea for deliverance, we may even be able to share his confident expectation that God will answer and does bless. Yet, when the psalmist turns his words against his enemies and asks God to "strike [them] on the jaw" and "break the teeth of the wicked," some of us will have more difficulty, because we feel constrained as Christians from demonstrating such desire for retribution on our enemies. We are not to retaliate with evil for evil but to return good for evil (Rom. 12:17–19). When slapped on one cheek, we are called to respond by turning the other (Matt. 5:39). We are to love our enemies and pray for them (Matt. 5:44). Such commands may leave us more than a little uncomfortable with the psalmist's violent desires for his enemies.

Let me offer two possible reactions to this lack of comfort we often feel. (1) If we are really honest with ourselves—down at the core of our being, where only we and God truly know ourselves—we will have to admit, I think, that sometimes we too feel the kind of anger (sometimes even hatred!) against those who have unjustly abused and belittled us. This is not simply an example (as it has sometimes been explained) of Old Testament, pre-Christ ignorance. It is not that the Israelites (whom the psalmist represents) just did not understand what God truly wanted because they had not yet experienced the gracious love and mercy of God poured out on sinful humanity through the work of Jesus. It is not simply that the Israelites were fiercely loyal to their nation as the one embodiment of the people of God and therefore viewed their own enemies as the enemies of God—and deserving of judgment. While there may be a germ of truth in these claims, it is just too easy to distort them and as a result to miss the challenge these verses make to our own moments of anger and hatred.

(2) We must take a closer look at how the Old Testament uses these particular phrases: "strike on the jaw" and "break the teeth." On at least two occasions (Job 29:17; Ps. 58:6), the image describes breaking the teeth of an attacking lion in order to free the prey from its grasp. In such a case the act is not conceived as retribution or vengeance but the necessary act to break the death grip and save the life of the victim. The psalmist of Psalm 3 feels encircled and constricted—approaching death. His call can be understood more as a cry for freedom than for vengeance on the enemy.

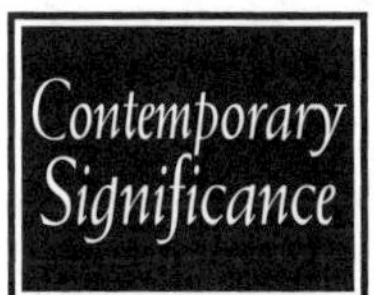

UNDER ATTACK. THIS psalm confronts us on a number of fronts. It challenges us with its clear message that the life of the faithful is *not* a life free from the pain of attack from those who oppose us. None of us desires to be attacked. None of us enjoys the experience when it happens. The attack on the psalmist, however, is of the most severe kind. Not only does it seek to destroy his dignity and honor, but it tries to undermine his very confidence in the good intent of God to bless and save.

Sometimes when we are under attack by a particularly proficient enemy—one who knows us well enough to recognize and exploit our weak spots—we can begin to question our own worth to others, to ourselves, even to God. We live in a world where verbal, psychological, and even physical abuse seem to be commonplace. Neither family nor friends, nor even the church, is above suspicion. The result of having our spirit violated by those we trust is more than anger; often our sense of self is undermined as well. As a result, many go about with questions concerning their value and worth. Often we *feel* wrong even when we are not. When we take stock of ourselves, we may not see much God would want to save. Our inward uncertainty becomes as strong and as destructive as the outer attacks of the enemy. We can be too easily persuaded that the enemy's line is right: "God will not deliver you."

At moments like these—and for some these moments can stretch on for a lifetime—we need to tap into the vision the psalmist holds on to in this psalm, namely, a vision of human honor and dignity that proceeds from God and can only be made real in the heart of each individual by God himself lifting up the head of the person under attack. As long as our dignity and honor come from what we are able to do and accomplish or from what others around us think, we are standing on shifting ground and are unprotected from attack. Human beings fail and public opinion—even that of our closest friends and family—is too often fickle. Only God provides the shield that is both before and behind. Only he is our glory and the lifter of our head.

From another direction, the enemy's shout challenges us by denying that God is willing or able to meet our need. The enemy's cry does not only mean that you are not worth saving; it can also be taken to mean that we cannot trust God to deliver.

Countering the enemy. The psalmist counters the claim of the enemy in ways that remain instructive to us. He relies on past experience of God's deliverance to provide the foundation of confidence for the present. It is here that the NIV translation of verse 4 somewhat obscures the point. What the psalmist is clearly saying is that whenever (in the past, present, and future) he calls on Yahweh, Yahweh always has answered and will answer him. This is not simply blind trust or even trust based on unconfirmed experience; rather, this is trust grounded on God's acts of deliverance.

Often in the middle of the fray it is difficult to remember how God has earlier acted to save us. The present is all-consuming and the danger too real and present. That is why we need other means of remembering who God is and how he has benefited us. Scripture is a key testimony to the faithful and gracious intent of God to save us. Reading Scripture brings us again and again into contact with the history of God's relations with humanity and the world. A wholistic reading of Scripture can leave us with no doubt that God invests humans with great dignity, honor, and purpose from creation to the end of Revelation.

It is also clear in Scripture that God's intention for humanity and the world is good—blessing. In all that he does, Scripture teaches us, God is working for the good of humanity, binding human beings ever closer into the ultimate blessing that is his intention for all creation. God will not be dissuaded or frustrated from accomplishing what he intends for humanity, even by human sin that seeks to destroy us from within or by human evil that seeks our destruction from without. As the psalmist concludes in verse 8, "From the LORD comes deliverance" (or better, "Deliverance *belongs* to the LORD"). He will not be denied.

Along with Scripture and its testimony to the goodwill of God and his power to save, we also need the community of the faithful to add their witness to the saving acts of Yahweh. Sometimes our ability to look to our own experience of the saving grace of God is weakened by the painful experience of the present. That is when we need others who can speak a word of hope, grace, and deliverance to us from *their own* experience. That is the power of community—of life together.

Finally, Psalm 3 challenges us to acknowledge our own moments of anger and hatred and calls us to turn them from cries of vengeance on *our* enemies into pleas for God to deliver the faithful and to establish his justice. When we have been wounded terribly, it becomes difficult—almost impossible, really—to distinguish our cries for justice (which honors the order and righteousness that God intends for our world) from our desire for vengeance (which satisfies our anger and assuages the pain deep within our *nepeš*).

The psalmist's pleas for God to strike the enemies on the jaw and break the teeth of the wicked has a self-serving edge. It is a cry for vengeance with which we have every right to be uncomfortable. Rather than justifying our own desires for vengeance in which our pain is balanced by exacting an equal or greater pain from another, it ought to drive us to seek the mercy of God that forgives and reconciles and restores the purpose he has for all humanity.

THE LAMENTS

While examples of the lament form occur throughout the book of Psalms, this category particularly dominates the first two-thirds of the canonical Psalter. As a result, this segment of the collection (Books 1–3 [Pss. 1–89]) perhaps reflects most clearly the initial painful response of Israel to the devastation of the Exile. While specific laments (whether individual or corporate) may reflect a variety of original settings and circumstances, the editorial decision to group them in such concentration permeates these first three books with the sense of sadness, longing, frustration, anger, and desire for vengeance that surely mirrored the experience of exilic Israel (see, e.g., Pss. 79; 89).

What is particularly true of these laments in the first three books is also true of the rest of the laments scattered throughout the Psalter. Some of them exhibit explicit awareness of the exilic experience (Pss. 74; 89; 137; cf. 107). Others, while originally referring to some distinctly different circumstance, have been adapted, either by their later use or by purposeful editorial reshaping, to make additional reference to the formative national experience of the Exile.

This is especially noticeable when an individual psalm of lament is redirected at the end by the addition of a corporate plea for restoration from Exile (cf. Pss. 14 [also 53]; 25; 28; 31; 69). This reuse or reshaping of such laments does not completely obscure or replace the original context of these psalms, but it does illustrate just how greatly Israel's experience of exile influenced her understanding of her emerging new identity in the exilic and postexilic periods. The psalms (and especially the laments) illustrate how a literature composed to speak to an earlier and different context could be adapted and reappropriated to speak anew to a later circumstance. This illustration serves to illumine the similar history of shaping and reshaping of sacred texts to meet the changing needs in the lives of the faithful.

The Form of the Lament

Because the lament is the dominant type of composition in the first three books of the Psalter, it is important to lay out what can be known about the lament form and how the laments are to be distinguished from the competing primary forms delineated by Gunkel and his successors: praise and thanksgiving psalms. In what follows, I will consider first the form of the lament as a genre category and then discuss the occasion of the laments, including the enemy and the speaker encountered in them.

At the most general level, the three major psalm-types (praise, lament, and thanksgiving) share a rather simple common formal structure. Each includes an introduction, a body, and a conclusion. While these formal elements are the same, however, it is the content of each section that distinguishes lament from praise, and both from thanksgiving.

Introduction. For the laments, the introduction is most often characterized by a first-person cry to God—an invocation—in which the distressed speaker (individual or corporate) calls on God directly to hear and respond to a plea for deliverance. "Give ear to my words, O LORD, consider my sighing. Listen to my cry for help, my King and my God, for to you I pray" (5:1–2). This cry frequently includes questions directed to God: "My God, my God, why have you forsaken me?" (22:1); "How long, O LORD? Will you forget me forever?" (13:1); or requests for divine action in behalf of the supplicant: "Contend, O LORD, with those who contend with me; fight against those who fight against me. Take up shield and buckler; arise and come to my aid" (35:1–2).

The introduction of the lament establishes the speaker's dependence on Yahweh and the expectation that he will deliver those who fear and trust in him. Even in the most pessimistic of laments (e.g., Ps. 88) this sense of dependence is displayed by the psalmist's reluctant willingness to carry the problem of a seemingly distant and hostile God directly to the divine source in hopes of a resolution. As desperate as the situation is, as little hope as there seems to be that God (who is steadfastly depicted as the enemy) will now turn in grace and deliverance, the psalmist of Psalm 88 (and all the other laments, I suggest) ultimately realizes there is no other alternative but to come to Yahweh. This states the dependence issue in its most stark and honest form, for even when there seems to be no hope, the psalmists continue their conversation with Yahweh—because there is no other, a mighty God to save.[14]

---

14. Israel's growing awareness that there is no other God but Yahweh on whom she could trust for deliverance is clearly exhibited in such passages as Ex. 20:3; Deut. 4:35, 39; 5:7; 1 Kings 8:60; Isa. 44:8; 45:5, 6, 14, 18, 22; 46:9; Dan. 3:29; Joel 2:27.

The other side of the introduction to the laments is that they also represent hope. With all their questioning frustration with the apparent delay in divine response, the psalm writers consistently expect Yahweh to act. They know he is a mighty God capable of saving;[15] they know his merciful character from long experience and anticipate an outpouring of his grace once more. We need to remember that these collected laments were gathered, copied, transmitted, and preserved throughout the centuries in order to serve as a resource to those who would read them, recite them, and pray them again and again.

These are not just records of historical suffering and frustration (although they do open a window on that experience). They function on one important level as instruction and models in carrying on a faithful conversation with the maker of the universe. As such they offer hope that in occupying a position of absolute dependence on Yahweh (what Israel called "fear of Yahweh"), people receive benefit from being at one with the purpose of God at work in the world.

Body. Having petitioned the attention and response of Yahweh in the introductory invocation, the laments now turn to the central and more specific concerns of their plea. Often the distinctive character of the body of a lament is marked by the rehearsal of a narrative of the suffering that the narrator is currently experiencing. Slander, sickness, sin, famine, political upheaval, and legal accusations can all be at the root of a lament's pain.

Ruthless witnesses come forward;
  they question me on things I know nothing about.
They repay me evil for good
  and leave my soul forlorn. . . .
But when I stumbled, they gathered in glee;
  attackers gathered against me when I was unaware.
  They slandered me without ceasing.
Like the ungodly they maliciously mocked;
  they gnashed their teeth at me.
—Psalm 35:11–12, 15–16

While the body of a lament most often gives an account of the distress the psalmist faces, that narrative can be punctuated with questions directed toward God's continued absence or delay.

O Lord, how long will you look on?
  Rescue my life from their ravages.
—Psalm 35:17

15. Cf. Isa. 45:22; Dan. 3:29.

But now, Lord, what do I look for?
My hope is in you.
—Psalm 39:7

How long will the enemy mock you, O God?
Will the foe revile your name forever?
Why do you hold back your hand, your right hand?
Take it from the folds of your garment and destroy them!
—Psalm 74:10–11

How long, O LORD? Will you be angry forever?
How long will your jealousy burn like fire?
—Psalm 79:5

Such verses capture the sense of dismay and longing that occupy the thoughts of the psalmists in distress, wandering between fear and hope. They acknowledge that Yahweh is a mighty God, righteous in his character, rejecting evil, and purposing good for his faithful people. Yet the present experience of the psalmist is of divine distance and delay in the face of continued suffering. These questions bring this tension to articulation with hope of breaking the impasse.

We also find, scattered through the narrative of suffering in the body of the laments, petitions that approach God for favor, deliverance, and retribution on the enemy. There is in these psalms a sense that all is not right, that the proper order of life needs to be reestablished by God. Since God is capable of restoring that order and yet delays, the psalmists feel out of favor with him. Thus, there are many pleas for Yahweh to regard the faithful and grant them his grace:

Restore us, O God;
make your face shine upon us,
that we may be saved.
—Psalm 80:3; cf. vv. 7, 19

But I pray to you, O LORD,
in the time of your favor;
in your great love, O God,
answer me with your sure salvation. . . .
Answer me, O LORD, out of the goodness of your love;
in your great mercy turn to me.
—Psalm 69:13, 16

Likewise, deliverance is never far from the psalmists' minds during the recitation of their narrative of suffering:

Come near and rescue me;
redeem me because of my foes.
—Psalm 69:18

Experience of suffering and divine distance drives the psalmists toward God rather than away from him. They seek to awaken God to their need, to hasten his approach, and to ensure his action in their behalf.

Finally, there are within the narratives of suffering frequent petitions for God's power to be expended in retributive actions against those who oppose the psalmist and frustrate the divine will in the world. The psalmists speak with unvarnished clarity of purpose:

May the table set before them become a snare;
may it become retribution and a trap.
May their eyes be darkened so they cannot see,
and their backs be bent forever.
Pour out your wrath on them;
let your fierce anger overtake them.
May their place be deserted;
let there be no one to dwell in their tents. . . .
Charge them with crime upon crime;
do not let them share in your salvation.
May they be blotted out of the book of life
and not be listed with the righteous.
—Psalm 69:22–25, 27–28

May my accusers perish in shame;
may those who want to harm me
be covered with scorn and disgrace.
—Psalm 71:13

While these may seem like harsh and vengeful words (and there may well be that edge to them at many points), their preservation and reuse over many centuries in Scripture has the effect of removing these words from their original setting of *personal* affront, anger, and desire to "get back at" the enemy.

As readers through the ages have looked in from the outside at these harsh statements, I think two things have happened. (1) A certain permission is granted to acknowledge honestly when such anger and vengeance well up inside us in response to the pain and injustice of our own experience. Too often the New Testament commandments to love our enemies and to do good to those who persecute us lead us to pretend (even to ourselves) that we never have an angry thought or vengeful moment against those who offend us and wound us deeply. As these psalms show us, that is probably not true. We are angry, we do hate—even violently sometimes—and to "stuff that anger," to deny that it even exists, is not Christian but a misguided attempt to hide who we in fact really are. It is something akin to claiming that we have not sinned, as 1 John 1:8–10 warns us. Permission to *acknowledge* our anger before God, however, is not license to *act* on our anger against others. Rather, as these psalms suggest, we should leave action against our enemies in the hands of God.

(2) These words force us to recognize that there are individuals and actions that stand in enmity and hostility against God's purpose for a whole world. We ought to be angry at evidences of evil, oppression, and injustice that violate persons (including ourselves) and tear down the structures of peace and wholeness that God wants to build into our daily existence. It is right to have righteous anger and indignation in such cases. The psalmists often equate their personal enemies with God's enemies. While this may seem self-serving—and we ought to be careful to avoid assuming that anyone who angers or offends us is an agent of evil and an enemy of God—the psalmists' words do indicate that they are aligning themselves with his redemptive purposes in the world. It is important for the psalmists to be for God rather than for self and against those who oppose and undermine God's will, and it should be important for us as well.

Conclusion. Having called God to attention in the introduction of these psalms and having poured out their hurt, anger, and hope in the body, the psalmists most often turn at the end to expressions of confidence and commitment:

> Though you have made me see troubles, many and bitter,
> you will restore my life again;
> from the depths of the earth
> you will again bring me up.
> You will increase my honor
> and comfort me once again.
> —Psalm 71:20–21

> The LORD has heard my cry for mercy;
> the LORD accepts my prayer.
> All my enemies will be ashamed and dismayed;
> they will turn back in sudden disgrace.
> —Psalm 6:9–10

These expressions of confidence flow out of the psalmists' understanding of the nature of Yahweh. He is not a God who desires evil for the faithful (5:4), nor is he weak and incapable of carrying out his will. Yahweh is loyal to his covenant promises. Thus, the psalmists' statements of assurance in the face of suffering testify to their faith and dependence on the powerful, loving character of Yahweh, who alone made the universe and sustains all that is in it.

In addition, the testimony of the broader community of faith helps to shore up confidence. When an individual feels tempted to fall into despair, the faith of the community bears testimony to the faithfulness of Yahweh that remains eternally active. This is no "pie in the sky" lack of realism but an act of faithful surrender to the God who is known in the spirit and heart of humans so that—all evidence to the contrary—such knowledge cannot be shaken.

This assurance of the commitment of Yahweh leads the lamenting psalmists to make commitments of their own. Often these commitments are as simple as promises to sing God's praises.

> I will sing to the LORD,
> for he has been good to me.
> —Psalm 13:6

> I will give thanks to the LORD because of his righteousness
> and will sing praise to the name of the LORD Most High.
> —Psalm 7:17

Elsewhere, however, this commitment takes on the more formal character of a vow or pledge for a public act of thanksgiving within the context of temple worship:

> I will sacrifice a freewill offering to you;
> I will praise your name, O LORD,
> for it is good.
> For he has delivered me from all my troubles,
> and my eyes have looked in triumph on my foes.
> —Psalm 54:6–7

> I am under vows to you, O God;
> I will present my thank offerings to you.
> —Psalm 56:12

> Then will I ever sing praise to your name
> and fulfill my vows day after day.
> —Psalm 61:8

> With my mouth I will greatly extol the LORD;
> in the great throng I will praise him.
> —Psalm 109:30

Most likely the occasion for fulfilling these more formal vows would be the offering of the thanksgiving sacrifice (Heb. *todah*) in the temple after deliverance from trouble was accomplished. The connection between plea for deliverance and vow to praise and to offer sacrifices in the temple is even more clearly established in the thanksgiving psalms (see the discussion of thanksgiving psalms in volume 2 of this commentary).

Occasion of the Laments

As far as we can determine them, the occasions that stand behind the biblical psalms of lament are considerably varied. In the individual laments spoken by a single narrator, we encounter at the very least situations of sickness (Ps. 6), public slander (31), false legal accusations (35; 109), general enmity (3; 13; 54; 86), poverty, exploitation, and oppression (52; 53; 102), and the consequences of personal sin (51). Among the communal laments we find circumstances of national distress, including siege by enemies (83), military defeat (74; 79; 80; 137), and general societal evil (10; 12; 82), as well as the effects of famine and drought (85).

It is possible and indeed likely that over the centuries of psalm composition, many other laments were composed in response to other difficulties of life. These other psalms have not survived, however, and that may be either because of the vagaries of transmission or else because of a purposeful process of selection in which a limited collection was created by choosing those psalms most revered and traditionally influential, or those whose character and subject rendered them most adaptable to a broad range of settings and purposes.[16] The occasions of the psalms are not exhaustive but rather suggestive, and they can be extended by analogy to other circumstances.

One must, however, take care to distinguish between the occasion of the suffering to which a particular psalm responds and the circumstance in which a psalm is performed—that is, the occasion *from which* it was produced in contrast to the occasion *for which* it was produced. While the goal of form criticism may seem ostensibly to be recovery of the first of these—the original experience that precipitated the psalm—it is in fact the latter situation that has often dominated form-critical discussion.

We might designate these two occasions the "original experience" and the "occasion of the performance." You can get an idea of the difference between these two occasions by considering the different treatments of the

---

16. There are a few other compositions of psalm-like nature that are known from other texts both within and outside the Old Testament. Within Scripture we find psalms in Jonah 2, Lam., and Hab. 3. Outside Scripture we know several additional psalms from the LXX Psalter and compositions from the Dead Sea *Psalms Scroll* (11QPs[a]).

Israelite monarchy represented by the books of Kings and the parallel accounts recorded in the Chronicler's work. Both share the same original set of experiences (the historical events of the monarchical period), but each has a distinct "occasion of performance," separated by at least a hundred and possibly more than 150 years. One has only to compare the narratives surrounding the transition of royal power from David to Solomon and the preparations for the building of the temple in 1 Kings 1–2 with the parallel narratives in 1 Chronicles 28–29 to observe the radically distinct "occasions of performance."

In reference to the psalms, it can make a dramatic difference in interpretation whether one considers each psalm a private poem composed by an individual for personal reflection and piety, or (as do Mowinckel and his followers) a liturgical composition created for performance within a yearly festival celebrating the enthronement of Yahweh. With the laments in particular, we can see how the original experience precipitating a psalm as well as the communal worship of Israel in which the laments were most likely performed each had an influence on how the psalm was structured and the content presented.

Identity of the Enemies

Scholars have debated the identity of the "enemies" who oppose the righteous in the lament psalms.[17] For the most part we can distinguish between the enemies described in the communal laments and those who populate the individual pleas for deliverance. In the former, the enemies are almost without exception non-Israelite opponents of the nation. As such they also are easily equated with enemies of Yahweh himself.

The situation is more complex in regards to the individual laments. Mowinckel and his followers have attempted to understand all the psalms as part of a national liturgy of enthronement of Yahweh in opposition to the cosmic forces of evil and chaos. In this view, all references to enemies, whether in individual or communal psalms, are ultimately references to these demonized cosmic forces that oppose and seek to undermine the stable creation established by Yahweh. But since Mowinckel's construction of an enthronement festival is problematic and not generally accepted as a persuasive explanation of the background of the psalms, this view of the enemies likewise has little support. It is true, however, that in those psalms where Yahweh's creative power is the focus, the defeat of these chaotic cosmic powers *is* celebrated (see esp. the *Yahweh malak* psalms, Pss. 93–99).

---

17. Kraus (*Psalms 1–59*, 95–99) offers a particularly lucid and helpful discussion of the topic.

In the individual laments one must be satisfied with a more diverse understanding of those who oppose the righteous. In some instances the wicked seem to be those who stand *outside* God's people and who oppose the foundations of Israel's faith. In other cases, the opponents are clearly part of the community of faith, for they participate in the various social institutions of Israel and often seek to employ them to the detriment of the psalmists. The conflict here is between different interpretations of the faith rather than between believer and unbeliever.

The same is true of legal conflicts in which the psalmist is accused in court or confounded through false testimony. The wicked are Israelites exploiting the traditional legal structures for their own benefit. The situation is akin to Jezebel's exploitation of the Israelite legal system through false testimony that condemned Naboth to death and cleared the way to Ahab's acquisition of Naboth's vineyard. Once again, the calumny of the enemy is heightened in these circumstances because they are part of God's people and yet are manipulating the covenant structures to oppress and defraud their fellow citizens.

In some psalms of internal Israelite affairs, class power and privilege are at issue. The psalmists on occasion take the ruling elite to task for their failure to protect the rights of the more helpless elements of society: the poor and needy, widows, orphans, and even resident aliens.

The interpretation of the enemies in the individual psalms is sometimes complicated by the long history of collection, reuse, preservation, and adaptation of earlier psalms for the needs and purposes of the exilic community. This can be seen particularly clearly in Psalms 9–10, where apparently original references to more localized Israelite enemies of the psalmist are reinterpreted as "the nations" who oppose the people of God (see comments on these psalms).

The upshot of this discussion is the realization that all the enemies of God's people are certainly not out there among unbelieving society. Often the righteous must acknowledge that their greatest opposition comes from within—from those who claim the faith and yet twist and distort their interpretation of the essentials of faith to accomplish their own personal goals and benefits. The psalmists, like Job, realize that often the righteous must remain faithful even when the community of faith refuses to acknowledge their righteousness. It can also lead us to understand how God can call faithful individuals to confront and challenge distortions of the faith accepted by the elite leaders or even by the majority of the community of faith.

Psalm 4

FOR THE DIRECTOR of music. With stringed instruments. A psalm of David.

[1] Answer me when I call to you,
O my righteous God.
Give me relief from my distress;
be merciful to me and hear my prayer.

[2] How long, O men, will you turn my glory into shame?
How long will you love delusions and seek
false gods? *Selah*
[3] Know that the LORD has set apart the godly for himself;
the LORD will hear when I call to him.

[4] In your anger do not sin;
when you are on your beds,
search your hearts and be silent. *Selah*

[5] Offer right sacrifices
and trust in the LORD.

[6] Many are asking, "Who can show us any good?"
Let the light of your face shine upon us, O LORD.
[7] You have filled my heart with greater joy
than when their grain and new wine abound.
[8] I will lie down and sleep in peace,
for you alone, O LORD,
make me dwell in safety.

THIS PSALM IS an individual lament (or perhaps better a plea for deliverance) like Psalm 3. The context of Psalm 4, however, is quite distinct from the personal attack that dominated the previous psalm. Here the motivating circumstance seems to be failure of crops as the result of some natural calamity—perhaps drought. Such distress, as frequently occurred in ancient Israel, raised questions about Yahweh's ability to provide agriculturally for his people and drove many into the arms of the foreign gods with their claims of prowess in agricultural (and human) fertility.

The psalmist rejects the fertility deities as false gods, counsels his people to remain confident in Yahweh, and appeals to Yahweh to demonstrate his good intent to his people by providing for their needs.

The Heading (4:0)

SEVERAL NEW TERMS appear in the heading of Psalm 4. The first word (Heb. *lamenaṣṣeaḥ*) appears to be a participle that refers to some liturgical officiant, here translated as "For the director of music."[1] The verbal form of this same root is used in Ezra and 1 Chronicles to describe the task given to some to provide supervision over various aspects of building the temple. In 2 Chronicles, the plural participle form *menaṣṣeḥim* ("supervisors") occurs in the context of temple building as well. By contrast, the LXX of the psalm headings consistently renders the term "for ever" (*eis to telos*), apparently taking the word from a related noun form (Heb. *neṣaḥ*) that emphasizes endurance. However, the appearance of the term in 1 Chronicles 15:21 alongside other phrases related to psalm headings[2] and in a context supporting the normal meaning of the term in the Chronicler's work ("to supervise") seems sufficient to settle the matter. Just who this director was and precisely what role he had are no longer clear. Suffice it to say it denotes some organized supervision of the musical component of temple worship.

The second new term is the Hebrew *binginot* ("with stringed instruments"). The general category of musical instruments associated with *binginot* probably included the more specific *nebalim* ("lyres") and *kinnorot* ("harps") mentioned elsewhere.

Once again the psalm is considered Davidic, although no attempt is made in the heading to associate this composition with a particular circumstance in his life (as was the case in Ps. 3). The psalm is another more generally realized plea for deliverance that is easily adapted to a variety of concerns and settings. It is divided into three segments by the appearance of *selah* at the end of the first two sections. The divisions thus produced (vv. 1–2; vv. 3–4; vv. 5–8) correspond (with one exception) to the more thematic division of the text. The thematic division between the second and third sections seems to come at the end of verse 5—after the string of imperatives directed to the

---

1. The term occurs in the headings of fifty-five psalms, beginning with Ps. 4 and ending with Ps. 140.

2. In 1 Chron. 15:20 we find the phrase *binbalim ʿal ʿalamot* ("with lyres according to alamoth"; cf. Ps. 46:1), and in 1 Chron. 15:21 the related *bekinnorot ʿal haššeminit lenaṣṣeaḥ* ("with harps, directing according to haššeminit"; cf. Pss. 6:1; 12:1). This would seem to confirm the connection of the meaning associated with *nṣḥ* in the Chronicler's work with the form employed in the psalm headings.

psalmist's opponents ("know . . . do not sin . . . search . . . be silent . . . offer . . . trust")—rather than with the *selah* at the end of verse 4. The three thematic sections are: invocation and critique (vv. 1–2), wise counsel (vv. 3–5), and expression of confidence (vv. 6–8).

Invocation and Critique (4:1–2)

ANSWER ME. The opening section of Psalm 4 is divided into a plea directed to Yahweh (v. 1) and a rebuke directed to the psalmist's own people (v. 2). The initial plea ("Answer me when I call to you") recalls the similar expression of confidence in 3:4. Here, however, the phrase functions more as a direct plea for divine response than a confident recollection of past deliverance. The psalmist sincerely wants relief from distress.

O my righteous God. This phrase is more literally translated "O God of my righteousness," and it assumes a legal setting where God is the judge who assesses circumstances and renders a verdict regarding the actions of the parties in relation to what is expected. A verdict of *ṣedeq* ("righteous") implies that the party so named has fulfilled appropriately the demands of rightness. Thus, in the psalmist's case, God is viewed as *already* having rendered a pronouncement in the psalmist's favor. Thus, the righteousness in this verse should be connected to the psalmist, not to God. In a sense the psalmist is saying: "O God, who knows and has proclaimed my righteousness, answer me when I call."

Give me relief from my distress. The psalmist describes his distress as restriction, being closed in, and he understands the desired relief in terms of expansive room. The Hebrew text for the latter ("give room") is a *perfect* verbal form in contrast to the *imperatives* that precede and follow it ("answer me . . . be merciful . . . and hear"). Some translations resolve the conflict by accommodating the perfect to the imperatives—as in the NIV: "Give me relief." Others retain the perfect and understand the phrase as parenthetical expression of the psalmist's recollection of past deliverance.[3] The latter option has the benefit of remaining faithful to the underlying Hebrew, although the meaning of the psalm is little affected regardless of which translation is chosen. Here it is not so much the surrounding of foes as it is the press of circumstances that causes the psalmist to feel hemmed in and restricted.

Be merciful to me. The Hebrew word translated "be merciful to me" is better rendered "be gracious to me." This is, perhaps, a subtle distinction, but this word carries the sense of generous provision. In some instances the thing provided is actually stated, as the children Yahweh graciously provided Jacob

3. Cf. Kraus, *Psalms 1–59*, 144: "—In (my) distress you created room for me—."

in Genesis 33:5. The participial form is used to mean "one who gives generously; generous person" (cf. Ps. 37:21, 26). While in a sense the psalmist does desire mercy from Yahweh, the use of that term in this context obscures the fact that what the psalmist seeks involves Yahweh's generous giving of something he needs—in this case, probably both divine attention to his cry and agricultural relief of the pressing drought.

Hear my prayer. The imperative "Hear!" (*šemaᶜ*) is regularly used as a call to attention. It means something like my old football coach's call, "Listen up, men!" It is the opening word of the traditional call to worship of the Jewish faith and provides the title by which it is known—the Shema: "Hear, O Israel: The LORD our God, the LORD is one" (Deut. 6:4). It is more than just a call to hear; it is also a call to respond in obedience. While this expression may seem a little presumptuous to use in addressing God, the psalmist is surely aware that Yahweh is free to act or not to act as he pleases. But in the midst of distress, the psalmist approaches God in no uncertain terms. The niceties of prerogatives and rank are set aside, and the psalmist approaches Yahweh directly, demanding his active response.

My prayer. As might be expected, the word for "prayer" (*tepillah*) occurs some thirty-two times in the Psalter. It appears in the psalm headings as the defining term of five psalms[4] and is often combined, as here, with verbs calling God to listen to or pay close attention to the speaker's plight.[5] In later times, prayer became a more regularized and formalized practice with a daily series of set prayers initiated by the Shema and involving the binding of small packets of Scripture verses called *tefillin* (from the same Heb. root as *tepillah*) between the eyes and on the arm in obedience to Deuteronomy 6:8 and 11:18. The prayer in Psalm 4, however, is more likely a special prayer directed specifically to the psalmist's current distress.

O men. The psalmist's concern now shifts from invoking the attention and gracious response of God to a critique of the sinful humans to whom the cause of the current distress may be traced. If this psalm is envisioned as presented in temple worship in the midst of a national crisis brought on by failure of crops because of drought, who might the adversaries described be? While the NIV takes the underlying Hebrew (*bene ᵓîš*) in its most general sense ("O men"), there is considerable evidence that here the phrase refers to those of elevated social rank and position in contrast to those of more humble station (*bene ᵓadam*; lit., "sons of a human"; cf. Ps. 62:9, where both terms are used in contrast to one another). It is these *bene ᵓîš*—that is, influential members of society—that the psalmist critiques in 4:2, since they are the ones who wield

4. Pss. 17; 86; 90; 102; and 142.

5. Other verbs used beside *šemaᶜ* include *ᵓzn* ("listen to") and *qšb* ("pay attention to").

the power to affect the nature of communal life that the *bene ʾadam* must simply accept or endure.

How long? A number of Hebrew phrases are translated in English as "How long?"[6] Most express the plaintive plea of the oppressed to God for deliverance from trouble. As normally used, these phrases express the speaker's dismay over God's continued delay in bringing deliverance and have the tone of chiding God and prodding him to action. The use of the phrase "How long?" in Psalm 4:2 runs counter to this normal usage. Outside this verse, when this phrase is used in the Psalms,[7] the question is always directed to God, protesting a delay in his action in behalf of the speaker. In the context of the preceding imperatives invoking Yahweh's aid, the reader/hearer might anticipate a similar movement here. Instead, the psalmist's word turns to question and condemns those who shame God by seeking "false gods."

My glory. According to the psalmist, the *bene ʾiš* are responsible for bringing "shame" on "my glory." There are two ways commentators have understood "my glory" in this text. Following the understanding outlined in response to the appearance of the term in Psalm 3:3, many have taken the reference here as a similar reference to human dignity or reputation. In this view the *bene ʾiš* have attacked the psalmist's dignity and reputation, and it is this attack from which the psalmist seeks deliverance.

Others, however, take "my glory" in 4:2 to refer to the psalmist's God, Yahweh. If this is the case, then the psalmist is not addressing a personal attack but the shame and reproach brought to the glory of Yahweh. How one understands "my glory," then, influences how one interprets the psalmist's critique of the *bene ʾiš* in the following phrases.

Delusions and . . . false gods. The adversaries are said to bring reproach upon "my glory" when they "love delusions and seek false gods." Actually, the Hebrew is more ambiguous than NIV would suggest, especially in regards to the second of these two phrases. "Delusions" is a translation of the Hebrew *riq*, which describes what is "empty" (such as a jar in Jer. 51:34) or done "to no profit."[8] While the term is nowhere outside this verse used to refer to false worship, it is an apt description of "empty, profitless" dependence on false deities who cannot save.

The second Hebrew phrase describing the failure of the *bene ʾiš* is (lit.) "you seek after a lie." On the surface, this might be taken to indicate the opponents'

6. The most prominent are *ʿad ʾanah*; *ʿad matay*; and *ʿad mah*.

7. Cf. Pss. 79:5; 89:46.

8. Lev. 26:16 on sowing seed; Lev. 26:20 on spending strength; Isa. 30:7 on trusting in Egypt's help; Ps. 2:1 on conspiring in rage; Ps. 73:13 on keeping the heart pure; and often with "labor" (Job 39:16; Isa. 49:4; 65:23; Jer. 51:58; Hab. 2:13).

predilection for falsehood, as some translations and commentators do. However, to "*seek* a lie" seems an awkward way to express "take refuge in slander."[9] Elsewhere in the Old Testament, humans are said to "speak" lies, never to "seek" them. Perhaps, then, this alternate construction deserves an alternate interpretation. To this end, it is important to realize that although the verb *bqš* ("seek") is regularly used for the common action of looking for a person or a lost item,[10] it can also be used in a more technical, religious sense to mean "seek divine assistance" or "enquire counsel of a deity" (often through prayer).[11] Couple this technical use of *bqš* with the fact that Amos uses *kazab* ("lie") as a disparaging reference to false/foreign gods,[12] and the NIV translation "seek false gods" presents an attractive possibility.

Such an interpretation suggests that the psalmist's opponents are condemned not because they have attacked the *psalmist's* reputation and honor, but because they have offended the *glory of Yahweh* when they sought relief from their agricultural problems by appealing for deliverance to false gods. In this case, the "lie" refers to pagan fertility deities who (falsely, in the psalmist's view) claimed power over the agricultural seasons as well as the productivity of crops, animals, and humans.

This latter translation and understanding have the added benefit of making better sense of the "right sacrifices" mentioned in verse 5 and the reference to "*their* grain and new wine" in verse 7. I will return to those issues in their proper place. *Selah* concludes the first major section of this psalm (see comments on 3:2).

Wise Counsel (4:3–5)

HAVING CONDEMNED THE opponents for seeking a solution to their difficulties by worshiping false gods, the psalmist now offers sage counsel for appropriate response in the circumstances. It seems clear that the psalmist assumes the opponents are within the covenant community of Israel when he advises them to "offer right sacrifices and trust in the LORD" (4:5). This makes their defection to the fertility gods even more offensive to the psalmist: In their desperation and fear, they have broken the covenant—sacrificed the very foundational relationship with Yahweh alone that set Israel apart from the

9. Kraus, *Psalms 1–59*, 148.

10. As when Saul and his servant seek the lost donkeys of Saul's father, Kish, in 1 Sam. 9:3–10:16.

11. Cf. Ps. 24:6, where *bqš* is paralleled by *drš*, the more usual term for inquiring of God; also Ps. 27:8; 105:4; 1 Chron. 16:11.

12. Amos 2:4. Cf. Ps. 40:4, where the NIV and others understand *śaṭe kazab* to mean "turn aside after a lie [false gods]."

pagan nations. The psalmist offers the opponents three pieces of advice—each characterized by imperatives and each composed of two balancing phrases.

1. God responds to the faithful (4:3). The psalmist begins the response in verse 3 by calling the wayward opponents to a new (or renewed) understanding of Yahweh's special relationship with those who remain faithful to him alone.

Know that the LORD. The psalmist tells the opponents what they should have known all along. The Hebrew word used in this imperative "know" (*ydᶜ*) is not simply intellectual knowledge about something or someone. It has an experiential edge sharpened through relationship.

Perhaps such knowledge is akin to comparing the knowledge one has of a spouse before the wedding and after thirty years of a marriage relationship. At the time of the writing of this psalm, Israel has been the covenant people of Yahweh for several centuries. That relationship implies growing knowledge through experience. The *bene ʾiš*, the psalmist says, should have known from their relationship with Yahweh what he expected of them in this circumstance. With this initial imperative, the psalmist challenges the opponents to reflect and acknowledge how their actions have taken them away from their covenant relationship with Yahweh alone.

The LORD has set apart . . . for himself. "Set apart" (*plh*) has the sense of "make a distinction between, deal differently with."[13] In the covenant, God has taken upon himself a special relationship with Israel. Throughout the Old Testament Israel confesses that Yahweh treats them in ways unlike the "nations"—those other peoples not bound to Yahweh through the covenant relationship. The distinctive nature of this covenant is that Israel experiences the presence of Yahweh among them. In Exodus 33:16, Moses pleads with Yahweh not to remove his presence from him and the people, for without Yahweh's presence, "What else will distinguish me and your people from all the other people on the face of the earth?"

The godly. The NIV of the Hebrew word underlying "godly" obscures somewhat the covenant context of the psalmist's concern. The term *ḥasid* does not mean simply "godly," although it certainly carries those overtones. A *ḥasid* is one who practices *ḥesed*, and *ḥesed* is fulfilling one's obligation to a relationship established—either formally or informally—by covenant. Family relationships, community responsibilities, covenant with Yahweh—all carried their obligations of loyalty and faithfulness. It is this loyalty and faithfulness to Israel's covenant with Yahweh that the psalmist has in view here.

---

13. Cf. Ex. 8:22; 9:4; 11:7, where Yahweh deals differently with the Egyptians and Israelites during the plagues.

It is this *ḥesed* that the *bene ʾîš* have failed to maintain when they turned for aid to the false gods of fertility.

The LORD will hear when I call. The psalmist goes on to cast his own lot with those who remain true to Yahweh alone. The confidence expressed here grows out of his assurance of the special relationship provided by covenant with God. Because of the distinctive relationship that Yahweh maintains with those who are faithful, the psalmist is certain—as the *bene ʾîš* cannot be—that Yahweh *will* respond.

2. Cultivate a proper attitude of humility. Having laid the foundation of covenant loyalty and expectant trust in Yahweh, the psalmist now cautions the opponents to consider how their breach of relationship places them and their community in jeopardy. He calls them to assume an attitude of humility and to take action to restore proper relationship with God.

In your anger do not sin. The more straightforward translation of the imperative of the Hebrew verb *rgz* is "tremble" (the NIV translates this as a prepositional phrase, "in your anger"). The majority of times this word appears in the Old Testament it means "to shake, tremble," usually in response to some fearful stimulus. The earth shakes with an earthquake or at the awesome presence of Yahweh. Humans also acknowledge their vulnerability in the presence of almighty God by trembling. The word captures a sense of instability. Only occasionally is this word interpreted as "rage, be angry"—assuming that trembling is a demonstration of tightly controlled rage.[14]

Commentators who understand the psalmist's plea to be for relief from the false accusations of the opponents usually interpret *rgz* as evidence of their malevolent anger and hostility toward the psalmist. The phrase "Be angry, but do not sin" is then understood as a caution for the opponents to curb their rage and leave the psalmist in peace.

If, however, the context is (as I have suggested above) the faithless response of the opponents to pursue false gods, then this caution flows naturally out of the psalmist's preceding acknowledgment of the special relationship that exists between Yahweh and those who remain faithful to him. The admonishment in this latter case is both a carrot and a stick—a promise and a warning—since Yahweh promises to keep those who trust him but metes out just punishment on covenant-breakers. The psalmist is then calling the opponents to acknowledge how their rebellion has placed them in an untenable position before Yahweh—a position in which they should wisely "tremble" and be careful not to repeat their sinful acts.

---

14. Even in these passages the meaning of *rgz* is rather obscure (cf. Gen. 45:24; Prov. 29:9; Ezek. 16:43).

A number of interpreters rearrange the words in this verse—primarily to restore poetic balance and parallel structure. The usual approach results in the following rendition: "Speak to your heart and do not sin, tremble on your bed and remain silent." This creates a twice-repeated presentation of *command—prepositional phrase—command*. While the symmetry is appealing, there is no textual evidence for this arrangement, and the resultant meaning is little affected. The NIV has wisely chosen to remain with the established text.

Search your hearts. This is an idiomatic translation of the Hebrew (lit., "speak in your heart"). The psalmist tells his opponents to carry on an inward deliberation in light of his admonition. The heart here is not the seat of the emotions, as we most normally consider it. Rather, the heart is the center of reflective thinking and consideration of one's true desires. It is in the heart that one plans and deliberates. The deliberations of the heart can be either good or evil, wise or foolish.[15] The New Testament demonstrates a similar understanding of the heart as the seat of good or evil deliberation when it records Jesus' saying: "The good man brings good things out of the good stored up in his heart, and the evil man brings evil things out of the evil stored up in his heart. For out of the overflow of his heart his mouth speaks" (Luke 6:45).

On your beds. The bed is often pictured as the place where reflection and meditation is done and plots are hatched. In Micah 2:1, the wicked are described as lying awake at night hatching evil plans that they hasten to put into action in the morning. A similar picture is presented in Psalm 36:4, where the wicked plots evil on his bed and "commits himself to a sinful course." The implication seems to be that even sleep offers no relief from the evil created by the wicked—the wicked are simply using the time to lay plans for tomorrow's misdeeds.

Here, however, the psalmist counsels these opponents of his to utilize their time to reflect deeply on their actions and their potential consequences in light of the picture of Yahweh as covenant God of the faithful. Rather than new plans for rebellion, such reflection will result rather in trembling and fearful silence.

Offer right sacrifices. The psalmist concludes the admonition of the *bene ʾîš* with encouragement to set their original wrong right with appropriate religious offerings to Yahweh. In view of the psalmist's earlier description of Yahweh as "God of my righteousness" (v. 1), the "right [*ṣedeq*, right/righteous] sacrifices" required of the opponents are to be understood as acknowledgments of "the justice proceeding from Yahweh"[16]—the reaffirmation of

15. Compare the opening description of the fool in Ps. 14:1, "The fool says in his heart, 'There is no God.' " The Heb. for "in his heart" is the same as in our passage.

16. Kraus, *Psalms 1–59*, 148.

covenant obligations to God. In contrast to their earlier seeking after false gods, the opponents ought instead to acknowledge the rightful claims of the covenant God, Yahweh, by making appropriate sacrifices to him.

Trust in the LORD. It is not enough to make ritual acknowledgment of the rightness of God's claims against his faithless people or to reaffirm through a sacrifice the covenantal relationship that exists between the people and Yahweh. Here the psalmist calls the faithless *bene ʾîš* to the sort of stance they should have assumed from the first—the stance the psalmist has taken all along. To put actual flesh on the bones of their sacrifices, the opponents must place their trust and hope for deliverance on Yahweh himself alone. With this admonition the second portion of the psalm comes to an end.

Expression of Confidence (4:6–8)

THE FINAL SEGMENT of the psalm turns from critique and counsel of the opponents to the psalmist's own affirmation of confident joy in the provision of Yahweh. He introduces this concluding affirmation of trust with the contrasting uncertainty of those who wonder, "Who can show us any good?" This question reveals a rather crass pragmatism that led at the beginning of this psalm to the callous disregard of covenant obligations and the pursuit of false hopes among the fertility deities. The "who" of this sentence clearly refers to the multiple gods and goddesses of the pagan pantheon—here viewed as a sort of competitive services register from which consumers are free to choose the best deal. Personal benefit and profit become the key to religious alliance and practice. "Which deity will provide me with what I need? That is whom I will serve." In contrast, the psalmist, even in the face of uncertainty, trusts in the steadfast love of Yahweh—a love that never ceases.

The light of your face. To see God's face is to be in his presence. When he hides his face, he cloaks his presence, and humans experience the terrible limitations of their own meager power in the presence of life's destructive possibilities. When God's face shines (using the imagery of the life-giving sun), humans experience the benefit and joy that his presence brings. That is what the psalmist seeks as the antidote to the current darkness: the very realization of the presence of God.[17]

You have filled my heart with greater joy. Note how the psalmist uses to great effect the repetition of terms throughout this psalm.[18] Here the heart of the psalmist is contrasted with the heart of the opponents. Whereas their

17. The phrase has many connections with the traditional Aaronic blessing recorded in Num 6:25–26. Cf. also Ps. 30:7; 67:1; 104:29.

18. "My cry" (vv. 1 & 3; NIV "my call"); "righteousness" (vv. 1 & 5); "hear" (vv. 1 & 3); "heart" (vv. 4 & 7); "bed/lie down" (vv. 4 & 8); "trust/safety" (vv. 5 & 8); "many/abound" (vv. 6 & 7).

hearts are filled with fear and rebellious plotting, the psalmist lays claim to a heart filled with joy from Yahweh that far exceeds any hope the opponents may have had for abundant grain and wine.

Their grain and new wine refer to the false hopes for release from drought or famine that have motivated the *bene ʾîš* to pursue the lies of the fertility deities. Even without the abundance promised by these lying gods, there is a joy in relationship with Yahweh that only the faithful can experience and understand.

I will lie down and sleep in peace. The psalmist's confidence in Yahweh is demonstrated by the ability to lie down and go to sleep peacefully even in the face of difficulty. There is an emphasis (using *yaḥad*) on the psalmist's capacity to lie down and to sleep at the same time. In contrast, the opponents are pictured lying wakefully and are counseled to use their time reflecting on their misdeeds (v. 4). The passage links this psalm back to Psalm 3, where a similar confidence is expressed in quite different circumstances (3:5).

For you alone, O LORD. The cause for the psalmist's relaxation is clear: Yahweh is the source of his sense of security. The emphatic use of the Hebrew *lebadad* ("alone") is intended to recall the opponents' rebellious failure to acknowledge their special covenant relationship with Yahweh (vv. 2–3). Their pursuit of false gods is a direct rejection of the realization that the psalmist affirms here: Yahweh *alone* is the true source of safety and *shalom*. He *alone* makes the psalmist "dwell in safety."

MANY ASPECTS OF this psalm enable it to exceed the bounds of its historical and social context and allow it to offer continued guidance to us so many centuries later. I choose to discuss here three emphases that I find particularly striking and central to the psalm's original meaning, and at the same time open interpretive windows into our own setting and time.

The danger of undue influence. The psalmist speaks in the earlier verses of this psalm of the *bene ʾîš*—the influential members of his society. It was these residents of the Israelite upper class—often wealthy, often descendants of the royal family, usually members of the ruling establishment—who set the tone and standards of Israelite life. They were the legal authorities responsible for the administration of justice. They were the guardians of culture and values. Through the priests they influenced the religious norms and practices of Israelite temple worship.

We know comparatively little about the popular religious practices of the common people—those who by the time of Jesus were known by the designation "people of the land." We sometimes attribute the introduction of foreign fertility worship into Israel to the rather untutored confusion of these uneducated masses, who are depicted as worshiping alongside Canaanites at rural open-air shrines and thus failed to distinguish carefully between fertility worship of their neighbors and Yahweh's demands for the exclusive loyalty of his people.

The psalmist, however, targets the influential members of society, not the common persons. These are people "in the know"; they influence and control society at the highest level. The psalmist accuses them of exercising misleading influence. The books of Samuel and Kings offer much confirmation for the psalmist's view. It is the kings who were regularly condemned for their adoption of Canaanite religious practices and for leading the people astray. The prophets certainly agreed that Israel's failure of commitment to her covenant with Yahweh could be traced to the highest levels of the ruling classes: kings, nobility, sages, and even priests.

The psalmist stands almost alone against the influential crowd, calling them to repentance and renewal. Rather than capitulating hopelessly to their overwhelming superiority of power and place, he offers a small but clear voice against the societal tide—a voice of commitment to the foundational covenant relationship with Yahweh. But rather than condemning and rejecting the power elite of the day, the psalmist's critique of the *bene ʾîš* recalls them to first principles and values. He does not wish to dismiss or destroy those who have abused their power to lead the people astray but desires to see them restored to their properly focused position of leadership.

The lure of a pragmatic faith. The psalmist points in 4:6, when the many are described as asking "Who can show us any good?" to the seductive lure of a faith founded on pragmatism. The core of the opponents' problem is that they understand religious worship and relationship with God to be a matter of personal benefit. The focus of faith for those so inclined has a pragmatic edge: What's in it for *me?* Show me the personal benefit!

Once faith came to be understood primarily in terms of personal benefit, pragmatics dictated that the Israelites shop around for the best deal. If the Canaanite deities claimed power over fertility and agricultural productivity, give them the sacrifice they require. Very quickly faith and religious practice become the means of manipulating God (or the gods!) to fulfill *my* needs and desires. The foundational purposes of the covenant—to know Yahweh and to walk in his ways—gets lost in the rush for personal benefit.

It is this core mindset that the psalmist critiques here. The opponents are more concerned with ending the drought and restoring agricultural stability than with maintaining faith with the covenant, so that they ignore the demands of loyalty to Yahweh alone and run to the false gods for relief.

Unlike Job, the psalmist's opponents do not understand that Yahweh is God and worth holding on to even in the midst of trouble and strife. Job held on to Yahweh not because of the benefit he received—he lost everything!—but because Yahweh was God; faced with that reality, Job could do no other.

Knowledge of the presence of God. In verse 3, the psalmist challenges the opponents to acknowledge that Yahweh has established a special relationship with those who remain loyal to their covenant with him. As I mentioned earlier, the key benefit of the covenant for Israel was their continued experience of the gracious presence of Yahweh with them. It is to knowledge of this fact that the psalmist calls the opponents with the demand "*Know* that the LORD has set apart the godly for himself." The opponents, in their pragmatic focus on self-benefit, have forgotten or ignored this foundational truth: Yahweh alone is their God, who is present with them *even in the midst of trouble.*

The Old Testament prophets also condemned the leaders of Israel for their lack of knowledge of God. The kind of knowledge of God that Hosea is after (cf. Hos. 2:20; 4:1, 6) is no intellectual understanding. It is rather a deep experiential knowledge that comes from continued intimate relationship with God. That is why the verb "know" (*yd*ᶜ) is regularly used throughout the Old Testament to describe intimate sexual relations. To develop such intimate knowledge of God requires continued experience of his presence. It is to this hope for intimate knowledge of God in the heart that Jeremiah points when he records God's declaration, "I will give them a heart to know me, that I am the LORD" (Jer. 24:7; cf. 31:34, "They will all know me, from the least of them to the greatest"). For the psalmist, then, it is this kind of "heart knowledge" of Yahweh gained through continued experience of his presence that gives the lie to the opponents' pragmatic attempt to manipulate the false gods for relief.

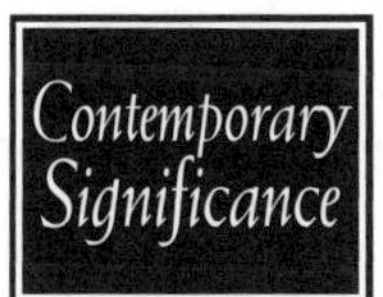

THE PRESENCE OF GOD. This psalm is actually a call to "practicing the presence of God." When Brother Lawrence wrote his small book with that title over a century ago, it offered the shockingly simple insight: that rather ordinary persons could experience God as present in the midst of the ordinary activities of their lives. The key to experiencing God is not withdrawal from ordinary life into the extraordinary life of prayer, meditation, and fasting offered by the monastery or convent. Rather, Brother Lawrence suggested, the key was to constantly place one's mind and heart upon God *in the midst of the ordinary* and so to transform one's common duties and activities into uncommon moments of prayer and communion with God. Knowing God, then, becomes an abiding conversation with the God who is always present and awaits only our acknowledgment of that presence through heartfelt communication with him.

Like the opponents in this psalm, we are often tempted to equate God's presence in our lives with experiences of personal benefit—or, in some instances, with the experience of punishment for some personal sin. As a result, when we experience pain and trouble and can discover no sinful reason for the experience, or when life simply runs on with an almost interminable sameness, we sometimes conclude that God is distant, removed, and unknowable—that "he is not working for us." Consequently we may feel free—sometimes almost driven—to discover what does work! Like the psalmist's opponents, we may find ourselves seeking a lie. No, not the ancient pagan fertility deities that challenged Israel's loyalty, but the things we hope will fill the void and end the pain. Money, power, sex, drugs, control, prestige, relationships are all things we turn to in order to provide a barrier against the droughts and famines of our lives.

What works for me. The strong and popular influences of our own society and time, such as the media, commercialism, politics, business, professional athletics, and even some forms of the church, have been caught up in this pragmatic focus on what works *for me*. We cannot avoid being bombarded through all our senses with the message that *we* are the center of our universe and that our purpose is to use any method available that promises the security and benefit we deserve. Too infrequently does God play any part in the pragmatic methodologies we use in our quest for personal benefit. When he does, there is often a manipulative edge to our approach. Like the psalmist's opponents, our sacrifices often seek to bend God to our will. "You have promised," we say, "therefore, you *must*. . . ."

By contrast, the ability to make the "right sacrifices" that the psalmist envisions grows from a right and intimate knowledge of the God to whom we offer our gifts. Taking our eyes off ourselves and our own benefit and placing our aim entirely on knowing God as he truly is and deserves to be known completely rewrite the equation of relationship with God so that personal benefit and pragmatism are no longer at the center of it.

Pain does not become pleasure, nor does hunger becomes satiety. God does not twist our world so that wrong becomes right. But with God at the center, there exists a rightness that is not obliterated by want or pain. It is not the kind of faith that rejoices in hurt, but a faith that faces the reality of pain with Job's steady confidence: "Though he slay me, yet will I hope in him" (Job 13:15).

Psalm 5

FOR THE DIRECTOR of music. For flutes. A psalm of David.

1 Give ear to my words, O LORD,
consider my sighing.
2 Listen to my cry for help,
my King and my God,
for to you I pray.
3 In the morning, O LORD, you hear my voice;
in the morning I lay my requests before you
and wait in expectation.

4 You are not a God who takes pleasure in evil;
with you the wicked cannot dwell.
5 The arrogant cannot stand in your presence;
you hate all who do wrong.
6 You destroy those who tell lies;
bloodthirsty and deceitful men
the LORD abhors.

7 But I, by your great mercy,
will come into your house;
in reverence will I bow down
toward your holy temple.
8 Lead me, O LORD, in your righteousness
because of my enemies—
make straight your way before me.

9 Not a word from their mouth can be trusted;
their heart is filled with destruction.
Their throat is an open grave;
with their tongue they speak deceit.
10 Declare them guilty, O God!
Let their intrigues be their downfall.
Banish them for their many sins,
for they have rebelled against you.

11 But let all who take refuge in you be glad;
let them ever sing for joy.

Spread your protection over them,
that those who love your name may rejoice in you.
12 For surely, O LORD, you bless the righteous;
you surround them with your favor as with a shield.

THIS PSALM IS another plea for deliverance—perhaps a morning prayer (v. 3)—grounded in the psalmist's unshakable confidence in the nature of God (esp. vv. 4, 12) and characterized by a series of studied contrasts between those who take refuge in Yahweh (with whom the psalmist identifies) and those who oppose the psalmist and God. Following the opening plea (vv. 1–3) and the thematic characterization of God as opposing evil (v. 4), the psalm is divided into four, two-verse stanzas alternating in their focus between the rebellious wicked (vv. 5–6, 9–10) and the hopeful righteous (vv. 7–8, 11–12). The psalmist concludes with confident hope for blessing and protection (v. 12).

The Heading (5:0)

ONCE AGAIN THE psalm is attributed to David with no further attempt to clarify the context of composition. Some note the psalmist's reference to the temple (v. 7) as an impediment to Davidic authorship of the psalm. The only new term introduced in the heading is the phrase *ʾel hanneḥilot*, which some take as description of a tune for accompanying the psalm (having to do with "the inheritance"), but which most commentators relate to the type of musical instrument to be used (usually "flutes").

Opening Plea (5:1–3)

THE PSALMIST BEGINS with a trio of imperatives in synonymously parallel phrases directing God's attention to the psalmist's "words" (*ʾamaray*), "sighing" (*hagigi*), and "cry for help" (*qol šawʿi*). The second of these nouns is part of a constellation of Hebrew words based on the root *hgh*. The basic sense of this root seems to be quiet murmuring or whispering to oneself or others that can be heard but not understood by those around. The murmuring is most often positive (as in meditation on the things of God, cf. Pss. 1:2; 35:28; 63:6; 71:24; 77:12; 143:5), but on occasion it can be construed negatively (the plotting of enemies, cf. 2:1; 38:12; the inability of idols to utter speech, cf. 115:7). Here in 5:1 and in 39:3, the only other occurrence of this particular noun from the common root, the word emphasizes the inward nature of the psalmist's murmuring prayer for deliverance. He calls on God to hear not only the clearly articulated and verbalized pleas but also to attend even to the inarticulate murmuring of an agonized soul.

The verbs used in this initial parallel construction support this interpretation. The first imperative calls God to "give ear" to the psalmist's spoken plea; the second requires God to "consider" or "perceive" what is not clearly spoken but remains trapped in the psalmist's heart; the final one demands that God carefully "listen" or pay attention to the psalmist's utterance, whether internally or externally expressed. Note that it is only in the third parallel phrase that the true nature of the psalmist's speech is made clear to be a "loud cry for help" (*qol šawᶜi*) rather than any other form of quiet meditation or reflection.

My King and my God. Immediately following the third parallel phrase of pleading, the psalmist introduces the first reference in the Psalter to Yahweh as "king." The Hebrew term *melek* was regularly used by Semitic-speaking peoples throughout the ancient Near East for the human monarch or ruler. In Psalm 2:2, the plural of *melek* refers to the "kings of the earth" who oppose Yahweh and his Anointed One. In 2:6, Yahweh terrifies his opponents by declaring, "I have installed my King [*melek*] on Zion," a clear reference to the divine authorization of the Davidic dynasty of Israelite kings. The word continues to appear throughout the Psalter with similar reference to foreign kings and the kings of Israel.

Our psalm, however, introduces a significant theme of the Hebrew Psalter: the recognition that Yahweh is both "God" and "king" of the psalmist individually and of Israel corporately.[1] Human monarchy assumed an important role in the history of Israel. The kings—in particular, David and Solomon—were viewed as providing needed order and stability for life, along with protection and security from foreign powers. Israel's appreciation of kingship and its benefits was always balanced, however, by a modicum of healthy skepticism. The abuses of royal power and position encountered during Israel's historical experience of monarchy are described in 1 Samuel 8:11–18 and proscribed in the Deuteronomic law.[2]

Many psalms, beginning with this one, recognize the limited nature of human kingship and acknowledge that only Yahweh deserves to be honored as eternal king, just in all his ways.[3] Yahweh's trustworthy kingship is the foundation on which the psalmist's cry for help is based.

---

1. See the discussion of "The Kingship of Yahweh in the Psalms," in "Theology of the Psalms," in vol. 2 of this commentary.

2. See esp. Deut. 17:14–20, where the prohibitions listed most nearly approximate the excess for which Solomon is condemned in 1 Kings 11.

3. Compare the sentiments of Ps. 146, where human rulership is denigrated (146:3–4) in comparison to the eternal reign of Yahweh (v. 10), who is described as performing appropriately the responsibilities of the oriental monarch of the ancient Near East (vv. 6–9).

In the morning. Perhaps the double reference in this verse to "morning" indicates that this psalm was intended to accompany the morning sacrifice.[4] It is not clear that this is the intent, however; perhaps the reference to morning is a sign of the earnestness of the psalmist, who rises early to entreat Yahweh for deliverance. The psalmist waits "in expectation," being confident that God will respond positively.

The Character of God (5:4–6)

THE PSALMIST FINDS the grounds of confidence to approach Yahweh in the very character of God himself. These two verses emphasize God's absolute rejection of evil and those who commit evil acts and initiate the alternating attention to the wicked and then the righteous that structures the psalm.

You are not a God who takes pleasure in evil. The psalmist begins with a phrase that describes the essential nature of Yahweh from which human consequences flow: God is incompatible with evil. Where God is, evil cannot coexist. For this reason it is best to take the second phrase of verse 4 as "evil cannot even visit with you." The Hebrew verb here translated "visit" (*gwr*; NIV "dwell") emphasizes the most tentative and impermanent of visitations. In contrast to the Hebrew *yšb* (more normally translated "take up residence, dwell"), *gwr* is often translated "sojourn" and is used throughout the Old Testament to describe temporary, nomadic camping in tents, with an emphasis on impermanence. One who resides in the sense of *gwr* is a temporary alien passing through rather than a permanent resident.[5] The psalmist's point is that God is so incompatible with evil that even the most temporary coexistence is utterly impossible.

It is this understanding of the essential nature of God that informs Israel's unique perception of the *holiness* of Yahweh. In general, the ancient Near Eastern concept of holiness was devoid of any essentially moral element. Holiness was defined by reference to the gods; to be holy was to be what the gods were. Morally, the ancient Near Eastern gods demonstrated no clear distinction from humans. They acted in anger, in lust, or for personal gain. They carried grudges and sought vengeance. They could lie, deceive, and manipulate. Their chief distinction from humans was that they were powerful and lived forever. Thus, they were considered the source of both good and evil in human experience. All that humans experienced—good or evil—was attributed to divine will and action, often completely unrelated to any human responsibility.

---

4. The daily sacrifice of a male lamb and a cereal offering with oil were offered both morning and evening.

5. See Gerald H. Wilson, "יָשַׁב," *NIDOTTE*, 2:550–51; A. H. Konkel, "גּוּר," *NIDOTTE*, 1:836–39.

Israel's understanding of the character of Yahweh broke with this long-standing tradition. As the psalmist's statements imply, Yahweh's holiness was defined by his essential character. Yahweh is eternal and powerful, but he is also essentially good and incompatible with evil. As a consequence, those who align themselves with evil will suffer the consequences of divine rejection. This forms the basis of the psalmist's confident belief that Yahweh will act to frustrate the psalmist's opponents. Where Yahweh is, the arrogant cannot stand. He "hates" those involved with evil deeds (v. 5). This is strong language but consistent with the psalmist's belief that Yahweh cannot coexist with evil or condone the acts of evildoers. Yahweh destroys "those who tell lies" and abhors "bloodthirsty and deceitful" persons (v. 6).

Hope for Deliverance (5:7–8)

BUT I, BY YOUR GREAT MERCY. Yahweh's holiness has two sides. Not only is it incompatible with evil, demonstrated by his rejection of evil and judgment of the evildoer; it is also characterized by his "relentless goodness" toward his creation and those humans who live in it. By relentless goodness I mean that from the beginning, God's only intent was and still is to bless his creation. Judgment and mercy, therefore, are not two competing characteristics of Yahweh but are two inseparable consequences of his holiness. Relentless goodness is the flip side of incompatibility with evil. "God is light; in him there is no darkness at all" (1 John 1:5).

God's holiness offers sinful humanity both its greatest problem and its greatest hope. Because a holy God cannot "wink" at sin or turn a blind eye to it, sinful humans find themselves under his judgment, in need of salvation and reconciliation. But because he is also relentlessly good, he has provided a way, first through Israel and ultimately through Christ, that they can be restored to right relationship with one another and with God in order to continue to receive blessing and not judgment.

Thus, when rightly viewed, Yahweh's holiness is not just the basis for his judgment on sin but is at the same time the foundation for his work of salvation. The key to what humans receive from God—judgment or mercy—is not the character of God but the nature of how humans relate themselves to him. Arrogant evildoers, who rebelliously align themselves with evil, receive the consequences of God's incompatibility with evil: judgment and rejection. But those who "fear the LORD"—and by this phrase Israel means to acknowledge absolute dependence for survival on the merciful holiness of God—receive spiritual restoration and blessing.[6]

6. See the discussion of "Fear of Yahweh" in the section on "Theology of the Psalms" in volume 2 of this commentary.

Verses 7–8 contrast the psalmist's anticipation of divine grace with the divine rejection depicted in the preceding verses. Because of Yahweh's abundant mercy, he dares to enter into the very presence of God in the temple, while the arrogant evildoers cannot even hope to visit with God. The psalmist desires to be led in ways made straight by a merciful God; the wicked, however, can only anticipate divine rejection and destruction. The contrast developed in these verses is reminiscent of Psalm 1, which maintains a similar tension between God's protection of the righteous and rejection of the wicked.

Because of my enemies. In addition to the description of the "straight ... way" of blessing prepared by a merciful Yahweh for those who fear him, these verses provide transition to the next segment of the psalm with this brief mention of "my enemies." It is because of the enemies that the psalmist must rely especially on divine mercy and guidance. Because of their opposition the psalmist's path has become twisted and unsure.

Judgment on the Enemies (5:9–10)

IT SEEMS CLEAR from the phrases used to describe the offense of the enemies that the psalmist is suffering malicious attacks and false accusations. The opening phrase can be rendered, "Nothing reliable exists in their mouth."[7] The word interpreted "can be trusted" in the NIV means "that which is firmly established, grounded."

Their heart is filled with destruction. This phrase is difficult, and the NIV is somewhat misleading. The normal Hebrew word for "heart" (*leb*) is not used here. In its place we find a noun of the root *qrb*. One noun of this root (*qereb*) describes the inward parts of a human or an animal, sometimes considered the seat of emotion or thought. Those who understand *qereb* to be the noun in this context assume it implies destructive anger or plotting on the part of the enemies.

An alternative is possible, and perhaps better. The same root *qrb* is most often related to spatial nearness or approach, with verbal forms expressing "draw near, approach"; at least one noun (*qerab*) carries the meaning "hostile approach" or "battle." In the context of this verse, it may well be preferable to translate the phrase "their approach is destruction." If so, the psalmist is not so much criticizing the inward character or plotting of the opponents as expressing dread at their very approach, for whenever they appear, destruction follows in their wake.

---

7. The psalmist alternates in this verse between singular and plural reference to the enemy. Here the third masculine singular pronoun ("his mouth") is used, while the very next phrase employs the third masculine plural ("their heart").

The last two phrases of verse 9 continue this unflattering portrait of the psalmist's enemies. Their throat is an open grave through which those they slander are brought to ruin and even death.[8] Their tongue is skillfully adept at smoothing the rough edges of falsehood so that it becomes palatable.[9] What powerful images of the deadly consequences of slander!

It is interesting to note in the Hebrew of these verses that while the psalmist refers to the enemies with plural pronouns, they are consistently viewed as sharing a single body part. They have only one mouth, one heart, one throat, and one tongue. This feature is irregular enough that it seems obvious the psalmist is seeking to portray his multiple enemies as a single entity acting in concert.[10]

Declare them guilty, O God! Having established the grounds for a case against the opponents before Yahweh, the psalmist, like some modern-day prosecuting attorney summing up before jury and judge, now demands a verdict appropriate to their offense. The psalmist desires that the enemies' slanderous attacks and rebellious plans will turn back on them.

An interesting contrast is created through the use of a phrase literally translated "in the multitude of," both here (v. 10) and earlier in verse 7. Here the opponents are to be judged by God "in [because of] the multitude of their sins." By contrast, in verse 7 the psalmist has hopes to enter the presence of God "in [because of] the multitude of your [Yahweh's] faithful mercy." The use of the same phrase in such different ways heightens the contrast the psalmist is establishing between the rebellious enemies and the righteous sufferer.

The appropriateness of the judgment the psalmist seeks is obvious from the use of the imperative "banish them." Together the enemies present a powerful opposing force. Not only does he desire that they fall prey to their own destructive plans, but he hopes Yahweh will destroy their ability to act in unity and thus blunt the effectiveness of their attack.

The psalmist concludes this plea for judgment against the enemies by characterizing their offense as more than a simple personal attack against him or a case of misunderstanding. The opponents are sinners, and their deeds are open rebellion against God himself. When evildoers falsely accuse the righteous, they violate the very nature of Yahweh (cf. vv. 4–5) and thus

---

8. There is an interesting parallel between this image and the Ugaritic myth of the god Mot (meaning Death), who is depicted spreading his lips from sky to earth in order to convey hapless humans to the abode of the dead through his open gullet.

9. The word translated in the NIV as "speak deceit" (*ḥlq*) is most often translated as "use a smooth tongue" in the sense of speak flattery or deceit.

10. This may explain the appearance in the first phrase of v. 9 of the doubly singular construction *pihu* ("his mouth").

deserve the judgment that proceeds from God's incompatibility with evil. In other words, the psalmist's demand for judgment is not so much a call for vengeance for a personal affront as it is a desire for the harmonious covenant relationship intended by Yahweh to be affirmed and established against all attack.

The Benefit of the Righteous (5:11–12)

THE PSALMIST INTRODUCES the final contrast with a description of the joyous response to deliverance by "all who take refuge" in Yahweh.[11] While the enemies will fall under the weight of their own rebellious plotting, those who revere Yahweh (v. 7) and make him their refuge (v. 11) will "be glad" and "ever sing for joy."

The theme of taking refuge in Yahweh is an important one in the Psalter and has already been initiated in the blessing that concludes Psalm 2: "Blessed are all who take refuge in [Yahweh]" (2:12). The immediate image evoked by these terms is that of fleeing to a fortress or place of security in time of trouble. Such trust is more than a temporary desire for protection or security. It evidences a willingness to commit one's whole destiny to God. As such this phrase is an appropriate equivalent of the more familiar "all who fear the LORD," for both communicate an awareness of one's absolute dependence on God's characteristic holy mercy—a mercy that is not deserved, cannot be presumed, and yet constitutes sinful humanity's only hope, no matter how firmly established they may be among "the righteous" (v. 12).

As the psalmist's imperative demands for judgment against his opponents in verse 10 follow a description of their character as grounds of judgment (v. 9), so here his description of the enduring joy of those who take refuge in Yahweh is followed by a request for divine protection. The image the psalmist presents has several possible antecedents. The NIV's "Spread your protection over them" is a rather expansive rendering of the much briefer underlying Hebrew *tasek ʾalemo*, which is more literally translated, "Cover over them." First Kings 8:7 uses the same words to describe the cherubim at the ends of the ark of the covenant in the Most Holy Place of the temple as spreading their wings to "cover over" the ark. The psalmist in Psalm 17:8 asks Yahweh to hide the one seeking refuge in him "in the shadow of your wings." In 91:4 we hear that Yahweh "will cover you with his feathers, and under his wings you will find refuge." The occurrence in these contexts of several parallel expressions and words—especially "take/seek refuge" (5:11; 17:7;

11. The verb *ḥsh* ("take refuge") is used twenty-five times in the Psalter, most in reference to finding security with Yahweh. The noun *maḥseh* ("refuge") appears an additional twelve times with similar reference.

91:2, 4, 9) and "shield" (*ṣinnah* rather than the more common *magen*; cf. 5:12; 91:4)—makes this an attractive connection.

Verse 12 returns to a sense of certainty and hope grounded in the character of God. As in verse 4, where the psalmist takes God's incompatibility with evil as grounds to anticipate divine judgment of the wicked, so here hope for blessing and protection of the righteous are grounded in the certainty that Yahweh is a God who blesses the righteous and surrounds them with favor like a shield. These two descriptions of the character of God (vv. 4, 12) bracket the core contrasts of the psalm (vv. 5–11) at the beginning and end as a sort of variation on the inclusio. It is this core understanding of Yahweh that stands at the heart of this psalm, and indeed of all the lament psalms. If there is any primary message here, it is that who God essentially is and how humans respond to that essence determine what humans ultimately receive from his hand.

PSALM 5 EMPHASIZES two concepts that contemporary humans—particularly those living in the decidedly Western context of the United States—have difficulty relating to: monarchy and divine holiness. This psalm presents these two themes (esp. the latter) as essential foundations for appropriate human understanding of and response to God.

The kingship of God. Those of us who have been shaped by the modern experience of democracy often have a difficult time understanding and appreciating monarchical rule. We prize individual freedom and choice and have a strong suspicion regarding any authority that is imposed or established without our consent. As enshrined in our foundational documents, authority to govern is conferred by those governed and is to be exercised for the benefit of those who confer it. If governance fails to provide the protections and benefits expected, the governed have the right to change the governing authority—whether peacefully by an elective process or violently by rebellion.

Ancient monarchy, by contrast, often seems grounded in autocratic, authoritarian, and unilateral rule by force. Dynastic rule eliminated any choice on the part of the governed, relying on heredity rather than ability, charisma, or promise of benefit. In ancient Egypt of the Old Kingdom, the king (or pharaoh) was believed to be divine—Horus, the son of the god Osiris, who ruled directly over humans. To resist his rule was to resist the cohesive order of the universe (know as *Maʿat*) and was consequently not only unwise but ultimately wicked.

At the opposite end of the Fertile Crescent in Mesopotamia, kings rarely considered themselves divine. They were viewed nevertheless as endowed with authority to rule, not by the people they governed but by the gods themselves. Although this might seem autocratic and oppressive—and it certainly lent itself to abuse on occasion—kingship in Mesopotamia always understood that part of its divine authorization was based on an expectation of benefit to be provided to those governed. In royal records, stelae, reliefs, and other documents, the kings often felt constrained to describe their reigns in terms of the benefit provided to the people and kingdom—even though annexed by military conquest. Key issues were order and justice, security (both national and personal), economic prosperity, and appropriate respect to religious shrines and worship—not too different from our contemporary expectations of government.

Israel's view of human kingship was not far removed from that of her contemporaries. In 1 Samuel we learn that Yahweh permitted kingship in response to needs expressed by the people. Kings were authorized by Yahweh and anointed as a sign of their choosing by God's prophet. They were expected to lead the people in the ways of Yahweh and had limits placed on their royal powers and freedoms.[12] Abuse of their prerogatives brought condemnation and punishment, as David's adultery with Bathsheba and Ahab's seizing of Naboth's vineyard both illustrate.

Thus, while the Israelite kings were not considered gods, they were divinely installed and authorized, and their responsibility was to God for the benefit of the people, not vice versa. Israel's ultimate experience of monarchy, however, was that human kings could not be relied upon to produce consistently the kind of security, prosperity, and spiritual balance that had been anticipated. Psalm 146:3–4 encapsulates the limitations of kingship Israel came to understand:

> Do not put your trust in princes,
>   in mortal men, who cannot save.
> When their spirit departs, they return to the ground;
>   on that very day their plans come to nothing.

Kings abuse their power, and even the best of them die, leaving their people an inheritance of turmoil and insecurity.

The way Israel came to resolve the problems generated by the failings of human kings was to shift their hope and trust to the divine rule of Yahweh. Psalm 146:5, 10 exclaims:

> Blessed is he whose help is the God of Jacob,
>   whose hope is in the LORD his God. . . .

---

12. See esp. Deut. 17:14–20.

The LORD reigns forever,
your God, O Zion, for all generations.

As Psalm 5:2 already acknowledges, Yahweh is both God and eternal King.[13] As king, he is able to do what human kings ultimately fail to accomplish—rule justly and righteously forever.

Responding to divine holiness. God's holiness can be a fearsome thing. Humans who come suddenly or unaware into the divine presence are shaken and must take precautionary action. Moses removed his sandals at the burning bush (Ex. 3); Jacob built an altar after realizing Yahweh was in the place he had spent the night (Gen. 28).

Throughout the Hebrew Bible Yahweh's holiness confronts sinful humans (and *all* are sinful!) with threat. After Moses desired the opportunity to see the defining essence of Yahweh ("Show me your glory," Ex. 33:18), God declined on the grounds that such full disclosure would destroy Moses ("No one may see me and live," 33:20). Isaiah had much the same experience when he saw Yahweh in the temple, surrounded by seraphim proclaiming God's holiness: "Woe to me! . . . I am ruined! For I am a man of unclean lips . . . and my eyes have seen the King, the LORD Almighty" (Isa. 6:5). Thus, as I suggested previously, God's holiness—his incompatibility with evil—presents sinful humans with their greatest problem: the destructive consequences of sin in the presence of holy God.

But judgment is not holy God's final word. At the burning bush Moses was not destroyed but provided a way to stand before Yahweh's holiness unharmed. God even answered Moses' later request to see God's glory as much as was possible: "When my glory passes by, I will put you in a cleft in the rock and cover you with my hand until I have passed by. Then I will remove my hand and you will see my back; but my face must not be seen" (Ex. 33:22–23).

Isaiah had a similar experience. Certain of imminent destruction, he experienced instead divine redemption and cleansing. His "unclean lips" were purified by a coal from the altar, and he was allowed to stand in the divine presence—even commissioned to do the divine will. This experience of unexpected, undeserved redemption by holy Yahweh provides shape to the whole book of Isaiah. In Isaiah 1–39, God's holiness is advanced as the basis of judgment against rebellious Israel. Isaiah's most frequent title for Yahweh,

13. As already mentioned in relation to Ps. 2, the kingship of Yahweh is sometimes connected to the future reign of the Messiah—the Anointed One—who will bring Yahweh's divine reign down to earth. See also the discussion of the kingship of Yahweh before Pss. 93–99.

"the Holy One of Israel," is regularly associated with oracles of judgment in these chapters, emphasizing his incompatibility with evil.

When, however, the reader crosses the boundary represented by Isaiah 40, a remarkable change occurs in how Yahweh's holiness is perceived. In chapters 40–66, the Holy One of Israel is connected with hope for redemption and oracles of salvation. "Your Redeemer [is] the Holy One of Israel" (Isa. 41:14).[14] It is attractive to connect this understanding of holy Yahweh as both judge and redeemer with Isaiah's own experience in the temple (Isa. 6:1–9), where he anticipated the judgment he knew he deserved but received instead redemption and grace.

It is this experience of divine holiness associated with redemption, grace, and salvation that drives home the inadequacy of a negative view of holiness as divine judgment against sin. It is that, of course, but Yahweh's holiness is so much more. In his holiness, God's relentless goodness toward all he has made is working itself out in benefit and blessing. That is why divine holiness remains not only sinful humanity's greatest problem, but it is at one and the same time its greatest hope. The Holy One who *judges* is also the Holy One who *redeems*! Israel comes ultimately to stake her life on that fact.

PERHAPS THE MOST important lesson contemporary humans can take from this psalm is that human hope is grounded in the essential character of God—a character that is constant and does not change regardless of the ebb and flow of human circumstances. The righteous—those who take refuge in God—find hope in God's holiness both because he is incompatible with evil *and* because he is relentlessly good.

We hope in God and find refuge there because, despite the rampant evil that characterizes our world and even gains a foothold in our own lives, God is not unconcerned with evil or injustice. Even less is he their author. That is why the faithful throughout the ages, when faced with the implacable evil of pain, suffering, oppression, and injustice, are able to call confidently on God for redress, as the psalmist does here. As Christians we may be somewhat disconcerted by the harsh imprecations heaped on the enemy by the righteous. We feel constrained to moderate our anger and sense of injustice after the words of Jesus, "Bless those who curse you" (Luke 6:28; cf. Rom. 12:14). But the psalmist's words call us to remember that Jesus was never afraid to call evil what it was or to take a firm stance of condemnation against

14. Cf. also Is. 43:14; 44:6, 24; 47:4; 48:17; 49:7; 54:5, 8; 60:16; 63:16.

all its forms. We too must take evil seriously, aligning ourselves with God's essential character of holiness.

We must also trust and proclaim the relentless goodness of God that will never allow evil to have the last word. The biblical message is consistent in affirming that the world as we know it is broken and does not represent the full intention of the creator. God is not the author of the evil we experience, nor is he unconcerned or unable to respond. The mystery of continued suffering and evil does not undermine the psalmist's confidence that God's full intent and purpose for humanity and all creation is good and blessing. Even Job ultimately confessed that the God he encountered was sovereign over the creation and worth holding on to despite the clamoring voices of pain and suffering.

In the final analysis, the psalmist sides with Job. His hope is grounded not in the swirling press of circumstance but on the unchanging sovereignty of holy Yahweh. Yahweh is the psalmist's king and God (v. 2), as he is ours. He is the king who establishes justice and security. He is the sovereign who leads us in the paths of righteousness and divine blessing. Let all who take refuge in him be glad!

Psalm 6

FOR THE DIRECTOR of music. With stringed instruments.
According to *sheminith*. A psalm of David.

1 O LORD, do not rebuke me in your anger
  or discipline me in your wrath.
2 Be merciful to me, LORD, for I am faint;
  O LORD, heal me, for my bones are in agony.
3 My soul is in anguish.
  How long, O LORD, how long?

4 Turn, O LORD, and deliver me;
  save me because of your unfailing love.
5 No one remembers you when he is dead.
  Who praises you from the grave?

6 I am worn out from groaning;
  all night long I flood my bed with weeping
  and drench my couch with tears.
7 My eyes grow weak with sorrow;
  they fail because of all my foes.
8 Away from me, all you who do evil,
  for the LORD has heard my weeping.
9 The LORD has heard my cry for mercy;
  the LORD accepts my prayer.
10 All my enemies will be ashamed and dismayed;
  they will turn back in sudden disgrace.

A STRIKING PLEA for deliverance, Psalm 6 employs a dramatic description of physical pain and anguish and the resulting emotional distress to good effect. It may be, as many suggest, that the psalmist's cause for distress is severe illness or debilitating disease, though such descriptions are sometimes used as metaphors for other kinds of suffering.

The psalm is divided into three main units. The opening segment (vv. 1–5) is directed to God, entreating his aid. This invocation is punctuated with almost desperate cries (vv. 3, 5). The psalmist turns in the second unit to a narrative description of the physical torment endured as a result of suffering

(vv. 6–7). This section concludes with a transitional reflection that the psalmist's pain is increased because of the opposition of enemies (v. 7). The final segment turns to a confrontation of the psalmist's foes, coupling a rejection of them with an assurance of God's willing deliverance (vv. 8–10).

The Heading (6:0)

MOST OF THE terms here are familiar from earlier psalms.[1] The only newcomer is the phrase "According to *sheminith* [*šeminit*]." The term is most likely musical, reflecting either a type of eight-stringed instrument or a particular instrumental tuning. As in most of the psalm headings, the reference to David comes after the liturgical instruction—perhaps an indication of the order in which the elements were added.

Invocation of God (6:1–5)

THESE FIVE VERSES where the suffering psalmist invokes Yahweh to come to his aid can be divided into three subsections, each exhibiting distinctive, parallel grammatical structures.

Do not rebuke me in your anger. The first subsection (v. 1) is composed of two lines of affirming parallelism employing negative jussives. Jussives are verbal forms that express the will of the speaker without resorting to the absolute demand associated with the imperative. An instructive example is the way Esther approaches the king in Esther 5. She wishes to invite Xerxes to a banquet she has prepared for him and asks him in this manner: "If it pleases the king ... let the king ... come today to a banquet I have prepared for him" (5:4). You don't command a king's attendance! You *request* it. The same is even more true of God. The psalmist requests Yahweh's response. To get this across in a negative expression is awkward: "O LORD, let you not ..."; thus, the NIV uses what could be taken mistakenly as a negative demand.[2]

The word translated "rebuke" comes from a verbal root that describes a process of legal argumentation by which one person is declared to be in the right. In a legal dispute, there are always two parties. For one to be declared right means the other must be proven wrong. Thus, the psalmist pleads that

---

1. Comments on "for the director of music" are found in the commentary on the heading of Ps. 4. For "with stringed instruments" see the heading of Ps. 4 as well. "A psalm of David" first appears in the heading of Ps. 3.

2. In Heb., negative commands or prohibitions are expressed neither with imperatives nor with jussives but with imperfect verb forms negated by the particle *lo*ʾ. The resulting construction means something like "Don't!" or "Don't even think about it!" The most familiar group of negative imperatives in the Old Testament are the Ten Commandments, where imperfects negated by *lo*ʾ are traditionally rendered "Thou shalt not. . . !"

Yahweh will not prove himself right at the psalmist's expense. As Job understood, however, it is ultimately futile to confront God in court, for God can only be shown to be in the right and his accuser in the wrong.

Discipline. The second jussive in the parallel phrase stresses the educational aspects of discipline and training. Here the picture is the training of an animal or a child. Such discipline can proceed from calm resolution and determination, but it can sometimes (when the subject being trained is balky and rebellious) derive from a core of hot anger. The psalmist again pleads that God will not allow the psalmist's rebellious actions to lead to angry discipline and rebuke.

Anger . . . wrath. The psalmist fears that the suffering he is experiencing results from divine anger or wrath. Thus, he pleads for Yahweh not to establish his case, for in doing so the psalmist will be shown in the wrong. Whether this indicates an awareness of guilt of some sort on the part of the psalmist is not clear, but Yahweh is viewed at once as both threat and hope. If the psalmist's malady is physical sickness, the ancient world often saw a direct connection between guilt and illness. Sickness was viewed as divine punishment for sin. For this reason the Pharisees asked Jesus about the man who was blind from birth: "Who sinned, this man or his parents?" (John 9:1–2). The two parallel Hebrew words for "anger" and "wrath" (*ʾap* and *ḥemah*) suggest an anger that is hot and poisonous in its intensity.

Be merciful to me. The second subsection of the first unit (vv. 2–3) is set off by a shift to true imperative forms followed by participial clauses introduced by the particle *ki* ("for") describing the state of the psalmist. The emphasis changes as well from the negative request that Yahweh refrain from discipline to more positive entreaties for divine action in mercy and healing. The opening phrase of the unit—"Be merciful to me, LORD"—uses the imperative of the verb *ḥnn* ("be gracious, show favor"). While the NIV is not wrong, it does obscure the psalmist's desire that God show gracious generosity and favor rather than what we normally think of as mercy.

For I am faint. In this positive plea, the psalmist's suffering functions more as a motivation for Yahweh's gracious action than as a description of divine punishment. Perhaps the problem confronting the psalmist is not the fact that Yahweh is punishing the psalmist's sin (though that remains a possibility) but that he has not acted generously to heal the psalmist and remove the suffering. The participle *ʾumlal* can be used to describe the "withering up" of vegetation (Isa. 16:8). The psalmist "shrinks up" both physically and spiritually (as those with severely debilitating disease so often do at the end).

Heal me. While is it not absolutely clear whether the sickness described is real or metaphorical, the psalmist continues to use the language of sickness and healing. In balance with the first phrase of this subsection, he uses a positive imperative followed by two matched participial phrases, both introduced by the initial particle *ki*. Withering away and on the brink of destruction, healing and restoration to health are the goal of the psalmist's desperate plea.

For my bones are in agony. The NIV of the underlying word, while capturing the anguish experienced by the psalmist, does not bring out sharply enough the sense of terror associated with the expression. Elsewhere the word translated "are in agony" (*bhl*) is rendered "terrified out of one's senses"; here it describes not just the agonizing pain of illness and disease but the suffocating fear that can attend deteriorating life force and loss of control. At the very core, in the "bones," fear has taken root that threatens to undo the psalmist.

My soul is in anguish. If the situation seems hopeless, it could always be worse! In the balancing participial phrase, the psalmist adds even more emphasis to the engulfing terror. Not only are the bones, the core of the physical self, terrified out of their senses; the very core of his being, the *nepeš*—that source of selfhood created by the divine animation of the physical body—is even more terrified (lit., "terrified out of its senses indeed!"). As the body fails, the psalmist senses even the animating life force provided by God slipping away.

How long! The first two subsections of the long invocation of Yahweh conclude in verse 3b with an anguished cry that both sums up the desperation of the psalmist and provides transition to the pleas of the final subsection. Having described graphically the terror and disintegration brought on by extended suffering, the psalmist realizes the only hope for healing is the gracious action of Yahweh to save. And yet, Yahweh does not act! The psalmist's question slips out, unguarded, almost an accusation: "But you, O LORD, how long?" (lit.). You can almost hear exclamation points after every word. God is able to save—he is the psalmist's only hope—and yet he continues to delay his response to the psalmist's cries.

Turn, O LORD, and deliver me. The third subsection (vv. 4–5) of the opening unit contains a series of three imperatives demanding divine action, followed by a justifying clause. The word "turn" (*šwb*) is regularly used to describe a change of action or direction. The prophets frequently use the term as a call to repentance.[3] In the wisdom literature, the idiom "turn [*šwb*] from evil" describes the characteristic stance of the righteous. Humans clearly need to repent and change direction, but the term is also used of God. Israel experienced that the mercy of Yahweh could lead him to respond to human

3. The New Testament word for repentance, *metanoia*, captures a similar sense of "changing direction."

repentance with a revocation of decreed judgment. Thus, Yahweh could himself "repent" and "change,"[4] and our psalmist entreats him to "turn" from his long inactivity and act graciously to save.

Deliver me . . . save me. The psalmist uses two further imperatives to entreat Yahweh's deliverance. The first of these has the sense of "withdraw" or "tear out" and is used in at least one context (Lev. 14:40–43) to describe the extraction of contaminated stones from a wall. Similarly, the psalmist desires to be "snatched out" of the engulfing circumstances. The second term is the more common word for "save, deliver, rescue; give aid."

Because of your unfailing love. The psalmist grounds his entreaty for divine action in the merciful nature of Yahweh and his "unfailing love [*ḥesed*]." His need is displayed for all to see but has yet to motivate divine response. His words shift the attack from hope for divine compassion to the essential character of Yahweh, upon which any compassion must be based. Because Yahweh is in his essence one who exercises committed and enduring faithfulness (*ḥesed*), he must act in the psalmist's behalf.

No one remembers you. The psalmist brings the final subsection of the opening unit to a close with a dramatic strategy to motivate God's action. The introductory particle *ki* ("for, because") governs two prepositional phrases that expand artfully on the same theme: If Yahweh continues to "forget" the faithful in this life, there will be no one left above ground to praise him! Certainly the psalmist is feeling forgotten by Yahweh and feels threatened by the approach of death and the oblivion that the Hebrew concept of Sheol, the abode of the dead, assumed. The Hebrew understanding of death and its aftermath held out little or no hope of resurrection into new life (that hope was a later development during the intertestamental period). The dead, regardless whether they were judged righteous or wicked, were thought to descend to Sheol, where they took up a grey, dusty, shadowy existence that admitted no possibility of relationship with God, no experience of blessing or punishment, and no hope of new life.

Unlike the Christian view of heavenly existence after death, there is no chorus of the faithful eternally singing the praises of God around his heavenly throne. Sheol is, by contrast, mute and silent. So the psalmist plays a trump

---

4. For passages about divine repentance using *šwb*, see Ex. 32:12; Job 6:29; Ps. 7:12; 90:13; Jer. 4:28; Jonah 3:9. Many find such changeability in God troublesome. We like to think of God as "the same yesterday and today and forever" (Heb. 13:8). Yet, change in God (from the human viewpoint) is the foundation of prayer and the source of human hope. The Old Testament's testimony that Yahweh does change—even repents [*šwb*]—forms a tension with the many descriptions of his sure and unchanging nature. This tension (or paradox) marks out the boundaries of faith and is intended to be held continually together rather than resolved in favor of one or the other feature.

card: If God wishes to hear the praises of the faithful, he must keep them alive now, with their voices primed with thankfulness for his deliverance!

The Torment of Suffering (6:6–7)

THE MIDDLE UNIT of Psalm 6 focuses on the suffering that torments the psalmist, using a constellation of less common vocabulary words. The extended suffering occasioned by Yahweh's delay of action has reduced the psalmist to nocturnal episodes of uncontrollable weeping and anguish.

I am worn out. The verb *yg*ʾ describes weariness resulting from hard labor and exertion. The psalmist's anguish and groaning are hard work and result in exhaustion. Weeping and tears dominate the night hours. The psalmist "swims all night long on my bed." Tears "drip down" (or "melt" like wax, another meaning of the Heb. word *śḥh*), soaking the bed. Such bouts of restless, uncontrollable weeping are often the end result of physical exhaustion and prolonged stress.

My eyes grow weak . . . they fail. Two verbs in parallel phrases describe the deterioration of the psalmist's eyes. The reasons provided for this failure do not include the extended weeping, however, but move the psalm in a different direction, providing transition from the description of the psalmist's pain to confrontation of his opponents. His eyes grow weak from "anger" (NIV "sorrow"), not weeping, and fail "because of all my foes." The shift of focus at least opens the possibility that the description of suffering from disease in Psalm 6 is used metaphorically for suffering experienced through the attacks of opponents.

Confrontation of Foes (6:8–10)

IN THE FINAL unit of Psalm 6, confrontation and rejection of the psalmist's enemies (vv. 8a, 10) bracket a strong affirmation of confidence in deliverance by Yahweh (vv. 8b–9). Just who these opponents might be is not clear. The psalmist describes them as those "who do evil" (*poʿale ʾawen*, terms reminiscent of Psalm 5:5, where Yahweh will not allow the arrogant to stand in his presence and hates all those "who do wrong [*poʿale ʾawen*]").

Away from me. The psalmist rejects any association with the opponents in the strongest terms. He seems not so much to be putting off attack as withdrawing from any hint of guilt that might be derived from association with those hated by God. The classic wisdom definition of righteousness is to "turn away from evil." Here the psalmist takes the righteous stance by demanding his enemies to "[turn] away from me."

The LORD hears. In the midst of confronting the enemies and sending them away, the psalmist offers up as a reason for his strong rejection and equally strong confidence that, despite the signs of long delay, Yahweh does hear the psalmist's plea and will deliver him. In a threefold affirming parallelism the psalmist expresses assurance that (lit. trans.):

> He hears, Yahweh, the sound of my weeping;
> He hears, Yahweh, my lament;
> Yahweh my prayer will receive.

Might this suggest that the primary offense of the enemies was their caustic assertion of the psalmist's guilt and that, therefore, Yahweh would not deliver?

All my enemies will be ashamed. The psalmist returns to the enemies with confidence that they will be shamed by being proven wrong. Yahweh will deliver the psalmist, and the opponents will receive a public comeuppance. The psalmist employs a series of wordplays in verse 11 to emphasize the point. As in verses 2c–3a he was terrified to the core by continued restraint of Yahweh in the face of the opponents' claims and the psalmist's worsening condition, so now the enemies will similarly be "greatly terrified" by Yahweh's action in the psalmist's behalf. As he pleaded with Yahweh to "turn [*šwb*] ... and deliver me" (v. 4), now the enemies "will turn back" (*šwb*) and "will be ashamed." Finally, although the psalmist (v. 3b) cried out in desperation "How long?" over the delay of God, now the enemies will experience divine judgment and shame "in sudden disgrace."

Bridging Contexts

A STUDENT OF mine who was journaling his way through the early psalms of the Psalter in response to a class assignment wrote in his journal: "What is it with these psalmists anyway? They're such a bunch of whiners!" It's true, isn't it? If all we had was the first book of the psalms (1–41), or even the first three books (1–89), our overwhelming impression would be one of lament—what my student called *whining*! The cumulative effect of reading through these psalms dominated by the lament can be a growing discomfort. The psalmists seem always to be hurting. Their view of the world is so dark and pessimistic. They are so demanding—seeking deliverance and redress from God. Where is the joy of the believer's life?

Rather than seeing these psalms as a mirror of our own experience or allowing them to challenge our own naive worldview, we can end up avoiding them as we might avoid a negative friend who is always depressed and threatens to drag us down every time we are together. But before we excise the psalms from our private and personal canon of Scripture or find ourselves hopping, skipping, and jumping through the Psalter in search of the more "positive parts,"[5] we must remember that the psalms, with all their whining, are no longer just the collected comments of a bunch of negative people. They have become in a strange way God's words *to* his people. No matter how uncomfortable they make us feel, they are still Scripture and must be included in what it means to study the "whole counsel of God."

In what follows, I will look at three aspects of Psalm 6 that can challenge us: a sense of rightness run amok, bargaining with God, and the rejection of evildoers.

Rightness run amok. Yes, the psalmists seem to complain a lot. This may in part be because the world in which they lived was filled with danger and threat, pain and suffering, attack and oppression. We know that because of war, plague, famine, and high infant mortality, the average life expectancy during good times in the ancient Near East was about forty years. That may be why forty years appears regularly in the Old Testament as the round number for a generation. So, for every person who reached the biblical ideal of seventy to eighty years (Ps. 90:10), many more failed to survive infancy.

And that was just the good times. In really bad periods of famine, drought, and rampant plague, average life expectancy could drop as low as eighteen years of age! Life *was* difficult for the psalmists and their world—far more difficult than anything we are likely to encounter in our technologically advanced modern world. Perhaps they had good reason to whine and lament.

But that is not the whole picture. The psalmists did not lament just the personal, individual, or societal suffering they saw and experienced. They also complained because it just did not seem right! The rightness that should have been an integral part of a world created by Yahweh seemed to have run amok in suffering, pain, injustice, oppression, and death. Life was not just difficult, it was not only painful, it was also very, very wrong.

With this sense of wrongness and injustice in the world, the psalmists did not respond as many do today. This pain was not something to be simply dismissed as part of the necessary fabric of a godless world of chance and accident. The psalmists' sense of rightness demanded that God act to reestablish his intended order. Thus, the psalmists felt free to ask, "God, what are you doing? Where are you?" By these tough questions hurled at God, the psalmists were aligning themselves with the tough-minded worldview that the world as we have it is not the world as it should be or as God intended. The world is broken and needs divine help to restore it.

Nor does the psalmist in Psalm 6 see the wrongness encountered in the world as something that ought to be glossed over. The psalmists call suffering

---

5. This is unfortunately what some modern hymnbooks do in their published responsive readings. Many of the more negative passages of the psalms are passed over and omitted.

"suffering" and oppression "oppression." They never try to explain it away or find ways to interpret it positively. They appeal to God to remove it and to restore his intended order in all life. They are not so unrealistic as to think such restoration will magically happen as they desire, but they are consistently clear in their affirmations that it ought to be so.

Bargaining with God. Another significant feature of Psalm 6 is the psalmist's rather transparent attempt in verses 4–5 to "bargain" with God. He builds the motivation for Yahweh's delivering action on the assumption that the psalmist has more to offer God alive than dead. This is a recurring, if not frequent, theme in the lament psalms. The psalmist here urges God to act because he is approaching death when it will no longer be possible either to praise God or to testify concerning his goodness to others.

This may seem like rather ineffective and self-centered pleading—and in a sense it is. It finds its more positive counterpart in the promise to praise God before the great congregation repeated in some lament psalms. While they may seem to border on manipulation, the psalmist's words do reveal a certain understanding of God and of the role of humans in relation to him. On the one hand, the psalmists acknowledge God as free to act in any way consistent with his essential holy nature.[6] He is free to deliver, so the psalmist is emboldened to hope for a change of circumstance. But God is equally free not to save.

On the other hand, the psalmist assumes that the proper role of humans—the role threatened by death—is to "remember" (*zkr*) God and to praise him. These two activities are important parts of congregational worship. If the psalms are any indication, Israel was constantly remembering her life before Yahweh and calling those memories to praise. It may be, as Kraus suggests,[7] that the psalmist here is mourning the loss of human meaning and purpose through remembrance and praise rather than attempting to "threaten" Yahweh by the potential loss of it.

Rejecting the evildoers. The psalmist's rejection of the evildoers in Psalm 6 seems less a response to endemic evil in the world than a reaction to those who seek to undermine his confidence in God's goodwill for the psalmist and all humans. The prolonged delay of divine response has left him vulnerable to this kind of attack.

In verses 1–3, the psalmist pleads for divine mercy rather than angry discipline and wonders at the end why God takes so long to answer. In the following verses (vv. 4–5), the poet comes face-to-face with imminent death and

---

6. See the discussion of divine holiness in the section on "Theology of the Psalms" in volume 2 of this commentary.

7. Kraus, *Psalms 1–59*, 162–63.

mourns the loss of life as well as the ability to praise the goodness of God. He is reduced to weeping in the next set of verses (vv. 6–7) and relates the cause of overwhelming sorrow to the attacks of the enemies. The psalmist then seeks to send away the evildoers who seek to undermine confidence:

> for the LORD has heard my weeping.
> 9The LORD has heard my cry for mercy;
> the LORD accepts my prayer.

As a result of Yahweh's faithfulness, the enemies will not be defeated or destroyed; instead, they will be ashamed and dismayed and made to withdraw in sudden disgrace. Rather than violent opponents, these people seem to me more like the friends of Job, who in their "comforting" actually undermined Job's confidence both in his own righteousness (already affirmed for the reader in God's conversation with the adversary) and in the beneficent goodwill and justice of God. The psalmist's rejection of the evildoers is not so much a rejection of them as it is a refusal to accept their negative message. Their resultant shame and dismay affirm Yahweh's power and will to save in the face of prolonged suffering and divine silence.

INTERPRETING PAIN AND SUFFERING. Often we try to interpret away the troublesome evidence of a world run amok by giving pain and suffering new and more palatable names, such as "divine discipline" or "test of faith" or "opportunity for growth." This they can be and certainly have been for many generations of the faithful. But the danger of such an approach is that it can dull our awareness of the "wrongness" of pain, suffering, and oppression. When they become just one more means God uses to accomplish his purposes, we fail to realize just how contrary to God's will and intention for his world and his people these evidences of evil really are.

We must realize with the psalmists that the experiences of personal pain—whether physical, emotional, or spiritual; the sense of the distance, even the absence of God in our lives; the alienation we feel from ourselves or from others; the resultant sense that we live in a hostile world—are all evidences that we live in a disordered world that is at present far less than the world God created. It is a world that in many ways defies the good intention of the creator.

To say with Joseph, "You intended to harm me, but God intended it for good" (Gen. 50:20) is far different from saying that God creates evil in order to accomplish good ends. To say with Paul that "in all things God works for the good of those who love him, who have been called according to his purpose" (Rom 8:28) is to affirm that evil, whether natural or human, physical or emotional, does not have the upper hand, but that God can reshape any evil we experience in order to bring forth good—in order to allow our broken lives and our disordered world to move back toward the fullness of his purpose.

Like the psalmist, let us mourn suffering, pain, oppression, and evil in all their forms rather than rejoice in them as divine punishment when they fall on one we think deserves it. Nor should we seek to explain such things away as discipline and guidance when we experience them ourselves. We can and should allow distress and oppression to provide opportunities to shape our dependence on God to create a fierce loyalty to him, but they remain evil just the same and do not become good by the fact that God can turn them to our good.

If, as the psalmist suggests, the chief role of humans is to remember and praise God, how is it possible to do that in the midst of personal pain and suffering? It is especially difficult when all the voices around us undermine our confidence—either with words that are too negative or with those that are too positive.

On the one hand, I am injured almost beyond repair by those who claim, "There is no way out. This pain is deserved. God does not care. God does not exist!" I have to admit that I have been too long ingrained in the faith from earliest childhood to be shaken, even in times of great trouble, by those who question whether God exists. God has existed for me from earliest memory. But I can, like so many in my culture, believe that God could not possibly care for one like me, and this fear can lead quickly to despair of any deliverance.

On the other hand, my confidence in God can be shaken by those who too easily seek to put some positive cast on my experience of pain. "God is in control. God is using these circumstances to punish or discipline you. Praise God for what is happening, for you will understand the purpose for it later." Far from helping me, such responses, while often well intended, can leave me with a sense of isolation. I am left with a feeling that my pain is not understood and is belittled. I cannot escape the gnawing feeling that this suffering, no matter how deserved, is nevertheless evil and ought not to be.

I meet regularly with a group of men who have experienced significant pain and trouble in their lives. The best solace we offer to one another is not to explain away the pain but to acknowledge its reality. We can hold up to one another our own experiences of divine grace within the continuing reality of suffering that marks our daily lives. The pain has not gone away, but God and his grace have become even more real to each of us as we acknowledge that God's will for us is not suffering and death but abundant life, lived in the light shining out of the darkness.

Psalm 7

A SHIGGAION OF David, which he sang to the LORD concerning Cush, a Benjamite.

1 O LORD my God, I take refuge in you;
save and deliver me from all who pursue me,
2 or they will tear me like a lion
and rip me to pieces with no one to rescue me.

3 O LORD my God, if I have done this
and there is guilt on my hands—
4 if I have done evil to him who is at peace with me
or without cause have robbed my foe—
5 then let my enemy pursue and overtake me;
let him trample my life to the ground
and make me sleep in the dust. *Selah*

6 Arise, O LORD, in your anger;
rise up against the rage of my enemies.
Awake, my God; decree justice.
7 Let the assembled peoples gather around you.
Rule over them from on high;
8 let the LORD judge the peoples.
Judge me, O LORD, according to my righteousness,
according to my integrity, O Most High.
9 O righteous God,
who searches minds and hearts,
bring to an end the violence of the wicked
and make the righteous secure.

10 My shield is God Most High,
who saves the upright in heart.
11 God is a righteous judge,
a God who expresses his wrath every day.
12 If he does not relent,
he will sharpen his sword;
he will bend and string his bow.
13 He has prepared his deadly weapons;
he makes ready his flaming arrows.

[14]He who is pregnant with evil
and conceives trouble gives birth to disillusionment.
[15]He who digs a hole and scoops it out
falls into the pit he has made.
[16]The trouble he causes recoils on himself;
his violence comes down on his own head.

[17]I will give thanks to the LORD because of his righteousness
and will sing praise to the name of the LORD Most High.

THIS PSALM IS a plea for deliverance from the psalmist's enemies, who are depicted as attacking him like ferocious beasts. Employing the legal motif of a law case argued in court before a judge, the psalmist appeals to Yahweh to base his judgment on righteousness alone and, therefore, to exonerate the innocent and to mete out judgment on the wicked.

Verses 1–2 open with an invocation to Yahweh encapsulating the psalmist's desperate need for deliverance. The psalmist concludes the psalm (v. 17) with thanksgiving and praise for anticipated deliverance, emphasizing the righteous character of Yahweh, which is the psalmist's basis for confidence. Between these extremes, the psalm is divided into four units: the psalmist's protestation of innocence (vv. 3–5); an appeal to Yahweh as righteous judge (vv. 6–9); a description of Yahweh's preparation for judgment (vv. 10–13); and a confident description of the anticipated fate of the wicked (vv. 14–16).

The Heading (7:0)

A NEW MUSICAL notation appears at the beginning of this psalm heading: "*shiggaion*" (*šiggayon*). By its position this is probably an ancient genre designation (see the discussion of "Types of Psalms" in the Introduction). Although some have tried to make a connection with the Akkadian *shegu* ("lament"), the exact nature of a *šiggayon* and what distinguishes it from other types of lament is uncertain. This is the only occurrence of the term in the Psalter, so we are unlikely to gain much more clarity in the future.

The heading also contains a historical notice suggesting a relationship between this psalm and a specific event in David's life. Unfortunately, "Cush, a Benjamite," concerning whom David is supposed to have sung this *šiggayon*, is unknown from the biblical corpus, so that the historical allusion must remain obscure. The use of the verb *šar* ("he sang") does suggest that for the person who appended this notice, David was considered author of this psalm.

Appeal to Yahweh (7:1–2)

THE PSALMIST IS in desperate straits and feels pursued by ravenous beasts who threaten to tear him apart. He "takes refuge" in Yahweh, using the words of promise first issued in 2:12 ("Blessed are all who take refuge in [the LORD]") and recommended as the source of gladness and joy in 5:11. Placing oneself in the protective care of Yahweh is foundation enough for confident hope for deliverance from the savage attacks of the psalmist's enemies. Consequently, he is able to call out to Yahweh to "save" and "deliver" him (see comments on Heb. *yšᶜ* ["save"] at 3:2 and *nṣl* ["deliver"] at 6:4), using common parallel words suggesting release from restriction and snatching out of extreme peril.

Tear me like a lion. The psalmist's images of impending destruction are graphic and extreme. This is no quiet, dignified death. It promises horrific rending and tearing as when lions gather to fight over their portion of recently taken prey. The terror is so great that the psalmist realizes that without the protection of Yahweh, there is no hope for escape.

Protestation of Innocence (7:3–5)

IF. VERSE 3 introduces the next major segment of this psalm—the psalmist's protestation of innocence. Similar concern to deny guilt is expressed in the Egyptian text sometimes referred to as "The Negative Confession of Sin."[1] The Egyptian speaker here is a deceased person who, upon approaching the scales of Maᶜat (where entrance to the afterlife is determined), directly declares his innocence of all wrongdoing through a series of negative claims: "I have not. . . ."

In our psalm, however, the psalmist's claims of innocence are couched in the form of a self-imprecation or self-curse. Confident of complete innocence, he is willing to accept dire consequences if any guilt can be proved. The passage is, therefore, divided into an "if" section (vv. 3–4), describing possible wrongs of which the psalmist claims innocence, and a "then" section (v. 5), where consequences of proven guilt are laid out. Verse 3 provides a more inclusive disclaimer of guilt ("If I have done this and there is guilt [*ᶜawel*] on my hands"), to which verse 4 provides specific examples ("done evil to him who is at peace with me or without cause have robbed my foe").

---

1. An English translation is available in Walter Beyerlin, "The Negative Confession of Sin (Book of the Dead, Saying 125)," *Near Eastern Religious Texts Relating to the Old Testament*, ed. W. Beyerlin et al., trans. John Bowden (OTL; Philadelphia: Westminster, 1978), 63–67.

The kind of guilt (*ʿawel*) envisioned stains the hands and may suggest some ritual hand-washing ceremony to demonstrate purity. The protestation takes in the extremes of avoiding conflict with the one "at peace with me" (*šolemi* ["one allied by covenant or treaty"]) as well as "my foe" (*ṣoreri*). In regard to the foe, the psalmist may well imagine circumstances under which "plundering" the enemy would be acceptable. Here, however, he maintains a higher standard under which even an enemy can only be attacked for cause.

Then. The "then" section of the psalmist's self-imprecation establishes a sort of balance with the opening plea for deliverance in verses 1–2. He uses the same Hebrew root *rdp* to describe the "pursuers" from whom he seeks refuge (v. 1) and the deadly "pursuit" by the enemies that he accepts as the just consequence of any guilt that might be established (v. 5). In verse 5, however, pursuit culminates in overtaking so that the fearful tearing imagined in verse 1 would become reality. The psalmist—safe in innocence—willingly submits to any penalty that a righteous judge would levy against the guilty parties in the case. Rightly judged, the psalmist will come forth unscathed while the false accusers will receive the appropriate punishment for their evil.

Let him trample my life. The psalmist returns in no less violent images to the feared consequence of pursuit described in the opening verses of the psalm. There the tearing and rending of wild beasts was imagined; here it is the trampling of the defeated foe in battle. The verb *rms* ("trample") can be used to describe the action of a potter mixing clay by foot (Isa. 41:25), a vintner crushing grapes (63:3), a crowd of people trampling a man (2 Kings 7:17), or horses trampling Jezebel underfoot (2 Kings 9:33).

The psalmist anticipates death from such trampling. Notice the progression in these verses. The enemies would "pursue and overtake" the psalmist's *nepeš* (NIV "me" in v. 5a, the distinctive self animated by God), "trample" his very "life" (*ḥay*) to the ground, and cause even his "glory" (*kabod*; NIV "me" in v. 5c) to dwell in the dust.[2]

Yahweh Called to Judgment (7:6–9)

HAVING ESTABLISHED INNOCENCE through this protestation, the psalmist now turns to Yahweh in his role of righteous judge. With an initial string of imper-

2. The NIV's translation of Heb. *škn* as "make [to] sleep," while certainly poetic and dramatic, obscures the point of the underlying Hebrew. There the meaning is certainly that the one who currently resides in the world of the living will take up residence (although a less permanent and substantial living) in the dust. It seems that something more than "sully my reputation" is called for by these phrases.

atives he calls on Yahweh to arise in righteous indignation and to assume his seat as judge. Surrounded by the assembly of all peoples, Yahweh, exalted over all, is ready to hear the case and render righteous judgment.

Arise, O LORD. Rising is a commonly expressed preparation for movement. It presumes a refocusing of energy and concern to follow a new course of action. Here the psalmist calls on Yahweh, wherever he has been previously involved, to refocus his concern on the psalmist's case and to prepare to act in judgment. The object of concern that he hopes will motivate Yahweh to new action is divine indignation against the arrogant violence of his enemies.[3]

Awake, my God. As in the preceding phrases, the psalmist calls God to renewed action. Since Yahweh neither sleeps nor slumbers (121:4), how can he awake? In reality, the psalmist is calling Yahweh to bestir himself in his behalf.

Decree justice. While the perfect verbal form used here may possibly continue the force of the preceding imperatives, it seems more likely that the psalmist is describing the grounds on which his hope for righteous judgment is founded. He is willing to take the risks implied in the protestation of innocence if the case can only be submitted to the scrutiny of a righteous judge. Who better than Yahweh, who has decreed justice and who will even judge the fate of nations (v. 8)? This is more than a simple track record of past just decrees. It is, as Job recognized, that the very concept and nature of justice is established by Yahweh himself. He defines justice, affirms it as righteous, holds humans to its standard, and consistently acts to uphold it.

Justice. The Hebrew word for "justice" (*mišpaṭ*) assumes, as one would expect, a legal setting such as is described in this psalm. In a case brought before a righteous judge, the first step is to hear the evidence brought by the contending parties. Then the judge proclaims *mišpaṭ*—a statement of what the appropriate course of action should have been for all parties in the case. Having established *mišpaṭ*, the judge proceeds to declare the relation of the contending parties to that standard. Righteous is the affirmation that one has fulfilled the demands of *mišpaṭ* (cf. v. 9) whereas the wicked have failed to measure up.

Judge me, O LORD! Before such a righteous judge (vv. 9, 11), the innocent need have no fear. So the psalmist calls out to be judged by Yahweh. The psalmist's "righteousness" and "integrity" leaves no doubt as to the

---

3. While the affirming parallel structure of the first two phrases of v. 6 might suggest that Yahweh's "anger" in the first phrase ought to be balanced by his "rage" in the second, the word for "rage" is consistently a negative emotion of arrogant pride, which seems best related to the enemies who immediately follow.

appropriate decision from a righteous judge—even one "who searches minds and hearts" (v. 9). Such a judge can be trusted to bring wickedness to its proper conclusion while making "the righteous secure" (v. 9).[4]

Minds and hearts. While "minds and hearts" is not a bad translation, the original Hebrew refers to "hearts and inward parts." The point is that God is able to scrutinize the interior thoughts and emotions of humans.

Make . . . secure is not so much a reference to security measures or protection as it is to providing a solid, unshakable foundation. Using this Hebrew word God is elsewhere said to create the unshakable underpinnings of the world, which cannot be moved.

Yahweh Prepares for Judgment (7:10–13)

THE GOD WHO judges righteously also metes out the consequences of that judgment. The psalmist describes how Yahweh, having declared *mišpaṭ*, now responds as a "shield" and defender for those proven to be righteous (the "upright in heart," v. 10). He also prepares to mete out judgment on the wicked. The psalmist clearly has personal enemies in view here. Though Yahweh has yet to act openly, he is "a righteous judge . . . who expresses his wrath every day."

Expresses . . . wrath. The NIV obscures somewhat the legal background of this term (Heb. *zaᶜam*), which might better be understood as "passes sentence." Yahweh is not a judge who only occasionally sits in courts and infrequently renders judgment. The psalmist's hope and claim are that Yahweh is constantly overseeing human affairs and declaring *mišpaṭ*. His case will not slide by unnoticed but will receive the attention it deserves.

If he does not relent. The word translated "relent" (*šwb*) here presents a bit of a theological quandary. When used of humans, the term is often translated "repent." The NIV avoids attributing repentance to God by using "relent" rather than the more problematic "repent," which might seem inappropriate of God.[5] But the phrase is used of God with sufficient frequency to suggest that in the mind of the Hebrews, God can be said to repent or at least to change a previous course of action.

We see God doing precisely this in Jonah 3:9, where the Ninevites' hope their repentance may spark a corresponding repentance in God (once again the NIV translates *šwb* as "relent"). The point is that, at least from the

---

4. The NIV has severely reordered this verse without much cause. The original order is "Let the evil of the wicked be at an end, but establish the righteous, O one who searches minds and hearts, O righteous God."

5. Others direct this phrase to the enemy of the psalmist (e.g., Craigie); still others omit the phrase altogether (e.g., Kraus).

human point of view, God seems on occasion to change his mind and to withdraw previously decreed disaster. This is the hope embodied in all prophetic pronouncements of doom. Such pronouncements, far from being fixed, unalterable predictions, encourage human repentance in the full hope that God himself will respond by replacing the decreed judgment with mercy.[6]

He will sharpen his sword. In this case, Yahweh prepares to mete out the punishment due from his righteous judgment of the psalmist's case. The images are militaristic: sharpening the sword, stringing and drawing the bow, and preparing to let fly with flaming arrows at the enemy.[7] This well-drawn portrait of the ready archer stops just short of release—bow straining, eye on the target; Yahweh is poised, ready to act. The picture encourages the enemies to reconsider their opposition in light of Yahweh's sure defense of the righteous.

The Fate of the Wicked (7:14–16)

FROM THE DAUNTING description of Yahweh as the implacable enemy of the wicked, the psalmist moves on to describe the fate of the wicked themselves. Heaping up words relating to conception and birth, the psalmist scorns the one who is "pregnant with evil" and trouble.[8] Such a one, saturated with evil, gives birth to a "lie" or "falsehood." Whether this refers to false accusations put forth by the psalmist's enemies or to an ironic declaration that their plans to defeat him will ultimately fail (cf. NIV "disillusionment") is not clear. The latter may be more likely in light of the pattern established in this segment to describe how the enemies' hostile intents recoil to their own detriment.

Pit. The enemy ultimately falls into the trapping pit prepared for the psalmist; that is, trouble and violence fall back on the head of their creator. Once again, this commentary on the hapless progenitors of the psalmist's woes serves as a warning to dissuade them from their path of violent attack.

---

6. The question of divine repentance is complicated by the fact that more than one Hebrew term is employed to describe divine repentance. One of the most important is the verb *nḥm*, which is also used of both humans and God to describe repentance or change of mind. In Num. 23:19, we hear that "God is not a [mortal] ... that he should change his mind [*nḥm*]." Elsewhere, however, Yahweh is described as willing to do just that (cf. Jer. 18:8, 10; 26:3, 13, 19; Joel 2:14; Jonah 4:2).

7. Others (e.g., Kraus) take this to be a portrait of the enemy preparing to continue attacks against the psalmist—an attack that will turn back in disaster on the attacker himself.

8. The first two phrases are in affirming parallelism, using two Heb. words for "be pregnant, conceive" (*ḥabal*, *harah*) for variation.

Concluding Praise (7:17)

THE PSALMIST CONCLUDES by returning to the theme of Yahweh's "righteousness." Yahweh is to be praised because he is a righteous judge, who can as a result be trusted to exonerate and uphold the righteous while punishing the wicked.

The LORD Most High. The divine title "Most High" (*ʾel ʿelyon* or simply *ʿelyon*) would seem in its origin to have assumed a range (or pantheon) of deities over whom Yahweh ranked as chief. This is not inconsistent with clear evidence of Scripture that throughout most of her history, Israel did not clearly deny the existence of other gods, although she understood Yahweh's claim on her to be one of absolute allegiance and exclusive loyalty.[9]

THE PSALMIST GLORIES in God's *righteousness*. The term is applied explicitly to God no less than three times in this psalm.[10] Sometimes we have difficulty being comfortable with the idea of righteousness. It can seem to be hard and inflexible. We often relate it in our minds to human self-righteousness—a decidedly negative term used to describe fanatics and self-assured persons we would rather not be around.

It is dangerous, however, to judge God's righteousness on the basis of rather limited and distorted human expressions of righteousness. His righteousness flows from that essential nature of holiness we discussed in relation to Psalm 5 (see comments). Righteousness is the demonstration—the living out, so to speak—of God's innate character of holiness. Because God is incompatible with evil and relentlessly good, he can do no other than uphold righteousness.

It is God's righteousness that enables the psalmist to trust in God as protective "refuge." Because God is holy and righteous, the psalmist can depend on him to uphold the righteous and protect them from the attacks of the wicked. As such, then, divine righteousness takes on a softer edge defined by divine mercy and blessing. The two consequences of divine holiness and righteousness—judgment and mercy—can never be severed but continue to exist in tension.

It is, of course, how humans respond to God that determines whether they experience mercy or wrath, judgment or grace. The psalmist knows this and is careful to affirm innocence in verses 3–5.

---

9. Cf. Gen. 14:18–22, where Abram identifies Yahweh with the god whom Melchizedek reveres as "God Most High [*ʾel ʿelyon*], Creator of heaven and earth."

10. See vv. 9, 11, and 17.

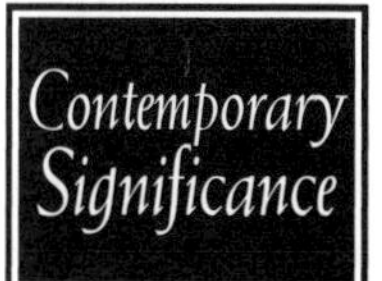

I WOULD LIKE to return to two images from Psalm 7 that I believe can help us transplant this psalm into the contemporary soil of our own time and place. The first image is the one with which the psalmist begins: the rather unexpected invitation to "take refuge" in God. The second is related to the first and actually forms the dominant theme that is viewed from a variety of angles throughout the whole psalm: the deep and sincere reflection on our character engendered by coming into the presence of God.

God is our refuge. How comforting it is to think of God as our "refuge." This is a theme that returns time and again throughout the Psalter. The psalmists invite us to understand divine righteousness as a source of confidence and comfort rather than of fear and dismay. Yahweh, the righteous judge, is our refuge, in much the same way that for Isaiah, Yahweh, the Holy One of Israel, becomes not the anticipated destroyer but the unexpected redeemer of Israel.[11]

Yet often, precisely when we need that refuge most, we feel unable or unworthy to enter in. A minister friend of mine was enjoying a long-term effective ministry when he received the call from the bishop. A woman in the minister's congregation had accused him of sexual improprieties and was threatening to sue. My friend knew the accusations were true, so he went down into his basement, pulled a gun out of the gun rack, and prepared to send a bullet through his heart to end his life.

Now my friend had been effectively preaching a message of a God of love and forgiveness for over twenty years! But in the hour of his own complete and utter powerlessness, his own faith was almost completely dismantled—he was unable to see beyond the God of judgment to the God of love offering refuge. Thankfully my friend survived. A providential phone call interrupted his plans and offered a new opportunity for counseling, healing, and restoration. But how many of us, faced by a crumbling world, fail to accept God's invitation of refuge and hope?

Our hesitation need not be the result of our own sense of unworthiness and sinfulness. Sometimes we, like the psalmist, are beset from without by false accusations, failed finances, abusive partners, and a myriad of other circumstances either within our control or not. The sense of guilt and shame

---

11. In the first half of Isaiah (chs. 1–39), the title "Holy One of Israel" is used of Yahweh primarily in oracles of judgment on Israel. In the latter half of the book (chs. 40–66), the title is unexpectedly connected with the hopeful designation "Redeemer," as in 41:14, "The LORD, your Redeemer, the Holy One of Israel."

we can feel at such times often creates an almost insurmountable barrier to entering the refuge of God.

I remember a woman who was going through a particularly painful divorce from an abusive husband, explaining how difficult it had become for her to attend worship services because all she could do, she said, was to sit in the back of the sanctuary and weep. Her pain was so great, her embarrassment over the failure of her marriage so strong, that she almost cut herself off from what should have been a healing, caring community—the church of God. At least she kept coming—even if all she could do was weep. How many of us would have this woman's courage? Or would we, like a wounded animal, crawl away to some remote hideout to heal or die on our own?

God *is* our refuge. He stands ready to deliver and to save. But a refuge must be entered before it is effective. Often our understanding of God's righteousness prevents us from taking that step. Too often we understand God's righteousness to mean that he judges not only our rebellious sinfulness but also our weakness and ineffectiveness as human beings. As a result, we do not take the steps to healing and wholeness that God provides.

Judge me, O LORD, according to my righteousness. The idea of God as refuge is a wonderful and important gift to all of us who live in the midst of a broken world (and that is all of us, whether we realize it or not). But sometimes we can take that refuge so for granted that we become almost exclusively focused on the sense of security, love, and acceptance that God provides. We forget that entering the refuge God provides means entering the presence of God himself, and that is not something to be undertaken lightly or unadvisedly.

The college at which I taught for many years announced a special chapel program. Rather than our usual format, the notice announced, this time we would have a "worship chapel." Now, I had thought that all our chapels had intended to be worship experiences, so I came with some curiosity to see what this special format might be. As it turns out, the worship chapel was spent entirely singing choruses of praise to God. Now I enjoy praise choruses—in a balanced sort of way—and I certainly sensed a genuine spirit of sincere praise in myself and my fellow worshipers. But I left that experience with a deep-seated suspicion that we had only partially worshiped—that something quite necessary and important was still missing.

As a child I remember singing the classic hymn "Rock of Ages." I envisioned being hidden in the cleft of the rock—covered over by the protective hand of God. In my youth I understood that God was protecting me from all those evils and attacks that came from without, and I took comfort in his divine care. Only much later, however (far too much later), I came to realize that God's hand was protecting me *from myself and the consequences of my own sin!*

I believe firmly that true worship incorporates acknowledging and repenting of sin. Only then do we realize how totally dependent on God and his gracious mercy we really are. This is one aspect of worship that the more liturgically oriented traditions often do better—leading worshipers through moments of corporate recognition, contrition, and repentance for sin. Then comes the undeserved affirmation: "You are forgiven!"

When I recognized my sin, I began to understand at last the full meaning of God's care and protection. Then I really began to read and understand the verses of this song: "Let the water and the blood, from thy wounded side which flowed, be of sin the double cure, save from wrath and make me pure." I am a sinner deserving of punishment and death, but in Christ a gracious God has provided a way for restoration and new life.

That is what the psalmist's protestation of innocence brings home to me. It is not just a rather brash claim of spiritual excellence and perfection. It is instead a clear recognition that taking refuge in the presence of God is not a condition to be entered into lightly. Coming into his presence should always force us to sober self-reflection and evaluation. It should not lead us too quickly or easily to absorption in the praise of our protector God. Instead, it should lead us first and always to acknowledge how much we need his divine gift of undeserved mercy and grace.

God does indeed offer refuge we can depend on. But being able to stand within the protective embrace of almighty God is not the assured result of our spiritual perfection and pride. It is instead the consequence of our recognition of our spiritual bankruptcy and our total capitulation to the immeasurable grace of our Savior and Lord. In the words of the wise woman of Tekoa, "God does not take away life; instead, he devises ways so that a banished person may not remain estranged from him" (2 Sam. 14:14). That is cause for hope and praise indeed!

Psalm 8

FOR THE DIRECTOR of music. According to *gittith*.
A psalm of David.

[1] O LORD, our Lord,
how majestic is your name in all the earth!

You have set your glory
above the heavens.
[2] From the lips of children and infants
you have ordained praise
because of your enemies,
to silence the foe and the avenger.

[3] When I consider your heavens,
the work of your fingers,
the moon and the stars,
which you have set in place,
[4] what is man that you are mindful of him,
the son of man that you care for him?
[5] You made him a little lower than the heavenly beings
and crowned him with glory and honor.
[6] You made him ruler over the works of your hands;
you put everything under his feet:
[7] all flocks and herds,
and the beasts of the field,
[8] the birds of the air,
and the fish of the sea,
all that swim the paths of the seas.

[9] O LORD, our Lord,
how majestic is your name in all the earth!

HAVING WENDED OUR way in five consecutive psalms (Pss. 3–7) through the dark valleys of lament and pleas for deliverance, we hear the strains of a joyful melody rising from just beyond the steep hill represented by Psalm 7, and we arrive at the crest to discover a welcome prospect of breathtaking beauty and awesome delight. Psalm 8 introduces us to the first experience of joyful praise and adoration in the Psalter. After this brief but brilliant chorus of praise, we will return again in the following psalms to the darkness of pain and the anguish of brokenness. But here in Psalm 8, if just for a moment, darkness and suffering are driven away by the commanding vision of the sovereign God of the created universe and his unfathomable care for humanity.

The psalm is enclosed with an inclusio of great power through which the psalmist proclaims the central message of wondrous awe that pervades the psalm (vv. 1a, 9). Between these two markers, the psalm contains three sections: (1) praise of the majestic power and protection of Yahweh displayed in creation (vv. 1b–2); (2) recognition of human frailty in the light of God's creative power (vv. 3–4); and (3) astonished acceptance of divine empowerment of humans and their resultant responsibility (vv. 5–8).

The Heading (8:0)

THE PSALM IS considered Davidic, although once again there is no particularly Davidic element within the psalm. The psalm seems to grow from awe-filled observation of the night sky—an opportunity the young David must have enjoyed on many occasions as a shepherd in the fields. "According to *gittith*" may indicate a musical tune, denote the type of instrument to be used, or perhaps refer to a ceremonial occasion.[1]

The Thematic Framework (8:1a, 9)

THE NAME OF GOD. The psalm begins and ends with the astonished exclamation: "O LORD [Yahweh], our Lord, how majestic is your name in all the earth!" In English translation, the opening phrase is rendered somewhat redundantly by the tradition of translating the divine name *yhwh* with the deferential "LORD" (in small caps). In this case the divine name is immediately followed by the phrase "our Lord," which employs the common word of respect (*ʾadonay*) and has the awkward effect in reading a translation of making the phrase repetitious.

This movement to replace the four letters of the actual divine name Yahweh (*yhwh*) with the respectful "Lord" is ancient and reflects Israel's concern to avoid any misuse of God's name as prohibited in the Ten Commandments (Ex. 20:7): "You shall not misuse the name of the LORD your God, for the LORD will not hold anyone guiltless who misuses his name." This distancing from the pronouncing of God's name had its effect on the LXX, where *yhwh* is regularly translated by the Greek *kyrios* ("Lord").

1. Kraus, *Psalms 1–59*, 180; Craigie, *Psalms 1–50*, 105.

Jewish respect for the name of God did not end here, however. Over time the word *ʾadonay* was elevated by its association with Yahweh to such a level of respect that a further distancing step was considered necessary. Currently among Orthodox Jews, *ʾadonay* in reference to God is used only in direct prayer to him. In reading Scripture or in conversation about God, Yahweh and *ʾadonay* are both avoided and are replaced with *haššem* ("The Name")—the ultimate form of circumlocution.[2]

Knowing that the psalmist is in fact saying "O Yahweh, my Lord" makes a much clearer connection between Yahweh and the "majestic name" the psalmist exalts. The gift of God's very name Yahweh to Israel in the Exodus event was an act of radical self-revelation by which he made himself known and accessible to the people he had taken as his own. This is not the hidden God of the laments but the God who displays himself to be seen in his creation—the God who wills to be known in his majesty by human beings and creation alike.

The "name" of God also is an extension of God himself. Where God chooses to place his name—in the land, in the temple, on his people—there God is also. The presence of his name lays claim to divine authority wherever it dwells. The opening phrase of the psalm, "how majestic is your name in all the earth," is parallel with the following phrase, "You have set your glory above the heavens." The result is a merism, in which "earth" and "heaven" mark out the two extremes of all that God has created and declare all to be permeated with the majestic name of Yahweh.

---

2. This process led over time to some rather subtle but far-reaching misunderstandings. Hebrew Scripture was originally written without vowels present—as a consonantal text. Various ways were developed to mark out the Tetragrammaton (the four letters of the divine name Yahweh), so that readers would not mistakenly pronounce it. Among the Qumran scrolls from the Dead Sea, Yahweh is often written in archaic Hebrew script that is visibly distinct from the later square Aramaic characters adopted for the transmission of the text and later for printed versions of the Hebrew Bible. When much later (between the fourth and seventh centuries A.D.) vowel points were inserted in the consonantal text of Scripture (above and below the consonants), the divine name was not at first provided with vowels. This indicated the name was not to be pronounced out loud. The consonants of the replacement word *ʾadonay* were placed in the margin to indicate the appropriate remedy: "Don't say Yahweh! Read instead *ʾadonay*." This was, however, very complicated, since the divine name occurs thousands of times in the Hebrew Bible. Still later, a less difficult shorthand method was adopted by placing the vowels of *ʾadonay* around the consonants of the divine name *yhwh* in the text. The resulting hybrid formation *yehowah* led ultimately to confusion when it was mistakenly taken as the correct pronunciation of the divine name. This confused reading remains with us today in many circles as Jehovah. It is clear, however, that the combined form was never intended to be read in this way but was simply an abbreviated way of warning the reader to respectfully replace the divine name with *ʾadonay*.

How majestic! The psalmist's response to the name of God displayed in creation is not one of fear but of adoration and amazement. The Hebrew term *ʾaddir* ("majestic") elsewhere describes a "mighty" ship (Isa. 33:21), a "leader" (Jer. 30:21), or "nobles" (Judg. 5:13). The common thread seems to be one of impressive—almost intimidating—power. It is a power that is visible, on display for all to see.

The Hebrew synonym *kabod* ("glory") describes the more inward, defining essence of an individual, whether human or divine. To see God's glory is to know him as he really is at the core of his being. To do so is fraught with as much danger as significance, because for sinful humans to know the holy God in this way is to risk the destruction of their very being that stands in such contradiction to the divine essence. By contrast, *ʾaddir* describes God's public side, God's willingness to be seen—God on display, so to speak. That public presence is for the psalmist impressive, awe-inspiring, even intimidating, but not particularly threatening or destructive; the psalmist is instead inspired to rejoice.

The Creative Power of Yahweh (8:1b–2)

THIS VERSE AND a half are extremely difficult to understand in the original Hebrew and therefore equally difficult to interpret regardless of the target language.

You have set your glory above the heavens. The difficulties begin with an awkward grammatical construction in the last half of verse 1. The verse begins with the normal relative particle "who, which," followed by an apparent imperative verb form, "give, set, place." The resulting phrase is not only awkward but ungrammatical.[3] Most solutions involve textual rearrangement or at least different division of words. One of the more popular is Mitchell Dahood's suggestion that these two words ought to be combined to make a form of the verb *šrt*, meaning "I will worship."[4] The phrase then describes the psalmist's resolve to adore Yahweh's glory rather than recognizes Yahweh's self-revelation in the heavens.

While this conjecture is appealing in some senses, because of the merism with the first half of verse 1 as well as an additional link with the phrase "you have set [ordained/established]" at the end of verse 2, it seems best to me to render this uncertain passage as in the NIV translation: "You have set your glory." In this way the psalmist makes a transition between the thematic

3. Kraus (*Psalms 1–59*, 178) gives a helpful summary of the various solutions offered along with associated bibliography.

4. Mitchell Dahood, *Psalms: Introduction, Translation, and Notes*, 3 vols. (AB; Garden City, N.Y.: Doubleday, 1966–1970), 1:49. More recently, P. Craigie (*Psalms 1–50*, 104–5) follows the same tack.

recognition of the divine glory of Yahweh that permeates all creation to the following contrast between the weak, dependent children and the powerful foes of the psalmist and God.

From the lips of children and infants. The NIV translation of the Hebrew term "mouths" with the more specific "lips" somewhat obscures the dual focus of the psalmist in this passage. The two types of children mentioned in this verse are distinguished by their youth. The second term (Heb. *yoneqim*) describes nursing infants or "sucklings"; the earlier term (Heb. *ᶜolelim*) is frequently coupled with sucklings and may be best translated "toddlers." For children (and especially "toddlers and nursing infants") the "mouth" is the source of nourishment. Toddlers and nursing children are particularly dependent on others for food and protective care. The psalmist uses this image of vulnerability and dependence to create a dramatic contrast with the presumed power of those who oppose God and his faithful ones. Mighty Yahweh, whose majestic power and glory are displayed throughout the creation, is able to build the innocent weakness of these dependent babes into a powerful opposition to his enemies.

In addition to gaining nourishment, the mouths of babes is the source of inarticulate murmuring and babbling. While no direct mention is made of speech here, it may well be that the psalmist—as many commentators presume—has also in mind how the rough, unschooled babblings of very young children can be an unexpected source of praise to their creator.

You have ordained praise. Scholars have offered a variety of opinions regarding what Yahweh fashions from the mouths of these "toddlers and nursing infants." The NIV's translation of the Hebrew *ᶜoz* as "praise" runs counter to the normal interpretation of this word as "power" or "strength." Although the LXX does render this word as "utterance of praise" (*ainon*), this meaning of *ᶜoz* is always associated with verbs of giving, which is not the case here. Taking it as praise probably derives from an understanding that humans *cannot* give "glory and strength" to Yahweh; therefore, this idiom must mean to give praise instead.[5] However, the psalmist's point is that God builds strong defenses out of human vulnerability and weakness rather than their praise. The recognition of one's own weakness is the starting point for recognizing dependence on the strength of God. This connects more directly with the central reflection on the unexpected elevation of humans by God that stands at the heart of this psalm.

Because of your enemies. It is to oppose the enemies of God that the frailty of human infants is fashioned into a powerful defense. In this context

5. The comments of Franz Delitzsch, *Biblical Commentary on the Psalms*, trans. Francis Bolton (Grand Rapids: Eerdmans, repr. 1970), 1:152, in this regard are well taken.

the opponents are emphasized to be the enemies of God ("*your* enemies," v. 2) rather than those opposing the psalmist. It is not unlikely, however, that here, as throughout the psalms, the psalmist is fluidly able to identify personal enemies with those hostile to God. This seems particularly appropriate in the reference to "the avenger" at the end of verse 2, which seems more appropriate as a response to real or imagined affronts from other human opponents. Placing the opponents on the cosmic level, however, does heighten the sense of divine strength employed to defeat them.

To silence. The verb "to silence" comes from the Hebrew root *šbt* ("bring to a stop/standstill/end; make disappear"). It is the same root from which the word "Sabbath" comes, as the day in which all work is brought to a standstill. While the translation "silence" works effectively in counterpoint to the babbling praise of the infants, the more likely intention in this context is that God is bringing his enemies to an end so that they will be no more.[6]

Human Frailty (8:3–4)

FROM THE HEIGHTS of heaven, where the glory of God is displayed across the night sky, the psalmist now comes down firmly to earth. The shift in context that occurs in verses 3–4 mirrors in reverse order the merism with which the psalm began. There the name of Yahweh was majestic "in all the earth" while God's glory was set "above the heavens." Here the psalmist begins with awed wonder at the creative power of Yahweh displayed in "the heavens" (v. 3) and is then drawn to reflect on the significance of earthbound humans (v. 4).

When I consider your heavens. The sense of reverie under the expanse of the night sky is finely drawn and produces a hushed and yet intense response of wonder: the myriad points of light—beyond the psalmist's ability to number—and the clockwork precision with which moon and stars turn and return again and again to mark out the months and years of human existence. While human generations come and go, moon and stars continue in their regular appearance and movement undisturbed or altered.

The work of your fingers. All this wondrous display the psalmist recognizes as the creative artwork of Yahweh. It is in fact Yahweh's heaven that the psalmist stands beneath. It is his possession by right of creation, as the possessive pronouns ("*your* heavens"; "*your* fingers") show. All this vast, enduring monument to the creative power and art of God is but child's play to the divine creator—spun off the tips of his fingers, without even breaking a sweat!

---

6. Or, perhaps, the image is a response to the restless conspiracy of the nations depicted in Ps. 2:1–3, whose murmuring is here both "silenced" and "stilled."

What is man. . . ? Have you ever taken your stand, as the psalmist does here, beneath the night sky and felt yourself dwarfed to insignificance by its almost unfathomable immensity? Glittering stars flung across the dark void of space, like some abstract painting. When the Hebrews wanted an expression for anything too vast to be counted or even comprehended, this was the image to which they turned. Centuries before David, another ancient saw in the night sky a divine answer to his desire for an heir. God told Abram, "Look up at the heavens and count the stars—if indeed you can count them. . . . So shall your offspring be" (Gen. 15:5). And ever after, whenever the roaming nomad Abraham slept under the stars, God's incomprehensible promise was renewed and displayed to his wondering eyes.

Our psalmist is driven by the experience of the magnificent night sky to acknowledge what humans spend much of their time denying in the daylight—that while humans have little authority and power in the ultimate scheme of the universe, evidence of God's power is ready at hand all around. In contrast to the enduring natural elements of the world, we humans come late on the scene, live fragile and troubled lives, and depart quickly, leaving behind little noticeable mark. The author of Ecclesiastes agrees: "Generations come and generations go, but the earth remains forever. . . . There is no remembrance of men of old, and even those who are yet to come will not be remembered by those who follow" (Eccl. 1:4, 11).[7]

Even the particular Hebrew term used here for humanity (*ʾenoš*) describes weakness and frailty. The Hebrews had other terms in their vocabulary arsenal to describe humans. The familiar and frequent *ʾadam*, which came to serve as the name for the first human, describes humans in more generic terms ("humanity, humankind"[8]), while the more specific term *ʾîš* describes the male of the human species. In poetic contexts (such as here in Ps. 8), *ʾîš* normally represents individual humans in their strength. By contrast, *ʾenoš* most often emphasizes human frailty, weakness, and mortality; thus, the use of that term here is no accident but intentionally stresses the distance the psalmist experiences, opening up between the glorious creator God, Yahweh, and his far less significant and less powerful human creatures.

The son of man. In the second phrase of verse 4, the psalmist parallels the first phrase affirmingly. To balance *ʾenoš* he uses the poetic variant *ben-ʾadam* ("son of man"). This phrase is often used in this fashion to parallel *ʾenoš* or the more generic *ʾadam*. If *ben-ʾadam* has any special thrust, it is probably to emphasize the fragile mortality of the human condition—much as does

7. The whole discussion in Eccl. 1:2–11 points up the contrast between the enduring natural process of the world, which continues unchanged from generation to generation, and the brief, fitful, unmemorable lives of human beings.

8. Cf. Gen. 1:26–27, where Yahweh creates *ʾadam* both male and female.

ʾenôš in this and other passages. Jesus' choice of "son of man" as his personal self-designation (in contrast to Messiah) is certainly revealing. By adopting this title as his own and connecting it as he does with the suffering servant of the latter half of Isaiah, he particularly identifies with the fragile weakness of mortal human beings, who are dependent for their very existence on the gracious mercy of God. In any case, the psalmist, by the use of these two words, drives home the frailty and limitation of humans in comparison to the awesome, universal, creative power of Yahweh displayed across the heavens.

By this subtle depiction of an awed human spectator dwarfed beneath the immense expanse of the glittering heavens, the psalmist brings the reader to the inward and outer point of the humble self-reflection to which the psalm has been moving along. In the studied and extreme contrast between the power, might, and majesty of Yahweh and the infinitely receding significance of humans, the psalmist lays the groundwork for the central message of the psalm. For ultimately Psalm 8 is *not* about divine power, or even human insignificance. It is much more about divine grace, empowerment, and resultant human responsibility.

That you are mindful . . . that you care. The psalmist's final thought is not "How great and magnificent you are, O God, and how puny we humans are by contrast." Instead, his central insight is that in spite of the incredible chasm that separates humans and their God, so that humans appear as but minuscule specks of dust on a rock revolving around one of thousands of stars in but one of countless galaxies flung across the universe, God is still mindful of humans and has the will, purpose, and incredible gifting for our lives. Out of sight is *not* out of God's mind as far as humans are concerned. In the world of human kings, a peasant subject might languish unknown and uncared for in the furthest reaches of the empire, but Yahweh remains mindful of all those whom he has made for a purpose.

The two terms the psalmist uses to indicate the interest and care with which God attends to his human creatures are instructive. The first comes from the Hebrew root *zkr*, which indicates "remembering, calling to mind." It is the way I recall and remember my son living in another state. The distance recedes as my mind calls him up and dwells in care on him. The second is from the root *pqd*, which can mean something like "hunt up, seek out; long for, take care of." It is as if God's calling to mind his human creatures sparks such a longing for them that he must seek them out and lavish care on them. What an incredible image of divine care and love!

Empowerment and Responsibility (8:5–8)

IT IS CLEAR from the beginning of Genesis that human beings are no accident or afterthought to Israel's God, in contrast to how they appear in the

Mesopotamian creation narratives. There, the younger Mesopotamian gods rebel at the hard work the ruling gods have imposed on them—digging the Tigris and Euphrates River valleys—and demand replacement laborers. You guessed it! Humans were created to relieve the gods of their labor and to serve the gods' needs.

In Genesis 1, however, the whole creation account moves from the beginning toward the creation of humans as God's culminating creative act on the last day. Only humans are uniquely created "in the image of God" (Gen. 1:26–27), set apart from the rest of animate creation by this distinctive relationship to the creator.

The creation account is clearly the text our psalmist has in mind here. Having read through the powerful description of Yahweh's creation of the natural order, the psalmist is amazed at the care lavished on the creation of humankind. Humans, who can seem so powerless and small in the scheme of things, are invested with stupendous worth and responsibility by the creator. Created in the very image of God, they are given responsibility to extend God's dominion and protective care over the rest of creation.

You made him. The psalmist lays out two ways Yahweh's creation of humans counters their seeming powerless insignificance. Having created them as weak and powerless creatures, with one foot firmly planted in the creaturely world they share with the other animated beasts created on the sixth day,[9] God goes on to plant the other human foot squarely and uniquely in the divine realm, both by the unique gift of the divine image and by the role of responsibility and authority given only to humans.

A little lower. The psalmist recognizes the dual distinction that accrues to humans in the creation narrative: honor and responsibility. God has made humans "a little lower than the heavenly beings"—a position of distinct honor. The phrase "heavenly beings" is an interpretive translation of the Hebrew word *ʾelohim* ("god, gods"). By form this word is a plural noun and appears regularly as the common reference to the multiple foreign deities worshiped by the polytheistic nations. In a rather unusual development, the same plural noun form is used throughout the Old Testament to refer to the one God of Israel, otherwise known as Yahweh.

---

9. In the account of the sixth day of creation in Gen. 1:24–31, humans share the same creative day with the other animated land beasts. This provides humans with a direct and close relationship with the rest of the created order of which they are also a part. It is also significant that no individual blessing is pronounced on the land beasts as occurs for the sea and air creatures in 1:22. This leaves the impression that the similar blessing to "be fruitful and increase in number" (1:28) covers *both* the beasts and humans—a further indication of humans' close and essential relationship to the rest of creation.

Between these two extremes are a number of occurrences of the plural noun form to describe what appear to be heavenly beings subordinate to Yahweh. It is not clear whether this use of *ʾelohim* indicates a tendency toward henotheistic belief—that while other gods exist, Yahweh is over all and demands Israel's absolute loyalty—or whether it had in Israel's mind already come to be purged of any connection to the pagan gods and more nearly approximated what we, following the lead of the author of Hebrews (Heb. 2:5–8), call "angels." The ambiguity inherent in the use of the word has led translators to a variety of options, such as "less than God" (RSV, cf. NRSV), "less than a god" (NJB, REB), and the NIV's "lower than the heavenly beings."

Regardless of the exact translation chosen, the meaning for humans is clear. God has bestowed the highest possible honor on an earthly creature by creating them only a little less elevated than beings that occupy the heavenly sphere. Whether that is God, a god, heavenly beings, or angels, humans have been catapulted far beyond their seeming weakness and insignificance—not by any value of their own but simply by the action of a free divine choice and grace that causes the human jaw to drop and the mind to reel. The honor and glory bestowed on humans is driven home unequivocally in the second half of verse 5: God's establishing of human status to a place just below the heavenly beings is certainly not a penalty. It is equivalent, says the psalmist, to being crowned "with glory and honor."

Crowned with glory and honor. Crowns in Israel were normally wreaths woven of flowers or palm branches. Israelite kings and priests wore a *nezer* crown, signifying their consecration to God. Other pagan kings were said to wear *ʿaṭarah* or *keter* crowns, a sign of royal authority. Crowns of the *ʿaṭarah* type, decorated with flowers, were worn at banquets as a sign of honor and elevation. It is probably this type of "crowning" (*teʿaṭṭerehu* in v. 5; derived from *ʿṭr*) that the psalmist envisions in this case—human beings exalted as a sign of divine favor with "glory" (*kabod*) and "honor" (*hadar*, "splendor, grandeur"). These are characteristics of God himself that adorn the frail humans created in his image and allow his power to be displayed through those creatures he has graciously chosen to extend his authority into the world.

The Hebrew term for "glory" (*kabod*) is most often used to describe the glory of God. Divine "glory" in this sense is the more inward, defining essence of God as he really is, as contrasted with "majesty" (*ʾaddir*, cf. 8:1). When the psalmist describes God as crowning humans with glory, the implication is that through their unique relationship to Yahweh humans come to share in their own inner being the image and essence of the creator that belies their outward appearance of weakness and insignificance.

You made him ruler. There is yet another way Yahweh uniquely distinguishes humans from the rest of creation. As he has set them apart by the glory and honor of his image, so he also sets apart humans by giving them responsibility over the earth. It is certain in my mind that the psalmist has the account of creation in Genesis 1:28 clearly in mind here. In the Genesis 1 narrative, humans stand uniquely between the rest of creation and the creator. As a sign of their inseparable link with the rest of animated creation, humans share the sixth day of creation with the land animals. Yahweh creates first land animals and then humans. Unlike the preceding fifth day, God pronounces no blessing following the creation of the land creatures (1:24–25), although he does make the previously repeated evaluation of his work, "and God saw that it was good." Following the creation of humans in 1:26–27, God does supply the blessing that was earlier omitted (1:28), by implication blessing both animals and humans together. The placement of this blessing *after* the creation of humans links them back to the preceding land creatures, of whom humans are considered an integral part. Like the animals, humans are part of the creaturely order and as such are dependent on the creating and sustaining mercy of God.

In the following verses of the Genesis narrative, however, it is humanity's distinction from the animals that is emphasized. Unlike the animals, humans share the divine image (1:26–27) and are given responsibility over the animals and the rest of creation (1:28). Like the animals humans are to be fruitful and multiply, but, rather than simply "filling the earth" as the animals are commanded, humans are to exercise divinely authorized responsibility over it. This role of responsibility sets humans apart from the rest of creation and emphasizes their essential unity with the creator from whom their responsibility and authority derives.

The word used in Psalm 8 to describe this human responsibility ordained at creation is the Hebrew verb *mšl* ("rule, govern; exercise dominion over," here with causal force meaning "make someone exercise dominion over"). This word can mean to provide structure, as the heavenly bodies "rule" over the night and day in Genesis 1:18, or to control, as when the husband is said to "rule" over the woman in Genesis 3:16. The clear implication of this particular Hebrew form is that human authority over the world is not autocratic but derived from the authority of the creator, with whom humans share a unique link. As a result, human authority is distinctly limited and directly responsible to God.[10]

10. The Genesis narrative uses two different words to describe the authority and responsibility of humans over creation. I will return to these in the Bridging Contexts section.

Under his feet. One symbolic act in the ancient Near East to indicate superiority over a defeated enemy was for the king to place his foot on the neck of the enemy lying prostrate at his feet. This act of humiliation of the enemy and exaltation of the king graphically displayed who was in control and who was not. Elsewhere the psalms use a similar image of making one's enemies a "footstool" (Pss. 99:5; 110:1). But here the prostration of the earth under the feet of the divinely elevated human, while a sign of likeness to God and distinction from the rest of creation, is *not* an indication of human strength, power, and unlimited authority. The earth is *placed* under human authority by God—not by human power. Any authority exercised by humans over the earth is distinctly limited, derived from God, and ultimately responsible to him.

The Thematic Framework Revisited (8:1a, 9)

O LORD, our Lord. Our psalm ends as it begins—in fulsome praise of the creating God, whose majestic name permeates all that he has made. Yet subtly our understanding of the ground for praising Yahweh has shifted from the first verse to the last. At the beginning our praise began by affirming the magnificence of the creator. At the end, we stand in awe at the unexpected grace that has elevated his human works to unimaginable heights of glory, honor, and responsibility; sharing God's image, we are also called to share his loving care for all he has made. This perspective can and must change how we look at the world of which we are at one and the same time integral parts and strangers passing through.

PSALM 8, IN all its brevity, is full of rich and complex insights into the nature of human beings and the intended shape of their relations to God and the created order. In this section I will carry our thinking and reflecting deeper into several of those rich insights and inquire how they continue to impact our own world. I will consider three concepts of such magnitude that books have been written expounding each one: (1) the gift of the divine name; (2) the implication of the creation of humans in the divine image; and (3) the meaning of God's command to humans to rule over the earth.

The gift of the divine name. In the Old Testament, a name, whether of humans or of God, is an extension of the one who bears it and often reveals something of the character of the person named. Jacob, whose name means "one who seeks to take the place of another," wrestles with himself and God at Wadi Jabbok and is renamed "Israel"—"one who struggles with or holds on to God" (Gen. 32:22–30). Hosea's three children by Gomer all have meaningful symbolic names (Hos. 1:4–9).

Likewise, God's gift to Israel (and to us) of his personal name Yahweh is meant to reveal something of his nature. As best we can recover at this late point, the Tetragrammaton *yhwh* represents a Hebrew verbal form (to be exact, a Qal imperfect third masculine singular, derived from *hwh*) and was probably originally pronounced *Yahweh*. As we will see shortly, this form of the name actually represents an abbreviation of the *full* divine name—an abbreviation spoken from the human point of view. The complete name of God was revealed at the Exodus (Ex. 3:14) by God himself in the more extended phrase *ʾehyeh ʾašer ʾehyeh* (two first-person imperfect verbs connected by the relative particle *ʾašer* ["who, what"]). Having revealed this longer form of his name, God immediately goes on to abbreviate it to the more manageable first-person form *ʾehyeh* ("I will be") and recommends that humans address him appropriately with the third-person form Yahweh ("Say . . . *yahweh* has sent me to you"; i.e., "Yahweh has sent me to you," Ex. 3:15).

Now, this type of imperfect verb form describes action that is not complete—either because it is continuing or because it still lies in the future. This distinction has given rise to two primary interpretations of the meaning of the divine name. Some have emphasized the continuing aspect of God and suggested the divine name recognizes that Yahweh is the God who is and continues to be. The resulting translation of the full name in Exodus 3:14 is often rendered, "I am who I am," and connections are made with the response of Jesus, who, when queried before the Sanhedrin whether he was the Messiah (Mark 14:62), replied "I am."[11] Using the form Yahweh, humans would speak of God as "he is."

Taking the more future-oriented interpretation of the imperfect leads in slightly different directions. The resulting translation is the familiar "I will be what I will be." Humans address God in the shorthand third-person form Yahweh as "he will be." Now, lest we think God is merely being arrogant and cryptic (e.g., "I will be whatever I want to be"), let me suggest three possible implications of the name so interpreted.

(1) The name offers to God's people *a powerful promise of continuing divine presence* in their lives. "I *will be*!" says Yahweh, and that is not a promise to be taken lightly. In the immediate context of Exodus, Yahweh promises to be with Moses, to speak through him, and to be with Israel as they flee and travel to the Promised Land. Throughout Israel's history, God's people acknowledge the constant and consistent presence of Yahweh in their

11. Greek, *ego eimi*.

midst—both in blessing and in punishment. Thus, one thing that Yahweh means by revealing his name to Israel is that he will "be with" his people from now on and into the future.

(2) Knowledge of Yahweh will grow and increase through *continued future revelation* of his nature and purpose. "I will be what I *will* be," Yahweh says. God did not hand Moses a tidy pamphlet entitled "Knowing God in One Easy Lesson." Instead, he invited Moses and all Israel to embark with him on a lifelong journey of discovery that proved to be considerably less than tidy. Israel acknowledged again and again throughout the Hebrew Bible that her understanding of God was incomplete at first and required centuries of refinement—through many experiences of joy and pain, freedom, bondage, and deliverance. Even Paul recognized the continuing growth in knowledge and understanding of God that awaits consummation in the last days: "Now I know in part; then I shall know fully, even as I am fully known" (1 Cor. 13:12).

(3) Although the gift of the name to humans is an incredible opportunity for access to God, God *nevertheless remains free from human manipulation and abuse*. Yahweh claims, "I will be what *I* will be." In the ancient world in which Israel lived, the name of the god was often a closely guarded secret employed in the deepest, most intimate recesses of the worship system. The name of a god provided access to the deity. Incorporated into incantations and rituals, the name could command the god's presence and force action. It was carefully protected, therefore, to prevent unauthorized use by enemies or the ignorant, who might create evil consequences by their unorthodox use of the god's name.

Yahweh's name was given to his people freely, and with that gift came open access to him. But the very name offered—Yahweh—provided protection from human manipulation and control. God would be what *he would be*, not what humans desired or sought to manipulate him to be. This rejection of human abuse may well lie behind the prohibitions against misuse of the divine name in the Ten Commandments, noted above.

It is the name Yahweh, with all its attendant mystery and revelation about the nature of Israel's God, that the psalmist of Psalm 8 pronounces "majestic." It is a majestic name for a majestic God, who promises to be with us, continues to reveal himself to us in each and every new circumstance, and yet remains forever beyond our power to control or manipulate to our own purpose.

The image of God. The awed amazement with which the psalmist reflects on the creation of humans by God is derived from a close and sensitive reading of Genesis 1. Humans are created with one foot firmly planted within the created order, sharing with the rest of animate and inanimate creation an absolute dependence on the gracious mercy of God poured out in life and sustenance. Unlike the rest of creation, however, humans, by virtue of being created in the image of God, share a unique relationship that binds them together with their creator while embuing them with responsibility for his creation.

Just what does it mean that humans bear the image of God? How do they display this image and what impact ought it to make on their relation to God, their fellow humans, and the rest of creation? These questions have no easy answers, but they are important foundations for understanding the whole biblical story—both Old and New Testaments.

Consider a few thoughts on what the image of God is *not*. The image has nothing to do with physical form. Humans are not like God because he has two legs, two arms, two eyes, a nose, and a mouth. Scripture teaches us that God is eternal spirit and not confined to physical form. It is true that God does occasionally appear in human form as an angelic messenger (Judg. 13) or mysterious wrestler (Gen. 32), and most supremely in the incarnation of divine Word in the human flesh of Jesus. However, Scripture always takes care to let us know that this physical form is not the full measure of God but is the result of divine accommodation—pouring his divine essence into a physical form that can be apprehended by humans. In other words, God is not limited to human form but humbles himself in the form of Jesus (Phil. 2:4–11) so that we may know him as fully as humanly possible.

Others have suggested that the essential link between humans and God that constitutes the divine image is human rationality. In this view, it is our ability to think, choose, and act freely on those choices that separates humanity from the animals and provides the essential link to God. While I believe there is a significant element of truth in this viewpoint, I believe it falls short of expounding the full meaning of the divine image that humans bear. Hebrew Scripture (and the New Testament as well) never emphasizes human rationality as the essential link with God. This focus on rationality as the unique connection between God and humans is more the result of the Enlightenment than biblical teaching.

To understand what is meant and implied by humans created in the divine image, we must begin by exploring the meaning and purpose of the image in the ancient Near Eastern context in which the creation narrative and Psalm 8 were written. In 1979 a Syrian farmer unearthed a statue while plowing his field.[12] The statue was a life-sized likeness of the Assyrian governor Hadadyisʿi and was inscribed with a bilingual inscription in Aramaic and Akkadian. The statue is of interest because it represents the only known text outside the

12. A. R. Millard and P. Bordeuil, "A Statue from Syria with Assyrian and Aramaic Inscriptions," *BA* 45 (1982): 135–41.

Bible where cognates of the same two terms employed in Genesis 1:26 to describe the "image" (*ṣelem*) and "likeness" (*demutaʾ*) of God borne by humans are found together. The statue is described in the text as the "image" and "likeness" of the king.

Evidently statues of kings similar to this image and likeness of the governor Hadad-yisʿi were set up in locations around the king's domain to provide a visible representation to the people of the distant and therefore effectively invisible king. The statue showed what the king was like, served as a constant reminder of his presence, and extended a claim of royal authority over the place where the statue stood.

Similar understandings were attached to the statues of the polytheistic gods and goddesses worshiped in the ancient Near East. While most people understood that the image was not really the god, it did show what the god or goddess looked like, provided a place of presence where the deity could be found and approached, and established a claim of divine authority over a locality and the people in it.

If we apply these insights to what it means for humans to be created in the image and likeness of Yahweh in Genesis 1, a significant role emerges. In Israel, any image or physical representation of Yahweh was expressly prohibited (Ex. 20:4–6). This must be related to the fact that Yahweh's image is to be borne *by his people*. Together humans are to represent and make known to the created order what God is like (cf. Matt. 18:20). And by humanity God's divine authority is to be extended to the rest of creation.

Such a view of the divine image impressed on humanity heightens the magnitude of human responsibility in creation. Humans are not merely servants of God created for his benefit. Rather, they are the very means through which God is to be revealed, mirrored, and known. They are the chosen regents through whom divine authority is mediated to the earth. It is this recognition that causes the psalmist to stand in awe and amazement beneath the glittering heavens. We will return in the Contemporary Significance section to consider the implications of this image and this responsibility for contemporary Christians.

Rulership and dominion over the earth. Human beings, who lack only a little from the heavenly beings, are established as rulers over the earth and have everything placed under their feet by God. This understanding of the role of humans appears to stand in subtle tension with the account in Genesis 1:26–28, to which it is surely a response. In Genesis, humans, having been created in the image and likeness of Yahweh, are told to "rule" (*rdh*) over the creatures and to "subdue" (*kbš*) the earth. Some interpreters have understood these two Genesis terms against a background of royal authority and prerogative and assumed that human dominion over the earth entails unlimited power and autocratic control. Such a view can lead to abusive relationships to the world and its creatures and has rightly been critiqued for its human-centered excesses and destructive consequences.[13] Such an understanding is not consistent, however, with the findings of a careful investigation of the use of these terms in the Old Testament.

The first term (*rdh*), rather than "have dominion," is better translated "exercise authority over." On a number of occasions in Kings and Chronicles, those who "exercise authority" are not kings at all but the king's appointed representatives, supervising the activities of the king's employees.[14] It is obvious that such appointed agents of the king exercise only such limited control as delegated to them by the monarch. They do not rule as they please or as benefits themselves but as profits the king's business.

Humans who abusively exercise the authority given them are subject to divine rebuke and condemnation (Lev. 25:43, 46, 53; Ezek. 34:4). Even kings exercise only limited authority derived from Yahweh. Psalm 72:8 prays to Yahweh that the Israelite king might "rule" or "exercise authority" from sea to sea, while 110:2 recognizes that it is Yahweh who allows the king to exercise authority against his foes. Yahweh gives the right to exercise authority to whom he wills and takes that right away from those kings (both foreign and Israelite) who abuse their power (Lev. 26:17; Neh. 9:28; Isa. 14:6; Ezek. 29:15). Clearly the authority associated with the Hebrew root *rdh* is not unlimited or autocratic; rather, it is authority granted by Yahweh, to be exercised in accordance with his will.

The second term (*kbš*) is most frequently taken to describe violent conquest and the subjugation of another. The violent nature is often related to the narrative in Esther 7, where an enraged king Xerxes, having just learned of Haman's attempt to manipulate the king and Persian law in order to commit genocide against Queen Esther's Jewish people, discovers Haman leaning on the queen's dinner couch to plead desperately for his life. Enraged, the king condemns Haman and cries: "Will you even attempt to *kbš* the queen in my own house?" Commentators usually interpret the king's accusation as one of attempted rape of the queen.

A closer look, however, is less than supportive of such a violent understanding of *kbš*. Fully one-third of all occurrences of this verb refer to the failure of Israelites to free fellow Israelite servants after the completion of their

13. Cf. Lynn B. White, "The Historical Roots of Our Ecological Crisis," in *Western Man and Environmental Ethics*, ed. Ian Barbour (Reading, Mass.: Addison-Wesley, 1973); Gerald H. Wilson, "Restoring the Image: Perspectives on a Biblical View of Creation," *Quaker Religious Thought* 24 (1990): 11–21.

14. See 1 Kings 5:16; 9:23; 2 Chron. 8:10.

required term of service. Here it is not the act of *kbš* that is condemned. To exercise such authority appears to be perfectly legitimate. Condemnation comes when legitimate authority is extended beyond acceptable limits. Another third of the occurrences of *kbš* have to do with the Promised Land being brought under the authority of Yahweh through the agency of Israel and David (Num. 32:22, 29; Josh. 18:1; 2 Sam. 8:11; 1 Chron. 22:18). Once again the emphasis is not so much on violent conquest and subjugation as it is on establishing divine authority by means of human agency. The remaining occurrences, while in more difficult interpretive contexts (cf. Est. 7:8; Mic. 7:19; Zech. 9:15), can each be understood as using a similar rendering: "bring under authority."

Thus, even these two foundational words in the original Genesis narrative do not provide warrant for autocratic human control and subjugation of the creation for human benefit. Humans are to exercise limited, divinely instituted authority and are to bring the whole cosmos under the authority of God. This interpretation of Genesis is consistent with the more subtle expressions of Psalm 8, where humans are made to rule by God, who likewise places all things under their feet.

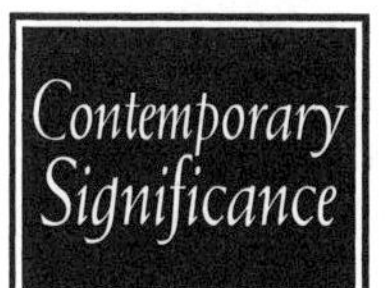

WHAT'S IN A NAME? Have you ever thought what it would be like to live with a name that expressed your character? Some early Quakers and Puritans bore names that marked out the faith of their parents. Faith, Hope, and Charity were common names as well as virtues. Less common but equally evocative were more stalwart designations like Prudence, Reliance, or Endurance. But even these names did not necessarily reveal the character of those who bore them.

If you were to bear a name that made known your innermost being, what do you think that name might be? What would it be like to have that character revealed every time Mom or Dad called you in for dinner? "Wishy-washy, come eat!" "Liar! It's time to go!" We so frequently cloak our real selves—revealing only what we believe will earn acceptance—that such rough exposure of our true identities might panic us. I know it would me! What would it be like to be known for what we really are—as we know ourselves within? Could we stand up to such fierce scrutiny?

It is an interesting exercise to think back through our lives and to decide what would be the names characterizing the various shifts and movements in our becoming who we are today. If we are honest, we would have to admit that our characters have grown and changed (not always for the better) under the events and pressures of life's journey. Choosing a name for those shifts and changes (as one would name a newborn child) can help us see more clearly the twists and turns that have brought us to where we now stand.

If you could choose, what name would you *want* to have applied to you? If you are anything like me, you have probably tried to live out many names—masks to hide the real you. But what name would you *like* to characterize your innermost being? The distance between who we would like to be and who we really are is often a cause for guilt and despair. We cannot be who we would like to be because our sinful selves keep getting in the way.

This psalm opens up a new window on who we really are. Although we see ourselves as weak [*ʾenoš*] and insignificant [*ben ʾadam*], God sees us as only a little lower than he himself. Although we are rebellious sinners, God in Christ has provided a way to change our names. We are no longer to be called enemies but friends of God. Christ has prepared the way for sinners to be known as *bene ʾelohim*—the "children of God" (cf. John 1:12).

Divine epithets. The emphasis on the divine name needs further application as well. Many names—epithets really—are used of God in the Old and New Testaments. Some, like *ʾelohim* or *ʾel*, are more generic terms for "God" and tell us little about who he is. Others combine these generic elements with designations that talk about how God is known—for example, *ʾel šadday* ("God who appears in the mountain regions"); *ʾel roʾeh* ("God who appears in a vision")—or describe relationships through which God is known—*ʾel ṣebaʾot* ("God of the [heavenly] hosts"); *ʾel ʾabot* ("God of the ancestors").

Other names directed to God are more concerned to encapsulate some understanding of his nature and character. Isaiah calls Yahweh *qadoš yiśraʾel* ("Holy One of Israel") and strings together the familiar series of descriptors in Isaiah 9:6: "Wonderful Counselor, Mighty God, Everlasting Father, Prince of Peace." The "fatherhood" of God has captured Christian imagination ever since Jesus made the familiar *Abba* ("Daddy") his preferred designation for God and invites his followers to do the same (cf. Matt. 6:8; John 20:17).[15] While the title "mother" is never applied *directly* to God in the Bible, feminine imagery does imply that God acts as a compassionate and caring mother, comforting and suckling her children (Ps. 131:2; Isa. 66:13).

What are some contemporary names we might use to describe the God of our experience? Twelve-step recovery groups encourage those seeking freedom from addictions and other destructive compulsive behaviors to turn their will and life over to the care of God "as you understand God." While

15. Cf. also Rom. 8:15: "For you did not receive a spirit that makes you a slave again to fear, but you received the Spirit of sonship. And by him [the Spirit] we cry '*Abba*, Father!'"

the final phrase is intended to maintain a necessary spiritual component of healing while avoiding conflict that can arise from the diversity of religious belief systems followed by attenders, there is an element of truth that mirrors my own experience of God. My understanding of God grows as I see him at work in my life day by day, shaping me into the person I am becoming.

Several years ago my church community participated in a pre-Easter Fifty-Day Adventure. One key element of this communal time of reflection, repentance, and preparation was to keep a daily list of "God sightings"—times and ways in which we saw God in the ordinary events of our daily lives. I was amazed by the effectiveness of this simple exercise. Simply by focusing my attention several times a day, I was able to become aware that God was present with me and was making himself known—if I would only look and listen.

I was even more impressed, however, that being able to see God present and at work was a choice I made to see certain events and circumstances as evidence of God's working. Rather than naming them "accidents" or "coincidences," I chose to see God at work in them and to acknowledge his will and purpose in my life. In such small ways we can provide shape and texture to our experience and understanding of the God who reveals himself to us.

All these names and epithets are descriptions of God developed from human experience and perspective. They represent ways men and women, ancient and contemporary, have tried to express their growing and changing understanding of the God who continually breaks into their lives. But our psalm speaks of a miraculous name that is not derived from human perception but is a gift of divine self-revelation. What a wonderful certainty—that God wants to be known by his creation, and in particular by his human creatures.

Creation is not a consequence of divine need. God is distinct from and independent of the creation. Even humans have not been created to fulfill a need of God. They have not been brought into being to serve God or to provide a conversation partner for an otherwise isolated deity. Before humans ever existed, God had the capacity within himself to communicate, commune, and deliberate, as the plural reference in Genesis 1:26 demonstrates: "Let *us* create humans in *our* image, in *our* likeness...." The role envisioned for humans from the first is not to serve God but to serve the rest of creation.

So, why the creation? If God is complete in and of himself, why was the creation necessary? Creation is the result—the necessary consequence—of a God of love, who desires to extend that love beyond himself, to make himself known. God created the cosmos, and in particular human beings, so that they might experience the benefit of knowing him and being in relationship with him. God is a God who desires to be known, and that is why his name is majestic in all the earth and his glory is set above the heavens. Paul recognizes this desire of God to be known in Romans when he says, "What may be known about God is plain to [humans], because God has made it plain to them. For since the creation of the world God's invisible qualities—his eternal power and divine nature—have been clearly seen, being understood from what has been made" (Rom. 1:19–20).

The divine name Yahweh revealed at the Exodus is one more evidence of this God who wants us to know him, who is reaching out to know us. The God who promises to be with us, to continually unfold himself to us in new and deeper ways of understanding, even while remaining ever free of human attempts to manipulate and distort him, is the God who made himself intimately and ultimately known in his Son, Jesus the Christ. Jesus said, "I and the Father are one" (John 10:30), and "Anyone who has seen me has seen the Father" (14:9).

Some of us have taken this identification between Jesus and the Father so seriously that Jesus, friend and Savior, begins to obscure God, Father and righteous judge. Our love and reverence of Jesus is certainly not wrong as long as we do not allow it to drive a wedge between our understanding of God based on the New Testament witness to Jesus and the God of grace, love, and power revealed throughout the Old Testament. The church has long recognized that it is impossible to distinguish between a gracious God of the New Testament and a wrathful Old Testament God. To do so is to fall into the same confusion as Marcion in the second century A.D.[16] The God who creates in Genesis, the God who saves in the Exodus, the God who calls to repentance in the prophets, the God praised in our psalm, is the same God revealed in Jesus of Nazareth, who has made himself known "at many times and in various ways" (Heb. 1:1–2).

Bearing the divine image. Since we bear the likeness of God—his very image—how are we to go about displaying it to the rest of creation? Clearly humanity through the ages has not been a very good paradigm of divine character. Yes, there have been moments of inspired behavior that approach the love and care of God, but for the most part humans present a poor picture by which to know and understand the creator.

True, the brokenness of humans and the whole creation because of the disobedience of humankind since Adam and Eve is the obvious explanation for human failure to rightly represent God to the world. The image borne by

16. Marcion, a bishop of the early church, believed that the God of the Old Testament was *not* the same God as in the New. He devised a heavily edited version of the Gospel of Luke and of the Pauline letters that supposedly omitted references to the Old Testament. Marcion was declared a heretic, and opposition to his truncated "canon" gave impetus to the efforts to define the limits of the authoritative collection of New Testament books.

humans has been tarnished and twisted almost beyond recognition. It is little wonder that when the world looks at the human condition and even the example of the Christian community, so many come to question whether God even exists.

But our brokenness is no excuse, because in Christ God has offered a remedy for human brokenness. In Christ we are spiritually empowered to look beyond ourselves and our own desires and to relate appropriately to other humans, both male and female, and to the rest of creation, animate or inanimate. We can participate in the restoration of the divine image that has been our purpose since the creation of the world.

Let us return to the question with which we began this section: How are we to go about displaying the divine image we bear to the rest of creation? For a hint we need to look briefly at the narratives of the creation of humans in Genesis 1 and 2.

In Genesis 1, God creates humans at the end of the creative period, and it is clear that humans are the point to which all creation has been moving since the beginning. This affirms the awed view of human elevation expressed in Psalm 8. The key passage is Genesis 1:26–27: "Then God said, 'Let us make man in our image, in our likeness, and let them rule over [the creatures].' So God created man in his own image, in the image of God he created him; male and female he created them." Let me draw three implications from these verses for how we display the divine image to the world.

(1) The image of God is a relational image realized in the appropriate interaction of multiple humans together and with their God. When God says "Let *us* create man in *our* image," he is not talking about other polytheistic deities. He does not mean angelic beings, nor is he using the royal plural as in "It is *our* decree. . . ." Whatever this plural in the mouth of God means, it at least implies that God has within his essential self the ability to commune with himself in a way that can only be mirrored in humans by relationship to another individual. To fully display God's image to the world, then, requires multiple humans. For this reason in Genesis 1:27, the poet artfully expands the creation of *man* into the creation of *humanity* with the affirmingly parallel phrase "male and female he created them."

The need for multiple humans to display God's image is confirmed in the distinct but complementary text of Genesis 2, when the *ʾadam* (human being), initially formed out of the ground, is declared by God himself to be "not good" in isolation, and God sets immediately about finding a human counterpart to provide the possibility of relationship and communion. An animal partner will not do.

Genesis 2 drives home the same point when the *ʾadam* is only complete and one when male and female are united together in right relationship. To paraphrase John Donne, "No *man* is an image entire unto himself." Only when we are enabled by God's power to relate together rightly—human to human, male to female—do we display the whole intended image of God.

(2) Plurality and gender diversity are not enough in the absence of right relationship. Our world is full of plural males and females struggling to defeat, control, or exploit each other. This is not the divine image. Sinful brokenness stands in the way of restored relationship in our world. But the church is called out of the world to be the place where the divine image is restored and fractured humanity can see a paradigm of God's people relating appropriately to one another regardless of race, gender, status, and so on. We can be "one in the Spirit ... one in the Lord." Although we are different members, we are all one body—and we pray that all unity will one day be restored.

(3) The fact that we as Christians are so like our world and not distinct is perhaps the greatest criticism that can be leveled against us today. We are no different in the way we dress, how we eat, where we live, what we say and do, how we marry, or how we divorce.[17] Psalm 8 calls us to allow an awe-filled glimpse of the majesty of the creator God to renew our sense of wonder and purpose to be the image of God that our world desperately needs to know.

17. In fact, a recent survey conducted by George Barna indicates that "born-again Christians" are more likely to divorce than unbelievers (27 percent for born-again Christians against only 24 percent of those not born again and 21 percent of agnostics and atheists). The survey was reported in *Southern California Christian Times*. Inland Empire Edition, 11/2 (February 2000): 1, 11–13.

Psalms 9 and 10

FOR THE DIRECTOR of music. To the tune of "The Death of the Son." A psalm of David.

9:1 I will praise you, O LORD, with all my heart;
I will tell of all your wonders.
2 I will be glad and rejoice in you;

I will sing praise to your name, O Most High.

3 My enemies turn back;
they stumble and perish before you.
4 For you have upheld my right and my cause;
you have sat on your throne, judging righteously.
5 You have rebuked the nations and destroyed the wicked;
you have blotted out their name for ever and ever.
6 Endless ruin has overtaken the enemy,
you have uprooted their cities;
even the memory of them has perished.

7 The LORD reigns forever;
he has established his throne for judgment.
8 He will judge the world in righteousness;
he will govern the peoples with justice.
9 The LORD is a refuge for the oppressed,
a stronghold in times of trouble.
10 Those who know your name will trust in you,
for you, LORD, have never forsaken those who
seek you.

11 Sing praises to the LORD, enthroned in Zion;
proclaim among the nations what he has done.
12 For he who avenges blood remembers;
he does not ignore the cry of the afflicted.

13 O LORD, see how my enemies persecute me!
Have mercy and lift me up from the gates of death,
14 that I may declare your praises
in the gates of the Daughter of Zion
and there rejoice in your salvation.

15 The nations have fallen into the pit they have dug;
their feet are caught in the net they have hidden.
16 The LORD is known by his justice;
the wicked are ensnared by the work of their hands.
Higgaion. Selah

17 The wicked return to the grave,
all the nations that forget God.
18 But the needy will not always be forgotten,
nor the hope of the afflicted ever perish.

19 Arise, O LORD, let not man triumph;
let the nations be judged in your presence.
20 Strike them with terror, O LORD;
let the nations know they are but men.
Selah

10:1 Why, O LORD, do you stand far off?
Why do you hide yourself in times of trouble?

2 In his arrogance the wicked man hunts down the weak,
who are caught in the schemes he devises.
3 He boasts of the cravings of his heart;
he blesses the greedy and reviles the LORD.
4 In his pride the wicked does not seek him;
in all his thoughts there is no room for God.
5 His ways are always prosperous;
he is haughty and your laws are far from him;
he sneers at all his enemies.
6 He says to himself, "Nothing will shake me;
I'll always be happy and never have trouble."
7 His mouth is full of curses and lies and threats;
trouble and evil are under his tongue.
8 He lies in wait near the villages;
from ambush he murders the innocent,
watching in secret for his victims.
9 He lies in wait like a lion in cover;
he lies in wait to catch the helpless;
he catches the helpless and drags them off in his net.
10 His victims are crushed, they collapse;
they fall under his strength.
11 He says to himself, "God has forgotten;
he covers his face and never sees."

12 Arise, LORD! Lift up your hand, O God.
Do not forget the helpless.
13 Why does the wicked man revile God?
Why does he say to himself,
"He won't call me to account"?
14 But you, O God, do see trouble and grief;
you consider it to take it in hand.
The victim commits himself to you;
you are the helper of the fatherless.
15 Break the arm of the wicked and evil man;
call him to account for his wickedness
that would not be found out.

16 The LORD is King for ever and ever;
the nations will perish from his land.
17 You hear, O LORD, the desire of the afflicted;
you encourage them, and you listen to their cry,
18 defending the fatherless and the oppressed,
in order that man, who is of the earth, may terrify
no more.

THESE TWO PSALMS introduce us to a phenomenon encountered several times within the canonical Psalter: Two adjacent psalms seem to have been read together as a single composition. Most often this special relationship is marked out by the second psalm lacking a heading while the heading of the first psalm does "double duty" for both. For the first time in Book 1 of the Psalter (except for the introductory Psalms 1 and 2), a psalm (Ps. 10) appears with no heading.

This lack of a heading for Psalm 10 may seem inconsequential by itself, but several other factors need to be pointed out. (1) A survey of the extant manuscripts of the Psalter scattered throughout the monasteries, museums, and libraries of the world reveals that many combine Psalms 9 and 10 into a single composition—evidently taking the lack of a heading in Psalm 10 as an indication these psalms are to be read as a unity.[1]

1. Research of this type was begun in the seventeenth and eighteenth centuries in response to growing awareness of the existence of numerous manuscripts of the Hebrew Bible and the New Testament scattered through monasteries and libraries throughout Europe. Comparison of these manuscripts with each other led to the discovery of thousands of variations in spelling, wording, and more extensive content, preserved by these

(2) In addition, careful observation of the Hebrew text of these psalms reveals the presence of an acrostic pattern also binding the two into one. The pattern begins with *aleph* in 9:1 and continues through the letter *kaph* in 9:18, giving two lines to each letter (except for the fourth letter, *dalet*, which is omitted, and toward the end where *yod* is given only one line while *kaph* has three).[2] Psalm 10 contains the final segment of the acrostic, beginning most clearly with the letter *pe* in 10:7, continuing through the final letter of the Hebrew alphabet (*taw*) in 10:17.[3] The central letters of the acrostic— *mem, nun, samek*—are not clearly displayed, perhaps having been obscured by whatever tradition chose to divide the original acrostic composition into two separate psalms.

(3) Finally, the LXX treats these two psalms as a single psalm of thirty-nine verses.[4] The acrostic is, of course, invisible in the Greek translation. As a result of the LXX's treatment, the enumeration of the psalms in the Greek Psalter disagrees with that of the Hebrew text (and the English, which follows the Hebrew) by one for most of the psalms. Both collections do preserve a total of 150 compositions; the Greek Psalter presents the Hebrew Psalm 147 as two psalms, numbered there as Psalms 146 and 147.[5]

What this ambiguity about the separation and combination of the texts of these two psalms suggests is the existence of alternative traditions regarding how this material should be read. In what follows, I will comment on the two psalms as a single composition, while also making a few comments about how reading them separately might affect interpretation.

---

texts; this fact led to attempts to collate, record, and categorize all these variants as the basis of textual studies. This was the beginning of modern, scientific text criticism, which seeks to establish the original version of the biblical text by comparing all variants and determining which one most likely represents the original reading. Two of the most exhaustive and painstaking attempts to collate variants in the texts of Old Testament manuscripts are Benjamin Kennicot, ed., *Vetus Testamentum Hebraicum cum Variis Lectionibus*, vol. 1 (Oxford: Clarendon, 1776), and Johannes Bernardus de Rossi, *Variae Lectiones Veteris Testamenti ex immensa Mss. editorumq. codicum* (Parmae: ex Regio Typographeo, 1784–1798).

2. These latter inconsistencies (in the *yod* and *kaph* verses) may have been affected by the division of the original poem into two parts, thus obscuring the acrostic nature of the whole.

3. The normal sequence of the Hebrew alphabet is disordered in Ps. 10 by exchanging the *pe* and *ᶜayin* verses.

4. On the basis of the Hebrew alphabet of twenty-two characters, one would anticipate a complete acrostic to contain some multiple of twenty-two verses—in this case forty-four, since each letter is represented by two verses of poetry. The lack of compatibility with this expected figure is further evidence of the disrupted nature of the acrostic of Pss. 9–10.

5. The schema of the two Psalters runs like this: (a) Pss. 1–8 are the same; (b) Hebrew Pss. 9 and 10 = Greek Ps. 9; (c) Hebrew Pss. 11–146 = Greek Pss. 10–145; (d) Hebrew Ps. 147 = Greek Pss. 146 and 147; Pss. 148–150 are the same. The Greek Psalter does, of course, include the additional Ps. 151, described in its heading as being "outside the number" of the traditional psalm collection.

Both psalms can be categorized as pleas for deliverance from "the wicked," although Psalm 9 introduces elements of anticipated thanksgiving. Structurally, Psalm 9 begins (following the heading) with (1) an expression of anticipated thanksgiving for deliverance (9:1–3); then alternates between (2) segments expounding Yahweh's role as judge of the "nations" (9:4–8, cf. 15–20) and (3) a more personally focused section acknowledging Yahweh as the "refuge" for those (including the psalmist) who trust in him (9:9–14); and (4) concludes with a description of retributive judgment meted out on the wicked (9:15–20).

Psalm 10 opens with (5) a plea to Yahweh to show himself in deliverance (10:1); then divides into (6) a long accusation of the arrogant wicked person who ignores God and oppresses the weak (10:2–11) and (7) a cry for Yahweh to arise and defeat the wicked (10:12–15); and (8) concludes by expressing confidence on the basis of the eternal kingship of Yahweh (10:16–18).

The Heading (9:0)

THIS PSALM IS attributed to David and classified in the most general sense as a *mizmor* ("psalm").[6] After the familiar opening reference to the "director,"[7] the phrase *ᶜalmut labben* is more difficult to access. The alternatives most often chosen are to read the phrase either as the name of a tune to which our psalm is to be sung (e.g., "Concerning the Death of the Son")[8] or as a reference to certain "female voices" employed in the performance. Neither alternative provides much insight into interpretation.

Anticipation of Thanksgiving (9:1–3)

I WILL PRAISE YOU. Like many of the laments, Psalm 9 includes an advance notice of thanks for deliverance and restoration. The Hebrew verb used here is usually translated "give thanks" rather than the NIV's "praise." A noun of the same root (*todah*) is used to describe the "thanksgiving sacrifice" offered in the temple to celebrate deliverance from trouble. It is the Hebrew verb *hll* (from which we get the word "hallelujah") that is more rightly rendered "praise." By "praise" the Hebrew normally means celebration of the exalted character and being of Yahweh, while "thanks" is normally a response to God's gracious acts of deliverance.

---

6. For both of these elements, see comments on the heading of Ps. 3.

7. See comments on the heading of Ps. 4.

8. Cf. NIV. Whether the tune name has any significance to the interpretation of the psalm is patently unclear. Since it is so obscure, it seems best not to make much of it.

It is clear from the body of the psalm that the psalmist is still suffering and that hope for deliverance still lies in the future; yet the psalm begins with this expression of confident thanksgiving. Often these notices of thanks scattered throughout the laments are understood as confident (almost naive) expectation based on past experiences of deliverance and an understanding of the character of Yahweh. Alternatively (and perhaps more likely), these can be understood as later proclamations of thanksgiving inserted into the original lament after deliverance had actually been experienced. As a result, we get to see the whole process of suffering, plea, deliverance, and thanksgiving telescoped in a single composition. The psalmist's thanks is unfolded in a series of affirming parallelisms, each reflecting a facet of the fullness of thanksgiving.

With all my heart. The depth of the psalmist's confidence and assurance is demonstrated by the fact that praise rises not from the lips—the external organs of speech—but from the totality of the psalmist's heart—the center of moral decision-making and trust. When Deuteronomy wants to speak of complete unification of purpose and full obedience, it admonishes the hearer to respond to God "with all your heart and with all your soul,"[9] knowing that it is out of the interior process of deliberation that the true nature of an individual is revealed. Humans look on the outside (and may therefore be persuaded by deceptive speech), but God looks on the heart and knows us as we really are. The psalmist, in spite of the lament yet to come, is unified of soul and purpose in deep thanks to Yahweh.

I will tell of all your wonders. The psalmist's praise is grounded in the "wonders" (i.e., wonderful works) of Yahweh—a reference to Yahweh's mighty acts in creation and history that exceed human ability to comprehend and understand. Consequently, they are "awesome" and "wonderful" and even "fearful" to the humans who experience them. The psalmist here vows to bear witness to the saving grace of Yahweh—probably a public profession within the temple worship service and perhaps in conjunction with offering the *todah* (sacrifice of thanksgiving).

I will be glad and rejoice. The psalmist piles up words for joyous thanksgiving to Yahweh. The psalmist will "be glad" (*śmḥ*) and will "rejoice" (*ʿlṣ*) as Hannah rejoiced (1 Sam. 2:1) as she turned her precious son over to Yahweh.[10]

I will sing . . . to your name, O Most High. Having declared God's saving grace to the gathered worshipers, the psalmist celebrates deliverance and, caught up in the festive occasion, breaks forth into songs of thanksgiving and

9. Cf. Deut. 4:29; 6:5; 10:12; 26:16; 30:2, 6, 10.

10. Hannah's song is also the model behind Mary's Magnificat in Luke 2, which evidences a similar attitude of deep joy and thanksgiving tied to the deliverance promised by the birth of Jesus.

praise. It is the name of Yahweh of which the psalmist sings, introducing a backward link to Psalm 8, where the majestic name of Yahweh was revealed in all the earth. Here the psalmist declares within worship the wondrous acts of God and sings out the name of Yahweh in the company of the faithful. Even before the appearance of Psalm 8, almost the exact same phrase as we find here concludes Psalm 7: "I . . . will sing . . . to the name of the LORD Most High" (7:17). As we continue in our analysis, we will explore whether there is further reason for grouping and arranging these psalms together.

My enemies turn back. The grammar of this phrase is open to varied interpretation. The verbal portion is a combination of a preposition (Heb. *be-*) and an infinitive. The resulting construction is a "temporal phrase" most often rendered, "When [my enemies] turn back. . . ." Taken this way, the anticipatory nature of the psalmist's thanksgiving is made more apparent: The psalmist *will* praise . . . *will* tell . . . *will* be glad and rejoice . . . *will* sing, *when* the enemies turn back. The psalmist's joy and thanks do not arise from an already accomplished fact of deliverance, but he looks forward gratefully to a future deliverance confidently awaited and expected. This gives more credence and urgency to the psalmist's cry in 9:13: "O LORD, see how my enemies persecute me!" This is suffering in the experience of it, not just recalled.

They stumble and perish. If we take the preceding phrase as a future temporal phrase, then the stumbling and perishing of the enemies describe the hope of the speaker as well. The forms can easily be taken as jussives expressing the will of the speaker ("Let them stumble and perish"). The NIV rendering as present imperfects must understand them as describing a future event understood as already occurring in the present. That is, the psalmist is so certain of Yahweh's deliverance that the enemies are seen as already stumbling and perishing.

Judge of the Nations (9:4–8)

VERSE 4 ACTS as a hinge, with verse 4a offering a concluding reason for the psalmist's opening praise ("my enemies turn back . . . *because* you have upheld my right"), while at the same time verse 4b introduces the theme of Yahweh as righteous judge that dominates the following section ("You have sat on your throne, *judging righteously*").[11] The psalmist uses perfect verb forms to describe Yahweh's activity of judgment as already decided but awaiting enforcement in the future.

---

11. If it were not for the alphabetic structure of the psalm (v. 4 forms the second line of the *bet* verse begun in v. 3), it would be tempting to divide verse 4 and allow the first half to close the opening section and the second half to open the next.

You have upheld my right and my cause. The legal term employed in the case of "my right" is the familiar Hebrew word *mišpaṭ* ("judgment, justice"), which describes the judge's determination of what *should have occurred* in a case before investigating how each party's actions measure up to that expectation. "Cause" is the Hebrew *din* ("verdict, sentence"), which refers to the judge's pronouncement of findings concerning all parties. That the psalmist refers to "my *mišpaṭ* and "my *din*" indicates confident assurance that Yahweh's judgment has already been decided in the psalmist's favor.

Your throne. The dominant emphasis in these verses is on Yahweh's character as a *righteous judge*. Judges are described as "sitting" in judgment, and while it is true that the word "throne" (*kisseʾ*) is most commonly used to describe the throne of the ruler, nowhere in Psalm 9 is the terminology of kingship (Heb. *mlk, melek*) used. It is not until Psalm 10:16 that Yahweh's kingship is explicitly declared. The term translated "reigns" in 9:7 is the common Hebrew word for "sit" (*yšb*), which the NIV has interpreted in light of the kingly role of Yahweh. This interpretive stance also appears in translating the Hebrew verb *din* ("judge, render judgment") by the explicit kingly term "govern." While this is not out of the realm of interpretive possibility, given the context of the combined psalm, it does distract from the primary emphasis on the role of Yahweh as judge that dominates the poet's mind here.

The theme of righteous judge also links Psalms 9–10 back to Psalm 7. There God judges the "wicked," who are envisioned for the most part as members of the psalmist's community who falsely accuse him. Psalms 9–10 expand the theme of divine judgment to include the "nations"—those non-Israelite peoples who attack and oppress God's people. (Note the juxtaposition of "nations" and "wicked" as recipients of divine rebuke and destruction in the affirmingly parallel phrases of 9:5.) Such an expansion allows the exilic community to read psalms that were originally more locally focused in the light of the more international setting of the Exile. What applied to the divine judgment of the more local wicked of preexilic Israel can now be applied to the wicked "nations" oppressing Diaspora Judaism.

In a series of parallel phrases, the psalmist describes the divine judgment on the opposing nations. Yahweh has "rebuked" and "destroyed" the nations (9:5), "endless ruin has overtaken" them, and Yahweh has "uprooted their cities" (9:6)—another indication these are nations and not localized enemies. As a result, in contrast to the eternal "name" of Yahweh (9:2), the "name" of the enemy is "blotted out ... for ever and ever" so that "even the memory of them has perished" (9:5–6). While this confident depiction of Yahweh as the remover of nations might refer to the defeat of the Canaanites in the Conquest, it might equally well describe the eventual fates of the Assyrian and

Babylonian empires from the view of exilic and postexilic Israel. Those wicked nations who destroyed Israel have themselves been destroyed by the mighty acts of God.

He has established his throne for judgment. The segment concludes with a recognition that Yahweh's judgment is no temporary, passing thing. Yahweh "sits [the more natural translation of *yšb* than the NIV's 'reigns'] forever," having set up his throne for the purpose of judgment. Thus, the psalmist can continue to rely on God's righteous judgment being meted out on the offending wicked. In phrases almost identical with those found in the important *Yahweh malak* Psalms 96 and 98, the expansive arena of Yahweh's judgment is driven home: "He will judge the world in righteousness; he will govern [better, 'render judgment on'] the peoples with justice" (cf. 96:13; 98:9).

A Refuge for the Oppressed (9:9–14)

CONFIDENT THAT YAHWEH is a righteous judge who eternally sits ready to pass judgment for the righteous and against the wicked, the psalmist is ready to proclaim him as trustworthy refuge and stronghold (cf. comments on "refuge" in 2:12; 5:11; 7:1) for those who are "oppressed" and "in times of trouble" (9:9). The same Hebrew word (*miśgab*) appears behind the NIV translation for both "refuge" and "stronghold" in this verse. This word describes a high, rocky spot that is inaccessible and thus provides protection from encroaching enemies. The NIV, while certainly more varied, obscures the bonded parallelism between the two halves of this verse. "Yahweh is a *refuge* for the oppressed, a *refuge* in times of trouble." The psalmist sees God as a remote and protected spot to which the psalmist can flee out of the press of trouble.[12]

Those who know your name. Verse 10 returns to the theology of the divine "name" that permeates the whole Psalter (see comments on the significance of the divine name in Ps. 8). Those who "know [the] name" of Yahweh are the covenant people who have received the revelation of God's name (Ex. 3; 6), who therefore share an intimate relationship with him and faithfully serve him alone. The affirming parallel lines of this verse provide further definition to this group with the phrases "trust in you" and "seek you." Knowing Yahweh is not simply a matter of mental cognition; rather, it involves complete reliance on Yahweh (instead of on self, others, power, wealth, etc.) and must be the pursuit of the heart rather than that to which one is driven by external pressure.

---

12. While it is suggestive that reference to Yahweh as "refuge"—using either of the terms (*ḥasah/maḥseh* or *miśgab*) previously encountered—does not occur in the third book of the Psalter (Pss. 73–89), it remains unclear whether this distribution is reflective of some larger editorial purpose.

The word *drš* ("seek") is regularly used in the Old Testament as a technical term to describe purposeful inquiry for divine guidance. Such inquiry signifies the inquirer's reliance on God and willingness to follow the way set out by him. The psalmist affirms that such people—who share an intimate relationship with God, trust in him fully, and seek his guidance—have never been forsaken by him (9:10). The eternal judge (9:7) is eternal refuge for the faithful and therefore the source of eternal trust and confidence in times of trouble.

Sing praises to the LORD. The hearers (and readers) of this psalm are now called to praise God because he is "enthroned" (again, a kingly interpretation of the verb "sit") as judge (cf. 9:7) and is a defender of "the afflicted" (9:12). Again using *drš*, which describes the faithful follower's intent to seek after Yahweh's guidance, the psalmist pictures God as one "who avenges blood"—who intently seeks out the bloody offenses perpetrated on his faithful ones.[13]

From the gates of death. The psalmist's confident description of Yahweh as refuge for the faithful concludes with a return to the reality of the present suffering. The persecution of the psalmist's enemies leaves the psalmist at "the gates of death" (9:13) and in need of divine salvation (9:14). Note the contrasting balance created by the use of the Hebrew *šaᶜare* ("gates") to describe both the fearful threat of death ("from the gates of death") and the joyful place of thanksgiving for deliverance ("in the gates of the Daughter of Zion"). God sits in judgment on the nations from Zion—a reference to Jerusalem and the temple where Yahweh "causes his name to dwell"—to whose gates the delivered psalmist wishes to return to sing praises.

Judgment on the Nations (9:15–20)

PSALM 9 CONCLUDES with a description of the divine retribution visited on the wicked as the just due for their violent oppression of the weak and needy. Once again the interplay in these verses between the "nations" and the "wicked" allows flexibility in understanding the enemy as the wicked individuals opposing the psalmist or as the evil nations oppressing Israel. One gathers the impression that an originally personal psalm has been adapted to speak to the situation of the exilic community by identifying the "wicked" with the "nations."

Ensnared by the work of their hands. Verses 15–16 are concerned with retributive justice applied to the enemy. They fall in the trap they have dug

13. The plural *damim* ("blood") is often used to describe violent blood-letting or murder (cf. 1 Sam. 25:26; 2 Sam. 16:7; 21:1).

or in the net arranged to snare others. This sort of "reap what you sow" consequence is seen as evidence of divine justice. Because God is just, evil will return on the head of the evildoer. It is clear from the concluding verses of Psalm 9 that this settling of accounts still remains to be accomplished. Evil has yet to receive its comeuppance from God. Yet, as in Psalm 5:4, the psalmist trusts in God's enduring character of justice and acknowledges that such a God will make things right.

In the midst of the psalm we find an unusual and rather disconcerting appearance of what is apparently a musical notation (v. 16)—"*Higgaion. Selah.*" We are familiar with *selah* from earlier occurrences (cf. comments in Pss. 3 and 4), where it coincides with structural divisions. Such structural function is far from clear in this instance, although it may be that some musical interlude is intended at this point. The term *higgaion* is more difficult. Elsewhere it describes the growl of a lion, human groans, or muttering while reading—even the cooing of a dove. Perhaps a low, indistinct sound is the common element. Kraus suggests that with *selah* a musical interlude may be intended at the end of a thematic section.[14]

Verses 17–18 set up a contrast between the wicked/nations and the needy, who rely on God. Those wicked nations who have forgotten God will themselves pass into oblivion in the grave (cf. 9:6), while the needy who feel as though God has forgotten them in the present can trust that forgetfulness and perishing are not God's final word for them. Their "hope" for deliverance will not be frustrated.

Let not man triumph. The concluding call for Yahweh to "arise" against the foes admits clearly that the hoped-for deliverance, however certain in the faith of the psalmist and the community, is still to come. God must yet be called to prevent the triumph of the wicked. Once again, it is the "nations" who are firmly in view here at the end. Whatever the original form of the psalm, it is now understood as a communal cry for deliverance from the oppression of the nations. As such it fits well the setting of the Diaspora community.

These last two verses (9:19–20) are framed in a way to emphasize the essential powerlessness of the wicked/nations as well as to strike a responsive chord with the preceding Psalm 8. When the psalmist pleads "Let not *man* triumph," he uses the same word *ʾenôš* as is featured in Psalm 8's amazed reflection, "What is *man*. . . ." In Psalm 8, frail, powerless, mortal *ʾenôš* is unexpectedly endowed with glory and honor by being placed as God's regent over the earth and its animal inhabitants. Here in Psalm 9, however, the same frail *ʾenôš* has perverted his divinely given role by dominating and oppressing weak and needy fellow humans.

14. Kraus, *Psalms 1–59*, 27, 196.

The psalmist's plea becomes more understandable in this light. Having perverted and exceeded their role—having assumed the prerogatives of God himself—the wicked/nations need a shock treatment ("Strike them with terror, O LORD"). They must be judged in the very presence of Yahweh himself—an encounter that will force them to acknowledge their true identity: *ʾenoš hemmah* ["They are but men"] (9:20), whose only hope of glory and power is that given by a gracious God to his trusting people (see also comments at the end of Ps. 10).

The end of Psalm 9 is marked once again by the enigmatic *selah*—clearly at the end of a thematic unit in this case. As it stands by itself, this psalm is a plea for deliverance marked by a steady confidence in the righteousness of God, which forms the basis of enduring trust in his judgment. The enemy in the psalm in its earliest form may have been a more localized "wicked" man who was oppressing the individual psalmist (note the first-person singular verbs and pronominal suffixes in 9:1–4, 13–14). But as the psalm progresses, the focus increasingly shifts to include the suffering community marked out by more generalized phrases such as "those who know your name," " those who seek you," "the needy," or "the afflicted."

The individual voice of the psalmist becomes the model of endurance and praise, which the community is called to emulate. The psalmist praises Yahweh and tells of his wonders, rejoicing in and praising his name (9:1–2), and then he calls the listening community to join in praise and proclamation among the nations (9:11). Just as the psalmist trusts that God's mercy will lift him up even from the "gates of death" itself, so the faithful community is assured that "the needy will not always be forgotten, nor the hope of the afflicted ever perish" (9:18). In this way the psalm is opened to continued interpretation and application in new circumstances.

The Arrogant Wicked (10:1–11)

LINKING BACK TO "times of trouble" mentioned in 9:9, Psalm 10 opens with agonized questions directed to God, revealing a sense of isolation and divine absence that contrasts with the confident affirmation of Yahweh as "refuge" in Psalm 9. Deliverance is not yet at hand in Psalm 10, and for the psalmist God seems hidden and removed (10:1). The questions and the attendant sense of abandonment set the stage for the long acrimonious description of the arrogant wicked that dominates 10:2–11.

In his arrogance. The wicked oppressors of Psalm 10 are primarily the more localized enemies of the community, identified with the "nations" only by a single subtle statement near the end of the psalm (10:16). The attitude of the domineering enemy is far removed from that of the awed and humbled *ʾenoš* of Psalm 8—and that seems to be the psalmist's point. Just as Psalm

9 seeks divine judgment forcing the power-hungry *ʾenôš* to acknowledge their powerlessness (9:20), so Psalm 10 calls for divine redress so that *ʾenôš* "who is of the earth, may terrify no more" (10:18).

Nothing will shake me. The description of the wicked is divided into two sections of five verses, each concluded by a quotation of "the wicked man" who arrogantly assumes his independence from divine scrutiny (10:6, 11). The first section (10:2–6) describes the arrogant pride of the one who considers himself his own law, devising schemes to hunt down the weak (10:2), satisfying the lusts of his heart (10:3), and finding no use for God (10:3b–4); yet he remains so prosperous that in his pride "he sneers at all his enemies" (10:5). The only conclusion such a person can make is that God is effectively inoperative (10:4), his laws can be breached with impunity (10:5), and indeed, "Nothing will shake me; I'll always be happy and never have trouble" (10:6).

God has forgotten. From this supposed unshakable foundation, the wicked one proceeds to even more violent conduct. Violent speech flows from his mouth (cursing, deceptions, threats, trouble, and evil [10:7]) and overflows into violent action (ambushing and murdering the innocent and helpless [10:8–9]). His victims are completely crushed beneath his power (10:10). Once again the wicked, experiencing no resistance from God, can only conclude, "God has forgotten; he covers his face and never sees" (10:11).

Plea for Deliverance (10:12–15)

THE PSALMIST'S RESPONSE to this finely drawn portrait of arrogant human self-determination is to suggest that it is divine absence or delay that has allowed opportunity for the wicked to work. The portrait was prefaced (10:1) with the psalmist's pointed questions regarding the reasons for God's delayed response to the pleas of the needy and the injustice of the wicked. Now he follows his critique with a call for divine action coupled with a second set of questions regarding the wicked's almost casual assumption of divine ignorance or unconcern (10:12–13).

The segment begins with the imperative phrase "Arise, LORD!" which along with other elements already mentioned links Psalm 10 back again to Psalm 9, where the same call concludes the psalm (9:19).[15] Again, the plea is that Yahweh end his period of apparent inactivity and act in judgment consistent with his righteous character, on which the psalmist depends. The

15. The same phrase occurs in 7:5; this serves as an additional tether binding Pss. 7–10 together into a thematic grouping. It is suggestive that nowhere else in the Psalter (or in the whole Old Testament, for that matter) do any occurrences of Heb. *qumah* ("arise") appear in consecutive psalms—let alone a grouping of psalms as here.

uplifted hand is often a symbol of engagement in battle and here parallels the act of rising as an indication of moving from inactivity to redemptive action in behalf of the psalmist.

Do not forget the helpless. The wicked enemy claims that God has forgotten and does not see the violence done to the helpless (10:11). The psalmist calls God to counter that claim as ill-founded and indicative of a deep misunderstanding of God. Almost in amazement the psalmist wonders aloud, "Why does the wicked man revile God? Why does he say to himself, 'He won't call me to account'?" (10:13). The first phrase ("revile God") refers back to 10:3, where the wicked in arrogance inverts the standards of morality by blessing the greedy and reviling Yahweh. The word translated "revile" (*nʾṣ*) means to treat irreverently or with disrespect.

The second phrase, "call ... to account" (*drš*), appears no less than five times in the combined psalm, with several different nuances. Only in the massive Psalm 119 (also an alphabetic acrostic) do as many occurrences of this term appear within a single composition (cf. 119:2, 10, 45, 94, 155). The basic meaning of *drš* seems to be "seek out; inquire (for guidance)." In 9:10 and 10:4, the term describes those who either willingly seek or arrogantly refuse to seek Yahweh in order to know his path. In the remaining three occurrences (9:12; 10:13, 15), the NIV resorts to other nuances to render *drš*. For 9:12, "one who *seeks out* blood guilt" becomes "he who avenges blood"—an appropriate variation that nevertheless obscures the ironic wordplays the psalmist is introducing in the combined psalm: God *seeks out* (and avenges) acts of blood guilt perpetrated on *those who seek* him by those who *refuse to seek* him and who think God *will not seek out* (or *avenge*) their wrongdoing.

In 10:13, 15, the NIV translates *drš* as "call to account" rather than the more straightforward "seek out/inquire." Again, while this is an appropriate, idiomatic variation, it fails to emphasize the wordplay the psalmist is making with this root.

Yahweh as Eternal King (10:16–18)

THE COMBINED PSALM concludes by acknowledging Yahweh as the eternal king, who rightly fulfills the role of the Near Eastern monarch as protector of the afflicted and defender of "the fatherless and the oppressed" (10:16–18). An unusual number of terms for these defenseless classes of persons who require the protection of the monarch are used in this psalm. Seven words are used, and in each case the first use of the term in the whole Psalter occurs in Psalms 9–10. These terms, translation, and appearance are: (1) *ʾebyon* ("poor, needy"; 9:18); (2) *dak* ("oppressed"; 9:9; 10:18); (3) *ḥelekah* ("victim, unfortunate person"; 10:8, 14); (4) *yatom* ("fatherless, orphan"; 10:14, 18); (5) *naqi* ("innocent"; 10:8); (6) *ᶜani* ("weak, wretched"; 10:2, 9); (7) *ᶜanawim* ("helpless, [one who knows he is] humble, gentle"; 9:13, 19; 10:12, 17).

Nowhere else in the Psalter does such a collection of these terms exist. Thus, one major concern of the psalmist appears to be revealed: the oppression of the defenseless people by the wicked *ʾenoš*, who deny the effective existence of God and forsake their divinely given role of extending God's care to the world (see comments on Ps. 8) in order to exploit and oppress those weaker than themselves. Since Yahweh is the eternal righteous king, he will take the side of the weak, defenseless, and oppressed in society against the wicked so that "*ʾenoš*, who is of the earth [i.e., is mortal and of limited power and authority], may terrify no more" (10:18).

OFTEN WE TEND to read the psalms as individual and isolated compositions. Psalms 9 and 10 suggest that may not always be the only or even the best approach. Clearly these psalms were originally part of a unified alphabetic acrostic and push us to acknowledge that what now appear to be separate though adjacent psalms may have greater connection and unity than we formerly supposed. This recognition begins to open us up to understanding the messages of individual psalms within a broader context—that of the whole Psalter. Form criticism seeks to realize this broader connection by comparing psalms of similar type from all over the Psalter; this attempt has resulted in many significant results.[16]

In the preceding commentary on the combined Psalms 9–10, I have repeatedly suggested that the understanding of a psalm owes much to its broader, local context made up of the surrounding psalms. Frequently the arrangement of psalms seems to be purposeful and influences the way in which themes, ideas, and language in any specific psalm are to be understood in the light of others. In what follows I will consider (1) the relationship that exists among Psalms 7–10, and (2) the effect of shifting from individual to societal and from monarchical to postmonarchical focus in these same psalms.

16. In the section on "The Theology of the Psalms" in vol. 2 of this commentary, I explore another aspect of this broader context by asking what the psalms—taken as a whole—have to say about God, humans, the world, and the relationship of all three. This biblical theological approach assumes that the teaching of Scripture must be drawn from the whole range of scriptural texts and documents and from an understanding built up that honors each and allows tensions perceived to stand as markers of the boundaries of faith.

The relationship of Psalms 7–10. We begin by considering the literary relationship that has developed for the grouping of Psalms 7–10. In discussing Psalms 9–10 we have seen bits of evidence linking those two psalms together as well as linking the combined psalm back to Psalms 7 and 8. What is the effect of reading these psalms within the broader context of this grouping rather than taking each psalm as a totally isolated experience? The cumulative effect, I suggest, is more than reading the four psalms in isolation.

With the exception of Psalm 8, all of these psalms are pleas for deliverance from trouble. Singly and together these compositions call on Yahweh to serve as refuge and defender of the faithful and to act as righteous judge in relation to the wicked. We can observe a shifting identification of the enemies from the more localized wicked who oppress the individual faithful person in Psalm 7 toward the more generalized criticism of the "nations"—the non-Israelite *goyim*—who are called to account for their treatment of the community at large (Pss. 9–10). Let's take a quick glance at this thematic development as we read these psalms alongside one another together with the admonition to "meditate day and night" (1:2).

(1) Psalm 7 describes divine judgment on the more localized wicked and promises to praise the name of Yahweh Most High because of his righteous judgment (7:11, 17). A slight openness is maintained toward more universal themes by 7:7–9, which describes Yahweh's judgment as directed toward the "assembled peoples" (*ʾummim* in v. 7; *ʿammim* in v. 8)—a clear reference to Yahweh's authority over both Israelite and non-Israelite nations. But by and large Psalm 7 is narrated in individual terms ("I" and "my"), and the enemy described is personal.

(2) Psalm 8 articulates the praise of the "name" of Yahweh that is promised at the end of the previous psalm (7:17). The psalmist envisions the name of creator Yahweh as extending above the heavens and majestically filling the earth. He stands in awe of the creative power of Yahweh and is amazed and humbled by the honor done to weak, mortal humans (*ʾenoš*), whom Yahweh "made to rule over the earth" (8:4–8). The clear implication of the tension maintained in this psalm—between human insignificance and divine power; human humility and divinely given glory, honor, and authority—is that any power exercised by humans in the world is *distinctly* limited by and derived from God. This view of humans as *ʾenoš* also offers an effective rebuke of the arrogance of the enemy in Psalm 7.

(3) In Psalm 9, the "wicked," who are also described as "only humans" (*ʾenoš*, 9:19–20), are gradually identified with the non-Israelite nations (*goyim*, 9:5–6, 11, 15, 19–20). These nations in control actively oppress the poor and the weak, eschewing any sense of humility and abusing their divinely given

responsibility, but according to Psalm 8 they exercise limited, derived authority. As a result the psalmist pleads for Yahweh to prevent their triumph and to teach them their appropriate station—that "they are but *ʾenoš*" (9:19–20).

(4) Finally in Psalm 10, Yahweh is celebrated openly as "King for ever and ever" (10:16)—a status implied earlier in Psalm 9 by the attention given to Yahweh's eternal throne and enthronement (9:7, 11). Yahweh's kingship indicates that human rulership can never be autocratic, self-limiting kingship but is always derived and divinely conferred responsibility to care for Yahweh's creation and to establish justice and equity. In the end (10:16–18) Yahweh is described as the eternal king, forever fulfilling the responsibilities of the ancient oriental monarch to protect the defenseless in society. This means that Yahweh is the only one who can be trusted to judge and to rule righteously. The final verse drives this home by affirming that Yahweh's rulership is necessary to displace wicked human powers "in order that *ʾenoš*, who is of the earth, may terrify no more" (10:18).

As a result of reading these four psalms as a thematic unit, a powerful message of divine power and human responsibility is displayed. This is not to say, however, that we only read these psalms rightly when we read them together. The ancient editors of the Psalter, who arranged the psalms in their present order, saw fit to preserve the psalms as individual compositions set off as such by spacing in the manuscripts and by providing many with psalm headings to mark them out as separate compositions. We have always revered and employed the individual psalms in this fashion—and we will (and certainly should) continue to do so. Each psalm has its own integrity, shape, and voice that ought to be heard and appreciated.

What I am suggesting here is not an exclusive way of reading the psalms but another way to appreciate the ensemble that the ancient editors created and arranged in the Psalter. In reading the whole Psalter as an ensemble, one hears new voices and new tensions between voices that offer new and challenging insights that are overlooked in isolation. It is something like hearing the overture to an opera on a CD collection of overtures and then hearing it as it was originally intended—as part of the whole work. The music can be appreciated either way, but with different effects and understandings. The same is true of the music of the psalms.

From individual to community and society. As we read Psalms 9–10 carefully, it seems clear that an originally individual psalm, in which the psalmist seeks deliverance from the oppression of personal attacks by localized enemies, has been adapted for later reuse by the community who employ the earlier words to reflect on their own struggle with national, non-Israelite enemies—the "nations" (*goyim*). We should not be surprised to learn that this kind of "rereading" or adaptation of earlier material to speak anew to a later circumstance is a common phenomenon in the psalms, and indeed in the whole of Scripture. Perhaps the most obvious cases in Scripture are the "rereading" given to the earlier monarchical history recorded in Samuel–Kings by the Chronicler and the reuse of Mark's Gospel by Luke and Matthew in the writing of their own accounts.

Be that as it may, clearly many of the psalms—particularly psalms of the individual—have been adapted to continue speaking long after their original setting and in very different circumstances. Sometimes this adaptation merely opens up an essentially individual composition to appropriation by a larger community, who together share similar experiences. This may happen in order to integrate the individual's experience into the practice of corporate worship,[17] but it may also be the result of adapting an earlier psalm to a postexilic context.[18] It is easy to see how the exilic community, living in a foreign land and under the pressure to assimilate to a foreign culture, would find ways to revitalize the earlier psalms from their national life. By reusing them, they maintained a continuity of identity with their past heritage and provided a hedge against assimilation's threat of total absorption. At the same time, the words of these psalms had to be understood as relating to the later circumstances of the community.

In the case of our combined psalm, the interpretive shift takes words originally directed to wicked oppressors within the nation of Israel as appropriate comments to apply to the non-Israelite nations oppressing the Jewish exiles. We see this particularly in Psalm 9, where passages condemning "the wicked" stand rather awkwardly connected with those about "the nations." Note 9:17, where the reference to "the nations" follows almost as an explanatory gloss: "The wicked return to the grave, all the nations that forget God."

In 9:15–16, the circumstance is reversed with "the nations" mentioned first, but in a context normally reserved for the more personal enemies of the individual:

> The nations have fallen into the pit they have dug;
> their feet are caught in the net they have hidden.
> The LORD is known by his justice;
> the *wicked is* ensnared by the work of *his* hands.

The singular noun, verb, and possessive pronoun italicized in the second half of this passage reflect the singular grammar of the original Hebrew. That the NIV chose to render these terms in the plural in order to agree more

17. In this regard see Pss. 31:23–24; 32:1, 11; 66:16; 77:13–20; 130:7–8; 131:3.

18. Cf. Pss. 14:7; 25:22; 53:6; 57:9; 69:34–36; 102:12–22, 28; 129:5–8; 144:14–15.

closely with the preceding comments on the nations illustrates just how rough the connection really is.

The same is true of 9:3–5a, where, following the description of the enemies and of Yahweh sitting in righteous judgment over them, one is almost surprised by the introduction of "the nations" into the discussion:

> My enemies turn back;
>   they stumble and perish before you.
> For you have upheld my right and my cause;
>   you have sat on your throne, judging righteously.
> You have rebuked the nations and destroyed the wicked.

THIS PSALM OFFERS us a couple of opportunities for practical reflection and application regarding our contemporary circumstances and environment. (1) How does the theological shaping of Psalms 7–10 impact our contemporary setting? (2) How might the interpretive shift that takes place in Psalms 9–10 from the concerns of the individual to that of the community, and from enemies within the community to national enemies without, find parallel and equivalence in our own day and time?

The shape of Psalms 7–10. Reading the combined Psalms 9–10 within the context of the larger consecutive grouping of Psalms 7–10 provides new insights regarding psalm interpretation as a whole and regarding understanding of the specific message of this psalm.

An interpretive approach. A unified reading mirrors a way of approaching other groups of psalms—and indeed the Psalter as a whole. The reading suggests a purposeful arrangement of these psalms in order to create an effect and to communicate a unified message.[19] The interpretive approach suggested includes the following elements: (1) Accept the integrity of each psalm and its ability to speak in its own right; (2) acknowledge that relationships exist (or at least may exist) among consecutive psalms as long as they are based not on fanciful connection but on clear evidence of linguistic and thematic connection; (3) ponder and meditate on these connections (as exhorted in Ps. 1), spending time with them and allowing impressions to build over time; (4) seek to articulate the connections observed in a persuasive way, allowing them to be checked by other interpreters' perceptions of

19. See the discussion of "The Shape of the Psalter" in volume 2 of this commentary and the various essays describing the shape of the individual books of the Psalter scattered throughout this two-volume work.

the same psalms. As we progress through this commentary, more psalms groupings will be considered and this interpretive process expanded.

Specific elements of the unified message. The combined Psalms 9–10 speaks a message that is consistent with the messages expressed by the individual psalms. It is a threefold message that speaks primarily to those *within* the community of faith, but also serves as a critique of those who stand *outside* that community and are often in opposition to it. The message is one of humility, limitation, and responsibility.

(1) Humility. The problem of the enemy of the psalmist and the community of the faithful in this psalm (and in the larger grouping of psalms) is a loss of proper perspective. The arrogant pride that marks the wicked in Psalm 10 in particular (10:2–11) has none of the sense of wonder and awe that marks the psalmist's encounter with the creator in Psalm 8. The *ʾenoš* of Psalm 10 has no use for God in his thoughts and considers God as a nonfactor in human existence (10:4, 11). Set immediately following the wondrous pronouncements of Psalm 8, this prideful dismissal of God is stated in its most shocking and extreme fashion. The result is as much a warning for the faithful not to allow the seeming absence of God (10:1) to erode confidence in his active concern and presence as it is a rebuke of the faithless for their ignorance and pride.

It is too easy to condemn those who rather brashly and vocally dismiss God as impotent or question his benevolent concern or existence. These are, of course, extreme cases that stand in stark contrast with the boundaries of faith. What is more difficult, however, is to escape what some call "functional atheism"—giving clear, positive affirmation to the existence of God and my need to rely on him while acting as if I have to care for my own needs on a day-to-day basis.

Such Christians often give an impression of having it all together, of being self-sufficient. They do not seem to need others and often talk of "victories" and almost never about "struggles, failures, or needs." I am speaking from firsthand experience here. For most of my life I have been addicted to "looking good and competent—even masterful." Any struggles I felt (and there were many) I kept well hidden inside myself. I built a tall and thick wall between those who knew me and that part of me I felt was unacceptable or suggested weakness. I thought I could rely on no one but myself to meet my needs and could only maintain relations with important others by manipulating what I let them know about myself. It took a major, world-shattering personal crisis to convince me that I *could not* do it on my own and that all my attempts at control were actually destructive hideouts preventing me from getting what I most needed and wanted.

It was only when my carefully constructed façade collapsed, revealing all the hurt and pain and confusion I had kept so well hidden for so many years, that I was able to experience the release that comes through admitting powerlessness and the inability to control even the smallest significant details of living. For years I had spent so much energy maintaining the wall that hid my secret self that I had little left for family, for work, or for relationships with others. I had become an extremely self-focused person, proud of my visible accomplishments and the influence I felt I had over others. I was proud, I was arrogant—and I was angry.

Let me explain. For years I seemed to have it all together: position, influence, accomplishment. But in reality the things that offered satisfaction often seemed to elude me. I had no self-love because I knew the struggling, manipulative individual who lurked behind my wall; I lived in constant fear of being unmasked and losing all that exterior façade on which I so depended. I had few truly close friends because I was unable to let any of them inside the wall to know me fully and deeply. I had to remain on guard and keep my distance. And so I was angry because, despite looking good on the outside, I could not have what I truly wanted: to be known as I truly am and to be loved and accepted as I truly am—warts and all.

This has been a very personal way of talking about the need for humility. As long as we humans think that we can or must exercise control over our lives, we remain forever unable to stand in awe before the majestic glory of God that fills the earth and transcends the heavens (Ps. 8). We are only able to glory in our own power and manipulative control, exercised for our own benefit. Or we live scared, angry lives, seeking to look competent while knowing inside just how far out of control life really is.

Humility is a scary thing because it admits to someone else that I am not in control in some part of my life. I am not talking of that sort of artificial humility we express when someone compliments us or honors us and we rather sheepishly respond with statements like: "It was nothing. I didn't do so much. Someone else could have done a better job." I mean the kind of soul-shattering humility that the lament psalms express when nothing stands between you and the bottomless abyss except God himself, and we cry out with Isaiah, "I am ruined!" (Isa. 6:5).

(2) Limitation. This kind of humility leads to (or, perhaps, arises out of) an awareness of the limitations that exist on human power. The psalmist concludes Psalm 9 with the plea for Yahweh to cause the wicked to "know they are but *ʾenoš*" (9:20). Psalm 10 concludes with the hope that Yahweh will establish his rule over the earth so that "*ʾenoš*, who is of the earth, may terrify no more" (10:18). In other words, the psalmist's experience of oppression at the hands of the wicked is a result of *ʾenoš* gone wrong—an abuse of the power and authority given to humans by God in Psalm 8. This divinely given power has been misdirected because of an arrogant and

prideful misunderstanding of how and why humans are to exercise that power. Only a return to a proper understanding of what it is to be *ʾenoš* can set things right.

I see two ways in which contemporary society tends to reflect the same misunderstanding of humanity that plagued the psalmist's opponents. The first is the approach of the committed atheist who denies the existence of God altogether, or of the less committed but more apathetic members of society at large who assume that if God does exist, he has no effective interest in or influence over the course of contemporary life. For both groups, human beings are on their own, left to their own devices to set their goals, devise morals, fulfill desires and dreams, and meet needs. Human will, intelligence, and ingenuity become the ultimate power and will in the world. Since there is no Higher Power and no ultimate truth or meaning, humans are free, like the wicked of Psalms 9–10, to exercise power and oppression for their own benefit. No one or nothing will ever call them into judgment.

Our psalm decisively undermines such a viewpoint by calling the reader back to the awe-inspiring encounter with God in Psalm 8. It is God who created the universe; human power is insignificant in light of the "finger play" of God that spun off the sun, moon, and stars without effort. It is God who set humankind in a position of authority and responsibility over the creation—it is no accident but part of his will and purpose. As a result, what humans do in and with the world, how they exercise the power delegated to them by God, is not a matter of indifference but of great significance. Ultimately, humans are limited regents responsible to God for their care of the creation and of all creatures within it.

(3) Responsibility. A second way contemporary society reflects a misunderstanding of human authority over the creation is seen in the widely held assumption that the creation is there to be exploited for human desire and benefit. While Psalm 8 remains silent on what limitations might be placed on human authority, Psalms 9–10 are not hesitant in filling in the blanks. Here it becomes clear that humans are *not* empowered to seek their own benefit, nor are they given power to rule autocratically as they see fit. Rather, humans have derived authority from God to see that the earth and its inhabitants are cared for and become fruitful. Human responsibility turns outward away from self-benefit to seek the wholeness of all creation.

Psalms 9–10 are especially concerned that those in positions of authority use their power and influence to seek justice and equity, defending in particular those individuals in society who have no access to power and representation: the widows, orphans, needy, weak, and so on. Rather than use power to ensure self-benefit and comfort, they are to support the cause of the poor and needy, eschewing the example of the arrogant wicked in Psalm 10 and following instead the model of Yahweh, who hears the desire of the afflicted and defends the fatherless and the oppressed (10:17–18).

Working as I have over the last several years in an urban environment, I have been made increasingly aware of the need for the church to become involved in justice and equity issues. The situation is certainly complex at best and is growing more so each year with the constant influx of ethnic-minority peoples into our cities. There are, of course, the more obvious ways of working for justice and equity, to which many churches give some recognition: legislative action to work for civil rights and public education and services, concern with rising crime, access to health facilities and care, the care and feeding of the homeless. These are all issues our society is seeking to address, and many churches are working to make an impact here.

But other issues are less obvious. How do the suburban churches filled with majority-culture Christians build bridges to the urban and inner-city congregations composed mostly of minority-culture persons, who struggle to maintain a Christian witness under difficult circumstances? For example, many urban ethnic-minority pastors lack adequate preparation for their ministerial roles. They are prevented by lack of financial resources, lack of educational preparation (many lack college degrees necessary to enroll in traditional seminary programs), time constraints (many are bivocational pastors, working at secular jobs to support their ministry), and lack of culturally appropriate programs of education. Most of these barriers can be removed by the application of money, influence, time, and advocacy—all of which most suburban congregations have in abundant supply.

The work of racial reconciliation is another silent issue in most suburban churches. It is true that many congregations do include persons of different ethnic and racial background in their membership. But usually the ethnic-minority persons are few and are accommodated to the majority culture that predominates. How can suburban churches develop significant, ongoing relationships with primarily ethnic-minority churches in the inner city? What creative activities can bring people together in ways that allow the building of relationships, two-way sharing of resources, and a real witness to the power of Christ to obliterate barriers of race, class, wealth?

To truly respond to the call of Psalms 9–10, those of us who are part of the dominant majority-culture churches must be actively seeking ways to stand with our minority brothers and sisters in Christ as well as the urban communities they and we seek to serve. Paul speaks to the kind of mindset and "heartset" that is needed in Philippians 3, when he describes how he came to consider all his personal status and attainment of privilege and influence to be worthless. Instead, he seeks to "know Christ and the power of his resurrection and the *fellowship of sharing in his sufferings*, becoming like him in his death" (Phil. 3:10, italics added). Whatever this means in full, it certainly means in part that positions of power, status, and privilege are to be foregone in order to participate in the sufferings of Christ, who loved the poor and needy and died to set all humans free from the power of self-focused sin and death. Taking our stance alongside the suffering, oppressed, and marginalized in our society is certainly one way to stand with Jesus over against the oppressive powers of our day. It is a way of showing solidarity with our urban brothers and sisters, who need our strength and care. And they will have much to teach *us* about the "fellowship of sharing in [Christ's] sufferings" along the way.

Individual to society. We have seen how Psalms 9–10 illustrate the way many psalms have adapted reflections of individual experience into the medium for corporate, communal expression. This occurs in this particular psalm, not as a matter of individual testimony *within* the community of the faithful (as we see elsewhere), but rather as an adoption of the individual's experience as the experience of the whole community. This is an important means of drawing the whole community into a common experience, providing real living experiences rather than abstract ones, and challenging those of the community who may not have encountered the experience of this specific individual. Let's consider two ways this kind of shift from individual to community speaks to our contemporary circumstance.

(1) Throughout the history of the church, hymn-writing has provided a way of transferring the experience of an individual to the community. Great hymns explore a whole variety of human experience—praise, lament, thanksgiving, confession, and so on. The last twenty years or so have seen a marked shift in many churches to the use of contemporary praise choruses rather than the classic hymns of the faith. One consequence of this shift has been that, because most choruses are concerned with a more limited spectrum of human experience (praise), the community gathered to worship is led to a rather one-sided experience of Christian faith. Early criticism of the praise-chorus movement, to the effect that they were superficial and did not reflect a sufficiently biblical foundation, was blunted by the introduction of more and more choruses relying primarily on scriptural texts (especially the psalms!).

But the problem is that even these biblically based choruses are selective—choosing bits of psalms rather than the whole. They are still praise-oriented, often ignoring those portions of psalms that reflect anger, confession, sin, and need. By quoting snippets of Scripture as they do, choruses can leave the impression that they provide a more comprehensive understanding of the Christian faith than their selective approach makes possible, leaving the singer and the community with the false impression that worship is only (or primarily) praise and thanksgiving.

Many of the older hymns drew on the psalms and other biblical passages and themes to provide the foundation of their reflections. Rather than quote Scripture directly, however, they sought to expound the scriptural themes and insights in ways that reflected their contemporary context. What we need is a new generation of hymn writers who will use their skills to translate the breadth of individual experience into communal moments of confession, lament, thanksgiving, confidence, and question as well as praise.[20]

(2) This shift to a societal focus raises another issue in interpreting the psalms in our own context. How do we relate our own national or societal circumstances to the words of the psalms? Often we forget that Israel was a "theocracy"—a nation bound by a covenant relationship to the rulership of God. Israel's covenant with Yahweh was established at Mount Sinai in the wake of their deliverance from Egypt, and through the law were established the contours of faith—love, loyalty, obedience—that were to govern the ongoing relationship. We err when we uncritically identify our own nation with the covenant "people of God" that Israel represented. The modern, secular nations—no matter how much they may claim to be "under God" and seek to encourage "Christian" values in society—are not bound by a covenant relationship to the one God of Israel.

The pains taken in the Western world to establish clear separation between church and state and the interpretation of what was originally a tolerance of varieties of *Christian* religious expression to mean toleration of religious pluralism in its extreme sense should make this abundantly clear. While I am not counseling intolerance toward other religious faiths in secular government affairs, I point this out to demonstrate that our government is not an apt parallel to the theocracy in Israel.

The shift of the psalmist's critique of the enemy from those within the covenant family to the "nations" who stand without gives us our clue. What I am suggesting is that most often our nation or society must be identified with those *goyim* who stood outside the covenant relationship with Israel's God. Our situation is much more like Daniel or Joseph seeking to influence Nebuchadnezzar or Pharaoh than it is like Nathan or Isaiah or Jeremiah calling David or one of the later kings of Israel and Judah to task for lack of loyal obedience to Yahweh.

---

20. I have been personally blessed by the work of Bryan Jeffery Leach, who has written numerous new hymns and additional verses to traditional hymns that reflect powerfully and artistically on the breadth of the human condition before God.

We certainly may be called to speak to other nations regarding human rights, oppression, exploitation, and lack of environmental concern. But we must always remember that our nation is one of these nations. The people of God can no longer be identified with any particular national entity or restricted to any national boundary. The process of dispersion that began with the exilic Diaspora of the Jews throughout the nations of the world was completed by the Christian promulgation of the gospel to the Gentiles—the Greek equivalent for and consistent translation of the Hebrew *goyim*—so that the distinction between the church and the world was no longer attached to racial, national, or even cultural heritage.

Like the disobedient humans who at the Tower of Babel had their languages confused and were dispersed through the world, so disobedient Israel was dispersed among the nations in the Exile, becoming a fragmentary people who gradually lost their memory of the ancestral Hebrew language except in ritual circumstances. The dispersion of the church to disciple "all nations" in obedience to the Great Commission (Matt. 28:18–20) parallels the creation command to "be fruitful and increase in number; fill the earth" (Gen. 1:28; 9:1), which was only forcibly accomplished in the Tower of Babel narrative (and only with destructive results because of the humans' resistance). The Christian Diaspora, so to speak, is an obedient response to God's will and contains in the gospel and the gift of the Holy Spirit the seeds of eventual reunification and restoration of all humanity as God intends and as Pentecost prefigured (cf. Acts 2).

Paul acknowledges and affirms this divine intention to reunite all humanity through the gospel when he proclaims that "there is neither Jew nor Greek, slave nor free, male nor female, for you are all one in Christ Jesus" (Gal. 3:28). He further points out how in Christ and his church "the dividing wall of hostility" between Jews and Gentiles has been destroyed (Eph. 2:11–22). After visiting the home of the Roman centurion Cornelius (Acts 10), Peter realizes God's inclusive intent to save when he declares: "I now realize how true it is that God does not show favoritism but accepts men from every nation who fear him and do what is right" (Acts 10:34–35).[21]

The consequence of this restructuring of God's people in Christianity away from a particular national identity to a multinational community of the redeemed is to demand that we, like the exilic community before us, read the

21. Cf. Rev. 7:9, where the "great multitude that no one could count, from every nation, tribe, people and language" stood before the Lamb, wearing white robes and declaring in the words of Ps. 3:8, "Salvation belongs to our God." Rev. 14:6 also describes an angel carrying the "eternal gospel to proclaim to those who live on the earth—to every nation, tribe, language and people."

messages of the psalms regarding the "nations" and the other enemies of Israel as words about those who oppose or oppress the community of faith or those faithful individuals who stand within it. In this regard we must include our own secular nation and society, with its obsession with self-determination and power, as standing outside the community of faith and in enmity with the kingdom of God.

Psalm 11

FOR THE DIRECTOR of music. Of David.

1 In the LORD I take refuge.
How then can you say to me:
"Flee like a bird to your mountain.
2 For look, the wicked bend their bows;
they set their arrows against the strings
to shoot from the shadows
at the upright in heart.
3 When the foundations are being destroyed,
what can the righteous do?"

4 The LORD is in his holy temple;
the LORD is on his heavenly throne.
He observes the sons of men;
his eyes examine them.
5 The LORD examines the righteous,
but the wicked and those who love violence
his soul hates.
6 On the wicked he will rain
fiery coals and burning sulfur;
a scorching wind will be their lot.

7 For the LORD is righteous,
he loves justice;
upright men will see his face.

THE PSALM IS an expression of confident trust in Yahweh in opposition to the pessimistic advice of those who think the present evil circumstances presage the imminent crumbling of the "foundations" of world order, so that the psalmist should flee to the hills in order to escape. The psalmist's reply in this psalm takes the following form: (1) In verses 1–3, he establishes a contrast between confidence that "refuge" is available in Yahweh (11:1a-b) and the fearful counsel to flee offered by his contemporaries (11:1c–3); (2) verses 4–6 constitute a description of Yahweh as righteous judge, examining both the righteous and the wicked and measuring out appropriate judgment on each; (3) the psalm concludes (11:7) with the affirmation of Yahweh's essential righteousness and love of justice, which provide the continuing basis of hope and a strong motivation for the "upright" to endure.

The Heading (11:0)

THE HEADING CONTAINS no new terms but is referred to "the director of music" and attributed to David.[1] The latter reference reestablishes the consistent Davidic character of the first book following the minor interruption occasioned by the lack of a heading in Psalm 10.

Refuge or Flight (11:1)

HOW THEN CAN you say to me? The psalmist establishes the confident tone of the psalm by creating a studied contrast between the consuming fear generated by those who counsel flight and the psalmist, who takes refuge in Yahweh. We have encountered the theme of refuge in Yahweh before in Psalms 2 and 7; it will appear regularly throughout the rest of the psalms (see comments on 2:12). Here the psalmist's confident reliance on the protective care of Yahweh in the face of trouble provides a calming center in the midst of the chaotic description that follows. As we will see later, his hope for refuge in Yahweh is related to the concluding observation that the "upright . . . will see his face" (11:7).

Flee like a bird. The fearful counsel the psalmist seeks to counter comes from those who expect the worst. It is unclear whether those who speak are themselves afraid or are sarcastically attempting to undermine the psalmist's confidence. The use of the phrase "to my *nepeš*" (NIV "to me") reflects an attempt to address and influence (here negatively) the deepest needs, desires, and hopes of an individual (see comments on 3:2). This supports the idea that the speakers are opponents rather than cosufferers of the psalmist; their purpose is not genuine concern for the psalmist's well-being but sarcastically chipping away at the foundation of his confidence and hope.

The sentence structure in the Hebrew text is difficult, terse, and spare, employing neither the preposition or the comparative structure reflected in the NIV translation. Woodenly rendered the text says, "Flee [to] your mountain, bird!" with the opening imperative appearing in the consonantal text as a masculine plural (but read in the marginal notes and by the vowels inserted as a feminine singular); the pronominal suffix on mountain is masculine plural, and the noun "bird" is feminine singular. A number of textual emendations

1. Consult the comments on the headings of Pss. 3 and 4.

have been attempted to smooth out the roughness. Most separate the masculine plural pronominal suffix (Heb. *-kem*, "your") from the phrase "your mountain" and understand these letters to be the freestanding preposition *kemo* ("like, as"). The resulting translation, "Flee [to the] mountain like a bird" is a modest and mostly reasonable emendation. It does, however, leave us with the problem that the imperative is either feminine singular (awkward unless the psalmist is a woman!) or masculine plural (in which case the quotation must be understood as taken from speech directed to the larger community rather than the psalmist in particular, as v. 1 seems to indicate: "to me").

A last possibility remains. Rather than separating the pronominal suffix as a freestanding preposition, some understand the letters of this suffix as a confusion for an original masculine plural ending on "mountain" (*hrym* ["mountains"] rather than *hrkm* ["your mountain"]). In this case, one can read the feminine singular imperative as responding appropriately to the feminine singular noun *ṣippor* ("bird") and render the phrase as a rather sarcastic remark directed to the singular psalmist: "Fly away to the mountains, [little] birdie!"

What Can the Righteous Do? (11:2–3)

SHOOT FROM THE **shadows.** The reason for the counsel to flee is elaborated in verses 2–3: The wicked are preparing an attack to destroy the upright. The metaphor employed is that of a sudden attack by an archer hidden in the dark. The "wicked" (plural) are viewed collectively as a unified assassin, bending a single bow, setting a single arrow to a single string, and releasing a destructive dart out of the darkness—a sudden, unanticipated attack. The real nature of the attack on the upright is left unstated, with the rest of the psalm implying only some miscarriage of justice that Yahweh is expected to examine and set right.

The upright in heart. As a designation for the faithful, "upright" (*yašar, yešarim*) occurs eighteen times in the psalms.[2] Of these occurrences, seven[3] add the additional qualifier we find in this verse: (lit.) "upright *of heart* [*leb*]." That the two phrases ("upright" and "upright of [in] heart") are synonyms for the same group of faithful followers of Yahweh is evident by their use at the beginning and end of our psalm (11:2, 7) for the same group of supplicants.[4] The term derives its meaning from the root idea of straightness—the opposite of crooked—that can be applied to straight, smooth roads or straight,

---

2. Pss. 7:10; 11:2, 7; 32:11; 33:1; 36:10; 37:14, 37; 49:14; 64:10; 94:15; 97:11; 107:42; 111:1; 112:2, 4; 125:4; 140:13.

3. Pss. 7:10; 11:2; 32:11; 36:10; 64:10; 94:15; 97:11.

4. In Ps. 37:14, *yašar* is linked with the word *derek* (in an additional expansion of the theme of uprightness) to describe those whose "way is upright."

direct persons. These people whose ways and hearts are "straight" are those attacked by the wicked but who will ultimately be justified by Yahweh.

When the foundations are being destroyed. The counsel to flee concludes with a pessimistic rhetorical question that all but admits defeat. The situation of uncontrolled violence on the righteous is so dismal that the pessimistic advisor understands the very foundations of society to have been laid in ruins. There is nothing left to rely on and no course of action left in the circumstances but to flee for one's life. In a world and society run amok, where the dignity of life is casually ignored and raw power rules in the place of justice, righteousness, and equity, what can a righteous person hope to do? In the face of such overwhelming odds, the advice is: "everyone for himself or herself." This is the ultimate reflection of self-interest and despair. "How little *you* are! How little (almost nothing) *you* can do! Take care of yourself first!"[5]

Yahweh the Examiner (11:4–6)

THE PANICKED DESIRE to flee in the context of the muddled and violent circumstance of the psalmist's present is countered by the resolutely calm description in verse 4. Yahweh is "in his holy temple," seated "on his heavenly throne." This picture serves two purposes. (1) It shows Yahweh enthroned, in control, and unperturbed by the apparent chaos unleashed in human affairs. This is not to say God is unconcerned by injustice and violence; his concern is amply illustrated in the rest of the psalm. But he is not undermined or panicked by the disorder and destruction that dismay humans; instead, he remains unshaken and eternally in power. This provides the psalmist and reader with a growing sense of confidence to counter the pessimism of the advisors.

(2) The psalm pictures Yahweh as a divine judge and examiner. As in 9:7–8, he sits down as judge and establisher of justice. From his vantage point in the heavens he is able to examine the chaotic human events on the earth and render righteous judgments. Nothing escapes his gaze.

The dual description of Yahweh as "in his holy temple" and "on his heavenly throne" is significant. The former is an indication of God's immanent presence among humans (most particularly the faithful), while the latter emphasizes the transcendent power and authority that separates him from the chaotic futility of human power. God is at once *among* his people, strengthening, empowering, and saving, and at the same time *above* all humans, ruling, examining, and rendering righteous judgment.

---

5. The NIV textual note offers an alternative reading of this phrase that is equally despairing: "What is the Righteous One [God] doing?" Others (e.g., Craigie, *Psalms 1–50*, 131, 133) suggest, "What has the righteous done [to deserve this]?"

He observes . . . his eyes examine. Employing two less common verbs (*ḥzh* ["see"] and *bḥn* ["examine"]), both of which occur far more frequently in the prophetic books than elsewhere in the Hebrew Bible,[6] the psalmist begins to shift the discussion away from the resolute presence of Yahweh in the face of human violence and its resultant chaos to a description of God's righteous judgment exercised over both the upright and wicked. From his heavenly vantage point God "observes" human affairs—in much the same way as he did before the Flood in Genesis 6 or at the Tower of Babel in Genesis 11—and "examines" them.

The prophets use *ḥzh* to describe the visionary process by which some of them receive divine communication and understanding regarding the circumstance and future of Israel. Nominal forms of this same root describe prophetic "visions" and in some occasions the person who received them.[7] Precisely how the prophetic aspect of this term might be operative in Psalm 11 is unclear, especially since it is God who "sees" or "observes" here. Perhaps the intent is to stress observation with perception or understanding as opposed to just seeing. How often do we *see* common items before some set of circumstances brings a sharper focus that adds a new and deeper *understanding* to our vision? When God sees humans, he perceives and understands what is going on and its deepest implications for life.

God's clear understanding and perception is brought out even more clearly by the term *bḥn*. The term signifies testing and examination and is used on at least one occasion to describe the "proof" of precious metals by smelting (Zech. 13:9). There is a certain scrutiny intended here that brings to light the good and distinguishes it from the bad.

The LORD examines the righteous. The righteous do not escape this examination. The NIV translation somewhat obscures the balance intended in verse 5. A better rendering in my opinion is: "Yahweh examines (both) the righteous and the wicked." His reaction to his examination of the wicked is immediately described in the second half of verse 5, while the fate of the righteous is delayed to the end of the psalm.

In response to the wicked the psalmist sets up an ironic tension through wordplay. Those (wicked) who "*love* violence" inspire *hatred* in the innermost

6. Of fifty-one occurrences of *ḥzh* in the Old Testament, twenty-six are found in the prophetic books and nine in the psalms, with thirteen in wisdom literature and the remaining three in the Pentateuch. The verb *bḥn* appears twenty-eight times in the Old Testament, with ten being in prophetic literature, nine in the psalms, six in wisdom literature, and the remaining three in Genesis and 1 Chronicles.

7. The noun "vision" is found in the titles of Isaiah, Obadiah, and Nahum. The title "seer" appears frequently in the Chronicler as well as in the prophets (Isaiah and Amos) and in 1 and 2 Samuel.

defining being of Yahweh ("his soul" [*nepeš*]).[8] While the attribution of hatred in God may raise uncomfortable questions for us as Christians who focus on the abundant and forgiving love of God poured out for all in Christ, we should not lose sight of two important considerations. (1) This very human insight about God reflects the very human nature of the psalms in their origin. These are the words of anguished human beings poured out honestly before God, so the selection of words and the attribution of negative human emotions to God begins in this human perspective. However, before we excise or consign to oblivion any description of God with which we feel uncomfortable (that is a pretty slippery way to define and understand God!), we need to acknowledge that these human words were transformed when they were recognized as the authoritative Word of God. Here the community of faith understood God to be speaking *to them* in ways that even the original authors of the psalms may not have understood or fully intended. We need, then, to be careful not to simply reject the uncomfortable but seek to understand it within the whole context of Scripture.

(2) There is a sense, is there not, that God does stand forever in an inimical relationship to those who "love violence"? Psalm 5:4 cautions us that Yahweh is "not a God who takes pleasure in evil; with you the wicked cannot dwell." Because of his essentially holy nature, God has no love for those who align themselves with evil. In the contrast between the "upright" and the "wicked," between those oppressed and those who love to oppress by violence, God is always on the side of the oppressed faithful and against the violent wicked. That is his nature; to expect differently would be to unweave the fabric of creation and to let in a chaos infinitely greater than that brought about by rebellious human violence. If in this contrast God loves the upright, what is left for the wicked but "unlove"? By this phrase, then, the psalmist affirms what we already know about God—he is adamantly and eternally opposed to those who use violence to oppress others and to further their own power and control.

Fiery coals and burning sulfur. Our analysis of the Hebrew verbs *ḥzh* ("see") and *bḥn* ("examine") led us to think of the Flood and the Tower of Babel narratives in Genesis. The destructive consequences poured out on the wicked as a result of this examination reminds us of another Genesis account: that of Sodom and Gomorrah (Gen. 18–19), where God destroyed those wicked cities by raining down fire and sulfur on them.[9] Here in Psalm

8. See the discussion of *nepeš* in the comments on Ps. 3:2.

9. In both Gen. 19:24 and Ps. 11:6, God rains "fire" (*ʾeš*) and "sulfur" (*goprit*). In Ps. 11:6, the term *paḥim* is rather awkwardly added just before *ʾeš*. It is generally agreed that this word (which normally means "leaves" of metal) should be emended by reversing the last two letters of the consonantal text to *paḥme* ("coals"), with the resulting construction translated as in the NIV's "fiery coals."

11:6 the violent wicked are expected to receive the same divine judgment as Sodom and Gomorrah—the epitome of perverted wickedness in the tradition of the Old Testament.

In addition to the obviously divine judgment suggested by the fire and sulfur raining down, the wicked will also experience the destruction of a "scorching wind" (11:6).[10] This devastating wind—perhaps equivalent to the modern sirocco—withers crops and dries up fragile water sources necessary for both animal and human consumption. The judgment is one of discomfort, which threatens life and well-being; this is the appropriate "portion of their [the wicked's] cup" (NIV "their lot"). Kraus refers this phrase to the contrasting "cup of salvation" and "cup of wrath" poured out by God on the righteous and wicked respectively.[11] This seems a proper background for the context of Psalm 11:6. Yahweh pours into the cup of the wicked the wine of his wrath, which they are forced to drink to the dregs with all the attendant destructive consequences (cf. Ps. 116:13; Isa. 51:17, 22–23).[12]

Affirmation of Yahweh's Righteousness (11:7)

OUR PSALM CONCLUDES by affirming Yahweh's righteousness and his love of justice. These twin attributes are in the foreground to provide the basis of the psalmist's confident hope in the face of the pessimistic undermining of the alternative voices in the psalm. Although the upright are under violent attack (11:2) and the foundations of society and order are crumbling away beyond the control of the righteous (11:3), the psalmist trusts in the established righteousness of Yahweh to examine all humans, whether righteous or wicked (11:4–5), and to deliver appropriate judgment to each (11:5–6). For this reason he can affirm Yahweh as "refuge" (11:1) in the midst of chaos and trust expectantly that the "upright ... will see his face" (11:7b).

VERSE 3 POSES the central reflective question of this psalm: "When the foundations are being destroyed, what can the righteous do?" It is clear that in the psalmist's mind there are only two responses to this question: Either one can flee to the mountains as the counselors suggest, or one can take refuge in Yahweh. Let's take a look at how Israel

10. Holladay connects the Hebrew *zalʿapah* with "rage" rather than "scorching" and understands the passage in 11:6 as a "whirlwind" (*CHALOT*, 89).

11. Kraus, *Psalms 1–59*, 204.

12. For related passages see Pss. 16:5; 23:5; 75:8; Jer. 25:15, 17, 28; Lam. 4:21; Ezek. 23:31–33; Hab. 2:16.

as a nation, or individuals within Israel, responded to the shaking of their foundations in both ways.

Flee to the mountains. Perhaps we ought first to ask what it means to "flee to the mountains." It is unlikely, given the metaphorical nature of this comment (in which the psalmist is asked to take on the role of a bird) that actual, physical flight was intended. It is possible to flee either inwardly or outwardly. I remember hearing a teenage girl who had been sexually abused over a number of years by an uncle describe how during each incident she floated out of her body and observed what went on almost dispassionately from a safe spot near the ceiling of the room. That is a classical description of disassociation—an emotional withdrawal from experiences too painful to bear—when one simply departs within oneself to a place that is more bearable, more safe. I wept when I heard this girl's story. I wept not only because of the destructive consequences of the horrific abuse she had suffered in her young life, but also because I myself had fled inwardly to escape fear and pain I had been unwilling to face.

If, then, we are not just thinking of physical flight, what are some examples of how Israel fled when her foundations were threatened? To go to the very beginning, Adam and Eve fled into denial, accusation, and recrimination. Because of their disobedience, the foundational relationships of the creation were twisted and broken. Relationship to God, relationship between humans themselves, and relationship between humans and the other creatures were perverted into self-seeking attempts to manipulate and control others for personal benefit. When confronted by the reality of their sin, Adam and Eve sought to cover up with a bunch of fig leaves and hid themselves from God in the shrubbery. Then when face to face with God, they tried to deflect attention and responsibility from themselves by pointing fingers at one another and even at God.

King Saul saw the foundations of his hope for a dynasty passed on to his son Jonathan crumbling under the weight of the people's preference for David as well as Jonathan's selfless love for David. Saul's fear that David would take the throne and bring his dreams to an end led him to anger, to violence, and ultimately to depression and madness. Unwilling to submit to the clear will of Yahweh, Saul sought violently to take matters into his own hands and to snuff out the life of his supposed opponent.

Called by Yahweh to prophesy against Nineveh, Jonah fled twice; first he ran physically on a ship from Joppa as far from God and Nineveh as the Mediterranean Sea would take him. At the end of his ministry, he fled again into bitter resignation on the hillside overlooking Nineveh—hoping for their destruction but expecting divine mercy and deliverance. After all, God ought to bless those who loved him and curse those who hated him. To forgive those who denied his very existence and who refused any obedience to him was to turn the foundational faith of Israel on its ear—to threaten to destroy any special relation that might exist between Israel and her God. "I knew it!" Jonah cried, "I knew you would forgive those undeserving pagans, and I wanted no part in it. I wanted them to get what they had coming: defeat, destruction, embarrassment, and pain. So, go ahead, save them if you must, but don't expect me to participate in any celebration." I suspect that Jonah would have received Jesus' command to "go and make disciples of all nations" with little joy and even less obedience.

Toward the end of the monarchical period, faced by the overwhelming military and political power of first Assyria and then Babylon, Judah fled into a false piety and a twisted interpretation of their covenant relationship with Yahweh to escape the threatened destruction of their foundational hopes and dreams. They were the "people of Yahweh," after all, chosen by him from all the families of the earth for special relationship. Hadn't he promised that the descendants of David would always rule over the kingdom? Didn't the temple of Yahweh in Jerusalem guarantee his continued presence with them? Didn't the daily sacrifices and other rituals fulfill their covenantal obligation to God? It was easy to believe that God would not allow his people to fall prey to the vicious pagan nations that surrounded her. With all her faults, wasn't Judah far better than those idol-worshiping foreigners? Surely Yahweh would not permit the ridicule of defeat to undermine his glory and honor.

As these examples illustrate, Israel knew well how to flee when her foundational hopes, traditions, dreams, and expectations began to be destroyed. Hiding behind denial and blame, seeking by anger and violence to undermine the opposition, dwelling in bitter resignation, and relying on a twisted and self-serving piety to manipulate God to their own ends, these individuals (and others like them) could flee from the threats to their personal foundations without ever taking a single physical step toward those distant mountains. Nevertheless, there are others in Scripture who provide a contrasting example of those who, when confronted by destructive threats, chose to take refuge in Yahweh. Let's look briefly at a few of these.

I take refuge. Just as fleeing need not be physical, so taking refuge may be metaphorical. It is possible to take refuge in God without entering a physical place of safety. I remember once being taught to use meditative visualization as a means of coping with stress. I was instructed to close my eyes and visualize a particular place from my past where I had felt safe and secure. My "safe place" was a childhood hiding place about ten feet up in a tree shrouded from view in a twisted mass of honeysuckle vines in which I had hollowed out a space where I could sit and look out over an adjoining field. My abiding impression was of peace and security, swathed in the shifting green shadows and filtering sunlight, and in season the sweet, fresh smell of honeysuckle blossoms filled the air. I learned that whenever stress mounted, I could mentally "go to my safe place" and experience a renewed sense of peace and relaxation without ever having to leave the place I was.

When God called Abraham and told him to sacrifice his "only son," Isaac, the secure foundations of his hard-won faith in Yahweh threatened to crumble. This was the child of promise, the means by which God had promised to give Abraham descendants and through whom blessing was to come to the whole world. Abraham could have fled physically or metaphorically in one of the ways I described above, but he did not. Instead, he packed up his donkey, took his beloved son with him, and walked straight into the refuge God provided on his way to Mount Moriah, where the sacrifice was to take place.

We know this because of the thematic repetition that characterizes the Genesis passage. In response to Isaac's innocent, yet telling, query to his father, asking where the sacrifice was that would go with the wood and the fire, Abraham replied, "God himself will provide the lamb for the burnt offering" (Gen. 22:8). After God did provide a ram, we are reminded twice at the conclusion of the narrative that "Abraham called that place The LORD Will Provide. And to this day it is said, 'On the mountain of the LORD it will be provided'" (22:14). Clearly Abraham's earlier reassurance of Isaac was no clever deceit, nor simply the wishful thinking of a desperate father. It was the result of Abraham's having come confidently into the refuge God provides and having found the assurance there that indeed Yahweh does provide, even when the foundations are being destroyed.

Like Saul above, King David faced the threat of having his kingdom snatched from him by a powerful rebel. The problem for David was that the armed enemy at the gates of Jerusalem seeking his life was his own beloved son Absalom. In the rush to flee the city before the forces of Absalom could trap him there and overwhelm him, David was approached by the priests bearing the ark of the covenant—the visible sign of God's invisible presence—to take it with them as an indication of Yahweh's support of the fleeing king against his rebellious son. Surely David was tempted to exploit this most important and holy religious object and its potent symbolism in his own behalf. Certainly God had promised to be with David, so why not make that presence visible by bringing the ark along?

But David's response is instructive—a clear indication that at this moment of high crisis and personal threat, he had already entered the presence of Yahweh for refuge. David said, "Take the ark of God back into the city. If I find favor in the LORD's eyes, he will bring me back and let me see it and his dwelling place again. But if he says, 'I am not pleased with you,' then I am ready; let him do to me whatever seems good to him" (2 Sam. 15:25–26). David surrendered to God's will and found refuge there.

In the New Testament Gospels, we find a similar example in Jesus. After some three years of public ministry, one day near Caesarea Philippi he took stock of how the multitudes in general and his closer disciples in particular understood his message and purpose. The matched questions, "Who do people say I am?" and "Who do you say I am?" (Mark 8:27, 29), brought a devastatingly disappointing response. The people as a whole had little understanding, at best associating Jesus with John the Baptist, or Elijah, or one of the ancient prophets. The disciples were almost equally clueless, although Peter did offer the inspired insight that Jesus was the expected Messiah. But even this understanding was far from complete, since he and the rest of the disciples anticipated a conquering, kingly Messiah, complete with defeat of the enemies of the Jews and an earthly kingdom with places of authority for each of the Twelve.

Jesus, however, understood that his role was to suffer and die a criminal's death—ridiculed, forsaken, and misunderstood. Certainly he was tempted by Satan in the desert to forsake suffering and use spectacular means to satisfy the people and usher in the kingdom. Yet the Gospels tell us that from that day on, Jesus resolutely set his face toward Jerusalem, teaching his disciples along the way that the Son of Man must suffer and die there. Jesus was able to continue this journey to Jerusalem without fleeing because he had already entered the refuge of God, from which he could accept the role of suffering service to others.

These three scriptural examples stand in contrast to the four earlier examples of those who fled when the foundations were being destroyed. These last three did not flee; rather, they entered the refuge that God provides in the midst of threat and destruction. By acknowledging the steady provision of God in a most horrific situation, by surrendering to God's will rather than exploiting the most holy religious rituals and traditions, or by assuming the role of suffering servant for others, these last three came into the presence of God and knew true refuge.

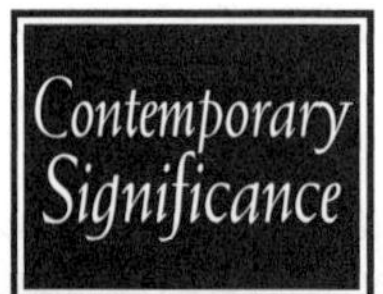

I TRUST YOU are already beginning to see how the links discussed above bridge their way into contemporary life and especially your own life. Often it seems today that we feel threatened (like the psalmist several millennia ago) in personal and communal ways with the apparent collapse of the foundations on which our lives have been built. We hear many voices around us declaring that the sky is falling or the world as we know it is heading for imminent demise, and we are counseled to flee for our lives.

The approach of the third millennium A.D. provided a recent example in this regard. We were warned continuously about the "Y2K millennium bug" that would create computer mayhem as older computer programs, designed to recognize years using only the final two digits, would be unable to distinguish the years 2000 and following from 1900 through 1999. As a result of this confusion, it was warned, major national and international computer systems could fail and important life-support systems (banks, government, utilities) would collapse. Although major efforts were expended to correct the bug, many claimed that there was little chance that all systems would be repaired before the turn of the century, and major governmental systems were admitted to be far behind the necessary schedule for completion.

Some predicted dire consequences—even a total collapse of metropolitan systems of order and a return to a self-sufficiency agrarian economy. A neighbor of mine, who is a computer programming consultant, said he would take a "cautious" approach by stockpiling a two- to four-week supply of cash, food, and other necessities and have them on hand when December 1999 rolled around.

Now that the millennium has arrived and all the dire predictions have proven largely unfounded, all this concern and furor seems far-fetched or even a little embarrassing to most of us; but every new century has seen its share of apocalyptic doomsayers who predicted the collapse of all order and the end of the world. Christians are particularly susceptible to this disaster mode of thinking. The prevailing sense that Christians are "in the world but not of the world," that we must exercise care not to have our morals and values shaped by the twisted values of the world, that our world is hurtling toward a cataclysmic end that will usher in the true "kingdom of God"—combined with a particular interpretation of eschatological and apocalyptic passages in Daniel, the prophets, and Revelation—have left many Christians anticipating the final conflict of God and good with Satan and evil. Thus, Christians remain susceptible to persuasive or even dramatic disaster thinking that predicts the imminent end of the world.

But apocalyptic eschatology is only one—although perhaps the most all-consuming—scenario in which contemporary Christians are confronted with the threat of the destruction of the familiar, orderly foundations of life. Other less cataclysmic circumstances produce a similar sense of threat of chaos. Let me mention a few of these situations and then return to consider how we can respond either by fleeing or by finding refuge in God.

The loss of personal identity. A friend operates a purebred cattle ranch in California. Most of his life has been focused on establishing and maintaining this lifelong dream. He and his family have made numerous sacrifices to make this dream possible. And they have had a fair amount of success, having developed a good reputation and a loyal following for their breed of cattle and their particular genetic strain.

But the last few years have begun to take their toll. Poor beef markets led to poor sales prices for their animals and less capital to develop and sustain their operation. My friend, who is now in his fifties and has two daughters of college age—neither of whom has evidenced interest in taking over the family operation—is faced with the reality of declining financial and physical resources to get the daily hard labor of ranching done. He is having to consider carefully and painfully whether it is time to lay down this dream.

My friend's circumstance mirrors on a personal scale the situation in the world of American agriculture at large. Long-term family farming operations are disappearing, brought down by hard markets, uneven competition with large conglomerate operations, and the loss of children to the cities and more lucrative and stable work. A way of life characteristic of the heartland of America and generations of farming families is passing away. How does one respond to the loss of such a foundational vision that gives identity to one's life? One does not just *do* farming or ranching, one *is* a farmer or rancher—usually living on the ranch or farm twenty-four hours a day. To now take on another line of work is to give up the old self and adopt a new identity—always a threatening process.

And it is not just farmers and ranchers who are being faced with such drastic identity changes today. With the advent of "downsizing" of the work force in many companies and "outsourcing" of production to other companies and countries, along with a shift to employing more temporary workers, many of our contemporaries have lost jobs that have provided a large source of their identity.

The threat of pluralism. Another change threatening our way of life is the increasing ethnic, cultural, and religious pluralism prevalent in our society—especially in the urban environment. We once could say "one nation, under God," think of the nation primarily as European, English-speaking (white, Anglo-Saxon, Protestant), and understand God in Judeo-Christian terms. Now, however, we need to face the fact that within fifty years people of color will be in the majority in our nation; already the Christian God bumps shoulders constantly in society and shares equal protection under law with the gods of the other nations and peoples.

That is a radical change in our culture and a threatening one—especially to the majority culture, who sees their influence not so slowly slipping away, to be replaced by a polyglot of competing cultural identities that are at best uncomfortable and often even hostile. And this change is not just an American phenomenon—it is mirrored in cities and nations around the world, where urbanization and globalization are producing rapid shifts to pluralism and the conflicts it ultimately brings.

The societal assault on Christian values. One last example of a threat to the foundations that is particularly unsettling to Christians is related to the example just cited. Because our nation was founded by a primarily Eurocentric culture, the early traditions, values, and principles reflected in society were largely influenced by Christian thought and practice. With the gradual increase in pluralism through the intervening centuries, rapidly increasing in our own time, cultural and value conflicts are also increasing. The response of society at large has been one of toleration on the one hand and individualism on the other. Note the typical response: "What's good for you is fine for you, and what's good for me is fine for me. You believe what you want, and I'll believe what I want." In other words, a common set of values and principles that governs society is no longer possible.

The situation has been magnified by the decidedly postmodern worldview that has made great inroads into cultural thinking today—particularly among the young. The postmodernist rejects the existence of absolute truth that can and should serve as the foundation of life in all cultures. They share an equal suspicion regarding rational, logical argumentation as a way of understanding truth because they have seen such argumentation manipulated to justify so many competing claims and viewpoints. The postmodernist rejects a common set of values and principles governing all humans and accepts rather that values are a personal matter shared by a larger community as the basis of communal existence—without having any absolute character.

Since there are no absolutes stemming from divine expectation in this system, values are simply what works for an individual, and societal norms are only the set of values that a group has agreed upon. As a result, almost anything goes—except criticism of someone else's values or beliefs. Tolerance is the only absolute in the postmodern arsenal, and the only attitude *not* to be tolerated is *intolerance.* The only exception to this general rule is directed toward the Christian faith, which in postmodern thinking is bound up with the domination of the majority culture and is guilty of the supreme intolerance. As such, the claims of Christianity must be undermined and rejected in order to establish the aura of tolerance that postmodernism requires.[13]

A result of this postmodern worldview over the last forty years, coupled with the increasing plurality in society and increased globalization of our

---

13. Other religions (such as Islam) are equally intolerant—claiming unique and absolute truth for their beliefs, but because they have not been traditionally associated with the dominant culture, there is less negative critique directed toward them.

awareness brought about by technological advances in media, has been a rapid breakdown in societal norms that reflected compatibility with the Christian worldview. With the exaltation of the individual self we have seen the breakdown of self-limitation or sacrificial service for the benefit of others; materialism and acquisition overwhelm spirituality, and immediate gratification is mirrored with our national race into credit card debt. Many other Christian principles, such as purity, chastity, stewardship, and care for the world, have suffered major attacks and setbacks as well.

How then does the church (or an individual Christian, for that matter) respond to a rapidly changing societal context in which primary Christian values are being attacked and rejected and in which Christians themselves are being subtly (and not so subtly) drawn into a web of assimilation and change that is contrary to their most cherished beliefs and values? We will return to consider that question below.

Fleeing or taking refuge. The three examples given above are intended as illustrations of major, enduring life changes that threaten to undermine the foundations on which our lives and identities are grounded. This list is not intended to be exhaustive—nor is it my intention to suggest that only events of such magnitude can have the effect of shaking our personal foundations. I do think, however, that a threat of this magnitude—systemic societal evil or disruption—is what the psalmist is talking about in Psalm 11. Considering how we respond to such threats, whether greater or smaller in magnitude, can be instructive.

According to this psalm, in such foundation-shaking circumstances we have two basic choices: Either we can flee to the hills, or we can take refuge in God. Let's see how these alternatives play themselves out in our own culture and context.

Survivalism. Our society often responds to foundational threat by some form of fleeing. Survivalists, for example, fearing increased governmental intrusion and the possibility of world collapse, sometimes flee physically into remote areas, where they can become a law unto themselves. They respond to what they see as governmental oppression by resisting taxes, setting up provisional governments, and in some instances even carrying out terrorist activities against the establishment.[14] Their withdrawal from mainline society is fear-based and demonstrates a desire to exercise self-determination and control.

Racial supremacy. Racial supremacy groups respond to a different set of stimuli. Anger and fear over a long history of racial prejudice and oppression of African Americans in this country and elsewhere led in the 1960s and

14. The bombing of the government office building in Oklahoma City is one example.

1970s to the creation of black pride/power groups, such as the Black Muslims and Black Panthers. Both groups were militaristic, promising to resist white oppression with force. On the other side of the racial barrier, white supremacy groups as old as the Ku Klux Klan and as new as the Aryan Brotherhood have responded to increasing racial plurality and the impending loss of white majority control with racial separation, denigration, and hostility. Violent language often breaks out into real violence against those who are not a part of the "white" race. Anger, hatred, and hostility characterize the most extreme forms of these movements, marking a withdrawal from society as a whole, a rejection of compromise and reconciliation, and the establishment of an exclusive, self-concerned community, erecting walls and barriers to protect those within.

Millennialism. As the year 2000 approached, we saw an increase of groups pronouncing doom and gloom and encouraging others to flee with them into some form of millennialism. Christianity has seen its own share of millennialist movements through the years. The Millerites, for example, put on white robes and congregated on hilltops anticipating the coming of Christ and the end of the age in 1844. Seventh-Day Adventism had its early origins in such anticipation of the "advent" of the Millennium. More recently the book *Eighty-Eight Reasons the Lord Will Return in 1988*[15] stirred millennial imaginations before being passed over by current events.

But Christians are not the only groups affected by millennial fervor. The tragic experience of the Heaven's Gate cult demonstrated the willingness of persons to flee their dissatisfaction with this present world into some other more perfect alternative existence or age. For the members of this group, that flight was accomplished by mass suicide in hopes of being translated to a spaceship hidden behind a passing comet. The spaceship would then transport the faithful to a new life removed from the oppressions and frustrations experienced here and now. All these groups, Christian and non-Christian alike, share an exclusive self-focus, a dissatisfaction with the present life, and a desire to flee to a better world.

Cultural isolation. Another form of flight is to create barriers of isolation around a community in order to preserve its distinctives from the onslaught of cultural pressure from the outside and to provide a united front for mutual protection against what is viewed as a hostile environment. Clear and extreme examples of such isolation in our society might be the Amish communities of Pennsylvania (and elsewhere) and the Hasidic Jewish communities throughout the world. These groups continue to live a separate life within larger society. Their distinctives of dress and custom are protected by limited

15. Later revised to *Eight-Nine Reasons the Lord Will Return in 1989*.

contact with outsiders and a strong sense of community loyalty and group identity. In some rare instances (such as the ultraorthodox Jewish communities in Israel), such groups may seek to impose their distinctive values on the larger society, but most often they are content to "live and let live," trading isolated self-determination for any influence on the world around them.

Cultural assimilation. But another way for the church and Christian individuals to flee the experience of conflict and oppression by a society that neither shares nor appreciates Christian values has been cultural assimilation. This approach rejects both the violent, angry resistance and rejection associated with supremacist withdrawal and the more passive withdrawal into isolated purity characteristic of the Amish communities. It refuses escape through millennial flight to another world. In this response, Christians give up those distinctives that separate them from society and thereby remove the cause of conflict and rejection. They accommodate themselves to the values and mores of society at large in materialism, sexuality, divorce, treatment of the poor, and so on. The lives of such Christians have ceased to be distinctive—to challenge the life of the non-Christian society around them. Such a life of cultural assimilation is safe and may be convenient and prosperous, but it is flight nevertheless.

All these (and others as well) are ways Christians are tempted to flee from the foundation-threatening pressures of life. Such avenues as we have discussed offer avenues of escape at the expense of Christian distinctives or the loss of Christian influence and testimony to the world we have been called to challenge with the word and love of God in Christ. Yet we are called by this psalm—and by Christ—to a "better way," the way of discovering refuge in God at the very moment that the foundations are being destroyed.

Finding refuge in God. Finding refuge in God obviously does not mean escape. It does not mean avoiding persecution or suffering. Jesus certainly found refuge in his Father, but he still experienced rejection by his enemies, abandonment by his disciples, and the cruel suffering and even death on the cross. I wonder how many other countless faithful followers have experienced this refuge throughout the ages? Stephen certainly did when he spoke God's truth to a hostile crowd who ultimately stoned him to death. Paul was able to accept his imprisonment on false charges in Rome as an opportunity to witness to the household guard of Caesar.

Corrie Ten Boom, faced by the madness that was Nazi Germany's mass murder of six million Jews, was able not to flee into self-preserving silence and passivity but took an active hand at hiding Jews, even though it ultimately meant imprisonment and the loss of much of her family in the concentration camps. In the same context, Dietrich Bonhoeffer also felt compelled to act against the madness by participating in a plot to assassinate Hitler. Imprisoned and ultimately executed for his part in that plot, Bonhoeffer's prison writings are ample testimony to the deep refuge he had found in God through Christ.

Thus, whatever else it means, taking refuge in God does *not* mean escape or avoidance of pain and suffering. Part of the reason for this is that fleeing is self-focused and self-concerned. We flee when we are concerned about protecting ourselves. By contrast, the kind of refuge that God offers calls us to give ourselves away: "For whoever wants to save his life will lose it, but whoever loses his life for me will save it" (Luke 9:24).[16] Taking refuge in God is other-focused. Those who enter that refuge hold on to God by letting go of self and thinking instead of others. That is why Christ chose to go forward from Gethsemane to the cross and death. That is why Stephen spoke the truth in the face of an angry mob. That is why Corrie Ten Boom and Dietrich Bonhoeffer were not dissuaded by the threat of imprisonment and death from acting in crazy circumstances not out of personal interest but for the good of others.

Such an understanding of taking refuge calls into question any response to crumbling foundations that is based on self-interest and avoidance of personal pain and suffering. In moments of personal or communal crisis—such as the approach of a new millennium or terrorist attacks on national icons—we need to be ready to speak a word of truth, comfort, and hope to a chaotic setting of doom and gloom, rather than withdrawing into our self-serving fantasies of a better world for the faithful.

We need to be actively seeking to alleviate the pain of those around us rather than escape ourselves. Rather than fearing the inroads that racial and cultural plurality are making into our own personal power and well-being, we should be involved in promoting racial reconciliation, celebrating ethnic diversity (and learning from it!), and working for equity, justice, and equal opportunity for those of any race and culture. The call to take refuge is not a call to hunker down and remain inactive until the danger passes. It is a call to realize that in Christ we have been given life so abundant and so eternal that we need not fear to give it all away.

16. Cf. the parallel passages in Matt. 16:25 and Mark 8:35.

Psalm 12

FOR THE DIRECTOR of music. According to *sheminith*. A psalm of David.

[1] Help, LORD, for the godly are no more;
  the faithful have vanished from among men.
[2] Everyone lies to his neighbor;
  their flattering lips speak with deception.

[3] May the LORD cut off all flattering lips
  and every boastful tongue
[4] that says, "We will triumph with our tongues;
  we own our lips—who is our master?"

[5] "Because of the oppression of the weak
  and the groaning of the needy,
I will now arise," says the LORD.
  "I will protect them from those who malign them."
[6] And the words of the LORD are flawless,
  like silver refined in a furnace of clay,
  purified seven times.

[7] O LORD, you will keep us safe
  and protect us from such people forever.
[8] The wicked freely strut about
  when what is vile is honored among men.

LIKE THE PRECEDING PSALM, Psalm 12 is a plea for deliverance, though here the psalmist speaks in the first-person plural ("we/us"), representing the community. Also like Psalm 11, evil appears endemic and the suffering of the faithful extreme. The psalmist's primary complaint has to do with lies and deceptively flattering speech with which the enemy maligns the weak and needy. Verse 6 draws a striking contrast between the deceptive words of the wicked and the flawless words of Yahweh.

The psalm opens with a description of what motivates the complaint (12:1–2) and continues with a plea for divine action, specifically directed to the offense of lying and deception (12:3–4). Yahweh promises intervention in behalf of the weak and needy (12:5), and the psalmist feels confident that Yahweh will deliver as promised—describing Yahweh's "flawless" words as the basis for that confidence (12:6–7). The psalm concludes by returning to the circumstances of oppression that occasion the complaint and serve as motivation for Yahweh's intervention (12:8).

The Heading (12:0)

THE HEADING REFERS this psalm to "the director of music"[1] and describes the psalm as a *mizmor* of David.[2] As in the heading of Psalm 6, the term *haššeminit* ("According to *sheminith*") most likely refers to an appropriate tuning of the harp to accompany the performance of the psalm.

Grounds of Complaint (12:1–2)

THE PSALMIST DRIVES home the description of the circumstances that occasion the complaint in the language of hyperbole. The godly no longer exist. The faithful have vanished. Lying and deception are universal. By this tactic the psalmist (who must be accounted among the "godly ... faithful") heightens the sense of oppression experienced (it's everywhere) and leaves God little choice but to act. The circumstance is similar to that in Genesis 18, where Abraham pleads with God for the deliverance of Sodom and Gomorrah from destruction if only ten righteous persons are found dwelling there—but none are found.

The psalmist's focus is on lying and deceit used to malign and exploit the weak and needy for the benefit of the deceitful. These manipulators of words place great stock in their ability to twist and control language for their own purposes (12:4); but in reality, says the psalmist, they speak not so much "lies" (which would use the Heb. *šeqer*) but *šawᶜ* ("deception," that which is "worthless" or empty of meaning). This sets up a contrast between the empty words of the boastful wicked and the "flawless" and effective words of Yahweh in 12:6.

Flattering lips. The Hebrew behind this phrase (*śepat ḥalaqot*) is both instructive and descriptive. "Flattering" is from the Hebrew root *ḥlq* ("make smooth"). A wooden translation might be something like "lips of smooth things" (cf. our own idiomatic expression "a smooth talker"). This phrase acknowledges that a persuasive command of the language is not always accompanied by a positive regard for the truth; one can manipulate truth to accomplish one's own ends. Thus, *śepat ḥalaqot* may mean "flattering lips," which shape speech to appeal to the ego of the listener, or "deceptive lips,"

1. See comments on the heading of Ps. 4.
2. See comments on the heading of Ps. 3.

implying speech that exploits the ambiguities and complexities of language to shade the truth. In either case the intent is to deceive.

Speak with deception. The NIV translation of this phrase (*beleb waleb yedabberu*) obscures an interesting idiomatic construction. Since the heart is, for the Hebrew, the seat of reflective thought and commitment, the idiom captures a particularly pernicious form of deception. These masterful speakers of the word speak from a "double heart." They do not say what they truly think or mean but hide the truth within them—in another heart, so to speak. In his brief but insightful volume on Hasidic Judaism, *The Way of Man According to the Teachings of Hasidism*, Jewish theologian Martin Buber suggests that the origin of all conflict between humans in this world is the result of

> conflict between three principles in man's being and life, the principle of thought, the principle of speech, and the principle of action. The origin of all conflict between me and my fellow-men is that I do not say what I mean, and that I do not do what I say. For this confuses and poisons, again and again.[3]

Plea for Deliverance (12:3–4)

INCENSED BY THE enemy's arrogant determination to manipulate language and thus to obscure truth, the psalmist pleads for a punishment worthy of the crime. Still operating in the realm of hyperbole, he demands that Yahweh remove the offending elements of speech: "May the LORD cut off all flattering lips and every boastful tongue" (12:3). This is a harsh punishment, to be sure, but one that metaphorically emphasizes the anger the psalmist (and those who have been maligned and deceived) feels for such unabashed disregard for the truth. The utter self-absorption of the wicked is reflected in the mirror of their own arrogant words as they are quoted by the psalmist to reveal their moral bankruptcy: "We will triumph with our tongues; we own our lips—who is our master?" (12:4). Notice the chiastic arrangement of these verses revealed by the ordering of the elements of speech. The psalmist's plea introduces first lips and then tongue, while the liars' boast reverses the order with "our tongues ... our lips."

We will triumph. The Hebrew behind the NIV's "triumph" is the Niphal imperfect of *gbr* ("be strong"). The wicked believe their mastery of deceptive language gives them power and leads to victory. That personal power comes at the cost of the truth and the exploitation of the defenseless is of no concern to them. Their trust in their ability to twist language to their own advan-

3. Martin Buber, *The Way of Man According to the Teaching of Hasidism* (Secaucus, N.J.: Citadel, 1966), 29.

tage is akin to some of the worst practices of lawyers to exploit the loopholes in legal statutes or to hide important conditions in the endless stilted and wilting officious prose and grammar in the "fine print" of contracts. The wicked described here are so confident in their mastery they feel invincible—completely in control and without limits. "As long as our lips are with us, who is our lord?"

This question is clearly intended to be rhetorical. The anticipated answer is, of course, "No one." As such it reveals the massive egos of the liars, who feel there is no one who can stop them, no one to whom they must bow. But in the context of Psalm 12, the question also serves ironically to set up the divine response in verse 5. While the wicked see no impediment to the free manipulation of language, the psalmist and the reader know another answer to the liars' puffed-up question. Who is their master? Yahweh is! And that is exactly what Yahweh demonstrates in the following verse.

Divine Response and Promise (12:5)

THE LIARS MAY consider the plight of the poor and needy whom they exploit a matter of little or no concern. But Yahweh takes his kingly role as protector of the defenseless seriously (see comments on 10:16–18). "Because of the oppression[4] of the weak and the groaning of the needy, I will now arise," says Yahweh (12:5). Yahweh—the divine king who sits in judgment in Psalms 9–10, who from his heavenly throne examines both righteous and wicked in Psalm 11, who has given feeble *ʾenoš* great honor and authority in Psalm 8—will enforce limitations on that power and authority when he arises to protect the defenseless "from those who malign them."

Confident Expectation (12:6–7)

HAVING HEARD DIRECTLY from God of his imminent response, the psalmist confidently drives home the contrast between the shifting, distorting, and ultimately powerless words of the wicked and the "pure utterances" of Yahweh that accomplish what they promise.[5] Using the analogy of the smelting

---

4. The Hebrew means more directly "destruction, devastation." See Craigie, *Psalms 1–50*, 136, for an excellent critique of Dahood's suggestion on the basis of Ugaritic that this term be translated "sobs." Dahood would have the parallel halves of this verse more identical in meaning ("sobs" vs. "groaning"). There is, however, no difficulty accepting the traditional understanding that God *sees* the "devastation" suffered by the weak and *hears* the "groaning" that oppression produces.

5. Cf. on this theme of the effective word of Yahweh in Isa. 55:11, where the Hebrew term for "word" is *dabar* in the singular rather than the plural of *ʾimrah* as here in Ps. 12. The theological understanding, however, is similar and supportive.

and purification of precious metal from the other base materials bound up in the ore, the psalmist describes the "words of the LORD" as "pure utterances,"[6] "refined silver,"[7] and "purified [washed, strained?] seven times."[8]

Between the last two phrases is a rather difficult passage (Heb. *baʿalil laʾareṣ*, lit., "at the entrance of the earth") that is variously rendered. Delitzsch takes *baʿalil* as "in a furnace," a move followed by most translators. Dahood and others take *laʾareṣ* to indicate the location or material of composition of the furnace: "a furnace in the ground" or "an earthen/clay furnace." Kraus, who leaves the passage untranslated, suggests a possible reference to a "procedure in the process of smelting" that is now obscure to us, or the incorporation into the text of an originally separate marginal note. Suffice it to say that the passage is difficult, but it does not undermine the primary metallurgical imagery and the picture of refined purity attributed to the words of Yahweh. This purity of the divine utterance shows up the self-focused and grasping nature of the liars' words, in contrast to the grandiose expectations expressed in 12:4.

The description in 12:6 is also intended to increase confidence in the faithful. That it accomplishes its purpose is demonstrated in the affirmation of trust declared in verse 7. Yahweh *will* watch over the weak and needy and *will* protect them "forever." Persuaded of the emptiness of the claims of the wicked, emboldened by the divine promise of protection, and convinced of the pure effectiveness of the divine words, the psalmist is confident that the faithful will be preserved in the midst of attack.

Reprise of Complaint (12:8)

THE PSALMIST CONCLUDES by returning to his earlier (12:1–2) grounds of complaint against the wicked. As yet they experience no limitation to their power to oppress but move about freely so that in the psalmist's present circumstance, human vileness is ascendant. The call to confident faith in divine protection comes from *within* the experience of oppression and (as in Ps. 11) offers a peace and security that is not based on the complete removal of evil and distress. The wicked still spout their boastful and misleading lies. They still strut about unhindered. But the faithful see through the eyes of the psalmist that Yahweh is the God of the pure, effective word, who takes the side of the needy when all others malign them. In the words of the New Testament, "If God is for us, who can be against us?" (Rom. 8:31).

---

6. More accurate than the NIV's "flawless," which draws from the evaluation of gemstones rather than the metallurgical context of this passage.

7. Once again the metallurgical imagery is clear.

8. This too is a metallurgical image, used in Job 28:1 of the purification of gold. It suggests the extreme care involved in sifting out true gold from any impurities in the ore.

THE CENTRAL IMAGE of this psalm is the spoken word. The contrast between the boastful, deceptive, self-serving words of the wicked and the pure, effective words of Yahweh is at the core of the psalmist's message.

The effective word. The spoken (and written) word plays an important role in the biblical context. In Bible times, the spoken word was thought to bear a greater significance than in our contemporary setting. Words were thought in some way to be "effective." That is, properly chosen and configured, they were thought to accomplish what they said. For this reason, on the one hand, curses were not simply cathartic venting of inner rage, as we might think of them today, but were dangerous attempts to injure another that had to be countered or protected against by some ritual or amulet. On the other hand, words spoken in blessing were not just expressions of wishful thinking but really added to the well-being and health of the one blessed.

This understanding of the effective word heightens the ironic tension in the story of Balaam (Num. 22–24), who, called by Balak, king of Moab, to curse the Israelites, was prevented by God from doing anything but blessing them. The sages also understood the importance of carefully choosing one's words in order to avoid the negative consequences unleashed by foolish or malicious speech (see, e.g., Prov. 15:1–2, 4, 28; 17:27; 18:6–8, 21; 19:5; 20:20; 21:23, 28).

The spoken word was also intended to reflect the inner character of the upright person. That is why malicious and deceptive speech, as in our psalm, was so destructive to human society and so contrary to the intention of Yahweh. Humans look at the outside and can be misled by cunning and deceitful words. God, however, sees the heart and judges the discrepancies that arise between word and spirit.[9] The "double heart" of which Psalm 12:2 speaks is the result of personal disintegration and gives rise to an equally disintegrated double talk. Thus, the sages consider integrity between heart and speech an essential foundation of wisdom: "My son, if your heart is wise, then my heart will be glad; my inmost being will rejoice when your lips speak what is right" (Prov. 23:15–16).

The kind of integrity the sages enjoin is ultimately reflected in the essential character of Yahweh. Yahweh is the only one who is truly transparent—not in the sense that all his motives are clearly understood, but in that there is no ultimate contradiction in him between thought and speech, word and

9. A number of proverbs condemn malicious and deceptive speech (see, e.g., Prov. 26:22–26).

action. In this role of the true and upright God, who can discern and judge any lack of integrity in humans, Yahweh is referred to on at least two occasions as the "God of truth" (Ps. 31:5; Isa. 65:16), and his distinction from deceptive humans is emphasized in Balaam's ironic preface to his second oracle, "God is not a man, that he should lie" (Num. 23:19).

To choose the way of the lie and deception is to reject decidedly the way of Yahweh and to opt instead for self-power and self-interest. This is essentially the pattern that disrupted and distorted the divine image humans were created to reflect from the beginning. The serpent's subtle distortion of the prohibition against eating the fruit of the tree—insinuating suspect motives to God (Gen. 3:4–5)—and the humans' use of self-deceiving words to justify their disobedience and to shift blame elsewhere (3:6, 10–13) are examples of the powerfully deceptive character of the separation *within* humans of truth and the lie, thought and motivation, self-will and the desire to justify one's chosen path to others—even to God. "All a man's ways seem innocent to him, but motives are weighed by the LORD" (Prov. 16:2; cf. 21:2).

Humans are not good judges of their own best interests because they are divided within themselves. "There is a way that seems right to a man, but in the end it leads to death" (Prov. 14:12; 16:25). God, by contrast, sees clearly human motives (16:2) and their most propitious path. "For a man's ways are in full view of the LORD, and he examines all his paths" (5:21).

While human words—whether truth or lie, blessing or curse—have an effect, they are not ultimately effective. I mean that while human words can help or hinder, wound or heal, they are ultimately unable to counter the creative and sustaining word of Yahweh. In the conversation between humans and God, Yahweh always has the last word. Job acknowledges this when he cries out, "Though one wished to dispute with [God], he could not answer him one time out of a thousand. . . . How then can I dispute with him? How can I find words to argue with him?" (Job 9:3, 14). Thus, the psalmist is confident that Yahweh will arise to protect the weak "from those who malign them" (Ps. 12:5). The boasters' words ultimately deceive only themselves. God is not misled or impressed but sits in judgment over this offense of truth, justice, equity, and the order of his creation.

Divine transparency. The "flawless" character of Yahweh's word, refined like the finest silver seven times, is more than an illustration of the ultimate effectiveness of the divine word. The point of the psalm is not just that God will have the last word. The purity of the divine word also illumines a certain *transparency* in God. What Yahweh says reveals his true character. God does not dissemble or deceive. He says what he means, and he does what he says. Therefore, not only can one trust Yahweh; one can also understand who God is by attending to his words. That is to say, God's word is more than powerful and effective—bringing to being and sustaining the whole creation from the beginning—it also reveals who he is.

In this matter of divine revelation, the fact of divine transparency—of integrity and truth in the divine utterance, so to speak—is of extreme significance. It is this fact that allows us truly to know him through his words. It is almost incredible when you think of it that God, the creator of the universe, condescends to make himself known to humans through the revealing Word of God, so that his glory in all its magnificence is truly displayed through the whole earth (Ps. 8). It is even more astounding that when the spoken word of revelation failed to win the hearts of a self-focused people, God sent a different kind of Word to carry the conversation through to its completion. It is Christ who embodies, in the most concentrated and all-consuming form, both the revealing and effective character of the divine word. It is in Christ that we see God face to face, knowing even as we are known. It is in Christ that the power of sin is broken and life once again overpowers death.

If the divine Word—whether spoken, written in Scripture, or incarnate in Jesus Christ—is the chosen means through which God has made and continues to make himself known to us, then truth and transparency (integrity) are at the root of who God is. If we, then, are to fulfill our role to reflect the image of the creator, then we too must reflect the same kind of "flawless" purity of speech as the psalmist ascribes to Yahweh. Thus, the description of Yahweh's pure word is not just a condemnation of the evil perpetrators of "double speak" in this psalm or anywhere in life. It is also a challenge to those of us who hunger and thirst after righteousness to speak with a unified heart that reflects our creator.

HOW DO WE bring this discussion down to the earth of our own time and place? I imagine that most of you (even those who are not the least bit imaginative) could provide me with a long list of ways that words are used deceptively and manipulatively for self-interest. It is usually easier to point to others in this regard. In what follows, therefore, I will try to lead us from looking outward at others to looking inward at our own lack of integrity in word and action.

A world of deceptive words. We are all aware of the misleading nature of advertising. Cigarettes promise implicitly to make you sophisticated, adult, independent, or "cool." No one mentions that they can kill you as well. The whole point of advertising is to exploit the ambiguity of language to create an attractive presence while downplaying or ignoring negative aspects of a product and staying on the legal side of speech. To be "legal," however, is not the same as being "straightforward" or "honest." Words don't always mean what they seem. "Pure" juice, for example, must only contain a small percentage of actual juice to pass the legal grade. The result of advertising is often persuasion by implication or innuendo or by highly selective, partial communication, with significant omissions. The standard Latin rejoinder or disclaimer *caveat emptor* ("let the buyer beware") demonstrates just how ancient this problem is.

Our legal system all too often exploits language. What is legal is not necessarily what is just or equitable. Laws supply a modicum of order to limit the chaos of human relationships. Certainly in our day much of the legal profession has become not defenders of justice but exploiters of what is legal. The obscure, technical language (legalese) employed to make legal definitions and documents as precise as possible has been proved time and again to be full of "loopholes"—situations not covered or left ambiguous. Much of the legal profession thrives on the mastery of this language and its ambiguities in order to exploit loopholes for their clients' (and their own) gain.

Of course, the Old Testament knows many examples of such legal maneuvering and shading of the truth—as well as outright lying. One drastic example is the story of Naboth's vineyard, in which Queen Jezebel corrupted the legal system in order to falsely accuse Naboth of a capital crime so that his execution would free up a prime vineyard he had previously refused to sell to King Ahab (1 Kings 21). This is another form of exploitation—to use plausible language to cloak falsehood so that truth is rendered powerless.

Advertising and law (and I should add politics here!) are only examples of the more obvious contexts in which language is exploited and twisted for gain. There are also those willing to cross the line of legality. Most recently I have heard on a number of occasions of companies who hid a request for "telephone service" in the small print on the bottom of what appeared to be a simple prize sweepstakes form. Those who signed up thought they were entering a sweepstakes to win a trip, or a vehicle, or some other attractive prize. Imagine their surprise when months later charges began to appear on their telephone bill for services they had unknowingly authorized by signing the sweepstakes form!

But not only do we live in a society that lies to us, but we lie to ourselves as well. Our streets are filled with people who refuse to know themselves or to accept the truth about the lives they have chosen to lead. One characteristic of compulsive personalities is an almost unlimited ability to deny the truth.

- I have not chosen wrongly, but I am a victim forced into this lifestyle by a hurtful society, parent, spouse, and so on.

- What I am doing is not so bad—especially when you compare it to what others are doing.
- If you had a spouse (job, problem) like mine, you would drink (smoke dope, act out sexually, etc.) too.
- No one is getting hurt here—we are all consenting adults.
- Drugs don't hurt me; they increase my acuity, enhance my performance, and help me cope with stress.

Most of us know someone who uses these types of blatant distortions to justify a path of destructive behavior. Perhaps we are there ourselves.

There are other, more subtle lies that we tell ourselves—punching holes in our lives and allowing the spirit of joy to drain inevitably away.

- I am not worth much.
- I can't do anything of value.
- I am unlovable.
- I am incompetent.
- I have to control my life and others to see that my needs are met.

These are all attitudes based on a series of foundational lies: Human beings have no worth other than what they make for themselves; that worth is dependent on how others value us; we are responsible to earn the acceptance of others. This kind of evaluation of self-worth leads to a life of deceit and manipulation. If my value is based on what others perceive about me, then I must always present an acceptable outside. Since I cannot always do that, then I must become better and better about hiding the truth about myself from those whose opinion I value and whose relationship I fear to lose.

This way of the lie is a set-up for failure. No matter how careful I am to separate the real me from the public me, I do not have enough energy to keep the wall in place at all times. The truth will get out—often with devastating results. Even if the carefully constructed façade never crumbles, the inner toll on integrity and the ability to share intimately with another is immense. We live life knowing it is all a lie. People only care for me because they don't know the real me. If they did, they would reject me, because the real me is unacceptable.

Often we try to downplay the importance of words. "Words are cheap," we say. "The end justifies the means, and it is okay to manipulate words (and people) for a good end." But there is always a price for deceptive words. The foremost is a loss of personal integrity and transparency. Deceptive, manipulative words build a barrier to being truly known—it creates a loss of intimacy. If we are not one within ourselves, how can we ever hope to fulfill the creation hope to become one with others? The Tower of Babel story in

Genesis 11 speaks of how God confused the rebellious humans' languages so that they no longer understood each other. As a result, they were unable to work together and were ultimately scattered across the face of the earth. In a similar way, loss of correspondence between inner reality and the spoken word leads to confusion and misunderstanding, with ultimate personal and societal fragmentation.

Finally, our own inability to speak the truth within ourselves or outside ourselves hampers our ability to know God truly. God reveals himself freely to us in his Word. He makes himself known as he really is. He desires intimate relationship with us. But as we already know, intimacy is a two-way street; it takes honesty, openness, and vulnerability on both sides. A parent unknowingly opens an ambiguously addressed e-mail message and discovers a note to a daughter or son indicating a ongoing struggle the child is experiencing (say with sex, or drugs, or alcohol). The parent may now know the child's inner secret, but there is no intimacy at all. Until the two (parent and child) are able to acknowledge the reality and communicate to one another openly about the circumstance, knowledge only builds a barrier to intimate relationship.

The same is true of our relationship to God. God wants to know us intimately. True, he omnisciently knows all there is to know about us. But he desires an open, vulnerable association with us in which we open our lives fully to him as he has opened himself to us in Christ's making himself vulnerable to misunderstanding, rejection, suffering, and even death. He wants us to know as we are known. More than just knowing him—as powerful as that is—God wants us to know ourselves and each other with that same vulnerability and transparency that led Christ to the cross in our behalf.

Psalm 13

FOR THE DIRECTOR of music. A psalm of David.

1 How long, O LORD? Will you forget me forever?
How long will you hide your face from me?
2 How long must I wrestle with my thoughts
and every day have sorrow in my heart?
How long will my enemy triumph over me?

3 Look on me and answer, O LORD my God.
Give light to my eyes, or I will sleep in death;
4 my enemy will say, "I have overcome him,"
and my foes will rejoice when I fall.

5 But I trust in your unfailing love;
my heart rejoices in your salvation.
6 I will sing to the LORD,
for he has been good to me.

PSALM 13 IS a brief poem of only six verses. But those verses plumb the depths of near despair before concluding with an unexpected confession of trust and confidence. The psalm is a lament characterized at the beginning by a series of four plaintive questions. Structurally the psalm falls into three stanzas, each composed of two verses: the initial series of questions (vv. 1–2), a plea for deliverance from approaching death (vv. 3–4), and a concluding expression of confidence and trust (vv. 5–6).

The Heading (13:0)

NO NEW TERMS appear in the psalm heading. The psalm is referred to "the director of music"[1] and described as a "psalm of David."[2]

1. See comments on the heading of Ps. 4.
2. See comments on the heading of Ps. 3.

Questioning God (13:1–2)

QUESTIONING GOD IS an ancient tradition in Israel. In Genesis 4, Cain responds to God's concern for the whereabouts of his brother, Abel, with a question of his own: "Am I my brother's keeper?" (4:9). Abram answers God's promise of great reward with the poignant question, "What can you give me since I remain childless and the one who will inherit my estate is Eliezer of Damascus?" (15:2). The greatest example of a questioner outside the psalms is Job, whose questions begin in Job 3 and are not quelled until God appears in chapter 38.

The questions at issue here are not simple requests for knowledge but express deep human misgivings about the character and activity of God and their effect on human life. This kind of questioning—flung in the face of God, as it were—is a product of and a response to the experience of the hiddenness of God, who refuses to appear and act as humans expect and desire.[3] Rather than information, these questions seek divine presence and action on the questioner's behalf. Such questions reveal a faith seeking to understand in the midst of painful experiences that shake the very foundation of believing.

How long? The four lines with which our psalm begins are each introduced with the same interrogative phrase, *ʿad ʾanah* (lit., "until where?"), translated as "How long?"[4] These questions are addressed directly to God, as the vocative use of Yahweh and the second-person verbs connected with God in verse 1 show. The questions express the sense that God has withdrawn from the psalmist's present experience and has hidden himself. God's failure to appear and act leads to a fear of abandonment—that Yahweh has forgotten the psalmist. Such divine forgetfulness threatens to undo him, because to be known and remembered by God is to be in the relationship of blessing (as Ps. 1:6 clearly suggests).[5]

The experience of God's absence has inward emotional effects on the psalmist. His sense of abandonment leads to inward "wrestling" with thoughts (13:2—"I take counsel within myself") and daily "sorrow" (*yagon*, "torment")

---

3. See the discussion of "Divine Hiddenness" in "The Theology of the Psalms" in vol. 2 of this commentary.

4. Several Heb. interrogative phrases are translated "How long?" in the psalms. These include: *ʿad ʾanah* ("until where?" cf. 13:1–3; 62:3); *ʿad mah* ("until what?" cf. 4:2; 74:9; 79:5; 89:46); *ʿad matay* ("until when?" cf. 6:3; 74:10; 80:4; 82:2; 90:13; 94:3); and *kamma* ("like/as what?" cf. 35:17; 119:84). All of these are understood as introducing questions of divine hiddenness and delay; thus, they are rendered as temporally concerned rather than questions of spatial or relational interest.

5. In this light, the promise in 1 Cor. 13:12 that we will "know as we are known" is a promise of being established in the protective care and blessing of God. To the contrary, the pointed rejection of the faithless at the end time—"I never knew you. Away from me, you evildoers!" (Matt. 7:23) is an ominous consignment to destruction.

in his heart. There are also external consequences since the psalmist—no longer convinced or certain of Yahweh's active presence in his behalf—wonders whether the enemy can be held at bay much longer (13:2).

Plea for Deliverance from Approaching Death (13:3–4)

THE PSALMIST'S SENSE of desperation is voiced in a series of pleas to God that expand in almost inexorable fashion:

> Look! Answer me, O Yahweh my God.
> Cause my eyes to shine[6] lest I sleep in death,
> Lest my enemy say, "I have overcome him!"
> (Lest) my oppressor rejoice that I am shaken.[7]

Without the hoped-for divine intervention, the psalmist can only anticipate rapid decline, defeat, and death.

Trust and Confidence (13:5–6)

THIS PSALM CONCLUDES with an unanticipated expression of trust and confidence. As unexpected as such a turn might seem in any individual lament psalm, it is actually more common than one would think for laments to turn to confidence at the end.[8] In this case the psalmist's trust is based on an understanding of the character of God as well as the psalmist's previous experience of goodness from Yahweh's hand.

Your unfailing love. The psalmist finds the grounds for hope in Yahweh's *ḥesed*—translated here as "unfailing love." The term has more of "loyalty" or "enduring allegiance" about it than the emotions we normally associate with "love." The context is one of commitment to a covenantal agreement between parties—perhaps a king and a vassal. The covenant partner who demonstrates enduring loyalty to the covenant relationship and faithfully fulfills his covenant obligations, not because he is forced to but because of a sense of commitment to the relationship—such a person is said to do *ḥesed* ("unfailing [covenant] love").

---

6. The picture is of the gradual glazing over of the eyes as death approaches and the life force begins to ebb. See also comments on Ps. 38:10.

7. This translation is mine. Rather than the NIV's "when I fall," the Heb. *ʾmwṭ* ("be made to stumble, totter, wobble") preserves the image of the imminent collapse of a tottering, stumbling person (because of the effects of illness, or physical attack?) or of a wobbling wall rendered unstable by an earthquake. The psalmist is only too aware of the stability provided by the sustaining presence of Yahweh—a concrete presence that the wicked in their arrogance and independence deny (cf. Pss. 10:6; 16:8; 30:6; 60:2; 62:6).

8. Consult the section on "Lament" in the introduction; also "The Laments" at the end of Ps. 3.

In the case of Yahweh and Israel, Yahweh has freely chosen to enter into a covenant relationship with Israel to be her God while she is his people. Yahweh chooses this relationship, not because of Israel's greatness but simply because he loves Israel and desires to fulfill faithfully the promises made to the patriarchs (Deut. 7:7–8). That is *ḥesed*. Even when Israel fails in her commitment to her covenant obligations (as in the monarchy before the Exile), her God remains faithful. Though he may punish Israel for her sins, he remains true to his purpose for her. That is why Israel can continue to hope for restoration in the face of the loss and destruction of the Exile. That too is why the psalmist can continue to hope for personal restoration even as death is at the door. Therefore, his heart can rejoice in Yahweh's anticipated salvation (Ps. 13:5), and he can sing songs concerning Yahweh's goodness (13:6).[9]

THE ABSENCE OF GOD. The human experience of God is fraught with paradox. God is totally other than humans, but he makes himself known within their world of experience. God is good and all-powerful, but he allows evil to happen. God is always present and knows all, but we often experience him as absent and inactive.

The biblical view of God mirrors that of human experience. Alongside texts of God's entry into the human world through creation, theophany, and wondrous works of deliverance, we discover testimonies to his hiddenness. A sense of divine abandonment is particularly well etched in Job. Job—whom we know from the beginning to be righteous—experiences loss after loss: possessions, family, health, and even reputation. His agonized search to find God in the mess his life has become and his desire to understand how divine presence and righteous suffering can possibly occupy the same place are met only by divine silence. For Job, God's purposes remain hidden while experience seems to contradict the traditional understanding of God's essential nature as incompatible with evil and relentlessly good.

Although God ultimately breaks his silence in the later third of the book, Job's experience of divine abandonment permeates the first thirty-seven chapters and resonates too clearly with human experience. Even when God does appear at the end of Job, his statements do little to answer the repeated question of Psalm 13: "How long?" Ecclesiastes is another book that agrees

9. Perhaps this is one of the "new songs" that respond to new acts of divine deliverance. See comments on 33:3.

that the purposes of God in the world of human experience are impossible to know. Experience shows that good and evil happen without regard for the recipient's righteousness.

Within the Psalter, divine hiddenness is a dominant theme in the first two-thirds. Both lament and thanksgiving acknowledge the reality of God's absence.[10] These psalms continued to play a key role in Israel's worship during the exilic and postexilic periods. The loss of the land and kingdom were significant blows to the identity of the Diaspora Jews, situations that needed to be squared with the understanding of God as powerful, present, and in control.

The arrangement of psalms of lament in the Psalter provides a literately structured response to the plaintive cries of lament: "How long?" Books 4 and 5 (Pss. 90–150) point the exilic community to a new source of hope: Yahweh is coming to judge the earth and to rule directly over humanity. Like Job, the faithful will hold on in the interim until Yahweh reveals himself and his Messiah in power.[11]

Christ too experienced abandonment by God. His suffering was particularly severe on the cross—because of the sheer pain of it, the loss of his disciple band, and the obvious failure of any broad-based human response to his earthly ministry. Jesus expressed his greatest pain in the words of Psalm 22:1: *ʾeli ʾeli lamah ʿazabtani* ("My God, my God, why have you forsaken me?").[12] Jesus' example shows that it is not wrong to experience the abandonment of God, nor is such an experience necessarily the result of personal sin. Often when one is most firmly in the center of God's purpose and will are attacks most severe and God seems most distant.

Like his Old Testament counterparts in the Psalter, Jesus stayed the course, choosing to remain faithful to the purposes of God throughout his suffering and death. We know that he was steeped in the Old Testament literature and used it to understand and articulate the character and purpose of his own ministry. He must have known the Psalter well—it is the most frequently quoted Old Testament book in the New Testament—and Psalm 22 in particular.[13] He must have drawn much strength, courage, and understanding from such texts.

---

10. See the section on "Lament" and "Thanksgiving" in the introduction.

11. See the section on "The Shape of the Psalter" in vol. 2 of this commentary.

12. Jesus' speech, reported in Mark 15:34, is Aramaic: *eloi eloi lama sabachthani*.

13. In the "Index of Quotations" provided in the Aland-Black-Metzger-Wikgren *Greek New Testament* (New York: American Bible Society, 1966), the Psalms are quoted over 400 times, and Ps. 22 appears twenty-four times, outstripped only by Ps. 110 with twenty-five quotations. The 400 plus citations occupy approximately ten columns in the "Index"—equaled only by Isaiah (ten columns) and almost twice as many as any other book.

Diaspora Judaism came to understand the pain of the Exile as redemptive suffering. We tend to consider the nation of Israel/Judah as a monolithic whole. We insist that the Exile was visited on the *whole* nation because of its sins. We forget that within this nation just prior to the destruction and captivity, there were many faithful followers of Yahweh who had not forsaken the covenant, who did not worship other gods, who worshiped Yahweh in spiritual truth and not empty rituals, and who upheld justice and compassion.[14] Yet these righteous ones found themselves torn from their land and taken away into exile along with their covenant-breaking neighbors! Where was the God of the righteous then?

It is true that a sort of community solidarity permeates the people of God in the Old Testament that runs counter to our Western sense of fierce independence. When Achan sinned (Josh. 7:1–11), we read that "Israel has sinned; they have violated my covenant"; thus, the entire nation suffered the consequent defeat at Ai. When David angered Yahweh by taking a census of Israel (2 Sam. 24; cf. 1 Chron. 21), the whole nation suffered the punishment of a plague.

So, in the aftermath of the Exile, when the Deuteronomic historians of Israel explained the loss of the kingdom and the land as the result of the sin of the nation, the answer must have been less than personally satisfying for those faithful followers of Yahweh, who found themselves suffering the consequences of national wickedness through no fault of their own.[15]

Throughout the centuries since, the convention arose of understanding the continuing suffering of Diaspora Judaism as redemptive, vicarious suffering by the faithful remnant for the sins of the whole community. This draws on Isaiah's four Servant Songs (Isa. 42:1–6[9]; 49:1–6; 50:4–11; 52:13–53:12), in which Yahweh's servant (variously identified as Israel, a faithful remnant, the prophet, or some future servant/messiah) suffers innocently for the sins of the people.[16]

---

14. When Jezebel threatens the life of Elijah the prophet because of the defeat and execution of the 400 prophets of Baal on Mount Carmel (1 Kings 18), he flees to Horeb to consult with Yahweh. When Elijah complains that he is the only faithful follower of Yahweh left in the whole land, Yahweh responds by revealing 7,000 persons who have not forsaken Yahweh to worship Baal (19:18). The later prophets also make it clear that within the sinful nation, there yet exists a "faithful remnant," loyal to Yahweh and his covenant.

15. A good example here is found in Dan. 9, where Daniel, an exemplary youth living in exile, turns his heart to pray for the forgiveness of the sins of his people and their ultimate restoration by God. The earlier narratives of the book describe how Daniel and his three friends (Shadrach, Meshach, and Abednego) suffer in exile although they remain radically faithful, even at the risk of torture and death.

16. The tendency in Christian circles to read these Servant Songs as predictions of the events in the life and death of Jesus obscures the original thrust of these passages to identify the servant with Israel (or the remnant) and thereby call them into a redemptive relationship to the whole nation and indeed the whole world.

In this regard the acute and tragic suffering of the European Jewish community under the Nazi program of exploitation and extermination during World War II has come to be called "the Holocaust," a reference to the completely burned sin offering offered yearly on the Day of Atonement for the sins of the nation. In this way the suffering and death of six and a half million Jews and their survivors has been interpreted as vicarious and redemptive sacrifice by the innocent for the sins of the world. This reinterpretation of the suffering of the faithful follows the lead of Job and Ecclesiastes in affirming that the absence of God is not a sign of his lack of power or concern. Nor is God's delay in coming a necessary indication of the wickedness of those who suffer in the interim. God is still God and worthy of worship and allegiance despite the inability of humans to comprehend human suffering fully.

RESPONDING TO A **sense of God's absence.** Many in today's world live out of a sense of abandonment. The existential philosopher Jean-Paul Sartre calls this sense of loss of the divine the "condemnation of freedom," because without God everything is permissible and nothing has any true significance or purpose. As a result, each human is "forlorn, because neither within him nor without does he find anything to cling to."[17]

There are several possible responses to this sense of abandonment. Some assume that God has withdrawn or hidden himself because *he doesn't want to associate with me*. This attitude assumes that *I am the root cause* of God's apparent absence. Many today struggle with such feelings of unworthiness, believing that abandonment by parents or even active abuse is the result of some wrong within themselves rather than brokenness within the parents or abusers. The psalmist of Psalm 13 talks of wrestling with thoughts and experiencing daily sorrow in the heart. Such inner turmoil often grows out of self-condemnation and can lead to anger, paralysis, and despair.

Others respond to the hiddenness of God by denying his existence altogether. If God is out of the picture, then humans are left entirely to their own devices. The only avenue available is to rely on self-power and self-control. When God is removed, we are left to make our own way in the world.

The third possible response is that mirrored in Psalm 13: to "wait" on God as an acknowledgment of our own powerlessness and dependence on

17. Sartre, *Existentialism* (New York: Philosophical Library, 1947), 25–27. See also the discussion in the Contemporary Significance section for Ps. 19.

him. This need not be silent suffering, for both Job and our psalmist fill the void with their questions and appeals to God. And that is as it should be. The continuing conversation, even though one-sided, affirms the relationship—just as a father estranged from his son (or vice versa) continues to write letters even when no response is received.

The lessons the Psalter offers regarding divine absence include the following.

- The experience of divine abandonment is real and painful and is rightfully brought to God in laments and questions. God is not offended by our honest questions or even our heated complaints. Both confirm our desire for relationship and our faith that all is not as it should be.
- Divine absence need not be seen as the result of some failing within ourselves. Even the righteous suffer, and indeed suffering without divine intervention can be understood as one of the hallmarks of faithful living.
- Suffering the absence of God can be redemptive as others are brought to realize through our experience that the painful realities of life do not deny the existence, power, and compassionate concern of our God.
- God is worth holding on to faithfully even when we do not experience him as present.

Regaining a sense of God's presence. Finally, we must consider some practical responses to the question: "When God is absent, how do we regain a sense of his presence?" I will offer three from personal experience.

Voicing our complaint. Whenever we experience God as absent, we must vocalize our experience openly and honestly. I am not speaking here of talking incessantly to our family and friends about how distant we feel removed from God or complaining about how alone we feel. I mean instead that we should talk openly and honestly *to God* about our sense of abandonment. I don't know what form this conversation may take for you, but personally I have found two avenues for carrying my own complaint directly to God.

One is through writing poetry that reflects the inward turmoil and anguish I am feeling. This is for me an effective way of opening up my spiritual and emotional wound to the sight of God. Journaling is a similar concrete way of expressing inner reflection in a less poetic form.

The other way I have conversed with an absent creator is through audible, spoken words. This is best pursued for me when I am alone—perhaps in the car or on a walk in the woods. I don't want to be observed by those who might fear I am becoming unhinged. But actually speaking the words I think and feel has a way of getting out of my head and objectifying them. It also gives God a certain presence as the one to whom I am speaking—walking alongside me or sitting in the passenger seat of my car. By voicing my complaints—really voicing them—I acknowledge a continuing connection with God where none is immediately apparent.

Getting out of ourselves. Another way to begin to restore a sense of God's presence is to turn my attention away from myself to others. When I focus on myself, I tend to increase my sense of isolation and aloneness. But when I turn my eyes and hands to others in compassionate caring and service, I bring them into my world and break my self-imposed silence. It is amazing how seeking the welfare of others opens me to the gracious action of God in their lives and ultimately in my own.

In the recent film *Life Is Beautiful*, a Jewish father who is taken to a Nazi concentration camp with his five- or six-year-old son chooses to carry on an elaborate fiction to protect his son from the desperate reality of their situation. They are in a competition to win an awesome prize and must be willing to suffer the constraints of the camp to ensure their chance of winning. The father mugs, spins tales, coerces the rest of the inmates into his conspiracy, and ultimately struts comically to his death in order to preserve the hope of his young son. Along the way the father communicates to his son, his wife, and other inmates that regardless of the ugly spin that humanity can put on it at times, life as God intends it is beautiful, and that beauty must be held on to even in life's darkest moments.

In the community of faith. Finally, when God is absent for me, it is possible to catch a glimpse of him—or at least a testimony of his presence—when I stand within the community of faith. When I sit or stand shoulder to shoulder with my fellow Christians in worship, I can hear songs of praise to God even when my own heart is silent. Communion with God's people is a down payment on the promise with which the psalmist concludes Psalm 13: "I trust in your unfailing love; my heart rejoices in your salvation. I will sing to the LORD, for he has been good to me."

Psalm 14

FOR THE DIRECTOR of music. Of David.

1 The fool says in his heart,
"There is no God."
They are corrupt, their deeds are vile;
there is no one who does good.

2 The LORD looks down from heaven
on the sons of men
to see if there are any who understand,
any who seek God.
3 All have turned aside,
they have together become corrupt;
there is no one who does good,
not even one.

4 Will evildoers never learn—
those who devour my people as men eat bread
and who do not call on the LORD?
5 There they are, overwhelmed with dread,
for God is present in the company of the righteous.
6 You evildoers frustrate the plans of the poor,
but the LORD is their refuge.

7 Oh, that salvation for Israel would come out of Zion!
When the LORD restores the fortunes of his people,
let Jacob rejoice and Israel be glad!

THE PSALM IS an extended meditation on the folly of the wicked, who deny the effective existence of God and expend their energies in corrupt lives dedicated to personal gain through the oppression of the poor. Although essentially a wisdom meditation and instruction, the psalm has been converted into a communal lament and plea for the deliverance of Israel from exile by the addition of a final verse (14:7). The poem is essentially composed of two stanzas of three verses each—the first describing the foolishness of evildoers (14:1–3) and the second giving the divine response about judgment on the wicked (14:4–6); it concludes with a communal hope for restoration from exile (14:7).

Psalm 14 is reduplicated with a few significant variations as Psalm 53. The latter psalm stands within what is called the Elohistic Psalter and affords us the opportunity to observe the distinctive preference in the later collection for the divine name *ʾelohim* over the Tetragrammaton Yahweh (see the comments on Ps. 53 for a discussion of this issue).

The Heading (14:0)

THE PSALM HEADING contains no new terms, being referred "to the director of music"[1] and attributed to David.[2] In the heading to Psalm 53, in addition to the designations mentioned above, the psalm is further described as a *maśkil* of David,[3] and a tune or harp-tuning for accompaniment (Heb. *ʿal maḥalat*) is also suggested.[4]

The Folly of the Evildoers (14:1–3)

THE FOOLISH WICKED are led astray by their arrogant assumption that there is no limit to their personal power and control. This is expressed in verse 1 by the quotation placed in the mouth of the "fool" (*nabal*):[5] "There is no God" (*ʾen ʾelohim*).[6] By taking this counsel "in his heart," the fool is deliberating in the center of moral and ethical decision-making. The point is that the corrupt action that follows is not the result of ignorance but of a knowing commitment to a lifestyle based on the false conclusion that God has no effective place in human life. Folly is then for the Israelites not simply uninformed stupidity but a moral decision for evil, which can, therefore, be equated with wickedness.

They are corrupt. Rejection of God leads to actions founded in self-interest and disregard for moral values. The corruption of the wicked has influence beyond them. The Hebrew for "corrupt" (*šḥt*) means "spoil or ruin (something); act ruinously" as well as the NIV's translation. The rebellion of the wicked infects for the worse the world in which they live.

---

1. See comments on the heading of Ps. 4.

2. See comments on the heading of Ps. 3.

3. See the discussion of *maśkil* in the comments on the heading of Ps. 32.

4. See comments on the heading of Ps. 53. The term *ʿal maḥalat* also occurs in the heading of Ps. 88.

5. This term appears frequently in Old Testament wisdom literature as the contrasting counterpoint to the "wise person" or "sage" (*ḥakam*).

6. Here, as elsewhere in the psalms, the psalmist is careful to use the more generic designation *ʾelohim* in the speech of unbelievers (whether Israelite or non-Israelite).

Their deeds are vile. As the NIV translates verse 1b, the two phrases describe the inner and outer effects of the fool's rebellious lifestyle. As corruption pollutes the inner world of the wicked, their deeds extend that infection to those outside. The second phrase (*tʿb*) has the basic meaning of "act abominably" and stresses the effects of the perpetrator's actions on others.

The LORD looks down. In a scene reminiscent of the introduction to the Flood narrative (Gen. 6:5–7, 11–13) and the Tower of Babel episode (11:5–7), God surveys the creation from his heavenly vantage point. Humans are so corrupt and have so corrupted their environment that there is no longer any "redeeming social value" expressed by their existence. The corruption described in Genesis 6:11–12 uses the same Hebrew verb as in our text, making the connection with Psalm 14 even more persuasive. These thematic and verbal links leave the reader of Psalm 14 with the clear implication that divine judgment is the only appropriate response to the completely corrupt lives of the foolish.

There is no one who does good. This summary phrase bears out the interpretation supplied by recourse to the Genesis texts. As with Lot and his family at Sodom (Gen. 18–19), so here God can find no righteous person to shield the wicked from divine judgment. Everyone has "turned aside." Clearly this must represent a hyperbolic emphasis on the complete bankruptcy of the fool's moral state; otherwise the narrator and those who agree would have to include themselves in this absolute decree of judgment. The phrase brackets the description of the divine scrutiny of the wicked both at the beginning (Ps. 14:2a) and in an emphatic form (which adds "not even one") at the end (14:3b).

Judgment on the Wicked (14:4–6)

THE FOOLISH WICKED are identified as "evildoers" (*poʿale ʾawen* ["those who do trouble, iniquity"]). Since *ʾawen* sometimes describes idolatry (cf. Hos. 12:12), "evildoers" may refer to those who worship idols, and the use of the verb *swr* ("turn aside") in 14:3 could be understood as turning from Yahweh to other gods (cf. Deut. 28:14, where *swr* is also used). The more general sense of those who do moral evil (= "wicked") seems more likely here, however.

Will evildoers never learn? Not only are the wicked enmeshed in evil deeds, but they lack a foundational knowledge of Yahweh that would allow them to relate to him properly. Rather than resistance to education and discipline (as the NIV's "learn" would imply), the wicked demonstrate a lack of experiential knowledge (Heb. *haloʾ yadeʿu* ["Don't they know?"]) that grows out of their rejection of Yahweh. Once again, this is no simple ignorance but an act of rebellious rejection of relationship with God. To "call on the LORD" (14:4) is another way of describing a relationship of interaction with him. It can mean appealing to God for help or invoking his presence in worship. The evildoers' refusal to call on Yahweh is equivalent to their failure to "seek God" in 14:2 and is characteristic of their life stance of denying his existence in 14:1.

They devour my people like bread. The effects of the evildoers' rebellion bleed out beyond their own relationship with Yahweh to infect their environment and those who share it. Their evil deeds are characterized as casual acts of self-focused consumption that nevertheless have ultimate consequences for those consumed. Eating bread is the basic act of self-nourishment and sustenance. It is engaged in constantly, day by day, and casually—with hardly any reflection. It is with an equally casual attitude that these evildoers "consume" God's people, described in 14:6 as the "poor."[7] Devouring the people is an image familiar from the prophet Micah (Mic. 3:3), who condemns Israel's ruling elite for their cruel exploitation of the people they should be protecting.

Overwhelmed with dread. Verse 5 exhibits some difficulties of interpretation. (1) It is not immediately clear in the Hebrew who it is that is "overwhelmed with dread" (*pḥd* ["trembling with fear/dread"])—the oppressed people or the oppressing wicked. The second half of the verse describes the cause of trembling as the presence of Yahweh with the righteous. This seems to suggest it is the evildoers who are fearful.[8]

(2) It is also unclear whether the occasion for fear is in the past (the verb is a perfect), present, or future. The arrogant attitude of the wicked seems to counter the possibility of a present visitation of Yahweh to strike fear into their hearts. Most commentators take the description as a hopeful envisioning of a future judgment that will give the wicked the knowledge they currently lack: "God is present in the company of the righteous" (14:5).[9]

The plans of the poor. The deeds of the wicked, once unleashed, bring shame on the plans of the poor. The wicked are clearly those who exercise societal power, and their godless perspective heaps ridicule on the oppressed poor, who seek to maintain a faithful relationship to Yahweh. Rather than being undermined, however, the poor discover what the evildoers can never know: that Yahweh is the refuge of the faithful.[10]

---

7. For a discussion of various terms for the oppressed, see comments on Ps. 10:11–18.

8. See the apt comments in Craigie, *Psalms 1–50*, 145, on Dahood's contention that this means "they have formed a cabal" (referring to the evildoers).

9. Cf. Craigie, *Psalms 1–50*, 148; James L. Mays, *Psalms* (Interpretation; Louisville, Ky.: John Knox, 1994), 83; Kraus, *Psalms 1–59*, 222–23; T. K. Cheyne, *The Book of Psalms or The Praises of Israel* (New York: Thomas Whittaker, 1895), 35; Derek Kidner, *Psalms*, 2 vols. (TOTC; Downers Grove, Ill.: InterVarsity, 1973), 1:79; J. W. Rogerson and J. W. McKay, *Psalms 1–50* (Cambridge Bible Commentary; Cambridge: Cambridge Univ. Press, 1977), 62.

10. See discussion of the theme of refuge in the comments on Ps. 5:11–12.

Hope for Restoration from Exile (14:7)

THE PSALM CONCLUDES with a previously unanticipated expansion of the perspective of the narrator to include the experience of the exilic community. From preoccupation with the nature and deeds of the wicked, the psalm turns decisively at the end to a communal expression of the desire for restoration. The idiomatic expression in the Hebrew is *mi yitten miṣṣiyyon yešuʿat yiśraʾel* ("who will give from Zion the salvation of Israel?"). This phrase expresses the ardent desire of the speaker that something take place—something like: "O that someone would give. . . ." This person is clearly Yahweh, who acts in Israel's behalf.

Out of Zion. Zion plays an important historical and theological role in the identity of the people of Israel. Geographically the place is identified with the hill on which the city of Jerusalem stands, although the exact location within the city is disputed. Some locate it in the city of David—the prominent rocky ridge extending south of the Temple Mount to the confluence of the Kidron and Tyropoeon valleys near the Pool of Siloam. Others identify Zion with the Temple Mount itself.[11]

Zion is associated with the establishment of Jerusalem as the capital of David's kingdom and as the center of the divine rule of Yahweh through the agency of the Davidic kings.[12] Zion is considered the "dwelling" of Yahweh,[13] his "throne,"[14] and the seat of his authority.[15] Yahweh rules from Zion,[16] blesses from Zion,[17] shines forth from Zion,[18] and sends help/salvation from Zion.[19] Yahweh loves Zion,[20] has chosen her for his own,[21] will have compassion on her,[22] and will ultimately restore/save her.[23]

Restores the fortunes of his people. The ardent desire of the community for salvation already knows the confidence of realization. Verse 7b is a temporal phrase normally translated "when [the LORD] restores. . . ." There is no

---

11. See the article on "Zion" in *ISBE*², 4:1198–1200.

12. See the discussion of Zion in the section on "The Theology of the Psalms" in vol. 2 of this commentary.

13. Cf. Pss. 74:2; 76:2; 132:13; 135:21.

14. Cf. Pss. 9:11; 84:7; 110:2.

15. Cf. Pss. 99:2; 110:2; 149:2.

16. Ps. 110:2.

17. Pss. 128:5; 133:3; 134:3.

18. Ps. 50:2.

19. Pss. 14:7; 20:2; 53:6.

20. Ps. 87:2.

21. Pss. 78:68; 132:13.

22. Ps. 102:13.

23. Pss. 69:35; 87:5; 102:16.

"if" here, only a certain future anticipated as coming. The NIV's translation of the Hebrew word *šebut* as "fortunes" chooses a less common rendering of the term. The more usual meaning attached is "captivity," as in Ps. 126:1—*bešub yhwh ʾet šebit ṣiyyon* ("when Yahweh brought back the captives to Zion")—indicates.[24] The most likely rendering of the phrase is "when Yahweh overturns the captivity of his people"—a clear reference to the "captivity" experienced in the Babylonian exile.

If this is indeed the most appropriate rendering, then this last verse likely reflects an adaptation of an earlier psalm so it could continue speaking to the exilic community of the faithful, who can no longer look to the established monarchy or temple worship associated with Zion as the symbol of unity and hope. Hence, the psalm in its latest form hopes for the *future restoration* of Zion and all it symbolizes as the source of divine salvation for the people of God. When this restoration is realized, then Jacob and Israel will rejoice and be glad.

DIVINE SCRUTINY. Psalm 14 describes Yahweh's observation of human activity on the earth, using a Hebrew idiom that emphasizes God's distance from the human sphere. Yahweh "looks down from heaven ... to see." The verb "looks down" (*šqp*) suggests looking down from a height, as the connection with "heaven" confirms.

This picture illustrates the keen awareness often expressed in the Old Testament in general and the psalms in particular of a transcendent God who remains hidden or absent from the world of human suffering. The image is often invoked in circumstances of great suffering and oppression, when God seems particularly distant from his people. The poet of Lamentation 3:50 vows to produce tears without end "until the LORD looks down [*šqp*] from heaven and sees." In Psalm 102:19–20 "the LORD looked down [*šqp*] from his sanctuary on high, from heaven he viewed [*nbṭ*] the earth, to hear the groans of the prisoners." Similarly the psalmist in Psalm 80:14, still smarting from the destruction of the Exile, calls on Yahweh to "look down [*nbṭ*] from heaven and see" the desperate plight of his people.[25]

Similar images of divine scrutiny of human activity from the heavens are found in the Tower of Babel narrative (Gen. 11:1–9), where Yahweh "came

---

24. The unknown word *šibat* should be emended to *šebit*, a cognate form of *šebut* ("captivity").

25. Although the verb *šqp* does not appear here, the use of *miššamayim* ("from the heavens") affirms the same perspective of divine scrutiny from above.

down to see"[26] the puny tower that the humans conceived as rising majestically into the heavens. In the Sodom and Gomorrah episode, Yahweh tells Abraham "I will go down and see" if the actual sin of these two infamous cities is as bad as the report he has received (Gen. 18:21).[27] In these last two instances God comes down not because of the suffering of the innocent but because of the sin and corruption of the wicked. The two go hand in hand, however—human evil and the suffering of the innocent. Where the one is, the other cannot be far behind.

Psalm 14 brings these both together. The absolute corruption of powerful humans (14:2–3) is matched by their exploitation of the poor (14:4). Thus, divine scrutiny becomes the opportunity for God to display both sides of his holy character: his implacable incompatibility with sin and evil and his relentless goodness toward those who fear him.[28]

Although God may often be experienced as absent, the psalmist affirms in this imaginative description that God nevertheless remains vigilant and aware of what goes on in the human world. Yahweh is not a God who slumbers (cf. 121:3–4), nor is he ignorant of what humans do. While the wicked fools may act as if "there is no God," the psalmist knows better. Yahweh's seeming inaction is not a result of any lack of knowledge. He is fully aware of what humans do and is prepared to act in behalf of his faithful ones.

The Old Testament offers a variety of interpretations of divine absence and delay, including: (1) permitting the faithful to be tested by their circumstances; (2) pointing out that the world in and of itself is not a reliable place on which one can depend; (3) leaving ample opportunity for the wicked either to repent or to cook their goose thoroughly. Note that God does not act impetuously against frivolous misdemeanors but arrays himself adamantly against well-established and entrenched evil—for which no excuse is available.

God of the poor and oppressed. Psalm 14 leaves no doubt where Yahweh's sympathies lie. In any conflict between oppressed and oppressor, God is always on the side of the righteous poor. Any delay in his acting cannot be the result of a lack of concern for justice, equity, and compassion. As the psalmist notes, "God is present in the company of the righteous. . . . The

---

26. Again, although the verb here is *yrd* ("descend, go down") rather than *šqp*, the perspective of divine scrutiny from a distance is identical.

27. The Flood narrative includes, of course, another example of divine scrutiny of human evil and consequent judgment. While God is described as "seeing" human wickedness and corruption in Gen. 6:5, 12, there is no mention of his "looking down from the heavens" in this case.

28. See comments on Yahweh's essential character as "holy" (*qadoš*) at Ps. 5:7–8.

LORD is their refuge" (14:5–6).[29] Therefore only "fools" would presume to think they can oppress the poor with impunity.

God's presence with the poor is no guarantee they will never experience suffering. But the psalm does provide comfort that they are on God's side as he is on theirs and that their suffering cannot be explained away (as Job's friends try to do) as the necessary consequence of unconfessed sin. The righteous do suffer. In fact, their suffering can even be seen as a measure of their righteousness, as Jesus triumphantly proclaims at the conclusion of the Beatitudes: "Blessed are you when people insult you, persecute you and falsely say all kinds of evil against you *because of me*. Rejoice and be glad, because great is your reward in heaven, for in the same way they persecuted the prophets who were before you" (Matt. 5:11–12, italics added).

Even though the righteous may understand their suffering as a badge of honor that places them in the company of God himself, this does not make their suffering any less objectionable to the oppressed poor or to their God. The oppression of the righteous is a sign that God's intended creation order has been corrupted and *his* plans "frustrated" as much as those of the poor (Ps. 14:6). That the poor can turn to the refuge of Yahweh in the midst of their oppression is a source of great comfort and joy. That they *must* (because of the oppressive acts of others) turn to Yahweh for protection is no joyful event, but it serves as the basis of divine judgment on the oppressors.

IDENTIFICATION WITH THE WICKED. What immediately comes to your mind as you read Psalm 14:1–6? Just who are the "evildoers" to whom God is so adamantly opposed here? If you are like me, you will probably admit that your initial reaction is to point to all those indications of evil deeds and persons *out there*, in the world outside yourself. That was how I first read these condemning words—they were directed to all the opponents of God who wreak havoc on the poor, powerless, defenseless, and righteous of the world. In the final analysis, I tend to identify myself with those oppressed ones with whom God is said to be present and a refuge (14:5–6).

We would probably not be all wrong to understand this psalm and our world in this way. There is much evil out there in the world—war, genocide,

29. See comments on the important theme of Yahweh as refuge at Ps. 5:11–12. The idea that Yahweh is *present* in the midst of the oppressed poor is similar to the more positive New Testament affirmation that "whatever you did for one of the least of these brothers of mine, you did for me" (Matt. 25:40), or, "For where two or three come together in my name, there am I with them" (18:20).

abuse, oppression, exploitation—that needs to be noted for what it is and confronted actively by all those who call the name of Christ. But what came to impress me more as I read this psalm over and over is the inclusive language employed throughout to describe those confronted by God. "There is *no one* who does good . . . *all* have turned aside, they have *together* become corrupt; there is *no one* who does good, *not even one*" (14:1d, 3, italics added). Those whom Yahweh scrutinizes from his heavenly vantage point are the "sons of men" (*bene ʾadam*), the most general and diffuse term for "human beings."

While the psalmist does recognize a small group of oppressed righteous whom God protects (14:5–6), the emphasis is clearly on the failure of humanity-at-large to fulfill the creation intention to be God's image.[30] The effect of this condemnation of all humans is akin to Paul's declaration that "all have sinned and fall short of the glory of God" (Rom. 3:23).[31] The judgment is inclusive, including you and me as well as those at whom we are wont to point the finger.

What strikes me, then, is the solidarity in which I stand with those I label "evildoers." This gives me pause—*should* give us pause—when I rush to take my place among the righteous and wait for God to bring down his judgment on my enemies. This failure of understanding is particularly acute, I believe, among those of us Christians who find ourselves blessed by happenstance of birth and circumstances to be part of the rich "first world." When we hurry to class ourselves with the righteous poor, we often fail to acknowledge the many ways our abundant lifestyle is founded on the exploitation of the "two-thirds" world who have so little.

Friends who have traveled in leadership positions among Christian communities of Africa, South America, and the Far East have confirmed my own conversations with Palestinian Christian friends on the West Bank. Inevitably these conversations lead to deep amazement on the part of these "two-thirds" world Christians about how those of us who have been given so much can still be so unaware and unconcerned for the needs and pains of those who live out their lives under oppressive governments and experience continuous poverty and exploitation.

These are certainly questions Jesus would want us to acknowledge and to seriously meditate upon. They are not easy questions with simplistic answers. But if we look carefully, we will have to admit that in many ways we are more closely related to the oppressive powerful than the exploited poor.

30. See the comments on the "image of God" in Ps. 8.

31. Cf. Rom. 3:9–12, where this very psalm passage is quoted in support of Paul's contention that Jew and Gentile alike stand under the judgment of God for sin. Similar sentiments are found in Ps. 143:2 and Eccl. 7:20.

This means that when we fail to acknowledge the suffering of the rest of our world, when we seek to preserve our own "favored status" at the expense of those who are less powerful than we are, when we simply try not to think too hard about how our abundance is related to the poverty of others, then the judging words of Psalm 14 are directed to us, not just those faithless, foolish, evildoers "out there."

Psalm 15

A PSALM OF David.

[1] LORD, who may dwell in your sanctuary?
Who may live on your holy hill?

[2] He whose walk is blameless
and who does what is righteous,
who speaks the truth from his heart
[3] and has no slander on his tongue,
who does his neighbor no wrong
and casts no slur on his fellowman,
[4] who despises a vile man
but honors those who fear the LORD,
who keeps his oath
even when it hurts,
[5] who lends his money without usury
and does not accept a bribe against the innocent.

He who does these things
will never be shaken.

THIS BRIEF POEM of only five verses provides instruction to those who desire to enter the presence of Yahweh in his sanctuary. It may well represent a type of priestly teaching presented to those approaching the Temple Mount in Jerusalem to encourage them to prepare physically and spiritually for their access to the "Holy Place" for worship.

Because of its brevity, the psalm has little obvious structure. It begins with a theme-setting question directed to Yahweh (15:1), continues with a series of eleven answers to the question describing the character and conduct of those who need not fear to enter God's presence (15:2–5b), and concludes with a summary statement of confidence (15:5c). While this psalm does not exhibit much connection with the vocabulary of the wisdom tradition, it does share the concern to teach the way of righteousness and demonstrates similarities with certain negative confession texts known from the wisdom literature of other ancient Near Eastern cultures.[1]

The Heading (15:0)

THE HEADING TO Psalm 15 simply describes this psalm as a "psalm of David."[2]

The Thematic Question (15:1)

THE OPENING QUESTION—twice repeated in slightly variant and expanding parallel format—initiates the theme of "dwelling" with Yahweh that provides the backdrop for the whole psalm. We have encountered this theme in 5:4, where the statement takes on a negative tone: "You are not a God who takes pleasure in evil; with you the wicked cannot dwell." Our psalm stands almost as a response to this earlier verse when it asks, "Who then *may* dwell with Yahweh?" Psalm 5 goes on to describe those wicked who are excluded from the divine presence while Psalm 15 takes pains to describe the character of those who can hope for admittance.

The idea of "dwelling" (*gwr*)[3] in the "sanctuary" (*ᵓohel* ["tent"]) of Yahweh is one that is repeated, especially in the first three books of the Psalter (Pss. 3–89). Beginning with 5:4, the theme appears nine times in eight psalms (5:4; 15:1; 23:6; 27:4; 39:12; 61:4; 65:4; 84:4, 10)—all within the first three books. Outside these books the less specific idea of living in Yahweh's presence appears in only two psalms (102:28; 140:13).

A variety of Hebrew words are translated "dwell, live, reside" in the Old Testament. The verb *gwr*, used here, emphasizes the more temporary or impermanent nature of residence in the divine presence. The noun derived from this same root (*ger*) describes a "resident alien," who possesses no right of place but resides because of the gracious permission of the landowner. This is a potent and appropriate image for humans dwelling in the presence of God.

This emphasis on the tentative nature of human residence in God's presence is heightened by the use of the Hebrew term *ᵓohel* ("tent") to describe the divine abode. The NIV's "sanctuary" assumes the identification of this "tent" with the movable shrine or tabernacle that moved with the wandering Israelites in their journey from Mount Sinai to the Promised Land and continued to house

1. See Text 31, "The Negative Confession of Sin (Book of the Dead, Saying 125)," in Walter Beyerlin, *Near Eastern Religious Texts Relating to the Old Testament* (OTL; Philadelphia: Westminster, 1978), 63–67.

2. See comments on the heading of Ps. 3.

3. See the comments on Ps. 5:4.

the ark of the covenant until the temple was built during the time of Solomon. The connection of the tent with the "sanctuary" of Yahweh is probably apt in this context since it is in the shrine that Yahweh's presence is sought and most sensed. Also the parallel phrase in 15:1b bears this connection out since it refers to taking up temporary residence (Heb. *škn*)[4] on Yahweh's "holy hill"—an obvious reference to the Temple Mount in Jerusalem.

Eleven Answers (15:2–5b)

HAVING SET THE scene and theme of the psalm, the psalmist now supplies eleven answers to the foundational questions of 15:1. With one exception, these answers are grouped in parallel pairs that expand on common perceptions from different angles. In the case of 15:4b, as we will see, there is but a single answer expanded by a second "advancing" line.[5] The parallel groupings do not always conform to the verse divisions imposed on the earlier poem (cf. 15:2c–3a). Together these answers offer a comprehensive, if not exhaustive, response to the central concern of the psalm: What style of living prepares one for living in the presence of Yahweh?

Whose walk is blameless and who does what is righteous. The first set of answers uses affirming parallelism to expand on the foundational characteristic of the faithful that underlies all the rest. The one who hopes to dwell in the divine presence is the one who maintains a blameless walk and lives righteously. The Hebrew *tamim* ("whole, entire; free of blemish") does not imply sinless perfection but a way of life that is "whole" by virtue of consistent dedication to the "way of the LORD." Those so dedicated will be judged as having fulfilled the demands of "righteousness." The Hebrew here is a legal term describing the appropriate course of action in a particular circumstance. The one who "does what is righteous" is declared guiltless in that case, if not sinless in all cases.[6] The contrast between the one who "does what is righteous" (*poʿel ṣedeq*) in this verse and the "evildoers" (*poʿale ʾawen*) of 14:4 is certainly intentional.

Who speaks the truth . . . and has no slander. To maintain the requisite "blameless" character, one must be careful to "speak the truth" both "in the heart" and in external conversation to and about others. The comparison can be freely drawn with those in 12:2 who lie to their neighbor, whose "flattering lips speak with deception." To speak the truth in the heart is to be

4. The use of *škn* also supports the tentative nature of human residence with Yahweh. This term describes the temporary dwelling in tents characteristic of nomadic populations without right of land ownership and therefore no fixed abode.

5. See the discussion of "The Art of Hebrew Poetry" in the introduction.

6. See the commentary on Ps. 4:1–2.

so integrated that inner thought and audible speech agree—creating a sort of transparency of being and purpose that allows others to know that "what they see is what they get." This sort of inner truth and integrity makes one's words reliable so that it is unthinkable that the distortions of slander should proceed out of the mouth of such a person.[7]

Who does his neighbor no wrong and casts no slur. Integrity and truthfulness have implications not only for personal character but also for how one treats others. This next set of parallel lines extends the discussion to relationships with the "neighbor" (*rea*ᶜ; *re*ᶜ*eh* ["friend, companion, comrade"]) and "fellowman" (*qarob* ["close associate"]). The description moves from general to specific statements. The one who wants to enter God's presence "does his neighbor no wrong" in the broadest sense, and more specifically "casts no slur" (lit., "does not raise reproach") on a close associate.

Who despises a vile man but honors those who fear the LORD. The fourth set of parallel lines offers the seventh and eighth answers in the form of opposingly parallel statements. On the one hand, the one who wants to approach God claims an attitude toward evil that mirrors that of God himself. To "despise" one who is "vile" (*nim*ʾ*as* ["the one rejected by God"]) is to align oneself with the God who takes no pleasure in evil (5:4) and with whom the wicked cannot hope to dwell (Heb. *gwr*). By contrast the second line indicates that the one who wants to approach God responds to those who fear Yahweh by honoring them.

Who keeps his oath. In the final set of three answers, the one who seeks to enter the presence of God carries piety to the level of personal limitation and sacrifice. The first answer (15:4c) has no parallel line but is extended through advancing parallelism. Not only is the faithful one truthful, but such a one is also willing to keep an oath even if it means personal hurt or loss. The picture seems to be one in which the individual is forced by circumstances to make a vow or oath that may not be to his own self-interest (e.g., a king forced to accept the obligations as a vassal to a conquering monarch). If opportunity later offers itself for the individual to reject the oath taken under duress (e.g., if the former overlord dies or his sovereign power grows

7. The phrase translated by the NIV evidences textual difficulty, mostly occasioned by the lack of clarity regarding the Qal perfect verb from *rgl*, which occurs only here in the whole Old Testament. Elsewhere this verb (related to the word "foot") occurs most frequently in the Piel stem, where it has the sense of "travel about; roam around." Dahood (*Psalms*, 1:84) suggests "trip over the tongue" as a possible meaning, as does Craigie (*Psalms 1–50*, 149). Kraus (*Psalms 1–59*, 225) thinks more of making "the rounds as a slanderer." The question is whether the verb itself bears the notion of slander or if that is an implication of the context. Perhaps we can use a rendering like "roams around *on his tongue*"—implying an inappropriate use of the tongue for gossip or slander.

weak), it might be assumed that the vassal would be only too ready to refuse to fulfill the unwelcome requirements. The one who desires to dwell in Yahweh's presence, however, must take even such difficult promises seriously. He will not change his vow even if opportunity affords the chance.

Such a person will also not seek to gain financial advantage over those in need by loaning money for interest (15:5). Lending money or goods for interest was commonly practiced in the ancient Near East, and Mesopotamian law codes such as that of Hammurabi (ca. 1792–1750 B.C.) were careful to set limits on interest rates[8] and defined the obligations of both debtor and creditor. While it remains uncertain, it is thought that *nešek* ("interest"), as in our psalm, means interest on money, while another term (*marbit*) describes the payment of interest on grain and other goods. The Deuteronomic law prohibits exacting interest from fellow Israelites while permitting such transactions with foreigners (cf. Ex. 22:25; Lev. 25:35–38; Deut. 23:19–20). Whether the legal requirements were ever followed in Israel is unclear, but the legal statutes themselves and the prophetic condemnation of abusive practices make it certain that some Israelites did charge interest to their fellows. In some cases, those who were unable to pay sold themselves or their children into slavery to meet their debts (Lev. 25:39; Neh. 5:5).[9]

Finally, the faithful one is willing to forego personal gain through bribes in order to maintain the transparency and integrity spoken of in 15:2–3a. Bribery—the giving of a gift or reward in order to influence legal judgment—is condemned in biblical law (Ex. 23:8). The one who takes a bribe is cursed (Deut. 27:25) and placed in such evil company as the wicked sons of Eli (1 Sam. 8:3), who were destroyed by God. The prophets condemn bribery that places the "innocent" (*naqi*)[10] poor at a distinct disadvantage in a legal system where money "talks" (Isa. 1:23; 5:23; Mic. 3:11). The practice is also mentioned in wisdom literature, which recognizes the pragmatic effectiveness of a bribe in opening doors for the giver (Prov. 17:8; 21:14) while at the same time understanding the essential perversion of justice that the practice entails (17:23).

Confident Summation (15:5c)

AT THE END, the psalmist sums up this question-and-answer exchange with a confident assessment: Whoever emulates the lifestyle approved in these

8. Hammurabi's Code sets the rate for money transactions at 20 percent while goods could return as much as 33.3 percent. In other circumstances interest rates go as high as 50 percent.

9. For further information, consult the articles on "Interest" in *ISBE*², 2:860, and *EDB*, 525–26, as well as the article on "Usury" in *ISBE*², 4:959.

10. Cf. comments on Ps. 10:16–18.

verses need never fear being "shaken" (*mwṭ*), a verb that describes the kind of insecurity experienced when one's feet are on rough, untrustworthy ground (Pss. 38:16; 66:9; 121:3), or especially when a person, building, or even the earth is shaken by earthquake or landslide (46:2). Trust in Yahweh provides the righteous with eternal security from such slippery slopes or shaken foundations (cf. 21:7; 55:22; 112:6; 125:1). In the end the psalm cuts two ways: On the one hand, it encourages the faithful hearer to emulate the lifestyle described so as to qualify for the blessing of Yahweh's presence; on the other hand, the final word assures those who attend to the psalmist's words that their trust is not in vain but issues forth in the firm and secure foundation of life.

APPROACHING GOD. Israel took approaching God in worship seriously. Entering the holy precincts of the temple was not something to be done thoughtlessly—preparation of body, mind, and spirit was necessary. Psalm 15 describes a moment of deep reflection that probably happened every time a worshiper approached the gateways to the Temple Mount. The psalm says in essence: "This is a holy place. You are coming to meet with Yahweh here. God is holy and incompatible with sin. Take stock of your life and the consequences of entering the presence of the holy God."

Israel's seriousness in approaching God is reflected in the theology and architecture of temple worship that gradually limited access the closer one approached the holiness of God. You might think of this as a series of concentric circles. The outer circle represents the world at large—what we might call the "profane" world, including all the unbelieving nations and peoples. The most central circle is the Most Holy Place—the inner shrine of the Jerusalem temple, where Yahweh came in his holy essence to be present with Israel.

Moving from the outside in, one passes through a series of circles representing increasing holiness and decreasing access to that holiness. From the profane world one moves to the nation (and land) of Israel, a kingdom of priests and a holy nation to Yahweh. Next is the holy city, Jerusalem, the one place within the land of Israel where Yahweh has especially caused his holy Name to dwell. Once in Jerusalem, one proceeds to the Temple Mount—Yahweh's "holy hill"—marked off from the rest of the city by its elevation, walls, and the demand (reflected in Ps. 15) for special preparation before entering. The next circle is the temple precinct circumscribed by walls and divided into areas of limitation (the Court of the Gentiles; the

Court of the Women; the Court of the Israelite Men). Immediately about the temple itself only priests and their Levitical assistants could officiate. The temple proper was limited to priests alone, and only the *high* priest was allowed to enter the Most Holy Place to meet with Yahweh—once a year on the Day of Atonement.

While the theology of temple worship places its emphasis on the temple itself as the place where Yahweh is fully present, Israel does testify in her narratives of the desert wanderings, and especially in the Holiness Code, to an awareness of Yahweh's special presence among the people themselves. For this reason it was necessary for the Israelites within the camp and outside the Tent of Meeting to take precautions not to offend the holiness of Yahweh who was present in the camp (Num. 5:3). Often those rendered temporarily unclean were removed from the camp until they could be restored to cleanness (cf. Lev. 13:45–46; 14:1–3; Num. 5:1–4). Even the common elimination of human waste was to be accomplished outside the camp and carefully regulated: "For the LORD your God moves about in your camp to protect you and to deliver your enemies to you. Your camp must be holy, so that he will not see among you anything indecent and turn away from you" (Deut. 23:14).

Just how strictly ritual purity regulations such as these were followed during the monarchical period remains unclear. But the incorporation of these legal texts into the canon of the Old Testament is an indication that exilic and postexilic Israel had a strong sense that God was constantly present in day-to-day life even outside the temple precincts and that as a result life was to take on a different—holy—character because of that presence.

We know that preparation for temple worship included such elements as prayer, fasting, and ritual cleansings. Each of these outer acts was to signify the inward reality of "fear of the LORD"—the appropriate acknowledgment of one's sin and complete dependence on the gracious mercy of God. The threat implied by bringing together in worship the holiness of Yahweh and the sinfulness of humans is clearly demonstrated by Isaiah's response to his vision of Yahweh in the Jerusalem temple (Isa. 6:1–9). Isaiah knew that for a sinful person such as him to come into the glorious presence of the holy God ("Holy, holy, holy is the Lord Almighty") was to risk well-deserved destruction ("Woe to me! . . . I am ruined!").

Thus, worship for the Israelites was more than just praise of Yahweh. It also involved recognition of one's sinful nature and repentance for it, petition for divine deliverance from the suffering occasioned by the brokenness of the world, along with thanksgiving for God's enduring faithfulness to his world and his purposes for it. These consistent themes of worship are addressed throughout the psalms.

PREPARING FOR WORSHIP. How do you prepare to worship God? I am talking here particularly of corporate worship, where the community of faith comes together into the presence of God. I can still recall some of the "rituals" of preparation from my childhood. First, there was the Saturday night bath—whether I needed it or not—akin to the ritual cleansing worshipers performed as they approached the Temple Mount. On Sunday morning we got dressed up in special clothing (suit and tie for me from an early age), marking out that this was not a day like other days. Even the ride to church was usually more subdued than our typical automobile excursions—we kids were aware that on Sunday a different standard of behavior was in effect.

When we arrived at church, we entered the "sanctuary," where subdued lighting, symbolic decor, and hushed voices signaled we had left the sphere of normal activity and entered the place of worship. As we waited for the service to begin, organ music played in the background and conversation was hushed, allowing for meditative reflection and prayer. The shift from our "normal" world to the "worship" world was unmistakable; even as small children we knew we were in "the house of God," preparing to encounter him through worship.

The situation has changed a great deal since my childhood. For one thing I bathe more frequently now than I did as a child, so a Saturday night shower doesn't seem so special! For another I now live in Southern California rather than Southeast Texas—I am sure regional culture is part of the change. But in general our approach to worship has shifted over the last forty years. The services I attend now are much less formal than those of my childhood. There is no special dress these days; most wear "California Casual" (which a friend defines sarcastically as "a clean pair of shorts"). We no longer enter a "sanctuary," but many worship in a gymnasium or multipurpose room with folding chairs rather than pews. The emphasis is on familiarity—nothing odd or strange to prevent anyone from feeling comfortable. This also affects the way community is expressed: for example, through the encouragement of normal greeting and conversation as those arriving move about in active fellowship.

It is interesting to note, however, that Psalm 15 does not focus on these forms of physical preparation for and style of worship. Instead, it emphasizes the twin aspects of personal integrity and appropriate relationship to others. The one who is ready to enter God's presence is *not* the one who has taken the prescribed ritual precautions or who knows how to adopt the requisite outer attitudes of worship. Instead, the one who lives a life of transparency, where one's inner thought is reflected truly in speech and deed—such a one is ready to meet God.

The kind of worship envisioned here breaks out of the confines of temple and Sabbath to infect the rest of the week and all of life. It is aware of God's presence day by day and not just at prescribed moments of worship. Here life becomes a form of worship in which ordinary human activities and relationships are invested with uncommon sacramental character. Honest words become the embodiment of our prayer, and loving relationships exalt our God in praise.

Martin Buber, the Jewish theologian known for his loving and challenging exposition of the faith of Hasidic Judaism, speaks of a way of life in which common human acts are transformed into significant service to God by the intention to live that act as a part of God's restoration of creation.[11] May we see God present in all our common moments of life and enter his presence as we intentionally dedicate our thoughts, words, deeds, and relationships to the restoration of his kingdom.

---

11. Buber, *The Way of Man*, 36–41.

Psalm 16

A MIKTAM of David.

[1] Keep me safe, O God,
for in you I take refuge.

[2] I said to the LORD, "You are my Lord;
apart from you I have no good thing."
[3] As for the saints who are in the land,
they are the glorious ones in whom is all my delight.
[4] The sorrows of those will increase
who run after other gods.
I will not pour out their libations of blood
or take up their names on my lips.

[5] LORD, you have assigned me my portion and my cup;
you have made my lot secure.
[6] The boundary lines have fallen for me in pleasant places;
surely I have a delightful inheritance.
[7] I will praise the LORD, who counsels me;
even at night my heart instructs me.
[8] I have set the LORD always before me.
Because he is at my right hand,
I will not be shaken.

[9] Therefore my heart is glad and my tongue rejoices;
my body also will rest secure,
[10] because you will not abandon me to the grave,
nor will you let your Holy One see decay.
[11] You have made known to me the path of life;
you will fill me with joy in your presence,
with eternal pleasures at your right hand.

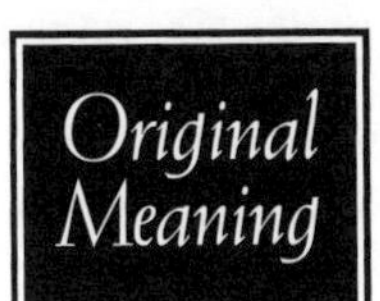

ALTHOUGH IT BEGINS with a brief petition ("Keep me safe, O God"), Psalm 16 is primarily a psalm of confident resting in God. Following the initial plea (16:1), the psalm continues with a profession of faith (16:2), a statement of the psalmist's refusal to worship other gods (16:3–4), a confident commitment to Yahweh (16:5–8), and (5) an expression of confidence and joy in Yahweh (16:9–11).

The Heading (16:0)

THE PSALM IS attributed to David and includes a new term, *miktam*, which appears elsewhere in the Psalter only in the five consecutive Davidic Psalms 56–60. Although a variety of explanations have been offered, the meaning of *miktam* remains obscure.[1] Probably the most influential suggestion is that of Mowinckel, who insists that the term is derived from a root meaning "cover" and should be understood as an "atonement psalm."[2] But such a designation seems out of sync with the content of this song, which has nothing to do with forgiveness of sin. More recently, several commentators have preferred an interpretation through the Targumim to an "inscribed stela."[3] The idea is that a standing stone inscribed with the content of this psalm would have been left in the temple as an offering gift. Since we have no evidence of such a practice in Israel, we should exercise caution in understanding the elusive meaning of the term.

The Initial Plea (16:1)

THE PSALM BEGINS with a petition for the protective care of Yahweh. As there is no real sense of distress exhibited in the rest of the psalm, the plea is more a desire for continued protection than for deliverance from specific trouble, as is borne out by the Hebrew word *šmr* ("watch, guard, keep"). Thus, the psalm has generally been understood as a psalm of confidence rather than a plea for deliverance. The psalmist realizes that the potential for suffering, attack, or failure is always present, and so he preemptively assumes a position of complete reliance on Yahweh as protective refuge.[4] This commitment picks up on the general description of the previous Psalm 15, especially the concluding promise that the one who emulates the character exhorted in the body of the psalm will enter God's presence and so "never be shaken" (15:5). The psalmist of Psalm 16 is laying claim to and accessing the refuge offered in that earlier psalm.

---

1. See the discussions in Kidner (*Psalms*, 1:38); Craigie (*Psalms 1–50*, 154); and Kraus (*Psalms 1–59*, 24–25) for further discussion.

2. Sigmund Mowinckel, *Offersang og Sangoffer* (Oslo: Aschehoug, 1951), 492.

3. See the discussion in Kraus (*Psalms 1–59*, 24) and Craigie (*Psalms 1–50*, 154).

4. See comments on Pss. 2:12 and 5:11–12. Kraus's assumption (*Psalms 1–59*, 235–36) of a context of fleeing to the sanctuary for refuge from one's pursuers seems overly specific, especially given the lack of a sense of threat and urgency in this psalm.

It is remarkable, although not unique, that the psalmist's words are here addressed to "God" (*ʾel*) rather than to Yahweh. The more generic form of address is occasionally used in the Psalter (cf. 17:6) and even dominates in the Elohistic Psalter collection,[5] but it is less than common outside that collection, particularly in the expression of petition.

Profession of Faith (16:2)

THE DEGREE OF variation represented by competing translations of verse 2 of this psalm indicates the extent of textual difficulty encountered in the Hebrew.[6] The issue concerns who is speaking in the confessional words of 16:2a (NIV "I said to the LORD"). The choice is between the first-person voice of the psalmist or the second-person voice of another. The choice made affects and is affected by the translation of verses 2–4, especially the understanding of who the "holy ones" (NIV "saints") and "glorious ones" are. In what follows, I will outline both viewpoints briefly, since the question is, in my opinion, almost impossible to resolve.

---

5. See discussion of the Elohistic Psalter in "The Shape of the Psalter" in vol. 2 of this commentary. The generic designation *ʾel* was employed as the name of the old high god of the Canaanite pantheon. By the time of the biblical period, El had become *deus otiosus*—the aged god who had in many senses been shouldered aside by the young god, Baal, who had arrived later in Canaan through the migration of Semitic peoples (Amorites) from the northeast by way of Mesopotamia at the beginning of the second millennium B.C. The character and activities of El and Baal are illuminated by the alphabetic cuneiform texts discovered at Ras Shamra, Syria, in the late 1920s. These texts reveal the existence of an extensive Canaanite kingdom known as Ugarit and provide our most thorough inside glance at Canaanite religious, political, and economic texts that have not been run through the negative sieve of biblical critique. For further information on Canaanite religion and the god El, consult P. C. Craigie and G. H. Wilson, "Religions of the Biblical World: Canaanite (Syria and Palestine)," *ISBE*[2], 4:95–101; F. M. Cross, *Canaanite Myth and Hebrew Epic* (Cambridge, Mass.: Harvard Univ. Press, 1973); M. H. Pope, *El in the Ugaritic Texts* (VTSup 2; Leiden: Brill, 1955).

6. The first difficulty is the verb translated in NIV as "I said." The Hebrew consonantal text is *ʾmrt*, which could be vocalized either as first common singular (*ʾamarti* ["*I* said"]); second masculine singular (*ʾamarta* ["*you* (masc.) said"]); or second feminine singular (*ʾamart* ["*you* (fem.) said"]). The base text of *BHS* (the standard critical edition of the Hebrew Bible) provides vowels for the consonantal text that fix the meaning of the word as the latter of these choices (second feminine singular). This choice is difficult to square with the larger context of the psalm, but it is even *more* difficult to explain away according to the normal principles of textual criticism, which assume that the more difficult reading is likely to be the earlier. It is almost impossible to explain why a scribe would alter an earlier first common singular form to reflect the second feminine singular.

Most translators have chosen to emend the base text of *BHS* to reflect the first common singular form found in many other Hebrew manuscripts and reflected in the translations of the Septuagint and the Syriac. A significant number of commentators, however, opt for the second *masculine* singular possibility.

I said to the LORD. If the first-person singular form is chosen, then verses 2–4 are the words of the psalmist and express an almost palpable sense of confidence in the protective care of Yahweh. Verse 2 becomes an extension of the confidence expressed in the last half of verse 1 and is an example of a towering profession of faith in Yahweh. Yahweh is the psalmist's "highest good" (lit. Heb., "[you are] my good—there is none above you").[7]

You said to the LORD. Craigie,[8] opting for the second masculine singular translation of the consonantal text ("you said"), discovers a balance between verse 2 "(you said) to Yahweh ..." and verse 3 "(you said) to the holy one ..." and takes even verse 2 as the statement of those who lack sufficient loyalty to remain faithful to Yahweh. Placing such opposite viewpoints in the mouth of a single speaker suggests a rather confused and syncretistic faith that offends the single-minded loyalty of the psalmist. In this view the "you" is speaking out of one side of his mouth by claiming loyalty to Yahweh, while at the same time proclaiming to the pagan deities his "delight" out of the other side. The harsh critique and disclaimer that follows in 16:4 then reflects the psalmist's absolute and personal rejection of such wishy-washy accommodation and stakes out his clear commitment to Yahweh alone.

Refusal to Worship Other Gods (16:3–4)

AS FOR THE SAINTS. Those who take verse 2 as the psalmist's direct address to Yahweh follow two different paths, depending on how they understand the word *qedošim* ("holy ones" in v. 3). Despite the fact that the normal Hebrew word designating the pious faithful is *ḥasidim*, many (including NIV at this point) take *qedošim* to mean "saints," understand verse 3 as a positive commendation of the "glorious faithful" in the land of Israel, and connect the verse with the preceding statements in 16:1–2. Other commentators, however, drawing on rather persuasive evidence that *qedošim* is a reference to the pagan Canaanite deities,[9] link verse 3 with the negative comments in the following verse 4. In this case, the expression of delight in the "holy ones" and "glorious ones" (16:3) becomes a negative example of false allegiance to

---

7. The pointing of the consonantal text as second feminine singular in *BHS* may reflect the contemporary understanding of the text. It may reflect an understanding of the word as referring to Israel speaking as the "bride" rather than the psalmist. The Targumim explain the feminine term as a reference to the psalmist's "soul" (*nepeš*), assuming that this feminine word has been omitted from the text. See the comments in F.-L. Hossfeld and E. Zenger, *Die Psalmen: Psalm 1–50* (Die Neue Echter Bibel; Würzburg: Echter Verlag, 1993), 110.

8. See Craigie, *Psalms 1–50*, 153–54, 157.

9. See the comments and bibliography cited in Dahood, *Psalms*, 1:87–88. The NJB and Craigie also follow this option, although without discussing the evidence.

pagan gods, which stands in sharp contrast with the proper commitment to Yahweh expressed in verse 1.

Sorrows . . . will increase. It is not clear whether the psalmist expresses a desire that those seeking other gods may suffer or is merely describing the consequences of their disloyalty to Yahweh.[10] Regardless, the opening statement of 16:4 disassociates the psalmist from the wrong-headed dependence on pagan deities characteristic of those described in 16:3. The worshipers of other deities are described as "running" urgently or excitedly after them. Their haste demonstrates their misguided need or joyous attachment to what is false. Rather than simply "sorrows," the verse describes the increase of their "painful sore spots," like bruises from blows or the sores of Job.

I will not. The loyalty of the psalmist to Yahweh is expressed by complete rejection of any involvement in the false worship of other gods. Two acts of worship are mentioned, both of which the psalmist eschews. (1) The first act is pouring out blood from the sacrificial victim as a sign of submission to a deity and as a plea for deliverance from divine wrath. The terms "libation" (a liquid poured out as an offering) or "oblation" (any act of worship or sacrifice) are often used to describe liquid offerings of wine or blood that were poured out as sacrifices to the deity. While Israelite priests did manipulate the blood of sacrificial offerings—putting some on the "horns" of the altar with their fingers, sprinkling the cover of the ark of the covenant in the Most Holy Place, and pouring the remainder at the "foot" of the altar—a distinction was always drawn between what Israel did with sacrificial blood and the "libations" of the pagans. The verb *nsk* ("pour out as a libation") is never used to describe Israel's manipulation of blood.

When Israelites "pour out" sacrificial blood, the word *špk* is used. Precisely what the difference in practice is remains unclear, but the prohibitions in the law (Deut. 12:16, 24; 15:23) against eating sacrificial blood suggests that the pagan blood libations involved ritual drinking of sacrificial blood—an act abhorrent to Israelites, who even followed rigid kosher rules in which blood was drained from meat used as food. It is thought that in Israelite religious practice, libations of wine may have substituted for blood libations.[11]

(2) In addition to rejecting the ritual pouring and drinking of sacrificial blood, the psalmist also indicates loyalty to Yahweh by refusing to "lift [take] up the names" of the pagan deities. The picture is one of the pagan worshiper lifting the libation cup to his lips to drink the sacrificial blood—here

---

10. The difference is between the Qal jussive (desire) and the Qal imperfect (consequence). For the verb in question, it is impossible to distinguish visually between these two forms.

11. Cf. Ex. 29:40; Lev. 23:13; Num. 15:5, 7, 10; 28:14; Hos. 9:4. See also the articles on "Libation" in *ISBE*[2], *EDB*, and *IDB*.

identified with the "names" of the pagan gods—in an act of allegiance and commitment to them. There is no evidence, however, that the phrase "lift up the name [of a deity]" is an idiom for a particular ritual act. Rather, it seems a simple reference to the frequent use of the divine name in prayer, ritual, and magical rites within the pagan cult.[12] The prohibition against abuse of the divine name Yahweh is an indication of the seriousness attached to the voicing of the divine name in Israel. Even the name Yahweh itself provides certain safeguards against such abuse.[13]

Commitment to Yahweh (16:5–8)

HAVING REJECTED ANY allegiance to pagan gods, the psalmist now recognizes Yahweh as "my portion" and "my cup." He lifts upon his lips the name of Yahweh rather than of other gods.

A delightful inheritance. The metaphor shifts and overlaps from the "portion" in the ritual "cup" to the "portion" (*ḥeleq*) of the land distributed by "lot" (*goral*) with "boundary lines" (*ḥabalim*), marking off the ancestral "inheritance" (*naḥalah*). These four terms are all associated with the distribution of the land to the tribes of Israel following the conquest of Canaan.[14]

The implication of the psalmist's memory of the land division is counter to the prevailing thought of some that the Canaanite deities were the powers at work in the fertility and prosperity of crops and herds by virtue of their long identification with the land. Many Israelites apparently turned to the established deities, thinking them more effective than Yahweh, who had only recently arrived as a deity. The psalmist, by contrast, knows that it is Yahweh who apportions the land to whom he will and who provides for its security and prosperity. Therefore, "lifting up the names" of the pagan deities is of no avail. The pleasant circumstances that surround the psalmist are the result of the blessing of Yahweh.

I will praise the LORD. As is usually the case, the NIV translates the Hebrew *ʾabarek* as "I will praise" rather than the more direct and literal "I will bless." While this interpretive move is nowhere (to my knowledge) explained, it may reflect a hesitancy to accept that humans are able to bless God, who is complete and ineffable in himself. The Hebrews, however, frequently speak of humans doing just that—blessing God. They had no difficulty in conceiving that humans could do more than simply express the awe and wonder of

12. See Hossfeld and Zenger, *Die Psalmen*, 111.

13. See the discussion of the divine name Yahweh in the Bridging Contexts section of Ps. 8.

14. See the discussion in Kraus, *Psalms 1–59*, 237–38. Cf. Josh. 13:23; 14:4; 15:13; 17:5; also Num. 18–21; 26:55; Deut. 4:21.

God's person and deeds that constitute the heart of praise. The Israelites understood that grateful humans desire to give to God something more than laudatory praise, and that is what blessing is all about—the desire to heap good and benefit on the one blessed.

We may debate theologically over whether these expressions of blessing have any effect on the complete, immutable God, but we cannot deny the ardent desire to give good to God that these expressions represent. To translate *brk* as "praise" deflects and obscures the issue and ultimately waters down the intent and purpose of the original Hebrew.

Who counsels me. In the preceding section, Yahweh was seen as the provider of the psalmist's secure and blessed environment. The boundaries of the psalmist's inheritance were assigned by God and fell in pleasant and delightful places (16:5–6). Now the psalmist acknowledges that Yahweh continues to provide counsel and instruction, remaining always at the psalmist's right hand. The verb "counsel" (*yʿṣ*) has the sense of "give advice, provide counsel." *The NIV Study Bible* notes an apt connection with the "way of life" that Yahweh makes known to the psalmist in 16:11. Again, though the psalmist's "heart"[15] is described as providing instruction (Heb. "chastise, discipline; teach, train") during the night, it is clear in the context that it is Yahweh who is shaping the psalmist in this way.

I have set the LORD always before me. Yahweh is counselor and instructor; now he is the psalmist's "guide." He is "before" the psalmist, leading in the secure path. The psalmist can trust this path because Yahweh is "at [his] right hand"—the place of support and protection (16:8b). As a result the psalmist is confident that "I will not be shaken" (16:8c)—the same kind of confidence expressed previously in 15:5. There an unshakable foundation was created by a pattern of life adhered to by those who would enter God's presence. Here in 16:8, the psalmist reaches this firm footing by acknowledging the continuous presence of Yahweh with the psalmist. The juxtaposition of these two psalms and these similar phrases and concerns leaves the impression that the narrator of Psalm 16 is claiming to have fulfilled the requirements set out in Psalm 15, so that Yahweh's presence is assured and the secure foundation of life attained.

Confidence and Joy in Yahweh (16:9–11)

MY HEART . . . my tongue. Because of that secure foundation, the psalmist sings out with a glad "heart" and a joyful "tongue." The NIV's reference to the

15. Actually, in the Heb., it is the psalmist's "kidneys" or "innermost recesses" (*kilyah/kilyot*) that do the instruction. Perhaps this is a description of some deep internal churning that provides insight and direction.

"tongue" interprets a difficult original context. The literal rendering of the Hebrew text is "my glory [*kebodi*] rejoices."[16] Some Hebrew manuscripts present a slightly different consonantal text, where the result would be *kebedi* ("my kidney") rejoices. The kidneys were considered inner indicators of human emotion and deliberation (cf. v. 7b). The NIV's translation relies on the Septuagint rendering.[17]

My body also will rest secure. If the NIV's use of the LXX is followed, the passage follows an instructive pattern. Inner joy (the heart) breaks forth into audible praise (the tongue), and emotional joy is grounded in the physical security of "the body" (16:9b). The phrase "rest secure" renders the Hebrew *yiškon labeṭaḥ* ("dwells in trust/safety").[18] The sense of security comes from the psalmist's "trust" in Yahweh, as becomes clear in the following verses.

The reason for the psalmist's feeling of security in Yahweh is introduced by the Hebrew particle *ki* ("because") in 16:10. The reasons given fall into three categories: (1) deliverance from death (16:10); (2) continued guidance (16:11a); and (3) the gift of divine presence (16:11b-c).

The psalmist is secure because Yahweh will not abandon him to "the grave." This is the third reference to *šeʾol*, the abode of the dead, in the Psalter.[19] To enter *šeʾol* was to depart from all forms of human existence and activity without hope of return. Although all humans eventually entered *šeʾol* through death, the only hope for escape from its clutches lay in the hands of Yahweh.

---

16. For a discussion of "glory, honor" in relation to human reputation and significance, see comments on 3:3–4.

17. The LXX reads *he glossa mou* ("my tongue").

18. The Heb.verb *škn* ("dwell") denotes a more temporary form of residence than the alternative verb *yšb* ("live/dwell"). The former is most frequently used to describe the nomadic life of tent-dwellers, who move about. The latter describes the contrasting settlement of those who farm the land and are therefore tied to it. Compare this verse with 4:8, where Yahweh is said to "make [the psalmist] dwell in safety." The verb employed in 4:8 is *yšb*, indicating more permanent residence (see comments on 4:8; also see G. H. Wilson, "ישׁב," *NIDOTTE*, 2:550–51.

19. The term occurs only sixteen times in the whole Psalter, with thirteen of these occurrences coming in the first three books (6:5; 9:17; 16:10; 18:5; 30:3; 31:17; 49:15; 49:14 [2x]; 55:15; 86:13; 88:3; 89:48). The remaining three (116:3; 139:8; 141:7) all are found in the fifth and final book. The Hebrew concept of the abode of the dead shares much with the general Mesopotamian view illustrated by such texts as "Descent of Ishtar to the Nether World," *ANETP*, 1:80–85. A place of dark, dusty, pale existence, *šeʾol* was considered the final resting place of *all* the dead, righteous and wicked, regardless of the moral evaluation of their life on earth. Like the Greek Hades, *šeʾol* was thought to lie underground toward the center of the earth, so that those who died went "down" to the "pit" to reach their final destination. Those who entered *šeʾol* did not return and so were barred from all human pursuits, including worship. See the articles on "Sheol" in *ISBE*², *IDB*, and *EDB*.

There is no clear belief in immortality or resurrection expressed here. Although Acts 2:25–31; 13:35–37 quotes this passage and interprets it to explain the resurrection of Jesus, the interpretation assumes that in its original context the psalm held out no hope of resurrection to David or other humans, only for the Davidic Messiah yet to come in Jesus. Thus, most likely the psalmist's immediate hope is for divine intervention to prevent death in his present circumstance.

Your Holy One. This phrase is variously understood, as the different translations attest. The underlying Hebrew word (*ḥasid* ["pious, devout, faithful one"]) describes the person who is consistently loyal in fulfilling the demands of the covenant—the practical equivalent of those "who fear the LORD." The translations vary in whether this term refers to the psalmist, who would thus be acknowledged as one of the pious believers, or to a more specific Holy One—the coming Messiah. The NIV's capitalization of the phrase indicates support for the latter interpretation—one that accords with the use of this passage in Acts 2 and 13 as part of an argument that understands the resurrection of Jesus as evidence that Jesus is *the* Holy One, since God did not abandon him to Sheol or allow him to "see decay."

However, most translations (rightly in my opinion) take the former tack and translate the phrase with some variation of "faithful servant" or "godly one." Thus, the use of the passage in Acts follows a more typological mode of interpretation, in which Jesus is understood as the ultimate "type" of faithful servant who was not abandoned by God to Sheol and decay.

Made known . . . the path of life. Besides being confident of divine deliverance from the threat of death, the psalmist is also assured of continued guidance on the right path. The revelation that is described could be a reference to the instruction provided by the preceding Psalm 15:5, which promises an unshakable place in the presence of God. Here the psalmist makes clear that the "path of life" is not some vague, impossible demand, but a path set out and made known by the God who is the psalmist's counselor and teacher (16:7)—who desires humans to know him and makes the path to his presence plain.

What the psalmist of Psalm 15 desired—to dwell in the presence of Yahweh (15:1)—the psalmist of Psalm 16 joyously anticipates as a promised reality. With death avoided and the way to God made clear, he can only rejoice at being filled (Heb. *śbᶜ* ["be satiated, satisfied"]) with joy and "eternal pleasures" in the divine presence.

The psalm concludes with a reference to the "right hand" of Yahweh (16:11) that balances the earlier mention of the "right hand" of the psalmist (16:8). As Yahweh stood always at the psalmist's right hand, present to guide and protect, so the psalmist is assured of being "forever" at the right hand of Yahweh to experience the benefits and blessings of his presence.

BOUNDARY LINES. The central imagery of Psalm 16 is drawn subtly from the narratives surrounding the apportionment of the land following the Conquest (cf. Josh. 12–24). This context provides understanding for the whole passage.

1. In the opening verses the psalmist denies any association with other gods, claiming to be bound exclusively to Yahweh (16:2–4; cf. Josh. 23:7–8, 15–16; 24:14–24).
2. In 16:5–6 the psalmist rejoices in the portion (*ḥeleq*)[20] assigned by lot (*goral*), whose boundary lines (*ḥabalim*)[21] shape the psalmist's inheritance (*naḥalah*).[22] The blessings of the land are firmly in mind (16:6).
3. The presence of Yahweh to counsel, instruct, and guide the psalmist dominates verses 7 and 8. Because of the divine presence the psalmist is unshakably confident (16:8; cf. Josh. 1:5; Pss. 15:5c; 25:12; 32:8).[23]
4. In verses 9 and 10 the psalmist uses language of security that is primarily associated with Israel's possession of the land (16:9b; cf. Deut. 33:12, where the same phrase—"rest secure"—is used as in Ps. 16:9b).

---

20. The term *ḥeleq* appears to intrude in this context between *menat* and *wekosi*. See Ps. 11:6, where the shorter phrase (without *ḥeleq*) appears with the meaning "[a scorching wind is] the portion of their cup [*menat kosam*]." The larger construction is an unusual example of a construct phrase in which a single construct noun (*menat*) is connected to *two* nouns in the absolute (*ḥelqi wekosi*). The use of the unusual form here allows the psalmist to refer to Yahweh both as the "portion of my allotment" (*menat ḥelqi*) and as the "portion of my cup" (*menat . . . kosi*).

Hosts were known to apportion drink into the cups of their guests. It is clear that they could show favor or displeasure by how liberally or meagerly they treated each guest. In Est. 1:7–8, King Xerxes was liberal with all his guests, ordering his servants to serve each guest as much royal wine as the guest wished. Elsewhere the "cup" (*kos*) can be a demonstration of divine salvation, anger, or wrath. It is possible that this may reflect a Near Eastern custom of kings dispensing judgment on those who had offended them by requiring them to drink a cup of poison. The insertion of *ḥeleq* in this context has the effect of shifting the imagery of divine favor from the *general* imagery of divine largess to the more specific notion of the apportionment of the land, where *ḥeleq* figures prominently.

21. The term *ḥebel* is normally employed in the singular form rather than the plural (*ḥabalim*), as here. The meaning is usually rendered "share"—possibly a smaller segment within a *ḥeleq* ("allotment"). Cf. Josh. 17:5 "allotment" of Manasseh. Cf. Ps. 78:55, where Yahweh "causes to fall for them an inheritance with a boundary" (*wayyapilem beḥebel naḥalah*).

22. All these terms are used extensively throughout the narratives of the allotment of the land among the tribes following the Conquest.

23. The presence of Yahweh with Israel to counsel, instruct, and guide is a clear emphasis of the Conquest and settlement narratives.

5. God shows the psalmist the path (or way) of life as opposed to the "way of death."[24] The necessity of choice between these two alternatives is characteristic of the exhortation of Deuteronomy, although there the emphasis is on "living long in the land" (cf. Deut. 4:40; 30:15–16).

Psalm 16 has taken these traditional images of hope in the land and subtly shifted them in order to spiritualize the land/inheritance imagery. Rather than focus on physical land, the psalmist attests that *Yahweh* is his "portion" and "cup." This shift reflects reinterpretation by the exilic or postexilic community, who no longer experience the land. It would be quite a statement to say that, even in exile, "the boundary lines have fallen for me in pleasant places; surely I have a delightful inheritance" (16:6). Such a declaration of faith is only possible for those who have learned by experience that the blessings of the presence of Yahweh are distinct from residence in the ancestral land and that the "path of life" can be walked even in a strange and alien land. Unlike the lamenting psalmist of Psalm 137 ("How can we sing the songs of the LORD while in a foreign land?" 137:4), the voice here acknowledges that wherever one finds the presence of Yahweh, "there is fullness of joy . . . pleasures forevermore" (lit. trans. of 16:11).

RESTING SECURE. WHERE do we find our security? Can we say along with exilic Israel that "the boundary lines have fallen for me in pleasant places"? As I drive around my neighborhood, I am surprised by the growing number of signs posted on residences announcing the installation of a protective "security system." Such signs are intended, of course, to forestall burglaries by announcing beforehand that any attempt at breaking in will set off an alarm and bring security forces to the scene. I have even noted "false" security cameras for sale in catalogs, intended to give the impression of security where none exists! In a society obsessed by the possession of "things," concern for security against robbery has grown to epidemic proportions.

And we live in a relatively secure society as a whole. While times and places within our society can be insecure, I would guess that most of you who

---

24. The phrase here uses the less common Hebrew word *ʾoraḥ* ("way, path") rather than the more usual *derek* ("way, path"). The phrase *ʾoraḥ ḥayyim* ("way of life") is found at Prov. 5:6a and 15:24, while the similar *ʾoraḥ leḥayyim* ("path *to* life") appears also in Prov. 10:17. The phrase *derek ḥayyim* appears in Prov. 6:23 and Jer. 21:8. The latter passage is closely related to the Deuteronomic exhortation, "I have set before you life and death . . . choose life" (Deut. 30:19). The Jeremiah passage reads "This is what the LORD says, See, I am setting before you the way [*derek*] of life [*ḥayyim*] and the way of death" (Jer. 21:8).

purchase and read this commentary do not live your lives in constant fear for your life and property. We may lock our doors regularly and even install a security system, but few of us have experienced the destabilizing effects of a burglary. Those among us who do are the exception rather than the rule.

This is certainly not the case in many areas of our world. Civil war, violent lawlessness, rampant poverty, debilitating drought, devastating earthquakes, and destructive storms are a way of life for much of the two-thirds world. And even parts of our own relatively secure society can experience the destabilizing effects of natural disaster—earthquake, tornado, hurricane, flooding, fire—and uncontrolled human evil (riots and destruction, terrorist bombings, public school shootings).[25] Is our security dependent on things or circumstances? Or, like the psalmist, is our assurance wholly in God, who is our portion and cup?

Psalm 16 testifies that even at the most unstable and threatening moments of our lives—when all other forms of security fail and leave us without defense—Yahweh is *still* our "portion and . . . cup." German theologian and pastor Dietrich Bonhoeffer experienced this overpowering presence of God while imprisoned and awaiting execution. Many of us have experienced the same assurance of divine presence even when the rest of our worlds are in turmoil: when our job is suddenly taken away at fifty-five years of age; when our husband dies and leaves us without protection in a hostile world; when our prodigal son leaves home to go to a foreign land. In these situations—and many others like them—Psalm 16 wants us to know that Yahweh is our "portion and . . . cup," our "delightful inheritance" with its boundary lines falling in "pleasant places."

In God's presence, the insecurities of life do not just disappear, but we are empowered in him to find the path of life *within* and *through* those painful times when we seem to approach the very gates of Sheol itself. In God's presence we discover there is "[fullness of] joy" and "eternal pleasures" (16:11).

In the original version of his hymn "Forth in Thy Name" based on Psalm 16:2, 8, and 11, Charles Wesley penned a song of commitment to find and respond to God's presence in everyday life and work. The hymn concludes with his summation of a life lived confidently in the awareness of God's presence now and forevermore (16:11) in the hopeful final phrase: "And closely walk with Thee to heaven." May we too discover and acknowledge God at our right hand—joy, pleasure, cup, and portion—as we journey through this life *with* him and *to* him.

---

25. During the process of editing this manuscript for publication, the World Trade Center Towers in New York City were blown up by terrorists (Sept. 11, 2001).

Psalm 17

A PRAYER OF David.

1 Hear, O LORD, my righteous plea;
listen to my cry.
Give ear to my prayer—
it does not rise from deceitful lips.
2 May my vindication come from you;
may your eyes see what is right.

3 Though you probe my heart and examine me at night,
though you test me, you will find nothing;
I have resolved that my mouth will not sin.
4 As for the deeds of men—
by the word of your lips
I have kept myself
from the ways of the violent.
5 My steps have held to your paths;
my feet have not slipped.

6 I call on you, O God, for you will answer me;
give ear to me and hear my prayer.
7 Show the wonder of your great love,
you who save by your right hand
those who take refuge in you from their foes.
8 Keep me as the apple of your eye;
hide me in the shadow of your wings
9 from the wicked who assail me,
from my mortal enemies who surround me.

10 They close up their callous hearts,
and their mouths speak with arrogance.
11 They have tracked me down, they now surround me,
with eyes alert, to throw me to the ground.
12 They are like a lion hungry for prey,
like a great lion crouching in cover.
13 Rise up, O LORD, confront them, bring them down;
rescue me from the wicked by your sword.
14 O LORD, by your hand save me from such men,
from men of this world whose reward is in this life.

You still the hunger of those you cherish;
their sons have plenty,
and they store up wealth for their children.
15 And I—in righteousness I will see your face;
when I awake, I will be satisfied with seeing
your likeness.

THE PSALM IS a plea for deliverance from the attacks of enemies who speak arrogantly against the narrator and seek to ravage like wild beasts. The psalmist claims innocence from all accusations and concludes with a confident anticipation of protection in the presence of God. Various phrases and themes link this psalm back to Psalms 15 and 16. All three seek the protective care of the divine presence (cf. 15:1; 16:8, 11; 17:15) and employ the same Hebrew verb *mwṭ* ("be shaken, slip"), a relatively rare word that elsewhere in the Psalter appears only in single separated psalms.[1] Likewise, the theme of taking "refuge" in Yahweh—using forms of the root *ḥsh*—binds this psalm with Psalms 16 and 18 (cf. 16:1; 17:7; 18:2, 31).[2]

The structure of the psalm is relatively simple: An initial plea is buttressed by the psalmist's claim of innocence (17:1–5); a second plea is supported by a description of the virulent attack by the enemies (17:6–12); and a final plea is accompanied by the psalmist's confidence in God's good intent for those whom he "cherishes" (17:13–15).

The Heading (17:0)

THE PSALM IS described as a "prayer of David" (*tepillah ledawid*), the first of five appearances of the term *tepillah* in the psalm headings (cf. the headings of Pss. 17; 86; 90; 102; 142).[3] Kraus considers the *tepillah* as a type of lament or

1. The Niphal verb occurs seventeen times in the whole Psalter (10:6; 13:4; 15:5; 16:8; 17:5; 21:7; 30:6; 46:5; 62:2, 6; 82:5; 93:1; 96:10; 104:5; 112:6; 125:1; 140:10).

2. Of the thirty-seven occurrences of verbal and nominal forms of the root *ḥsh* in the Psalter, only here does the root appear in three consecutive psalms. On three other occasions *two* consecutive psalms are affected (Pss. 36:7 and 37:40; 61:3, 4 and 62:7, 8; 141:8 and 142:5). These other groupings may be significant as well. See comments on these specific psalms.

3. The heading of Ps. 86 is identical to that of Ps. 17: *tepillah ledawid*. While Ps. 142 is also attributed to David, the initial designation of the composition is as a *maśkil*, with the term *tepillah* appearing only at the end of the heading following a historical note. Ps. 90 is

entreaty either for oneself or in intercession for others, a description supported by most occurrences of the term in the Psalter.[4]

Plea and Claim of Innocence (17:1–5)

FROM THE BEGINNING, Psalm 17 is couched in the voice of the innocent sufferer. The commentators are generally agreed that the difficult Hebrew phrase in 17:1a (*šimᶜah yhwh ṣedeq*, lit., "Hear, O Yahweh, what is right") ought to be interpreted in light of the parallel phrase in 17:1b to be the psalmist's plea that Yahweh pay attention to his cause or just plea.[5] The LXX renders the phrase *dikaiosyne mou* ("my righteousness"). As Dahood recognizes, the parallel with "my cry" (*rinnati*) indicates some audible cry to God for redress.[6] In verse 1 Yahweh is called to "heed" (*šimᶜah*) and "pay attention" (*haqšibah*) and "listen" (*haᵓazinah*), since the psalmist's declaration is without deceit.

My vindication. The psalmist is confident that when Yahweh hears his case and renders judgment, the psalmist will be found to have fulfilled the requirements of "justice" (*mišpaṭ*).[7] As a result he anticipates that complete "vindication" (NIV's translation of *mišpaṭ*) will proceed from Yahweh, because the righteous judge (cf. 7:11) will hear the case and "see what is right" (17:2b)

Examine me. The psalmist invites divine scrutiny and examination, confident there is no fault to be uncovered. The reference to testing "at night" has led some to suspect a context of "incubation" in the temple by one seeking refuge from false accusations.[8] The two outer images of probing and testing (Heb. *bḥn* and *ṣrp*) are drawn from the context of metallurgy and the refining of ore, while "examine" (*pqd*) has the sense of close inspection or scrutiny. The psalmist expects to survive this divine critique, for there is no

---

designated a "prayer of Moses" (*tepillah lemošeh*), while Ps. 102 is styled more generally as a "prayer of the afflicted one. . ." (*tepillah leᶜani. . .*). The plural form of the noun (*tepillot*) appears in the postscript concluding the second book of the Psalter: "This concludes the prayers of David son of Jesse" (72:20).

4. Kraus, *Psalms 1–59*, 26. The term is often coupled in the bodies of the psalms with an imperative verb of hearing, entreating divine attention to the psalmists' pleas (cf. 4:1; 17:1; 39:12; 54:2; 55:1; 61:1; 65:2; 84:8; 86:6; 102:1; 143:1).

5. *BHS* suggests a variety of possible emendations, including: *yhwh ṣaddiq* ["righteous Yahweh"], *ᵓel ṣaddiq* ["righteous God"], or *ᵓel ṣidqi* ["God of my right"]. In any case the sense seems to be a plea that Yahweh take the innocent suffering of the psalmist seriously.

6. Dahood, *Psalms*, 1:93.

7. For a discussion of the legal character of *mišpaṭ* and other related terms, see comments on Pss. 4:1–2; 7:6–9.

8. Cf. comments of Kraus, *Psalms 1–59*, 245–246; Rogerson and McKay, *Psalms 1–50*, 71 in this regard.

condemning evil to be found[9]; he has been careful "that my mouth will not sin" (17:3c).

The examination moves from the "heart" (17:3a) to the "mouth" (17:3c) to the outward actions (17:4). In all these the psalmist claims to have avoided sin—a sign of true integration, that thought, word, and deed coincide. Thus, his earlier claim that the plea for vindication does not "rise from deceitful lips" will be proved true by the divine investigation.

As for the deeds of men. This initial phrase sets the stage for the discussion that follows in the remainder of 17:4–5. As far as concern with human activity (Heb. *lipᶜullot ʾadam*)[10] goes, the psalmist claims righteousness. The picture is that of Yahweh, enthroned in the heavens and looking down on his creatures as at the Tower of Babel (Gen. 11) or before the Flood (Gen. 6) in order to scrutinize their activity.[11] Each individual is examined, and judgment is passed. In this great examination, the psalmist confidently expects to pass without doubt.

By the word of your lips. In contrast to the "deceitful lips" mentioned earlier (17:1), the psalmist understands the words of Yahweh's lips as the essential guide for a life that avoids the path of violence[12] and keeps firmly to Yahweh's way. As in the preceding psalm, it is Yahweh who provides the traveler with the accurate roadmap to life and joy (16:11).[13] The final statement of 17:5 ("my feet have not slipped") may function either as fur-

---

9. The theme of divine examination is also prominent in 11:4–5, where Yahweh "examines" (*bḥn*) the righteous and the wicked, with the result that the wicked are found wanting and judged with "fiery coals and burning sulfur" while the "upright" will see the face of God (11:7).

10. The background is similar to that in Prov. 24:12, where God is also depicted as "weighing the heart" of those who deceitfully claim innocence by way of ignorance and concludes with the admonition, "Does not he who weighs the heart perceive it? Does not he who guards your life know it? Will he not repay each person according to what he has done?" This proverb and Job 34:11 are the only places outside Ps. 17:4 where the Hebrew noun *poᶜal* ("deed, deeds") is used together with *ʾadam* ("humans"). The weighing of the heart is also known in Egypt, where the heart of the deceased is weighed in a scale against the "feather" of Maᶜat to determine whether or not the deceased is worthy of entering the afterlife. As in Israel, the heart is the center of moral deliberation and is thought to be the place where wrong decisions or sins piled up, thus weighing the heart down.

11. Cf. also Pss. 7:9; 9:7–8; 11:4–6; 14:1–2 for similar images of divine examination.

12. Cf. Craigie, *Psalms 1–50*, 163, "robbers' roads."

13. The psalmist employs some literary variation in describing "ways" confronting humans. The "ways of the violent" (*ʾorḥot pariṣ* in 17:4c) seems to denote a bare track through the wilds where "ravenous beasts" (*pariṣ*—cf. v. 12 later in this psalm, where the enemies are characterized as "lions hungry for prey"; see also Isa. 35:9, where *pariṣ* is paralleled by "lion") or "robbers" (cf. Jer. 7:11) lie in wait. By contrast, the "paths" (*maᶜgelot*) of Yahweh are the more frequented wagon tracks of commerce, where the safety of numbers provides security.

ther evidence of the psalmist's loyal adherence to the teaching of Yahweh or as a grateful acknowledgment of the security provided by divine guidance.

The Enemy Attack (17:6–12)

THE PSALMIST RETURNS once again to plea for a divine hearing. He makes an audible cry to God (lit., "I have cried aloud to you"), confident that God will "answer" (*ᶜnh*), "give ear" (*nṭh* ["stretch out, extend (his ears)"]),[14] and "hear" (*šmᶜ*) the psalmist's speech.

The wonder of your great love. The NIV follows the majority of commentators in emending the initial verb in verse 7 (*plh* ["separate, divide, treat differently"]) to reflect the Hebrew verb *plʾ* ("show wonder; do marvelously"). Many Hebrew manuscripts contain this emended reading, which seems to make better sense in the context. God is the one who makes known the incomprehensible character of his enduring, loyal love and concern (Heb. *ḥesed*).[15]

Deliverer of those who seek refuge. The Hebrew term behind the NIV's "you who save" (*mošiaᶜ* ["one who saves, savior, deliverer"]) has a robust history.[16] In the Deuteronomic legislation, the word is used at first (Deut. 22:27) to mitigate the guilt of a betrothed woman, accosted and raped in the open countryside, because even though she resisted and screamed, there was "no one to deliver her" from her attacker. Subsequently, as one of the curses for disobedience to the covenant, the Israelites are warned (Deut. 28:29, 31) that they will be afflicted by God so that there will be "no one to deliver you" from the divine wrath.

In Judges, *mošiaᶜ* assumes a more technical usage, where it is used to describe the judges, who are also called "deliverers" (cf. Judg. 3:9, 15) raised up by God. The process continues in Samuel–Kings, with several passages in which *mošiaᶜ* has clearly become the more technical designation "deliverer" (1 Sam. 14:39; 2 Kings 13:5).

Prophetic evidence outside of Isaiah is mixed, with two passages where verbal force seems warranted (Jer. 30:10; Zech. 8:7) and two others where "deliverer" seems more appropriate (Jer. 14:8; Hos. 13:4). Isaiah has by far the most occurrences of *mošiaᶜ* in Old Testament literature, all but one (Isa. 19:20)

---

14. A graphic image of straining to hear a faint or distant sound. Like a horse whose ears turn in order to locate and draw in a sound or a human cupping the hand to the ear to maximize the reception of sound, God is depicted as straining to hear—wanting to hear the psalmist's plea.

15. See the comments on *ḥesed* at Ps. 13:5–6.

16. See comments on Ps. 3:1–2.

falling within the last twenty chapters of the book.[17] All eight occurrences assume the quality of a quasi-title for Yahweh, such as "Deliverer, Savior," and are paralleled in many instances by other divine titles such as "Holy One of Israel" and "Redeemer."

The four occurrences of *mošiaᶜ* in the book of Psalms share the ambiguity observed in the rest of the Old Testament. In Psalm 18:42, the phrase most closely parallels the Deuteronomy passages with its conviction that the wicked can expect no "deliverer" to arise in their behalf. In the remaining three passages (7:10; 17:7; 106:21), the nominal phrase seems more likely, although a verbal rendering is not impossible.

The upshot of this investigation is that by crying out to Yahweh, the Savior of those who seek refuge, the psalmist is invoking a long heritage of relationship between Yahweh and Israel. Whenever Israel cried to Yahweh, acknowledging his power over her, Yahweh responded as *mošiaᶜ*. When, by contrast, Israel refused to obey Yahweh, there was no deliverer (Heb. *ʾen mošiaᶜ*) for Israel, and Yahweh sold them into the control of other nations—a pattern clearly illustrated by the opening chapters of the book of Judges (esp. Judg. 2:10–3:4).

The psalmist who claims a guilt-free relation with God is confident that Yahweh as *mošiaᶜ* will rescue him from "those who rise up against" him. Yahweh will deliver by his "right hand" (*yamin*, 17:7b)—another link back to Psalm 16, where this word occurs twice (16:8, 11). Here it refers to the powerful presence of Yahweh to protect and save.

Keep me as the apple of your eye. The psalmist now introduces two images of the protective care and concern of Yahweh. The first relates the psalmist to the pupil of the eye (Heb. *ʾišon bat ᶜayin* ["little man of the daughter of the eye"]—NIV "apple of your eye"), which is to be carefully guarded from injury. On several occasions while I was wearing hard contact lenses, I developed corneal scratches. The resulting searing pain and burning effectively illustrated to me the zealous care we exercise to protect these delicate but essential parts of our body.

The second image is the desire to be hidden "in the shadow of [God's] wings." This image refers in the most general sense to the protection of small birds under the wings of their hovering parent (cf. Isa. 34:15). Jesus uses such an image in the New Testament to describe his desire to protect Israel—a desire frustrated by her rejection (Luke 13:34).[18] Others take this image to refer to the wings of the cherubim spread across the cover of the ark of the

---

17. The term *mošiaᶜ* occurs a total of thirty-three times in the Old Testament. Of these, eight (about 25 percent) appear in Isa. 43–63 (cf. 43:3, 11; 45:15, 21; 47:15; 49:26; 60:16; 63:8).

18. Cf. Ruth 2:12; Pss. 36:7; 63:7.

covenant, which stood in the Most Holy Place within the Jerusalem temple.[19] This image then would be a picture of seeking refuge in the temple—in the presence of Yahweh—since only the high priest could enter the Most Holy Place of the temple.

Perhaps more convincing in this connection is the discovery of a covenant context for these verses.[20] Using language drawn from two great songs reflecting on Israel's history with Yahweh—the "Song of the Sea" in Ex. 15:1–18 (esp. vv. 11–13)[21] and the "Song of Moses" in Deut. 32—the psalmist clearly marks out that Israel's foundation of hope is in Yahweh's faithful and enduring loyalty to his people, which in the past led to deliverance and continues to hold out hope to those who have kept their feet on Yahweh's paths (Ps. 17:5; cf. 16:11a).

The imperative verbs pleading for deliverance now slip into the declarative perfects and imperfects that describe the enemies who "assail" the psalmist on every side (17:9). The enemies are *ʾoyebay nepeš* ("enemies of my soul [*nepeš*]"), who seek to destroy his animating life source.

The continuing description of the wicked in 17:10 is plagued by the difficulty of the opening phrase: *ḥelbamo sageru* (lit., "their fat they have closed in"). *BHS* suggests an emendation to *ḥeleb libbamo* ("the fat of their heart"—assuming a loss by reason of haplography of the repeated consonants -*lb*-). This emended phrase—which appears also in Ps. 119:70 (*ṭapaš kaḥeleb libbam* ["the fat of their heart is unfeeling"])—is then taken to mean (as in the NIV) that the enemies' hearts are "callous" and uncaring.[22] Craigie resists emendation and renders the original text "became rebellious," drawing (rather tenuously in my opinion) on Deuteronomy 32:15 ("Jeshrun grew fat and kicked") as an indication of rebellion.[23]

Verse 11 offers several difficulties. The first word *ʾaššurenu* is unintelligible as it stands and requires some emendation, as the notes in *BHS* indicate.

---

19. See comments of Kraus (*Psalms 1–59*, 248–49).

20. See Craigie, *Psalms 1–50*, 163.

21. In the "Song of the Sea" Yahweh is celebrated for his deliverance of Israel and is declared the incomparable "wonder working" (Ex. 15:1; cf. Ps. 17:7) God who saves by his "right hand" (Ex. 15:6, 12; cf. Ps. 17:7), and through his enduring loyalty (Ex. 15:13; cf. Ps. 17:7), guides his people to his "holy dwelling" (Ex. 15:13; cf. Ps. 15:1, where a different but similar idiom is employed).

22. A similar image of the fat heart closed to God is found in Isa. 6:10, although it uses a different idiom (the Hiphil of the verb *šmn* ["make fat"]).

23. It is clear that Jeshrun is a symbol of rebellion in the Deuteronomy passage. But it is not clear that "fatness" is an indication of rebellion on its own. It is the "kicking" along with further description of Jeshrun "abandoning" and "rejecting" God (Deut. 32:15c-d) that confirm rebelliousness. In our psalm there is no such further confirmation.

One option is to transpose the final two vowels to achieve the consonantal form *ʾšrwny* (rather than *ʾšrynw*). The resultant fully pointed Hebrew verb *ʾiššereni* (a Piel perfect of *ʾšr* ["step, lead, restrain, reprove"]) is taken to relate to the Greek rendering *ekballontes me* ("cast me out").

These calloused enemies "surround" (*sebabuni*)[24] the psalmist with a fixed purpose (Heb. "they have set their eyes"). Their goal is (lit.) to "stretch out (a tent) on the earth." This phrase is difficult since the verb is normally used of "pitching" a tent. Most commentators take the phrase as a reference to some hostile activity toward the psalmist, such as "throwing ... to the ground" (NIV) or "pitching" out. The use of the term "pitching out" by some commentators offers the impression that this translation is derived from the idiomatic use of *nṭh* to describe the usual process of setting up a tent—and thus lends weight to the translation "throw down; pitch out." It must be recognized, however, that the convergence of the ideas "set up a tent" and "throw out" only occurs in the *English* word "pitch" and should not be transferred unthinkingly to the Hebrew *nṭh*. One does not "throw" a tent to set it up, but "stretches" it out or "stakes it down." The meaning of the term in 17:11 ought to be found within this semantic range as well.

The translation is made more difficult by the lack of pronominal suffix on the verb to indicate to whom the action is directed. Most commentators assume it is the psalmist who is affected. It is certainly not unambiguous. It is feasible that it is the enemies themselves who desire to "spread out in the land," as they have already "surrounded" the psalmist. If, however, it *is* the psalmist who is addressed here, it would seem that some translation such as "stake (me) out on the ground (like a tent)" might more appropriately render the idiom.

A lion hungry for prey. The surrounding enemies are like hungry lions moving in for the kill, crouching in ambush (Heb. *mistarim* ["secret places"]). The initial word of verse 12 (*dimyono* ["his likeness"]) speaks of the opponents of the psalmist in a collective singular in order to make the connection with the ravening lion image. Like the lion, the enemies passionately long to "tear in pieces; rend prey."

---

24. The Hebrew manuscripts preserve a tension between the Ketib (what is written in the consonantal text) and the Qere (an alternative pronunciation indicated by vowel pointing and marginal notes). In this case, the Ketib preserves the probable form *sebabuni* with a first common singular pronominal suffix ("they have surrounded *me*"), while the Qere indicates a similar form *sebabunu* with a first common *plural* pronominal suffix attached ("they have surrounded *us*"). If the plural suffix was original, it would offer evidence of a later adaptation of this psalm to speak to the larger community. It seems best to me, however, to continue with the singular reference at this point.

Final Plea (17:13–15)

THE PSALMIST SLIPS back into the imperative mode of speech abandoned previously at the end of verse 8. With a series of four quick imperatives, he initiates the final plea for deliverance from the surrounding enemies.

Rise up. The first imperative calls Yahweh to action in the psalmist's behalf. From his seat on his throne of judgment, Yahweh is to stand in order to render judgment and enforce it.

Confront. Next, the psalmist pleads with Yahweh to confront the enemy troubling him. The enemy is still considered in the collective sense, as the singular suffixes indicate (*panayw* ["his face"], 17:13b).

Bring them down. With the third imperative, the psalmist wants Yahweh to force the enemy to bend their knee to Yahweh's will.

Rescue. The final imperative brings the plea to the psalmist's primary point: deliverance. This theme, coupled with a sense of confidence, dominates the remainder of the psalm.

From such men. Verse 14 is difficult and has sparked considerable discussion, particularly over the form and translation of the initial word *mimtim*. Delitzsch suggests the verse is linked with the last imperative in the preceding verse and thus parallels the phrase, "Deliver my *nepeš* from the wicked (by) your sword." Our phrase would thus be understood something like: "(Deliver my *nepeš*) from dead men (by) your right hand." Craigie instead separates the phrase from the preceding one, repoints the form in question as *memitam* (from *mwt* ["kill; cause to die"]). His emendation does little to improve the situation, in my opinion, and Delitzsch ought to be followed, as the NIV does.

The repetition of *mimtim* introduces the continuation of the psalmist's thought that Yahweh should deliver the psalmist's *nepeš* "from men of this world whose reward is in this life."[25] The resulting poetic composition follows a fairly regular pattern:

> Save my *nepeš* from the wicked (with) your sword,
> (Save my *nepeš*) from mortals (with) your hand, O Yahweh,
> mortals with a brief life-span, whose portion is in life (alone).

This kind of stair-step pattern, with each line linking back to the preceding but adding some new progression, is not uncommon in the poetry of the psalms (see esp. 93:3–4).

---

25. The contrast between these wicked enemies who find their "portion" (*ḥeleq*) in this life and the fervent psalmist of Ps. 16, for whom Yahweh is "my portion [*ḥeleq*] and my cup" could not be greater!

More difficulties arise in the continuation of verse 14. The initial word appears with alternate Ketib form (indicated by the written consonants) and Qere form (indicated by vowel points). The Ketib (Heb. *ṣepinka*) is an unknown and probably corrupt form, while the Qere (Heb. *ṣepunka*) is found in a number of Hebrew manuscripts. The passive participle *ṣepunka*, however, is singular ("Your hidden thing, treasure") while the verbal construction that follows anticipates a plural form ("You fill *their* belly"). This is usually explained by understanding *ṣepunka* as a collective referring (as in the NIV) to those whom Yahweh values. Such ones will not experience want but will have their bellies filled and will see their children satisfied as well.

This reflection on the faithful care and concern of Yahweh for his "treasure" leads at last to the psalmist's concluding expression of confidence. As in the preceding sequence of psalms (esp. Pss. 13–16, but beginning perhaps as early as Ps. 11), the resolution of his hope is in coming near to Yahweh and experiencing the secure blessing of the divine presence. The psalmist recognizes that it is only the "righteous" who can stand in Yahweh's presence (17:15; cf. 16:11) and who can hope to "be satisfied with seeing" the likeness of God. As Yahweh "fills" those who are his "treasure" and "satisfies" (*śbʿ*) their children, and as the narrator of Psalm 16:11 hopes to be "filled" (*śbʿ*) by God, so the faithful psalmist will receive as reward of enduring faithfulness the satisfaction (*śbʿ*) of seeing God.[26]

The theme of coming into the divine presence was introduced in Psalm 11:7, where we heard the affirmation "the LORD is righteous, he loves justice; upright men will see his face." Psalms 11 and 12 provide contrasting examples of the "faithless" and the "faithful" response to this earlier observation. In 14:5, the theme is renewed when we learn that "God is present in the company of the righteous." Psalm 15 then describes the character of the one who would enter the divine presence, and Psalm 16 lays claim to the kind of righteous loyalty to Yahweh that allows the psalmist to experience "joy in [Yahweh's] presence" (16:11). Now, Psalm 17 concludes with the fervent anticipation that the righteous psalmist will see God's face and be satisfied (17:15).

SEEING THE PRESENCE OF GOD. The heart of Psalm 17 is expressed in the psalmist's final anticipation of seeing the "face" of God and of experiencing satisfaction (17:15). This desire is the subject of conflicting presentation in the Old Testament, such that further exploration is necessary. On the one hand to "seek" or to "see" God's face is

26. See the section on "Dwelling in the Presence of God" in "The Theology of the Psalms," in vol. 2 of this commentary.

viewed positively as the appropriate goal of the righteous. In Psalm 105:4, the faithful are encouraged to "seek his face always."[27] Similarly, in 2 Chronicles 7:14 Yahweh promises that when his rebellious people "humble themselves and pray and seek my face and turn from their wicked ways," he will hear, forgive their sin, and heal their land.

Such passages affirm that to "seek the face of God" is to seek him *earnestly*, willing to submit to his will.[28] In this context, seeing God's face is to experience his presence in blessing. When Yahweh "makes his face shine" on his people or "turns his face toward" them, the result is blessing.[29] By contrast, when God hides his face, his presence is removed in judgment.[30]

Despite this positive aspect of seeing God's face, numerous passages point instead to rather fearful consequences. Jacob, having wrestled all night with "a man" at the Wadi Jabbok, comes away from the experience rejoicing that unexpectedly "I saw God face to face, and yet my life was spared" (Gen. 32:30). Similarly, when Moses beseeches Yahweh to allow him to see the divine glory, Yahweh allows him to see only the back of God, for "you cannot see my face, for no one may see me and live" (Ex. 33:20–23; cf. also Isaiah's fear in Isa. 6:5).

These contexts point out the fearsome—even potentially deadly—consequences of seeing the face of God. The Exodus passage is particularly curious in light of the repeated tradition in the Pentateuch that Moses did indeed, in his many encounters with the deity, see Yahweh "face to face."[31] The solution to this apparent difficulty is perhaps to be found in Numbers 12:8, where Yahweh says of Moses, "With him I speak face to face, clearly and not in riddles; he sees the form of the LORD." Apparently, Moses' seeing Yahweh "face to face" meant that God was *directly present* with him, not that Moses saw the very visage of God. Rather, Moses was allowed to see the "form" of God—his shape. As in Exodus 33, Moses is permitted to see as much of Yahweh as is humanly possible without being destroyed. In this sense it was also possible to say to the Israelites at Sinai that Yahweh "spoke to you face to face out of the fire on the mountain" (Deut. 5:4)—meaning that God spoke directly to them in person while shielding them from the destructive consequences of their sin coming into contact with his glory.

So Israel understands that under certain circumstances it is not only possible but even desirable to "see the face of the LORD." Seeking Yahweh's face is encouraged because it results in an outpouring of divine blessing. This is not to deny, however, that in other circumstances the face of Yahweh continues to

---

27. Cf. also 1 Chron. 16:11.
28. Cf. 2 Sam. 21:1; Pss. 24:6; 27:8; 119:58; Hos. 5:15.
29. Cf. Num. 6:25–26; Pss. 67:1; 80:3, 7, 19; 119:135.
30. Cf. Deut. 31:17–18; Job 34:29; Ps. 15:1.
31. Cf. Ex. 33:11; Num. 12:8; Deut. 34:10

retain its destructive potential. The key in Israel's understanding is how one approaches God. Unlike the wicked, who falsely persuade themselves that "God covers his face and never sees" their evil (Ps. 10:11), Israel affirms that only the "upright ... will see his face" (11:7). Thus, the psalmist is able to approach God with words that approximate those used by Yahweh himself to describe Moses in Numbers 12:8: The psalmist will see God's "face" (in the sense of apprehending him directly) and will also be satisfied with seeing his "likeness."

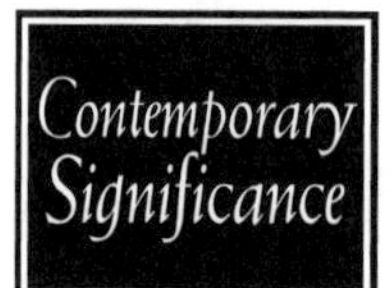

LIKE ISRAEL, WE Christians also desire to see God face to face and in Jesus—God incarnate—we are allowed to see as much of God as is humanly possible without destruction. Jesus, who is the very image of the Father (John 10:30; 2 Cor. 4:4; Col. 1:15) is the means by which believers can see the face of God (John 14:9; 2 Cor. 4:6).

The New Testament witness also understands that the "face of God" has fearsome potential for judgment. In 1 Peter 3:12, we learn that "the face of the Lord is against those who do evil" (a quote from Ps. 34:16), while in Revelation 6:16, the unbelievers of the earth, confronted by a day of judgment, plead to the mountains: "Fall on us and hide us from the face of him who sits on the throne and from the wrath of the Lamb!"

By contrast, the faithful are treated to a description of the new Jerusalem, where God and the Lamb reign forever. "No longer will there be any curse. The throne of God and of the Lamb will be in the city, and his servants will serve him. They will *see his face*, and his name will be on their foreheads" (Rev. 22:3–4, italics added). In other words, the New Testament preserves the same tension as the Old between those who will experience the face of God as judgment and the faithful who discover both blessing and satisfaction when God's face shines on them.

But how can we today experience the same satisfaction in seeing God's face that the psalmist records? Let's draw several short lessons from the text of Psalm 17.

An integrated life. Unlike the enemies who attack, the psalmist claims a life of integrity. Day and night, in thought, word, and deed, the psalmist holds fast to Yahweh's paths, never slipping. What a challenge this is in our world today, where we are constantly tempted to compartmentalize family life from work life, our personal faith from "what works" with others, principled ethics from what gets the job done. At the beginning of his important book *Does God Need the Church?* Gerhard Lohfink tells how in the aftermath of World War II he joined the Catholic Integrated Community [*Katholische Integrierte Gemeinde*], a development from "the Catholic youth movement to find a new way toward a living Church in face of their horror that the Holocaust could occur in a Christian Europe."[32] Ever since that time Christians have had to struggle with what it means that such atrocities against fellow humans can occur in societies that consider themselves Christian.

We know that the need for integration is a crucial component for emotional, psychological, and spiritual well-being and wholeness. Yet we constantly find ourselves pressured to do what works rather than what we know is right. We are told that what we believe is a matter of personal opinion, ought to be kept to ourselves, and should have little influence on how we must act in the "real world." As a result, there is little sense today that a *Christian* life can be clearly distinguished from the lives of unbelievers who surround us. A recent survey has demonstrated the disturbing truth that the highest rate of divorce today is among those who identify themselves as conservative, evangelical Christians![33]

A powerful illustration of the difference between a fragmented life and integrated life is offered by the film *The Apostle*. The main character—played by Robert Duvall—is a successful Pentecostal pastor who has long juggled his enthusiastic evangelism and preaching with a hidden life of womanizing and alcohol abuse. When, however, he discovers his disenchanted wife has embarked on an affair of her own, he flies into a drunken rage and beats his wife's lover to death with a baseball bat. Fleeing the scene of the crime, he hides himself in the backcountry of Louisiana, first working as a manual laborer but increasingly drawn to minister to the needs of local people by reviving a defunct church.

This new ministry becomes a means of personal redemption as God enables the "apostle" to reintegrate his inner and outer worlds around his repentant faith in God and his desire to bring others to redemption. At the end of the film, having submitted himself to the demands of the legal system, the "apostle" is seen working on a chain gang while encouraging the other convicts with his enthusiastic presentation of God's power and grace unleashed in broken lives like his own.

Psalm 17 cautions us that failure to maintain integrity of thought, word, and deed has disastrous consequences. Where do we find the power to live such integrated lives in our fragmented and compartmentalized world?

Grounded in the Word. The psalmist realizes that true transparency of self must be grounded in God's Word. "By the word of your lips I have kept

32. Gerhard Lohfink, *Does God Need the Church? Toward a Theology of the People of God* (Collegeville, Minn.: Liturgical Press, 1999), vii, esp. n. 2.

33. The survey was conducted by the George Barna Research Group and was reported in *Southern California Christian Times,* 11/2 (February 2000): 1, 11.

myself from the ways of the violent. My steps have held to your paths; my feet have not slipped" (17:4–5). The Word of God made flesh in Christ and witnessed to in Scripture is both the criterion of divine examination (17:2–3) and the guide to the path of Yahweh (17:5). An integrated life is a life that is willing to stand under the judgment of Scripture and to guide its faltering steps by the same.

I am dismayed at the high degree of biblical illiteracy evident among the freshman college students who populate my introductory classes. Most are fine young men and women with a strong faith and a desire to serve God. But few have more than a passing awareness of the content and teaching of Scripture—especially the Old Testament. Without that foundation it is hardly surprising that many of them struggle to live lives in which knowledge, faith, and praxis are integrated. They know that smoking is addictive and can kill them, but smoking is on the rise anyway among our Christian teenagers and young adults.

Most know the biblical teaching and standards for sexuality, but many have simply given up the struggle and seek to justify their "natural need" for sexual expression without regard to marriage or commitment. They are not alone. I know too many pastors and leaders whose positions have been lost and families and congregations shattered because of an inability to properly relate one's sexual drive and the life of faith. Scripture—honestly encountered and humbly apprehended—can confront our falsehood and lead us once again to the paths of righteousness.

Out of this world. Finally, Psalm 17 helps us to see that the power to live transparent lives of integrity comes when we find our satisfaction *outside* of this world. Verses 14–15 make this clear with an important contrast between the "men of this world whose reward is in this life" and those like the psalmist, who are satisfied with seeing God's likeness.

The NIV translation of the former group ("men of this world") obscures a powerful rendering of the Hebrew (*mimtim . . . mimtim meḥeled ḥelqam baḥayyim*). Taken from the root *mwt* ("die; death"), the plural noun *metim* emphasizes the *mortal* nature of those who are described almost literally as "dead men."[34] These emphatically mortal humans are bound to their worldly existence because their "reward [*ḥeleq*] is in this life."[35] By studied contrast, the psalmist finds satisfaction in seeing the "face" and "likeness" of God (17:15).

---

34. Cf. NRSV, NJB, "mortals"; NAB, "dead men."

35. Note esp. the contrast between the "this worldly" perspective of the wicked in this psalm and the "other worldly" focus of the psalmist in 16:5, for whom Yahweh is both "portion" (*ḥeleq*) and cup.

When we look to this world for our satisfaction, we are doomed from the outset to frustration and disillusionment. The author of Ecclesiastes searched far and wide and taught the futility of human endeavor and reliance on wealth, status, and power. The rewards of this world are short-lived and soon left for others to enjoy. Even respect and reputation are fleeting, and Job's quest for divine vindication could not last. But Job, Ecclesiastes, and the author of our psalm all agree, each in his own way, on the only source of continuing satisfaction. Ecclesiastes calls it "fear of God"—acknowledgment that one is ultimately and completely dependent on the gracious mercy of God (Eccl. 12:13). Job lays down his defenses and demands when confronted at last by the undeniable presence of the Almighty—"My ears had heard of you but now my eyes have seen you" (Job 42:5). Job's response affirms the hope of the psalmist that the righteous will see God's face and find satisfaction there (Ps. 17:15).

Psalm 18

FOR THE DIRECTOR of music. Of David the servant of the LORD. He sang to the LORD the words of this song when the LORD delivered him from the hand of all his enemies and from the hand of Saul. He said:

1 I love you, O LORD, my strength.

2 The LORD is my rock, my fortress and my deliverer;
my God is my rock, in whom I take refuge.
He is my shield and the horn of my salvation,
my stronghold.
3 I call to the LORD, who is worthy of praise,
and I am saved from my enemies.

4 The cords of death entangled me;
the torrents of destruction overwhelmed me.
5 The cords of the grave coiled around me;
the snares of death confronted me.
6 In my distress I called to the LORD;
I cried to my God for help.
From his temple he heard my voice;
my cry came before him, into his ears.

7 The earth trembled and quaked,
and the foundations of the mountains shook;
they trembled because he was angry.
8 Smoke rose from his nostrils;
consuming fire came from his mouth,
burning coals blazed out of it.
9 He parted the heavens and came down;
dark clouds were under his feet.
10 He mounted the cherubim and flew;
he soared on the wings of the wind.
11 He made darkness his covering, his canopy around him—
the dark rain clouds of the sky.
12 Out of the brightness of his presence clouds advanced,
with hailstones and bolts of lightning.
13 The LORD thundered from heaven;
the voice of the Most High resounded.

14 He shot his arrows and scattered the enemies,
great bolts of lightning and routed them.
15 The valleys of the sea were exposed
and the foundations of the earth laid bare
at your rebuke, O LORD,
at the blast of breath from your nostrils.

16 He reached down from on high and took hold of me;
he drew me out of deep waters.
17 He rescued me from my powerful enemy,
from my foes, who were too strong for me.
18 They confronted me in the day of my disaster,
but the LORD was my support.
19 He brought me out into a spacious place;
he rescued me because he delighted in me.

20 The LORD has dealt with me according to my
righteousness;
according to the cleanness of my hands he has
rewarded me.
21 For I have kept the ways of the LORD;
I have not done evil by turning from my God.
22 All his laws are before me;
I have not turned away from his decrees.
23 I have been blameless before him
and have kept myself from sin.
24 The LORD has rewarded me according to my
righteousness,
according to the cleanness of my hands in his sight.

25 To the faithful you show yourself faithful,
to the blameless you show yourself blameless,
26 to the pure you show yourself pure,
but to the crooked you show yourself shrewd.
27 You save the humble
but bring low those whose eyes are haughty.
28 You, O LORD, keep my lamp burning;
my God turns my darkness into light.
29 With your help I can advance against a troop;
with my God I can scale a wall.

30 As for God, his way is perfect;
the word of the LORD is flawless.

He is a shield
  for all who take refuge in him.
31 For who is God besides the LORD?
  And who is the Rock except our God?
32 It is God who arms me with strength
  and makes my way perfect.
33 He makes my feet like the feet of a deer;
  he enables me to stand on the heights.
34 He trains my hands for battle;
  my arms can bend a bow of bronze.
35 You give me your shield of victory,
  and your right hand sustains me;
  you stoop down to make me great.
36 You broaden the path beneath me,
  so that my ankles do not turn.

37 I pursued my enemies and overtook them;
  I did not turn back till they were destroyed.
38 I crushed them so that they could not rise;
  they fell beneath my feet.
39 You armed me with strength for battle;
  you made my adversaries bow at my feet.
40 You made my enemies turn their backs in flight,
  and I destroyed my foes.
41 They cried for help, but there was no one to save them—
  to the LORD, but he did not answer.
42 I beat them as fine as dust borne on the wind;
  I poured them out like mud in the streets.

43 You have delivered me from the attacks of the people;
  you have made me the head of nations;
  people I did not know are subject to me.
44 As soon as they hear me, they obey me;
  foreigners cringe before me.
45 They all lose heart;
  they come trembling from their strongholds.

46 The LORD lives! Praise be to my Rock!
  Exalted be God my Savior!
47 He is the God who avenges me,
  who subdues nations under me,
48 who saves me from my enemies.

You exalted me above my foes;
from violent men you rescued me.
49 Therefore I will praise you among the nations, O LORD;
I will sing praises to your name.
50 He gives his king great victories;
he shows unfailing kindness to his anointed,
to David and his descendants forever.

PSALM 18 IS a close copy of the composition that appears in 2 Samuel 22:1–51. There, as here, the psalm is described as David's melodic response to the divine deliverance from "the hand of all his enemies," including Saul (2 Sam. 22:1; cf. Ps. 18:0). The psalm is an extended hymn of praise to Yahweh for his deliverance of the psalmist from a host of enemies. The theme of Yahweh as "rock," "fortress," and "refuge" appears at significant points throughout the psalm (18:2, 30–31, 46).[1]

Structurally, the psalm falls into five sections: an introduction of praise for Yahweh's deliverance (18:1–3), a narrative in almost mythic terms of Yahweh's saving acts in behalf of the psalmist (18:4–19), a passage of instruction in which the personal righteousness of the psalmist provides guidance for the reader/hearer (18:20–29), a description of victory over the enemies in which the psalmist's commitment to Yahweh serves as an example to the reader/hearer (18:30–45), and a conclusion that returns to praise of Yahweh (18:46–50).

The Heading (18:0)

THE PSALM IS referred to "the director of music" and is attributed to David.[2] David is further qualified by the term "servant of Yahweh" (*leᶜebed yhwh*)—a phrase most commonly associated with Moses throughout the Old Testament but referring exclusively to David in the psalms (here; 36:0).[3] This phrase

1. For a discussion of the importance of Yahweh as "refuge" in the Psalter, see the section on "Yahweh as Refuge" in "The Theology of the Psalms" in vol. 2 of this commentary.

2. See comments on the headings of Pss. 3 and 4.

3. The phrase *ᶜebed yhwh* appears twenty-two times in the Old Testament. Of these occurrences, seventeen refer to Moses as the "servant of the LORD" (Deut. 34:5; Josh. 1:1, 13, 15; 8:31, 33; 11:12; 12:6; 13:8; 14:7; 18:7; 22:2, 4, 5; 2 Kings 18:12; 2 Chron. 1:3; 24:6). Of the remaining five appearances of the phrase, two refer to Joshua (Josh. 24:9; Judg. 2:8), two to David (Pss. 18:0; 36:0), and one to the "blind servant" (probably Israel) of Isa. 42:19. It is true that the *idea* of servant to Yahweh is expressed in other contexts in the Old

conveys a relationship of great strength and loyalty and confers on the bearer an elevated authority of declaring the divine word and leading God's people.

The heading also includes a historical statement (almost identical to 2 Sam. 22:1)[4] that connects the psalm to David's experience of deliverance from his enemies through victory over them. The psalm heading differs from 2 Samuel 22:1 in two minor respects. (1) The opening phrases of the psalm heading employ the *ʾăšer* clause pattern common to a number of historical statements in the headings (*ʾăšer dibber lyhwh* ["who spoke to Yahweh"]), while in 2 Samuel a more narrative construction is used ("and David spoke to Yahweh"). As a result, in each case the psalm is bound more closely into its broader context. Psalm 18 is usually included in the category of psalms known as "royal psalms."[5]

(2) The other variation between the two versions of the psalm is even more minor. Second Samuel 22:1, in referring to David's deliverance from Saul, repeats the phrase "from the palm [*kap*] of Saul" used in the previous reference to the enemies ("from the palm [*kap*] of all his enemies"). Psalm 18, however, offers a stylistic variation in reference to Saul by using the frequently parallel phrase "from the hand [*yad*] of Saul."

Whether or not David actually composed this hymn is a matter of conjecture, with commentators taking either position. The language of the psalm is for the most part too general to allow specific connection with identifiable

---

Testament, using the word *ʿebed* in connection with various pronominal suffixes (e.g., *your* servant; *my* servant), but the use of the whole phrase as a *title* (as in our passage) is less frequent and is dominantly applied to Moses. The idea of servanthood to Yahweh is particularly connected with the prophets, who are often called "*my* servants" (2 Kings 9:36; 14:25; Isa. 20:3; Dan. 6:20; etc.). See the articles on "Servant of the Lord" in *IDB*, *ISBE*², and *EDB*, and the extensive bibliographies included there. For Isaiah, it seems clear that the Servant of Yahweh in Isa. 42:18–19 refers to the deaf, blind, and faithless in Israel. But the subtle shifting back and forth that takes place in the Servant Songs (42:1–9; 49:1–7; 50:4–11; 52:13–53:12), from the servant as Israel, or the prophet, or a faithful remnant, or a future individual lends greater ambiguity than might be expected to the interpretation of this passage. On these songs, see H. H. Rowley, *The Servant of the Lord and Other Essays on the Old Testament* (London: Lutterworth, 1952), 1–88.

4. Shemaryahu Talmon, in his article "*Pisqah beʾemṣaʾ pasuq* and 11QPs[a]," *Textus* 5 (1966): 11–21, suggests that blank spaces preserved in the text of the Hebrew manuscripts of the Old Testament (and esp. in Samuel–Kings) are intended to point the reader to additional texts expanding on the preceding narratives. Some of the texts Talmon suggests are out of the Psalter. In the case of Ps. 18 = 2 Sam. 22, it would seem that the expansive psalm has at last been incorporated directly into the narrative context. See also Brevard S. Childs, "Psalm Titles and Midrashic Exegesis," *JSS* 16 (1971): 137–50, and Wilson, *The Editing of the Hebrew Psalter*, 73–75.

5. See the section on "Royal Psalms" at the end of Ps. 2. For a discussion of the interpretation of the royal psalms, see the Bridging Contexts section of Ps. 20.

life-settings. That the narrator is a king of Israel is suggested by verses that mention "ruling over nations" (18:43, 47), Yahweh's giving victory to "his king" (18:50), and references to God's "anointed, to David and his descendants forever" (18:50). While these references suggest a king as speaker of these verses, other verses indicate some caution in too easy an identification with David. In 18:6, Yahweh is described as hearing the psalmist's cry of distress "from his temple." If this means the earthly temple constructed by Solomon, the psalm would reflect a context subsequent to the death of David, or else it must be explained as a later interpolation.

Additionally, the psalmist's radical protestations of innocence in 18:20–24 seem difficult to square with David's sin with Bathsheba (which forms the presumed backdrop for Ps. 51) and with 1 Chronicles 22:7–9, where David is described as a "man of blood" and was prevented by God from building the temple.

Introductory Praise (18:1–3)

THE PSALMIST BEGINS with first-person address of his love to Yahweh, "I love you, O LORD" (18:1),[6] and then continues in the third person to heap up epithets of Yahweh that call forth the psalmist's praise. Yahweh is the psalmist's strength (*ḥizqi*), rock (*salʿi*), fortress (*meṣudati*), deliverer (*mepalṭi*), rock of refuge (*ṣuri ʾeḥeseh bo*), shield (*maginni*), horn of salvation (*qeren yišʿi*), and stronghold (*miśgabbi*). All these epithets respond to Yahweh as source of refuge, protection, and deliverance. The theme of "refuge in Yahweh" is a prominent one in the Psalter and began as early as 2:11. Psalm 18 brings together in the space of these two verses almost all of the phrases characteristic of this theme.[7] I will comment briefly on each term that appears here for the first time.[8]

My strength. The psalmist considers Yahweh to be the source of "strength." Later in the psalm, he describes how Yahweh enables him to perform all the feats necessary for effective and successful action in battle. The

6. This first-person address is missing in the 2 Sam. 22 version of this psalm, which begins directly with the descriptive phrase: "The LORD is my rock."

7. See comments on 5:11. No other psalm brings together as many of these phrases as does Ps. 18, but several do offer significant concentrations. See esp. Ps. 144, where five of these eight terms appear (*ṣuri* in 144:1; *meṣudati* in 144:2; *miśgabbi* in 144:2; *mepalṭi* in 144:2; *maginni* in 144:2) along with the additional epithet *ḥasdi* (144:2, "my faithfully loyal one"). Ps. 31 also brings together a number of these terms, including *ṣur* (31:2), *meṣudah* (31:2, 3), *salʿi* (31:3), and adds *maʿoz* ("mountain stronghold," 31:2, 4). Ps. 71 also includes three of these terms (*ṣur*; *salʿi*; *meṣudah*) in a single verse (71:3), while adding *maʿon* ("hidden lair, den," possibly to be read *maʿoz*, as in 31:2).

8. For the term "shield," see the commentary on Ps. 3:3.

term employed here in this opening phrase appears only here in the Old Testament, so its meaning is somewhat obscure. It does, however, come from the common Hebrew root *ḥzq*, which bears the meaning "be strong, hard." The sense is to have a "tough, enduring" quality.

My rock. The two Hebrew terms employed in this passage for "rock" (*selaᶜ* in 18:2a; *ṣur* in 18:2b) offer little to separate them and are often used in parallel constructions. If there is any distinction, it seems to me that *selaᶜ* more frequently suggests larger, more massive natural structures such as crags, cliffs, and mountainsides, while *ṣur* can more often refer to lesser features like boulders. This is, however, not a consistent distinction, and there is much overlap between these two terms. The image of God as "rock" is common in the Psalter and stresses two aspects of his protective care for humans who trust in him. (1) God as rock provides a firm, unshakable place for those who rely on him. (2) More specifically related to this passage, God is the inaccessible rocky crag or mountain hideaway in which the beleaguered psalmist can rest secure from all attacks.

My fortress. Hebrew *meṣudah* ("fortress," 18:2a), like the references to God as rock, conjures up visions of a remote mountain stronghold in inaccessible terrain that inhibits hostile attack by its very isolation and harsh environment. Closely related is *miśgab* (18:2c), which denotes a rocky high spot used as refuge. I am reminded of the massive fortress of Masada[9] on a rocky plateau overlooking the Dead Sea, or a variety of cliff dwellings and caves along the walls of the twisting wadis (stream beds) that wind their way down from Jerusalem to the Jordan River near Jericho. Archaeological surveys have uncovered numerous such sites that were inhabited from prehistoric times into the Middle Ages. Such remote locations afforded security to outlaws as well as to refugee citizens under attack by enemy forces.

These hideouts were used regularly by Jewish rebels and zealots from the time of the Maccabean revolt in the second century B.C. through the first and second Jewish rebellions in the first and second centuries A.D. In the Middle Ages, Christian monks and hermits gravitated to these remote sites, seeking the solitude that allowed their personal search for prayer, meditation, self-sacrifice, and ultimate union with God. The monastery of St. George still stands in the Wadi Qelt, halfway between Jerusalem and Jericho.

God has become for the psalmist a place of security equal to one of these rugged, isolated, and inaccessible mountain fortresses. He can withdraw to God in the same way as those under attack can withdraw to their hidden caves to avoid discovery by their enemies.

---

9. From the related Aramaic word *meṣada* ("fortress").

My horn. The image of the "horn" (*qeren*) refers to animal horns used either as musical instruments or as containers for liquids—especially oil for anointing those selected for divine purposes. The horn was often a symbol of strength, power, and victory, perhaps because animals contested other animals by butting and thrusting horns at them. To "exalt the horn" of someone (1 Sam. 2:1, 10) is to augment their power so that they secure victory. On the contrary, to "cut off the horn" (as in dehorning cattle) is to limit one's effectiveness in battle and to bring about defeat (Jer. 48:25). To envision Yahweh as the psalmist's "horn" is to understand that Yahweh is the source of power and strength that ensures the psalmist's ultimate victory against his foes.

My deliverer. Yahweh is the one who helps the psalmist "evade" or "escape" those who attack; he is the psalmist's "deliverer" (from *plṭ* ["effect escape, help to escape"]). Including this verse, the participle form occurs five times in the Psalter (18:2, 48; 40:17; 70:5; 144:2), on each occasion emphasizing the character of Yahweh as deliverer of the oppressed. The appearance of other forms of this same root and stem in eleven other passages indicates the importance of this theme in the psalms.[10] Outside the Psalter, comparable forms are found only four times—twice in the parallel context (2 Sam. 22:2, 44) and once each in Job 23:7 and Micah 6:14.

Chiastic structures. These eight terms (strength, rock, fortress, deliverer, rock, shield, horn, stronghold) are artfully arrayed in a complex literary structure, in which each of the first four terms in 18:1–2a is paralleled by one of the four terms that follow in 18:2b-c. Some of these connections are more obvious. "Rock" (*salᶜi*, 18:2a) is related to "rock" (*ṣuri*, 18:2b), while "fortress" (*meṣudati*, 18:2a) is linked to "stronghold" (*miśgabbi*, 18:2c). Moving from these clear relationships, it is not difficult to recognize that "strength" (18:1) is also related to "horn" (symbol of "power" in 18:2c), and "deliverer" (18:2a) must be connected to the remaining term "shield" (18:2c).[11] These terms are introduced in an order that produces a complex chiastic relationship.[12] After the first set of terms are introduced,

strength rock fortress deliverer

10. The Piel imperative of this same root appeared in 17:13 ("rescue") and is found as well in three additional psalms (31:1; 71:4; 82:4). The Piel imperfect of this verb appears eight times in the Psalter (18:43; 22:4, 8; 37:40 [2x]; 43:1; 71:2; 91:14).

11. As Yahweh "helps (the psalmist) escape" the attacks of the enemy, so a shield "helps (the bearer) escape" the arrows, spears, and swords of the opponents.

12. See the discussion of *chiasm* in the section on "Poetry of the Psalms" in the introduction.

the related terms are so arranged that the two inner terms (rock = rock; fortress = stronghold) are moved to the outside, while the outer terms (strength = horn; deliverer = shield) are moved to the interior and even transposed with each other, forming the following chiastic relationship:

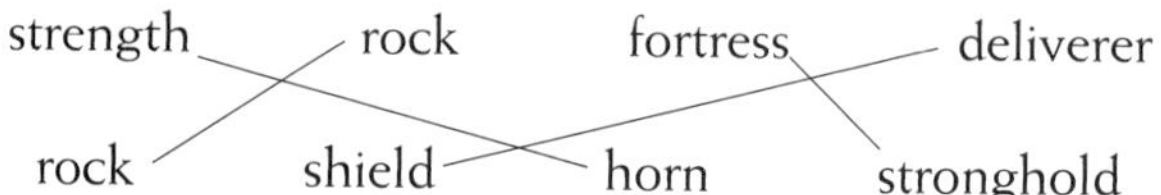

The complexity of the relationship illustrates the poetic artistry characteristic of ancient Hebrew poetic technique.

I call to the LORD. The introductory verses draw to a conclusion with a summary statement that prefigures the outcome of the psalm. The psalmist calls on Yahweh in time of need and experiences divine deliverance. While bringing the introduction to a close, this verse also provides transition to the description of distress that follows.

Narrative of Deliverance (18:4–19)

THE NARRATIVE BEGINS with a generalized description of distress (18:4–6), continues with a theophany (18:7–15), and concludes with a description of divine deliverance (18:16–19).

Distress. The attack experienced by the psalmist is life-threatening. While we gain no specifics from the description, it is clear that he understands the circumstance as being bound over to the power of death. Twice the phrase "cords of death" appears (18:4a, 5a), along with the similar image of the "snares of death" (18:5b). The psalmist feels bound and trapped, being drawn helplessly toward death, and he needs God to act as deliverer or liberator, one who helps him to escape from these entanglements. The alternative image of the rushing torrents of the sea (or perhaps the tumbling waters of a flash flood in a normally dry wadi) drives home the threat the psalmist feels. Life is going under, and only Yahweh can save.

When the psalmist calls, Yahweh hears and responds (18:6). God is depicted as enthroned in the temple (18:6c)—possibly a sign that the psalmist's cry is understood as prayer uttered during temple worship. The mention of the temple,[13] as noted above, makes it less likely that the psalm was composed by David as the heading supposes—unless the temple is envisioned as the *heavenly* abode (or palace) of God rather than the earthly tem-

13. On two occasions in 1 Sam. (1:9; 3:3), the term *hekal* is used to describe "Yahweh's temple" at Shiloh. While it is *possible* this may be a reference to the tabernacle tent, it is equally possible that the reference is to a more permanent shrine building associated with Shiloh, a precursor to the later Solomonic temple.

ple. That Yahweh is viewed as coming down through the clouds (18:9), thundering from heaven (18:13), and reaching down from on high (18:16) would seem to lend weight to this latter interpretation.

Theophany. The narrative of deliverance now moves to an extended theophany,[14] in which the approach of God into the profane world of human existence is described with all its fearsome effects. The awesome power and majesty of the divine glory entering the human world is not business as usual. God's holy otherness places sinful humanity under threat, and even the created order suffers by direct exposure to his presence. The created world cannot contain the creator, and its usual laws and order are stretched to the breaking point by this divine intrusion.

The earth trembled and quaked. Earthquake imagery paints a fearsome scene of Yahweh's coming. God is the creator of the earth—the one who set the foundations that render it stable—and when Yahweh comes in anger (18:7c) or in judgment, the very stability of the earth, on which humans rely, is shaken to its core.

Smoke rose from his nostrils. The psalmist mixes several images in the attempt to stress the awesome and frightful power of righteous God in judgment on human evil. Here, in an almost dragonlike picture, God in his wrath breathes out smoke and fire, pouring out a "consuming fire" of coals from his mouth. It would be easy to assume that the smoke and fire are indications of God's anger and wrath poured out on sinful humans. However, we should exercise some caution here. The consuming fire is not so much an indication of divine wrath as it is a sign of the complete "otherness" that sets God apart from humans.

He parted the heavens and came down. As often in theophanic passages, Yahweh is depicted as coming from a distance—here, from "the heavens."[15] The verb rendered "parted" (*nṭh*) is among the more confusing forms in the Old

---

14. The term *theophany* (from the Greek *theophaneia* ["appearance of God"]) refers to primarily literary descriptions of God being manifested in the realm of human awareness. Sometimes this divine manifestation is accompanied with a spoken word of revelation. Often God's presence has a fantastic and catastrophic effect on the creation, indicating the awesome power, glory, and otherness of God. The mountains "melt like wax," seas "boil," lightning flashes, winds roar. Such theophanies are most common in the Old Testament (cf. Deut. 33:2; Judg. 5:4–5; Ps. 68:7–18; Hab. 3:2–19), although they are not unknown in the New Testament—especially in Revelation (e.g., Rev. 1:12–16). See also the pertinent articles on "Theophany" in *IDB*, *ISBE*², and *EDB*.

15. Coming "down" from the heavens is perhaps one further indication that the reference to the "temple" in 18:6 should be taken as meaning the heavenly abode of God rather than the Jerusalem temple. Elsewhere Yahweh is said to come from the desert of Seir and Teman (regions associated with Edom to the east of the Dead Sea) or from Mount Sinai (cf. Deut. 33:2; Judg. 5:4; Hab. 3:3).

Testament, since in some circumstances (such as here) only one of its three root consonants remain. Fortunately, the word occurs frequently enough that its varied forms are generally recognizable. The term describes the act of stretching something out—as a tent in erecting it or two hands in a dramatic gesture. Here it is as if Yahweh "parts" the heavens as one opens up a bead curtain by holding back the two sides with outstretched hands. Whether the psalmist has a specific storm phenomenon in mind is unclear, but Yahweh's entrance from the heaven is clearly related to the storm imagery that follows.[16]

Dark clouds. The Hebrew *ʿarapel* (NIV "dark clouds") on many occasions catches the forbidding gloom that attends and shrouds the presence of God (Ex. 20:21; Deut. 4:11; 5:22; 1 Kings 8:12) when he appears to humans. Such foreboding clouds are certainly part of the storm imagery the psalmist is using here. But as we will see in the Bridging Contexts section, the clouds serve a dual purpose: dramatically introducing the gathering gloom of impending judgment, yet protecting humans from the destructive power of Yahweh's consuming fire.

Mounted the cherubim. The storm imagery directed to Yahweh here has connections with broader ancient Near Eastern texts describing the pagan storm deities—in particular, Baal. Craigie[17] goes so far as to suggest our text is an adaptation of the Canaanite themes surrounding the struggle of the chaotic gods Yam (Sea) and Mot (Death) with Baal. In his view the adaptation has shifted this cosmic struggle to the more specific hopes for deliverance from the psalmist's distress. This stretches the imagery further than it was intended to go, but there is no doubt about association with storm imagery. Yahweh mounts[18] a cherub and flies. He "soars" on the "wings of the wind" (*kanpe ruaḥ*).[19] Note especially how the biblical passages claim Yahweh's authority over the power of the storm at the expense of the pagan deities who supposedly rule it. Note here Psalm 68:4, which uses

---

16. Cf. similar imagery of Ps. 97:1–6.

17. Cf. Craigie, *Psalms 1–50*, 173–74.

18. The NIV translation "he mounted" seems to assume the Hiphil stem, while the traditional text is pointed as a Qal. The Qal is usually translated "ride" while the Hiphil is normally rendered "mount (or cause [someone else] to mount) in order to ride." Elsewhere Yahweh is described as "riding on the clouds" (cf. Deut. 33:26; Ps. 68:4; 104:3). This has led some to assume that the "cherub" mentioned in 18:10 is actually a reference to the storm clouds, which serve as the divine chariot of God (see esp. Ps. 104:3). The NIV, however, has rendered the singular Heb. noun *kerub* as a plural (*kerubim*). This indicates the NIV translators understand the term to refer to the cherubim that stand on the ark of the covenant and between which Yahweh is understood to sit, or to the cherubim that bear the stormy throne chariot of Yahweh in Ezekiel (cf. Ezek. 1, where the beings are called "living creatures," and Ezek. 10, where they are identified as "cherubim").

19. See also Ps. 104:3.

the common Canaanite epithet of Baal[20]—"(the one) who rides on the clouds"—and immediately counters with the qualification "his name is the LORD."

He made darkness his covering. Again, as in verse 9, darkness obscures the approaching deity. That this cloaking of God is intentional rather than accidental is implied by the active verb *yašet* (from *šyt* ["set, appoint"]) as well as the accompanying noun that the NIV translates "his covering" (*seter*). The straightforward meaning of this noun is "hiding place," implying an intentional secrecy on God's part. This is part of the gracious mystery of God. In coming near to make himself known, God conceals himself both in mystery and grace. God is more than we can know in our limited, sinful humanity. Thus, he allows us to see as much of him as we can bear while obscuring what would overwhelm and ultimately destroy us.

The brightness of his presence. Additional storm phenomena are described as accompanying Yahweh's approach. Hail (18:12b), lightning (18:12b, 14b), and thunder (18:13a) are viewed as the weapons and war cry of the divine warrior[21] to route his enemies. Lightning bolts are also mentioned as the weapons of the Canaanite storm deity Baal and are depicted in stylized fashion on various reliefs and stelae from Ras Shamra.[22] Yahweh arrives to confront his enemies and shoots hail and lightning bolts at them like "arrows" (18:14a). The enemy, thus confronted, is scattered and routed.

The valleys of the sea were exposed. The mythological character of the theophany is revealed as the language of divine conflict slips over into the cosmic struggle between Yahweh and the chaotic waters of creation. The shift in verse 15 connects the enemies against which Yahweh comes with the waters of the earth that are forced to withdraw before the majestic power and

---

20. This phrase occurs in reference to Baal in the Canaanite literature from Ugarit. A generous sampling of these texts can be found in Beyerlin, *Near Eastern Religious Texts Relating to the Old Testament*, esp. 196, 198, 199, 205.

21. For more background on Yahweh as warrior, see Patrick D. Miller Jr., *The Divine Warrior in Early Israel* (Cambridge, Mass.: Harvard Univ. Press, 1973); Tremper Longman III, "The Divine Warrior: The New Testament Use of an Old Testament Motif," *WTJ* 44 (1982): 290–307; Tremper Longman III and Dan G. Reid, *God Is a Warrior* (Grand Rapids: Zondervan, 1995).

22. Ras Shamra is the modern name of the location on the coast of northern Syria where the first discoveries were made of clay tablets written in an alphabetic cuneiform Canaanite language closely akin to ancient Hebrew. The language was subsequently called Ugaritic, after the ancient Canaanite city Ugarit, which was uncovered through archaeological excavations on the spot. For an example of a stele bearing the image of Baal with lightning bolts, see the illustration in Beyerlin, *Near Eastern Religious Tests Relating to the Old Testament*, 212. A photo of the same stela can be seen in *ANETP*, vol. 1, #136.

onslaught of Yahweh. As they flee, the "valleys of the sea" are exposed to sight, and the "foundations of the earth"[23] are revealed.

A common Near Eastern motif is the cosmic struggle between the ancient gods of the chaotic waters (Apsu and Tiamat) against the younger gods of order and stability. The defeat of the ancient gods by the younger was the first step toward stability and order that made human existence on the earth possible. In the Old Testament, these ancient myths have been reinterpreted in light of Yahweh's role as sole deity and creator. Yahweh is the one who divides the waters and sets the boundaries they are not to pass.[24] Elements of struggle between Yahweh and the chaotic ancient waters are retained in such poetic contexts as our present psalm and others (e.g., 74:12–14; 89:9–10; 93:3–4; 124:4–5).[25]

Deliverance. The final segment of the narrative shifts the focus from the power of Yahweh displayed in the storm and in his successful conflict with the chaotic waters to the psalmist's personal experience of deliverance. This connection is made by viewing the distress as being overwhelmed by "deep waters," from which Yahweh extracts the psalmist (18:16). These threatening "waters" are identified with his real enemies 18:17—those "who were too strong for me." Yahweh, however, is the psalmist's "support" (18:18b), and he swoops "down from on high," like some rescuing helicopter, to pull[26] the despairing psalmist to safety.[27]

That the psalmist considers the circumstances desperate is indicated by the use of the term *ʾed* ("[final] disaster") to describe the impending doom represented by the enemies' confronting attack (Heb. *qdm* ["confront, oppose"]; cf. 18:5b, where the "snares of death" confront the psalmist). Yet Yahweh leads

---

23. The imagery is of the stable foundation or pillars on which the whole earth is viewed as resting. Ordinarily these foundations were covered by the waters of the seas and are related to the "foundations of the mountains" that were shaken by Yahweh's approach in 18:7b.

24. In the Genesis account of creation (Gen. 1), the earth is initially chaotic ("formless and empty," 1:2) and associated with the ancient waters (the "deep" [*tehom*], mentioned in 1:2, is linguistically related to the name Tiamat). It is Yahweh who acts on the waters to limit them and provides a secure and stable environment for human life (1:6–13).

25. Outside the psalms this struggle is also reflected in Job 38:8–11; Isa. 51:9–10; Jer. 5:22; Hab. 3:8–10.

26. This rare Heb. verb (*mšh*) is used elsewhere only in the parallel passage in 2 Sam. 22:17 and in Ex. 2:10, where it provides the etymology of the name Moses (Heb. *mošeh*).

27. I am reminded of graphic photos of the removal of U.S. personnel from Saigon at the end of the Vietnam War. As the enemy closed in, one particularly striking picture shows an American helicopter hovering above the U.S. embassy compound while desperate individuals huddle below, awaiting their turn to be lifted out to the waiting aircraft carriers at sea. The scene is heavy with gloom and near panic, with the helicopter offering the only hope of escape.

the psalmist out into a "spacious place," a place with breathing room, where the strictures of siege and attack are removed (18:19a).

Because he delighted in me. Divine aid is the consequence of divine "delight" in the psalmist. Yahweh has a relationship of protective joy with him. This awareness forms a transitional bridge with the following confessional section. Here rescue depends on an attitude of divine delight and pleasure; in what follows, divine pleasure with humans rests on a foundation of righteousness and loyalty—characteristics that Yahweh possesses innately as part of his essential character but which humans are called to emulate in response to divine love.

Instruction in Righteousness (18:20–29)

THESE TEN VERSES admonish the readers/hearers to enter into a relationship of righteous loyalty to Yahweh so that they too might experience divine delight and deliverance. The section is further divided into three subsections that alternate between the personal experience of the psalmist (vv. 20–24, 27–29) and more general instruction to the faithful (vv. 25–26).

Personal righteousness. The first subsection is clearly marked off by an inclusio of almost identical verses at beginning and end (18:20, 24),[28] which set out the primary theme of the whole larger section: Divine deliverance is a consequence of personal righteousness, loyalty, and cleanness of hands. This is intended to encourage those who hear to use the psalmist's experience as a guide in order to experience divine deliverance in their own lives.

Between the two elements of the inclusio, the psalmist protests innocence in relation to Yahweh's demands. He has kept loyalty to Yahweh by having "kept his ways" and not "turned from him" (18:21). More specifically he claims adherence to the "laws" (*mišpaṭayw*) and "decrees" (*ḥuqqotayw*) of Yahweh—a clear reference to the Mosaic law (18:22). Finally, the psalmist assumes a position of ultimate satisfaction of divine expectation that is styled as "blameless" avoidance of "sin." While this does *not* assume absolute

---

28. The opening phrases form affirming parallelism with a chiastic arrangement of members:

> The LORD has dealt with me according to my righteousness;
> according to the cleanness of my hands he has rewarded me.

The concluding phrases mimic the first but with subtle alterations. The secondary verb "reward" is shifted to replace the initial verb "dealt." The loss of "reward" in the secondary phrase is compensated by the introduction of the new phrase "in his sight."

> The LORD has rewarded me according to my righteousness,
> according to the cleanness of my hands in his sight.

perfection, it does imply a serious dedication to righteousness and availing oneself of the remedies for sin and restoration of relationship set out in the Mosaic law.

Admonition to the faithful. The second subsection (18:25–26) uses the device of repeated reciprocity to encourage the faithful to adopt a fruitful relation to Yahweh. The basic premise is that since one receives from Yahweh what one gives to Yahweh, it is best to choose a lifestyle that issues forth in blessing rather than disaster. The subsection is marked by a shift to second-person direct address to Yahweh.

Using a series of balanced phrases introduced by the Hebrew particle *ʿim* ("if") and continuing with nouns followed by verbs of the same root, the psalmist drives home the intimate relationship between human character and divine response. To the "faithful" (*ḥasid* ["one who is loyal to covenant obligations"]) Yahweh demonstrates faithfulness (from *ḥsd* ["show oneself faithful"]). To the "blameless" (*gebar tamim*) he is "blameless" (from *tmm* ["show oneself blameless"]) in return. To the "pure" (*nabar*, from *brr*) Yahweh is also "pure" (from *brr*). By way of contrast, however, to those who are "crooked" (*ʿiqqeš*), Yahweh shows himself to be "shrewd" (from *ptl*).[29]

Personal empowerment. The third subsection (18:27–29) offers a series of summary statements that move the discussion from the more general acknowledgment of the previous section that Yahweh is the hope of the faithful (18:25–26) to the more specific and personal recognition that Yahweh is indeed the psalmist's own source of strength against the enemy. These three verses are each introduced by the particle *ki* ("for, because"), providing the grounds for the confidence previously expressed.

The first statement (18:27) employs the characteristic wisdom contrast between the "righteous/humble" and the "wicked/haughty" to make transition from the earlier general reflection on Yahweh's caring response to the faithful to the more personal experience of the psalmist. Yahweh "saves the humble but brings low ... [the] haughty."

Using two independent images—light within darkness and the necessary courage to face battle—the psalmist now attests personally to Yahweh's empowerment in the face of difficult and threatening circumstances. In the darkest night, Yahweh supplies the psalmist's lamp with oil so that the resulting light turns back the darkness.[30] It is like an endless supply of batteries to

29. Here the repeated reciprocity between noun and verb is broken at last—perhaps as an illustration of the broken relationship created by human "crookedness."

30. It is interesting that here both "lamp" and "darkness" are considered possessively by the use of the first-person singular pronominal suffix ("my"). This emphasizes the psalmist's personal experience of deliverance from trouble.

keep the flashlight going when one is lost in the dark woods, or like a ready supply of firewood to keep the wolves at bay while sending out signals to the rescue party. For the soldier faced by a whole enemy troop or the attacker scaling the wall of a fortress bristling with soldiers, Yahweh supplies the energy and courage to move forward against seemingly insurmountable odds.

The Way of Victory (18:30–45)

A CHANGE FROM first-person direct address to third-person description of God signals the shift to the fourth major section of the psalm: a description of the victory that the faithful experience when they trust in the "perfect way" of Yahweh. The section is introduced by verses 30–31, which return to the major themes of refuge and God as "rock" (*ṣur*) with which the psalm began (18:1–2). Note how reference to God as rock returns also at the beginning of the final section of the psalm (18:46), suggesting a purposeful structural function for this theme.

His way is perfect. As the psalmist claims to have followed the righteous paths set out by Yahweh (18:21), so Yahweh perfectly fulfills what is expected of the divine covenant partner. His "way" of dealing with humans and the world cannot be faulted—Yahweh is *tamim* ("whole, complete, intact, integrated"), just as the psalmist has claimed to be *tamim* (18:23). This means Yahweh can be trusted to do what he says, to act according to his promises and commitments. The synonymously parallel second phrase bears this foundation of trust out even further, since each word of Yahweh is also "flawless" (18:30b ["refined for purity, tested"]).[31]

Shield . . . refuge. Because of the integrity of God's way and the purity of his word, he can be trusted as a shield and refuge by those who bind themselves to him by righteousness and "cleanness of hands" (cf. 18:20–24). To these faithful ones, Yahweh proves to be a faithful deliverer and shield (cf. 18:25–27). Yahweh is the rock who provides refuge for those who trust in him (18:31; cf. 2:12). The psalmist's confidence in Yahweh is expressed in the form of two rhetorical questions: "Who is God besides [*mibbalᶜade*][32] Yahweh? And who is the Rock except [*zulati*][33] our God?" The obviously anticipated

---

31. Note the connection with Ps. 17:3, where the psalmist calls on Yahweh to "test" the psalmist's faithfulness. In both cases the verbal root *ṣrp* is used so that Yahweh's word has been "tested" (*ṣarup*) and found true. Yahweh provides the paradigm for the psalmist's own character.

32. This comparatively rare preposition occurs only seventeen times in the Old Testament, and only this once in the psalms. The basic meaning is "apart from" or "except for."

33. Another relatively rare preposition that occurs only eighteen times in the whole Old Testament. This is the only appearance in the psalms. The preferred meaning is "except, besides."

answer is "No one!" Yahweh is the only trustworthy source of refuge and deliverance available to the faithful.

Arms me with strength. God as "rock," "refuge," and "shield" are not fuzzy, pious, hopeful concepts to the psalmist; they are grounded in the harsh and yet practical context of real-world experience. God here is not a vague, "pie-in-the-sky-by-and-by" future hope but an effective reality of strength and deliverance here and now. Along with giving strength, Yahweh also provides sure footing in the conflicts of life (18:32b–33). In 17:5, the psalmist refers to surefootedness as a sign of commitment to Yahweh. Here it is Yahweh who makes the psalmist nimble like a deer in rough terrain.

The image the psalmist chooses—perhaps from personal experience, perhaps from poetic empathy—is almost a divine "boot camp" for warriors. As Paul in Ephesians 6:10–18 admonishes the faithful to take advantage of the full array of spiritual armor available from God in their fight against the spiritual powers of this world, so the psalmist envisions a divine program of training and equipping that will enable the faithful to turn back enemy onslaughts and achieve victory over them. While this psalm expresses David's response to divine deliverance from his enemies, to focus only on this experience misses the intended admonition of the faithful through the ages to allow God to train and prepare them for the struggles they face.

Here those struggles are styled as military conflicts requiring physical battle with sword, bow and arrows, agility, and endurance. But as we have seen from Paul's passage on spiritual armor, these conflicts may be spiritual as well. Certainly the reason this psalm was reused, preserved, and passed on was its ability to continue to speak to a variety of persons and contexts of conflict—whether physical or emotional, military engagement or spiritual conflict. We will return to this subject in the section on Contemporary Significance

He trains my hands for battle. The psalmist considers Yahweh the source of strength, endurance, agility, and skill in battle. He uses a variety of images to drive this home. Not only does Yahweh strengthen the narrator's arms (18:32a), but he also makes his feet agile like the deer so that he is secure in precarious places (18:33). The psalmist is empowered to bend the powerful compound bow[34] to do battle. He is protected by Yahweh's "shield of victory" (or "salvation," 18:35a), and God himself supports the weary warrior in the midst of the fight (18:35b-c).

You broaden the path. Even the path the psalmist takes during the conflict is guarded and guided by God. In a play on the psalmist's earlier acknowledgment that Yahweh's "way" is "perfect" (*tamim* in 18:30a), it is now Yahweh

34. Compound bow // bow of bronze (see Craigie, *Psalms 1–50*, 176).

who, during the heat of battle, makes the psalmist's "way" "perfect" (*tamim* in 18:32b). The immediate context implies that Yahweh is protecting the psalmist's every move in battle so that he is preserved from deadly mistakes of movement and judgment. In the middle of hand-to-hand combat it is easy to slip or to move without thinking into a restricted position that prevents effective fighting and gives the opponent the advantage. God is watching the psalmist like a fellow soldier to see this does not happen. This interpretation is supported by the parallel thought in 18:36, where Yahweh broadens the terrain so that the psalmist's footing remains sure.

I pursued my enemies. The psalm now moves from a section of "you" language, describing Yahweh's equipping of the psalmist, to "I" language, detailing his use of that equipping to defeat the enemy. The psalmist "pursues" (*rdp*), "overtakes" (*nśg*), "destroys" (*klh*), and "crushes" (*mḥṣ*) the enemy so that they fall at his feet—either dead or in an act of submission (18:37–38).[35]

You armed me with strength. The psalmist returns to a recognition that any accomplishments of strength on the battlefield are the results of divine empowerment. "You" language returns, and the theme of divine strengthening first encountered in 18:32a is reprised, so that the defeat and submission of the enemies is ultimately God's accomplishment (18:39–40a).

I silenced my foes. The final phrase of verse 40 returns to "I" language and both concludes the preceding section (18:39–40) and prepares for what follows. The verb used here (*ṣmt*) ought to be translated "I silenced them [those who hate me]" rather than the NIV's "I destroyed [them]." Yahweh's

---

35. It is worth mentioning that the sequence of verbs employed in this description of the empowered psalmist defeating the enemy, which the NIV translates as a description of a *past* event remembered, are actually imperfect verb forms (or perhaps cohortatives?), which normally express incompleted action, usually in the future—a fact noted by only few commentators (see, e.g., Kidner, *Psalms*, 1:95–96). Delitzsch (*Psalms*, 1:265) suggests (perhaps rightly) that the context is retrospective, so that while the narrative with imperfects assumes an immediacy of narrative as if it is currently happening, the actual events are still past. [Bruce K. Waltke and M. O'Connor, *An Introduction to Biblical Hebrew Syntax* (Winona Lake, Indiana: Eisenbrauns, 1990), ß 31.2b, call this type of imperfect *customary non-perfectives*.] However, one ought to at least consider the possibility that the psalmist is here anticipating *future* victories yet to be realized. Part of the pressure to understand these verses as already past comes from the identification of this psalm with David's deliverance from his enemies, as indicated in the heading (18:0) and by the connection with the parallel psalm in 2 Sam. 22. It is also true that the parallel text in 2 Sam. 22 creates an unambiguously past reference by supplying significant verb forms with what are traditionally pointed as *waw* consecutives. However, the contrast created by this alternative text only serves to emphasize the alternative possibility introduced by the psalm where consecutive imperfects are not used. This would seem a conscious decision on the part of the redactor who produced the text, whether the psalm is prior to the 2 Samuel text or dependent on it. Without these links, it would not be unnatural to assume that here the author is speaking of the future rather than the past.

empowerment of the psalmist, their forced submission, and their inability to flee have resulted in the psalmist's experience of "silencing" the foe who had previously taunted. In verse 41, these defeated and silenced enemies are effectively muffled again as their pleas for help—even to Yahweh himself—go unheeded. They are left vulnerable to the attack of the psalmist, who describes his victory in the "I" language of 18:42.

I beat them as fine as dust. The background of the images used in this verse is not certain but sounds like a potter beating up old pots into powder in order to reconstitute it as clay once more (cf. Ps. 2:9), although the winnowing of wheat to separate it from the chaff also seems to fit the "blowing in the wind" image. Craigie's "pulverized"[36] is graphic but does not exactly capture the nuance of the verb *šḥq*, which describes an act of "grinding" a substance (such as incense) into powder rather than beating it.

The parallel phrase is rendered difficult by confusion regarding the verb *ʾariqem* ("empty, pour out"), which 2 Samuel 22:43 reads as *ʾadiqqem* ("crush, pulverize"—a more exact parallel with the preceding phrase). Where the dust in the first phrase is blown away "on the wind," it is "wet clay, mud, potter's clay" that is either "poured out" or "crushed" in the street. Some translators take the latter to mean "trampled under foot."[37] It seems to me that the psalmist is mixing metaphors here—describing the fineness of the pulverized material by reference to the fine dust blown about by the desert sirroco and then reverting to a wet clay image in the following line. Regardless, the idea of destroying and discarding the enemy is complete.

You have delivered me. Note the literary pattern that is well established by the time the reader reaches this verse. In a series of "you" statements the psalmist describes Yahweh's saving and equipping acts (cf. 18:35–36, 39–40, 43). Then in each case he moves to describe a personal experience of the consequences of this divine empowerment (18:37–38, 41–42, 44–45), the first two of which are marked by repeated "I" language.

Here divine deliverance has led to unanticipated authority over the defeated enemy, who are understood as defeated "nations" for the first time. The narrator becomes—by Yahweh's empowerment—the "head of nations" and is served by peoples he did not even know existed! Here the narrator begins to be identified in a "kingly" way. He is "head of nations," and people "serve" and "obey" (*šmᶜ*)[38] him. Foreigners "cringe" (lit., "feign submission"),

36. Cf. Craigie, *Psalms 1–50*, 168.

37. Kraus, *Psalms 1–59*, 254–55.

38. The construction is difficult here—Kraus (ibid., 256) even suggests that it be "set aside" altogether. The parallel in 2 Sam. 22 has *lišmoaᶜ ʾozen* ("as soon as the ear hears"; Qal infinitive construct) instead of the more obscure *lišemaᶜ ʾozen* ("report of the ear; hearsay"; see *CHALOT*, 377) in the present text.

"lose heart" (lit., "wither, fall like leaves") before him, and come "trembling from their strongholds" (lit., "dungeons").[39] The picture is of a conquering king receiving the submission of his enemies.

Conclusion of Praise (18:46–50)

THE PSALM CONCLUDES with a song of praise to Yahweh for deliverance and victory. This section begins by referring to Yahweh as the psalmist's "rock" (*ṣuri*), linking back to the opening lines of the psalm (18:2) as well as to the opening of the previous section (18:31), and bringing this important theme of the psalm to an appropriate end.

Once again the section moves back and forth from "he" language describing Yahweh's role as deliverer/empowerer (18:46–48a, 50), "you" language praising Yahweh directly (18:48b–49), and "I" language expressing the narrator's firm commitment to praise and exalt God (18:49). The conclusion revisits the major themes of the psalm, including Yahweh as "rock" and the author of victory (18:46, 47, 50) and the narrator empowered by God to subdue and rule over the enemy (18:48b, 50). Here, finally, the narrator is specifically identified with kingship and David (18:50). This concluding phrase (also present in 2 Sam. 22) leaves uncertain whether the kingly figure intended is actually David or a member of the Davidic dynasty who occupies the throne at a particular point in time. The last phrase "to David and his descendants forever" tends to support the latter understanding.

The psalmist's promise to "sing praises to" the name of Yahweh among the nations (18:49) mirrors the similar promises made in 9:11 and 57:9 and the comparable commitment to praise Yahweh "before the gods" in Psalm 138. While this promise could certainly reflect preexilic concern to attest loyalty to Yahweh in Israel surrounded by the pagan nations, the sentiment clearly took on heightened significance for the exilic community, who were "scattered among the nations" (cf. Pss. 44:11; 106:27; Ezek. 20:23) and who struggled with what it meant to continue to "sing the songs of Zion" and "the LORD's songs" while in captivity in foreign lands (cf. Ps. 137). While the appearance of this theme in clearly exilic contexts does not mean that our present psalm was composed to speak to the community of exiles, it surely represents one important reason why Psalm 18 was treasured and preserved by those who had experienced a similar call to commitment in the face of conflict with pagan religion.

---

39. Perhaps the image here, rather than defeated enemy, is of prisoners set free, who come forth from their captivity uncertain of the present circumstances and their future.

DIVINE OTHERNESS. WHEN the psalmists employ fearsome imagery to capture the radical "otherness" that marks God's approach to the sphere of human existence, they often emphasize the effects of God's presence on the physical creation. Mountains smoke and melt, the earth quakes, and even the seas recede as if seeking to avoid the holy God. In these descriptions the psalmists are communicating several truths about the world in which we live.

(1) Creation is *not* the creator but can in fact be threatened by God's approach and presence. Like the humans who reside within it, the physical earth is corrupted by evil and subject to the judgment of God's essential holiness—with its incompatibility with evil. While Genesis 1–11 makes it clear that the earth only came to its corrupted state as a result of human evil and disobedience, the earth is seen as vulnerable to the powerful presence of holy God.

This vulnerable "otherness" is also seen in the fact that the earth owes its very existence and continuation to the mercy and grace of the creator God. The fact that when Yahweh comes, the very foundations of the earth are shaken to their core, illustrates that the continued existence of the earth is wholly dependent on the will and purpose of God.

The fearsome phenomena that attend Yahweh's coming have much in common with the judgment unleashed on the earth by God in the Flood (Gen. 6–9). When God saw that humans were unremittingly evil (6:5) and that the whole earth had been infected by their violence (6:11–12), he determined to release the chaotic waters above and below the earth—waters he had restricted at creation in order to provide the secure environment that allows humans to thrive. The decision to flood the earth was in essence a decisive act of *uncreation*. The chaotic waters threatened to undo the tenuous stability represented by the earth and demonstrated decisively that the protective environment depends entirely on God's gracious will. The approach of the righteous God into a decidedly unrighteous world presents much the same threat.

(2) By undoing the stability of creation, God is undermining any false sense of reliance by humans on their seemingly secure environment. In the words of the old spiritual, "This world is not my home, I'm just a passin' through!" Humans must hold existence in this world lightly and rely on God alone rather than any stability the world may seem to represent.[40]

40. This may also help explain the existence of destructive natural phenomena in the world. Tornadoes, hurricanes, earthquakes, and the like drive home convincingly that our world is not ultimately a stable environment we can rely on. As a result, we are driven to place our trust in God alone.

(3) Another image of divine "otherness" is the psalmist's use of the "consuming fire." Elsewhere in Scripture, the biblical writers acknowledge that God is in his essential character a "consuming fire."[41] When Deuteronomy 4:24 affirms that "the LORD your God is a consuming fire, a jealous God" (quoted in Heb. 12:29), it is saying something akin to Yahweh's own declaration to Moses in Exodus 33:20: "You cannot see my face, for no one may see me and live." Yahweh is righteous, holy, wholly other, and absolutely incompatible with evil and sin.[42] Thus, the problem of how sinful humans might come unharmed into the presence of a holy God necessitated—in Israel's historical understanding—the institution of sacrificial worship intended to atone for sin and to make continued communion with God possible.

Despite the promise of divine forgiveness and restoration of relationship held out in Israel's temple worship system, Israel never forgot the fearful aspect of coming unprepared into the presence of God. While Moses might visit with Yahweh "face to face" (Ex. 33:11; Deut. 34:10), others found the prospect daunting. Jacob was shaken after realizing God was at Bethel (Gen. 28:10–19), and the people of Israel who gathered at Mount Sinai were so terrified by the appearance of the glory of Yahweh on the top of the mountain (with theophanic smoke, fire, and quaking) that they refused to speak with him directly ("face to face") but sent Moses as their intermediary (Ex. 20:18–21; Deut. 5:4–5).

Jewish tradition tells us that even the high priest, who entered the Most Holy Place once a year to deliver the blood of the sin offering to the atonement cover of the ark of the covenant, must have done so with fear and trembling. He wore bells attached to his garments to indicate to those outside (should they cease to jingle) if he was struck down by God and needed to be hauled out by the ever-present rope tied around his ankle. Entering God's presence was (and still is) serious business and is fraught with danger for the sinful, unwary, or unaware.

Rather than just a sign of divine displeasure, then, it is this inherent danger of coming into the presence of Yahweh that the psalmist captures in these tense images of a God breathing smoke and fire, shaking the foundations of the earth with his coming. Even at his most beneficent, Yahweh is no one to be trifled with or approached lightly.

Light within darkness. The psalmist effectively uses the interplay between light and darkness to demonstrate the dual nature of Yahweh's essential holiness. On the one hand, the dark clouds in which Yahweh cloaks himself

41. Ex. 24:17; Deut. 4:24; Isa. 33:14; Heb. 12:29.

42. See also comments on Ps. 5:4–5.

represent the impending judgment against sinful humans. God's withdrawal from full and open fellowship with them is a consequence of human disobedience and sin. Thus, humans no longer enjoy direct communion with their maker. Because the gloom obscures his essence, there is a sense of mystery and foreboding that attends the experience. Also, because the gloom shrouds the destructive potential of a full encounter with God, the deepening gloom can have a fearsome quality to those who deserve judgment (cf. Jer. 13:16). In some of the prophets, the fixed phrase "a day of clouds [*ᶜanan*] and gloom [*ᶜarapel*]" represents Yahweh's coming judgment (Ps. 97:2; Ezek. 34:12; Joel 2:1–2; Zeph. 1:15–17).[43]

On the other hand—and in this context perhaps more important—this darkness has the effect of protecting sinful humans from the destructive consequences of the glory of God. It is a gracious act for God to come so close to humans without injuring them. Notice how Psalm 18 juxtaposes Yahweh's covering himself with darkness (18:11) and the brightness that breaks through the clouds before him (18:12). Even in the threatening gloom, the brightness of God's essential being is not completely obscured. In his coming, all is not darkness and obscurity, but his glory shines through to offer glimpses of his character and hope for deliverance.

I remember experiencing several near complete solar eclipses. As the disk of the moon began to obscure the sun, natural light began to fade into a murky dusk. Shadows on the ground rippled and quavered. Eventually only the corona of the sun could be seen around the edges of the disk. Yet it could not completely subdue the sun's brightness, which continued to break out at the edges so that an observer had to take care to watch the whole process indirectly or through a special coated glass to avoid getting one's eyes burned.

Similarly, the darkness that shrouds Yahweh only serves to emphasize the brilliance of the radiance cloaked within. No one is left wondering whether God is present or not or what his true nature might be. As John says of Jesus, "In him was life, and that life was the light of men. The light shines in the darkness, but the darkness has not [overcome it].... The true light that gives light to every man was coming into the world" (John 1:4–5, 9).[44]

The God who responds. The central part of Psalm 18 (vv. 20–29) embodies the psalmist's confidence that Yahweh will respond with deliverance.

---

43. Isaiah 60:1–3 uses the term *ᶜarapel* to establish a hopeful contrast between the other nations, who are covered with the gloom of God's judgment, while Israel anticipates the rising of Yahweh's glory over them.

44. The translation is a slight modification of the NIV translation. At the end of verse 5, the NIV translates "darkness has not understood it," rather than the more common translation "darkness has not overcome it."

These verses make clear Israel's understanding that Yahweh was a God who shaped his interaction with humans to *their* needs and character. Yahweh was not a "one-size-fits-all" kind of God but one who allowed his own people to influence how their relationship with God worked itself out.

For Israel Yahweh was not static, fixed, or predictable. This does not mean that God was constantly changing, but it does mean he revealed himself to be neither capricious nor whimsical. His essential core is stable: Yahweh is "holy." As I have indicated elsewhere,[45] Israel understood this essential character of God to hold in tension two inseparable components. God is at once and always incompatible with evil, yet relentlessly good. Nevertheless, human experience of God is varied and changing. For example, it took Israel several centuries to win her way from polytheism (belief in many gods who demand my allegiance) through henotheism (belief that many gods exist but only one demands my allegiance) to true monotheism (belief that only one God exists and demands my allegiance). Along the way Israel's experience of God was constantly growing.

In 18:20–29, the psalmist declares an obvious reciprocity between the way we relate ourselves to God and the way he in return responds to us. This is first marked out by the inclusio that frames the first four verses of this section. "The LORD has dealt with me according to my righteousness; according to the cleanness of my hands ..." (18:20). God responds appropriately to human character—in this case responding to the psalmist's righteousness with deliverance.

This initial affirmation is borne out in the continuing verses. Yahweh responds faithfully to the faithful, shows blamelessness to the blameless, and manifests purity to the pure. Character anticipates a balanced divine response. The crooked, however, find God to be shrewd, and the proud find themselves humbled by God.

This sort of reciprocal relationship between human character and divine response is sometimes called retribution—a type of understanding commonly associated with many of the proverbs. "The eyes of the LORD are everywhere, keeping watch on the wicked and the good" (Prov. 15:3). "Whoever gives heed to instruction prospers, and blessed is he who trusts in the LORD" (16:20). "The LORD detests the thoughts of the wicked, but those of the pure are pleasing to him" (15:26). "The LORD is far from the wicked, but he hears the prayer of the righteous" (15:29; cf. 10:27; 11:4, 8, 19–20.)

Against any sort of slavish cause-and-effect understanding—such as promulgated by "prosperity preachers" of our current context—Job and Ecclesiastes (and even some of Proverbs) offer full and effective defense. Job

45. See comments on Ps. 5:4–5.

demonstrates decisively that righteousness is no assurance of prosperity or even good health or reputation. Ecclesiastes concurs: "There is something else meaningless that occurs on earth: righteous men who get what the wicked deserve, and wicked men who get what the righteous deserve. This too, I say, is meaningless" (Eccl. 8:14).

The ultimate conclusion of these wisdom works is that wisdom and righteousness are the only way of life, even if they do not lead to prosperity. Job finds God worth holding on to even in the midst of his painful suffering and loss (Job 42:1–6). Ecclesiastes concludes that in the end, the whole duty of humanity is to "fear God and keep his commandments" (Eccl. 12:13). And even the Proverbs distinguish between the benefit of righteousness and the passing blessings of wealth and security: "Better a little with the fear of the LORD than great wealth with turmoil" (Prov. 15:16); "better a little with righteousness than much gain with injustice" (16:8).

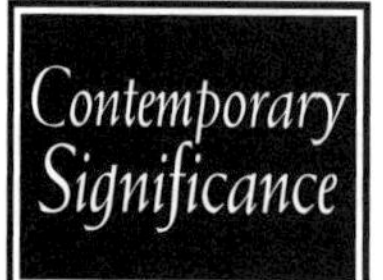

FACING THE QUAKES. Growing up in southeast Texas, I had a lot of experience of hurricanes and floods but none of earthquakes. While attending Fuller Seminary in Pasadena, California, however, I had the disconcerting experience of surviving the 1971 earthquake in Los Angeles—a major one and my first. I remember awaking in the early dawn unaware of what had wakened me. I was impressed by an absolute silence. Then the quiet was shattered by a loud chorus of barking dogs near and far, and almost immediately the first rolling wave of the earthquake began to shake our apartment.

I immediately knew—no questions asked—that this was an earthquake. I sprang from the bed and the first thought in my mind was to save the two tall dresser mirrors that I had delayed for some months attaching to the walls. As I leapt about in pursuit of my rescue task, the room tottered and shook. I could hear things crashing and banging in the other rooms. Then the mirrors toppled off the dresser and one smashed against my knee as they fell to the floor.

Almost as soon as it began, the quake was over (although those few seconds seemed like an eternity to me), and the apartment settled back down into an uneasy quiet—except for the continued barking of dogs. I discovered my wife—a fifth-generation native Californian, mind you—standing appropriately in the doorway of our bedroom with a look composed of a little fear and a lot of amusement at my frantic antics, now that the danger had passed.

During the next few days we cleaned up our apartment, where the contents of shelves had been emptied on the floor and even the eggs in the door of the refrigerator had all been cracked by the fierce shaking. I particularly remember the momentary panic that attended each aftershock that came over the next few weeks. I certainly can relate to the psalmist's description of the trembling and quaking of the earth down to the foundations of the mountains.

I think many of us today have real difficulty imagining the presence of God in such earthshaking and awe-inspiring terms. In many contemporary congregations God through Jesus has become a familiar friend rather than a holy God. We seem to jump up and down singing praises rather than prostrate ourselves, struck dumb by the awesome presence of God.

While I do think it is important for our contemporary culture to understand that God is our helper and friend, I also think something essential is lost when we *never* experience the shock of God's holy presence as did Moses (Ex. 3:1–6), Jacob (Gen. 28:10–22), Isaiah (Isa. 6:1–9), and Paul (Acts 9:1–19). God is, of course, a friend who loves and comforts us, but he is also the holy God, who knocks our socks off and shakes us to our very foundations. We need to experience God as both if we are to keep our faith in the right perspective.

The fearsome display of theophany warns us not to place too much confidence in our seemingly secure environment. God is not the world and at best has only an uneasy relationship with the world. Ultimately, the world as we know it must be done away with and renewed in order to make way for "a new heaven and a new earth" (Rev. 21:1), which will allow humans and God to coexist together forever.[46]

According to my righteousness. The psalmist (18:20–24) expects to be treated by God in accord with his righteousness. Such a claim may make many of us uncomfortable, who understand with Paul that "there is no one righteous, not even one" (Rom. 3:10). Several Old Testament writers affirm similar convictions: "No one living is righteous before you" (Ps. 143:2); "there is not a righteous man on earth who does what is right and never sins" (Eccl. 7:20).

In this context it seems clear that our psalmist's claim of righteousness is no pretension of absolute sinlessness but is instead a claim of having assumed the appropriate attitude of "fear of Yahweh." Those who fear God know that they are ultimately dependent on his gracious mercy for life and continued preservation. Truly relying on God in this way is taking the path of Yahweh—

46. Gerhard Lohfink, *Does God Need the Church?*, discusses how in Revelation creation imagery of the heaven and earth surrounded by continuing threat of the chaotic waters is reenvisioned as a new heaven and earth in which the chaotic waters are no longer present: "The first earth had passed away, and there was no longer any sea" (Rev. 21:1).

a way that leads to life. This kind of reliance on God is the Old Testament equivalent of faith in the righteousness that comes from God (Rom. 4:6–25).

Our righteousness counts for something. It may not pay off in wealth and pleasure. We may not achieve all our goals, satisfy our desires, or rise to great influence and power. But the blessing of God's presence in our lives is in direct proportion to our acknowledgment of absolute dependence on him. God does deliver the righteous—although not always *from* their troubles, always *to* renewed experience of the joy of his indwelling spiritual presence. As Job and the Proverbs attest, that is the better way, the way of life.

He makes my way perfect. Related to the psalmist's confession that God responds "according to my righteousness" (18:20–24) is the further admission that it is Yahweh and not the psalmist who "makes my way perfect." (18:32b). The psalmist does not claim sinless perfection, but he relies on Yahweh's gracious provision. In the commentary I indicated that this phrase, linked with the following verse, suggests nimble surefootedness. However, the connection with Yahweh's "perfect way" and "flawless word" in 18:30 implies that much more is at stake here than simply secure footing. It implies that for those who trust and rely on the equipping power of Yahweh to confront and defeat the powers that oppose them, Yahweh makes their path a "blameless" way that mirrors the path of God himself.

That is the gospel message unleashed in an Old Testament idiom! What we cannot do for ourselves—make our path perfect—God can and will do for us. Faith, trust, commitment, and reliance can turn our fumbling steps into a "way" to the fulfillment of God's purposes for us.

Psalm 19

FOR THE DIRECTOR of music. A psalm of David.

1 The heavens declare the glory of God;
the skies proclaim the work of his hands.
2 Day after day they pour forth speech;
night after night they display knowledge.
3 There is no speech or language
where their voice is not heard.
4 Their voice goes out into all the earth,
their words to the ends of the world.

In the heavens he has pitched a tent for the sun,
5 which is like a bridegroom coming forth from his pavilion,
like a champion rejoicing to run his course.
6 It rises at one end of the heavens
and makes its circuit to the other;
nothing is hidden from its heat.

7 The law of the LORD is perfect,
reviving the soul.
The statutes of the LORD are trustworthy,
making wise the simple.
8 The precepts of the LORD are right,
giving joy to the heart.
The commands of the LORD are radiant,
giving light to the eyes.
9 The fear of the LORD is pure,
enduring forever.
The ordinances of the LORD are sure
and altogether righteous.
10 They are more precious than gold,
than much pure gold;
they are sweeter than honey,
than honey from the comb.
11 By them is your servant warned;
in keeping them there is great reward.

12 Who can discern his errors?
Forgive my hidden faults.
13 Keep your servant also from willful sins;
may they not rule over me.
Then will I be blameless,
innocent of great transgression.
14 May the words of my mouth and the meditation of
my heart
be pleasing in your sight,
O LORD, my Rock and my Redeemer.

THIS PSALM IS an awe-filled description of the cosmic self-revelation of God through his creative acts (particularly the heavens) and his gracious instruction in Torah. The lofty praise with which the psalm begins leads at the end to a down-to-earth prayer for forgiveness and personal alignment with God's will and pleasure. Verses 1–6 share a common interest in the creative revelation of Yahweh in the heavens, moving from general description (vv. 1–4; heavens, skies, all the earth) to more specific focus (vv. 5–6; the sun in its circuit through the heavens). The second half of the psalm again shares a common theme of the self-revelation of Yahweh in Torah while offering two subsections that consider, respectively, God's revelation through Torah (vv. 7–11) and human response to that revelation (vv. 12–14).

The Heading (19:0)

THE PSALM IS referred to "the director of music"[1] and attributed to David as a "psalm" (*mizmor*)[2]; no new terms are introduced.

Revelation of God in the Heavens (19:1–4b)

THE HEAVENS DECLARE. The psalm opens not with praise, nor even a call to praise God, but with a description of the proclamation of praise by the products of his creative power—in particular, "the heavens." What we usually recognize as inanimate creation is here given life and voice as the heavens and skies "declare," "proclaim," and "pour forth speech" in praise of the creator. The first two of these verbs are participial forms while the third is an

1. See comments on Ps. 4.
2. See comments on Ps. 3.

imperfect verb form. The participles emphasize the continuously ongoing nature of the proclamation made by the heavens, but the imperfect, in its expression of incomplete action, also indicates that the praise is not ended but continues. This is, then, a continual outcry of nature to God from the moment of creation until now and on into the future.

The first two lines (19:1) are affirmingly parallel in a chiastic arrangement.

The heavens	declare	the glory of God
the works of his hands	proclaim	the skies

The next two lines form also affirming parallelism but without any chiastic features.

Day to day	they pour forth	speech
night to night	they display	knowledge

The parallel members in these verses are instructive (as they were originally intended to be, I am sure). "Heavens" and "skies" are clearly references to the creation account, although the NIV's choice to render the Hebrew *raqia*ᶜ as "skies" rather than the more usual and accurate "firmament" obscures that connection. Together the two terms clearly allude to the creation narrative. In the beginning, God created the "heavens and the earth" (Gen. 1:1)—a merism for everything. Then, as one of his first creative acts, God set up the "firmament" (1:6) to separate the chaotic waters from one another.

The Hebrew term *raqia*ᶜ ("firmament") reflects an ancient understanding of cosmology (the formation and structure of the world) that differs from our modern scientific view. The *raqia*ᶜ is a sort of upside-down bowl that sat on the circular, plate-like earth to form a sealed environment in which human, animal, and plant life were secure. God created this arrangement at the beginning to bring order to the chaotic waters, which were limited by his decree to prescribed boundaries above and below the earth. The celestial objects (sun, moon, stars, etc.) were thought to be fixed in the *raqia*ᶜ and to move about there.

The chaotic waters could be let in through the "windows of heaven" as rain or storms, or they could rise as springs and subterranean torrents from beneath the earth. In the Mesopotamian account of creation,[3] the chaotic waters are thought to be ancient gods of inertia (Tiamat and Apsu) who fight a losing battle with the younger, more active deities led by Marduk. After the

3. There are many English translations of the Mesopotamian creation and flood texts. See, e.g., *ANETP*, 1:28–39; Beyerlin, *Near Eastern Texts Relating to the Old Testament*, 80–99.

ancient water deities are defeated, Marduk splits the body of Tiamat and creates the firmament, separating the waters above and below the earth.

The Flood account in Genesis 6–9 describes how these chaotic waters threatened to "undo" creation by dissolving the limiting boundaries. In the Mesopotamian account, once the waters were unleashed (by an angry god), they were soon out of control, and the gods—part of creation themselves and, therefore, under threat of annihilation as well—cowered behind the walls of their heavenly abode, screaming "like dogs" as they awaited their destruction. This does not happen in the biblical narrative, however, because of God's complete control and gracious mercy. The concluding promise of Genesis 9:12–17 offers the reassurance that humanity never need fear this kind of ultimate threat from the chaotic waters again. Whether one assumes this kind of cosmological description indicates the biblical authors' limited, prescientific understanding of their world or uses poetic imagery and license, it is important to recognize the powerful images associated with this cosmological understanding.

Thus, the psalmist here is not just reflecting on the impressive expanse of the heavens but shows an understanding that goes all the way back to the creation of the universe. It carries with it not only awe at the glorious majesty of the heavens and the splendid sun that dominates the day[4] but is also aware (cf. the term *raqia*ᶜ) of the protective grace of God that the firmament has silently and effectively extended since God formed it.

The work of his hands. The parallel lines of verse 1 also have the interesting effect of bringing together the "glory of God" declared by the heavens with "the work of his hands" proclaimed by the skies. The term *kabod* ("glory") in reference to God normally describes that awesome and innate essence of God that is so intensely "other" than human experience that it is described as brilliant light or a consuming fire (cf. 18:8), which at once awes and threatens to destroy the beholder. Here, however, it is the visible, created work of God's hands that are equated to his "glory." In some strange way the heavens, the sun, and the protective firmament are part of that glory—or at least reflect it for understanding human eyes to see.

Day and night. The story the heavens have to tell is not confined to daylight hours. Although the magnificence of the sun is in the foreground of verses 4b–6, it is clear that the psalmist, like the author of Psalm 8, has also spent time gazing at the far-flung stars and planets of the night sky. The heavenly message is unimpeded and continues to sound twenty-four hours a day, seven days a week, for eternity. Their nightly "display" (from *ḥwh*

---

4. For a similar reverie on the *night* sky, with the resultant realization of divine grace and mercy poured out on humans, see Ps. 8.

["announce, inform"]) is "knowledge," equivalent to the daytime "speech." The parallel Hebrew constructions "day after day" and "night after night" emphasize the continuity of revelation as one day passes the message of divine glory to the next day and each night receives its abiding knowledge from those preceding, representing an unbroken chain of communication going back to creation.

No speech or language. The NIV's translation of verse 3 represents a subtle departure from the norm of commentators. The usual tack is to take these lines as connecting back to the preceding verses and stress the silent character of the heavenly proclamation. They testify to the glory of God without using voice or words that any human could hear. The NIV shifts the nuance and connects verse 3 with what follows. Rather than emphasizing the silence of communication, the phrase now becomes an indication of the all-pervasive extent of the testimony. The "speech" and "language" in question in this interpretation is no longer the mute testimony of the skies but the receptor language of the far-flung human race. There is no part of humanity—whatever the language—that has escaped the proclamation of the heavens about their creator.

Either translation is possible, and the NIV has the added benefit of according well with Paul's similar treatment of revelation through creation (Rom. 1:18–23), where because of the pervasive testimony of creation throughout the earth, no human anywhere has any excuse for failing to recognize God. However, the use in Psalm 19:3 of the same Hebrew word for "speech" that appears clearly linked to the heavens in 19:2a would seem to bring the decision down on the side of the more traditional understanding.

To the ends of the earth. While the link with Romans 1 may not be explicitly made in 19:3, it is certainly established by 19:4. Although the speech, words, and voice of the heavens are inaudible, they nevertheless do have a "voice" (*qaw*)[5] that can be perceived in all the earth and "words" that extend their testimony to the ends of the world. The section concludes with the insistence that the revelation of God through the soundless testimony of the heavens and firmament is all-pervasive and available to all humanity.

The All-Seeing Sun (19:4c–6)

IN THE MIDDLE of verse 4, the psalm takes a new turn by introducing an extended metaphorical description of the sun. In the present context, this

5. The lexicons provide only the meaning "cord, line" for this noun. Dahood (*Psalms*, 1:121–22), however, supplies persuasive support for a cognate noun *qaw* with the meaning "call, sound, proclamation." This would accord with the LXX and Vulgate renderings, meaning "sound." Alternatively, it may be that the *lamed* of the more regular Heb. word *qol* ("voice," which appears in 19:3b) has dropped out of the consonantal text.

description represents a move from the more general "works" of God—heavens, firmament—to a specific example of those works. The shift is akin to a *metonymy*, a literary device in which a part is introduced as representative of the whole. The sun is a part of the heavenly features through which the glory of God has been displayed and communicated since the beginning.

This metaphor assumes that the sun resides in a tent pitched in the heavens by God; then the biblical poet mixes metaphors by viewing the sun first as a bridegroom (19:5a) and then as a mighty man running a race (19:5b).[6] The shifting metaphors make a gradual progress—from residing in the tent (19:4c), to departing from the pavilion (19:5a), to running a course (19:5b), and finally to the sun's trip through the whole "circuit" of the heavens (19:6).

Bridegroom and champion. The "triumphant sweep"[7] of the sun through the heavens displays the glory of God like a bridegroom, who, dressed in his greatest finery and beaming with the joy of the occasion, leaves his "pavilion" (*ḥuppah*).[8] The public nature of such an occasion would involve the whole village population in the celebration, emphasizing the impossibility of missing the event—or, by parallel, the revelation of God. Not to be present at such an occasion would require studied indifference or active enmity toward the family of the bridegroom. God, in his creation of the heavens and the sun, is making himself known to all on just such a scale of joy and glory.

The sun is also likened to a "champion" (*gibbor*, "warrior, mighty man"), who rejoices to "run his course." The NIV'S rendering of "champion" and "course" implies a preset course such as a race. Perhaps a better image (although a less refined one) is of the warrior, who, having worked himself up into an energetic frenzy oblivious to the possibilities of personal injury, rushes headlong toward the enemy in a battle lust that approximates a joy to be active at last after the anxious tensions of waiting. For a warrior people—as the Hebrews certainly were—this sort of fearless indifference to personal safety and joy of battle was a sign of a great warrior. An enemy must prepare for the onslaught while respecting such signs of bravery, and companion warriors will follow the mad rush of such a "champion" into the

---

6. Or perhaps a warrior running to battle or a messenger carrying a report.

7. See *NIVSB*, footnote to 19:4b–6.

8. The *ḥuppah* is perhaps to be connected with the "canopy" under which the Jewish rite of marriage is performed even today. The event has been popularized in theater and motion picture productions of *Fiddler on the Roof* and *Yentl*. Alternatively, the event may describe the moment in the marriage preparations when the groom leaves his home accompanied with all his friends (and indeed the whole village) to proceed through the streets to the home of his bride's family in order to deliver the bride price and receive the father's permission to marry. The joy and attention focused on the bridegroom at either of these occasions would supply an appropriate image for the psalmist.

crush of battle. Once again the psalmist chooses an image for divine revelation that cannot be ignored. God is visible in his creative works and can only be ignored to one's own peril.

Nothing is hidden. This second section of the psalm draws to a close with a pointed reminder to the reader/hearer that as the sun's circuit arcs over all human activity, nothing escapes the watchful eye of the God who created the sun. The sun moves from one end of the heaven to the other, and its heat both warms and illumines all that humans do and say. The psalmist possibly intends a subtle reminder in the use of the phrase "from its/his heat." The underlying Hebrew word can mean both "heat" and "warmth," or in many instances "rage" or "anger"—including that of God in judgment (cf. Jer. 30:23; 32:31–32; 33:5; Ezek. 25:14; 36:6). The sun, then, with its constant scrutiny of human activity from its position in the heavens not only provides welcome warmth but also represents the possibility of divine judgment for sin.

Thematic progression. At this point the thematic progression that stitches the varied elements of this psalm together becomes clear. In the first segment the reader/hearer learns that the works of Yahweh reveal the creator to all who can see them—whatever their language or race. No human has any excuse for failing to recognize the authority of the creator God. In the second section, the glorious sun, which also mirrors God's glory, constantly arcs overhead so that none escape the blessing or judgment implied by its heat. This leads almost naturally to the third section, which introduces the Torah of Yahweh that is intended as guide (19:7–10), warning (19:11a), and reward (19:11b).

Revelation Through Torah (19:7–11)

THERE IS CONSIDERABLE discussion regarding the unity of the psalm, whether the creation imagery (19:1–6) fits with the Torah concerns of the second half of the poem (19:7–11). For some, this earlier component is an adapted Canaanite hymn to the sun,[9] in which the sun, worshiped as a deity by the Canaanites, is clearly marked out as a creature—only one among many of the "works of the hands" of Yahweh. The tendency in recent years, however, has been to accept the unity of Psalm 19, recognizing that sun and law/justice are commonly associated in the ancient Near East, where the sun deity (Utu, Shamash) is indeed the god of justice.[10]

---

9. Dahood, *Psalms*, 1:121; cf. the comments in Craigie, *Psalms 1–50*, 179–80; Kraus, *Psalms 1–59*, 272.

10. Cf. Nahum Sarna, "Psalm XIX and the Near Eastern Sun-God Literature," in *Papers of the Fourth World Congress of Jewish Studies* (Jerusalem: World Union of Jewish Studies, 1967), 171–75.

For those called to know God through his creative works, the divine scrutiny illustrated by the constant arcing of the sun overhead implies the need for a guide in order to satisfy God's will and expectation. The psalm now moves to consider how the Torah (the law) fulfills the role of admonition and guide to reward (19:11), through which Yahweh's will is revealed to those who fear him. The section consists, for the most part, of a series of adjectives describing the character of Torah, each accompanied by a verbal phrase revealing how Torah impacts the life of the faithful. Along the way Torah is paralleled by a series of nouns and phrases that artfully vary and expand on the concept. The same group of related terms is constantly repeated in Psalm 119, where one of these terms appears in almost every line of that extended acrostic poem.[11]

Perfect ... reviving. The first statement is the most programmatic and general. The *torah* ("law") of Yahweh is "perfect" (*tamim*, "whole, complete; without blemish/anything lacking"). This essential wholeness of Torah is the basis of all the other characteristics: trustworthiness (19:7c), rightness (19:8a), radiance (19:8c), purity (19:9), certainty (19:9c), and righteousness (19:9d). Similarly, the effect on the believer is also more general and foundational: Torah causes the whole "being" (*nepeš*; NIV "soul")[12] of the believer to "turn/return."

Many commentators take this Hiphil participle of *šwb* to mean "restore, revive," ignoring one of the more common uses of the verb to describe human repentance and obedience to God and his Torah. This predilection of the commentators is perhaps the result of an assumption that God—honoring free will in humans—does not manipulate or cause humans to "repent." While "restore, revive" is a possible translation here, it seems to me that the poet may well have intended a double meaning, suggesting to the astute reader that the Torah not only *revives* but also calls the faithful to *repent* and *return*. This certainly is compatible with the attitudes revealed in 19:11, where Torah "warns," and in the final section of the psalm, where the narrator feels the need to seek divine forgiveness from both willful and unintentional sin (19:12–13).

---

11. See the discussion of "Acrostic Psalms" in the section on "The Poetry of the Psalms" in the introduction. Of the six terms expounding the concept of divine guidance associated with Torah in Ps. 19 (*torah*, *ᶜedut*, *piqqudim*, *miṣwot*, *yirᵓat yhwh*, and *mišpaṭim*), five occur in the first seven verses of Ps. 119—and in the same order as in our psalm (*torah*, *ᶜedut*, *piqqudim*, *miṣwot*, and *mišpaṭim*). The phrase "fear of Yahweh" (*yirᵓat yhwh*) does not appear in Ps. 119, although references to "*your* [Yahweh's] fear" do occur at 119:63, 74, 79, 120—though not as a description of Torah. In addition to the terms in Ps. 19, Ps. 119 also includes the word "decrees" (*ḥuqqim*) in 119:5 and often.

12. The NIV's "soul" is misleading. See the discussion of *nepeš* in the comments on Ps. 3:1–2.

Trustworthy . . . making wise. Because God's Torah is "perfect" (complete, lacking nothing), it can be trusted to form the firm foundation of human life, providing sure guidance on the way Yahweh knows and blesses (cf. Ps. 1:6). In this case, the term chosen to characterize the Torah is *ᶜedut* ("testimony, warning sign"; NIV "statutes").[13] Like a highway sign notifying drivers of winding roads or treacherous conditions ahead, the Torah is provided to "warn" the faithful of dangerous and slippery conditions that confront them (cf. 19:11a). God's "testimony" is "trustworthy" (from *ʾmn*, "faithful, proved to be reliable").

The sure guide and protective admonition that the Torah represents is useful—even necessary—to instruct simple, naive youth (Heb. *peti*). Here the psalmist is not talking of those who are mentally challenged but of youths who are still so inexperienced and untutored that the options of life leave them confused and in danger of making destructive choices. These are not arrogant, rebellious "fools" (Heb. *kesilim*), but well-intended persons who do not yet possess sufficient experience of life to understand the ramifications and consequences of decisions. For these persons earnestly seeking guidance, the Torah serves to "make them wise."[14]

Right . . . giving joy. In the third set of terms, Torah is likened to undeviating "precepts" (*piqqudim*) that, if followed, lead one straight to the goal of faithful living. The noun *piqqud* is related to the verb *pqd* ("search, appoint, assign, order") and has the meaning of "orders" or "directions" that guide one, like a road map or verbal directions that allow you to find a place you have never visited before. The directions provided by God's Torah are not misleading but are "straight" and do not lead astray. Again, the present characterization grows out of the preceding two. Because God's word in Torah is "whole" and "complete" (19:7a-b), it is also "reliable" and "trustworthy" (19:7c-d), and thus it can provide "undeviating" guidance to life (19:8a). This guidance is not viewed as restrictive but "gives joy to the heart."[15]

Radiant . . . giving light. Reconnecting with the sun imagery in the previous section, the psalmist now describes the "commands" of Yahweh as

13. The noun *ᶜedut* (related to the noun *ᶜedah*, "testimony") is completed by the abstract ending *-ut* and is considered singular, with an distinctive plural—*ᶜedot*. The traditional translation of *ᶜedut* has been "testimony"—though testimony with a decidedly warning edge (cf. Holladay, *CHALOT*, 266). The term is used to describe the tablets of the Ten Commandments (Ex. 31:18; 32:15; 34:29), the ark of the covenant that contains the tablets (Ex. 25:22; 39:35), and, particularly in the psalms, the Torah in general (Pss. 78:5; 81:6; 119:88; 122:4).

14. This is a factitive function of the Hiphil, in which the state described in the Qal ("be wise") is established in the Hiphil ("make wise").

15. Cf. comments on Ps. 9:1–3.

"radiant" and "giving light to the eyes" (19:8c-d). The term the NIV renders as "commands" is actually in the Hebrew a singular form.

God's command is "radiant"—a term sometimes describing purity. As Dahood has shown,[16] this word is often connected with the sun, both in the Canaanite literature from Ugarit and in the Bible itself.[17] A sort of clear, brilliant, pure light is surely intended. This radiance provides light for the eyes of the faithful, lighting their way.[18] To "give light to the eyes" can also mean enliven or restore life, since the eyes dim or lose their light in death (cf. Ps. 13:3; Eccl. 12:3).[19] That a more intellectual form of enlightenment is intended is not so clear.[20]

Pure . . . enduring forever. The psalmist now departs from the pattern established in the preceding verses. That pattern can be described as: *Torah synonym + Yahweh + adjective + factitive participle + noun affected.* In the first four sets, this pattern is followed exactly, and the visual similarity of the phrases is heightened by the use of Hiphil and Piel participles, beginning with the consonant *m-*. Because of the factitive nature of these participial forms (i.e., make to return, make wise, make joyful, enlighten), the following nouns are objects of the participles, indicating the elements affected by the verbal action (i.e., self, naive youth, heart, eyes). In the fifth phrase, however, the participial pattern is altered by the use of a Qal form that does not carry the same factitive function. The following word (*laᶜad*) is an adverb, describing the duration of the preceding verbal action: "enduring *forever*."

These distinct variations from what precedes suggest something different is going on in this passage. This is borne out by the use of *yirʾat* ("fear") as the opening noun of the phrase. In all the preceding phrases, the opening nouns are synonyms linked to Torah. Here, however, the noun is not a Torah word or synonym but a characteristic of the faithful believer. To "fear Yahweh" is to assume an appropriate attitude of humility, loyalty, and absolute dependence on Yahweh. *BHS* recognizes the contrast this term represents and

---

16. *Psalms*, 1:123.

17. Dahood mentions *UT*, 1005:2–4; see Song 6:10, along with our psalm.

18. Illumination is also linked with Yahweh in the great and traditional Aaronic blessing instituted in Num. 6:22–26, "The LORD bless you and keep you; the LORD make his face shine upon you and be gracious to you; the LORD turn his face toward you and give you peace." Cf. also the brief allusion to this blessing in Ps. 67:1. The phrases of this blessing could be taken to reflect sun terminology and movement. Cf. the Egyptian "Hymn to the Aton," celebrating the life-giving power of the sun disc worshiped by the pharaoh Akh-en-aton (ca. 1365–1348 B.C.).

19. The dimming of the eyes is also associated with grief—an experience not far removed from death itself (cf. Job 17:7; Ps. 88:9; Lam. 5:17).

20. See Craigie, *Psalms 1–50*, 182.

suggests an emendation to a word for "speech" (ʾ*imrat*)—another suitable synonym for Torah (cf. Ps. 119:38).[21]

While this is not an impossible emendation, the variation in the participial pattern already signals that we should look at the introduction of "fear of the LORD" more carefully. Rather than continuing a list of characteristics of Torah, the psalmist apparently begins to bring the response of the faithful into view by inserting a clear reference to the enduring blessing of the fear of Yahweh that "purifies" the faithful. The adjective *ṭehorah* can mean "pure, clean, genuine," but it often has the more specific connotation "be *cultically* clean." If "fear of the LORD" results in cultic purity and the consequent ability to stand in the presence of Yahweh "forever," this is strong encouragement for the faithful listener to adopt this most appropriate attitude.

Ordinances . . . sure and altogether righteous. The broken pattern continues into the next phrase. The first part of this phrase reverts to the previous pattern of *torah synonym* + *Yahweh*. The "ordinances" (*mišpaṭim*) of Yahweh is a legal term, which describes a judge's statement of what *should* have taken place in a particular case. As a description of Torah, it implies that this instructive guide to life is God's own statement of what is appropriate in human conduct. A *mišpaṭ* is not just a divine or royal demand—that is, what God wants. Rather, a *mišpaṭ* is a judgment—by no less than God himself—of what *ought* to occur, of what is right.

One of the most difficult aspects of pagan, polytheistic religion in the ancient Near East was the lack of assurance about what the god (or gods) demanded. As the myths from Egypt to Mesopotamia illustrate, the gods were notoriously changeable and could manipulate, trick, and overpower one another; thus, humans could never be certain which god would rule at the moment or what exactly that god might demand. Consequently, although there *were* certain protocols governing human behavior in relation to the gods, the demands of the gods could change from situation to situation.

The matter was complicated further by the lack of any moral superiority to humans among the gods. The ancient gods of polytheism operated with just as twisted a moral standard as humans. They lied, cheated, stole, were sexually promiscuous, and generally outdid their human servants with their lack of consistent morality. They were distinguished from humans by only two major characteristics: They were powerful, and they lived forever. Therefore, whatever the gods demanded had to be obeyed because they had the power to make human existence miserable, and there was no hope of outliving them.

---

21. See also the comments in Dahood, *Psalms*, 1:123–24; Kraus, *Psalms 1–59*, 268.

By contrast, our psalmist says, Yahweh (who is one and unopposed) has given in his Torah a "sure" (*ʾemet*) judgment (*mišpaṭ*) of what constitutes right human behavior. The term *ʾemet* carries a sense of "reliability, permanence, continuity, faithfulness, and fidelity." These are no "wishy-washy" commandments subject to change at the divine whim, but secure and permanent statements of what ought to be. Not only are these *mišpaṭim* considered judgments rather than statements of divine will ("I want..."), but together they represent a "righteous" standard (Heb. *ṣadequ yaḥdaw*). This does not mean that the way of life to be lived by these standards is righteous (although it certainly is), but that the standards themselves are righteous.

Here again the psalmist breaks with the former pattern by introducing a Qal perfect verbal construction rather than the expected participle. The use of the perfect, with its expression of completed action, suggests that the righteous standard of Yahweh's *mišpaṭim* is an accomplished certainty that can be relied on. Since the term "righteous" is a legal one, meaning "judged to have performed what is appropriate in a case under consideration," the *mišpaṭim* of Yahweh are not expressions of divine whim but sure guides to appropriate human behavior.

More precious than gold. Surely a divinely given Torah such as the psalmist describes in these verses—a Torah that is "whole" and "complete" (19:7a-b), that is "reliable" and "trustworthy" (19:7c-d), that provides "undeviating" guidance to life (19:8a), and that is "consistent" and "altogether righteous" in its demands (19:9c-d)—is a precious resource for humans who are struggling to know how to live appropriately in a difficult world. Thus, in 19:10 the psalmist heaps up praise for the value of God's Torah in terms of precious metals ("gold" and "pure gold") and "gourmet delectables" (or perhaps "simple pleasures"?) of the day ("honey" and "honeycomb").

The section concludes with a statement that rounds out the Torah's value while it finishes off the whole Torah section. Yahweh's Torah is considered of such importance and value because it both warns (Heb. from *zhr*)[22] and guides the faithful, keeping them on the path of life and reward (19:11). The psalmist uses the term "your servant" to designate the one or ones who will benefit from the admonition and guidance of divine instruction. While this

---

22. A common modern Israeli warning sign bears a declaration from the same root: *zehirut*! Warning! But it is interesting to note that the root of this participle is also found in the noun *zohar*, yet with an alternate meaning of "shining, splendor." One of the most significant works of Jewish kabbalistic mysticism from the Middle Ages is known by this title *HaZohar* (*The Splendor*), since it records visions of the splendor or the glory (*kabod*) of Yahweh himself. In light of the linking in this psalm of the revelation of God in the heavens and the sun with the revelation in the Torah, the use of this root is suggestive, if not significantly developed.

expression may seem to be a general reference to any faithful believer, the subsequent use of the same phrase in 19:13 makes it clear that the psalmist probably intends this as a self-designation.

The discipline of Torah is twofold: "stick and carrot," admonition and reward. The former is clearly represented in the words of Torah itself while the latter is suggested by the psalmist's own words in the preceding section. As a "reward" the psalmist probably has in mind a "great result" (Heb. *ʿeqeb rab*) of adherence to the demands of God's instruction rather than a promise of great wealth, pleasure, or prosperity. The term *ʿeqeb* describes an "end" or "result" while leaving the nature of that result undefined.

Human Response (19:12–14)

HAVING WONDERED AT the revelation of God declared through heavens and sun and having rejoiced in the admonition and guidance offered through God's Torah, the psalmist turns at last to the appropriate human response of those who adopt the proper attitude of "fear of the LORD." For the first time a personal note clearly enters the psalm as the psalmist employs first-person singular pronouns and verbs to express contrition for sin and hope for forgiveness.

Who can discern his errors? This final section begins with a thematic rhetorical question acknowledging the difficulty of discerning unintentional offenses that one might commit. The term for such offenses (*šegiʾot*) appears only here in the Hebrew Bible but comes from a verbal root (*šgg*) that is more common and carries the meaning "to commit error or sin inadvertently."[23] The implication seems to be that for these inadvertent sins, there is little to do but to trust in the mercy of Yahweh.

The psalmist seeks divine assistance to avoid both "hidden faults" (19:12b) and "willful sins" (19:13a) that threaten to rule over Yahweh's servant. In contrast to the unintentional errors of 19:12a, these offenses seem to be active choices for disobedience and rebellion against God. Thus, "hidden faults" are probably offenses kept secret by the sinner rather than the kind of unknown sin covered by *šegiʾot*. By contrast, "willful sins" are open acts of rebellion known to all in society. The psalmist realizes the potential for such acts of willful rebellion and self-power that have come to the point of ignoring the sanctions even of societal morality to become ruling influence, undermining all areas of life.

Blameless and innocent of great transgression. The psalmist's goal is never sinless perfection but avoiding "great transgression" (*pešaʿ rab*) against God.

23. The NIV translation of this verb in Job 12:16 seems to imply deliberate deception.

There was a certain acceptance of the sinful nature of humanity, for which the Israelite sacrificial system offered remedy and restoration to right relationship with God and other people. Humans can no more achieve sinlessness than they can avoid breathing. Even if one could keep the law precisely and avoid all known sin, there were always those *šegiʾot*—those inadvertent errors of which one is unaware. In this context, the psalmist's hope to become "blameless" (from *tmm*, "be finished, complete; blameless")[24] should be taken as a desire for "completeness" and "wholeness," just as the Torah of Yahweh is "perfect" or "whole" (*tamim*, 19:7a). The wordplay employing the root *tmm* for both Torah and hopeful psalmist is unmistakable. Those who stake their lives on the complete guidance provided by God's instructive Torah will also achieve the kind of wholeness of relationship that avoids willful disobedience.

The words of my mouth and the meditation of my heart. I have often heard this final plea for acceptance used before preaching—and I have used it myself—as a way of submitting one's own words to the mysterious scrutiny of God with whose will and desire the speaker wishes to be aligned. These words carry much the same weight here at the end of Psalm 19. Some commentators want to attach this plea exclusively to the words of this psalm, suggesting the psalmist is seeking divine affirmation and confirmation of the instruction offered here. That may well be true, although I think it does not prevent a broader function as well.

This final verse provides an especially apt conclusion to the theological movement we have observed in this psalm, knitting together its otherwise disparate parts. Because Yahweh is unmistakably revealed in the heavens, humans have no excuse for not acknowledging him. As the sun arcs overhead bathing all in its heat and scrutinizing all that humans do, so humans cannot escape divine awareness (and judgment) of what they say and do. Yahweh has not left humans in the dark as to what he expects of them but has provided complete admonition and guidance in his Torah. Those who follow this guidance can avoid "great transgression" and experience the kind of wholeness of relationship that God intends. In this light, the final plea is the psalmist's attempt to achieve alignment with God's will through inner ("meditations of my heart") and outer ("words of my mouth") integrity. The psalmist is submitting all to the will and purpose of Yahweh.

The final statement, then, is more than a plea for hearing this psalm. It is as well a model of the kind of submission to the will of God admonished in the whole psalm. There is implied in this submission a recognition of a need for personal deliverance and redemption. Yahweh is the speaker's "Rock"

---

24. The verbal form is unusual and unexpected. A few manuscripts read *ʾettam* instead, which would be the regular Qal imperfect form for this verb.

(Heb. *ṣuri*)[25] and "Redeemer" (Heb. *goʾali*), the one in whom the psalmist's hope resides. The use of this "rock" terminology clearly links the words of Psalm 19 back to the theme of refuge that dominates Psalm 18, where the word "rock" appears no less than three times (18:2, 31, 46) in structurally significant positions.[26]

Other verbal linkages connect these psalms as well. In 18:30 we learn that God's "way is perfect [*tamim*; cf. 19:7]" and "the word [*ʾimrah*][27] of Yahweh is flawless," while in 18:32 the speaker hopes his way will be made "perfect" (*tamim*; cf. 19:13c) by God. The *NIV Study Bible* notes that Psalm 19 "completes the cycle of praise—for the Lord's saving acts, for his glory reflected in creation, and for his law" that was begun in Psalm 18.

THE HEAVENS ARE TELLING. Austrian composer Franz Joseph Haydn (1732–1809), in his oratorio *Creation* (*Schöpfung*), included a movement based on Psalm 19 that has outstripped the larger composition in fame and recognition. The magnificent strains of orchestral instruments ("The Heavens Are Telling") join with the combined choral voices to create a splendid aural painting of the heavenly testimony to God's glory that lies at the heart of this psalm.

Psalm 19 is only one place in which the theme of heavenly witness is mentioned. In a variety of passages Israel has explored the role of the heavens in revealing the will, purpose, and nature of Yahweh. In what follows I will consider what Israel understood the heavens to declare.

Creative power. Most obviously, an open gaze at the grandeur of the night sky brought Israelite psalmists to a keen awareness of Yahweh's creative might. Psalm 8 figures prominently in this regard with its awe-filled reverie on the starry expanse of the heavens. But other psalms join the chorus of praise as well (cf. 57:5, 11; 108:5; 113:4; 148:13), and in particular the final Hallel of the Psalter (Pss. 146–150) becomes a crescendo of praise in which the heavens are joined by all creation in praise of their creator.[28] Indeed, the

---

25. See discussion of terms related to the theme of refuge in the comments on Ps. 18:1–2.

26. In addition to the three occurrences of *ṣur* ("rock"), the synonym *selaʿ* ("rock") also occurs in 18:2.

27. If the suggestion to emend *yirʾat yhwh* ("fear of the LORD") in 19:9 to *ʾimrat yhwh* ("word of the LORD") is correct, then the verbal connection with 18:30 is more precise. Even without the exact parallel, however, the use of this synonym for Torah in 18:30 (cf. 119:38) still connects with the strong context established in 19:7–11.

28. Cf. Jer. 32:17: "Ah, Sovereign LORD, you have made the heavens and the earth by your great power and outstretched arm. Nothing is too hard for you."

narratives of Genesis 1–2 are in one sense an expanded testimony to God as creator of heavens and earth and everything in them.

Relentless goodness. Alongside Yahweh's creative power, the heavens testify readily to his consistently good intention for his creation in general and its human inhabitants in particular. Jacob invokes the "blessings of the heavens above" as a sign of Yahweh's beneficent care for his people (Gen. 49:24–25).[29] Deuteronomy understands that the abundant rain from the heavens is an indication of God's blessing (Deut. 28:12). The New Testament understands this divine desire to do good as extending to the unbelieving world when Jesus calls his followers to mirror the love of God, who "causes his sun to rise on the evil and the good, and sends rain on the righteous and the unrighteous" (Matt. 5:45).

Divine judgment. The heavens also reveal the judgment of God on a sinful world. The heavens participated in the judgment unleashed in the Flood when the chaotic waters above the firmament poured down through the windows of heaven on the polluted earth (Gen. 7:11–12). At Sodom and Gomorrah it was "burning sulfur" that fell from the heavens as a consequence of divine judgment on the wicked cities (Gen. 19:24). In Deuteronomy 11:16–17, the shutting off of the heavens "so that it will not rain and the ground will yield no produce" becomes divine judgment for Israel's going after other gods. Though fools may persuade themselves that God is so far removed in the heavens that he neither sees nor is concerned with human life (cf. Job 14:21; 22:14; Pss. 4; 14; 94:7), God does look down from his heavenly vantage point to see and respond to all that humans say and do.

Enduring faithfulness. Also associated with the heavens is the enduring character of Yahweh's faithfulness. The heavens that antedate the creation of humans stand as a paradigm of endurance, so that it is said of David: "I will establish his line forever, his throne as long as the heavens endure" (Ps. 89:29). Of Yahweh's decrees and promises we learn: "Your word, O LORD, is eternal; it stands firm in the heavens. Your faithfulness continues through all generations" (119:89–90). As the heavens stand firm above the earth since the beginning of creation, providing the protective environment in which humans can live, so Yahweh's word is eternally trustworthy—present to lead and guide.

Demythologizing the cosmos. In a more subtle fashion the heavens in Israelite Scripture proclaim that Yahweh is the only true God. In the pagan world of the ancient Near East the heavenly bodies—sun, moon, stars—were

---

29. Jacob's blessing to his sons recalls the blessing he received from his father Isaac: "May God give you of heaven's dew and of earth's richness—an abundance of grain and new wine" (Gen. 27:28).

divine beings who exercised power over their own realms and over humans. In Psalm 19, however, the sun appears not as an independent deity but as one of the "works of [God's] hands" who carry out his bidding. The same is true in Psalm 8, where moon and stars appear as objects of creation—mere "finger play" (8:3) for the creator, Yahweh. A similar move takes place in Psalm 18, where the "seas"—understood in pagan Mesopotamian myths to be ancient gods of chaos who struggled for control of the universe with the younger gods—are described as inanimate elements of creation subject to the will and purpose of Yahweh.[30] By removing the polytheistic element of creation the biblical poets emphasize the sovereignty of Yahweh over the created universe. In this way the heavens with all their features testify to the glory and creative might of the one who made them (cf. Rom. 1:20).

Protective care. Equally subtle is the way the heavens by their very existence declare the protective care and concern of God for his creatures. The use of the term *raqia*ᶜ ("firmament"; see comments on 19:1) links the heavens in Psalm 19 to the protective envelope created at the beginning by the creation of the *raqia*ᶜ (NIV "expanse"; NRSV "dome") to hold back the chaotic waters above the earth so that a hospitable environment for life could exist (Gen. 1:6–10). That this *raqia*ᶜ effectively holds off the destructive powers of chaos is confirmed in the Flood narrative, where the waters are allowed to break through these restraints and threaten to undo creation altogether. The firmament's continued existence signifies to the observant psalmist that Yahweh continues to protect and care for his creation and its creatures.

Ultimate instability. Finally, the heavens—even with all their endurance and protective care—are only objects of the creation and not the source of ultimate hope. Isaiah describes the ultimate destruction of the heavens and the earth in order to point his people to the only true source of salvation and hope—Yahweh himself: "Lift up your eyes to the heavens, look at the earth beneath; the heavens will vanish like smoke, the earth will wear out like a garment and its inhabitants die like flies. But my salvation will last forever, my righteousness will never fail" (Isa. 51:6). Peter picks up the same theme in the New Testament, where he describes "the day of God and ... its coming. That day will bring about the destruction of the heavens by fire, and the elements will melt in the heat" (2 Peter 3:12).

---

30. This is not to suggest that the psalms are not able on occasion to exploit the ancient creation myths of chaotic waters struggling for control. Elsewhere Yahweh is described as defeating the seas or crushing the sea serpent Lotan (cf. Job 26:12–13; Ps. 74:13–14; 93:3–4). For Yahweh's creation and control of the seas, see Job 7:12; 36:30; Ps. 33:7; 89:9; 95:5; 146:6; Prov. 8:29.

The heavens, then, testify by their own impermanence to the eternality of the God who made them and continues to exist forever. As a result, those who fear Yahweh and trust in him need not fear "though the earth give way and the mountains fall into the heart of the sea, though its waters roar and foam and the mountains quake with their surging" (Ps. 46:2–3).

In all these ways the heavens declare the glory of God, pointing those who will listen to hope in the creator of heaven and earth and all that is in them.

Torah as guidance and blessing. Too often Christians think of the Old Testament Torah (law) as legalistic restrictions of behavior that must obeyed under pain of divine punishment. In this viewpoint Christ has freed us from bondage to the law of obedience to the law of grace—we are saved *not* because we keep the law but because we believe in (rely completely on) the saving death of Jesus Christ. While the statement above concerning the Christian view of grace is accurate, the view of the law described is too narrow and one-sided to capture the robust understanding of Torah that characterized Israel at her best. As Psalm 19 suggests, Israel proclaimed the Torah to be no onerous burden but instead the source of wisdom (19:7), joy (19:8b), and light (19:8d). Torah is both precious (19:10a) and pleasurable (19:10c).

It is this broader understanding of Torah that makes the traditional translation "law" such an inadequate interpretation of this complex concept. We tend to equate Torah and law on a one-to-one basis that leads us frequently to misunderstand what Israel experienced through her long acquaintance with Torah. Formed from the Hebrew root *yrh* ("instruct, teach"), *torah* in wisdom literature embodies the corpus of instruction that provides guidance for those who are serious to live lives of wisdom. Rather than "law," the term is more properly understood as "instruction" or "guidelines." While it is true that Yahweh in the Old Testament promulgates commandments, statutes, and ordinances for Israel to obey, the choice of the term *torah* to characterize this body of tradition shows that Israel understood its *primary* function to be one of guidance in right living.

It is this character of Torah that occupies the attention of the psalmist in Psalm 19. The purpose of Torah is to "warn" the faithful servant of Yahweh (19:11a) to remain on the path that leads to "reward" (19:11b). By its guidance, one is empowered to understand one's errors and to avoid "hidden faults" or "willful sin" (19:12–13a). Rather than restriction, Torah offers freedom from the rule of sin and consequently escape from divine judgment (19:13b-c).

The appropriate response to Torah, according to the psalmists, is "delight" (1:2; 119:70, 77, 92, 174) and "love" (119:97, 113, 163), not some grim-lipped adherence. It is through the Torah that life is preserved (119:93, 149,

156).[31] It is little surprise that the later postbiblical celebration of the end of the yearly Torah reading cycle and the beginning of the next was called Simhat Torah ("Joy of the Torah"), emphasizing the joy the Jewish community experiences in having the Torah to guide their lives before God. The Torah scroll is paraded around the synagogue, accompanied by joyous singing and dancing. This joyous and festive night follows immediately on the heels of the solemn New Year observance, Rosh Hashanah—a week of fasting, reflection, and repentance culminated by Yom Kippur (the Day of Atonement). The contrast could not be more radical, and yet the linkage of these occasions is highly important as repentance (Rosh Hashanah) leads to forgiveness and restoration (Yom Kippur), followed by joyous celebration of the means of continued communion with God (Simhat Torah).

Christians need to incorporate this broader, more positive view of Torah into their understanding of the Old Testament law. Rather than a heavy burden, rightly understood, the law was the guide to continued life and restoration of communion with the holy God. Jesus responded primarily to misinterpretation and abuse of God's law when he criticized the teachers of the law and the Pharisees for piling up burdens on those seeking to approach God. He expressed his acceptance of the validity of the Torah when he declared he had not "come to abolish the Law or the Prophets ... but to fulfill them" (Matt. 5:17).

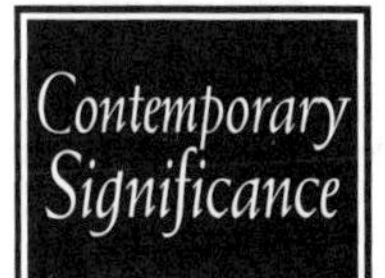

JUST HOW DOES the Old Testament Torah relate to us as Christians? Although Jesus respected God's law and claimed to fulfill rather than abolish it, the early church ultimately agreed that keeping the Jewish law was not a requirement for Gentiles (non-Jews) to become faithful followers of God in Jesus.[32] With the eventual waning of the Jewish church, keeping the Old Testament law became a moot question for the vast majority of Christians who were and continue to be Gentiles.

Paul's treatment of the Old Testament law clearly suggests that it has its place in revealing sin and—through the impossibility of keeping it—driving believers to rely through faith wholly on the gracious mercy of God. This is a view that Jesus seems to share when, in the Sermon on the Mount,

31. See also in this regard, Ps. 119:25, 37, 107 ("Preserve my life according to your word"); 119:50, 154 ("Preserve my life according to your promise"); 119:88, 159 ("Preserve my life according to your love").

32. See the developments as described in Acts 8–15, esp. the culminating decision expressed by James and the elders of the Jerusalem church in 15:12–29.

he proclaims the impossible command: "Be perfect, therefore, as your heavenly Father is perfect" (Matt. 5:48). The implication seems to be that the law demands perfection, and since no human (other than Christ himself) can fulfill that demand, then all must trust solely on the forgiveness extended by God through Christ.

So where does that leave the law for Christians? Do we ignore it altogether as an antiquated way of life intended only for ancient Israel (and contemporary Jews) and superseded by the freedom of grace? Or do we seek to distinguish between the more universal commandments (which we keep) and the "culturally bound" requirements (which we don't)? How can the view of Torah offered in Psalm 19 provide guidance for our Christian lives today?

In regards to the first prospect, if Christ has "fulfilled" or "completed" the law, this *does not mean* that the Old Testament Torah was some sort of defective system unable to accomplish what God intended. The Torah was God's word for Israel. Jesus accepted the Torah (and indeed the whole Old Testament) as God's authoritative word for himself and his followers. Torah led those who related themselves rightly to it into a proper, restored relationship with Yahweh. This is not defective. It may not be the "fullness" of God's revelation, but it rightly accomplishes what God intended it to do.

The view of Torah offered in Psalm 19 is an important help in understanding what it was intended to accomplish. Torah both warns and guides. It marks out boundaries of faithful living and raises an alarm when those boundaries are violated. Torah does not expect absolute perfectionism. Psalm 19 assumes the existence of unintentional sin (19:12–13). Torah, however, provides a guide for avoiding "willful sins" and "great transgression" against God (19:13) and offers a way for restoration of communion for the repentant.

If we think of Torah in this way, as a gracious admonition and guide, then it is like the protective firmament mentioned in 19:1, which provides a shield against destructive chaos. Torah marks out the boundaries of holy living in the presence of a holy God. Torah is not a way to gain God's gracious presence but is a response to the reality of the holy God dwelling *already* in the midst of his people.

Even as Christians who are recipients of the covenant of grace, we understand that there is still an expectation of holy living for the faithful. James declares that "faith without deeds is dead" (James 2:26); that is, saving faith will always issue forth in right living. Paul consistently follows his proclamation of salvation by grace through faith with clear admonition to holy living. Like Israel, then, Christians need admonitions and guides for right living.

There are those within our Christian communities who are more than willing to tell us exactly what constitutes faithful living. It might be a particular view of creation, or the infallibility of Scripture, or even a certain stance on abortion or capital punishment. This can become a new sort of legalism—a belief that adherence to this standard constitutes a clear sign of faith. Those who believe as I do are "in"; those who do not are "out." The analogy of the Torah offers caution. The Torah was not an entrance examination to determine who was in or out. Rather, Torah was a way of life taken by those already committed to Yahweh. Torah served as a response of faith, not a sign of faith.

How does the Torah lead to right living? Through some sort of slavish obedience? Jesus counsels us no when he admonishes his followers to have a righteousness that "surpasses that of the Pharisees and the teachers of the law" (Matt. 5:20). The Pharisees excelled in seeking and demanding perfect adherence to the Torah. How could anyone hope to *surpass* their efforts? Jesus' point is that the law is not about sinless perfectionism but about acknowledging sin and committing one's way wholly to God. Psalm 19 agrees when its references to inadvertent sin put legalism in its place. Torah drives those who know they are sinners to rely only on the gracious mercy of God. That is the Old Testament gospel—not that humans can keep the demands of Torah perfectly but that God graciously provides a way for sinners to be restored to right relationship with him.

Finally, how can keeping the law be a delight? Is not any restriction on our personal freedom a painful burden that must be borne, not enjoyed? Would not the greatest joy and satisfaction come from being entirely free to pursue our own desires and purposes without restriction? In this regard the comments of Jean Paul Sartre, one of the greatest articulators of existentialist philosophy, are significant. According to Sartre humans are absolutely free and yet "forlorn." Both freedom and forlornness are the result of the fact (in Sartre's view) "that God does not exist and that we have to face all the consequences of this."[33] Furthermore, Sartre claims that existentialists

> think it very distressing that God does not exist, because all possibility of finding values in a heaven of values disappears along with Him; there can no longer be an *a priori* Good, since there is no infinite and perfect consciousness to think it. Nowhere is it written that the Good exists, that we must be honest, that we must not lie; because the fact is we are on a plane where there are only men. Dostoevsky said, "if God didn't exist, everything would be possible." That is the very starting point of existentialism. Indeed, everything is permissible if God does not exist, and as a result man is forlorn, because neither within him nor without does he find anything cling to.[34]

---

33. Jean Paul Sartre, *Existentialism*, 25.

34. Ibid., 26–27.

If God does not exist, there is no purpose or value in life. Humans are absolutely free to choose to make of life (or not to make of it) whatever they choose.

This circumstance leads Sartre to conclude that humans are "condemned to be free. This means that no limits to my freedom can be found except freedom itself or, if you prefer, that we are not free to cease being free."[35] Absolute freedom is "condemnation" because there is no meaning or purpose behind anything humans do. Only the existence of some mind or purpose beyond humans themselves can give meaning to life. That is God. For Sartre God does not exist.

But in the world of Israel, where God does exist, Torah is a delight because it offers shape, meaning, and purpose to life. It offers guidance for appropriate relation to God. I remember working one summer in a factory that made corrugated cardboard boxes. The process of printing, cutting, folding, gluing, stacking, and shipping boxes of a variety of shapes and purposes was fascinating for a summer employee who did not have to look forward to a long career of box-making.

But I remember a day when I arrived at work for the night shift only to discover that the machine to which my crew had been assigned had broken down and was in the process of being repaired. I found myself left with nothing to do for almost a whole eight-hour shift from 11 P.M. to 7:00 A.M. I could not go home since I had to stand by in case the machine went on line again. Never have I spent a more "forlorn" eight hours! I was free, but I had no purpose or direction to order my time. I spent most of my shift trying to look busy sweeping nonexistent dust particles from one part of the shop to another. I was almost delighted the next night to resume the monotonous and tiring labor of stacking endless piles of boxes as they came off the line.

Humans are not left alone and forlorn with no purpose or meaning in life. God's Word—his Torah—is a delight because through it we discover who God is and how to assume our place within his creation—a place of unexpected honor, responsibility, and communion with him.

---

35. Jean Paul Sartre, *Being and Nothingness: An Essay on Phenomenological Ontology* (New York: Philosophical Library, 1956), 440.

Psalm 20

FOR THE DIRECTOR of music. A psalm of David.

1 May the LORD answer you when you are in distress;
may the name of the God of Jacob protect you.
2 May he send you help from the sanctuary
and grant you support from Zion.
3 May he remember all your sacrifices
and accept your burnt offerings. *Selah*

4 May he give you the desire of your heart
and make all your plans succeed.
5 We will shout for joy when you are victorious
and will lift up our banners in the name of our God.
May the LORD grant all your requests.

6 Now I know that the LORD saves his anointed;
he answers him from his holy heaven
with the saving power of his right hand.
7 Some trust in chariots and some in horses,
but we trust in the name of the LORD our God.
8 They are brought to their knees and fall,
but we rise up and stand firm.

9 O LORD, save the king!
Answer us when we call!

LIKE PSALM 18 before it and Psalm 21 immediately after, Psalm 20 is one of the "royal psalms"[1] and is explicitly concerned with the military activities of the Israelite king.[2] In this psalm the people (or perhaps more specifically, the army) speak to the king in a long

1. See the section on "Royal Psalms" in the introduction and at the end of Psalm 2.

2. Note the explicit mention of the king in 18:50; 20:9; 21:1, 7. The related designation for the king ("his anointed") also appears in 18:50 and 20:6.

series of jussive forms[3] (20:1–4, 5b), expressing their desire for divine assistance and ultimate victory. A number of commentators note the similarity of setting to the events described in 2 Chronicles 20. It seems that at the time of an impending military campaign, it was not unusual for king, people, and army to seek divine assistance through prayer, fasting, and temple liturgy. Our psalm represents one such liturgical entreaty of divine assistance. In its original setting, the psalm would have functioned as a sort of pledge of loyalty by the army to their ruler before embarking on a military campaign.

Although the king is an important focus of the psalm, he remains silent (unless 20:6, with its first-person address, can be construed as the king speaking). Otherwise, this voice is that of a representative individual[4] who speaks with assurance of Yahweh's divine intervention in the king's behalf.

Structurally, the liturgy in this psalm falls into four parts: hopes for divine intervention and victory (20:1–5), assurance of divine support (20:6), confession of trust in Yahweh (20:7–8), and a final plea directed to Yahweh (20:9). The term *selah* appears at the end of 20:3 but provides no obvious structural function.[5]

The Heading (20:0)

NO NEW TERMS are introduced in the heading of this psalm. Like Psalms 19 and 21, Psalm 20 is referred to "the director of music" and is attributed to David as a "psalm" (*mizmor*).[6] While the psalm is attributed to David, the reference in 20:2a to the "sanctuary" (*qodeš*),[7] coupled with "Zion" (20:2b), and mention of the king's "sacrifices" and "burnt offerings" (20:3)—if these are to be taken as indicating the Jerusalem temple—suggest a date *after* the time of

3. The NIV interprets these nine imperfect forms as jussives expressing the will of the speaker. The particular forms in question, however, demonstrate no distinctively jussive features and may be taken as typical imperfects with equal justification if the context warrants. If the forms were taken this way, the army would be expressing confidence that Yahweh *will* assist the king in achieving victory, rather than expressing their hope and desire that he do so.

4. See *NIVSB*, 804, drawing on 2 Chron. 20, which suggests a "Levite."

5. For a discussion of the term *selah*, see comments on Ps. 3.

6. See comments on the headings to Pss. 3 and 4 for further discussion of these terms.

7. The *BHS* apparatus suggests an emendation to *miqqodšo* ("from *his* holy place"), which could refer to the temple but might also be construed to indicate Yahweh's "holy dwelling." The mention of "from Zion" in parallel to "holy place" strengthens the case for the temple being intended, in my opinion, as does the following reference to the king's sacrifices and burnt offerings (20:3). While it is not impossible for sacrifices to have been offered other than in the temple at this time, the most natural referent for these activities and for this language is the Jerusalem temple.

David. There are no specific indications within the psalm itself to clarify the date or suggest a historical setting.

Hope for Divine Intervention and Victory (20:1–5)

A STRING OF eight imperfect forms linked in pairs dominates the first section of the poem. Most likely these imperfects are to be rendered as jussives, although there is no formal distinction between jussive and imperfect in these particular forms. The phrases are addressed to the king—who is spoken of with second-person pronouns as "you"—and express the desire of the army or the people that Yahweh intervene in the king's behalf. The linked pairs ask for divine hearing and protection (20:1), divine help and support from the temple (20:2), God's favorable response to the king's offerings and sacrifices (20:3), and successful fulfillment of the king's military plans for victory (20:4).

May the name of the God of Jacob protect you. The assembled people seek protection for their king (and themselves) in the "name of the God of Jacob" (20:1b). The phrase "the God of Jacob" appears eighteen times in the Old Testament—twelve of them in the Psalter.[8] In Exodus 3:6, 15, the phrase is clearly connected with the revelation of the divine name Yahweh.[9] The shorter phrase "God of Jacob" is an abbreviation of the longer reference to "the God of your fathers—the God of Abraham, the God of Isaac and the God of Jacob" (cf. Ex. 3:15).

Obviously the psalmist finds a sense of security in having access to the divine name and the God it represents. While this is the only time the entire phrase "*name* of the God of Jacob" occurs, the "God of Jacob" does appear several times in situations of protection. In Psalm 46:7 and 11, the God of Jacob is Israel's "fortress" (*miśgab*).[10] In 76:6, he stops the attacking power of horse and chariot with his rebuke. In 81:1, he is called upon as Israel's "strength."

Help from the sanctuary ... support from Zion. The people seek help and support for the king "from the sanctuary" and "from Zion." The linking of these two places suggests the psalmist has the Jerusalem temple in mind

---

8. See Ex. 3:6, 15; 4:5; 2 Sam. 23:1; Isa. 2:3; Mic. 4:2; and Pss. 20:1; 24:6 [cf. NIV note]; 46:7, 11; 75:9; 76:6; 81:1, 4; 84:8; 94:7; 114:7; 146:5. The Isaiah and Micah passages are duplicate quotations. In Exodus, the phrase is part of the longer patriarchal formula "the God of Abraham, the God of Isaac, and the God of Jacob." According to Ex. 3:15, God tells Moses, "This is my name forever, the name by which I am to be remembered from generation to generation." The phrase also occurs four times in the New Testament—three times in the parallel passages in Matt. 22:32; Mark 12:26; Luke 20:37, where it refers to Ex. 3:15, and once in Acts 7:46.

9. For further discussion of this event, see comments on 8:1, 9.

10. For discussion of this and other terms for fortresses and strongholds, see comments on 9:9–14.

as the place where supplications to Yahweh can be made and divine assistance received. While some think Zion originally referred to the prominent ridge (south of the present temple mount) on which the original Jebusite city conquered by David stood, the term has also been associated with the hill on which the Solomonic temple was erected.[11] Later (presumably during the exilic period, when access to Jerusalem was restricted) "Zion" came to be identified with the whole of Jerusalem, the "holy city." In this psalm, however, the more narrow reference to the Temple Mount seems appropriate—perhaps an indication that the temple was still present and in operation when the psalm was written. If so, the psalm is a preexilic poem.

By seeking God's help and support from the temple on Zion, the speakers may be anticipating that the ark of the covenant will go forth from there to lead the army into victorious battle against the enemy as it had prior to the monarchy (cf. Num. 10:35; Josh. 6; 1 Sam. 4:3, 5). After the construction of the temple, the ark of the covenant assumed its place in the inner niche of the temple. There is evidence, however, that it was taken from there to lend support to Israel's army in military campaigns (cf. 2 Sam. 11:11). Such a procession featuring the ark would be calculated to provide visible confirmation of the invisible presence of Yahweh with the troops and would give strength and courage to their efforts.

Sacrifices and . . . offerings. Kings played an important religious role in offering sacrifices. Saul offered sacrifices in preparation for battle (1 Sam. 13:8–10).[12] David and Solomon both were prominently involved in religious worship and sacrifice (2 Sam. 6; 24:18–25; 1 Kings 3; 8:62–63), as were the kings of Israel and Judah after them (2 Kings 16:12, 15; 2 Chron. 29:21–23; 31:3; 35:16). In this psalm the people want God to "remember"[13] that the king has fulfilled his obligations of sacrifice in temple worship. They want God to "accept" the king's offerings for sin so that no barrier prevents divine support for his activities. In this context, the "desire of [the king's] heart" (Ps. 20:4a) and "all [the king's] plans" (20:4b) surely refer to the mutual hopes of king, people, and army for success in the coming battle.

---

11. See comments on 14:7. This hill should be identified with the Temple Mount on which the Islamic shrines the Dome of the Rock and the Al Aksah Mosque presently stand.

12. Although Saul's sacrifices earned Samuel's condemnation here, there is no clear indication that it was the general practice of kingly sacrifices that was at fault; rather, Saul allowed his anxiety at the massing troops of the enemy to push him to override the expectation that he wait until Samuel arrive. As in the prophets at a later date, it was not sacrifices themselves but the attitude in which they were offered that rendered them illegitimate.

13. See the discussion of divine remembering in the commentary on Ps. 13:1–2. To be "remembered" or "known" by God is to be in the appropriate relationship of blessing that Ps. 1:6 contrasts with the "perishing" state of the wicked.

Shout for joy. Anticipating positive divine response in the form of a victorious military campaign, the speakers vow a joyous and noisy victory celebration.[14] The word translated "when you are victorious" is the same word frequently taken as "salvation, deliverance" (*yešuʿah*). On a number of occasions this word (along with the related nouns *yašaʿ* and *tešuʿah* and the verb *yšʿ*) clearly exceeds the sense of deliverance and achieves the more fulsome meaning of "victory."[15] It is interesting to note, however, that the use of this particular term, "victory," rather than being a human accomplishment and potential source of pride, is always swallowed up in *divine deliverance*. To proclaim "Victory!" is to acknowledge at one and the same time that "Yahweh has delivered me."

The second half of this celebratory response is somewhat obscured by a spot of difficult Hebrew. The verb translated in the NIV as "lift up our banners" is otherwise unknown in the Hebrew Bible or elsewhere. The meaning used here is derived from a noun (*degel* ["banner"]) that shares the same root, with the idea of "lifting up" being supplied for an interpretive understanding of the context.[16]

All your requests. The opening section of the psalm concludes with a summary phrase encapsulating the speakers' hopes for a positive divine response to "all [the] requests" for divine assistance for the king and the army expressed throughout these verses. It is hoped that Yahweh will "fill up/make full; fulfill" (*mlʾ*)[17] all that the king requests.[18]

---

14. Many commentators take the imperfect verb forms in 20:5a-b as a continuation of the jussive mood established in the preceding verses and concluded by the final expression in verse 5: "May Yahweh grant all your requests." If this interpretation is correct, then this passage would be rendered "Let us sing aloud in praise of your victory! Let us do homage to the name of our God!" (Rogerson and McKay, *Psalms 1–50*, 90); or perhaps, "May we shout for joy in your victory and raise a banner in the name of our God" (Craigie, *Psalms 1–50*, 184). Dahood (*Psalms*, 1:127) also reflects this tendency with a more subjunctive interpretation: "That we might exult in your victory, and in the Name of our God hold high the banners."

15. Besides the present passage, compare Pss. 18:35; 44:3, 6, 7; 118:15; 144:10; Hab. 3:8.

16. See the discussion in Dahood (*Psalms*, 1:128), Kraus (*Psalms 1–59*, 278), and Craigie (*Psalms 1–50*, 184). Kraus, drawing on the LXX rendering *megalynthesometha* ("we will be magnified") assumes a possible transposition of the letters *-d-* and *-g-* with a resultant Hebrew form *nagdil* (Hiphil imperfect of *gdl*) or *negaddel* (Piel imperfect of *gdl*), but ultimately opts for a more severe revision to *nagil* (Hiphil imperfect of *gyl* ["rejoice; exult"]), entirely on the basis of parallelism.

17. Another factitive use of the Piel, in which the meaning of the Qal stem ("be full") is brought to fruition in the Piel ("make full/fulfill").

18. The term "request" is appropriate here since the noun shares the root with the verb "ask, request." This is different from what one might "desire" (Heb *ḥepeṣ*, *taʾawah*, or *raṣon*). In 21:2, Yahweh is said to have "granted [the king] the desire [*taʾawah*] of his heart"—a distinctive phrase that nonetheless links back to the similar idea expressed in 20:4a (where "desire" does *not* actually appear in the Hebrew text).

Assurance of Divine Support (20:6)

NOW I KNOW. A distinctive and singular voice now breaks into the communal recitation of hope that has characterized the psalm thus far. The first-person verb here is also a perfect form (from *ydᶜ* ["to know"]). It is introduced by the temporal particle *ᶜattah* ("now"), which provides transition to this new section. The nuance of the perfect of *ydᶜ* implies a knowledge that has come to a finished understanding rather than an ongoing, developing knowledge. The one who knows in this way knows certainly and is able to communicate the results of that knowledge with assurance, like the speaker in our psalm.

The identity of this speaker is not clear from the context. Drawing on the similar context of 2 Chronicles 20, many commentators assume the speaker to be one of the Levites serving in the temple, who here speaks prophetically to assure king and people of a positive divine response and certain victory. It is generally assumed that some Levites bore the responsibility to provide a divine word in response to the supplications and requests of worshipers—including the king. Scholars point to various passages in the psalms as examples of this kind of prophetic proclamation in temple worship (cf. Pss. 110:1–2; cf. 60:6–8; 85:8–13).[19]

The LORD saves. The proclamation of salvation is offered in terms that assume its certainty. The key verb "saves" (*yšᶜ*) describes an action that is fixed and complete. This speaking of a future act as if it were already completed is sometimes called the "prophetic perfect," in which "the certainty of being answered realises the fulfilment in anticipation."[20] Thus, this verb could have been translated "has given victory," following the pattern established for "when you are victorious" in 20:5.[21] The solo speaker envisions the coming victory as an accomplished fact and communicates this certainty to the gathered and expectant worshipers. Whether this proclamation represents a ritual assurance or comes as the result of some particular oracular inquiry for the will and word of Yahweh is uncertain.

His anointed. The king is identified as God's "anointed" (*mašiaḥ*)—a Hebrew term that begins as simply a description of those anointed with oil

---

19. There is a slight possibility that the speaker in this verse might be the king referring to himself in the third person as Yahweh's "anointed." If so, the verse would represent the king's humble acknowledgment of his dependence for success and victory on the "salvation" that comes from God alone.

20. Delitzsch, *Psalms*, 1:294.

21. The NIV's inconsistency in translating forms of the root *yšᶜ*, even within the context of the same psalm, illustrates the difficulty and even "slipperiness" of deciding between the alternatives of "victory" and "salvation/deliverance" in each instance. In many (if not *most*) passages "salvation/deliverance" provides an adequate translation with good meaning.

as a sign of their selection for special purpose but develops over time as a special title or designation, "Messiah," for the divinely empowered, Spirit-filled royal leader, who will ultimately judge the nations and bring God's kingdom on earth. This reference links our psalm back to Psalm 2:2, where the same term appears in a context of conflict and deliverance. There the "Anointed One" is described as God's "Son," established as king in Zion by Yahweh, who laughs at the puny plots of opposing kings and warns them to submit to the rule of his kingly Son. The placement of Psalm 2 as an untitled psalm at the beginning of the Psalter has provided it with a significance beyond its original setting and has in the postexilic shaping and reading of the psalms rightly focused attention away from the failed human role of the kings to the future hope of the coming messianic ruler.[22]

Our present passage, in its original context during the monarchical period, stands between these two extremes. The title seems to have assumed some august elevation by its association with the person of the king but has not yet exceeded those bounds to focus attention on the coming Messiah. As long as a human ruler was present to provide a focal point for present hopes, the sense of need for a future cosmic deliverer was blunted. I will return in the discussion of Bridging Contexts and Contemporary Significance to consider how this term—and, indeed, all of the royal psalms—might be read differently after the demise of the kingship during the Exile.

He answers him. The promised deliverance and victory is understood as an answer to the intercessory plea with which the psalm began. In 20:1, the gathered supplicants expressed their hope: "May the LORD answer you when you are in distress." Now the prophetic voice assures the gathered body that Yahweh indeed "answers [the king] from his holy heaven" (20:6b). That the complete answer in terms of realized victory still anticipates the future is confirmed by the concluding words of the whole psalm (20:9b), where the gathered supplicants, despite the assurances of the prophetic speaker, are still hoping for the promised divine answer as they cry out: "Answer us when we call!"

But here the people and king are assured of Yahweh's complete support and the certain victory that is to be claimed. Yahweh's answer will come from his "holy heaven" (his divine abode), in the form of "the saving power of his right hand"—the symbol of power and authority unleashed in behalf of the king.

---

22. See the pertinent discussion in the sections on the "Royal Psalms" at the end of Ps. 2 and the section on "Messianic Reinterpretation" in "Theology of the Psalms" in vol. 2 of this commentary.

Confession of Trust in Yahweh (20:7–8)

HAVING RECEIVED THE prophetic promise of divine support and victory, the assembled people affirm their trust and dependence on Yahweh in a set of opposingly parallel lines contrasting the fate of those who trust in their own strength with those who hope in Yahweh. The verb translated "trust" (*zkr*) is a Hiphil first-person plural, describing the people's commitment to Yahweh (20:7b; cf. Isa. 26:13). The verb is supplied in the first half of the verse by implication. The literal Hebrew reads something like: "These in chariotry, these in horses, but we in the name of Yahweh our God place our trust." *Zkr* has the meaning "cause to remember, call to remembrance; acknowledge." The point is that while others rely on the trappings of military power and success, the Israelites remind themselves that their only hope is in the "name" of their God, Yahweh.

By trusting in "chariots" and "horses" the misguided opponents are relying on the most advanced and effective forms of warfare available in contemporary society. Ironclad chariots pulled into battle by seasoned war-horses were terrifying in their ability to break up massed troops and make them vulnerable to the attack of trained foot soldiers following in the destructive wake of the chariots. In their early contacts with the Philistines and other advanced enemies, the Israelite spear-wielding infantry was at a decided disadvantage—especially on the flat plains, where chariots were particularly effective.[23]

By the time of Solomon, however, Israel had adopted the chariot as the standard of effective warfare, and Solomon was known for his massive chariot forces. Our psalm cautions both king and people from equating victory with superior equipment and fighting personnel. Even early Israel—outnumbered and overpowered by superior weaponry—found ways to limit the effectiveness of chariotry and to win lopsided victories against their better-trained and better-equipped foes.

In this section of the psalm, the Israelites—king, army, and people—affirm their faith that victory is dependent on the power and authority of Yahweh. Those who trust only in their military superiority are doomed to fall (20:8a). In contrast, those who trust in Yahweh "rise up and stand firm" (20:8b). Once again, it is the "name" of Yahweh that provides the protective power the supplicants seek (20:7b; cf. 20:1b).

---

23. A review of Israel's early successes against the Philistines reveals a strategic use of restricted terrain—hill country, mountain passes, narrow valleys, or river crossings—where the horse-drawn chariot was least effective.

Final Plea (20:9)

THE PSALM CONCLUDES with a final plea that draws together the intercessory and personal prayers of the assembly. The "victory" or "salvation" of the king (20:9a) is the foundation of communal security and is the answer to the prayer raised from the first. In their pleas that Yahweh "answer" them (20:9b), the supplicants are recalling their opening plea for the king (20:1a) as well as the divine promise of deliverance in 20:6b. This final plea serves almost as a concluding Amen, proclaiming as it were, "Let what has been asked and promised truly become reality!" This last verse contains the only specific reference to the king in the psalm, although the previous use of "his anointed" and the reference to military activity left little doubt before.

THE SPECIFIC FOCUS of Psalm 20 on intercession for the Judahite king and hope for victory in a military campaign highlights the difficulty of interpreting such "royal psalms" for contemporary application. Both historically and culturally this psalm and its contents remain distant and alien to many contemporary readers, who have little or no experience of monarchy in general or of the Davidic monarchy in particular. Should this psalm be viewed only as a historical example of how Judahites prayed for their king before a military engagement? Is it correct to apply this psalm to the cosmic struggle of the coming Messiah with the forces of evil? Ought we extend our interpretation to serve as a model for intercession for national leaders facing similar conflicts in the present? Or is there an appropriate way to apply this psalm to the life of *any* member of the faithful community of God who faces difficult struggles today? Let's consider each of these options in order.

Historical description. It is certain that this psalm provides us with a glimpse of the interaction of king, people, and temple personnel in temple worship. That the kings offered sacrifices on many occasions and sought divine support for military engagements is well documented throughout the Old Testament.[24] This psalm provides us with a window into a particular liturgical moment in worship where intercession, assurance, and petition interweave. Historians seeking to reconstruct the role and function of kings in temple worship find this composition a helpful source of data.

---

24. 1 Sam. 13:5–10 (Saul); 2 Sam. 6:17–19 and 24:18–25 (David); 1 Kings 3:3–4, 15 and 8:62–63 (Solomon); 12:31–33 (Jeroboam); 22:1–40 (Ahab of Israel and Jehoshaphat of Judah); cf. 2 Kings 3:26–27 (king of Moab).

But is historical description the *only* value that still attaches to Psalm 20? Are we done once we have speculated on what the psalm reveals about the function of Judahite kingship? I think not! The fact that these 150 cultic poems have been preserved as holy Scripture is a testimony to their multivalent vitality. The shift to holy Scripture has changed their character from historical snapshots to the source of God's continuing word to his people. In this text we still hear God speaking a formative word to his people—to us.

Messianic hope. Another way of interpreting this psalm (and the other royal psalms)—a way that moves beyond historical description to allow the composition a continuing voice—is to understand its words as directed not to one of the historical kings of Judah but to the future "anointed [one]" (20:6), the Messiah. The shift from *historical* king to *apocalyptic* Messiah is a move that took place in the postexilic period when hopes for reestablishing the Davidic monarchy were slim. Rather than relegate these royal psalms to the archive, they were instead reinterpreted to refer to the future "shoot ... from the stump of Jesse" (Isa. 11:1)—a divinely empowered ruler who would accomplish what none of the historical kings had ever done. The Messiah would defeat God's enemies decisively and establish God's direct rule over all the earth.

That the New Testament interpreted many of the royal psalms as references to Jesus *the* Messiah is confirmed by Acts 2:30–35, where Psalms 110 and 132 are interpreted as speaking of Jesus, and Hebrews 7:11–25, where Psalm 110 is again interpreted as referring to Jesus as a "priest ... in the order of Melchizedek." It is certainly valid to find in Jesus the fulfillment of the Old Testament hopes directed toward the Davidic kingship. What the human kings were unable to accomplish, Jesus carried to fruition. What the kings represented at their best, Christ epitomized in his life and work and will fulfill in the Second Coming as victorious Lord.

But if this were the *only* appropriate way to read these psalms—as having exclusive reference to the future Messiah (identified by Christians with Jesus)—then the psalm would once again be cut off from the present and would serve as in the first interpretive method to focus our attention exclusively on what the New Testament writers taught about Jesus. The only difference is that our focus has now been redirected from the distant past to the unspecified future.

Present-day national leaders. A third way of interpreting royal psalms in general and Psalm 20 in particular is a way that refocuses the teaching of the psalm firmly into the present. This approach draws an analogy between the ancient kings of Judah and present-day national leaders. The idea is that these leaders share similar contexts and concerns and that the psalms addressed to one are applicable to the other.

There is, however, a difficulty in any easy equation of the context and nature of Israelite monarchy and contemporary national leadership—a difficulty illustrated by Psalm 20. No nation today can lay exclusive claim to the identity of the Old Testament people of God. Even to understand the United States as a nation "under God" and, therefore, specially blessed by him is fraught with conflicts and contradictions. Nowhere is this more clearly displayed as in our own Civil War, where two parts of the same "Christian nation" found themselves at war with each other, both invoking the blessing of the same God in its behalf. Whereas Israel was called by God to be a kingdom of priests and a holy *nation*, the church—which most closely approximates the New Testament reflex of the people of God—are faithful followers called out *from all nations* to form the transnational body of Christ in service to the world. While individual nations may more or less reflect the values and purposes of God's kingdom, no single nation can claim that identify exclusively as its own.

As a result, to identify the leader of any one nation as the modern equivalent of the king of God's people is subject to dangerous misunderstanding and distortion. The primary purpose of the kings of Israel and Judah (a purpose they too often failed to pursue) was to lead the people in the ways of Yahweh (cf. Deut. 17:14–20; 1 Sam. 12:19–25); who can say as much for any national leader today?

The assumption that it is possible to equate the contexts of the Davidic kings and modern national leaders is misguided. It is true that there may be similarities and that there may be ways that psalms like Psalm 20 can guide us in regard to modern leaders, but no easy transference is possible. Just consider the implications of such statements as those in 20:4 and 20:5c if applied uncritically to modern national leaders: "May [God] give you the *desire of your heart* and make *all your plans succeed*.... May the LORD grant *all your requests*." Such hopeful desires make no sense in our modern secular state.

The existence of such longing in Psalm 20 assumes that the people's hopes and desires are bound up in that of their leader, that both people and leader are together the people of God, and that together they are seeking to carry out God's will on a national level. It is unwarranted and unwise to make that assumption about most of our national leaders regardless of their spiritual commitment, and it is equally futile to claim that about our nation as a whole. Any attempt to apply Psalm 20 to the situation of modern national leaders must proceed cautiously and take these caveats into consideration.

Members of the community of God. Our final option is to apply the words of this psalm to any member of the community of God who shares an analogous context of struggle. What justification can I give for such an interpretive move? For one thing, note the fluid interconnection in the Old

Testament between king and people. The king is not only leader but also representative of his people. The sins of the king are visited on his people,[25] and it is the people's loyalty to Yahweh that is expected to keep the king in office.[26]

It is also clear from the role of David in the Psalter that he serves as a model of appropriate piety for all the faithful. While there continues to be doubt whether David actually composed all the psalms that bear his name in their headings, the effect of associating his name with these compositions—in particular, those with historical notices of events in his life—is to make these psalms representative responses to life experiences that can provide models of response to our own circumstances. If David responded to circumstances in his life with the words of these psalms, what better way for me to respond here and now?

Thus, if David the ideal king can provide a model for ordinary believers, then the royal psalms with their pictures of royal life and spirituality can also serve as ways of understanding our own response to God. In this psalm we may see ourselves both as intercessors for others who suffer and as sufferers in need of intercession. In the final call for the salvation of "the king," we (like the narrator of old) can find hope for our own deliverance: "Answer us when we call!"

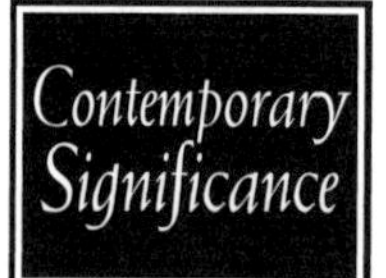

IF WE ACCEPT the rationale outlined above that it is appropriate to apply this psalm to the needs and experiences of any member of the community of faith, what does Psalm 20 teach us? In what follows, I will reflect briefly on four aspects of this poem that open up insights for contemporary Christians seeking their way before God.

Trusting the name of Yahweh. The dominant theme of the psalm is a call to "trust in the name of the LORD" (20:7b). At the beginning the hope is expressed that "the name of the God of Jacob" will protect the faithful one (20:1b), so that "the name" of God brackets the whole composition at beginning and end. The "name of God" is of course *yhwh*, as 20:7b makes explicit. The divine name associated with these four letters (the Tetragrammaton) is taken from the narrative in Exodus 3:1–16, where, at the burning bush, God reveals to Moses and the Israelites for the first time his personal name.[27] The

25. Cf. 2 Sam. 24, where David's decision to make a census of fighting men results in divine punishment of all Israel by the outbreak of plague.

26. 1 Sam. 12:20–25.

27. See the comments on the divine name at 8:1 and in the Bridging Contexts section to that psalm.

full name of God revealed at this point is the Hebrew phrase *ʾehyeh ʾăšer ʾehyeh* ("I will be what I will be"; Ex. 3:14). Yahweh is an abbreviated form of this name from the human point of view and means "He will be. . . ."

By the gift of this name Yahweh provides special access to his people and reveals his essential character. He promises in this name to be with and for his people, to continue to reveal himself over a lifetime of experience with Israel, and yet to remain free from any attempts to coerce or manipulate his action.[28] To "trust in the name" of Yahweh, as Psalm 20 affirms, is to accept the character of God revealed in this name, to commit to relationship with Yahweh, and to accept the implications of that relationship.

Yahweh is the God who delivered Israel from bondage in Egypt. He cemented a covenant relationship with his people on Mount Sinai—a relationship that demands that Israel be loyal to him, trust in his protective care, and bring equity, justice, and compassion in relation to other members of the covenant family. Like Israel and her king, we are called to trust in the God who has delivered us and has called us into a covenant relationship of loyal commitment and trust.

Help from the sanctuary, from Zion. When the psalmist speaks of "help from the sanctuary," most likely the ark of the covenant is in mind. Brought up to Jerusalem by David and ensconced in the Most Holy Place of Solomon's temple, the ark signified the invisible presence of Yahweh in the midst of his people. The help envisioned may well be the movement of the ark from its resting place in the temple to lead the Israelite army into battle with their foes.[29] Help from the sanctuary is Yahweh himself coming to the aid of his people against their enemies.

Remembering sacrifices and burnt offerings. As mentioned in the Original Meaning section, the kings were known to offer sacrifices and burnt offerings in the context of temple worship. The king is implied to have fulfilled his covenantal responsibility by offering scrupulously "burnt offerings"

---

28. The implications of the divine name Yahweh are discussed in the Bridging Contexts section of Ps. 8.

29. The ark certainly was employed in this fashion during the conquest of the land (Joshua) and was lost during the time of Samuel after it had been carried into battle with the Philistines (1 Sam. 4–6). The assumption of the priestly bearers of the ark, who carried it out of the city in order to accompany David when he fled Jerusalem before the forces of his son Absalom, was that the ark implied the presence of Yahweh with the side that possessed it. David clearly distanced himself from that theology when he sent the ark back to the temple with the declaration: "Take the ark of God back into the city. If I find favor in the LORD's eyes, he will bring me back and let me see it and his dwelling place again. But if he says, 'I am not pleased with you,' then I am ready; let him do to me whatever seems good to him" (2 Sam. 15:25–26). This is the kind of trust Psalm 20 describes.

to remove sin and "sacrifices" or voluntary "gifts" to Yahweh that celebrated restoration of right relationship. Again, it is the inward reality of right relationship that Yahweh remembers rather than the abundance of sacrifices offered.[30] Rather than taking this to mean that God remembers how we make sacrifices (of time, money, suffering, etc.), this passage is talking about fulfilling our covenantal responsibilities of relationship to God. Have we acknowledged our sin and turned from it? Are we experiencing and celebrating a renewed and restored relationship with God? God "remembers" us when we are on the way of faithful loyalty to him and when we daily seek him with body, mind, soul, and spirit.

We may think that it takes restrictions on ourselves—fasting, living in poverty, risking our lives, giving our lives to full-time ministry, performing heroic acts—to earn us special merit, that gets us remembered. This psalm suggests it is rather the consistent attention to the small, common acts of fellowship, obedience, and relationship that keeps us in the mind of God.

The desire of your heart. Does it make you feel somewhat uneasy that the psalmist longs for God to grant the desire of king's heart? I wonder if the psalmist would have asked the same thing immediately following David's affair with Bathsheba? It scares me to think that God might grant the desires of my heart, because my heart is too often distorted by inappropriate wants and cravings that could have disastrous consequences. If all my plans succeeded, there could be hell to pay!

The key to understanding how the psalmist can say this is related to where this hopeful longing stands within this psalm. Immediately preceding is the indication that the king had fulfilled rightly his covenant obligations of removing sin and celebrating communion with Yahweh (20:3). Immediately following is the psalmist's concluding contrast between two attitudes of trust: those who trust in human military power (chariots and horses) and those who trust instead in "the name of the LORD" (20:7). In this context, therefore, the psalmist's hope is no *carte blanche* for the king to achieve every goal and fulfill every desire. Instead, it is grounded in the realization that desires that grow out of right relationship with God and that lead one to trust only in Yahweh are desires that are in line with the will of God himself.[31]

It is also important to note that the Hebrew here does not contain the word "desire." That is an interpretive expansion on the literal Hebrew expression: *yitten leka kilbabeka* ("May he give to you according to your heart"). This suggests that what God gives is dependent on the nature of the heart of the recipient. Elsewhere when this phrase *ke* + *lebab* ("like [your/his] heart") is used,

30. Cf. Lev. 26:27–30; 1 Sam. 15:22–23; Amos 5:21–25.

31. Cf. Mark 11:24.

it implies that a parity is being established with the heart mentioned. Since the original form of Psalm 20 was addressed to the Davidic king, this phrase is used to describe an essential parity between David and the heart of God when David is first anointed as king: "The LORD has sought out a man after his own heart" (1 Sam. 13:14). In the following chapter the armor-bearer of Saul's son Jonathan follows his master into a risky engagement with an expression of solidarity: "Do all that you have in mind. . . . Go ahead; I am with you heart and soul [lit., according to your heart]" (14:7).

That one's heart is not always a good model for such solidarity is confirmed in the Deuteronomic recommendation that any soldier who is afraid to go into battle should be allowed to return home to avoid the chance "that his brothers will be become disheartened too [lit., like his heart]" (Deut. 20:8). Similarly, we learn that in his later years Solomon's heart was turned by his foreign wives so that it was not "fully devoted to the LORD his God, as the heart of David his father had been" (1 Kings 11:4). The identical phrase is also used in 1 Kings 15:3 to describe the failure of Abijah to follow in the spiritual footsteps of David.

In Psalm 20, then, what God gives has a certain parity with the heart of the recipient. If, like his father David, the king's heart is "like the heart of God," then his plans will succeed and his requests be granted. If, however, like Solomon, his heart is not like that of David and of God, he can expect judgment, like that visited on Solomon and Abijah.

Thus, giving to us according to our hearts does not mean giving us whatever we desire. It means that as our heart is aligned with or against God's will and purpose, we can expect to receive accordingly blessing or judgment. Rather than an invitation to license, this is a wake-up call to bring our hearts into alignment with the will and purposes of God. The rest of Psalm 20 offers two indications of how this might be accomplished: Pay regular and close attention to matters of restoration and communion, and put your trust in Yahweh alone (20:7–8).[32]

32. This kind of trust is what the Old Testament calls "fear of the LORD." Such "fear" is far from terror; rather, it describes the core realization that in all aspects of life one is absolutely dependent on Yahweh alone.

Psalm 21

FOR THE DIRECTOR of music. A psalm of David.

1 O LORD, the king rejoices in your strength.
How great is his joy in the victories you give!
2 You have granted him the desire of his heart
and have not withheld the request of his lips. *Selah*
3 You welcomed him with rich blessings
and placed a crown of pure gold on his head.
4 He asked you for life, and you gave it to him—
length of days, for ever and ever.
5 Through the victories you gave, his glory is great;
you have bestowed on him splendor and majesty.
6 Surely you have granted him eternal blessings
and made him glad with the joy of your presence.
7 For the king trusts in the LORD;
through the unfailing love of the Most High
he will not be shaken.

8 Your hand will lay hold on all your enemies;
your right hand will seize your foes.
9 At the time of your appearing
you will make them like a fiery furnace.
In his wrath the LORD will swallow them up,
and his fire will consume them.
10 You will destroy their descendants from the earth,
their posterity from mankind.
11 Though they plot evil against you
and devise wicked schemes, they cannot succeed;
12 for you will make them turn their backs
when you aim at them with drawn bow.

13 Be exalted, O LORD, in your strength;
we will sing and praise your might.

PSALM 21 STANDS in its present context as a response to the promise of divine intervention and victory in Psalm 20. As in the former psalm, Psalm 21 still anticipates victory (21:8–12) and praises Yahweh for his promised support and strength (21:1, 13).

A number of elements link Psalms 20 and 21 together. In addition to the emphasis on divine promise of victory using the Hebrew noun *yešuaᶜ* ("salvation, deliverance; victory") and verbs of the root *yšᶜ* ("save, deliver; make victorious"; cf. 20:5, 6, 9; 21:1b, 5a), both psalms refer to "the king" (20:9; 21:1). Thus, both are included among the lists of "royal psalms."[1] In both psalms Yahweh's "right hand" effects the king's deliverance (cf. 20:6; 21:8), and Yahweh's "strength" is celebrated (*geburah* in 20:6; *ᶜoz* in 21:1; *ᶜoz* paralleled by *geburah* in 21:13). Finally, the theme of "trust in . . . the LORD" is sounded in 20:7 and resounded in 21:7.

Structurally, Psalm 21 is framed by twin references to praise of Yahweh's "strength" (21:1, 13), which set the tone of the psalm throughout. The psalm is then divided into two sections of five verses each: God's positive blessings on the king (21:2–6) and his negative confrontation of the enemy (21:8–12). In the center of the psalm, between the two extended sections, stands the confession of the king's trust in Yahweh, grounded in an acknowledgment of Yahweh's strength poured out in blessing on his king and resulting in judgment on the enemy nations. The complete structure of the psalm can be outlined as follows: introductory praise of Yahweh's strength (21:1), Yahweh's blessing on the king (21:2–6), the king's confession of trust in Yahweh (21:7), Yahweh's judgment of the enemy (21:8–12), and concluding praise of Yahweh's strength (21:13).

The Heading (21:0)

LIKE PSALMS 19 and 20 before it, Psalm 21 is referred "to the director of music" and attributed to David as a "psalm" (*mizmor*). No new terms are introduced in the heading.[2]

1. Scholarly lists of the "royal psalms" exhibit much agreement and only slight variations of contents. According to Hermann Gunkel (*The Psalms* [Philadelphia: Fortress, 1967], 23), the list includes Pss. 2; 18; 20; 21; 45; 72; 101; 110; 132; and 144:1–11. Artur Weiser, *The Psalms*, 45, cites Pss. 2; 18; 20; 21; 72; 89; 101; and 110. According to Gerhard von Rad, *Old Testament Theology*, trans. D. M. G. Stalker (2 vols.; New York: Harper, 1962, 1965), 1:319, note 1, the royal psalms are Pss. 2; 18; 20; 21; 45; 72; 89; 101; 110; and 132. For a discussion of the interpretation of royal psalms, see the Bridging Contexts section of Ps. 20.

2. For discussions of the pertinent terms, see comments on the headings to Pss. 3 and 4.

In Praise of Yahweh's Strength (21:1)

AS PSALM 20 ends with direct mention of the king (20:9) for whom the gathered assembly seeks divine deliverance, so Psalm 21 begins with a similar reference to the king (21:1) rejoicing in the strength of Yahweh, which provides the king with victories. The appearance at the end and beginning of the identical term *melek* ("king")[3] links these two psalms together—this time in a relationship of plea (Ps. 20) and response (Ps. 21). The king rejoices in the deliverance promised in Psalm 20.

It is not clear from Psalm 21 whether the king has already experienced the salvation promised in Psalm 20. In fact, the opposite seems to be true, since 21:8–12 anticipate a divine reckoning with the enemy that lies in the future. Perhaps Psalm 21 represents a liturgical response to the *promise* of deliverance and victory rather than to the *fulfillment* of that promise. Having heard the prophetic decree of victory in 20:6, the king responds in joyful trust, looking forward to fulfillment.

Blessing on the King (21:2–6)

DESIRE OF HIS heart . . . request of his lips. The king is a model of integrity; what he desires in his heart he requests with his lips. Inward motivation and outward speech agree. This is the same kind of integrity of inward and outward being that is exhorted in the concluding plea of Psalm 19:14, where spoken words and heart meditation also agree.

The king's desire for deliverance is an intense and eager desire, parallel to the kind of desire that drives a groom to negotiate an engagement for the woman he wishes to marry. The term translated "request" in 21:2b is related to the verbal root *ʾrś* ("become betrothed, arrange an engagement"). The link between "desire" and "request" seems to be that of a potential groom, for whom "desire" for a woman leads to negotiation ("request") for engagement. Inward motivation and outer action are of a piece. In the case of the king described here, words of the mouth and

---

3. The term "king" (*melek*) occurs some sixty-four times in the Psalter in singular and plural forms. Of these, three are abstract mentions of kings in the most general sense, twenty-six describe foreign kings, fourteen are references to Israelite rulers, and twenty-one call Yahweh/God king. It is most interesting to note that there is no reference to Israelite monarchs using the term *melek* after the third book of the Psalter (i.e., after Ps. 89). David does appear in the headings of a number of psalms in the fourth and fifth books and is explicitly mentioned in the text of Pss. 122:5; 132:1, 10, 11, 17; 144:10. He is even called God's "anointed one" (132:10, 17), but never is he, or any other Israelite ruler, called *melek*. For more on this, see comments on Ps. 2.

meditation of the heart must be pleasing to Yahweh since both are "granted" (cf. Ps. 19:14).[4]

Blessings and . . . a crown. Yahweh's response to the king's integrity pours out in blessing. The psalmist uses a wordplay for those who have been reading their way through the consecutive Psalms 17–21. When he says that God "welcomes" (from *qdm* ["confront; meet"]) the king (21:3), the psalmist is using a word that has appeared three times with a very different meaning in Psalms 17 and 18 (cf. 17:13; 18:5, 18). In those earlier contexts, the confrontation described was a negative and threatening one. In 17:13 it is the enemies who are "confronted" by Yahweh and brought down. In 18:5 the "snares of death confront" and threaten to overwhelm the psalmist. In 18:18, once again the powerful enemies "confront" the psalmist, seeking to defeat him. As a result of this more normal use, the choice of *qdm* in the present context is a bit jarring and unexpected. But the psalmist uses the tension created to confound the reader's expectations and heighten the sense of blessing and joy that attend Yahweh's "confrontation" of the faithful.

The "crown [*ʿaṭarah*; perhaps better, 'wreath'] of pure gold" that the king receives is to be distinguished from the coronation crown (*nezer*, from the root *nzr* ["to set apart, dedicate to God"]). The crown or wreath (of flowers, leaves, or sometimes gold)[5] represented by *ʿaṭarah* is a gift of honor given to visiting dignitaries or guests at banquets. This rich gift, then, is a sign of the honor bestowed on the king by God—an open sign of divine approval for all to see.[6]

Life . . . glory . . . splendor and majesty. The psalm now turns to a more specific description of the blessing and honor poured out on the king by Yahweh. The king has asked for life, and God has given him abundant, long-lasting life. The descriptive *ʾorek yamim* ("length of days") already means *long* life, and the psalmist adds to that *ʿolam waʿed* ("for ever and ever"), so there can be no doubt that Yahweh more than fulfills the king's hopes and expectations.[7]

---

4. The NIV's translation of Ps. 20:4a as "May he give you the desire of your heart" would seem to indicate a close and possibly intended link with 21:2a, "You have granted him the desire of his heart." However, the earlier verse translates a very different Hebrew phrase from the later one. Ps. 20:4a is more literally translated, "May he give you according to your heart," which is less similar to 21:2 than appears from the translations. See comments on 20:4 for a discussion of the meaning of that phrase.

5. Although the Heb. word has traditionally been translated "pure/fine gold," Holladay (*CHALOT*, 290) suggests a possible identification with *olivine chrystoline*, a semi-precious stone used for ornamentation in the ancient world.

6. See comments on Ps. 8:5.

7. While it is not clear that the term carried the modern sense of "eternity," it certainly implied a length of time far in excess of the normal life expectancy of individuals. Coupling that extreme time period with yet another term for long time span, *ʿad* ("yet, still"; NIV "eternal" in v. 6), heightens the sense of permanency intended.

Divine support issues in more than life for the king. God's presence also ensures "victory/deliverance," which enhances the king's stature and reputation with his people and with neighboring nations. Thus, the king is also said to receive from Yahweh "glory," "splendor," and "majesty." "Glory" (*kabod*) is human dignity, reputation, and honor recognized by public opinion.[8] "Splendor" (*hod*) refers more to impressive bearing than reputation, while "majesty" (*hadar*) refers to splendid dress and ornamentation.[9] Because of Yahweh's support, the king enjoys good public opinion as well as regal bearing and impressive dress.

Eternal blessings. The "rich blessings" bestowed on the king beginning in 21:3 are summed up as this section comes to a close. Note how the term "blessings" envelops the description of divine grace at beginning (21:3) and end (21:6), giving shape and closure to the passage. The "rich" blessings of 21:3 become (lit.) "blessings continuing into the future" in 21:6, and these continuing blessings are linked with the "joy of [God's] presence" (21:6b).

Confession of Trust (21:7)

VERSE 7 OCCUPIES the center point of the psalm and provides transition from the positive blessings of God on the faithful king to the negative judgment of God on the enemies. The distinctive nature of the verse is revealed by the appearance only here of third-person reference about Yahweh rather than the second-person address to him that dominates the rest of the psalm. In this central verse, the king responds to the description of divine blessing and presence with a confession of trust in Yahweh.

This confession of trust is introduced by the Hebrew particle *ki* ("for, because")—an indication that his trust is grounded in the evidence of divine support provided by the preceding rehearsal of blessings. The king understands these blessings as evidence of Yahweh's "unfailing love" (*ḥesed*), which denotes faithful loyalty to obligations assumed through a covenant relationship. The king (like the faithful intercessors of 20:7) trusts Yahweh because Yahweh has proven himself generous in blessing and because he is fiercely loyal and faithful to his covenant with king and people.[10] Thus, the king is confident he will never be "shaken" (21:7).

---

8. See comments on Ps. 3:3–4.

9. See Holladay, *CHALOT*, 77, for entries on both *hod* and *hadar*. Both terms are used in reference to the king in 45:3, while *hadar* along with *kabod* ("glory") is one of the gracious gifts of God on all humanity (8:5).

10. Exactly which covenant relationship the psalmist has in mind here is not immediately clear. If it is the Sinai covenant between Yahweh and all Israel, then the king is con-

Divine Judgment on the Enemy (21:8–12)

THE PRESENCE OF God is a two-edged sword. For the faithful who trust in him, God brings blessing and salvation, while for the rebellious who resist his rule, God's coming means judgment. In 21:8–12, the psalmist describes the hoped-for consequences of Yahweh's "appearing" (21:9a) on the enemy. That we are beyond the king's reflective confession of trust is indicated by the return to second-person direct address of Yahweh ("your enemies," "your foes").

Yahweh will "lay hold, seize" his opponents (an unusual translation of *timṣa*ʾ ["will find"]),[11] and his presence will become for them a time of destruction rather than blessing. Their end is described in terms of a "fiery furnace" that consumes them as a consequence of divine wrath.[12] The fire illustrates the destructive consequence of rebellious humans coming into the presence of the theophanic glory of God.[13] God—through a consuming fire—is depicted as "swallowing up" and "consuming" his opponents.

Their descendants ... their posterity. The destruction is viewed as so total that the enemies' descendants will be destroyed as well. Rather than later divine attacks on the descendants, this probably means that as a consequence of the complete elimination of the present generation of rebellious enemies, future generations will never come into existence.[14]

---

fident that Yahweh will protect his people by supporting the king against his enemies. If it is the Davidic covenant, then the king is basing his confidence on Yahweh's promise of an eternal kingdom for David and his descendants. It may well be that both covenants stand behind the confidence expressed in this psalm.

11. Holladay (*CHALOT*, 209) offers the meaning "to meet by chance (what presents itself to one)" for the phrase *timṣa*ʾ *yad*. Alternatively, the nuance of "seek out" might fit the context.

12. The return in the second half of v. 9 to third-person reference about Yahweh ("*his* wrath") leads *BHS* to suggest this half verse is a later gloss.

13. For further discussion of theophany, see comments on 18:7–15.

14. The parallel structure of 21:10 is an artful example of the subtle expressions of affirming parallelism.

Their fruit	from the earth	you will destroy
and their seed	from human beings	

The verb "destroy" that concludes the first line also governs the thought in the second. The subtle shifting between "fruit"—indicating the coming to fruition of their hopes for descendants—and "seed"—suggesting the beginning point from which posterity proceeds—encapsulates the whole process of begetting descendants from beginning to end. In addition, the juxtaposition of "the earth" (as the physical environment) and "human beings" (as the social environment) heightens the sense of the loss that the disappearance of future generations will make in the world.

They cannot succeed. That the catastrophic fire is apocalyptic imagery is suggested by the return in 21:11 to the psalmist's real-life context. Surrounded by enemies who "plot evil" and "devise wicked schemes," the psalmist is confident they will not succeed in their plans.[15] The defeat pictured in these verses, however, is military defeat, when the enemies "turn their backs" and flee because of the supportive strength of Yahweh (21:12). Yahweh is here the "divine warrior,"[16] who stands beside the king with "drawn bow" to frustrate the plans of the enemy.

Concluding Praise of Yahweh's Strength (21:13)

LIKE SO MANY psalms, Psalm 21 ends as it began, with a renewed promise of praise for Yahweh's "strength" that supports the king and gives him victory. The final call is for Yahweh to be "raised up" or "exalted" because of his many acts of "strength." The communal nature of this praise becomes clear in the second half of the verse, where the voice of the people breaks out in their promise to "sing" (a cohortative, meaning "let us sing") and "praise" ("let us praise") Yahweh's "might" (*geburah*).[17] Like Psalm 20, Psalm 21 is ultimately a psalm of the people who entreat God concerning the king's need of divine help from Yahweh against his enemies.

THE VICTORIES YOU GIVE. The first section of Psalm 21 is bracketed by the appearance of the identical term (*bišuᶜatka*) at beginning (21:1) and near the end (21:5). The presence of this word provides a thematic focus for this section on the action of Yahweh in behalf of king and people. The NIV translation of this word as "victories" in both cases has applied interpretive pressure on the understanding of *bišuᶜatka* in two ways.

(1) The term in the Hebrew is a singular noun, not plural as the NIV renders it.[18] The plural rendering flies in the face of the text and tends to generalize the king's experience of victory away from any particular historical

15. The circumstance of conspiring nations joining together to attack "the king" of Yahweh is reminiscent of Ps. 2, although the words used are distinctive.

16. For further discussion of the "divine warrior," see comments on 18:13. Cf. also Longman and Reid, *God Is a Warrior*, passim.

17. The use of *geburah* at this point links Ps. 21 back to the "saving power [*gebura*]" of Yahweh's "right hand" in 20:6 (cf. also 21:8, "right hand").

18. Most other translations employ the singular: e.g., NRSV "help" (21:1, 5); NJB "saving help" (21:1, 5); REB " victory" (21:1, 5).

circumstance (no longer recoverable) to which the original psalm might be responding. Such a shift from particular to general is consistent with the messianic reading of the royal psalms characteristic of the NIV.

(2) The base Hebrew noun *yešuʿah* more commonly means "salvation" or "deliverance" than "victory." The use of "victories" rather than the more common "salvation" or "deliverance" is also consistent with the NIV's messianic reading of the psalm. Since the Messiah *brings* salvation and deliverance rather than receives it, as does the king in Psalm 20, the shift to "victory" allows the king to appear to participate in the "victories" given through the power of God. The problem of such a rendering, in my opinion, is that it is not comfortable with the text and undermines the original, premessianic reading of the psalm.

This rendering also obscures the connection that links Psalms 20, 21, and 22 together. In Psalm 20 the people who are interceding for the king anticipate a resounding shout of joy *bišuʿateka* (lit., "when you are delivered," 20:5).[19] A singular voice confidently proclaims, "Now I know that the LORD saves [*hošiaʿ*] his anointed" (20:6). Psalm 21 then describes the king rejoicing in the "salvation" provided by Yahweh (21:1, 5). The certainty of divine deliverance that marks these two psalms provides stark contrast with the *failure* of divine deliverance expressed in the plaintive cry with which Psalm 22 begins: "My God, my God, why have you forsaken me? Why are you so far from my salvation [*mišuʿati*; NIV saving me]?" (22:1).[20]

What gives the king joy at the beginning of Psalm 21 is the deliverance provided by Yahweh, not the victory he himself accomplishes with divine empowerment. This interpretation is more consistent with the opening phrase of 21:1, where the king rejoices in Yahweh's strength, not his own! It also fits well with the king's spoken "request" (for deliverance?) in 21:2b and provides a strong foundation for the king's "trust" in Yahweh that completes the section (21:7). While it is true that the final section of this psalm depicts military action that might seem appropriate for a "victory" celebration, it is Yahweh who is seen to defeat the enemy, and it is Yahweh whose strength is exalted at the close.

At the time of your appearing. Psalm 21 concludes with what might be called a "proto-apocalyptic" description of divine judgment on God's enemies by a consuming fire. Judgment by fire is a common image in the Old

19. In this instance the NIV also translates with "victory" rather than "salvation/deliverance" but shifts the nominal construction into a temporal phrase that would be more likely with an infinitive construct.

20. The theme of deliverance (using two other Heb. roots) dominates the first two-thirds of Ps. 22 (*plṭ* in 22:4, 8; *nṣl* in 22:20; *yšʿ* also appears in 22:21). For further discussion of the linkage between Pss. 21 and 22, see comments on Ps. 22.

Testament,[21] and Yahweh himself is on a number of occasions called a "consuming fire," a probable reference to the essential character of Yahweh and its destructive potential for those who see or approach it.[22] I call this passage *proto*-apocalyptic because the Old Testament image of a consuming fire most often anticipates the destruction of immediate enemies rather than an eschatological consummation. While it is true that the prophetic oracles were looking into an indeterminate future at the time of their pronouncement, most had already seen fulfillment by the time of inscripturation, and only a few have clearly shifted their focus to the eschatological end times.[23] That an apocalyptic interpretation ultimately ruled the day is indicated by an apparent allusion to these verses in James 5:3 in a clear context of eschatological consummation.[24]

Like the "consuming fire," the image of a fiery furnace is also used of divine judgment or testing. A variety of Hebrew words are translated "furnace"—probably describing different kinds of furnaces employed for various purposes. The smoke rising from the destruction of Sodom and Gomorrah is described in Genesis 19:28 "like smoke from a furnace." Since this term is also used in Exodus as the source of soot employed by Moses to create the plague of boils (Ex. 9:10, 18), it may describe the kilns in which mud bricks were fired.

As a place of testing for Israel, Egypt itself is called on several occasions an "iron-smelting furnace [*kur habbarzel*]" (Deut. 4:20; 1 Kings 8:51; Jer. 11:4). Elsewhere the term *kur* appears as an indication of divine testing (Prov. 17:3; 27:21; Isa. 48:10) or judgment (Ezek. 22:18, 20, 22). In these instances *kur* is connected with various metals that undergo refinement through smelting: gold (Prov.17:3; 27:21); silver (Isa. 48:10); silver, copper, tin, iron, and lead (Ezek. 22:18, 20, 22). In the narratives of Daniel, Shadrach, Meshach, and

---

21. Cf. Lev. 9:24; 10:2; Num. 11:1; 16:35; 21:28; Deut. 5:25; Judg. 9:15, 20; 2 Kings 1:10, 12, 14; Job 15:34; 20:26; Pss. 21:9; 78:63; 106:18; Isa. 10:17; 26:11; Jer. 17:27; 21:14; 49:27; 50:32; Lam. 4:11; Ezek. 15:7; 19:12, 14; 20:47; 23:25; 28:18; Hos. 8:14; Amos 1:4, 7, 10, 12, 14; 2:2, 5; Obad. 18; Nah. 3:13, 15; Zeph. 1:18; 3:8; Zech. 9:4.

22. Cf. Ex. 24:17; Deut. 4:24; 2 Sam. 22:9; Ps. 18:8; Isa. 30:27; 30:30; 33:14. Consuming fire can also have positive connotations. When used of sacrifice, it can represent the means by which right relationship is restored between sinful humans and God (cf. Lev. 6:10; 2 Chron. 7:1). Compare also the New Testament references in Heb. 10:26–27; 12:29.

23. See esp. Zeph. 1:18; 3:8, where consuming fire is clearly associated with "the day of the LORD's wrath" and is intended as judgment of "the whole world" (Zeph. 1:18b; 3:8d).

24. K. Aland, M. Black, B. Metzger, *Greek New Testament* (New York: United Bible Society, 1994), lists James 5:3 as a quotation of Ps. 21:9: "Now listen, you rich people, weep and wail because of the misery that is coming upon you. Your wealth has rotted, and moths have eaten your clothes. Your gold and silver are corroded. Their corrosion will testify against you and *eat your flesh like fire*. You have hoarded wealth in the last days" (James 5:1–3).

Abednego are thrown by the king of Babylon into a "blazing furnace" [Aram. *ʾattun nuraʾ*], which the king intends as judgment but God uses as a test of their faithfulness.[25]

The term employed for "furnace" in our passage is the Hebrew *tannur*, which most often describes an oven for baking.[26] On the two occasions other than our psalm that the NIV translates this term "furnace," divine judgment is clearly in mind. In Isaiah 31:9, Assyria will panic and flee before the supernatural intervention of Yahweh, "whose fire is in Zion, whose furnace is in Jerusalem." Malachi offers a distinctly eschatological and apocalyptic setting when he declares: "'Surely the day is coming; it will burn like a furnace. All the arrogant and every evildoer will be stubble, and that day that is coming will set them on fire,' says the LORD Almighty, 'Not a root or a branch will be left to them'" (Mal. 4:1).

The concept of a fiery furnace as an image of the eschatological judgment reappears in the New Testament. Jesus tells two parables of the end times in Matthew 13—one of pulling out weeds at "the end of the age" (13:37–43) and the other describing the separation of good and bad fish (13:47–50). Both conclude with similar warnings that the wicked will be thrown into "the fiery furnace, where there will be weeping and gnashing of teeth" (cf. 13:42, 50).

The use in both Old and New Testaments of similar images of fiery eschatological judgment emphasizes the continuity that binds these two scriptural collections together. Such continuity of image, theme, and message flies in the face of any attempt to distinguish between Old and New Testaments by claiming the former proclaims a message of wrath and judgment while the latter is exclusively focused on gracious mercy and salvation.

The New Testament, of course, is a gospel of God's gracious mercy poured out abundantly in Jesus Christ on those who will receive it. But the New Testament, even from the mouth of Jesus himself (Matt. 13:42, 50), makes it abundantly clear that God is still in his essential nature a "consuming fire" (Heb. 12:29), who cannot be trifled with—a consuming fire who can receive the sacrifices of the repentant and turn them into restoration. But at the same time God's consuming fire *must* consume those who align themselves with evil and refuse to accept his mercy. The eschatological warning of both Testaments is unmistakable: Those who persist in resisting God's will and purposes will suffer the same fate as stubble consigned to the furnace or dross left behind in the refining process.

---

25. Cf. Dan. 3:6, 11, 15, 17, 19, 20, 21, 22, 23, 26.

26. For *tannur* as "oven," see Ex. 8:3; Lev. 2:4; 7:9; 11:35; 26:26; Neh. 3:11; 12:38; Hos. 7:4, 6, 7; Lam. 5:10. The term also appears in Gen. 15:17, where it describes the smoking "fire pot" by which Yahweh indicates his commitment to the covenant established with Abraham.

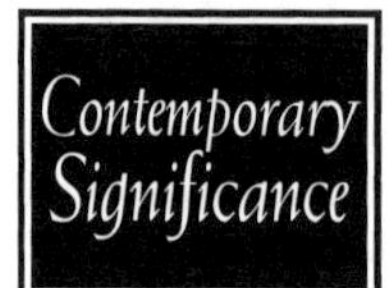

AS IN PSALM 20, the picture and attitude of the king serve as an appropriate model for the individual believer seeking guidance for his or her own life.[27] Characteristic of Israelite kingship was a tension that most of us face almost daily. If you look at the early narratives of the origins of Israel's monarchy, this tension is very apparent. The kings constantly struggled with competing demands. On the one hand, the people wanted them to become political and military leaders winning victories against Israel's enemies. On the other hand, God reluctantly called them while demanding them to forego the normal kingly reliance on military, political, and financial power in order to lead the people in the ways of Yahweh.

The stories of Saul illustrate just how difficult it was to keep these demands in proper perspective. Twice God rebuked Saul through Samuel for failing to remember his proper role. Early on Saul failed to trust in Yahweh by waiting for Samuel's appearance before a battle. Instead, seeing the enemy troops massing and his own fearful army dwindling away, he manipulated the sacrificial offering in order to ensure military victory (1 Sam. 13:1–15). Later Saul allowed himself to be swayed by popular pressure into resisting the complete annihilation of the Amalekites as demanded by Yahweh (15:1–34). In both instances Saul saw victory and popular acceptance as more important than leading the people to fear Yahweh and rely on him alone. Thus, the kingship was taken away from Saul and his family (15:17–26).

The same tension is evident in the description of appropriate kingship found in Deuteronomy 17:14–20, where God permits kingship with a series of limiting caveats. The king must be a native Israelite. He must not multiply horses, wives, gold, or silver. Moreover, he must refer often to the law of Yahweh and live carefully by it. Under these conditions, God promises, "he and his descendants will reign a long time over his kingdom in Israel" (17:20).

The references to horses, wives, gold, and silver, while not immediately clear, are nevertheless fairly transparent in their intent. Horses were the essential component for creating a corps of horse-drawn chariotry—the A-bomb of military technology of the day. In essence the kings were being told *not* to rely on military power!

Multiple marriages were the means by which ancient kings cemented political treaties and relationships with foreign nations. Such treaties helped to normalize relationships and provided weaker powers with strong partners with whom to resist the pressures from the major powers bearing down on them. By rejecting such political maneuvering, the kings were asked to give up another source of kingly power in favor of reliance on Yahweh alone.

---

27. See the discussion in the Contemporary Significance section of Ps. 20.

The final reference to gold and silver is by now more clear. Financial power has always been one of the necessary trappings of political and military power. How else can a king pay and supply a standing army? How else can great building campaigns be carried forward? Once again the kings of Israel were expected to eschew one of the most important features of national leadership—financial power.

Rather than the usual forms of kingly power, therefore, the kings were required to bind themselves to keep the law of Yahweh and to rely on him alone. It is no accident that Deuteronomy 17:14–20 reflects clearly and negatively on the kingship of Solomon, who served at once in Israel as the great king of wisdom and the epitome of folly (1 Kings 9:1–11:13). Solomon's kingship violated all three of the expectations laid down in Deuteronomy 17. He amassed a huge chariotry force by trading horses throughout the Near East. His large number of wives is well known—many of whom (like the daughter of Pharaoh) were political marriages as described above. And Solomon's opulent wealth was legendary. Massive amounts of gold and silver—derived through a harsh taxation policy—shored up his military expansion, political relationships, and economical development.

Yet, this great royal power was not matched by an equal dedication to the law of Yahweh. Solomon's folly led him to introduce foreign worship in Jerusalem, by which the people were led astray from loyalty to and reliance on Yahweh alone. For this reason much of his kingdom was taken away from his descendants.

We face similar tensions in our own lives on a daily basis. Constantly we must choose between self-power and relying on Yahweh alone. We want to be in control of our lives, and we want to take the credit for the victories we achieve. Yet we are too often forced to admit—by circumstances, by our own failures—just how little control we really have over our lives. We cannot even control our own desires or discipline our use of time, money, or the TV! How can we hope to exert influence on our children, world politics, natural forces, or even the drunken driver careening along the highway?

Many twelve-step programs incorporate an admission of "powerlessness" as the first step of the program: "Admitted we were powerless over [our compulsions], that our lives had become unmanageable." Rather than fostering despair, however, the program moves on to a second step: "Came to believe that a *power greater than myself* could restore me to sanity." And the third step models a life-saving step from "I am able" to "He is able," when it says: "Made a decision to turn my will and my life over to God. . . ."

Psalm 21:1–7 mirrors just such a recognition of personal powerlessness and a turning to the power of God. It is in this context of surrender that the translation of *yešuᶜatka* in verses 1 and 5 should take its meaning. The subtle difference between the NIV's "victories" (implying an accomplishment of the king) and the alternate rendering of "salvation" or "deliverance" (implying the powerful action of Yahweh) is important. The whole context here is one of trust in and reliance on the "strength" of Yahweh (21:1). The real actor in these verses is Yahweh, not the king. Yahweh gives salvation (21:1, 5a), grants the desires of the king's heart and the request of his lips (21:2), crowns the king (21:3), gives abundant life (21:4), and provides the king with divine presence (21:6). King has only to ask (21:2, 4), and God responds. In such a context of divine power, it seems most appropriate to translate *yešuᶜatka* as "your salvation" or "your deliverance" rather than "victories."

Similarly, in our own lives such a subtle difference can make a world of difference in how we perceive God working in us. Do we understand our victories—however great or small—as God's deliverance? Or do we see our own power and ability in our accomplishments? An excerpt from the Third-Step Prayer of Alcoholics Anonymous walks a narrow line between personal victory and divine deliverance: "Take away my difficulties that *victory* over them might bear witness to those I would help of *your* power, *your* love, and *your* way of life." Victory here, as in Psalm 21, is divine deliverance. It is God who takes away our difficulties, and our testimony is to his power made manifest in our weakness.[28] Ask any recovering addict how they can resist their addictive compulsions, and they will tell you, "I can't. God can, if I let him!"

When the king (and we) surrender our weakness to God's strength, we experience not only "salvation" but "eternal blessings" (21:6a) as well. Those blessings include divine honor, symbolized here by a "crown of pure gold," and the gift of "glory . . . splendor and majesty" (21:5).[29] As mentioned in the comments on 21:2–6, these three are visible ornaments of royal power and public prestige: public dignity, regal bearing, and splendid dress. They are transitory and passing glories, which may fade and vanish with age or loss of power and wealth. But the psalmist promises the king "*eternal* blessings" (21:6), which are filled out in the following verses: the joy of God's presence (21:6b), God's unfailing love (21:7b), and an unshakable foundation (21:7c). These gifts cannot be taken away as long as the king (and we) trust in Yahweh (21:7a).

---

28. See 2 Cor. 12:9–10.

29. The divine gifting described in 21:3–5 has much in common with God's exaltation of humankind in Ps. 8:5. These passages share three root words: "crowning;" "crown" (8:5, *ᶜṭr*; 21:3, *ᶜaṭeret*); "glory" (8:5, *kabod*; 21:5, *kabod*); and "honor/majesty" (8:5, *hadar*; 21:5, *hadar*). With the emphasis on "ruling" in 8:6, it may be that the psalmist of 21:3–5 had these images of divine gifting in mind in describing the blessing poured out on the king.

As I read again and again through the verses of Psalm 21, phrases from the great traditional hymn "How Firm a Foundation" begin to echo through my mind. To my knowledge this hymn is nowhere claimed to be based on Psalm 21, but the more I listen, the more connection I can see. "How firm a foundation ... is laid for your faith.... Fear not, I am with thee, O be not dismayed, for I am thy God, I will still give thee aid; I'll strengthen thee, help thee, and cause thee to stand, upheld by my gracious, omnipotent hand.... That [trusting] soul, though all hell should endeavor to shake, I'll never, no, never, no, never forsake!" Note again the psalmist's praise in 21:13:

Be exalted, O LORD, in your strength;
 we will sing and praise your might.

Psalm 22

FOR THE DIRECTOR of music. To the tune of "The Doe of the Morning." A psalm of David.

1 My God, my God, why have you forsaken me?
Why are you so far from saving me,
so far from the words of my groaning?
2 O my God, I cry out by day, but you do not answer,
by night, and am not silent.

3 Yet you are enthroned as the Holy One;
you are the praise of Israel.
4 In you our fathers put their trust;
they trusted and you delivered them.
5 They cried to you and were saved;
in you they trusted and were not disappointed.

6 But I am a worm and not a man,
scorned by men and despised by the people.
7 All who see me mock me;
they hurl insults, shaking their heads:
8 "He trusts in the LORD;
let the LORD rescue him.
Let him deliver him,
since he delights in him."

9 Yet you brought me out of the womb;
you made me trust in you
even at my mother's breast.
10 From birth I was cast upon you;
from my mother's womb you have been my God.
11 Do not be far from me,
for trouble is near
and there is no one to help.

12 Many bulls surround me;
strong bulls of Bashan encircle me.
13 Roaring lions tearing their prey
open their mouths wide against me.

14 I am poured out like water,
and all my bones are out of joint.
My heart has turned to wax;
it has melted away within me.
15 My strength is dried up like a potsherd,
and my tongue sticks to the roof of my mouth;
you lay me in the dust of death.
16 Dogs have surrounded me;
a band of evil men has encircled me,
they have pierced my hands and my feet.
17 I can count all my bones;
people stare and gloat over me.
18 They divide my garments among them
and cast lots for my clothing.

19 But you, O LORD, be not far off;
O my Strength, come quickly to help me.
20 Deliver my life from the sword,
my precious life from the power of the dogs.
21 Rescue me from the mouth of the lions;
save me from the horns of the wild oxen.

22 I will declare your name to my brothers;
in the congregation I will praise you.
23 You who fear the LORD, praise him!
All you descendants of Jacob, honor him!
Revere him, all you descendants of Israel!
24 For he has not despised or disdained
the suffering of the afflicted one;
he has not hidden his face from him
but has listened to his cry for help.

25 From you comes the theme of my praise in the
great assembly;
before those who fear you will I fulfill my vows.
26 The poor will eat and be satisfied;
they who seek the LORD will praise him—
may your hearts live forever!
27 All the ends of the earth
will remember and turn to the LORD,
and all the families of the nations
will bow down before him,

[28]for dominion belongs to the LORD
and he rules over the nations.

[29]All the rich of the earth will feast and worship;
all who go down to the dust will kneel before him—
those who cannot keep themselves alive.
[30]Posterity will serve him;
future generations will be told about the Lord.
[31]They will proclaim his righteousness
to a people yet unborn—
for he has done it.

A POWERFUL INDIVIDUAL psalm of deep lament, Psalm 22 shares a number of connections with Psalms 69, 70, and 71 toward the end of the second book of the Psalter. In particular Psalms 22 and 70–71[1] share similar phrases. The similarities include: (1) the plea that Yahweh "be not far" from the narrator (22:11, 19; 71:12); (2) reference to divine support from the psalmist's birth (cf. 22:9–10; 71:6); and (3) the plea for quick relief (22:19; 70:1, 5; 71:12). In the New Testament, Psalm 22 is used on a number of occasions to interpret the suffering and death of Jesus, and he himself quotes portions of its text from the cross.[2]

In my reading of Psalm 22, I have divided the text into three balanced sections of ten verses introduced by the thematic verse 1. Each of the larger sections must be further divided as well, with internal divisions being indicated by certain repeated features. The first two sections focus on the psalmist's complaint, while the final section features the psalmist's promise to praise Yahweh for deliverance and salvation. The psalm can be outlined as follows: thematic introduction (22:1); the silence and absence of God (22:2–11)—divine silence (22:2–5) and divine absence (22:6–11); vicious attacks by humans (22:12–21); promise of praise (22:22–31)—promise and call to praise (22:22–24) and vow of continued praise (22:25–31).

---

1. For the evidence suggesting that Pss. 70 and 71 should be read as a single unified composition, see comments on Ps. 70.

2. Ps. 22 figures in New Testament interpretation of Jesus at Matt. 27:35, 39, 43; John 19:23–24, 28. For Jesus' use of this psalm while on the cross, see Matt. 27:46.

The Heading (22:0)

THE HEADING BEGINS with a reference "for the director of music" and concludes with the common description "a psalm of David."[3] Between these elements appears the new phrase *ʾayyelet haššaḥar* (lit., "according to the Doe of Dawn")—a probable reference to the ancient tune to which the composition was to be sung.[4]

Thematic Introduction (22:1)

MY GOD, MY God, why have you forsaken me? The opening words of this psalm have become so familiar to us from Jesus' use of them (in an Aramaic version)[5] from the cross that it is difficult for us to separate them from that much later context and read them as an integral part of Psalm 22. If we read these words *only* as words about Jesus, we ignore the original and continuing word of God to *us* this psalm in its entirety represents. These opening words encapsulate the thematic agony of the first two-thirds of this psalm. The psalmist feels totally abandoned. The use of the perfect verb *ʿazabtani* ("you have forsaken me") with its sense of completed action makes God's abandonment seem more complete and final—an act accomplished in the past with effects extending into the present and beyond.

So far from saving me. The last half of verse 1 is awkward. The questioning "why" of the first half of the verse must be taken to refer also to *both* of the remaining phrases, while the plaintive "so far" of the second phrase must also govern the last phrase. The interpretive rendering of the rather difficult literal Hebrew can be illustrated below, where the italics in parentheses represent words that are not in the original text but are supplied to clarify the meaning. (Delete the parenthetical phrases to get a sense of the literal Hebrew text.)

> Why have you forsaken me?
> (*Why are you*) so far from my deliverance?
> (*Why are you so far from*) the words of my groaning?

---

3. For discussion of these two more common elements of the psalm headings, see comments on Pss. 3 and 4.

4. The NIV's translation "To the tune of 'The Doe of the Morning,'" makes the interpretation as a tune explicit and further understands the reference to "the dawn" more generally to indicate "the morning." For a more detailed discussion of tunes in the psalm headings, see J. F. A. Sawyer, "An Analysis of the Context and Meaning of the Psalm Headings," *Transactions of the Glasgow University Oriental Society* 22 (1967–68): 26–38. For this specific element, see also Kraus, *Psalms 1–59*, 30.

5. Jesus' speech, reported in Mark 15:34, is Aramaic: *eloi eloi lama sabachthani*.

Such ellipses of significant material from parallel lines is not uncommon in Hebrew poetry, but it often renders the interpretive task more difficult and ambiguous.

The NIV's "saving me" renders a noun construction (*mišuʿati*; lit., "from my salvation/deliverance") as a verbal phrase. While this clarifies the meaning in the context, it obscures the connection that exists between this phrase and the thematic use of the same noun (*yešuʿah*) in Psalms 18, 20, and 21.[6] In those passages the term speaks of the "deliverance" that Yahweh has given his king or that is anticipated as sure to come. The use of the term in the present psalm creates a stark contrast as the psalmist agonizes over clear evidence that Yahweh is "far" from providing "deliverance."

The Silence and Absence of God (22:2–11)

THE FIRST MAJOR section of the psalm emphasizes the theme of abandonment through two sets of contrasts between the psalmist's current sense of God's complete absence and past reports of God's very present help in time of trouble. The first contrast focuses on God's *silence* (22:2–5) while the second is concerned with his *failure to act* (22:6–11). The NIV marks these contrasts by the use in both instances of the expression "yet you . . ." (22:3a, 9a) to introduce the earlier experience so contrary to the psalmist's own.[7]

You do not answer. When God does not reply to the psalmist's repeated cries, it is not because he is unable to speak or is unaware of the psalmist's plight. Divine silence is for the psalmist an example of the mysterious exercise of God's free will. It is this difficult circumstance—that God is aware and could answer but does not—that fuels the psalmist's painful confusion and dismay. Note the intentional contrast between the psalmist's almost garrulous attempts to persuade God with many words (22:1b–2: "my groaning," "I cry out," "[I] am not silent") and God's complete silence (22:2a: "you do not answer").

Note also the further contrast established between the psalmist's present experience of abandonment and the reports of Yahweh's earlier quick response to the cries of the "fathers" (22:5). When the ancestors of Israel cried out for help, God not only heard but answered and acted. The ances-

6. The noun appears as "victory" in 18:50; 20:6; 21:1, 5. Consult the commentary on these verses for further discussion of the linkage of this theme.

7. There is no Hebrew equivalent of "yet" in the text of 22:3a. In 22:9a the author does use the Heb. particle *ki* ("but") to express the adversative sense of the passage that follows. Both passages use the pronoun *ʾattah* ("you") as part of the introduction, linking the two together and clarifying the adversative sense of the first passage by the clearly adversative character of the second.

tors were "not disappointed" (22:5), as the psalmist is. The fact that Yahweh is the Holy One[8] who "is seated [on] the praises of Israel" (22:3)[9] implies there is no failure of faithfulness on Israel's part that might explain any lack of divine responsiveness. Israel trusted (22:4a, 4b, 5b)[10] Yahweh, and that trust was rewarded when God "delivered" them from their distress (22:5). Once again the contrast between God's past active deliverance and the present experience of his complete silence and absence heightens the psalmist's confusion and pain.

I am a worm and not a man. The contrast continues and is heightened in the second set of oppositions offered. The psalmist's situation feels even more desperate than that of the ancestors, and yet Yahweh still does nothing. He feels reduced and degraded below the status of a human being by the taunts of his enemies as well as the lack of divine concern. The "worm" (*tolaᶜat/toleᶜah*) is a destructive creature mentioned in agricultural contexts.[11] In Jonah 4:7, the worm is significant by virtue of its *in*significance. Jonah is chided for having more concern for the plant destroyed by the worm than for the inhabitants of Nineveh, who stood to lose their lives because of their sins. Jonah would have God destroy the insignificant worm to preserve his comfort, but he would not intercede to seek forgiveness for the Ninevites in order to save them.

Like Jonah, the opponents viewed the psalmist as worthy of destruction. They express "scorn" (*ḥerpah*), they "despise" (*bzh*), "mock" (*lᶜg*), and "insult" (*pṭr*) the psalmist, they "wag their heads" in ridicule (22:6–7). Their public articulation of scorn once again emphasizes the contrast between the psalmist's experience of abandonment and God's deliverance of the ancestors.

---

8. For a discussion of the meaning of *qadoš*, see comments on Ps. 5:7–8.

9. This is the more natural reading of the Heb. behind the NIV's "you are enthroned as the Holy One; you are the praise of Israel." The verb for sitting (*yšb*) is a Qal active participle here, indicating that Yahweh is continuously and currently sitting. The nuance behind the NIV's "enthroned" suggests that others are placing God on the throne. The further question concerns whether the verb is to be attached with what precedes or what follows; the Hebrew accentuation groups the verb with what follows. The noun the NIV renders "praise" is actually a plural ("praises"), although some Hebrew manuscripts exhibit the singular form. All this suggests that the better translation is to understand the first phrase as an affirmation of Yahweh's essential character as Holy One, while the second phrase describes his continual resting on the throne provided by the praises of a faithful Israel. While the phrase "sitter of the praises of Israel" may seem awkward to us, this is an acceptable way to say "sitting *on* the praises. . ." in Hebrew.

10. It is certainly significant that this verb of trust is used three times within four consecutive phrases (22:4–5), emphasizing the "trust" in Yahweh that characterized Israel's faithful reliance on their God.

11. Cf. Ex. 16:20; 25:4; Deut. 28:39; Jonah 4:7.

He trusts[12] in the LORD;
 let the LORD rescue[13] him.
Let him deliver him,
 since he delights in him.

Although the Hebrew behind "trust" in this verse is not the same as in 22:4–5, the ideas are parallel and link the two passages together. Like the ancestors the psalmist relies on Yahweh, but unlike them he experiences no divine protection and deliverance. Moreover, the public taunts of the enemy grind this home in the most painful way possible.

You made me trust in you. The study in contrasts is not over yet. Again the psalmist shifts to second-person address of Yahweh, introduced with the phrase "yet you" (22:9).[14] This leads to the final contrast between the psalmist's present circumstance and past experience. In a passage much like 71:5–6, the psalmist recalls events of birth and early childhood as evidence of absolute trust and commitment to Yahweh. Yahweh is depicted as the midwife (from *gḥh* ["draw out (from the womb)]") upon whom the child is "cast out/down" from the mother's womb.[15] The helpless infant must rely on the waiting midwife to catch it as it departs from the protective care of the mother's womb into the harsh realities of life. Because of the infant's helplessness, the psalmist finds it appropriate to acknowledge that Yahweh "made me trust" while at his mother's breast (22:9b) so that his commitment to Yahweh as "my God" dates "from my mother's womb" (22:10b).

This sense of early protective care contributes to the growing feeling of abandonment that permeates the psalmist's present. As near as the midwife must be to catch the birthing child, as close as a nursing infant must feel snuggled to its mother's breast, so far does the psalmist feel from the God who

12. The verb translated "trust" here is difficult. The form in the text (*gol*) makes no sense here. According to the Greek, Syriac, and some versions of the quote in Matt. 27:43, the word should probably be taken as *gal*, from the Heb. *gll* ("roll away"). In this context it has been understood metaphorically to mean "roll away (a concern)" onto Yahweh. Kraus (*Psalms 1–59*, 292) suggests the Aramaic targum read an original *yagil* ("he shrieked ecstatically/wildly for joy").

13. Cf. 22:5, where the ancestors' trust leads to Yahweh's "rescuing" them, using the same verb (*plṭ*).

14. See footnote 7, above.

15. Two Heb. words are used here to describe the mother's womb: *beṭen* (22:9a, 10b) and *reḥem* (22:10a). The first—often translated "belly"—is most likely a reference to the internal "womb" or "uterus" in which the child is carried during the gestation period. The second—usually translated "womb"—is more likely a reference to the birth canal or vagina, as the rather crude soldiers' of Judg. 5:30 suggests: *raḥam raḥamatayim* ("a *reḥem* or two for each").

still delays to act. "Don't be far from me," he cries (22:11a)[16] as trouble closes in and he realizes "there is no one to help." The opening phrases of verse 11 constitute the first plea in the psalm and give voice to the sense of abandonment that has been building.

Vicious Attacks by the Enemies (22:12–21)

THE PSALMIST'S ENEMIES are depicted as fearsome beasts that surround him and cut off all escape. The animals are introduced in a particular order—bulls (22:12), lions (22:13), and dogs (22:16)—that is reversed in the plea for deliverance: dogs (22:20), lions (22:21a), and wild oxen (22:21b). Bashan (22:12), where the bulls originate, was a lush region in the north Transjordan, east of the Sea of Galilee and known for its well-fed cattle.[17] The lions are caught in the midst of a grisly meal, "tearing" (*ṭorep*) at their prey and "roaring" (*šoʾeg*) to warn off any competitors.

The fierce attack reduces the psalmist to fear and weakness. The signs of physical weakness are common ones. His strength departs like water "poured out" on the ground (22:14a), so that his body feels awkward and out of control ("all my bones are out of joint"). Similarly, the psalmist's heart (courage) melts away like wax before a fierce flame (22:14c-d). He feels weakened by fear (22:15a, "dried up like a potsherd") and has a bad case of "cotton mouth" (22:15b, "my tongue sticks to the roof of my mouth"), fearing the approach of death (22:15c).

They have pierced my hands and my feet. Evil men surround the psalmist like "dogs" (22:16a-b), but the result of this attack is a matter of debate. The primary Hebrew text reads "like a lion [are] my hands and my feet." This makes little sense in the context. Considerable literature has been generated, and a variety of emendations has been suggested to resolve the issue. Various Greek, Latin, and Syriac versions offer translations suggesting "seek to bind" or "pierce."[18] The latter option resonates, of course, with the crucifixion of Jesus, though the supporting evidence is not particularly strong.

The psalmist's desperate circumstances are illustrated by the physical deterioration of the body—the bones stand out through the skin. The enemies, anticipating the fast-approaching end, "stare" and "gloat"[19] and even

16. This cry—"Don't be far removed!"—will return again at the end of the second major section of the psalm (cf. 22:19).

17. Cf. Deut. 32:14; Ezek. 39:18; Amos 4:1.

18. See the discussion with a thorough bibliography of resources in Craigie (*Psalms 1–50*, 196).

19. The sense of "gloat" is not derived from the Hebrew verb *rʾh* ("look, see"), but is an interpretive rendering from the context.

raffle off the hapless psalmist's clothing before he is dead.[20] The similarity to events surrounding the crucifixion, where soldiers raffle off Jesus' garments while he is dying on the cross, have been noted at least since the collection of traditions on which the Gospel accounts are based (cf. Matt. 27:35; Mark 15:24; Luke 23:34; John 19:23–24).

Be not far off. The second stanza of ten verses closes as does the first—with the plea that Yahweh "be not far off" (22:19a; cf. 22:11a). Verse 19 is introduced by the second-person pronoun *weʾattah* ("and you"), so that the conclusion of this stanza links back to the internal divisions of the first stanza, where the pronoun *ʾattah* was twice used to introduce structural contrasts (cf. 22:3, 9). This subtle literary shaping helps unite the first two stanzas, with the common theme of complaint, in distinction from the final stanza, with its emphasis on praise.

Whereas stanza 1 ushered in despair and additional complaint, stanza 2 shifts at the end to a direct and succinct plea for deliverance. The desperate nature of the circumstances becomes apparent in the urgency with which the psalmist calls for aid. As a soldier surrounded and about to be overwhelmed by the enemy in close hand-to-hand combat might call out to his comrades for assistance, the psalmist calls out to God for deliverance: "To my aid, hurry!" (lit. trans., 22:19b).[21]

Deliver my life from the sword. In the two verses that follow this initial plea, the psalmist continues to seek rescue first from the more general threat of "the sword" (22:20a) and then from each of the metaphorical categories of attackers envisioned at the beginning of the stanza: dogs (22:20b; cf. 22:16a), lions (22:21a; cf. 22:13a), and wild oxen (22:21b; cf. 22:12).

My precious life. The precious character of the psalmist's life that hangs so precariously in the balance is stressed by the use of the more unusual word *yaḥid* ("only")[22] to expand on the parallel "my being." The "only child"

---

20. Since the Heb. of this passage simply reads "*they* will stare," it is possible that the antecedent of "they" is "bones" rather than "enemies." Although the plural of "bones" is by form feminine in this verse while the pronoun is masculine, the singular "bone" (*ʿeṣem*) is masculine and appears with both masculine and feminine plural forms. In this interpretation, the verse would read: "I can count all my bones, and they gaze and stare back at me."

21. The NIV's "come quickly to help me," while accurate enough, is a bit pallid to catch the real urgency and desperation behind this plea. A similar imperative phrase (*leʿezrati ḥušah*) directed to God in desperate circumstances is found also in Pss. 38:22; 40:13; 70:1, 5; 71:12; and the similar phrase *ḥušah li* ("hurry to me") appears at 141:1. (See the discussion of this phrase in the comments on Pss. 70 and 71, where it provides a connecting link between these two psalms.)

22. The term *yaḥid* is most often used to describe an "only child"—such as Isaac (Gen. 22:2) or (in the feminine) the only daughter of Jephthah (Judg. 11:34).

is normally referred to in contexts of threat or mourning for the loss of a precious child.[23]

Promise to Praise (22:22–31)

THE FINAL STANZA of ten verses turns decisively toward praise. The stanza is subdivided into two segments, each introduced by a second-person address to Yahweh promising to proclaim praise to the psalmist's fellow worshipers in the temple (cf. 22:22, 25). Both promises are followed by a passage in which Yahweh is mentioned in the third person, and others are encouraged to praise him by a rehearsal of reasons he is praiseworthy (cf. 22:23–24, 26–31).

I will declare your name to my brothers. The first subsection of this final stanza begins with a vow to declare Yahweh's name to the psalmist's brothers in worship.[24] A subtle wordplay is introduced with the verb *spr* ("count, recount, declare") to describe the psalmist's proclamation of the goodness of Yahweh in the temple. This same verb form appeared in 22:17a at the moment of despair when the psalmist was "counting" the bones that poked through his emaciated body. That temple worship is intended is clearly indicated by the phrases "in the congregation" (22:22b) and "in the great assembly" (22:25b). Note also that to "declare the name of the LORD" is equivalent to "praising the LORD," as the use of these phrases in parallel implies. To make known the name Yahweh is to reveal something about his praiseworthy character.

You who fear the LORD. The psalmist's promise to praise Yahweh now becomes a call to others—that is, the psalmist's fellow worshipers—to join in the praise of Yahweh. Those who "fear the LORD" (i.e., those who adopt the appropriate attitude of trust and dependence on him[25]) are further identified as the "descendants [*zeraᶜ*] of Jacob" and the "descendants [*zeraᶜ*] of

---

23. Note esp. the story of the near sacrifice of Isaac in Gen. 22, where the preciousness of Isaac—who came late in life to Abraham and Sarah and who represents their only hope for the fulfillment of the divine promises—is emphasized by the piling up of words in the description: "Take your son, your only son [*yaḥid*], the one you love, Isaac, and sacrifice him" (lit. trans.). Other uses of the term are found in Ps. 25:16; Isa. 6:26; and in the narrative of Jephthah, who having vowed to sacrifice the first thing that greets him as he returns home from a victorious campaign, is shocked when his only daughter (*yeḥidah*) runs out of the house to meet him (Judg. 11:34).

24. For a discussion of the name of Yahweh and its significance to Israel, see comments on Ps. 8.

25. For a discussion of the meaning of "fear the LORD," see the section on "Theology of the Psalms" in volume 2 of this commentary.

Israel" (22:23b-c). Three imperative verbs enjoin the gathered worshipers to glorify Yahweh: "Praise him," "honor him," and "revere him."[26]

The reasons for Yahweh's praiseworthiness are clearly related to the psalmist's need to experience the presence of God and the assurance of his concern for the psalmist's plight. His hope and assurance are grounded in Yahweh's past history of action for those who are afflicted.

In this reflective meditation on Yahweh's faithfulness the psalmist affirms that God has never "despised or disdained the suffering [*ᶜenut*][27] of the afflicted one [*ᶜani*]." The ordering of this verse, with the two negative verbal phrases, each with its own negative particle (*loʾ*), loaded up front in the verse, emphasizes the unbelievable quality of Yahweh's failure to act in behalf of those who call on him. This has the effect of strengthening the ground of hope while at the same time heightening the pain of the psalmist's experience of abandonment in the opening lines. This tension between hope and despair is carried on into the second half of the verse, where Yahweh is said not to have "hidden his face" from the afflicted but to listen "to his cry for help"—both statements at odds with the psalmist's own experience to this point.

The theme of my praise. This is certainly a nice turn of phrase, but it is not a direct rendering of a clear underlying Hebrew. It is rather an interpretive understanding of the slight awkwardness encountered in the more literal rendering, "From with you [is] my praise in the great assembly." Dahood's creative suggestion that the Hebrew be repointed and understood as a verb based on the noun "one hundred" and meaning "say 100 times" is amusing but not worthy of serious consideration. Craigie is certainly more nearly right in recognizing that only some prophetic experience within the context of worship can explain the psalmist's sudden shift from despairing language at the beginning of the psalm to the affirmations of complete assurance in 22:24–26. Either the psalmist has heard some priestly/prophetic pronouncement of deliverance or has had a renewed personal experience of the presence and mercy of Yahweh in the midst of worship. It is in this sense, then, that the psalmist can say that "my praise" is "from you [the LORD]"—either as a pronouncement from God or from being in his presence.

---

26. The last imperative construction (*guru mimmennu*) is more accurately taken as "be afraid because of him" and is in this context a variation on the more common expression employing *yrʾ* (cf. 22:23a).

27. This Hebrew noun *ᶜenut*—formed by an abstract ending (*-ut*) on the same root (*ᶜnh*) as the following noun *ᶜani*, does not appear elsewhere. Holladay (*CHALOT*, 278) suggests it should rather be read as the infinitive construct of the verb *ᶜnh* ("answer"). In that case the whole phrase would be translated: "He has not . . . disdained *to answer* the afflicted."

The return in 22:25 to direct address to Yahweh signals the second subsection in this final ten-verse stanza. Once again the worship context is made explicit with the mention of the "great assembly" (22:25a; cf. "congregation" in 22:22b) and the psalmist's promise to fulfill vows (22:25b; cf. the promise to praise in 22:22b). The reference to "those who fear you" also refers back to the same group called to join in the psalmist's praise in 22:23a.

They who seek the LORD will praise him. The concluding praise section of the psalm (22:26–31) moves out in almost apocalyptic fashion to describe the global effects of Yahweh's righteous rule. The themes addressed include: (1) the welfare of the poor who are satisfied (22:26a); (2) the submission of the nations to the rule of Yahweh (22:27–28); (3) the leveling of society in acknowledged dependence on Yahweh (22:29); (4) the continued praise and proclamation of the righteousness of God (22:26b, 30–31). The psalmist envisions a future in which the current state of affairs is turned on end and the true purposes of Yahweh are realized in the world of human events. God comes near, and humans—rich or poor, Israelite or non-Israelite—will acknowledge his lordship and bow before him.

The poor will eat and be satisfied. The "poor" are the *ᶜanawim*, those whose rights are denied in an oppressive society—the weak, the widow, and the orphan, who have no one to offer protection and advocacy.[28] The synonymous parallelism of 22:26 links these forgotten ones with those "who seek the LORD" (*dorešayw*)[29] and praise him in the second half of the verse. By means of this linkage the psalmist marks out these despised and exploited members of society as the seriously faithful, who because of their fragile circumstances have been led into the appropriate acknowledgment of their absolute reliance on the provision of Yahweh. It is this awareness and acceptance of dependence that constitutes the primary meaning of the Israelite concept of "fear of the LORD"—the attitude that dominates the remainder of the psalm.

All the ends of the earth. The psalmist emphasizes the universal, apocalyptic vision with this all-encompassing phrase. Each of the thirteen occurrences of this phrase in the Old Testament—all in poetic contexts—is tinged with apocalyptic expectation. The tribe of Joseph will "gore" the nations at the *ends of the earth* (Deut. 33:17). Yahweh will shatter all opposition and judge

---

28. See the discussion of various categories of oppressed persons in the comments on 10:16–18.

29. The verb *drš* is the most usual way of expressing a religious inquiry into the will and purposes of God—normally involving formal ritual at the worship place. Such inquiry is not just casual questioning but represents a careful, intentional attempt to seek out and understand God's will.

the *ends of the earth* (1 Sam. 2:10). Yahweh's salvation will extend out to include the nations at *the ends of the earth* (Ps. 67:7; 98:3; Isa. 45:22; 52:10; Jer. 16:19). Israel through her king will rule to the *ends of the earth* (Pss. 2:8; 72:8; Mic. 5:4; Zech. 9:10). Yahweh is the acknowledged creator of the *ends of the earth* (Prov. 30:4), gives it to whom he wills (Ps. 2:8), and retains the right of authority and judgment over it (1 Sam. 2:10; Jer. 16:19).

That the ends of the earth can "remember" and "return" to Yahweh indicates that it is the scattered inhabitants of the earth whom the psalmist really has in view. Those sinful nations who at the tower of Babel (Gen. 11) were scattered across the face of the earth are here envisioned as drawn, as if by a magnet, to worship Yahweh in fulfillment of the promise to Abraham in Genesis 12:2–3, that through him and his descendants "all the families of the earth" would find blessing.[30] The hope expressed here is for the ultimate fulfillment of God's purposes for Israel through the restoration of his creation. This acknowledgment of Yahweh's authority through obedience and worship is only right, the psalmist suggests, because "dominion [*hammelukah* ("position or right of kingship")] belongs to the LORD and he rules over the nations" (22:28).

The rich . . . will feast and worship. In an intentional contrast that constitutes a sort of merism with the "poor" in 22:26a, the psalmist introduces the "rich of the earth," who both eat like the poor and worship like the families of the earth in 22:27b. These linkages draw the whole passage together into a literary unity. The purpose is to indicate that all humanity—Israelite or non-Israelite, rich or poor—will acknowledge the rulership of Yahweh and bow to it.[31] The latter part of verse 29 makes this dependence clear. As in Ecclesiastes 3:18–21; 9:1–6, "all who go down to the dust[32]. . . who cannot keep themselves alive" (Ps. 22:29) refers to all humanity, who are ultimately absolutely dependent on Yahweh for the very breath that sustains life.

---

30. In Gen. 12:3 it is the (lit.) "families of the earth" (*mišpeḥot haʾadamah*) who find blessing through Abram, while here it is the "families of the [non-Israelite] nations" (*mišpeḥot goyim*) who come to worship Yahweh. The similarity, while not precise, is sufficient to link these two ideas together.

31. There may also be an intended reference to the eschatological feast (Isa. 25:6; Luke 14:15), in which all the faithful—rich or poor, Jew or Gentile—will participate on an equal footing.

32. "Going down" or "returning" to the dust is a common metaphor for death in the Old Testament (cf. Gen. 3:19; Job 17:16; 34:15; Pss. 90:3; 104:29; Eccl. 3:20). The abode of the dead, Sheol, was thought to be "down" under the surface of the earth, and in broader ancient Near Eastern mythology was thought to be a lightless place, where everything was covered with dust. The Gen. 2–3 account of creation and fall links the dust image with the earthen material from which God is said to have created the first humans. Death, then, is understood as a return to the preanimated state.

Posterity will serve him. The final subsection of the last stanza describes a continuing proclamation of Yahweh's righteousness coupled with endless praise (22:30–31). In an awkward but clear reference back to 22:23, where the "descendants" (lit., "seed") of Jacob and of Israel are called to honor and fear Yahweh, the word "seed" (NIV "posterity") is again used in 22:30 to describe those who will continue to "serve" Yahweh into the future.

The remainder of verse 30 is more difficult, with the LXX and other versions suggesting a variety of minor textual emendations. As it presently stands, the Hebrew text reads something like, "It will be recounted concerning my Lord to a generation." In this case the beginning of 22:31 would be "They will come and they will declare. . . ." Some commentators, sensing the awkwardness of the reference to "a generation," include the first word of verse 31 ("they will enter") in some adapted form at the end of verse 30 and interpret the emended phrase as "to a coming/future generation." This seems to be the route taken by the NIV. Other commentators, linking this half verse with what follows in verse 31, interpret the passive verb "will be told" as an active form and read the whole phrase as "[posterity] will tell the coming generation about my Lord; they will declare his righteousness to a people yet to be born." This does, however, involve considerable adjustment to the underlying consonantal text—albeit relatively minor ones.

The path followed by the NIV seems a reasonable response to the text and produces a kind of attractive progression if not exact parallelism. After a more general opening statement "Posterity [seed] will serve him," the psalmist describes two stages by which the proclamation of Yahweh's righteousness is made known. First, God's faithfulness is recounted (presumably by the psalmist's own generation) to the coming generation; these in turn proclaim it to "a people yet unborn." By this means the psalmist fulfills the "vow" mentioned in 22:22, 25.

For he has done it. God's righteousness is not simply a quality of character but the result of having done something. Once again it is necessary to recall that the Hebrew word "righteousness" is essentially a legal term, which describes the status of the one who has been determined by a judge to have done all that is proper in a particular circumstance or case.[33] Therefore, when used of God (or of humans, for that matter) righteousness never describes a sinless quality or attitude but is an evaluation of one's course of action. Thus, it is entirely understandable in this context to conclude this description of Yahweh's righteousness by proclaiming, as the psalmist does, "for he has done it." Yahweh has in all things fulfilled the demands of appropriate action in relation to his creatures and all creation.

---

33. See comments on "righteous; righteousness" in 4:1–2.

PSALM 22 AND JESUS. In the opening paragraphs, I spoke briefly regarding the difficulty of interpreting this psalm in contemporary Christian circles other than as a prediction of the suffering and death of Jesus on the cross. The use of the psalm to understand the death of Jesus is well entrenched since the New Testament writers initiated the movement.

According to the indices of Old Testament quotations, allusions, and verbal parallels in the United Bible Societies *Greek New Testament*,[34] Psalm 22 is referred to some twenty-four times in the New Testament. Three of the four direct quotations listed and fourteen of twenty allusions/parallels are found within the narratives of Jesus' passion and crucifixion, indicating that this psalm had already been received as an important resource for understanding and explaining the suffering and death of Jesus at an early date. This is certainly true. Jesus himself affirmed that connection when he chose verse 1 as his statement of agony from the cross. Nevertheless, I caution against any exclusive understanding of Psalm 22 only in light of Jesus.

One negative tendency of such an exclusive approach to this psalm has been to mine the psalm for its prophetic references to Christ while ignoring its long history within the community of faith *before* Jesus knew or used it. It is because of this long history of meaning in the community of faith that Jesus understood it to have special significance to his own life, ministry, and death. Only as we understand what the psalm means on its own are we better able to understand why Jesus chose these words to reflect his own agony of abandonment by his Father at the final moment of crisis represented by the cross.

Far from being just a prediction of events surrounding Jesus' death, the psalm reflects a model of response to abandonment and divine delay with which Jesus could identify and by which he could open windows for others into his own spiritual conflict. By quoting just verse 1 of this psalm, Jesus could draw on a long history of awareness on the part of his listeners who knew how the first nineteen verses illustrate the struggle of the faithful sufferer who waits for deliverance by God. It is important to realize that even the New Testament writers were able to read Psalm 22 as encouragement to the faithful in their contexts of suffering.[35] If we read this psalm *only* as pre-

---

34. Barbara Aland, Kurt Aland, Johannes Karavidopoulos, Carlo M. Martini, Bruce M. Metzger, *The Greek New Testament*, 4th rev. ed. (New York: United Bible Societies, 1994), 887, 895. The indices list four direct quotations (Matt. 27:46; Mark 15:34; John 19:24; Heb. 2:12), and twenty allusions or verbal parallels.

35. Cf. esp. Rom. 5:5; Phil. 3:2; 2 Tim. 4:17.

diction of Christ, we obscure our own obligation to see and hear ourselves in these words. That is certainly what Jesus did and what he calls us to do—to identify with the pain of those, including himself, who have come under the weight of the seemingly unconquerable distance that can separate God from his faithful one(s) in a time of deep suffering.

Eschatological vision of hope. The psalmist's faithful response to the absence of God is placed within a broader context of an eschatological vision of hope. In the midst of fulfilling a vow of praise "in the congregation"—a praise grounded in the past history of Yahweh's faithfulness even in the face of his absence (22:22–24)—the psalmist suddenly shifts gears with a remarkable profession: "My praise in the great assembly [is] from with you!"[36] This phrase is remarkable because the psalmist realizes that even when Yahweh is most distant and entirely absent from our experience, the ability to praise him is a testimony to his enduring presence with those who fear him. The very ability to praise comes from God himself.

This realization catapults the psalmist from a historical reflection to a vision of eschatological hope. Note how the verbs suddenly shift to the future and remain there until the end of the psalm. Note also the universal and eschatological tone that invades his hopes. The poor will eat and be satisfied; all the "ends of the earth" will turn to Yahweh; the "families of the nations" will submit to his rule. Thus, in the final analysis, the problem of divine absence in the face of righteous suffering is resolved through recourse to eschatological hope. The move is similar to that of apocalyptic, where a situation of "primary deprivation" without hope of present deliverance leads to apocalyptic thinking in which God will ultimately set all things right and honor the faithfulness of those who suffer and even die.

This kind of resolution acknowledges that our present world does not coincide with the will and purposes of God for his creation. It admits the possibility that faithful living may *not* result in deliverance—that suffering and death are realities for the faithful. But, at the same time, it also understands that present suffering and evil will not *ultimately* prevent the fulfillment of God's plans. God still rules over his creation, and his word accomplishes what he purposes. This kind of praise that accepts the real potential for death of the faithful aligns itself with the true nature of God and does not pragmatically adopt the ways of the world as an action plan in the face of divine absence. The faithful psalmist remains loyal and takes solace in the knowledge that regardless of the personal outcome, God's will *will* be done.

36. This literal Heb. translation is rather interpretively rendered in the NIV as, "From you comes the theme of my praise in the great assembly."

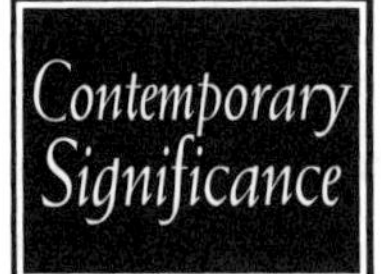

WORMS, DOGS, LIONS, AND OXEN. Psalm 22 offers insight into how the act of oppression has the effect of dehumanizing both oppressed and oppressor. Because of the relentless attacks of the enemy, the psalmist feels less than human—even a worm. When I was a college freshman, years before recent attempts to eliminate the dehumanizing effects of college "hazing," all freshmen were required to wear beanies in school colors from school opening until homecoming in November. The beanies were called "slime caps" because, according to upperclassmen, freshmen were slime—the only form of life known to be insignificant enough to crawl under the belly of a worm without touching it! "Slimes" were expected to do work for upperclassmen on request and could be required to drop and do pushups if caught not wearing a cap.

I never thought of all this "hazing" as dehumanizing or oppressive at the time. We freshmen knew that we were equal to—no, even better than—any upperclassman, and we took pains to show them so in organized and unorganized contests (some of which got way out of hand). The beanies that were intended to mark us out as "slime" also had the opposite effect of building freshman community and esprit de corps. I have to admit that I did my share of "slime baiting" when my junior-year roommate turned out to be an unsuspecting slime! It was not until some of the extreme hazing carried out by a fraternal organization led to the illness and death of a pledge that the administration (and we, I must admit) began to recognize the destructive potential present in such activities.

The psalmist felt dehumanized by the attacks of the enemies—reduced to a despised worm, mocked, scorned, and insulted by "all who see me" (22:6–7). The ridicule of the enemy even twisted the devastating experience of divine abandonment into a proof of God's lack of care for the psalmist. Their searing taunts (repeated by Christ's detractors as he hung on the cross) assumed God had no interest in the psalmist and no intention to deliver: "He trusts in the LORD; let the LORD rescue him. Let him deliver him, since he delights in him" (22:8). As a "worm," the psalmist felt beyond the care and concern even of God.

But the enemies do not escape their own scathing attack. By tearing at the psalmist, they have thrown off the last vestiges of the divine image that exalts humanity[37] and have adopted the methods of carnivorous beasts. God's original intention for irenic relations between humans and beasts has been disrupted by the human choice for evil, and it results in Genesis

37. See comments on 8:3–8 and compare the creation narrative in Gen. 1:26–31.

9 in a fearful stand-off in which both humans and beast tear and kill one another. Humans have given up their divine distinctives to become like the beasts, and God holds both accountable for their murderous acts (9:1–6). Like the post-Flood humans, the psalmist's enemies are described as carnivorous beasts rending and tearing their prey. In their violent pursuit of him they have dehumanized themselves along with their prey and brought down divine condemnation on their own heads.

In our sinful relationships with others, we are often tempted to view them as less than human. In lust we can make others objects that we can use to satisfy our desires. In pursuit of our ambitions our competitors can too easily become rungs to be stepped on as we move "up." When we use others in this way, we actually give up our exalted status (tarnished though it may be by sin) as the image of God and choose to take our place among the beasts.[38]

The psalmist offers one significant counterpoint to the enemies' dehumanizing attack. From the moment of birth Yahweh has valued and supported the psalmist. Verses 9–11 are an interesting blend of protective care and vulnerability. The birth of a child was a time of great vulnerability in the ancient world. Infant mortality was high and still births common.[39] God is depicted as the midwife who sees that the child is born safely and nourished by the mother. These verses demonstrate the importance of his presence from the earliest moment of life, as is the vulnerable child's necessary dependence on God for birth and continued life. This is no insignificant beast left to bear its young on its own, whose offspring must fend for themselves from an early age. This is a cherished and protected human child, who is "cast upon" God from birth and is made to trust in him (22:9–10).

Worship and hope. In the midst of despair the psalmist offers two avenues of hopeful response. (1) The first appears again and again in the psalms and

---

38. While Ps. 22 asks simply for deliverance from the beastly enemies, it is clear elsewhere that when we dehumanize ourselves to act like the beasts, the punishment we receive is in accord with our new status. One is not able to use reason to restrain an attacking lion but must resort to violence in order to save the life of the one attacked. For this reason the psalmists in Pss. 3:7 and 58:6 plead for God to "break the teeth" of the enemy who have the faithful in a death grip.

39. Note how in the Atrahasis Epic, when unlimited procreative abilities led the rapidly expanding human population into conflict with the gods, the ultimate solution to the conflict (after interim attempts through plague, drought, and famine had failed) was brought about by decreeing limitations on human procreativity. That these limitations included barrenness, miscarriage, still births, and high infant mortality rates indicates these phenomena were widespread facts of life in the ancient world.

will be treated only briefly here: The psalmist finds support and hope in the worshiping community of the faithful. The enemy may dehumanize and threaten death, but in the congregation of the faithful God's righteous power is still proclaimed. When our faith is undermined by our circumstances and we are tempted to despair altogether, sometimes our only remaining hope is to place ourselves within the worshiping community of God's people. There he is praised even if we are unable to praise him. There the mighty acts of God are proclaimed even when we cannot see them. There God is present though he remains absent from our own experience.

(2) The second avenue is the way of hope laid out in the eschatological promises at the end of the psalm. Despite all evidence to the contrary in our own world of experience, God is still on his throne (22:3), and the whole of creation is moving inexorably toward the conclusion of his purposes for it. That purpose is good and praiseworthy (22:3b, 25–26)—the submission of all earthly powers to his own (22:27–28), the leveling of rich and poor in their common realization of their absolute dependence on him (22:26, 29), and an endless future proclamation of God's righteousness to unborn generations (22:30–31).

How do you respond to the apparent absence of God in our world—the endless dehumanization of others in war and genocide, the exploitation of the poor by those in power, the lustful twisting of divinely gifted persons into objects of sexual fantasy? In a whimsical but bitter mood long ago, I composed a little poem that captured my frustration as youthful idealism eroded into adult realism.

Is mankind kind? Or would you mind,
If I altered the meter to call him maneater?
Not neater or nicer, a constant surpriser
is man, Kind he's not, nor selfless. What
we need I am sure is a Manicure.

Psalm 22 assures us that the "cure" is at hand. God is present and working for the good purposes for which he created us and the world. That purpose cannot be frustrated but will be accomplished in God's time. The call in the words and images of this psalm is for us to persevere in faithful reliance on God *precisely when he seems most distant*!

The faith modeled by Jesus on the cross was no fairweather religion that trusted in God when the going was good. Neither was it a faith that fled like the disciples when confronted by the harsh realities of rejection, persecution, and indeed execution. His was a faith that experienced the worst the world had to offer—knew what it was to feel abandoned by God—and yet just when it was darkest, as life was slipping away, he was able to proclaim with a final certainty: "It is finished!" (John 19:30). This was not a cry of defeat but of victory—a realization that the purpose of God for the creation was made whole in the work of his faithful Son. Having won his way through to the end, Jesus surrendered his spirit into the hand of God the Father (Luke 23:46).[40] Psalm 22, with its hopeful vision of a future restored to its original purposes, encourages us to do the same.

---

40. Jesus' final word in John's Gospel is the Greek *tetelestai* ("It is finished"). The word is a perfect passive from *teleo*. The perfect tense in Greek expresses an action completed in the past with results continuing into the present. The Greek word is akin to the Hebrew verb *šlm*, which it often translates in the LXX. The Hebrew carries the force of "be/make whole/complete." The root is commonly used to describe the "peace offering" (*šelamim*), which might better be understood as a sacrifice that celebrates the *restoration* of life to proper relationship with Yahweh.

Psalm 23

A PSALM OF David.

[1] The LORD is my shepherd, I shall not be in want.
[2] He makes me lie down in green pastures,
he leads me beside quiet waters,
[3] he restores my soul.
He guides me in paths of righteousness
for his name's sake.
[4] Even though I walk
through the valley of the shadow of death,
I will fear no evil,
for you are with me;
your rod and your staff,
they comfort me.
[5] You prepare a table before me
in the presence of my enemies.
You anoint my head with oil;
my cup overflows.
[6] Surely goodness and love will follow me
all the days of my life,
and I will dwell in the house of the LORD
forever.

THIS IS, OF course, one of the most familiar and favored poems in the entire book. Such familiarity often heightens the difficulty of commentator and reader alike to read the psalm anew and to prevent traditional understandings from blinding them to the depths of meaning the psalm offers. At its heart Psalm 23 is an expression of confidence in the protective care of Yahweh, upon whom the psalmist expresses absolute dependence. In this regard the psalm is a fitting response to the themes introduced in Psalm 22, where the narrator calls contemporary Israel to acknowledge their dependence on Yahweh (22:23, 27–29) and vows to praise his name (22:22; cf. 23:3) in the midst of the congregation and to future generations (22:30–31).

Psalm 23 presents a sort of "sandwich" structure, with sections referring to Yahweh in the third person occurring before (23:1–3) and after (23:6) a central section using second-person address of God (23:4–5). A fuller structural outline of the psalm includes an introduction establishing the shepherd images and the theme of trust (23:1), Yahweh's leading his "sheep" into abundant life (23:2–3), Yahweh's providing his "sheep" with secure life (23:4), Yahweh's blessing of the trusting faithful (23:5), and a concluding expression of confidence (23:6).

The psalm also presents an assortment of themes and images that continue to reappear in the following collection of Psalms 24–30. Chief among these is the emphasis on the "house" or "dwelling" of Yahweh, where the psalmists hope to find protection and security. This concern surfaces in the liturgical preparations to enter the temple precincts recorded in Psalm 24, the expression of love for Yahweh's dwelling place in 26:8, the psalmist's earnest seeking to dwell in the house of Yahweh in 27:4–5, the lifting up of one's hands toward Yahweh's "holy place" in 28:2, the acknowledgement of all who are in the temple of Yahweh's glorious kingship in 29:9, and finally the heading linking Psalm 30 to the "dedication of the temple." This constellation of recurring themes in so many adjacent psalms can hardly be coincidence and must be explored as each psalm is considered.

The Heading (23:0)

NO NEW TERMS appear in the heading to Psalm 23, which is described simply as a "psalm [*mizmor*] of David."[1]

Introduction (23:1)

THE OPENING VERSE establishes the dominant theme of the first four verses. That Yahweh is "shepherd" is consistent with claims elsewhere that he is "king," since ancient Near Eastern monarchs also described themselves as shepherding their people and understood their gods as fulfilling this role as well.[2] As shepherds, such kings understood their responsibility to provide protective order for their people and to administer just and effective laws.

It is especially significant within the continuing context of the consecutive Psalms 18–23 that the singular voice of the psalmist is associated—

1. See comments on the heading to Ps. 3.

2. A number of texts make this connection clear. See, e.g., the following pages in Beyerlin, *Near Eastern Religious Texts Relating to the Old Testament*, 13, 15, 26, 28, 40, 46, 102, 107, 137, 143. The prologue to Hammurabi's Law Code makes the connection of shepherd and king especially clear.

whether in reality or imagination—with the model king, David, who is particularly known for his shepherd experiences.[3] That David, who understood himself to be the shepherd of Israel and who was acknowledged by the people as such, should speak of Yahweh as "*my* shepherd" (23:1) is a way of acknowledging that Yahweh is indeed the power behind the throne of David (and all the kings of Israel and Judah), and that in reality Yahweh is the true king of Israel. This theme finds its way throughout the remote corners of the Psalter, but it is especially prevalent in the final two books and concentrated in the *Yahweh malak* psalms in Book 4.[4]

I shall not be in want. The focus of the word "want" is not so much on the idea of "desiring" something as on "lacking" something needed. The psalmist does not mean that Yahweh shepherds us by giving us everything we desire. Rather, those who trust in Yahweh as sheep do in a shepherd will never lack for whatever they *need*. The NIV's translation "I shall not *be in* want" succeeds in clarifying the true meaning of the phrase. In the verses that follow, the psalmist illustrates how the shepherd-God supplies abundantly all that his trusting people need.

Abundant Life (23:2–3)

THE SHEPHERD LEADS his sheep in pleasant places full of all the necessities of life: green pastures of grass and quiet streams providing water for drinking. Those who have visited the undeveloped lands of the Bible will know just how unusual this picture is. At best the land is a dry, rocky set of rolling hills covered with a sparse and tough grass. Water sources are few and often seasonal. Shepherds had to be ready to take their flocks on long migrations from one source of grazing and water to another.

The psalmist paints a scene of abundant life in three descriptive statements—each speaking of the shepherd in the third person and employing an imperfect verb form.[5] The shepherd causes the sheep to lie down, makes

---

3. Cf. 1 Sam. 16:11, 19; 17:15, 20, 34–37; 2 Sam. 7:7–8; Ps. 78:70–71.

4. See the discussion of the *Yahweh malak* psalms in the introduction and in the commentary on Pss. 93, 95–98.

5. It is striking that all three imperfects also occur in one of the "factitive" or "causative" stems—indicating the shepherd's influence and authority over the flock. The normal "causative" stem is the Hiphil, which most often infers applying some causative effect on someone else. For example, the verb *yd*ᶜ ("know"), when used in the Hiphil stem, means "to cause (someone else) to know (something)" and is often translated "make known, reveal." In comparison, the usual "factitive" stem is the Piel (although the Hiphil can also take on this force). The factitive stem normally occurs with a "stative" verb that describes existing in a state rather than accomplishing some action. An example of a stative verb would be "rest" rather than the active verb "run." The factitive form of the stative verb just mentioned

them approach quiet waters carefully, and leads them faithfully on the correct paths. All three images emphasize the shepherd's role as provider.

Obviously grass and water are the sheep's staff of life, and the shepherd knows how to find them both and leads the hungering, thirsty sheep to them. Although "paths of righteousness" may have an unusual ring to our ears, it can mean no more than the "right path," that is, the one that gets you where you need to go. The ambiguity of language and context, however, allows a moral quality to creep in. If the shepherd and sheep are images of a life fully dependent and trusting on Yahweh, then "paths of righteousness" take on the meaning of a way of life that fulfills God's expectation for his follower. The sheep are not left to their own devices but are led by God himself to take the correct path—the one that gets the sheep where they need to go.

For his name's sake. The shepherd (God) acts in ways that reveal and confirm his character and nature. In the Hebrew culture, a personal name was often thought to reveal the character of the individual named.[6] God's revelation to Israel of his personal name Yahweh at the time of the Exodus gave her unprecedented knowledge of his nature and access to him. This knowledge and access had to be protected by the prohibition against abusive use of the divine name.[7] Closely related to this idea is the concept of reputation. To have a "name" is to bear a *good* reputation,[8] while to be disreputable is to have no name at all (Job 30:8). Here, however, the shepherd/Yahweh acts to benefit the sheep, not just in order to preserve his character or reputation but in a way that is consistent with the nature the name reveals.

Secure Life (23:4)

FROM A LIFE of abundant ease, the psalmist moves to a description of fearful threat. In the migration through the spring landscape in search of ever-elusive grass and water, the flock must pass at times into and through the deep, rugged wadis—dry stream beds cut through the semidesert hills by the seasonal torrents unleashed by the winter rains. The air in the bottom of these wadis is heavy with the rising heat of the day, and the canyon depths are swathed in dark shadows as the rising cliff walls exclude the distant sun. At

---

would be "make/cause to rest." The primary distinction between causative and factitive stems is that the former occurs with *active* verbs, while the latter occurs with *stative* verbs. Both stems emphasize that the subject of the verb is exercising decisive influence over someone else, as in the case of our verse.

6. Cf. the extended discussion of the idea of "name" in the comments on Ps. 8.

7. Cf. Ex. 20:7; Deut. 5:11.

8. Cf. Prov. 22:1, where "good name" (i.e., good reputation) translates the Hebrew *šem* ("name"), with no modifiers attached (cf. also Eccl. 7:1).

this moment of crossing the wadi floor, the pleasant scenes of green pastures and still waters seem far removed—there is no grass or water, the heat can be oppressive, and the whole flock must struggle up the steep sides of the canyon to resume its journey toward the next feeding place.

Valley of the shadow of death. There is some evidence in Hebrew for the use of hyperbolic word constructions such as this one to express the superlative—the most extreme. The Hebrew word *ṣalmawet* is apparently a combination of two words: *ṣel* ("shadow") and *mawet* ("death"). Together these words express the superlative—in this case, something like "the shadowiest of all shadows." Thus, contemporary translations tend to replace the traditional translation with the more prosaic "deepest shadow."[9] The LXX (*skias thanatou*) shows that the literal meaning was not entirely lost on the readers, and it is probable that the author of Psalm 23 used the phrase purposefully to emphasize the danger and threat that confronted the flock in crossing these wadis.

I remember hiking down Wadi Qelt from Jerusalem to Jericho with a friend. A narrow, ancient Roman aqueduct, still flowing with water, clung to the canyon wall at a height of several hundred feet. We began our journey following the rugged footpath on the opposite canyon wall, dipping at points to the bottom of the wadi and back up the other side. It took only about two such trips down into the shadowy depths of the stifling heat at the wadi bottom (and this was in the early morning!) and scrambling back up the steep limestone wall to regain the path, before we overcame our natural reluctance of heights and continued our journey walking along the outer rim of the aqueduct—or, in the most narrow portions, in the aqueduct itself.

Even so my two-liter bottle of water was depleted halfway through our journey. When we stopped at St. George's monastery to replenish our supply, the water tap in the courtyard first emitted only steam, and then a grudging stream of almost boiling water. I had enough trouble dragging myself up and down those rocky hills. I cannot imagine the difficulty of herding a whole flock of sheep through the "valley of the shadow of death."

---

9. The article on "Shade; Shadow" in *ISBE*[2] is a good place to start in the exploration of the phrase "shadow of death." Note the contrasting view presented in the article on "Shadow" in *IDB*, where the attempt is made to derive *ṣalmawet* from a root *ṣlm*. In either case, the meaning is the same. We encounter similar examples in contemporary expressions such as "a killer face" or a "tie to die for."

In another example of this kind of superlative, the word "God" is also used to this end in Jonah 3:3, where the size of the city of Nineveh is described as *ʿir gedolah leʾlohim* (lit., "a great city unto God"). The idiomatic meaning of the phrase is clearly to emphasize the superlative size of the city "a *really* big city!" or more irreverently "a *by God* big city!"

I will fear no evil. Despite the oppressive and threatening setting, the psalmist/sheep is unafraid. Because he fears Yahweh, he need not fear anything else. The rugged circumstances offered every reason for fear. On my personal journey down Wadi Qelt, dehydration was a real possibility. I also remembered halfway through the trip that this was the remote location on the way "down from Jerusalem to Jericho" that Jesus' Good Samaritan saved the life of the man who had been robbed and left for dead by thieves (Luke 10:25–37). The psalmist's very real reasons for fear fade, however, in the presence of the shepherd/Yahweh.

Your rod and your staff. The psalmist of Psalm 22, when taunted by foes crying "He trusts in the LORD; let the LORD rescue him" (22:8a), responds with an affirmation of trust and confidence: "You who fear the LORD, praise him! . . . For he has not despised or disdained the suffering of the afflicted one; he has not hidden his face from him but has listened to his cry for help." Similarly, our psalmist knows that it is the presence of Yahweh's rod and staff that vanquishes fear before the dependent flock. Life with the shepherd is secure; the rod and staff will guide and protect.

Both terms employed here are variously translated in different contexts. Either can be called a "staff, (walking) stick" for support while walking, presumably used by the shepherd to guide the movement of the flock by pushing and striking the sheep. If there is any clear distinction between the two, it is likely that "rod" (*šebeṭ*) is a shorter, mace-like implement that could be used as a striking weapon for raining heavy blows against enemy or attacking beast. "Rod" can also assume in royal contexts the meaning "scepter" and becomes a visible ornament of kingly authority. Graphic depictions of such royal scepters—usually a short, rod-like handle with a heavy striking knob at the end—appear frequently in the paintings and reliefs of the ancient Near East. By contrast, the "staff" (*miš^cenet*) more frequently suggests a longer, supporting staff and is associated on occasion with the support of the sick or elderly.[10]

The "comfort" these implements provide is the reassurance of guidance in correct paths to abundant food and water, and of protection by the shepherd from the dangers and enemies encountered on the way between areas of pasturage. As the sheep trust the shepherd, so the psalmist encourages the reader to join in trusting Yahweh.

---

10. Related words including *miš^can* (2 Sam. 22:19; Ps. 18:18) and *maš^cen, maš^cenah* (Isa. 3:1) affirm the meaning of support. For *miš^cenet*, see Ex. 21:19; Judg. 6:21; Zech. 8:4. A ruler can also use a *miš^cenet* (Num. 21:18), although whether this is simply a walking stick or a royal scepter is uncertain.

Blessed Life (23:5)

DESPITE THE ATTEMPTS by some commentators to understand verse 5 in the context of the shepherd's relation to the flock,[11] it seems more likely that here the image shifts in order to connect the psalmist's message to the human audience explicitly. The image shifts, therefore, from the joys and threats of the migrating flock to the new picture of the beleaguered faithful affirmed and honored by God in the very presence of the enemy. In these verses, Yahweh is no longer shepherd but assumes the role of host, while the trusting follower sits as honored guest at his table. The picture is one of the realization of ultimate communion with God himself.[12]

To accept another as a guest at one's table was to set aside enmity and to assume responsibility for the safety of the guest while in your dwelling. To sit at Yahweh's table is to enjoy fellowship and communion with him. To do so "in the presence of my enemies" is to have one's special relationship to God declared publicly in a context of divine blessing and security.

Dwelling in Yahweh's House (23:6)

NOT ONLY DOES the psalmist sit as an honored guest at table with God, but he looks forward in confidence to dwelling in Yahweh's house forever. This theme of residing with Yahweh, while not common, does occur with enough frequency in the psalms to make it remarkable.[13]

What might it mean to dwell in the house of Yahweh? (1) The idea of taking refuge in the temple comes to mind, in connection with the use in 23:6a of the verb *rdp* ("pursue after"). It is from such pursuit by a "blood avenger" that one might flee to the temple and claim asylum by grabbing the horns of the altar.[14] Here, however, the term is used to describe the relentless pursuit of the psalmist by the "goodness and mercy" of God. In this view the psalmist, pursued by enemies, takes refuge in the temple and there experiences the relentless goodness and mercy of Yahweh. The earlier reference to

---

11. By this interpretation the table is some form of mobile feeding unit employed in the desert or a sort of "staff" employed by the shepherd, while the act of anointing is a type of medical treatment for sick sheep. Cf. Ludwig H. Köhler, "Psalm 23," *ZAW* 68 (1956): 227–34.

12. Several commentators, including Dahood (*Psalms*, 1:147–48) and Kraus (*Psalms 1–59*, 308), make reference to the passage from the Amarna letters in which a local prince pleads with the Egyptian authorities: "May it please him to give gifts to his servant while our enemies look on." It may be this kind of visible and public evidence of divine support and acceptance that the psalmist anticipates.

13. See Pss. 26:8; 27:4; 36:7–8; 52:8; 65:4; 84:1–4, 10–12; 92:12–14, for examples of similar imagery.

14. Cf. Ex. 21:13–14; 1 Kings 1:50–53; 2:28–30.

sitting at table in the presence of the enemy thus describes the circumstance of the one in asylum who receives the protection and care of God while the enemy looks on.[15]

(2) While the idea of refuge or asylum is certainly a plausible response to this passage, it is not the only one. Dahood thinks of "eternal happiness in God's celestial abode" after the troubles of this life. While it is true that God's "house" may refer to his heavenly dwelling,[16] such an other-worldly view is unlikely in this context. More attractive is Craigie's recognition of Exodus themes in the language of the psalm. For Craigie, the transition from shepherd/sheep to host/guest turns on the recognition of a common "wilderness wandering" motif. As the sheep are guided in their trek through the desert by the caring shepherd, so Israel was guided through the Exodus wanderings by Yahweh, who provided their needs. Craigie particularly notes the similar language in Psalm 78:19, where Yahweh is described as "spreading a table in the desert" (cf. 23:5) as he provided for the Exodus Israelites.

Craigie goes on to connect this backward glance at the Exodus with anticipation of future eschatological feasting at God's table.[17] To me it seems more likely that the twin themes of provision in the desert and anticipation of dwelling in the temple resonate most strongly with the experience of exilic pilgrims on their journey (whether actually or mentally) from their Diaspora homes to celebrate communion with God and his gathered people in the Jerusalem temple. To these travelers—pointed toward the temple—the images of the guiding, protective shepherd and of the provisioning Exodus God offer the hope necessary to sustain them during their rough pilgrimage to Jerusalem and their lives in exile as well.[18]

Thus, these exilic pilgrims, with their remembrance of the past and anticipation of the future, provide the necessary "glue" to bind the two halves of Psalm 23 together—provision in the desert and dwelling in God's house. Regardless of which interpretation one assumes, to dwell with God is a potent image of eternal security and ongoing relationship.

---

15. See Kraus (*Psalms 1–59*, 308–9) as a recent proponent of this view.

16. For further information on the various uses of the Hebrew word *bet* ("house"), consult Wilson, "ישׁב," *NIDOTTE*, 2:550–51.

17. The eschatological banquet theme is mentioned in the prophets (Isa. 25:6) and figures prominently in the New Testament teaching of Jesus as well (cf. Luke 14:15).

18. This connection with pilgrimage to the Jerusalem temple is particularly interesting in light of the following Ps. 24:3, with its emphasis on preparing to "ascend the hill of the LORD . . . [and] . . . stand in his holy place."

AS NOTED ABOVE, the theme of approaching and dwelling in the house of God binds together Psalms 23–30. In this group of psalms, the desire to dwell with God is related to Exodus and pilgrimage themes that were particularly meaningful to the exilic Jewish community, who lived far away from the spiritual center of their faith—the second temple in Jerusalem. These Diaspora Jews lived in a hostile foreign environment, where their faith was constantly being stretched and challenged by threats of destruction (cf. Esther; Dan. 3; 6) or where they were tempted to assimilate to the majority culture (cf. Dan. 1). Their faith was sustained—at least in part—by the hope of standing within the temple precincts and experiencing the communion of worship with the international fellowship of Diaspora pilgrims.

The idea of being able to *dwell eternally* in the temple, rather than worshiping only sporadically there on a pilgrimage, must have communicated the most fervent hope of the faithful exilic Jews, who lived at such great distance from this central, unifying image of the faith.[19] It is little wonder that these images exercise such power in the Old Testament writings. As far as the Psalter goes, it is interesting to note that most of the references to "dwelling" in the house of Yahweh occur in the first three books of the collection (Pss. 1–89).[20] Let's explore further this magnificent image of residing in the presence of God.

House as temple. It is clear that the hope expressed is to dwell in the temple and not simply to be with God in his heavenly dwelling. In 27:4 and 65:4 the "house" (*bet*) of Yahweh is parallel with the more explicit word *hekal* ("temple, palace").[21] In 26:8, the house is the "place where your glory dwells"—an allusion to the presence of Yahweh's *kabod* in the Most Holy Place. Finally, the psalmist in Psalm 84 refers to the altar and singing praises (84:2–4), both indicating that the temple of Yahweh is in mind.

The temple is a symbol of Yahweh's presence with Israel. It is here that God "comes down" in a special way to be with his people. It is here that

19. See here Ps. 84:1–10, where once again the Jerusalem temple is the longed-for goal of pilgrimage.

20. Cf. Pss. 23:6; 26:8; 27:4; 36:7–9; 52:8; 65:4; 84:1–4, 10–12. The only occurrence outside these books is found in 92:12–14: "The righteous will flourish like the palm tree, they will grow like a cedar in Lebanon; planted in the house of the LORD, they will flourish in the courts of our God. They will still bear fruit in old age, they will stay fresh and green."

21. Ps. 65:4 further identifies this *hekal* as *qedoš* ("holy"), making the connection with temple even more clear.

they can approach him, knowing they will find him. As Psalm 24 so appealingly describes, the temple is the place where a prepared people (24:3–6) and a mighty, victorious God converge in worship. To be present in the temple is to be before God—to have access to him in lament, praise, and thanksgiving. To be ever dwelling in the temple, then, means to remain always in God's caring and effective presence—to escape the sense of distance and absence that must have plagued the days of the exilic Jewish community living at great distance from the spiritual center the temple afforded and in the midst of often dangerous and hostile circumstances.

Temple as place of refuge. The Deuteronomic legislation provided that those who were fleeing vengeance for a death they had accidentally caused could find asylum in a "place" Yahweh would designate. Certain cities are listed as places of refuge to which such persons could flee.[22] That Jerusalem—and in particular, the altar of the temple—became one of these places is implied, though never stated unambiguously. According to Exodus 21:14, should a person guilty of deliberate murder seek asylum inappropriately, the authorities should "take him away from my altar and put him to death" ("my altar" implies the temple was considered a place of asylum). The narratives in 1 Kings regarding how both Adonijah and Joab sought asylum by seizing the "horns of the altar" in the Jerusalem temple lend weight to this view.[23]

Certain other passages in the psalms reflect this understanding of the temple as providing protective refuge for those pursued by vengeful enemies. When Yahweh is described as "covering with his wings" those who seek refuge, there may be more in view than the protective care of a mother fowl for her offspring. The wings may well be a reference to the cherubim whose spreading wings overshadowed the ark of the covenant in the temple.[24] Psalm 36:7–8 brings together these two images of refuge under the wings and dwelling in the house of God: "Both high and low among men find refuge in the shadow of your wings. They feast on the abundance of your house." While it seems unlikely that the ark itself could have served as the place of refuge—since access to the Most Holy Place and the ark was limited to the high priest alone—this metaphorical use of the ark as place of asylum is understandable since it was the place where forgiveness was extended through the yearly sacrifice of the sin offering for all the people.

---

22. Cf. Num. 35:6–32; Deut. 19:1–13; Josh. 20:1–9; 21:13, 21, 27, 32, 38, where the pertinent legislation is given and the cities chosen listed.

23. 1 Kings 1:50–53; 2:28–35. The story of Joab's execution after seeking asylum in the temple fulfills the demand of Ex. 21:13–14, since Joab was guilty of deliberate and premeditated murder of Abner and Amasa (1 Kings 2:31–33).

24. See comments on 5:11–12.

In this light the picture in 23:5–6 of the beleaguered psalmist being treated with great honor and care "in the presence of my enemies" may refer to the experience of one's enjoying asylum in the temple while enemies waited for an opportunity to carry out their vengeance. In the legislation concerning cities of refuge, the one who sought refuge was safe as long as he remained in the designated city. The refugee had to remain there until the death of the current high priest,[25] but then he could return home with impunity.

Dwelling as more than asylum. Although the idea of temple as refuge lends a certain light on the interpretation of these passages, dwelling in the house of God seems to mean more than a place of security from pursuing enemies. Note how the psalmist desires to "dwell in the house of the LORD *forever*," which suggests more than escaping an immediate threat. Dwelling in God's house is viewed in these passages as an expansive rather than a restrictive experience.

One does not just escape vengeance and impending death but experiences abundance and delight: "[People] feast on the abundance of your house; you give them drink from your river of delights" (36:8). Yahweh is here viewed as opulent host who exercises liberal hospitality to his guests, who are honored to have been chosen to live with God and who are "satisfied with the goodness" of Yahweh's house. Dwelling in God's house, therefore, is an experience of blessing and honor as well as protection. In this context, Psalm 23's spread table, anointed head, and overflowing cup are the gracious ministrations of a welcoming host, who lavishes honor, care, abundant goodness, and protective care on his guest.[26]

Ongoing experience of God himself. Dwelling in God's house is also an opportunity to experience God intimately on an ongoing basis. The one who sits at table with the divine host is treated to a feast of the presence of God as well as to gourmet table delicacies. Psalm 27:4 captures this hope magnificently when the psalmist declares: "One thing I ask of the LORD, this is what I seek: that I may dwell in the house of the LORD all the days of my life, to gaze upon the beauty of the LORD and to seek him in his temple." Dwelling with Yahweh affords the guest opportunity to experience the "beauty" (*noᶜam*) of God. The Hebrew word *noᶜam* comes from the root *nᶜm*, which has the meaning "be pleasant, delightful" rather than the visually pleasing effect that

---

25. Cf. Num. 35:25; Josh. 20:6.

26. See also 84:10–12: "I would rather be a doorkeeper in the house of my God than dwell in the tents of the wicked. For the LORD God is a sun and shield; the LORD bestows favor and honor; no good thing does he withhold from those whose walk is blameless. O LORD Almighty, blessed is the man who trusts in you."

we normally associate with "beauty." Coming to Yahweh's house is not only escape *from* enemies; it is escape *to* the very presence of God himself.[27]

The source of light and life. To come to the dwelling of God is to approach the very source of light and life. Where Yahweh dwells, there his "glory" penetrates and illuminates everything (26:8). On one level, the desire to live in the house of Yahweh is a plea for direct access to God. Along with constant view of the "delightfulness" of Yahweh, the guest in God's house has the ability to "inquire" of God for guidance (27:4). Such guidance allows God's guests to prosper on the way that God knows (1:6). They are described as flourishing trees; "planted in the house of the LORD, they will flourish in the courts of our God. They will still bear fruit in old age, they will stay fresh and green" (92:13–14).[28]

The hope expressed in Psalm 23 to "dwell in the house of Yahweh *forever*" is grounded in the belief that Yahweh is the source of life and light and that to dwell with him is to have eternal access to these resources. Thus the psalmist of Psalm 36:7, 9 declares: "How priceless is your unfailing love! ... For with you is the fountain of life; in your light we see light."

In other words, the desire to dwell in God's house is more than just a hope to escape from the threats of our enemies. It more importantly involves coming into and remaining in the presence of God's glory with all the necessary implications of personal preparation. Being in God's presence implies the ability to gain divine guidance in following the way of Yahweh as well as to experience the blessing of the divine hospitality: abundant provision, steadfast love, forgiveness, protection, light, and life. In a sense, dwelling with God is to experience what Paul speaks of as the mature Christian's goal: to see God face to face and to know him fully as one is first known by him (1 Cor. 13:12).

PSALM 23 OFFERS several images of life with God that can have significant impact on how we live our contemporary lives of faith. In what follows I discuss three of these that I consider reflective of the heart of this psalm.

Life as pilgrimage. The idea of pilgrimage through dangerous territory to the house of God is subtly interwoven with the images of shepherd and flock. Pilgrimage was certainly one of the foundational elements of Israelite identity,

27. The temple is the "place where [God's] glory dwells" (26:8), and to dwell there is to live within the glow of God's true essence.

28. See also 52:8: "I am like an olive tree flourishing in the house of God; I trust in God's unfailing love for ever and ever."

even before the Exile. Israel remembered her earliest ancestors as "wandering Arameans" (Deut. 26:5) who survived the sojourn in Egypt before receiving the Promised Land. Abraham too left home and family to travel endlessly in search of the new home God had promised. After the Exodus, Israel as a nation experienced forty years or more of wandering before entering the Promised Land.

During the Exile the exilic community came to think of their life outside the land as a new form of Egyptian bondage and their hoped-for return as another Exodus. With the rebuilding of the second temple as a spiritual center for Diaspora Judaism, pilgrimage to Jerusalem became an important way to maintain a universal Jewish identity. Worship in the temple provided an important opportunity for an international community of Jews to come together in an expression of unity: the worship of the one true God, Yahweh.

Pilgrimage to the Promised Land reinforced the exilic Jews' sense of temporary residence in the lands of exile. They were "passing through" and looking forward to reaching the land promised to their ancestors. The pressures of living in a hostile, non-Jewish environment were similar to those dangers confronted by pilgrims on their way to the Jerusalem temple. Continued focus on the goal kept both sets of pilgrims—real and metaphorical ones—faithful to Yahweh in difficult circumstances. The psalms of pilgrimage, with their attention to faithful living in the midst of the dangers of the journey, spoke to the needs of the everyday life of the exiles.

Pilgrimage remains an apt image for our continuing lives as Christians before God. It assumes that where one is now is not where one is heading. Hebrews 3 talks of the goal of God's people as entering into the "rest" intended by him since the creation of the world and symbolized by the Sabbath rest he instituted at the beginning (Gen. 2:1–3).

The kind of rest envisioned both in Hebrews and Genesis is not the kind of rest that restores the energy of one tired out by labor. God was not exhausted by his creative labors. Rather, he rested on the seventh day because he was done; creation was complete and whole with nothing lacking or omitted.[29] This is the kind of rest the author of Hebrews has in mind: to enter into the state of whole, complete life intended by God at the beginning: "For anyone who enters God's rest also rests from his own work, just as God did from his" (Heb. 4:10).

Like the believers whom the author of Hebrews addresses, life as we now know it does not conform to the "rest" intended by God. We stand in what some theologians like to call the "already but not yet." Through the saving grace unleashed by Jesus we have begun to experience the reality of the restoration of the world to its original creation intention. Our inward selves

---

29. Cf. Heb. 4:3, 10.

are being transformed into the likeness of Christ. Our relationships with others are founded on self-giving love (*agape*) rather than personal benefit. Even our relationship to animate and inanimate creation can be restored to God's original intention of providing protective care and making fruitful.[30] Through Christ's victory, the kingdom of God has *already* broken in among us, and life is being transformed and restored.

Nevertheless, the world at large is *not yet* the place of completeness and wholeness that the author of Hebrews envisions in the hoped-for "rest." Like the heroes and heroines of faith described in Hebrews 11, we have yet to experience the fullness of what has been promised. We still see much in life—even in ourselves—that confirms the brokenness and incompleteness of life, that denies the very concept of "rest" as God intended it in Genesis 1. We live as strangers in a strange land, travelers on the way, not at home here but testifying to the reality of the future rest that has invaded our lives and urges us on to its ultimate completion at the "day of Christ."

Setting a table before us. The central image of Psalm 23 is the prepared table, a symbol of honor and provision. The fact that the table is prepared "in the presence of my enemies" accords well with verse 4 about the protection afforded by the shepherd's rod and staff while traveling through the valley of the shadow of death. It also fits with the discussion of pilgrimage, in which life lived in the presence and power of God is life lived in a world that is *not yet* restored to the wholeness God intends. As a result, the faithful, though experiencing divine presence and reward for their faithfulness, are still among enemies.

We need to acknowledge to ourselves and to others that being in Christ does not mean that the troubles, cares, pains, and dangers of this world are simply removed from us. We remain "in the presence" of our enemies. We need also, however, to ask and constantly remind ourselves in what ways, day by day, God is setting a table for *us* in the presence of our enemies.

As a practical example, I remember when I was, for an extended period of time, underemployed. Finances were tough, and for a variety of reasons it did not seem likely that circumstances would change soon. The year was coming to an end, and Christmas was looming with the unwelcome prospect of a meager celebration overshadowed by concerns to make ends meet. I remember feeling inadequate and guilty that my failures were affecting my wife and children in ways I felt they did not deserve. I began to wonder where God was in all this.

Two things happened at that time that I equate with God's preparing a table for me in the presence of my enemies. My enemies were mostly of my

30. See comments in Gerald H. Wilson, "Renewing the Image: Perspectives on a Biblical View of Creation," *Quaker Religious Thought* 24 (1990): 11–21.

own making—fear, guilt, shame, anger. But one afternoon I arrived home from my part-time job to find a package of wrapped Christmas presents on my doorstep. No note identified the giver—it was not family—but there was something for each member of the family. They were simple things—a pair of socks for me—but these simple gifts demonstrated that we were loved and cared for by both God and his people. I suddenly felt as if the welcoming oil of God's anointing had been poured in abundance over my head.

Just a few days later an anonymous money order arrived in the mail. Again, no one ever claimed responsibility. But it was enough to take the edge off the anxiety that surrounded us and allowed us to enter the Christmas season with a renewed sense of joy in the expected advent of God's greatest gift.

Acts like these are confidence-builders that set aside the taunts of our enemies. When we have sinned and are seeking to rebuild broken lives in the community of faith, the handshakes of friendship, the hugs of caring, the invitations to social occasions and fellowship, and the opportunity to serve others and God all give testimony that God is at work in us and for us. When we have lost for whatever reason the trappings of social success and acceptance, we need signs that our brothers and sisters in Christ love us and care for us, as does Christ himself. These acts of love become tables prepared by God (and his people) in the presence of our enemies, who want to tear us down and shatter our hopes. I challenge you to seek to become a "caterer" at the table God prepares for those who are surrounded by enemies.

Dwelling in the house of God. Related to the idea of pilgrimage through a strange and hostile land is the hope to dwell forever in the house of Yahweh, his temple. That house is, of course, the end goal of the exilic pilgrimage. It also provides a potent metaphor for the goal of restoring God's original intention for the world and its inhabitants that becomes the ultimate hope of both Judaism and Christianity. In the temple the faithful come together in God's presence to experience unity and communion, wholeness and peace.

How then do we today dwell in the house of God? Is this only a future hope, a sort of wishful thinking? Or can we take up residence here and now? Must we wait until the final apocalyptic consummation of the world, the defeat of evil once and for all? Or is there a sense that our residence in the dwelling place of God is in the face of and in spite of the very real and ongoing evidence of world evil?

As long as we think of the "house of God" as a *place*—whether in time or outside of time—we are probably doomed to wait in vain for its appearance. As long as we are looking for an experience that takes us out of the pain and uncertainty of living, we will not know what it means to dwell in God's house forever. But as Psalm 23 shows us, dwelling in God's house does not mean some sort of translation out of our circumstances of pain. Instead, it means to dwell with God in the very presence of our enemies! It is possible, says the psalmist, to experience the gracious presence of God and to receive the abundance of life he offers in the midst of life as it presently is. That is the *already* breaking into the *not yet*.

Let me suggest a few practical ways we can dwell in God's house here and now. (1) If such dwelling means to be in God's presence and to see his gracious beauty, then we need to find ways to acknowledge that presence in the small, seemingly insignificant happenings of everyday life. Most often it is a *choice* we make to acknowledge that God is present and active around and in us. To stop and admit that the chatter of a small child's voice in the bushes outside our window is a testimony to the goodness of God; to acknowledge that the compassion that pours out of us for a person in pain is a link to the compassion of God himself; to allow ourselves to be angry at the violence and injustice that fills our world—these are ways of entering God's presence and dwelling with him. When a sunset reminds us of the creative and sustaining power of God; when the hassles of the long commute remind us how far the brokenness of our world is from God's intention; when we open our innermost secrets to the judging, healing, forgiving eyes of our maker—then we know God is among us and we are with him.

(2) Another way I have found essential to maintaining an awareness of my presence in the house of God is to unite consistently with the family of faith in the broadest range of worship experiences. When, like the ancient exilic pilgrims to the temple, I stand in the fellowship of believers to acknowledge that all aspects of my life are under the care and sovereignty of God, then I am reminded that God is here among us in spite of (and even *in*) our joys and pain, suffering and death, marriage and divorce, sickness and health. Worship with the community of faith (whether inside or outside the church building) helps me to stitch together all the competing and conflicting aspects of my life into a whole lived in the presence of God. Worship is not for me an escape from the threatening pressures of my world by fleeing into the protective arms of my Savior. Instead, worship is a moment in which I gain the perspective that God is indeed with me in the midst of my daily hassles and failures.

(3) Finally, I dwell in God's house and in his presence whenever I unite with him and his people in service to his world. God loves his world—the poor, the suffering, the animals, the environment. God desires justice, equity, compassion, and generosity. If we are dwelling in his house and seeing God as he truly is, then we cannot help but know these things and seek to live them out as well. Whenever we bring love, caring, joy, restoration, forgiveness, salvation, and hope to God's creation and its inhabitants, we are dwelling with him and he with us.

Psalm 24

OF DAVID. A psalm.

1 The earth is the LORD's, and everything in it,
the world, and all who live in it;
2 for he founded it upon the seas
and established it upon the waters.

3 Who may ascend the hill of the LORD?
Who may stand in his holy place?
4 He who has clean hands and a pure heart,
who does not lift up his soul to an idol
or swear by what is false.
5 He will receive blessing from the LORD
and vindication from God his Savior.
6 Such is the generation of those who seek him,
who seek your face, O God of Jacob. *Selah*

7 Lift up your heads, O you gates;
be lifted up, you ancient doors,
that the King of glory may come in.
8 Who is this King of glory?
The LORD strong and mighty,
the LORD mighty in battle.
9 Lift up your heads, O you gates;
lift them up, you ancient doors,
that the King of glory may come in.
10 Who is he, this King of glory?
The LORD Almighty—
he is the King of glory. *Selah*

FROM THE NEED for provision in the desert and the desire to "dwell in the house of the LORD" expressed in Psalm 23, Psalm 24 moves to the city of Jerusalem and the approach to the temple itself. If Psalm 23 alludes subtly to the pilgrimage of members of the exilic or postexilic Jewish community through the dangerous "valleys" to the delights of the holy city, then Psalm 24 describes the convergence on the house of Yahweh of the seeking people.

The liturgical character of the psalm appears clearly in its antiphonal question-and-answer structure. Whether the disparate sections of the psalm constitute the actual progressive elements of a temple liturgy[1] or simply bring ancient liturgical remnants together in a literary construction[2] is impossible to determine. There is, however, almost universal agreement on the structural division of the psalm. Three elements describe the essential building blocks of the psalm: an introductory affirmation of Yahweh's universal authority expressed by his creative establishment of the cosmos (24:1–2); an "entrance liturgy," which declares standards for those who want to approach Yahweh's "holy hill" upon which the temple sits (24:3–6); and a processional in which the "King of glory," "the LORD Almighty," enters the gates of the temple precincts (24:7–10). While these three segments are generally accepted, the significance of the arrangement is variously understood and forms the real crux of the interpretation of the psalm.[3]

The Heading (24:0)

THE HEADING CONTAINS no new terms but, like Psalm 23, is simply described as a "psalm of David."[4]

Yahweh's Creative Authority (24:1–2)

THE INTRODUCTORY VERSES affirm the authority of Yahweh over the whole earth, its contents and inhabitants, by employing creation terminology. Because he created it, the earth belongs to Yahweh. The paralleled words "earth" (*ʾereṣ*) and "world" (*tebel*) are a standard word pair, appearing often together.[5] This pairing appears in several related types of contexts. In certain

1. See Kraus, *Psalms 1–59*, 311–12, for this view.

2. See Craigie, *Psalms 1–50*, 211, for this view.

3. The appearance of the technical term *selah* accords with the proposed structure since it stands at the conclusion of both second and last sections. This may perhaps suggest a closer relationship between the first and second sections, since no *selah* intervenes.

4. For a discussion of both these terms, see comments on the heading of Ps. 3, where both occur for the first time. There is no immediately apparent significance for the variation in order of these two terms (*mizmor ledawid* in Ps. 23 vs. *ledawid mizmor* in Ps. 24), although the former arrangement occurs far more frequently (30 times) than the latter (only 6 times). If the psalm actually incorporates a liturgy for entering the temple precincts, this raises serious questions with the traditional attribution to David associated with the psalm heading.

5. The pair appears some twenty-five times in the Old Testament: sixteen times outside the Psalter (1 Sam. 2:8; 1 Chron. 16:30; Job 34:13; 37:12; Prov. 8:26, 31; Isa. 14:21; 18:3; 24:4; 26:9, 18; 34:1; Jer. 10:12; 51:15; Lam. 4:12; Nah. 1:5) and nine times within it (Pss. 19:4;

passages "earth" and "world" emphasize the stable character of the cosmos Yahweh creates and sustains. "The foundations of the earth are the LORD's; upon them he has set the world" (1 Sam. 2:8). "Tremble before him, all the earth! The world is firmly established; it cannot be moved" (1 Chron. 16:30).[6]

In other contexts, the emphasis is on the authority that attaches to Yahweh as the creator of the cosmos. "The heavens are yours, and yours also the earth; you founded the world and all that is in it" (Ps. 89:11). "Let all the earth fear the LORD; let all the people of the world revere him. For he spoke, and it came to be; he commanded, and it stood firm" (33:8–9).[7]

Closely related to the authority derived from his role as creator of the cosmos are those passages that describe Yahweh as judge over the creation and its inhabitants. "My soul yearns for you in the night; in the morning my spirit longs for you. When your judgments come upon the earth, the people of the world learn righteousness" (Isa. 26:9). "He comes to judge the earth. He will judge the world in righteousness and the peoples in his truth" (Ps. 96:13; cf. 98:9).[8] Because Yahweh creates and sustains the world, it is *his* in the sense that it depends totally on him for its continued existence—and he exercises authority and judgment over it.

The final group of passages employing *ʾereṣ* and *tebel* describe the fearful effects of the theophanic approach of the creator God into his fallen creation.[9] "The mountains quake before him and the hills melt away. The earth trembles at his presence, the world and all who live in it" (Nah. 1:5). "Tremble before him, all the earth!" (1 Chron. 16:30). "Your lightning lit up the world; the earth trembled and quaked" (Ps. 77:18).[10]

The earth is the LORD's. In 24:1–2, it is the stabilizing influence of Yahweh's creative and sustaining power that is primarily in view, with the

---

24:1; 33:8; 77:18; 89:11; 90:2; 96:13; 97:4; 98:9). The concentration of five occurrences (89:11; 90:2; 96:13; 97:4; 98:9) at the end of Book 3 and the beginning of Book 4 of the Psalter is suggestive of editorial concern and affirms the link between the *Yahweh malak* psalms (93; 95–99) and the questions regarding the demise of the Davidic covenant raised in Ps. 89. For further discussion, see comments on Pss. 89–99 and the various essays on the shape of the Psalter offered throughout this two-volume commentary.

6. For other examples of this emphasis on stability and security using *ʾereṣ* and *tebel*, see Jer. 10:12; 51:15.

7. For other passages in this vein, compare Ps. 24:1; 90:2; Prov. 8:26, 31.

8. Other passages describing Yahweh as judge of the earth include Job 34:13; Isa. 26:18; 34:1–17.

9. For additional discussion of theophany, see comments on Ps. 18:7–15.

10. For other theophany passages employing *tebel* and *ʾereṣ*, see Ps. 97:4. Human sin and evil also leave their negative imprint on the world as Isa. 24:4–5 indicates: "The earth [*ʾereṣ*] dries up and withers, the world [*tebel*] languishes and withers, the exalted of the earth languish. The earth is defiled by its people."

extended concern to affirm his authority over what he has created. It is likely, however, that a theophanic approach of Yahweh is just under the surface of these opening verses. This explains the importance in verses 3–6 of one's preparation for approaching "the holy place" and the description in verses 7–10 of the coming of Yahweh himself, the "King of glory." The psalm points out that the stability and security of the creation cannot be isolated from right relationship with Yahweh. As a result, one must prepare for his coming.

Everything in it. It is not just the earth over which God exercises authority, but all that is in it. The Hebrew *meloʾah* is more literally "its fullness" or "what fills it." The phrase occurs in a number of contexts that make it clear that God has authority over and concern for *all* creation: inanimate and animate, vegetation, animals, and humans—all are dependent on the creator for life and existence.[11] This concern has implications for how we relate ourselves to the physical creation in which we live. I will return to this issue in the Contemporary Significance section.

He founded it upon the seas. Creation imagery clearly and appropriately dominates these opening verses. God's authority over the earth and all its contents is derived from the fact that he created them. As a result, all creation is completely dependent for its very existence on his continuing mercy and grace. A similar thought is expressed in 135:6: "The LORD does whatever pleases him, in the heavens and on the earth, in the seas and all their depths."

In the creation narratives of ancient Mesopotamia, the seas and waters (actually, "rivers") played an important role. The ancient chaotic waters were gods who resisted the creative movement toward stability and order associated with the younger gods. Creation took place in a context of divine struggle, in which the younger gods were the ultimate victors. Marduk, who led the younger gods to victory, used the bodies of defeated water gods, Apsu and Tiamat, to set the protective boundaries of the inhabitable world.[12] As in the biblical narrative, the chaotic waters were banished to below the earth and above the heavens, where the gods controlled their introduction into the world as rain coming down or springs bubbling up.

---

11. The Heb. *meloʾah* (or with a masculine pronoun *meloʾo*) appears most frequently with the noun *ʾereṣ* ("earth, land"; cf. Deut. 33:16; Isa. 34:1; Jer. 8:16; 47:2; Ezek. 12:19; 19:7; 30:12; 32:15; Mic. 1:2), though on two occasions it is connected with *tebel* ("world"; Pss. 50:12; 89:11). In addition, the term appears three times with *yam* ("sea"; Pss. 96:11; 98:7; Isa. 42:10) and once with *ʿir* ("city"; Amos 6:8).

12. Translations of the various Mesopotamian texts of creation can be found in a variety of sources listed in most commentaries on the early chapters of Genesis. The two most significant resources are Beyerlin, *Near Eastern Religious Texts Relating to the Old Testament*; Pritchard, *ANETP*.

In Canaanite myth, Yam (the Hebrew word for "sea") is one name for the water god who struggles with Baal for control of the world; Yam's alternate name is Judge Nahar (from the same Hebrew word for "waters" that appears in Ps. 24:2). This suggests that the Hebrews "demythologized" the Canaanite myths by removing the divine element associated with these chaotic waters subdued by Yahweh at creation.[13] The connection in Psalm 24 is clear. Yahweh's authority and concern for his creation is displayed in his subduing the chaotic waters that threaten the world and in his establishing the earth securely upon waters held in check only by his power. All creation is dependent on the mercy and grace of Yahweh, who alone sustains "all things by his powerful word" (Heb. 1:3).

Preparation to Enter the Presence of God (24:3–6)

HAVING AFFIRMED THE creative power and continuing authority of Yahweh over the whole world, the psalm now turns its gaze on the creature who would enter the presence of this creator God. The liturgical nature of the psalm becomes clearer in a series of antiphonal questions and answers. Many commentators have pictured a throng of pilgrim worshipers approaching the Temple Mount in Jerusalem, preparing to go up to participate in worship. We know that the southern approach to Herod's temple was perforated with numerous small ritual baths in which the worshipers would cleanse themselves before approaching the holy precincts.

Who may ascend the hill of the LORD? The questions spoken here are intended to cause those who seek entrance to reflect humbly on their need for repentance and divine mercy. The liturgy is not so much a self-righteous declaration of innocence as it is a solemn admission of dependence on the merciful grace of the God, whom the worshiper approaches. It may well be that a priest (or priests) calls out these questions to those preparing to enter the temple precincts.

The setting is particularly fitting for exilic and postexilic pilgrims reaching the end of their long journey through treacherous lands and over dangerous seas to arrive at this moment of communal worship with an international fellowship. Having come from diverse nations and having survived the many perils of the journey, they were especially well situated to acknowledge—as the opening verses of the psalm do—that Yahweh is the creator Lord of the whole cosmos and all it contains.

---

13. Ugaritic texts describing the struggle between Baal and Yam are part of the Baal-Anat cycle (I AB–VI AB). English translation of these often fragmentary texts are available in *ANETP* and Beyerlin, *Near Eastern Religious Texts Relating to the Old Testament*.

Clean hands and a pure heart. The standard for approaching the presence of Yahweh is high but not as impossible as it might at first seem. One must first have "clean" hands. The term "clean" (*naqi* ["innocent"]) appears by far most frequently in the phrase *dam naqi* ("innocent blood"), which refers to those who are killed when they do not deserve to be. "Clean of hands" (*naqi kappayim*) would seem to mean those whose palms are "free" of the blood of such innocent victims. It is an outward measure of character and righteousness. Such people are "free" or "exempt" from guilt (and therefore punishment).

A "pure heart"[14] shifts the issue of righteousness before God from external action to the interior nature of the person. Much as in the Sermon on the Mount (Matt. 5–7), right relationship with God is determined not by obedience to an external law alone but by integrity, in which the outward acts of an individual are consistent with and flow out of an inner attitude of dependence on God. "Man looks at the outward appearance, but the LORD looks at the heart" (1 Sam. 16:7).

Does not lift up his soul to an idol. The underlying Hebrew of *BHS* says literally, "... has not lifted up *my* soul [*napši*] to emptiness." Most Hebrew manuscripts, however, read "*his* soul" (*napšo*) instead. A better rendering of *nepeš* is "self, essential being"[15] rather than the traditional but misleading "soul." Craigie translates the word as "mind," seeking to focus on the interior allegiance of the worshiper to idols but misleading once again by the almost exclusive association of "mind" with mental processes.

The *nepeš* is much more than mind or soul. It is the essential integrated being that is sustained in life by the animating breath/spirit given by God. To speak to the *nepeš* is to seek to influence that person at the level of deepest concern. To "lift up one's *nepeš*" is to offer[16] one's deepest commitment of the whole self to—in this case—"emptiness." On the three other occasions (all in the Psalms) when one is described as "lifting up the soul," it is always to Yahweh that the offering of self is made, and it is especially telling that Psalm 25 begins by proclaiming absolute loyalty to Yahweh: "To you, O LORD, I lift up my *nepeš*," as if to offset by stark contrast the treacherous picture of 24:4.

---

14. The kind of "purity" that *bar* suggests is that accomplished by "sorting" or "sifting out" so that only the good remains. "Sort, sift" is, in fact, the meaning of the verb *brr*, from which this adjective is derived.

15. For a discussion of the meaning of the term *nepeš*, see comments on 3:1–2.

16. To "lift up" has overtones of worship and praise, as numerous references to "lifting up the hands" in worship to Yahweh make clear. See e.g., Pss. 28:2; 63:4; 134:2; Lam. 2:19; 3:41. Worship is also characterized by lifting up "hearts" (Lam. 3:41) or a "cup of salvation" (Ps. 116:13) in other passages.

The "emptiness" to which the integrated worshiper avoids offering himself or herself is most likely (as the NIV indicates) a foreign deity or idol. We have already seen the propensity of the psalmists to cloak references to foreign gods in terms of shame, delusion, and falsehood (4:2). As Dahood points out, a whole collection of passages confirms that *šawᵓ* ("emptiness, vanity, falsehood") was often used in this manner.[17] Again, in a context of pilgrimage to Jerusalem from exile in foreign lands, this standard of absolute loyalty to Yahweh in the face of a real pressure to assimilate to foreign religious practices (cf. Dan. 3; 6) makes good sense.

He will receive blessing. The worshiper whose inner and outer worlds are integrated in loyalty to Yahweh "receives blessing from the LORD" (24:5). The wordplay that develops between this phrase and the preceding verse (24:4b) is subtle (especially in English translation) but significant. Instead of "lifting" (*nśᵓ*) himself to an idol (24:4b), the approved worshiper will "lift" (*nśᵓ*) himself to Yahweh (cf. 25:1). As a result, the integrated worshiper "receives" (*nśᵓ*) blessing from Yahweh. The Hebrew root *nśᵓ* also plays a prominent role in the final section of Psalm 24, where it appears no less than four times in the liturgy concerning the "lifting up" of the gates and doors of the temple precinct at the approach of Yahweh the king.

Vindication. Along with blessing, the approved worshiper receives *ṣedaqah* ("righteousness, justice, what is right") as well. The word *ṣedaqah* is a legal term that denotes a ruling by a judge regarding what should have occurred in a case under judgment. One who has fulfilled properly the expectations of justice in a case is declared *ṣaddiq* ("righteous"). The judge's statement of what should have occurred is *ṣedeq* ("justice, righteousness"). When one is declared *ṣaddiq*, then one receives *ṣedaqah*, a public acknowledgement of compliance with the expectations in the case—or, as NIV puts it, "vindication." In the case of the pilgrim approaching the temple precincts, the declaration gives permission to enter into God's presence. The fact that this permission comes from "God his Savior" emphasizes that "righteousness" is granted by God, not earned by faultless compliance with external law.

Such is the generation of those who seek him. The final verse of this section can be taken as an admonition that the reader follow the path just described so as to be included in the "generation" characterized by seeking God. But this verse might also be considered the affirming liturgical response of the pilgrims as they dedicate themselves to the pursuit of right relationship with Yahweh.[18] The connection of the psalm to pilgrimage is strength-

---

17. Dahood lists Ps. 26:4; 31:7; 119:37; Jonah 2:8.

18. For the former view, see Kraus, *Psalms 1–59*, 311–15. The latter understanding is expressed by Craigie, *Psalms 1–50*, 213.

ened by the use here of the two verbs of "seeking"—*drš* and *bqš*—that Kraus calls "technical terms for the pilgrimage to the sanctuary."[19]

The King of Glory Comes (24:7–10)

HAVING GAINED ADMISSION to the temple precincts, the gathered pilgrim worshipers anticipate the arrival of Yahweh himself. While on one level this might indicate that Yahweh had gone forth previously to lead the army of Israel to victory over the enemy, it also communicates the continuing sense that the temple can never fully contain the glory that is Yahweh; rather, it serves only as the meeting place of God and humans. As the divine "dwelling," the temple is the place where Yahweh *temporarily* resides among his people and is the center from which he makes forays into his world.[20]

Who is this. . . ? The final four verses of the psalm (24:7–10) constitute an antiphonal liturgy of question and answer performed at the gates of the temple precinct. This ritual enactment has traditionally been associated with the return of the ark of the covenant—the visible sign of the invisible presence of Yahweh—from military victory. The language of verse 8 in particular accords well with this military tone: "The LORD strong and mighty, the LORD mighty in battle." The name "Yahweh of hosts" (*yhwh ṣebaʾot*; NIV "the LORD Almighty") is also associated with Yahweh's military leadership (24:10b). In this view, the victorious throng accompany the ark to the gates of the temple compound and demand entrance in a ritual liturgy calculated to emphasize the glory, strength, power, and majesty of their victorious God.

The repeated ritual questions from within the temple precincts—"Who is this king of glory?"—are not real questions of identity but serve only to delay entrance so that the claims of Yahweh can be repeated in ever more exalted form in the following verses until there can no longer be any doubt that "the LORD Almighty—he is the King of glory!" (24:10). The repeated pronouncement of "glory" in demand, question, and answer has the effect of exalting the glory of the divine king, Yahweh.[21]

The acknowledgment of Yahweh as "king" during the period of Israel's monarchy would certainly have had a different effect than the same claim made during the exilic or postexilic period, when human monarchs no longer

---

19. Kraus (ibid., 314) provides the following references in support of his claim: Amos 5:5; 2 Sam. 21:1; Hos. 5:15; 2 Sam. 12:16.

20. On the various terms used to describe Yahweh's residence among humans and the implications for understanding the relative permanence of his appearance with them, see the article on "ישׁב," *NIDOTTE*, 2:550–51.

21. See the discussion of "The Kingship of Yahweh in the Psalms," in the section on "Theology of the Psalms" in vol. 2 of this commentary. See also the comments on 5:1–3.

existed. As long as human kings ruled over the day-to-day affairs of Israel, there must always have been some overlap and conflict with the affirmation that Yahweh is king. Precisely to what extent human and divine kings were identified in Israel remains unclear. We do know that in the ancient Near East at large, kings were often considered the representatives on earth of the divine king. In places like Egypt and (later) Mesopotamia, the human king came to be considered divine—a god in his own right. While it is doubtful that Israel ever understood human rulers in the latter light, certainly the kings of Israel and Judah often found it difficult sharing authority with Yahweh, and conflicts consistently arose around their inability to submit their own will to that of God.

In the post-monarchical period, this claim that Yahweh is king must have taken on a decidedly different ring. Human kingship had proved itself ultimately a failure at ensuring the security and identity of the nation. Its collapse in defeat and exile raised strong questions and stringent critique of the validity of the very idea of human kings. People reached the conclusion that human kings were an ambiguously negative institution, tolerated only so long as subordinated under the kingship of Yahweh; this led to the erosion of the significance of human kingship and the exaltation of the divine kingship of Yahweh. As long as Yahweh is king, his faithful followers can live under the human rulership of any number of foreign monarchs and still maintain their loyalty and allegiance to the one true king, Yahweh.

In the present context, however, together with the preceding section setting standards for the entrance of worshipers into the presence of Yahweh, this final liturgy of divine entry into the temple represents in dramatic form the essential convergence of God and human that temple worship enacted at its core. When humans, rightly prepared in heart and action, wait for Yahweh in worship, the "King of glory" comes! That is the essential mystery of worship that this psalm celebrates. In the house of God, Yahweh deigns to be present with "the generation of those who seek . . . your face."

Lift up your heads, O you gates. Lifting up the head is a sign of joyous anticipation and hope. When one lifts one's own head, it is sign of the hope and joy that characterizes the person's outlook. When one lifts another's head, it is an indication of offering hope and joy where there is none. In 3:3, when God lifts the head of the struggling psalmist, God offers hope and joy in the midst of a threatening setting.

In our passage, the gates are instructed to lift up their heads, metaphorically announcing the hope and joy that approaches the gathered worshipers in the person of the victorious king, Yahweh. There is no evidence—archaeological or otherwise—that gates in the temple actually "lifted up." As far as we know, they rotated horizontally on pivots in door sockets. The demand, then, is metaphorical, to announce the occasion of joy while at the same time asking for entrance.

You ancient doors. The Hebrew behind "ancient" is the venerable *ᶜolam* ("eternity, long time"). The period of time that *ᶜolam* represents can extend into the distant past or into the future. God is "from *ᶜolam* to *ᶜolam*" (90:2)—as close as Hebrew comes to talking about "eternity." The references in 24:7b, 9b to "doors of *ᶜolam*" may suggest the doors' antiquity (e.g., NIV "ancient doors") or their enduring character (e.g., REB "everlasting doors"). Kraus suggests a less likely alternative that *ᶜolam* here refers to the transcendent doors of the heavenly dwelling of Yahweh.[22] Regardless, the venerable doors of the temple are challenged to provide access in expectant hope and joy to the glorious divine warrior king, who comes to his worshiping people.

THE EARTH IS YAHWEH'S. What does it mean that "the earth is the LORD's"? The construction used here for the possessive is the familiar preposition *le* + *yhwh*, which is most often rendered "belongs to Yahweh." The context in Psalm 24, however, suggests that what is at stake is not just a claim of divine possession or ownership. Such ownership could be the result of divine conquest and domination—as when a human king takes a vulnerable land and makes it his subordinate vassal.

When, however, verse 2 goes on to make a connection between Yahweh's creation of the cosmos and his ongoing relationship to the world and its contents, the psalmist is pointing beyond God's dominating authority to his essential role in the very origin of the world and its continued existence. What he is saying is not that we are Yahweh's world because he has taken it for his own by power of conquest, but that the world must acknowledge its absolute dependence for being, sustenance, and continued existence on its creator and sustainer—Yahweh alone.

There is no other alternative, since there is no independent existence apart from Yahweh. To deny that all life relies totally on the sustaining power of God's hand is to act the fool and to join those rebel nations of Psalm 2, whose futile determination to cast off divine rule brings such robust guffaws from the lips of Yahweh enthroned on high. To rebel as if one could be independent of God is to opt for "nonbeing" and is ultimately "ridiculous." When God withholds his power, everything withers, fades, languishes, and comes to nothing (104:27–30).

22. Kraus, *Psalms 1–59*, 315.

The Lord comes to judge the earth. God's relation to the world as its creator also means he has the right of judgment over it. This relationship of creation and judgment is most clearly expressed in the *Yahweh malak* psalms (Pss. 93; 95–99), which celebrate Yahweh as creator, king, and judge of the earth. "In his hand are the depths of the earth, and the mountain peaks belong to him. The sea is his, for he made it, and his hands formed the dry land" (95:4–5). "Say among the nations, 'The LORD reigns.' The world is firmly established, it cannot be moved; he will judge the peoples with equity. Let the heavens rejoice, let the earth be glad . . . they will sing before the LORD, for he comes, he comes to judge the earth. He will judge the world in righteousness and the peoples in his truth" (96:10–11, 13).

The coming of Yahweh as king, then, as at the end of Psalm 24 and in the *Yahweh malak* psalms, is coupled with anticipation of judgment on the earth and its peoples. As Psalm 24 implies, Yahweh's coming will issue either in great rejoicing for those who acknowledge their dependence on Yahweh and seek him rightly (24:3–6) or in judgment for those who do not.

Everything in the world. It is not just the earth that belongs to Yahweh, but everything in it as well. That implies that God has authority over everything in the world and that his concern is not just with human beings, or with their salvation, but with the *shalom*/well-being of the whole cosmos—animal, vegetable, and mineral.

This concern of Yahweh for the *whole* world is reflected in the legal traditions concerning the welfare of animals and the soil itself. God's law provided for humane treatment of animals. An ox forced to grind grain in a mill could not be muzzled (Deut. 25:4). Rest was required for donkey and ox as well as humans on the Sabbath (Ex. 23:12; Deut. 5:14). The land was to be given rest every seventh year. Human blood spilled on the earth was not a matter of indifference but corrupted and polluted the land so that it was no longer useful. Pollution by human violence reached such extremes before the Flood that the deluge was as much a cleansing of the earth as a punishment of the human perpetrators (Gen. 6:5–13). Such divine concern for creation should have significant influence on how we relate to the nonhuman environment in which we live. I will return to this issue below

LIVING IN GOD'S WORLD. If the earth is Yahweh's because he created it, sustains it, cares for it, and judges it, we as believing followers of the creator should think in specific ways about the world and relate ourselves appropriately to it. Neither we nor the cosmos has any independent existence outside God's will and power. To think, then, that we can act in ways that do not concern the creator or that how we use or abuse the creation is a matter of indifference to God is to join the fool in Psalm 14 in the self-deceptive denial of the existence of God.

The fact that the world is *God's* creation and possession undermines all human pretensions to ownership. Israel understood this when she promulgated the Jubilee legislation. Every fiftieth year, this statute demanded, all debts were to be cancelled, and all property—in particular, land—was to revert to its original tribal allotment.[23] This served to prevent any tribe or clan from becoming inordinately rich or powerful by accruing land to the detriment of others. It is not clear whether the Jubilee restoration of property ever occurred, but the effects on social relationships would be immense. The very existence of the legislation indicated the ideological understanding that the land could not in reality be possessed but only held as an agent of God.

In a different but related statute, all agricultural lands—regardless of ownership—were required to lie fallow every seventh year. This allowed the land itself to rest from labor, indicating once again that the land was not at the control and service of Israel but under the authority of Yahweh. Those who held the land did so under God's authority and were responsible to him for the use they made of it.

The undermining of human ownership runs counter to the basic principles of capitalism, where ownership of property and the means of production are key ingredients of cornering a market, increasing demand, and commanding profitable prices. The financial news continues to be full of reports these days of attempts to monopolize commodities and products, create artificial scarcity, and thus create windfall profits. The ability of individuals or associations to manipulate or control a market is greatly inhibited when the world is seen as belonging to God.

It is *the world* that belongs to Yahweh, not just Israel. This means that God's concern for the well-being of his creation extends far beyond the borders of the covenant people to include the Gentiles, the animals, and even physical creation. As God's agents in the world, we are called to view the cosmos with God's eyes, not through the lens of our own self-interest. How can we stockpile surplus grain when other countries are starving their way through drought? Is it ethical to allow companies to sell disease-resistant, genetically manipulated grain to Third World countries when the grain will not reseed itself, locking farmers into an endless return to the suppliers for the seed? While it is true that ethical questions are often raised and debated, it is still surprising just how often the primary justification given for decisions and actions is "national interest." We have a long way

23. See this Jubilee legislation in Lev. 25.

to go to see the world as God's world and to work for the benefit of the whole cosmos.

When the world is God's, we are called to rely on him rather than our own power to control, exploit, and use the world to protect and benefit ourselves. In the Sermon on the Mount, Jesus calls us to give up an attitude of anxious striving and to depend on the care of God (Matt. 6:25–34). Psalm 104 makes much the same point by describing how Yahweh makes the earth fruitful so that plants, animals, and humans are satisfied with good things (104:10–16, 24–30). All are utterly dependent on his caring, for "when you hide your face, they are terrified; when you take away their breath, they die and return to the dust. When you send your Spirit, they are created, and you renew the face of the earth" (104:29–30).

When we realize that our life is in God's hands, we are emboldened to make decisions about our finances, relationships, and even the environment that are based on the well-being of the cosmos, not just personal benefit or concern. Like Christ, we should be willing to take on self-limitation, even suffering and death, in order to work for the restoration of all God's world. Then and only then will we truly be able to say: "The earth is the LORD'S, and everything in it, the world and all who live in it."

Psalm 25

OF DAVID.

1 To you, O LORD, I lift up my soul;
2 in you I trust, O my God.
Do not let me be put to shame,
nor let my enemies triumph over me.
3 No one whose hope is in you
will ever be put to shame,
but they will be put to shame
who are treacherous without excuse.

4 Show me your ways, O LORD,
teach me your paths;
5 guide me in your truth and teach me,
for you are God my Savior,
and my hope is in you all day long.
6 Remember, O LORD, your great mercy and love,
for they are from of old.
7 Remember not the sins of my youth
and my rebellious ways;
according to your love remember me,
for you are good, O LORD.

8 Good and upright is the LORD;
therefore he instructs sinners in his ways.
9 He guides the humble in what is right
and teaches them his way.
10 All the ways of the LORD are loving and faithful
for those who keep the demands of his covenant.
11 For the sake of your name, O LORD,
forgive my iniquity, though it is great.
12 Who, then, is the man that fears the LORD?
He will instruct him in the way chosen for him.
13 He will spend his days in prosperity,
and his descendants will inherit the land.
14 The LORD confides in those who fear him;
he makes his covenant known to them.
15 My eyes are ever on the LORD,
for only he will release my feet from the snare.

[16]Turn to me and be gracious to me,
  for I am lonely and afflicted.
[17]The troubles of my heart have multiplied;
  free me from my anguish.
[18]Look upon my affliction and my distress
  and take away all my sins.
[19]See how my enemies have increased
  and how fiercely they hate me!
[20]Guard my life and rescue me;
  let me not be put to shame,
  for I take refuge in you.
[21]May integrity and uprightness protect me,
  because my hope is in you.

[22]Redeem Israel, O God,
  from all their troubles!

THE TWENTY-TWO VERSES of this psalm form an alphabetic acrostic poem (one that begins each verse with successive letters in the Hebrew alphabet[1]). The final verse (25:22) stands outside the acrostic pattern since it follows the *taw* line (25:21). This verse also introduces the communal concerns of Israel into an otherwise individual composition, which is probably a way of adapting an earlier psalm to the needs of the postexilic Diaspora community.[2] Kraus takes the verse as a later addition,

---

1. For further discussion of the alphabetic acrostic form, see the section on "Hebrew Poetry" in the introduction. The acrostic in Ps. 25 is clearly defective in verse 18, which should begin with the Hebrew letter *qop* but starts with the word *reʾeh* instead. For this reason *BHS* suggests an emendation to *qešob* ("be attentive") or *qeḥah* (from *lqḥ*, "take"), although without textual support. Similarly Kraus (*Psalms 1–59*, 319) emends to *qešar* ("have regard"). Charles A. Briggs (C. A. Briggs and E. G. Briggs, *A Critical and Exegetical Commentary on the Book of Psalms*, 2 vols. [ICC; Edinburgh: T. & T. Clark, 1906–1907], 1:229) connects the existing text *reʾeh* with a possible original *qrʾ* ("meet"), with the understanding that the original *qop* was omitted by confusion with the following *reʾeh* that appropriately begins the *reš* line in verse 19. The latter explanation has the strength of plausibility and is picked up by Craigie (*Psalms 1–50*, 17). The *waw* verse also is reconstructed out of the short partial v. 5b, where a few manuscripts supply the word with an initial conjunction *w*- ("and").

2. Hossfeld and Zenger, *Die Psalmen*, 163, also understand the verse, and thus the final form of this psalm, as a response to the postexilic setting.

while Craigie connects it with a postexilic acrostic tradition in which the *waw* line is "suppressed" and a final line added (cf. Ps. 34).[3]

Beyond the obvious shaping of the acrostic method, the structure of the psalm is more difficult to determine. There is a clear alternation between second-person direct address of Yahweh and third-person narrative about him, with verses 1–7, 11, 16–22 falling into the former category and verses 8–10, 12–15 representing the latter. Taking into consideration these changing indications of second- and third-person reference to Yahweh along with thematic shifts, the structure of the psalm can be described as follows: statement of trust (25:1–3), plea for deliverance (25:4–7), praise for Yahweh's faithfulness (25:8–10), pivotal prayer for forgiveness (25:11), confidence of those who fear Yahweh (25:12–15), individual plea for deliverance (25:16–21), and communal plea for redemption (25:22).

The Heading (25:0)

NO NEW TERMS appear in the heading of Psalm 25. The psalm is the first in a grouping of four consecutive psalms (Pss. 25–28) that are identically and simply attributed to David.[4]

Statement of Trust (25:1–3)

THE PSALM BEGINS with a confident declaration of trust in Yahweh (25:1), followed immediately by a plea that the speaker not be "put to shame" or defeated by the enemy (25:2). This plea does not undermine the statement of trust because it is grounded in the theological observation that follows in verse 3; because Yahweh will never allow those who trust in him to be put to shame, the psalmist is free to claim personal application of that truth. Unlike the treacherous idol worshiper of 24:4, he declares, "I lift up my *nepeš*"[5] to Yahweh, who alone is trustworthy (25:1).

Do not let me be put to shame. Shame here is not just an inward feeling but an outward experience of public embarrassment. The enemies of the psalmist seek a public condemnation that is undeserved. I am reminded of the public humiliation demanded of the adulteress Hester Prynne by the Puritan community in Hawthorne's *The Scarlet Letter*. Having borne a child out of wedlock while her husband was away, Hester was required to wear visible on her bodice a scarlet A, signifying her sinful state, and was to be followed

3. See Kraus, *Psalms 1–59*, 317; Craigie, *Psalms 1–50*, 277. In *BHS*, the line is suggested in the apparatus at 25:5c by adding the conjunction to the word *ʾotka* ("you") with the support of a few manuscripts. See also the comments of Hossfeld and Zenger, *Die Psalmen*, 161.

4. See comments on the heading of Ps. 3.

5. See comments on *nepeš* in Ps. 24:4.

about through the streets by a drummer boy constantly announcing her presence to the disapproving public. Similarly, in our psalm the enemies are not satisfied with a private put-down but desire the whole community to join in their ridicule and stigmatizing of the psalmist.

Although the same verb (*bwš*) is employed three times in verses 2–3, the difference in the forms employed is significant. In verse 2 the psalmist uses a negative jussive form (*ʾal ʾebošah*) to express the *desire* that Yahweh will not allow the psalmist to be shamed. In verse 3, however, the forms are both imperfects (*loʾ yebošu; yebošu*), indicating the psalmist's *certainty* that Yahweh does not allow those who trust in him to be shamed.

Plea for Deliverance (25:4–7)

SHOW ME YOUR WAYS, O LORD. The second-person address of Yahweh continues, but a series of imperative forms signals the shift from declaration of confidence to plea for deliverance. The section is subdivided into two parts: verses 4–5, focusing on divine instruction in the "ways" of Yahweh; and verses 6–7, stressing the theme of divine remembrance. Together the two pieces describe the psalmist's humble teachability (25:4–5), acknowledgment of sin (25:7), and complete reliance on the undeserved mercy of God (25:6–7).

The "ways" (*derakeyka*) and "paths" (*ʾoreḥoteyka*) of Yahweh are here viewed as many and not one. This acknowledges that the one "way" of righteousness before Yahweh envisioned in Psalm 1:6 is actually composed of many moments of decision and faithfulness. The psalmist is not left alone on this journey but can trust Yahweh to guide and instruct along the way. Like the shepherd of Psalm 23, Yahweh leads the one who trusts in him along the correct paths (from *drk*, "cause me to walk"). Craigie understands this latter verb to imply that God supplies the strength to follow the path made known by God—something like "enable me to walk."[6]

Guide me in your truth. Rather than the NIV's "truth," the underlying Hebrew word (*ʾemet*) is better translated "faithfulness," the same basic meaning associated with the word in 25:10. The primary idea is of enduring reliability that can be trusted—not just rightness. The psalmist wishes to be guided faithfully through the myriad circumstances of life, able to rely at every turn on the consistent presence of Yahweh.

My hope is in you. The psalmist again claims the foundational truth of verse 3 by identifying fully with those who "trust" in Yahweh and consequently need not fear being put to shame. The completeness of his trust is confirmed by its continuous nature: "all day long."

6. Craigie, *Psalms 1–50*, 219.

Remember ... your great mercy and love. The psalmist does not trust in personal integrity and sinless righteousness but grounds all hope in the "great mercy and love" of God. "Great mercy" (*raḥameyka*) is related to the noun *reḥem* ("womb, uterus") and is taken to mean "the feelings of a mother to the child in her womb," hence, "compassion, mercy." Elsewhere Yahweh is spoken of as having given birth to Israel/Ephraim and having such motherly feelings that he is unable to give the child up (Jer. 31:20; Hos. 11:1–8). It is to this bond of "motherly love" that the psalmist appeals rather than to any generalized idea of compassion.[7]

In addition to Yahweh's tender compassion, the psalmist also relies on his "love" (*ḥesed*).[8] More accurate than the NIV's translation "love" (for which *ʾahabah* is a more common Hebrew alternative) is the rendering "enduring (covenant) loyalty." This is the kind of loyalty that grows out of a bond of commitment. God's covenant with Israel demonstrated his willingness and purpose to bind himself to her in an unbreakable (on *his* part) relationship of committed loyalty. This *is* love, not of an emotional sort but of a settled and accepted decision. Such commitment endures—"for they are from of old" (25:6b)—and can serve as the foundation for the hope for deliverance that the psalmist expresses.

Remember not.[9] In verse 6 the psalmist calls Yahweh to "remember" his compassion and enduring covenant loyalty, on which he grounds all hope of deliverance. In verse 7, however, the psalmist entreats Yahweh *not* to remember his youthful indiscretions and rebellious ways. Whether this refers to the sins of immaturity that the psalmist has outgrown or is a reminder of sins of "long-standing" (as the NIV study notes suggest, as a parallel to Yahweh's enduring compassion) is not immediately clear. In any case, the psalmist does not dismiss such sin as inconsequential. At the central point of the psalm (25:11), he confesses "great" iniquity and seeks forgiveness from God. Rather than simple "forgetfulness," he is asking God not to allow these confessed sins to stand in the way of divine deliverance. When set opposite one another in the balance, he is confident that Yahweh's enduring loyalty and compassion will outweigh his long-standing sin.

In Praise of God's Faithfulness (25:8–10)

A SHIFT TO third-person reference about God signals the beginning of a new section. The content shifts as well from plea to descriptive praise of Yahweh for his enduring love and faithfulness (25:10a). This section responds point

7. See comments on *reḥem* at 22:9.
8. See comments on *ḥesed* at 6:1–5.
9. See comments on "remembering" at 8:3–4.

for point to the pleas in verses 4–7 (instructive guidance, enduring mercy, and love), grounding confidence in the characteristic nature of God.

Good and upright is the LORD. The preceding section concluded with the plea for Yahweh to respond to the psalmist's request "for the sake of your goodness" (25:7).[10] The essential character of God governs his willingness to instruct and guide his people (25:8–9), and to do so with enduring loyalty and faithfulness (25:10). To be "upright" (*yašar*) is to be "straight, level; undeviating." Like the shepherd of Psalm 23, Yahweh is the trustworthy guide who knows the terrain and provides the guidance the psalmist seeks in 25:4–5. Yahweh instructs[11] sinners in "his ways" (cf. 25:4), guides (*drk*, cf. 25:5a), and teaches the "humble."[12] The "ways" (*ʾorḥot*, cf. 25:4b) of Yahweh are governed by his "loving" compassion (*ḥesed*, cf. 25:6b) and "faithfulness" (*ʾemet*, cf. 25:5a) directed toward those who "keep" his covenant and testimonies.

The Pivotal Prayer (25:11)

THIS CENTRAL THEMATIC verse is marked out by another shift in person—in this case, to second-person direct address of Yahweh. "For the sake of your name,[13] O LORD," the psalmist cries, using a form of phrase that recalls both the similar conclusion of verses 4–7 (the only previous second-person section) and 23:3 ("He guides me in paths of righteousness for his name's sake"). What the psalmist seeks here, however, is less guidance than forgiveness of "iniquity" (*ʿawon* ["intentional sin; action that is crooked or wrong"]).[14]

Those Who Fear Yahweh (25:12–15)

FOLLOWING THE PIVOTAL confession of sin, the psalm shifts once again to the third person, indicating a new section. These verses describe the blessings that accrue to those who "fear the LORD" (25:12a, 14). Moving from the singular reference in 25:12 ("he who fears the LORD") to the plural reference

---

10. The NIV's "for you are good, O LORD" (*lemaʿan ṭubeka yhwh*) obscures the later connection of this phrase with *lemaʿan šimka yhwh* ("for the sake of your name, O LORD") in the central thematic verse 11.

11. This is the same Heb. root from which the noun *torah* ("instruction, law") is derived. With the reference to Yahweh's "covenant" and "testimonies" in 25:10b (cf. NIV "demands of his covenant"), it is clear that adherence to the Torah is expected.

12. For a discussion of the various categories of oppressed persons, see comments on 10:16–18.

13. For an extended discussion of the divine name, see comments on 8:1.

14. See the discussion of various expressions for sin in the section on "The Theology of the Psalms" in vol. 2 of this commentary. The idea of "crookedness" associated with *ʿawon* stands in direct contrast to the claim that Yahweh is *yašar* ("straight") in 25:8.

in 25:14 ("those who fear him") has the effect of linking the experience of the psalmist to the more general experience of the community to which he speaks. The section moves in two directions: It admonishes the larger community to adopt the stance of fearing Yahweh, and it provides a foundation for the psalmist's confidence of deliverance, since he claims the kind of total reliance on Yahweh that fearing him entails (cf. 25: 15a).

Who . . . is the man that fears the LORD? Those who fear Yahweh experience the kind of instructive guidance the psalmist seeks (25:4–7) and confidently anticipates (25:8–10). Yahweh is an intimate confidant and reveals (cf. the request in 25:4a) his covenant (25:14b; cf. 25:10) to those who fear him (25:14). They need not struggle to understand how to fulfill his expectations but are directly and clearly instructed in the appropriate way.

Fear of Yahweh is an attitude that acknowledges one's absolute dependence on Yahweh for mercy, forgiveness, and continued existence. The psalmist stakes out a claim for such dependence with his statement in 25:15: "My eyes are ever on the LORD, for only he will release my feet from the snare."

The Final Plea (25:16–21)

THE FINAL SECTION of the psalm is marked out by another shift to second-person direct address of Yahweh, accompanied by a new string of seven imperative verb forms that signal the psalmist's final plea for deliverance.

Turn . . . and be gracious. The initial phrase seeks to redirect Yahweh's attention to the psalmist's plight. The psalmist is "lonely"[15] and "afflicted,"[16] feels beset by multiplying "troubles"[17] and "anguish," and wants to experience God's gracious deliverance.

The root cause of this distress becomes clear in 25:18, where it is traced to the psalmist's sin. This understanding illumines his description of "troubles of [the] heart" (25:17a), which are seen more as a result of the inner turmoil (cf. *ʿamali*, 25:18a) of guilt and shame than the fear of attack by enemies. The admission of "sin" links back to the psalmist's plea (25:7) that Yahweh

15. On *yaḥid*, see comments on Ps. 22:20. Here the emphasis of this word seems to be more on isolation and the resultant vulnerability experienced.

16. See comments on the various types of oppressed persons mentioned in the psalms at 10:16–18.

17. The NIV is reading the verb connected with this noun ("they have widened," from *rḥb*) as "increased; multiplied"—a translation not entirely appropriate for this word. The form presents problems because the verb is masculine plural while the supposed subject is feminine plural. *BHS* suggests an emendation to the masculine singular imperative form and reads it as a plea to Yahweh to "make wide" the "strictures" of the psalmist's heart.

not remember long-standing sin and to the pivotal confession and plea for forgiveness in 25:11.

See . . . my enemies. While the preponderance of the psalm is concerned with the painful consequences of the psalmist's own sin, the enemies briefly mentioned in 25:2 now reappear greatly increased, both in number and in intensity. They hate the psalmist with a "fierce" hatred. The Hebrew *ḥamas* ("violent") normally refers to bloodletting of a particularly offensive kind. It was this kind of violence that so corrupted the earth in Genesis 6:11–13 that Yahweh decided to cleanse the earth through the Flood. From this kind of active hatred the psalmist requires divine protection and deliverance (25:20a).

Let me not be put to shame. The psalmist returns to the theme with which the psalm began—the psalmist's hope to escape public shame and ridicule (25:1–3). Laying claim to the promise declared in those earlier verses—"no one whose hope is in you will ever be put to shame"—he reiterates absolute dependence on Yahweh: "I take refuge in you . . . my hope is in you" (25:20c, 21b).

May integrity and uprightness protect me. The question we must ask here is whose "integrity and uprightness" is at issue. If the phrase refers to Yahweh, the psalmist is trusting in the Lord's characteristic nature to provide deliverance and safety. Already the trait of "uprightness" has been attributed to Yahweh in 25:8, where it is coupled with "goodness." It may be that, having run to Yahweh as refuge, the psalmist is now expressing confidence that God will surely protect those who trust in him; he will live up to the promises made earlier in the psalm.

But perhaps the psalmist's own integrity and uprightness is under consideration. If so, he is saying that hope for deliverance is dependent on his fulfillment of expectations as laid out in this psalm. Because he is humble, contrite, confessing sin, and relying completely on God's gracious mercy, the psalmist can confidently anticipate deliverance. While it is difficult to determine which of these interpretations is to be preferred, the linkage of this reliance on integrity and uprightness with the opening line of Psalm 26—"Vindicate me, O LORD, for I have led a blameless life"—seems to confirm the latter as more likely.

Communal Plea for Redemption (25:22)

WE COME AT the end of Psalm 25 to the additional *pe* verse that stands outside the acrostic form (which ends in v. 21 with the *taw* verse). This final verse shares with the preceding section the use of second-person address of Yahweh and the use of an imperative verb form, "redeem." The verse broadens the narrow focus of the psalm by identifying the pleas of the individual psalmist with the communal concern for the redemption of Israel "from all their troubles."[18] As Hossfeld and Zenger note, this final phrase is most likely a postexilic addition to the psalm, or even more likely, as Craigie points out, evidence of a postexilic shaping of the whole psalm that intentionally adapts the singular sentiments of the earlier psalm to serve the needs of the later worshiping community.[19]

A COVENANT FOR SINNERS. The central theme of Psalm 25 is finding the "way" (or "ways") of Yahweh. Notice how many times "way/ways" or "paths" appear in this psalm (vv. 4a, 4b, 7, 8b, 9b, 10a, 12b). Finding the way of Yahweh means experiencing deliverance, prosperity, and divine grace. Closely related to the theme of the "way" is the idea of "covenant," by which the path and its demands are made clear (vv. 10b, 14b).

It is remarkable that in Psalm 25, contrary to normal expectation, the covenant the psalmist anticipates is not a relationship predicated on absolute perfection of obedience but is from the outset a "covenant for sinners." In 25:7, the psalmist acknowledges sinful acts of long-standing, hoping that Yahweh will no longer "remember" them. In 25:8 he goes on to declare that one indication of Yahweh's "good and upright" character is the fact he "instructs *sinners* in his ways." God's purpose is to bring sinners into the covenant, and to this end he provides the necessary guidance and instruction to make their participation possible.

This idea of a "covenant for sinners" is borne out by the Old Testament narratives of the lives of those we might tend to consider "saints." Abraham, Jacob, David, Gideon, and Samson were all "sinners" who nonetheless found themselves bound graciously into a covenant relationship with Yahweh. Abraham with his constant confusion of self-interest and divine promise; Jacob's numerous attempts to manipulate and control the gift of divine blessing; David and his abuse of kingly power for personal gain and gratification; Gideon's creation of seductive idols to lead the people astray; Samson's self-destructive pursuit of love in the arms of the enemy—none of these "sinners" could undermine God's purpose to establish and flesh out a relationship of salvation with his people. God relentlessly pursues these and other sinners. He instructs them in his ways (25:8b, 12:b), guides them in what is right

18. Actually the Heb. reads "all *his* troubles" rather than the NIV's "*their* troubles."

19. See Hossfeld and Zenger, *Die Psalmen*, 163; Craigie, *Psalms 1–50*, 221–22.

(25:9a), teaches them his way (25:9b), confides in them (25:14a), and makes his covenant known to them (25:14b).

If we are not talking about sinless perfection, then what *are* the characteristics of those whom God pursues in these verses? Perhaps the overarching description is "humble" (25:9). Yahweh "guides" and "teaches" the humble—those who acknowledge their need and reliance on him. Such humble persons are also characterized by the "fear of the LORD" (25:12a, 14a), another way of describing an attitude that acknowledges one's absolute dependence on Yahweh alone for life, salvation, and continued sustenance.

Those humble sinners who fear Yahweh also hope and trust only in him (25:2a, 3a, 5c, 15, 20c, 21b). It is important to note that it is "hope" and "trust" that link the humble sinners to the covenant with God, not sinless obedience. Here is a clear statement of the gospel of grace in the heart of the Old Testament! When the psalmist declares that "all the ways of the LORD are loving and faithful for those who keep the demands of his covenant" (25:10), we immediately think of the law and the necessity of keeping its commandments. But the broader context of this psalm chips away at our traditional view of an Old Testament covenant of law and sharpens our vision of a covenant of grace offered to sinners in *both* Old and New Testaments. The Torah is then the guidebook by which "sinners" are led into a covenant of grace, acknowledging their sinfulness and relying wholly on the gracious mercy of God for salvation.

God responds to such humble sinners who rely wholly on him in gracious ways. He is loving and faithful to them (25:10), forgiving their iniquity (25:11) and taking away all their sins (25:18b). In addition, God frees sinners from the snares that entangle them (25:15), graciously removes the anguish they experience (25:17), and protects them from public humiliation and shame (25:2–3, 20).

Such a gracious, divine response to sinners is far from our normal understanding of the Old Testament covenant of law. But it is the usual understanding of God's enduring faithfulness and steadfast love described in the psalms. Compare, for example, the heart of Psalm 103 with its testimony of a gracious God: "He does not treat us as our sins deserve or repay us according to our iniquities. . . . As far as the east is from the west, so far has he removed our transgressions from us. As a father has compassion on his children, so the LORD has compassion on those who fear him" (103:10, 12–13). God is the God of *both* Old and New Testaments, both of Israel and of the church. We should not be surprised if his message of grace and salvation fills the pages of the former covenant as well as the latter.

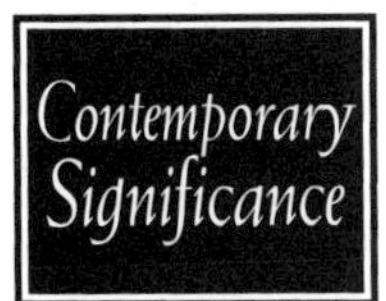

THE "COVENANT FOR SINNERS" that Psalm 25 describes is a divine gift for which I am personally grateful. I find I often identify most with those Old Testament characters who struggled honestly and faithfully with their doubts, fears, and inward demons. I am thankful that God calls sinners into relationship with himself, that he forgives our sin, and that he releases us from our anguish as well as the snares that bind and hinder us.

Jesus brings much the same message in his earthly ministry. When confronted by the Pharisees over his association with "tax collectors and 'sinners,'" Jesus replied pointedly, "It is not the healthy who need a doctor, but the sick. I have not come to call the righteous, but sinners" (Mark 2:17; cf. Matt. 9:12–13; Luke 5:31–32). Jesus did not mean to say that the Pharisees were without sin and, therefore, without need of repentance. His point was that all were sinners and equally in need of God's gracious salvation. The only thing that separated the Pharisees and the "sinners" with whom Jesus associated was that the latter were humble enough to admit their need and to trust wholly in God's gracious forgiveness.

The Pharisees, by contrast, trusted in their ability to meet the demands of the law and thought, therefore, that they had no need for divine mercy and grace. The message of both Old and New Testaments is clear: Those who enter the eternal kingdom of God's grace are those who acknowledge their sin and trust in the gracious mercy of God while surrendering self-power and pride. May our eyes ever be on Yahweh, for only he will release our feet from the snares of life (cf. 25:15).

Psalm 26

F DAVID.

[1] Vindicate me, O LORD,
for I have led a blameless life;
I have trusted in the LORD
without wavering.
[2] Test me, O LORD, and try me,
examine my heart and my mind;
[3] for your love is ever before me,
and I walk continually in your truth.
[4] I do not sit with deceitful men,
nor do I consort with hypocrites;
[5] I abhor the assembly of evildoers
and refuse to sit with the wicked.
[6] I wash my hands in innocence,
and go about your altar, O LORD,
[7] proclaiming aloud your praise
and telling of all your wonderful deeds.
[8] I love the house where you live, O LORD,
the place where your glory dwells.

[9] Do not take away my soul along with sinners,
my life with bloodthirsty men,
[10] in whose hands are wicked schemes,
whose right hands are full of bribes.
[11] But I lead a blameless life;
redeem me and be merciful to me.

[12] My feet stand on level ground;
in the great assembly I will praise the LORD.

THIS PSALM IS a prayer for redemption founded on an extended protestation of personal innocence, which the psalmist invites the penetrating gaze of divine scrutiny to confirm and honor. Psalm 26 shares with Psalm 25 a concern with vindication (cf. 25:21 and 26:1–3) and is linked with the sequence of Psalms 23–30 through a common focus on the "house" or "dwelling" of Yahweh.[1] Psalm 25 assures those who trust wholly in Yahweh and allow his instruction to guide them in the way of righteousness that they can be confident of divine deliverance. Psalm 26 responds to that assurance by laying out the psalmist's case for having led such a humble (26:2),[2] innocent (26:1a, 3b, 6a, 11a), and trusting life (26:1b) as Psalm 25 describes.

The voice of the individual dominates Psalm 26 (cf. first-person language throughout). God is consistently addressed in the second person. The body of the psalm is bracketed (26:1, 11) by a plea for vindication/redemption grounded in the psalmist's claim of a "blameless life." The motif of worshiping in the sanctuary is key to the understanding of the psalm, especially in the central vow to offer praise around the altar and the expression of love for the temple.[3]

More than many psalms, Psalm 26 demonstrates the tension that can exist between a psalm's original intent and its subsequent reuse in the more literary context of the Psalter. Its original context appears to be that of an individual seeking asylum in the temple. Its structure can be understood in this light: plea for vindication (26:1; cf. 26:11), submission to divine examination (26:2–7), prayer for continued dwelling in God's presence (26:8–11), and statement of confidence and praise (26:12).

Placed within the literary context of an extended group of psalms (Pss. 23–30) concerned with approaching and dwelling in the house of Yahweh, however, Psalm 26 takes on a slightly altered function and significance. It continues to speak to the postexilic community, expressing the love and awe of the successful pilgrim who, having entered the temple in the throng of worshipers, is overwhelmed and convicted of the necessity of a blameless life separated from association with the wicked. The "bloodthirsty" sinners (26:9) offer an apt parallel to the pagan communities in which most of the exilic Diaspora found themselves. In this way an essentially Palestinian psalm has been renewed to continue to speak with power to generations whose experience is far removed from the original setting.

---

1. See comments on dwelling in the house of Yahweh at 23:6.

2. We may find it difficult at first to recognize humility in what may seem like a rather brash and prideful statement of complete innocence, but it *is* there. Especially the call for Yahweh's scrutiny is a moment of humble submission to divine authority. One does not lightly open the dark inner recesses of one's being to God's gaze, for the consequences of sin are real and God's mercy is very necessary, as the psalmist clearly recognizes in 26:9–11.

3. The motif of taking refuge in the sanctuary may play a role in the background of this psalm, esp. in the central expression of the psalmist's fear of being dragged away from it among the sinners who deserve punishment. Alternatively, this may represent the fear of the exilic community of being judged along with the foreign nations among whom they lived. See comments on taking refuge in the temple at 2:12.

The Heading (26:0)

NO NEW TERMS are introduced in the heading to Psalm 26, which is the second of four consecutive psalms (Pss. 25–28) to be attributed simply to David.[4]

Plea for Vindication (26:1)

THE NIV'S "VINDICATE ME" is an interpretive rendering of the Hebrew *špṭ*, which more literally means "judge me." While the ultimate result of the examination is the declaration of the psalmist's "blamelessness," the invitation to judge prepares the way for the following verbs of examination and scrutiny in 25:2 (*bḥn* ["test"]; *nsh* ["examine"]).[5] The psalmist is calling for examination, confident that his life meets the standards of righteousness required for vindication.

I have led a blameless life. The psalmist's claim to have led a blameless life is not an assertion of sinless perfection.[6] It is rather a claim to possess the appropriate attitude of "fear of God"—the awareness of one's sinfulness and absolute dependence on divine mercy—that constitutes the essential relationship with God that defines human righteousness in Israel's understanding. "Fear of the LORD" is not fear or terror, but it does have fearful overtones. Fearing God is having a clear understanding who God is and how my own sinful nature places me in deadly conflict with his nature, and it is knowing that my only hope is divine grace and mercy. Thus, when the psalmist goes on to describe the basis of his claim of "blamelessness," it is this attitude of dependence that we must keep in mind.

I have trusted in the LORD without wavering. The psalmist's expression of firm trust in Yahweh must be understood against the background of the fear of Yahweh just outlined. Verse 1 defines the kind of "blameless life" that will survive Yahweh's scrutiny *not* in terms of sinless perfection but as "unwavering trust" in God. Literally, the psalmist declares, "I have trusted in Yahweh; I will not wobble." This is not just a past act of firm trust but a lifestyle that will continue unshaken into the future.

Submission to Divine Examination (26:2–7)

TEST ME ... **try me** ... **examine**.... The repeated synonyms for testing drive home the psalmist's willing submission to God's examination.[7] The closest parallel to this threefold repetition of testing occurs in 17:3, where

---

4. See comments on the heading of Ps. 3.

5. See further comments on divine testing and scrutiny at 11:4 and 17:3.

6. See comments at 15:2–5.

7. See comments on divine examination at 11:4–6 and 17:1–5.

two of the three verbs are the same as used here (cf. *bḥn* ["probe"] ... *pqd* ["examine"] ... *ṣrp* ["test"] ... in 17:3 with *bḥn* ["test"] ... *nsh* ["try"] ... *ṣrp* ["examine"] in 26:2).[8] The context in Psalm 17 is similar, for there too the psalmist invites divine scrutiny and affirms innocent behavior (cf. 17:3–5).[9] Yahweh looks on the interior motivation of humans insofar as he examines the psalmist's "heart" (lit., "my kidneys")[10] and "mind" (lit., "my heart," which in Hebrew is the center of reflection and decision making). By offering thesc parts of life to the divine gaze the psalmist is demonstrating complete openness.

Your love is ever before me. Once again Psalm 26 links back to Psalm 25 by the use in the two halves of this verse of God's *ḥesed* (NIV "love") and his *ʾemet* (NIV "truth). In 25:10, these terms define the "way" of Yahweh in which the psalmist sought to walk: "All the ways of the LORD are *ḥesed* and *ʾemet* for those who keep the demands of his covenant." Here the psalmist claims to be walking continually[11] in the presence of Yahweh's *ḥesed* and *ʾemet*.[12]

As discussed in Psalm 25, these two terms mean something more than the NIV translation immediately suggests. *Ḥesed* describes the fierce loyalty and commitment that marks Yahweh's loyalty to his covenant relationship with his people (and ought to mark his people's relationship to him). Similarly, *ʾemet* is not merely "truth" but an "enduring faithfulness," as the NIV renders it in 25:10. Clearly the foundation of the psalmist's hope and security is not personal integrity and sinlessness but Yahweh's fierce loyalty and enduring faithfulness, which provide a way for essentially sinful humans—who acknowledge their complete dependence on Yahweh's mercy and grace—to continue to walk in his presence.

I do not sit with deceitful men. In a passage reminiscent of 1:1, the psalmist introduces a "negative confession" or "protestation of innocence" similar to that found in Psalm 15 in preparation for entering the temple precincts. By offering

---

8. The root *bḥn* ("test, examine, probe") appears twice in 11:4–5; also alongside the verb *pqd* in Job 7:18.

9. Note the similar thought expressed in different words in 17:5, which declares: "My feet have not *slipped*" (*bal namoṭu*); cf. 26:1: "I have trusted *without wavering*" (*loʾ ʾemʿad*).

10. It is interesting that the kidneys figured prominently in the ritual of sacrifice practiced throughout the ancient Near East. When animals were sacrificed, the kidneys and the surrounding fat were burned on the altar to the deity. Because of their inaccessibility deep in the inner recesses of the abdominal cavity, the kidneys provided an apt metaphor for the deep inward recesses where humans sought to hide their sin.

11. The Hithpael stem in which the verb *hlk* appears here can emphasize the repeated nature of an action, as in Esther, when Mordecai constantly walks back and forth before the house of women where Esther is being kept because he is concerned for her welfare and wants to know how she is faring (Est. 2:11).

12. The term *ḥesed* appears as well in 25:6 and 7; while *ʾemet* is found in 25:5.

specific examples of innocent behavior, he is expanding on the preceding claim, "I walk continually in your truth" (26:3b). Like 1:1 the protestation is a series of statements disassociating the psalmist from certain categories of persons: "deceitful men",[13] "hypocrites,"[14] "the assembly of evildoers,"[15] and "the wicked." Unlike Psalm 1, there is no attempt here to describe progressive enmeshment with evil (cf. 1:1, "walk ... stand ... sit"). Rather, by a repeated alternation between perfect and imperfect verb forms, the poet stresses past, present, and continuing avoidance of evil associations—(lit.) "I have not sat ... I will not consort ... I have hated ... I will not sit."[16]

I wash my hands in innocence. Even today at the approaches to the Western Wall[17] in Jerusalem, provision is made for worshipers to wash their hands before entering the holy space demarcated by barriers. We also know that the southern steps leading up to the Temple Mount contained numerous "ritual baths," where worshipers could cleanse themselves before entering to worship. The claim to have washed one's hands adds support to the interpretation of Psalm 26 as being related to pilgrimage and temple worship.

While not identical, the word "innocence" (*niqqayon*) is from the same root as the term translated "innocent" (*neqi*) in 24:4. Innocence is associated

---

13. The word used for "men" here appears only in plural forms; its singular form is unknown. The term means distinctly male in gender rather than a more generic "human." The word appears most frequently in phrases such as *mete mispar* ("a countable [small] number of men") and *mete meᶜaṭ* ("a few men"), which emphasize small numbers. The phrase *mete šawᵓ* appears in Job 11:11, describing the category of males characterized by falsehood.

14. The term *naᶜalamim* is not well understood. The form is a Niphal participle masculine plural from the root *ᶜlm* ("hidden"). The force of the Niphal stem in this case appears to be passive, so that the literal sense of the word is "those who are hidden." In 1 Kings 10:3, the singular *neᶜalam* describes the difficult philosophical issues raised by the Queen of Sheba in her conversation with Solomon, for whom no matter was too *difficult* to interpret. The implication seems to be issues whose true nature is not immediately apparent on the surface. In relation to humans, this may mean those who are not transparent in their relationships with others, who keep their true feelings and motives hidden.

15. A wordplay may be at work in the use of the term *mereᶜim* ("evildoers"). The similar word *mereᶜim* ("intimate, close friends") shares the identical consonantal text and differs only in a single vowel point.

16. The whole confession is bracketed at beginning and end with verbs of sitting that exhibit the same alternation between perfect-imperfect, past-future: "I have not sat ... I will not sit." This gives the whole statement a sort of completeness of effect.

17. The Wailing Wall is the western supporting wall of the Temple Mount, on which the temples of Solomon and Herod originally stood. Since access to the top of the Temple Mount (now the site of the Islamic shrines the Mosque of Omar and the Al Aksah Mosque) is officially prohibited for Orthodox Jews, the Western Wall provides the closest encounter now available with the ancient temple. As a result it has become a particularly revered place of worship for the international Jewish community.

with the "hands/palms" (24:4, *neqi kappayim*; 26:6, *ʾerḥaṣ beniqqayon kappay*). The identical phrase found in 26:6 occurs also in 73:13, where (as in 24:4) "innocent hands" are associated with a "pure heart."[18] The linkages between these three passages add weight to the idea of a pilgrimage/temple context and provide additional support for thematic linkage of Psalms 23–30.

I go about your altar. Now prepared to enter the temple precincts by the ritual cleansing of the hands, the pilgrim psalmist walks about the altar while "proclaiming aloud" the praise of Yahweh and telling his "wonderful deeds"[19] (26:7). Like the even more cryptic passage in 118:27 ("with boughs in hand, join in the festal procession up to the horns of the altar"), this verse may open a vague window on the practice of worship in the temple. The psalmist's participation in the ritual act of circling the altar and proclaiming praise (26:7) leads directly to the central profession of love for Yahweh's house that stands at the heart of this psalm (26:8).[20]

Standing in the Presence of Yahweh (26:8–11)

I LOVE THE house where you live. Caught up in the act of temple worship (perhaps for the first time, if these are truly the words of a postexilic pilgrim), the psalmist is filled by a sense of love for the temple as the place where God and humans come together.[21] The successful completion of the long journey to Jerusalem, the excitement of joining with the international community of the faithful, and the wonder of sinful humans being allowed to stand in the very presence of the glory (26:8b) of Yahweh[22] are almost overwhelming. That the temple is the "house" where Yahweh's glory "dwells" is clearly established by a variety of passages (esp. 2 Chron. 7:1–3; Ezek. 43:4–5; 44:4). Ezekiel also speaks of praising the "glory of the LORD" in his dwelling place (Ezek. 3:12), while Psalm 29:9 records the response of the

18. Although the Hebrew words for "pure" employed in these verses are not from the same root (24:4, from *brr*; in 73:13, from *nkh*), the thought world expressed is similar. The connection of a pure heart and innocent hands in the context of worship preparation is striking and certainly is a way of stressing inward and outward integrity.

19. See the discussion of the "wonderful works of Yahweh" in the commentary on Ps. 9:1–3.

20. Circling about a central cult object is also part of the *Haj* ("pilgrimage") in Islam. There the faithful individuals join with the large international congregation of pilgrims in circling the Kaaba—the sacred shrine in Mecca—as one of the first activities of the pilgrimage experience.

21. Cf. Ps. 24, where the two halves bring together the worshiping community and the victorious God.

22. For a further discussion of the "glory" of God, see "Responding to divine holiness" in the Bridging Contexts section on Ps. 5.

company of gathered worshipers to the theophanic approach of Yahweh as storm: "and in his temple all cry, 'Glory!'"[23] The reference in 26:8 to the "house" of Yahweh links this psalm backward and forward with the group of thematically related Psalms 23–30.

Do not take away my soul along with sinners. If this is understood as the voice of one taking asylum in the temple, then the plea is that the psalmist will be judged worthy of refuge and be allowed to remain in the temple. We know that once an individual had claimed asylum in the temple, a determination had to be made as to the legitimacy of the request. If it was determined to be a just request, the individual was allowed to remain until the trial date; if not, then asylum was denied and the individual executed.[24] Thus, the psalmist's plea not to be taken away along with sinners speaks to the possibility of being declared guilty and asylum being denied.

In the literary context of the postexilic community, the "bloodthirsty"[25] schemers and bribers from whom the psalmist wishes to be disassociated would be understood as (1) the pagans among whom the exiles lived, and (2) those elements of the Jewish community who had accommodated themselves to pagan society in ways detrimental to their own people.[26] The verb "take away" (*ʾsp* ["gather as in harvest"]) clearly refers to divine action rather than human agency. This allows the broader interpretation that the psalmist desires to be distinguished from those whom God judges and destroys. The psalmist's final plea for redemption (26:11), based on a "blameless life," fits this context as well.[27]

---

23. See my discussion of the temple as Yahweh's dwelling, "ישׁב," *NIDOTTE*, 2:550–51.

24. Cf. Ex. 21:13–14; 1 Kings 1:50–53; 2:28–30.

25. The expression *ʾanše damim* appears five times in the biblical text: four times in the Psalter (Pss. 26:9; 55:23; 59:2; and 139:19), and once in Prov. 29:10. Perhaps this term originally described those who wished to consummate a blood vendetta upon an *innocent* person seeking asylum. By the time of the postexilic period, these passages would have been broadened to include all those who represented enemies of God (see esp. Ps. 139:19–22). David is called a "man of blood" twice by Shimei son of Gera, descendant of Saul, as David fled Jerusalem before the troops of Absalom (2 Sam. 16:7–8). This accusation attempts to put David into the category of the *ʾanše damim*, who are guilty of spilling innocent blood. Later, David's desire to build a temple for Yahweh is frustrated because, according to Yahweh, David has poured out blood (*damim*) before God in his many military campaigns (1 Chron. 22:6–10; 28:3). He is not, however, called a "man of blood" in this context.

26. See, e.g., the venal judges who seek to seduce Susanna in the Apocryphal additions to Daniel.

27. One other piece of evidence in support of a postexilic reading of the psalm is the use in 26:12 of the term *maqhelim* (NIV "great assembly"). Although the noun is a plural form, the NIV chooses to translate it as a singular reference to the gathering at the Jerusalem temple. Might this plural form instead refer to the plural "places of assembly" among the exilic communities (i.e., the synagogues)?

I lead a blameless life. The psalmist returns to the protestations of innocence with which he began (cf. 26:1). If his plea for divine examination issues in the expected decree of vindication, then the recognition of a blameless life lays the sure foundation of hope for redemption ("redeem me")[28] through divine grace.

Confident Expectation (26:12)

THE PSALM ENDS—as do many of the laments and pleas for deliverance—with a statement of the psalmist's firm conviction that God will act in his behalf. Elsewhere we hear of the fear engendered when the narrator's feet are in danger of "slipping" (cf. Deut. 32:35; Pss. 17:5; 37:31; 73:2; 121:3); like a mountain climber crossing a snowy crevice on an aluminum ladder, each step is precious. Here, however, because of God's protective guidance the psalmist's feet "stand on level ground" (26:12), and all fear of slipping is gone. As a result, the psalmist's praise of Yahweh wells forth in the "great assembly" (lit., "assemblies").[29]

VINDICATE ME. The idea of vindication (26:1) is associated with judging. In Psalm 26 the verb used is *špṭ* ("judge"), the same root behind the name of the "judges" (*šopeṭ/šopeṭim*), who delivered Israel during the period of the settlement. The NIV translates this verb as "vindicate" (cf. also 1 Sam. 24:15; Pss. 35:24; 43:1). The thinking behind this translation is that when the innocent are "judged," they will be declared "not guilty" in public and thus experience vindication. But it is possible for a person judged to be declared "guilty," so the translation as vindication is interpretive and dependent on the interpreter's reading of the individual context.[30]

Perhaps more clearly related to the idea of "vindication" is the verbal root *ṣdq* ("declare righteous"; cf. Job 11:2, "Is this talker to be vindicated/declared

---

28. The link between this singular plea for redemption and the similar plural plea at the end of the preceding Ps. 25:22 ("redeem Israel, O God") is clear. In the postexilic reading of such psalms, singular voices could be understood as mirroring the collective concerns of all Israel.

29. The NIV's translation of *maqhelim* as "great assembly" flies in the face of the fact the word is plural and the adjective "great" does not appear here. It is at least possible that the postexilic pilgrim, anticipating ultimate return to the Diaspora setting removed from the Jerusalem temple, here promises to spread praise of Yahweh among the exilic gathering places—the synagogues.

30. The near synonym *dyn* ("judge, decide") is also translated "vindication" by the NIV in Gen. 30:6; Pss. 54:1; 135:14.

righteous?"). Nouns from the root *ṣdq* are translated by the NIV as "vindication" or "vindicator" in Psalms 24:5; 35:27; Isaiah 50:8; 54:17; Jeremiah 51:10. Obviously, when a person who claims to be innocent is declared "righteous" in a legal decision, vindication has taken place.

The whole idea of "vindication" is that a *public* acknowledgment of righteousness takes place. The central struggle of the poetic sections of Job is for a public acknowledgment of Job's righteousness. Job is willing to lose all—family, possessions, health, even life—if only God will appear and acknowledge to Job's friends what he (and the reader) already know to be true, namely, that Job is "blameless and upright." This public pronouncement does finally take place for Job (Job 42:7–9), but only after he is confronted by God himself and forced to admit that his desire is of little consequence in light of God's awesome presence in all his glory (42:1–6).

Although vindication is clearly a desire of the psalmist and has often sustained martyrs willing to die rather than give up their faith, both Job and Daniel warn the faithful that in some circumstances, public acknowledgment of righteousness may be impossible. Daniel's three friends Shadrach, Meshach, and Abednego articulate this clearly when, faced by the blazing furnace, they refuse to bow to idols with a radical affirmation of their faith: "If we are thrown into the blazing furnace, the God we serve is able to save us from it, and he will rescue us from your hand, O king. But *even if he does not*, we want you to know, O king, that we will not serve your gods or worship the image of gold you have set up" (Dan. 3:17–18, italics added). As it turns out, the three men are saved and their faith is vindicated, but their statement clearly separates their faithfulness from any necessary public vindication.

Divine scrutiny. The psalmist invites divine examination, confident of his blameless character. This motif appears in other psalms as well (e.g., 7:6–9; 11:4–6; 14:2–3; 17:2–5). God is judge, who knows the outer acts and inward thoughts of humans; thus, he is able to determine without error the relation of each human to *mišpaṭ*—what ought to have occurred in each circumstance. See the discussion of "Yahweh the Examiner" in the comments on Ps. 11:4–6.

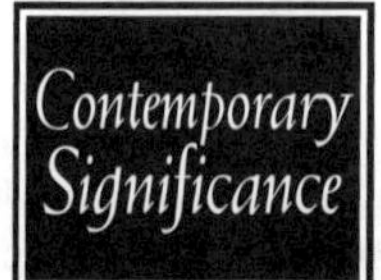

LIVING A BLAMELESS LIFE. The psalmist claims to have led a "blameless" life (26:1, 11). As we have already seen, this does not mean a perfectly sinless life but a life grounded in "fear of the LORD"—acknowledgment of one's absolute dependence on the gracious mercy of God (cf. comments on 26:1, 11). The psalmist unpacks to an extent what it means to live "blamelessly." Let us consider these attitudes and actions and consider how they might relate to our own attempts to live faithful lives before God.

Trust in Yahweh without wavering. The first element of blameless living is an attitude of unwavering trust in God. This foundational attitude undergirds all we think, say, and do. Unwavering trust enables us to do things we might not ordinarily attempt. Sometimes this may mean we remain still and wait for God rather than relying on our own strength (cf. 27:14). Other times it might encourage us to leap out in faith.

When my son was about two years old, he took swimming lessons. I can still remember him standing dripping wet on the side of the pool, preparing to leap into the pool where I waited to catch him. His eyes shifted back and forth from the water to my eyes, and then he jumped, arms straining to reach mine. I pulled him into my arms and felt him shivering more with excitement than the cold. That took a lot of trust, and I was amazed to think he trusted me so much. Later that trusting leap communicated such confidence to my son that he demonstrated little fear of the water and was likely to plunge into the water at any time, even without anyone to catch him. Trust can give us the confidence to attempt things that seem beyond us.

Walk continually in your truth. The second element the psalmist describes in a blameless life is related to the first. An unwavering trust in God leads one to shape one's life continually by recourse to God's "truth." Again, we must remember that the Hebrew word *ʾemet* has more the sense of "enduring reliability" than what we normally think of as "truth." This is supported by the use of *ḥesed* ("lasting loyalty") in the preceding parallel line. Yahweh is trustworthy because all his dealings with us are characterized by "lasting loyalty" and "enduring reliability."

What makes for a blameless life, however, is to commit oneself to a continual relationship with this reliable God. The psalmist claims to "walk around continually," immersed in the reliable character of God. This kind of relationship rubs off on others so that they too become reliable, loyal individuals. May it be so with us.

Avoiding evil associations. In contrast to continual association with a reliable God, the psalmist avoids enduring linkages with those whose lives repudiate the faithfulness displayed by God. We are not talking about causal or even redemptive association here. Clearly Jesus purposefully associated with "sinners" as a way of revealing God's love for them while calling them to repentance and salvation. The verbs employed in these verses of Ps. 26 (*yšb* ["sit, dwell]; *bwʾ* ["enter in, have dealings with"]) describe more extended, intimate relations. If one is walking "continuously" in the presence of God's reliable love, then the lifestyle of the deceitful, hypocrites, evildoers, and the wicked is no longer attractive.

I love the house where you dwell. The one who lives a blameless life loves the dwelling place of God. Immersing oneself in the things of God and avoiding those things that counter or undermine his purposes make entering his presence more appealing. As the Gospel of John affirms, "Everyone who does evil hates the light, and will not come into the light for fear that his deeds will be exposed. But whoever lives by the truth comes into the light, so that it may be seen plainly that what he has done has been done through God" (John 3:20–21).

Where we live and where we spend our time has a lot to say about who we are and what we value. Do we love the house where God dwells? Or are we content to rub shoulders with the rich and famous, who seek pleasure, power, and wealth as the defining values of their lives? This psalm calls us to reflect on our own lives. If we were to open our lives up to the honest examination of heart and mind described in 26:2, would we find the same indicators of a blameless life that the psalmist claims? What changes would you have to make to be able to say, "I walk continually in relationship with your enduring reliability"?

Living a confident life. The psalmist is so confident that we may wonder how we could ever gain such confidence in our own acceptability to God. Whenever we are forced (usually against our will) to take a close look at the interior reality of our lives, we may not see much of enduring value there. Thankfully, however, we are not talking about earning God's acceptance through perfectly righteous behavior. We know enough if we are honest to dismiss that possibility from the start. Our only hope is the same kind of "unwavering trust" our psalmist speaks of in 26:1.

Our trust should be in what Paul calls "the righteousness from God" (Rom. 3:5, 21–24)—the righteousness God confers on those who accept salvation offered through Jesus Christ. Such righteousness (*dikaiosyne*) is a legal term similar to that used in the Old Testament (*ṣedaqah*). Humans receive "righteousness" from God in that they are declared "not guilty" by God and thus legally "justified."[31] As Romans 5:1–5 makes abundantly clear, this righteousness gives us confidence to stand in the presence of holy God without fear and to anticipate with great joy "the hope of the glory of God."

---

31. The Greek verb for "justify" (*dikaioo*) has the same sense of "acquitted, declared not guilty" associated with the Heb. verb *ṣdq*.

Psalm 27

OF DAVID.

1 The LORD is my light and my salvation—
whom shall I fear?
The LORD is the stronghold of my life—
of whom shall I be afraid?
2 When evil men advance against me
to devour my flesh,
when my enemies and my foes attack me,
they will stumble and fall.
3 Though an army besiege me,
my heart will not fear;
though war break out against me,
even then will I be confident.

4 One thing I ask of the LORD,
this is what I seek:
that I may dwell in the house of the LORD
all the days of my life,
to gaze upon the beauty of the LORD
and to seek him in his temple.
5 For in the day of trouble
he will keep me safe in his dwelling;
he will hide me in the shelter of his tabernacle
and set me high upon a rock.
6 Then my head will be exalted
above the enemies who surround me;
at his tabernacle will I sacrifice with shouts of joy;
I will sing and make music to the LORD.

7 Hear my voice when I call, O LORD;
be merciful to me and answer me.
8 My heart says of you, "Seek his face!"
Your face, LORD, I will seek.
9 Do not hide your face from me,
do not turn your servant away in anger;
you have been my helper.

Do not reject me or forsake me,
O God my Savior.
10 Though my father and mother forsake me,
the LORD will receive me.
11 Teach me your way, O LORD;
lead me in a straight path
because of my oppressors.
12 Do not turn me over to the desire of my foes,
for false witnesses rise up against me,
breathing out violence.

13 I am still confident of this:
I will see the goodness of the LORD
in the land of the living.
14 Wait for the LORD;
be strong and take heart
and wait for the LORD.

PSALM 27 IS in the final analysis a psalm of confidence (cf. 27:3d, 13a), although at its core it remains a desperate plea for divine presence in the midst of attack. The psalm is bracketed by declarations of confident trust (27:1–3, 13–14), which surround a central search for divine presence and deliverance (27:4–6, 7–12). In its concluding exhortation to "wait for the LORD; be strong and take heart and wait for the LORD" (27:14), the psalmist enjoins the reader to the same pattern of faithful endurance that he models in the body of the psalm: In the face of suffering and attack, the faithful continue to trust in Yahweh rather than their own devices.

The contrast between absolute confidence and desperate pleading is characteristic of many of the laments or pleas for deliverance in the Psalter and must have resonated strongly with the situation of the postexilic community, who treasured, preserved, and transmitted these psalms to subsequent generations. The central part of Psalm 27 shares the thematic interest in "dwelling in the house of the LORD" that characterizes the whole group of Psalms 23–30.[1] Structurally the psalm exhibits four sections: confidence in Yahweh against the enemy (27:1–3), the desire to dwell in the house of Yahweh (27:4–6), plea for deliverance from enemies (27:7–12), and confidence and encouragement (27:13–14).

1. Ps. 27:4–6; cf. 23:6; 24:3–6; 26:8; 28:2; 29:9; 30:0; see comments on 23:6.

The Heading (27:0)

PSALM 27 IS the third consecutive psalm to be attributed simply to David.[2] There are no new terms introduced in the heading.

Confidence in Yahweh (27:1–3)

YAHWEH IS DESCRIBED as the psalmist's "light," "salvation,"[3] and "stronghold of ... life."[4] In the affirming parallelism of verse 1, the first two phrases ("my light and my salvation") are paralleled by the expanded phrase "stronghold of my life," suggesting that these three terms provide nuances to the psalmist's understanding of Yahweh's protective role. Yahweh is the illuminating light that vanquishes the "[deep] shadow of death" (23:4) threatening the psalmist. That light marks out the "paths of righteousness" (cf. 23:3; 25:4, 9), along which God leads the faithful. Yahweh is also the life-saving stronghold that delivers the psalmist from the attacks of his enemies. Because of that guidance and protection, he is unafraid (27:1:b, d; cf. 23:4).[5]

The protective presence and care of Yahweh encourages the psalmist to stand confidently firm in the face of enemy attack (27:2–3). His enemies are depicted as ravening beasts seeking to "devour my flesh" (27:2), as an enemy military encampment (27:3a), and as declaring an all-out war (27:3c). In spite of the severity of the attack, the psalmist remains confident and unafraid, certain that the enemy attack will "stumble and fall" (27:2d).[6] The NIV's translation of *boṭeaḥ* as "I am confident" rather than the more usual "I am trusting" obscures the connection between this phrase and similar uses of the verb *bṭḥ* ("trust") in 25:2 and 26:1. The participial form used here emphasizes the immediate and continuing trust the psalmist is placing in Yahweh.

---

2. See the discussion of Davidic attribution in the introduction and comments on the heading of Ps. 3.

3. As we have seen in other contexts, *yešaᶜ* can also mean "deliverance." Cf. comments on the related word *yešuᶜah* at 3:1–2.

4. For a discussion of the concept of "refuge" and the terms related to it, see comments on 5:11–12; see also section "Refuge in the Psalms" in "Theology of the Psalms" in vol. 2 of this commentary.

5. When the psalmist in 27:1b, d asks, "Whom shall I fear ... of whom shall I be afraid?" the obvious answer is "Fear Yahweh, not humans!"

6. To "stumble" is the prelude to disaster as our psalm and the similar context in Ps. 9:3 ("My enemies turn back; they stumble and perish before you") indicate. In contrast, those who trust in Yahweh do *not* stumble or fall. "Though he stumble, he will not fall, for the LORD upholds him with his hand" (Ps. 37:24); "Great peace have they who love your law, and nothing can make them stumble" (119:165).

Desire to Dwell in the House of Yahweh (27:4–6)

I SEEK ... **that I may dwell in the house of the LORD.** The psalmist's deepest desires are to "seek" Yahweh and to "dwell" in his presence forever. The connections with the preceding group of psalms are obvious. Seeking Yahweh's face (27:4, 8) was the primary characteristic of the generation to be admitted to the holy hill of Yahweh in 24:6.

The idea of "seeking" Yahweh described here through the two parallel verbs *šʾl* ("ask") and *bqš* ("seek")[7] may have a more technical and ritual flavor than is immediately apparent. To ask of Yahweh and to seek his face can imply formal, ritual actions of seeking divine guidance within the context of worship.[8] To seek God in this way is not a matter of unfocused searching but a sign of commitment to the way of life he demands and provides. To "seek" false gods (as in 4:2) is to commit oneself to them. The faithful generation is made up of those who seek the face of Yahweh and commit themselves to him alone.

To gaze upon the beauty of the LORD. The psalmist is almost obsessed with Yahweh and wants always to be in his presence. Ancient monarchs were known on occasion to grant extravagant requests to their subjects. King Xerxes was so taken by Queen Esther that he invited her to ask what she wanted "even up to half the kingdom," and it would be given to her (Est. 5:3, 6). If asked such a question by Yahweh, the king, our psalmist has a ready reply: He wants to "dwell in the house of the LORD all the days of my life" (27:4). The psalmist desires to see firsthand the gracious kindness[9] of Yahweh, the host.

Dwelling in the house of Yahweh is not just an experience of aesthetic delight in the gracious hospitality of God. There is a protective benefit to the nearness of God. As the psalmist puts it, "He will keep me safe[10] ... he will hide me[11] ... in his dwelling[12] ... his tabernacle." Even at the moment of

---

7. The second occurrence of "seek" in v. 4 results from emending the Hebrew text *lebaqqer* ("inspect sacrifices") to *lebaqqeš* ("seek") by connection with the verb *ʾabaqqeš* ("I will seek") earlier in the verse.

8. See comments on *bqš* at 4:1–2, and especially footnote 11.

9. The emphasis in the phrase *benoʿam yhwh* (NIV "beauty of Yahweh") is on the gracious kindness of Yahweh as host, not the physical or essential beauty. One can observe kindness and grace as well as beauty.

10. A Qal imperfect from *ṣpn* ("store up, treasure; hide, shelter").

11. A Hiphil imperfect from *str* ("hide, secret").

12. The word is from *sukkah* "[temporary] shelter" with the unusual third masculine singular pronominal suffix *-oh* attached. Coupled with the parallel noun *ʾoholo* ("his tent") these phrases may refer to the mobile "tabernacle" shrine mentioned in the Exodus narratives. It is unlikely that these references to the "tent" reflect a premonarchical origin for this psalm. Certainly in its final form the composition is aware of the temple (cf. *hekalo* in 27:4). It is through the use of these terms that the psalmist brings the memory of the Exodus together with the current experience of pilgrimage to the temple.

greatest nearness to God there is a continuing awareness of the threat that life in the psalmist's world offers.

High upon a rock. Shifting metaphors, the psalmist describes Yahweh's protection in new terms: "[He will] set me high upon a rock." The Hebrew *ṣur* ("rock") more frequently refers to large boulders. God is frequently considered the psalmist's "rock" and as such provides firm footing and protective covering.[13] Being "set high" (from *rwm*) on a rock prepares the way for the image of the exaltation (also from *rwm*) of the psalmist's head above the enemies in 27:6. To be protected by Yahweh in the presence of the enemy (cf. 23:5) is to be exalted by association.

Will I sacrifice ... I will sing. Protection and exaltation lead to praise. Freed from fear of the enemy by the presence of Yahweh, the psalmist is free to sing praises and to offer sacrifices of thanksgiving to God.

Plea for Deliverance from Enemies (27:7–12)

A SHIFT TO second-person direct address of Yahweh signals the beginning of the next section of the psalm. The appearance of a string of imperative and negative jussive forms characterizes the psalmist's plea for deliverance laid before Yahweh.

Hear my voice. As in most pleas for deliverance, the section begins with the psalmist's entreaty to be heard ("Hear ... O LORD"). This cry underscores the reality of his suffering in spite of a strong confidence in Yahweh's saving nature. One does not cry out for relief when Yahweh is currently delivering or has already delivered.[14] The rest of the plea is divided into a desire for divine presence in the face of God's seeming absence (27:8–10), a desire for divine instruction in the right way (27:11), and a desire for divine vindication in the face of "false witnesses" (27:12).

Seek his face. Despite the textual difficulties in this passage,[15] it is clear that the psalmist is here expressing the heartfelt desire to come into the

---

13. See esp. comments on 18:1–3, where this term and others relating to the theme of refuge are discussed.

14. Note that the psalmist's cry to be heard mimics the fundamental call to Israel to hear and obey Yahweh (*šemaᶜ yiśraʾel* ["Hear, O Israel. . ."], Deut. 6:4; see also Deut. 4:1; 5:1; 6:3; 9:1; 20:3, most of which appear to be section headings recalling the primary call in 6:4). Outside the Psalter the phrase is used of Yahweh only in Deut. 33:7 ("Hear, O LORD, the cry of Judah"). Within the Psalter, the exact phrase *šemaᶜ yhwh* occurs only twice; here and in Ps. 30:10 ("Hear, O LORD, and be merciful to me"). A similar use of the alternative form of the Qal imperative (*šimᶜah*) does occur once in 17:1 ("Hear, O LORD, my righteous plea"); on five other occasions similar constructions appear, although with significant variations in order (cf. 39:12; 84:8; 102:1; 130:2; 143:1). This seems a rather audacious use of the imperative to call Yahweh to obedience to *his* covenant obligations.

15. Literally, the text reads, "Of you has said my heart, "Seek *my* face!""

presence of Yahweh. What the heart has communicated as its deepest desire ("Seek his face!"), the psalmist has acted upon ("Your face, LORD, I will [continue to] seek").[16]

Do not hide your face from me. The psalmist's search can only succeed if Yahweh continues to allow himself to be known. In 27:5 the psalmist hoped Yahweh would "hide me in the shelter of his tabernacle," allowing him to live in God's protective presence. Now, having gained access to the house of Yahweh, he pleads that the divine host will not absent himself.

Do not . . . forsake me. In two parallel lines the psalmist entreats Yahweh not to turn him away in anger or to reject and abandon him.[17] The prospect of divine abandonment is even more difficult because of his past experience of Yahweh as "my helper" (27:9c) and "my Savior" (27:9e). Despite the continued experience of divine absence, the psalmist is confident this is not proof of abandonment but of Yahweh's remaining a firm hope—even when parents might fall away (27:10).

Teach me your way. Resuming a theme characteristic of this collection of consecutive psalms (Pss. 23–30), the psalmist seeks divine instruction ("teach me")[18] and guidance ("lead me")[19] in the proper "way" (27:11).[20] Here the reason for finding the right path is related to the enemy attack that the psalmist is experiencing. The enemies are described as "my oppressors" (27:11), "foes" who desire the psalmist's defeat (27:12a), and "false witnesses . . . breathing out violence"[21] (27:12b-c). This verse makes the original setting of the psalm seem like a case of false accusation in the courts. This gives further definition to the "evil men" of 27:2, who advance like a ravenous horde of locusts to devour the psalmist, and the "enemies"

---

16. The psalmist's "seeking" Yahweh connects back to his earlier "seeking" to dwell in Yahweh's house in 27:4, but it also provides links to the approved "generation of those who seek him" in 24:6.

17. The string of negative jussive forms ties the whole entreaty together as a unit.

18. Cf. the similar use of the verb "teach, instruct" in 25:8, 12, to describe the instruction of both sinners and the one who fears Yahweh in the right "way."

19. The verb "lead" appears also in 23:3.

20. The "straight path" the psalmist seeks has thematic linkages throughout this group of psalms, beginning with the "paths of righteousness" in 23:3. The "straight path" of 27:11 is also reminiscent of the "level ground" on which the psalmist confidently stands in 26:12, since both use the same Heb. word *mišor* ("straight, level").

21. The Hebrew is difficult and interpreted variously as "a violent witness" (Hosfeld and Zenger, *Die Psalmen*, 174 [*Gewaltzeuge*]), "raging" (ibid., 173 [*wüten*]), or the NIV's "breathing out violence"—the last two both taking the word from the root *ypḥ* ("gasp for breath; groan") or *pwḥ* ("blow; blast"). The "violence" these enemies breathe out is the Heb. *ḥamas* ("violence that spills blood"). See also 25:19, where this same word describes the "fierce" hatred the enemy has for the psalmist.

of 27:6 in whose presence he is exalted by the protective presence of Yahweh.

Confidence and Encouragement (27:13–14)

I AM STILL CONFIDENT.[22] In this final section the psalmist returns to the confident stance of verses 1–3. He "believes" or "is convinced" that he will see the "goodness of the LORD[23] in the land of the living"—a clear reference to an expectation to be delivered in this life.[24]

Wait for the LORD. The psalmist's final word is an encouragement to the reader/listener to take heart from his experience and to wait confidently for God's deliverance in similar circumstances. Verse 14 is bracketed at the beginning and end with the identical phrase "wait for the LORD" (*qawweh ʾel yhwh*)—the repetition making the emphasis plain. There is a sense of tense, anxious expectation in *qawweh*—a sort of sitting on the edge of your seat. In between these repeated encouragements stands an exhortation to a confident attitude among those who wait expectantly.

The two verbs "be strong" (*ḥzq*) and "take heart" (*ʾmṣ*) are the same used in Joshua to encourage the Israelites as they cross the Jordan River to take the Promised Land.[25] The resonances with the conclusion of the Exodus wanderings and the anticipation of entering the Promised Land serve again

---

22. The base text underlying *BHS* (i.e., Codex Leningradensis) begins 27:13 with the Heb. word *luleʾ* ("unless"), which normally introduces a protasis clause responding to a preceding apodosis (if) clause. Because no apodosis is present prior to this verse and because the peculiar marking of this word in the Masoretic Text indicates strong suspicion regarding its presence—a suspicion confirmed by its absence in a number of manuscripts—most commentators and translations omit it entirely.

23. The more unusual form *ṭub* ("goodness, well-being, success") links Ps. 27 back to 25:7 and forward to 31:19, which also describe the goodness of Yahweh. That goodness (using the more common form) appears also in 23:6 and 25:8.

24. The phrase "land of the living" occurs some fifteen times in the Old Testament, seven of which are in Ezekiel (Ezek. 26:20; 32:23, 24, 25, 26, 27, 32), four in the Psalms (Pss. 27:13; 52:5; 116:9; 142:5), two in Isaiah (Isa. 38:11; 53:8), and one each in Job (Job 28:43) and Jeremiah (Jer. 11:19). In all cases it clearly refers to this present life as opposed to the vague nonexistence of Sheol.

25. Coupled as imperatives of encouragement these verbs occur twelve times in the Old Testament: once when God directs Moses to encourage Joshua (Deut. 3:28), three times in Moses' actual instructions to Joshua (Deut. 31:6, 7, 23), five times in Joshua's instructions to Israel in the conquest of the land (Josh. 1:6, 7, 9, 18; 10:25), twice as David encourages Solomon to complete the building of the temple (1 Chron. 22:13; 28:20), and a final time in Hezekiah's instructions to his troops in the face of the Assyrian invasion (2 Chron. 32:7). These verbs are also paired in slightly different constructions in 2 Chron. 11:7; 13:7; Ps. 31:25; Isa. 35:3; Nah. 2:1, and these roots occur together as nouns in Isa. 28:2 and Amos 2:14.

to connect this psalm with the continuing motif of wandering and pilgrimage characteristic of the whole group of Psalms 23–30.

A NEW EXODUS. The Exodus theme is prominent in a number of psalms, especially in the fourth book of the Psalter (Pss. 90–106). Here in Psalm 27, a subtle reference to the dwelling of Yahweh as *sukkah* ("booth, temporary dwelling") and *ʾohel* ("tent")[26] suggests a connection with the desert wandering of the post-Sinai Israelites. In the exilic and postexilic periods, the Diaspora community, drawing on the prophets, understood their captivity as akin to the period of bondage in Egypt. In Isaiah 48:10, the prophet refers to the testing of Israel by exile as a "furnace" of affliction—an image commonly used to refer to Egyptian bondage.[27] The desert wandering on the way from Egypt to Canaan is used as an image of the return from exile in Isaiah 43:16–21.

This connection of two periods of bondage outside the Promised Land—Exodus and Exile—is intended as a message of hope. As God was not prevented by the power of Egypt from calling his people to himself and providing them with a secure future, so the exiles could trust that God's power was sufficient to recall and reestablish them from exile.[28]

Seeking Yahweh's face. The psalmist vows to seek Yahweh's face (27:8) in terms that describe a wholehearted commitment to God, usually in a time of great difficulty. David, confronted by a three-year-long famine devastating the land, "sought the face of the LORD" in order to avert the famine and the sure destruction it threatened (2 Sam. 21:1). Hosea 5:15 explains that the destruction of Israel and Judah at the hands of Assyria was intended to convince them of their guilt so that "they will seek my face; in their misery they will earnestly seek me."

The phrase "to seek God" is often used for a technical "inquiry" of the deity to determine the appropriate response in one's present circumstances. The Hebrew word ordinarily used for "seek" in such cases (*drš*, "inquire about; seek information about") is not the one used in our text. Rather, our text has the Hebrew verb *bqš*, which means "request, ask for." This verb can also mean "entreat, plead for," as in the book of Esther when Haman "pleads for his

26. The NIV's translation of *ʾohel* as "tabernacle" interprets the term here as a reference to the *miškan* ("tabernacle"), which is also called the "Tent of Meeting" (*ʾohel moʿed*).

27. Egypt is called an "iron-smelting furnace" in Deut. 4:20; 1 Kings 8:51; Jer. 11:4.

28. See comments on 23:5–6 and the Bridging Contexts and Contemporary Significance sections for this psalm.

life" after his plot against the Jews was revealed to King Xerxes (Est. 7:7; cf. also 5:6, noted above, where the word "request" is the nominal form *baqqaša* of the same root *bqš* and is paralleled by the noun *šaʾelah* ["petition"]). In Psalm 27:4 these same two roots express the psalmist's desire to dwell in Yahweh's house: "One thing I ask [*šʾl*] of the LORD, this is what I seek [*bqš*]."

The implication of 27:8 is that the psalmist is not making an inquiry of Yahweh but is earnestly pleading for the "face" of Yahweh itself—his very presence. What he desires more than anything, requests, and pleads is for Yahweh to be present with him. Thus, the next verse continues: "Do not hide *your face* from me" (27:9). In this light, when David "seeks the face of the LORD" because of the famine, he is not seeking understanding but the reassuring presence of God, who has not abandoned him even in the midst of suffering. Similarly, God through Hosea wants his people to realize their sin through the punishment of exile and to seek, plead for, and desire more than anything the presence of God among them.

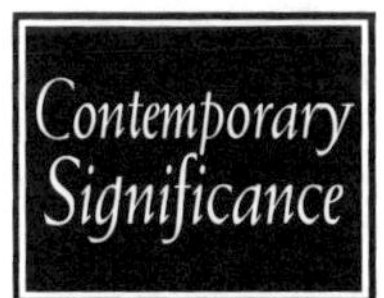

THE STRONGHOLD OF **my life.** How do we find a rock solid place of confidence when all else is swirling about us? It is this ability to stand confidently that sets the faithful apart and gives testimony to the presence of God in our lives. Where or to whom do you go when life seems too much to handle? Perhaps to your spouse or a close friend, a trusted minister, your parents? For the psalmist, God is the stronghold of his life—the secure place when all else fails.

Too often human relationships fail—because they are human. Many of us have felt betrayed or abandoned by friends, spouses, and even parents. The statistics are not good. Divorce is on the increase even among "born-again Christians."[29] Prominent news reports have detailed instances of physical, emotional, and sexual abuse of children by religious leaders and Christian parents. When we place our hopes and reliance on fallible human beings, we are bound to experience failure. When all our human resources are so unreliable, where do we turn for unshakable support?

According to our psalmist, Yahweh is the one reliable support—the one who accepts us even "though my father and mother forsake me" (27:10). There is no more crushing experience than for a child to be abandoned by his or her parents. Orphan children—even those adopted by loving and caring families—are often obsessed to know why their birth mother

29. See the report of George Barna in *Southern California Christian Times* 11/2 (February 2000): 1, 11.

"abandoned" them. Were they so unlovable, unwanted, that even their mother gave them away? The recent legislation to open adoption records to such adult orphans, even against the wishes of the birth parents, illustrates the obsessive power such questions hold. But God is ultimately the only reliable source of care and acceptance. Many abandoned children who have been unable to answer the questions of their birth and loss of parental love have found in God a loving parent who does not forsake them.

Besides being our secure refuge, God is also "light." Light illumines the darkness. We know scientifically that darkness is the absence of light. Where light is, darkness cannot exist. We use flashlights only when it is dark and we need to find our way or know what is around us. We don't have "flashdarks" that dispel light!

As a child I remember a powerful fear of the dark. We lived in a country setting, and at night there were no streetlights to dilute the absolute blackness. On occasion I would be sent at night on an errand to our barn—maybe fifty yards from the house. I remember running as fast as I could between house and barn to spend as little time as possible in the dark.

Two Sunday comic strips have done an especially good job of exploiting childhood fears of the dark. In one, my favorite, *Calvin and Hobbes*, the main characters, a small boy and his stuffed tiger, often find themselves marooned on the boy's bed while "monsters" whisper in the dark under the bed, hatching plans to get them. In the other, *Bloom County*, one of the children has a closet where all his anxieties live in the dark, threatening on occasion to break out in monstrous form to consume him.

Like our fears, these monsters and anxieties thrive in the dark, but they cannot survive in the light. Like a flashlight pointed at a persistent noise, light shows up our fears for what they really are. Imaginary monsters and inflated anxieties are reduced to reality. God, then, is for the psalmist (and for us) the light that illumines our way and reveals our fears and enemies for what they truly are in the light of God's power and care. This is not to say that all our fears are groundless or figments of our imaginations. The psalmist's enemies are very real. But God provides refuge in the face of real attacks and struggles.

Waiting for God. One of the most difficult aspects of faithful Christian living for me has been waiting for God. Too often I am impatient and want God to act *now*, on my schedule. Most often that is not how it happens. Waiting takes strength and demonstrates trust, courage, and endurance. Andrew Murray's collection of thirty-one daily meditations on the theme of waiting on God was particularly helpful to me in a time of personal difficulty. I have returned to this classic treatment many times. In response to this passage from Psalm 27:14, Murray writes:

> "Be strong and of good courage [NIV take heart]." These words are frequently found in connection with some great and difficult enterprise, in prospect of the combat with the power of strong enemies, and the utter insufficiency of all human strength. Is waiting on God a work so difficult, that such words are needed. . . ? Yes, indeed. The deliverance for which we often have to wait is from enemies, in whose presence we are so weak. The blessings for which we plead are spiritual and all unseen—things impossible with men—heavenly, supernatural, divine realities. Our heart may well faint and fail.[30]

The words "be strong and take heart" are words of challenge and encouragement to soldiers just before engaging in battle. This is how Moses and God exhorted Joshua before leading Israel into battle (Deut. 31:7, 23; Josh. 1:6, 7, 9, 18). In the same manner Joshua encouraged Israel before they faced the enemy (Josh. 10:25). David used these words when strengthening Solomon to assume the leadership of the kingdom (1 Chron. 22:13; 28:20), and so king Hezekiah exhorted his military officers when Sennacherib besieged Jerusalem (2 Chron. 32:7). These are words of preparation for action. Too often we find action preferable to waiting! Like Saul, we would rather take matters into our own hands and face the enemy boldly in our own strength rather than wait for God (1 Sam. 13:1–15).

Waiting on God is hard work. Yet, it is one way—perhaps the only way—of demonstrating God's strength manifest in our weakness. Whenever we rush frantically about trying to "do it" on our own, we in effect become "functional atheists," denying by our actions that God is active in our lives. Often to admit that we are powerless is the first step toward acknowledging God's strength unleashed in our lives. The well-known serenity prayer is one expression of this need to rely on God: "God, grant me the serenity to accept the things I cannot change, the courage to change the things I can, and the wisdom to know the difference." Acceptance is not resignation or despair but a step of trust and commitment. It means acknowledging my need to rely on God alone. It is an expression of the confidence that the psalmist of Psalm 27 mirrors in 27:13: "I am still confident of this: I will see the goodness of the LORD in the land of the living." He says this in the presence of enemies, even though God is not immediately apparent (27:7–9).

Sometimes this kind of confidence requires a different way of seeing. C. S. Lewis tells of his experience standing in a dark potter's shed on a sunny day. Through a chink in the wall a sunbeam probed its way into the dark interior of the shed. Lewis suggests it is two quite different things to look at the

30. Andrew Murray, *Waiting on God* (New York: Revell, n.d.), 46–47.

beam of light and how it interacts with the dark, illuminating only a small part of the shed, or to step into the light and look along the beam to its source.[31] Waiting for God is like standing in the dark but looking along the beam of light that comes from God. Knowing the source of light gives us confidence that outside the darkened sheds that describe our lives, light bathes the whole landscape. Light will not be overcome by the dark but will vanquish it. It is that kind of vision of God that gives us the courage to wait in confidence.

---

31. C. S. Lewis, "Meditation in a Toolshed," *God in the Dock* (Grand Rapids: Eerdmans, 1970), 212–15.

Psalm 28

OF DAVID.

1 To you I call, O LORD my Rock;
do not turn a deaf ear to me.
For if you remain silent,
I will be like those who have gone down to the pit.
2 Hear my cry for mercy
as I call to you for help,
as I lift up my hands
toward your Most Holy Place.

3 Do not drag me away with the wicked,
with those who do evil,
who speak cordially with their neighbors
but harbor malice in their hearts.
4 Repay them for their deeds
and for their evil work;
repay them for what their hands have done
and bring back upon them what they deserve.
5 Since they show no regard for the works of the LORD
and what his hands have done,
he will tear them down
and never build them up again.

6 Praise be to the LORD,
for he has heard my cry for mercy.
7 The LORD is my strength and my shield;
my heart trusts in him, and I am helped.
My heart leaps for joy
and I will give thanks to him in song.

8 The LORD is the strength of his people,
a fortress of salvation for his anointed one.
9 Save your people and bless your inheritance;
be their shepherd and carry them forever.

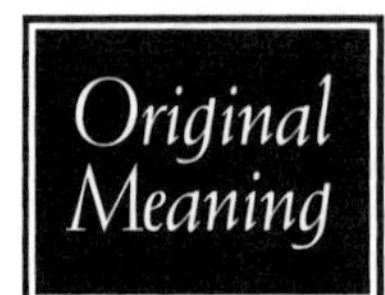

THIS BRIEF PSALM of only nine verses is a plea for deliverance by someone suffering the malice of enemies. The psalmist feels close to death (28:1) and seeks retribution from God on those who attack (28:3–5). The final two verses reinterpret the individual expressions of the original psalm to the corporate needs of the community—probably an indication of the reuse of this composition among the exilic and postexilic Diaspora. The psalm shares numerous links with the preceding group of Psalms 23–27 (esp. 27) and concludes with a plea for Yahweh to be Israel's "shepherd"—a plea that forms a sort of parenthesis around Psalms 23–28.[1]

The structure of the psalm exhibits four sections: an opening plea for deliverance (28:1–2), a call for retribution on the enemy (28:3–5), praise for deliverance (28:6–7), and a call for communal deliverance (28:8–9).

The Heading (28:0)

PSALM 28 IS the last in a series of four consecutive psalms (Pss. 25–28) that are simply attributed to David.[2] No new terms are introduced in this heading.

Opening Plea for Deliverance (28:1–2)

DRAWING ON THE characteristic silence and lack of aural acuity associated with deafness, the psalmist entreats Yahweh not to "turn a deaf ear" to the psalmist's cries. If God does "remain silent," the psalmist will "be like" those who descend to death in Sheol. He entreats Yahweh as "my Rock" (28:1), a characterization that links back to 27:5 and the picture there of being placed "high upon a rock" for protection. God is the psalmist's secure high place.

Hear my cry for mercy. Having established a context of need in verse 1, the psalmist proceeds to the plea proper in verse 2. The plea is for divine "favor"[3] and for "help," accompanied by a gesture of supplication—lifting up the hands[4] toward the temple (28:2).[5]

---

1. See comments in the *NIV Study Bible* notes to Ps. 28.

2. See comments on the heading of Ps. 3.

3. The NIV has "mercy" here. There is a subtle but significant difference to my way of thinking in "mercy" and "favor." The former is unmerited and undeserved, while the latter may be based on some perceived reason—such as Job's righteous behavior.

4. The lifting of the hands to God is a gesture of prayer (141:2) and can be associated either with praise (63:4; 134:2) or supplication (28:2; Lam. 2:19; 3:41).

5. The reference in this verse is to the "rear room of the temple where the holiness of Yahweh resides." The term *debir* is employed more generally in the ancient Near East to designate the rear room or inner niche "of a Syrian type of temple," which later came to be called in Hebrew parlance the "Holy of Holies"—*qodeš haqqedašim* (Holladay, *CHALOT*, 66; the NIV translates this phrase as "the Most Holy Place").

Call for Retribution (28:3–5)

DO NOT DRAG me away.[6] In a plea reminiscent of 26:9, the psalmist seeks to distinguish himself from the wicked and to avoid the punishment he thinks they so richly deserve.[7] The enemy are the "wicked" and "those who do evil," who use a facade of cordiality to mask an inner attitude of malice.[8] The lack of transparency exhibited by these opponents contrasts unfavorably with the expectation expressed for those who fear Yahweh in such passages as 17:3; 19:12–14; 26:2. God looks on the heart and expects one's attitudes, desires, and commitment to reflect consistency with one's outwardly observable actions.[9]

Repay them for their deeds. The psalmist is now free to call for divine judgment on the evildoers. In what is apparently an economic idiom, God is asked to (lit.) "pay them according to the work they have done." Wages are tied to performance, and in this case we already know the quality of the work of the "evil*doers*." The psalmist employs a chiastic construction surrounding an inner parenthetical expression that makes the evil character of the work explicit and the anticipated judgment clear.

Give-to-them according-to-their-work
(according to the perverseness of their deeds)
according-to-the-works-of-their-hands give-to-them.

The psalmist's plea for retribution on the enemy concludes in 28:4d with a summation that parallels and balances 28:4a (lit.): "Cause their deeds to return upon them."[10]

---

6. The verb "drag" is the Hebrew also employed in Gen. 37:28 to describe Joseph's brothers "dragging" him roughly out of the pit in order to bundle him off into slavery with the Midianites.

7. As mentioned in relation to 26:9 (see comments), there may be a connection here with the idea of asylum in the temple. If the one seeking asylum was determined to be guilty, he would be "dragged" out of the temple and executed. Here the psalmist disassociates himself from those who would suffer such a fate.

8. For similar attempts to disassociate from wicked persons, see 1:1; 26:4–5, 9 and comments. The word that the NIV translates "cordially" is *šalom*, the common word for "peace; wholeness; well-being." The point seems to be that the evildoers outwardly express concern for the well-being of their neighbor, but in their hearts they desire to hurt him.

9. The same demand for transparent consistency between one's inner attitudes and outward actions motivates much of the Sermon on the Mount (Matt. 5–7), where Jesus heightens the demand of righteousness associated with the Pharisees by pointing away from external obedience to the law to the inner attitude of repentance and reliance on the mercy of God.

10. The Heb. *gemul* is often translated "reprisal, reward," but as a contextual interpretation from a root meaning "deeds, doings" (Holladay, *CHALOT*, 62).

The justification for the psalmist's request follows in 28:5 and demonstrates a remarkable parallel with the request itself. The evildoers are to be condemned not simply because of their evil works, but because they demonstrate utter disregard and appreciation for the works of Yahweh himself. The deeds of Yahweh that are ignored are described in terms immediately parallel to the description of the enemies' evil works. They disregard the "works of the LORD" and ignore "what his hands have done" (lit., "the deeds of his hands"). As a consequence of their rejection of him, Yahweh will treat them like a conquering king treats a rebellious city: He will "tear them down" and will "never build them up again."[11]

Praise for Deliverance (28:6–7)

THE PSALMIST EXPERIENCES the certainty that Yahweh has indeed heard his plea for divine favor. This certainty is expressed in words that almost exactly parallel the plea itself in 28:2. Because of this assurance he "blesses"[12] Yahweh and promises to give praise in song (28:6–7).

The LORD is my strength and my shield. We have seen the ideas of Yahweh as "strength" and "shield" combined before (see 18:2). There, however, "my strength" was expressed by the less common Hebrew word *ḥezeq*[13] rather than by *ʿoz*, as here.[14] God is often acknowledged as the "shield" of the faithful in the psalms.[15] The psalmist is aware of past experiences of Yahweh's strengthening and protective presence that encourage continued trust—"my heart trusts in him" (28:7b). The verb "trust" (*bṭḥ*) is a perfect form that might better be rendered in this context "has trusted" or "has come to trust," describ-

11. While this passage probably was not *originally* intended to speak to the exilic destruction of the Jerusalem temple, it likely resonated in a reverse manner with the postexilic Jewish community and came to express a sort of appropriate hope for retribution against those who "tore down" the temple and "did not rebuild it." The shift to communal language in the final verses of the psalm (28:8–9) suggests this individual plea for deliverance was reinterpreted in light of the exilic experience. Cf. also Jer. 1:10, where two of the same verbs (*hrs* ["overthrow, throw down"] and *bnh* ["build"]) are used to describe God's judgment and restoration.

12. Once again the Hebrew psalmist has no problem envisioning humans "blessing" God. The NIV's consistent translation of *brk* in this kind of context is "praise." This may indicate some theological hesitation on the part of the NIV translators to describe humans as capable of blessing the almighty, immutable, unchanging, and entirely complete Yahweh (see the comments on 16:5–8).

13. This is the only occurrence of *ḥezeq* in the whole Old Testament.

14. Holladay (*CHALOT*, 269) suggests that in some cases *ʿoz* may mean "fortress" rather than "strength" (cf. Ps. 59:18).

15. See comments on Ps. 3:3 for further discussion of "shield." Yahweh is also described as *magen* in 3:4; 7:10; 18:2, 30; 33:20; 59:11; 84:11; 115:9, 10, 11; 119:114; 144:2.

ing a completed event with effects remaining to the present. As a result of this confident trust, the psalmist finds help from Yahweh—a theme that connects Psalm 28 back to 27:9, where Yahweh is the psalmist's "helper," and forward to 30:10, where God is "my help."

The psalmist's "heart" not only trusts as a foundation of deliverance (28:7b) but also rejoices, exults, or "leaps for joy" as a consequence of that deliverance (28:7c). The joyful praise comes forth in the form of a song of thanksgiving, a motif that again links this psalm back to 27:6 and forward to 30:12. Since we know that the sacrifice of thanksgiving was often accompanied by a public recitation of a psalm of thanksgiving, it may well be that verses 6–7 encapsulate the intent and content of that public declaration. This may explain the shift into a third-person description of Yahweh instead of the direct address earlier in the psalm.

Call for Communal Deliverance (28:8–9)

PSALM 28, LIKE many individual psalms in the Psalter, exhibits at its end a shift from purely individual to more communal concerns. If one accepts the recommended emendation in *BHS* of the awkward prepositional phrase *lamo* ("to him") to the more understandable *leᶜammo* ("to his people")[16] evidenced in other Hebrew manuscripts, then the individual image of Yahweh as the psalmist's "shield" (28:7) has been expanded to include the whole community in 28:8. This sort of movement is often associated with postexilic adaptation of earlier individual hymns to speak to the needs and issues of the exilic Diaspora community, although nothing in these final verses necessitates an exilic viewpoint.

His anointed one. God is the "fortress of salvation"[17] for his "anointed one." We have encountered previous references to God's "anointed one," beginning in 2:2 and continuing in 18:50 and 20:6. Those earlier passages have demonstrated the complex of concepts that surround this designation, including divine election for service; the covenant of kingship between God, David, and the Davidic dynasty; and the anticipated deliverer known as "*the* Messiah."

Precisely which of these concepts is operative in these final verses of Psalm 28 is difficult to determine. If the reference is part of the early, preexilic context of the original psalm, then it probably refers to the Israelite king currently in power or, more generally, to all such kings. If, as seems more

---

16. This could be explained as an *aural* copying error since *leᶜammo* and *lamo* are so close in sound.

17. The term *maᶜoz* ("fortress") also appears at 27:1; 31:2, 4; 37:39; 43:2; 52:7; 60:9; 108:9. The word *yešuᶜot* ("salvation, deliverance") is often translated "victory, victories," as the earlier use in 18:50 demonstrates.

likely, the concern with the "anointed one" is part of the postexilic adaptation of this psalm, then it most likely refers to the coming Messiah through whom Yahweh will save his people and bless his inheritance (28:9a). Regardless of which scenario is original, it is clear that the postexilic community would have come to associate this statement with their hopes for the anticipated saving appearance of the Messiah.

Save your people and bless your inheritance. The final entreaty slips over into direct address of Yahweh again and acknowledges that Israel is Yahweh's "people"—an inalienable "inheritance" dependent on him for their blessing. As the psalmist sought earlier to bless Yahweh (28:6), so Israel now seeks blessing from him. One's "inheritance" (*naḥalah*) is that property acquired during a lifetime that cannot be taken away but remains to be passed on to one's descendants. Israel is God's "inheritance" in the sense that they are his possession, and no one else can lay any claim on her.

Be their shepherd. The picture of the divine shepherd returns for the first time since its introduction in 23:1. This term is used of God only one additional time in the Psalter (80:1). The effect of the linkage between Psalms 28 and 23 is to mark off these psalms "as a collection linked by many common themes."[18]

Carry them forever. The image of God as shepherd is merged here with the image of Yahweh as the servant God who carries his people rather than be carried by them. Isaiah 46:1–2 ridicules those who entrust their lives to idols that must be carried from place to place by their worshipers. Instead, Israel is called to trust Yahweh who has carried *them* from their birth and will continue to do so until their old age (46:3–4). Isaiah 63:9 again recalls that Yahweh "in his love and mercy ... redeemed them; he lifted them up and carried them all the days of old." This reference to the "days of old" may well reflect the account in Deuteronomy 1:31, which reminds the Israelites how Yahweh carried them in the desert during the Exodus wandering—another intriguing link to the Exodus-pilgrimage tension discerned in Psalms 23–30.[19]

RETRIBUTION. THE PSALMIST calls on God to judge the evildoers according to their deeds (28:4–5). The idea of retribution—that what one does ultimately determines how God responds—is commonly expressed in biblical wisdom literature, especially Proverbs. There we encounter the expectation that because Yahweh has created the world,

18. See the *NIV Study Bible* note on this verse.

19. See comments on 23:6.

there must be a certain orderliness about the cosmos that distinguishes clearly between the righteous and the wicked, the wise and the fool. The wise and righteous can anticipate divine blessing while the fool and wicked can expect God's judgment.

While this general concept is repeatedly affirmed in the proverbs and psalms, the nature of divine blessing is debated within the wisdom books themselves. Some passages suggest that wisdom/righteousness leads to prosperity and wealth.[20] Other passages, however, make it clear that divine blessing is not always synonymous with economic abundance or even robust health.[21]

Our psalm aligns itself with the point of view that God judges the wicked and upholds the righteous. Interestingly, divine judgment is described as appropriate pay for work performed—a sort of biblical equivalent of marketplace economics, where certain jobs or professions are more highly paid because of market demand. Those with essential or highly prized tasks can demand higher wages or greater benefits while those in less influential positions are more poorly paid. In an age where entertainers and professional athletes receive multimillion dollar contracts while teachers and laborers receive far less, the motivational force behind salary differential cannot be said to be the lasting and innate value of the work itself but the perceived marketplace value—which job has the potential for greatest financial return for those who pay the bills.

In our psalm, it is interesting to note the kinds of "work" for which the psalmist's enemies are condemned. It is not that these are murderers or thieves—there is no indication of physical assault or robbery. Instead, they are described as "two-faced" or deceptive in their relations with others. They "speak peace" (NIV "speak cordially") to their neighbors—expressing a concern for others' well-being—while actually harboring resentments and "malice" toward those they address. This is an interior attitude of self-focus and self-concern that is not visible to those around about. Yet lack of integrity in inner thought and outer expression is one of the sinful attitudes commonly addressed in the psalms.[22]

Clearly such deception undermines the foundation of intimate relationship. To cloak one's inner thoughts and feelings behind a deceptive exterior is to deny others access to the real person. Humans can dissemble with one another and succeed in hiding their true selves and motivations for a while at least, but God is not deceived since he looks on the heart and knows all the plans and motivations of his creatures. Even in the world of human

20. Cf. Prov. 10:3, 16, 22; 11:19; 12:21; 13:21, 25; 14:11; 15:6; 16:20.

21. E.g., Prov. 11:4, 28; 15:16; 16:8, 16, 19; 19:1; 22:1; 28:6.

22. Cf. Pss. 5:9; 17:3, 10; 28:3; 55:21; 58:2; 62:4.

relationships, hidden motivations and attitudes often are revealed through actions more than words. Malice in the heart will ultimately inform what the hands do.

Not only do the enemies "do evil," allowing their true nature to work itself out in their deeds; they also have no respect for what God is about. This is hardly surprising since what God desires and works for is the ultimate restoration of right relationship human to human and all humans with their God. God's work is most often diametrically opposed to the deceptive practices of the enemies. The holy God takes care to make himself fully known to his creatures, both in his deeds and in the explicit revelation of his innermost character. God is holy, hating evil and desiring only good for his creatures. God is compassionate, just, merciful, and forgiving to those who acknowledge their dependence on him. God desires an intimate relationship grounded in integrity and sharing of the interior life. God shares himself and expects the same in return.

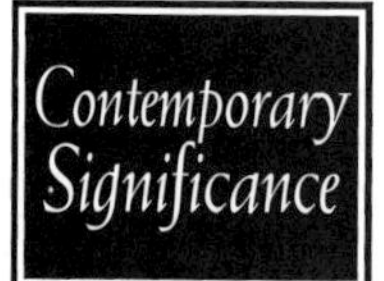

SUFFERING AMONG THE WICKED. For exilic Israel the idea of the innocent being dragged off to suffer along with the wicked was a real experience. Too often we think of the nations of Israel and Judah as monolithic wholes who broke their covenant with Yahweh and *deserved* to be carted off into exile, far from all that was familiar and comforting. We forget that there remained within the nation a faithful remnant who believed the words of the prophets and entrusted themselves completely to God, similar to the seven thousand faithful at the time when Elijah believed himself to be alone—those who had never bowed to Baal or kissed him (1 Kings 19:1–18). During the Exile, these faithful few did not experience the deliverance hoped for but found themselves dragged away into captivity along with the sinful many, who had rejected Yahweh's warnings. They experienced the same suffering—the dislocation and loss—that the faithless community as a whole deserved.

Those faithful innocents in exile had a choice: to understand their suffering among the wicked as happenstance (i.e., the accidental results of the vagaries of existence outside the control of an uncaring or unjust God), as evidence of deserved punishment for some sin hidden from themselves, or as evidence of a divine calling for the righteous few to suffer vicariously for the sins of the wicked many. The message of Job comes across clearly here. The righteous do suffer, but not for any hidden sin unknown even to themselves. God is still to be acknowledged as just and compassionate while the suffering faithful continue to rely wholly on him.

The suffering servant of Isaiah—whom Jesus took as the foundational model for his own ministry of suffering and death for the sins of his people—was first and foremost a call to the faithful few to adopt the role of vicarious sufferers for the sins of the many. In so doing, they were to act redemptively for the forgiveness and redemption of the people as a whole. It was only because they were ultimately unable (or unwilling) to fulfill this role completely that God himself, incarnate in Jesus, accomplished the vicarious and redemptive suffering for all humanity that made possible the restoration of God's original creation intention.

I said this view of vicarious suffering was a choice. The exilic faithful could have (and I suppose many did so) wallowed in their self-pity, refusing to accept any solidarity with their suffering community and demanding divine explanation for an essentially unjust act.[23] They could also have looked inward, accusing themselves of imaginary sin to explain their suffering.

We have to admit if we are honest that we have the same choices when confronted with suffering and brokenness today. God's purpose in calling his church "out"[24] of the world is not to escape its brokenness and pain. He has called us out in order to experience a new wholeness and to experience the world's brokenness for what it really is: a direct contradiction of God's intention for humanity and his whole creation. Armed with this knowledge and with the power of his Spirit sustained within the fellowship of believers, we have been sent back to the world—with the "mind of Christ Jesus"—to make its suffering our own and so to redeem it.

Whenever we love instead of hate, when we exchange self-protection for risky compassion, when we allow our hearts to be broken by the suffering of the world around us, we turn our own senseless suffering not into a cry of anger, but into a plea for unity and restoration. Then we are able to cry out with the psalmist in 28:6–7:

> Praise be to the LORD,
> for he has heard my cry for mercy.
> The LORD is my strength and my shield;
> my heart trusts in him, and I am helped.
> My heart leaps for joy
> and I will give thanks to him in song.

---

23. The lamenting cries of Pss. 89 and 137 fall into this category of complaint.

24. The New Testament word for "church" is the Greek *ekklesia*, "those called out."

Psalm 29

A PSALM OF DAVID.

[1] Ascribe to the LORD, O mighty ones,
 ascribe to the LORD glory and strength.
[2] Ascribe to the LORD the glory due his name;
 worship the LORD in the splendor of his holiness.

[3] The voice of the LORD is over the waters;
 the God of glory thunders,
 the LORD thunders over the mighty waters.
[4] The voice of the LORD is powerful;
 the voice of the LORD is majestic.
[5] The voice of the LORD breaks the cedars;
 the LORD breaks in pieces the cedars of Lebanon.
[6] He makes Lebanon skip like a calf,
 Sirion like a young wild ox.
[7] The voice of the LORD strikes
 with flashes of lightning.
[8] The voice of the LORD shakes the desert;
 the LORD shakes the Desert of Kadesh.
[9] The voice of the LORD twists the oaks
 and strips the forests bare.
And in his temple all cry, "Glory!"

[10] The LORD sits enthroned over the flood;
 the LORD is enthroned as King forever.
[11] The LORD gives strength to his people;
 the LORD blesses his people with peace.

AT THE HEART of this brief psalm of eleven verses is a powerful and artistic description of the theophanic appearance of Yahweh in the devastating power of a thunder and lightning storm (29:3–9). The poetry of the psalm is particularly characterized by repetition and expansion of words and ideas: The phrase "the voice of the LORD" appears no less than seven times; "ascribe to the LORD" occurs three times; the divine name Yahweh ("LORD") appears four times at the beginning (29:1–2), balanced by four times at the end (29:10–11). Indeed, the divine name appears at least once in every verse except the central one (29:6), and most often twice.[1]

Other phrases, such as "shakes the desert," "breaks the cedars," "thunders," "sits/is enthroned," appear twice. Far from dulling appreciation of the psalm's artistry, the repetition effectively builds excitement and intensity as the reader along with the poet is caught in the midst of the shattering pyrotechnic display of a rattling thunderstorm with repeated flashes of lightning and ear-splitting thunderclaps.

The central focus of the psalm is on the revealing "voice" of Yahweh, who makes his glorious kingship over the whole earth known through this powerful display. In the face of this disturbing display of the power of God who sits enthroned as king, the faithful can only bow in worship (29:1–2) and proclaim along with the thunderous voice of God, "Glory!" (29:9). At points the psalm takes on almost mythical overtones, as it depicts Yahweh's power over the "mighty waters" (*mayim rabbim*) and the "flood" (*mabbul*), whose chaotic force he restrained in the Genesis creation and Flood narratives.[2]

The structure of the psalm falls into three major divisions: the call to worship and testimony (29:1–2), the theophanic appearance of Yahweh in the storm (29:3–9), and the acknowledgment of Yahweh's enthronement as king (29:10–11).

The Heading (29:0)

NO NEW TERMS appear in the heading to Psalm 23, which is described simply as a "psalm [*mizmor*] of David."[3]

Call to Worship and Testimony (29:1–2)

IN VERSES 1–2 the "mighty ones" are three times called to "ascribe to the LORD" the glory[4] and strength due his name. The NIV's choice of the translation "mighty ones" for *bene ʾelim* (lit., "sons of gods") obscures the fact that *ʾelim* is the plural of the common ancient Near Eastern word for "god" (*ʾel*).

---

1. Altogether Yahweh appears either singly or in combination with other words a total of eighteen times in the eleven verses of the psalm, leaving no doubt that the psalmist's focus is on the majestic power of the being of Yahweh and on his name.

2. By "mythical" I mean having to do with those narratives that intend to explain the origins of the universe and humanity—frequently in highly poetic language. The Genesis accounts of the creation and Flood share with similar ancient Near Eastern texts a focus on chaotic waters that must be controlled within boundaries before secure human existence can be assured. By being described as "enthroned over the flood," Yahweh is proclaimed as the authoritative ruler of the chaotic waters and creator of a stable universe.

3. See comments on the heading to Ps. 3.

4. See the initial references to *kabod* in the comments on Pss. 3 and 8.

The term *ʾelim* appears only four times in the Hebrew text of the Old Testament, twice alone (Ex. 15:11; Job 41:25) and twice in the phrase *bene ʾelim* (Pss. 29:1; 89:6; cf. also *ʾel ʾelim* in Dan. 11:36). The Exodus passage clearly refers to the pagan "gods," who are negatively compared to Yahweh: "Who among the gods is like you, O LORD?" In a similar passage, Psalm 89:6–7 asks: "Who in the skies above can compare with the LORD? Who is like the LORD among the *bene ʾelim* [NIV heavenly beings]? In the council of the holy ones God is greatly feared; he is more awesome than all who surround him." Job 41:25 (MT 41:17) depicts the rising of leviathan to the surface of the ocean as so fearsome that even the *ʾelim* (NIV "the mighty") are afraid.

While this phrase may well have been reinterpreted as Israel's monotheistic understanding of Yahweh grew, it seems clear that the original reference was to those "other gods" worshiped by the pagans—gods who could not compare to the majestic, powerful, and authoritative creator, Yahweh. Even if this invocation to the "gods" is understood metaphorically, its underlying purpose is to enhance the majesty of Yahweh at the expense of foreign deities, who are here called to proclaim the glory and strength "due his name" while bowing down in worship of his holiness (29:2).

The "glory" and "strength" that the *bene ʾelim* are to ascribe to Yahweh make this opening segment of Psalm 29 a fitting counterpoint to the entrance liturgy of 24:7–10. There the "King of glory" is welcomed into the temple precincts as the conquering ruler, who is "strong" and "mighty," "mighty in battle." Here in Psalm 29, Yahweh (described in verse 10 as "enthroned as King forever") approaches in theophanic splendor (29:2) and is received by those within the temple with the cry "Glory!" (29:9).

Splendor of his holiness. The divine "splendor" (*hadrat qodeš*; "splendid holy attire") that the psalmist mentions is a visual splendor associated with clothing and befitting the rank and character of the one who wears them. In Proverbs 14:28, this term describes the grand garments of a king. This visible reference to the holy splendor of Yahweh's attire leads the psalm a step closer to his theophanic appearance that dominates verses 3–9. When Yahweh appears in all his glory, the pagan deities can only acknowledge his glory and strength and humbly bow in worship. This acknowledgment of Yahweh's glory by the deities sets the standard for those human worshipers who will later experience God's theophany in the temple and, like their divine counterparts, can only respond with their own awe-filled cry of "Glory!" (29:9).

Theophany of Yahweh in the Storm (29:3–9)

PSALM 29 STANDS as a response to the plea in Psalm 28 that Yahweh not remain silent (28:1). Notice how the phrase "the voice of the LORD" appears seven times in 29:3–9, clearly making this the major theme of this middle section. Yahweh speaks as he comes in response to the psalmist's plea for deliverance.

The God of glory thunders. The emphasis on the "voice of the LORD" is also connected with the imagery of the thunderstorm, associated with the theophany of Yahweh in these verses. Such imagery is common in theophany passages.[5] Here the voice of Yahweh does not *speak* but *thunders* (29:3) in a powerful, majestic voice (29:4) that "shakes" the earth (29:8), "breaks the cedars" (29:5), and "twists the oaks" (29:9). Although these last two phenomena are associated in our psalm with the "voice" of Yahweh, they may well be the result of other storm-related events, such as wind and lightning.

Cedars of Lebanon . . . Desert of Kadesh. The descriptive phrases of the theophany picture a massive storm originating over the Mediterranean Sea (29:3), moving ashore at the heavily forested Lebanon range to the far north of Israel (29:5–6), and then across the Desert of Kadesh associated with the ancient city of that name (29:8).[6] During the reign of Solomon, this area was under the control of Israel.

Cedars. The cedars of Lebanon were well known in the ancient Near East as the largest, most spectacular stand of trees in the region. The trees supplied building materials for structures throughout the Mediterranean, from Egypt to Mesopotamia. In the Mesopotamian tale of Gilgamesh and Enkidu, the forests of Lebanon were considered sacred to the gods, who used the cedars for the construction of their own dwellings. The forests were guarded by the great monster Huwawa, who gave Enkidu a mortal wound but was ultimately defeated and killed by Gilgamesh.[7] Solomon imported cedars from Lebanon for use in the building of his palace and the Jerusalem temple (1 Kings 5:6–10; 7:1–12).

The power of Yahweh is displayed in the storm's power to "break" the strong and lofty cedars of Lebanon. We lived for twelve years on a well-wooded lot, surrounded by tall pines, cedars, oaks, birches, and maples. Several winters ago, during a particularly strong windstorm, a sixty-foot blue spruce toppled in the middle of the night, fell across a power line, and came to rest on our garage, damaging only a few shingles. Not long after that, I awoke after another windstorm to find a huge pine had collapsed on our paved parking pad. I must admit that we no longer rest easily when winds

---

5. See the discussion of theophany in the comments on Ps. 18:4–19; compare other theophany passages such as 18:7–15 and 77:16–19.

6. Ancient Kadesh was located inland, about equidistant from Damascus to the south and Aleppo to the North. Rather than a "desert" of sand, the area might better be called an unoccupied "wilderness" or steppe—alternative translations of the Heb. *midbar*.

7. The narratives of Gilgamesh and Enkidu are available in various translation. See, e.g., *ANETP*, 1:40–75.

begin to blow. We have seen their power and its consequences on our trees. We have also seen the path of destruction taken by a tornado that touched down in a nearby wooded area—snapping off large trees far above ground as if they were toothpicks or pencils. This must have been the picture our psalmist had in mind. Even the tallest, strongest, most majestic cedars of Lebanon were no match for the power of Yahweh.

He makes Lebanon skip like a calf. Not only the wind, but also the thunder attends the theophanic approach of Yahweh and his "voice." The powerful claps of thunder shake the very earth under the psalmist and all those who await God's coming in the temple. The thunder causes the whole Lebanon range of mountains and its southernmost peak, Sirion,[8] to "skip like a calf ... like a young wild ox" (29:6). While in some theophanic passages this shaking of the earth may seem to describe earthquake or even volcanic activity (cf. 18:7), for the most part it is the powerful explosion of thunder that seems to be behind the narrator's experience here (cf. 77:16–19), as the sevenfold repetition of the "voice of the LORD" makes clear.

Twists the oaks. The most straightforward translation of the phrase *yeḥolel ʾayyalot* would be "cause deer (pl.) to writhe/tremble [in fear/childbirth]" because "bring to labor" is the normal meaning of the Polel form of the verb *ḥyl*. Some Hebrew manuscripts, however, read "trees" instead of "deer," an interpretation that more closely parallels the second half of the verse, "strips bare the forests."[9]

And in his temple all cry, "Glory!" The pinnacle and climax of the theophany comes at the height of the storm's power, as all those gathered in the temple worship Yahweh with a loud acclamation of "Glory!" With this shout the worshipers fulfill the call of the opening verses: "Ascribe to the LORD ... glory and strength ... due his name." This cry of acknowledgment is wrested from them almost against their will as the blasting, crashing, flashing display of divine power cannot be denied. All tremble! All worship! All know the glory of Yahweh!

Yahweh's Enthronement as King (29:10–11)

HAVING COME IN splendor and power across the "mighty waters" (both the chaotic floods of creation and the Mediterranean Sea are in view here), having left the northern mountains of Lebanon with devastating evidence of his

---

8. Another designation for Mount Hermon (cf. Deut. 3:8–9).

9. The difficulty is compounded by the fact that the plural of the word "forest/thicket" (*yaʿar*) is normally masculine (*yeʿarim*) rather than feminine as the form used here (*yeʿarot*). *BHS* offers another possible emendation of this word to *yeʿalot* "(female) mountain goats," a reading that would parallel the "writhing deer" version of the first half of this verse.

power, and having entered the temple to loud acclamations of his glory, Yahweh now "sits [down] enthroned as King forever." In the temple, the ark of the covenant in the Most Holy Place served as the place where the invisible God of Israel sat with his people—enthroned between the wings of the cherubim as Israel's king.

Enthroned over the flood. In a reference to his control and limiting of the chaotic waters at creation, Yahweh is described as mounting his throne "over the flood." Beside this single occurrence of *mabbul* ("flood") in Psalm 29:10, the term appears twelve times—all within the Genesis Flood narrative and all referring to the threatening, chaotic waters that Yahweh subdued once and for all.[10] This exercise of divine authority and control over the chaotic forces threatening to undo creation and human existence established once and for all that Yahweh is the cohesive power that holds the universe together. He is the "eternal King," on whom all human hopes are pinned. For this reason, whenever Yahweh's "kingship" is celebrated, images of his creation might and control can never be far behind. Note, for example, the creation images that abound in the collection of *Yahweh malak* psalms (Pss. 93; 95–99).[11]

Gives strength . . . blesses his people. Having assumed his rightful place as eternal king, Yahweh becomes the source of confident hope for his people. The end of Psalm 28 proclaims Yahweh as "the strength of his people" (28:8), and the people plead for Yahweh to "save" them and "bless" them (28:9). Now, at the end of Psalm 29, the enthroned Yahweh has come as his people desired to give "strength to his people" and to "bless his people with peace" (29:11). In a fitting convergence of the pilgrimage motif observed throughout Psalms 23–29, those who have come so far seeking Yahweh have found him. He has come revealing himself as their King and Savior, and he blesses them with peace.

HENOTHEISM AND MONOTHEISM. Verse 1 reveals an inconsistency of translation that deserves comment. The NIV chooses to translate the Hebrew phrase *bene ʾelim* as "mighty ones," obscuring the fact that the more direct rendering would be "children of the gods," or at the very least "heavenly beings." The term *ʾelim* is the masculine plural form of the noun *ʾel* ("god"), a term regularly employed in the Canaanite language of

10. The word *mabbul* occurs in Gen. 6:17; 7:6, 7, 10, 17; 9:11 [2x], 15, 28; 10:1, 32; 11:10.

11. It is no accident that the closest theophanic parallel to Ps. 29 is Ps. 93—the lead-off psalm of the *Yahweh malak* collection. See discussion of the Yahweh *malak* psalms in the section on "Psalm Types" in the introduction.

Ugarit to refer to a single deity or to serve as the name of the chief Canaanite god, El. The NIV is inconsistent in its translation of this word, recognizing the primary meaning "gods" in Exodus 15:11, while preferring "heavenly beings" in Psalm 89:6 and "mighty [ones]" in Job 41:25 and Psalm 29:1. This inconsistency may demonstrate a reluctance on the part of the translators to admit the possibility that Israel may have acknowledged the existence of other deities alongside Yahweh. At the least the NIV obscures the possible reference to other gods and downplays Israel's awareness of them.

It is clear, however, that Israel employed terms like this—*ʾelim* ("gods"), *bene ʾelim* ("children of the gods"), and related uses of *ʾelohim* ("gods")[12] and *bene ʾelohim* ("children of God/the gods; heavenly beings"; cf. Job 1:6; 2:1)[13]—because she was immersed in a culture dominated by polytheistic belief systems and often struggled with pressure to conform. We know that Israel struggled with the temptation to worship gods other than Yahweh down to the exilic period, at which time (and *only* then) did absolute monotheistic belief in the existence of Yahweh alone take root firmly in the exilic community. Since that time belief in other gods has had no attraction to the Jewish community, who had been well trained by the prophets that there was no other god besides Yahweh and that to worship other deities as if they did exist was foolishness and risked complete separation from their covenant relationship with the one true God.

But prior to the Exile, Old Testament texts give us ample evidence that Israel not only acknowledged the existence of gods other than Yahweh but ran frequently after them, seeking benefit and blessing by offering allegiance to them. It is possible that some of these early Israelites were plain and simple *polytheists*—believing that many gods existed and that a person had to deal with all of them in order to gain the most benefit and avoid danger and hurt. Such Israelites would have "covered all the bases" by worshiping other deities along with Yahweh. These polytheistic Israelites incurred the wrath of the Israelite prophets, who castigated them for their lack of covenant loyalty to Yahweh alone and ridiculed them for creating and worshiping deities that did not in reality exist or have the ability to save (cf. Isa. 40:18–20; 41:21–24; 43:9–20; 46:3–7; Dan. 5:23; Hos. 4:12).

---

12. The noun *ʾelohim* is a masculine plural form and is used so frequently for the multiple gods of the polytheistic nations that only a few examples are given here (e.g., Ex. 15:11; 23:32–33; Deut. 6:14; 8:19; Pss. 82:1; 86:8; 95:3; 96:4; 97:7, 9; 135:5; 136:2; 138:1). The most striking feature in Israel's use of this term is that the plural form came to be used when referring to the one God of Israel. In these cases, the singular nature of God was clearly indicated by the use of masculine singular verbal forms!

13. The NIV even more interpretively translates *bene ʾelohim* as "angels," while supplying a textual note to the more direct rendering "the sons of God."

But many of these earlier Israelites were probably not polytheists but what are called *henotheists*. Henotheism—a word derived from the Greek *hen* ("one") and *theos* ("god")—describes a belief system in which many gods are thought to exist, although only one has claim on my absolute loyalty. Many of Yahweh's demands for Israel's allegiance can be read in this vein, that is, as stopping short of unambiguous monotheism. Note, for example, "You shall have no other gods *before* me" (Ex. 20:3), which demands that Yahweh occupy first place among whatever deities are acknowledged to exist. References to Yahweh as *ʾel ʿelyon* ("the Most High God") also imply that there are other gods over whom Yahweh is dominant. Yahweh is explicitly said to be "exalted [or feared] above all gods" in passages such as 1 Chronicles 16:25; Psalms 95:3; 96:4; 97:9; and Daniel 11:36–37.

The admission that other gods existed although Yahweh claimed exclusive allegiance may explain why the kings of the northern kingdom considered themselves Yahweh worshipers (as demonstrated by their habit of giving their children names honoring Yahweh) while allowing the worship of other deities among the mixed Canaanite/Israelite people of their kingdom.[14] The same could have been said for Solomon, who remained a Yahweh devotee while allowing the construction of temples in Jerusalem for the gods of his many wives.

As stated above, it was not until the prophetic critique of the causes of the exilic destruction of the nation and temple that the Diaspora community as a whole moved toward unambiguous monotheism. This was certainly not immediate. Even Psalm 137, brimming with the pain of the Exile, wonders: "How can we sing the songs of the LORD while in a foreign land?" (137:4), questioning whether God can compete with the deities of the victorious Babylonians outside his own "turf." Only gradually were the Disapora faithful able to understand that God was still operative among the exiles (cf. Ezekiel), that the cause of the Exile was no weakness on God's part but a sign of his strength in using other nations to punish his rebellious people, and at last that Yahweh was indeed the "King over all the earth" because he made it.

Yahweh and the storm. Here Yahweh is depicted in terms of the power of the storm (cf. also Deut. 33:26; Pss. 68:4–10; 104:3–4). Many ancient Near Eastern deities were associated with the power of the storm. In Egypt, Amun was the great storm god who provided rain for crops and animals alike. Closer to home, the Mesopotamian god Hadad and his Canaanite reflex Baal are both depicted as riding on the backs of bulls, clutching light-

---

14. Some scholars have suggested that the northern kings kept the early capital Tirzah as a center of exclusive Yahweh worship while Samaria allowed worship of multiple deities for the mixed population of the kingdom.

ning bolts in their hands. Like Yahweh, Baal is also said to "ride on the clouds" when he brings the rain.[15]

Whether you think that Israel transplanted entrenched Canaanite fertility images associated with Baal to their own nomadic desert warrior God, Yahweh, when they entered and settled down in the land of Canaan, or whether you see these similarities of depiction between Baal-Hadad and Yahweh as theological claims that it is in fact Yahweh and *not* Baal-Hadad who brings the rain that sustains the crops, the comparisons are striking. The former response might lead to syncretism and confusion of Baal and Yahweh, while the latter is more clearly a rejection of the Canaanite deity and firm allegiance to Yahweh alone. These niceties of detail, however, would probably have been lost on the general population, with the result that Yahweh was probably worshiped alongside the Canaanite deity and in many instances identified with him.

THE DEMONSTRATION OF GOD'S POWER. One of the vivid memories I retain from seven years of living in Athens, Georgia, is of incredible displays of lightning during passing thunderstorms. The sky would grow increasingly dark during the day, and then bolts of lightning would begin crashing down, followed by peals of thunder and torrents of rain. The lightning included jagged filaments of light connecting earth and sky as well as blinding "sheet lightning," which lightened the whole terrain while thunder boomed almost simultaneously.

It was during one such storm that my son—who was then about seven or eight and an inquisitive boy by character who loved to observe nature in all its forms—sat cross-legged on the carpeted floor of our family room, just inside the sliding glass door that opened on to our patio, fascinated by the powerful display outside. As he sat enthralled with his nose practically plastered to the glass door, suddenly a tremendous flash of sheet lightning exploded just outside with a blast of thunder that shook the whole house. In an immediate and involuntary response, my son did a back flip across the carpeted family room and landed gasping in the middle of the room, his wide eyes transfixed by the pouring rain outside the patio door. As he lay there, a single word escaped his lips: "Wow!"

The worshiping psalmist and all those around in the temple respond to the display of Yahweh's power with a similar mixture of fearful amazement

---

15. See the Aqhat Epic, in which Baal is described as "the Rider of the Clouds," in *ANETP*, 1:127.

and fascinated wonder. Their words may carry a more theological edge than my son's "Wow!" but their explosive pronouncement of "Glory!" (29:9) exhibits a similar response of fascinated awe and fearful distance. It took a while for my son to return to business as usual that day, and I think he has continued to think of lightning differently ever since. What changed for him in that moment was his sudden new appreciation of the destructive potential of the powerful display. In that convulsive back flip, he acknowledged that the object of his fascination had also the power to harm—lightning was nothing to be fooled around with. It was more than just a beautiful display; it was uncontrollable power with the ability to destroy!

How long has it been since you were overwhelmed in this way by a sense of God's powerful presence? Too often today God has become our "buddy" and "pal." As Christians we sometimes become so comfortable with the salvation we have received in Christ that we forget just how undeserved it is. When we focus on God only as Redeemer, Savior, and friend, and not as powerful God, creator, and hater of sin and evil, it is easy (often unintentionally) to emasculate our understanding of God until he is like our human buddies and pals who accept us as we are and do not challenge us to change.

Isaiah did not equate the saving nature of God with "buddy-ship"! When he saw that "Holy, holy, holy is the LORD Almighty" (Isa. 6:3), he did not grin and slap God on the back. He didn't even give him a friendly hug or handshake. Rather, he found himself prostrate on the ground, fearful even to look at God. This believing priest, who had performed all the required rituals of cleansing and preparation to serve God in the temple, was forced in this moment of revelation to acknowledge the deep-seated lack of holy character that separated himself from holy God, an emptiness that deserved divine judgment.

Similarly, Simon Peter in the New Testament found himself overwhelmed with such a clear sense of God's power that resided in Jesus that he was knocked to his knees. After a long and unsuccessful night of fishing, an exhausted Peter responded rather reluctantly to Jesus' request that he "put out into deep water, and let down the nets for a catch" (Luke 5:4). Peter had no expectation that the endeavor would have any more success than the previous night's hard work, but he complied simply because it was Jesus who asked. Suddenly the nets were overflowing, and the boat was so full of fish that it was in danger of sinking. And where was Peter? Not slapping Jesus on the back and laughing about his good fortune; instead, he found himself flat on his face at Jesus' feet,[16] acknowledging his sinfulness: "Go away from me, Lord, I am a sinful man!" (5:8).

---

16. Prostrate in the slippery fish bottom of the boat, Peter had to acknowledge that he too was one of the "fish" Jesus had come to catch!

When we really see God as he is—when his power and holiness is displayed for us—there should be no other appropriate response but to get on our knees in acknowledgment of just how far our lives, even at their very best, are removed from the holiness of God and just how undeserved is the gracious love and salvation that God pours out on us day by day.

Praise to the Lord, the Almighty, the King of creation!
O my soul, praise him, for he is thy health and salvation!
All ye who hear, now to his temple draw near;
Join me in glad adoration![17]

17. From the hymn "Praise to the Lord, the Almighty" by Joachim Neander, 1650–1680, translated by Catherine Winkworth, 1827–1878. Taken from *The Covenant Hymnal* (Chicago: Covenant Press, 1973), 29.

Psalm 30

A PSALM. A song. For the dedication of the temple. Of David.

1 I will exalt you, O LORD,
for you lifted me out of the depths
and did not let my enemies gloat over me.
2 O LORD my God, I called to you for help
and you healed me.
3 O LORD, you brought me up from the grave;
you spared me from going down into the pit.

4 Sing to the LORD, you saints of his;
praise his holy name.
5 For his anger lasts only a moment,
but his favor lasts a lifetime;
weeping may remain for a night,
but rejoicing comes in the morning.

6 When I felt secure, I said,
"I will never be shaken."
7 O LORD, when you favored me,
you made my mountain stand firm;
but when you hid your face,
I was dismayed.

8 To you, O LORD, I called;
to the Lord I cried for mercy:
9 "What gain is there in my destruction,
in my going down into the pit?
Will the dust praise you?
Will it proclaim your faithfulness?
10 Hear, O LORD, and be merciful to me;
O LORD, be my help."

11 You turned my wailing into dancing;
you removed my sackcloth and clothed me with joy,
12 that my heart may sing to you and not be silent.
O LORD my God, I will give you thanks forever.

PSALM 30 IS a fitting summation of the group of psalms extending from Psalm 23 through 29. Like the majority of those psalms, this one is a lament or plea for deliverance.[1] Its heading links the psalm to the temple—one of the central themes in this group.[2] In addition, the psalm has numerous thematic and verbal resonances with the preceding psalms—especially Psalm 27—that will be mentioned below.

The psalm falls into three unequal portions: an introductory declaration of intent to praise Yahweh with a general statement of the reason for praise (30:1–3); a widening call to the reader/listener to join the psalmist's praise (30:4–5); and an extended narrative of the psalmist's changing circumstance (30:6–12), which encompasses a collapse into dismay (30:6–7), a plea for deliverance (30:8–10), and the divine response remembered with joy (30:11–12).

The Heading (30:0)

FOR THE MOST part the heading includes familiar terms: "psalm" (*mizmor*), "song" (*šir*), "of David."[3] The heading does, however, include a unique phrase describing the purpose for which the psalm was supposed to have been composed: "For the dedication of the house [NIV temple]."

The word for "house" (*bayit*) in this context is ambiguous and is sometimes taken to refer to the "royal palace."[4] Yet in addition to this usage, the noun *ḥanukkah* ("dedication") is most frequently used to refer to the dedication of the temple altar (Num. 7:10, 11, 84, 88; 2 Chron. 7:9), only once the "wall of Jerusalem" (Neh. 12:27). The cognate verb *ḥnk* ("dedicate") twice mentions the dedication of a common soldier's house (Deut. 20:5), once encourages dedicating a child at the start of life (Prov. 22:6), and twice refers specifically to dedicating the "house of the LORD/God" (1 Kings 8:63; 2 Chron. 7:5). The use of *habbayit* ("*the* house") and the position of Psalm 30 at the end of the collection of Psalms 23–30 with their emphasis on the house of Yahweh, makes it most likely that the Jerusalem temple is intended here.

---

1. The core psalms of this group are all pleas for deliverance (Pss. 25; 26; 27; 28), while threat and divine deliverance figure prominently in Ps. 23 as well.

2. Just what dedication of the temple this has in view remains obscure—whether that of the original Solomonic temple, the restored exilic temple, the rededication in the time of the Maccabean revolution, or some other moment of purification.

3. For *mizmor* and *ledawid* see comments on the heading of Ps. 3. This is the first occurrence of the simple *šir* in a heading (see also headings to Pss. 45; 46; 48; 65–68; cf. also the heading of Ps. 18).

4. See the NIV textual note.

Declaration of Praise (30:1–3)

THE PSALMIST BEGINS with a declaration of intent to praise Yahweh and gives his reason behind this praise. The language used is that of exaltation ("I will exalt you, O LORD"). Just as Yahweh "exalted" the psalmist upon a secure rock (27:5) so that the psalmist's head is "exalted" above his surrounding enemies (27:6), so now the psalmist seeks to "exalt" Yahweh by making known his saving acts. To exalt Yahweh in worship is a common theme in Hebrew poetry and is usually associated with praise for his acts of deliverance. In the Song of the Sea (Ex. 15), Israel "exalts" Yahweh for their deliverance from the Egyptians (cf. 15:2). In Isaiah 25:1, Israel's exaltation of Yahweh introduces a list of the ways Yahweh has faithfully "done marvelous things ... planned long ago."[5] Exalting Yahweh was accomplished through praise (Ex. 15:1 and Isa. 25:1 both link exaltation and praise), especially of the divine name (Pss. 34:3; 145:1).

You lifted me out of the depths. The psalmist cites his experience of deliverance for which he praises Yahweh. Yahweh has "lifted" (from *dlh*) the psalmist "out of the depths." The counterbalance provided through the use of the parallel verbs "exalt" (*rwm*) and "lift" (*dlh*) become more clear as one considers them from the point of view of the speaker. "Exalt" involves motion *up and away from* the speaker—as if one were pushing a small child up on to a high rock to safety in rising waters (cf. 27:5). By contrast, "lift" describes motion *up from below and toward* the speaker. The verb *dlh* can describe "drawing water" from a well (Ex. 2:16, 19; Prov. 20:5)—as one would pull a person in danger of drowning out of the raging water with the aid of a rope. It is interesting to note in this regard that the phrase reported in the NIV as "out of the depths" is supplied interpretively, since there are no corresponding words in the Hebrew text.

Did not let my enemies gloat. No clear picture is gained of the psalmist's opponents in this psalm. This single reference would classify them as the type of people who hang around those in difficulty or suffering in order to "rejoice" over their downfall. In this case, "to gloat" translates the Hebrew phrase *śimmaḥ li* ("allow to rejoice concerning me"). Similar concern expressed with this phrase appears in 35:19, 24, 26; 38:16.[6]

You healed me. The psalmist's suffering may have been occasioned by a desperate illness. Certainly there is a sense of having been delivered from

5. See also, Pss. 34:3; 99:5, 9; 107:32; 118:28; 145:1 where the exaltation of Yahweh plays an important role.

6. The NIV also uses the term "gloat" in 22:17 to interpret the phrase *yabbiṭu yirʾu bi* ("they look, they see me").

death's door. The psalmist "called . . . for help" and was answered with divine healing. Yahweh "brought [the psalmist] up" from Sheol, the abode of the dead, and caused him to live from among those "going down into the pit."[7] The use of the participle "those going down" in this latter phrase emphasizes the immediacy of death. The psalmist appears almost to have been plucked out of the line of those currently waiting to enter Sheol.

Call to Join in Praise (30:4–5)

THE PSALMIST NOW calls on the listening/reading "saints"[8] to join in the praise of Yahweh—another indication that the setting of the psalmist's recitation is likely temple worship. The saints are called to "sing" (more accurately, "play music")[9] and "praise" (more accurately, "give thanks to") Yahweh's "remembrance, reminder" (*zeker*; often God's "name" is what reminds one of another, as the NIV suggests). These two acts of worship return at the conclusion in 30:12.

His anger lasts only a moment. The psalmist's call to praise flows from the awareness that Yahweh's final word is never lament and suffering but deliverance for his faithful ones. The reference to the limits to divine anger are intended as occasion for hope, especially for those who endure faithfully even in the face of suffering. The use of the image of divine anger in this context implies that the psalmist may be relating the suffering he has experienced to divine action, possibly as the result of his sin.[10] The only failing attributed to the psalmist in this psalm is the smug sense of false security mentioned in 30:6–7. The psalmist assures the enduring faithful (the "saints") that divine displeasure is not an eternal fixture of life, but the tears of suffering will ultimately resolve into morning shouts of joy. Tears are "permitted to stay the night"—like a particularly unwelcome guest—but must be on their way by morning.

---

7. The phrasing is a little awkward, but not impossible. The prepositional phrase *miyyorede* (following the Ketib and other versions) "from those who go down" might also mean "more than those descending." The *bor* "pit" (like the hole into which Joseph's brothers threw him before selling him into slavery, Gen. 37:22) is often used as a parallel to Sheol.

8. This is from the same root as *ḥesed* ("enduring covenant loyalty") and emphasizes enduring loyalty and faithfulness to the covenant demands rather than what we normally associate with "holiness; piety; sainthood."

9. The verb *zmr* appears again at the end of this psalm (30:12) and has occurred previously with this same sense in 27:6 (cf. also 28:7).

10. See the comments on the interconnectedness of sin and sickness in the Israelite understanding in the comments on 6:1–5.

The Psalmist's Narrative (30:6–12)

IN THE REST of the psalm, the psalmist gives an account of the changing mental and emotional processes that accompanied his downfall and deliverance. It is not often that we find such a clear and linear description of the circumstances behind lament and thanksgiving.

Collapse into dismay. The psalmist begins with an almost naive sense of safety and security: "When I felt secure . . ." (30:6). The phrase "I will never be shaken" (*bal ʾemmoṭ*) directly relates to other passages in the psalms that make use of this idiomatic expression. When used of humans, this phrase is often connected with a sense of dependence on and trust in Yahweh (15:5; 21:7; 55:22). Confidence comes as a result of Yahweh's power and his will to save. However, the phrase can also express a false sense of security, based on a rejection of Yahweh and a will to self-power that is doomed to failure (10:2–6). The key distinctive between these two uses of the idiom is the *attitude* of the human described: whether one of fear of Yahweh, acknowledging absolute dependence on him, or rejection of Yahweh, seeking to exert self-control of one's world. The former attitude leads to a firm and secure footing in life, while the latter will ultimately fall.

When you favored me. The tension between real and false security is played out in verse 7. Verse 5 might seem to imply that divine "favor" is a fixed certainty since it is said to last "a lifetime." Yet the true key to the psalmist's security is Yahweh himself. When Yahweh "favors" the psalmist, all is secure; but when Yahweh "hides his face," the psalmist collapses in dismay. Following on the heels of the rather arrogant profession of confidence in 30:6, verse 7 drives home the conditional nature of security. Security is as much an attitude of dependence as it is a circumstance of protection. Trusting in Yahweh and relying on him come what may provide security that is ultimately independent of every circumstance.

You made my mountain stand firm. This phrase is difficult, as commentators note. Some scholars assume a comparative phrase and emend the first-person pronominal suffix to a masculine plural construct ending, with a resulting translation "more than mountains of power." This would also necessitate understanding the psalmist as the object of the preceding verb "you made [me] stand." Kraus emends this verb to a first-person singular form, "I was made to stand." While precise translation may elude us, the sense of confident security remains clear, especially by way of contrast with the sense of dismay that follows immediately at the end of the verse.

You hid your face. To "hide the face" is an image for the withdrawal of divine presence and support that appears frequently both inside and outside the Psalter. God's withdrawal is most commonly associated with his "anger" over human sin[11] and leaves humans feeling rejected by God, isolated, and vulnerable to attack by their enemies. The realization of divine absence expressed in 30:7 leaves the psalmist feeling "dismayed," although the Niphal of the verb *bhl* usually means something stronger—more like "terrified, out of one's senses."[12] The sense of abandonment experienced here relates to the similar feeling in 27:9, where the psalmist pleads, "Do not hide your face from me, do not turn your servant away in anger."

Plea for deliverance. The awareness of vulnerability leads the psalmist to seek deliverance and divine favor. In a move reminiscent of 6:5 and 88:11, the psalmist questions whether there is any "gain"[13] to God in the psalmist's impending death, since all possibility of lifting praise to Yahweh is cut off by descent into Sheol.[14] The NIV's translation of the Hebrew *bedami* as "in my destruction" takes the phrase from a root *dmh* ("be destroyed"), rather than the alternate root *dmh*, meaning "be silent,"[15] or from the noun *dam*, meaning "in my blood." This obscures a possible wordplay in 30:12, where the psalmist refuses to be silent (*yiddom*)[16] and instead makes music in thanks to Yahweh.

---

11. On a very few occasions, *humans* are said to "hide their face" from God—usually out of fear of judgment deserved for their sin (cf. Ex. 3:6; Rev. 6:16). Even more rare is the use of the phrase for Yahweh "hiding his face" from human sin as a way of *mercifully* not acting in judgment (Ps. 51:9). Far more frequently, however, Yahweh hides his face as an act of judgment and rejection that leaves the human to face alone the consequences of sin and the lack of divine protection. See particularly the passage in Deut. 31:17–18, in which Yahweh prophesies to Moses concerning the disloyalty of Israel that will lead to divine rejection, so that the people of Israel will say, "Have not these disasters come upon us because our God is not with us?" (See also Deut. 32:20; Job 13:24; 34:29; Pss. 13:1; 27:9; 44:24; 69:17; 88:14; 102:2; 104:29; 143:7; Isa. 50:6; 54:8; 57:17; Jer. 33:5; Ezek. 39:24, 29; Mic. 3:4.)

12. Holladay, *CHALOT*, 34.

13. This term normally has negative implications and is often translated "illegal" or "dishonest gain" (e.g., Ex. 18:21; 1 Sam. 8:3). The word is related to the verb *bṣʿ* ("cut off") and may refer to a portion of a larger whole that is "cut off" as the individual's portion in a transaction. One could imagine that as various economic commodities were transferred through "middle men," the original value could be greatly reduced by each person "cutting off" a portion (whether openly or surreptitiously). It would seem that the word was not considered universally evil or negative, since it is here applied to the "gain" or "profit" that God might receive through human praise.

14. The "pit" (*šaḥat*) into which the psalmist fears descending here is different from the "pit" (*bor*) mentioned in 30:3. The *šaḥat* is a trap dug to capture animals, while the *bor* is a cistern intended to capture rainwater. Either could be used as an image of the burial pit in which a dead body was placed and, by extension, Sheol, the abode of the dead.

15. See Holladay, *CHALOT*, 72.

16. The interpretation of this passage continues to be difficult because of the varieties of meaning attached to the root *dm*. On the one hand the root *dmm* means "perish, be destroyed" while the similar root *dmm* can mean "stand still, be motionless" and the related root *dmh* can mean either "be like" or "be silent."

The rhetorical questions at the end of 30:9—each assuming the answer "No!"—realize that the only "profit" that humans represent to God lies in their praise and acknowledgment of his faithfulness.

Hear, O LORD. In what appears to be an abbreviation of the more extended cry in 27:7,[17] the psalmist seeks to gain Yahweh's ear and favor. He desires Yahweh to appear as "helper" (*ʿozer*), a term related to that used in 27:9 (*ʿezrati*). The similar phraseology serves once again to link Psalm 30 with Psalm 27.

Divine response remembered with joy. Psalm 30 concludes with the psalmist's joyful memory of deliverance realized. His rites of mourning have become instead a "circle dance" like the Hora, while God is depicted as replacing the psalmist's mourning clothes with a festal garment.

That my heart may sing. In response to these changed circumstances, the psalmist is unable to remain silent (*loʾ yiddom*) but breaks forth in a song of thanksgiving. This passage is difficult because of the lack of clarity regarding the relationship of words in the first half of the verse. The first verb means "he/it will play music [to] you." The subject is unclear and is most often supplied by emending the following noun *kabod* ("glory") to *kabedi* ("my kidney/ innermost part"), which the NIV specifies even further to "my heart." According to the *BHS* note, however, the Syriac version reads both verbs in the first half of this verse as first-person singular forms: "I will make music/sing (to) you" and "I will not remain silent."

This opens the intriguing possibility that the word *kabod* is not the subject of the preceding verb but the exclamation "Glory!" that is set to music in praise of Yahweh. In this case, the psalmist exclaims: "I will play/sing out to you 'Glory!' and I will not remain silent." Such a public acclamation of Yahweh's glory would link this verse back to 29:9, where those in the temple respond to the signs of Yahweh's theophanic approach in the storm with a similar cry. At the end of Psalm 30, the psalmist concludes with a promise of eternal praise of Yahweh.

COMING INTO THE PRESENCE OF A HOLY GOD. At first glance this seems a strange psalm to be titled "For the dedication of the temple." There is little recognizable about the temple in this thanksgiving psalm. It is almost enough to make us say there must be some

17. See comments on 27:7 for additional discussion of this type of cry and its relationship to the central call for Israel to hear and obey Yahweh.

mistake here! Surely the heading has arrived at its present position through some obscure and erroneous process.

But let me offer two suggestions as to how Psalm 30 *can* be seen to address the approach to holy God who is present in his holy temple. (1) We can read this psalm in connection with Psalm 29. There we see the worshipers of God overwhelmed by the theophanic appearance of Yahweh in the thunderous display of the storm. As God becomes most present, as his holiness breaks powerfully into the human world with fearsome consequences (29:3–9), the unison response of the worshiping congregation is almost torn from their throats as they together cry "Glory!" (29:9). If the above interpretation of 30:12 is accurate, the author of Psalm 30 echoes this earlier cry with a parallel vow: "I will play/sing out to you, 'Glory!' and I will not be silent!" This linkage places Psalm 30 squarely into the context of temple worship, so that the psalm itself becomes part of the psalmist's testimony in the congregation of the faithful—testimony that fulfills the vow to proclaim Yahweh's *glory*.

(2) The second way to see Psalm 30 in a temple context is to examine again the psalmist's exhortation in verse 5 of the "saints" of Yahweh, who are charged to "sing to the LORD . . . praise his holy name." He is standing in the midst of the congregation of the faithful as they join in the worship of Yahweh. The temple is not far away but surrounds this gathered band of worshipers, who respond joyfully to the testimony of God's faithfulness. Envisioning a temple context for this psalm allows us to understand the central tension—between the psalmist's changing sense of confidence and dismay—in a new light.

The Jerusalem temple was a source of great confidence for the Davidic dynasty and the people they ruled. As the place where Yahweh chose to enthrone his name, where God came down to be especially present in the Most Holy Place, where God's gracious forgiveness and mercy were delivered through the sacrificial system, and where people experienced communion with God through the sacrificial meal, the temple represented the promise of divine presence with and for Israel. Where Yahweh was present with his people, there was no room for fear. Where Yahweh was present, the rage of the nations was cause for divine laughter and scoffing (2:4).

Particularly in its association with the Davidic dynasty the temple became a source of great confidence and hope. We can see that hope expressed both in David's charge to Solomon to build the temple (1 Chron. 22:6–10) and in Solomon's prayer on the occasion of the dedication of the temple, to which the heading of Psalm 30 refers (2 Chron. 6:14–42). In the first passage David recounts to Solomon the promise of Yahweh that Solomon will be the one to build a house for Yahweh's name, while Yahweh will "establish the throne of his [Solomon's] kingdom over Israel forever" (1 Chron.

22:10). In Solomon's dedicatory prayer, the king calls on God to fulfill his promise:

> Now LORD, God of Israel, keep for your servant David my father the promises you made to him when you said, "You shall never fail to have a man to sit before me on the throne of Israel, if only your sons are careful in all they do to walk before me according to my law, as you have done." And now, O LORD, God of Israel, let your word that you promised your servant David come true. (2 Chron. 6:16–17)

The temple, then, is linked in Israel's mind with the promise to David of an eternal dynasty of Davidic descendants. Although this promise was given on the condition of continued obedience (as the 2 Chron. passage indicates), it was easy for Israel ultimately to assume a direct connection of temple, sacrifice, and worship with God's promise of continuing security.

The degree to which the Judahites came to trust in the presence of the temple can be seen in Jeremiah's well-known temple sermon.[18] Yahweh sent Jeremiah to stand in the gate of the temple and to call to repentance those passing by on their way to and from worship. His words make it clear that the people were trusting in the presence of Yahweh's temple to protect them from harm.

> Do not trust in deceptive words and say, "This is the temple of the LORD, the temple of the LORD, the temple of the LORD!" If you really change your ways and your actions and deal with each other justly . . . if you do not follow other gods to your own harm, then I will let you live in this place, in the land I gave your forefathers for ever and ever. But look, you are trusting in deceptive words that are worthless.
>
> Will you steal and murder, commit adultery and perjury, burn incense to Baal and follow other gods you have not known, and then come and stand before me in this house, which bears my Name, and say, "We are safe"—safe to do all these detestable things? (Jer. 7:4–10)

The Jerusalem temple is a place where God and Israel agree to meet for the forgiveness of sin and the celebration of ongoing communion; it is no amulet to ward off evil. God's promises of presence and protection are tied in Jeremiah's sermon to the fulfillment of Israel's covenant responsibilities to both God and humans. If Israel fails to keep her obligations, then the divine presence and power can be withdrawn and sinful Israel abandoned to the consequences of her rebelliousness. Ezekiel depicts the moment when the glory of Yahweh—the evidence of his presence with Israel—departs in disgust

---

18. The sermon appears in two versions: Jer. 7:1–15 and 26:1–6.

from the Most Holy Place and leaves his people to the merciless attacks of the Babylonian armies (Ezek. 10–11).

Psalm 30 drives home the tension that exists whenever one places a false sense of security in God's protective power. When one thinks it is possible to separate out the essential minimum of response to God from a wholehearted realization of dependence on him in all of life's moments, deceptive seeds are planted. Israel thought it was enough to have the temple and to regularly offer sacrifice and worship in the name of Yahweh; then the rest of her life was of little matter. She could live a compassionless, self-focused life of injustice and exploitation; she could worship other gods and yet stand in the Jerusalem temple completely convinced of her invulnerability because of God's presence in the temple. The Exile, however, finally convicted Israel of what they should have known all along: that Yahweh is a jealous God[19] and that enduring faith in him involved the "fear of the LORD"—the recognition and acceptance of absolute dependence on his mercy and grace in all of life.

When sinful people come into the presence of holy God—whether in the temple or elsewhere—they are driven to their knees in acknowledgment of their sin and its deserved judgment. Isaiah's response to his vision of holy Yahweh in the temple (Isa. 6:1–9) is an illustrative example, but so is the reaction of Samson's father, Manoah, to the departure of God's messenger in the flame of a sacrifice (Judg. 13:19–22). So the sudden shift in Psalm 30:6–7 from smug confidence to utter dismay is characteristic of those from whom God has withdrawn his protective power in order to teach them their vulnerability and to call them into a renewed relationship of complete dependence on him.

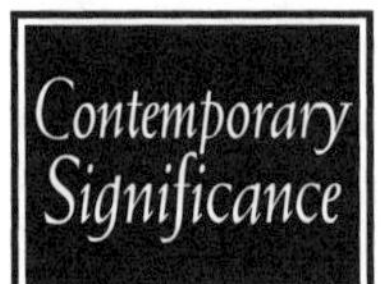

FROM SECURITY TO DISMAY, AND BACK AGAIN. Psalm 30 is a song for the vagaries of life. It knows God as both closely attentive and pointedly distant. The psalmist within this brief psalm explores the frigid hinterlands of divine absence as well as the sunny heights of God's gracious presence. This is, of course, nothing particularly new for the biblical psalms of thanksgiving, but Psalm 30 is particularly adept in its expression of the ease with which we can slip from security to dismay, and it is also particularly clear in locating the impetus behind this shift in the attitudes and perceptions of the human heart.

The psalmist declares, "When I was untroubled ... I thought, 'I shall never be shaken'" (30:7 JPS), and the awareness of divine grace was very real and

19. Cf. Ex. 20:5; 34:14; Deut. 4:24; 5:9; 6:15; Josh. 24:19.

present. Yet, all it took to bring this sense of eternal security crashing down was for the psalmist to run headlong into the experience of God's absence: When God hid his face, "I was terrified," the psalmist wails (30:8 JPS). For most of us, life is full of similar moments when our awareness of God's presence waxes and wanes. I am talking about our *awareness of God* here, not the *reality* of his presence or absence. God is always present, whether we realize it or not. This psalm, however, illustrates how our feelings, our perceptions, can either strengthen or undermine our confidence in facing the circumstances of our lives.

Clearly our perceptions are not always the best judge of reality. God is present even when we doubt it or cannot perceive him. That reality is not changed by our being aware or unaware. Nevertheless, our reaction to our circumstances can be immensely altered by our sense of God's presence or absence. As the psalmist indicates, the ability to perceive God at work in the midst of a troubled time made all the difference in the world. Wailing turned to a dance of joy, and rich festal garments replaced sackcloth and ashes.

In Philippians 4, Paul talks in a similar way about learning to be "content" in whatever circumstance he might find himself:

> I am not saying this because I am in need, for I have learned to be content whatever the circumstances. I know what it is to be in need, and I know what it is to have plenty. I have learned the secret of being content in any and every situation, whether well fed or hungry, whether living in plenty or in want. (Phil. 4:11–12)

We know Paul experienced great extremes throughout his ministry. Moments of great response to his teaching were followed by times of equally great rejection, when his life was in danger and he was run out of town on a rail. There were joyous relationships of mutual caring and support (like Priscilla and Aquila and the church at Philippi), countered by other contacts where Paul was suspected, criticized, and belittled. What then was Paul's "secret," which enabled him to remain content even in times of severe suffering, oppression, and want?

Philippians 4:13 describes clearly the source of Paul's continuing confidence and contentment: "I can do everything through him who gives me strength." The apostle had found a way to focus on the power and strength of God, not his own weakness or the nature of his current circumstances. It was not Paul's circumstances that gave him confidence or inspired dismay; it was his reliance on the strength of God, who undergirded him in Christ Jesus.

In a different context but with similar effect the author of Hebrews exhorts his readers to avoid the love of money, but to "be content with what you have"

(Heb. 13:5). Often we love money and strive after it because of the false sense of financial security it seems to offer, or the power it gives us to manipulate our circumstances and exercise control over our lives. However, Psalm 30, Paul, and the author of Hebrews all agree in cautioning us not to find our security in any circumstance, fickle feeling, or human source of power that seems to offer us control of life. Instead, true contentment—the lasting strength to stand up with confidence in any circumstance—comes only from God, about whom the author of Hebrews goes on to say: "The Lord is my helper; I will not be afraid. What can [anyone] do to me?" (Heb. 13:6).[20]

These Scriptures call us, then, to ground our hope and confidence in God alone. Psalm 30 goes further to say that even when God is not particularly apparent or our circumstances suggest he is distant or absent, even then our only hope is to place our trust in him. This placing of our lives in the hands of God is the attitude of submission that the Old Testament knows as "the fear of the LORD." When we acknowledge that without God life is formless and void, when we admit our own powerlessness, when we acknowledge that he alone has the power to save, then regardless of its circumstances, life with God at the center can be marked with enduring contentment.

20. The author of Hebrews offers two quotations from the Old Testament in Heb. 13:5b–6: the first from Deut. 31:6, the second from Ps. 118:6–7.

Psalm 31

FOR THE DIRECTOR of music. A psalm of David.

1 In you, O LORD, I have taken refuge;
let me never be put to shame;
deliver me in your righteousness.
2 Turn your ear to me,
come quickly to my rescue;
be my rock of refuge,
a strong fortress to save me.
3 Since you are my rock and my fortress,
for the sake of your name lead and guide me.
4 Free me from the trap that is set for me,
for you are my refuge.
5 Into your hands I commit my spirit;
redeem me, O LORD, the God of truth.

6 I hate those who cling to worthless idols;
I trust in the LORD.
7 I will be glad and rejoice in your love,
for you saw my affliction
and knew the anguish of my soul.
8 You have not handed me over to the enemy
but have set my feet in a spacious place.

9 Be merciful to me, O LORD, for I am in distress;
my eyes grow weak with sorrow,
my soul and my body with grief.
10 My life is consumed by anguish
and my years by groaning;
my strength fails because of my affliction,
and my bones grow weak.
11 Because of all my enemies,
I am the utter contempt of my neighbors;
I am a dread to my friends—
those who see me on the street flee from me.
12 I am forgotten by them as though I were dead;
I have become like broken pottery.

13 For I hear the slander of many;
there is terror on every side;
they conspire against me
and plot to take my life.

14 But I trust in you, O LORD;
I say, "You are my God."
15 My times are in your hands;
deliver me from my enemies
and from those who pursue me.
16 Let your face shine on your servant;
save me in your unfailing love.
17 Let me not be put to shame, O LORD,
for I have cried out to you;
but let the wicked be put to shame
and lie silent in the grave.
18 Let their lying lips be silenced,
for with pride and contempt
they speak arrogantly against the righteous.

19 How great is your goodness,
which you have stored up for those who fear you,
which you bestow in the sight of men
on those who take refuge in you.
20 In the shelter of your presence you hide them
from the intrigues of men;
in your dwelling you keep them safe
from accusing tongues.

21 Praise be to the LORD,
for he showed his wonderful love to me
when I was in a besieged city.
22 In my alarm I said,
"I am cut off from your sight!"
Yet you heard my cry for mercy
when I called to you for help.

23 Love the LORD, all his saints!
The LORD preserves the faithful,
but the proud he pays back in full.
24 Be strong and take heart,
all you who hope in the LORD.

THIS PSALM IS a plea for deliverance from the intrigues, plots, and conspiracies of an enemy (31:13, 20). The psalmist appeals to the "God of truth" (31:5) for protection from the "lying lips" (31:18), arrogant speech (31:18), and "accusing tongues" (31:20) of his opponents. Yahweh is envisioned once again as the "strong fortress" and "refuge" (31:1–4), by which the beleaguered psalmist is protected from attack and preserved from the personal shame (31:1, 17) that results from being publicly slandered (31:13).

The psalm moves between the experience of extreme anguish (31:9–13) and the realization of great confidence and trust in the power of Yahweh to save and protect (31:6–8, 14–15, 21–22). The first three verses are similar to 71:1–3, where almost identical words appear, although expanded at points by additional phrases.[1] This confirms the psalmists' practice of drawing on a treasury of psalmic resources and reworking them to serve in new contexts and for new purposes.

The psalm divides into six sections: a plea for deliverance from a trap set by the enemies and Yahweh is seen as refuge (31:1–5), a statement of commitment and confidence (31:6–8), the primary plea for mercy with a description of the psalmist's weakness and anguish (31:9–13), a statement of trust and anticipation of deliverance from enemies (31:14–18), a proclamation of God's goodness (31:19–20), and a call to praise Yahweh (31:21–24).

The Heading (31:0)

NO NEW TERMS appear in the heading to Psalm 31. The composition is described simply as a psalm (*mizmor*) of David and referred to "the director of music."[2]

Plea for Deliverance (31:1–5)

THIS FIRST SECTION is dominated by the psalmist's concern to find refuge in Yahweh. The related terms pile up in these verses ("refuge" in 31:1, 2, 4; "rock" in 31:2, 3; "fortress" in 31:2, 3), emphasizing this theme of reliance and trust that underlies the whole psalm (see comments on the refuge theme in 2:12; 5:11; 7:1; 9:9). Once again it is clear that to "take refuge in the LORD"

---

1. This circumstance is, of course, more complex than can be briefly stated. Through 31:2a the two psalms are practically identical. From that point the two diverge more significantly, each offering phrases not appearing in the other but maintaining a progression of similar phrases.

2. See comments on these terms in the headings of Pss. 3 and 4.

constitutes a step of faith and trust in the face of a reality of threat, oppression, and suffering. To take refuge in Yahweh is to trust that Yahweh affirms the righteousness of the faithful and to hope confidently that he will indeed act to establish that essential righteousness publicly.

That those who put their trust in Yahweh continue to suffer is the whole point of the lament psalms. The righteous cannot hope to avoid suffering and oppression from the hand of the wicked, but they face such suffering in full dependence that Yahweh's righteousness (31:1) mirrors and affirms their own, and in trust that divine righteousness will ultimately fill the earth, revealing wickedness for what it is and affirming the righteous who endure faithfully. This does not represent hope for a "quick fix" or "pain avoidance" but is an example of aligning oneself with what is true and right regardless of the painful consequences.

Deliver me in your righteousness. The narrator wants Yahweh to demonstrate divine righteousness by bringing him into safety and security. There are a number of words translated "deliver" or "save" in the Old Testament. The one used here (*plṭ*) has the meaning "help someone to escape, bring into security." Besieged by the arrogant, lying words of the wicked, the psalmist feels insecure and threatened, and he petitions Yahweh for the sense of security and safety that the divine refuge offers. At the same time, the narrator can hope for divine response because Yahweh is righteous (31:1) and will determine the truth (31:5) of the circumstances surrounding the psalmist, revealing the prevarication of the enemy.

Let me never be put to shame. Most often we think—at least I know *I* do—of shame as a feeling, an emotion. As such, shame can be denied or submerged in the inner person so that those outside never know what we are feeling. In the Hebrew context of Psalm 31, however, shame is not so much a feeling (although feelings must have been involved) as it is an outward, visible circumstance of public disgrace. The kind of attack the narrator experiences is not just an attempt to make him feel bad, but the enemy tries to discredit him in the public arena.

To seek (as the psalmist does) "never [to] be put to shame" cannot mean complete escape for a lifetime from any public reproach. Our psalm makes it clear that the psalmist already experiences the contempt of the neighborhood (31:11) and physical infirmities that lead to avoidance by friends and slander by many (31:11–13), who use the common association of sickness with sin to raise questions about his righteousness. What the psalmist desires, then, is not avoidance of such shame but an ultimate clearing of the slate and a public vindication of truth and righteousness. In such a circumstance, there is no longer any possibility of public misperception; all things will be made transparently clear.

As a result, the tables will be turned on those who lead the attack on the psalmist. He wants their twisting, distorting manipulation of truth to be made known so that *they* will be put to shame—not by feeling bad but by public disgrace (31:17). Thus, his plea that the enemy "be put to shame" is not simply a cry for vengeance—to "pay them back" for a personal offense; rather, it is a desire that Yahweh's righteousness be unavoidably and undeniably mirrored in the realm of human affairs, with consequent affirmation of the righteous and condemnation of the wicked.

Turn your ear to me. I am reminded of the small child sitting on her mother's lap while her mother is in conversation with a friend. After several attempts to interrupt the conversation to gain her mother's attention, the child reaches out a hand, pulls the mother's face close to her own, and says in a most plaintive voice, "Mommy, you're not *listening* to me!" The psalmist's plea similarly demands God's full, undivided attention to a desperate situation that requires immediate action (*meherah* in 31:2 ["come quickly, hurry"]).

Be my rock . . . a strong fortress. Having proclaimed from the first line a willingness to take refuge in Yahweh, the psalmist now calls on Yahweh to be what the psalmist has trusted him to be: the place of security and protection from the enemy. He desires to experience in reality, in the present, the sense of a secure place from which to face the attacks of the wicked. The picture is of a remote rocky crag or a well-protected military outpost in rugged mountain terrain. From behind such removed and impregnable defenses the psalmist is content to watch the futile plots and machinations of the enemy played out.

Since you are my rock and my fortress. In an odd progression, the psalmist goes on to admit that the "refuge" hoped for is in reality already present. This tension between desperate desire for and confident experience of divine deliverance and protection is characteristic of many (if not most) of the laments. The psalmists constantly float back and forth between confident reliance on Yahweh's care and protection and desperate pleading that hoped-for deliverance will quickly materialize. I think this affirms that their chief desire was for an abiding sense of spiritual and emotional protection by God rather than for complete escape from all hurt and attack. The psalmists were far too astute observers of human affairs to anticipate such unlikely results. What this psalm seems to seek is enduring courage and a sense of divine presence in the face of ongoing struggle and strife.

For the sake of your name. Having already labeled God as righteous (31:1) and preparing to link Yahweh with the epithet "God of truth" (31:5), the psalmist now grounds his plea for deliverance on the essential characteristics of God that constitute his public reputation, so to speak: "If you, God, wish to live up to your reputation of righteousness and truth, you will not allow falsehood to bring down the righteous!"

Lead and guide me. The psalmist employs the imagery of the hunted animal pushed by pursuing hunters toward a hidden trap that will capture him. Surrounded by enemies, he feels the need of divine guidance to avoid rushing headlong into those hidden pitfalls. On the way to the secure stronghold, the pursued warrior may have to thread his way through a minefield laid by his enemies, who hope to destroy him before he can reach the safety of refuge.

Into your hands I commit my spirit. The psalmist makes an act of commitment into the hand of the God of truth, whom he trusts to redeem the faithful. It is notable that it is the "spirit" (*ruaḥ*) that the psalmist surrenders to Yahweh, not the "soul" (*nepeš*). The *nepeš* describes the animated physical being that constitutes a living person. At creation God breathed his own "breath of life" (*nišmat ḥayyim*) into the inanimate body of the first human, so that the being became a *nepeš ḥayyah* ("a living being," Gen. 2:7). Elsewhere this animating "breath" (*nešama/nišmat*) that emanates from God is identified with the spirit of God (*ruaḥ*) that sustains humans during their lives and returns to God upon their death.[3]

To commit one's "spirit" to God is not simply to trust for physical deliverance of the physical being or *nepeš*, but it is to make the ultimate surrender of the very animating force of life into the care of the God from whom it comes and who may sustain or remove it as he pleases. The psalmist's act of commitment, coming as it does at the end of the opening plea, reflects complete surrender of self-control and submission to God's will.[4]

Commitment and Confidence (31:6–8)

THIS NEXT SECTION flows out of the statement of commitment expressed in 31:5. Verse 6 contrasts the futility of trusting in gods other than Yahweh ("cling to worthless idols") with the psalmist's own confident reliance on Yahweh ("I trust in the LORD"). The phrase "worthless idols" (*hable šawʾ*) is

---

3. In Job the identification of these terms is esp. clear, when "spirit of God" (*ruaḥ ʾel*) is paralleled with "breath of the Almighty" (*nišmat šadday*) on two occasions (Job 32:8 and 33:4). See also Job 34:14, where spirit and breath are linked. Eccl. 12:7 and Ps. 146:4 describe the departure of the *ruaḥ* at death. Eccl. 12:7 goes so far as to note the spirit returns to God, "who gave it." In a clear reference to the account of creation in Gen. 2, Zech. 12:1 declares that Yahweh "forms" (using the same Heb. verb *yṣr* as in Gen. 2:7 to describe the forming of the first human by God from clay) the *ruaḥ* "of man within him."

4. In Luke's passion narrative, Jesus at the last gives himself up into the care of God with the words of this psalm: "Father, into your hands I commit my spirit" (Luke 23:46). In Acts 7:59, Stephen commits himself into the care of Jesus with much the same words.

instructive. The Hebrew combines two words—"nothingness, void" and "worthless, in vain, false"—to refer rather obliquely but pointedly to the ineffective emptiness of idols on which the wicked rely. The remaining verses celebrate the psalmist's assurance of Yahweh's love (31:7) and deliverance ("you have not handed me over to the enemy," 31:8).

In this context, the psalmist's confidence seems to be derived from past experiences of deliverance that offer new hope for the present. The anticipation of glad rejoicing is the result of Yahweh's previous attention to the affliction and anguish of the psalmist and the resulting deliverance from the enemy. Consequently, Yahweh's effective presence and action contrasts favorably to the empty void represented by the false gods. Yahweh "saw . . . and knew" (31:7) and has already acted in ways to free and liberate the oppressed narrator (31:8).

Hand. The psalmist sets up a nice contrast using the phrase "in/into the hand of. . . ." In verse 5, he surrenders to the protective care and control of Yahweh with the phrase "into your hand I commit my spirit." This section describes Yahweh as providing protective care for the psalmist by not surrendering him "into the hand" of the enemy. The phrase occurs again in 31:15, where he acknowledges once more that hope for deliverance is "in your hands." The striking phrase with which verse 8 concludes ("[you] have set my feet in a spacious place") offers an effective response to the hemmed-in feeling that dominates the darker moments of the psalm.

Plea for Mercy (31:9–13)

THE PSALMIST RETURNS briefly in 31:9 to the plea for deliverance with which the psalm began (cf. vv. 1–4). But here the plea introduces an extended narrative of suffering that serves as the motivation for divine deliverance. The description uses images of drastic physical deterioration, which might be associated with symptoms of extreme illness as analogies to the painful waning of life force as the result of constant attack from without.

My eyes grow weak with sorrow. The deterioration of eyesight may be the result of old age or sickness, or (as here) irritation and anger (see comments on 6:7). It is not so much sickness or sorrow that has brought the psalmist so low but anger and irritation over false accusations and a negative public perception that saps his will to live. The NIV expands the second phrase ("my soul and my body") by adding a synonym "grief" that does not appear in the Hebrew; the term *kaᶜas* ("irritation, anger") in the second line does double duty for both phrases.

The psalmist's desperate sense of extremity is revealed in verse 10: "My life is consumed [better, 'finished, completed, brought to an end'] by anguish and my years [are brought to an end] by groaning." "Strength fails" and bones "grow weak."

Because of all my enemies. The reason for the rapid deterioration of physical health and the waning of the will to live now becomes clear. It is the attacks of enemies and the "utter contempt of . . . neighbors" that weigh the psalmist down. Even those who claim to be friends avoid him in the street so that he feels forgotten—cast off like a broken piece of pottery.

For I hear the slander of many. The reason for all this treatment of the psalmist is the slanderous reports being made by many. The disgraceful public shame the psalmist experiences is falsely induced, but it produces a context of contempt in which the psalmist feels terrified, under attack, and threatened.

Trust and Anticipation of Deliverance (31:14–18)

WHAT A DIFFERENCE a conjunction and emphatic word position can make. Following the intense description of the demoralizing situation the psalmist faces, verse 14 begins with the common conjunction *waw* and the first-person singular pronoun: *wa*ʾ*ani* ("and I"). The placement of the pronoun at the beginning is an emphatic move and indicates a strong response to what has preceded. It is appropriately rendered by the NIV's "But I," although it is difficult to render the emphasis intended here. It is as if he says: "Contrary to what one might expect under the circumstances, I do not despair, *but I* surrender in trust to the hand of God" (31:14–15), naming Yahweh as the only source of hope.

My times are in your hands. The use of "time/times" in this sense is more than a remark on the passage of time. Underlying the psalmist's surrender is an understanding of life as made up of a series of decisive moments in which a person can take either appropriate or inappropriate direction, depending on how he or she responds to the circumstances. One response is to seek to control and manipulate the situation to one's advantage. That is clearly what the psalmist's opponents are doing. The other way is to surrender one's personal will to the power and authority of God, as the psalmist seeks to do in 31:15.

This is no simplistic fatalism in which the psalmist, confronted by life-threatening circumstances, simply shrugs and says, "Whatever!" Rather, it is a call to the righteous to become people who "understand the times" (cf. 1 Chron. 12:32; Est. 1:13)—to be perceptive observers of life and sensitive to the character and purpose of God, and to respond appropriately in each "time." The psalmist's confidence that Yahweh remains powerful over all the discordant activities of the enemies permits him to eschew frantic attempts to shore up personal interest, and instead to take up residence in the secure stronghold Yahweh provides.

Let your face shine. The presence of God is a radiant glory that stamps its impress on those who perceive it. After spending forty days and nights in the presence of Yahweh, Moses' face glowed in a haunting reminder of his divine encounter (Ex. 34:29–35). The treasured Hebrew benediction (Num. 6:24–26)[5] uses the phrase "[May] the LORD make his face shine upon you" as a graphic image of divine blessing and grace. Elsewhere we learn that to see the divine face is to risk death (Ex. 33:18–33). To anticipate coming into the glorious presence of Yahweh without harm is the ultimate hope of grace and divine favor (cf. Isa. 6:1–9).

Let me not be put to shame. The psalmist returns to the theme of the opening verses—the desire not to remain publicly disgraced. Like Job, the psalmist hopes to experience ultimate vindication when God appears to set all things right. Job did receive a sort of vindication in the final chapters of that book, but our psalmist is still waiting divine action.

Desire for a righteous public settlement of affairs, where truth is known and parties judged according to their relation to it, leads the psalmist to plead that the lying enemies receive "the shame" they have falsely heaped on the psalmist's head (31:17). As he feels brought low to the point of death by the enemies' vicious plotting, so he envisions their strident voices as silenced once and for all in death (31:17–18).[6]

Along with the reference in 31:13 to slanderous plots directed toward the psalmist, the notice about the "lying lips" of his enemies makes it clear that their offense is false and arrogant speech, by which they seek to undermine the reputation of the righteous. The personal experience of the psalmist is broadened in 31:18 to include the righteous in general, preparing the ground for the shift to communal perspective that takes place in 31:19–20, 23–24.

Proclamation of God's Goodness (31:19–20)

THE POEM SHIFTS at this point into the mode of praise. These two verses have the effect of generalizing the circumstances of the psalmist to incorporate the whole community of the faithful. His experiences are seen not as

---

5. The Numbers passage is the only occurrence of the phrase outside the Psalter. Within the psalms the phrase occurs at 4:6; 31:16; 67:1; 80:3, 7, 19; 104:15; 119:35, and it is consistently associated with divine favor and blessing (see also comments on 4:6).

6. Sheol is the abode of the dead and is viewed as a place of passive silence and resting. Craigie (*Psalms 1–50*, 262) notes connections between death and silence in 94:17 and 115:17.

isolated personal events but as part of the great tapestry of dealing between God and his faithful people. As God has stored up goodness for those who fear him, so goodness is in store for the suffering psalmist.

In the sight of men. The psalmist has hope of *public* vindication and restitution to counter the destructive slander that has led to public condemnation and disgrace. Those who take refuge in Yahweh, as the psalmist has from verse 1, can anticipate that God's stored-up goodness will be bestowed "in the sight of men," not simply kept secretly in escrow. It is important for communal well-being and wholeness that righteousness be recognized and praised while falsehood is recognized and condemned.

In the shelter of your presence . . . in your dwelling. Again the idea of refuge returns with the introduction of the new image of "shelter" or secret hiding place. Yahweh hides the faithful in the place of his own transcendent presence. The NIV's "shelter" is a bit weak. The sentence employs both the verb *str* ("hide, conceal") and the noun *seter* ("hiding place") to describe not just a shelter but a place of concealment from the psalmist's besieging troubles.[7] The human experience of God is that while he comes graciously to humans, he is not at their beck and call but comes on his own terms and in his own time. God often seems inaccessible and removed—transcendently "other." When hidden with God in the divine "hiding place," the faithful need not fear the scheming attacks of the wicked. Not only are they protected by God, but they are also removed and distanced from the fray.

The term translated "dwelling" (*sukkah*) is most often used to describe a temporary "lean-to" or "booth." As such, the *sukkah* (plural *sukkot*) has lent its name to the Feast of Booths (Succoth), which remembered the Israelites' nomadic journey from Egypt to the Promised Land.[8] In God's dwelling, he protectively gathers the faithful as a treasure to be preserved from robbers and thieves. The verb used for this protective act (*ṣpn*, NIV "keep safe") is the same one used in 31:19 to celebrate the goodness Yahweh has "*stored up* for those who fear" him. As Yahweh amasses a vast treasure of goodness from which he graciously blesses the faithful, so the faithful are drawn together in his presence, safe from the schemes and plans of the wicked.

---

7. The theme of God as "hiding place" links this psalm to the following one, where God is once again viewed as protective place of concealment from trouble. Cf. 32:7, where the same Heb. term (*seter*) is used of God.

8. It is generally agreed that the Feast of Booths reinterprets an originally agricultural feast in which the *sukkot* were temporary shelters built to shade workers during the grain harvest. This early festival was given new life and purpose by making it the time for recalling the nomadic escape from Egyptian bondage. A similar transition can be seen taking place in the Feast of Weeks, an original agricultural festival mentioned as such in the Old Testament but transformed in later years into a remembrance of the giving of the law on Mount Sinai.

Call to Praise (31:21–24)

IN THIS SECTION praise of Yahweh remains the psalmist's aim (as in the preceding verses). Here, however, the focus returns to his more specific context, as evidenced by the use of first-person singular pronouns "I" and "me" throughout. If in the former passage the psalmist was generalizing to include a larger group of believers in praise, now the object is to give testimony to this larger group from his own experience. We see in passages like these somc hints of normal practice in temple worship. The individual worshiper brought personal concerns to worship but interacted frequently with the larger gathered community through calls to join in praise or moments of personal testimony directed to the congregation.

It is interesting that the NIV chooses to render the Hebrew passive participle as "Praise be...." A more natural translation—especially if humans are in view—is "Blessed be...." Perhaps the NIV translators were somewhat wary of suggesting that Yahweh—envisioned as complete within himself—can be additionally *blessed* by humans. This misses the point of the psalmist's statement, however, which is looking at this exchange of blessing, if you will, from the human side. The psalmist desires to pour out abundant blessing on Yahweh, who has shown such grace to the psalmist. It is not a question of theology (i.e., *can* humans actually bless God?), but of anthropology (i.e., the grateful being turns wholeheartedly to the creator in a desire to return the blessing received).

He showed his wonderful love. The Hebrew underlying the rather simple English translation "showed" is full of meaning. The Hiphil verb form is used in this case to capture the sense "reveal, make known." Moreover, the root of the verb *plʾ* has the basic sense "to be too hard or difficult; to be extraordinary, astounding." Together, Hiphil verb form and verbal root combine to provide a meaning far beyond "show." God has shown his faithfulness (Heb. *ḥesed*) in an astonishingly unexpected way, which is almost impossible for the recipient to believe.

The psalmist goes on to describe this astounding demonstration of divine faithfulness. Surrounded—as if in a besieged city—by the false accusations and distorted perceptions of friend and foe alike, he felt beyond divine help. "I am cut off from your sight!" he cried.[9] He was so far gone that God could

9. The sort of personal reflection out of a specific context described in this verse with the Heb. phrase *waʾani ʾamarti be-*... occurs three times in the psalms (Pss. 30:6; 31:22; 116:11; cf. also Isa. 38:10). That two of three occurrences should be found in adjacent psalms is suggestive. In Ps. 30 the reflection comes out of a sense of well-being (NIV "When I felt secure..."), while Ps. 31 reflects a situation of stress and confusion (NIV "In my alarm..."). Ps. 116 employs the same wording as 31:22 (NIV "In my dismay...") for a similar context of distress.

not even see him, let alone help. "Yet"—such a powerful little word, which reveals that human perceptions are often mistaken and that the psalmist's feeling of defeat is not *yet* the final word—when all seemed lost and beyond the redemptive power of Yahweh, Yahweh heard the cry for help. The psalmist has no need to carry the narrative further to describe God's saving intervention. It is enough to know that he *heard*, for, having heard the cry of the faithful, divine action cannot be doubted.

In the final verses, the narrator once again addresses the congregation of the faithful, drawing them into the experience of deliverance and praise (31:23–24). Those addressed are variously called "saints" (*ḥasidim*), "the faithful" (*ʾemunim*), and "you who hope in the LORD" (*meyaḥalim* is better translated "wait for, endure"). The psalmist counsels these people to "love the LORD" and to "be strong and take heart."

These are characteristics to possess in the face of difficulty and attack—the same words Joshua used to prepare the people of Israel for their campaign against the inhabitants of the Promised Land (Josh. 1:6, 9). The readers of this psalm would likely have recalled those circumstances as one example of the way Yahweh has shown his faithfulness in an astonishingly unexpected way (Ps. 31:21). Likely they would have remembered the concluding exhortations of Joshua 1:9: "Have I not commanded you? Be strong and courageous. Do not be terrified; do not be discouraged, for the LORD your God will be with you wherever you go." With this allusion to Joshua, the psalmist drives home the message of personal experience by relating it to a classic example taken from Israel's formative historical traditions. As Yahweh acted for Joshua, he has acted for me, and we can trust him to act again.

THE FEAR OF SHAME. As I said earlier, we often think of shame as a *feeling* of wrongness or disgrace. Psychologists today attempt to distinguish between *shame*—an *undeserved* sense of wrongness often put upon us by other people or situations beyond our control—and *guilt*—an *appropriate* sense of wrongness resulting from our own wrong actions. While this may be a helpful distinction in the progressive outworking of a counseling process, it is usually difficult to make in common practice. The Hebrew words that stand behind the Old Testament concept of shame similarly make no attempt to distinguish undeserved *shame* from justified *guilt*.

The Hebrew concept of shame is also less an emotion or feeling than a situation of public condemnation and approbation. At the core, what is involved in our passage (and in the many other places where shame is considered in the psalms)[10] is a tension between public perception and what the psalmist knows to be reality. The community may think he has sinned, been defeated, and been forgotten or rejected by God. They may even reject God altogether and think the exercise of power by the wicked is more effective than the righteous person's enduring dependence on Yahweh. Thus, the psalmist may experience the reproach, ridicule, rejection, condemnation, and oppression of the community while remaining in reality faithfully dependent on Yahweh and feeling personally righteous.

Once again significant links between the lament psalms and Job are clearly drawn. Job is convinced of his own righteousness and seeks above all to have that righteousness vindicated in public by God himself. If God would only come to answer Job's questions, God would have to declare him in the right, leaving no public doubt of his faithfulness (Job 23:1–7; 31:6). Similarly, our psalmist is falsely accused and publicly condemned although in reality innocent of these misperceptions.

While law courts are charged with determining the true state of affairs and rendering judgment to contending parties according to their relationship to that truth, justice is too easily perverted by falsehood and bribes or by the inability of humans—judges and general public alike—to look beyond the outward appearances to perceive the inward reality. God, however, looks on the heart and passes judgment based on a person's true inward being. Thus the innocent psalmist, like Job, wants God to come in judgment, knowing that then the righteous will be vindicated and the wicked condemned.

Alignment with the essential righteousness of Yahweh. The psalmist teaches the reader an important but difficult lesson. It is necessary to align oneself with the essential righteousness that characterizes Yahweh even if it does not pay off in benefit. That is another way of saying that commitment to the way of Yahweh is costly.

There was a tendency in Israel to assume that commitment to relationship with Yahweh meant immediate reward and benefit in the temporal world. The Deuteronomic law code seems to imply this with statements like: "If you fully obey the LORD your God and carefully follow all his commands I give you today, the LORD your God will set you high above all the nations on earth. All these blessings will come upon you and accompany you if you obey the LORD your God" (Deut. 28:1–2). There follows in the text a whole series of immediate, physical benefits promised to the obedient Israelites:

---

10. Cf. Pss. 4:2; 25:2, 3, 20; 31:1, 17; 34:5; 35:4, 26; 40:14, 15; 44:7, 15; 53:5; 69:6, 7; 70:2, 3; 71:1, 13, 24; 78:66; 83:16; 86:17; 89:45; 97:7; 109:28, 29; 119:6, 31, 46, 78, 80; 127:5; 129:5; 132:18.

fruitfulness of humans, animals, and crops; defeat of enemies; abundant prosperity (Deut. 28:3–14).

Much of the biblical wisdom literature—especially Proverbs—takes the same tact. The wise/righteous prosper while fools/wicked perish. It is this assumed cause-effect relationship between righteous obedience and divine blessing that underlies the community's critical scorn for the psalmist's circumstance. If the righteous prosper, then the corollary must also be true that those who do not prosper must not be righteous. Thus, the psalmist's claims of innocent suffering fall on deaf ears; the circumstance of suffering have already established the case—guilty!

The testimony of this psalm, however, puts the lie to this common misperception that obedience leads unquestionably to benefit and prosperity. The psalmist (like Job) knows the inward reality of innocence and yet experiences suffering and public ridicule. The lesson is twofold: that the righteous *can* and often *do* suffer, and that the blessing of righteousness must be understood as different from the physical benefit and prosperity commonly anticipated.

Even some of the Proverbs (although only a few) understand this. "Better a poor man whose walk is blameless than a rich man whose ways are perverse" (Prov. 28:6). "Better a little with the fear of the LORD than great wealth with turmoil" (Prov. 15:16).[11] Sometimes public reputation is considered more important as a sign of divine blessing than wealth. "A good name is more desirable than great riches; to be esteemed is better than silver or gold" (Prov. 22:1).[12] When one's reputation is wrongly endangered (as in our psalm), that is the ultimate cause of shame and disgrace. One might be willing to suffer poverty, oppression, sickness, and even death if only one is publicly recognized as a righteous woman or man. To have this last shred of human dignity destroyed as well is the ultimate human defeat. That is why the psalmist hopes for divine vindication.

THE POWER OF CONTEXT. The contemporary cry is "Location! Location! Location!" In sales—especially real estate—location is considered "everything." The context in which a house is located determines value, desirability, and ultimately makes or breaks the sale. So, at least the real estate salespersons would have us believe.

11. Cf. also Prov. 3:14; 15:17; 16:8, 16, 19; 17:1.

12. See also the biblical books of Job and Ecclesiastes for a contrasting view to this general pattern.

Context is also considered important for understanding the value of our lives. What do you do? How much do you make? Where do you live? Do you have a vacation home? What kind of car do you drive? How many vehicles do you own? Where do your children go to school? Where do you buy your clothes? Whom do you count among your friends? Often these criteria drive our perception of our value and worth. They are the ways we have come to understand and identify ourselves and others. And if our context should change—a job lost, a spouse dead or divorced, a moral failure tarnishing a reputation—then our value is tarnished as well.

The flip side of the fear of shame that is at the center of our psalm is the pursuit of status, image, and reputation. We seek success, often measured by public approval. When that carefully constructed image is shattered by any number of unexpected reversals, it can feel suspiciously like life is no longer worth living.

He was a respected and successful Christian with an international reputation. He was well liked at work, in the community, and among his friends. He was "moving up" into areas of authority and responsibility. But when his private moral demons became public, it became devastatingly painful for his wife, children, family, and friends. As new revelations became known day after day and the circle of awareness grew, a lifetime of defense mechanisms began to fail—denial, excuses, anger, minimizing, rationalizing, compartmentalizing.

In private he huddled in a near fetal position in the grips of an almost uncontrollable tremor and shake. In public, by some incredible exercise of will over body, he was able to master the tremor and appear almost normal, except, perhaps, to a careful observer. But inside his hollow eyes, his mind was consumed with a single thought: how a high-speed automobile collision could relieve his wife, family, and, most important, of course, himself from the near lethal agony of the consequences of his own sin and public humiliation.

In moments like these, our perception of our circumstances seem to say there is no way out; all is hopeless. This is particularly true in the out-of-control times of public disgrace and shame. It is understandable that we allow our circumstances to determine our perception of reality and hope, since our whole identity is so often based on visible externalities and how others view us. When our outer world collapses and the world and our friends turn the cold shoulder of disapproval, it is easy to buy the majority view that we are not worth knowing or saving. Like the man I described above, we can see no hope and may contemplate, or even act on, a desperate need to escape from uncontrollable pain.

The psalmist expresses just such desperation. Surrounded like a besieged city, the psalmist cries out, "In my alarm I said, 'I am cut off from your sight!'"

(31:22). The context of ridicule, approbation, and disgrace led the psalmist to believe he was beyond the caring of God, alone and helpless. But human perspectives are distinctly limited, and our context is always a slippery foundation for personal identity, value, and hope. The psalmist's experience in immediate response to the desperate cry is that Yahweh unexpectedly hears and responds in mercy. In what appeared to be hopeless circumstances, God arrives to provide refuge and hope.

How do we catch on to this hard, new perspective—one that evaluates personal value and hope not on public opinion or circumstance (both of which are beyond our ability to control)? Our psalmist discovered a way to dwell in the shelter of the divine presence even when all hell had broken loose in his circumstance and his personal context offered no reasonable hope for escape. In what follows, I will offer two suggestions for how the psalmist was able to do this: (1) He discovered a foundation of personal identity, value, and hope that was independent of any context or circumstance; (2) he learned the lesson of surrender that the newfound identity made possible.

Clinging to the God of truth. The psalmist learned that human perception is a dangerous basis on which to ground one's understanding of the present context or one's hope for the future. The very human perspective of his antagonists, even though grounded on common traditional understanding affirmed by society at large, was confounded by his own intimate knowledge of the truth—the psalmist was righteous. Similarly, however, his own very human interpretation of the immediate context—an interpretation that led to despair—while based on a clear evidence of the contemporary realities, was equally erroneous in the end because Yahweh was present and was providing a secure dwelling for the psalmist in his presence.

The man I described above, who in despair at his public disgrace and steadily deteriorating circumstances saw no way out, was thankfully wrong! A loving friend recognized the signs of despair and got the sufferer into counseling. Another gracious and caring friend supplied the funds to make extended treatment possible. A gracious Christian community received the wounded man and his family with redemptive love and restoration.

Our own interpretation of our context can be dangerously wrong. Where we see no God, God nevertheless hovers lovingly just outside our peripheral vision. Within a despairing context we need to discover a perspective of truth that exceeds our own limited understanding of reality. We need to see ourselves and our circumstances through the eyes of "the God of truth" (31:5), who looks beyond the temporary externals to see the eternal verities that work for redemption. Only with this true vision as our foundation can we discover what has been waiting for us all along—the secure dwelling of God, the rock and refuge in the midst of trouble.

Sometimes it is possible to gain this true perspective from the wisdom and encouragement of others in the community of faith. Sometimes it comes by reading the Scriptures and taking to heart the visions of God's sovereign authority over the universe. Always, however, it is the convincing work of the Spirit that opens our eyes and hearts to the divine refuge that stands waiting for us to enter in. If you would give the Spirit occasion to speak thus to you, if you would be challenged to see through God's eyes in the midst of personal pain and an impossible present, I would invite you to read again and again through the psalms—which by their history of composition, collection, and canonization offer personal, communal, and spiritual testimony to the refuge of God.

Into your hand I commit my spirit. Out of this new perspective of truth that derives only from the God of truth comes a newfound ability to surrender—not to despair and hopelessness, but to a secure trust in God.

When our circumstances seem troublesome or even hopeless, often we feel driven to take control to find our own way out of the mess. Our inward mechanism says something like: "I cannot trust anyone else to take care of my needs. If my need is to be met in this circumstance, I must find a way to do it myself. If I cannot find a way to do it myself, then it is hopeless."

The psalmist, in spite of the aggressively negative attacks of the enemy and in spite of equally pessimistic personal doubts, was ultimately able to see the situation through the eyes of the God of truth and surrendered in commitment to the refuge of God. The author of the Gospel of Luke records these words from Psalm 31:5 as Jesus' last utterance from the cross (Luke 23:46).

It seems clear that it is not merely these few words that Jesus and the Gospel writer wished to bring to the reader's attention, but the whole context of Psalm 31 in which they originally stood. In a position of public condemnation and shame, perceived by the surrounding community to have been a criminal, a charlatan, and a failure, Jesus made his last speech the words of this psalm. At the very point of death, when no immediate or future worldly restitution could have set things right, Jesus committed himself to the redemptive care of the "God of truth," who saw through all the twisted and distorted human words and perceptions to the reality of the world and the heart of the dying man hanging on the cross.[13]

---

13. The phrase "God of truth" is a singular one. Similar phrases occur only in Isa. 65:16 and 1 Esdras 4:40. The Hebrew of the former (*ʾelohim ʾamen*) is not an exact reflection of the Hebrew of our psalm (*ʾel ʾemet*). In Isaiah the phrase is often translated "faithful God." The 1 Esdras passage in the Greek is an exact reflection of the LXX of Ps. 31:5 (Gk. *ho theos tes aletheias*). By contrast, the Isa. 65:16 passage in the LXX is rendered *ton theon ton alethinon*.

Luke's Christ, surrounded by taunting enemies and fearful, doubting disciples, enters into death as an act of commitment to the righteous God of truth, who alone can be trusted to vindicate the enduring faith of the righteous. With these words Christ slipped, not down from the cross to avoid death (as his sneering detractors tempted him to do), or to assume without further suffering his rightful role as messianic king, but into the secure refuge of God that even death could not shake or overthrow.

Like Jesus, we cannot assume that committing our spirits into the hand of the God of truth will result in deliverance from suffering and death. Indeed, to commit one's spirit in this way is to give up any control or expectation over the outcome of life and to trust in the redemptive love of God, come what may. It is this giving up that makes it possible in the final analysis to enter the refuge of God. The taunts and ridicule do not disappear. They simply pass by without harm because we have passed beyond caring. The one who gives up life finds it. And in surrendering our claim to what we had thought to be life, we discover the true nature of living in the power of God alone and in his presence.

Psalm 32

OF DAVID. A *maskil.*

1 Blessed is he
whose transgressions are forgiven,
whose sins are covered.
2 Blessed is the man
whose sin the LORD does not count against him
and in whose spirit is no deceit.

3 When I kept silent,
my bones wasted away
through my groaning all day long.
4 For day and night
your hand was heavy upon me;
my strength was sapped
as in the heat of summer. *Selah*
5 Then I acknowledged my sin to you
and did not cover up my iniquity.
I said, "I will confess
my transgressions to the LORD"—
and you forgave
the guilt of my sin. *Selah*

6 Therefore let everyone who is godly pray to you
while you may be found;
surely when the mighty waters rise,
they will not reach him.
7 You are my hiding place;
you will protect me from trouble
and surround me with songs of deliverance. *Selah*

8 I will instruct you and teach you in the way you
should go;
I will counsel you and watch over you.
9 Do not be like the horse or the mule,
which have no understanding
but must be controlled by bit and bridle
or they will not come to you.

[10]Many are the woes of the wicked,
but the LORD's unfailing love
surrounds the man who trusts in him.

[11]Rejoice in the LORD and be glad, you righteous;
sing, all you who are upright in heart!

AS A PSALM of thanksgiving coupled with instruction encouraging the reader not to resist the guidance of Yahweh but to trust fully in him, Psalm 32 is divided into five segments: a proclamation of blessing (32:1–2), the narrator's personal example (32:3–5), exhortation with personal testimony (32:6–7), admonition against resisting God's instruction (32:8–10), final call to praise (32:11). While the term *selah* appears three times within the psalm, it only imperfectly relates to the proposed structure of the composition (see comments on *selah* at Ps. 3.)

Thematically Psalm 32 links back to Psalm 31 through the use of "hiding place" terminology in 32:7 (cf. comments on 31:20) and links forward to Psalm 33, which has no heading of its own.[1] Psalm 32 concludes with an exhortation to "rejoice" and "sing" directed to two groups: the "righteous" (*ṣaddiqim*) and the "upright in heart" (*yišre leb*). Psalm 33 opens with a similar exhortation to "sing" directed to the same two groups (*ṣaddiqim* and *yešarim*). The remainder of Psalm 33 can be understood as an appropriate response to these two exhortations by the whole worshiping community.

The primary focus of Psalm 32 is on the salutary effect of confession of sin that leads to divine forgiveness and restoration.[2] The instructive exhortation in 32:8–10 flows from the wisdom tradition and is taken by some scholars to be the words of the psalmist to the reader out of personal experience. Others understand this passage to report *divine* encouragement—perhaps reminiscent of a priestly oracle given to the supplicant in the temple (see comments below).

The Heading (32:0)

THE PSALM HEADING marks the first appearance in the Psalter of the Hebrew term *maśkil* in a heading (a noun based on the verb *śkl*, "make someone

1. See the discussion of untitled psalms in the section on "The Shape of the Psalter" in vol. 2 of this commentary. Cf. Gerald H. Wilson, "The Use of 'Untitled' Pss. in the Hebrew Psalter," *ZAW* 97 (1985): 405–13.

2. Ps. 32 is the second of seven penitential psalms in the Psalter (Pss. 6; 32; 38; 51; 102; 130; 143).

keen/clever; instruct").[3] The term is well known in the wisdom literature, where it is frequently used to mean "instruct, make perceptive," but is occasionally taken to mean "have success, be prosperous." While the idea of instruction is appropriate for the context of Psalm 32 and is reflected in the instructive style of Psalm 78 as well, the other eleven psalms so designated cannot by the widest stretch of imagination be called instruction. Kraus suggests that a *maśkil* is a song that has been "artistically molded" according to "the principles of wisdom," searching for "the fitting, uplifting, mighty word that is suitable for the object to be sung about and to be praised."[4] As such, the term is more an evaluation of the artistic merit of a psalm than an attempt to categorize it.

The fact that the following Psalm 33 has no heading of its own suggests a possible tradition for the combination of Psalms 32 and 33 (as seen previously with Pss. 9 and 10). Here, however, there is no clear evidence of original unity, so that any connection is more one of theme, imagery, and purpose than actual composition.[5]

Proclamation of Blessing (32:1–2)

THE PSALM BEGINS with a twofold repetition in verses 1–2 of the Hebrew term *ʾašre* ("blessed")—the same word that begins the whole Psalter (1:1). The poetic structure of these two verses is primarily affirming, with *ʾašre* in verse 1 introducing two participial phrases that describe the blessed person: "whose transgressions are forgiven, whose sins are covered." In verse 2 *ʾašre* is used, and the first following phrase, while not grammatically parallel to the two participial phrases just noted, is thematically parallel: "whose sin the LORD does not count against him." Each of these three phrases employs a distinctive term for human sin: "transgression" (*pešaʿ* ["rebellion against God"]), "sin" (*ḥaṭaʾah* ["turning away from the true path"]), and "sin" (*ʿawon* ["distortion, perversion, evil, disrespect for God"]).[6]

The second phrase in verse 2 does not parallel the preceding lines either grammatically or thematically. Instead, it leads the blessing to its conclusion with a declaration of the kind of human character that justifies the gracious forgiveness and blessing promised. The person who can anticipate Yahweh's forgiveness is the kind of person "in whose spirit is no deceit." The

---

3. The term appears in 14:2; in the headings, it appears an additional twelve times (Pss. 42; 44; 45; 52; 53; 54; 55; 74; 78; 88; 89; 142).

4. Kraus, *Psalms 1–59*, 25.

5. See my comments on the connections between Pss. 32 and 33 in my discussion of Ps. 33; also in Wilson, *The Editing of the Hebrew Psalter*, 174–76.

6. See Craigie, *Psalms 1–50*, 266; Kraus, *Psalms 1–59*, 369.

phrase also prepares the way for what follows in the personal narrative section. There we find flesh put on the bones of a spirit without deceit. Forgiveness comes to the one who confesses sin completely and openly without deceit or reservation.[7]

A Personal Example (32:3–5)

IN THESE THREE verses, the psalmist describes a personal experience that moves from initial resistance to confession (32:3–4) to reluctant but complete admission of sin (32:5). The two movements in the narrative—first resistance, then confession—are accompanied by contrasting descriptions of the consequence of the psalmist's attitude.

When I kept silent. First, the psalmist refuses to admit sin, preferring to remain silent. But resistance led to what appears to be inward turmoil and agony. The psalmist's "bones wasted away" (32:3), indicating an interior pain that set him groaning day and night (32:3–4). The result of the inward conflict was a loss of strength, as if wilting from a summer drought. Those who have experienced extreme bouts of depression probably recognize the symptoms here. An interior darkness opens up that threatens to swallow the sufferer. A normally energetic person can be reduced to inactivity—feeling almost drugged and unable to lift a finger to move.

Your hand was heavy upon me. The cause of the agony is clear to the psalmist: Unconfessed sin leads to divine disapproval. He can find no escape from this sense of God's judgment—even enmity—either day or night (32:4). In Psalm 31, the narrator, although affirming innocence, experienced a similar agony because of the false accusations of friend and foe. Eyes, soul, and body grew weak; life was consumed with groaning; strength failed and bones grew weak (31:9–10). There the cause was the psalmist's enemies (31:11), not God. Remarkably, the innocent suffering psalmist was able to trust God for deliverance and find refuge in the midst of trouble. But here in Psalm 32, the guilty narrator finds no release from the agony of guilt, because God's judgment leaves no refuge to flee to!

---

7. An interesting assimilation of texts apparently takes place in the LXX version of Ps. 32. There the Greek text reads, "there is no deceit *in his mouth*" rather than the Hebrew's "in his spirit." This seems to modify the original text toward Isa. 53:9, "nor was any deceit in his mouth." In the Greek text, the two Heb. words for "deceit" (*remiyyah* and *mirmah*) are translated by the same Greek word: *dolos*. In the New Testament, 1 Peter 2:22 clearly quotes from Isa. 53:9 as illumining the model of Christ we are to emulate. In Jesus' first encounter with Nathanael (John 1:47–51), he praises Nathanael as "a true Israelite, in whom there is nothing false." The theme of lack of deceit as praiseworthy was certainly well established by the time of Christ.

The linkage of sin and sickness is apparent here as well as in Psalm 31. It was commonly understood that sin could bring divine retribution in the form of physical illness. Thus, the illness of the narrator of Psalm 31 gave ample justification to enemy or friend alike to assume the worst: God was judging the psalmist for sin. But the psalmist took care to indicate that to the contrary, the suffering experienced was the result of false accusation by malicious humans.

In Psalm 32, however, the community perception is closer to the truth—the psalmist *has* sinned, with illness as the consequence. It is interesting that the suffering appears less as the result of divine assault than the outworking of the psalmist's own repressed guilt. This is perhaps too modern an interpretation, but one with which many moderns are thoroughly familiar. The destructive effects of repressed and unexpressed emotions and anxieties can be powerfully experienced in physical pain and psychological disintegration.

Then I acknowledged my sin to you. Having descended into the depths both physically and emotionally, the psalmist is, by some unrevealed change of attitude, mind, or will, able at last to reveal his hidden sin to God. Once the cover-up is over, the resulting release is immediate. The response to the psalmist's confession is not further punishment but complete divine forgiveness (32:5). Not only is his sin forgiven, but even the guilt is "lifted away" (NIV "you forgave"), using the beautiful image of removing the terrible crushing weight of guilt like a boulder. We will consider implications of this idiomatic phrase in the Bridging Contexts section.

Exhortation and Personal Testimony (32:6–7)

HAVING LAID OUT personal experience as evidence, the psalmist now calls his readers/hearers to apply these insights to their lives through personal action. The exhortation in these two verses is styled as direct address to God (note the second-person masculine singular pronouns), but the purpose is clearly to encourage humans to seize on the hope engendered by the psalmist's experience of divine grace extended in response to honest confession, so that they too will approach God in prayers of open confession.

While you may be found. There is a sense of realistic urgency in the psalmist's call to prayer. While God is always present with humans, he is not always available to be found by them. Reluctance to confess leads to delay and compounds the possibility of human error. God does not make himself readily available to those who seek him only in times of extreme distress. The psalmist's exhortation is that a relationship of trust and reliance on God must be built in times of relative peace and security, so that when the "mighty waters" of trouble come, the one who has an established pattern of communication with Yahweh will not be overcome.

Once again, as throughout the psalms, note that the coming of trouble to the righteous is assumed. The psalmists are realists, who base their understanding and hope on the real experience of life with all its diversity. The assurance given here is that a firm foundation will enable those who are prepared to face the onslaught without being toppled.

You are my hiding place. The psalmist continues the sideways exhortation of the reader/hearers by addressing to Yahweh a personal expression of confidence in the protective care of God. The "hiding place" terminology (*seter*) directs us back to the strong refuge motif that dominated Psalm 31. As there, the psalmist of Psalm 32 encourages the audience to trust that Yahweh provides protection in the midst of trouble; God will "guard/protect" him from trouble (32:7). God surrounds the faithful, not with strong defensive walls, as might be expected, but with "songs of deliverance." It is as if the confident songs of those who have placed their trust in Yahweh soar upward to form an impenetrable barrier to repulse the enemy.

Admonition and Instruction (32:8–10)

AS SUGGESTED ABOVE, there is some debate as to who is speaking in these verses, with some opting for God and others for the psalmist. The former is made difficult by the third-person reference to Yahweh in verse 10: "The LORD's unfailing love surrounds the man who trusts in him." The latter interpretation is hindered by the use in verse 8 of the second-person singular pronouns to reflect the addressee of the exhortation. If the psalmist were instructing a larger audience in the temple, it would seem more likely to employ plural pronouns in direct address.

It is true, however, that the initial verb in verse 9—a Qal jussive directed to the listener—is second-person *plural*. This raises a third possibility (mentioned by some[8]) that these statements may represent a priestly oracle of deliverance delivered to the psalmist (thus in the singular) in the temple as a direct message from God. If this is the case for verse 8, the plural in verse 9 suggests that the psalmist is using a traditional adage to connect individual personal experience to the experience of the listening community.

Horse and mule. The psalmist appeals to the image of two common beasts of burden to make his point. Horses and mules have no moral sense to guide them in decision-making, in plotting out the righteous way. Their movements must be controlled and limited by the use of "bit and bridle." The verb translated in the NIV as "have [no] understanding" (*byn*) is commonly used in wisdom literature to describe those who are perceptive, having clear

8. See Craigie, *Psalms 1–50*, 267; Kraus, *Psalms 1–59*, 371.

understanding that informs right decision-making. Clearly, animals like the horse and mule lack this kind of perception, relying on instinct, ingrained training, or human control to direct their paths.

The readers, therefore, are warned not to deaden their perceptive senses so that they end up resisting the divine will and must be disciplined by the "many woes" (32:10) that come on the wicked. By contrast, those wise ones who trust in Yahweh find themselves surrounded by his "unfailing love." Once again the faithful are protectively surrounded by Yahweh. In 32:7 "songs of deliverance" provided the shield against the enemy. Here the same verb for "surround" is employed (*sbb*), but it is God's enduring covenant love (*ḥesed*) that provides the barrier.

Final Call to Praise (32:11)

THE SONG CONCLUDES with a call to praise Yahweh. As noted earlier, two groups are identified as being summoned: the "righteous" and the "upright of heart." These two groups are the ones blessed in the opening verses because their sins have been forgiven. There is no sense that "righteousness" in this context assumes absolute purity and sinlessness. These are righteous because they have trusted Yahweh and been willing to confess their sins openly and completely to him, as the psalmist eventually did (32:5). Such righteousness is not earned by blameless human comportment but is granted by a gracious God in response to human trust and surrender.

This final verse, with its invocation to praise Yahweh, provides the occasion for the voicing of praise in the following Psalm 33. What the psalmist exhorts here, the voices of the next psalm fulfill (see comments on Ps. 33). This is not to say this verse does not function perfectly well as the conclusion to Psalm 32—it certainly does that as well. Joy, ecstatic shrieking, and singing are all appropriate responses for those who experience the faithful love of God poured out on them. This word picture gives us a brief window onto the celebratory worship of ancient Israel. No solemn, staid occasion this! The milling throngs, overcome with the wonder of God's love, parade about leaping and dancing, shrieking and singing in a marvelous cacophony of uninhibited and infectious praise.

BEARING THE RESPONSIBILITY OF GUILT. As mentioned in the comments on 32:5, the psalmist's confession brings an experience of release from guilt that is likened to "lifting" a crushing weight that has pinned him down. There is more to this image of "lifting away the guilt" than immediately appears on the surface. This idiom occurs numerous other times in the Old Testament, beginning with Cain's plaintive cry, "My guilt is greater than I can bear" (Gen. 4:13, lit. trans.), and it continues through the prophets.[9] The consistent meaning of the phrase is "to bear (responsibility of) guilt." That is clear in Cain's situation, though he feels the weight of his responsibility. In Exodus 28:38, Aaron is said to "bear the guilt" involved in consecrating profane items to the service of God. The Leviticus passages use the phrase to conclude specific legal circumstances with the judgment that a person "will be held responsible" for the guilt of his actions.

That it is possible for someone to bear responsibility for the guilt accruing from the actions of another is illustrated in Numbers 30:15, where a husband who fails to nullify his spouse's vow in a timely manner is held responsible for any guilt that may result. In a contrasting manner, Ezekiel 18:19 describes circumstances in which a son is not to be held responsible for the guilt of his father.

The affirmation in our passage that God "lifted up" the guilt of the psalmist's sin is part of a broader use of this idiom in relation to God. In Exodus 34:7; Numbers 14:18; and Micah 7:18, Yahweh bears responsibility for the guilt of Israel. Like the husband of Numbers 30:15, he assumes responsibility for the actions of his spouse, whether right or wrong. For this reason Isaiah (Isa. 33:24) can say (using the passive form of the same idiom) that the sins of those who dwell in Jerusalem (lit.) "will be lifted up" or borne by God himself.

Of course the ultimate example of God's "lifting up" or "bearing the guilt of our sin" is accomplished in the work of Jesus. Hebrews 9:28 most nearly approaches the Old Testament idiom when it declares "so Christ was sacrificed once to take away the sins of many people;[10] and he will appear a second time, not to bear sin, but to bring salvation to those who are waiting for him." Paul, in a less direct allusion, makes a similar point: "God made him who had no sin to be sin for us, so that in him we might become the righteousness of God" (2 Cor. 5:21).

As the Old Testament people of God realized, when they confessed their sin openly and faithfully, God did through the sacrificial system what they could never do for themselves. As he did in Jesus, he himself bore the responsibility for their sin, lifted up the crushing stone of guilt that pinned them

---

9. See, for example, Gen. 4:13; Ex. 28:38; 34:7; Lev. 5:1, 17; 17:16; Num. 5:31; 14:18; 30:15; Isa. 33:24; Ezek. 4:4, 6; 18:19; 44:10, 12; Mic. 7:18.

10. This seems a clear allusion (if not a direct quote) of Isa. 53:12, where the alternate phrase "lift up sin" is used at the end of the fourth Servant Song (52:13–53:12): "For he *bore the sin of many*, and made intercession for the transgressors." First Peter 2:24, in the midst of a discussion of the crucifixion drawing extensively on Isa. 53, agrees that "he himself [Jesus] *bore our sins* in his body on the tree" (italics added in both references).

down, and ushered them into the "glorious freedom of the children of God" (Rom. 8:21).

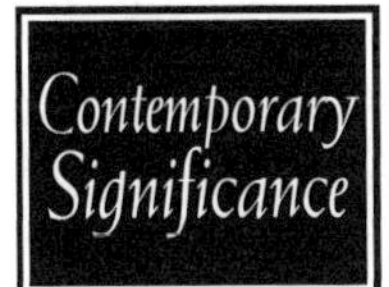

CONFESSING SIN. At the heart of Psalm 32 is the act of confession of sin. Not only does the psalmist confess to God (32:5), but he makes that confession within the hearing of the worshiping congregation. It is the opening of his heart to God that ultimately works forgiveness and restoration (32:5, 7), but there is also an important dynamic at work in his constant movement from God to the worshiping community. For the psalmist to make public confession in this way is both instructive to the community (32:1–2, 6, 8–10) and supportive of him as the community surrounds him with "songs of deliverance" (32:7c, 11).

Public confession remains an uncomfortable and therefore infrequent experience for modern (esp. Protestant) Christians. Particularly in North America two elements collide to inhibit our willingness to admit our faults even among our fellow Christians. (1) The first is the fierce independent streak that characterizes much of our society. We are at some levels consumed with a concern for personal privacy. What I do is my business and no concern of yours.[11]

This desire—even demand—for personal privacy is closely linked to the sense of radical tolerance that permeates society. What is "good" for you is okay with me as long as you demonstrate the same tolerance for what I consider "good" for myself. Such a dynamic of privacy makes us increasingly unwilling to divulge our most private issues and concerns to others and makes us uncomfortable to intrude into the inner privacy of others. The result is often a rather superficial relationship with others, in which only the most obvious or innocuous elements of our lives are shared.

---

11. In a strange way the Internet is eroding this cult of privacy. In order to explore the labyrinthine contents of the Web, one must submit all sorts of personal information to Web providers in order to be fully connected. "Cookies"—placed on our computers by persons unknown to us—track our moves, communicating to marketers, merchandizers, and system administrators our viewing preferences and our buying tendencies. Yet we put up with this intrusion because the Internet offers an illusion of anonymity since we can cloak our identity to other users with whom we come in contact. The illusory nature of this sense of privacy and anonymity is nowhere better illustrated than in the use of the Internet at work. Recent actions by employers to track employee Internet and e-mail usage, resulting in disciplinary actions and even dismissals for excessive use of the Web during work hours, accessing inappropriate (esp. pornographic) sites, or objections to the amount and content of e-mail messages, have made it clear that use of the Web, far from being private and secure, is subject to the scrutiny of many others.

(2) The second element that stands in the way of public confession is a sense of perfectionism that pervades much of Western Protestantism. Our desire to be completely independent leads us to assume that we *ought* to be perfectly able to accomplish our goals, fulfill our needs, and reach our dreams. We *should* have the self-discipline to overcome our shortcomings and lead full and satisfying lives. All too often, however, our lives are marked by failure, dissatisfaction, lack of self-control, and an erosion of confidence in our ability to meet our own needs or those of the ones we love.

Our obvious (at least to ourselves) failure to live up to the "shoulds" and "oughts" of our lives, instead of leading most of us to confess our weakness and need, causes many of us to hide our failings behind a façade of apparent success, happiness, and control. Twelve-step groups are full of people who followed their sense of powerlessness and fear of being discovered as they really were into years of hiding their fears in a variety of destructive behaviors: alcoholism, drug addiction, sexual compulsion, eating disorders, gambling addiction, and many, many others.

Those of us who make our home within the church have fared little better. The cults of independence and perfection have prevented many a struggling evangelical Christian from admitting his or her fears, failures, and helplessness until the crisis was so great that it could no longer be denied and broke out with the utmost devastation for all those concerned.

Those who have passed through this dark and painful tunnel and emerged at last on the other side, forgiven and restored to their faith in God, almost unanimously speak of having learned the value of confession and accountability within a supportive community of loving, caring fellow strugglers in life. The "fifth step" of Alcoholics Anonymous says, "Admitted to God, to ourselves, and to another human being the exact nature of our wrongs." That is confession, and these people have found it to be a powerful necessity for life lived truly and faithfully. Having a support group or community of faith willing to hear your wrongs as fellow sinners rather than perfectionist judges, a group willing to share from their own less-than-perfect struggles the experience, strength, and hope they have gained from relying on God's power, has broken through years of helplessness and denial to offer freedom from a lifetime of compulsive behaviors that no human power within or without could ever have relieved.

Our psalmist confides, "[When] I acknowledged my sin to you and did not cover up my iniquity ... you forgave the guilt of my sin" (32:5). God bore the guilt of the psalmist's sin himself—lifted it up and bore it away! That is a very New Testament concept deeply embedded in the Old Testament consciousness of the psalmist. John says it in similar words, "If we confess our sins, he is faithful and just and will forgive us our sins and purify us from all unrighteousness" (1 John 1:9). I have found that confession to God and another human being, freely given and freely received, is an important step in freedom from the bondage of sin that gains immeasurable strength from our fear and hiding. May you find such an accountability person or group in your own life, and may you take it as God's calling to you to be a faithful and trustworthy hearer for those who need your loving ear.

Psalm 33

1 Sing joyfully to the LORD, you righteous;
it is fitting for the upright to praise him.
2 Praise the LORD with the harp;
make music to him on the ten-stringed lyre.
3 Sing to him a new song;
play skillfully, and shout for joy.

4 For the word of the LORD is right and true;
he is faithful in all he does.
5 The LORD loves righteousness and justice;
the earth is full of his unfailing love.

6 By the word of the LORD were the heavens made,
their starry host by the breath of his mouth.
7 He gathers the waters of the sea into jars;
he puts the deep into storehouses.
8 Let all the earth fear the LORD;
let all the people of the world revere him.
9 For he spoke, and it came to be;
he commanded, and it stood firm.
10 The LORD foils the plans of the nations;
he thwarts the purposes of the peoples.
11 But the plans of the LORD stand firm forever,
the purposes of his heart through all generations.

12 Blessed is the nation whose God is the LORD,
the people he chose for his inheritance.
13 From heaven the LORD looks down
and sees all mankind;
14 from his dwelling place he watches
all who live on earth—
15 he who forms the hearts of all,
who considers everything they do.
16 No king is saved by the size of his army;
no warrior escapes by his great strength.
17 A horse is a vain hope for deliverance;
despite all its great strength it cannot save.
18 But the eyes of the LORD are on those who fear him,
on those whose hope is in his unfailing love,

[19]to deliver them from death
and keep them alive in famine.

[20]We wait in hope for the LORD;
he is our help and our shield.
[21]In him our hearts rejoice,
for we trust in his holy name.
[22]May your unfailing love rest upon us, O LORD,
even as we put our hope in you.

THIS PSALM IS a hymn of praise to Yahweh, celebrating his righteous character, creative power, and sovereignty—qualities that make him the only reliable foundation for trust and hope. As a communal hymn of praise and rejoicing, Psalm 33 roots out of the command in 32:11 that the "righteous" (cf. 32:11 and 33:1) and the "upright in heart" (cf. 32:11; 33:1) "rejoice" and "sing." In its present position, and especially without its own psalm heading, Psalm 33 is bound closely to the preceding psalm and provides the song of rejoicing requested there.

Structurally the psalm is divided into four major sections: invocation to praise (33:1–3), motivation for praise (33:4–11), exhortation to trust Yahweh (33:12–19), and concluding affirmation of trust and hope (33:20–22). Because of its twenty-two verses, Psalm 33 is sometimes classified as an "acrostic song"[1] or an "alphabetizing" song[2] that conforms its length to the number of letters in the standard Hebrew alphabet, though it does not seek to begin each verse with successive letters of the alphabet (as do the acrostic songs).[3]

The lack of a psalm heading in this psalm is noteworthy, especially since it is only one of two psalms in Book 1 of the Psalter (Pss. 1–41, considering Pss. 1 and 2 as introductory) that do not have any heading. All the remaining thirty-seven psalms in this book are referred to David, and most have other indications of psalm type and musical performance notes included. As mentioned elsewhere, psalms without titles are frequently combined with the preceding psalm in the ancient Hebrew manuscripts, yielding a single

1. See Kraus, *Psalms 1–59*, 374.

2. See Craigie, *Psalms 1–50*, 271.

3. For discussion of the acrostic psalms, see the section on "The Poetry of the Psalms" in the introduction. For a brief discussion on this psalm, see Craigie, *Psalms 1–50*, 271. For further literature on the subject see J. M. Vincent, "Recherches éxégetiques sur le Psaume 33," *VT* 28 (1978): 442–54.

composition. This is true of Psalm 33—at least ten ancient Hebrew manuscripts combine Psalms 32 and 33.[4]

In some cases (e.g., Pss. 9–10 and 42–43) the combination of such psalms seems to reflect an original unity. But that does not seem to be the case here; the two compositions seem distinct enough to warrant composition as separate psalms. However, the tradition for combination of these two originally distinct psalms certainly recognizes the verbal, grammatical, and thematic links that connect them. I will mention these as the commentary on these verses proceeds.

Invocation to Praise (33:1–3)

THE OPENING INVOCATION is made up of six half-verses, five of which are governed by second-person plural imperatives calling the reader/listener to praise Yahweh. The verbs describe various aspects of music-making, both instrumental and vocal, that must have played a regular part of worship in the Jerusalem temple. The righteous and upright are called to "sing joyfully," "praise ... with the harp," "make music ... on the ten-stringed lyre," "sing ... a new song," "play skillfully," and "shout for joy." The scene is a noisy, joyous occasion with musicians, singers, and worshipers joining together in raucous praise.

Sing . . . a new song. The Hebrew phrase "sing to the LORD a new song" (*širu lyhwh šir ḥadaš*) appears as the opening phrase of the important enthronement Psalms (Pss. 96; 98) as well as the opening phrase of Psalm 149. Outside the Psalter, the identical phrase occurs only in Isaiah 42:10, where it introduces a song in praise of Yahweh's "new" acts of deliverance.

Somewhat different references to a "new song" appear also in 40:3 ("He put a new song in my mouth, a hymn of praise to our God") and in 144:9 ("I will sing a new song to you, O God"). In the New Testament, a "new song" figures in the eschatological context of Revelation 5:9 and 14:3 in celebration of the eternal deliverance accomplished by the Lamb that was slain. Kraus, drawing on the use in Revelation, understands this "new song" to represent "that last, all-encompassing hymn that breaks out of the category of space and time."[5] Craigie emphasizes instead the continuing use of the phrase in the Psalter to designate "the ever-new freshness of the praise of God in his victorious kingship."[6] Longman connects this phrase closely to the theme of Yahweh as "divine warrior."[7]

4. See the discussion of "untitled psalms" in Gerald H. Wilson, *The Editing of the Hebrew Psalter*, 173–81.

5. Cf. Kraus, *Psalms 1–59*, 375.

6. Cf. Craigie, *Psalms 1–50*, 272.

7. See Longman, "The Divine Warrior," 290–307; cf. Longman and Reid, *God Is a Warrior*, 45, 191.

It does seem that a "new song" is a logical response to a "new act" of deliverance. For such new joy, the old expressions of joy just will not do! New praise must find its way to the singing lips and playing fingers. It also seems understandable that by association, the ultimate eschatological act of deliverance requires the ultimate "new song," as Revelation recounts.

Motivation for Praise (33:4–11)

IN THE SECOND major section of the psalm, the psalmist lays out in sixteen lines the motivating reasoning behind the call to praise. The motivation falls into three categories: the right and faithful *character* of God (33:4–5), the powerful and creative *word* of God (33:6–9), and the enduring and unshakable *purpose* of God (33:10–11).

The right and faithful character of God. The first motivation for praising Yahweh is grounded in his essential character. What God says is "right and true." The NIV evidently uses these two words to get at the full meaning of the single Hebrew word *yāšar* ("straight, level, right"). The plural of the same word is used to describe the "upright," who are called to praise Yahweh in 33:1. Moreover, Yahweh is characterized by being "faithful" (*ʾemunah* ["steadiness, reliability, honesty"]) in all he does (33:4). Because Yahweh is upright and reliable, he also loves righteousness and justice in the world he has created,[8] and his own dealings with his creatures and creation demonstrate his "unfailing love" (*ḥesed*) to them.

The powerful and creative word of God. From this foundation of the trustworthy character of Yahweh that fills his creation with his "unfailing love," the psalmist turns to God's creative word (vv. 6–9). In a clear reference to the creation narrative of Genesis 1, the description focuses on the power of Yahweh's *spoken* word to call things into existence. The passage is composed of a series of four examples of affirming parallelism, the first and last of which emphasize that spoken word (vv. 6, 9):

> By the word of the LORD were the heavens made,
> their starry host by the breath of his mouth. . . .
> For he spoke, and it came to be;
> he commanded, and it stood firm.

Between these outer "bookends" are two verses that emphasize, on the one hand, the amazing power of God in gathering and controlling the mighty

8. For a discussion of the terms "righteous, righteousness" and "justice," see comments on 4:1–2; 7:6–9.

oceans like water in a jar (33:7),[9] and, on the other hand, encourage the hearers to respond to this evidence of Yahweh's creative power with appropriate dependence ("fear the LORD") and respect ("revere him").[10]

The enduring and unshakable purpose of God. Having explored God's righteous character and creative power as reasons to praise him, the psalmist moves on to the last motivation. The righteous God who creates with power stands firm in his purpose despite the opposing plans of the nations around Israel. The purposes of Yahweh are enduring and will not be frustrated.

Verses 10–11 demonstrate a careful and balanced structure to highlight the contrast between the fleeting and ineffective "plan" (*ʿaṣat*) and "purposes" (*maḥšebot* ["plans, schemes, plots"]) of the opponents and the enduring "plan" and "purposes" (*ʿaṣat* and *maḥšebot*) of Yahweh. It is clear that Yahweh is the one in control as he "foils" the plan and "thwarts" the purposes of his opponents. By contrast, his plan and purposes are enduring, standing firm forever through all generations.

Exhortation to Trust Yahweh (33:12–19)

THE THIRD MAJOR segment of the psalm contains sixteen lines, like the preceding segment. The first verse (33:12) links back to the preceding discussion by using singular forms of the same nouns used to describe the "nations" (*goyim*) and "peoples" (*ʿammim*) whose futile plans and purposes were frustrated by the sovereign will of Yahweh (v. 10). The singular "nation" (*goy*) and "people" (*ʿam*) in verse 12 refer to Israel in her status as one of the nations populating the world created by Yahweh. As such, Israel's plans and purposes are subjected to the same sovereign will of Yahweh as the rest of the nations.

Israel's unique status, however, is set out forcefully by the use of the introductory word "Blessed" (*ʾašre* ["happy, blessed"]). Israel is "blessed" above all other nations because the righteous God who created the world and exercises sovereign control over the peoples within it has chosen Israel for special relationship—to be their God.[11] Israel, by divine election, has become

9. There may also be echoes here of Yahweh's primeval defeat of the chaotic waters at creation by which the enduring stability of the world was ensured, but that struggle is not foregrounded (cf. Ps. 93).

10. The idea of "fearing" God can sometimes be troubling. It is clear from a thorough study of this phrase and concept that it does *not* mean "be afraid"; rather, it is an idiomatic expression carrying the weight of "maintain the appropriate relationship and attitude of absolute dependence on and loyalty to Yahweh." See the discussion of "Fear of Yahweh" in the section on "The Theology of the Psalms" in vol. 2 of this commentary.

11. This theme is esp. significant in the Pentateuch (cf. Gen. 17:7; Ex. 6:7; Lev. 11:45; 22:33; 25:38; 26:12; Num. 15:41; Deut. 29:13), but also appears in the prophets (cf. Jer. 7:23; 11:4; 30:22; Ezek. 36:28).

God's "inheritance" (*naḥalah*)—a reference to land or property possessed in perpetuity by a family and which is inalienable and cannot be taken away.

This rehearsal of the "blessed" status of Israel is the first step in exhorting the listeners to trust in their God. The remainder of the section builds on this beginning in three movements that balance those of the preceding section: Divine scrutiny holds humans to the standard of Yahweh's righteousness (33:13–15); reliance on human power is doomed to failure in comparison to the power of Yahweh (33:16–17); and Yahweh's purpose for those who hope in him is deliverance (33:18–19).

Divine scrutiny. In 33:4–5, the readers of the psalm were motivated to praise Yahweh for his upright and faithful character, which "loves righteousness and justice." Now we learn that this righteous God looks down from his heavenly vantage point to scrutinize the hearts and actions of humankind. This image of heavenly observation and critique is common in the Old Testament, beginning as early as the Flood account (Gen. 6) and the Tower of Babel narrative (11:5). The upshot of such heavenly observation is usually evaluation and critique of those observed, and often judgment.

Elsewhere, the divine scrutiny seems to be connected with imagery of the sun, which rises over the earth by day, exposing all to the brilliance of its rays.[12] In both Egypt and Mesopotamia, the god of the sun was considered the god of justice because of his ability to dispel darkness and reveal all the actions of humans. In the face of such divine scrutiny there is no escape. Yahweh sees all—even the inward thoughts of the heart that he "formed" (*yṣr* ["shape, form (as a potter shapes clay)"]). Thus, the "plans" and "purposes" of humans (cf. 33:10–11) are transparent to him, as is their willingness or lack of willingness to trust in him.

The futility of self-reliance. The myth of human power is now debunked, with the purpose of encouraging the reader/listener to place trust and hope in the power of Yahweh rather than the futile pretense of self-power. The psalmist draws on the imagery of war and battle to make his point. While the size of an army is a significant factor in any engagement, it is vain to assume that superior numbers will inevitably provide victory. The books of Joshua and Judges are clear evidence of a small force empowered by God to defeat larger armies. By contrast, the books of Kings offer sufficient proof of the futility of relying for victory on superior numbers and military equipment. For example, in the account of the death of Ahab in 1 Kings 22, despite joining forces with the king of Judah against their mutual enemy and despite disguising himself so that no one would

---

12. Pss. 19 and 104 are sometimes mentioned in this regard. The heavenly scrutiny of God is also mentioned in 14:2 and 53:2. In 85:11, "righteousness looks down from heaven."

know he was the king, Ahab was killed by the arrow of an archer who "drew his bow at random."

The divine purpose of deliverance. The psalmist turns in this third segment to consider how God's purpose and plan for "those who fear him" are "to deliver them from death and keep them alive in famine" (33:18–19). As Yahweh scrutinizes all humans from above, knows their plans and purposes, and foils those who rely on self, so "the eyes of the LORD" observe those who depend wholly on him in order to act for their deliverance. Once again it is important that the quality expressed by the "fear" of Yahweh is not fear or terror but an awareness of one's absolute dependence on him. It is willingness to give up self-reliance and self-power in order to become "those whose hope [from *yḥl*; better translated 'those who patiently wait'; cf. 31:24] is in his unfailing love."

Concluding Affirmation of Trust (33:20–22)

THE PSALM CONCLUDES with a communal affirmation of trust in Yahweh, using vocabulary that links back to the immediately preceding section on the one hand, and all the way back to the concluding verses of Psalm 32 on the other. In the first case, the concluding affirmation is begun and concluded with references to hopeful "waiting" on Yahweh, which links to the mention in 33:18 of "those who wait hopefully for [*meyaḥalim*; NIV "whose hope is in"] his unfailing love." In the concluding affirmation, the first reference to "waiting" employs the Hebrew verb *ḥkh* ("wait patiently for," 33:20). This verb does not relate directly to the verb *yḥl* used in 33:18, but the appearance of *yḥl* at the end of the affirmation (33:22) indicates the same semantic range is intended for both verbs in this context.

Additional verbal links to the preceding section are found in the repetition in 33:22 of the important word *ḥesed* (NIV "unfailing love") that appears as well in 33:18. In the earlier verse we learn that Yahweh's eye is on those who wait hopefully for his unfailing love. In the concluding line of the final affirmation of trust, the speakers cry out, "May your unfailing love rest upon us, O LORD, even as we wait hopefully for [NIV put our hope in] you" (33:22). The community of faith lays claim to what has been promised, that Yahweh knows the heart of and delivers those who place their reliance wholly on him.

As far as links back to the conclusion of Psalm 32 are concerned, two are most persuasive. (1) The term "unfailing love" (*ḥesed*) occurs as part of the invocation to praise Yahweh, which concludes the previous psalm (32:10) and which Psalm 33 seems designed to fulfill. (2) Yahweh's *ḥesed* is said to surround the one "who trusts in him" (32:10). In the concluding affirmation of Psalm 33, we hear the community who waits hopefully for the promised deliverance declare: "In him our hearts rejoice [cf. 32:11], for we trust in his holy name" (33:21).

Our help and our shield. Yahweh is the trusting community's "help" and "shield." The former term is used frequently in the psalms to describe Yahweh's role as protector of those in trouble.[13] As such there is no inherent sense of inferiority in the designation "helper," as might be assumed in our culture of job classifications where the term is often used to describe subordinate groups of assistants. Here the word means one who supplies desperately needed service and is almost equivalent to the term "deliverer."

The shield described by *magen* is one of several types of movable protective shields used by soldiers in the ancient Near East (see comments on 3:3–4). The speakers trust Yahweh because he provides the kind of protective covering in the midst of the fray that a shield provides the soldier in combat.

WAITING FOR GOD. Psalm 33 teaches one of the cardinal lessons Israel had to learn again and again throughout her long history with God: Deliverance belongs to Yahweh (3:8), and salvation comes to those who "wait hopefully" for Yahweh rather than those who trust in any form of human power. The supreme example of this need to trust Yahweh in contrast to relying on human power is the picture of Israel between the Egyptians and the Red Sea in Exodus 14. Aware of the approaching Egyptian chariot forces behind them and with all escape seemingly cut off by the expanse of the Red Sea before them, the people panic and complain to Moses: "It would have been better for us to serve the Egyptians than to die in the desert!" (14:12).

Moses, able to see with the eyes of God, responds serenely, "Do not be afraid. Stand firm and you will see the deliverance the LORD will bring you today. The Egyptians you see today you will never seen again. The LORD will fight for you; you need only to be still" (14:13–14). At this point the impossible happens: The sea opens up to allow the Israelites to pass through to safety, while the pursuing Egyptians, blinded by their seeming invincible military power, are destroyed pursuing their enemies into the sea.

Hopeful waiting—faithful endurance—rather than panicked action is the appropriate stance of God's people. Joshua and his followers had to march around the seemingly impregnable fortress of Jericho *seven times* before the

13. See 20:2; 30:10; 54:4; 70:5; 72:12; 107:12; 121:1, 2; 124:8; 146:5; esp. 115:9, 10, 11, where the phrase "he [Yahweh] is their help and shield" is employed as a repeated refrain. Verbal forms of the same root appear in 79:9; 109:26; 118:13; 119:86,173.

walls came tumbling down and the city was given into their hands (Josh. 6). The Aramean general Naaman similarly had to bathe himself *seven times* in the Jordan river before his leprosy was removed (2 Kings 5). By contrast, Saul was rejected as king when, confronted by the massing enemy and the gradual depletion of his own ranks, he failed to wait for the coming of Samuel before offering sacrifice to entreat Yahweh's favor in the upcoming battle (1 Sam. 13).

Such waiting is a sign of surrender to the power of God rather than trusting in human strength and power. David manifested a similar trust and willingness to wait when he fled Jerusalem before the attacking forces of his rebellious son, Absalom. As he departed the city, the priests joined his retinue carrying the ark of the covenant as a sign of God's invisible presence with the forces of the king. David sent the priests and the ark back to the city with this declaration of his willingness to wait on God's restoring purposes: "Take the ark of God back into the city. If I find favor in the LORD's eyes, he will bring me back and let me see it and his dwelling place again. But if he says, 'I am not pleased with you,' then I am ready; let him do to me whatever seems good to him" (2 Sam. 15:25–26).

The psalms are full of exhortations and descriptions of waiting hopefully for God.[14] These references are particularly concentrated in Books 1 and 2 of the Psalter, where lament dominates and confidence and trust form an important aspect of the psalmists' message. Despite suffering, struggle, and pain, Yahweh remains worthy of trust and is the only sure source of hope.

THE ENDURING DESIGN **of God.** I have mixed emotions about revealing that I once owned a 1976 Fiat Sport Coupe. When I bought the car, it was only three years old—bright orange with black pin-striping. It was a sporty little four-speed that appealed to my still youthful visions of driving a fast car. But over the years (I kept it for thirteen!) my sporty car began to deteriorate. It went through a cycle of replacement parts: starter, alternator, two fuel pumps, another starter. All this was made more difficult and expensive by the fact that Fiat dealerships had been phased out in the United States, and the available parts inventory was decreasing year by year. Along the way, one cynical mechanic told me what he thought FIAT really meant: "Fix It Again, Tony!"

14. This is but a partial listing of the many references to waiting/hoping for God in the psalms: 5:3; 25:3, 5, 21; 27:14; 31:24; 33:18, 20, 22; 37:7, 9, 34; 38:15; 42:5, 11; 43:5; 52:9; 119:166; 130:5, 7. At least four Heb. verbs are at work here: *ṣpḥ* ("make long, endure, wait"); *qwh* ("wait eagerly"); *yḥl* ("wait, hope"); and *śbr* ("hope, wait").

Toward the end I was reduced to pulling used parts off two wrecked vehicles I had discovered rusting in a friend's hazelnut orchard. As the collapsing car became subject to increasingly frequent and inconvenient breakdowns, I was at last convinced to trade it in for a newer vehicle. I still remember the grins and smothered laughter among the car sales personnel after I drove my once prized Fiat Sport Coupe up to the dealership—clutch slipping, exhaust smoking—and gladly took the $100 they offered me for it.

Something of the same scenario has repeated itself with almost every car I have owned. None was made to last forever! I am convinced that autos are produced with planned obsolescence. Designs change; equipment fails, necessitating replacement parts or replacement vehicles. I have grown to understand that one does not place trust in a car, no matter how new or well maintained it may seem to be.

I particularly like the way the Jewish Publication Society translation of Psalms renders Psalm 33:11: "What the LORD plans endures forever, what He designs, for ages on end."[15] Unlike the Detroit auto manufacturers, God's designs are not subject to planned obsolescence. What God designs and makes endures.[16] Psalm 33 celebrates the enduring quality of God's creation and makes it the foundation of trust and hope. But it is not the enduring creation—as lasting and stable as it appears to be—that fills the psalmist with trust. It is, instead, the creator God himself who inspires hope and confidence. As Psalm 102:26–27 says, even the enduring earth and heavens will eventually "wear out like a garment" that God casts aside as no longer useful, but the creator God, who was there before the foundation of the earth, remains the same.

All human plans, purposes, and sources of power are ultimately subject to futility because of the transient nature of humans. People come and people go, but in the great scheme of the cosmos, they leave little lasting impression.[17] But God endures and is therefore trustworthy.

It is not just God's longevity that renders him worthy of trust. It is his essential righteousness that stands at the center of the psalmist's confidence. It is not just because God is eternal that the psalmist trusts him, but because

---

15. *The Book of Psalms: A New Translation According to the Traditional Hebrew Text* (Philadelphia: Jewish Publication Society of America, 1997).

16. See Ps. 102:26–28.

17. The challenging poem of Eccl. 1:3–11 clearly teaches what our psalmist acknowledges, that human endeavor and power is a futile source of confidence and trust. "What has been will be again, what has been done will be done again; there is nothing new under the sun. Is there anything of which one can say, 'Look! This is something new'? It was here already, long ago; it was here before our time. There is no remembrance of men of old, and even those who are yet to come will not be remembered by those who follow" (1:9–11).

"the word of the LORD is right and true; he is faithful in all he does. The LORD loves righteousness and justice; the earth is full of his unfailing love" (33:4–5). An evil god who was eternal would inspire neither confidence nor trust, only fear. Yahweh, however, is a God who "loves righteousness and justice." This does not mean simply that he loves those who do righteousness and justice (although that is also true). It means that God's essential character is grounded in justice and righteousness; it is who he is at his core, he can do no other.

The pagan gods of the ancient Near East had no such essential commitment to righteousness and justice. They are often depicted as combating, conniving, tricking, and overpowering one another to get their way. Yahweh, on the contrary, is committed to do what is right and just. He can be trusted to act in ways that are consistent with this essential character.

Even more, however, the psalmist trusts Yahweh because of clear evidences of God's loving care for his people. As the Jewish Publication Society translation puts it: "The earth is full of the Lord's *faithful care*" (33:5b). This is a grand translation of the Hebrew word *ḥesed*, which captures the enduring commitment and love that is so essential to its meaning. God is trustworthy, not just because he is eternal or because he is committed to righteousness and justice, but foremost because he daily evidences his "faithful care" throughout the world he has made.

Psalm 34

OF DAVID. When he pretended to be insane before Abimelech, who drove him away, and he left.

1 I will extol the LORD at all times;
his praise will always be on my lips.
2 My soul will boast in the LORD;
let the afflicted hear and rejoice.
3 Glorify the LORD with me;
let us exalt his name together.

4 I sought the LORD, and he answered me;
he delivered me from all my fears.
5 Those who look to him are radiant;
their faces are never covered with shame.
6 This poor man called, and the LORD heard him;
he saved him out of all his troubles.
7 The angel of the LORD encamps around those who fear him,
and he delivers them.

8 Taste and see that the LORD is good;
blessed is the man who takes refuge in him.
9 Fear the LORD, you his saints,
for those who fear him lack nothing.
10 The lions may grow weak and hungry,
but those who seek the LORD lack no good thing.

11 Come, my children, listen to me;
I will teach you the fear of the LORD.
12 Whoever of you loves life
and desires to see many good days,
13 keep your tongue from evil
and your lips from speaking lies.
14 Turn from evil and do good;
seek peace and pursue it.

15 The eyes of the LORD are on the righteous
and his ears are attentive to their cry;
16 the face of the LORD is against those who do evil,
to cut off the memory of them from the earth.

[17]The righteous cry out, and the LORD hears them;
he delivers them from all their troubles.
[18]The LORD is close to the brokenhearted
and saves those who are crushed in spirit.

[19]A righteous man may have many troubles,
but the LORD delivers him from them all;
[20]he protects all his bones,
not one of them will be broken.

[21]Evil will slay the wicked;
the foes of the righteous will be condemned.
[22]The LORD redeems his servants;
no one will be condemned who takes refuge in him.

PSALM 34, LIKE the preceding Psalm 33, has twenty-two verses, indicating its relationship to the Hebrew alphabet of twenty-two letters. Unlike the earlier "alphabetizing" song, however, Psalm 34 is indeed a full-blown acrostic psalm, albeit a somewhat imperfect one. The verse that should begin with the letter *waw* (the sixth letter in the Hebrew alphabet) is missing, and an additional verse beginning with the letter *pe* is included at the end (34:22). The addition of a final *pe* verse is not unique, appearing also in Psalm 25 and in a medieval Hebrew version of Sirach 51, a much earlier Hebrew version of which has been discovered in broken form in the Qumran *Psalms Scroll* designated 11QPs[a].[1]

The normal explanation of the additional verse in psalms like these is to observe that the expansion shifts the center of the acrostic to the twelfth letter of the alphabet (*lamed*) and so allows one to take the beginning (*aleph*), middle (*lamed*), and final (*pe*) letters to form the Hebrew verb for "learn, teach" (*ʾlp*). This structure becomes apparent only to the most astute observer and is one more evidence of the painstaking care exercised by the poets who constructed alphabetic acrostics. In any account, since the *waw* verse is missing in Psalm 34, the normal explanation does not fit, so the circumstances are left unexplained.

The psalm begins with an invocation to praise Yahweh along with the psalmist (34:1–3); it is followed by his personal testimony of deliverance

1. James A. Sanders, *The Dead Sea Psalms Scroll* (Ithaca, N.Y.: Cornell Univ. Press, 1967), 117.

and confidence (34:4–7). The body of the psalm is a series of proverbial instructions encouraging faithful reliance on Yahweh (34:8–22).

The Heading (34:0)

PSALM 34 IS the fourth of thirteen psalms that seek in the heading to connect with a specific event in the life of David.[2] Most of the incidents mentioned in these headings are known from elsewhere in the Old Testament narrative, though a few (e.g., Pss. 7; 60) are not recognized outside the reference of the particular psalm heading. In the case of Psalm 34, the incident seems to parallel 1 Samuel 21:10–15, when David feigns madness while in the court of the Philistines. The passage in Samuel uses the name Achish for the Philistine who "drove him away" rather than Abimelech, as in the psalm heading. Attempts to explain the discrepancy are speculative. Other than the historical reference, the psalm is simply attributed to David.[3]

Invocation to Praise Yahweh (34:1–3)

THE PSALM PROPER begins with an invocation to praise Yahweh, in which the psalmist first proclaims personal determination to "extol," "praise," and "boast in" Yahweh (34:1–2) and then invites the listener/reader to join in "glorifying" and "exalting" the name of Yahweh along with him. The poetry of these verses is generally affirming parallelism, although the grammatical structure of each line varies significantly. The first three lines (34:1–2a) follow the theme of the psalmist's personal praise of Yahweh, while the fourth line (34:2b) shifts to the invitation of a larger audience, which dominates the remainder of the invocation. The purpose of praise is subtly hinted at in the second line of verse 2, where those called to join the psalmist's praise are called "the afflicted,"[4] suggesting it is deliverance from oppression that occasions the psalmist's joy.

The series of terms used to express praise and glorification of God are suggestive and not exhaustive. The first (from *brk*) is probably best rendered "bless" rather than the NIV's "extol," which has limited meaning to most readers today.[5] The second verb (from *hll*) occurs in the reflexive Hithpael stem that sometimes means "praise oneself (i.e., boast)." Here the idea of boasting is carried over but is directed away from self to God. This publicly

2. The other twelve psalms are 3; 7; 18; 51; 52; 54; 56; 57; 59; 60; 63; 142.

3. See comments on the heading of Ps. 3.

4. See discussion of terms for the poor and oppressed in the comments on 10:16–18.

5. See comments regarding a reluctance to depict humans as able to "bless" God at 31:21–24.

expressed pride in Yahweh has the goal of encouraging the afflicted and providing cause for rejoicing (34:2).

The actual invitation to praise calls the hearers to join the psalmist to "glorify" (*gdl*; lit., "make great") and "exalt" (*rwm*, "raise up, exalt") Yahweh and his name together. This is one of the chief objects of communal worship. The commitment to continual praise of God was likely part of the ongoing service of temple worship. The Qumran scrolls describe a twenty-four-hour system of organization by which someone was always studying and expounding Scripture.[6] The opening verse of Psalm 34 suggests something like this for the continual praise and exaltation of Yahweh.

Personal Testimony of Deliverance (34:4–7)

THE PSALMIST HERE presents a personal testimony of deliverance by Yahweh, interwoven with encouragement to others to entrust themselves to his care. The movement from specific personal testimony to general exhortation occurs twice in these four verses: specific testimony (34:4), general exhortation (34:5), specific testimony (34:6), general exhortation (34:7).

I sought the LORD. The term translated "sought" (*drš*) is never used of seeking someone or something whose location is unknown. When one seeks God in this fashion, one does so knowing full well where he is, but is seeking either a restored relationship with him or, most commonly, information, guidance, or direction from him. This seeking may be accomplished through prayer or by some more technical means, such as the casting of the Urim and Thummim or receiving the word of a prophet. Such seeking is serious, purposeful searching, not confused wondering or wandering. The psalmist's search was rewarded by an answer from God and deliverance from "all [his] fears."

Those who look to him are radiant. The psalmist's personal experience of deliverance leads to a general conclusion that those who trust Yahweh will experience the same. They radiate joy in a tangible, visible way.[7] In some

---

6. "And where the ten are, there shall never lack a man among them who shall study the Law continually, day and night, concerning the right conduct of a man with his companion. And the Congregation shall watch in community for a third of every night of the year, to read the Book and to study Law and to pray together." From the *Community Rule* (also called the *Manual of Discipline*), column VI. Translation is from Geza Vermes, *The Dead Sea Scrolls in English* (New York: Penguin, 1968), 81.

7. The Heb. for "radiate"(*nhr*) also occurs in Isa. 60:5. While it is tempting to connect this description of radiance as the result of looking to Yahweh, with the similar description of Moses descending Mount Sinai with a radiant face because of his close contact with God, the Heb. phrase used in the latter case ("the skin of his face shone," lit. trans. of Ex. 34:29) is distinct from that used in Ps. 34:5.

sense this radiance stands in contrast to the possibility of shame that is to be avoided. The faces of those who are radiant because of their trust in Yahweh "are never covered with shame" (34:5).

This poor man called. The psalmist returns to the description of specific deliverance, assuming the identity of the *ʿani* ("poor person; weak, helpless") whose desperate cry has been met with divine deliverance (34:6). In describing Yahweh's salvation, he introduces a phrase that will return twice later in the psalm: "He saved him out of all his troubles" (cf. 34:17, 19); in these latter two verses it is generalized to the experience of the "righteous" and becomes the dominant theme of the proverbial section of the psalm.

The angel of the LORD encamps around those who fear him. Once again the psalmist shifts from personal experience to a general encouragement of the listening community. As he has experienced the responsive deliverance of Yahweh, so the community can anticipate divine protection from "the angel of the LORD" in response to their attitude of dependence ("fear him").

The "angel of the LORD" occurs some fifty times in the Old Testament, with 80 percent in the historical books. Seven more appearances occur in the Prophets (one in Isa. 37:36; six in Zech. 1, 3, and 12), and the three remaining occurrences are in the Psalter; once here and twice in the following psalm (35:5, 6).[8] The angel of Yahweh is a rather enigmatic figure in the Old Testament. He often appears in human form to deliver messages from God or to carry out Yahweh's purposes on earth. There is some tendency in these narratives to equate this angel with God himself, so that often it is difficult to draw a clear, distinctive portrait of the angel.

In most passages in which the angel of Yahweh is mentioned, he serves as a divine messenger mediating communications between God and humans. This is clear, for example, in the story of Hagar in the desert (Gen. 16), Abraham when asked to sacrifice Isaac (Gen. 22), Moses at the burning bush (Ex. 3), and Balaam (Num. 22). On occasion the angel of Yahweh appears as a fearsome avenging angel delivering divine wrath. Consider the role of the angel in 2 Samuel 24 (cf. 1 Chron. 21), when he afflicted the people of Jerusalem with plague at God's command, or in Isaiah 37:36 (cf. 2 Kings 19), where he "put to death" 185,000 Assyrian soldiers (again probably by plague) besieging Jerusalem. In Zechariah 12 the angel of Yahweh is depicted as going before the restored people of God to destroy their enemies.

---

8. It is most suggestive that the only two occurrences of the angel of Yahweh in the Psalter occur in adjacent psalms. We will consider the relationship of these two psalms as the commentary proceeds.

It is perhaps this last image that informs the picture presented in Psalm 34 (and in 35:5–6). The angel of Yahweh encamps around God's people, surrounding them with divine protection from their enemies. In 35:5–6 he drives away the psalmist's enemies and pursues them as if to destroy them in battle. The role of the angel in the Balaam narrative (Num. 22) as he stands in the way of Balaam with sword drawn to bar his approach to curse Israel may also feed into the traditional understanding of the angel of Yahweh as the protector of Israel. The view of the angel moves from the most general understanding as a divine functionary communicating the divine will to humans, to an avenging angel of God who metes out punishment on earth, to a protecting angel who creates a shield around those whom Yahweh would make secure.

Proverbial Instruction (34:8–22)

VERSE 8 SETS the tone for the following collection of proverbial aphorisms that make up the remainder of the psalm. This verse is an exhortation to discover the goodness that Yahweh represents and to "take refuge in him." That verses 8–22 form a collection is indicated by the use at beginning (34:8) and end (34:22) of the parallel phrase "take refuge in him" as a pair of boundary bookends (inclusio). The former is an exhortation to trust Yahweh while the latter is a promise of divine protection. Together these statements bind the varied proverbial statements into a unity and provide a thematic cohesion that links them together.

Fear the LORD. From the opening exhortation to "taste" (i.e., prove by experience) Yahweh's goodness, the psalmist moves to a set of two proverbial statements (34:9–10) focused around the common phrase "lack nothing/no good thing." Those who "fear the LORD" receive what they need from him. The second proverb draws on the animal world for confirmation. The young lions may be unable to meet their own food needs and thus "grow weak and hungry," but those who "seek [*drš*] Yahweh" as the psalmist "sought" (*drš*) him (34:4) will lack nothing.

I will teach you. Having established "fear of the LORD" as the foundation of security, the psalmist lays out for the reader/listener the nature of this most important relationship (34:11–14). He assumes the classic wisdom role of the teaching parent and calls his readers to come as children to be instructed in what it means to demonstrate the appropriate "fear of the LORD."[9] In the following verses, those who wish to experience long life (34:12) should

9. See the discussion of "Fear of Yahweh" in the section on "The Theology of the Psalms" in volume 2 of this commentary.

avoid malicious slander and lies (34:13) and should "turn from evil and do good"[10] (34:14), seeking diligently after wholeness.[11]

The eyes [and ears] of the LORD. The next two verses (34:15–16) provide contrasting examples of Yahweh's response to the righteous and those "who do evil" (contrary to the exhortation in 34:14). The eyes and ears of Yahweh are attentive to the needs of the righteous, while the wicked can anticipate only opposition from God, which will result ultimately in their complete eradication from life and even from "memory" (34:16). The verses encourage the hearers to follow the path of "fear of the LORD" laid out in the preceding verses.

He delivers them from all their troubles. Verses 17–20 are linked together by the repeated concept "deliver from all troubles" (34:17, 19). It is the deliverance of the "righteous" (34:17, 19) that is at issue here. These verses are intended to be an encouragement to those experiencing opposition and oppression that Yahweh is aware of their trouble and will act to deliver them. When the righteous cry out, Yahweh hears and acts in their behalf (34:17).

These verses also exhibit an interesting wordplay using the Niphal participle of the verb *šbr* ("be broken"). Yahweh is "close to the brokenhearted" (34:18; Heb. *nišbere leb*) and will protect the bones of them so that "not one of them will be broken" (34:20; Heb. *loʾ nišbarah*). The wordplay serves to bind these verses (34:17–20) together as a unit. Those who fear Yahweh can trust that their cries will come to the attention of a watchful God, who will oppose the wicked and deliver the righteous.

Evil will slay the wicked. The psalm concludes with a final contrast between the wicked and the righteous in the classic tradition of wisdom literature. In an interesting way in verse 21, it is "evil" itself that brings about the downfall of the wicked, who are identified here with the "foes of the righteous" (34:21). While it is not unambiguously stated *how* evil slays the wicked, the parallel line suggests that it is their evil acts (their failure to fear Yahweh and turn from evil) that leads to divine condemnation.

By contrast, those who "take refuge in" Yahweh (34:22) need not fear condemnation. Because they fear Yahweh and eschew evil, he will redeem them. This verse, with its reference to taking refuge in Yahweh, brings the series of proverbial exhortations begun in 34:8 to a close. As we have seen,

10. In wisdom literature, this is frequently the definition of right human relationship to God and others.

11. The term behind my use of "wholeness" and the NIV's translation "peace" (34:14) is *šalom*, which is regularly translated as "peace" but means far more than the cessation of war and conflict. The word has overtones of "completeness" and means to assume the kind of "right" relationship to God, the world, and others that establishes an appropriate balance that can only be understood as "wholeness."

what might appear to be an unorganized series of aphorisms does exhibit a certain order. The hearers are encouraged to take refuge in Yahweh (34:8) and to assume the appropriate dependence on him embodied by "fear of the LORD" (34:9). This all-important relationship of "fear" is defined as turning from evil (34:11–14), and the consequences of the response of righteous and wicked are illustrated (34:15–22) in order to encourage the righteous that dependence on Yahweh is the only hope for redemption.

BLESSING YAHWEH AT ALL TIMES. The poet begins this psalm with the express purpose of "blessing" God. How, we might ask ourselves, is it possible for finite human beings to "bless" God in any way? Is not God complete in himself and unaffected by our praise? Is not praise actually directed at the well-being of those humans who profess their intent to bless God? Perhaps "blessing" is just another way of saying "praise"—meaning to proclaim the praiseworthy character, attributes, and deeds of God. This appears to be what the NIV translators suggest by their regular translation of the Hebrew verb *brk* ("bless") as "praise" (or "extol" in 34:1) whenever it is found on the lips of humans and directed to God.

The Old Testament authors and writers—and particularly the psalmists—would seem to disagree. While they have in their vocabulary lists perfectly good and frequently used phrases to express "praising" God—verbs like *hll* ("praise"), *gdl* ("make great"), and *rwm* ("exalt")—they persist in using *brk* ("bless") in reference to God. This suggests they desired with this term to express their determination to do something more than just talk *about* the wonderful deeds and marvelous character of God. They intended to make clear their desire and purpose, even their determination, to return to God the blessing they had received from him. The kind of blessing God gives to his people calls forth a response in kind.

Leave it to the philosophers to debate the logic or rationality of humans blessing God. The psalmists are determined to do just that—to give good back to the king of the universe. That they believed in the power of the spoken human word to do good or harm is illustrated by the way in which many passages that hint of humans cursing Yahweh have been altered to remove any offense. Take, for example, the pointed encouragement by Job's wife that he should end all pretense at integrity and "curse God and die!" (Job 2:9). While the clear import of the passage is that Job is exhorted to *curse* God so that the resulting destruction would end his suffering in death, the underlying Hebrew text reads *barek ʾelohim wamut* (lit., "bless God and die"). Because the Old Testament scribes were uncomfortable allowing a word for "curse"

(*ʾarur*; *qll*) to be directed to God, they replaced cursing with blessing here and elsewhere.[12] In other words, if curses against God were thought capable of doing harm to him, surely human blessings of God were considered equally capable of doing good.

By participating in the blessing of God, humans are aligning themselves with the purposes and plans of the deity rather than ranging themselves against them. While it may be theologically correct to say that God is unchanged by our blessing or cursing, it is certainly true that when his creation returns divine blessing, his purposes are brought to completion in a way that is not possible without that response.

A prototype of the Beatitudes? I am struck when I read this psalm at its similarity with the New Testament Beatitudes (Matt. 5:3–12). In both it is the persecuted who receive the kingdom of God. In Matthew's treatment of the Beatitudes it is those who acknowledge their spiritual poverty and who are persecuted because of righteousness who enter the kingdom of God (Matt. 5:3, 10). The parallels with Psalm 34 are clear. On the one hand, Yahweh "is close to the brokenhearted and saves those who are crushed in spirit" (34:18). On the other hand, "the eyes of the LORD are on the righteous and his ears are attentive to their cry.... The righteous cry out, and the LORD hears them; he delivers them from all their troubles" (34:15, 17).

Other parallels are apparent as well. In the Beatitudes, those who "hunger and thirst after righteousness" will be filled (Matt. 5:6), while in Psalm 34, "those who fear [Yahweh] lack nothing ... those who seek the LORD lack no good thing" (34:9–10). Matthew 5:9 speaks of a blessing on "the peacemakers," while Psalm 34:14 encourages the righteous to "turn from evil and do good; *seek peace* and pursue it." The Beatitudes encourage the "pure in heart" (Matt. 5:8), while this psalm commends those who "keep [their] tongue from evil and [their] lips from speaking lies" (Ps. 34:13).

The parallels are not all exact, of course, but the tenor of the two passages is remarkably similar. Blessing from God comes to those who eschew the power tactics of the world and rely wholly on God as refuge. Such people suffer persecution and want in worldly measure but are filled with the blessings that come only from God. The conclusions of both passages are telling. For Matthew those who are insulted, persecuted, and falsely accused for the sake of Christ are blessed because their reward is great in heaven. Psalm 34 similarly concludes that although "a righteous [person] may have many troubles ... the LORD redeems his servants; no one will be condemned who takes refuge in him" (34:19, 22).

---

12. See Job 1:5, 11; 2:5; see also the related passage in 1 Kings 21:10, 13, where Naboth is sentenced to death for blasphemy after being falsely accused of (lit.) "blessing" God.

A RIGHTEOUS MAN MAY HAVE MANY TROUBLES. The psalmist has an intense desire to bless God "at all times" (34:1). That may seem an easy task when all is going well and life is experiencing the abundant blessing of God. But what about when life is full of trouble and pain? Satan makes almost the same point when he says about Job to God: "Does Job fear God for nothing? ... Have you not put a hedge around him and his household and everything he has? You have blessed the work of his hands, so that his flocks and herds are spread throughout the land. But stretch out your hand and strike everything he has, and he will surely curse [bless][13] you to your face" (Job 1:9–11).

The psalmist wants to make it clear that those who are called to bless Yahweh are not those who are beyond suffering and pain. To the contrary, they are described as the "poor" (34:6), those who take "refuge in him" (34:8, 22), who "cry out" under oppression (34:6, 15, 17). They are "brokenhearted" and "crushed in spirit" (34:18), who must rely on God to "redeem" them (34:22) and save them "out of all [their] troubles" (34:6, 17, 19). They are the ones who in the *midst* of their trouble experience the blessing of Yahweh. Psalm 1 tells us that divine blessing comes to the one who avoids evil associations and delights in God's *torah*, receiving nourishment and guidance from that law on the way that leads to life. Here it is the one who "fears the LORD" who experiences blessing.

Once again, to "fear God/Yahweh" is to pare life down to its essential core: acceptance that one is completely dependent on God's gracious, undeserved mercy. To experience that mercy in the midst of trouble is to know the "blessing" our psalmist describes. To "lack nothing" (34:9) or "no good thing" (34:10) certainly does not mean never to be in want or never to suffer pain and uncertainty. If that were the case, the psalmist would never speak of the blessed ones as the poor who call on Yahweh for deliverance from their troubles. Blessing comes precisely from acknowledging one's dependence on God—that he alone is the refuge the psalmist seeks.

We too often identify divine blessing with "getting the goods" in one way or another. "How blessed" we think is the one who is financially secure or well respected, or whose family is well balanced and happily trouble free. We thank God for the blessings of health, comfortable living, and even national security. In doing so we rightly acknowledge how much all aspects of our lives depend on God.

---

13. The Heb. text here reads *yebarakeka* ("he will bless you"), although the text clearly requires "curse."

The trouble is that we may come to associate divine blessing *exclusively* with such external evidence. The people of Jesus' day struggled with this sort of thinking. If a child was born blind, it had to mean that someone had sinned, because certainly God would not visit such pain and suffering on the righteous (John 9:1–12). Jesus' answer is shocking, both to his hearers and those of us who read the account now: "Neither this man nor his parents sinned ... but this happened so that the work of God might be displayed in his life" (9:3). The blind man was not suffering as the consequence of his sin but so that his suffering could serve a deeper divine purpose and significance.

This does not mean that we never suffer as a consequence of our own distorted decisions and sinful actions. Certainly alcoholism, uncontrollable rage, deceit, sexual promiscuity, and dishonesty—to name but a few of our sinful failings—can pay back severe and destructive consequences on us and all those around us. But to equate all suffering with the consequences of sin is to miss the point Jesus made so long ago, both in the account of the blind man and in the Beatitudes: The righteous suffer undeservedly,[14] but in their suffering they have opportunity to glorify God and to receive his blessing!

14. Of course, I am not denying that in some sense "none is righteous, no not one" (Ps. 14; 53) and that all sinners deserve divine punishment for their failings.

Psalm 35

Of David.

1 Contend, O LORD, with those who contend with me;
fight against those who fight against me.
2 Take up shield and buckler;
arise and come to my aid.
3 Brandish spear and javelin
against those who pursue me.
Say to my soul,
"I am your salvation."

4 May those who seek my life
be disgraced and put to shame;
may those who plot my ruin
be turned back in dismay.
5 May they be like chaff before the wind,
with the angel of the LORD driving them away;
6 may their path be dark and slippery,
with the angel of the LORD pursuing them.
7 Since they hid their net for me without cause
and without cause dug a pit for me,
8 may ruin overtake them by surprise—
may the net they hid entangle them,
may they fall into the pit, to their ruin.
9 Then my soul will rejoice in the LORD
and delight in his salvation.
10 My whole being will exclaim,
"Who is like you, O LORD?
You rescue the poor from those too strong for them,
the poor and needy from those who rob them."

11 Ruthless witnesses come forward;
they question me on things I know nothing about.
12 They repay me evil for good
and leave my soul forlorn.
13 Yet when they were ill, I put on sackcloth
and humbled myself with fasting.

When my prayers returned to me unanswered,
14 I went about mourning
as though for my friend or brother.
I bowed my head in grief
as though weeping for my mother.
15 But when I stumbled, they gathered in glee;
attackers gathered against me when I was unaware.
They slandered me without ceasing.
16 Like the ungodly they maliciously mocked;
they gnashed their teeth at me.
17 O Lord, how long will you look on?
Rescue my life from their ravages,
my precious life from these lions.
18 I will give you thanks in the great assembly;
among throngs of people I will praise you.

19 Let not those gloat over me
who are my enemies without cause;
let not those who hate me without reason
maliciously wink the eye.
20 They do not speak peaceably,
but devise false accusations
against those who live quietly in the land.
21 They gape at me and say, "Aha! Aha!
With our own eyes we have seen it."

22 O LORD, you have seen this; be not silent.
Do not be far from me, O Lord.
23 Awake, and rise to my defense!
Contend for me, my God and Lord.
24 Vindicate me in your righteousness, O LORD my God;
do not let them gloat over me.
25 Do not let them think, "Aha, just what we wanted!"
or say, "We have swallowed him up."

26 May all who gloat over my distress
be put to shame and confusion;
may all who exalt themselves over me
be clothed with shame and disgrace.
27 May those who delight in my vindication
shout for joy and gladness;

may they always say, "The LORD be exalted,
who delights in the well-being of his servant."
28 My tongue will speak of your righteousness
and of your praises all day long.

PSALM 35 FALLS generally into the category of psalms known as prayers for deliverance. It contains extensive descriptions of the attacks of the enemies, punctuated with personal pleas for deliverance and personal anticipations of praise. The voice of the psalm is singular, sparking speculation that the narrator is intended to be the king responding to some national crisis.[1] While the identification is not certain, there are moments throughout the psalm in which the perspective is broadened to include the worshiping community (35:18, 27).

A series of direct quotations characterizes the poem, placed in the mouths of various parties, including God (35:3), the psalmist (35:10), the enemy (35:21, 25), and the worshiping community (35:27). This allows the psalmist to reveal the inner reflections of the protagonists to the reader and probes deeper than the surface description of observable action and reaction.

Craigie[2] suggests dividing the text into three major sections (35:1–10, 11–18, 19–28), which, with some refinement below, offers a helpful understanding of the movement of the psalm. It begins with a plea for divine action and deliverance that employs phrases familiar to both legal (*ryb* ["present a lawsuit"; NIV "contend"]) and military (*lḥm* ["engage in battle"; NIV "fight"]) conflict (35:1–3). The psalm then describes enemy attacks in terms of military battle (35:4–8), using the second of the two images introduced in the opening plea. Craigie's first section concludes with a personal response and promise of praise (35:9–10).

The idea of legal conflict dominates the next section, describing "ruthless witnesses" who maliciously attack the psalmist (35:11–16). Craigie's second section is concluded by a personal plea and promise of praise (35:17–18).

The final section is punctuated with the term translated by the NIV as "gloat over me" (35:19, 24, 26). This section describes the arrogant twisting of the truth by the psalmist's enemies, who assume they have gained the upper hand over him (35:19–27). This unit is, in my opinion, directed more generally to cover both the military and legal opponents described in the pre-

1. Cf. esp. Craigie, *Psalms 1–50*, 285.
2. Ibid.

vious sections. Like the preceding sections, this one concludes with a personal plea for deliverance (35:22–25) and a promise to praise (35:28). In this case, plea and promise are separated by an extended request for retribution to fall on the psalmist's enemies (35:26–27).

The Heading (35:0)

THIS PSALM BEARS no new terms in its heading and is simply designated with the single term "to David."[3]

Plea for Divine Action and Deliverance (35:1–3)

THE PSALMIST BEGINS by requesting that Yahweh respond to the psalmist's enemies in a style of confrontation related to their attack (legal and military): Yahweh should "contend" with those who "contend" and should "fight" with those who "fight" (35:1). The remainder of the introductory plea describes the anticipated action of Yahweh in more militaristic terms. The psalmist views Yahweh almost as a bodyguard, who in the midst of close combat in battle is called to "take up shield and buckler,"[4] to "brandish spear and javelin"[5] against his enemies.

I am your salvation. In response to the psalmist's cry, Yahweh runs through the fray, spear and shield in hand, to defend the psalmist's life. As he does so, Yahweh's ringing voice is heard above the din of battle, shouting "I am your salvation!" This encourages the beleaguered psalmist to hang on until deliverance arrives.

Military Attack (35:4–8)

WITH THE ASSURANCE of Yahweh's approach ringing in the ears, the psalmist turns to a plea for retribution on those who "seek my life [*nepeš*]" (35:4).[6] Using a series of jussive verb forms that express the will of the speaker, the psalmist wants Yahweh to mete out appropriate punishment on those who oppose and seek to destroy the faithful narrator.

---

3. See comments on the heading of Ps. 3.

4. The *magen* was a smaller, round shield worn on the arm and preferred by those wielding swords for the mobility it offered. The *ṣinnah* was a larger, rectangular shield behind which those wielding spears could hide most of their body while thrusting out at the enemy (see also comments on 3:3–4).

5. The *ḥanit* is a shorter, thrusting spear used in close combat. The meaning of *segor* is debated, with some suggesting a double axe, and others the "socket" from which a throwing spear (or javelin) is launched. If the latter is true, the image is a *metonymy* in which the part is used to express the whole; thus the NIV's "javelin." See "Spear" in *EDB*, 966.

6. For a discussion of the Heb. word *nepeš*, see comments on 3:1–2.

This call for retribution begins with the desire that the enemy experience the kind of complete public "disgrace" and "shame" encountered in Psalm 31.[7] As we saw there, this is not simply a desire to strike out and hurt the enemy but signals the psalmist's hope that the real world reflect the righteous order characteristic of holy Yahweh and that the inward truth of human character, normally known only to God, be made manifest in public.

The psalmist goes on to describe the anticipated retribution in terms reflective of guerilla warfare. Those who plot his ruin will "be turned back" like an unsuccessful attack (35:4). Like chaff blown by the wind,[8] they will be driven away and pursued through the night down "dark and slippery" paths by the "angel of the LORD."[9]

Verses 6–7 illustrate the retributive expectations of the psalmist. Punishment received is equivalent to the offense committed. Those who plotted his "ruin" (*raᶜah* in 35:4) will themselves be overtaken by "ruin" (*šoʾah* in 35:8). Those who hid a net to entrap him (35:7) will be entangled themselves (35:8). Those who dug a pit for him (35:7) will fall into it instead (35:8).[10]

Response and Promise of Praise (35:9–10)

THE FIRST MAJOR section of the psalm concludes with the psalmist's personal response to the anticipated salvation of Yahweh (cf. 35:3, 9) by promising to rejoice and praise God. His *nepeš* (NIV "soul"), which has been under

---

7. See the discussion of "shame" in the comments on 31:1–5, 17–18 and in the Bridging Contexts section for that same psalm.

8. This verse mixes agricultural and military metaphors. Chaff is the husk of harvested grain that is separated from the useful kernel by beating or running over the grain with a sledge. The grain is then tossed into the air during a breeze so that the lighter chaff is blown away and the heavier kernels fall to the ground to be collected.

9. See comments on 34:7.

10. The Heb. of 35:7–8 is particularly disjointed and difficult. The NIV assumes the transposition of the Hebrew word *šaḥat* ("pit") from its awkward position in the first phrase of verse 7 (where it precedes *rešet* ["net"]) to a more appropriate position in the second phrase, where it provides the missing object of the verb "dig." Some (e.g., Kraus, Craigie) omit the Heb. *ḥinnam* ("without cause") from the second phrase as repetitive. Dahood (*Psalms*, 1:211–12) postulates (rather weakly) on the basis of Ugaritic a root for the same word that means "stealthily." The final phrase of verse 8 is equally debated. The existing Heb. provides the difficult "into ruin let him fall into it"—the double preposition being particularly awkward. To restore the retributive balance of "ruin . . . net . . . pit," some suggest reading the Heb. text of *bešoʾah* ("into ruin") as *baššuḥah* ("into the pit"). The NIV's "into the pit, to their ruin" is a conflation of these two options. Dahood suggests the Heb. word *šoʾah* (usually translated "ruin") can have the sense of "pit."

attack, will sing God's praises, and his *ʿaṣmot* (NIV "whole being"; lit., "bones") will testify to Yahweh's saving grace. Once again we must remember that there is no intention to distinguish between the eternal, imperishable "soul" and the mortal, perishable "body" here. Unlike the Greeks, the Hebrews understood human life to be composed of a physical body animated by the divine spirit. Such an animated person was a *nepeš* or a *nepeš ḥayyah* ("living being"). At death, the animating spirit returns to God and the person embarks to the grey existence of Sheol, the abode of all the dead. So *nepeš* and *ʿaṣmot* are two different ways of looking at the same experience of being a physical human being.

The various verbs used to express the psalmist's testimony of rejoicing and delight emphasize a visible and audible expression of joy in a public setting. By this celebration he gives testimony to the deliverance set in motion by Yahweh. That testimony is encapsulated in the exclamation preserved in 35:10: "Who is like you, O LORD?"—a rhetorical question with only a single obvious answer: "No one!" Yahweh is unique among the gods in this context because of his concern and action to rescue the poor and needy from their powerful oppressors (35:10).

Legal Conflict (35:11–16)

THE PSALMIST NOW describes a situation of confrontation in a legal setting. He is opposed by "ruthless witnesses." The term *ḥamas* (NIV "ruthless") regularly connotes violence that results in bloodshed.[11] What is depicted, then, is damaging false testimony in a case involving the death penalty. The accused is confused by cross-examination because the questions asked assume knowledge of which the psalmist is ignorant (35:11)—a sure sign of his innocence.

The psalmist's distress at this legal attack is increased by the opponents' callous disregard for his favorable treatment of them in the past. They repay his goodness with evil. The classic exemplary tale of "repaying evil for good" is found in 1 Samuel 25, where David, although living as an outlaw on the run from Saul, has treated the property of the wealthy Nabal (whose name means appropriately "fool") with respect. When David sends men to Nabal

11. This kind of testimony is explicitly forbidden in Ex. 23:1, and in Deut. 19:16–19 provision is made that when such a "violent, ruthless, malicious" witness is found out, the penalty that would have been imposed on the innocent party is to be carried out on the witness instead. For this kind of "violence" God brought the great Flood to cleanse the earth (Gen. 6:11, 13), which is understood to have been "filled" and "polluted" by human bloodletting. The prophets also regularly condemn *ḥamas*. Cf. also Ps. 27:12, where "false witnesses" (*ʿede šeqer*) are described as "breathing out violence" (*wipeaḥ ḥamas*).

requesting food and supplies, they are summarily dismissed. As David prepares to attack and destroy Nabal, the latter's intelligent wife, Abigail, sends needed supplies to David (unknown to her husband) and is able to avert certain disaster. To return evil for good, then, is one of the greatest insults imaginable and is a sign of great disrespect, insolence, and rejection of one's authority.[12]

They . . . leave my soul forlorn. Several alternatives have been proposed for the awkward Hebrew *šekol lenapši* (lit., "grief of childlessness of my soul"). Dahood suggests a Shaphel verb form from *klh* ("be spent, destroyed"), while Kraus and Craigie[13] prefer to read *śaku* ("they lie in wait for," from *śkh*), understanding the final lamed of *šekol* as dittography from the following *lenapši*. As there is no clear resolution, the NIV has opted for a creative rendition of the original Hebrew.

I put on sackcloth. The psalmist describes an earlier time of exemplary intercession on the behalf of the false witnesses when they were ill. Whether all the witnesses were ill at the same time, or this is metaphorical description of the psalmist's blameless behavior, or even whether this reflects a beneficent attitude toward the accusers is uncertain. The point remains, however, that the psalmist claims to be innocent of any offense that explains the opponents' hostile attitude.

This description allows us to observe some of the primary customs associated with intercessory prayer for illness. The psalmist puts on mourning garments ("sackcloth"), fasts as an indication of humility, offers prayer for healing, and continues to mourn for an extended period when no immediate healing is perceived (35:13–14). His sincerity is illustrated by comparison to the deep personal mourning for a friend, brother, or even one's mother. He bows down in grief and weeping (35:14). The depth of sincere suffering that the psalmist endures in intercession for those who are not even close friends or family members heightens the sense of amazement and offense at the opponents' baseless attacks.

When I stumbled. Like vultures gathering around a fallen animal, waiting for an opportunity of weakness, the opponents are delighted when the psalmist stumbles. There is no indication of moral failing to justify their attack—only a moment of vulnerability. The vicious character of their opposition is revealed by the nature of their actions. They are "gleeful" for the opportunity to strike (35:15); they "attack" when the victim is unaware of their

---

12. Prov. 17:13 describes the lasting effects of such insolent disregard on the perpetrator: "If a man pays back evil for good, evil will never leave his house" (cf. also Ps. 38:20; Jer. 18:20).

13. Dahood, *Psalms*, 1:213; Kraus, *Psalms 1–59*, 391; Craigie, *Psalms 1–50*, 285.

presence (35:15);[14] they continue their attacks "without ceasing" (35:15);[15] they "maliciously mock" the psalmist (35:16);[16] and they "gnash their teeth" (35:16) like threatening beasts of prey.[17]

Personal Plea and Promise of Praise (35:17–18)

THE DESCRIPTION OF the legal attack against the psalmist concludes with a plea for divine rescue that develops the picture of the attackers as beasts of prey introduced in 35:16. He wishes to be saved from the "ravages" of the attackers, characterized as acting like "lions" (35:17). The psalmist questions "how long" God can view the enemies' depredations and sit still without acting.[18]

My precious life. This stylish and artful word (*yaḥid*) presents the image of a precious, only daughter, which depicts the psalmist's life as it hangs tenuously in the balance. The word emphasizes the precious, irreplaceable character of that child. To consider the impact of this word, look at the story of Abraham's near-sacrifice of Isaac in Genesis 22. Having just received Isaac as the fulfillment of God's promise of a son and a down payment of descendants without number, Abraham is told to "take your son [*ben*], your only son [*yaḥid*] Isaac, whom you love," and sacrifice him (22:2). Each term piles up, adding to the irreplaceable preciousness of the child now called into threat by God's command. In our psalm, the psalmist calls on God to deliver his "only daughter" from the clutches of the ravaging enemy. The parallel in the preceding line makes it clear that *yaḥid* refers to his life (Heb. *napši*).

Plea leads to thanksgiving as the psalmist promises to offer the testimony of thanksgiving in the corporate setting of temple worship. The "great

---

14. This verse is difficult, esp. the word *nekim*, since it occurs nowhere else. A variety of solutions have been suggested, ranging from reading *nkym* as *nkrym* (*nekarim* = "strangers"; see Kraus, *Psalms 1–59*, 391) to Dahood's reading as *nkym* (*nokim* = "smiters"; see Dahood, *Psalms*, 1:213). Craigie's replacement of *nkym* by *tkym* ("oppressor") has the support of the Dead Sea manuscript 4QPs[a] (Craigie, *Psalms 1–50*, 285).

15. The attackers *qareʿu* ("tear up, tear away, tear apart"), perhaps referring to the effects of slander on the victim, although Kraus (*Psalms 1–59*, 391) prefers *qrṣ* ("wink [in derision]"; cf. 35:19) or *qrʾ* ("cry out").

16. The preceding phrase is another difficult one, with no satisfactory solution.

17. Perhaps here an equivalent of our phrase "baring the fangs" like a beast of prey, either in anger or in anticipation of tearing into a victim.

18. There is some discussion regarding the precise meaning of the term translated by the NIV as "from their ravages" (Heb. *miššoʾehem*). Dahood (*Psalms*, 1:214) assumes a connection with the same root as employed in *šoʾah* (v. 8) and suggests the meaning "from their pits." Kraus (*Psalms 1–59*, 391) draws on the parallel with "lions" in the next line to suggest an emendation to *miššoʾagim* "their roars." The NIV assumes an unusual masculine plural form of the feminine noun *šoʾa* ("ruin, devastation") or a related masculine noun form.

assembly" is the community gathered for worship. He will offer praise among God's people made vast by their gathering together to praise their God.

Let Them Not Gloat Over Me (35:19–27)

THE PSALMIST NOW enters into a series of pleas for deliverance (35:19–21), vindication (35:22–25), and retribution (35:26–27) directed toward those who rejoice (Heb. *śmḥ*; NIV "gloat" in 35:19, 24, 26) over the psalmist's distress. Once again he characterizes these attacks as baseless (35:19; cf. 35:7).[19] To "wink the eye" (*qrṣ ʿayin*) is to act and to speak duplicitously, making insinuations that impact others negatively (cf. Prov. 6:13; 10:10; 16:30).[20] The psalmist's enemies are hostile and present false testimony, claiming to be eyewitnesses (Ps. 35:20–21).

The caustic exclamation "Aha! Aha!" attributed to the false opponents, flows from a sense of having the upper hand and is, therefore, a public form of "finger pointing," which intends to cause public shame and disgrace of the individual. This phrase is almost always placed in the mouth of enemies and detractors (cf. Job 39:25; Pss. 35:21, 25; 40:15; 70:3; Ezek. 25:3; 26:2; 36:2).[21]

O LORD, you have seen this. The psalmist employs a subtle wordplay in appealing to God. The false witnesses had claimed to be firsthand witnesses of his disgrace when they said "With our own eyes we have seen it" (35:21). Now the psalmist appeals to the superior vision of Yahweh: "O LORD, you have seen this." Because Yahweh sees and knows the truth, the psalmist pleads for him to break silence and to draw near to confound the false testimony of the enemies.

The psalmist pictures Yahweh as both deciding judge and star defense witness (or perhaps defense attorney) coming to the witness box to speak in behalf of the psalmist. As Yahweh "awakes" (35:23) and "rises,"[22] he will

---

19. Verse 19 consists of two affirming parallel lines in which the two verbs (*yiśmeḥu* ["rejoice/gloat"] and *yiqreṣu* ["wink"]) are both governed by the single negative particle *ʾal* ("not" at the beginning of the first line). In this case both verbs would be jussives expressing the will of the speaker, "Let them not. . . ." Alternatively, the second verb can be seen as independent of the negative particle, thus serving as a relative clause, so that the second line can be translated: "My unjustified haters who wink the eye." In either case the meaning is essentially the same.

20. The NIV's "maliciously" is not in the Hebrew text but is an interpretive translation of the consistently negative meaning of the idiom.

21. The psalmist's detractors are also said to "gape" (lit., "make wide against/concerning me their mouth")—a visible distortion of the mouth in a public display of pretended astonishment or dismay intended to ridicule the object of scorn.

22. "Awake" and "arise" are not intended to suggest divine slumber; rather, they express the psalmist's desire that Yahweh stir himself up from apparent inactivity to actively accomplish his deliverance.

"defend" the psalmist and will "contend" (*ryb* ["present my law case"]) with the enemies. The narrator desires divine vindication through a public discrediting of the false testimony of the opponents.

The cry "vindicate me!" (35:24) is actually a plea for Yahweh to render judgment, declaring the appropriate course of action in the present circumstances. The psalmist is confident that he will be proved righteous or innocent of all claims and is equally sure that any cause for the enemies' "gloating" will be destroyed (35:24). When Yahweh makes the truth known, the enemies will be unable to continue their ridicule of the psalmist (35:25), nor will they be able to accomplish what they desire (35:25).[23] Their claim to have defeated and "swallowed up" the psalmist (35:25) will be nullified.

May all who gloat over my distress. The psalmist now moves into the final stretch of the psalm by turning to a plea, not for personal deliverance, but for personal vindication through the meting out of appropriate retribution on the enemy. In a series of jussives, he desires that justice be served by allowing the false witnesses to experience the public discrediting and disgrace they had planned for him. Through the use of the theme of "gloating" (*śmḥ* ["rejoice"]), this final thrust is linked back to the beginning of this section in 35:19 and the subsequent plea for vindication in 35:24 so that the whole section forms a unified structural element in the psalm. The plea that the false witnesses experience the "shame" and "disgrace" appropriate to their acts (35:26) further links this section back to the request expressed in 35:4.

Internally, the repetition of "exalt" and "delight" provides unity to this segment and allows for a subtle, ironic contrast between those who "exalt themselves" (35:26) and those who exclaim "The LORD be exalted" (35:27). The psalmist makes more positive comparison between those who "delight" in his vindication (35:27) and those who declare that Yahweh "delights in the well-being of his servant" (35:27)—an obvious reference to the psalmist.

My tongue will speak of your righteousness. The psalm concludes with the hopeful psalmist promising to testify regarding Yahweh's righteousness that has vindicated him against the false witnesses. He will proclaim praises to Yahweh "all day long." The verse forms a fitting conclusion to Psalm 35 but also provides appropriate transition to Psalm 36, which declares the righteousness of Yahweh, who provides refuge to the righteous (36:5–9) and presides over the downfall of the wicked (36:1–4, 11–12).

---

23. To speak to one's *nepeš*, as here, is to reflect on one's most deeply held desires and convictions (see comments on 3:1–2).

THE INCOMPARABILITY OF YAHWEH. The central part of Psalm 35 turns on a rhetorical question ("Who is like you?") that the psalmist utters in response to God's anticipated retribution against his enemies (35:10). The obvious answer is "No one!" which serves as the immediate foundation for the confidence that Yahweh is able to deliver. There is no other god like Yahweh, who can match his power or inhibit his action in the psalmist's behalf.

As a reference to the incomparability of Yahweh, the Hebrew phrase "Who is like you?" (*mi kemoka*) occurs elsewhere in Scripture and in the psalms (cf. Pss. 71:19; 89:8; Isa. 44:7; Jer. 49:19; Jer. 50:44).[24] In other contexts, that incomparability is expressed in a less interrogative style, with declarations such as "There is none like ..."; "There is no god like ..."; "No one is like ..."; and so on. These declarations range from affirmations of Yahweh's incomparability to other deities in a polytheistic (or at least henotheistic) environment[25] to clear statements of Israel's ultimate insight that Yahweh is the *only* God.[26]

But just what is it that sets Yahweh apart and above all others? A variety of characteristics are mentioned. Some have to do with Yahweh's mighty *deeds*. He is the worker of incomparable deeds and wonders (71:19; 86:8), who is able to accomplish what he announces beforehand (Isa. 44:7). A related characteristic is Yahweh's exalted power (Job 36:22; Ps. 89:6).

God is also set off by his essential *character* of righteousness (Ps. 71:19), holiness (Ex. 15:11), glory (Ex. 15:11; Ps. 113:5), and majesty (Ex. 15:11; Deut. 33:26). Yahweh is faithful (Ps. 89:8) and keeps his promise to David (1 Kings 8:23 = 2 Chron. 6:14). He helps the poor, needy, and powerless (1 Kings 8:23 = 1 Chron. 6:14; 2 Chron. 14:11; Ps. 35:10; 113:5), mercifully forgives sin, and does not remain angry forever (Mic. 7:18). In Job 36:22, Yahweh is celebrated as incomparable teacher—a probable illusion to his superior wisdom. Elsewhere it is his enthronement above all nations, and even the earth itself that sets Yahweh apart.

The psalmists and others draw great solace from their insight that Yahweh is *not like* the gods of the other nations, or even like human kings or sages. The venality and fickleness of the gods of Mesopotamia is well known. It is not just

24. The phrase can also be used of humans, marking out their superiority to others (cf. Deut. 33:29; 1 Sam. 26:15).

25. For references to the incomparability of Yahweh to other gods in a polytheistic or henotheistic context, see Ex. 15:11; Deut. 33:26; 1 Kings 8:23 = 2 Chron. 6:14; Pss. 86:8; 89:6, 8.

26. Proclamation of the exclusive existence of Yahweh is the intent of 2 Sam. 7:22 = 1 Chron. 17:20.

the matter that various gods and goddesses opposed and sought to undermine one another. The greatest difficulty lay in the fact that the individual deities were inconsistent in their dealings with humans. They could be tricked, misinformed, or emotionally manipulated so that they could swing in a moment from beneficent care to harsh punishment of their followers. All one's careful worship and supplication could be undone in a moment's pique.

Thus, it was great comfort for Israel to know that Yahweh is not like the gods of the nations. Not only is he superior in power and might, but he is also consistent in his essential character of holiness, justice, and mercy. But this confidence did not mean that Israel always understood how her experience of Yahweh squared with her profession of his consistent character. Job certainly felt abused and abandoned by God when his own righteousness was not publicly acknowledged. The author of Ecclesiastes also found it nearly impossible to understand how the prosperity of the wicked and poverty of the righteous could reflect the justice of a holy God. But both these authors, despite their dark and incisive critiques of the painful realities of their respective worlds, stop short of a final condemnation of God. For the narrator of Ecclesiastes, life—even with its pain and uncertainties—remains the gift of God, and wisdom is still its own reward (Eccl. 5:18–20; 8:7–10). And for Job, Yahweh remains holy God, wholly in control. Despite Job's (and our) frequent inability to understand his way in the world, God still remains worthy of our trust even while his absolute power is unquestioned.[27]

It is important, nevertheless, that our psalmist couches the incomparable nature of God not only in terms of power and might but also in terms of Yahweh's care and rescue of the poor and needy from those who overpower and rob them (35:10). In the final analysis, God's trustworthiness is the result of his incomparable power used for the benefit of the powerless. God is so superior in all things that he has no need to use power for self-interest, but he is free to champion those who have no power at all. This is the hope Israel clings to, and this is the hope that remains for us as well.

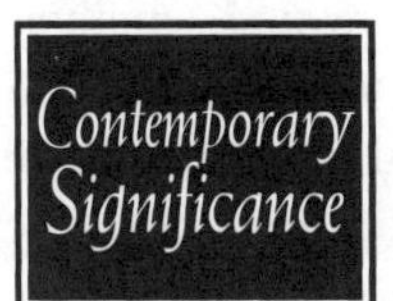

A DESIRE FOR PUBLIC VINDICATION. As in other psalms already commented upon,[28] the desire for public vindication plays an important role in Psalm 35. The psalmist's hope for public shame and disgrace to come upon the enemy (35:4), or even for slippery pathways

27. The psalmists—esp. in the laments—often reflect a similar awareness of the inconsistencies of life in relation to their profession of Yahweh's character.

28. See esp. the comments on public vindication in the Bridging Contexts section of Ps. 26.

to lead them ultimately to ruin (35:4–8), may make us uncomfortable when we compare Jesus' admonition to "love your enemies." Our difficulty may be eased somewhat if we understand that what the psalmist really desires is a public "setting things right." He is confident that if Yahweh were to act as judge in the public forum of the city gate (where many cases were tried), the psalmist would be declared in the right while his detractors would receive their public comeuppance. In such a case, for righteousness to be declared means someone else must also be determined "guilty." This is, then, not so much a case of wishing your enemy ill as it is a desire for righteousness and justice to prevail with all its necessary consequences.

In fact, the psalmist's desire for vindication ultimately turns away from self-seeking altogether. More than his personal vindication, condemnation of the enemy leads to public acclamation of the righteousness of *God*. The point of the public discrediting of the wicked is that others will see God at work and thus proclaim: "The LORD be exalted, who delights in the well-being of his servant" (35:27). The psalmist will offer public testimony: "Who is like you, O LORD?" (35:10); "my tongue will speak of your righteousness and of your praises all day long" (35:28). Public testimony to God's righteousness will match and even outstrip public ridicule and public vindication (35:18, 28).[29]

The psalm cautions us to be clear about our motives when we seek public vindication for ourselves and even wish for the downfall of our detractors. God is not in the vengeance business. Instead, he is concerned to set things right. When we ask God for vindication, we may get more than we ask for! If God were to judge all wrong and sin in the world, he would have a few things to deal with in our own lives. Perhaps this is where Jesus' admonition to "love your enemies" and "do good to those who abuse you" comes from. Ultimately, there is not so much separating us as we might think. We are all sinners in need of God's gracious mercy and forgiveness. When we call down divine judgment on them, we may find ourselves in the dock as well.

Again, this is not to say we should discount the psalmist's words altogether. There is innocent suffering that needs to be confronted and judged. We ought not to turn a blind eye on injustice or oppression, whether directed to ourselves or others. But the psalmist reminds us that what is finally at stake is not *our* reputations or even our well-being but *God's* glory and righteousness. To pray that he will set things right is to admit our own culpability in the "unrightness" of the world around us and to cast ourselves on him—both for forgiveness and for deliverance.

---

29. Twelve-steppers have a way of putting this in the Third Step prayer: "Take away my difficulties that victory over them may bear witness to those I would help of your power, your love, and your way of life."

Psalm 36

FOR THE DIRECTOR of music. Of David the servant of the LORD.

1 An oracle is within my heart
concerning the sinfulness of the wicked:
There is no fear of God
before his eyes.
2 For in his own eyes he flatters himself
too much to detect or hate his sin.
3 The words of his mouth are wicked and deceitful;
he has ceased to be wise and to do good.
4 Even on his bed he plots evil;
he commits himself to a sinful course
and does not reject what is wrong.

5 Your love, O LORD, reaches to the heavens,
your faithfulness to the skies.
6 Your righteousness is like the mighty mountains,
your justice like the great deep.
O LORD, you preserve both man and beast.
7 How priceless is your unfailing love!
Both high and low among men
find refuge in the shadow of your wings.
8 They feast on the abundance of your house;
you give them drink from your river of delights.

9 For with you is the fountain of life;
in your light we see light.
10 Continue your love to those who know you,
your righteousness to the upright in heart.
11 May the foot of the proud not come against me,
nor the hand of the wicked drive me away.
12 See how the evildoers lie fallen—
thrown down, not able to rise!

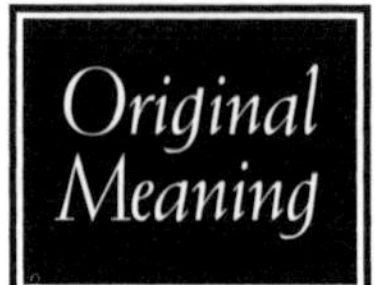

A BRIEF PSALM of only twelve verses, Psalm 36 offers confidence to withstand the proud and arrogant evil of the wicked because of a divine revelation of the all-encompassing love of Yahweh for those who know him. In its central theme concerning the downfall of evildoers, Psalm 36 is related to Psalm 37. The concluding declaration of Psalm 36 ("See how the evildoers lie fallen") prepares the way for the more extended description of the destruction of the wicked that occupies much of Psalm 37.

Structurally Psalm 36 falls into four sections: the opening description of the ignorant and arrogant wicked (36:1–4), the contrasting revelation of the boundless love of Yahweh that provides both protection and abundance (36:5–9), the psalmist's plea for the continued outpouring of divine love and protection (36:10–11), and the concluding call for the reader/listener to share the psalmist's confidence in the ultimate fall of the wicked (36:12).

The Heading (36:0)

THE PSALM IS referred to "the director of music" and attributed to David.[1] Between these two familiar terms stands the second of only two appearances in the psalm headings of the phrase *leᶜebed yhwh* (lit., "of the servant of Yahweh"). In the Old Testament this phrase is applied to David only here and in the heading to Psalm 18.[2] The majority of such references are to Moses, the servant of Yahweh. The attachment to David of an epithet so strongly associated with Moses may well suggest that a messianic interpretation of David (perhaps filtered through the Servant Songs?) is already in operation here rather than a straightforward, historical one.[3]

The Arrogant Wicked (36:1–4)

THE PSALM OPENS with what the NIV calls "an oracle" or, perhaps better, "prophetic utterance" (*neʾum* ["whispering, declaration, decision"]).[4] This Hebrew word has become a fixed technical term usually referring to

1. See comments on the headings of Pss. 3 and 4 for these terms.

2. For the statistics on the use of this expression, see note 3 in the discussion of Ps. 18.

3. It is tempting to suggest this association of David and servant of Yahweh in the psalm headings might explain the source of Jesus' own adoption of the suffering servant as the model of his messianic role. Jesus was certainly well immersed in the psalms and often used them to interpret his own life and ministry (cf. his quotation of portions of Ps. 22 from the cross).

4. The word "oracle" is normally the translation applied to the Hebrew term *maśśaʾ* ("carrying, burden; pronouncement, oracle").

prophetic utterances in response to divine revelation or insight. It is frequently accompanied by other prophetic formulae, such as *koh ʾamar yhwh* (lit., "Thus says Yahweh"), and is normally placed at the conclusion of prophetic oracles (although it can be found at beginning or middle as well).

The use of *neʾum* implies that the psalmist is acting as a prophet to communicate insights provided by divine inspiration. In relation to David, we find *neʾum* twice in 2 Samuel 23:1 to introduce his "last words" (2 Sam. 23:1), a poetic encapsulation of the Davidic covenant that is styled as a prophetic pronouncement: "The Spirit of the LORD spoke through me; his word was on my tongue. The God of Israel spoke, the Rock of Israel said to me . . ." (23:2–3). Clearly David is in some sense considered a "prophet," although he is infrequently depicted fulfilling the classic roles of that office.[5] The Dead Sea *Psalms Scroll* (11QPs[a]), a collection of psalms from the last third of the Psalter interspersed with psalms not included in our canonical book of Psalms, includes these last words of David toward the end of that collection and in association with a prose account of his writings that also assumes he was inspired by God.[6]

Rather than a typical oracle of judgment or deliverance as encountered in the Prophets, Psalm 36 might better be called an "insight" into the fate of the arrogant, self-motivated, and self-focused wicked, who exhibit no "fear of God" and yet often seem to prosper regardless. It is this insight into human affairs that the psalmist seeks to communicate.

No fear of God. The psalmist describes the overarching condition of the sinful wicked in terms of rebellious indifference: "There is no fear of God before his eyes." One would anticipate from the NIV that the underlying Hebrew is the classic phrase *yirʾat elohim*, which constitutes the primary Israelite understanding of an appropriate relationship to God.[7] That is *not* the case here, however. Instead we find the Hebrew phrase *paḥad ʾelohim* ("trembling/terror of God").

This choice of words seems deliberate. They are parallel to those of the classic phrase but are clearly distinct from them. The Hebrew *yirʾah* in the classic phrase does not have the sense of "terror, fear" but signifies a realization of one's absolute creaturely dependence on Yahweh for one's continued

5. See in the New Testament Acts 2:30.

6. 11QPs[a], col. 27. The account known as David's Compositions attributes to David a total of 4,050 psalms and songs for various occasions and purposes. The account also claims divine inspiration for these compositions: "And Yahweh gave him a discerning and enlightened spirit so that he wrote. . . . All these he wrote through the discernment that was given him from before the Most High."

7. See the discussion of "Fear of Yahweh" in the section on "The Theology of the Psalms" in vol. 2 of this commentary.

existence. It is an outgrowth of true humility and proper recognition of the limits of human power and control. By contrast, *paḥad* does connote abject fear or terror accompanied by trembling. In other words, the wicked in this psalm so little understand Yahweh that they misunderstand appropriate relation with him as "terror" or "trembling" rather than absolute dependence. Regardless, the psalmist notes, they do not even adopt this decidedly reduced understanding of Yahweh in their practice. Clearly, they do not humbly acknowledge their dependence on Yahweh, but neither are they afraid of him.[8]

The rest of the description in 36:2–4 records the descent into wickedness that this negative foundation of misunderstanding and arrogant rebellion causes. Since the wicked have no true understanding of Yahweh or of their dependence on him, their view of self is so inflated they are unable to recognize or acknowledge their own sin (36:2). This leads to speech that is "wicked and deceitful," manipulating and distorting truth (36:3). Without a wise understanding of God and self, the wicked are inhibited from doing good (36:3). As a result, even time normally spent in rest and recuperation is occupied with plotting evil (36:4). The descent is completed with the realization that the wicked are completely "committed" to a sinful course (*ʿal derek loʾ ṭob*; lit., "on the way not good"; NIV "to a sinful course," 36:4). The descent of the wicked offers an instructive parallel to the admonition in Psalm 1:1, and the committed path of the sinner is the same path that "perishes" in 1:6.

The Boundless Love of Yahweh (36:5–9)

THE PSALMIST NOW turns to a contrasting portrait of Yahweh's boundless love that provides a sure foundation for those who acknowledge their dependence on him. Employing an intricate merism,[9] he praises Yahweh's love that fills the whole of creation—reaching from heaven (36:5) to earth (35:6), and on earth expanding from the mighty mountains[10] to the great deep

8. It is also interesting to note that the psalmist does not relate the wicked's fear to Yahweh, as in the classic phrase *yirʾat yhwh*, but uses instead the more generic divine epithet *ʾelohim* ("God"). It is common practice in the psalms to avoid placing the divine name Yahweh in the mouth of unbelievers or severe sinners. Instead, the psalmists often substitute *ʾelohim*, possibly indicating the lack of understanding such people have of the true nature of Yahweh and at least protecting the divine name from association with such profane belief.

9. See the discussion of poetic technique in the section on "The Poetry of the Psalms" in the introduction.

10. The Heb. *harre ʾel* literally means "mountains of God." On occasion, however, the generic terms for god/God (Heb. *ʾel*; *ʾelohim*) are used as emphatic particles with the sense of "really big!" (cf. Jonah 3:3, "and Nineveh was a great city *to God*" probably means "and Nineveh was a *really big* city!").

(36:6).[11] Along the way, the psalmist brings together Yahweh's "love" (*ḥesed* ["covenant loyalty"]) with his "faithfulness" (*ʾemunah*), "righteousness" (*ṣidqah*), and "justice" (*mišpaṭ*) to form a complete and secure foundation for human trust and dependence. The ignorant wicked know so little about Yahweh that they trust only in self-power and the illusion of self-control. The psalmist—and those who hear—have confidence to let themselves go into the loving, faithful, righteous, and just arms of God, who is concerned with the welfare of humans but preserves "both man and beast" (36:6).

How priceless is your unfailing love! Despite the passing mention of Yahweh's righteousness and justice (36:6) as important foundations of trust, it is clearly Yahweh's "unfailing love" (36:5, 7, 10) that occupies the psalmist here. The enduring love that filled heaven and earth in verse 5 is proclaimed as "priceless" in verse 7. The precious character of that love is understood in terms of its effects on humans. It is a source of protection and refuge for "both high and low among men" but goes far beyond this to provide "abundance" of delight. This description borders with the paradisiacal pleasures of the creation, but it also connects with the eschatological banquets anticipated in the last times.[12] Humans are welcomed like honored houseguests and treated to all the abundance and pleasure the householder can afford.

Not only does Yahweh's love provide abundant pleasures, but it also offers access to the life-sustaining refreshment of the "river of delights" (36:8) and the "fountain of life" (36:9). The paradisiacal connections are even more explicit in the reference to Yahweh's "river of delights" (*naḥal ʿadaneka*). The second word here is the same word (*ʿeden*) that provides the name for the paradisiacal garden from which the four rivers flow to provide life-giving water to the earth (Gen. 2:8–14).[13] Eschatological concerns return in the reference to the "fountain of life" (*maqor ḥayyim*), which is closely related to the "spring of living water" (*meqor mayim ḥayyim*) in Jeremiah 2:13; 7:13—a picture of Yahweh as the source of life, which the Israelites are accused of having forsaken in favor of leaky cisterns dug by their own power.[14]

In your light we see light. The experience of God on these terms is enlightening. The ignorance and arrogance attributed to the wicked in

---

11. The second term in the initial merism (NIV's "skies") is the Hebrew *šeḥaqim*. The word is normally associated with the heavenly phenomenon of clouds. Holladay (*CHALOT*, 366), however, suggests a connection with (clouds of) dust. This would make the double merism more complete and exact: "heavens . . . dust (of earth); mountains . . . deep."

12. Cf. Gen. 2; Isa. 5:7; 25:6; 55:2; 58:14; Matt. 8:11; 22:1–14; Luke 13:29; 14:16–24.

13. Cf. also the related imagery surrounding the "river of the water of life" in Rev. 22:1–2.

14. See the discussion of "living water" in the Bridging Contexts section below. For Jesus' use of related ideas, see his discussion with the Samaritan woman in John 4.

verses 1–4 are washed away in a flood of awareness of the trustworthy character of Yahweh. The dark of doubt is driven away by the light of God's love revealed.

It is possible once again to find connections between God's light and both creation and eschatological imagery. Light is, of course, the first act of creation, distinct from sun, moon, and stars, vanquishing darkness and beginning the defeat of chaos (Gen. 1:1–5). In Revelation 21:23–24, the new Jerusalem is lighted by the glory of God and the Lamb, no longer requiring the pallid illumination provided by sun, moon, and stars. The light of divine illumination opens the eyes of the psalmist and those who follow his lead to the amazing abundance of Yahweh's life-giving love, which eludes the blind and ignorant wicked.

Plea for Yahweh's Continued Love (36:10–11)

THE CONTRAST BETWEEN the arrogant wickeds' ignorance of the true character of Yahweh and the enlightened believers' confident acceptance of him as the source of abundant delight and even life itself leads inexorably to the psalmist's plea that Yahweh establish the reality of that divine love in the present world of his own experience. Again, it is Yahweh's *ḥesed* that the psalmist wishes to continue (36:10). But in the present circumstances it is the righteous outworking of that love in the protection of the "upright in heart" and the judgment of the wicked (36:10–11) that he invokes. Trusting in the abundant goodness of Yahweh as the source of life, the psalmist can also trust that the present preeminence of the arrogant wicked is not God's plan and will. Thus, in calling for divine action to set things right, he is at once expressing his personal desire and aligning that personal desire with the will and purpose of Yahweh.

The psalmist's prayer includes the desire not to be overwhelmed and subdued beneath the power of the wicked ("May the foot of the proud not come against me"[15]) as well as the hope not to be "driven away." While the precise meaning of the last phrase is not clear, it may be that the psalmist is continuing the imagery of the "fountain of life" from the earlier verses, so that his desire is not to be driven away from watering at the source of life, as a herd of sheep might be driven from the watering troughs at a well by competing shepherds.[16] At any rate the psalmist desires not to be driven from God by the apparent upper hand enjoyed by the wicked.

---

15. For placing one's foot on an enemy as a sign of conquest and subjection, see comments on 8:6; 110:1.

16. Cf. the conflict between the herdsmen of Lot and Abraham in Gen. 13; also Moses' rescue of the daughters of Reuel from the local shepherds in Ex. 2:16–19.

Final Call to Confidence (36:12)

THE PSALMIST CONCLUDES with the prophetic vision that corresponds to the "oracle" proclaimed in the opening verse. In his mind's eye God has implanted a vision of the fall of the wicked that gives the lie to their apparent present dominance and power. This vision, following on the body of the psalm, is actually a call to confidence in the enduring love of Yahweh. Those who see as the psalmist sees, in the light of Yahweh's love, will commit themselves in trust to the true source of all life.

THE HEAVENS AND THE EARTH. The initial description of Yahweh's enduring *ḥesed* is couched in terms of a sweeping description that brings together the farthest reaches of the heavens (36:5) and the depths of the earth (36:6). As noted above, the connection of these two extremes forms a merism with the intent of embracing the whole of creation as the arena of God's concern and control. This is particularly clear in the opening verses of Genesis 1, where God is described as having "created the heavens and the earth" (Gen. 1:1)—meaning everything.

As creator of everything, Yahweh is viewed as *above* or *outside* his creation and apart from it. Yahweh is enthroned above the heavens (Isa. 21–23); his heavenly abode is viewed as resting on the chaotic waters subdued at creation and relegated to fixed and limited locations above the heavens and below the earth. This reference is, of course, to the ancient cosmology in which the flat plate of the earth and seas is overarched by the inverted bowl of the "firmament" (*raqiaᶜ*) and together form a sealed and protective environment by which the chaotic waters are held off and the rest of creation allowed to exist.[17] Unlike the gods of Mesopotamia and Egypt, who derive their existence by sexual means from *within* creation,[18] Yahweh stands outside, calls creation into being, and is unthreatened by any threat to its continued existence. By contrast, in Mesopotamia, when the Flood comes and threatens to dissolve all creation, the gods are depicted as cowering defenseless behind the walls of their palaces, whimpering "like dogs" because the end of creation means their end as well. By contrast Yahweh

17. In this understanding, the Flood (Gen. 6–9) is a threat of *un*creation, in which the chaotic waters above the earth rain down and those beneath the earth bubble up to flood and dissolve the tenuous protective habitat of humanity and all creation.

18. In Mesopotamia, the chaotic primeval waters Apsu (male) and Tiamat (female) give birth to the younger gods, while in Egypt it is the earth Geb (male) and heavens Nut (female) that accomplish the same feat.

in the midst of the raging flood remains—to adopt the words of an old Bob Dylan song—"unconcerned."[19]

God is creator of heaven and earth—all that is; he remains outside his creation and yet is deeply involved in it both as its sustainer and judge. As Isaiah 40:22–23 puts it: "He sits enthroned above the circle of the earth, and its people are like grasshoppers. He stretches out the heavens like a canopy, and spreads them out like a tent to live in. He brings princes to naught and reduces the rulers of this world to nothing." God remains in control of his creation; this is cause for great confidence for the psalmist, who trusts that Yahweh will ultimately set all things right.

This setting of all things right is envisioned in Revelation as a *re-creation*. There God "makes all things new" by creating a "new heaven and a new earth" (Rev. 21:1–5), in which the fallen nature of *this* world is renewed to its original intention. In such a new creation, with a new heaven and earth, the psalmist can envision a future in which "the evildoers lie fallen—thrown down, not able to rise" (Ps. 36:12). Along with the psalmist and the author of 2 Peter, we too can look "forward to a new heaven and a new earth, the home of righteousness" (2 Peter 3:13).[20]

The water of life. The psalmist speaks in reverential tones of experiencing the hospitality of the divine house of Yahweh (36:8–9) and of sharing the refreshment offered by the host: restorative drink drawn from God's "river of delights" and the "fountain of life." The paradisiacal nature of these water sources has already been explored, but there are a few further connections to be made here.

First, "living water" (*mayim ḥayyim*) most often refers to flowing water taken from streams or rivers or to water drawn from spring-fed pools. This kind of living water was distinguished from standing water left in jars, gathered in cisterns, left standing by rainfall in stagnant pools, or even drawn from a well. The distinction was particularly important in the laws of ritual purity and cleansing. Only "living water" had the property of cleansing from uncleanness. For this reason ritual baths had to be provided with some access to living water in order to maintain their cleansing property and status. Often a channel of living water would be directed from a stream or spring to the site of the bath so that a small amount could be let into the chamber pool before each supplicant entered for cleansing.[21]

---

19. "When He Returns," words and music by Bob Dylan (Special Rider Music, 1979).

20. Cf. 2 Cor. 5:17: "Therefore, if anyone is in Christ; [there] is a new creation; the old has gone, the new has come!"

21. Such arrangements are noted at Qumran as well in the ritual baths uncovered in private houses from the Second Temple period in Jerusalem.

In his encounter with the Samaritan woman (John 4:7–30), Jesus alludes to the common act of drawing water from a well and providing drink for a stranger to offer the woman the hospitality of God's house described in this psalm. "If you knew ... who it is that asks you for a drink, you would have asked him and he would have given you living water" (John 4:10). At first the women takes Jesus' statement at its natural level and questions where he could secure such "fresh water" since he doesn't even possess the means of drawing from the well at hand. But Jesus deepens the conversation by pointing to a spiritual meaning: "Everyone who drinks this [well] water will be thirsty again, but whoever drinks the water I give him will never thirst. Indeed, the water I give him will become in him a spring of water welling up to eternal life."

Living water has been transformed into a "spring of water ... [of] eternal life" (equivalent to *maqor ḥayyim* in Ps. 36). Jeremiah employs a similar phrase (*meqor mayim ḥayyim* ["spring of living water"]) to speak of Yahweh as a "spring of living water" that Israel rejected in favor of cisterns dug by their own hands (Jer. 2:13; 7:13). The woman understands the allusions in Jesus' conversation and immediately asks to receive what Jesus is offering.

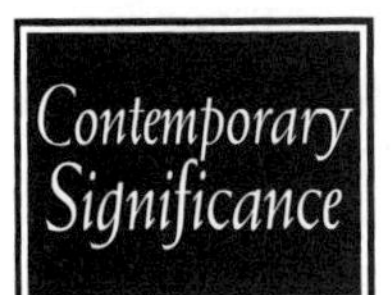

THE APPARENT SUCCESS **of the wicked.** The fact that the wicked prosper while the righteous suffer continues to bother us as much as the psalmist. We long for a world of true retribution, where what one sows is what one reaps. At least we think we do. This longing is actually a sign of our recognition that God is incompatible with evil and that any world he created *ought* to reflect his rejection of wickedness and blessing on the righteous. He is not a God "who takes pleasure in evil" (Ps. 5:4). How could it be otherwise?

Such reflections on what *ought to be* in the clear, hard light of what *is* can lead to conflicts of Joban proportions. Like Job, the faithful can be driven to confront God with our questions. But, unlike Job, we can also be tempted to anger, bitterness, cynicism, and despair. We can even be tempted to give up on God, his world, even life.

The psalmist of Psalm 36 offers one way forward beyond cynicism and despair. It is only one way, because Job and Ecclesiastes find other, darker avenues of faith in the face of suffering and apparent meaninglessness. Here, however, the psalmist offers a vision of a future in which God's original intention for his creation actually works. In that future, the wicked "lie fallen—thrown down, not able to rise!" (36:12). Although the world is currently broken, suffering under the consequences of human sin and evil, the time will come, says the psalmist, when God will set all things right and the wicked will get their just due.

This may seem to some a rather weak "pie in the sky by and by" platitude—a sort of pious wishful thinking that refuses to see or acknowledge the twisted state of the world we live in. But the psalmists are fully aware of human evil that permeates the world without and infects their inward beings as well. In addition, there is no clear evidence in Psalm 36 that the psalmist expects to experience this setting of all things right in his own lifetime.

In this psalm the vision of the fallen wicked is an affirmation of the integrity of God—the God whom the psalmist trusts despite the current situation. The poet finds the strength to live today, not in some hoped-for future, but in the ongoing provision of God for the faithful; his unfailing love provides refuge as well as the abundant delights of God's house. When we choose to live our lives focused on some future, heavenly hope—no matter how blessed or true—we fail to understand or to take hold of the hope this psalmist brings, and we fail to experience the hospitality of God breaking through into our here and now.

The hospitality of God. I remember being invited to a wedding in Bethlehem at the height of the Palestinian Intifada. My wife joined the women preparing the bride for the ceremony by creating intricate henna designs on her hands and palms. I sat with the men at the bridegroom's house as they prepared and walked with them to the home of the bride's father to present the traditional bride price. After the wedding at the Church of the Nativity, we joined the festivities at the home of the groom's family. The whole of Bethlehem seemed in attendance, treated to food and drink in abundance. As the only nonlocals present, my wife and I were treated to hospitality unlike any we had experienced before. We were given positions of honor close to and in plain view of the head table, where the newly wedded couple were enthroned. Our plates were never allowed to remain empty, and our cups were constantly filled with refreshment.

The hospitality within was in studied contrast to the evidence of continuing hostility from without. Israeli troops constantly patrolled the streets in their jeeps, stopping guests to question them and generally intruding their presence into an otherwise joyous occasion. It made me wonder whether Roman troops had done the same at that wedding so long ago in Cana of Galilee (John 2). I was also reminded how the Gospel writers often used wedding celebrations like the one I experienced as images of God's abundant hospitality.

As we sit in God's house surrounded by joy, celebration, and the abundant gifts of his grace, may we not be too distracted to see the hostility that still lurks outside—hostility that is contrary to God's ultimate purposes, hostility that will one day be overthrown, "thrown down, not able to rise." This awareness should, I think, push us in two directions. (1) It ought to encourage us with the hope that God is not a God who takes pleasure with evil and that we can trust that he is even now working to make all things new and right. (2) It ought to admonish us to confront evil where it exists and to take our place in the overthrow of suffering, pain, sorrow, sin, and hatred—all the hostilities of this world that intrude on the joyous celebration of God's kingdom.

Psalm 37

OF DAVID.

1 Do not fret because of evil men
or be envious of those who do wrong;
2 for like the grass they will soon wither,
like green plants they will soon die away.

3 Trust in the LORD and do good;
dwell in the land and enjoy safe pasture.
4 Delight yourself in the LORD
and he will give you the desires of your heart.

5 Commit your way to the LORD;
trust in him and he will do this:
6 He will make your righteousness shine like the dawn,
the justice of your cause like the noonday sun.

7 Be still before the LORD and wait patiently for him;
do not fret when men succeed in their ways,
when they carry out their wicked schemes.
8 Refrain from anger and turn from wrath;
do not fret—it leads only to evil.
9 For evil men will be cut off,
but those who hope in the LORD will inherit the land.

10 A little while, and the wicked will be no more;
though you look for them, they will not be found.
11 But the meek will inherit the land
and enjoy great peace.

12 The wicked plot against the righteous
and gnash their teeth at them;
13 but the Lord laughs at the wicked,
for he knows their day is coming.

14 The wicked draw the sword
and bend the bow
to bring down the poor and needy,
to slay those whose ways are upright.
15 But their swords will pierce their own hearts,
and their bows will be broken.

16 Better the little that the righteous have
than the wealth of many wicked;
17 for the power of the wicked will be broken,
but the LORD upholds the righteous.

18 The days of the blameless are known to the LORD,
and their inheritance will endure forever.
19 In times of disaster they will not wither;
in days of famine they will enjoy plenty.

20 But the wicked will perish:
The LORD's enemies will be like the beauty of the fields,
they will vanish—vanish like smoke.

21 The wicked borrow and do not repay,
but the righteous give generously;
22 those the LORD blesses will inherit the land,
but those he curses will be cut off.

23 If the LORD delights in a man's way,
he makes his steps firm;
24 though he stumble, he will not fall,
for the LORD upholds him with his hand.

25 I was young and now I am old,
yet I have never seen the righteous forsaken
or their children begging bread.
26 They are always generous and lend freely;
their children will be blessed.

27 Turn from evil and do good;
then you will dwell in the land forever.
28 For the LORD loves the just
and will not forsake his faithful ones.
They will be protected forever,
but the offspring of the wicked will be cut off;
29 the righteous will inherit the land
and dwell in it forever.

30 The mouth of the righteous man utters wisdom,
and his tongue speaks what is just.
31 The law of his God is in his heart;
his feet do not slip.

[32] The wicked lie in wait for the righteous,
seeking their very lives;
[33] but the LORD will not leave them in their power
or let them be condemned when brought to trial.

[34] Wait for the LORD
and keep his way.
He will exalt you to inherit the land;
when the wicked are cut off, you will see it.

[35] I have seen a wicked and ruthless man
flourishing like a green tree in its native soil,
[36] but he soon passed away and was no more;
though I looked for him, he could not be found.

[37] Consider the blameless, observe the upright;
there is a future for the man of peace.
[38] But all sinners will be destroyed;
the future of the wicked will be cut off.

[39] The salvation of the righteous comes from the LORD;
he is their stronghold in time of trouble.
[40] The LORD helps them and delivers them;
he delivers them from the wicked and saves them,
because they take refuge in him.

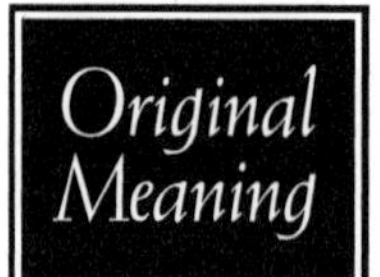

AS AN ALPHABETIC acrostic poem, Psalm 37 is the last of four such compositions in Book 1 of the Psalter (Pss. 9–10; 25; 34; 37). After this psalm we must wait until Book 5 (Pss. 107–145), where another four acrostic compositions appear (Pss. 111; 112; 119; 145).[1] In Psalm 37, each letter of the Hebrew alphabet appears only once and in traditional order, with each letter introducing a unit of four lines[2]—usually a two-verse stanza.

1. See the discussion of acrostic psalms in the section on "The Poetry of the Psalms" in the introduction. This balanced distribution of the acrostic psalms in the first and last books of the Psalter is a strong indication that wisdom interests have played an important role in shaping the final form of the canonical book of Psalms.

2. Except in the case of the *ḥeṭ* stanza (vv. 14–15), which has six lines, and the *nun* stanza (vv. 25–26), which includes five lines.

The psalm is an instructional poem, incorporating numerous recognizable proverbial sayings into a relatively loose framework that explores two major themes: the problem of the apparent prosperity of the wicked and the need for the faithful to trust Yahweh and to find refuge in him. These two concerns circle around one another throughout the psalm without any clear sense of thematic development. In its present position following Psalm 36, it is difficult to avoid the conclusion that Psalm 37 is intended to expand on 36:12 to "see how the evildoers lie fallen—thrown down, not able to rise!"

While it is difficult to isolate structural sections in the psalm, there are some subtle clues in the appearance of repeated phrases that punctuate the composition at various points and offer a way of dividing the poem into segments. The primary phrase repeated at intervals is the promise that the wicked "will be cut off" (*krt* in 37:9, 22, 28, 34, 38). In all instances but the last, this phrase is coupled with the positive promise that the faithful "will inherit the land" (37:9, 22, 29, 34). Using these repeated phrases as markers, we can divide the psalm into six sections: call to trust Yahweh in spite of the prosperity of the wicked (37:1–11), the ultimate fate of the wicked (37:12–22), the blessings of the faithful (37:23–29), contrasting presents (37:30–34), contrasting futures (37:35–38), and confidence in Yahweh (37:39–40).

The Heading (37:0)

THE PSALM IS simply attributed to David, with no other additions.[3]

Call to Trust Yahweh (37:1–11)

DO NOT FRET. Verses 1–2 establish the perspective and tone that dominate the entire psalm. They admonish the reader/listener not to be concerned because of the apparent success and invulnerability of the wicked, because their ultimate destiny is defeat and destruction. The phrase "do not fret" (*ḥrh* ["be angry, indignant; fly into a passion"]) appears three times in this section, once at the beginning and twice near the end (37:7, 8).[4] We must not let the seeming prosperity of the "wicked" and "those who do wrong" undermine our trust in the just character and sovereign power of Yahweh. The "fretting" that is discouraged is not just moral indignation but a desire that the cohesive moral power of the universe, which Yahweh represents, remains intact.

3. See the discussion of attribution to David in the comments on the heading of Ps. 3.

4. Compare this verse with the similar aphorism in Prov. 24:19: "Do not fret because of evil men or be envious of the wicked." The two verses agree in all particulars in the Hebrew except in the identification of the group that is not to be envied. In Prov. 24:19 that is the "wicked" (*rešaᶜim*) while in Ps. 37:1 it is "those who do wrong" (*ᶜośe ᶜawlah*).

They will soon wither. As encouragement to his readers/listeners the psalmist offers a striking image taken from the local agricultural experience of shepherds roaming the countryside in search of grass for their animals. With the onset of the early spring rains, the arid hills spring quickly into a lush green covering of grass. Almost as quickly, however, the heat of late spring and summer parch this fodder into a brittle brown. The wicked ought not cause undue concern because their prosperity is just as tenuous as the spring grass that is "here today, gone tomorrow." The image of withering grass recurs frequently in the psalms—most often as an indication of the tenuous, transient nature of human life in contrast to the eternal constancy that is Yahweh.[5]

Following the negatively stated admonition of verse 1, the psalmist shifts (37:3–6) to a series of positively stated imperative directives to the hearers. They are called to "trust" (37:3, 5) in Yahweh, "dwell" (37:3) in the land, "delight" (37:4) in Yahweh, and consequently "commit" (37:5) their way to him. As a result of turning their negative anger into passionate commitment to Yahweh, they will receive from God security and safe pasture (37:3),[6] the "desires" (*mišʾalot*, from *šʾl* ["the thing asked for, requested"]) of their hearts (37:4), and clear, public vindication against the wicked (37:6).

A pair of balanced statements, each involving two positive imperatives and the call not to fret (37:7–8), leads to a clear statement of the future destiny of the wicked (37:9). The psalmist cautions the reader to "be still" and "wait" for Yahweh rather than fret over the successful schemes of the wicked (37:7). In the balancing verse the reader must "refrain from anger" and "turn from wrath" since fretting can only lead to evil (37:8).

This unit concludes with the basis of a positive response to the psalmist's demands. In two balanced verses, he repeats the opening theme with a negative and positive inducement to the reader. The evil have only "a little while" before they are "cut off" and are "no more," but the "meek" who "hope in the LORD" will "inherit the land" (37:10–11).

---

5. See 37:2; 90:5; 92:7; 102:11; 103:15; 129:6, of which four are located in the important and formative Book 4 of the Psalter (Pss. 90–106). The other occurrence besides our psalm (129:6) is an apparent allusion to Isa. 37:27 = 2 Kings 19:26 (or perhaps vice versa). Outside the Psalter the image of withering grass appears in Job 8:12; Jer. 12:4; and frequently in Isaiah (Isa. 15:16; 37:27; 40:6, 7, 8; 51:12). Jesus used the image in his Sermon on the Mount (Matt. 6:30) as an admonition not to worry excessively (cf. Luke 12:28); it also appears in 1 Peter 1:24 as a quote from Isa. 37:27. In Rev. 8:7, a third of the grass of the earth is burned up when the seventh seal is opened.

6. The Heb. *reʿeh ʾemunah* ("consistent/reliable pasture") is an apparent reference to the withering grass image used in verse 2. Although the wicked can anticipate only divine judgment and ultimate destruction, those who trust Yahweh can look forward to secure and abundant pasture for their flocks and themselves.

The Ultimate Fate of the Wicked (37:12–22)

THE CONCLUSION OF the opening section provides the transition to the second, which describes the ultimate futility of the plots and schemes of the wicked and assures the faithful that Yahweh's righteous sovereignty is still in charge. Four illustrations of the futility of the wicked's attempts at self-power (37:12–13, 14–15, 20, 21–21) bracket a contrasting exhortation to righteousness and blamelessness (37:16–19). The purpose is to contrast the secure future of the righteous with the certain disappearance of the wicked.

While the wicked may plot against the righteous (37:12) and even cause them trouble and pain ("gnash their teeth at them"),[7] Yahweh remains unimpressed and unconcerned, even laughing at their pretense to power—in much the same way the enthroned God of 2:4 emitted a deep mocking guffaw from the heavens at the rebellious imaginings of the kings of the earth. God knows, as the psalmist understands and declares to the hearer, that the days of the wicked are already numbered (37:13). The wicked may draw their sword and bow to oppress the poor and needy (37:14), but the evil they intend will return on them decisively (37:15).

Better the little. The psalmist turns to the proverbial roots of wisdom to supply illustrations of the better way and better hope that attend the righteous. Stringing together a series of aphorisms similar to those found in Proverbs, he develops contrasting consequences of the diverging ways of the wicked and the righteous.

The initial aphorism is of the "better this . . . than that" variety common to Proverbs,[8] and it sets the theme for the collection: "Better the little that the righteous have than the wealth of many wicked; for the power of the wicked will be broken, but the LORD upholds the righteous" (37:16–17). The opponents of the psalmist are wealthy, many, and powerful. By contrast the author and the other righteous have little and are powerless. Nevertheless, it is the righteous who ultimately have the better end of the bargain. The wealth and power of the wicked will avail them nothing, while the righteous poor can anticipate divine aid.

---

7. Here and in Lam. 2:16, apparently the baring of the teeth in a snarl as a beast of prey menaces its intended victim. Cf. Ps. 112:10, where the image seems more like the baring of the teeth in a grimace of pain, although the snapping of an injured animal at those who approach may also fit. In the New Testament (predominantly in Matt.), the phrase occurs for the most part in tandem with tears ("weeping and gnashing of teeth") and seems to rely on the image of suffering and pain rather than being a predator.

8. Cf. Prov. 3:14; 8:19; 12:9; 15:16, 17; 16:8, 16, 19, 32; 17:1, 12; 19:1, 22; 21:9, 19; 22:1; 25:7, 24; 27:5, 10; 28:6. Prov. 15:16 offers a close parallel to our verse: "Better a little with the fear of the LORD than great wealth with turmoil" (cf. also 16:8; 28:6).

The second aphorism expands on the positive expectations of the righteous initiated at the end of the first. Like the wicked, the righteous find their days numbered and "known to the LORD" (37:18; cf. 37:13). There is, however, one significant difference. Yahweh knows just how many days the wicked have before judgment comes, while "the blameless" live out their days under the watchful care of God, "and their inheritance will endure forever." In a play on the "withering" fate of the wicked in 37:2, the psalmist describes the hope of the blameless in related terms: "They will not wither" like the wicked but will enjoy abundance in a time of want (37:19).

The third aphorism hammers home the tentative existence of the wicked by using another agricultural image. The verdant green fields—symbolic of the temporary success of the wicked—will "vanish like smoke" (37:20). This may refer to an unexpected and uncontrolled grassfire that destroys a farmer's crops, as when Samson set fire to the Philistine fields by turning loose foxes in the fields with firebrands tied to their tails (Judg. 15:1–5). It may alternatively suggest a purposeful burning of stubble after the harvest to prepare the land for the next cycle of planting.[9]

In the fourth and final aphorism in the series, the contrast is between the generosity of the righteous and the self-focused greed of the wicked, who "borrow and do not repay" (37:21). This section concludes with the second repetition of the structural tension between the wicked, who are "cut off," and the righteous, who will "inherit the land" (37:22).

The Blessings of the Faithful (37:23–29)

THE PSALM NOW moves from a description of the ultimate fate of the wicked to a consideration of the blessings that accrue to the faithful. Again, a series of extended proverb-like compositions, each consisting of four poetic lines, explore the subject. The overarching theme is the security of those who trust in Yahweh.

The first aphorism introduces the theme with the image of the protective care of Yahweh along the "way" or "path" of the righteous, making each step sure and firm and offering a steadying hand should the righteous stumble (37:23–24). As the righteous "delight" in Yahweh and commit their "way" to him (37:4–5), so Yahweh "delights" in the "way" of the righteous and makes their "steps firm" (37:23).

---

9. Isa. 47:14 and Mal. 4:1 both indicate that such a custom of burning stubble was practiced in Israel; each uses the practice as a potent symbol of judgment. The insubstantial character of smoke that quickly dissipates is also known elsewhere in Scripture. See Ps. 102:3 and Isa. 51:6 and the related reference in Ps. 68:2.

Though he stumble. It is not likely that the "stumbling" and "falling" mentioned here describes moral failure, from which Yahweh would then be seen as protecting the unrighteous. Rather, it likely refers to troubles encountered along the "way" that threaten to undo the righteous. Yahweh protects them so that even when they are knocked down by enemies or circumstances, they are not prostrated but are set on their feet once again. I recall once watching a group of Hasidic Jewish theology students accompanying their venerated *ṣaddiq* ("righteous one") through the streets of the Old City of Jerusalem. They surrounded their aged leader on every side with their care and concern, holding his elbows to steady him over the rough cobblestones and clearing the way before him. This is the kind of picture the psalmist paints of Yahweh's attentive care for the righteous.

I have never seen the righteous forsaken. As is usual in the biblical wisdom tradition, the narrator-sage of our psalm grounds his teaching in an aphorism of observation and experience (37:25–26). While experience confirms God's radical faithfulness to the righteous as well as the insubstantial nature of the wealth and power of the wicked, the psalmist speaks in these verses in a traditional form of testimony; these words should not be interpreted to mean a naive assumption that the righteous never hurt or suffer want. To the contrary, the whole psalm and much of canonical wisdom literature respond to the reality of the righteous suffering and the inexplicable prosperity of the wicked. In a sense, what the psalmist reports is not naive unreality but an inner vision of the true reality that accords with Yahweh's character and purpose—the reality that must ultimately arrive.

Dwell in the land. The third and fourth aphorisms in this section are linked by the promise that the faithful will "dwell in the land forever," which brackets the beginning and end (37:27, 29). The third aphorism (37:27–28) also recalls the similar admonition and promise offered in 37:3: "Trust in the LORD and do good; dwell in the land and enjoy safe pasture." The comparison of these two verses provides some interpretation of what the psalmist meant by "turn from evil." The parallel phrase in 37:3 suggests that the way to eschew evil is to acknowledge the inadequacy of one's own power, and to "do good" means placing one's trust in Yahweh alone. The poet also includes an element of justice in understanding the responsibility of the faithful (37:28). Those who adopt this position of absolute dependence may not avoid all suffering, but they are assured they will "dwell in the land forever" (37:27, 29).

In this last phrase in 37:27, "dwell" (*škn*) emphasizes a relatively settled residence that follows a period of nomadic wandering.[10] Coupled with the word

10. For further discussion of the meaning of this verb and related noun forms, see Gerald H. Wilson, "שׁכן," *NIDOTTE*, 4:109–11.

"forever" (*le^colam*), the phrase provides a contrasting description of a final settling down after a long period of instability. Perhaps the poet wants to contrast this coming to stability with the dissolution of the wicked's apparent stability into nothingness ("vanish," 37:20; "be no more," 37:10; "not be found," 37:10, 36).

This second collection of aphorisms ends much as does the first collection—and the introductory admonition as well. As in those earlier cases, we read a contrasting description of the fate of the wicked, who are "cut off," and the righteous, who will "inherit the land" (37:28–29). In this case, however, it is the "offspring" of the wicked who will experience obliteration. This gives us a reverse hint as to how the psalmist understands that the righteous can hope to dwell forever—through their descendants. The wicked, however, have no such hopes, since even their children will be cut off.[11]

Contrasting Presents (37:30–34)

THE STUDY OF contrasts between the righteous and wicked continues with a third, briefer set of aphorisms. An extended wisdom saying about the present reality of the righteous (37:30–31) is immediately followed by a contrasting picture of the devious plots of the wicked (37:32–33). The righteous person "utters wisdom, and his tongue speaks what is just" (37:30). He takes an unshakable stance on the firm foundation of the law of God so that "his feet do not slip" (37:31). The wicked, by contrast, are preoccupied in attacking the righteous (37:32), thinking to kill them from ambush or to defeat them in court. Yahweh will prevent either harm from overtaking those who trust him (37:33).

The psalmist exhorts the faithful to "wait" patiently for Yahweh while keeping "his way" (37:34). Despite what seem to be contrary indications in the present circumstance, they are to trust that Yahweh will ultimately act. The psalmist then encourages the righteous by assuring them that they will "see" when the wicked are "cut off" (37:34).

Contrasting Futures (37:35–38)

JUST AS THE righteous and wicked occupy conflicting positions in the present, so the future holds much the same in store. In response to the promises declared in 37:34 (that the righteous "will inherit the land" while the wicked "will be cut off"), the psalmist offers another personal observation that confirms the promise. He has "seen" the prosperity of the wicked that seemed

11. Cf. the later statements of 37:37–38 to the effect that while there is "a future" for the righteous "man of peace," the "future of the wicked will be cut off." In light of the statement about the offspring in 37:28, most likely the later statement should be understood as a reference to the end of the line of posterity.

rooted and grounded like a flourishing tree established in its native soil (rather than a transplant that might be expected to struggle) suddenly, unexpectedly, disappear. Contrary to all expectations, he "was no more" and "could not be found" (37:35–36).[12]

The psalmist then calls the reader/listener to share in the observation. If they will but "consider the blameless" (37:37) and "observe the upright," they will reach the same conclusion: "There is a future for the man of peace," but the "future of the wicked will be cut off" (37:38).

Confidence in Yahweh (37:39–40)

EXPERIENCE AND OBSERVATION confirm the promise of Yahweh. Wisdom teaching provides the firm foundation for present assurance, enduring faith, and future hope. The psalm concludes with a triumphant declaration of confidence and commitment that breaks loose from the traditional language of the sages and wisdom. Once again the theme of Yahweh as "refuge" and "stronghold" of the righteous takes the stage.[13] Because the body of the psalm is preoccupied with the eventual defeat and demise of the wicked, the conclusion offers a hopeful way forward.

As in Psalm 31, these verses do not envision a complete escape for the righteous from oppression or suffering at the hands of the wicked. Rather, it offers those who take refuge in Yahweh a place of security *in the midst* of suffering and applies spiritual balm to the anguished souls of the righteous as they affirm and reaffirm that Yahweh is the helper of the righteous (37:40). He does not wink at the wicked and is powerful to establish his will and purpose in the world. This gives a meaning and purpose to righteous suffering that transcends any hope for escape; they suffer *for* Yahweh, understanding their pain as the badge of enduring faithfulness.[14]

THE SUCCESS OF THE WICKED. The heart of Psalm 37 is focused on the apparent success of the wicked in the psalmist's world. From the opening admonishment not to "fret because of evil men," the psalmist makes clear that his righteous contemporaries must have been doing precisely that: looking with pained disbelief at how the evil

12. Cf. 37:10, where the disappearance of the wicked is promised in very similar terms. Experience confirms promise. What has been observed before offers the foundation for hope in the present circumstances.

13. See esp. comments on Ps. 31.

14. See comments on 44:22.

doings of the wicked seemed to go unpunished while the righteous suffered under their power. The consternation of the righteous grows out of their understanding of God and the world—a view that is often called "retribution." Since God is not "a God who takes pleasure in evil" (5:4), one would expect that the wicked and righteous will each receive their just rewards from his hand. Indeed, many psalms expect or even celebrate just that. But in our present psalm, this expectation of retribution—reaping what one has sown—has *not* been fulfilled. Thus, the psalmist offers the admonition not to fret simply because the evil are not receiving their just due.

The assumption of retribution is particularly prominent in some of the biblical wisdom literature and is often considered a chief characteristic of the wisdom worldview. Examples of retribution can be found in the opposingly parallel aphorisms of Proverbs,[15] the speeches of Job's friends,[16] and in many psalms.[17] The idea of retribution had its limits even within the wisdom literature, however. Observation and experience—two vital elements in the wisdom worldview—also uncovered *violations* of the expected retributive norms, in that the righteous did not always prosper, while the wicked often did.

Proverbs takes note of these facts in such observations as: "Better a little with righteousness than much gain with injustice" (Prov. 16:8); "how much better to get wisdom than gold, to choose understanding rather than silver!" (16:16); "better a poor man whose walk is blameless than a rich man whose ways are perverse" (28:6). Such sayings make it clear that righteousness is not synonymous with wealth or prosperity and that the righteous and wise often experience poverty of circumstances.

Job and Ecclesiastes make similar observations about the breakdown of retribution, and they do so in much harsher terms than Proverbs. "In this meaningless life of mine I have seen both of these: a righteous man perishing in his righteousness, and a wicked man living long in his wickedness" (Eccl. 7:15); "there is something else meaningless that occurs on earth: righteous men who get what the wicked deserve, and wicked men who get what the righteous deserve. This too, I say, is meaningless" (8:14). Job in particular speaks in eloquent tones about the incongruity of wicked persons who live long, prosperous, and secure lives without any interference or judgment from God.[18]

Thus, the psalmists are not alone in their critique of retribution, nor are they alone in their "fretting." They join a long heritage of sages who place

---

15. See, e.g., Prov. 10:16, 22; 11:19, 21, 28; 15:6, 16; 16:20; 21:6; 22:16; 23:4–5; 24:19–20; 28:8, 20, 25.

16. See, e.g., Job 4:7–9; 8:1–7, 20; 11:13–20; 15:20–35; 18:5–21; 20:4–29.

17. See, e.g., Pss. 1; 5:4–7; 7:14–16; 34:6–7, 15–16.

18. See, e.g., Job 21:7–16; 24:1–12. It is true that elsewhere Job seems to expect divine judgment ultimately to fall on the wicked (cf. 24:18–24; 27:13–23).

their observations in tension with the more naive expectations of retribution. In so doing the psalmists cast their lot with those who acknowledge a world run amok—in which the expected principles of a holy God no longer operate unerringly day by day. In this world the righteous suffer while the wicked seem to prosper with impunity.

Such a view is clearly described in 73:2–11, which begins with the words: "But as for me, my feet had almost slipped; I had nearly lost my foothold. For I envied the arrogant when I saw the prosperity of the wicked." The psalmist goes on to describe the seemingly carefree and blessed existence of those who oppress the poor and thumb their noses at God—assuming he has no knowledge or concern about their wickedness. This disparity between what is and what ought to be has created a spiritual crisis for the psalmist, who almost loses faith in God.

I find it interesting that the Hebrew behind the word translated "prosperity" in 73:3 is *šalom*, the word we normally associate with "peace." As this particular context makes clear, *šalom* has a much broader range of meaning and includes such nuances as "wholeness, soundness, completion, well-being, safety, security" as well as "prosperity." Peace in this sense is much more than the cessation or lack of war. It describes the secure, blessed existence that can only come from the hand of God and which mirrors God's original intention for all creation. No wonder the psalmist of 73:2 (and of 37:1) is so dismayed when the wicked experience a "wholeness" and "prosperity" out of bounds with their deeds.

It is also telling that Psalm 37 employs this same word *šalom* twice to define the ultimate reward of the *faithful*: "The meek will inherit the land and enjoy great peace" (37:11); "consider the blameless, observe the upright; there is a future for the man of peace" (37:37)." It is *šalom*, this kind of God-given complete and secure wholeness, that characterizes God's intention for his world and those who fear him. It is the seeming usurpation of this blessed state of wholeness precisely by those who stand squarely against all that God represents that constitutes the psalmist's greatest problem—a problem that nearly causes the narrator of Psalm 73 to stumble.

The response of the psalmists (along with the sages) is twofold. (1) The success of the wicked is never allowed to undermine their confidence in God's justice and goodness. They continually view this inexplicable state of affairs as a reversal of his intention and purpose that must ultimately be set right. This is no unrealistic, wishful thinking but a sincere commitment to an understanding of divine character that remains unshaken. God is incompatible with evil and must judge it—if not now for some mysterious reason, then in some unspecified future.

(2) In spite of the faithful endurance (or enduring faithfulness) of God's people, in the midst of a topsy-turvy world retribution clearly does not always work. As tempting as it might seem to throw off the bonds of faith and to adopt the cynical, self-serving practices of the wicked in hopes of sharing in their "prosperity," the psalmists—and Job and Qohelet—agree that such a path leads only to destruction. Better, they say, a *little* (or even great suffering) with righteousness than the empty prosperity of the wicked.

Canonically, these two viewpoints are permitted to stand side by side without resolution. That is because both represent true understandings of God and his world. Retribution keeps its eyes firmly fastened on the character of holy God and the knowledge that righteousness and justice are his final word. The counter view plants its feet firmly in the here and now, realizing that because God places a premium on human free will and because that will often opts for self-will and evil, the world as we know it does not reflect his purpose or intention. The former view counsels the faithful not to give up on God but to endure faithfully to the end. The latter understanding cautions us against equating righteousness with wealth or suffering with sin. It also opens a window on a new value system that finds the relationship with God engendered by righteous living a far superior treasure than wealth, power, or even health could ever offer.

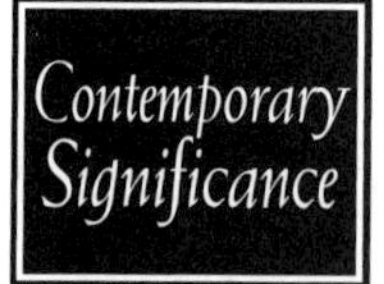

OUR WORLD IS not so different from that of the psalmist in Psalm 37. Everywhere we look, those who deny or ignore God seem to enjoy easy lives of prosperity and security. While billions of the world's poor struggle to survive, those in power grow ever richer, virtue is mocked, and injustice and license permeate the highest levels of society. And lest I join a self-righteous chorus condemning "them," I must admit the myriad of ways I choose each day to participate in the distorted society of which I am a part: seeking self-will, self-power, self-comfort, and ease.

The realization of this darkness without and within can tempt us to view God as the "big fix," which can take us out of our suffering and pain. During one particularly difficult period I was earnestly seeking God's presence in my life through prayer, meditation, Scripture—certainly not bad things in themselves. Yet God continued to seem distant and absent. One day, however, I realized what I was doing. I was making God into a "big fix" to take me out of my misery. I wanted an ecstatic experience with God that would so fill me with his spiritual presence that I would no longer be aware of the suffering that surrounded me and filled me. I was shocked by the realization of how similar my desire for God was to the need of the addict for a narcotic high or an alcoholic haze that obliterated—even for a moment—the pain of the real world.

When I set aside this unrealistic view of relationship with God, I began, little by little, to experience the presence of God *within* the distorted world in which we live. Our rampant evil has twisted God's creation almost beyond recognition, but it has not been able to run God out of the world. I found that throughout each day I could maintain a running conversation with God—a conversation that was often angry and sarcastic on my part, but a real communication nevertheless with God in my world.

Often, when confronted by evil in our world without and within, we look to God for escape. When, like the psalmists, we find our circumstances remain unchanged, God can seem distant, absent, and unconcerned. Our praises to the just and righteous God, creator of the universe, can seem forced and hollow. The continued presence of evil, pain, and suffering in spite of our prayers and praises can lead us to contorted, hurtful logic in order to maintain our belief in a righteous, powerful God. "We must have sinned. We must have failed. God must be testing us or teaching us some great and difficult truth!" The great and difficult truth God is teaching us is this: Life in a world thoroughly corrupted by human evil is going to remain difficult and painful! God cannot remove us from the pain of living without removing us from living itself.

As I learned, our failure to acknowledge the distorted and fallen nature of the world in which we live can dull us to the richness of relationship with God, which can blossom even in the midst of pain. Fretting about what is an essential characteristic of a fallen world is to seek to change the unchangeable. This is not to say that we should not seek to confront and eliminate suffering and injustice wherever we find it. To struggle against evil in all its forms is to remain faithful to the vision of a holy God, who calls us to be holy as well. But to think that by our efforts we can eradicate evil once and for all is to put ourselves in the place of God, which will in turn distract us from hearing God's word delivered by the psalmist: "Do not fret because of evil men.... The salvation of the righteous comes from the LORD; he is their stronghold in time of trouble. The LORD helps them and delivers them ... because they take refuge in him" (37:1, 39–40).

Psalm 38

A PSALM OF DAVID. A petition.

1 O LORD, do not rebuke me in your anger
or discipline me in your wrath.
2 For your arrows have pierced me,
and your hand has come down upon me.
3 Because of your wrath there is no health in my body;
my bones have no soundness because of my sin.
4 My guilt has overwhelmed me
like a burden too heavy to bear.

5 My wounds fester and are loathsome
because of my sinful folly.
6 I am bowed down and brought very low;
all day long I go about mourning.
7 My back is filled with searing pain;
there is no health in my body.
8 I am feeble and utterly crushed;
I groan in anguish of heart.

9 All my longings lie open before you, O Lord;
my sighing is not hidden from you.
10 My heart pounds, my strength fails me;
even the light has gone from my eyes.
11 My friends and companions avoid me because of
my wounds;
my neighbors stay far away.
12 Those who seek my life set their traps,
those who would harm me talk of my ruin;
all day long they plot deception.

13 I am like a deaf man, who cannot hear,
like a mute, who cannot open his mouth;
14 I have become like a man who does not hear,
whose mouth can offer no reply.
15 I wait for you, O LORD;
you will answer, O Lord my God.
16 For I said, "Do not let them gloat
or exalt themselves over me when my foot slips."

[17]For I am about to fall,
and my pain is ever with me.
[18]I confess my iniquity;
I am troubled by my sin.
[19]Many are those who are my vigorous enemies;
those who hate me without reason are numerous.
[20]Those who repay my good with evil
slander me when I pursue what is good.

[21]O LORD, do not forsake me;
be not far from me, O my God.
[22]Come quickly to help me,
O Lord my Savior.

THIS PSALM IS a lament,[1] a plea for deliverance from trouble—in this case, severe physical anguish and suffering that the psalmist acknowledges as the consequences of personal sin (38:3–4, 18). The debilitating suffering provides the occasion for attacks by his enemies, and even the psalmist's friends and acquaintances are withdrawing their support (38:11–12). The psalm begins with an invocation of Yahweh to withdraw his physical rebuke (38:1–4); it continues with a narrative of the psalmist's anguished suffering (38:5–20), twice punctuated by personal address to Yahweh (38:9, 15–16); and it concludes with a final plea for deliverance (38:21–22).

Because of its twenty-two verses, the psalm falls into that category that Craigie and Kraus have called "alphabetizing" psalms, although it shows no evidence of any acrostic pattern.[2] Further, there is no suggestion of the traditional language or concerns of wisdom normally associated with the acrostic psalms.

The Heading (38:0)

IN ADDITION TO the familiar attribution to David,[3] the heading includes the technical term *lehazkir* ("cause to remember"; NIV "a petition"), which also

1. It is traditionally included among the seven penitential psalms: 2; 32; 38; 51; 102; 130; and 143.

2. See Craigie, *Psalms 1–50*, 271; Kraus, *Psalms 1–59*, 374. Kraus's term "acrostic songs" is confusing and may be the result of unwieldy translation. Beyond the number of verses, Craigie also mentions the "considerable regularity of the internal structure and balance" of the psalm as characteristic of this category.

3. See comments on the heading of Ps. 3 for discussion of this term.

appears in the heading of Psalm 70. Delitzsch calls attention to 1 Chronicles 16:4, where Levitical singers are appointed by David to serve before the ark of the covenant "to make petition [*lehazkir*], to give thanks [*lehodot*], and to praise [*lehallel*] the LORD, the God of Israel." These three terms relate clearly to major form-critical categories of psalms: lament, thanksgiving, and praise. Delitzsch further suggests that psalms such as 38 and 70 accompanied the memorial (Heb. *ʾazkarah*) sacrifice, in which a portion of the offering was burned on the altar, sending smoke into the heavens to recall the offerer to the mind of Yahweh.[4] Our psalm, however, demonstrates little evidence of a cultic connection.

The Invocation of Yahweh (38:1–4)

VERSES 1–4 ESTABLISH the perspective and tone for the remainder of the composition. The psalmist experiences physical suffering as the rebuke of Yahweh for personal sin. He does not deny the assumed accusation but freely admits his guilt (38:3–4).

The affirming parallelism of the first two lines sets out the picture of Yahweh as teacher/instructor who "rebukes" (or "reproves, sets right") and "disciplines" (or "teaches") the psalmist. The setting is less the courtroom than the classroom, and Yahweh is less a judge than a teacher correcting a student. This nuance is important in that the description of divine discipline in the following verses is severe, but the underlying theme of instruction provides hope of ultimate improvement and deliverance.

From the psalmist's view Yahweh is acting out of "anger" and "wrath," regular terms used to describe the experience of God's displeasure with human sin. However, the atmosphere of instruction fostered here provides a context that somewhat mitigates the harshness of divine anger/wrath by understanding it as a part of divine instruction.

The discipline God metes out is expressed in terms of an attack with "arrows." Rather than a strictly military image, the arrow most likely represents the onset of a particularly virulent and painful physical ailment. The Canaanite god Resheph is known as an archer whose arrows bring pestilence.[5] It may also be the pain, inflammation, and suffering associated with wounds from poisoned arrows that the psalmist has in mind.[6] It is clear, in any case, that the psalmist understands this attack as from God, whose "hand has come down upon" him (38:2).

---

4. Delitzsch, *Biblical Commentary on the Psalms*, 1:20.

5. Craigie, *Psalms 1–50*, 303; Kraus, *Psalms 1–59*, 411.

6. Cf. Job 6:4 and 34:6, where Job equates God's attack with the poison of arrows and the "incurable" wounds they left behind.

The consequences of this divine attack is a rapid decline of the psalmist's physical health. The exact nature of the ailment has been variously diagnosed,[7] but Craigie is probably correct in assuming that this approach is misleading.[8] The enduring power of the psalm that led to its preservation over time is probably its ability to mirror the painful circumstances of a variety of ailments experienced by penitents, who can see themselves in the words of this psalm. Craigie's suggestion that the litany of complaints in Psalm 38 may well represent not a single disease but "a lifetime of disease in the person of the poet" is instructive.[9]

The effects of the disease are all-consuming. The psalmist's "body" has "no health" (*metom* ["uninjured spot"]) at all (38:3), and his "bones" have "no soundness" (*šalom* ["wholeness, completeness"]). This alternation likely describes inner as well as outer physical pain and deterioration. Add to this the psychological torment of "guilt" (38:4), and the psalmist's absorption by disease is complete.

Narrative of Suffering (38:5–20)

AFTER THE INITIAL and most general description of the psalmist's experience of pain and its origin in sin, he provides an extended narrative of suffering in more specific detail. This account encompasses sixteen verses and can be divided into two parts: verses 5–10, where the focus is on the physical consequences of suffering; and verses 11–20, where relational effects between the psalmist and friends or enemies are explored.

Physical consequences. The description uses language of extreme gangrenous infection. The afflicted psalmist's diseased body exhibits "wounds" or sores that emit a foul odor (38:5). They "fester and are loathsome." The sickening smell of diseased flesh must have surrounded him and has influenced the reaction of friends and companions, who avoid contact (38:11).

The psalmist is "bowed down" (*ʿwh* ["become agitated?"]) and "brought very low" by this malady (38:6); he experiences searing back pain as well (38:7).[10] It is not clear whether this is another symptom—the doubling over because of pain in the abdominal region—or whether he is adopting the position and attitude of mourning prostration. In any case, he acknowledges the suffering as a consequence of personal sin and "folly" (*ʾiwwelet*

---

7. Kraus (*Psalms 1–59*, 411–12) takes the symptoms to suggest leprosy.

8. See Craigie, *Psalms 1–50*, 303–4.

9. Ibid., 304.

10. The reference to the "back" (*kesel* ["loins, area around kidneys"]) may indicate kidney pain or disease. The pain is described as burning ("searing").

["impious foolishness"]),[11] to which he now responds with mourning and repentance.

The psalmist feels "feeble and utterly crushed," and he is able to respond only with inarticulate groans and sighs (38:8–9). The longing desire he is unable to express God is still able to understand (38:9), since it "lies open" and "is not hidden" from him. This first subsection of the narrative concludes with a picture of the psalmist in desperate straits—perhaps nearing death. A wildly beating heart, general weakness, and glazed vision herald the end.[12]

Relational consequences. The psalmist's condition has disruptive effects on relationships with others. Those whom he might count as positive relationships—friends, companions, neighbors—distance themselves "because of my wounds" (38:11).[13] At the same time, his opponents consider the sickness an opportunity to take advantage of. They are mentioned in terms already encountered in 35:4 and 37:32: "those who seek my life" and "those who would harm me."[14] They plot the ruin of the narrator, using threats and deception (38:12).[15]

I am like a deaf man ... a mute. The psalmist—beset within and without, consumed with the pain of disease and of deteriorating relationship—is unable (or unwilling) to respond to the attacks of his enemies (38:13–14). We have no indication of the content of these attacks other than the vague reference to "slander" in 38:20, so we remain uncertain whether the accusations are false, or perhaps true but a harsh public airing of the details of the psalmist's sin. In any case, the psalmist assumes the demeanor of the deaf who cannot hear the words of his detractors. Since he clearly does hear the enemy's attacks, it may well be that the deafness is a way of shutting out what cannot otherwise be avoided. Similarly, the psalmist makes no reply, acting as if mute.

---

11. This word occurs over twenty times in Proverbs.

12. The verb translated as "pounds" is the unusual Pealal stem and has the meaning "keep on moving back and forth, beat violently (of heart)" (Holladay, *CHALOT*, 255).

13. Lit., "my contact, blow; mark, disease" (from the root *ngᶜ* ["reach, touch, strike"]). When an illness is thought to be a divine attack, then the marks of the disease are considered blows or bruises.

14. See comments on 35:4; also 3:1–2.

15. The NIV has broken up the existing Heb. sentence to provide a set of three balanced and parallel lines, following the accentuation of the Hebrew text (lit. trans.):

> They set traps, those who seek my life
> and those who would harm me speak threats
> and deceptions all day long they plot.

The last phrase in particular seems awkward, and the first word ("deceptions") might best be taken with the preceding phrase, "and those who would harm me speak threats and deceptions." For the use of the Heb. verb "murmur, meditate, plot," see comments on 1:2 and 2:1.

You will answer, O Lord my God. Unable to answer his accusers, the psalmist waits for Yahweh to act as defender and vindicator (38:15). He is confident that Yahweh will prevent his enemies from "gloating" (*śmḥ* ["rejoice over"]) over his misfortune or pressing their advantage to completion during this time of weakness ("when my foot slips," 38:16). The narrator feels at a crisis point ("about to fall")[16] and is wracked with pain (38:17). This sense of vulnerability and lack of control leads him at last to the full confession of sin and an expression of remorse.[17]

This section of the psalmist's narrative concludes with a complaint regarding the opposition. Here the description seems to move beyond the circumstances of illness to encompass more long-standing enmities. These numerous and "vigorous enemies" (38:19) are not simply opportunists taking advantage of a moment of vulnerability but implacable opponents, who seek to counter the psalmist's every attempt to do "good" with a disproportionate and baseless response of "evil" (38:20).

If the aura of disease seems to recede into the background at this point, it may indicate that the disease motif is employed as imagery to speak to difficult and painful circumstances of physical, emotional, and relational disintegration growing as the result of personal sin and guilt. There is the connection of feeling overwhelmed by outside forces beyond one's control.

Final Plea for Deliverance (38:21–22)

THE PSALMIST RETURNS at the end to directly address Yahweh, pleading for God's immediacy of presence in deliverance. The sense of forsakenness (lit., "don't abandon me") and isolation from God ("be not far from me") are coupled with the language of urgency ("come quickly to help me") to emphasize the psalmist's vulnerability and imminent doom. At the bottom of personal resources and hope, he recognizes that Yahweh is synonymous with salvation: "O Lord my Savior."

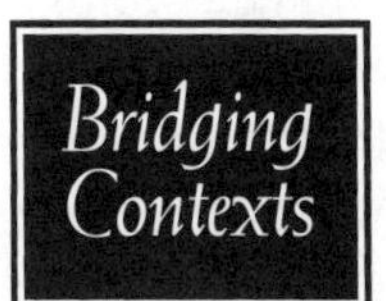

MY LORD, MY SALVATION. Although God is, at the beginning of this psalm, the source of the psalmist's rebuke for sin (38:1–4), by the final lines he has become both Lord and salvation. The term used for "salvation" here is *tešuᶜah*, the less common of two nouns of

16. The Heb. of this phrase, *leṣelaᶜ nakon* ("for stumbling I am established"), suggests the stumbling of the victim is permanent and imminently final.

17. For a discussion of the different nuances represented by *ᶜawon* and *ḥaṭṭaʾat*, see comments on 32:1–2.

similar meaning drawn from the verb *yšᶜ* ("help, deliver, save"). The more common of the two (*yešuᶜah*) has the broader pattern of meaning encompassing "help given, deeds of help," and by extension "salvation." The word in our text is more narrowly focused on the end product of "deliverance" or "salvation."[18] The two are, however, closely related and together provide a context of meaning that sheds light on our psalm.

The particular turn of phrase that characterizes the faith of our psalmist is to acknowledge that God is "my salvation" (38:22; NIV "Savior"). This final cry is directed to God but is done within the hearing of the community of faith, so that it bears the earmarks of both plea for divine response and testimony of faithful reliance. The psalmist is both in need of divine deliverance (calling for it) and acknowledges that there is but one source of hope (the delivering God). A similar realization appeared at the end of Psalm 37, where we hear that "the salvation [*tešuᶜah*] of the righteous comes from the LORD" (37:39).

The fifty-seven occurrences of these two related nouns are scattered throughout the Psalter and punctuate all five books.[19] Within these occurrences the following pattern emerges. Humans are called to acknowledge that Yahweh/God is the only sure source of salvation or deliverance.[20] Beginning with the clear proclamation in 3:8 that "salvation belongs to the LORD" (lit. trans.), the psalmists continue with affirmations such as "the salvation of the righteous comes from the LORD" (37:39); "you are the rock of my salvation" (89:26, lit. trans.); "say to my soul, 'I [Yahweh] am your salvation'" (35:3). Salvation is so much the possession of Yahweh alone that it can be spoken of as *his* salvation: "My heart rejoices in your salvation" (13:5); "The LORD has made his salvation known and revealed his righteousness to the nations . . . all the ends of the earth have seen the salvation of our God" (98:2–3).[21]

Along with this acknowledgment of God's saving power comes the admission that all human attempts to save ultimately fail. In simple terms, "human salvation is worthless" (60:11 = 108:12, lit. trans.). Or in the words of 33:16–17: "No king is saved by the size of his army; no warrior escapes by his great strength. A horse is a vain hope for deliverance [*tešuᶜah*]; despite its great strength it cannot save." Similar sentiments are found at the conclusion of the

18. In military contexts both words can be translated "victory," although to do so often obscures linkages and wordplays being created with other forms of the root *yšᶜ*.

19. It is interesting that *tešuᶜa* occurs (thirteen times) only in Books 1, 2, and 5 (i.e., not in Pss. 73–106). By contrast, *yešuᶜa* occurs forty-four times in all five books of the Psalter.

20. See, e.g., 3:8; 35:9; 37:39; 51:14; 71:15; 74:12; 80:3; 88:1; 98:3, 4; 118:14; 119:41; 140:7; 149:4.

21. See also 9:14; 70:4; 91:16; 96:2; 106:4; 119:41, 123, 166, 174.

Psalter: "Do not put your trust in princes, in mortals, in whom there is no salvation [*tešuʿah*]" (146:3).[22]

Not only do the psalmists recognize the inadequacy of human power to save and call on Yahweh as the only trustworthy source of deliverance; they also feel called to testify to their experience and knowledge of God in the worshiping congregation. Psalm 40:9–10 is particularly clear in this regard: "I proclaim righteousness in the great assembly; I do not seal my lips, as you know, O LORD. I do not hide your righteousness in my heart; I speak of your faithfulness and salvation. I do not conceal your love and your truth from the great assembly." This kind of testimony is, of course, at the heart of the psalms. Whenever the psalmists describe or proclaim the deliverance they experience, they are giving voice to this witness.[23]

There is one last, darker aspect of the psalmists' awareness that salvation belongs to Yahweh. If salvation is God's possession, if it is in some sense particularly *his*, then it is in his control and not simply at the beck and call of humans—no matter how righteous they may be. This awareness of the freedom of God to give or withhold his deliverance is not as clearly expressed in the psalms as in, let's say, Job, Ecclesiastes, or the prayer of the three friends of Daniel (Dan. 3:16–18). It is in the final analysis not deliverance but *God* whom the three friends of Daniel, the psalmists, and Job seek to know and experience. It is this realization that lies behind the psalmist's exclamation at the conclusion of Psalm 38, "O Yahweh, my salvation!" (pers. trans.). Even if the desired deliverance delays or does not come, God is the continuing source of hope and salvation, now and into the future.

GUILT AND HEALING. Often the awareness of our sin leads to an attack from without. When our own sensation of guilt is heightened, every word of attack and criticism can seem true. For our psalmist, the acute sense of guilt and divine displeasure that dominates the opening lines (38:1–8) leads to a moment of capitulation. His strength is spent, all hope of self-deliverance is gone, and his heartfelt longing is laid before God, the only source of hope (38:8–10).

22. The translation is mine. It is esp. interesting that here at the end of the Psalter we find a phrase that recalls and reaffirms the statement with which the collection began. At the end of Ps. 3 the reader is called to acknowledge that "salvation belongs to Yahweh" (3:8a, my translation).

23. See, e.g., 9:14; 13:5–6; 35:9–10; 51:14; 68:19; 71:15; 96:2; 116:12–14.

At this point—when all hideouts are dismantled and reality rushes in—guilt threatens to overwhelm the psalmist like a tidal wave (38:4), so that he is left vulnerable and defenseless in hopelessness against the attacks of friend and foe alike. Especially when they are made public, moments of moral failure can lead to debilitating consequences. The public today thrives on the fall of heroes, or just good men or women gone wrong. Perhaps it is a way of excusing our own failings, but we are often drawn to the scene of sinful collapse like vultures surrounding a dying animal—unwilling to depart until every recess has been revealed and every bone picked clean.

Such public outcry and continuing humiliation can lead to the destruction of useful human beings and prevents their rehabilitation. Fear of public exposure and its consequences to sinner and family alike can delay the acknowledgment of sin until it becomes a festering sore that can no longer be contained, so that it breaks out with the most destructive consequences possible. Often Christian leaders enmeshed in moral failures feel unable to confess their sin or to seek help, because of their fear of public humiliation for themselves as well as the innocent members of their family. Some even choose suicide rather than confession.

Our psalm helps us to see that acknowledging sin is the only way out of this trap of fear and destruction. The phrase used in Twelve-Step circles is true: "We are only as sick as our secrets." As long as we refuse to acknowledge our sin, we feed the fear that controls us and allow it to work its destructive way within and without. Confessing our sin to God and even a single trustworthy person can have the effect of removing the power our secrets wield over us. It does not mean that the destructive consequences set in motion by our sinful actions can always be fully avoided. We may still have to restore what we have taken or pay the legal price of our acts. We may have to deal with the destructive results of an adulterous affair and work long and hard to rebuild lost trust and effectiveness. But confession can remove the fear of discovery and enable us to accept the forgiveness of God.

This is especially true when those who know our secrets have themselves experienced the gracious forgiveness of a merciful God and thus can lead us to hear the power behind the simple passage from 1 John 1:9: "If we confess our sins, he [God] is faithful and just and will forgive us our sins and purify us from all unrighteousness." Psalm 38 cautions those of us who sin not to let our fear of discovery and the attacks of those who are looking for a chance to humiliate us prevent us from acknowledging our sins and experiencing the gracious forgiveness of God.

Nevertheless, the psalm also calls those of us who too often join the humiliating catcalls of the crowd to be examples of those who lend a caring and listening ear. We can be examples of God's forgiveness unleashed among his faithful community—examples who can encourage those with hidden sin to acknowledge their need for confession and restoration. Only in such a community can we really reflect the wholeness of God, who desires *all* to know their sin as well as to experience his forgiving power. Otherwise, Christ our Lord has gone to the cross in vain!

Psalm 39

FOR THE DIRECTOR of music. For Jeduthun. A psalm of David.

1 I said, "I will watch my ways
and keep my tongue from sin;
I will put a muzzle on my mouth
as long as the wicked are in my presence."
2 But when I was silent and still,
not even saying anything good,
my anguish increased.
3 My heart grew hot within me,
and as I meditated, the fire burned;
then I spoke with my tongue:

4 "Show me, O LORD, my life's end
and the number of my days;
let me know how fleeting is my life.
5 You have made my days a mere handbreadth;
the span of my years is as nothing before you.
Each man's life is but a breath. *Selah*
6 Man is a mere phantom as he goes to and fro:
He bustles about, but only in vain;
he heaps up wealth, not knowing who will get it.

7 "But now, Lord, what do I look for?
My hope is in you.
8 Save me from all my transgressions;
do not make me the scorn of fools.
9 I was silent; I would not open my mouth,
for you are the one who has done this.
10 Remove your scourge from me;
I am overcome by the blow of your hand.
11 You rebuke and discipline men for their sin;
you consume their wealth like a moth—
each man is but a breath *Selah*

12 "Hear my prayer, O LORD,
listen to my cry for help;
be not deaf to my weeping.

For I dwell with you as an alien,
a stranger, as all my fathers were.
13 Look away from me, that I may rejoice again
before I depart and am no more."

AS A PLEA for deliverance from divine rebuke for sin, Psalm 39 shares many connections with Psalm 38. Both psalms speak of divine "rebuke" and "discipline" (cf. 38:1; 39:11) for sin as "blows," "wounds," or "bruises" (cf. 38:11; 39:10) from the "hand" of God (cf. 38:2; 39:10). In both psalms the narrator acknowledges personal sin as the cause of divine judgment (cf. 38:4–5, 18; 39:8, 11) and adopts an attitude of silent waiting in the presence of detractors (cf. 38:13–16; 39:1–3, 8–9). Both stress—although in different ways—the tenuous nature of human life (cf. 38:10, 17; 39:4–6, 11).

This silent waiting for God is also mirrored in the opening verses of Psalm 40, and confession of personal sin figures prominently in both Psalms 40 and 41 (cf. 40:12; 41:4). These connections, along with the reappearance of the theme of sickness in Psalm 41, suggest that these four psalms have been stitched together to form the conclusion to book 1 of the Psalter.[1]

Psalm 39 falls into four sections: a personal meditation on the agony of silent waiting (39:1–3), a direct address to Yahweh regarding the frailty of human life (39:4–6), an acknowledgment of sin (39:7–11), and a final plea for deliverance (39:12–13). The term *selah* appears twice (39:5, 11) but does not coincide with the obvious literary structure of the poem.

The Heading (39:0)

MOST OF THE terms in the heading are familiar from earlier psalm headings ("For the director of music ... psalm of David").[2] The one new term, "for Jeduthun," appears also in the headings of Psalms 62 and 77. Jeduthun is one of three choir leaders appointed by David to lead temple worship (cf. 1 Chron. 16:41–42; 25:1, 6; 2 Chron. 35:15). If this reference suggests authorship, it raises questions regarding the meaning of the frequent reference to David in the psalm headings. We cannot be certain whether the intent is to acknowledge Jeduthun as author of the psalm and David as the one authorizing it or perhaps giving it a "Davidic" style, or whether David

1. See comments on "The Shape of Book 1" at the beginning of Psalm 1.
2. See comments on the heading of Pss. 3 and 4 for discussion of these terms.

is the author and Jeduthun the "style" or the one responsible for its performance. It is difficult to making any absolute claims about these types of statements in the psalm headings.

The Agony of Silent Waiting (39:1–3)

IN WORDS REMINISCENT of Jeremiah (Jer. 20:9) and Job (Job 2:11–13), the psalmist speaks of a period of silent waiting during suffering, followed by impassioned speech. In Psalm 38:13–14 the psalmist played deaf and mute in the face of the attacks of the enemy. Here, although the wicked are present, his silence seems directed more toward God's disciplinary punishment. On the one hand, his silence is an attempt to harden himself against relentless attacks by ignoring them; on the other hand, the psalmist remains silent to avoid having to admit sin or to acknowledge the justice of God's treatment (39:1–2) in the presence of the wicked (39:1).[3]

It is difficult to know just what words the psalmist kept from speech that might be considered "sin" (39:1).[4] If we are to suppose these words are recorded in the body of the psalm, there is nothing there that exceeds the bounds of numerous similar complaints throughout the psalms. The psalmist merely acknowledges the frailty of humans and requests divine deliverance. What is so "sinful" about that? Perhaps, then, the sinful words remain unspoken, so that what eventually escapes his lips are not those originally intended words but new insights gained during the self-imposed period of silent meditation.

The key may be found in 39:2, where the psalmist says that silence—"not even saying anything good"—only increased his anguish. In this event the speech he "muzzles" (i.e., keeps in check) would be a caustic diatribe against the "wicked" who are "present." The struggle is, then, between striking out verbally at the wicked or alternatively speaking something "good" (39:2).

The psalmist's silent meditation leads to a sense of divine compulsion to speak that cannot be denied. This is a familiar experience among the

---

3. While Jeremiah experienced a similar extended period of silence, his eventual outbreak was into prophetic speech rather than a personal complaint to God. It is true, however, that the words that surround Jeremiah's description and provide its literary context are just such a complaint to God (Jer. 20:7–10). It is the parallel attempt to bottle up words that are burning to be spoken that connects Jeremiah and the psalmist (and to some extent Job).

4. The NIV of 39:1a breaks into two phrases what is in the Hebrew essentially a single statement: "I said, 'Let me guard my ways from sin with my tongue.'" The difference is subtle, but it refocuses the whole thought around the idea of careful speech rather than a more general "watching of the ways." The statement employs the cohortative form of the verb, which expresses self-encouragement and exhortation to a course of action rather than a more declarative determination.

prophets, who often feel compelled to proclaim the "word of the LORD."[5] The "fire" that makes the psalmist's heart "hot" (39:3) is a graphic way of depicting an internal anguish as a result of keeping silent (cf. Jer. 20:9). The inner turmoil ultimately forces him to break his self-imposed silence (39:3c) with the "good" word of the body of the psalm. The prophetic parallels, however, make it clear that the heat behind the psalmist's words is a sort of divine compulsion rather than his own human anger and irritation.

The Frailty of Human Life (39:4–6)

THE RELEASE OF the anguish of meditative silence comes with an expression of the frailty of human existence. Rather than a diatribe against evil or even an anguished complaint to God, the psalmist offers an informed meditation on the fragility of human life that parallels similar insights found in Psalms 8; 90; 104, and others.

The psalmist wishes to know the "end" of his life and the "number" of his days (39:4), not in order to have mastery over life but to gain an appropriate appreciation for the tenuous and fragile nature of human existence. Elsewhere the fragility and brevity of human life is contrasted with the enduring power and eternality that is God.[6] Here, however, no such contrast is exploited. Yahweh does supply the hope of the psalmist, but he makes no attempt to stress God's superior strength and endurance. In a sense he has already gained the perspective requested in 39:4 and knows that human life is "fleeting"[7] (39:4), a "mere handbreadth" (39:5),[8] its span of years "as nothing" (39:5).[9]

This new perspective leads to a pessimistic evaluation of human life and its lasting accomplishments that is reminiscent of Ecclesiastes; it even uses the central, defining concept of that book. In the summing phrase of verses 4–5, the psalmist concludes that "each man's life is but a breath" (39:5c)—a conclusion that provides the foundation of the evaluation in verse 6. The NIV's translation of the word "breath" (*ḥebel*) obscures the clear connection with the teaching of Ecclesiastes, where that same word is translated "meaningless," as in Ecclesiastes 1:2 (cf. 12:8):

"Meaningless! Meaningless!"
  says the Teacher,

---

5. See, e.g., Jer. 20:7–10, as well as the comments in Amos 3:8: "The lion has roared—who will not fear? The Sovereign LORD has spoken—who can but prophesy?" The book of Jonah is an extended picture of the futility of trying to escape the divine call to prophesy.

6. Cf., e.g., Pss. 8; 102; 144; 145; 146.

7. Heb. *meh ḥadel* ("how close to an end") or perhaps "how forsaken [by God]."

8. Heb. (lit.) has "a few spans of four fingers."

9. Heb. (lit.) has "my duration [is] as if it does not exist."

"Utterly meaningless!
Everything is meaningless."[10]

It seems that the psalmist's evaluation of brief human existence is not so much that it is insubstantial in length—that point has already been made—but that it is ultimately just as insubstantial in accomplishment and consequence.[11]

The continued thought in verse 6 focuses—as does Ecclesiastes—on the empty accomplishment of human endeavor. Humans walk back and forth as "phantoms" (*ṣelem* ["image"]),[12] a term employed for statues of gods and kings in the ancient Near East and particularly used in Genesis 1:26–27 to describe the creation of humans in the "image" (*ṣelem*) and "likeness" (*demut*) of God. The implication is that humans are not "the real thing" but only an empty copy of themselves. As the images of the false gods in Isaiah cannot move, take care of themselves, or save those who worship them, so these empty human "images" can accomplish nothing consequential on their own.[13] Their "bustling" is as vain as their compulsion to accumulate wealth is futile (39:6).[14]

Acknowledgment of Sin (39:7–11)

HAVING ESTABLISHED THE frailty of human life and the futility of human endeavor, where can the psalmist turn for effective help? He finds hope for deliverance from sin and the "scorn of fools" in Yahweh (39:7–8). Deliverance comes at the price of confession of sin (39:8, 11), and the psalmist acknowledges that the suffering endured is from God (39:9–11) and is intended as "rebuke and discipline" (39:11). It is this knowledge that has prevented him from voicing a complaint before the wicked (39:9; cf. 39:1–2); the punishment was deserved and just.

In verse 11 the psalmist ties divine "rebuke and discipline" together with the earlier theme of human frailty. The futility of human endeavor—the

10. The Heb. is *habel habalim ... habel habalim hakkol habel*, where the phrase *habel habalim* is a superlative expression that means "the greatest of all possible *habalim*." Traditionally the term has been translated "vanity."

11. The final phrase of v. 5 is difficult and somewhat uncertain. Taken literally it means something like "surely every vanity of every man takes a stand." Many Heb. manuscripts omit the first *kol* ("every") as is in the case of the repetition of this phrase in 39:11. If we take the lead of that second phrase, we might render 39:5 as: "Surely every human being that stands upright is meaningless." A very harsh evaluation!

12. See the discussion of the "image of God" in the comments on Ps. 8.

13. Cf. Isa. 44:9–18.

14. An agricultural image coupled with the following verb "gather." The phantom men "pile up" as if gathering grain into piles in the field, while others will "gather" the collected grain into their storehouses.

inability of humans to secure even their own wealth—is understood here as consequence of divine discipline.

Final Plea for Deliverance (39:12–13)

THE PSALMIST CONCLUDES with a final plea to Yahweh for deliverance. God is called to listen attentively (39:12) to his cry and weeping. In an interesting development, he assumes the humble role of a resident "alien" (*ger*) and "stranger" (*tošab*), both terms indicating a class of non-Israelites permitted to reside rather tenuously in the land. Because of divine discipline, the psalmist, like the "alien" and "stranger," understands the tenuous, vulnerable hold on life a sinner experiences and longs for restoration of the secure relationship God promises the faithful. His desperate state is encapsulated in verse 12: Unless Yahweh relents and ends the punishment, he has no hope but to depart and be no more.

LIVING AS AN ALIEN AND A STRANGER. The psalmist's reference to the "alien" and "stranger" necessitates further comment. Both terms indicate a class of non-Israelites who were traditionally permitted to reside among God's people within the Promised Land, but they had no "inheritance" (tribal allotment of land) like the children of Israel. These alien residents could experience a degree of harmony with the native inhabitants but enjoyed few rights of land ownership or the normal civil protections of Israelite society.[15] The Old Testament uses various terms to refer to non-Israelites living within the covenant community.

(1) Alien (*ger*). In the most limited sense a *ger* was a person attached to an Israelite household but not a member of the actual family. He or she could be an employee or a servant. Elsewhere the word describes a nonnative resident of a town or region. In this sense it describes the Israelite patriarchs themselves as they traveled in foreign lands (1 Chron. 16:19; Ps. 105:12). As a consequence, Canaan is sometimes called the "land of sojourning" (*ʾereṣ magur*), because the ancestors of Israel lived there for an extended time as "aliens."

Such "sojourners"—whether the patriarchs or later non-Israelites—could settle down only with permission of local rulers and enjoyed few rights. As a result, they were vulnerable in society and catalogued along with exploited

15. A helpful article on the Old Testament concept of the alien or stranger is found in "Sojourner; Alien; Stranger," *ISBE*², 4:561–64.

elements of society (including servants, hirelings, the needy, poor, orphans, and widows). Nevertheless, Israel is cautioned not to treat aliens as they had themselves been treated. Mosaic legislation accorded aliens a modicum of security and certain rights within Israelite society (fair trial, participation in temple worship, the Day of Atonement, the right to glean along with other poor elements of society). Aliens could even be envisioned as achieving sufficient wealth and position that native Israelites might serve them (Lev. 25:47–55). But this was only possible when such aliens completely identified with the covenant community. This meant a close association with Israel in which aliens demonstrated a commitment to Yahweh and the spiritual values of Israel.

(2) The second term is the Hebrew *tošab*, a noun derived from the verb *yšb* ("sit, dwell, take up residence"). This word occurs in only thirteen places in the Old Testament and is always paired with a second term (such as "hireling" or *ger*), so that its individual meaning and distinction remains unclear.

(3) In addition to these two terms found in 39:12, two other Hebrew words describe non-Israelites whose place within the covenant society was even more negatively evaluated and thus tenuous. A "foreigner" (*nokri*; derived from *nkr*, "to be unknown, unrecognizable") describes a person living within Israel who was nevertheless ethnically distinct from the Israelites (cf. the reference to the Jebusites as *nokrim* in Judg. 19:12). Theologically, a *nokri* is the spiritual opposite of the faithful member of the covenant community and is thus viewed as a serious threat to Israelite life and worship (Zeph. 1:8; Mal. 2:11). Such "foreigners" were not allowed to eat the Passover, and animals from their flocks were considered unsuitable for Israelite sacrifices. Because *nokrim* were not part of the covenant community, prohibitions against charging interest did not apply to them; it was also acceptable to sell animals to them that were inappropriate for Israelite consumption.

(4) The *zar*, like the *nokri*, was considered an outsider to the Israelite household and was viewed with suspicion. The noun derives from *zwr*, meaning "to turn aside, depart, deviate"; thus, a *zar* is someone adamantly opposed to Israelite covenant faith. In the plural, *zarim* can refer to enemies of the whole nation (cf. Isa. 1:7; 29:5; Jer. 5:19; 30:8; Ezek. 7:21; Hos. 7:9). Both the *zar* and *nokri* resided within Israel but refused closer association with Israelite faith or religious practices. Their more resistant and even hostile attitude toward Yahweh and the covenant faith made association with them dangerous and thus socially proscribed.

The psalmist draws on the experience of non-Israelite "aliens" and "strangers" as an analogy of the kind of painful barriers sin has erected between himself and God. While all around the covenant people were enjoying close association with one another and with God, the sinner felt immense distance blocking all hope of contact. He also imaginatively connects the sense of isolation and societal suspicion experienced by the patriarchs in their wanderings to the sense of rejection—by self, others, and God—that the person enmeshed in transgression often feels.

MUZZLING THE TONGUE. Often pain (regardless of its source), whether externally or internally motivated, can cause us to lash out. I remember smashing my thumb with a badly aimed blow of a hammer, and my pain, wanting a cause other than myself to blame, overflowed with loud and caustic exclamations as I threw the hammer violently to the ground unaware and unconcerned whether anyone was in my line of fire. In some television and movie presentations, a stock dramatic scene presents a woman in the midst of labor contractions lashing out fiercely at her husband, who wants only to help. Similarly, in moments of psychic or emotional pain many of us tend to strike out at others as a way of diverting ourselves from our own discomfort and passing the blame and pain on to others.

In the midst of the pain brought on by personal sin, "muzzling the tongue" (as our psalmist describes) can be either a good or a bad thing. (1) On the good side, the one who stifles the knee-jerk response to lash out at others can enter into a state of "meditative silence," where the interfering "noise" generated by oneself and others is lessened. When we actually "listen" to what our pain is telling us, we can often hear what God wants us to hear and learn in and through the pain. Silence in the face of pain can be a way of culling out the "bad" from the "good"—avoiding self-justification or attacks unleashed on others.

When I truly listen to my pain and the anger it generates, I often discover that it is greater than the circumstances justify or is misdirected. I have begun to evaluate my anger against a scale of 1 to 10. If the circumstance seems to merit an anger level of 4, yet I am responding at level 9 or 10, then I know there is something at work other than the circumstance I am acknowledging. Too often the difference is the result of old wounds submerged and never dealt with, a sense of personal sin or guilt I am unwilling to admit, or fear of rejection or vulnerability. These hidden factors elevate my anger as a way of masking myself and pushing others (including God!) away from intimate relationships in which resolution can occur.

Meditative silence can allow us time to reflect on the real reasons behind our anger and pain before our lashing out jeopardizes relationships by distorting and confusing the real issues involved. Time taken in truly listening can help us understand what God wants us to hear and declare from this painful circumstance. This is not to say that all painful circumstances are brought on us by God to teach us a lesson. In Psalm 39, the psalmist's pain is the result of personal sin. But within each circumstance, regardless of its origin, there is an understanding that leads to the "way of God" *from* that place.

(2) On the bad side, muzzling the tongue can be a way of not acknowledging the truth—God's truth—about our situation. Not to acknowledge our own sin can lead others to the wrong conclusion about our suffering rather than accepting the just nature of God's discipline.

In this psalm, the psalmist was tempted to remain silent, "not even saying anything good" (39:2). But the pressure to speak out built up until it was an unstoppable force that broke free of his restraints. If the interior of the psalm is any indication, the irresistible message that ultimately escaped from his lips was a declaration of the frailty of humans in contrast to the complete adequacy of God. His suffering was not the result of divine weakness but of human sin. Indeed, the psalmist's only hope is in Yahweh, who is both discipliner and Savior.

This true word flows out of the meditative silence that precedes, and it rightly situates the psalmist's pain in the context of sin and divine discipline. It communicates to those who surround the poet—friend and foe alike—that God is a God of both justice and salvation, who hears the prayers of those who acknowledge their sin and call on him. When we experience pain—of our own or other's making—we need to reflect, as does the psalmist, in order to make our spoken response a true one that acknowledges our frailty and our need for God's salvation.

Living as resident aliens. Sin separates from God. At the end of Psalm 39, the psalmist, having acknowledged his sin, admits how great a distance this transgression has created between himself and the holy God. He feels like an "alien" and a "stranger" in God's presence, and this sense of distance is the cause of weeping (39:12) and a desire for change.

While I cannot speak for you, I can acknowledge that my own bouts of sinning have resulted at times in a sense of deep alienation from God—a self-imposed distance that appears at times almost insurmountable. I am too unworthy for divine care, too deeply enmeshed to honestly admit my condition, or too weak to return to the path of holy living on my own. In this state I can understand what the psalmist means by "dwelling with [God] as an alien, a stranger." I have traveled on occasion in other countries in which the language and culture was far removed from my own. I have felt the distance that crops up when everyone else knows how to act, speak, and respond to every circumstance, but I feel like an uncultured and ineffective boob, an object of amusement and scorn, who cannot hope to move acceptably in that society.

Sin, says the psalmist, creates this kind of distance with God. God is the one who scourges the psalmist with blows from his hand (39:10)—who rebukes, disciplines, and consumes the wealth of humans. Yet God is also the one to whom he cries for deliverance. This humble recognition that God is at once judge and deliverer is what the Old Testament means by the "fear of the LORD"—the admission that one has no hope in self or others but only as God offers it. This kind of fearful vulnerability is what the psalmist means by dwelling as an "alien [and] stranger" before God. And it is this kind of awareness and vulnerability that places you and me in the position of acceptance at which God can act as salvation and deliverance.

Psalm 40

FOR THE DIRECTOR of music. Of David. A psalm.

1 I waited patiently for the LORD;
he turned to me and heard my cry.
2 He lifted me out of the slimy pit,
out of the mud and mire;
he set my feet on a rock
and gave me a firm place to stand.
3 He put a new song in my mouth,
a hymn of praise to our God.
Many will see and fear
and put their trust in the LORD.

4 Blessed is the man
who makes the LORD his trust,
who does not look to the proud,
to those who turn aside to false gods.
5 Many, O LORD my God,
are the wonders you have done.
The things you planned for us
no one can recount to you;
were I to speak and tell of them,
they would be too many to declare.

6 Sacrifice and offering you did not desire,
but my ears you have pierced;
burnt offerings and sin offerings
you did not require.
7 Then I said, "Here I am, I have come—
it is written about me in the scroll.
8 I desire to do your will, O my God;
your law is within my heart."

9 I proclaim righteousness in the great assembly;
I do not seal my lips,
as you know, O LORD.
10 I do not hide your righteousness in my heart;
I speak of your faithfulness and salvation.

I do not conceal your love and your truth
from the great assembly.

[11] Do not withhold your mercy from me, O LORD;
may your love and your truth always protect me.
[12] For troubles without number surround me;
my sins have overtaken me, and I cannot see.
They are more than the hairs of my head,
and my heart fails within me.

[13] Be pleased, O LORD, to save me;
O LORD, come quickly to help me.
[14] May all who seek to take my life
be put to shame and confusion;
may all who desire my ruin
be turned back in disgrace.
[15] May those who say to me, "Aha! Aha!"
be appalled at their own shame.
[16] But may all who seek you
rejoice and be glad in you;
may those who love your salvation always say,
"The LORD be exalted!"

[17] Yet I am poor and needy;
may the Lord think of me.
You are my help and my deliverer;
O my God, do not delay.

LIKE PSALMS 37, 38, and 39, Psalm 40 is a plea for deliverance from suffering as the consequence of personal sin. Because the final five verses of this psalm are practically identical with the whole of Psalm 70, some have considered the psalm a composite psalm, in which two distinct compositions have been imperfectly joined.[1] Others consider the first sixteen verses of Psalm 40 to have been written to incorporate the verses from Psalm 70.[2] In this case the final composition, while not entirely original, exhibits an intentional and thoroughgoing unity. Still others consider

1. Cf. Cheyne, *The Book of Psalms*, 108, who sees as many as three poets at work in Ps. 40. Dahood, *Psalms*, 1:245, and Kraus, *Psalms 1–59*, 423, also fall into this category.

2. See the comments in Craigie, *Psalms 1–59*, 313–14.

Psalm 40 to be the original version of the psalm, a portion of which was then adapted at a later date for use as Psalm 70, where it functions as an introduction to Psalm 71.[3]

The question of the original form of Psalm 40 probably cannot be resolved, although it certainly seems possible—upon examination of the whole Psalter—that bits and pieces of psalmic compositions (whether large or small) were reused and recombined in new and later compositions. This process seems to have been common and did not seem to decrease the value of the compositions made up of parts of previous works. In the commentary that follows, I assume a unity of Psalm 40 and seek to understand and expound the movement of the whole.

Besides the more obvious division between the thanksgiving of the first twelve verses and the lament of the final five verses (the ones parallel to Ps. 70), there is little consensus about the structure of this psalm. It begins with a description of past deliverance experienced by the psalmist (40:1–4), continues with an avowal of personal faithfulness and witness (40:5–10), offers a transitional description of the need for divine aid (40:11–12), and concludes with a plea for speedy delivery (40:13–17).

The Heading (40:0)

NO NEW TERM appears in the heading to Psalm 40, which is referred to "the director of music" and described as both Davidic and a *mizmor*.[4]

Description of Past Deliverance (40:1–4)

THE THEME OF "waiting" for Yahweh in the midst of trouble that began in Psalm 37 and continued through Psalms 38 and 39 is sounded once again in 40:1.[5] It seems significant that the enduring expectancy commanded in 37:34, affirmed by the psalmist's commitment in 38:15, and reflected in the narrative of Psalm 39, should reach such a definite conclusion in the emphatic construction of 40:1. The use of the Piel infinitive construct of *qwh* ("wait for") together with the Piel perfect of the same root adds strength and emphasis to the action described. Whereas in the former psalms Yahweh's response was

---

3. Craigie adopts this position, ibid., 314. Rogerson and McKay also argue for the unity of Ps. 40, *Psalms 1–50*, 191. See also comments on Ps. 70, below.

4. See comments on the headings of Pss. 3 and 4 for discussion of these terms.

5. Two Hebrew verbs underlie this theme of waiting. The first (*yḥl*) carries the primary sense of *endurance*, the willingness to "hang in there" faithfully for a long time (37:7 [as emended in *BHS*]; 38:15). The second (*qwh*) emphasizes *intent expectancy*, as if the thing hoped for is about to happen *now* (37:34; 40:1). The two words are paralleled in 130:5, indicating that both endurance and expectancy are part of waiting for Yahweh's deliverance.

anticipated and hoped for, here it is an experienced reality: "He turned to me and he heard my cry."

He lifted me. The psalmist proceeds to describe in imaginative terms the deliverance experienced. The sufferer has been lifted from the slippery muck and mire where no secure footing is possible and has been placed on the solid rock—"a firm place to stand" (40:2). I am reminded of the opening scenes of a motion picture about World War I called *The Blue Max*. In these scenes, a young German infantryman is enmeshed in the muck and mire of seemingly endless trench warfare and looks up from his muddy fox hole into a pristine blue sky to see a biplane engaged in a dogfight with the enemy. In the next scene, our young soldier has volunteered for flight training!

It is this contrasting sense of hopeless and helpless enmeshment in the slime and then being transported to a secure and safe (and clean) environment that the psalmist captures in these opening verses. Yahweh is deliverer! This brings a "new song" to his lips (40:3)[6] in response to this new act of divine deliverance. This new song is a "hymn of praise" (*tehillah*); note that the plural form of this word (*tehillim*) forms the Hebrew title of the whole book of Psalms. In an unusual way, then, the psalms—whether lament or praise, thanksgiving or wisdom—are considered a collection of "new songs" that break from the thankful heart of a delivered people.

Many will see and fear. The purpose of the new song is testimony. It will draw others to "fear" Yahweh. The paralleling in this verse of the phrase "fear [Yahweh]" with the later "put their trust in [Yahweh]" supplies important clarification to our understanding of this significant theological concept. When Israel talks about fearing Yahweh, she decidedly does *not* mean to be afraid of him. This is particularly clear in Exodus 20:20, where Moses tells the children of Israel at Mount Sinai: "Do not be afraid. God has come to test you, so that the fear of God will be with you to keep you from sinning." They are not to "be afraid," and yet the purpose of God's coming is that they should learn "the fear of God."[7]

In our passage, the positive content of fearing Yahweh is put forward as "trust" in him (40:3) and is clarified further by the blessing in 40:4: "Blessed is the [one] who makes the LORD [Yahweh] his trust, who does not look to the proud, to those who turn aside to false gods." Those who fear Yahweh (who assume the appropriate relationship of loyalty and dependence) are contrasted with those who "look to the proud" and "turn aside to false gods"

---

6. See comments on 33:3 for discussion of the phrase "new song."

7. For further discussion of the concept of the fear of Yahweh, see comments on Ps. 34 and the section on "The Fear of Yahweh" in "The Theology of the Psalms" in vol. 2 of this commentary.

(lit., "go astray after a lie")—both references to forsaking Yahweh to worship other gods. Perhaps the primary hope the psalmist holds out for divine mercy is that while he has indeed sinned, he has not forsaken Yahweh like those who no longer "fear him." Fearing Yahweh, then, does not expect perfect sinlessness but demands a baseline loyalty and dependence on him that brings the sinner back again and again to seek God's forgiveness and blessing.

Avowal of Personal Faithfulness and Witness (40:5–10)

AS IS OFTEN the case in the biblical psalms, the aphoristic blessing in 40:4 both illuminates the call to fear Yahweh in the preceding verses and opens the way to the psalmist's affirmation of faith in the verses that follow. This transition is accompanied with a change in his grammatical reference to Yahweh from third person to second person, signifying direct address in 40:5–10.

In this new section the psalmist testifies to the "wonders" Yahweh has done (40:5–6) and declares personal loyalty to him (40:7–10). The "wonders" of Yahweh are too numerous to detail (40:5) as his plans for us are too vast to enumerate.

There is a bit of awkwardness in this section, and most translations have availed themselves of some rearrangement of the words—most relatively minor. Literally the Hebrew goes something like this:

> Many (things) you have done, you (yourself)
> O Yahweh, my God, your wonders and your plans for us.
> There is none to arrange them for you (*or* compare to you,
>   *or* call you to account)[8]
> If I should (attempt to) make them known or declare them,
> They are too vast to number (*or* to tell).[9]

Sacrifice and offering. Verses 6–8 are often taken as a general condemnation of the sacrificial system of Israelite temple worship and are compared with such passages as 1 Samuel 15:22; Jeremiah 6:20; and Amos 5:22. More contemporary commentators resist the idea that the psalm definitively rejects sacrifice, preferring to understand these verses in some other way. Kraus speaks of a shift in emphasis from sacrifice to the song rather than the rejection of sac-

8. The verb used here (*ʾrk*) can be variously translated. It has the base meaning of "arrange in lines" and by extension comes to describe "drawing up in battle formation" and then "to confront someone." Another possibility seized upon in many translations is the idea of comparison derived from placing things alongside one another. This last possibility, despite its popularity, seems less likely in this context than the idea of confronting God or calling him to account for the plans he has made for human beings.

9. The word in question here is the Heb. verb *spr*, which appears here as *missapper* and can be translated either "count" or "relate/declare/tell."

rifice.[10] Craigie explains the tension as the result of liturgical movement in which the king participated, who, having offered sacrifices at the appropriate point of the liturgy, moves on to another part of the liturgy in which "the offering of sacrifices alone was not enough; more was required of him."[11]

Of these three possibilities (rejection of sacrifice, shift of emphasis to the song, and liturgical movement), the view of Kraus seems more persuasive—at least in a modified form. If Psalm 40 and its statements about sacrifice are taken to be a response to life after the destruction of the temple and the cessation of the sacrificial system, then the shift of emphasis is more understandable and even necessary. We know that after the destruction of the second temple by the Romans in A.D. 70, the rabbis taught that the lack of sacrifice could be compensated for by study of the Torah, faithful prayer, fasting, and deeds of kindness.[12]

Perhaps another way to understand these seemingly harsh words about sacrifice is to take them as referring only to the specific experience of the psalmist and as another example of the incomparable wonders performed by Yahweh. In this case the psalmist is testifying that rather than demanding gifts and sacrifices as payment for the psalmist's sin, what Yahweh really wanted was "open [pierced] ears" of the psalmist attentive to God's instruction (40:6) and a heart willing to allow the *torah* ("law") to guide it (40:8).

What appears to be a clear affirming parallelism in the first and third lines of 40:6:

> Sacrifice and offering you did not desire ...
> burnt offerings and sin offerings you did not require

is rather awkwardly interrupted by the difficult phrase: "but my ears you have pierced" (*ʾoznayim karita li*). Kidner mentions a possible connection with the ceremony in which a servant attached himself to his master in perpetuity by having an awl driven through one ear into the door post (Ex. 21:6), but he prefers the alternative translation of the verb *krt* as "dug," as in digging a well.[13] This would yield the sense of "open up" ears or "dig (new) ears" so

---

10. See Kraus, *Psalms 1–59*, 427.

11. See Craigie, *Psalms 1–50*, 315.

12. Cf. various treatments of the subject in the Babylonian Talmud, including *Berakot* 15a-b; 17a; *Sukkah* 49b; *Baba Batra* 9a; *Menaḥot* 110a; cf. also *ʾAbot de Rabbi Nathan* 20a. One related question in light of the evidence of the Dead Sea Scrolls for the continued fluidity of the Psalter collection into the second half of the first century A.D. is: Which destruction of the temple and resulting lack of temple sacrifice does the psalm reflect? That by the Babylonians in 587 B.C.? Or the Roman destruction of A.D. 70?

13. Derek Kidner, *Psalms*, 2 vols. (TOTC; Downers Grove, Ill.: InterVarsity, 1973), 1:159.

that one can hear.[14] The new openness acquired by the psalmist through God's action is apparently mirrored in his willingness to do the divine will (40:8), occasioned by a new awareness that sacrificial ritual is not enough to satisfy Yahweh.

The balanced affirming parallelism represented by the outer lines of verse 6 need further comment. The forms of sacrifice mentioned combine to form a sort of merism[15] intended to encompass the whole of sacrificial ritual and experience. The first two forms of sacrifice—*zebaḥ* and *minḥah*—are essentially positive sacrifices, celebrating communion with God through a shared meal in the first instance and by means of a grateful gift to God in the second. The second two forms—*ʿolah* and *ḥaṭaʾah*—describe offerings primarily designed to remove the effects and consequences of human sin. The *ʿolah* is the whole "burnt offering," in which no communion meal is possible because the whole offering is burned on the altar to God. The *ḥaṭaʾah* is clearly identified by its name as a "sin offering." These two sets of offerings, then, mark the opposing ends of the spectrum of sacrificial experience in Israel, implying in this context that it is the entire sacrificial system that is at issue here, not just certain sacrifices.

In the scroll of the book. Having established in the preceding verses that God's *desire* and *requirement* is an inner awareness and attentiveness rather than the fulfillment of external ritual, the psalmist now claims personal adherence to that ideal. He is one who responds to the wonderful works of Yahweh with inner commitment (40:8) and outer testimony (40:9–10).

Verse 7 remains somewhat enigmatic because of a lack of clarity regarding the identity of the "scroll." Besides this verse, this phrase occurs only in two other contexts in the Old Testament. The first refers to the "scroll" in which Baruch son of Neriah recorded the prophecies of Jeremiah in order to present them to the king of Judah after Jeremiah had been prohibited from prophesying. The king burned that scroll so that Jeremiah had to record his prophecies a second time (Jer. 36). The second is found in Ezekiel 2–3, where Ezekiel is presented with a "scroll" containing words of "lament and mourning and woe" from God. The prophet is instructed to eat this scroll and then to proclaim the words it contains to the rebellious people. If these two uses define "the scroll," it contains the words of God as revealed to the prophets.

Other possibilities offered by commentators include: (1) a scroll containing the petition of the psalmist that was laid up in the temple to serve as

14. Craigie (*Psalms 1–50*, 313), referring to Delitzsch, suggests a possible understanding of *krh* ("pierce"), meaning that "God's word penetrates deafness."

15. See comments on merism in the section on "The Poetry of the Psalms" in the introduction.

a testimony when the plea was later fulfilled,[16] (2) a scroll of Mosaic Torah,[17] (3) a scroll containing an account of the psalmist's "debit" because of sin,[18] (4) a scroll detailing the responsibility of kings in Deuteronomy 17:14–20 (assuming the royal character of this psalm),[19] or (5) a personal copy of the scroll mentioned in Deuteronomy to which the king committed himself at his coronation.[20] The wild divergence in interpretation illustrates the ambiguity of this phrase and leaves us with no sure way to determine its meaning in this context.

Whatever solution one chooses, it seems clear that the psalmist, having experienced a new awareness and understanding as the result of divine opening of his ears (40:6), now perceives the "scroll" as speaking directly to his circumstance (40:7). As a result he becomes willing to do Yahweh's will (40:8). The "scroll," then, challenges the psalmist to internalize Yahweh's instruction in his heart and to "proclaim righteousness in the great assembly" (40:9). The remaining verses of this section repeat his commitment not to conceal this newfound understanding but to proclaim Yahweh's righteousness to the faithful community (40:9b–10).

This leads me to believe that what the psalmist perceived in the "scroll" was the reality of his sin and the righteousness of Yahweh's punishment. If so, then these verses are tantamount to a confession of sin—the psalmist does not conceal Yahweh's righteousness but proclaims it—coupled with an affirmation of Yahweh's faithfulness, salvation, love, and truth (40:10). Thus, whereas the psalmist was tempted to explain away the suffering experienced as undeserved and therefore to cast aspersion on God, the change of heart wrought by his new understanding led to confession, submission, a desire for obedience, and a public acknowledgment of divine righteousness.[21]

Proclaim righteousness. The psalmist's determination to proclaim Yahweh's righteousness to the congregation of the faithful is the practical equivalent to the New Testament proclamation of the gospel. The underlying Hebrew verb (*bśr*) means "to bring (in this case *good*) news," which is the primary meaning of the Greek underlying the word "gospel" (*euangelion* ["good

16. See Kraus, *Psalms 1–59*, 426; Mays, *Psalms* (Interpretation; Philadelphia: Westminster, 1994), 168.

17. See Cheyne, *The Book of Psalms*, 111; Rogerson and McKay, *Psalms 1–50*, 193.

18. See Dahood, *Psalms*, 1:246.

19. See Delitzsch, *Biblical Commentary on the Psalms*, 39–40; Craigie, *Psalms 1–50*, 314.

20. See Kidner, *Psalms*, 1:160; *The NIV Study Bible*, 826.

21. The similarity to the situation in Ps. 39 is remarkable. There the psalmist initially resists speaking out until compelled to by the inner working of God. The psalmist then confesses sin and justifies the disciplinary punishment and rebuke of God to those who are observing his distress.

news"]).[22] The psalmist does not keep the "good news" of God's righteous and faithful saving love under wraps but publishes it abroad.

Not conceal. The psalmist's struggle is intensified by the variety of ways used to describe his temptation to conceal the righteousness of Yahweh. He did not "seal" his lips, "hide" God's righteousness, or "conceal" (lit., "efface"[23]) Yahweh's faithfulness and truth.[24]

The Need for Divine Aid (40:11–12)

AFTER ESTABLISHING A foundation of personal faithfulness, the psalmist appeals to Yahweh for mercy, asking God to apply in his case those very characteristics of "love" (*ḥesed*) and "truth" (*ʾemet*) that he so freely praised in the congregation of the faithful (40:9–10). In 40:9, the psalmist has declared, "I do not seal my lips" from testifying to the wonderful acts of Yahweh; now he appeals to Yahweh, "Do not withhold your mercy from me."

This appeal also includes the psalmist's desperate circumstances as justification for divine deliverance, using imagery normally reserved for descriptions of pounding surf. Many troubles "without number" and "more than the hairs of my head" surround the psalmist while his own sins overtake him like waves crashing down on a shipwrecked survivor in the open sea. The tumult is so great that, like the imperiled swimmer, he is no longer able to see beyond the immediate life-threatening circumstances (40:12). Isolated and desperate, the psalmist is on the brink of losing all hope ("my heart fails").

22. In fact, the LXX translates *bśr* in this verse with a form of *euangelizo*, the verbal cognate of *euangelion*.

23. The term "efface" (from the Old French *effacer* ["remove the face"]) means to remove something that exists by destroying or obliterating it. Archaeology frequently uncovers examples of effacing, such as statues with their features chiseled off, reliefs with names expunged, etc. One of the more famous examples is the movement by Akhenaton (born Amenophis IV), the "heretic king" of Egypt from 1363 to 1347 B.C., to have the name of his father, Amenophis III, removed from all honorific reliefs around the nation because that name honored the old god Amun, whom Akhenaton had rejected in favor of the sun disk, Aton. I have often wondered what part the result of this censorship process, with its visible devastation of the reliefs, played in Akhenaton's decision to build a new capitol for his reign at Ikhnaton—modern day Tel el-Amarna. Recent accounts of the destruction of 1,500-year-old statues of the Buddha at the order of the Taliban rulers of Afghanistan follow this same pattern of obliteration. The Old Testament practices its own form of literary "effacing" when it replaces the divine name element Baal in human personal names with the caustic judgment Bosheth ("shame"): e.g., Ishbaal, "Man of Baal" (1 Chron. 8:33; 9:39), the son of Saul, becomes Ishbosheth, "Man of Shame," in other texts (cf. 2 Sam. 2:8 and twelve other times).

24. It is interesting to note that all the verbs used to describe attempts at concealment begin with the Heb. letter *kaph*. This type of alliterative wordplay calls attention to the verbs and intensifies their effect on the alert reader.

Speedy Delivery (40:13–17 = 70:1–5)

AS A CONCLUDING plea for deliverance, the psalmist uses five verses that are—except for a few significant variations—identical with the freestanding Psalm 70. By its position before Psalm 71 (which has no psalm heading), Psalm 70 serves as an introduction to the far more extended plea for deliverance in the following psalm.[25] There has been considerable debate concerning which version of these verses (40:13–17 or 70:1–5) is earlier, with most concluding that Psalm 70 is an original, independent poem adapted for use at the end of Psalm 40. This seems a more persuasive argument than the alternative explanations offered for splitting these verses off from an original context. There is also a great deal of verbal linkage between Psalms 70 and 71 that suggests an intimate association between them (see comments on 70–71).

Moreover, the one significant variation of 40:13–17 from the parallel verses of Psalm 70 seems to support the view of Psalm 40 being a later adaptation. Consider the following comparison of the verses in question:

Ps. 40:17	*Ps. 70:5*
Yet I am poor and needy;	Yet I am poor and needy;
may the Lord think of me.	*come quickly to me, O God.*
You are my help and my deliverer;	You are my help and my deliverer;
O my God, do not delay.	O LORD, do not delay.

The italicized portion highlights the variant renderings offered by these two psalms. Psalm 40 is distinguished not only by its use of distinctive words here but also by a rather abrupt shift from direct address of Yahweh in the second-person singular (initiated in 40:5 and continuing without break to this point) to an internal reflective reference to Yahweh in the third-person singular. This does not seem as natural as the consistent address of Psalm 70. The abrupt shift in 40:17 can be explained as a way of fitting these verses into the "new" context of Psalm 40 by adapting this verse to reflect the third-person reflective mode with which the psalm begins (cf. 40:1–4, in which Yahweh is also referred to in the third person).

A second variant in 40:13 is consistent with an adaptation of these verses to the context of Psalm 40. The lack of an imperative verb at the beginning of 70:1 leaves the reader to supply the lack from the urgent imperative *ḥušah* ("hasten") in the second line.[26] This establishes a mood of rather demanding urgency that is repeated in 70:5 and again in 71:12. By contrast, the use in 40:13 of the much less demanding verb in initial position (*rṣh* ["be

25. See comments on Pss. 70–71 for a discussion of how those two psalms work together.

26. See the comments of Marvin E. Tate, *Psalms 51–100* (WBC; Dallas: Word, 1990), 203.

pleased"]) reduces the sense of urgency and heightens the element of humble entreaty that is appropriate for one seeking removal of the consequences of personal sin.

Verses 13–17 bring Psalm 40 to a conclusion in an unexpected fashion. The earlier part of the psalm was directed to the psalmist's testimony to the faithfulness of God before the congregation and desire for deliverance from the unspecified troubles that have resulted from sin. Now, without previous mention, these final verses focus on his enemies, whom the psalmist wants Yahweh to recompense for their attacks. What seems natural and integrated in the context of Psalms 70–71 here seems an unanticipated change. The one link with the earlier portion of Psalm 40 is the continuing theme of trusting Yahweh, mirrored by the psalmist's patience in 40:1 and exhorted of the reader in 40:3–4. In this context, 40:16—"May all who seek you rejoice and be glad in you; may those who love your salvation always say, 'The LORD be exalted!'"—is seen as a blessing on those who trust in Yahweh (cf. 40:4).[27]

WAITING PATIENTLY. As noted above, the theme of waiting for divine deliverance binds together Psalms 37–40. There are two kinds of waiting envisioned here. (1) The first (associated with *yḥl*) emphasizes patient endurance over a long time. Such waiting assumes that God does not always act quickly but that his deliverance is sure and worth waiting for. The noun *toḥelet* is built on this root and describes one's enduring hope and expectation that does not fade over the long haul (39:7).

(2) Along with this durable waiting, the psalmists encourage expectant anticipation. It certainly seems possible that those exiles of the Diaspora looking to the Psalter for encouragement that God would deliver them might grow weary with the long wait and might see their confidence erode. Thus, the second verb (*qwh*) speaks to the need to maintain anticipation and expectation in the face of a long delay. Those who ultimately experience the salvation of God are those who endure faithfully *and expectantly*. This kind of waiting is akin to that exhorted of the ten virgins waiting for the coming of the bridegroom in Matthew's parable. All ten virgins endured until the coming of the bridegroom. All ten virgins fell asleep while the waiting drew out overnight. But only five of the virgins endured expectantly as indicated by

---

27. For more detailed discussion of 40:13–17, see comments on 70:1–5. A comparison of these verses illustrates the complexity of understanding the dynamics of what is generally understood to be an Elohistic Psalter (Pss. 42–83), in which the divine name *yhwh* is often replaced by the less specific and more generic designation *ʾelohim*. It is difficult, if not impossible, to discover any consistent method in these variations.

their readiness with extra oil. Those who endured expectantly were prepared when the bridegroom came to usher them into the banquet, while the others missed out on the festivities (Matt. 25:1–13).

Stuck in the muck. Deliverance in Psalm 40 is viewed as being set on a secure rock with firm footing (40:2). This is not an uncommon image for salvation and is often associated with the need for room and stability in hand-to-hand military combat. Here, however, the picture is that of one hopelessly bogged down in miry muck, like a truck stuck up to the hubs in mud.

The psalmist is seeking deliverance from sin (40:12), so it is interesting to see how its consequences are described as being mired down in a slippery place, with no secure footing or ability to escape. Several images are attached to the vocabulary used here. (1) One appears to refer to the clay (*ṭîṭ/ṭîṭîm*) pounded out into a smooth surface in building village streets.[28] While in most circumstances this must have provided a relatively hard surface, on occasions of rain or perhaps the spilling of blood in battle, the clay could become slippery and muddy (cf. Zech. 10:5).

(2) A second image connected with the slippery mire is the shifty sediments of the sea bed. Isaiah 57:20 describes the restless sea that tosses up slimy seaweed (*repeš*) and mud (*ṭîṭ*). Similarly, Psalm 69:14 describes the desperate plight of one who is sinking into the mire (*ṭîṭ*) while the sea waves crash over him.[29]

(3) The final image associated with slippery mud refers to the sediment left in the bottom of an abandoned cistern or pit. Jeremiah 38:6 describes the circumstances in which the prophet was abandoned to die by his enemies in a cistern having "no water in it, only mud [*ṭîṭ*], and Jeremiah sank down into the mud." When the king learned of Jeremiah's fate, he sent men with ropes to draw him up out of the muck and mire of the pit. Similarly Joseph's brothers threw him into an empty cistern before drawing him out in order to sell him to passing Midianites (Gen. 37:19–28).[30] Lamentations 3:53 describes the poet being thrown into a cistern and left to die while the "waters closed over my head." Apparently these accounts draw on a common practice of

28. Cf. 2 Sam. 22:43; Ps. 18:42; Mic. 7:10; Zech. 9:3; 10:5, all of which use the noun *ṭîṭ* as in Ps. 40:2. A similar reference using *ḥomer* instead of *ṭîṭ* is found in Isa. 10:6. In other settings *ṭîṭ* can describe the clay used by potters: Nah. 3:14, "Work the clay [*ṭîṭ*], tread the mortar [*ḥomer*]"; Isa. 41:25, "like a potter treading the clay [*ṭîṭ*]."

29. Earlier in the same psalm a similar setting uses the uncommon term *yawen* to describe the same kind of ocean mire into which the psalmist fears sinking (69:2). The only other occurrence of *yawen* is in 40:2, where it appears in the construct phrase with *ṭîṭ*: *miṭṭîṭ hayyawen* ("muddy muck"?).

30. Jer. 41:4–9 describes the use of a cistern as a repository for bodies resulting from slaughter.

using cisterns for imprisonment. Isaiah uses the image to envision the eschatological capture of the kings of the earth, who "will be herded together like prisoners bound in a [pit]" (Isa. 24:22), while in Zechariah 9:11, God offers hope to exilic Israel when he promises, "I will free your prisoners from the waterless pit."

Of these three related images employing *ṭîṭ/ṭîṭîm* the last seems most appropriate as the background of Psalm 40:2, where the term "slimy pit" is used.[31] Sin casts a sinner into a pit from which there is no escape. Secure footholds are gone on slippery ground so that the sinner is threatened with submersion and death.

A new song. See the discussion of "new song" in the comments on 33:3.

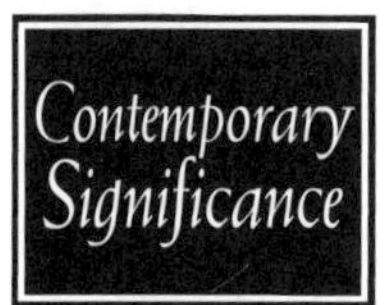

I DO NOT seal my lips. At the heart of Psalm 40 stands the narrator's self-description as one who has proclaimed *God's* "righteousness in the great assembly" (40:9). Immediately preceding this claim is the rather enigmatic statement of 40:7–8: "Here I am, I have come—it is written about me in the scroll. I desire to do your will, O my God; your law is within my heart." These earlier verses seem to reflect the self-awareness of the Judahite kings that they were bound in covenant relationship with Yahweh through their ancestor David and that their responsibilities were recorded in a "scroll" that each king was to keep with him for ready reference and reminder.[32] The purpose of the scroll was to keep the monarch grounded in spiritual reliance on Yahweh rather than on military, political, and financial power. It was also intended to encourage him to "revere the LORD his God and follow carefully all the words of this law and these decrees" (Deut. 17:19). Obedience to these decrees was the condition of long and continued rule.

Immediately following these verses recalling the "scroll" and the covenant relationship on which the kingship is founded, the speaker—who must be the king—describes in repeated terms how he has proclaimed righteousness in the great assembly. In his mind this must be appropriate fulfillment

---

31. The phrase is perhaps better rendered "desolate pit," according to Holladay (*CHALOT*, 356).

32. This scroll is mentioned in Deut. 17:18–20: "When he takes the throne of his kingdom, he is to write for himself on a scroll a copy of this law, taken from that of the priests, who are Levites. It is to be with him, and he is to read it all the days of his life so that he may learn to revere the LORD his God and follow carefully all the words of this law and these decrees and not consider himself better than his brothers and turn from the law to the right or to the left. Then he and his descendants will reign a long time over his kingdom in Israel."

of the expectations laid out in the scroll. The righteousness proclaimed is not that of the king but of God. Even in the midst of trouble occasioned by his own sin (40:12), the king takes care to make sure that the gathered people know that God is in the right.

Like the king and like the narrator of the preceding Psalm 39, we often have a tendency to remain silent while suffering the consequences of our own sin. Perhaps we are afraid of public condemnation, or we think our failure may undermine the confidence or faith of others, or perhaps the wicked will see our punishment and be encouraged to strengthen their ridicule and opposition. For whatever reason, however, we hesitate to make our failings known, preferring to "put a muzzle" on our mouths (39:1), or in the words of 40:9, to "seal [our] lips" rather than to speak openly and honestly.

While such self-imposed silence may save us some public embarrassment, it does so at the cost of much inner anguish and destruction (as 39:2–3 notes). It also has the negative effect of obscuring or effectively denying the "righteousness of God" that Psalm 40 proclaims. First John 1:8–10 is straight to the point: "If we claim to be without sin, we deceive ourselves and the truth is not in us.... If we claim we have not sinned, we make [God] out to be a liar and his word has no place in our lives."

The psalmist/king does not seal his lips but proclaims God's righteousness in the great assembly. This means acknowledging the sinfulness that justifies God's discipline. Only by confession is the narrator able to proclaim God's "faithfulness and salvation" (40:10). To deny his own failing is to "conceal [God's] love and ... truth" from those who most need to hear it. When the psalmist goes on to plead for divine mercy and forgiveness in 40:11, he knows that it is the very "love and ... truth" that he proclaims in confession that saves him. Similarly, 1 John encourages the reader: "If we confess our sins, he is faithful and just and will forgive us our sins and purify us from all unrighteousness" (1 John 1:9).

While the 1 John passage does not spell out how to carry out the confession—privately or publicly—Psalm 40 leaves no doubt that the proclamation of God's righteousness is a public act within "the great assembly." What are our great assemblies today? Is it the congregational worship service? The Sunday school class or Bible study/support group? I tend myself toward the latter, although appropriate moments of confession in congregational worship are important reminders to all those present that those gathered are no sinless perfectionists but sinners forgiven by God's grace. Like the king, it is not enough for us to "hide [God's] righteousness in [our] heart" (40:10a); it needs to be spoken abroad.

Our communities of worship and faith must take care that the important role of confession as a means of proclaiming God's righteousness, truth, and salvation does not become the exclusive domain of Twelve-Step groups and other psychological support groups. We need to be able to say to one another and to those who stand outside looking in: "I am poor and needy [and a sinner]; may the LORD think of me. You are my help and my deliverer; O my God, do not delay" (40:17).

The author of Hebrews (10:1–10) quotes a variant of Psalm 40:6–8 in support of the contention that Jesus has fulfilled the purpose of the Old Testament sacrificial tradition. Although the law requires animal sacrifices to be made (10:8), bulls and goats are unable to take away sin (10:3). Jesus, about whom it is written prophetically in the "scroll" of the Old Testament (10:7), came to do God's will by offering himself as the perfect sacrifice for those who believe throughout all time (10:9–10). It is interesting to note that the author of Hebrews, who is describing Jesus as the fulfillment of the Old Testament law, stops his quotation of Psalm 40:10 short of the statement in the latter half of the verse, "your law is within my heart" (40:8b).

Psalm 41

FOR THE DIRECTOR of music. A psalm of David.

1 Blessed is he who has regard for the weak;
the LORD delivers him in times of trouble.
2 The LORD will protect him and preserve his life;
he will bless him in the land
and not surrender him to the desire of his foes.
3 The LORD will sustain him on his sickbed
and restore him from his bed of illness.

4 I said, "O LORD, have mercy on me;
heal me, for I have sinned against you."
5 My enemies say of me in malice,
"When will he die and his name perish?"
6 Whenever one comes to see me,
he speaks falsely, while his heart gathers slander;
then he goes out and spreads it abroad.

7 All my enemies whisper together against me;
they imagine the worst for me, saying,
8 "A vile disease has beset him;
he will never get up from the place where he lies."
9 Even my close friend, whom I trusted,
he who shared my bread,
has lifted up his heel against me.

10 But you, O LORD, have mercy on me;
raise me up, that I may repay them.
11 I know that you are pleased with me,
for my enemy does not triumph over me.
12 In my integrity you uphold me
and set me in your presence forever.

13 Praise be to the LORD, the God of Israel,
from everlasting to everlasting.
Amen and Amen.

PSALM 41 STANDS as the last psalm of the first book of the Psalter (Pss. 1–41), and the doxology that stands at the end of the psalm (41:13) actually serves as the conclusion for the whole book.[1] This psalm is a complaint in response to the malicious plotting of the psalmist's enemies during a debilitating sickness. The illness has reduced his capacity to respond effectively to hostile innuendo, has raised his enemies' hopes for an imminent demise, and offers them (and even some friends) opportunity to plan for personal benefit in the vacuum left by his impending death. The psalm has particular poignancy since it is attributed to David, who late in his reign experienced a lengthy illness marked by similar plotting and intrigue by his associates and family. Whether or not David actually wrote this piece, it serves appropriately to mirror his experience and to conclude the first, most Davidic book of the Psalter.

The psalm is composed of twelve verses (omitting the doxology in 41:13, which concludes Book 1 of the Psalter), which are divided into four stanzas of three verses each, with the thematic movement of the psalm following the same division: the foundation of confidence (41:1–3), the complaint (41:4–9, two stanzas), and final plea and confidence (41:10–12).

The Heading (41:0)

NO NEW TERMS appear in the heading to Psalm 41. The poem is referred to "the director of music" and is described simply as "a psalm of David."[2] Omitting Psalms 1 and 2 as introductory and recognizing the tradition of linking psalms without headings with the preceding psalm (as in the case of Pss. 9–10; 32–33), Psalm 41 marks the conclusion of the first long run of entirely Davidic psalms (Pss. 3–41). Beginning with Psalm 42, a person other than David appears in the attribution of the psalm heading ("Sons of Korah"). In this literary context, Psalm 41 raises the specter of the king's illness and approaching death, and the change from Davidic psalms to the first Korahite collection creates an unsettled sense of transition and potential chaos in the reader.

The Foundation of Confidence (41:1–3)

THIS FIRST STANZA begins with the important Hebrew word *ʾašre* ("blessed, happy"), which also marks the beginning of the whole Psalter in 1:1.[3] While

1. See the discussion of "Concluding Doxologies" in the "The Poetry of the Psalms" in the introduction.

2. See comments on the headings of Pss. 3 and 4 for discussion of these terms.

3. See the remarks there regarding the importance of *ʾašre* in binding Pss. 1 and 2 together as an introduction to the Psalter.

the term is employed elsewhere in the psalms,[4] its appearance here, at the beginning of the last psalm of Book 1, seems hardly fortuitous.[5] This term here seems intentionally positioned to cause the reader to reflect back to the opening blessings in Psalms 1 and 2 and to read the present psalm—with its rather tenuous portrait of a king at risk—against that more powerful earlier picture of the king as established and empowered by God presented in Psalm 2.

As noted by others,[6] the placement of Psalm 2 suggests a messianic interpretation, in which human hopes are no longer to be pinned on a human kingship but on an anticipated "Anointed One," who will be divinely empowered to fulfill the role that the Israelite monarchs failed to satisfy. In this light, the positioning of Psalm 41 at the end of this Davidic collection tends to support a messianic reading of the royal psalms by highlighting the vulnerability of the human king, who can be undone by sin, illness, and disease, and for whom the whispering conspiracy of enemies and close associates is no laughing matter (cf. 2:4; 41:4–9).

Regard for the weak. The blessing is invoked on the one "who has regard for the weak." This phrase has certainly two (and possibly three) levels of meaning. (1) The blessing is a rather backhanded (and not so subtle) plea for deliverance. The suffering narrator turns out, as the psalm progresses, to be "the weak" in need of Yahweh's attentive "regard." By this blessing, then, God is reminded both of the psalmist's need and of God's power to save.

(2) On another level, however, the blessing serves as a *basis* for deliverance. In this reading the psalmist is the one who has regard for the weak, and because of that compassionate concern, Yahweh ought to deliver him from trouble as well. Lest we think of the psalmist as engaging in tit-for-tat theology ("I do, therefore I get"), we should remember that the *ʾašre* blessing is regularly employed to encourage and inculcate desired behavior rather than to reward it. That is why *ʾašre* is so often used in the proverbial literature as a motivation to right action.

The same is true of the promise that concludes verse 1: "The LORD delivers him in times of trouble." Such statements are not simplistic rewards but are teaching models marking out the path of righteousness that is consonant

4. A complete listing includes 1:1; 2:12; 32:1, 2; 33:12; 34:8; 40:7; 41:1; 65:4; 84:4, 5, 12; 89:15; 94:12; 106:3; 112:1; 119:1, 2; 127:5: 128:1, 2; 137:8, 9; 144:15; 146:5.

5. The impression of significance is enhanced by the realization that the term also occurs in the final psalms of Books 3 (89:15) and 4 (106:3) and brackets the concluding psalm of Book 5 (144:15; 146:5).

6. Craig C. Broyles, *Psalms* (NIBC; Peabody, Mass.: Hendrickson, 1999), 41–42.

with the will and pleasure of God. Such statements express the psalmist's confidence and are intended to bolster the commitment of the reader to God's way of "regard" for the weak.

Just what is this "regard" for the weak that is encouraged? The Hebrew word that underlies "regard" is *maśkil* (from *śkl*, "understand, gain insight to"). Rather than a sense of "compassionate concern" that might be expressed with the Hebrew verb *rḥm*, *maśkil* is a term associated with the wisdom tradition and reflects a perceptive ability to know the right response in a given situation—here, the treatment of the weak.[7] In 1 Samuel 18:14–15, David's perceptive ability to know how to engage in battle worried Saul, who feared David would turn his skill against Saul. Amos 5:13 uses the term to describe the person who is wise enough to know when to keep quiet in a difficult time.

A related noun (*śekel*) is used in David's encouraging words to his son Solomon as the time approaches for Solomon to succeed him as king. David prays, "May the LORD give you discretion [*śekel*] and understanding [*binah*] when he puts you in command over Israel, so that you may keep the law of the LORD your God" (1 Chron. 22:12). Here the type of perceptive ability to know the right course of action is attached to the necessary characteristics of the ruling monarch. In the light of the positioning of this psalm at the end of Book 1 of the Psalter, it seems more likely that some translation like "savvy" (ability to know what to do and when) is more accurate than (compassionate) "regard."

The LORD will protect him. The one who knows how to deal appropriately with the weak can anticipate appropriate treatment from Yahweh when weakness overtakes him. The remainder of this section describes the ways Yahweh will uphold the psalmist in illness. The description is divided into protection from external foes and troubles (41:2) and protection from the internal ravages of disease (41:3). Yahweh will "protect" the narrator and "preserve his life." Yahweh "will bless him"[8] in the land and "[will] not sur-

---

7. Actually, the masculine singular form of the participle occurs most frequently in the psalms (seventeen times, of which thirteen are genre designations in psalm headings, transliterated in the NIV simply as *maśkil*, e.g., 32:0). Outside the Psalter, the term most regularly occurs in wisdom literature (Job 22:2; Prov. 10:5, 19; 14:35, 15:24; 16:20; 17:2; 21:12). Two appearances of the Hiphil masculine plural participle (*maśkilim*) occur in Dan. 12:3 and 10, where they describe a group of faithful believers privy to important esoteric knowledge about the end times.

8. The verb "bless" (*ʾšr*) is from the same root as the opening word of the psalm (*ʾašre*). The NIV follows the LXX in translating this verb in the active voice. In the Heb. of the MT, the word is pointed as a Pual (passive) verb form and would be translated "(so that) he will be blessed. . . ."

render him"[9] to his foes. In addition, Yahweh will not allow sickness to undermine him. He will "sustain" the sick person on the sickbed[10] and will "change" the patient's bed as well.[11]

The Complaint (41:4–9)

A SHIFT FROM a third-person reference to Yahweh to a second-person address signals the beginning of the second section of the psalm. Two stanzas of three verses each expound the malice and calumny of the psalmist's enemies (41:5–6) and friends (41:9), who speak false cheer to the patient (41:6), spread groundless rumors, and plot together to take advantage of the situation (41:7–8). The section is introduced (41:4) by the psalmist's confession of sin and a plea to Yahweh for mercy. The description of the enemies' malice thus serves as illustration of the experience of suffering that might encourage divine mercy.

When will he die? The enemies anticipate the psalmist's death as imminent and expect his "name" to perish. The preservation of a man's name was an important aspect of Israelite belief. The reference is probably to the horror of dying childless—with no (male) descendant to carry on the family name. Abram's prickly response to God's greeting and promise in Genesis 15:1–2 illumines the great value placed on progeny to secure one's future place in the world. Equally as pointed is the extreme to which the law of levirate marriage[12] was willing to go in order to ensure the "name of the deceased" would not be cut off (Deut. 25:5–10).

In the same vein, the story of Tamar (Gen. 38), who, following the death of her husband, saw one of his brothers die as he attempted to fulfill the obligation of the *levir*, emphasizes the importance of preserving the name of

---

9. In the Heb., the phrase is the jussive ("let *you* not surrender him"), indicating a shift from description of divine protection into a plea for deliverance directed to God himself. The NIV follows the recommendation of *BHS* and reads the phrase as "he will not surrender him." The emendation seems reasonable to me.

10. The Heb. for "sickness" here comes from the verb *dwh* ("menstruate") and normally describes the "sickness" associated with a menstrual flow. For the Israelites, menstruation was considered polluting, rendering the woman unclean and dictating withdrawal from public association. Here the term seems to be used to suggest an ailment with particular public approbation, in which case the protective care of Yahweh to hold the patient supportively would be remarkable, since any contact with the unclean person would render the other unclean as well.

11. The Heb. verb for "change" here (*hpk*; NIV "restore") probably means to turn the pallet/mattress over or to air it out rather than changing soiled bedclothes, as we might expect a nurse to do. Alternatively, it might mean to reorient the bed so that the sick person can have a change of view. Either is a way of comforting the ill.

12. This common expression for the Israelite practice designated by the verb "fulfill the responsibility of the marriage of a brother-in-law" is taken from the Latin word *levir* ("brother-in-law").

the deceased. When her father-in-law, Judah, refused to offer his third and only surviving son to fulfill the levirate obligation, Tamar disguised herself as a prostitute in order to become pregnant by her father-in-law and thus preserve her husband's name at the extreme risk of her own reputation and life. The evaluation of Judah—"She is more righteous than I"—leaves no doubt that such extreme action was considered warranted in light of the importance of preserving the name. If the author of Psalm 41 is David or a later Davidic king, death without a male heir would not only mean the end of a dynasty and the obliteration of the "name" of the deceased, but it would offer opportunity to other contenders to the throne to gain power for themselves and their descendants.

United against the psalmist, foe and friend alike use the power of language to create a distorted picture of reality that fuels their fantasies and encourages their hopes. They "speak falsely" (41:6), "gather slander" (41:6), "whisper together" (41:7), and verbalize their worst imaginings (41:7–8), assuming that the "vile disease" will finish the patient off (41:8).

Even my close friend. The malice extends even to those whom the psalmist has counted as close associates. This passage is well known from Jesus' use of it at the Last Supper to predict Judas's coming betrayal (John 13:18). Not only was Jesus familiar with this psalm, but he was well read in the whole collection of psalms that existed at his time and studied them for insights into his own role and circumstances.[13] The estrangement and betrayal he experienced with Judas (and ultimately with all the disciples, who forsook him) found clear resonances with the sense of isolation and suffering expressed in Psalm 41. The sharing of bread was one of the most intimate moments in Israelite life, and meals were a time in which participants set aside all enmity and hostility. This being the case, betrayal by one who had "shared bread" was particularly distressing. The fact that it was "*my* bread" that was shared also suggests that the psalmist had supplied the repast, which thus heightens the sense of betrayal by the guest's ingratitude.

Has lifted up his heel. Commentators are not certain whether this phrase refers to an actual symbolic act of public rejection or whether it is simply an idiomatic expression for betrayal. A related idiom—"put one's foot on the neck of another"—describes a symbolic act of victory and subjugation of an enemy, so there may be some actual action involved here. Others suggest a cunning wrestling move or a "great kick" in a fight as the basis.[14]

---

13. See the discussion of "Jesus' Use of the Psalms" in the section on "The Theology of the Psalms" in vol. 2 of this commentary.

14. Cf. V. H. Koov, "Heel," *IDB*, 2:577; Delitzsch, *Biblical Commentary on the Psalms*, 48. Dahood's translation—"spun slanderous tales"—relies on unusual interpretation of the words based on related Ugaritic terminology. See Craigie's comments, *Psalms 1–50*, 319.

Koov mentions that the Hebrew behind the phrase "lifted up" (*gdl*) "is never used in the OT in the sense of 'lift up' or 'raise,' but always 'to act proudly,' 'to magnify oneself.'" He suggests that *ʿaqeb* ("heel") has been displaced from the end of verse 11 and should be eliminated.[15] Koov's conclusion seems apt, regardless of which alternative one chooses: "The emphasis would seem to be that one, with whom one was bound by a covenant of peace, who partook of one's bread, had violated the laws of hospitality, and had turned on his host."

Final Plea and Confidence (41:10–12)

HAVING POURED OUT a complaint of isolation and betrayal, the psalmist now seeks mercy from God and restoration to health. The plea for divine mercy relates back to verse 4, where he recalls a previous request for mercy in the face of sin. But he broadens its appeal in light of the merciless attack of the opponents depicted in the intervening verses. The psalmist's hope is not only for forgiveness and restored health but also for being requited against the enemies—balancing the account sheet between them.[16]

I know that you are pleased with me. The psalmist expresses a rather unexpected and audacious confidence in the pressing circumstances. Not only will Yahweh act to deliver, but he is actually "pleased" with the psalmist. He knows this because God has not allowed the enemies to triumph regardless of his extreme vulnerability. As a result, he dares to hope that God will honor his continued "integrity"[17] by taking a firm grasp[18] so that the sufferer is assured of a continued place in God's "presence."[19]

The Doxology (41:13)

VERSE 13 PRESENTS the first of four similar doxologies that function editorially to mark the conclusion of the first four books of the Psalter. This verse marks

---

15. Koov, "Heel," 2:577; Kraus, *Psalms 1–59*, 430, agrees.

16. Note the caustic irony of the wordplay between the treacherous "close associates" (*ʾîš šelomi* ["the one at peace/one/unity with me"]) and the anticipated pay back (*ʾašallemah* ["let me pay them back"]). The psalmist wishes to "settle account" with the enemies once and for all.

17. In light of the psalmist's confession of sin (41:4), *tom* cannot indicate moral perfection here but a way of commitment and integrity of purpose.

18. The picture is of one holding fast to an object so tightly that it cannot be lost because of unsettling circumstances or direct attack. I am reminded of the ball carrier in football plunging into the line hugging the ball to his chest in both arms to avoid an inadvertent fumble or being stripped of the ball by an opposing player.

19. The Heb. *nṣb* emphasizes the firmness and enduring quality of the thing/person set up and established. For a discussion of dwelling in the presence of Yahweh, see "Dwelling with Yahweh" in "The Theology of the Psalms" in vol. 2 of this commentary.

the end of the first Davidic collection of psalms (Pss. 3–41). The NIV's consistent translation of the Hebrew *baruk* (from *brk*) as "praise be ..." obscures the fact that this is not an attempt to praise God but is rather an outpouring of the human desire to give back to God in blessing. The difference may seem subtle, but it is significant. To *praise* God is to call others to awareness of God's great character, awesome power, and merciful benefactions to humans—a worthy activity. To *bless* God is a expression of the human desire to return goodness to God—in some way to give goodness and benefaction back to God himself. Although theologically we may bridle at the audacious idea that we might have anything to add to the complete and perfect wholeness that God is in and of himself, that is not really the point. What is at issue, and what is expressed in this doxology, is an *attitude* of wholehearted giving to God.

God of Israel. The concern with the God of the community betrays the secondary nature of this doxology in relation to Psalm 41, which is wholly focused on the experience and concerns of the individual. The doxology—particularly in concert with the other concluding doxologies—encapsulates the heart of a whole people, who out of a combined, national experience of suffering and restoration in the Exile have assembled this collection of psalms as an example and encouragement of their desire to bless Yahweh.

From everlasting to everlasting. The Hebrew *ʿolam* has the sense of a long time or time immemorial rather than the more precise term "eternity." It does have the effect, however, of removing this blessing of God from any specific attachment to an event or experience. This is no tit-for-tat blessing that responds to God's gifts by returning the favor. It is, instead, the outflowing of the recognition of God's essential worthiness within himself—without regard to his acts of gracious mercy and blessing on humans. From before he was known to humans until after there is no more knowing, God remains worthy of blessing.

Amen and Amen. This final phrase denotes an affirmation and acceptance of what has gone before. Related to the verb *ʾmn* ("be stable, firm, trustworthy, reliable"), the word expresses agreement and solidarity with an oath or a curse—"this is my position as well," "may this curse happen to me if I fail to keep my obligation." The Hebrew term comes over into Christian usage through the Greek transliteration *amen* and reflects similar usage in the New Testament. Jesus used the term to affirm the truth of his teaching by introducing statements with "Amen, Amen, I say to you..." ("Truly, truly..."). Jesus is also called "the Amen" (Rev. 3:14), affirming the truth of the testimony of his life and ministry. Nowadays "Amen" is a standard closure to public or private prayer, indicating personal or corporate alignment with the sentiments or commitments expressed. In some congregations, an outspoken "Amen!" is one audible way of expressing agreement with and encouragement of the speaker.

Blessed. As noted above, Psalm 41 begins, as does the whole Psalter, with a promise of "blessing." The term *ʾašre* is less common than the usual word for bless, *baruk*.[20] It evokes a circumstance of "wholeness, health, prosperity, balance." The one who is *ʾašre* experiences life as God intended it from the beginning. This does not deny that the world in which such blessed persons move and breathe is decidedly corrupted and removed from God's original intention. But it suggests that Israel believed it was to possible to experience this kind of blessed wholeness, here and now.[21]

The distribution of *ʾašre* throughout the Psalter is interesting.[22] Of particular note is its occurrence at the "seams" between the five books. We find *ʾašre* in Psalms 1 and 2 at the beginning of the Psalter, in Psalm 41 at the end of Book 1, in Psalm 89 at the end of Book 3, in Psalm 106 at the end of Book 4, and Psalms 144 and 146, which bracket the end of the final book (145), just before the concluding Hallel (146–150).[23]

Although *ʾašre* is most often associated with the biblical wisdom tradition, none of these "seam" psalms (except for Ps. 1) is particularly characteristic of wisdom. Psalms 2; 89; and 144 are "royal psalms" while Psalm 106 is a historical confession of Israel's sin in a Deuteronomic mode, and Psalm 146 is a praise hymn with connections to the *Yahweh malak* collection. By contrast, most of the other psalms that use *ʾašre* do display wisdom characteristics.[24] This suggests that nonwisdom compositions with *ʾašre* statements may have

---

20. The term *ʾašre* occurs over forty times in the Old Testament (twenty-five of these within the psalms), while *baruk* appears over seventy times (only seventeen of these in the psalms), a Qal passive participle.

21. For further discussion of *ʾašre*, see comments on 1:1 and 2:12.

22. The word *ʾašre* appears at 1:1; 2:12; 32:1, 2; 33:12; 34:8; 40:4; 41:1; 65:4; 84:4, 5, 12; 89:15; 94:12; 106:3; 112:1; 119:1, 2; 127:5; 128:1, 2; 137:8, 9; 144:15; 146:5.

23. I can offer no adequate explanation for the omission of *ʾašre* from the concluding psalm of Book 2 (Ps. 72). However, it is striking in this regard that when the kingly figure who is the focus of Ps. 72 is promised blessing by all the nations, that blessing employs a verb from the same root as *ʾašre* (72:17b). When, however, the nations are promised blessing from the king, it is the root *brk* that is used (72:17a), a probable reference to the covenant with Abraham/Israel in Gen. 12:1–3, where all the families of the earth will find blessing (*brk*) in their relationship to Abraham and his descendants.

24. See esp. Pss. 32 and 34 with their aphoristic instruction (binding the titleless Ps. 33 between them); Ps. 94 is also aphoristic and concerned with instruction; both Pss. 112 and 119 share the acrostic form that is associated with wisdom; Pss. 127 and 128 are both clearly wisdom instruction. The exceptions to the rule of wisdom connection are Pss. 40; 65; and 84, although 84 does include a "better than" statement (84:10), often part of wisdom aphorisms.

been adapted as part of the final wisdom editing to which the whole Psalter seems to have been subjected.[25]

The placement of these psalms with their emphasis on "blessing" and "wholeness" at the seams of the Psalter has the effect of following up on the introductory exhortation of Psalm 1 that those who follow the "way" that God knows experience the healing restoration of his intention and purpose in their lives. A return to this important structural theme at these important junctures drives home the intent of the final editors that the psalms are to be read within the new context provided them in the arrangement of the canonical Psalter. While each composition still retains its integrity as an individual expression of faith, the whole concert of songs together provides another way of hearing God's word within these human words as each individual expression is heard alongside of and in tension with other expressions that mark out the boundaries of faithful life before Yahweh.

Having regard for the weak. According to Psalm 41, it is the one who has regard for the "weak" who experiences the blessing of restored wholeness that *ʾašre* offers. But just who are the *dallim* whom the NIV here calls the "weak"? In most occurrences of this word, the connotation has more to do with a lack of financial resources than with physical weakness.[26] In Ruth 3:10 the term is contrasted in parallelism with *ʿašir* ("wealthy") to describe the two categories of "young men" whom Ruth resisted running indiscriminately after. The tension with the rich is particularly clear in Proverbs: "The wealth of the rich is their fortified city, but poverty is the ruin of the poor [*dal*]" (Prov. 10:15). "Wealth brings many friends, but a poor man's friend deserts him" (19:4). "He who is kind to the poor lends to the LORD, and he will reward him for what he has done" (19:17). "A rich man may be wise in his own eyes, but a poor man who has discernment sees through him" (28:11).[27]

Elsewhere the lack of resources possessed by the *dal* is noted. "A generous man will himself be blessed, for he shares his food with the poor" (Prov. 22:9). "Nebuzaradan the commander of the guard left behind in the land of Judah some of the poor people, who owned nothing; and at that time he gave them vineyards and fields" (Jer. 39:10).[28] Despite their lack of financial and

---

25. See the discussion of wisdom shaping of the Psalter in Wilson, "The Shape of the Book of Psalms," 129–42.

26. The word *dal* occurs in Gen. 41:19; Ex. 23:3; 30:15; Lev. 14:21; 19:15; Judg. 6:15; Ruth 3:10; 1 Sam. 2:8; 2 Sam. 3:1; 13:4; 2 Kings 14:14; 25:12; Job 5:16; 20:10, 19; 31:16; 34:19, 28; Pss. 41:1; 72:13; 82:3, 4; 113:7; 141:3(?); Prov. 10:15; 14:31; 19:4, 17; 21:13; 22:9, 16, 22; 28:3, 8, 11, 15; 29:7, 14; Isa. 10:2; 11:4; 14:30; 25:4; 26:6; Jer. 5:4; 39:10; 40:7; 52:15, 16; Amos 2:7; 4:1; 5:11; 8:6; Zeph. 3:12.

27. See also Job 34:19; Prov. 22:16.

28. Cf. Lev. 14:21; Prov. 19:17.

other resources, it appears that the *dallim* were not entirely destitute. Others could exploit them by stealing their grain (Amos 5:11), and Leviticus 14:21 implies they had the wherewithal to be required to provide sacrifices of a male lamb, one-tenth an ephah of choice flour mixed with oil, and additional oil as well.[29]

Although the primary connotation of *dal* seems to be lack of resources, in a few contexts another nuance seems appropriate. In 2 Samuel 13:4, *dal* describes a visible change of features in response to Amnon's obsessive preoccupation with his half-sister, Tamar. The NIV's "haggard" tries to capture this meaning. A similar use of *dal* occurs in the description of the seven lean cows in Pharaoh's dream, which were "scrawny [*dallot*] and very ugly and lean" (Gen. 41:19). Again, in 2 Samuel 3:1, the term describes the declining strength ("grew weaker and weaker") of the house of Saul in its competition with the rising house of David. On the basis of such nuances it is possible to justify the NIV's translation of *dal* in Psalm 41:1 as "weak," although that is not the most common rendering.[30]

It was the king's responsibility to ensure the rights of the *dallim* and to provide equity for them. "If a king judges the poor with fairness, his throne will always be secure" (Prov. 29:14). "A ruler who oppresses the poor is like a driving rain that leaves no crops" (28:3). "[The king] will take pity on the weak and the needy and save the needy from death. He will rescue them from oppression and violence, for precious is their blood in his sight" (Ps. 72:13–14).[31]

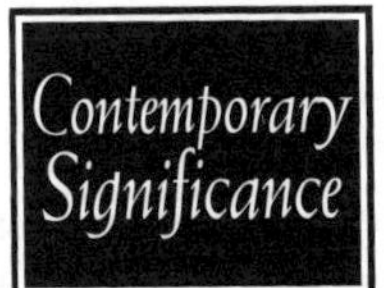

REGARD FOR THE WEAK. If having regard for the weak is commended to the reader of Psalm 41 and if the consequence of such regard is to experience the restoration of wholeness signified by *ʾašre*, how can we respond with such regard today? Let me suggest three aspects of what it means to regard the poor/weak in our own time.

(1) The first element of having regard for the *dallim* is to know how to offer the right and appropriate response in our contacts with them. As we noted on verse 1, the participle *maśkil* [NIV "regard"] speaks of having insight and understanding into the appropriate response to the "poor/weak" rather than

29. Job 20:19 may imply that some *dallim* had houses that could be taken from them.

30. In contrast, the NRSV reads Ps. 41:1 as "consider the *poor*," while NJB conflates the two possibilities to get "cares for the *poor* and the *weak*." Cf. also Judg. 6:15, where Gideon resists God's call to leadership by claiming: "How can I save Israel? My clan is the weakest [*baddal*] in Manasseh, and I am the least in my family."

31. Cf. Ps. 82:3–4; 113:7.

just compassionate concern. Often concerned people fail in their attempts to minister to others because they do not take the time to know whom they are trying to serve and what their needs really are. This kind of understanding requires time in order to build relationships with persons, often in an entirely different cultural setting. It may require us to sit down, shut up, and really spend time listening until others are willing to share their thoughts, fears, and needs.

When we think we can decide from the outside what problems beset a person or community and when we come with a unilaterally determined "program" to solve their problems, we are likely to offend and alienate those we seek to serve rather than gain their confidence and support. As codirector of a Christian nonprofit organization concerned to develop programs of education for ministry for members of underserved ethnic communities in a major urban center, I found myself sitting around a table with representatives of nine educational institutions and of an equal number of Christian service organizations, and with numerous representatives of urban ethnic churches and communities.

One of the first insights we gained was that academic professors and administrators—largely men and mostly from majority culture institutions—were skilled and comfortable with roundtable discussions, pushing forward viewpoints, mustering arguments, and persuading consent. We talked all the time and expected others to adopt our ground rules whenever they broke in to counter our arguments or to express their own views. Soon we realized, however, just how one-sided our "conversation" had become. Those we had invited to the meetings to speak for the ethnic minority communities were not comfortable with this kind of dialogue and remained strangely silent. After some discussion among ourselves, we agreed to sit down, keep quiet, invite input from others, and listen quietly until they began to talk and share. Only after extended silence and patient waiting did the circumstances begin to shift and the real voices of the urban communities emerge. Our hearts had always been in the right place, but first we had to learn the right way to approach and know those we wanted to collaborate with.

(2) The idea of collaboration implies the second aspect of "regarding the poor/weak." If we are truly committed to those we consider "poor" or "weak" and if we truly want to labor together with them in redemptive ways, we must acknowledge our essential unity with them. This is the message communicated by Psalm 41 when it moves immediately from encouraging the cultivation of regard for the weak to an exposition of the psalmist's own weakness that pled for the regard of God. The one who has regard for the weak will

be blessed because God will protect and bless him (41:2), sustain him on his sickbed, and restore him (41:3).

We are not so different from those we are called to serve. I am reminded again of Jesus' confrontation with the Pharisees over his association with "sinners" (Matt. 9:9–13). Jesus replied to their criticism: "It is not the healthy who need a doctor, but the sick. But go and learn what this means: 'I desire mercy, not sacrifice.' For I have not come to call the righteous, but sinners." The Pharisees needed to learn that they had much in common with those they called "sinners." In fact, it was this common bond that offered them their greatest hope; Jesus had come to save all who acknowledged their sinful condition and need. These Pharisees, however, were missing out on his offer because they could not see or accept their oneness with the tax collectors and sinners.

(3) Acknowledging our essential unity with the "poor" and "weak" leads us to the third aspect of "regard." When we build listening, hearing relationships that allow us to truly know and understand those we seek to serve and when we acknowledge our own needs and desires are essentially the same, we learn that service is a two-way street. As our Christian nonprofit organization began to listen to the urban ethnic minority communities, we discovered there was much they had to offer and teach us. They had insights into the distorted systems of this world that we in our privileged status had not even begun to consider. They had developed strength and patience bred only of struggle and suffering.

I found myself drawn to bring together some of the insights from this fruitful collaboration with my ongoing study of the psalms and was amazed to see how the modern urban experience was reflected in the experience of the righteous sufferers of the psalms. Equally amazing—and frightening—was the realization of how much I had in common with the "enemies" in the psalms, who were the "haves" of their day and who participated explicitly or complicitly in the exploitation of the *dallim* of their context. This is a lesson I would not likely have sought out by myself. But it has changed the way I look at the psalms, and I have my urban brothers and sisters to thank for the insight.

A life of personal integrity. Psalm 41 also encourages us to adopt a lifestyle marked by personal integrity. The kind of integrity intended by the Hebrew word *tom* (41:12) is more than just a matter of character, although character is obviously important. It is the psalmist's integrity that leads to being "upheld" by God and "set" in his presence forever. That is a kind of integrity I would like to have. But how do I go about doing that? I am an imperfect human with a track record of sin, so how can I ever hope to attain such a standard of integrity or even "blamelessness," as the underlying Hebrew word is often translated?[32]

Although many of the occurrences of *tom* receive the English translation "blameless" or "innocent," only a few appear in contexts that allow us to make a judgment about the basic and original meaning of the term. In Genesis 20:5–6; 2 Samuel 15:11; and 1 Kings 22:34 = 2 Chron. 18:33, events occurred that might or did cause harm, but the participants were declared "blameless" or "innocent" because *there had been no premeditation or intent to harm* behind their action. This is, perhaps, most clear in the incident in 1 Kings, where the king of Israel is killed by an arrow unleashed by an archer in indiscriminate fire—without intentional aiming—in the heat of battle. It is said that the archer shot his arrow *letummo* (NIV "at random") and thus hit the king (who was in any event disguised!) without any specific intention of doing so.

Similarly, Abimelech pleads his innocence (NIV "I have done this with a clear conscience [*betom lebabi*]") in Genesis 20:5–6, since he had taken Sarah from Abraham when they concealed their marriage relationship and claimed to be brother and sister. Likewise, the two hundred guests of Absalom, invited to a gathering in order to buttress his growing opposition to his father, David, "went quite innocently [*letummam*], knowing nothing about the matter" (2 Sam. 15:11). So this kind of "integrity" does not mean that no action resulting in harm occurred. A wife was taken and her virtue threatened. A king was threatened, and a rebellion fomented. But the participants are declared "innocent" or "blameless" because they lacked premeditation and intent.

Integrity of this sort involves no deceit, but it does involve integration of thought, word, and deed. When we have this kind of integrity, we say what we mean, and our words and actions reflect what is actually in our hearts and minds. We are all of a piece and transparent. This is a difficult practice to accomplish, especially when we fear how others will respond to what we think and feel. Perhaps we do need to reflect on our thoughts and emotions before giving them free rein. That is certainly what Psalm 39 seems to counsel when the psalmist talks about putting "a muzzle on my mouth" (39:1).[33]

Psalm 41 offers two further insights into the kind of integrity that leads to being upheld by God. (1) This kind of integrity is more than just a passive characteristic one can bear. It is a consistent way of acting—a life path,

32. The noun *tom* is related to the adjective *tam*. Both are often translated as "blameless" or "innocent." Cf. Gen. 20:5, 6; 25:27; 2 Sam. 15:11; 1 Kings 9:4; 22:34; 2 Chron. 18:33; Job 1:1, 8; 2:3; 4:6; 8:20; 9:20, 21, 22; 21:33; Pss. 7:8; 25:21; 26:1, 11; 37:37; 41:12; 64:4; 78:72; 101:2; Prov. 2:7; 10:9, 29; 13:6; 19:1; 20:7; 28:6; 29:10; Song 5:2; 6:9; Isa. 47:9 for the varied nuances of these words.

33. See comments on Ps. 39:1 and the Contemporary Significance section of that psalm.

so to speak, that has its beginning and end in God. There may be individual stumbles along the way, but the integrated person is the one whose eyes remain firmly fixed on the goal. It is this person who can cry out with the psalmist: "Search me, O God, and know my heart; test me and know my anxious thoughts. See if there is any offensive way in me, and lead me in the way everlasting" (139:23–24).

(2) This kind of integrity involves taking a stand in the strength of God. Psalm 41 describes this process as "in my integrity you uphold me and set me in your presence forever." The second of these two verbs (*yṣb*) is most often used in contexts where a firm stance in resistance to someone or something is intended. This is so in a military context of the soldier taking the stance for action against the enemy. One may rise and stand about, using the more common verb *ʿmd*. But *yṣb* conjures up in my mind the crouching soldier, sword and shield in hand, bracing for the clash with the onrushing enemy.

So Psalm 41 promises that the person of integrity will experience the upholding hand of God, providing bracing support in times of struggle, and will also be empowered by God to face the attack of the enemy. Such integrity does not mean "aloofness" or being above the fray. Instead, it pictures those willing to take a stand in the power of God to confront, resist, and counter wrong and injustice wherever it exists. It is out of this kind of integrated life that true regard for the weak is possible.

The Shape of Book 2 (Pss. 42–72)

BOOK 2 OF the Psalter begins much as Book 1 ends, with lamenting and pleas for deliverance. Book 1 concluded with a sense of human weakness facing extinction, and yet a contrasting hope for restoration by God, who would yet set the psalmist in his presence forever. Book 2 begins in the combined Psalms 42–43 with a longing for restoration by God, in which the psalmist's disquieted soul is balanced by confident trust in God, the Savior (42:5, 11; 43:5).

Psalm 44 introduces a query addressed to God and founded on the perception that God had been faithful in delivering the ancestors in ways the current generation has not experienced. Denying any sin or guilt to explain God's abandonment, this psalm calls on God to rise and act according to his past record and covenant responsibilities. The query continues in the background behind the celebration of the royal wedding described in Psalm 45. The obvious emphasis of this royal psalm is that the king is honored and elevated, protected by Yahweh, and guaranteed a lasting reputation and reign.

Psalms 46–48 continue in this vein, proclaiming God as refuge and security for the city of God that will not fall (46). The nations of the world will be subdued and will acknowledge the sovereignty of God's kingship (47). Psalm 48 celebrates the security of Zion and God's temple. The next psalm concludes this grouping with an exhortation not to fret about evil days and wicked people because poverty and suffering are no indication of God's lack of love and care. He will in fact redeem the life of the faithful from the grave (49:15).

Against this background of expectation of divine action to redeem his people from their trouble, Psalms 50–53 add a new dimension by introducing a call for the people to confess their sin. This is initiated in Psalm 50 by discussing the nature of true sacrifice and its link to any expectation of salvation (50:7–15, 23). Psalm 51 is a model confession of sin, intended to "teach transgressors [God's] ways" so that sinners will turn back to him (51:13). True sacrifice requires such confession, revealing a "broken spirit; a broken and contrite heart" (51:17) as the foundation of divine acceptance. This new attitude of confession leads in Psalm 52 to a contrast of the fates of the arrogant evil and those who "trust in God's unfailing love for ever and ever" (52:8). The former are snatched up and uprooted while the faithful are deeply rooted in the life-giving soil of God's house. Psalm 53 concludes this section by describing the destruction of the foolish evildoers who deny God's effective existence, but it closes with a plea for "salvation for Israel ... out of Zion" and restoration.

Following on the plea at the end of Psalm 53, the next six psalms (54–59) hammer the theme of restoration relentlessly. Toward the end of this group the tone takes on a more universal edge as the psalmist vows to praise God's deliverance "among the peoples" (57:9). Further, he is called to defeat the "gods/rulers" of the world (58) so that all humanity will know that "there is a God who judges the earth" (58:11). This group ends with a call for God to rouse himself and punish the nations so the "ends of the earth" will know that God rules over Jacob (59:5, 13).

In an almost shocking response to this clamor for divine deliverance and judgment of the nations, Psalm 60 offers instead a shattering experience of divine rejection. Deliverance is not forthcoming; instead, divine anger has shaken the land and God's people experience "desperate times" (60:3). This psalm goes on to declare that any reliance on human power is doomed to failure since the world belongs to God and he is the only reliable source of victory (60:11–12).

This rejection marks a turning point in Book 2. The remaining twelve psalms manifest a parallel growth between a developing reliance on God alone and an increasingly inclusive attitude toward the "peoples of the earth." An opening plea for deliverance is voiced from "the ends of the earth" (61:2), a possible allusion to the Diaspora community. This plea gives way almost immediately to expressions of confidence in God, who alone provides "rest" and "salvation" (62:1–2, 5–6) and whose "love is better than life" (63:3).

Psalm 64 sounds another plea for deliverance and protection but introduces a new reference to humankind who will learn to fear God (64:9). The positive nature of this inclusion of humankind gradually develops over the next few psalms as plea (64) turns to praise (65–68). God's goodness will inspire awe in "those living far away ... where morning dawns and evening fades" (65:8). "All the earth" will bow down to God and praise his "awesome ... works" (66:3–4). God's gracious blessing is desired so that his "ways may be known on earth, [his] salvation among all nations" (67:2). As a result, "all the peoples" will praise God, and "all the ends of the earth will fear him" (67:3–4, 7). This section concludes with Psalm 68 as it celebrates the triumphant rule of Yahweh over the earth so that his enemies are defeated, his temple is established, and all the kingdoms of the earth submit to him.

Praise begets a renewed and confident plea for deliverance (Pss. 69–71), in which the restored fortunes of the exilic communities are in view (69:35–36) and Yahweh is seen as the only hope of restoration (71:5). Although

God has made his people "see troubles, many and bitter" because of their sin, he "will restore [their] life again" (71:20). In conclusion, Psalm 72 offers prayer for the empowerment of the king for an eternal reign of justice and equity. On the one hand, this hope reflects the ideology of the Jerusalem Davidic dynasty and represents the hope that the promise of universal rule offered in 2:8 will be passed on and realized in subsequent generations of Davidic kings. This certainly illustrates the hopes of many in the Diaspora after the demise of the monarchy at the hands of the Babylonians. As we will see at the end of Book 3 (Pss. 73–89), these hopes were harshly crushed and led to great confusion and frustration on the part of those who had invested so much in the descendants of David.

However, the seeds of a different interpretation are already laid in the psalms leading up to the end of Book 2. Following as it does on the increasingly inclusive and universal tone of Psalms 65–68, Psalm 72's plea for the king and the king's son easily flows over into eschatological hope and expectation that exceeds the promise of the historical kingship. This king "will rule from sea to sea" (72:8); "his name [will] endure forever," and "all nations will be blessed through him" (72:17)—a culmination of the universal implications of God's original promise to Abraham (Gen. 12:3). This eschatological reading of the royal psalms is perhaps part of the most subtle shaping of the Psalter in its final stages. This is a point to which I will return in the section on "The Shape of the Psalter" in volume 2 of this commentary.

Psalms 42 and 43

FOR THE DIRECTOR of music. A *maskil* of the Sons of Korah.

42:1 As the deer pants for streams of water,
so my soul pants for you, O God.
2 My soul thirsts for God, for the living God.
When can I go and meet with God?
3 My tears have been my food
day and night,
while men say to me all day long,
"Where is your God?"
4 These things I remember
as I pour out my soul:
how I used to go with the multitude,
leading the procession to the house of God,
with shouts of joy and thanksgiving
among the festive throng.

5 Why are you downcast, O my soul?
Why so disturbed within me?
Put your hope in God,
for I will yet praise him,
my Savior and 6 my God.

My soul is downcast within me;
therefore I will remember you
from the land of the Jordan,
the heights of Hermon—from Mount Mizar.
7 Deep calls to deep
in the roar of your waterfalls;
all your waves and breakers
have swept over me.

8 By day the LORD directs his love,
at night his song is with me—
a prayer to the God of my life.

9 I say to God my Rock,
"Why have you forgotten me?

Why must I go about mourning,
    oppressed by the enemy?"
10 My bones suffer mortal agony
    as my foes taunt me,
saying to me all day long,
    "Where is your God?"

11 Why are you downcast, O my soul?
    Why so disturbed within me?
Put your hope in God,
    for I will yet praise him,
    my Savior and my God.

43:1 Vindicate me, O God,
    and plead my cause against an ungodly nation;
    rescue me from deceitful and wicked men.
2 You are God my stronghold.
    Why have you rejected me?
Why must I go about mourning,
    oppressed by the enemy?
3 Send forth your light and your truth,
    let them guide me;
let them bring me to your holy mountain,
    to the place where you dwell.
4 Then will I go to the altar of God,
    to God, my joy and my delight.
I will praise you with the harp,
    O God, my God.

5 Why are you downcast, O my soul?
    Why so disturbed within me?
Put your hope in God,
    for I will yet praise him,
    my Savior and my God.

SEVERAL FACTORS SUGGEST that these two psalms should be read as a unified composition. (1) Psalm 43 has no heading to separate it from Psalm 42. This may indicate that, like Psalms 9 and 10, there was a tradition for reading Psalms 42 and 43 together. (2) This idea is confirmed by a number of ancient manuscripts of Psalms that do write these two psalms as one. (3) The two psalms share a repeated refrain that appears regularly in a combined composition (42:5, 11; 43:5), dividing the whole into three segments of relatively equal size. (4) Finally, note the close parallel between 42:9, where the psalmist cries out to God, "Why have you forgotten me? Why must I go about mourning, oppressed by the enemy?" and the similar passage in 43:2, "Why have you rejected me? Why must I go about mourning, oppressed by the enemy?"

Together these two psalms form a lament and plea for vindication from oppression by one's enemies. Without 43, Psalm 42 is decidedly more muted, offering no resolution to the narrator's suffering except for the hope expressed in the refrain: "Put your hope in God, for I will still praise him, my Savior and my God" (42:5, 11). Psalm 43 adds a strong plea for vindication, coupled with the anticipation of approaching God's holy place to sing praises (43:1, 3–4).

As a single composition, the unified psalm offers the following three sections, each concluded by the familiar refrain that drives a muted sense of hope: The psalmist longs to meet God and to relive the lost joy of communion within the festivities of temple worship (42:1–5); downcast and removed from the temple, he feels overwhelmed and forgotten by God—taunted and oppressed by his enemies (42:6–11); he pleads for vindication, seeking divine guidance for a return to the temple and the joyful presence of God (43:1–5).

Several themes and motifs recur through this combined psalm. (1) Memory plays an important role as the psalmist "remembers" (42:4) the lost joys of temple worship, then "remembers" (42:6) the lost presence of God while feeling "forgotten" (42:9) by God, who should be both rock (42:9) and stronghold (43:2). (2) A second theme revolves around the absence of God. "When can I go and meet with God?" asks the psalmist (42:2). In response, the enemy twice taunts the distraught psalmist, "Where is your God?" (42:3, 10). As a result, he feels "forgotten" (42:9) and abandoned by God. The psalms conclude, however, with a joyful anticipation of being led once more into the temple, up to the altar, even to God (43:3–4), so that the opening longing is fulfilled by the end of Psalm 43.

The alert reader will note—even in English translation—a radical change in reference to God beginning with this psalm and continuing through Psalm 83. The significant difference observed between this group of psalms and those that precede and follow is in the name applied to the deity. Outside this group, the use of the direct divine name Yahweh ("LORD") is by far the most common designation. In Psalms 42–83, however, the more generic designation Elohim ("God") outstrips the appearance of Yahweh. While the reason for this difference is not yet satisfactorily explained, it is common to refer to this segment of the larger collection as the "Elohistic Psalter" because of the predilection for Elohim.[1]

The Heading (42:0)

THE HEADING MARKS the first appearance in the Psalter of an attribution to anyone other than David. Of the forty-one psalms of the first book, only Psalms 1; 2; 10; and 32—the first two introductory, the second two with traditions of combination with preceding psalms—have no heading. At the opening of Book 2, however, a series of eight psalms (including Ps. 43 as part of Ps. 42) bear attributions to "the Sons of Korah."[2] Korah was one of the Levitical musicians placed in charge of temple worship by David and Solomon.[3] The first mention of the Levitical musicians is intriguing in light of the psalm's focus on the joys of temple worship and the psalmist's longing to experience it once more. This suggests a probable exilic or postexilic date for this psalm in its present form.

The remaining terms of the heading are familiar from earlier appearances. It is interesting to note that the term *maśkil* appears in the headings of the three consecutive Psalms 42–45 (considering 43 together with 42) that begin the second book of the Psalter.[4]

Longing to Meet God (42:1–5)

FEW IMAGES IN the Psalter exceed the beauty of the opening lines of this psalm. The "soul" (*nepeš*) of the psalmist "pants" for God like a deer for scarce water in the midst of drought. Here Yahweh is seen as the source of life and refreshment that satisfies the longing of the psalmist to "meet with God." The emphasis is not just on his utter dependence on God for life (while that is, of course, assumed); it is rather the joy and pleasure of being in God's presence that the psalmist misses and longs to restore.

Often we fail to recognize how delightful and pleasant temple worship was for the participants. Taking our cues from the critical comments of the prophets seeking to correct inappropriate or abusive forms of worship, we too often think that temple worship consisted of lifeless repetition of empty ritual seeking to manipulate God to human purposes. Or, perhaps we are

---

1. See further discussion of the Elohistic Psalter in "The Shape of the Psalter" in vol. 2 of this commentary.

2. The Korahite psalms include Pss. 42, 44–49; 84–85; 87–88 (eleven altogether).

3. The information regarding the Levitical organization of temple worship is complex at best. The pertinent passages include 1 Chron. 6:16–44; 15:5–24; 16:41–42; 25:1–8.

4. For comments on *maśkil*, see comments on Ps. 32.

unable to relate to the system of blood sacrifice that predominated and tend to evaluate the whole experience as rather crude and primitive. But Psalm 42 clearly exhibits the sense of joy, praise, and spiritual connection with God that must have characterized the best of Israelite worship. Surely those responsible for temple music—as the Sons of Korah were—knew the power of music to lead the congregation and individuals within it into a deeper connection and lasting relationship with their God.

The living God. God is on occasion characterized as the "living God" (42:2). In what sense this is to be taken is not completely clear. Is God "living" in contrast to the pagan deities whom the prophets denigrate as having no life at all? Or is the reference more to God as the source of life? In the present context the latter seems more likely.

The image of thirst is instructive. The deer "thirsts" for streams of water as the psalmist's soul "thirsts" for God. Streams of running water that continue to flow even during the dry seasons are often called "living waters" since they are the source of life. The psalmist is most likely drawing that parallel here. He longs for God as the source of life. This is confirmed by the appearance in 42:8 of the almost identical phrase "the God of *my life*." The only difference is the addition of the first-person singular pronominal suffix to the word "life." While commentators suggest emending one text or the other for consistency, it seems appropriate to me to allow each to stand, with the second adding further definition to the first.

Meeting with God. God and not temple worship is the true source of the psalmist's life. It is God's presence for which he longs, and he laments the loss of that presence in corporate worship here. A literal rendering of the Hebrew—"When will I enter and see the face of God?"—makes this more clear. To "see the face of God" often refers to approaching God in the temple. In 43:3–4, the psalmist explicitly anticipates approaching "your holy mountain" and coming "to the altar of God, to God, my joy and my delight"—clear references to worship in the temple.

Where is your God? The psalmist longs to be with God and to worship him in the temple, but he is prevented and remains distant. This psalm does not provide us with a clear reason for his inability to participate in temple worship. The taunts of the enemy ("Where is your God?") and the implication of verse 5 that he is located outside the land of Israel at the source of the Jordan River lends itself to an exilic interpretation. The psalmist—a member of the Levitical musicians carried into exile—remembers the glorious worship of the past and longs to approach God in the festive rituals as before.

While such an interpretation is certainly compatible with the psalm, it may also be that the psalmist is hindered from worship for some other less drastic reason, such as sickness.[5] It does not seem possible to decide the issue, and it may well be that an earlier, preexilic psalm has been retained here precisely because it continues to resonate with the lives of the exilic and postexilic community.

These things I remember. As noted above, memory plays a significant role in the combined psalm. The psalmist in isolation longs for God's presence and remembers how that presence was joyfully experienced in communal worship. The lack of such occasion now represents the lack of divine presence that the occasion offered. The true heart of Israelite worship is revealed here. The joyous, festive rituals of music, processions, and sacrifice provided opportunity to come face to face with God. That continues to be the true aim of worship: to know and stand before God.

Why are you downcast? The first segment concludes with the introduction of the refrain. The refrain acknowledges the psalmist's suffering and sense of longing but does so with a challenging set of parallel questions intended to cast the present circumstances in a hopeful light. Tears have been the psalmist's "food" (42:3) because of the absence of God. The refrain embodies a sort of "self-talk" in which the psalmist recalls the ground for faith and hope. God is "my Savior," and therefore there is reason for hope and for praise.

Overwhelmed and Forgotten (42:6–11)

PICKING UP ON the terminology of the refrain, the psalmist acknowledges his "soul is downcast within" him. But immediately the refrain follows into a new terrain of hope: "Therefore I will remember you . . ." (42:6). Rather than remembering the "things" of worship in which the presence of God could be experienced, he now remembers God himself—the living God, the source of life and hope.

From the land of the Jordan. This reference seems to intend a location to the north, outside the land of Israel, toward the source of the Jordan River. Whether the place is the real setting of the psalmist or a metaphor for isolation, distance, or exile is uncertain. But the implication is clear: Prevented by distance (physical, emotional, or spiritual) from participating in the restoring worship of the community, the psalmist turns to the author of life himself.

Deep calls to deep. In a rather enigmatic mixing of water metaphors, the psalmist combines reference to the chaotic waters subdued at creation (the "deep"), the tumbling waterfalls of the source of the Jordan ("the roar of your waterfalls"), and the threatening pounding of ocean waves to depict an over-

---

5. Kraus, *Psalms 1–59*, 325.

whelming sense of oppression. These powerful waters have swept over and threaten to carry him away.

The LORD directs his love . . . his song is with me. In the midst of the drowning flood, God throws the psalmist a lifeline. Swept away, taunted that God is not present, longing to see God but far removed from all the familiar and comforting rituals that made God seem so real, he discovers an island in the midst of the sea. God is the "Rock" who provides firm footing and protection.

In the midst of the swirling turmoil of suffering, the psalmist encounters something almost unexpected. His thrashing hand grips the line of God's "love [*ḥesed*]" (42:8), God's faithful, committed, covenant love that endures forever. It is no accident that here alone in this first psalm of the Elohistic Psalter, the name of Israel's covenant God, Yahweh ("LORD"), appears. It is as if the two belong together; Yahweh and *ḥesed* cannot be separated. The "living God" of 42:2 becomes the "God of my life" in 42:8, and a song wells up within the psalmist, even in the midst of the dark.

Compare this verse with the bitter response of the exile in 137:4: "How can we sing the songs of the LORD while in a foreign land?" Yet our psalmist is able to find a song and to sing it out in response to the saving act of Yahweh that reaches into the isolated darkness of the flood. A similar understanding that God is not absent in the midst of trouble but continues to stand with us wherever we are is expressed in the powerful words of Psalm 139:7–12.

> Where can I go from your Spirit?
>   Where can I flee from your presence?
> If I go up to the heavens, you are there;
>   if I make my bed in the depths, you are there.
> If I rise on the wings of the dawn,
>   if I settle on the far side of the sea,
> even there your hand will guide me,
>   your right hand will hold me fast.
> If I say, "Surely the darkness will hide me
>   and the light become night around me,"
> even the darkness will not be dark to you;
>   the night will shine like the day,
>   for darkness is as light to you.

Why have you forgotten me? Still, no matter how powerful, the song does not remove the darkness, nor does it take away the suffering. God is the rock,[6] the island of safety in the storm, but the psalmist still feels forgotten,

6. See comments on "rock" in Ps. 18.

longing for God's presence. Mourning and mortal agony are still real experiences, and the enemy's taunt still has power: "Where is your God?"

Psalm 42 draws to an end with the repetition of the earlier refrain. Left as it is, the psalm offers but a somber hope, of a song breaking into the darkness and yet unable to vanquish the dark as does the light of Jesus in John's Gospel. In a sense, the song testifies to the light, but the psalmist must still wait in the darkness.

Plea for Vindication and Joyous Return (43:1–5)

WITH THE ADVENT of Psalm 43, we hear for the first time a plea to God for vindication and deliverance. The series of imperatives directed to God ("vindicate ... plead ... rescue") makes clear transition from the lament that dominated Psalm 42. The first two imperatives suggest a legal context, but note that the opponents described are "an ungodly nation" (43:1). Thus, it is perhaps better to understand the pleas as expressing the desire that the psalmist's hope and faith in God—in spite of the evidence of circumstance and the repeated taunts of the enemy—will be rewarded and publicly acknowledged.

In this context, the question as to why God, the stronghold, has rejected the psalmist (43:2) takes on a different tone than the similar passage in 42:9, where he simply laments without much hope of deliverance. In 43:2, following the imperative plea for vindication and before the following imperatives seeking divine light and guidance (43:3), his sense of rejection and suffering become an integral part of motivating God to action.

Send forth your light and your truth. The true goal and purpose of the combined psalm now becomes clear. At the beginning of Psalm 42, the psalmist, like a deer panting for water, longs to come into God's presence and remembers those passionate moments of temple worship when it was possible to come before God in festive joy. Now, in Psalm 43, we learn that his goal has never changed. He seeks divine light and truth to provide guidance for a return to God's holy hill and dwelling: the temple with its altar.[7] James Mays speaks of anticipated pilgrimage from exile to participate again with the community of worship in Jerusalem.[8] God's light and truth are the necessary companions on the way to ensure safe arrival.

The poet pictures with relish the consequence of a return to the temple: approaching the altar for sacrifice—the equivalent of coming into God's

---

7. The Heb. term used for "dwelling" here is *miškan* ("temporary dwelling"), often referring to the portable "tabernacle" used for worship by the tribes of Israel during the desert wandering. The use of the term here in conjunction with the reference to "your holy hill" is clearly intended to indicate the Jerusalem temple.

8. Mays, *Psalms*, 174–75.

own presence ("to God, my joy and my delight")—and praising God to the tune of the harp. In this joyous concluding context, the final repeated refrain seems much less somber and clearly more hopeful. The reader is lifted out of the darkness of suffering by the guiding light that restores the faithful to the faithful, loving presence of Yahweh.

THERE ARE MANY interesting themes that could be explored in this psalm. I will limit my comments to two that particularly stand out: remembrance and forgetting, both divine and human; and the importance of communal worship as a response to individual suffering.

Remembrance and forgetting. Memory has a particularly important role in the life of Israel and the Hebrew Bible. The primary terms employed—the verbal root *zkr* and all its related nouns—appear more than 350 times, scattered throughout the Old Testament from Pentateuch through Prophets and Writings. When one includes other idiomatic expressions (such as "bring to mind" or "keep in your heart") that do not use *zkr*, concern with memory is even more endemic.

As these idiomatic expressions suggest, "remember" in the Old Testament may mean something akin to our sense of "recall." But memory for Israel is never as simple as bringing to mind a set of feelings or facts. Almost without exception, a call to remember is at the same time a call to action. Israel is called to remember Yahweh in order to remain faithful to him. She is to remember the commandments and keep them. She must remember Yahweh's wonderful acts and give praise for them. She should remember how Yahweh delivered her in spite of her lack of righteousness and be humbly dependent on him. Memory is never passive but requires an active response to what is remembered. To remember Yahweh is to ground one's life in and on him and so to draw all one's life decisions and actions out of that foundation.

That is one reason why forgetfulness is so tragic and so often condemned in the Old Testament. It does not usually represent simple, passive loss of memory; rather, it describes a willful resistance or rejection of memory and a consequent failure to act appropriately. To forget Yahweh is to resist making the connection between who he is and how one is to act in response. It is to act as if Yahweh has no claim on me that embodies this sort of forgetfulness. It is as if one could wipe out of mind—unlearn, so to speak—all the history built up between two friends and to act as if you were "just another person" with whom I have no connection. The enormity of such failure to remember God is mirrored in the prophets' horrific condemnation of Israel as one who, having known Yahweh as no other nation, has nevertheless forgotten Yahweh so completely that "there is . . . no acknowledgment of God in the land" (Hos. 4:1).[9]

More than just a call to action, memory in Israel is also a form of proclamation and testimony. Israel is to remember God's wonderful acts and proclaim them aloud among the worshiping congregation in the temple. They are to testify among the nations to God's gracious dealings with them. Memory in Israel is not a private act of momentary recall but a continuous communal rehearsal of divine faithfulness. Much of temple worship seems to have been focused around proclaiming the mighty acts of God and offering thanksgiving and praise for them.

Memory has the power to preserve. Ecclesiastes laments the ultimate loss of individual human identity in death because "there is no remembrance of men of old, and even those who are yet to come will not be remembered by those who follow" (Eccl. 1:11). The tragedy of being forgotten led to the institution of the levirate marriage, in which the widow and brother of a childless person would join in an attempt to raise up a memorial child to preserve the name of the deceased. The constant repetition of the names of the ancestral progenitors of Israel—Abraham, Isaac, and Jacob (I would remember Sarah, Rebekah, and Leah and Rachel as well!)—is a clear method of remembering and thus preserving the lives and contributions of the "fathers."

Memory was also an important part of preserving religious and communal traditions. The book of Esther reminds us of the perceived importance of recording significant events in the lives of kings by describing the Book of the Remembrance of the Affairs of the Days, in which Mordecai's actions to save King Xerxes from a coup were recorded. In an oral society, memory is a necessary component of preserving and transmitting community and religious traditions. Early on Israel was instructed to remember the commandments and to transmit them to subsequent generations. Particularly significant traditions were to be written down (e.g., the commandments, reduced to writing by Moses). We raise plaques, endow buildings and scholarships, and carve headstones to remember those who have gone before. Israel raised cairns of stones, pillars, and altars and repeated the names and exploits of humans and of God to preserve for generations to come the "faith of the fathers."

Hebrew (and ultimately Christian) Scripture is an extension of this need to preserve and transmit the wonderful works of Yahweh and by so doing to proclaim his faithfulness to future generations. The act of proclamation and

9. Cf. also Isa. 17:10; 51:13; Jer. 2:32; 3:21; 13:25; 18:15; Ezek. 22:12; 23:35.

transmission is also an act of commitment, by which the proclaimer binds himself or herself to the one proclaimed. Once again, to forget Yahweh is not simply to lose memory of God's name, deeds, and commandments, nor even to fail to call him to mind. Forgetting God is a willful act of "unlearning," whereby rebellious humans reject what they have known and—through lack of commitment, disobedience, and refusal to transmit the truth—seek to create a world in which God does not act or even exist. Such humans are able to cry (as the enemies do in our psalm): "Where is your God?"

Life together. Israel knew the importance of community life and worship. The psalms are replete with examples of communal laments, communal praise, and communal thanksgiving. Worship was more than a number of individuals coming together. They came together to lament or celebrate their lives together. Yes, the psalms do contain as well many examples focused on the experience of the individual: laments, praise, thanksgiving, instruction. The individual is not simply swallowed up in society, but neither is society disbanded in favor of the individual.

What is interesting to me is how often individual laments, praise, and thanksgiving are broken into by reference to the community of faith or the congregation of worship. Psalm 31 is a good example of this widespread phenomenon. The narrator spends twenty-two verses describing an individual experience of trouble and suffering in which "I" and "my" dominate. Then, at the end (31:23–24), the tide turns abruptly, and he speaks outside himself to others. "Love the LORD, all his saints! The LORD preserves the faithful, but the proud he pays back in full. Be strong and take heart, all you who hope in the LORD." Perhaps some later editor has modified an originally completely individual lament to address a broader community. But the effect of this movement—regardless of its origin—is to place the individual in the midst of the worshiping congregation.

This phenomenon is so common within the psalms it cannot be accidental but must reflect Israel's understanding of the important interweaving of individual and community in worship.[10] The individual who has been delivered by God from trouble brings sacrifices of thanksgiving to the temple and stands among the congregation proclaiming his faithfulness. The one who still suffers does not sing laments in isolation but proclaims his or her need in the congregation and seeks hope there.

There is strength in numbers. The individual can encourage, challenge, or admonish the community toward faithfulness, endurance, or repentance. The community can provide a collective memory of the mighty acts of God that exceeds the memory or experience of one and provides the continued

10. Cf. Pss. 30; 32; 34; 52; 64; 66, for just a few examples.

context for enduring faith, hope, and love. For someone to be cut off from this experience of communal worship (as our psalmist is) is to be cut off from the sustaining ground of faith and hope and to be left to one's own poor devices to survive. Many don't.

That is why the psalmist "longs" to return to God's holy mountain and to the divine altar, and that is why he remembers with poignant sadness parading through the streets of Jerusalem with the multitudes on their way to the house of God.[11] This is not simply an example of getting carried away in a crowd! It is rather a deep awareness of the joy and necessity of connecting with something that is beyond oneself—even beyond oneself and God. To become a part of the family of worshiping believers is to become part of a sustaining community that stretches back for millennia and will stretch forward into the future until our Lord returns!

REMEMBERING AND FORGETTING in the context of worship. We bought our home from Paul and Wilma. He had taught for years at the local private Christian college. They lived in the retirement manor across the street from the college and often walked the two-mile loop that passed our home. Many times in the first years we lived here, we would discover Paul and Wilma working among the plants in our yard. The place had become such a part of who they were that it was hard for them to realize it was no longer theirs.

On a number of occasions we sat together, and Paul and Wilma would remember what life had been like at the college when they first moved here so many years before. Paul's teaching had been his life; the house and the gardens had been Wilma's domain. Over time, however, it became clear that Paul's memory was slipping. I took him to faculty lunch at the college one day, and while he enjoyed himself immensely, he could not remember where on campus his office had been or even what he had taught.

It soon became clear that Paul was suffering the effects of advancing Alzheimer's disease. Before long his memory failed completely. I visited him several times in the care center, but he never knew me. While he remained a sweet personality, he was ultimately unable to communicate or recognize his daughter or even Wilma, his companion of so many years. You may know

---

11. Compare the similar sentiments expressed by the author of Ps. 84, whose soul "yearns, even faints for the courts of the LORD" (84:2), who envies the sparrow because she can continually nest in the dwelling place of God (84:3), and who "would rather be a doorkeeper in the house of my God than dwell in the tents of the wicked" (84:10).

personally the pain of being forgotten by a parent or spouse who has been affected by Alzheimer's. The sense of loss and abandonment is palpable and can serve as some background for understanding the loss experienced by the psalmist, who feels forgotten by God (42:9).

All the lament psalms mirror this sense of abandonment by God to some degree or another. From the common sense of "Why do you delay when I need you?" as in this psalm, to the ultimate abandonment expressed in Psalm 22 or especially Psalm 88, the psalmists in trouble consistently sense that God is far away and slow to act. Help never comes quickly enough for the one in pain. Two bouts with kidney stones separated by twelve years have left me with the indelible impression of interminable waits at hospital admission desks, filling out forms doubled over with the pain, waiting to be admitted so I could be medicated to relieve the pain.

But I have to admit that the second bout went better than the first in some ways. This was partly because I recognized the symptoms at first onset and knew what to expect. I also knew that the pain would eventually come to an end when the stones passed. Finally, I knew that medication would ease the pain in the interim. Memory provided me with a sense of confidence to face a difficult future without panic. That is how memory functioned for the poet in our psalm. As he pours out his soul (42:4) in anguish, he remembers "these things"—the festive joy of coming into the presence of God. When his soul is downcast (42:6), he remembers God.

How do we counter the defeating sense of being abandoned by God? The psalmist holds out one effective way: to *remember* the times when God has been present with us, to recall those times when we came joyfully into his presence in the company of the faithful. A journal of life moments with God can be a treasure of remembrances that God has been with us and working through us even though the present may be difficult and God may seem impossibly distant.

The psalmist suggests another way to remember God's faithfulness: to long for and avail ourselves whenever possible of opportunities to stand together with those who are worshiping God. Even if we feel distant or abandoned, the celebration will have the effect of renewing our certainty and hope. To reverse Job's saying (Job 42:5), when it is no longer possible to see God with our eyes, sometimes it is necessary to hear of him by our ears. One of the roles of the worshiping congregation is to worship when I cannot, to celebrate the resurrection of Christ when I am mourning the death of a loved one or struggling with my own sin. The congregation is to declare the wonderful works of God even when I can no longer see him or sense his presence.

I remember returning to my congregation one Easter Sunday morning from a long time of being physically, emotionally, and spiritually distant. I entered that service not knowing what to expect—more than a little afraid. But as the service unfolded around me, I turned from being a spectator to become a participant as the redeeming truth that is Easter was relived again just for me in my ears, my eyes, my mind, and my heart. He had arisen! And he is arisen *for me*!

There is great danger in forgetting God, his mighty works, and the worshiping community of faith. Our society stands ever ready to taunt us, using the words of the psalmist's enemies, "Where is your God?" That they can even raise this question is a testimony to their powerful commitment to forgetfulness and ignorance. Ours is a world that does not wish to remember God. And the danger is that the world and our friends who are of the world can easily persuade us that there is no deliverance from our fears that we do not create for ourselves. It is easy in the face of the painful vagaries of life to conclude that we are on our own—life is what you make of it!

How often have we heard this sort of self-determinism *out there*? The problem is that, in my experience, human society—or even the individual representatives of that society—have been woefully unequal to the task of making meaning out of life. If we are really on our own, as the psalmist feels and our world claims, then we are indeed in deep trouble and have every right to despair. The danger of buying into the world's evaluation is that it doesn't work and threatens to overwhelm us with its chaotic waves and breakers, as the psalmist suggests.

That is why community worship is such an important part of the life of the faithful. The Israelites knew that and longed for those occasions when they could come together in celebration and in praise, repentance, and thanksgiving. Worship together is a place of memory. Together we call to mind what it is so easy to forget alone—that God is good and that his steadfast love endures forever for those who trust in him. Corporate worship counters our society's message of forgetfulness and sends a message both outwardly and inwardly that we are not alone. Worship is a place for testimony and celebration. It is a time for confession and forgiveness. It is a place where we remember the past, receive power to face the present, and conceive hope for tomorrow.

Why are you downcast, O my soul?
  Why so disturbed within me?
Put your hope in God,
  for I will yet praise him,
  my Savior and my God.

Psalm 44

FOR THE DIRECTOR of music. Of the Sons of Korah. A *maskil.*

1 We have heard with our ears, O God;
our fathers have told us
what you did in their days,
in days long ago.
2 With your hand you drove out the nations
and planted our fathers;
you crushed the peoples
and made our fathers flourish.
3 It was not by their sword that they won the land,
nor did their arm bring them victory;
it was your right hand, your arm,
and the light of your face, for you loved them.

4 You are my King and my God,
who decrees victories for Jacob.
5 Through you we push back our enemies;
through your name we trample our foes.
6 I do not trust in my bow,
my sword does not bring me victory;
7 but you give us victory over our enemies,
you put our adversaries to shame.
8 In God we make our boast all day long,
and we will praise your name forever. *Selah*

9 But now you have rejected and humbled us;
you no longer go out with our armies.
10 You made us retreat before the enemy,
and our adversaries have plundered us.
11 You gave us up to be devoured like sheep
and have scattered us among the nations.
12 You sold your people for a pittance,
gaining nothing from their sale.

13 You have made us a reproach to our neighbors,
the scorn and derision of those around us.
14 You have made us a byword among the nations;
the peoples shake their heads at us.
15 My disgrace is before me all day long,
and my face is covered with shame
16 at the taunts of those who reproach and revile me,
because of the enemy, who is bent on revenge.

17 All this happened to us,
though we had not forgotten you
or been false to your covenant.
18 Our hearts had not turned back;
our feet had not strayed from your path.
19 But you crushed us and made us a haunt for jackals
and covered us over with deep darkness.

20 If we had forgotten the name of our God
or spread out our hands to a foreign god,
21 would not God have discovered it,
since he knows the secrets of the heart?
22 Yet for your sake we face death all day long;
we are considered as sheep to be slaughtered.

23 Awake, O Lord! Why do you sleep?
Rouse yourself! Do not reject us forever.
24 Why do you hide your face
and forget our misery and oppression?

25 We are brought down to the dust;
our bodies cling to the ground.
26 Rise up and help us;
redeem us because of your unfailing love.

IT IS CERTAINLY no accident that the first *corporate* prayer for help in the Psalter follows immediately upon the combined Psalms 42–43 with its pregnant description of an individual in crisis upheld by the memory and reality of God's presence in the communal worship of Israel. Psalm 44 operates out of the same sense of bewilderment at the absence of God in a time of extreme need that characterizes the earlier two psalms.

By effect of its position, Psalm 44 extends the sentiments of the earlier psalms to the life of the community and makes more clear that the context against which all are to be read is the exilic experience of Israel.

McCann has pointed out a persuasive set of literary links connecting these three psalms that suggest purposeful arrangement: "These links suggest in each case that the trouble of the 'I' and the expressions of hope in Pss. 42–43 ... are meant to be understood in light of the experiences of exile and dispersion that lie at the heart of [Ps. 44]."[1] While this does not mean that Psalms 42 and 43 were *composed* during the exilic period, it does suggest that the postexilic community came to see their own experience of dislocation and humiliation reflected in these psalms, even though they may have been written in an earlier time. As a result, when the individual in Psalms 42–43 longs to return to the temple and experience the joy of God's presence there, he is heard to speak for the whole community in exile, who shares similar longing for restoration.[2]

Psalm 44 is arranged in five segments: the testimony of the ancestors (44:1–3), a contemporary appropriation of the tradition (44:4–8), a description of present suffering (44:9–16), a protestation of innocence (44:17–22), and a plea for deliverance (44:23–26). A major disjuncture of mood and viewpoint takes place after the first two segments and is marked by the appearance of the term *selah*.

The Testimony of the Ancestors (44:1–3)

PSALM 44 BEGINS almost as if the author had been reading Psalms 42–43! There the individual in crisis turned to the community of faith to remember those elements of past experience that affirmed God's continued presence and good intent to his people. The present psalm begins with a community's rehearsal of the ancestral history of God's saving grace—what is commonly called "salvation history," those events in Israel's history understood to be God's special working with and for her. In this case the rehearsal is primarily concerned with the conquest of the land of Canaan as described in the book of Joshua.

We have heard with our ears. The psalm begins by referring to the constant repetition of the patriarchal history and the mighty acts of God enjoined on Israel in the Deuteronomic literature. "Only be careful, and watch

1. J. Clinton McCann, "Books I-III and the Editorial Purpose of the Psalter," in *The Shape and Shaping of the Psalter*, ed. J. Clinton McCann (Sheffield: JSOT Press, 1993), 102.

2. "When Ps. 42–43 is read in light of Ps. 44 ... it takes on a collective orientation. The [repeated] refrain in Pss. 42–43 becomes an example for the postexilic community of how to face the problem of exile and dispersion" (ibid., 102–3).

yourselves closely so that you do not forget the things your eyes have seen or let them slip from your heart as long as you live. Teach them to your children and to their children after them" (Deut. 4:9).[3]

Israel took this injunction seriously, as demonstrated by the many rehearsals of the primary saving events of her history scattered through the Old Testament.[4] Indeed, in a real sense, the Old Testament itself is the ultimate fulfillment of Israel's commitment to preserve this testimony to God's mighty acts in her behalf.[5] Short of direct perception of God or of his incarnation in Jesus Christ, this testimony—whether spoken or written, proclamation or Scripture—continues to be the primary witness to God throughout the generations.

Job, for example, testifies, "I know that you can do all things; no plan of yours can be thwarted. . . . My ears had heard of you but now my eyes have seen you" (Job 42:2, 5). Jesus declares, "Anyone who has seen me has seen the Father" (John 14:9); and "blessed are those who have not seen and yet have believed" (20:29). The Gospel of John concludes, "Jesus did many other miraculous signs in the presence of his disciples, which are not recorded in this book. But these are written that you may believe that Jesus is the Christ, the Son of God, and that by believing you may have life in his name" (20:30–31). Despite the direct inward working of the Holy Spirit in our lives, we as the Israelites of old are still dependent on the testimony of those who have gone before—especially as embodied in the Scripture of Old and New Testaments.

You drove out. The psalmist, speaking for the community of faith, describes how the recorded and transmitted history of God's activity with the ancestors of the faith provides the foundation of confidence to present believers. God's mighty acts in behalf of the "fathers" are well known—here, the narratives recorded in the first half of Joshua. God displaced the inhabitants of Canaan and "planted our fathers . . . and made our fathers flourish" (44:2).

Not by their sword. The conquest of the land and the establishing of Israel in it were acts of divine grace, not events of national accomplishment. It was God's arm that brought victory,[6] not the sword and arm of the Israelites.

You loved them. The reason God acted in behalf of the Israelite ancestors is encapsulated in this brief phrase. The scriptural basis for this conclu-

---

3. Cf. Deut. 6:6–7, 20–23; 11:18–21.

4. See the formative essay by Gerhard von Rad, "The Form-Critical Problem of the Hexateuch," in *The Problem of the Hexateuch and Other Essays* (London: SCM, 1984), 1–78.

5. This rehearsal took a variety of forms but generally included deliverance from Egypt and the gift of the land of Canaan. In some cases the account begins with the call of Abraham (cf. Josh. 24:2–13; Ps. 105); in others it extends to the monarchy and perhaps even the Exile (Ps. 107).

6. Cf. Josh. 23:9; 24:12–13.

sion is provided in Deuteronomy (e.g., Deut. 4:37–38; 7:7–8; 9:4–6), where Israel is told that Yahweh has chosen them freely, not because of their greatness or righteousness but because he *loved* them and had a promise to keep.

Our psalm shifts the ground a bit by moving away from the "love" terminology of Deuteronomy (with the root *ʾhb*) to speak instead of God's being favorable to his people (using the root *rṣh* ["be pleased with, accept favorably"]). The distinction is subtle but significant. The Deuteronomy accounts understand God's actions in Israel's behalf as entirely unmerited favor, the result of Yahweh's love for Israel and his free choice to bless her. The choice of terms in Psalm 44 at least admits the possibility that God's choice of Israel was founded in his pleasure with her—a conclusion that can lead to misunderstanding and disappointment.

Contemporary Appropriation of Tradition (44:4–8)

THIS SECTION DEPICTS the community of faith doing what Psalms 42–43 has recommended. Faced with a contemporary context of suffering, the people *remember* past evidence of Yahweh's good intent and powerful action in behalf of their ancestors and in these verses seek to follow the advice of the repeated refrain of Psalms 42–43: "Put your hope in God, for [we] will yet praise him, [our] Savior and [our] God." Having reviewed the ancestral traditions, the community now adopts and professes those traditions as their own.

You are my King and my God. Contemporary Israel reaffirms in the present the ancient commitment of the ancestors to Yahweh alone. The single voice that speaks at this point may well be the king who, by naming God, acknowledges that any human efforts at rulership and control must submit to the ultimate sovereignty of God. The singular voice reappears again and again in what follows (cf. vv. 6, 15–16) so that the king is pictured as leading the people in recognizing the absolute dependence of human kingship on the gracious mercy of God.

Who decrees victories. The king (44:4) and then the people (44:5) acknowledge that God is the source of any victories over their foes.[7] This draws, of course, on the preceding description of the conquest of Canaan, which testified that God was the one who actively drove the inhabitants out before the armies of Israel. When the king declares that neither his bow nor

7. The Heb. term here translated "victory(ies)" is (along with its verbal cognate *yšʿ*) more usually rendered "salvation" or "deliverance." For example, the repeated refrain of Pss. 42–43 employs the same word to describe God as "Savior" (42:5, 11; 43:5). In some more military context (as in Ps. 44), victory seems an appropriate rendering, although "deliverance, salvation" are often used with good effect and equal sense in other translations—e.g., the rendering of 44:4b as "who ordains Jacob's rescue" (Kraus, *Psalms 1–59*, 443).

his sword (44:6) are adequate guarantees of victory without God's presence, he is appropriating the core theological expression of the earlier conquest: "Be strong and courageous. Do not be terrified; do not be discouraged, for the LORD your God will be with you wherever you go" (Josh. 1:9). In Psalm 44:8, both people and king affirm in their praise that God is the one deserving credit for any victory they experience.

Description of Present Suffering (44:9–16)

THE WORD *ʾap* ("also, yet"), with which verse 9 begins, introduces a radical shift in the tone and content of the psalm. It must in the context be translated as a strong "but now," marking extreme contrast with what has preceded. In verses 1–8 all had been confidence and assurance. As Israel's ancestors had experienced God's powerful support in battle with their enemies, so the present community of faith could anticipate his engagement in their behalf. The song of anticipated victory was already floating on their lips.

But now. Israel's experience did not live up to her expectation. Victory eluded them, and the reality of defeat took its place. Community and king alike felt rejected by God and humiliated by his obvious absence. While it is not possible to offer certainty regarding the setting for this lament (some suggest a preexilic defeat by Israel's enemies while others opt for a late Maccabean date),[8] the description suggests severe destruction, societal dislocation, and even deportation (44:11). Regardless of its origin, the psalm would have resonated with the ongoing circumstance of the Diaspora community. In particular, the phrase "scattered ... among the nations [peoples]" is used throughout the Old Testament to refer to the dispersion as a result of the Exile.

With harsh and pointed language, the psalmist leaves no doubt that the cause of Israel's suffering and disgrace is God himself. The emphatic litany of "You!" with which each verse (and some half-verses) begins in 44:9–14 is the result of a whole series of second-person singular verbal forms in the Hebrew text, all directed to God. God has rejected and humbled his people. He has caused them to retreat and be plundered. God gave them up and scattered them. He sold them for no personal profit and made them a reproach and a byword among the nations.

This is a strong view of God—just as strong, in fact, as the view expressed in the opening historic recollection. Israel's troubles are not the result of a weak God unable to cope with the superior threats of the enemy. God is entirely *able* to deliver and save his people. That is why the suffering that the believing community experiences creates such a dilemma. The problem is not a lack of

8. For a variety of options for dating, see Kraus, *Psalms 1–59*, 445–446; Craigie, *Psalms 1–50*, 332–33.

power, but why God has failed to act. As a result of this way of thinking, God is seen as the active force behind all the woe that has come upon his people.

You have made us a reproach. The embarrassing words of shame and disgrace pile up in the last verses of this segment like a cairn of stones intended to mark the scene of some scandalous infamy or like the piles of flowers left at the scene of a tragic and shattering death. Israel's neighbors, the surrounding nations and peoples, look on in amused glee at her misfortune. Reproach, scorn, derision, byword, shaking of the head—the words gather in heaps to mark the shame of God's people. Thus, it is entirely appropriate that the singular voice of the king breaks out in verse 15, lamenting the disgrace that is too much to bear. As the public and military representative of the nation, he must bear the brunt of ridicule that attends defeat.

Those who reproach and revile me. It seems likely that some of the king's reproach comes from his countrymen, who blame failure on his weak and ineffective military leadership. These reproach the king "because of the enemy" (44:16), to whose vengeful attacks they feel especially vulnerable. The enemy seeking revenge may be one of the major powers of Mesopotamia who historically ended the northern and southern monarchies of Israel. Assyria and Babylon were both harsh in their treatment of conquered peoples, as the Assyrians' practice of impaling captives alive and the deportation of defeated peoples from their homelands by both these nations demonstrate. But there is also ample evidence in the Old Testament how the lesser powers surrounding Israel took opportunity at the defeats administered by the Mesopotamian powers to take revenge on their former overlords. Psalm 137's castigation of Edom for their part in the destruction of Jerusalem (137:7) provides a good illustration of this.

Protestation of Innocence (44:17–22)

ALL THIS HAPPENED **to us.** The real reason for the community's dismay now becomes apparent. The narratives of Joshua and Judges, to which the opening verses of this psalm allude, describe the structural cycle of apostasy, defeat by enemies as divine punishment, repentance, and deliverance by divinely appointed leaders that characterized Israel's early life in the land. The accounts of Samuel and Kings show that the monarchical period was no different, with kings being evaluated as evil or good according to their adherence to the Deuteronomistic criteria of avoidance of idols and reverence for the one true temple in Jerusalem.

If anything, the opening verses of Psalm 44 downplay the ongoing struggle Israel experienced between her frequent episodes of disloyalty to Yahweh and the resultant oppression by foreign powers. Consequently, the picture of the Conquest is somewhat idealized. The theme of the Deuteronomistic History recounted in Joshua through 2 Kings is that the Exile was divine punishment for Israel's failure to maintain absolute loyalty to Yahweh alone as demanded by her covenant with him. That understanding permeates the whole Old Testament narrative from Pentateuch through Prophets and Writings, including many of the psalms (see esp. Ps. 106).

The new departure in this segment is not that Israel suffers defeat and exile. It is not even that the Exile is attributed to God. The Deuteronomistic History and viewpoint had already driven both those points home forcefully. Where Psalm 44 departs is in the community's earnest protestation of innocence of any guilt that might justify the punishment meted out in the Exile.

We had not forgotten you or been false to your covenant. The accusations leveled at Israel elsewhere in the Old Testament are here flatly rejected. Like Job, the lamenting people deny any disloyalty to God or breech of his covenant. Not only have they remained externally observant ("our feet had not strayed from [God's] path"), but they were inwardly faithful as well ("our hearts had not turned back"). This is no pretension of absolute sinlessness but honest affirmation of their commitment to covenant relationship with God and their ongoing intention to remain faithful. In their understanding of the covenant they had fulfilled their obligations and were entitled to be declared "righteous."

But you crushed us. They had remained faithful to God, but now he seems to be dealing faithlessly with them. They are left in desperate straits by what they can only construe to be the action (or restraint) of their God. The terms used to describe their plight are harsh and extreme: "crushed," "a haunt for jackals [a depopulated area, hostile to all civilized human life]," "covered . . . over with deep darkness [*ṣalmawet* ('shadow of [as dark as] death')]."[9] The radical nature of the threat highlights the discontinuity Israel feels regarding her faithfulness to covenant demands.

If we had forgotten. Israel's consternation is not the result of any naive assumption of unconditional divine support for the nation. She understands clearly and well that breech of covenant obligations would deserve such rejection and suffering as she now experienced at the hand of God. But

9. *Ṣalmawet* esp. connotes desperate, threatening circumstances. The most familiar appearance of the term is Ps. 23:4, where it is traditionally translated "[valley of] the shadow of death." The term appears in Ps. 107:10, 14; Isa. 9:2; Jer 2:6; Amos 5:8 as a description of extreme threat to life. Two appearances in Job (Job 3:5; 10:21) speak of the "land of darkness and *ṣalmawet*" in ways that approximate Sheol, the Hebrew abode of the dead. Thus, to be covered with "deep darkness," as in our passage, is to experience the ultimate threat of death.

search as she might, Israel is unable to discover in herself any faithlessness commensurate with the punishment received. She has *not* "forgotten the name of [her] God."

Once again we return to the theme of remembrance and forgetting that was so central to Psalms 42–43. Although the typical reticence of the Elohistic Psalter avoids the direct use of the divine name Yahweh at this point, the community of believers confesses her loyalty to "the name" of the covenant deity. Her memory (and active obedience), however, is met in her estimation with divine forgetfulness (44:24) and rejection (44:9), even though she has scrupulously avoided the cardinal sin of worshiping any god other than Yahweh (44:20).

Would not God have discovered it? Refusing to rely on her own protestation of innocence alone, the community calls on the covenant God to bear witness himself. It is impossible to hoodwink God, they declare. Their innocence or guilt is open to divine scrutiny, and they are confident he will admit their innocence. This Job-like subpoena for God to enter the witness box affirms the credibility of their case. Who would rely on falsehood before the God who knows even the inner thoughts and motives (44:21) of humans?

For your sake we face death all day long. Here lies the key affirmation and understanding of the psalm, subtly but powerfully expressed. Without this anguished acknowledgment, we would be tempted to spend our time criticizing the lack of self-awareness that stands behind the community's naive and misguided attempt to claim innocence. We would like to prove them guilty so as not to have to accept as our own their recognition that to be the chosen people of God entails undeserved suffering. That is at the core of what Israel is saying in verse 22. We are innocent, faithful to you alone, and yet we are becoming martyrs *for your sake*.

> Here too experiences of the individual laments have been adopted: the [righteous] must suffer much (Ps. 34:19)—it is an essential mark of his existence that (without mention of guilt) enmities and torments assail him (cf. Ps. 22). This interpretation ties the uniqueness of election to the mystery of the suffering of the righteous.[10]

Plea for Deliverance (44:23–26)

WITH TYPICAL LANGUAGE intended to rouse the hearer to action, the beleaguered community makes its desire for deliverance known. They want God to bring this period of extended rejection to an end (44:23; cf. 44:9). They

10. Kraus, *Psalms 1–59*, 448.

want his forgetfulness, which led to their current misery, replaced by active memory (44:24).

Our bodies cling to the ground. One last description of the people's personal desperation punctuates this concluding plea. Defeated Israel is forced prostrate in the dust by her conquering enemies. Using terms reminiscent of the creation narrative in Genesis (Gen. 2:24), the psalm describes the bellies of the prostrate Israelites "clinging" (*dbq*) so closely to the ground as to become united with it—perhaps an oblique reference to returning to the dust in death (cf. Gen. 3:19; Job 34:15; Ps. 104:29).

The psalm concludes with a final entreaty for God to "rise up" and redeem his suffering people (44:26). In the end, confident of her own innocence in covenant obligations, Israel calls on God to respond with the sort of "unfailing love" (*ḥesed*) that characterizes his commitment to covenant relationship with his people. While willing to accept the mystery of righteous suffering, they are not without hope that God will ultimately set things right. This hope betrays a conviction that God's final purpose is a restored creation environment in which righteousness begets blessing and not cursing. Resigned to the "real world" where all is not as it should be (44:22), Israel still hopes for an earlier experience of this renewed kingdom of God in which she can participate in the reconciliation of all things.

THE SUFFERING OF THE FAITHFUL. Psalm 44 raises a difficult and often troubling question: "What place does suffering have in the life of the faithful?" The Old Testament provides sufficient data to suggest that, at least at one significant level, Israel believed that the faithful ought not to suffer. One tributary of this idea can be traced to the wisdom tradition that Israel shared with the broader ancient Near East. This rather international wisdom viewpoint held to a particular philosophy of life with a series of interlocking beliefs or principles: (1) The world as created by God is characterized by a divinely instituted order; (2) it is possible for humans to perceive and understand this order through observing life and accumulating experience; (3) the wise (those who choose to live in accord with this order) are blessed and prosper in life while the foolish (those who choose to live contrary to this order) are cursed and perish. This last principle is known as "retribution"—the crop one harvests depends on the kind of seeds one plants.

A second contributor to the common attitude that the faithful ought not to suffer derives from the more distinctly religious sphere of Israelite life. In this view, it is the covenant relationship between Israel and Yahweh that determines the experience of blessing or cursing in the life of the community. According to the formulation of this viewpoint in Deuteronomy, the primary obligations laid on Israel by the covenant were: (1) to maintain absolute loyalty to Yahweh alone, avoiding entanglements with any other deities, and (2) to obey the commands of the Torah that instructed Israel how to fulfill her covenantal role as the "holy nation" of Yahweh. As a result of this covenant commitment, the righteous community (when Israel kept these commandments) received blessing and prosperity, while disobedient (or wicked) Israel could anticipate cursing, oppression by foreign powers, and ultimate perishing.[11]

These two ways of thinking, while originally distinct, intersected with one another in a variety of ways and over time joined to form a common belief system in which wisdom and Torah are identified, while the wise and foolish become synonymous with the righteous and the wicked. The combined form of worldview still believed that the righteous (wise) prospered while the wicked (fools) perished. The beauty of the system is its apparent simplicity: Follow the leading of wisdom, keep the commandments, and blessing and benefit will result. However, it became increasingly clear to some observers that life did not always turn out that way.

The biblical wisdom literature contains within itself evidence of a thoroughgoing critique regarding the viability of this simple viewpoint with its confident reliance on the working of retribution. While we cannot be certain about all the factors involved in precipitating this discussion, we can suggest at least two that must have played an important role: the suffering of the righteous, and the collapse of the monarchy and the loss of national identity in the Exile.

(1) As far as individual suffering was concerned, many cases could be readily explained as the result of personal folly or sinfulness. Even as late as the time of Jesus sickness, mental disorder, and other forms of physical suffering were often attributed to sinfulness (see John 9:2).

The book of Job, however, pointedly disputes whether all examples of suffering can be traced to individual sinfulness. Although Job's friends repeatedly attempted to convince him to confess some hidden sin, to accept the possibility of inadvertent sin unknown to himself, or even to acknowledge his suffering as divine discipline to bend him to God's purpose, Job maintained his innocence. And the reader knows what the friends could not have known, that in the opening dialogue between Satan and God, Job had already been declared righteous by none other than God himself. Job's suffering then must be explained in some other way.

---

11. See the explicit laying out of blessing for obedience and cursing for disobedience in Deut. 28.

But Job is not ultimately a book about the reason for the suffering of the righteous. The *fact* of such suffering is assumed and used to highlight a deeper question that underlies the book: "Is a God who allows the righteous to suffer worthy of continued loyalty and worship?" The final chapters of the book answer that question with a resounding "Yes!" while allowing the "why" of righteous suffering to remain as a divine mystery exceeding the bounds of human resolution.

As a consequence of the growing realization that the righteous can also suffer regardless of their righteousness, biblical wisdom had to conclude that since suffering does not negate the reality of the blessing of remaining faithful to God, the blessing of wisdom and righteousness must be understood in ways that transcend the traditional anticipation of a pleasant, honorable, and prosperous life.

> Better a little with the fear of the LORD
> than great wealth with turmoil. (Prov. 15:16)
>
> Better a little with righteousness
> than much gain with injustice. (Prov. 16:8)
>
> How much better to get wisdom than gold,
> to choose understanding rather than silver! (Prov. 16:16).
>
> Better to be lowly in spirit and among the oppressed
> than to share plunder with the proud. (Prov. 16:19)
>
> Better a poor man whose walk is blameless
> than a rich man whose ways are perverse. (Prov. 28:6)

(2) The communal suffering of Israel in exile occasioned another attack on the traditional view of retribution. The primary response came in the reinterpretation of Israelite history by what has come to be known as the Deuteronomic History. This history, stretching from Joshua through 2 Kings, understands the crux of the Exile to be Israel's failure as a community of faith to fulfill her covenant obligations of loyalty to Yahweh and obedience to the Torah. As a result, the exilic destruction and dispersion is understood as the deserved fulfillment of the curses of Deuteronomy 28:15–68 poured out on a wicked and rebellious nation.

This viewpoint permeates the prophets, who condemn the nation for its faithlessness and pronounce the coming judgment of the Exile as just and deserved. In the exilic period itself, voices like Ezra (Ezra 9:5–15), Nehemiah (Neh. 1:5–11), and Daniel (Dan. 9:4–19) acknowledge that Israel's sin stands behind the Exile and recognize that the way back to restored fellowship with Yahweh comes only through repentance, confession, and renewed obedience to the Torah. A number of the psalms reflect a similar evaluation of the exilic experience and hope for restoration (cf. Pss. 106:40–47; 130:8).

In the present psalm, however, we encounter a very different evaluation of the experience of military defeat and exile in the community. The community of faith believes that victory over their enemies can only be accomplished by the power of God working with them. They believe from past history and experience that God is *perfectly able* to deliver—then or now. While it is clear that the lamenting community understands the suffering they are undergoing to have been brought on them by the rejection of God, nowhere do they acknowledge any failing of covenant responsibility. "We had not forgotten you or been false to your covenant!" they cry (44:17). The fact that they now experience defeat and exile rather than victory can only mean, therefore, that God for some inscrutable reason of his own has given them up into the power of their enemies.

It is in this context of feeling abandoned and rejected by God for no apparent reason or fault of their own that the community of faith makes an amazing step of understanding—not *complete* understanding, mind you, but understanding that shapes their will to commit themselves in a new and painful way: "Yet for your sake we face death all day long" (44:22). The "yet" that begins this statement gives the whole a similar flavor to Job's reply to his friends: "Though he slay me, *yet* will I hope in him; I will surely defend my ways to his face" (Job 13:15). Regardless of the pain that attends their faith, the community remains committed to Yahweh, and this commitment was "for your sake"—that is, because of their firm commitment to God rather than their own benefit. According to James L. Mays,

> "For your sake" meant they could see no other meaning and purpose in their confession and trust than that they were accounted as sheep for slaughter. But that minimal and doleful interpretation of their suffering opens on the prospect of an understanding of suffering as a service to the kingdom of God. The prospect leads to the suffering servant of Isa. 53, to Jewish martyrs, and to the cross of Calvary. The apostle Paul will later quote verse 22 to a persecuted congregation of early Christians (Rom. 8:36) to persuade them to understand their suffering in the light of the death and resurrection of Jesus Christ.[12]

12. Mays, *Psalms*, 179–80.

TOO OFTEN OUR first reaction to Psalm 44 is to dismiss the protestation of innocence as a rather deceitful manipulation of God by a people in a state of deep denial. After all, we say, "all have sinned and fall short of the glory of God" (Rom. 3:23). But before we simply reject the community's claim of innocence out of hand, we need to consider several obviating factors.

(1) As mentioned above, the community's protest is no claim of complete sinlessness but a claim to have fulfilled their essential obligations to the covenant. Even the covenant code itself understood that individual sin and corporate guilt would occur and thus offered appropriate methods of restitution. The sacrificial system provided for the whole-burnt offering as a means of atoning for sin, whether individual or corporate. Indeed, the yearly offering on the Day of Atonement assumed that the sins of the nation could be removed by sincere repentance and renewed commitment accompanied by the prescribed sacrificial ritual.

We might not understand or be completely comfortable with this sacrificial method of removing ongoing sin, but most of us would have to admit that accepting the sacrificial death of Christ as Savior has not yet perfectly removed all our tendencies toward selfishness, anger, lust, greed, and other more subtle forms of sin. I am grateful to know that my moments of weakness and failure, while serious in their own right and in need of repentance and confession, do not drive an irreparable wedge between myself and God. I am glad that my commitment to Christ (and his to me) can begin here and now where I imperfectly stand and proceed with God's grace and the strengthening of his Spirit to refine me to become more like my Lord and Savior.

(2) The speakers do not stand alone in their claims. Most notably Job also claims to suffer without justification. While his friends try valiantly to dissuade him from what they perceive to be false claims, the book in no way undermines his essential uprightness of character—a righteousness confirmed by God himself in the opening dialogue with Satan and reconfirmed by God's concluding evaluation that the friends "have not spoken of me what is right, as my servant Job has" (Job 42:7). Moreover, other psalms find it possible to make similar claims of innocent suffering (see esp. Pss. 7:3–9; 18:20–24; 26:1–12, where some equally extreme claims of personal innocence before God are offered).[13] These powerful protestations of innocence are strongly stated and may give us the impression of manipulative distortion and

13. Cf. also the royal promises in Ps. 101.

willful self-denial. We should exercise caution, however, in dismissing these claims so lightly.

One main reason to avoid simply categorizing these claims of innocence as deceitful or misguided is the recognition that a decisive shift has taken place in the interpretation of the psalms when they were included as part of holy Scripture. What were originally human psalms composed by individuals to express human thoughts and emotions directed to God have, by the process of preservation, selection, transmission, and arrangement in the canonical book of Psalms, been transformed into the Word of God *to us*. In these words we hear God speaking to us, and we must learn to listen attentively to get that message rightly. If we dismiss these psalms too lightly as the product of sinful humans that we ought simply to ignore, we may find ourselves picking and choosing which bits of Scripture we will pay attention to. Then we run the danger of missing the hard truth that is spoken to us in psalms like this one.[14]

(3) As a final consideration, we have our own contemporary experience as proof that the innocent suffer through no fault of their own. The Nazi Holocaust, in which six and a half million Jews and millions of others lost their lives for no other reason than that they had the wrong ethnic background, is the most commonly cited example. But we have only to look at the "Killing Fields" of Southeast Asia, the civil-war-induced famines in Africa, the abuse of African Americans, native Americans, and other racial groups in our own heritage, and the persecution of Christians and other religious groups at the hands of totalitarian regimes around the world to know that "innocence," however defined, is no shield against persecution, abuse, or injustice.

Our own personal experience may illumine less pervasive examples of undeserved suffering and persecution. A Christian professor I know taught for seven years at a major secular research university. During that time he published as expected, received consistently positive evaluations, and seemed on track to receive tenure. About a year and a half before he could enter the

---

14. This is unfortunately the path most often chosen by responsive readings included in hymnals. The psalms are regularly used in this reading because of their obvious affinity to liturgical recitation in worship. But most commonly, the psalms are presented in a cut-and-paste format, with the positive sections foregrounded and most harsh, vengeful, and negative elements excised and removed. How often, for example, have you heard Ps. 137 read with the "baby smashing" passage left intact? This smacks of something far less than hearing the "full counsel of God." Perhaps we simply have not suffered often and deeply enough to really understand what God is saying through these difficult portions. There is a degree of needed honesty involved in praying through the psalms from beginning to end—"warts and all," as the *Rule of Saint Benedict* suggests.

tenure process, it became clear that his colleagues were not comfortable with his evangelical stance, and his evaluations began to reflect unanticipated questions about his suitability for the position. At last, the year before he would have entered the tenure process, he was informed by his department chair that his contract would not be renewed for the coming year, thus avoiding any requirement to provide written justification or adequate documentation for the termination.

This professor chose to see this series of events as an opportunity to move on to a new phase of ministry in his life. But for a long time it left a bitter taste of injustice, and the question "Why?" surfaced often. This was no personal holocaust, but it was a painful experience of rejection and suffering, with many negative consequences for himself, his wife, and his children. Many of you perhaps have similar experiences of rejection, harassment, oppression, or abuse that you can insert in place of this one. So the sentiments of this psalm are not so alien to us as they might first seem. Although as Christians we have often been well-schooled by a particularly strong sense of humility to accept almost any type of suffering as "deserved," I think most of us would have to admit there are times we would like to cry out with Psalm 44: "All this happened to us, though we had not forgotten you or been false to your covenant."

Once we admit that the innocent *can* suffer and acknowledge that there are times when we *do* understand the pain in our life to be undeserved, we are ready to learn the central lesson of Psalm 44. The lamenting community does not merely acknowledge its innocent suffering and resign itself to it as the result of the mysterious purpose of God. Instead, they give meaning to their suffering by recognizing it is not simply unexplained injustice that must be borne and survived; rather, it is part of what it means to be like God, to "share in the sufferings of Christ," so to speak; their suffering was "for [God's] sake."

As Mays reminded us earlier, the suffering of the innocent has a long heritage that goes back to the suffering servant of Isaiah 53, who, though innocent, suffered and died for the sins of his people.[15] Others, such as Daniel and his friends, were falsely accused and suffered because of their loyalty to Yahweh. Hebrews 11:35b–38 describes the faithful who were persecuted, tortured, and killed for their faith.

This kind of understanding of suffering—that the suffering of innocent Christians for their faith is part of what it means to be godlike[16]—puts flesh

15. In actuality there are four "Servant Songs" in Isaiah (Isa. 42:1–4; 49:1–6; 50:4–11; 52:13–53:12) that describe the suffering of the "servant of the LORD."

16. Cf. Rom. 8:17; 1 Peter 4:12–15.

on the bones of several difficult statements in the Gospels. In response to the inquiry of the disciples regarding who had sinned in the case of the man born blind, Jesus replied, "Neither this man nor his parents sinned . . . but this happened so that the work of God might be displayed in his life" (John 9:3). The man's blindness was not the consequence of punishment for sin, nor was it the meaningless result of happenstance. The man's lifelong suffering was given new significance by understanding it as an opportunity for "the work of God [to] be displayed in his life."

In a similar but slightly different response to the approaching death of his friend Lazarus, Jesus proclaimed, "This sickness will not end in death. No, it is for God's glory so that God's Son may be glorified through it" (John 11:4). Lazarus did die (though the episode did not end in death), and the suffering of his family was acute. But this painful loss, far from being pointless, was a significant opportunity for the glory of God and his Son to be made manifest.

It is interesting that in both New Testament accounts just mentioned, the same Greek grammatical construction[17] describes the future glorification of God in these events. This construction regularly indicates an unrealized contingency or possibility. The implication is that these events of suffering offered *opportunities* for the "work of God" to be demonstrated or the "Son of God" to be glorified through them. The result is a future potential and not a sure thing. It would have been possible for the sufferers and those around them to see only meaningless suffering and pain.

The same potential exists in our moments of innocent suffering. We may be tempted to vent our rage, seek revenge, or play the victim—and this psalm certainly encourages us to speak our pain and confusion honestly and bluntly to God, holding nothing back. But verse 22 offers us the opportunity to transform our meaningless pain into an opportunity to glorify God. How we choose to respond to undeserved pain is a "kingdom moment," a moment to reflect values that are not of this world but come only by the power and strength of God.

I am reminded in this context of the rather curious admonition in the Sermon on the Mount. There, in the midst of the account in Matthew 6, Jesus warns his listeners to get their life priorities straight. "Therefore I tell you, do not worry about your life, what you will eat or drink; or about your body, what you will wear. Is not life more important than food, and the body more important than clothes?" (6:25). Now, Jesus is not talking about excess or abundant possessions. He is not encouraging us to cut back and live a simple life. He is talking about *basic necessities of life*—food and clothing. Yet he

17. The construction is a Greek purpose/result clause, using *hina* plus aorist subjunctive.

says we ought not be anxious if we have nothing to eat or to wear. That is pretty radical and extreme, if you ask me![18]

Following the interpretation of these statements in Matthew to its extreme conclusion provides encouragement to those who are forced to choose between the kingdom of God and life in this world: a choice modeled by those martyrs—Jewish and Christian, ancient and modern—who have chosen the way of suffering and death rather than recanting their faith or accommodating their belief to the demands of physical necessity. There are times when dying is more important than all that physical life has to offer. There are times when one must lose his or her life in order to find it. I am thankful that Jesus believed this radical truth and acted on his belief.

---

18. Matthew 6 goes on to encourage its readers to trust in God and rest in the assurance that he knows their needs and will provide for them. The subtle radicality of the statement in 6:25, however, plants seeds that will ripen into a crop that can sustain those who are faced with decisions even more agonizing and far-reaching than those posed in Matthew 6. At its core, this statement says something like: "Isn't there more to life than eating? Isn't there more to the body than clothing?" I want to cry out, "No! I can't live without eating. I can't survive without protecting clothing." Followed to its logical (and I would suggest intended) conclusion, this statement tells me that there are some things worth going naked and starving for.

Psalm 45

FOR THE DIRECTOR of music. To the tune of "Lilies." Of the Sons of Korah. A *maskil.* A wedding song.

1 My heart is stirred by a noble theme
as I recite my verses for the king;
my tongue is the pen of a skillful writer.

2 You are the most excellent of men
and your lips have been anointed with grace,
since God has blessed you forever.
3 Gird your sword upon your side, O mighty one;
clothe yourself with splendor and majesty.
4 In your majesty ride forth victoriously
in behalf of truth, humility and righteousness;
let your right hand display awesome deeds.
5 Let your sharp arrows pierce the hearts of the king's enemies;
let the nations fall beneath your feet.

6 Your throne, O God, will last for ever and ever;
a scepter of justice will be the scepter of your kingdom.
7 You love righteousness and hate wickedness;
therefore God, your God, has set you above your companions
by anointing you with the oil of joy.
8 All your robes are fragrant with myrrh and aloes and cassia;
from palaces adorned with ivory
the music of the strings makes you glad.
9 Daughters of kings are among your honored women;
at your right hand is the royal bride in gold of Ophir.

10 Listen, O daughter, consider and give ear:
Forget your people and your father's house.
11 The king is enthralled by your beauty;
honor him, for he is your lord.
12 The Daughter of Tyre will come with a gift,
men of wealth will seek your favor.

[13] All glorious is the princess within her chamber;
her gown is interwoven with gold.
[14] In embroidered garments she is led to the king;
her virgin companions follow her
and are brought to you.
[15] They are led in with joy and gladness;
they enter the palace of the king.

[16] Your sons will take the place of your fathers;
you will make them princes throughout the land.
[17] I will perpetuate your memory through all generations;
therefore the nations will praise you for ever and ever.

ONE OF THE more unusual psalms in the Psalter, Psalm 45 is a hymn in praise, not of God, but of the Israelite king. As the heading of this royal psalm[1] indicates, the composition seems to have a royal wedding in mind. The psalm praises the "royal bride" as well as the king and concludes with hopes for the continued dynastic succession of Davidic kings (45:16–17).

A curious mention of God in the midst of the psalm (45:6) raises some question as to how this composition was interpreted in the postmonarchical period, when the dynastic hopes of the Davidic line had come to an end. The continued inclusion of such a specifically royal psalm in a postexilic Psalter must have become a mysterious anachronism unless new ways of interpreting it had developed. One possible way forward was to understand the wedding as that between God as groom and Israel as his bride. The messianic overtones of such a passage embodied Israel's continuing hopes for a Davidic descendant who would usher in the eternal kingdom of God.

Structurally the psalm falls into four sections: a self-aware introduction in which the psalmist describes the scribal task (45:1), praise of the king as groom in second-person direct address (45:2–9), praise of the royal bride in which reference to the king becomes third-person description (45:10–15), and a concluding hope for continuing dynastic succession through sons and the psalmist's promise to perpetuate the king's memory (45:16–17).

---

1. See the section on "Types of Psalms" in the introduction. For a discussion of the interpretation of royal psalms, see the Bridging Contexts section of the commentary on Ps. 20.

The Heading (45:0)

THE PSALM SHARES in its heading three terms with the preceding Psalms 42–43 and 44. All are introduced with a reference to "the director of music,"[2] all are designated as part of the first Korahite collection[3] (Pss. 42–49), and all are called *maśkil*.[4] In addition, the heading to Psalm 45 exhibits several uncommon phrases. The first (*ʿal šošannim*) appears to be a reference to the tune to which the composition is to be sung.[5] The word *šošannim* (appearing for the first time here but also occurring in the heading to Ps. 80) is the plural of the singular noun *šušan* ("lily, lotus blossom"), which appears in the heading to Ps. 60. The final new phrase is the combination of *šir* ("song")[6] and *yedidot* ("beloved [ones]; love") and seems to describe the focus of the psalm's content in praise of the royal wedding (thus the NIV's "A wedding song").

The Introduction (45:1)

THE PSALM OPENS with the psalmist's declared purpose to write verses "for" (or perhaps "about" or "concerning") the king. His heart has been "stirred" by a "good word/thing"—perhaps an indication of a poet's sense of being inspired to write pleasing poetry.[7] He pictures a moment of recitation of the finished work before the king. The idea of poetic inspiration is carried on into the description of his "tongue" as "the pen of a skillful writer." This phrase brings together the written and oral elements of poetry in the ancient world. While poems may have been composed with pen, they were created for public vocal performance. Perhaps the king is the poet's patron, who has commissioned this poem for his wedding day.

In Praise of the King (45:2–9)

THE PSALMIST'S INSPIRED "good word" begins with an extended section both praising the king and encouraging him to exercise his majestic power and splendor in the service of "truth, humility and righteousness" (45:4). The anticipated result of this display of kingly power is the defeat of his enemies (45:5) and the establishment of an eternal kingdom of justice and peace

---

2. See comments on the heading of Ps. 4 for further discussion of this term.
3. See comments on the heading of Ps. 42.
4. See comments on the heading of Ps. 32.
5. See the discussion on "The Psalm Headings" in the introduction.
6. See comments to the heading of Ps. 30, where this term first occurs. This is the second occurrence of *šir* in the Psalter; the headings of Pss. 46 and 48 also contain the word.
7. The NIV's "noble theme" is perhaps overly interpretive.

(45:6). The major portion of the description is bound at beginning and end by verses that proclaim the king's excellence over other humans (45:2, 7). His elevated character is related to a special divine "anointing" (45:2, 7)[8] and "blessing" (45:2).[9] In a dry and dusty land such as Israel, the pouring of oil on the lips and fragrant oil on the head would be means of attending to the needs and pleasures of an honored guest.[10] Here the king's lips have "grace" poured out upon them—probably an artful reference to a gifted ability for graceful speech.[11]

The most excellent of men. The king is praised as "most excellent" of the *bene ʾadam* ("human beings"; lit., "sons of man").[12] The basis of his exceptional excellence is not character or deeds but "beauty" of physical appearance, as the Hebrew verb *yph* indicates.

Gird your sword upon your side. The call to militant action against the king's enemies that begins here and continues to its resolution in 45:6 is at first glance directed to the king, who is expected to conquer. This is indeed the understanding of most commentators and may well be the correct one. One feature of these four verses, however, raises the question whether in fact *God* might be the one called to action here. In a literal reading of verse 6, it is explicitly God's throne that is established and his kingdom over which a "scepter of justice" will rule. God is referred to in this verse with the same second-person singular pronouns "you" as appear in the preceding verses 3–5. The language in those verses is similar to that applied elsewhere to God in his militant role of protector of his people and of his covenant.

Thus, while it is clear in 45:2 that God blesses the king and in 45:7 that God sets the king above his companions, the situation is much less clear in

---

8. The use of the translation "anointing" in both these cases hides the fact that different Heb. words are used. The first anointing—of the king's lips—in 45:2 translates the Hebrew *huṣaq* (from *yṣq* ["be poured out; be emptied out"]). The second anointing—with the "oil of joy"—in 45:7 translates the more traditional verb of anointing *mešaḥaka* (from *mšḥ* ["anoint"]). The verb *yṣq* is used for pouring out oil as a ritual act or libation (Gen. 28:18) or for pouring out oil on the head of a priest for consecration (Lev. 21:10), but it can also describe the "pouring out" of molten metal for casting (1 Kings 7:23, 24, 33).

9. The idea of eternal blessing for the king has surfaced previously in Ps. 21:6, where the phrase *berakot laʿad* ("eternal blessings") is used rather than *berakka ʾelohim leʿolam* ("God has blessed you forever"), as here.

10. Cf. Ps. 23:5; Eccl. 9:8; and the anointing of Jesus referred to in Luke 7:46.

11. See also Ps. 41:8, where the Heb. can be translated "a vile word pours forth from/on him," rather than the NIV's "a vile disease has beset him."

12. See the discussion of the term *bene ʾadam* in the comments on Ps. 4:1–2. The phrase *bene ʾadam* occurs twenty-one times in the Psalter. That the phrase appears in 21:10 is another link between that psalm and Ps. 45. The singular phrase *ben ʾadam* occurs only three times in the Psalms (Pss. 8:4; 80:17; 146:3).

the intervening verses. In a strange way, the militant language of royal majesty that would naturally be associated with the human king following verse 2 bleeds over into the kingly power of God to defeat the king's enemies. This may well reflect the cultural confusion that often existed in Israel between the acts of the king and the acts of God. Or, alternatively, it may be a later, postexilic shifting of expectations for human rulers to the divine king, Yahweh, in light of the failure of the Davidic monarchy in the Exile. Such elements of ambiguity allow passages like this one to be exploited messianically. Note how 45:6–7 is referred to Jesus in a messianic sense in Hebrews 1:8–9.

Clothe yourself with splendor and majesty. In another link to Psalm 21, the same words used in 21:5 to describe the divinely bestowed gifts of "splendor" (*hod*) and "majesty" (*hadar*) given to the king are used in 45:3 to picture the garments in which the king is to clothe himself as he departs for battle with the enemy. In the former passage, God grants the king "victory" and bestows "splendor and majesty." Here the king is to put on "splendor and majesty" and to "ride forth victoriously."[13]

Truth, humility, and righteousness. The power and majesty of human kingship in Israel was to be harnessed to the purposes of Yahweh. These three goals of the king's militant action against the enemy are not, perhaps, what one might immediately expect in reference to the king's victory. They represent a distinctive shaping of Israel's understanding of what is important—indeed essential—in life before Yahweh. "Truth" (*debar ʾemet*; lit., "word of truth") has more the sense of "enduring reliability, firmness" than simple accuracy.[14] The king's lips have earlier been "anointed with grace" (45:2), and here he is expected to pursue "a word of truth."

"Humility" (*ʿanwah*) is the true knowledge of one's appropriate status before God. When Isaiah comes into the presence of God (Isa. 6:1–9), he prostrates himself as a sinner before holy Yahweh. When Jacob realizes he has been in the presence of God unawares, he consecrates an altar at Bethel (Gen. 28:16–17). This sort of recognition of one's humble stature before God (cf. Ps. 8) is not abject groveling but is akin to the requisite attitude of "fear of the LORD" that describes Israel's understanding of a proper relationship to God. This is not "terror" but a recognition of one's dependence on the gracious mercy of Yahweh. Similarly, humility means recognizing Yahweh's infinitely exalted majesty above all human pretensions to pomp and status.

---

13. The term for victory in 45:3 (from *ṣlḥ* ["be prosperous, successful"]) is different from the noun used in 21:5 (*yešuʿah* ["salvation, victory"]).

14. See also comments on 19:9 for the meaning of this word in the Psalter.

This is an important counterpoint to the previous descriptions of the king's power, splendor, and majesty (45:3).[15]

"Righteousness" (*ṣedeq*), like the previous two terms, describes an important relationship to the exercise of kingship in Israel. A legal term, *ṣedeq* describes the status of having fulfilled all expectations in a particular matter under scrutiny.

These three characteristics—"enduring reliability" (*ʾemet*), "acceptance of one's true status before God" (*ʿanwah*), and "complete performance of one's obligations" (*ṣedeq*)—are important counterbalances to the ancient view of kings and kingship as capricious, prideful, and autocratic in the exercise of power.

Display . . . pierce . . . fall. The psalmist expresses three hopeful wishes for the success of the king's campaign against his enemies. He desires the king's "right hand" to "display awesome deeds."[16] Also, he hopes the king's "sharpened arrows" will find their way into the hearts of his enemies.[17] Finally, "nations" will fall under his feet.[18] It is the psalmist's expectation that these "awesome deeds" will result in the establishment of God's eternal "kingdom."

Your throne, O God. The introduction of the word "God" (*ʾelohim*) into the psalm at this point is rather unexpected. In the string of second-person singular pronominal references beginning at 45:2 and continuing to this point, the human king would seem to be in view. The direct address of God forces us to reflect back on the previous verses and consider whether the militant language in 45:3–5 in fact refers to *God's actions* in behalf of the king. Alternatively, it has be suggested that *ʾelohim* is here an epithet intended to describe the king's status as divinely authorized ruler.[19]

---

15. This is only the second occurrence of *ʿanwah* ("humility") in the Psalter. The first (and only other occurrence of the term in the whole Old Testament) is in 18:35. The closely related term *ʿanawah* (also "humility") appears in Prov. 15:33; 18:12; 22:4; Zeph. 2:3.

16. A difficult phrase with a literal meaning of "your right hand will instruct you (with) awesome works." One would usually expect *others* to be instructed, but here the activity seems to turn back upon the agent.

17. Another difficult passage. As most commentators note, the verse seems to have been disarranged here and must be transposed to make good sense. A verb is apparently missing from the phrase about "sharpened arrows in the hearts of the king's enemies." Perhaps the verb "they will fall" does double duty—here and in the second phrase about "nations will fall under you."

18. The word "feet" does not appear in the Heb. text, which joins the preposition "under" with the second masculine singular pronominal suffix.

19. The recognition of kings as gods was known in the ancient Near East, with examples in Egypt, where the pharaohs were thought to be Horus, and in Mesopotamia, where divine authorization of kingship on occasion bled over into divine kingship. In the "Curse of Agade" (*ANETP*, 2:204–15), the Akkadian king Naram-Sin seems to have taken on the prerogatives of divinity—an act that led to the fall of the Akkadian Empire according to later Sumerian commentators.

You love righteousness. It is clearly the king in 45:7 who loves righteousness and hates wickedness. The rather awkward juxtaposition of "God, your God" is characteristic of the Elohistic Psalter, where the frequent absence of the divine name Yahweh leads to some awkward redundancies (presumably the first *ʾelohim* replaces what at one time was *yhwh*).

With its references to anointing—in this case, with the "oil of joy"[20]—and the exaltation of the king above his "companions," verse 7 serves as a fitting balance to verse 2, where similar concerns began this section. Here the exaltation of the king is linked to his attitude toward righteousness and wickedness: He loves the one and hates the other. Righteousness (*ṣedeq*) and wickedness (*rešaᶜ*) describe contrasting courses of action. Unlike "good" (*ṭob*) and "evil" (*raᶜ*), which refer to abstract concepts, *ṣedeq* and *rešaᶜ* are legal terms that describe proper and improper conduct in a particular case.[21]

Robes ... palaces ... music. Verses 8–9 highlight the rich garments, opulent surroundings, festive music, and prestigious company gathered for the wedding ceremony of the king. Myrrh, aloes, and cassia are all aromatic preparations from resin, wood, and dried flowers respectively. Ivory palaces (i.e., adorned with carved ivory panels)[22] provide a rich setting while stringed instruments (cf. 150:4) play background music.

Daughters of kings. The daughters of kings often played an important political role in the ancient Near East by cementing relationships between nations through marriage. Solomon was known for such arrangements and even married Pharaoh's daughter as part of an alliance with Egypt (1 Kings 3:1; 9:16). The traditional translation "royal bride/queen" (*šegel*) is perhaps more elevated than the root of this word indicates. The verb *šgl* has strong implications of sexual intercourse and was considered so obscene to the Masoretes—who transmitted the text of the Old Testament and provided the system of vowels to fix its meaning—that they regularly substituted the less offensive *škb* ("lie with") as a marginal note (cf. *BHS* at Deut. 28:30; Isa. 13:16).

---

20. "Oil of joy" occurs again only in Isa. 61:3, where it provides a strong contrast to mourning. There those exiles who are grieving in Zion will receive "a crown of beauty instead of ashes, the oil of gladness [joy] instead of mourning, and a garment of praise instead of a spirit of despair." The Hebrew *śaśon* carries the meaning "exulting joy" and is often linked with *śimḥah* ("celebration").

21. See comments on "righteousness" and other related legal terms at 7:6–9.

22. Ivory imported from Africa or India was employed throughout the ancient Near East for ornamentation of buildings (as carved plaques) or furnishings. Solomon had an "ivory throne" decorated with lions and a calf (1 Kings 10:18–20). Ivory components from similar thrones have been uncovered at Samaria and Nimrud. Ahab was reported to have built an "ivory house" (1 Kings 22:39). Because of its expense, ivory was associated with great wealth and royalty. Pictures of carved ivory plaques can be seen in *ISBE*², 2:940–43.

As a result, Holladay suggests the alternate translation "favorite of [the] harem."[23]

Gold of Ophir. The royal bride is adorned with opulence. Gold of Ophir was a rare commodity (Isa. 13:12), imported into Israel by ships that sailed from Ezion Geber, a port at the northern end of the Gulf of Aqabah (1 Kings 9:26–28; 22:48), to a destination variously conjectured to be India, Africa, the Arabian peninsula, or even South America.[24] Gold of Ophir came to be the standard for gold of purity and quality. Most likely the bride's gold ornamentation consisted of rings, bracelets, arm bands, necklaces, earrings, and a crown.

In Praise of the Bride (45:10–15)

THE DIRECT ADDRESS of the psalm now shifts to the bride, who is depicted as a "daughter" forsaking her people and the house of her father to assume her role as wife to the king. Again, if this is a marriage to a foreign princess, then the image is an accurate one of the daughter who lived at far remove from family and national culture as part of a political marriage.

The impending marital relationship depicted in a few words is instructive. The king "craves"[25] the bride's "beauty," while the bride is counseled to "worship" (*ḥwh*) the king because he is her "lord." This rather one-sided relationship is consistent with what is known of the ancient Near East during this period and would be even less remarkable if Holladay's suggestion that *šegel* means "favorite of the harem."[26]

Further encouragement is offered the future bride, in that her new status will command respect from visiting dignitaries, bringing gifts.[27] She will move in the upper echelons of society and will receive the flattering attentions of the wealthy.

The rich and glorious attire of the bride (here called *bat melek* ["daughter of the king"]; NIV "princess") is recounted. Clothed in rich brocades interwoven with gold and in embroidered cloth,[28] the bride "is led [*ybl*] to the

23. Holladay, *CHALOT*, 361.

24. See the articles on "Ophir," *EBD*, 783; *ISBE*[2], 3:607–8.

25. The kind of craving depicted by *ʾwh* is usually of a bad kind (Holladay, *CHALOT*, 6), but certainly not some elevated aesthetic appreciation. The intent is to speak of the basic physical and sexual attraction.

26. The LXX translates *šegel* with *basilissa* ("queen"), so the process of reinterpreting the unacceptable term had already begun.

27. The "Daughter of Tyre" is representative of the kind of dignitaries that would attend such an occasion. Tyre had long and close relationships with the kingdom of Israel from the time of David and Solomon.

28. These words describing clothing are difficult to bring precision to and are often translated differently in different contexts.

king," a verb that most often describes bringing something as a gift, sacrifice, tribute, or even booty.[29] The bride's companions are similarly "led" (*ybl*) to the palace of the king—probably to remain as the new wife's attendants. This heightens the sense of a political arrangement rather than a marriage of equals or even a love match.

The King's Future (45:16–17)

THE POEM CONCLUDES as the bride and her entourage enter the king's palace. Besides the possibility of political alliance with another nation, the marriage also represents the potential for dynastic succession through the production of sons (45:16), who will "take the place" of the king's fathers. This description of dynastic succession seems to presume a long line of royal antecedents preceding the present king. This undermines confidence in identifying David as recipient of this psalm and points to some later monarch of the northern or southern kingdom. The king's sons will be given various duties during the life of the king in order to prepare them to rule after their father.[30] The term used here for "prince" (*śar*) does not exclusively refer to nobility but indicates an official position as representative of the king.

Perpetuate your memory. In the final verse, the possible confusion of God and king, mentioned in connection with 45:6, returns. On the surface it seems easy to assume that the psalmist is promising to keep the king's memory alive in subsequent generations through the vivid descriptions of this song. In this scenario the king is the one who will receive the praise of the nations "for ever and ever." The issue is not as simple as it may appear, however. An investigation of the use of the Hiphil of the verb *zkr* (i.e., "call to remembrance") along with the noun *šem* ("name," a word is present in the Heb. but not reflected in the NIV) tells us five other occurrences refer to the name of Yahweh (Ex. 20:24; Ps. 20:7; Isa. 12:4; 26:13; Amos 6:10), while several other refer to the other human or divine beings (Ex. 23:13; Josh. 23:7; 2 Sam. 18:18; Isa. 49:1).

Add to this the fact that in the psalms the image of "the peoples" (*ʿammim* ["peoples"], not "nations" as in the NIV) "praising" someone is *always* a reference to praising Yahweh. Thus, the reason for questioning who is in view in this verse is apparent: king or God? On the one hand, this phrase may display the close relationship that existed in the minds of king and people between kingship and divine rulership. In Egypt and Mesopotamia, kings

---

29. For varied uses of *ybl*, see Isa. 18:7; 23:7; 53:7; Hos. 10:6; Zeph. 3:10.

30. Absalom, e.g., used his position as the king's son to curry favor with disaffected elements and to build his own power base in opposition to his father (cf. 2 Sam. 15:1–6).

were known to assume divinity for themselves and were often worshiped[31] as gods by the people. While this was clearly never the case in Israel, the dividing line between king and God was often obscured, particularly in the exalted imagery of the psalms.

On the other hand, this concluding verbiage may reveal a postexilic exploitation of the ambiguities of the text to reinterpret this royal wedding song as a reference to the coming messianic Son of God, who is also seen as blurring the line between divine and human kingship. I will return to this issue in the Bridging Contexts section.

PSALM 45 EXHIBITS such a narrowly restricted "setting in life"—the wedding ceremony of a human king of Israel or Judah—that it raises in a radical way the question of how this kind of psalm could continue to function fruitfully in the later Diaspora community among exiles who had little or no hope that the Davidic kingship would ever be resumed. How could a psalm that focused on a ceremony that had not been enacted for hundreds of years still speak meaningfully to those for whom a royal wedding could have been only a nostalgic memory of times long past? Surely such a culturally and temporally conditioned poem could only continue to have power if its words and images were reinterpreted in ways that linked with the needs and hopes of the contemporary society. What evidence is there that Psalm 45 (and other psalms in the canonical Psalter, for that matter) was subjected to such a reinterpretive reading?

J. Clinton McCann shows how such a rereading of older psalms took place.

> These psalms can continue to be expressions of hope and confidence; however, the expressions of hope become two-edged when they occur immediately following Pss. 42–44; that is to say, the traditional hope embodied in the royal psalms, Zion songs and enthronement songs is modified and reoriented by the literary context. In order to survive the crisis of exile and dispersion, Israel had to profess that God was, in some sense, still its "refuge and strength" (Ps. 46:2), its "secure height" (Ps. 46:8, 12; 48:4), and "a great king over all the earth" (Ps. 47:3); however, such professions had to be understood differently when Israel spoke them no longer from the secure height of Zion but rather from a position of having been "cast off" (Pss. 43:2; 44:10) and "scattered . . .

31. Cf. 45:11, where the word translated "honor" is in reality the Heb. verb form *hištaḥwi* means "worship."

> among the nations" (Ps. 44:12). The arrangement of the Korah psalms, in which Pss. 42–44 introduce Pss. 45–49, thus assisted the community to face the disorienting reality of exile and also to affirm that hope was still possible. The old words (Pss. 45–49) can still have meaning; but they must be heard in a new context—a context that includes an awareness of the reality of exile and dispersion (Pss. 42–44).[32]

What happens, then, in the new context of the Exile is that Yahweh's kingship was understood as distinct from the experience of human kingship, which had been lost. God's kingdom was *not* synonymous with the kingdoms of Israel and Judah. His kingdom continued as present and future hope even though the human kingdom had collapsed.

This new context necessitated a reinterpretation of the divine promises to David and his descendants. What was one to make of the covenant that affirmed an "eternal throne" for the Davidic dynasty when that dynasty was already deposed and swallowed up in exilic Diaspora? The response of exilic Israel/Judah was primarily to push those hopes into the future. In a move we now call messianism, the Diaspora community, taking hold on one of the titles associated with divine authorization of the kings, began to look for a Messiah, a future descendant of David, who would reestablish an earthly kingdom that would never fail.

These hopes for a future "Anointed One" affected the way the psalms of kingship were read and understood. References to ancient kings in a now defunct kingdom were resignified to speak of a future one who would come to accomplish what all those former rulers had been unable to do: to fulfill the expectations of God and lead his people rightly in the paths of Yahweh. His kingship, supported by God, would never fail. A recent monograph by Christoph Rösel[33] argues persuasively that these future hopes for the "Messiah" stand behind the shaping of the early collection of Psalms 2–89.

In these psalms it seems clear that the hopes of the exiled people was for an ultimate reestablishment of the Davidic dynasty. This is cogently argued in the royal psalms that stand at the seams of this combined collection of the first three books (Pss. 2; 72; 89).[34] These three psalms provide an interpretive shape to the combined collection that recalls the divine covenant with David (Ps. 2) with its continued benefits and responsibilities for his royal descendants (Ps. 72) and concludes with an anguished plea to Yahweh for the restoration of the monarchy that has collapsed in the Exile (Ps. 89). In the

32. McCann, "Books I-III and the Editorial Purpose of the Hebrew Psalter," 102.

33. Christoph Rösel, *Die messianische Redaktion des Psalters: Studien zu Enstehung und Theologie der Sammlung Ps. 2–89* (Stuttgart: Calwer Verlag, 1999).

34. See comments on the royal psalms in "Types of Psalms" in the introduction.

context of the Exile, then, these royal psalms were reinterpreted as expressions of a hopeful future in which God's anointed king would once again rule over an eternal kingdom.

The messianic development of the Psalter does not stop here, however, but takes one additional step: the shifting of hopes for kingly rule to Yahweh himself. This final move associated with the final form of the Psalter is most evident as we move across the boundary separating the early collection of Books 1–3 and enter the later terrain of the last two books (Pss. 90–150). These two segments of the Psalter (Pss. 2–89 and 90–150) use contrasting techniques of editorial arrangement and give evidence of the earmarks of independent circulation.[35] The latter two books were added to the first three as a sort of response to the plea for restoration of the kingdom in Psalm 89—a response that immediately points the way to the collection of *Yahweh malak* psalms at the heart of Book 4.[36] The result is to direct the exilic reader away from hope for the reestablishment of the human Davidic kingship to the rule of Yahweh himself.

This apparent thematic shift is confirmed by a particularly interesting distribution of significant vocabulary relating to kingship. In the first three books, the Hebrew word *melek* ("king") is used in four ways: (1) for kings or kingship in the most general and abstract sense; (2) for the kings of the foreign nations; (3) for the kings of Israel and Judah; and (4) finally for Yahweh himself as king. But when we study the last two books, we discover an interesting change. While *melek* is used as before to describe kingship in general, foreign kings, and Yahweh as king, its use in relation to the kings of Israel/Judah *is entirely lacking*! This can be no accident but must reflect a changing understanding of kingship among those who appended this final segment to the growing Psalter collection.

Alongside this striking change in the use of *melek*, two other terms applied in the first three books to the human kings of Israel/Judah—*ᶜebed* ("servant") and *mešiaḥ* ("anointed one, messiah")—continue unabated into the last two books. The effect of these phenomena is to distance the Davidic kings from rulership associated with *melek* while emphasizing that Yahweh himself is the eternal *melek* of the faithful. At the same time the role of eschatological Messiah (*mašiaḥ*) and Servant (*ᶜebed*) who ushers in the kingdom and reign of Yahweh is emphasized.[37]

35. See the discussion in "The Shape of the Psalter" in vol. 2 of this commentary.

36. See the treatment of the *Yahweh malak* psalms in "Types of Psalms" in the introduction.

37. See Gerald H. Wilson, "Psalms and Psalter: Paradigm for Biblical Theology," in *Biblical Theology: Retrospect and Prospect* (Downers Grove, Ill.: InterVarsity, forthcoming). See also the discussion of this matter in the Bridging Contexts section of the commentary on Ps. 2.

What we see, then, is a two-stage reinterpretation of royal psalms such as Psalm 45 in the final form of the Psalter: a first stage reflected in Psalms 2–89, in which hopes for the reestablishment of the Davidic monarchy are pushed into an eschatological future, and a second stage reflected in the final form of the Psalter, in which the descendant of David is understood as the "anointed servant" who ushers in the direct rule of Yahweh himself.

HOW ARE WE in the twenty-first century to interpret and apply this alien psalm celebrating the marriage of a Davidic king millennia ago in a kingdom that no longer exists? There are two ways this ancient psalm can still have impact on Christians today.

Historical insight. Historically, the monarchy was an important part of Israel's experience of themselves and of God. The kings, and especially David, provided continuity and unity that gave expression in the real world to the divine promise to make Abraham a great nation and to give them a land. To gain insight into such an important and formative historical phenomenon is no mean feat and ought to be welcomed. Psalm 45, with its open window on the marriage of the king, gives us just such an opportunity of insight. Among the historical insights offered, I will select just three.

The intrusion of God. It is impressive just how much God is a part of this moment of public ceremony. Both king and princess, bridegroom and bride, are called to remember that God is the source and continuing support of their honored election. While history is clear that kings and queens often forgot God in their efforts to control and manipulate circumstances to their benefit or that of their offspring, at this moment of high ceremony God was called to mind as author and finisher of the monarchical faith.

Dynastic concern. Behind the pomp and circumstance of marriage joy, behind the language of religious fervor or romantic relationship, the concern with dynastic succession always lurks close by. The prominent place afforded this dynastic concern emphasizes the importance of children for the continuation of the royal line. This concern continues in a way the similar concern of the patriarchs and their barren wives for children to fulfill the divine promise of a multitude of descendants and a great nation. God's promise to David of an eternal throne necessitated a continual sequence of male heirs to take their seat. For dynastic memory to be perpetuated "through all generations" (45:17) required future Davidic kings.

The expectation of integrity and justice. This poem for the marriage ceremony of the king contains expectations and exhortations for justice and equitable rule. We do not read here only a joyous celebration of romantic love. The marriage also presented an opportunity for the king and his bride to commit themselves to the important aspects of royal rule: justice, equity, truth, humility, righteousness as the foundation of the continuing dynasty, even more than splendor, majesty, excellence, and grace.

Historically, then, this passage can help us to evaluate similar moments of political celebration. Is God a vital part of what is done? Is he really the author and finisher of our public and political endeavors? How would an awareness of his presence and expectation change the way we do business? Insofar as our governments and political figures are not theocracies or servants of God (as Israel and the kings of Israel were considered), what might that say about our reliance on them? How might we honor them without mindless trust? How can we hold them accountable without unrealistic expectations? Where is the appropriate measuring stick of equity and justice for our leaders?

Eschatological anticipation. As we have seen, when the extended exile began to render the monarchical themes and hopes of Psalm 45 obscure and even obsolete, the Diaspora community found new meaning in the eschatological reinterpretation of the kingly imagery of this psalm and others. The ambiguous statement in 45:6, "Your throne, O God, will last for ever and ever," seems to equate the bridegroom king with God himself. It is true that this verse may be a later insertion, intended to balance the preceding celebration of the king's majesty, splendor, and victorious might with a more humble acknowledgment that Yahweh alone represents the true and eternal king. It may reflect back to the affirmation in 44:4 that "you are my King and my God." Nevertheless, the presence of this ambiguous statement in Psalm 45 allows the possibility that the king, who appears here to be called "God," is in fact being understood as the anointed one who is to come—the Messiah, who will usher in God's kingdom. If so, then the marriage ceremony may well already be understood as between Messiah and the people of God, as in the later understanding of this psalm.

Surely we are now free to understand that the hopes and expectations that Israel pinned on the monarchy and the Davidic kings were ultimately carried to completion and fulfillment in the work and person of Jesus, the Messiah. What the human kings were unable to accomplish because of their moral, ethical, or physical failings, Jesus picked up and righteously completed. Thus, it is appropriate to understand the hopes and expectations expressed here as having their fulfillment in Christ's work. He is "the most excellent of men," the one whom God has blessed forever (45:2). He rides "forth victoriously in behalf of truth, humility and righteousness" (45:4). God will perpetuate his memory "through all generations" (45:17).

While these are not rightly prophetic predictions of Jesus, they are true words directed toward his fulfillment of the kingly role envisioned in this ancient, historical psalm. Thus, we can celebrate along with our ancient Judahite brothers and sisters the glory, majesty, splendor, and victory of God's king.

Psalm 46

FOR THE DIRECTOR of music. Of the Sons of Korah.
According to *alamoth.* A song.

1 God is our refuge and strength,
an ever-present help in trouble.
2 Therefore we will not fear, though the earth give way
and the mountains fall into the heart of the sea,
3 though its waters roar and foam
and the mountains quake with their surging. *Selah*

4 There is a river whose streams make glad the city of God,
the holy place where the Most High dwells.
5 God is within her, she will not fall;
God will help her at break of day.
6 Nations are in uproar, kingdoms fall;
he lifts his voice, the earth melts.

7 The LORD Almighty is with us;
the God of Jacob is our fortress. *Selah*

8 Come and see the works of the LORD,
the desolations he has brought on the earth.
9 He makes wars cease to the ends of the earth;
he breaks the bow and shatters the spear,
he burns the shields with fire.
10 "Be still, and know that I am God;
I will be exalted among the nations,
I will be exalted in the earth."

11 The LORD Almighty is with us;
the God of Jacob is our fortress. *Selah*

THIS IS A psalm of radical trust in the face of overwhelming threat. While the specific cause of threat is never clarified, it does seem to have to do with the uproar of pagan nations (46:6) and wars that Yahweh brings to an end (46:9). The psalm has a more universal tone, beginning with the cosmic, mythic turmoil of chaotic waters before creation (46:2–3) and continuing to Yahweh's ending of wars "to the ends of the earth" (46:9). Throughout all this threat and upheaval, God is—as the psalm insists from the opening lines—"our refuge and strength, an ever-present help in trouble." Although this psalm stands within the so-called Elohistic Psalter, the divine name Yahweh appears three times in this short psalm (vv. 7, 8, 11). The first and last of these are in the repeated refrain, while the second is part of the call to trust Yahweh that begins the final section of the psalm.

Psalm 46 breaks fairly easily into three sections, the latter two marked by a repeated refrain and all three exhibiting a concluding *selah*.[1] Thematically these sections include a radical trust expressed in cosmic, mythic terms (46:1–3), an assurance of Yahweh's protective presence (46:4–7), and a call to trust Yahweh who causes wars to cease (46:8–11).

The Heading (46:0)

THE HEADING OF Psalm 46 directs the psalm to "the director of music"[2] and is attributed to the "Sons of Korah," the fourth consecutive psalm (considering Pss. 42–43 as a single composition) to do so. In addition, the heading includes a probable song tune (*ᶜal ᶜalamot*)[3] and concludes with the general genre designation *šir*[4] ("song").

Radical Trust in Yahweh (46:1–3)

THE OPENING SECTION affirms a radical trust in the protective strength of God in terms that hark back to the theme of "refuge" especially characteristic of psalms in Book 1 of the Psalter,[5] but also found throughout the Psalter.

---

1. For further discussion of *selah*, see comments on Ps. 3.

2. See comments on the heading of Ps. 4, where this term is first used.

3. See the discussion of the psalm headings in the introduction. As *BHS* notes, a few manuscripts and versions suggest a possible emendation to *ᶜalmut*, as in the heading to Ps. 9 (see comments). At least one old Greek version suggests a form from *ᶜolam* ("forever"). The term *ᶜal ᶜalamot* appears also in 1 Chron. 15:20 in a description of the duties of temple musicians, who are "to play the lyres according to *ᶜalamot*." The general Heb. noun *ᶜalmah* (pl. *ᶜalamot*) means a "girl of marriageable age" or a "young woman before the birth of her first child" (Holladay, *CHALOT*, 274). The term in the psalm heading may refer to a song tune or perhaps to a particular high sound to be adopted in singing.

4. See comments on the heading to Ps. 30. Ps. 45 is also called a *šir*, although there the term may be connected with the additional designation *yedidot*.

5. See comments on 2:12; 5:11. The word "refuge" appears in approximately 35 percent of the psalms in Book 1, in contrast to 25 percent in Book 2, 5 percent in Book 3, 18 percent in Book 4, and 13 percent in Book 5.

The ideas of God's providing "strength" (*ʿoz*) and being a "fortress" (*miśgab*) are related in the earlier appearance of this theme as well as in this psalm ("strength," 46:1; "fortress," 46:7, 11). He is described as an "ever-present help," which in Hebrew (*nimṣaʾ meʾod*) means something like a help that "can be found when you need it."

The radical confidence of the psalmist is exhibited in an ability to stand without fear in the face of what constitutes a threat of uncreation. In the ancient Israelite cosmology (cf. Gen. 1 and elsewhere in the Old Testament), Yahweh established the stable environment for human existence—the earth—at creation by an act of sovereign control and limitation of chaotic waters. He established an orderly universe by creating and enforcing boundaries for these waters so that dry land appeared as a place where humans and land animals could live.[6]

The Flood (Gen. 6–9) threatened to dissolve creation order into precreation chaos by allowing these restricted waters to exceed and ultimately erase their established boundaries. Similarly here in Psalm 46, human existence would be threatened with dissolution if the roaring, surging seas and waters were able to topple (*mwṭ*)[7] the mountains into the sea so that the earth would "give way."[8] In the Mesopotamia account of the Flood, the gods cower in fear behind the walls of their heavenly abode as the chaotic waters—unleashed in a fit of pique against humans—threaten to destroy the gods as well. In Psalm 46, however, the psalmist claims a confident trust in Yahweh that allows contemplation of the ultimate destruction of creation without fear.

God's Protective Presence (46:4–7)

THE MOOD OF the poem changes noticeably as we move beyond the first *selah* into the second section of the psalm. From the roar of the rushing waters tearing at the coastline and toppling mountains, we come to the more peaceful description of the well-watered "city of God" (46:4). The

---

6. See 74:12–17.

7. The verb *mwṭ* is often used in the psalms to indicate the potential for disastrous falling. The affirmation that "I will not be moved" is one of the greatest claims of assurance expressed in the Psalter. Here the psalmist's confidence even exceeds this traditional hope for certain stability in the midst of the storm of life. Even if all stability and firm footing is removed, the psalmist will not be afraid. Cf. Pss. 15:5; 16:8; 21:7; 30:6; 55:22; 62:2, 6; 66:9; 93:1; 96:10; 104:5; 112:6; 121:3; 125:1.

8. The Heb. is less than clear. The consonantal text (*hmyr*) is variously taken as *hamir* (Hiphil infinitive from *mwr*) with the meaning "change," or as *himmor* (Niphal infinitive from *mwr*) with the meaning "quake, shake."

river is almost placid by contrast to the raging waters of the previous verses. Rather than destruction, this river offers rejoicing through the irrigation canals drawn from its main channel.[9] The contrast must be intentional and heightens both the sense of threat in the first stanza and the countering calm of the second.

The city of God is clearly a reference in the psalmist's mind to Jerusalem,[10] and the "holy place where the Most High dwells" is the temple. The promised presence of Yahweh in and with Jerusalem is a source of renewed confidence for Israel—even in the face of the onslaught of attacking enemies (46:6). "God is within her, she will not fall" is an assertion of absolute confidence that could be misleading if not coupled with covenant loyalty and obedience. Jeremiah calls his contemporary Jerusalemites to task for assuming too much when they rely on the temple to save them, crying, "The temple of the LORD, the temple of the LORD, the temple of the LORD!" (Jer. 7:2–15), as if the mere presence of the temple was a talisman to ward off evil rather than a place to humbly meet and worship God (cf. Pss. 74 and 137, where the destruction and loss of Jerusalem and the temple are very real experiences).

However, with this obvious caveat in mind, the psalmist affirms that unlike the mountains in 46:2 that topple (*bemoṭ*) into the sea, the city of God bolstered by his saving presence "will not fall" (*bal timmoṭ*). Since God is an "ever-present help" (46:1), he will help her quickly (the apparent emphasis of "at break of day"). Like the surging waters in the opening verses (*yehemu* ["they roar"]), nations may raise an uproar (*hamu*),[11] but kingdoms fall before the withering voice of Yahweh (46:6.

9. There may be some attempt to evoke the abundant watering associated with the river that flowed through the Garden of Eden (Gen. 2:10). It is also worth noting that in the Canaanite religious texts from Ugarit, Judge Nahar/River is one of the watery opponents who must be defeated to establish order. Here the river is harnessed to the good of the city of God. See comments on 36:8; 65:9. Note the studied contrast between this psalm and Ps. 137, where the "rivers of Babylon" offer occasion only for regret and anger over the destruction of Zion/Jerusalem, the city of God. The irrigation canals are also mentioned as a source of abundance and life in 1:3.

10. While the identification of the "city" with Jerusalem might be questioned on the basis that no such "river" is present in the City of David, the mythic language of the text overrides these concerns. See the discussion of Mays, *Psalms*, 185, regarding how "symbolic language used in the ancient Near East to imagine and speak about the dwelling place of the gods" included the presence of a stream that flowed from the "cosmic mountain where this dwelling was." Since Jerusalem is the dwelling place of the one God, Yahweh, it is described in the symbolic terms used for this cosmic city.

11. The vocabulary is different, but the imagery is similar to that of the raging, conspiring nations in 2:1.

This second section of the psalm concludes with the first statement of a refrain repeated at the end of the psalm: "The LORD Almighty[12] is with us, the God of Jacob is our fortress" (46:7, 11). The emphasis on the presence of Yahweh with his people as "fortress" (*miśgab*) links back to the opening affirmation (46:1) that Yahweh is refuge, strength, and "ever-present help."[13]

Trusting Yahweh (46:8–11)

THIS FINAL SECTION continues the theme of trust in Yahweh introduced at the beginning of the psalm (46:1) and renewed in the first refrain (46:7). The invitation to "come and see the works of the LORD" introduces a series of affirmingly parallel lines describing militant actions with an edge of violence. These acts have the effect of making "wars cease [*šbt*]"[14] throughout the earth (46:9) by destroying the necessary implements of war (here symbolized by "bow," "arrow," and "shields").[15] These works of God are reasons for horror to those who want to rule the earth with military might.

Be still, and know that I am God. The voice of the triumphant warrior God breaks into the scene in the first person, challenging foe and faithful alike. God's demand—"Cease! Desist!" (or perhaps the military counterpart, "Attention!")—calls all combatants to stop their fighting and pay attention. Only when they stop their struggles can they acknowledge that Yahweh is God (46:10). Yahweh proclaims his exalted status ("I will be exalted") before

---

12. The noun *ṣabaʾ* (pl. *ṣebaʾot*) is drawn from the same root as the verb *ṣbʾ* ("go to war; serve as soldier"). The *ṣabaʾ*, *ṣebaʾot* are the individual and massed military personnel necessary to carry out the campaigns of the king. In reference to Yahweh, the "host" are probably the heavenly beings who do his will (the angels), or in some cases the stars. Israel did consider Yahweh as king and therefore understood that he undertook military action as warrior against the enemy and for the protection of his people. The term *ṣebaʾot* in reference to Yahweh occurs some fifteen times in the Psalter, in eight psalms (24:10; 46:7, 11; 48:8; 59:5; 69:6; 80:4, 7, 14, 19; 84:1, 3, 8, 12; 89:8). In these appearances, the term is often associated with the kingship of Yahweh (cf. 24:10; 48:8; 84:3).

13. Refuge, strength, and fortress all come together in Ps. 59:16 and Jer. 16:19. The comparison of these texts with our psalm is instructive. In both Ps. 59 and Jer. 16, "refuge" is connected with the additional phrase "in time of distress" (*beyom ṣar/ṣarah*), a phrase that, while not identical with "in trouble" (*beṣarot*), has much in common with it. The conjunction of these four elements—refuge, strength, fortress, and trouble—suggest a traditional association on which all these passages draw.

14. The root underlying "make cease" (*šbt*) is the same as that behind the word "Sabbath" (*šabbat* ["day of rest"]).

15. The NIV's "shields" requires an emendation of the text from *ʿagalot* ("wagon carts") to an irregular form from *ʿagilah* ("round shield). Because of this difficulty, the word is sometimes taken as "chariots" (cf. the NIV text note; but see Holladay, *CHALOT*, 264). Perhaps Yahweh is here viewed as destroying the "wagons" carrying supplies to the military campaign.

all present. His exaltation is to be complete: among the "nations" (*goyim*) and in the whole "earth" (*ʾareṣ*).

The LORD Almighty is with us. The psalm concludes with the repetition of the refrain, driving home the primary theme of the psalm: Yahweh is indeed the refuge, strength, and fortress of the faithful, who can remain confident in his protective care—even in the face of a crumbling world (46:2–3) or rampant military attack (46:8–9).

THE CITY OF GOD. Reference to "the city of God" (or of Yahweh) occurs only seven times in the whole Old Testament; all but one of these appearances occur within the Psalter, and four within Book 2 (Pss. 42–72).[16] The city of God/Yahweh is clearly identified in Psalm 48: "As we have heard, so have we seen in the city of the LORD Almighty, in the city of our God" (48:8); in this psalm we also learn that the city is identified with "[God's] holy mountain ... Mount Zion" (48:1–2), an obvious reference to Jerusalem.

Because Jerusalem is Yahweh's special city, he is expected to protect her and her inhabitants from attack. According to 48:3, "God is in her citadels; he has shown himself to be her fortress." Although the city is itself a fortified place, God is the ultimate place of security, who will protect his city and its inhabitants. This view was especially important in relation to the growing sense of invulnerability that seems to have grown up in the Zion theology of Jerusalem.

Based on promises like that expressed in 48:8—"As we have heard, so have we seen in the city of the LORD Almighty, in the city of our God: God makes her secure forever"—some Judahites refused to accept the possibility that Jerusalem could be conquered by foreign troops. Jeremiah's sermon at the temple was directed at precisely this sort of false hope: "Do not trust in deceptive words and say, "This is the temple of the LORD, the temple of the LORD, the temple of the LORD!" (Jer. 7:4). Those who trusted in the invulnerability of Jerusalem because it was the site of Yahweh's temple would be sadly disappointed when he allowed Babylonian troops to overrun the temple and Jerusalem because of the sins of the covenant people.

The destruction of Jerusalem and the temple was a painful moment of identity crisis for those carried into exile by the Babylonians. The pain of loss continues to echo in the agonized cry of Psalm 137:5–6: "If I forget you, O Jerusalem, may my right hand forget its skill. May my tongue cling to the roof

16. The occurrences are Pss. 46:4; 48:1, 8 (2x); 87:3; 101:8; Isa. 60:14.

of my mouth if I do not remember you, if I do not consider Jerusalem my highest joy."[17] Even in the Exile Jerusalem was held in such great esteem that it became the focus of pilgrimage from the far reaches of the Diaspora at great cost and greater risk to life and limb.[18] Jerusalem became the spiritual center of a nation scattered among all the nations.

The esteem of Jerusalem and the theological struggle to explain how the promises of eternal protection and care such as in 48:8 could stand alongside the destruction of both temple and city led ultimately to the vision of the eschatological "new Jerusalem." Ezekiel envisioned an eschatological restoration of people, land, city, and temple (Ezek. 37–48). Other prophets contributed to this growing eschatological expectation.[19] Jerusalem will become the gathering place where the nations of the world will learn of Yahweh and his law (Jer. 3:17). The city will be rebuilt into a thriving center and will never fear destruction again: "It will be inhabited; never again will it be destroyed. Jerusalem will be secure" (Zech. 14:11).

This hope for return and restoration is, of course, central to the eschatological hopes of Diaspora Judaism and its messianic hopes. The Messiah, a descendant of the Davidic line, would defeat Israel's enemies and usher in the kingdom of God, in which a restored Jerusalem would provide the center from which God's reign would go forth over all the earth. In Christian circles, as this vision of the Messiah was attached to the dying and rising Jesus, the future hope for the restored city of God was spiritualized even further to become an experience of God that is outside time and space. Revelation takes up this theme once again as the combined Testaments come to their close: "And he carried me away in the Spirit to a mountain great and high, and showed me the Holy City, Jerusalem, coming down out of heaven from God" (Rev. 21:10).[20]

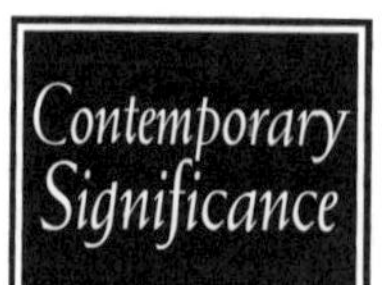

HE MAKES WARS TO CEASE. This passage makes it clear that God judges those who make war on the earth and that his ultimate goal and plan is to make "wars cease to the ends of the earth." We sometimes get so caught up in our just-war theories and what we see as the necessity of fighting fire with fire, pragmatically using violence to put down

17. See also 74:1–8.

18. The Psalms of Ascent (Pss. 120–134) are considered by many to be songs sung by pilgrims on their way to Jerusalem. On the dangers of pilgrimage, consider Ps. 107.

19. Cf. passages such as Isa. 44:26–28; 45:13; 58:12; 60:10; 66:20; Jer. 3:17; 33:7; Dan. 9:25; Joel 3:1, 20; Mic. 4:2; Zech. 8:3–4, 22.

20. Cf. Rev. 20–22 for the extended description of the Holy City, the new Jerusalem.

what we see as greater violence, using the ways of the world in our attempts to bring God's kingdom closer, that we forget that war and its violent consequences are not a part of the world that God intends.

This will not be an antiwar tract—although I do think that the Quakers, with whom I have been associated for the last fourteen years, have a radical peace testimony that needs to be heard. But I do want all of us to listen carefully to the condemnation of war this passage brings, and I want us all to realize that when we participate in war, we are not participating in God's creation intention but something that grew out of human sin and disobedience. We are not even participating in something that will last—wars will cease to the ends of the earth!

Be still. There are many ways to say "be still" in the Old Testament—a variety of Hebrew words are translated in this way.[21] But the term used in 46:10 (*rph*) has the sense of "cease and desist," like a parent separating two struggling children or a teacher breaking up a fight in the schoolyard. It does not mean to be quiet or calm as much as it means to stop what you have been doing and be still. Only when we cease our own frantic activity can we begin to experience God's acting for us. Only then, says the psalmist, can we know that he is God.

We will not fear though the earth give way. Psalm 46 begins with lack of fear in the face of the dissolution of the world and ends with confident stillness in the face of rampaging wars to the ends of the earth. In between lies the reason for this calmness—the place of eternal standing where God himself dwells, the fortress God provides, the city of God that will not fall (46:4–5). This kind of confidence is remarkable. We are not talking about confidence in the face of minor disturbances or setbacks here. Nor are we thinking of major, painful life losses—the death of a loved one, horrific degenerating disease, and the like.

As terrible as these may be, they pale in significance before the fearful prospect the psalmist portrays. What he describes is not just an earthquake such as have recently devastated parts of the world. It is rather the dissolution of the world and life as we know it in what amounts to a moment of uncreation. At creation, God placed boundaries on the chaotic waters, restricting them so that dry land could appear and provide living space for animals and humans. Here the psalmist is declaring that even if the chaotic waters were to break forth and dissolve creation order back into chaos, there would be no reason for fear.

---

21. See the following passages that in the NIV contain the phrase "Be still": Ex. 14:14 [*ḥrš*]; Neh. 8:11 [*hsh*]; Ps. 37:7 [*dwm*]; Ps. 46:10 [*rph*]; Jer. 47:6 [*dwm*]; Zech. 2:17 [*hsh*].

That is remarkable, particularly because the ancient Israelites were not well known for a robust belief in life after death. They thought instead of death as marking the end of effective existence for humans and animals alike (Eccl. 3:19–21; 9:3–4). One could no longer praise God in death, nor did the dead experience the wonders of God or his love and faithfulness (Ps. 88:10–12). This view makes the claim of the psalmist even more poignant since it is not mitigated by an expectation of resurrection or eternal life.

This passage reminds me of Jesus' statements in the Sermon on the Mount: "Therefore I tell you, do not worry about your life, what you will eat or drink; or about your body, what you will wear. Is not life more important than food, and the body more important than clothes?" (Matt. 6:25). Like the psalmist, Jesus has pared life down to its bare minimum—the basic necessities of food, drink, and protective clothing—and says, "Don't worry!" if even these are lacking. Don't worry even if you are dying of hunger, thirst, or exposure. Don't fear even if the world and life as we know it disintegrates around you! That is radical faith—faith I am not sure I can always match.

Typically, Jesus provides the clarifying word for me here. And even his answer is subtly expressed in a question that makes us reflect more intensely on the interrelationship of life and faith. "Is not life more important than food, and the body more important than clothes?" The NIV translation of this verse supplies an interpretive addition that obscures in my opinion the true point of Jesus' statement. In the NASB and NRSV the word "important" is omitted so that the result is something like, "Is not life more than food, and the body more than clothing?" The introduction of the word "important" has the unfortunate effect of reducing Jesus' point to an issue of relative importance. Of course life is more important than food, and the body is more important than the clothes one puts on. But that is *not* what Jesus asks.

Jesus' question is: "Is not life *more than food* and the body *more than clothing?*" And the obvious answer is "No!" in both instances. Life cannot be sustained beyond a short period without food (and particularly without drink). Nor can we survive long without protective clothing except in the most moderate of climates (which ancient Israel was not). This contradiction forces us to look behind Jesus' words for his real meaning—and we find it in the radical assumption that he modeled in his own life and ministry. There is something more important in life than living itself. In other words, there is something worth *dying for*! That is why Christ went to the cross.

We face death and the dissolution of the world, not because we are assured of a new life after death—some "pie in the sky by and by" hope of heaven. We live faithfully in the face of the ultimate threats of life because God is at the core the food and drink that make our lives worth living. Without him, life is simply a series of breaths taken without meaning, gourmet meals consumed as a distraction from the emptiness of a self-focused existence.

Life with God is not dependent on life as we know it—or even on the universe as we know it. Life with God transcends our need to life here and now at any cost. Life lived in the power of God's refuge and strength becomes *eternal life*—not just life that hopes to be restored in some future perfect existence, but life that is not threatened by the imperfection of our world or even by the dissolution of all we know.

"The LORD Almighty is with us; the God of Jacob is our fortress."

Psalm 47

FOR THE DIRECTOR of music. Of the Sons of Korah.
A psalm.

[1] Clap your hands, all you nations;
shout to God with cries of joy.
[2] How awesome is the LORD Most High,
the great King over all the earth!
[3] He subdued nations under us,
peoples under our feet.
[4] He chose our inheritance for us,
the pride of Jacob, whom he loved. *Selah*

[5] God has ascended amid shouts of joy,
the LORD amid the sounding of trumpets.
[6] Sing praises to God, sing praises;
sing praises to our King, sing praises.

[7] For God is the King of all the earth;
sing to him a psalm of praise.
[8] God reigns over the nations;
God is seated on his holy throne.
[9] The nobles of the nations assemble
as the people of the God of Abraham,
for the kings of the earth belong to God;
he is greatly exalted.

THIS BRIEF PSALM is a celebration of the kingship of Yahweh, who rules over the whole earth (47:2, 7; cf. 46:10). Most form-critical scholars include this psalm among the so-called "enthronement" psalms.[1] As it stands, it provides an appropriate response to calling Israel and the struggling nations (in 46:10) to "Stop!" (their warfare) and acknowledge

1. Cf. J. D. W. Watts, "Yahweh Malak Psalms," *TZ* 21 (1965): 341–48; Gerhard von Rad, *OTT*[2], 1:363, note. Other psalms included in this form-critical category are Pss. 93; 96–99; 149.

that Yahweh is God (and king). In Psalm 47, the pagan nations (*goyim*),[2] defeated in Psalm 46, are called to submit to the rule of Yahweh and to join in festive praise to Yahweh, clapping their hands and raising their voices in song along with all "the kings of the earth" (47:9). Peoples of all ethnicity (*leʾummim*) and heritage (*ʿammim*) join in the celebration as well. Psalm 47 gives voice to the exaltation envisioned in Psalm 46, when Israelite and non-Israelite together join in the praise of Yahweh, signifying the reunification of the world nations under the kingship of Yahweh.

The psalm downplays political aspects of Yahweh's rulership over the earth by using words to describe the non-Israelite peoples of the world other than the usual *goyim* ("nations"). The NIV's translation of the various terms used in this psalm obscures the fact that the more politicized term *goyim* occurs only in 47:10, where Yahweh's actual rulership is mentioned. In the rest of the psalm, the term *ʿam/ʿammim* ("people/peoples") occurs four times (47:1, 3, 9) and *leʾum/leʾummim* ("tribe/tribes") appears once (47:3).[3] As a result, Psalm 47 has the effect of emphasizing the reunification of the world peoples rent asunder at Babel (Gen. 11) and envisions a restoration of God's original creation goal for all humanity.

Structurally the poem falls into two stanzas of ten lines each: a stanza in praise of Yahweh for subjecting the pagan peoples under Israel (47:1–5), and a stanza in praise of Yahweh as king over the earth (47:6–9).[4] Each stanza is introduced by an imperative call to praise Yahweh ("Shout . . . with cries of joy," 47:1; "Sing praises," 47:6); each refers to the kingship of Yahweh over "all the earth" (47:2, 7); each describes the subjection of the "nations" (*ʿammim/leʾummim* under Israel in 47:3; *goyim* under God in 47:8);

2. The NIV's translation choices in this psalm obscure the different Heb. words that lie behind the translation "nation(s)." It is more usually the term *goy/goyim* that is translated "nation(s)." This word does appear in 47:8 (and is the only word translated "nations" in Ps. 46:6, 10). However, the NIV also translates the word *ʿammim* (more commonly and accurately rendered "peoples") as "nations" in 47:1, 3, 9a, 9b. In addition, the less frequent word *leʾummim* (normally an "ethnic community") is translated "peoples" in 47:3b. While these words for people groups are not always clearly distinguished in Old Testament usage, the following relationships usually are implied. The term *goy* describes a national entity that is an amalgamation of a number of tribes and ethnic communities. By way of contrast *leʾummim* designates an ethnically related "people group." Within such a people group, *ʿam* describes the extensive descendants of an eponymous ancestor (such as Israel or Abraham). The latter term is sometime exchanged for *šebeṭ* or *maṭṭeh* ("tribe"), although *ʿam* clearly intends a larger group.

3. See previous footnote.

4. Although there is a *selah* at the end of v. 4, this does not seem to correspond with the literary and logical division of the psalm.

and each concludes using the verb *ᶜlh* to describe the ascension/exaltation of Yahweh as king (47:5a, 9d; cf. 46:10).[5]

The Heading (47:0)

THERE ARE NO new terms in the heading of Psalm 47. The psalm is referred to "the director of music"[6] and is attributed to the "Sons of Korah."[7] It is also called a "psalm" (*mizmor*).[8]

Yahweh Subdues the Nations (47:1–5)

CLAP YOUR HANDS. While it may seem obvious to the reader that "clapping the hands" is an act of joyous response, the circumstance is more complex than first imagined since the specific idiom employed here (*taqaᶜ kap*) normally means "to strike hands" with another individual as confirmation of a bargain or contract between parties (like a handshake).[9] Clapping hands as an indication of joy and appreciation (as our applause at a performance) usually involves the verb *mḥ*ʾ rather than *tqᶜ*.[10] Clapping the hands does express malicious joy over the downfall of another or a sign of anger or judgment, but this usage regularly goes with the verb *spq*.[11] It is true that in Nahum 3:19 the phrase *taqaᶜ kap* is generally understood to denote clapping *"for joy"* over the fall of Assyria, but an alternate meaning in keeping with the verb's usual connotation is possible.[12] I suggest, therefore, that *taqaᶜ kap* in our passage does

---

5. While Ps. 46 employs the more standard verb for exaltation (*rwm*) and Ps. 47:9 uses the more general verb *ᶜlh* ("go up, ascend"; probably in a purposeful wordplay with the "ascension" image in 47:5), Ps. 47 still serves as an appropriate response to the anticipation of divine exaltation in 46:10.

6. See comments on the heading of Ps. 4.

7. See comments on the heading of Ps. 42.

8. See comments on this term at the heading of Ps. 3.

9. See Prov. 11:15; 17:18; 22:26. In one text the NIV translates *taqaᶜ kap* as indicating ridicule (Nah. 3:19), but this passage can also be understood as saying: "All those who hear the report about you will confirm a contract against you, for against whom has not your constant evil taken surety?" That is, all those nations forced by Assyria to give surety (through tribute or ransom) would jump at the chance to return the favor to their fallen enemy.

10. See Ps. 98:8; Isa. 55:12.

11. See Num. 24:10 Lam. 2:15, where *spq* occurs with *kap* ("hand"); in Jer. 31:19 it is the "inner thigh" or "sexual organ" that is struck; finally in Job 34:26, 37, where the verb stands alone. On one occasion (Ezek. 25:6) the verb *mḥ*ʾ with *yad* seems to indicate ridicule.

12. Note the comments on Nah. 3:19 in footnote 9, above, where I suggested the usual meaning for *taqaᶜ kap* in this passage, namely, to make a contract. If this is adopted as plausible, then as far as Ps. 47 goes, we would need to find a meaning other than "applause" or "signify joy." The idea is that these peoples of the earth are called to "strike an agreement"

not mean "clap the hands *for joy*"; rather, in keeping with its regular usage, the "nations" are being called to come to agreement regarding their relationship to Yahweh, God of Israel.

All you nations. As noted above, the "nations" here are actually "the peoples" (*ʿammim* rather than *goyim*). The use of the less political term emphasizes the reconciliation of humanity (separated by their rebellion at the Tower of Babel in Gen. 11) rather than the amalgamation of political states. The political element is not dismissed altogether since *goyim* ("nations") is used in 47:8a, where God is said to reign "over the nations." However, the use of less national vocabulary shifts the emphasis away from conquest toward restoration of Yahweh's original creation intention for all humankind.

The LORD Most High. It is fitting in this context of universal sovereignty where all humankind is called to acknowledge the kingship of Yahweh, God of Abraham, that the title "Most High" (*ʿelyon*), with its implication of superiority over the lesser gods of the pagan world, should be applied to Yahweh. To acknowledge Yahweh as *ʿelyon* is to submit to his authority, as the whole psalm demands. This Most High God is also declared "awesome" (lit., "worthy of fear"),[13] employing the common Israelite designation for the appropriate human relation to Yahweh—a relationship of humble awareness of absolute dependence on his merciful and sustaining power. In this psalm the call to submit to Yahweh in this fashion is extended beyond Israel to the whole of humanity.

The great King over all the earth. This "Most High" and "fear-producing" God, Yahweh, is here proclaimed to be more than the national God of Israel, taking his place among the panoply of national deities worshiped in the ancient Near East. Yahweh is a "great King [a commentary on *human* kingship] over all the earth" (*ʿal kol haʾareṣ*). Therefore, all people ought to acknowledge his authority.

He subdued [peoples]. In an unexpected way Yahweh is said to have "subdued [peoples] under us" (47:3a). Here the national identity of Israel—as the means through which humanity was to be restored to unity before Yahweh—does come to the foreground. In what apparently is an adaptation of the theme of divine subjection of the world to humans in 8:6, Israel is recognized as the entity through which human submission to Yahweh will be realized. The theme is also characteristic of the narratives of the conquest of

---

(by shaking hands in affirmation) among themselves, or with Israel, to stand under the kingship of Yahweh—as the assembled nobles of the "peoples" become the people of the God of Abraham in 47:9.

13. On the topic of the "fear of Yahweh," see comments on 2:11 and 15:4.

the land, when Yahweh drove out the peoples of the land of Canaan before the Israelites and gave them the land as an "inheritance."[14]

God has ascended. The first stanza concludes with a description of the joyous "noise" that surrounds Yahweh's "ascension" (47:5). The NIV pictures a procession of the ark of the covenant to the temple (cf. 24:7–10).[15] Yahweh goes up in the midst of great tumult and the sounding of the traditional ram's horn. This reference to God's "ascension" or "going up" is paralleled at the end of the second stanza by a reference to God's "exaltation."

Yahweh Rules as King (47:6–9)

THE SECOND STANZA focuses on the kingship of Yahweh. Although Yahweh has already been designated "king" in 47:2b, the second stanza reiterates this fact three times (47:6b, 7a, 8a) and mentions his enthronement as well (47:8b).

Sing praises. The praiseworthy nature of Yahweh's kingship is emphasized by the repeated commands to praise him at the beginning of this stanza (47:6). Five times the readers/listeners are instructed to "make music"[16] for God "our King."

God reigns over the nations. When the psalmist proclaims "God reigns" (*malak ᵓelohim*), the proclamation adapts a common exclamation almost exclusively associated with the divine name Yahweh. On nine occasions in the Old Testament Yahweh is proclaimed king, using some form of this phrase (*malak yhwh* in Isa. 24:23; 52:7; Mic. 4:7; *yhwh malak* in 1 Chron. 16:31; Pss. 93:1; 96:10; 97:1; 99:1; or *yimlok yhwh* in Ex. 15:18; Ps. 146:10). On one occasion the phrase "your God" replaces the divine name (Isa. 52:7). But the replacement of the name Yahweh by the alternative generic designation *ᵓelohim* occurs only in this psalm—in the context of the Elohistic Psalter.

Yahweh, who was "exalted in the earth" in Psalm 46:10, is now declared "king of all the earth" (47:7) and as reigning "over the nations" (47:8)—using

---

14. The theme of Yahweh's giving the land of Canaan to the Israelites "as an inheritance" is prominent in the Pentateuch (cf. Ex. 32:13; Lev. 20:24; Num. 34:2; Deut. 4:21; cf. also Josh. 11:23).

15. See *The NIV Study Bible*, 833–34, note on 47:5–6.

16. The NIV's translation of *zmr* as "sing praises" ignores the fact that the term has more to do with playing an instrument than producing vocal music. The fifth occurrence of the term in Ps. 47:7b instructs the reader/listener to "play for him a *maśkil*." The great variety of translations exhibited by the versions and commentaries reveals the relative uncertainty regarding the meaning of this term that appears in the headings of some thirteen psalms (32; 42; 44; 45; 52; 53; 54; 55; 74; 78; 88; 89; 142), all but one of which fall within the confines of Books 1–3 of the Psalter. The more general designation is as a "didactic psalm," but others, referring to method of composition or performance, prefer an "artful/skillful psalm." (Cf. the extended discussion in Kraus, *Psalms 1–59*, 25–26.)

the term *goyim* for the first and only time in this psalm. The two words describing Yahweh's dominion (*ʾereṣ* and *goyim*) point back to the exaltation of Yahweh "among the nations [*goyim*]" and "in the earth [*ʾereṣ*]" in 46:10 and further links Psalms 46 and 47 together.

Seated on his holy throne. Yahweh is pictured as an oriental monarch seated on his throne to grant audience and to judge.[17]

The nobles of the nations assemble. Once again it is the *ʿammim* ("peoples") who gather before Yahweh, not the *goyim* ("nations"), as in the NIV. These representatives of the peoples assemble before Yahweh *ʿam ʾelohe ʾabraham* ("the people of the God of Abraham"). Some commentators[18] assume a haplography and restore the preposition *ʿim* ("with") before *ʿam*, so that the representatives are "with" the Israelites. The emendation is often justified by the LXX, which includes the preposition *meta* ("with") but omits any reference to the "people" (*ʿam*). Rather than a haplography, however, this may well suggest that the LXX translators, faced with the same consonantal text as preserved in the MT, simply took a different interpretive path than the Masoretes, who later supplied the vowel points in the Hebrew text. Confronted with a single *ʿm*, the LXX read *ʿim* = *meta*, while the Masoretes read the *ʿm* as *ʿam* ("people").

If the representatives of the "peoples" stand before Yahweh "the people of the God of Abraham," this suggests that the pagan peoples *have become* the people of God (perhaps insert the word "as"), and the scattering at the Tower of Babel has been reversed. If the representatives merely stand "with" the people of God, the point is similar but less powerfully made.

The psalm ends with the exaltation of Yahweh. The kings of the earth in their submission to Yahweh have become his possession (47:9),[19] and there are no longer any who compete with the divine authority of Yahweh as King. The exaltation of Yahweh is related to his ascension to the throne by the use of the verb of the root *ʿlh* to describe both events (cf. *ʿalah* in 47:5a and *naʿalah* in 47:9). Yahweh is king over the whole earth, all the peoples of the earth acknowledge him, and God's original creation intention is now restored.

---

17. The reference to Yahweh's "holy throne" is reminiscent of Isaiah's vision of Yahweh enthroned in the temple with the seraphim calling out "Holy, Holy, Holy!" (Isa. 6:1–9). The image of Yahweh "sitting on his throne" also appears in 1 Kings 22:19 = 2 Chron. 18:18.

18. Kraus, *Psalms 1–59*, 466, and Craigie, *Psalms 1–50*, 347, are two examples.

19. The Heb. text actually contains the word *maginne* ("shields of. . .") rather than "kings of. . . ." *BHS* suggests a possible emendation to *signe* (an initial *mem* and *samek* are similar and often confused in handwritten script; "governors/rulers of. . ."). It is, of course, possible that the psalmist intended "shields of the earth" to be an image of the militant power of kings who have submitted to Yahweh here.

KING OF ALL THE EARTH. To understand the hope for universal restoration of humankind reflected in Psalm 47, it is first necessary to trace the path of disintegration that led from creation to the psalmist's (and our own) more fragmented contemporary circumstances. How is it, we are asking here, that humankind came to such a sorry and fractured pass, characterized by sin, hostility, and self-focused isolation? Why do the nations as described in the Scriptures represent a state of existence counter to God's intention? And how will the fractured world of human relations ever be reassembled and restored to wholeness?

(1) *A unified creation.* We must start with creation, where we find in the complementary narratives of Genesis 1 and 2 an account that emphasizes the original unity of humanity (and indeed the whole of creation) as God purposed and created it. Genesis 1 envisions humanity, both male and female, in all its diversity, together harmoniously reflecting the divine image to creation and extending the authority of Yahweh to it. Genesis 2, with its plaintive cry that the Adam alone was "not good," is followed by the search for an "appropriate counterpart" to overcome this deficit. This beautifully affirms the teaching of Genesis 1 that it is in harmonious living that males and females together display the divine image and fulfill God's purposes for humankind.

(2) *The disruption of sin.* But the original intention of unity and harmony is not our experience of human relationships, nor was it the experience of the biblical authors and editors. The description of the Fall in Genesis 3 and the remaining narratives of Genesis 4–11 drive home the theological understanding that the human choice for disobedience and sin disrupted the original unity and harmony of creation and have continued to infect the whole of the cosmos.

The first man's response to the divine confrontation over the eating of the forbidden fruit is instructive. The description of the woman—the man's appropriate counterpart in Genesis 2—was "bone of my bones and flesh of my flesh" (2:23), an affirmation of essential unity confirmed by the concluding observation that the two "will become one flesh" (2:24). In the divine confrontation, the man's evaluation changes from "bone of my bone and flesh of my flesh" to "[that] woman" (3:12)—accompanied, I am sure, with the requisite finger-pointing to indicate the distance that now separates the pair. As a result of sin, the original unity and harmony is destroyed, as evidenced by the anticipated hostility between humans and beasts (3:14–15), the expected subjection of a woman to her husband

(3:16), and the enmity relationship that grows up between humans and the earth (3:17–19).

(3) *Continued expansion.* Having been unleashed in the world because of human disobedience, sin and evil continue to spread their influence beyond the first generation with the murder of Abel by Cain (Gen. 4:1–16) and culminate in the complete corruption of all humanity and the whole earth just prior to the Flood (6:1–13).

The Flood unleashes the chaotic waters restricted by God at creation and threatens to allow God's corrupted creation to return to the chaos from which it began. But the Flood also reduces human evil, cleanses the corrupted earth, and allows a new start for humankind. The respite from sin is short-lived, however, and soon after the Flood abates, sin is on the rampage again, having survived the trip in the ark (Gen. 9:20–27).

(4) *The Tower of Babel.* By the time we reach the end of the first eleven chapters of Genesis, sin has again established a dominant foothold among humanity—a humanity depicted as at once unified ("the whole world had one language and a common speech," Gen. 11:1) and still disobedient. Choosing to remain together to build a city and a reputation for themselves rather than fulfilling God's decree that they scatter and fruitfully fill the earth, humans once again incur God's judgment, who confuses their languages and forcibly scatters them over the face of the earth (signifying the creation of a diverse world humanity, separated into hostile people groups and all suffering the debilitating consequences of sin and disobedience).

(5) *The need for restoration.* Genesis 1–11 leaves humanity as a whole in a desperate state. Infected by sin and evil, all humanity stands under the judgment of holy God and in hostile relations with one another and the earth. How is it possible for this broken world to be mended? The opening verses of Genesis 12 offer Israel's understanding of the divinely instituted solution to the problem of humankind. In the call of Abraham God prepares a way for all humanity to return to right relationship with him and one another. "I will make you [Abraham] into a great nation [Israel], and I will bless you; I will make your name great, and you will be a blessing. I will bless those who bless you, and whoever curses you I will curse; and all peoples on earth will be blessed through you" (12:2–3). Through Israel, then, the whole of humanity is to find a way out of the curse of sin into the gracious blessing of God.

(6) *A light to the nations.* Israel's responsibility is to be the channel through which all the peoples of the earth come to know the blessing of Yahweh. The prophets affirm this when they exhort Israel to fulfill her role as "light

for the Gentiles [*goyim*], that you may bring my salvation to the ends of the earth" (Isa. 49:6).[20] The prophets also envision an eschatological end time when Jew and Gentile alike will acknowledge the sovereignty of God and join together in praising him. This eschatological time of unity is described in terms of harmonious relationships between humankind and beast, which signify the restoration of God's original creation purposes for the cosmos (cf. Isa. 2:2–4; 11:6–7; 65:25; Mic. 4:1–4).

(7) *New creation.* God's ultimate purpose, according to this important Old Testament thematic strand, is to bring about the restoration of his original creation intention by redeeming the human race and by re-creating the harmony and unity with which the cosmos began. Insofar as Psalm 47 anticipates a day when all the peoples of the earth will join with Israel as the people of God to praise Yahweh as king over the whole earth, it is this eschatological consummation of God's purpose that the psalmist holds in mind.

HOW DO WE today join in this anticipated reunification of God's fractured creation? Unity and harmony certainly do not seem to characterize much of our contemporary world, let alone the Christian church. Genocide rules the relations of people groups from Malaysia, to Africa, to the Balkans. The hostility of nations is a recognized factor in international relations and still dominates the politics of the Holy Land. What hope can we have of anything different? Or must we just settle for the reality of the moment? Psalm 47 offers a perspective of hope for those of us who may be enmeshed in the myopic view of the contemporary world and all its brokenness.

God reigns. The foundation of the psalmist's hopefulness is a vision of God as king. God's kingship is for the psalmist a present reality rather than a future possibility: *God is king* of all the earth![21] He has *already become king* in the present.[22] He has *already* taken a seat on his royal throne and continues

20. The phrase "light to/for the Gentiles/nations" [*leʾor goyim*] occurs three times in Isaiah. The first two (42:6 and 49:6) use the term *goyim*, which the NIV translate as "Gentiles" (meaning non-Jewish nations). The third is found in Isa. 51:4, where the word *ʿammim* ("peoples") is used instead. The Greek translation of *leʾor goyim* (*phos ethnon*) appears only once in Acts 13:47, where the Isa. 49:6 passage is quoted. Although some would consider this passage a reference to Yahweh's suffering servant, or the Messiah, or even Jesus, it seems clear that Isaiah intends Israel to understand that this responsibility is also hers.

21. Using the phrase *ki melek kol haʾareṣ ʾelohim* to emphasize both the present and continuing nature of Yahweh's rule.

22. Employing the perfect *malak ʾelohim ʿal goyim* to stress the completion of the act of becoming king in the present.

to be enthroned there.[23] This enthronement of God flies in the face of the seeming independent action of kings and nations. All actions of those who think themselves free and autocratic rulers, of nations who play world politics with their own self-interest in mind, are unable to alter or frustrate God's plan to redeem humanity and to restore his creation.

Despite their pretense to power and freedom, "the kings of the earth *belong to God*" (47:9). While this does not mean that every action undertaken by rulers and nations—whether evil or good—is set into motion or predestined by God, it does mean that God's purposes are not deterred by kingly pretensions or the politics of nations. God's purposes move unhindered to their completion despite the chaotic brokenness of our world. God subdues the nations and provides Israel with its true inheritance.[24]

A commitment to unity and to praise. When Psalm 47 calls "all you nations/peoples" to clap their hands and praise God, it calls them to a covenant of unity with the rest of the world. If "clapping hands" is a sign of reaching an agreement, the picture is one of the diverse nations of the world coming together in agreement to praise the God of Israel.

Christians are those who have been called into a new relationship of unity and praise in Jesus Christ. The event of Pentecost, in which God-fearers from all over the world and representing speakers of diverse languages were all empowered by the Holy Spirit to understand the mighty works of God in their own language, is a sign that the divisions of the Tower of Babel are being overcome in Jesus and that humanity is being reunified (Acts 2:1–21).

Clearly distrust, suspicion, prejudice, anger, and hatred between individuals and races have not been entirely removed, but the early church was remarkable for its ability to draw together a diverse group of Gentile believers into a fellowship of unity and praise. Whenever human beings are enabled by the Spirit of God to "do nothing out of selfish ambition or vain conceit, but in humility consider others better than" themselves (Phil. 2:3); when humans with all their fears and prejudices are able to declare with Paul, "There is neither Jew nor Greek, slave nor free, male nor female, for you are all one in Christ Jesus" (Gal. 3:28), then the redeeming grace of God has broken in among us and begun setting things right. We will not see the completion of that restoration until the last day, but the in-breaking of God's kingdom into our contemporary lives is enough reason to join the chorus of unity and praise this psalm exhorts.

---

23. Again, the use of the perfect tense *yašab* signifies God's enthronement as an accomplished fact, not a hoped-for future event.

24. A probable reference to the conquest of Canaan, in which Yahweh drove out the resident nations to provide an "inheritance" for Israel.

Psalm 48

A SONG. A psalm of the Sons of Korah.

1 Great is the LORD, and most worthy of praise,
in the city of our God, his holy mountain.
2 It is beautiful in its loftiness,
the joy of the whole earth.
Like the utmost heights of Zaphon is Mount Zion,
the city of the Great King.
3 God is in her citadels;
he has shown himself to be her fortress.

4 When the kings joined forces,
when they advanced together,
5 they saw her and were astounded;
they fled in terror.
6 Trembling seized them there,
pain like that of a woman in labor.
7 You destroyed them like ships of Tarshish
shattered by an east wind.

8 As we have heard,
so have we seen
in the city of the LORD Almighty,
in the city of our God:
God makes her secure forever. *Selah*

9 Within your temple, O God,
we meditate on your unfailing love.
10 Like your name, O God,
your praise reaches to the ends of the earth;
your right hand is filled with righteousness.
11 Mount Zion rejoices,
the villages of Judah are glad
because of your judgments.

12 Walk about Zion, go around her,
count her towers,
13 consider well her ramparts,
view her citadels,
that you may tell of them to the next generation.

[14]For this God is our God for ever and ever;
he will be our guide even to the end.

PSALM 48 FALLS into the category of psalms often called "Zion Songs" because they celebrate the glory and honor of Mount Zion—the hill on which Jerusalem and the temple stood—as the place chosen by Yahweh to be the defining point of his presence with and among Israel. "Mount Zion" is mentioned twice (48:2, 11) and "Zion" once (48:12), and the repetition of the words for city (*ᶜir* in 48:1, 8 [2x]; *qiryat* in 48:2)—which in 48:1 are identified with God's "holy mountain"—affirm this focus emphatically.[1]

Psalm 48 demonstrates a number of links with Psalms 45–47. Yahweh is called the "Great King," as in 47: 2. The theme of the "city of God" (48:1, 8) that dominates Psalm 48 was introduced in 46:4. God is called Yahweh Almighty (*yhwh ṣebaʾot*, 48:8), an epithet also used in the repeating refrain of 46:7 and 11. Yahweh is the "fortress" (*miśgab*, 48:3) of Zion, similar to "our fortress" in 46:7, 11. "Kings" flee before the power of Yahweh (48:4–7) as they submitted to his rule in 47:9. Like the memory of the glory of kingship in 45:17, the memory of the glory of Zion will be passed on to future generations (48:13).

The psalm is divided into four stanzas, two on each side of a central verse providing the thematic statement of the whole composition. The sections of the psalm thus revealed are: the presence of Yahweh in Zion (48:1–3), defeat of Zion's opponents (48:4–7), eternal security of Zion (48:8), worshipers celebrating Yahweh's mighty acts in behalf of Zion (48:9–11), and declaration to future generations (48:12–14).

The Heading (48:0)

THE HEADING TO Psalm 48 contains no new terms. It is designated a "song" and a "psalm."[2] Like the rest of the compositions in this first grouping in Book 2, Psalm 48 is attributed to "the Sons of Korah."[3]

---

1. Zion is variously identified with Jerusalem, the city of God, and with a hill/mountain on which Jerusalem or the temple was situated. Zion is viewed as the seat of human and divine kingship—the former associated with the palace and the latter with the temple.

2. For "song," see comments on the heading of Ps. 30; for "psalm," see comments on the heading of Ps. 3.

3. See comments on the heading to Ps. 42.

The Presence of Yahweh in Zion (48:1–3)

THE PSALM BEGINS typically for a song in praise of Yahweh. Yahweh is "great" (cf. 48:2d) and "worthy of praise" (lit., "the one who is being praised"). The reference to the "city of our God" and "his holy mountain" appear simply as the location of those who praise—or perhaps emphasize the presence of God with his people that calls forth praise.

It is only in verse 2 that the focus on the city/mountain where Yahweh makes himself present becomes clear. Rather than praiseworthy deeds and attributes of Yahweh, it is the beauty and lofty impregnability of Zion that occupies the attention of the psalmist (48:2). As in 47:7, where Yahweh was celebrated as "King of all the earth," so Mount Zion as the seat of his rule is the "joy of the whole earth," continuing the theme of the universal kingship of Yahweh initiated in 44:4. Mount Zion is compared with the most inaccessible reaches of Mount Zaphon[4]—in Canaanite religious thought the abode of the primary Canaanite deity El. Yahweh, who is "Most High" over all other deities (46:4; 47:2), has his own lofty abode, from which he exercises his universal dominion over kings, nations, and the whole earth.

God is in her citadels. While the focus of the psalm remains firmly fixed on Zion/Jerusalem, the praise of Yahweh continues subtly to undergird all. As in Psalm 46, where the presence of God within the "city of God" prevents her from falling (46:4–5), here it is because Yahweh is "in" the city and its citadels[5] that the city is secure and worthy of awe-filled praise. Yahweh "has shown himself" as the city's "fortress" (*miśgab*) or mountain hideout.[6] The "fortress" connection links Psalm 48 back to the refrain of Psalm 46 (46:7, 11), where Yahweh Almighty, the God of Jacob, is also celebrated as Israel's "fortress."

The Flight of the Foes (48:4–7)

BECAUSE OF THE presence of Yahweh Zion stands firm in the face of the enemy. The opposing kings are depicted as joining forces for a combined attack (48:4), reminiscent of the conspiracy of the "kings of the earth" against Yahweh and his anointed described in 2:2. The joint approach of these opposing kings is described with a not-so-subtle wordplay. The verb that describes their "advance" (*ʿbr*) is used in many contexts to describe "transgression" of the law or a king's command. Thus, those who advance in hostility on the city of God are simultaneously labeled "transgressors."

---

4. See the articles on "Zaphon" in Bible dictionaries, such as *EBD* and *ISBE*[2].

5. The "citadel" is the fortified area of a city, where a last stand is made in case of an attack. It most often occupied the highest ground and was therefore the most defensible position in the city.

6. For discussion of the various terms for refuge, fortress, etc., see comments on Ps. 20.

The approaching enemy is astonished and rendered numb by what they see. Whether it is the lofty, fortified city itself (as the NIV implies) or the presence of Yahweh within her that stuns the enemy host is uncertain.[7] The response of the enemy to what they see—whatever it might have been—is described in a series of verbs and expressions indicating astonishment and terror: "astounded," "in terror," "seized" with "trembling" and with "pain," like a woman in childbirth (48:5–6). The end result is total destruction of the enemy army like a fleet of ships sent to the bottom of the sea in a hurricane gale (48:7).[8]

Thematic Center (48:8)

WHAT A DIFFERENCE perspective makes! The enemy hosts look on Mount Zion, tremble, and flee to their destruction. By contrast, the psalmist and his readers look at the "city of our God" and find enduring security. This firm confidence provides the heart of Psalm 48 and can only be attributed to an awareness of Yahweh's presence in the midst of his holy city. This confidence is based on past tradition handed down in what the readers "have heard," but this transmitted tradition has been reaffirmed through what "we have seen."[9] This thematic center of confidence is picked up again at the end of the psalm, when the psalmist encourages the readers to pass on their perspective of Zion and her ramparts and citadels to "the next generation," so that they too may be confident in God's enduring presence as protector and guide (48:12–14).

The Worship of Praise (48:9–11)

THE SETTING OF the psalm within temple worship becomes explicit by the mention of the "temple" in 48:9. The term used here (*hekal*) is also used to refer to the "palace" of the human king, while the alternative term *miqdaš*

---

7. The pronoun "her" that the NIV inserts to suggest the object of the enemy's vision is the city itself is not in the Heb. text (cf. the corner brackets around this word in the NIV).

8. "Ships of Tarshish" are mentioned on several occasions in the Old Testament (1 Kings 10:22; Ps. 48:7; Isa. 23:1, 14; 60:9; Ezek. 27:25). The references indicate Tarshish was most likely a port city on the Mediterranean Sea, usually located in Spain (some suggest the port Tartessos). Solomon was said to have assembled a large fleet to ply the Mediterranean for the rich materials needed to support his many building projects (1 Kings 10:22). A fleet of ships built by King Jehoshaphat (2 Chron. 20:37) was completely destroyed in a storm as in our text (cf. also the endangerment of Jonah's ship by storm on its way to Tarshish in Jonah 1:3ff.).

9. The transmission of traditions to future generations as a source of continued encouragement is an important part of many psalms. See esp. Pss. 22:30; 48:13; 71:18; 78:4, 6; 79:13; 89:1; 102:18; 145:4.

("sanctuary") defines the temple more in terms of its sacral function. The emphasis here, then, is on the temple as the abode of God—the place where he is present among his people as king.

We meditate on your unfailing love. Within the temple—in the palace of the divine king at the heart of Mount Zion—the gathered worshipers are supremely aware of Yahweh's "unfailing love" (*ḥesed*)—his enduring faithfulness to his covenant obligations. When the people "compare or ponder" (NIV "meditate") Yahweh's *ḥesed*, there is *no* comparison—so that his "praise reaches to the ends of the earth."

God's "name" (48:10) is, of course, Yahweh, and knowledge of this personal name provides special access to his people. That name also reveals the character of the one who bears it.[10] His superiority is demonstrated in two ways: his righteous deeds ("your right hand is filled with righteousness") and his "judgments."[11] Because of Yahweh's righteous judgments the whole of the Israelite nation—from the central capital city, where the temple stood, to the scattered villages in the countryside—rejoice. The movement described here matches that exhibited in the preceding verse—from central temple to "the ends of the earth."

Future Hope (48:12–14)

THE PSALM CONCLUDES with a mental tour of the defense works of Zion: "her towers," "her ramparts," and "her citadels." These impressive battlements are impressive enough to inspire confidence, but it is the God who dwells within Zion and guides her who forms the basis of the psalmist's proclamation of confidence to future generations. Yahweh is the eternal God who guides his people like a shepherd (cf. Ps. 78:52; also Isa. 49:10; 63:14).[12]

---

10. For discussion of God's name, see comments on Ps. 8.

11. See comments on legal terms such as *ṣedeq* and *mišpaṭ* at 4:1–2 and 7:6–9.

12. This final phrase of this psalm (*ʿal mut*) is difficult in this context and deserves comment (see Kraus, *Psalms 1–59*, 472, 476–77). The word *mut* is apparently the infinitive construct of the verb *mwt* ("die"). The NIV's "even to the end" draws on this meaning, although this rendering with the preposition *ʿal* is awkward (something like "upon, against, concerning dying"). Since the similar phrase *ʿalamot* is found in the heading of Ps. 46, where it is treated as a reference to a tune for singing, the critical apparatus of *BHS* suggests that *ʿal mut* was similarly a part of the heading of Ps. 49 (appearing between "sons of Korah" and "psalm") that has been misplaced. A. R. Johnson, "The Role of the King in the Jerusalem Cultus," in *The Labyrinth*, ed. S. H. Hooke (New York: Macmillan, 1935), 92, understands the phrase as a reference to the Canaanite deity of death, Mot, and translates: "May he [Yahweh] lead us against 'death.'"

THE CITY OF GOD. Our usual impression of the Old Testament period is of a rather rural, nomadic society of shepherds and villagers eking out a sparse existence. In reality, the ancient Near East was significantly urbanized from a very early period, with evidence of expansive, walled cities going back into the fourth millennium B.C. Ancient Israel was no stranger to this pattern of urban living, having her roots in the Mesopotamian region during the time of great cities and cultural development (the third millennium B.C.). By the time the ancestors of Israel traveled through Canaan on their way to Egypt (ca. 2000–1700 B.C.), the region was already dominated by numerous walled cities that controlled the trade routes and exploited the economic productivity of the surrounding areas.

The Egypt of Israel's experience (second millennium B.C.) was also largely urbanized, with significant cities dating to the late fourth millennium or at least the early third. Thus, it is no surprise that once Israel settled the land of Canaan and gained military and political control of the region, her early kings (David and Solomon) moved quickly to develop an urban-based society with strategic cities providing protection and administrative oversight for the outlying villages.

Of these early Israelite strongholds, surely pride of place and reputation go to Jerusalem, the strategically chosen capital city from the time of David. This ancient Jebusite town stood in a sort of Canaanite "no man's land" between the southern and northern Israelite tribal groupings. These two associations of tribes, called at some times "Judah" (south) and "Ephraim" (north), had long histories of relative independence from one another, so that the monarchical unification of these two regions was always tentative and uneasy. David's choice of Jerusalem was politically astute in that it was a site well situated between the north and south and without specific association with either. From Jerusalem David was able to pull the two groups together into a firm alliance that Solomon ultimately inherited and developed.[13]

Jerusalem served the purpose of a political and military administrative center. David apparently envisioned the city as a point of religious unification

13. Ultimately the coalition was only temporary. The texts of Solomon's reign suggest rather uneven treatment of the two regions by the Judahite king. Forced labor and heavy taxation in support of Solomon's building campaigns appear to have fallen disproportionately on the northern tribes. Thus, when Solomon died, his successor, Rehoboam, was faced by an embassy of northerners seeking assurances that these uneven treatments would cease. Rehoboam's arrogant rejection of their concerns led to the immediate succession of the northern tribes to form the kingdom Israel, under the leadership of Jeroboam I. Thus the division of the kingdom (only an 80- to 120-year "experiment") was a reversion to earlier associations of loyalty with a long history antedating the monarchy.

to hold the kingdom together spiritually as well. His concern is exhibited both in his early determination to bring the ark of the covenant into the city as an indication of God's presence with the new king and nation and in his later plan to build a temple for Yahweh in Jerusalem (done by Solomon). The construction of that temple also parallels the general ancient Near Eastern pattern of deities associated with cities that were their special abode and where their chief temples were located. Cities related to deities in this way were thought to experience special protection and benefit.

While in Mesopotamia the polytheistic nature of society and culture permitted the existence of numerous cities with competing patron deities, the monotheistic state of Israel ultimately decreed that the one true God, Yahweh, could have a temple—and thus a special relationship—with only *one holy city*. Although biblical texts (and archaeology) suggest that Yahweh could be worshiped in a number of locations during the united monarchy and even in the southern kingdom of Judah after the split, royal ideology gradually became more insistent that true worship was possible in Jerusalem alone. This conclusion was probably hastened by the conflict that arose with the "sin of Jeroboam," who built alternate temples at Bethel and Dan to prevent citizens of the northern kingdom from being influenced by Judahite ideology when they traveled to Jerusalem for worship. This event, perhaps more than any other, acutely raised the question of where Yahweh could be worshiped; that is, "Where is the city of Yahweh?"[14]

From the time of David and Solomon the "city of Yahweh" becomes increasingly identified with Jerusalem. In some cases the site is associated with Mount Moriah, where Abraham proved his faithfulness by his willingness to sacrifice his only son, Isaac (Gen. 22).[15] The association of deities and holy mountains is a long-standing practice, and Israel early associated her experience of Yahweh with mountains of historical significance to her national faith journey. There is, of course, Mount Sinai, where the law was received, and Mount Horeb, where both Moses and Elijah heard the voice of Yahweh. These two mountains were often identified in Israel's thinking.

Along with Mount Moriah, Mount Zion (or just Zion) is often identified with the location of Jerusalem and the temple.[16] The comparison of

14. Although accused of worshiping Baal, Jeroboam and his northern successors probably continued to think of themselves as worshipers of Yahweh, as the use of the Yahweh elements in the names of their children indicates.

15. The reference to "his holy mountain" in 48:1 may be either to this association or to the later mention of Mount Zion (48:2).

16. Note the mention of Mount Zion in 48:2, 11, and 12. The name "fortress of Zion" may have been a original Jebusite designation of the site that was subsequently taken over by David and Israel (cf. 2 Sam. 5:7).

Mount Zion and Mount Zaphon in 48:2 drives home the connection of Zion as the abode of Yahweh. Mount Zaphon—a mountain on the coast of the Mediterranean north of Israel—figured prominently in Canaanite mythology as the mountain abode of Baal.[17] By the comparison, the psalmist is claiming equal or even greater glory and stature for Jerusalem/Zion as the abode of Yahweh.

A series of psalms in the Psalter in honor of Zion were probably particularly revered by pilgrims during the exilic period (cf. 137:3).[18] According to the theology of these psalms, Mount Zion has been chosen by Yahweh (87:2; 132:13) as the place where he will be particularly present with Israel (46:4–5; 48:3). As a result of God's choice and presence, Zion is protected (46:5; 48:8) and her inhabitants blessed (84:4), so that it is an honor to be recorded as a citizen of Jerusalem (87:5–6). In Psalm 132, the election of Zion as Yahweh's eternal throne is connected with the promise to David of a continuing dynasty (132:11–18).[19]

Reliance on the invulnerability of Zion/Jerusalem because of Yahweh's special relationship to the city and the Davidic dynasty got Judah into trouble when she failed to take the prophetic critique of her failure to live up to the demands of the law. Following the Exile, hope for the reestablishment of Zion/Jerusalem became a cornerstone of the Diaspora community's eschatological expectation.

SEEING IS SOMETIMES a choice we make. This is particularly true of seeing the mighty acts of God in our support. C. S. Lewis talks about stepping into a beam of light penetrating a dark potter's shed and looking along the beam to its source.[20] Often we have to take such conscious steps to change our perspective in order to see God at work. When some Judahites looked at the ramparts and citadels of Jerusalem, I suspect they were filled with wonder and pride *at their own human accomplishments!* The psalmist saw something far different—the wondrous work of Yahweh to draw together and protect his people.

---

17. Because of its prominence and visibility for long distances, the mountain and its name became ultimately the Heb. designation for the northern direction (*ṣapon*). In this regard, see the article on "Orientation" in *ISBE*².

18. Among these psalms are usually included Pss. 46; 48; 76; 84; 87; 122; and 132.

19. The passage on the promise to David appears in response to a sense of abandonment and hope for restoration (cf. 132:1–4, 10). Cf. comments on the term *melek* in the Bridging Contexts section of Ps. 2.

20. C. S. Lewis, "Meditation in a Toolshed," *God in the Dock*, 212–15.

The psalm suggests that the advancing enemy saw much the same as the psalmist, yet as these troops approached the city, they were astounded and fled in terror. Now, surely these same troops had torn down the walls of many a conquered city, whose fortifications far surpassed those of Jerusalem. What sent them running back down the wadis away from the holy city of Yahweh? Rather than human endeavor, they saw the works of God and his protective care arrayed against them.

When we rely on our own works, it is all too easy to become filled with pride and to come falsely to trust in ourselves rather than God. Such an approach to life is doomed to failure from the start. The most powerful leaders have been removed from office by election, coup, or even death. The most brilliant minds have been subdued by a stroke or Alzheimer's. The strongest body can fall prey to accident or disease. No matter how impressive our battle works, they are an empty hope unless God is there.

As we have heard, so have we seen. What is it that changes our perspective like the psalmist's to see the mighty acts of God at work in our world? How do we step into Lewis's sunbeam to see God as the source? Our psalm suggests that our eyes can be opened when we listen to the testimony of past generations and allow that witness to shape and direct our vision.

"As we have heard," says the psalmist, "so have we seen" (48:8). Picture a group of pilgrims who have lived their whole lives at long remove from Jerusalem in the farthest reaches of the Diaspora. Now they are at last on the way to worship in Jerusalem. All their lives they have heard of the holy city of Yahweh: its history, its theology, its grandeur, the hope it represents. But now they are almost there, approaching the first overlook to catch a glimpse of their long-awaited goal. Do you think that when they crest the last hill for their first look, they will be disappointed? Absolutely not! It is only after having lived several months in its twisting streets, contending with the heat and garbage and traffic—after the "new" has worn off—they might begin to ask what was so special about this hot, dusty, crowded place.

I myself have been there for that first glimpse, the first look at the city of Jerusalem, and I can tell you that I was not disappointed a bit! My heart welled up within me as I saw the walls of the Old City and the domes of churches and buildings within it. Even though the walls are Byzantine or later and even though few of the standing structures go back to the time of David or even Jesus, it did not matter. I was overwhelmed with a sense of awe at being at last in this special place.

What is it that gives this place—not particularly grand or astounding in human terms—such a special significance? It is the testimony of those who have gone before about the acts of God that have taken place within its walls. I had been prepared by those who had gone before to look for the acts of God there—to recall the ways God had redeemed his people, including me.

What are the Jerusalems of our own lives? Where has God erected ramparts and citadels for our protection? When have our enemies been turned back through the power of God? How can we step into the light to see and acknowledge that God is at work in our mundane lives, caring, protecting, and saving? The Old Testament narratives as a whole, and the psalms in particular, provide us with ready examples of common human beings confronted by the extraordinary presence of God in their lives. Drawing on the examples of these ancient witnesses, we may be emboldened to see God at work in our own lives.

Tell the next generation. It does not end there, that is, with our realization of God at work in our lives. Sight is confirmed in speech as our tongues are loosed to join the growing testimony of the faithful. "Walk about Zion, go around her, count her towers, consider well her ramparts, view her citadels" (48:12–13). I remember walking the walls of the Old City alone and marveling at the new sights I was seeing. But the experience was incomplete until I could share it with someone else. I still have my journals and slides and have probably bored far too many family members and friends with accounts of my visits (perhaps you have done the same), but my own understanding was only fully confirmed when I articulated it in word and writing. I was joining with the psalmist and all the other psalmists and Old Testament writers in trying to pass on the experience of God revealed in a new and unexpected way.

A movement is afoot in our own time to encourage parents and grandparents to record their life memories and experiences for future generations. There are seminars and workshops to offer practical ideas and support for those who wish to leave a legacy for their immediate family and future generations. I wish my own maternal grandfather had left such a testament. As a child he moved by buckboard from Tennessee to Texas and grew up to become a cotton farmer during the post-Civil War period. He was a marvelous storyteller, but his stories are now silenced and lost.

I also wish I knew more about his spiritual history. I know he was a strong Baptist deacon. I remember stories of how he and my grandmother supported and nurtured an African American congregation during a time when such contacts were not common and were generally disapproved. But beyond the sketchiest outline, I know little. And now that my own parents are dead, I have little chance to reconstruct an intimate portrait of their spiritual origins and journey and how they influenced my own.

Such testimony is important for "the next generation" because they help to shape the way they see God at work in their own lives. When we talk about how God has been active in our own decision-making and in chastening instruction, and when we talk about how our knowledge and experience of God's presence have not always been crystal clear, we are providing a perspective by which our children and their children can encounter God in the common events of their lives. We can describe the ramparts, the citadels, and the towers that can become their personal experience of God's protective care.

Our guide even to the end. One of the testimonies I hope we make clearly to the next generation is that God is our guide. The Hebrew behind the NIV translation here is a verb. Rather than the noun "guide," what the Hebrew says is that our God will "lead us along" into the future. This is no signpost or person pointing us the way we should go. God is one who guides us along—going with us into whatever the future may hold. In a sense, I suppose, Jesus performs this function of "guide" when he comes among us—first in human flesh and then in his Spirit—to lead us.

This kind of leader may prod, cajole, encourage, and entice us to action, but he is always there with us. He does not abandon us but comes along with us. I don't know about you, but that comforts me. It is as if the tour company assigns a guide to us to go along to show us the way, briefing us on the history and culture of the spot, smoothing our passage, answering our questions, and informing us of the customs we need to know in order to get the most out of our experience. This is far different from receiving a map and a pamphlet with brief entries on the sights and sites and a promise for the bus to meet us at the other end of the route.

God leads us along "even to the end." Again the Hebrew is expressive. The phrase *ʿal mut* is apparently a form of the verb "die." Although the construction is a bit awkward, the general force seems clear: God leads us even to the point of death. The NIV's "even to the end" seems to water that down unnecessarily. Thankfully God does lead us, going with us, even to the point of death. Jesus again is the appropriate model in his willingness to become human and to be like us "to death—even death on a cross!" (Phil. 2:5–8).

Psalm 49

FOR THE DIRECTOR of music. Of the Sons of Korah.
A psalm.

1 Hear this, all you peoples;
listen, all who live in this world,
2 both low and high,
rich and poor alike:
3 My mouth will speak words of wisdom;
the utterance from my heart will give understanding.
4 I will turn my ear to a proverb;
with the harp I will expound my riddle:

5 Why should I fear when evil days come,
when wicked deceivers surround me—
6 those who trust in their wealth
and boast of their great riches?
7 No man can redeem the life of another
or give to God a ransom for him—
8 the ransom for a life is costly,
no payment is ever enough—
9 that he should live on forever
and not see decay.

10 For all can see that wise men die;
the foolish and the senseless alike perish
and leave their wealth to others.
11 Their tombs will remain their houses forever,
their dwellings for endless generations,
though they had named lands after themselves.
12 But man, despite his riches, does not endure;
he is like the beasts that perish.

13 This is the fate of those who trust in themselves,
and of their followers, who approve their sayings. *Selah*
14 Like sheep they are destined for the grave,
and death will feed on them.
The upright will rule over them in the morning;
their forms will decay in the grave,
far from their princely mansions.

[15]But God will redeem my life from the grave;
he will surely take me to himself. *Selah*

[16]Do not be overawed when a man grows rich,
when the splendor of his house increases;
[17]for he will take nothing with him when he dies,
his splendor will not descend with him.
[18]Though while he lived he counted himself blessed—
and men praise you when you prosper—
[19]he will join the generation of his fathers,
who will never see the light of life.

[20]A man who has riches without understanding
is like the beasts that perish.

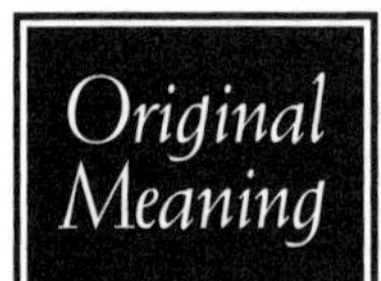

THE CONCERNS AND vocabulary of the wisdom tradition clearly mark Psalm 49 as a "wisdom psalm."[1] The primary concern or "riddle" (*ḥidah*) "expounded" here (49:4) is the apparent injustice of a world in which wicked fools prosper while the righteous wise live in poverty. This psalm shares with Job and Ecclesiastes a hard-won and enduring faith in Yahweh that rejects any easy or naive assumption of retribution in which wealth, prosperity, and ease of life can be associated with divine blessing for righteous living, while poverty is considered the consequence of sin.

The poem begins by addressing "all you peoples" (*kol haᶜammim*), an audience that links Psalm 49 back to the universalizing concerns of Psalms 46 and 47 (cf. esp. 47:1, 3, 9). Having come under the universal rule of the great king (46:8–10; 47:3, 7–9), the high and low, the rich and poor, are called to consider the conundrum of the prosperity of the wicked. The following treatment warns those who rely on their wealth as a sign of God's blessing and approval and encourages those whose righteousness has yet to issue forth in temporal prosperity that they should endure faithfully. This problem flows logically from the fact that if Yahweh indeed reigns, how can injustice remain?

The psalm is composed of three sections: an introduction in which the psalmist proposes to provide wisdom and insight into the vexing riddle at hand (49:1–4), a stanza exploring the futility of human reliance on wealth (49:5–12), and a final stanza describing the fate of those who trust in themselves (49:13–20). Both stanzas conclude with similar refrains (49:12, 20) that

1. See the discussion of wisdom psalms in "Types of Psalms" in the introduction.

subtly move the argument of the psalm from realization that wealth is no hedge against death (49:12) to the concluding implication that "understanding" is superior to wealth, since understanding God offers the only real hope of redemption.

The Heading (49:0)

THE HEADING OF Psalm 49 introduces no new terms, being referred to "the director of music," attributed to the "Sons of Korah," and labeled a "psalm" (*mizmor*).[2]

The Sage's Introduction (49:1–4)

THE PSALMIST BEGINS with a pluralized form of the classic opening to the Shema—Israel's call to faith—"Hear!" (*šimᶜu*). In the Shema (Deut. 6:4), Israel is called to acknowledge the unity and universal rule of Yahweh ("The LORD our God . . . is one") and to obey his commandments. In our psalm, it is the plural "peoples" of the earth who are called to hear, subtly driving home the universal perspective offered in 47:9, where "the nobles of the [peoples] assemble as the people of the God of Abraham."

It is also interesting to note that the language used here in the plural is characteristic of the singular pleas for deliverance often directed to Yahweh at the beginning of the laments (cf. 54:2). By using the language of lament, the psalmist sets the tone for the exploration of injustice and the call to enduring faith that follow.

Those called to hear are also described as those "who live in this world" (49:1b). The "world" (*ḥeled*) intended here is the world of *time*—akin to the Greek concept of *aion* ("the world at this time)" rather than *kosmos* ("the world in space"). That is, the emphasis is on those who live in this transitory age. The passing nature of human life is an important aspect of the psalmist's argument since wealth and ease have no eternal significance to those who pass away.

Low and high. Those called to hear and acknowledge the wisdom of the psalmist's words represent all aspects of human society, as the two merisms used in 49:2 indicate.[3] They are "low and high,"[4] "rich and poor."[5] The

---

2. See comments on the heading of Ps. 4 for "the director of music," on the heading of Ps. 42 for "the Sons of Korah," and on the heading of Ps. 3 for *mizmor*.

3. For comments on the poetic technique of merism, see "The Poetry of the Psalms" in the introduction.

4. In this combination, *bene ʾadam* seems to designate "simple folk; peasants" while *bene ʾiš* describes "children of the elite." Cf. 62:9, where the same opposition of classes occurs. In its singular form *ben ʾadam* has the more universal sense of "human being."

5. See comments on 10:16–18 for the various terms for the poor and oppressed.

opposition of privileged and oppressed, rich and poor, sets the stage for the discussion that occupies the body of the psalm.

My mouth will speak words of wisdom. Like the sages of Proverbs, Ecclesiastes, and Job, the psalmist places great stock on the educational character of the wise utterance. Like Qohelet, the self-conscious narrator of Ecclesiastes, the psalmist makes explicit the didactic purpose of the instruction. He desires to "give understanding" (49:3), drawing insight from deep within ("from my heart"). Since the heart is the seat of moral reasoning and decision-making, such "heart talk" is neither emotional nor intellectual claptrap but represents the deep and enduring outflow of the moral character of the speaker.

Proverb . . . riddle. The psalmist promises to give attention to the traditional forms of wise speech and instruction—the "proverb" and the "riddle" (49:4). There is little in the rest of the psalm that conforms to this expectation, although the repeated refrain (49:12, 20) may well represent a core proverbial saying that the psalmist uses to hammer home the main theme. The rest of the discussion is more like the extended discussion of Proverbs 1–9 or the narrative of Ecclesiastes than proverbial instruction.

The "riddle" (*ḥidah*) can approximate our modern-day puzzles or brainteasers used primarily for entertainment. The classic biblical example is the interchange between Samson and his wedding guests in Judges 14. Samson's riddle ("Out of the eater, something to eat; out of the strong, something sweet") was based on a set of events known only to him and so was a "sure thing." After wheedling the answer from Samson's bride-to-be, the guests replied with a stinging riddle of their own: "What is sweeter than honey? What is stronger than a lion?" The obvious answer—love—stabbed Samson with the knowledge that his beloved had betrayed him. This leads to his poetic but straightforward reply: "If you had not plowed with my heifer, you would not have solved my riddle."

Besides this entertaining form of the *ḥidah*, the term occasionally refers to difficult language or topics that require deep insight to resolve. It is probably this kind of philosophic discussion that took place when the Queen of Sheba tested Solomon's reputed wisdom with "riddles" (*ḥidot*). Undoubtedly this second meaning of *ḥidah* is operative in our psalm, with the difficult topic of discussion being the contradiction encountered when those who are wicked enjoy ease and prosperity while the righteous suffer oppression and want. A similar concern occupies the author of Psalm 73, who almost loses faith because of the seeming injustice that results from the prosperity of the arrogant wicked.

The Futility of Human Wealth (49:5–12)

WHY SHOULD I FEAR? The apparent collapse of righteous order that the prosperity of the wicked seems to herald does not undermine the psalmist's confidence in the ultimate good intent of God for the righteous. He acknowledges the reality of "evil days" and the corrupting influence of the crowd of "wicked deceivers" (*ᶜawon ᶜaqebay*),[6] who press their view of the efficacy of wealth (49:6) and use it to intimidate and oppress the poor.

The fear such a position could (and did) bring to the righteous poor is countered effectively by the psalmist's long view—the awareness of the cold, hard truth expressed in the following verses: "No man can redeem the life of another or give to God a ransom for him—the ransom for a life is costly, no payment is ever enough—that he should live on forever and not see decay" (49:7–9).[7] The Old Testament law instituted a process of "redemption" whereby persons and animals dedicated for sacrifice to God (usually the firstborn) could be released from this obligation by a payment. It was also common to pay "ransom" to free captives taken in war. Any such payment to God in order to free a human from the obligation of death is impossibly expensive and doomed to failure from the start. As the psalmist shows later (49:15), only God has the right and the wherewithal to redeem a human life.[8]

Wise men die. The psalmist poses the question of the value of human wealth in its starkest terms. For all their prosperity, wicked fools come inexorably to their end in death—just like the impoverished sage. The rich might argue that their wealth buys much comfort, pleasure, and control, but the singing sage replies that such power is illusory and pales beside the steady faithfulness of the poor, who have been forced by circumstance to acknowledge what is truly of ultimate value and pleasing to God. Such faithfulness is pared to its essentials since, like Job and the impossible demand of the Sermon on the Mount, it acknowledges that life is more than food and the body more than raiment (Matt. 6:25). The wealth of the wicked will pass to others after their inevitable deaths; rather than living forever in their

---

6. The phrase is difficult, with a literal meaning "the crooked activity of my heel," which makes little sense. *BHS* suggests an emendation to *ᶜoqebay*, a participle meaning "those who deceive me."

7. The phrase translated "redeem" (from *pdh*) normally refers to an act of paying to redeem humans or animals who by law belong to Yahweh (cf. Ex. 13:13). The related noun "ransom" (*koper*) means a price paid to release a captive or seized property. Both terms are used in vv. 7–8.

8. This psalm may well form the background of Jesus' teaching in Matt. 16:26 (Mark 8:37): "What good will it be for a man if he gains the whole world, yet forfeits his soul? Or what can a man give in exchange for his soul?"

magnificently constructed mansions, all the deceased will call the grave their eternal home (Ps. 49:11a).

The naming of lands after oneself (49:11b) was a prerogative normally reserved for conquering kings. Here the rich practice the naming of lands in a vain attempt to ensure some immortality for themselves. The psalmist ironically observes that the only land they will continue to possess after death is the tombs in which they are buried.

Man . . . is like the beasts that perish. The theme of the futility of relying on human riches is driven home in encapsulated form by the first occurrence of the refrain that later concludes the psalm (49:12, 20). In the LXX and the Syriac version, verse 12 is identical with verse 20, exchanging the phrase "without understanding" (*welo˒ yabin*) for verse 12's "does not endure" (*bal yalin*). The textual tradition is varied at this point, but it seems preferable to maintain the distinctive readings between these two verses with their added meanings. In the first the point is that riches do not guarantee endurance. The second suggests it is not riches themselves that are the issue but the lack of understanding that so often accompanies them. In either case, those with riches and those without join the beasts in their ultimate vulnerability to death (49:12b).

The Fate of Those Who Trust Themselves (49:13–20)

THE SECOND STANZA begins with a descriptive heading that sets the scene for what follows: "This is the fate of those who trust in themselves." Until now it has been the power of wealth that was trusted, but the subtle shift indicates the real issue, namely, the attitude of self-reliance that refuses to acknowledge dependence on Yahweh alone. It is this latter acceptance of one's absolute dependence on the undeserved mercy of Yahweh that is at the core of Israel's understanding of "the fear of the LORD." Such fear—which is considered the requisite attitude of the righteous—is not terror but submission of one's whole being to the vulnerable state of Yahweh's control. This is what the arrogant rich lack in our psalm—the willingness to give up control and to allow Yahweh to rule.

Like sheep.[9] Like trusting sheep who follow their shepherd to pasture, those who trust in themselves find their true shepherd in Death, who leads

9. Verse 14 is particularly difficult as the number of suggested emendations in the *BHS* textual apparatus indicate. Besides the ambiguous meaning of the verb *r˓h* ("lead to pasture/graze upon"), the major difficulties include (1) whether the verb translated "rule" is to be taken from the root *rdd* or from *yrd* ("go down [to Sheol"]); (2) whether the enigmatic *weṣuram* ("and their rock") ought to be emended to *yeṣuram* ("their form/shape") or *ṣuratam* ("their design/plan"); and (3) whether the infinitive construct form *leballot* ("waste away, decay") ought to be emended to *liklot* ("perish").

them to pasture in Sheol. Picking up on a certain ambiguity within the verb "lead to pasture" (*rʿh*), which can also mean "graze," the NIV and other commentators find a more sinister wordplay in the text. Rather than just leading these unperceptive sheep to pasture, Death will in fact "graze on them"—violating the role of shepherd as protector of his flock.[10]

The upright will rule. Not only will the rich find their hopes dashed when they descend to Sheol as food for Death, but the tables will also be turned as they discover themselves ruled over by the "upright" (*yešarim*). As well as an admonition to the rich who trust in their wealth and power, this verse offers encouragement to the righteous poor, who have been experiencing fear and deception in their oppression by the rich (49:5). Whether this ruling is thought to take place before death or in some retributive form of afterlife is unclear.[11]

The reversals of the expectations of the rich continue with the decay of their bodies in the grave (49:14c; cf. 49:9) and their loss of their "princely mansions" (49:14d; cf. 49:11, 16b).

God will redeem my life from the grave. This verse has traditionally been taken as an affirmation of confidence made by all the faithful poor who have been oppressed by the arrogant rich. The result is a studied contrast between the dashed hopes of the rich, who trust in themselves but can find no way to extend life or avoid death, and the faithful poor, who cast themselves totally on the strength and care of Yahweh. These latter *will* experience the redemption that the rich so fruitlessly seek.

Despite this longstanding tradition of interpretation, I find it tempting to understand these words not as the affirmation of the faithful but as a quotation of the futile hopes of the wicked.[12] The sense then is: "Their bodies rot in the grave, *although they had confidently proclaimed*, 'God will redeem my life from the grave; he will surely take me to himself.'"

Do not be overawed. In a backward glance at the intimidation of the poor described in 49:5, the psalmist counsels the reader/listener not to be "overawed" (lit., "don't be afraid"; cf. 49:5) at the increasing wealth of another individual (in contrast with their own continuing poverty). The reasons he gives for this have nothing to do with the very real prospect of oppression

---

10. In Canaanite mythology, the god of Death, Mot, receives the dead into the netherworld by swallowing them. He is graphically described as "one lip to earth and one to heaven, he stretches his tongue to the stars. Baal enters his mouth, descends into him like an olive-cake, like the yield of the earth and trees' fruit" (IAB, ii).

11. If the verb "rule" (*rdd*) is instead taken to be from *yrd* ("go down"), the phrase may refer to the descent of the wicked rich directly to Sheol. In this case the question of the upright ruling over the arrogant rich is removed.

12. See Craigie, *Psalms 1–50*, 360.

by the *nouveau riche*, who use their disdain as a way of distinguishing between themselves and the poor from whom they have only recently come. Rather, he gives two reasons.

(1) Wealth is a temporal distinction limited to this life; neither wealth or "splendor" (*kabod* ["glory"])[13]—that recognizable dignity or honor a person receives in public circles—is of any value in the grave. This seems to leave enjoyment here and now as the primary purpose for amassing wealth. (2) The psalmist's second reason cuts at the root of the misguided assumption that wealth is an indication of divine affirmation and blessing. Although the rich person's inward self-estimation (*nepeš*) of his own blessedness is matched by public perception ("men praise you when you prosper"), neither has effect on the estimation of God.

Man . . . is like the beasts that perish. The final message is emphasized at the conclusion by the subtle adaptation of the refrain in 49:12. In its first sounding the refrain simply indicated that riches have no staying power and cannot help one avoid the inevitability of death. Here, however, the substitution of *welo᾽ yabin* ("and does not understand") for the earlier *bal yalin* ("will not endure") indicates that it is the *attitude* of the rich and not the riches themselves that constitute the fatal error. The rich lack an awareness of their absolute dependence on Yahweh in life and in death—they lack any fear of Yahweh—which in turn leads the psalmist to describe them as "like the [unthinking] beasts that perish" (49:21b).

THE IDEA OF redemption or ransom was relatively common in ancient Israel. There are at least three Hebrew verbs (and related nouns) associated with the concept: *kpr* ("cover over, appease, atone for"), *g᾽l* ("buy back, redeem"), and *pdh* ("ransom, redeem"). *Kpr* is largely used for atonement for sin, though the noun *koper*, which appears in our passage, is translated several times as "ransom," and on other occasions as "bribe."[14] *G᾽l* is concerned primarily with the redemption of property (as in the story of Ruth, Naomi, and Boaz), in the sense of buying back tribal property that has passed on to another. *Pdh*, the most common root, describes a process of replacement of persons with a payment of money and is thus more closely related to what we might understand as "ransom." It is this latter term that figures most prominently in our psalm (49:7, 8), along with the noun *koper* (49:7).

13. For comments of the meaning of *kabod*, see discussion at 3:3–4.

14. For "ransom," see Ex. 21:30; 30:12; 25:21–22; Job 33:24; Ps. 49:7; Prov. 13:8; 21:18; Isa. 43:3. For "bribe," cf. 1 Sam. 12:3; Job 36:18; Prov. 6:35; Amos 5:12.

The most frequent use of *pdh* is in the constellation of verses dealing with the phenomenon of the "redemption of the firstborn." In Exodus, the Israelites are instructed to consecrate to Yahweh "every firstborn male. The first off-spring of every womb among the Israelites belongs to the LORD, whether man or animal" (Ex. 13:2). Parents were to teach their children that this act of consecration was a response to the deliverance of Israel from the hand of Pharaoh by means of the death of all the firstborn of men and animals (13:14–15). The firstborn of livestock "belong to the LORD" and are to be sacrificed to him. The exceptions permitted are firstborn donkeys[15] and human children, both of which were to be "redeemed" (13:12–13). While the purpose of this consecration of firstborn children to Yahweh is not completely clear, it was viewed as a serious duty not to be shirked (22:29; 34:19–20).

In Numbers, the redemption of firstborn Israelites takes a new turn with the dedication of the Levites as a special tribe of servants to Yahweh, who hold no tribal allotment of land and are supported through the sacrifices and gifts of the other tribes. The initial consecration of the Levites is connected with the redemption of the firstborn Israelites in Numbers 3, when Yahweh commands a count be made of "all the firstborn Israelite males who are a month old or more" (3:40). The Levites (who have already been counted) are then taken by Yahweh "in place of all the firstborn of the Israelites" (3:41). When the count is completed, the number of firstborn exceed the number of Levites by 273, so that a redemption payment was required at the rate of five shekels each (3:42–51).

The circumstance returns again in Numbers 8:15–19, where it is acknowledged that the Levites are a special group of Israelites "who are to be given wholly to [Yahweh]" (8:16) and who have been taken "in place of the firstborn, the first male offspring from every Israelite woman" (8:16). The firstborn were originally dedicated to Yahweh because they were delivered from death by the grace of Yahweh during the Passover, and their lives were thus "set apart" for Yahweh's purposes (8:17). The substitution of the Levites for the firstborn may indicate that before the official priesthood existed, the consecration of the firstborn to the service of Yahweh may have filled this gap.[16]

In the final stage of the canonical Old Testament, the question of the consecration of the firstborn son to Yahweh was resolved by "redemption" either by a substitutionary sacrifice of a lamb (Ex. 13:12–13) or for a financial consideration (Lev. 27:6; Num. 3:46). It remains unclear, however,

15. Perhaps donkeys were redeemed because of their economic importance as pack animals among the early nomadic Israelites.

16. Hannah's dedication of Samuel to lifelong service of Yahweh may reflect such an understanding.

whether originally the consecration of firstborn sons was understood as a sacrifice, as was demanded for livestock. The lack of surprise evidenced by Abraham in response to Yahweh's command to sacrifice his firstborn son, Isaac, in Genesis 22 suggests such sacrifices may not have been unheard of. The practice is known as late as the monarchy (1 Kings 16:34; 2 Kings 3:27; Mic. 6:7). The whole idea of "redemption"—that is, paying a substitutionary price to withdraw the firstborn—suggests that sacrifice may have been an original understanding in some circles.

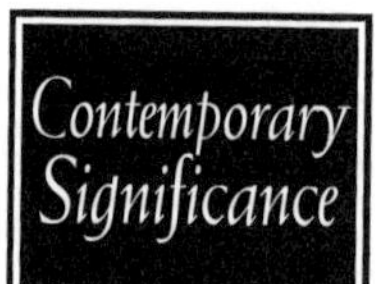

WHO ARE THE ARROGANT WICKED? Sometimes it can be a dangerous thing to allow the words of the psalmists to become the word of God to us. When that strange transformation takes place, we often find those human words of complaint coming back at us in uncomfortable ways. That is particularly true for me with the psalmist's complaint against the abusive and arrogant rich, as in this psalm. Having worked for several years in a Christian nonprofit organization concerned to develop programs of education for ministry for underserved ethnic minority communities in an urban setting, I am more and more often brought up short by the realization of how much I really have and possess in relative standards.

When I really admit it, I must acknowledge that I live among the privileged few of the world. Our standard of living here in the Eurocentric Western Hemisphere is among the highest anywhere. Our *wants* may be many, but our actual *needs* are few. I have never been hungry, unclothed, or constantly threatened. Disease is an infrequent visitor, and medical services plentiful. I may complain over rising costs, but resources are abundant and available for my use.

I said it is dangerous to hear the psalms as God's word to me because it opens my eyes to new perspectives I would not choose on my own. I would rather identify with the voices of complaint in the psalms: the abused, struggling have-nots, under constant pressure from without and plagued by doubts within. But my life is a bit too easy to fit many of these situations. Thus, my tendency is to *spiritualize* the sufferings and complaints of the psalmists. Who are my *spiritual* enemies? How am I suffering *spiritually*? How can I turn the attack of the powerful abusers into an attack against my Christian beliefs and principles by unbelievers?

The problem in this approach is that it silences the voices of those who are truly suffering want, pain, abuse, exploitation, and so on. It lets me off the hook by preventing me from having to acknowledge how in many ways my own consumerism and materialism feed the cycle of abuse in which the rich few live well off the misery of the poor many. That is why I need to hear the psalms not only as my words or as words that I can appropriate as my own, but as God's words—challenging me and confronting me with my complicity in the exploitation of others that my ease of living is grounded in.

Perhaps you are like me, spiritualizing the psalms and so masking the real challenge they speak to us from the mouths of others and the mouth of God. If so, I pray that God will send an uncomfortable spirit to convict both of us that he is a God who upholds the cause of the poor. "Blessed is he who has regard for the weak" (41:1).

The measure of life. The heart of Psalm 49 focuses on the riddle of the kind of awe we accord the ostentatiously rich. Often entertainers and athletes experience veneration far beyond what should be expected. There is a cult of envious fascination with the rich and famous. Even as the tabloids play out all the sordid aspects of their lives, we still believe there is something magic and special about those public figures who have the nerve and the wealth to live life on their own selfish terms. A certain part of us would like to do it too.

Nevertheless, Psalm 49 assures us that our awe and fascination are misplaced. There is nothing particularly special about the rich and famous. As the poet puts it: "But man, despite his riches, does not endure; he is like the beasts that perish" (49:12). Those golden people, with all their money and worldly power, are just a bunch of animals that die just as you and I do. In fact, says the psalmist, if we have the benefit of wisdom and perception, we are far better off than they could ever be. Without understanding they simply die like beasts. "But God will redeem my life from the grave; he will surely take me to himself" (49:15).

It is not clear whether the psalmist is speaking of a developed understanding of life after death. As 49:10 indicates, even the wise cannot live forever and enjoy the wealth they establish. Thus, if all humans die and are unable to avoid death despite great wealth and power, then what is left to measure the value of a life? We cannot look to some eternal future but must make our estimation on the basis of this life, the here and now. There are, then, two ways to measure the value of such a life. (1) The first is on the basis of wealth amassed, pleasure explored, and power wielded. But these are short-lived and unlasting. They cannot be taken with us and lose all value to us when we are gone (49:11, 16–19).

(2) The other way to evaluate a life is on the basis of faithfulness. Whether one is high or low, rich or poor, wise or foolish, the proof of a life well spent is this: "In what/whom do you trust?" Those who trust in themselves and wealth or power are doomed to the decay of death. Those who, however, trust in God will find their significance there. The former way is folly, says

the psalmist, and doomed to perish, while the way of enduring trust is for the psalmist the way of wisdom honored by God. What I cannot redeem for myself, God redeems for me (49:15).

The costly ransom of a life. What I cannot do for myself, God does for me. And nowhere does the idea of redemption of human life by God work itself out more clearly than in the work of Jesus Christ. Jesus is himself the costly price of redemption for human life. In the LXX of Psalm 49:7, the Hebrew verb *pdh* ("redeem") is rendered by the Greek *lytroo* ("to free by paying a ransom, redeem"). The noun form related to this verb (*lytron* ["price of release, ransom]") is used in the New Testament to describe the work of Jesus in our behalf. "The Son of Man did not come to be served, but to serve, and to give his life as a ransom for many" (Matt. 20:28; cf. Mark 10:45; 1 Tim. 2:6; Heb. 9:15). The impossibly high cost of redemption is acknowledged in Matthew 16:24: "What good will it be for a man if he gains the whole world, yet forfeits his soul? Or what can a man give in exchange for his soul?" (16:26).

In a way similar to Psalm 49, the Matthew passage encourages us not to trust in our own ability (through power, wealth, etc.) to save lives but to take up our cross in faithful service to God—in effect, to "lose" our lives as the key to finding them (Matt. 16:24–25). The reward for such a move of reliant trust in God is the "reward" each will receive from God when the Son of Man comes.

This is a message that we who have so much need to hear. All that we have and are can never be enough to pay God the price of our lives. Recent attempts on the part of certain groups to demand "restitution" for wrongs perpetrated on them or their ancestors at an earlier date provide another image alongside the idea of "redemption." Both redemption and restitution seek to set an equivalent financial value on some abstract experience: wartime atrocities, national bias, and exploitation of a minority group. Whenever we try this, we discover just how impossible it is to place a price on human dignity or on a human life. Just how much money can take away the horror and indignity of being forced into prostitution for enemy troops? How much is a couple of centuries of exploitation worth?

The innocent death of Jesus on behalf of sinful humanity was such an event of inequity. How do we pay God back for that? What price can you place on God's taking the punishment for a world's misdeeds? The price he has paid in Jesus is far too high for any hope of restitution. Our spotty attempts at good living won't even pay off the interest. Thankfully God does not ask for repayment—only acceptance of the redemption he has made possible for us. May we have the wisdom to take it.

Psalm 50

A PSALM OF Asaph.

1 The Mighty One, God, the LORD,
speaks and summons the earth
from the rising of the sun to the place where it sets.
2 From Zion, perfect in beauty,
God shines forth.
3 Our God comes and will not be silent;
a fire devours before him,
and around him a tempest rages.
4 He summons the heavens above,
and the earth, that he may judge his people:
5 "Gather to me my consecrated ones,
who made a covenant with me by sacrifice."
6 And the heavens proclaim his righteousness,
for God himself is judge. *Selah*

7 "Hear, O my people, and I will speak,
O Israel, and I will testify against you:
I am God, your God.
8 I do not rebuke you for your sacrifices
or your burnt offerings, which are ever before me.
9 I have no need of a bull from your stall
or of goats from your pens,
10 for every animal of the forest is mine,
and the cattle on a thousand hills.
11 I know every bird in the mountains,
and the creatures of the field are mine.
12 If I were hungry I would not tell you,
for the world is mine, and all that is in it.
13 Do I eat the flesh of bulls
or drink the blood of goats?
14 Sacrifice thank offerings to God,
fulfill your vows to the Most High,
15 and call upon me in the day of trouble;
I will deliver you, and you will honor me."

[16] But to the wicked, God says:

"What right have you to recite my laws
or take my covenant on your lips?
[17] You hate my instruction
and cast my words behind you.
[18] When you see a thief, you join with him;
you throw in your lot with adulterers.
[19] You use your mouth for evil
and harness your tongue to deceit.
[20] You speak continually against your brother
and slander your own mother's son.
[21] These things you have done and I kept silent;
you thought I was altogether like you.
But I will rebuke you
and accuse you to your face.

[22] "Consider this, you who forget God,
or I will tear you to pieces, with none to rescue:
[23] He who sacrifices thank offerings honors me,
and he prepares the way
so that I may show him the salvation of God."

THE FIRST PSALM in the Psalter attributed to Asaph, Psalm 50 breaks the string of Korahite psalms that began with Psalm 42–43. Following Psalm 50, the second great collection of "Davidic" psalms is introduced in Psalm 51 and extends (with the exception of Pss. 66 and 67) to the single Solomonic Psalm 72 at the conclusion of Book 2. Although Psalm 50 is part of the so-called Elohistic Psalter (Pss. 42–83), the divine name Yahweh does appear once in 50:1.

Thematically Psalm 50 shares links with the group of psalms beginning with Psalm 46 and is concerned with the security of Zion/Jerusalem. Psalms 45–50 flow out of the rather jarring juxtapositioning of Psalm 44, with its plaintive acknowledgment of the collapse of the Davidic monarchy in the Exile (44:9–14, 20–21), and Psalm 45, with its festive celebration of the wedding ceremony of the king. Yet in the arrangement of these two psalms, it becomes clear that the older psalm of celebration has been subtly reinterpreted in light of the exilic experience to offer renewed hope that *God's* throne "will last for ever and ever" (45:6). As a result, Psalm 45 takes on a messianic edge and Psalms 46–49 increasingly turn the reader's eyes to God, who is the mighty fortress in whom the exilic community must place their trust.

Psalm 50, then, describes the theophanic approach of Yahweh into the Jerusalem temple in order to judge Israel according to their covenant obligations. This emphasis on the covenant (explicitly mentioned in 50:5, 16) may explain the inclusion of the name of the covenant God, Yahweh, in 50:1. The psalm is divided into three sections: (1) an introduction in which Yahweh appears to judge his people (50:1–6), an accusing speech to the people counseling more reliance on God than sacrifice (50:7–15), and a harsh condemnation of the "wicked," who forget God but who are nevertheless called to return to covenant faithfulness (50:16–23).

The Heading (50:0)

THE PSALM IS the first to be attributed to Asaph (*leʾasap*). The remaining Asaphite psalms are grouped together in Psalms 73–83 at the beginning of Book 3 of the Psalter (Pss. 73–89) and at the conclusion of the so-called Elohistic Psalter (Pss. 42–83). Asaph is the chief of the Levitical singers (along with Heman and Jeduthun)[1] mentioned in 1 Chronicles 6:39 as being put in charge of the "service of song" in the Jerusalem temple and in 16:1–4 as being appointed to "minister before the ark of the LORD, to make petition, to give thanks, and to praise the LORD, the God of Israel" (16:4). Besides the mention of Asaph, the heading contains only the most general genre designation *mizmor* ("psalm").[2]

God the Judge (50:1–6)

THE INTRODUCTORY PASSAGE sets the scene for the two divine speeches that occupy the body of the psalm. God (identified as Yahweh only in the opening verse) comes in theophanic glory (50:3) to sit as judge (50:4, 6) over his covenant people (50:5, 16). At the same time his appearance is linked with sun imagery (50:1–2), a not completely unexpected phenomenon since the sun is often linked with judgment in the ancient Near East.[3]

---

1. Heman appears in the heading to Ps. 88, while Jeduthun is found in the heading to Ps. 39. Because the latter psalm also contains an attribution to David (*ledawid*), some question whether the reference to Jeduthun is an attribution of authorship or some type of musical direction (cf. 1 Chron. 16:41–42).

2. See comments on the heading to Ps. 3.

3. Sun imagery is used of Yahweh in other Old Testament contexts (e.g., Pss. 19; 37; 84:11; 104:1–3). For more on the connection of the sun and judgment in the ancient Near East, see comments on Ps. 19.

The Mighty One, God, the LORD. A rather awkward series of divine epithets opens the section. In actuality the Hebrew brings together the most common general terms for God in the ancient Near East (*ʾel* and *ʾelohim*) with the personal name of Israel's God, Yahweh (*yhwh*). The effect is to identify Yahweh with these more general terms as a way of saying that the God whom you worship as *ʾel* or *ʾelohim* is in fact Yahweh. This is most interesting in light of the fact that Psalm 50 stands within the Elohistic Psalter, where the divine name Yahweh is thought to have been replaced by the more general terms/names for God: *ʾelohim* and *ʾel*.

Speaks and summons the earth. This introductory passage is surrounded by a split merism of "earth" (50:1) and "heavens" (50:6), both in the context of speaking. In 50:1, Yahweh "speaks" and "summons" the whole earth, using another merism: "from the rising of the sun to the place where it sets."[4] In the heart of the section (50:4), the two ends of the merism are brought together as the purpose of the divine summons—delayed since verse 1 by the theophanic appearance of Yahweh (50:2–3)—is resumed through the use of the identical verb "summons." In 50:4, Yahweh summons both heavens and earth[5] as witnesses in the case against his people. The testimony itself is given in the final verse of the section: in relation to his covenant people, Yahweh is without fault—"righteous," as the heavens declare (50:6).

God shines forth. In the middle of issuing the divine subpoena, the psalmist pauses to make way for the theophanic appearance of God. God "shines forth" from Zion, a place that plays an important thematic role in Psalms 48–53.[6] The Zion theme is also linked in Psalm 48 (48:2, 11, 12) with the "city of God" and "divine king" themes (48:2, 8) characteristic of Psalms 46–48, suggesting that the whole group extending at least from Psalms 46 through 53 share interlocking themes and interests.

Zion is described as "perfect in beauty" (*miklal yopi*),[7] an indication of the high, even aesthetic regard held for the Temple Mount and the temple precincts located there. Great love and emotion are directed toward the spot, as a survey of the psalms mentioning Zion will affirm.

---

4. For a discussion of the poetic feature of merism, see comments on "Techniques of Hebrew Poetry" in the introduction.

5. Note how the reference to "heavens above, and the earth" chiastically reverses the order of elements in the split merism that surrounds this section—"earth" (50:1b) and "heavens" (50:6a).

6. The place name Zion (*ṣiyyon*)—a reference to the hill in Jerusalem on which the temple stood—appears some thirty-nine times in thirty-one psalms. Within Book 2 of the Psalter (Pss. 42–72) Zion appears eight times in six psalms: 48:2, 11, 12; 50:2; 51:18; 53:6, 65:1, 69:35. The largest collection of Zion psalms is found in Book 5 (Pss. 107–150), where thirteen psalms have the term fourteen times.

7. The abstract noun *miklal* is related to the verbal root *kll* ("make complete, perfect").

Our God comes. From the splendor of Zion and in the splendor of his glory, Yahweh "comes" into the sphere of human experience associated—as often in theophany—with fire and storm. "A fire devours before him"[8] and "around him a tempest rages." God will no longer remain silent—here God's silence represents not a withdrawal of support but a delay of judgment (cf. 50:21)—but will speak his case.

He summons. God's subpoena is for both witnesses (heavens and earth)[9] and defendants ("my consecrated ones," 50:5) to gather for the hearing of the case. Having served as witnesses to the original covenant agreement between Yahweh and Israel (Deut. 4:26), heavens and earth are now called to return as witnesses for the prosecution. That the matter is concerned with the covenant is made explicit in 50:5, where the accused are introduced as "my consecrated ones [*ḥasiday* is more accurately "my faithful ones"—those who practice *ḥesed*[10]], who made a covenant with me by sacrifice."

Righteous judge. The testimony of the heavens is made explicit as the first section of the psalm concludes. God—who is accuser and judge in these proceedings—is declared by the primary witness (we are probably to assume the "heavens" speak for the "earth" as well) to be "righteous," having fulfilled appropriately all the obligations taken on himself in the covenant agreement. Knowing this from the outset leaves no question but that covenant failure can only be the result of Israel's faithless behavior.

The First Accusation (50:7–15)

THE FIRST ACCUSATION is a parody of the Shema, the essential call to acknowledge Yahweh as the one and only God to whom Israel gives allegiance and obedience (Deut. 6:4). The call begins with an imperative of the verb *šmʿ* ("Hear!")[11] and concludes with the pronouncement, "I am *God*, your God" (*ʾelohim ʾeloheka ʾanoki*), an Elohistic Psalter version of the more usual proclamation "I am *the* LORD *[Yahweh]*, your God" (cf. Ex. 20:2; Deut. 5:6), associated

8. The obvious connection between the appearance of Yahweh and consuming fire and storm is the theophany at Sinai (cf. Ex. 24:17, where the phrase "consuming fire" occurs).

9. The heavens and earth are called as witnesses to Yahweh's covenant with Israel in Deut. 4:26; 30:19; 31:28 (cf. Isa. 1:2). In a more general sense heavens and earth can testify against an accused person in court (cf. Job 20:27).

10. There may be an element of *irony* or *sarcasm* intended here, since the continuation of the psalm shows that some of those who profess by their sacrifices to be *ḥasidim* are judged to be "wicked."

11. Since in the psalm the subject of the imperative is the feminine noun *ʿammi* ("my people") rather than the masculine noun *yiśraʾel* ("Israel"), as in the classic expression of the Shema in Deuteronomy, the imperative here takes a feminine singular form.

with the promulgation of the law on Mount Sinai.[12] By bringing together in this way both Shema and the giving of the law, the psalmist emphasizes the core of the covenant tradition as allegiance to Yahweh alone and obedience to his covenant demands.

It is the intersection of faithfulness to the covenant demands and sacrifice that are at issue in the remainder of the psalm. It is clear that sacrifices are being made in abundance (50:8). God does not "rebuke" (*ykḥ* ["reproach, reprove; give judgment"]) Israel for failing to sacrifice at all. Indeed, her sacrifices are "ever before me" (50:8). It is, however, Israel's *understanding* of sacrifice that appears to be defective.

In this first section, the problem seems to be that those who sacrifice believe their sacrifices are *essential* to God—that in some sense their sacrifices meet a need that God has. It was common in the Mesopotamian context—from which the Israelite patriarchs came and drew their sacrificial experience—to consider sacrifice as *dullu* ("service"), through which humans fulfilled their obligation to provide the gods with three meals a day. For this reason, the great Sumerian scholar A. Leo Oppenheim titled an important section on the sacrificial system "The Care and Feeding of the Gods."[13]

Such a view of sacrifice Israel ultimately rejected, although the number of times that this type of critique is offered in the Old Testament[14] and the harshness with which it is expressed leave the impression that many in Israel must have agreed with the general Mesopotamian view that sacrifice met the needs of God and offered an opportunity for humans to manipulate him.

I have no need. God's immediate and almost caustic response gives the lie to the idea that he has any need that a sacrifice can address. (1) The first reason is a matter of possession. Since the whole world is God's domain and all the creatures—animal or human—within that domain are his as well (50:10–11), the idea that bulls and goats (50:9) sacrificed by humans can add anything to God is viewed as patently ridiculous.

(2) The second reason goes to the heart of the common view of sacrifice as feeding the deity: God derives no nourishment from the sacrifices Israel

---

12. Although the similar phrase *ʾani yhwh ʾeloheykem* (with a different first-person pronoun and the second-person *plural* pronoun on the word "God") is used frequently in Exodus (e.g., Ex. 6:7, 16:12), Leviticus (esp. frequent), Numbers (e.g., Num. 10:10, 15:41), and even appears in Deut. 29:6, the form mimicked in Ps. 50:7 is directly related to the form used in the introduction of the Sinai narrative (Ex. 20:2; Deut. 5:6). Here the form is *ʾanoki yhwh ʾeloheyka*, as in Ps. 50.

13. A. Leo Oppenheim, *Ancient Mesopotamia: Portrait of a Dead Civilization* (Chicago: Univ. of Chicago Press, 1977), 183–98.

14. Other passages rejecting such a view of sacrifice are: Isa. 1:11–15; Jer. 7:21–23; Hos. 6:6; Amos 4:4–5; 5:21–25; Mic. 6:6–8.

offers (50:12–13). They were never intended as meals presented to him but are a mechanism for human benefit—agreed-upon acts by which humans acknowledge and repent of sin, give thanks for divine deliverance, and celebrate communion with a God who is present with them. For this reason God is depicted as almost venomously castigating his people: "Do you really think that I eat the flesh of bulls or drink the blood of goats?" (50:13); "I am not hungry!" he cries (50:12).

The section concludes with an exhortation to right sacrifice. The point of offering "thank offerings" is that such sacrifices acknowledge the offerer's absolute dependence on Yahweh's grace and mercy. It is this humility and dependence that is at the core of a right understanding of sacrifice. Such humility will see sacrifice for what it really is: an outward indication of one's inner allegiance to Yahweh and obedience to his covenant demands. Such people will "fulfill [their] vows" (50:14) to God and will experience the deliverance they seek (50:15).

The Second Accusation (50:16–23)

FROM EXHORTATION THE psalmist turns to confrontation. This time the accused are called the "wicked" (*rašaᶜ*). These are, however, still within the covenant people of Israel and give at least lip service to the covenant (50:16b-c). Their wickedness is that they lack the inner commitment to Yahweh that would give their ritual sacrifice meaning. In reality, their actions show that they "hate [God's] instruction and cast [Yahweh's] words behind [them]" (50:17).

The psalm offers six examples of covenant-breaking wickedness, presented in synonymous pairs. (1) They make friends with thieves and throw in their lot with adulterers; (2) they use their mouths for evil and hitch up their tongue to deceit; (3) they speak against their brother[15] and slander their mother's son. The first two are clear examples of covenant-breaking since they contravene two of the Ten Commandments (against theft and adultery). For the others, however, the case is less explicit. To "use the mouth for evil" is certainly negative and appears as an admonishment in many proverbs. But the phrase is too general to isolate a specific covenant command that is violated here. Similarly, the term used here for "deceit"

15. The construction in the Heb. is awkward. The phrase literally means something like "you dwell/sit with your brother you speak." *BHS* suggests emending *tešeb* ("dwell") to *bošet* ("shame") so the phrase would be translated, "shame you speak with/against your brother." The NIV has taken "dwell" as having a continuous effect. The parallel phrase is more clear: "with/against the son of your mother [= your brother] you give stain/fault." However, *dopi* ("stain") occurs only here in the whole Old Testament and must remain uncertain.

(*mirmah*) is never employed in the legal collections in the Pentateuch. Deceit is, of course, roundly condemned in the Psalms, Proverbs, and the Prophets.

The final two statements lack sufficient clarity to determine what specific covenant command the poet had in mind, if any. "Slander" is prohibited in Leviticus 19:16, but the idiom used there (*halak rakil* ["go about as a slanderer"]) is not related to Psalm 50:20b (*dopi*). In a general sense, the psalmist envisions failure to maintain relationships of honesty and respect—even with one's closest kin—as evidence of the erosion of covenant loyalty among those who offer sacrifice and speak of allegiance to Yahweh but "cast [his] words behind [them]" (50:17).

I kept silent. The wicked foolishly think they have God as confused about their true motives as their human contemporaries. Because God has done nothing to strike them down, they assume he is unconcerned, or even worse, that he is "altogether like" them (50:21).[16] God's reference to his "remaining silent" (*heḥerašti*) links back to 50:3, where Yahweh's approach in the theophany puts an end to his silent restraint (*ʾal yeḥeraš*).[17] The hope that the wicked have avoided divine notice is a false one. Despite any earlier delay, Yahweh intends to make his true nature clear to all. He "will rebuke" the wicked and "accuse"[18] them to their face (50:21).

Consider this. The wicked are admonished to take careful stock of God's warning—to let it seep down into their awareness and understanding until they really get it. The verb "consider" (from *byn* ["perceive, understand"]) implies clear, deep understanding. It is one of the favorite verbs the sages use in wisdom literature to describe understanding. It is a call beyond assumption and speculation to real knowledge of God.

The psalmist exhorts the people to adopt a renewed understanding of sacrifice and to offer evidence of one's inner reliance on Yahweh alone.

---

16. The Heb. phrase combines the Qal infinitive construct and the first-person singular Qal imperfect (*heyot ʾehyeh*) as an emphatic expression: "[you thought] I am indeed [like you]."

17. The fact that the earlier passage uses the negative particle *ʾal* rather than the more common *loʾ* suggests the verb form it negates (*yeḥeraš*) should be read as a jussive expressing the will of the speaker ("let him not remain silent") rather than a straightforward future declaration ("he will not remain silent"). It is the following description of the theophany that has persuaded the NIV that the whole passage should be read as actuality and not hope.

18. The final image (*ʾeʿerkah*) is a military expression of drawing up one's battle line across from the enemy troops. Picture, if you will, the Israelite army (1 Sam. 17:1–11) confronting the Philistines across the Elah Valley, with the giant champion Goliath strutting up and down challenging the Israelites to send out a champion for individual combat, and you may have some idea of the situation envisioned here.

The very fact of exhortation suggests that the "wicked" are (1) part of the covenant community (not pagan nations) and (2) are not beyond redemption (since they are offered a chance to change). They are further identified as those "who forget God" (50:22). In Deuteronomy Israel is counseled repeatedly not to forget Yahweh and his covenant.[19] Failure to remember Yahweh would lead to rejection and destruction (Deut. 8:19; 32:18–19). In Judges 3:7 it was Israel's "forgetting" Yahweh by worshiping pagan deities that led God to surrender them into the power of the king of Aram Naharaim.[20] The prophets also use the phrase to condemn Israel for following pagan gods[21] and to justify God's punishment through the Exile.

It is not entirely clear, however, that worship of pagan deities is behind the forgetting of God here. In a similar context in Psalm 78, we learn that Israel was to pass along the traditions of Yahweh's deeds and commandments to subsequent generations so that "they would put their trust in God and would not forget his deeds but would keep his commands" (78:7). Instead, Israel "did not keep God's covenant and refused to live by his law. They forgot what he had done, the wonders he had shown them" (78:10–11). Again, five times in Psalm 119 it is God's law, decrees, and precepts that the psalmist vows never to forget (119:61, 83, 93, 109, 141). While it is true that worshiping pagan deities was a serious breach of Israel's covenant obligation to be loyal to Yahweh alone, the more general statement would remain an effective admonition far into the postexilic period, when Israel had at last learned the lesson of absolute monotheism.

I will tear you to pieces. Forgetting God has severe consequences. The image used for divine judgment is that of a ravening beast tearing its helpless prey. God will tear his forgetful people to pieces (*ʾeṭrop*), "with none to rescue."[22] The latter phrase is combined with forms of *ṭrp* on four occasions as an apparent idiom for impending judgment or disaster. In Micah 5:8, it is exilic Israel itself who will act like wolves turned loose on the pagan sheep among whom they are living. In Psalm 7:2, it is the enemies who threaten to tear the psalmist to pieces with no hope of rescue. In the two remaining

---

19. Cf. Deut. 4:9, 23, 31; 6:12; 8:11, 14.

20. The usual idiom in Judges is "to forsake" (*yaʿazbu*) Yahweh (cf. Judg. 2:12; see also 1 Sam. 12:9).

21. Cf. Isa. 51:13; 65:11; Jer. 2:32; 23:27; Hos. 2:13; 13:6. See also Ps. 106:13, 21, where the golden calf incident during the Exodus wanderings is attributed to Israel's having forgotten "the God who saved them" and "what he had done."

22. The kind of tearing that *ṭrp* describes is always associated with wild animals (cf. Gen. 37:33; 44:28): most often the lion (Pss. 17:12; 22:13; Ezek. 22:25; Hos. 5:14; Nah. 2:12), but occasionally the wolf (Gen. 49:27; Ezek. 22:27).

occurrences, God is the one who threatens to tear his people to pieces as punishment for their sin (here and Hos. 5:14).[23]

He who sacrifices thank offerings honors me. What the wicked must understand and accept is that sacrifice is not a form of self-expression or self-power but a way of acknowledging thanks to God. Giving thanks requires admitting dependence on the one who delivers. It means knowing one cannot save oneself. Giving thanks acknowledges what God has already done in the past and, at the same time, "prepares the way" for future deliverance.

The phrases "who sacrifices thank offerings" and "honors me" link back to the end of the first accusation (50:14–15), where God has counseled the readers in similar language that thank offerings based on a clear understanding of one's dependence on God would lead to deliverance. These two sections of admonition, then, have the same goal and purpose, namely, to turn those who have forgotten God back to him and to enliven their inner attitude of dependence on him, which gives true meaning to their otherwise empty sacrifices.

THE COVENANT LAWSUIT. Psalm 50 constitutes a "covenant lawsuit" brought by Yahweh against his "consecrated ones, who made a covenant with me by sacrifice" (50:5). This sort of legal proceeding is well attested in the Old Testament—particularly in the Prophets—as a means by which God airs the failures of Israel and justifies his judgment on the nation. The verb *ryb* and related nouns (*rib* ["dispute, lawsuit"]; *ribah* ["legal case, speech in a case"]; *meribah* ["dispute"]) do not appear in Psalm 50, but the elements of a legal conflict are undeniably present.

Examples of such disputes are found in Genesis 13:7–8 in the conflict over water rights between the shepherds of Abraham and Lot, in the similar quarrel between the servants of Isaac and the herdsmen of Gerar (26:19–22), and in Jacob's dispute with Laban over the theft of Laban's *teraphim* (31:36). These examples suggest the public nature of the *rib* and its disputatious character, in which conflicting viewpoints are presented for resolution (Isa. 50:8).[24]

A *rib* includes several elements: Parties to the conflict are summoned in court (Ps. 50:1–5; Hos. 4:1); witnesses are called to observe the execution

23. The phrase is reminiscent of Amos's prophecy that only a remnant of Israel would survive the Assyrian conquest like a couple of leg bones or a piece of an ear left over from the carcass of a devoured sheep (Amos 3:12).

24. Legislation governing the *rib* is found in Ex. 21:18; 23:2, 3, 6; Deut. 17:8; 19:17; 21:5; 25:1.

of justice in the case (Ps. 50:1; Mic. 6:1–2); a judge sits to hear the evidence and to render judgment (Deut. 19:17; 25:1; 1 Sam. 24:15; 2 Sam. 15:1–4; Isa. 3:13); the opposing parties present their cases (Isa. 41:21); after all testimony has been heard, the judge pronounces a *mišpaṭ* ("judgment"), in which the parties are declared "righteous" if they have fulfilled the demands of justice and "wicked" if they have not.

A special form of the *rib* is the divinely initiated lawsuit. In these cases, Yahweh participates as complaining party, prosecuting attorney, and deciding judge.

> The LORD takes his place in court;
> he rises to judge the people. (Isa. 3:13)
>
> Woe to him who quarrels with his Maker,
> to him who is but a potsherd among the potsherds on the ground.
> Does the clay say to the potter, "What are you making?"
> Does your work say, "He has no hands"? (Isa. 45:9)
>
> "Therefore I bring charges against you again,"
> declares the LORD.
> "And I will bring charges against your children's children." (Jer. 2:9)[25]

The prophets used this common form of legal proceeding to drive home the seriousness of Israel's failure to keep the covenant. The *rib* allowed God to have his day in court when the people would rather ignore their responsibilities and take divine silence (cf. Ps. 50:21) as a sign of approval, lack of concern, or even divine weakness. The promulgation of the lawsuit ends Yahweh's silence decisively with a public accusation of guilt (50:3–6, 21b).

An adaptation of the divine lawsuit against Israel forms the basis of Job's demand to see God. Here the lawsuit is turned on its head as Job seeks to take Yahweh to court for breach of covenant.

> Oh, that I had someone to hear me!
> I sign now my defense—let the Almighty answer me;
> let my accuser put his indictment in writing. (Job 31:35)
>
> I will say to God: Do not condemn me,
> but tell me what charges you have against me. (Job 10:2)
>
> Hear now my argument;
> listen to the plea of my lips. (Job 13:6)
>
> Will the one who contends with the Almighty correct him?
> Let him who accuses God answer him! (Job 40:2)

25. See also Hos. 12:2; Mic. 6:2.

Job even raises the issue of God's multifaceted participation and the way it effectively undermines "due process."

> How then can I dispute with him?
> How can I find words to argue with him?
> Though I were innocent, I could not answer him;
> I could only plead with my Judge for mercy. (Job 9:14–15)
>
> He is not a man like me that I might answer him,
> that we might confront each other in court.
> If only there were someone to arbitrate between us,
> to lay his hand upon us both,
> someone to remove God's rod from me,
> so that his terror would frighten me no more.
> Then I would speak up without fear of him,
> but as it now stands with me, I cannot. (Job 9:32–35)

The divine lawsuit consistently accuses Israel of failure in her covenant responsibilities. Often this failure is described as a misuse or misunderstanding of the sacrificial system. Hosea's *rib* begins with an extensive list of covenant wrongdoings (Hos. 4:1–6), but later the true nature of sacrifice is brought to the fore: "For I desire mercy, not sacrifice, and acknowledgment of God rather than burnt offerings" (6:6). Amos is even more caustic in depicting Yahweh's rejection of empty sacrifice: "I hate, I despise your religious feasts; I cannot stand your assemblies. Even though you bring me burnt offerings and grain offerings, I will not accept them. . . . Away with the noise of your songs! I will not listen to the music of your harps. But let justice roll on like a river, righteousness like a never-failing stream!" (Amos 5:21–24).[26]

It is this failure of understanding regarding the true nature of sacrifice that dominates Psalm 50. Israel is condemned not because they fail to offer sacrifices and offerings (50:8), but because they seek to exploit in their abundant sacrifices a supposed need of God. Because she believes God *needs* her sacrifices, Israel believes he can be manipulated by abundant gifts with no regard for the spiritual condition or intent of the offerer. Not so, rejoins God. Sacrifice fills no lack in the creator of the world, to whom all belongs. Sacrifice is for the benefit of the offerer. It is a reflection of the attitude of the offerer and, rightly given, "honors" God (50:23a) while opening the door for God's gift of salvation. Clearly it is not the sacrifice that accomplishes salvation but God, in response to the offerer's attitude of thanksgiving and praise.

---

26. See also Jer. 6:20.

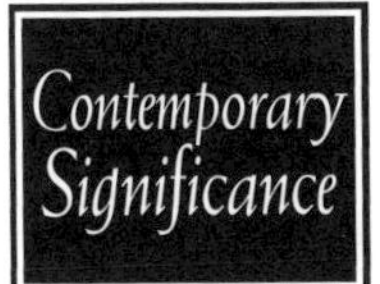

RIGHT WORSHIP AND RIGHT CONDUCT. Psalm 50 admonishes the covenant people "to consider" their failings in worship and in conduct—their relationship to God and to their fellow humans. This is, of course, the summary of "the Law and the Prophets," according to Jesus (Matt. 22:35–40). Right worship, says the psalmist, consists in acknowledging that we have nothing to bring to the creator of the universe that is not already his. Added to this is the realization that God does not need our sacrifices, but that they are entirely for *our own* benefit.

As far as conduct goes, God through the psalmist takes the "wicked" to task for assuming their acceptance of the covenant makes no restrictions on their abuse of their neighbors. Theft, adultery, verbal abuse, deceit, and slander are unfortunately the common practice of those who claim to adhere to the covenant (50:16–20). God wants a different sort of activity from his people.

Honor me. Psalm 50:23 reads: "He who sacrifices thank offerings honors me, and he prepares the way so that I may show him the salvation of God." The first part is directed to the question of worship. Right sacrifice intends to honor God rather than manipulate or exploit him.

How is it that our own worship *honors* God? Is it enough to offer abundant words of thanksgiving and praise? It depends, I believe, on what motivates our words. Words are cheap and often deceptive. Do we praise God because it makes us feel good? Or do we praise him because we realize just how little we deserve the salvation God offers and how radically he has invaded and changed our lives? Is it enough to fill the air with waving hands and swirling choruses if we are not concerned with truth, equity, justice—and are unwilling to work for it? Does our praise honor God when our congregations forget whole segments of society?

Let's not mistake praise and thanks for worship. They are vital parts of worship, but *only part*! True worship requires the fear of Yahweh, acknowledgment of sin, and petition of forgiveness. Then our thanksgiving and praise will be sincere. True worship involves opening our eyes to see the hurts of the world outside our gathering place. It means acting on what we see. Then our praise will have meaning beyond our own well-being and will sound with new sweetness in God's ears.

Prepare the way. The second half of the concluding admonition is directed to the one who "prepares the way" (50:23b). The Hebrew behind this expression requires some explanation lest it be confused with the more familiar phrase regarding the one who "prepares the way" of the Lord (Isa. 40:3; Mal. 3:1). The passages in Isaiah and Malachi use the verb *pnh* ("turn aside, cause to turn") and suggest a road-building effort in which the terrain is altered by bulldozing hills and filling valleys so that the "king's highway" may go on without obstruction.

That, however, is not the idiom used in Psalm 50:23. Here the Hebrew verb is *śym* ("set, put, establish"). The picture is more of the athlete's determined fixation on the goal or finish line. The focused concentration, no deviations to left or right, characterize the one who has "fixed his path" in the way 50:23 intends. The one who runs or walks with this kind of fixed determination will see "the salvation of God." Such a one does not "forget God," nor does he or she need to fear being torn to pieces with no one to rescue (50:22).

Paul talks of such disciplined focus in Philippians 3:8–14: "I consider everything a loss compared to the surpassing greatness of knowing Christ Jesus my Lord, for whose sake I have lost all things. . . . Forgetting what is behind and straining toward what is ahead, I press on toward the goal to win the prize for which God has called me heavenward in Christ Jesus."

Psalm 51

FOR THE DIRECTOR of music. A psalm of David. When the prophet Nathan came to him after David had committed adultery with Bathsheba.

1 Have mercy on me, O God,
according to your unfailing love;
according to your great compassion
blot out my transgressions.
2 Wash away all my iniquity
and cleanse me from my sin.

3 For I know my transgressions,
and my sin is always before me.
4 Against you, you only, have I sinned
and done what is evil in your sight,
so that you are proved right when you speak
and justified when you judge.
5 Surely I was sinful at birth,
sinful from the time my mother conceived me.
6 Surely you desire truth in the inner parts;
you teach me wisdom in the inmost place.

7 Cleanse me with hyssop, and I will be clean;
wash me, and I will be whiter than snow.
8 Let me hear joy and gladness;
let the bones you have crushed rejoice.
9 Hide your face from my sins
and blot out all my iniquity.

10 Create in me a pure heart, O God,
and renew a steadfast spirit within me.
11 Do not cast me from your presence
or take your Holy Spirit from me.
12 Restore to me the joy of your salvation
and grant me a willing spirit, to sustain me.

13 Then I will teach transgressors your ways,
and sinners will turn back to you.

[14] Save me from bloodguilt, O God,
the God who saves me,
and my tongue will sing of your righteousness.
[15] O Lord, open my lips,
and my mouth will declare your praise.
[16] You do not delight in sacrifice, or I would bring it;
you do not take pleasure in burnt offerings.
[17] The sacrifices of God are a broken spirit;
a broken and contrite heart,
O God, you will not despise.

[18] In your good pleasure make Zion prosper;
build up the walls of Jerusalem.
[19] Then there will be righteous sacrifices,
whole burnt offerings to delight you;
then bulls will be offered on your altar.

PSALM 51 IS the fourth of seven so-called "penitential psalms" in the Psalter (Pss. 6; 32; 38; 51; 102; 130; 143), in which confession and repentance from personal sin is the focus of the composition.[1] This psalm also introduces the second collection of "Davidic psalms," which extends (except for Pss. 66–67) from Psalms 51–70/71 (at the end of Book 2).

In its discussion of God's lack of delight in sacrifice and burnt offerings (51:16), the psalm shares connections with the similar discussion in 50:8–14. Like Psalm 50, the present one does not absolutely reject sacrifice but looks forward at the end to the restoration of "righteous" sacrifices and burnt offerings that *will* delight Yahweh in a restored Jerusalem (51:19; cf. 50:14, 15, 23). In its desire for forgiveness for sin and its concern to instruct sinners in the way of Yahweh that leads to restoration, Psalm 51 also has links with Psalm 25.

In its present position in the Psalter the psalm stands as an individual response to the exhortation with which Psalm 50 concludes: "He who sacrifices thank offerings honors me, and he prepares the way so that I may show him the salvation of God" (50:23). Psalm 51 lifts up a "thank offering" of confession and an amended life made possible by a "broken and contrite

1. See the comments on Ps. 6.

heart" (51:16–17), and it seeks the restoration of "the joy of your [God's] salvation" (51:12).

Structurally, the psalm may be divided into six parts: an opening plea for forgiveness from sin (51:1–2), a confession of sin (51:3–6), a plea for cleansing from sin (51:7–9), a plea for spiritual restoration (51:10–12), a vow of praise and public contrition (51:13–17), and a concluding expanded plea for the restoration of Zion/Jerusalem and "righteous" sacrifice (51:18–19). This latter section may well have been added to an essentially individual psalm in order to reflect the needs of the exilic community, who had lost Jerusalem and the temple and were struggling to understand what constituted "righteous sacrifice" in their new circumstance scattered among the nations, far from their ancestral home.

The Heading (51:0)

THE HEADING BEGINS with the familiar reference to "the director of music" and is described as a "psalm" (*mizmor*) of David.[2] In addition to this more usual information, the heading also includes a historical notice that interprets this psalm as a response to God's confrontation of David through the prophet Nathan over David's sin of adultery with Bathsheba.[3]

Plea for Forgiveness (51:1–2)

THE PSALMIST APPEALS to the "unfailing love" (*ḥesed*)[4] of God as the basis of hope for forgiveness. Although he has failed through sin, Yahweh does not fail but continues in his commitment to sinful humans who acknowledge their sin and rely on God's merciful forgiveness and love. This is the required attitude of dependence that Israel refers to with the phrase "fear of the LORD." The forgiveness sought is described in a series of imperative verbs for cleansing: "blot out" (*mḥh*),[5] "wash away" (*kbs*),[6] and "cleanse" (*ṭhr*).[7] It is certainly possible that this concern with cleansing reflects a ritual activity in the temple.

---

2. See comments on the heading of Ps. 4 for "the director of music" and on the heading of Ps. 3 for *mizmor* and the reference to David.

3. The first historical notice in the psalm headings appears in the heading to Ps. 3 (see comments).

4. See comments on 5:7, where this term first appears.

5. The image is that of wiping off dirt from the mouth (Prov. 30:20) or from a dish (2 Kings 21:13).

6. This verb describes the activity called "fulling," in which materials were cleaned by tramping on them in water since no soap was available for the process.

7. "Sweep/scour clean." When used with the preposition *min* as here, the term often refers to *cultic* cleansing in preparation for participation in temple ritual.

We know that worshipers immersed themselves in ritual baths carved in the limestone at the southern approach to the Temple Mount. Some such ritual of confession, repentance, and cleansing may be in mind here.

Along with the three verbs for cleansing, the psalmist uses three nouns for sin: "transgressions" (*pešaʿ*), "iniquity" (*ʿawon*), and "sin" (*ḥaṭṭaʾt*).[8] Rather than focus on specific types of sin, the use of all three terms seems intended to be comprehensive, so that the psalmist's confession is far-reaching and complete. This interpretation is confirmed in verse 3, where he admits his sin by referring only to the first and last categories previously mentioned (*pešaʿ* and *ḥaṭṭaʾt*), indicating the whole constellation of sin is intended, not just these two categories.

Confession of Sin (51:3–6)

I KNOW MY TRANSGRESSIONS. The psalmist does not simply express awareness of sin with these words but *contrition*—sorrow and a commitment not to repeat the offense. His claim that the sin is against Yahweh "only" may seem to belittle the offense against Bathsheba, against her husband, Uriah, or against society as a whole. But the intent is perhaps to heighten the sense of offense by acknowledging that ultimately violations of the covenant are offenses against God himself and are judged by divine sanction rather than societal acceptance or disapproval alone. The measure of the psalmist's sin in this case is "what is evil in [God's] sight" (51:4)—a much higher standard than the world holds.

You are proved right. Unlike Job, the psalmist freely acknowledges the justice of the divine accusation: God is "proved right"[9] and "justified."[10] Once again—as often in the psalms—God is seen as both the accuser bringing the charge ("when you speak") and the judge rendering the verdict ("when you judge").

Sinful at birth. By way of contrast to God's righteousness, the psalmist now concedes that his sin proceeds from a longstanding sinful nature. Rather than a clear articulation of the theological principle of "original sin" (though not incompatible with such a view), he recognizes that sin has had long-term and far-reaching influence in his life. This is honest self-evaluation that

---

8. These three terms for sin also appear in 25:7, 11 (see comments on those verses; see also "The Theology of the Psalms" in vol. 2 of this commentary).

9. The verb *ṣdq* ("be in the right/be righteous; have a just case") is a legal term affirming that the one who brings a case to court has fulfilled all the obligations of the circumstance under consideration. See comments on the related legal terms at 4:1–2; 7:6–9; 9:4–8.

10. This may well be another term with legal overtones, as a pronouncement of innocence in a trial.

does not minimize the significance of sin by considering it an anomaly in an otherwise unblemished life. The psalmist does not appeal the judge's decision in the law case but accepts the judgment, acknowledges the rightness of it, and prepares to respond with contrition.

Truth in the inner parts. In his expressions of self-awareness, the psalmist exhibits the kind of transparency God desires: He wants "truth [*ʾemet*] in the inner parts." The word *ʾemet* emphasizes reliability and trustworthiness over absolute accuracy. God is seeking a person whose external profession is consistent with the inner reality of his or her being that is often kept hidden away "in the entrails" (*baṭṭuḥot*; NIV "in the inner parts"; see comments in Bridging Context section). This kind of vulnerability allows God to transform one's inner self by teaching "wisdom in the inmost place" (51:6b). The psalmist affirms that appropriate revelation of the inner self requires divine wisdom.

Plea for Cleansing (51:7–9)

HAVING CONFESSED SIN, the psalmist now seeks the kind of cleansing from its effects that will allow restoration of relationship with God. The passage ends (51:9) with the psalmist's desire that God no longer take account of his sin, thus allowing relationship to continue. The passage is marked by the use, in reverse order, of the same terms for cleansing in the opening section. There we saw "blot out," "wash away," and "cleanse"; here we have "cleanse,"[11] "wash," and "blot out." The result is a sort of chiastic arrangement of elements.[12]

The term translated "cleanse" in NIV is actually a form of the Hebrew verb *ḥṭʾ* ("sin"), which in the Piel (as here) means "to free from (the effects of) sin." Branches of the "hyssop" plant[13] were apparently bound together to form an aspergillum, which was dipped in water and used in rituals of cleansing to sprinkle water on the persons or items requiring purification. This more formal ritual of cleansing is accompanied by "fulling" in order to make them "whiter than snow." Perhaps the two references are to inner (invisible) cleansing and outer (visible) purification.

To be cleansed of sin and its consequences is to experience joy and restoration. The painful effects of sin are here equated with the crushing of bones.

---

11. The artful variation in this phrase demonstrates the skill of the poet. In the first instance (51:2b) the noun "sin" (*ḥaṭṭaʾt*) is used with the verb "cleanse" (*ṭhr*). In the second passage, two verbs are used: "free from sin" (*ḥṭʾ*) and "be clean/pure" (*ṭhr*). Each expression uses the same roots, and the correspondence of form and meaning is unmistakable.

12. For a discussion of chiasm, see the section on "Techniques of Hebrew Poetry" in the introduction.

13. Probably a reference in the Old Testament to members of the marjoram and thyme families of aromatic plants rather than the actual hyssop plant, which does not grow outside southern Europe. See the articles on "Hyssop" in *EBD* and *ISBE*[2].

And since it is God who has done the crushing, clearly sin has damaged the psalmist's relation with God as well. He now seeks restoration of relationship and realizes that it will only happen if God takes the extraordinary step of "hiding his face" from his sins. To "hide the face" normally implies divine anger and rejection of the sinner (cf. 13:1; 27:9). When God hides his face, the psalmist feels abandoned and distressed (30:7; 143:7). Here, however, he pleads with Yahweh to "hide his face"—not from the psalmist but from his *sins*. Such an act implies that God chooses not to take one's failings into account but to "blot them out" (51:1, 9). Such restoration is entirely in God's hands and is predicated on the "unfailing love" and "compassion" of Yahweh (51:1).

Plea for Spiritual Restoration (51:10–12)

CONFESSION AND RITUAL cleansing are necessary steps to restoration of relationship with God. But any complete and continuing reconciliation requires a renewal of the inward spirit from which human purposes and actions flow. In these verses, the psalmist emphasizes the need for a transformed inner attitude characterized by a "pure heart," a "steadfast spirit," and a "willing spirit." These characteristics are indications of enduring change and transformation that provide the firm foundation for continuing relationship with God.

Having undergone both inner and outer cleansing as well as a lasting transformation of the spirit, the psalmist can now hope to be sustained by the lasting experience of the presence of Yahweh. The continued empowerment of the divine Holy Spirit and the renewed assurance of deliverance combine to provide a sustainable hope (51:11–12).

Vow of Praise and Public Contrition (51:13–17)

FOR ISRAEL AND the psalmist, confession and restoration are never simply private acts but involve the redeemed in public acts of joyous proclamation and response. Here the psalmist's anticipation of deliverance leads to vows of public acts of praise and contrition that provide instructive exhortation to right actions for other sinners (51:13). "Transgressors" (*pōšeʿim*) and "sinners" (*ḥaṭṭaʾim*) will learn the "ways" of Yahweh by learning of the psalmist's transformation through God's redeeming grace. Deliverance from "bloodguilt"[14] loosens his tongue to joyous proclamations of public praise (51:14–15).

---

14. "Bloodguilt" is the guilt that derives from "murder"—the shedding of an innocent person's blood. If the connection with the Bathsheba incident is taken seriously, then the sin at the core in *this* verse is the killing of Uriah the Hittite rather than the adulterous affair with Uriah's wife.

You do not delight in sacrifice. A second bit of instruction embedded in the psalmist's vows strikes the same theme as the first (51:16): What God desires is *inward change*, marked by truth, wisdom, and a broken, contrite heart. Here, as in the Prophets (and Ps. 50), the object is not the absolute rejection of all substitutionary animal sacrifice (although the seeds of that later realization are planted here). The psalmist instead intends to demonstrate forcefully what sacrifice is really about and what gives true efficacy to the outward, ritual acts. The groundwork for Christian sacramental theology—and indeed the radical critique of that theology by nonsacramental groups such as the Society of Friends (Quakers)—is laid by the realization that it is the inward reality that is effective, not the symbolic outward signs.

Plea for Restoration of Zion (51:18–19)

MAKE ZION PROSPER. For the first time in this psalm the theme of Zion enters the picture (51:18). The picture presented here—of the broken walls of Jerusalem being rebuilt like the broken and contrite heart of the psalmist—is one that stands contrary to the Davidic context presumed in the heading. The concern expressed for the rebuilding of Jerusalem has the effect of adapting this individual plea for deliverance to the circumstance of the exilic Jewish community, while the mention of Zion links Psalm 51 back to 50:2 and 48:2, 11–12. As the psalmist seeks through confession and contrition to stimulate the restoration of right relationship with God, so the exilic community sought through the words of this psalm to confess their sin and to lay the groundwork for the restoration of the sacrificial system, through which they had known continued forgiveness, renewal, and communion with their covenant God, Yahweh.

Righteous sacrifices. While the emphasis of the original psalm is on the transparent congruity of an inward relationship to God that validates one's outward acts, it may well be that the exilic community read those verses about the spiritualizing of sacrifice as indicative of their own situation, where temple ritual was precluded because of its destruction. The hope expressed at the end of the psalm, then, is that with the restoration of the walls of Jerusalem and the temple itself, "righteous sacrifices"—sacrifice consistent with the picture presented in Psalms 50 and 51—will once again be offered and be acceptable to Yahweh.

Note how these final verses respond to the earlier statements of 51:16–17 by utilizing the same terminology in the context of restoration. In 51:16, Yahweh does "not delight in sacrifice," nor does he "take pleasure in burnt offerings." By contrast, however, in 51:18–19 it is Yahweh's "good pleasure" that will lead to the restoration of Jerusalem and his "delight" in "righteous sacrifices" and "burnt offerings." In this way the exilic community reaffirms their understanding that it is the inner attitude of sin that invalidated the sacrificial system of Israel and led to the demise of the kingdom in exile. It will be renewal of the inward life of repentance and faith that will restore the covenant community in its relationship with God.

TRUTH IN THE INNER PARTS. God wants a kind of transparency in the lives of his people. The instruction to assume an attitude of intimate vulnerability with God uses two unusual terms to get the idea across. The first (*baṭṭuḥot*; NIV "inner parts," 51:6) occurs only here and in Job 38:36, making its meaning somewhat obscure.[15] The second is more common but in a very different context, so that the meaning here is an extension from the more normal usage. This word (*satum*; NIV "the inmost place"), a passive participle from the root *stm*, is more commonly used to describe the "plugging up" of available water sources (wells, springs, channels) to prevent their use by another party. In this way the wells dug by Abraham were "plugged up" by Philistines who became jealous of the growing wealth of Isaac (Gen. 26:15, 18).[16]

Stopping the wells that supplied cities was one way of crippling the power of the enemy (2 Kings 3:19, 25). While such damage could sometimes be repaired, much effort would have to be diverted to the task, and in some cases the trouble might not prove worth the effort. In a slightly different way, during the days of the invasion of Sennacherib's Assyrian army, Hezekiah had all the available water sources in Judah "plugged up" so that the invading troops would be deprived of their support (2 Chron. 32:3–4).

Perhaps the most famous example of stopping up a water source is the diversion of the waters of the Gihon Spring into a pool within the walls of Jerusalem, also accomplished by Hezekiah (2 Chron. 32:30).[17] The water sources were not permanently plugged so that no water flowed at all but were

---

15. Most translators interpret the noun *ṭuḥah/ṭuḥot* in Job 38:36 as "inner parts" (cf. Ps. 51). This means they interpret the parallel word in Job (*śekwi*) in an analogous way as referring also to some inward and invisible process (NIV "the mind"). Others suggest an alternate translation in which *ṭuḥot* means "the ibis (bird of Thoth)" and the second noun is a reference to another kind of bird (Holladay, *CHALOT*, 351, "cock"). This latter move reduces support for the traditional interpretation "inner parts" in Ps. 51.

16. In Nehemiah, it is the breaches in the walls of Jerusalem that were "plugged up" by the returnees.

17. Many relate this account to the building of Hezekiah's Tunnel, which diverted water from the Gihon Spring to what is now call Siloam's Pool. Others, however, identify Hezekiah's work with the surface trench covered with stones that skirts the southern part of the Ophel hill to bring water to the same pool.

diverted and visible access concealed from the enemy. This use of *stm* to describe the hiding of water sources in order to keep them from the view of the enemy brought on a whole new set of meanings related to the verbal root.

The new nuance is found most openly in God's word deflating the ego of the king of Tyre in Ezekiel: "Are you wiser than Daniel? Is no secret [*satum*] hidden from you?" (Ezek. 28:3). Through the power of God, Daniel was, of course, the master interpreter of dreams that had stumped all the sages and diviners of the king. So here *satum* refers to "secret things" hidden from general knowledge. Daniel also figures prominently in this developing nuance of the term when it is used to describe the "plugging up" of the words of the divine vision that were to be sealed until the end time: "The vision of the evenings and mornings that has been given you is true, but seal up [*setom*] the vision for it concerns the distant future" (Dan. 8:26). "But you, Daniel, close up [*setom*] and seal [*waḥatom*] the words of the scroll until the time of the end" (12:4; cf. 12:9).

Both these nuances have in common the willful "plugging up" and "hiding away" of something to prevent it being accessed by someone else. The Philistines plugged up Abraham's wells, just as the later kings plugged up and hid the water sources of their defeated enemies. Hezekiah plugged up the visible water sources of the land and diverted their waters to hidden reservoirs to prevent enemy use.

The use of this term in Psalm 51 is based on analogy. God seeks open access to those parts of our lives that we have chosen to keep deeply hidden within our inner world. The kind of "hiding" implied by the use of *stm* emphasizes the willful "holding back" of one's true self from God or others. By hiding, we protect ourselves from the vulnerability of being truly known. The psalmist clearly has sin in mind as part of the secret hidden away within and carefully shielded from the gaze of others.

The confessing nature of Psalm 51 runs counter to this kind of self-protective secrecy. The psalmist "unplugs" the inner barriers and allows the streams of honest self-reflection and self-revelation to flow again. It is this transparency that God desires and that in the end leads to the restoration of "the joy of [God's] salvation" (51:12).

Inner validation of outward ritual. The dynamic revealed in the psalmist's discussion of "righteous sacrifices" has much in common with the kind of transparency described in the section on personal openness just noted. What gives the rituals of worship and sacrifice meaning is the *inward* reality of the relationship from which they flow. Without "a broken and contrite heart" on the part of the offerer, God finds no pleasure in sacrifice and burnt offerings.

The Jewish community of the late first and second centuries A.D. found this principle vital to their continuing religious faith and identity. Prior to A.D.

70, the second temple as redesigned and expanded by Herod the Great served as the spiritual center of the Diaspora Jews scattered throughout the world. Many made a pilgrimage to Jerusalem and the temple in order to worship at least once in their lifetime in the holy shrine, in consort with a universal brotherhood of Jewish believers. The destruction of the temple brought this kind of worship experience to an end. From that day to this, there has been no holy place where the rituals of sacrifice could be performed and participated in. How did that affect the Jewish concept of sacrifice?

Well, in the aftermath of destruction of the temple in A.D. 70 the sacrificial system ceased to operate. The priestly class who had participated in the Jewish revolution against Rome were prohibited from exercising power, and the influential leadership of Judaism passed to the sages in the Great Bet Din (House of Judgment) at Yavneh. There, under the leadership of Yoḥanan ben Zakkai, the sages began to develop plans to enable Judaism to adjust to its new circumstance. In the face of the loss of sacrifice, Yoḥanan and his followers determined that sacrifice could be replaced by the pivotal acts of devotion, prayer, fasting, and the giving of alms. Thus, the sages came to the same conclusion as did Psalm 51: It is the inner relationship of the believer to God that gives value to the outward acts. When the outward acts of worship are prohibited, the inward reality still finds a way of acceptable expression.

Obviously, Christian sacramental theology developed further in this same direction. In many circles, the Christian sacraments are explained as the "visible sign of an invisible reality." Different Christian groups have placed varying degrees of emphasis on the practice of the sacraments and their efficacy. Some have gone so far as to declare baptism a necessary step in the salvation process. At the other extreme is the radical testimony of the Society of Friends (Quakers), who resist the performance of *any* outward rituals (including the usual sacraments), holding that it is inward spiritual baptism or inward spiritual communion that is the important reality. In fact, Quakers say, it is possible for the physical acts to assume such importance in the minds of believers that the inward reality of true relationship with God is neglected or even lost. In such cases we come full circle to return to the situation described in Psalms 50 and 51.

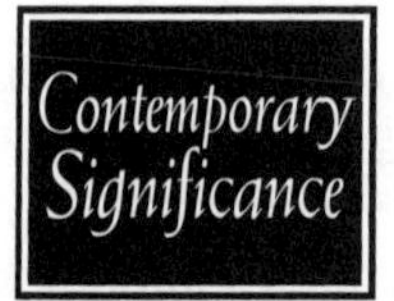

TRANSPARENCY. In the case of Psalm 51, the kind of transparency the psalmist exhorts is involved with the acknowledgment and confession of personal sin. Confession of our wrongs to another person can be difficult for us to do.

Knowing our sin. First, we often remain so personally unaware that we do not even recognize sin when it happens. Anger has been a slippery emotion for me. My family did not do anger well. It just wasn't allowed. I now find that when I feel anger, I am frequently misled because the anger I feel is usually a cover-up for some other emotion I would rather not admit (fear, guilt, shame, sin, vulnerability). The first step I must take is to identify the true source of the anger I am feeling. Often I am unaware up to this point of what is really bothering me. Like the psalmist, I must first "know my transgressions" before I can act to deal with it.

Once I have acknowledged my failing—whatever it may be—I usually have to go through a time of having it "always before me" before I can really respond to it. Knowing my sin doesn't mean a willingness or the power to confront it effectively. Often I enjoy basking in the anger (and the sense of self-justification it breeds) too much to want to give it up. Admitting sin and working on it is painful, and I don't like to face pain. Usually, however, once I have chewed on it for a while, I am finally able to get around to doing something about it. I get so sick of seeing it out there in front of me that I at last consent to let it be gone.

Psalm 51 adds several aspects of knowledge that come with awareness of personal sin. When we finally acknowledge our wrongs, we frequently realize our failure is in relation to God. Rather than some twisted human relationship we might explain away as someone else's fault ("They make me so mad!") or an unavoidable consequence of human nature ("Hey, it is just human to cheat [steal, lie on my taxes, etc.]!"), we must admit that our sin is the result of our sinful rejection of the "way of God" for our lives. Our refusal to accept our position as a beloved child of God leaves us relying on our own human abilities to manipulate, intimidate, deceive, and overpower others in order to get what we think we need. So God is really at the bottom of all our sin—whenever we allow ourselves to get down to the bottom of it.

Not only is sin against God, but it also has a long history in each of us. The psalmist expresses this by saying, "Surely I was sinful at birth, sinful from the time my mother conceived me" (50:5). Whether we want to accept the theological position of "original sin" and all its implications, most of us must admit that there is not a time before which our motives were pure, unselfish, and undistorted. We may explain our choices and responses in life as under the influence of family or society contexts, and these do have great effects on who we are and who we become. Regardless of the influences on our lives, we know that we have been essentially self-absorbed and self-centered for as far back as we can remember. We are the center of our universes, and all others are evaluated as they enter our orbit in regards to how their presence affects our hopes, dreams, and sense of physical and spiritual well-being.

To find the roots of sin is not to solve it. Ask any drug addict, alcoholic, or sex addict whether knowing the sociological roots of his or her habit makes beating the addiction any easier. But it can help us see the grounds for the distorted choices and decisions we make and can aid us in building the resolve to break this chain of negative consequences by making different choices in the future.

Cleansing my sin. Once we know our sin and hold it before ourselves, once we acknowledge its roots in the failure of our relation to God, and once we understand the long-term influences and consequences, we are ready to experience the cleansing God offers. The New Testament puts it this way: "If we confess our sins, he is faithful and just and will forgive us our sins and purify us from all unrighteousness" (1 John 1:9).

This kind of cleansing involves certain action steps. One of the first is to make amends for wrongs done—to set things right. To acknowledge I lied (stole, cheated, etc.) is a first step. To confess this failure to God and another human is another step forward, but the kind of "cleansing" the psalmist mentions, where "joy and gladness" return, requires taking responsibility and seeking to set things right. Such attempts may not always be accepted graciously by the injured party, but we are seeking not to escape anger, shame, or humiliation but to become a participant in the restoration of God's world by undoing as much as possible our own evil distortions and twistings.

Sin has consequences. Confession does not erase the effects of our wrongs. Even forgiveness does not necessarily remove the pain. The psalmist indicates this by his statement: "Let the bones you [God] have crushed rejoice" (51:8). Crushed bones may "rejoice," but they may never be whole again. The effects of sinful choices and evil living may never fully depart from us, any more than the effects of long-term alcoholism or drug addiction or of AIDS contracted from an uncontrolled life of sexual addiction. Our rejoicing may have to be expressed alongside the lasting consequences of our sin.

A new inward person. Awareness, confession, and restitution are not lasting unless accompanied by an inward spiritual change. Attempting to change behavior is often an ineffective way to combat entrenched sin. It is true, however, that as an interim step behavioral modification can provide the needed change of context to allow spiritual change to gain a foothold. That is why mature members of Twelve-Step groups are frequently heard to counsel newcomers to "act as if; fake it until you make it"—that is, assume the processes and acts of recovery even when belief in God or the effectiveness of the steps is still lacking.

Nevertheless, lasting restoration and recovery can only be achieved on the basis of a renewed spiritual relationship with God. We cannot recreate a "clean heart" within ourselves. Only God can regenerate a heart and renew a spirit. The psalmist is right in saying, "Grant me a willing spirit, to sustain me" (51:12b). Even the power to *desire* restoration and utter the words of confession that begins this process of renewal—that power comes from God, not ourselves.

The value of sin. The New Testament talks about the "wages of sin" (Rom. 6:23), but what is the *value* of sin? Most of us think of our sin as being utterly bereft of worth. That is one reason why we hesitate to confess our sin or acknowledge our struggles to others. But confession of sin can be the foundation of teaching and example (Ps. 51:13). Denying sin or covering it up (plugging up the well) prevents any others from drinking at the well of our experience and gaining the life-giving insights we have to offer.

There is another kind of negative assessment made of this kind of self-protective secrecy. By keeping the hidden waters to themselves, the Israelites intended to deny their enemies its life-giving properties. But when we hide our failings in our innermost secret places, we are denying others the benefit of our experience. Let's realize that our struggles revealed may embolden them to acknowledge and confess their own. Our experience of salvation, forgiveness, and restoration can encourage them that they too can be forgiven and restored, that they too can experience the "joy of [God's] salvation." The one true value invested in our forgiven sin is this possibility of testifying to the gracious mercy of God. This testimony is the proper response to God's re-creation of our inward persons and will be the means by which we will "teach transgressors [his] ways" so that "sinners will turn back to [him]" (51:13).

Psalm 52

FOR THE DIRECTOR of music. A *maskil* of David. When Doeg the Edomite had gone to Saul and told him: "David has gone to the house of Ahimelech."

1 Why do you boast of evil, you mighty man?
   Why do you boast all day long,
   you who are a disgrace in the eyes of God?
2 Your tongue plots destruction;
   it is like a sharpened razor,
   you who practice deceit.
3 You love evil rather than good,
   falsehood rather than speaking the truth.

Selah

4 You love every harmful word,
   O you deceitful tongue!

5 Surely God will bring you down to everlasting ruin:
   He will snatch you up and tear you from your tent;
   he will uproot you from the land of the living.

Selah

6 The righteous will see and fear;
   they will laugh at him, saying,
7 "Here now is the man
   who did not make God his stronghold
but trusted in his great wealth
   and grew strong by destroying others!"

8 But I am like an olive tree
   flourishing in the house of God;
I trust in God's unfailing love
   for ever and ever.
9 I will praise you forever for what you have done;
   in your name I will hope, for your name is good.
   I will praise you in the presence of your saints.

PSALM 52 PRESENTS an instructive observation of life with encouraging comments. While not traditionally classified as a wisdom psalm, it does share with the earlier wisdom composition Psalm 49 a concern with the arrogance of the wicked and their reliance on wealth rather than on God (52:1–7; cf. 49:6–20). Like Psalm 49 and the wisdom literature in general, the present psalm describes the contrasting lives and consequences of the wicked and the righteous. As a result, while it is not explicitly instructive like Psalm 49, Psalm 52 does offer instructive insights by its comparison of the two ways of righteousness and wickedness.

Psalm 50 introduced God as judge over his covenant people, condemning them for their false reliance on self and empty sacrifices while they deceive and exploit their fellows (50:7–21). In Psalm 51, then, David provided the model for the whole community (51:18–19) of the contrite sinner who confesses sin (51:3–6) and seeks spiritual restoration of relation with God (51:7–12), which validates the external ritual of cleansing and sacrifice (51:16–17). Now Psalm 52 offers the cautionary contrast between the arrogant evil person, who will be "snatched up" by God, "torn away . . . uprooted from the land of the living" (52:5), and the righteous person, who flourishes like an olive tree in the house of God (52:8).

The psalm is divided into three segments: the arrogance of the wicked and divine judgment (52:1–5), the response of the righteous (52:6–7), and the trust and praise of the psalmist (52:8–9).

The Heading (52:0)

PSALM 52 CONTINUES the second collection of Davidic psalms (Pss. 51–65, 68–70/71) and initiates a subgroup of this collection as the first of four consecutive psalms (Pss. 52–55) classified as *maśkil*.[1] Like Psalm 51, Psalm 52 bears a historical statement linking it with a specific event in the life of David—in this case, the narrative in 1 Samuel 22:9–10, where Doeg the Edomite informed Saul that David had received assistance from the priestly family of Ahimelech of Nob. Saul, who feared the growing popularity of David, condemned Ahimelech and his family to death for aiding David. When none of Saul's associates would carry out the execution, Doeg accepted the commission and killed eighty-five priests of Yahweh and slaughtered the whole town of Nob—men, women, and children.

1. The first *maśkil* in the Psalter is Ps. 32 (see comments on the heading of this psalm). A small collection of *maśkilim* begins the second book of the Psalter, including the Korahite Pss. 42–43, 44, 45.

Psalm 52, then, is thought to represent David's response to these events. The boasting "mighty man" (52:1), whose "tongue plots destruction" (52:2), would be Doeg, whose accusations led to the deaths of so many. The reference in 52:8 to the "house of God" (i.e., temple) leads some to question whether the psalm could have been written by David.

The Arrogance of the Wicked (52:1–5)

THE PSALMIST MUST have felt under attack by those who knew well how to control and manipulate language with destructive effectiveness. His enemies are so identified with their reliance on controlling speech that in the end they cannot be distinguished from their activity; that is why he calls them "O you deceitful tongue!" (52:4b). They have become what they do so well. The arrogance and evil intent of these enemies come together when they feel free to "boast"[2] of their evil "all day long" (52:1b). That is, the wicked are so confident in their ability to control that they are either unaware or unconcerned that their pride and evil activity together make them "a disgrace in the eyes of God" (52:1c).

Like a "sharpened razor" that can do good or evil depending on the one who wields it, the tongue has the power to lacerate and to destroy. Here the tongue of the wicked takes on almost a life of its own as it plots out its destructive course.[3] Its deceptive power to lie and mislead is put in the foreground here, as "deceit" and "falsehood" are the operative terms (52:2c, 3b, 4b). For the psalmist, the practice of deceit is not a shrewd political or business technique but an admission of having sold out to evil and falsehood in contrast to holding to good and truth.[4] The same kind of inner–outer transparency described in Psalm 51 (albeit of a *negative* kind, in this instance) is characteristic of these arrogant opponents: Their outward activity is truly reflective of their inward abandonment of God and his commitment to truth.

The final result of the enemy's arrogant falsehood and deceit is harsh judgment from the "God of truth" (Ps. 31:5). Using particularly strong language evocative of the destruction of houses and city walls (*ntṣ* ["demolish, tear down"]; *nsḥ* ["tear down"] in 52:5) as well as of the tearing of people away from their dwellings, the psalmist drives home the enormity of the consequences of the enemy's deceptive lifestyle.[5] The judgment is maxi-

2. This form is from *hll* ("praise") in a reflexive stem that means "praise oneself."

3. The tongue plots "destruction," although the Heb. word (*hawwah/hawwot*) can also mean "threats" (cf. 38:12), a translation that would fit the context of controlling speech well.

4. Cf. the New Testament discussion of the power and abuse of the tongue in James 1:26; 3:5–9; 1 Peter 3:10.

5. These kinds of images would certainly have spoken to the exilic community as the ultimate punishment from God for failure to rely on him.

mized in conclusion as the wicked are described as being torn out by the roots from the land of the living. The picture of a plant being ripped from the life-giving soil stands in contrast with the later description of the psalmist as an "olive tree flourishing in the house of God" (52:8).

The Response of the Righteous (52:6–7)

THE FALL OF the deceitful wicked provides an object lesson the righteous can take to heart. The "fear" that is produced is not abject terror but the appropriate fear of Yahweh, which characterizes what Israel understands to be the right relationship of dependence on and loyalty to Yahweh and his unfailing love. That the destruction of the wicked is the consequence of their lack of trust in God is explicitly stated in the mocking laughter of the spectators: He "did not make God his stronghold but trusted in his great wealth" (52:7). Behind the laughter, however, stands a clear admonition not to follow this path to destruction.

Trust and Praise of the Psalmist (52:8–9)

THE PSALMIST CONCLUDES with a picture of expectant hope and confidence in the blessing of Yahweh on those who trust in him. Unlike the wicked who will be pulled up, roots and all, out of the nourishing soil of the land of the living (52:5), the psalmist will be like a tree planted deep in the life-giving earth of Yahweh's own dwelling, flourishing with abundant foliage (52:8). This blessing of Yahweh's continued presence is linked to the psalmist's trust "in God's unfailing love [*ḥesed*]."

Trust and blessing shift over to praise and hope in the final verse. While in the mind's eye and heart the psalmist stands flourishing in Yahweh's presence, in the context of the real world the vicious words of the wicked still have their effect. Thus, in the midst of praising God "forever" for his deeds (52:9a), the psalmist continues to "hope" for the fulfillment of the envisioned judgment and blessing. His hope is in the divine "name" Yahweh—which intriguingly does not occur in this psalm of the Elohistic Psalter[6]—and in the evidence of God's actions on behalf of his faithful ones.[7] As often in the

---

6. This final verse evidences some difficulty in translation and some phrases may have been omitted. The Hebrew says: "I will praise you forever for what you have done, and I will expectantly await your name because it is good before your saints." The NIV assumes the opening verb of praise also governs the final phrase "before your saints."

7. Rather than "saints," the word *ḥasidim* has to do with fulfilling *ḥesed* ("covenant loyalty and love"). A better translation would be those who live out enduring loyalty to their covenant relationship with Yahweh.

psalms, the psalmist's promise of praise is not a private act but a communal testimony performed "in the presence of [Yahweh's] saints" (52:9c).

THE FLOURISHING TREE. Although there is some evidence that ancient Israel was far more forested than is the contemporary land, the presence of flourishing trees was still a sign of divine blessing for those who had a history of nomadism and were living on the fringes of a settled agricultural society. Particularly the "olive tree" (*zayit*) with its precious fruit was considered a sign of secure fortune and well-being. The olive and its oil provided the basis of food, medicinal treatment, luxurious ointment, and spiritual light and anointing. The cedar was prized for its use in building and was especially associated with the divine garden of God.[8]

Several biblical contexts present the picture of a flourishing tree as a symbol of the blessing of the righteous. Especially in Psalm 1:3 and Jeremiah 17:8, which are close in vocabulary, we see independent developments of a common exemplar. In both these passages the "tree" is mentioned in its most generic form (*ʿeṣ*) rather than one of the more specific varieties (*ʾerez* ["cedar"]; *zayit* ["olive"]). Both describe divine blessing as a well-tended tree intentionally transplanted near an irrigation canal. The result of abundant water is in both cases verdant foliage, consistent fruit in abundance, and lack of concern about drought. In each case, the blessing of the righteous is paralleled by the sad state of the wicked, depicted in contrasting terms of nonproductive dryness.[9]

The similarity of these two passages suggests a common metaphor within Israelite society. Similar images describe Israel as both blessed and punished by God: "The LORD called you [Israel] a thriving olive tree with fruit beautiful in form.... Let us destroy the tree and its fruit; let us cut him off from the land of the living" (Jer. 11:16, 19). "I myself will take a shoot from the very top of a cedar and plant it ... it will produce branches and bear fruit and become a splendid cedar.... All the trees of the field will know that I the LORD bring down the tall tree and make the low tree grow tall. I dry up the green tree and make the dry tree flourish" (Ezek. 17:22–24). The splendid green tree, carefully tended by abundant water, is thus a sign of God's care and

8. Cedars of Lebanon were shipped throughout the ancient Near East for building projects, and Canaanite mythology associated Lebanon and its cedars with the divine forests protected by the fearsome dragon Huwawa (cf. the Gilgamish Epic).

9. In Jeremiah, the context of the wicked is the "wastelands/desert," which is "parched," "a salt land where no one lives" (Jer. 17:6). For Ps. 1 the wicked are rootless "chaff that the wind blows away" (Ps. 1:4).

provision for his faithful people. To the contrary, the wicked and those who turn away from Yahweh can expect drought and ultimate destruction.

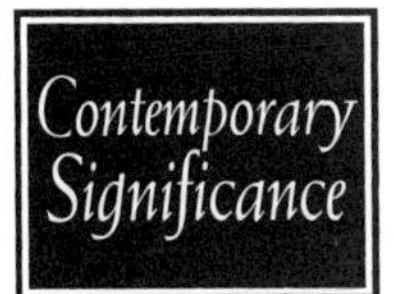

FEAR AND LAUGHTER. Most of Psalm 52 focuses on admonitions to the arrogant wealthy. The rather sarcastic taunts of the opening verses ("you mighty man . . . who are a disgrace in the eyes of God"; "you love every harmful word, O you deceitful tongue!") sets the tone for the section. The arrogant boasting of the wicked provides a negative model for the righteous, who at the end quietly profess dependence on and trust in God's unfailing love (52:8). The brash, caustic boasters lash out right and left with their lacerating tongues, loving every minute of the mayhem they cause. Yet all their destructive activity leads to no lasting security, because "surely God will bring [them] down to everlasting ruin" (52:5a). Their trust in wealth and their ability to destroy all opposition (52:7b) are completely undermined by their failure to "make God [their] stronghold" (52:7a). Those who would destroy all others will themselves be snatched up, torn out, and uprooted "from the land of the living" by God (52:5).

The decreed destruction leads righteous observers to two contradictory reactions: fear and laughter. (1) The *fear* they experience is not the kind of terror the arrogant wicked would have registered had they been sufficiently wise and aware. Rather, it is the fear of Yahweh—that appropriate relationship to God characterized by the quiet response of trust and dependence by the well-planted olive tree in the concluding verses of the psalm.[10] Thus, the instructive contrast of the psalm is emphasized again. The wicked trust only themselves and their own power; the righteous trust in Yahweh alone. The righteous know that were it not for the gracious mercy of God, their end with be the same as the wicked. There is a touch of vulnerability in their "fear," as there is any time we sense just how utterly dependent we are on something beyond our control: the skilled and attentive pilot of the aircraft we ride, the essential medication that keeps us alive, the holy God who undeservedly forgives and sustains us.

(2) The response of the righteous to the destruction of the wicked is tinged with *laughter* as well. It is not the nervous kind of laughter one produces when threatened, nor the vicious type of laughter that bursts out at the

10. That the "fear of God/Yahweh" does not mean being afraid of God is confirmed by Ex. 20:20, where Moses exhorts the Israelites who are cowering before the theophany on Mount Sinai: "*Do not be afraid*. God has come to test you, so that *the fear of God* will be with you to keep you from sinning."

expense of another. Rather, this laughter is the spontaneous relief we experience when we realize the fate of someone else will pass by us. The fear that acknowledges dependence on God leads to laughter of escaping the judgment of the wicked. The righteous know their trust is in God and not themselves. Even though self may consistently fail, God will not. One need not experience the rooting out reserved for the wicked but can look forward with joy and laughter to flourishing like a green olive tree in the house of God.

The key is trust in God rather than in self. The metaphorical olive tree is dependent on the care of the one who planted it and tends it. A tree cannot get up and move closer to the water source; it must depend on the care of the gardener to provide for its needs. When planted in the right spot, the tree sends down it roots deep into the life-giving resources of the stream. If we too are to be olive trees planted in the house of God, we must become lively and fruitful when we send down our roots into the life-giving source that God provides in his unfailing love.

Psalm 53

FOR THE DIRECTOR of music. According to *mahalath.* A *maskil* of David.

1 The fool says in his heart,
"There is no God."
They are corrupt, and their ways are vile;
there is no one who does good.

2 God looks down from heaven
on the sons of men
to see if there are any who understand,
any who seek God.
3 Everyone has turned away,
they have together become corrupt;
there is no one who does good,
not even one.

4 Will the evildoers never learn—
those who devour my people as men eat bread
and who do not call on God?
5 There they were, overwhelmed with dread,
where there was nothing to dread.
God scattered the bones of those who attacked you;
you put them to shame, for God despised them.

6 Oh, that salvation for Israel would come out of Zion!
When God restores the fortunes of his people,
let Jacob rejoice and Israel be glad!

PSALM 53 IS a close duplicate in verses 1–5a and 6 to the earlier Psalm 14:1–7. One set of variations between these two compositions is due to the use in Psalm 53 of the divine epithet *ʾelohim* instead of the Tetragrammaton *yhwh* that appears in Psalm 14 (cf. 14:2 = 53:2; 14:4 = 53:4; 14:7b = 53:6b). This is often taken as one of the clearest evidences of the existence of an Elohistic Psalter extending from Psalms

42–83, in which it is supposed that the divine name Yahweh has been suppressed and replaced by *ʾelohim*.[1] The most significant variant observed between these psalms lies in the comparison of 14:5a–6 with 53:5b-d (see below).

Like Psalm 14, our current psalm is an extended wisdom meditation on the folly of the wicked, who deny the effective existence of God and live corrupt lives through the oppression of the poor. The meditation is divided into three stanzas, with a concluding single verse. In this case, however, because of the textual difference in 53:5, the second stanza is composed of only two verses (53:4–5) rather than three as in stanza one (53:1–3) and in Psalm 14. Verse 5 is expanded in Psalm 53 to include four lines rather than the two lines found in 14:5. This effectively balances the two lines of 14:6 that are not included in Psalm 53.

Thematic structure follows the poetic structure with a description of the foolishness of evildoers and the divine response (53:1–3), a depiction of divine judgment on the wicked (53:4–5), and an expression of communal hope for restoration from exile (53:6).

The Heading (53:0)

THE HEADING SHARES with the more simple heading of Psalm 14 a reference to "the director of music" and attribution to David.[2] It expands those simple components with one new term—a possible tune or tuning for harp accompaniment (*ʿal maḥalat*) that occurs elsewhere only in the heading to Psalm 88. In addition, the poem is acknowledged as a *maśkil*,[3] the second of four consecutive psalms that bear this designation in their headings (Pss. 52–55).[4] Psalm 53 is the third psalm attributed to David in the second collection of Davidic psalms (Pss. 51–71).[5]

---

1. See discussion of the Elohistic Psalter in the opening comments to Pss. 42–43 and in "The Shape of the Psalter" in vol. 2 of this commentary.

2. See comments on the heading of Ps. 4 for "the director of music" and on Ps. 3 for psalms of David.

3. See comments on the heading of Ps. 32.

4. The heading of Ps. 88 shares two terms in common with that of Ps. 53: *ʿal maḥalat* and *maśkil*. Ps. 88, however, is not Davidic, being doubly attributed to Heman the Ezrahite and the Sons of Korah. See also comments on the heading of Ps. 88.

5. The second Davidic collection is composed of twenty-one psalms, of which eighteen bear Davidic attributions in their headings. The other three psalms (66, 67, and 71) are bound into their Davidic context in other ways: Pss. 66 and 67 by thematic connections with the surrounding psalms as well as the use of similar terms in their headings, and Ps. 71 by being read together with the preceding Ps. 70 (attributed to David).

The Folly of the Evildoers (53:1–3)

SEE THE COMMENTARY on 14:1–3 for discussion on these verses.

Judgment on the Wicked (53:4–5)

FOR 53:4, SEE comments on 14:4. Having described the corruption of human beings (*bene ʾadam* in v. 2) in terms that seem absolute, the psalmist now indicates there are those "poor" who are oppressed by the powerful fools and who receive divine care and protection. As a result, the wicked are condemned for treating the poor as consumable objects.

It is in 53:5 that the greatest variation from Psalm 14 occurs. A careful comparison of the Hebrew text of these psalms offers tantalizing clues that a faint or fragmentary text may have lain behind one or both of these textual versions.[6] Despite clear and distinctive divergence in wording at this point, the main thrust of the parallel passages remains the same: The wicked who refuse to acknowledge Yahweh—either in actuality or practicality—will be overwhelmed with dread and destruction by the very one whose existence they deny. God is the protector of the poor and will bring to judgment the oppressive deeds of the wicked.

In Psalm 14, the emphasis is placed on the protective power of God in behalf of the poor, while in Psalm 53, God's power is unleashed in judgment on the wicked. One way of reading the rather enigmatic phrase "there was nothing to dread" (53:5b) is that destruction came on the wicked when they least expected it—out of the blue, so to speak—that is, when everything seemed to be going their way. Another way to understand this phrase is to see the wicked as becoming so paranoid under the divine attack that they will see destruction everywhere, constantly glancing over their shoulder anticipating the next attack.

In a passage reminiscent of the well-known "dry bones" passage (Ezek. 37), the scattered bones depict the spiritual death of the wicked and their rejection

---

6. Note these comparisons:

Ps. 14	Ps. 53
šm pḥdw pḥd	*šm pḥdw pḥd lʾ hyh pḥd*
ky ʾlhym bdwr ṣdyq	*ky ʾlhym pzr*
ʿṣt ʿny	*ʿṣmt ḥnk*
tbyšw	*hbšth*
ky yhwh mḥshw	*ky ʾlhym mʾsm*

The additional phrase in the first line of Ps. 53 above (*lʾ hyh pḥd*) might easily have been omitted from Ps. 14 by haplography—the eye of the reader having skipped from the first *pḥd* to the second. The rest of the texts show relative balance in number of words, and some suggestive parallels: *ʿṣt* - *ʿṣmt* and *tbyšw* - *hbšth*.

by God. In Ezekiel, the dead bones of the Israelites, judged for their sin, in the Exile, are regathered, reknit, clothed with new flesh and skin, and reenlivened to live new life before their God. In Psalm 53, the reverse is envisioned for the wicked—scattered bones, the horrible effects of spiritual abandonment.

Communal Hope for Restoration (53:6)

SEE COMMENTS ON 14:7. As in Psalm 14, our present version concludes with an expression of the hope of the community for restoration. Once again, the NIV's translation of the Hebrew *šebut* as "fortunes" rather than the more common (and more likely) "captivity" obscures the link this verse makes with the exilic community. It also avoids the clear implication that, at least in its present form, the psalm reflects a period far later than the time of David.

LOCATION! LOCATION! LOCATION! Because Psalms 14 and 53 represent close duplicates, they provide us an opportunity to consider how the same psalm might function in an alternate literary context. Psalm 14 immediately follows Psalm 13, a plea for deliverance from arrogant enemies, who anticipate with rejoicing the psalmist's imminent fall (13:2c, 4). In Psalm 13, the psalmist is "wrestling" with thoughts of possible defeat and divine abandonment (13:1–2) but is able at the end to "trust in [Yahweh's] unfailing love" for salvation (13:5). In this context, Psalm 14 provides an encouraging vision of the end of the arrogant fools who deny the power of God and (like the enemies of Ps. 13) consume the poor. The unique portion of 14:5 (which does not occur in Ps. 53) reassures the suffering poor that despite the attacks of the enemy, "God is present in the company of the righteous" to strike dread into the hearts of their foes. Following on the heels of this assurance, Psalm 15 then offers the psalmist's commitment to a life of righteous integrity that qualifies him for the divine presence promised in 14:5 and which consequently "will never be shaken" (15:5c).

By way of contrast, Psalm 53 stands linked together with the preceding Psalm 52 as a combined description of corrupt humanity, who deserve God's judgment. This excursus on human evil is set in motion by the confessional Psalm 51, where the narrator learned the benefits of deep, cleansing confession before God. Toward the end of that psalm, he responded to the hope of restoration to "the joy of [God's] salvation" (51:12) by announcing his intention to "teach transgressors your ways" so that "sinners will turn back to you" (51:13). This commitment to teach transgressors is the appropriate kickoff for the strong pictures of human evil in Psalms 52 and 53, which graphically depict the arrogance and folly of the wicked and the futility of their hopes to escape God's scrutiny and judgment.

As a contrasting positive example standing at the juncture of these two descriptions of evil lies the calm, quiet, confident picture of the flourishing olive tree enjoying a fruitful life within the protective care of God's house (52:8–9). After the vow to teach transgressors is fulfilled in Psalms 52–53, Psalm 54 returns to the plea to enjoy the salvation of God envisioned in 51:12.

Scattered bones. We are horrified by the idea of cannibalism, yet we are strangely fascinated at the same time. Hollywood has learned to exploit this morbid obsession with productions featuring urbane killers like Hannibal "the Cannibal" Lector in *Silence of the Lambs* and the even more tortured sequel *Hannibal*. Cannibalism in times of stress—especially during long sieges of towns—was known in the ancient Near East and is mentioned in the Old Testament.[7] Our own history of Western expansion has its dark accounts of the Donner expedition snowed into the northern California mountains with insufficient supplies.

Two passages in Psalm 53 lend themselves to the suggestion of cannibalism. The first is most clear—the reference in 53:4 to the evildoers who "devour my people as men eat bread." The idea of cannibalistic savagery as a metaphor for the exploitation of the poor and powerless is found in 27:2 and even more graphically in Micah 3:1–3. It is as if one felt they could gain increased personal power by consuming the flesh of one's enemy, an apt image to apply to the vicious attacks by the rich on those less powerful persons they felt free to manipulate at will.[8]

The second image is less specific and is capable of varied interpretation. It is only in connection with the first image that the association with cannibalism may come through. I am talking of the image of the scattered bones of the wicked mentioned in 53:5. The image of scattered, fleshless bones appears elsewhere as the aftermath of a military defeat so great that the dead were left behind to waste away unburied. That is certainly the case in the famous "valley of dry bones" passage in Ezekiel 37.[9] But connected with the preceding verse, the scattered bones of 53:5 allow a subtle interpretation. Those who

---

7. Cf. Deut. 28:53; Jer. 19:9; Lam. 2:20; Ezek. 5:10; Zech. 11:9.

8. In certain headhunting societies, the idea existed that by eating the flesh or certain significant organs (like the heart) of the defeated enemy, one could gain some of the characteristics of the enemy for themselves or reduce the power of vengeance.

9. Scattered bones also figure in Ezek. 6:5, although there the bones of dead bodies are used to profane pagan holy places, rendering them useless for future worship (cf. 2 Kings 23:14). In Jer. 8:1, the disinterred bones of the kings and officials of Judah are scattered and exposed as a way of dishonoring them because of their faithless worship of other gods.

consume the flesh of the poor will themselves be consumed by the wrath of God so that their scattered bones will provide mute testimony to those who follow of both their sin and the appropriateness of their punishment.

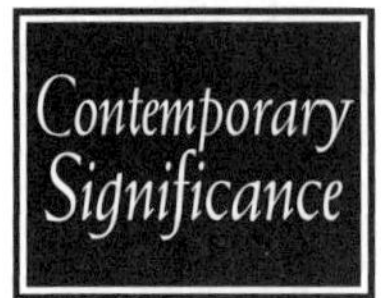

INCONSPICUOUS CONSUMPTION. Once again I need to be careful, I think, not to identify too easily with the exploited poor in this passage. I would be hard put to describe any exploitation I experience in the relatively easy existence I have today as "being devoured ... as men eat bread." That seems a pretty extreme evocation for the kind of manipulation society puts me through.

Now there are those in my society who *are* being consumed in a radical way, such as throw-away children and young men and women forced into the sex trade to satisfy the lusts of those who have no care for them other than as a source of momentary power and pleasure. Such individuals have become the equivalent to consumable products like bread or water, milk and potatoes to satisfy an appetite. Drug addicts, enslaved to cravings that submerge all aspects of their lives to the need to feed the addiction, fall into the same category of expendable persons, whose only role is to provide power and money to those who supply the drugs.

If I am not one of those throw-away people exploited as an object for my potential to satisfy another's need, I can identify with their pain and hate the circumstances that continue their exploitation, and I can work to redeem a society so lost that it "devours" its weak and helpless "like men eat bread." But I must be careful not to feel justified by my anger and freed by my energy. I need to realize just how complex and convoluted life is today, so that my own complicity in the exploitation of others is not always obvious to me or to anyone else. Just where does that silk shirt I enjoy so much come from? Who made it? Are they enslaved workers in an urban sweatshop? Where does our retirement fund place its investments?

The situation requires lots of care and energy, and we will probably never be able to know for sure. But as we learn, these kind of decisions do not seem to me insignificant. Our own consumption—conspicuous or otherwise—often does come at the price of exploiting others, eating them as if they are bread. We must be challenged by this psalm, and others like it, to reflect deeply and carefully on how our lives participate directly or indirectly in the exploitation of those the world considers expendable because they are, for the most part, invisible to us. There *are no expendable people to God!* And if we claim to be God's people, there should not be any for us either.

Psalm 54

FOR THE DIRECTOR of music. With stringed instruments. A *maskil* of David. When the Ziphites had gone to Saul and said, "Is not David hiding among us?"

1 Save me, O God, by your name;
    vindicate me by your might.
2 Hear my prayer, O God;
    listen to the words of my mouth.

3 Strangers are attacking me;
    ruthless men seek my life—
    men without regard for God. *Selah*
4 Surely God is my help;
    the Lord is the one who sustains me.

5 Let evil recoil on those who slander me;
    in your faithfulness destroy them.

6 I will sacrifice a freewill offering to you;
    I will praise your name, O LORD,
    for it is good.
7 For he has delivered me from all my troubles,
    and my eyes have looked in triumph on my foes.

PSALM 54 IS a plea for deliverance and shares with Psalms 52 and 53 the theme of enemies who have no regard for God (cf. 52:7; 53:1, 4; 54:3). This psalm revolves around 54:4, which carries the major theme: "Surely God is my help; the Lord is the one who sustains me." References to God's "name" as the basis of the psalmist's hope for deliverance bracket the psalm at the beginning (54:1) and end (54:6), and the divine name Yahweh itself stands at the end (54:6), despite the fact this psalm is part of the so-called Elohistic Psalter.[1] Concern with the divine

1. For further discussion of the Elohistic Psalter, see comments on Ps. 42. The reference in 54:4 to "the Lord" (*ʾadonay*) may also represent a "replacement" of the divine name *yhwh*. Over time in the Jewish community, the convention gradually arose—out of respect for the divine name and the desire to avoid abusing it—that when *yhwh* was encountered in the text, the word *ʾadonay* was spoken instead. See comments on the divine name in Ps. 8.

name also links this psalm with 52:9, which expresses similar confidence in the name.

Surrounding the central verse, the psalm is divided into two segments of three verses each (54:1–3, 5–7). The structure of the psalm can be described as follows: invocation of God to hear and save (54:1–2), description of the psalmist's plight (54:3), thematic statement of confidence (54:4), plea for retribution on the enemies (54:5), and vow of sacrifice and praise (54:6–7).

The Heading (54:0)

NO NEW TERMS appear in the heading of Psalm 54. The composition is referred to "the director of music" and attributed to David.[2] Like Psalms 52 and 53 before it and the following Psalm 55, the present one is called a *maśkil*.[3] The musical direction "with stringed instruments" (*binginot*) appears here for the first time since Psalms 4 and 6. The term also appears in the heading to Psalm 55.[4]

A historical notice connects Psalm 54 with the event in 1 Samuel 23:19–29, when the Ziphites informed Saul that David and his men were hiding in their territory and promised to turn him over to Saul. Nothing in the psalm specifically relates to those events, but the general concern about being attacked by "ruthless men" (54:3) and slanderers (54:5a) is compatible with the kind of attack experienced in 1 Samuel 23.

Call for Hearing and Deliverance (54:1–2)

THE PSALM BEGINS with a plea for God to "save" the psalmist "by [his] name." In this context God's "name" is synonymous with his "might" (*geburah*), as indicated by the parallel positions of the two phrases "by your name" and "by your might" in 54:1. For the Israelites, the name reveals the essential character and nature of the bearer; thus, with respect to God, the name reveals the power and authority of God himself. It is through the power and authority to which the name points that he acts to deliver and to judge.

Along with deliverance, the psalmist also desires "vindication." This translation of the underlying Hebrew word (*dyn* ["judge"]) is interpretive in that it assumes that when God judges the psalmist, he will be found righteous and thus vindicated. Along with "vindication," the psalmist seeks a hearing from

---

2. See comments on the heading of Ps. 4 for "the director of music" and on Ps. 3 for psalms of David.

3. See comments on this term at its first appearance in Ps. 32.

4. Indeed, the first four terms in the headings of Pss. 54 and 55 are identical: *lamnaṣṣeaḥ binginot maśkil ledawid* ("To the director of music. With stringed instruments. A *maśkil* of David").

God who is judge. His plea that God "hear" (*šmᶜ*) and "listen" (*ʾzn*) are attempts to gain access to a judge to hear the plaintiff's case.

The Psalmist's Plight (54:3)

THE PSALMIST VIEWS his circumstance as desperate—even life-threatening ("seek my life").[5] The attackers are called *zarim* ("strangers") and *ᶜariṣim* ("ruthless persons"). Normally a *zar* is a non-Israelite who does not share in Israel's covenant relationship with Yahweh, an interpretation that seems uncomfortable with the identity of the Ziphites, who were residents of Judah. Perhaps the intent is to use a particularly harsh term to describe fellow Israelites in order to emphasize just how far they had removed themselves from true covenant relationships. The term *ᶜariṣim* is often used in parallel with *zarim* to describe the fear-inducing opposition of foreign nations (cf. Isa. 25:5; Ezek. 28:7; 31:12), but it can also describe particularly "ruthless" attackers.[6]

Without regard for God. The attackers are not only strangers to covenant relationship and particularly ruthless; they also live with no regard for God. Like the "fool" in Psalm 53, these enemies refuse to acknowledge the authority of God over their lives. The phrase translated "without regard for God" is more literally rendered "they do not set God before them." The picture is akin to that of following a trailblazing guide—setting that person in front and keeping one's eyes fixed on that leader in order to know the right way. These attackers refuse to keep their eyes on God but seek to follow their own ruthless devices. Therefore, the psalmist feels confident to bring them into Yahweh's court for redress.

Statement of Confidence (54:4)

THE CENTRAL MESSAGE of the psalm is confidence in God as the psalmist's "help" and "sustainer" (lit., "prop, support"). Unlike the enemies, who ruthlessly "seek" to do harm to the psalmist's *nepeš*, God is the psalmist's "helper," who "props up" or "provides support" for him.

---

5. The "life" the enemies seek is the psalmist's *nepeš*—that animated being sustained by Yahweh's Spirit. This integrated person—body, mind, and spirit—is under attack.

6. The appearance of both *zarim* and *ᶜariṣim* suggests the original emphasis of the psalm was on attacks by foreign nations. This indicates the historical notice in the heading has adapted the original psalm to speak to the circumstances of the conflict between David, Saul, and the Ziphites. See the comments on this subject in Marvin Tate, *Psalms 51–100* (WBC 20; Dallas: Word, 1990), 46, 48, and Joachim Becker, *Israel deutet seine Psalmen: Urform und Neuinterpretation in den Psalmen* (Stuttgart: Verlag Katholisches Bibelwerk, 1967), 64–65. Tate agrees that Ps. 54 may be an adaptation of an earlier lament to the needs of the postexilic community. Becker claims that Ps. 54 is one of seventeen or so psalms that have been so reinterpreted.

Plea for Retribution (54:5)

OUT OF THIS confident expectation that God is helper and sustainer, the psalmist is able to seek the setting right of wrongs. In verse 5 he asks that God the judge render justice on his enemies by allowing the evil they intend for him to "recoil" on them. The enemies here are further called "slanderers" (*šoreray*)[7]—an accusation that fits the legal setting noted previously.

In your faithfulness. The psalmist anticipates the destruction of the enemy as a result of God's "faithfulness" (*ʾemet* ["truth"]). The idea behind *ʾemet* is more than veracity or accuracy. It is rather the sense of endurance and commitment. God is to be trusted not because he is correct and accurate but because he is enduringly committed and worthy of secure reliance.

Vow of Sacrifice and Praise (54:6–7)

AS IN MANY laments, this psalm concludes with a vow to offer sacrifice and praise. The mention of sacrifice does point back to the concern with right sacrifice in 50:7–15, 23 and 51:16–17, 19. However, here the psalmist raises no question concerning the desirability of sacrifice.

I will praise your name. The psalmist vows to praise Yahweh's name, picking up on the opening theme that it is the power of God's "name" that delivers. Here the divine name is specifically stated and commended because "it is good"—a link with the similar statement in 52:9. The sacrifice and praise were likely offered in the context of temple worship—or in the postexilic context, during a pilgrimage to Jerusalem or in local synagogue worship.[8]

He has delivered me. The psalm's final word is one of confident expectation of deliverance, stated as an accomplished fact. Either this is a sign of a reworking of the original lament after deliverance had been experienced, or else the psalmist's confidence is so strong that deliverance is assured. The last phrase of the psalm is more vague and general than the NIV has interpreted it: "My eyes have looked in triumph on my foes." The literal statement is "and at my enemies my eyes have looked." But since the context is one of rejoicing over the defeat of the enemy, the NIV interpretation seems appropriate.[9]

---

7. While this term has traditionally been translated more generally as adversary, Dahood's study (*Psalms*, 2:25–26) is probably correct in identifying the more accurate nuance "slanderer."

8. Following the destruction of the second temple by the Romans in A.D. 70, it became generally accepted Jewish practice to understand that attention to Torah, prayer, and almsgiving could "substitute" for ritual sacrifice until the temple would be rebuilt and sacrifice restored.

9. See Tate, *Psalms 51–100*, 48.

THE GOD WHO is over against us. According to this psalm, the enemies ultimately fail because they are "without regard for God" (54:3). As noted above, this phrase in the Hebrew means something like "they do not set God before them." While this may have the effect of saying "they do not keep their eyes on God," or perhaps "they don't follow the path blazed by God going before," the linking of this verse with verse 4 raises another interesting possibility. In verse 4, God is called the psalmist's "helper" (*ʿozer*). We find a similar combination of two words—*ʿezer* ["helper"] and *kenegdo* ["like one over against him"]—in the description of Adam's needed counterpart in Genesis 2:18. There God viewed the newly created human being as "not good"—that is, not yet complete—because there was not yet a "helper" (*ʿezer*) to provide the necessary relational counterpart (*kenegdo*; NIV "suitable for him").

After no suitable *ʿezer kenegdo* was found for the Adam among the animals (Gen. 2:19–20), God divided the originally created Adam into two parts, forming one into a woman and bringing her back to the man, Adam. The man, now clearly identified as male, acknowledges the woman as "bone of my bones and flesh of my flesh" (2:23), and the passage concludes with the beautiful admission that when these two beings—who had originally been one—come together in appropriate relationship, the completion of the *ʾadam* ("human being") is assured (2:24–25).

Thus, in the creation account, the appropriate relationship of man and woman realizes God's intended completeness for humanity. In this relationship there is no implied inferiority of the woman, since she is made of the same stuff as the original Adam. Also her role as *ʿezer kenegdo* cannot be taken as subordinate, since the term "helper" (*ʿezer*) is used elsewhere in Scripture to describe *God himself* as the "helper" of humankind. The woman, then, is viewed as fulfilling the role of God in completing the ability of humankind to relate appropriately among itself as God is able to relate fully within himself.[10]

Now we know (from Scripture and from our present experience) that male and female did *not* continue long to relate appropriately as God

---

10. Whatever else God's use of the plural self-reference in Genesis means (Gen. 1:26; 3:22; 11:7), it certainly implies that he has the capability to commune/relate within himself, which can only be paralleled among humans by relationship between/among independent human beings. Note in this regard the subtle confirmation of this in Gen. 1:27, where the creation of the Adam moves from "God created the Adam in his own image" to "in the image of God he created *him*" to "*male and female* he created *them*." This implies that there is something essential in *both* male *and* female that, when rightly related together, allows human beings to reflect the image of their creator.

originally intended and that the fall of human beings into sin and disobedience led—along with other consequences—to the destruction of the *ᶜezer kenegdo* relationship (Gen. 3). But our psalm passage suggests that God still stands ready to provide the necessary relationship to make humans whole. God is our helper, says the psalmist, if only we will "set him over against" ourselves.

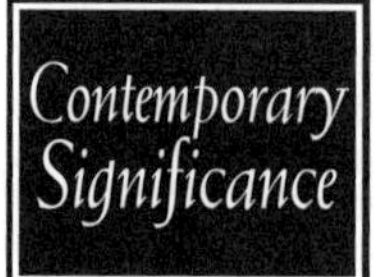

KEEPING GOD OVER against us. How do we do what the enemies of this psalm did not? How do we "set him [God] before [or over against] us"? On the one hand, there is the expectation of keeping our eyes fastened on God. If God is the one who is over against or in front of us, our vision ought always to be focused on him. It is somewhat like two lovers alone at a restaurant table—hands clasped across the tablecloth, eyes locked together as if no one else is in the room. That kind of focused gaze on God reminds me of the old gospel hymn, "Turn your eyes upon Jesus. Look full on his wonderful face, and the things of earth will grow strangely dim, in the light of his glory and grace."

Placing our gaze fully on God changes the way we see the rest of the world. When we look steadfastly at God, we find he is a God of justice and equity, a God who takes no pleasure in evil, the creator God who cares for the *whole* creation animate and inanimate, animal and human. Scrutinizing God in this way means we can no longer make light of his power and glory, nor can we ignore the call to participate in the restoration of the world. Our relationships will and must change; we will and must seek justice and equity as God does; we will and must respond to the whole creation in ways that seek its best interests rather than ours.

When the enemies of Psalm 54 set their eyes other than on God, they fail to see his "glory and grace." Without him in sight, they are able to disregard him and join the fool of 53:1 in saying, "There is no God." Ignoring his path, they feel free to become completely corrupt and without any good (53:1–4). In order to follow God's path, the path described in 1:6 as "the way of the righteous," we need to keep our eyes on him. Like the small child following his mom through the crowded shopping mall, a moment's distraction can mean the difference between arriving safely in his mother's wake or wandering the mall/world tearfully in search of her.

When we keep our eyes on God and allow him to be the helper who stands over against us, we can know the kind of fulfillment that even our most intimate human connections fail to provide. When our trust in human companions is betrayed (cf. 55:12–14), when our leaders fail (cf. 146:3–5), and even when our parents abandon and abuse us (cf. 27:7–10), God is there to hold us up and sustain us (54:4).

Knowing what we are praying for. Some of the prayers of the psalmists may bother us more than a little. Often they ask God for public redress of their wrongs in violent terms. "Let evil recoil on those who slander me; in your faithfulness destroy them" (54:5). Whatever happened to "love your enemy, do good to those who persecute you"? We feel constrained by our Christian principles to avoid spilling out anger and hurt on those we consider our enemies. Often we feel more than a little bit superior to these pre-Christian, Old Testament psalmists and their vengeful ways.

Let's stop before we get too smug, however, and realize two things. (1) Those words of anger and vengeance are, strangely enough, God's Word to us! What they teach us, I think, is *not* to go around hating our enemies, but to acknowledge that we sometimes (perhaps even often) *do* hate those who hurt us and wish them hurt in return. The recent execution of an infamous mass murderer is a case in point. Interviews with family members of those slain often expressed anger and rage and the desire to see the killer suffer as their lost loved ones suffered. They wanted to be there to see the lethal injection given, to witness the demise of the one they had named evil incarnate. If we convict the psalmist of wrong for these words of angry desire for vengeance, we will most likely have to convict ourselves as well before our lives are over.

These words of pain and rage challenge us to admit our own rage and hatred rising out of our vulnerability and impotence to stop the hurt and pain that consume those things, ideas, and people we hold so dear. These words also challenge us to acknowledge—in the absence of our own pain—that many others in our world have experienced life so abusive and anguished that they could pray these angry psalms without blinking an eye. Talk to some of the survivors of the Nazi Holocaust or those who experienced the abuses of apartheid in South Africa. Ask the families of the victims of revolutionary zeal in Chile and Nicaragua, mainline China, or the killing fields of Cambodia, and you will find they understand the words of these psalms in ways you and I never could. These words crack open a window to a true world that we may not want to admit exists—whether inside or outside of ourselves—but it is a world that our God knows and shares the pain it reveals.

(2) We need to realize that whenever we ask God to set things right, establish justice, vindicate the righteous, and bring an end to evil, we are actually joining the psalmists' pleas for God to bring destruction on the wicked. It is a bit naive of us to believe in a holy and righteous God who is incompatible with evil and to ask him to enter our world decisively in order to end the effects of evil, and to ignore the fact that such a clean-up would have

negative consequences for anyone and everything infected by wickedness. Both Old and New Testaments are clear in telling all who listen to them that aligning oneself with evil has destructive consequences. All those passages about fire and brimstone, divine judgment, eternal damnation, and hell are surely not there by mistake. Nor are they just the wishful thinking of angry, hateful people, who want to exercise destructive power over others.

Even when we ask for personal vindication rather than judgment on others, there is still a cutting edge to our request. To ask the judge to decide between two parties means that when one wins, the other loses; when the one is declared righteous, the other must necessarily be wicked. For us to be declared right means that others must be declared wrong and suffer the consequences of their wrongdoing.

It is interesting to me, however, that we never hear Jesus asking for personal vindication, but only for forgiveness. On the cross, rather than asking for God's angels to prove to his detractors that he was truly the Son of God, Jesus instead asks his Father to forgive those who have brought him to death, "for they do not know what they are doing" (Luke 23:34).[11] So we should be careful what we pray for, because we may get more than we bargain for.

---

11. Similarly, Job's demand for personal vindication is at first ignored until he is brought by the glory and grace of the God who comes to stand over against him to an admission that his personal vindication is of little account and in fact entirely unnecessary any longer (Job 42:1–6). When vindication does come for Job, it is after his confession to God has rendered it moot, and it is coupled with a prayer of intercession for the friends who, although declared wrong in comparison to Job, are nevertheless valued by God. The full restoration of Job is reliant on his giving up his claims against his friends by praying for them.

Psalm 55

FOR THE DIRECTOR of music. With stringed instruments. A *maskil* of David.

1 Listen to my prayer, O God,
do not ignore my plea;
2 hear me and answer me.
My thoughts trouble me and I am distraught
3 at the voice of the enemy,
at the stares of the wicked;
for they bring down suffering upon me
and revile me in their anger.

4 My heart is in anguish within me;
the terrors of death assail me.
5 Fear and trembling have beset me;
horror has overwhelmed me.
6 I said, "Oh, that I had the wings of a dove!
I would fly away and be at rest—
7 I would flee far away
and stay in the desert; *Selah*
8 I would hurry to my place of shelter,
far from the tempest and storm."

9 Confuse the wicked, O Lord, confound their speech,
for I see violence and strife in the city.
10 Day and night they prowl about on its walls;
malice and abuse are within it.
11 Destructive forces are at work in the city;
threats and lies never leave its streets.

12 If an enemy were insulting me,
I could endure it;
if a foe were raising himself against me,
I could hide from him.
13 But it is you, a man like myself,
my companion, my close friend,
14 with whom I once enjoyed sweet fellowship
as we walked with the throng at the house of God.

15 Let death take my enemies by surprise;
let them go down alive to the grave,
for evil finds lodging among them.

16 But I call to God,
and the LORD saves me.
17 Evening, morning and noon
I cry out in distress,
and he hears my voice.
18 He ransoms me unharmed
from the battle waged against me,
even though many oppose me.
19 God, who is enthroned forever,
will hear them and afflict them— *Selah*
men who never change their ways
and have no fear of God.

20 My companion attacks his friends;
he violates his covenant.
21 His speech is smooth as butter,
yet war is in his heart;
his words are more soothing than oil,
yet they are drawn swords.

22 Cast your cares on the LORD
and he will sustain you;
he will never let the righteous fall.
23 But you, O God, will bring down the wicked
into the pit of corruption;
bloodthirsty and deceitful men
will not live out half their days.

But as for me, I trust in you.

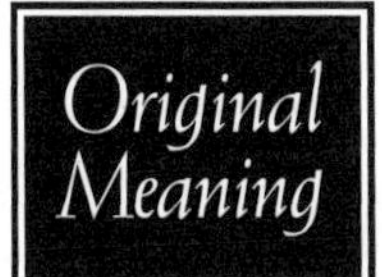

LIKE PSALM 54 before it and the several psalms succeeding it,[1] Psalm 55 is a plea for deliverance from the attack of one's enemies.[2] It is particularly poignant since it seems to respond to the hurt of betrayal by a close friend (55:12–14, 20–21). This fact has led some to connect the psalm to Judas's betrayal of Jesus.[3] Others, drawing on the similarity of 55:6–8 with Jeremiah 9:1–2 and the description of faithless friends in 9:4–6, even suggest Jeremiah as author or at least the inspiration for this psalm.[4] Identification of the betrayer as Ahithophel, the wise counselor of David who defected to Absalom,[5] does not fit well with the contents of the psalm. Most commentators are content to leave a final identification of the faithless friend unresolved.

Numerous difficulties and uncertainties beset the text of this psalm, as evidenced by the extensive textual apparatus in *BHS* and the considerable variations in the translations.[6]

The structure of Psalm 55 is less clear than for some of the laments. After a brief invocation of God to hear (reminiscent of 54:2), the body interweaves descriptions of emotional distress as the result of attack with pleas for divine action against the enemy and confident trust in God. For the purpose of discussion the psalm may be divided into the following sections: invocation of God (55:1–2a), a description of the psalmist's distress (55:2b–8), a plea for divine judgment on the enemy (55:9–11), the faithless friend (55:12–14), a renewed call for judgment of the enemy (55:15), a statement of confidence (55:16–19), a reprise of the faithless friend (55:20–21), and a call to confident trust in God (55:22–23).

1. The following psalms of lament include individual complaints (Pss. 56–57; 59; 61) and more general or communal complaints (Pss. 58; 60).

2. In this psalm, the psalmist's words are called "my prayer" (55:1a) and "my plea/lament" (55:1b).

3. At least one manuscript of the Latin Vulgate makes this connection explicit in the heading to this psalm: "The voice of Christ against the chiefs of the Jews and the traitor Judas" (see J. W. Rogerson and J. W. MacKay, *Psalms 51–100* [Cambridge Bible Commentary; New York: Cambridge Univ. Press, 1977], 29).

4. The notion is widespread and mentioned in commentators as diverse as Delitzsch (*Psalms*, 156), Rogerson and McKay (*Psalms 51–100*, 32), Tate (*Psalms 51–100*, 55), and Mays (*Psalms*, 207)—to name a few.

5. See representative comments in Delitzsch and Tate.

6. A thorough treatment of the textual variations and possible resolutions is found in Tate, *Psalms 51–100*, 51–54.

The Heading (55:0)

NO NEW TERMS appear in the heading of Psalm 55. The complete heading is identical to the opening four words of the heading of Psalm 54 (see comments there). This psalm is the fifth one in the second Davidic collection, which begins in Psalm 51 and extends through Psalm 71. It concludes the group of four *maśkil* psalms that began with Psalm 52. The immediately following Psalm 56 initiates a new group of five psalms (56–60), each of which is categorized as *miktam*.[7]

Invocation of God (55:1–2a)

A TYPICAL PLEA for God to hear the psalmist's complaint opens the psalm. The phrases are already familiar from the similar plea voiced in 54:2.[8] Here in Psalm 55, the psalmist stylishly alternates the positive pleas for divine hearing and response on the periphery ("listen," v. 1a; "hear ... answer," v. 2a) with the negatively expressed request that God "not ignore"[9] his "plea" (*teḥinnah*, v. 1b). As the psalmist in 54:2 sought vindication more than just a hearing, so the speaker of 55:1–2 desires God to "answer."

The Psalmist's Distress (55:2b–8)

THE PSALMIST'S CIRCUMSTANCE is dominated by mental and emotional turmoil. The latter half of verse 2 is made difficult by two uncommon verbs (*rwd* and *hwm*), and debate continues over the defining roots and their meaning in this context.[10] Despite the difficulties, the atmosphere of personal pain and uncertainty remains clear. The last half of verse 2 seems to go with verse 3. The "voice" of the enemy could be the "battle cry" of the surrounding attackers

---

7. For a discussion of groups of psalms marked by the use of identical terms in successive psalm headings, see Wilson, *The Editing of the Hebrew Psalter*, 155–67.

8. In Ps. 54, the phrase "hear [*šmʿ*] my prayer, O God" is paralleled by a second phrase employing the alternative verb "listen" (*ʾzn*). Here in Ps. 55, however, the alternative expression appears in the first phrase: "Listen [*ʾzn*] to my prayer, O God."

9. The root meaning of *ʿlm* is "hide"; in 55:1 it speaks reflexively of "hiding oneself." The sense is to "avoid" someone or something (here the psalmist's lament) so as not to deal with it. In this light the NIV's "ignore" seems accurate.

10. The debate over *ʾarid* is whether to derive the form from *rwd* ("roam about"), indicating restlessness of spirit, or from *rdd* ("trample, subdue"), suggesting oppressive thoughts. The LXX translation "to give pain to, grieve" suggests the Heb. *rʿʿ*, which has no support in the textual tradition. The NIV translates the verb as if third person plural, with the psalmist's "thoughts/concerns" as the subject, rather than the first person-singular found in the text. For *ʾahimah*, the question is whether to take the form from *hwm* ("murmur, be distracted"), in which case the verb is a cohortative ("let me be distracted") and awkward in the context, or from *hmh* ("groan, growl"), indicating the psalmist's verbal expression of pain.

or just the constant sniping of the psalmist's detractors (cf. 55:12). The word that the NIV takes as "stares" occurs only here in the Old Testament and thus is difficult to interpret, with some commentators understanding the meaning as "pressure."

The root of *yamiṭu* (NIV "bring down") is well known with the meaning "shake, quake, move" and is commonly used in the psalms to speak about either shaken or unshakable foundations.[11] The Hiphil stem with this root, however, occurs only here and in 140:10, where the meaning is equally unclear. The NIV incorporates the most general sense of moving into its translation. The enemy's angry attack against the psalmist is described with the verb *śṭm*, normally rendered "bear a grudge against, harbor animosity toward." Other commentators translate this verb as "hunt," "persecute," or even "revile."[12]

My heart is in anguish. The descriptions of inner turmoil continue as the psalmist's heart "writhes" in anguish under the assault of "terrors of death,"[13] "fear and trembling," and "horror."[14] The attack begins from without (lit., "falls upon me"), infects the inner emotions (lit., "enters into me"), and flows on to overwhelm the psalmist (lit., "covers me").

I would fly away. The distress is so great and so all-consuming that the psalmist wishes only to flee. His agitated inner deliberation reveals a desperate edge, while the desire to take on the wings of a "dove" (*yonah*) in order to fly away to a secure place of rest[15] is reminiscent of the attempt of Jonah (whose name is the word for "dove" [*yonah*]) to flee the call of Yahweh by taking a boat from Joppa to the farthest reaches of the Mediterranean Sea (Jonah 1:1–3). Wild "doves" often nested in remote and inaccessible cliffs in more deserted regions—thus the psalmist's image of fleeing to the security and rest of the desert.[16]

---

11. Cf., e.g., Pss. 10:6; 13:4; 15:5; 16:8; 21:7; 30:6.

12. See the discussion in Tate, *Psalms 51–100*, 52.

13. Here, as in 23:4, *mawet* ("death") is probably used as an intensifying element—"deadly terrors" or "ultimate terror." It may be that *mawet* is the result of dittography, repeating the latter part of the preceding word, *ʾemot*.

14. This last term has the meaning "shaking, shuddering," but it is used here with the verb *ksh* ("cover over, overwhelm," as with waves of water). Perhaps the image is of shudders "flowing over" the whole body.

15. The Heb. behind the translation "be at rest" is the verb *škn* ("dwell, settle down, nest"). The term is most often used to emphasize the temporary residence of nomadic peoples in tents and to describe the nesting of birds in the wild. See Wilson, "שׁכן," *NIDOTTE*, 4:109–11.

16. The Heb word *yonah* designated a variety of bird types of the family of small pigeons, only one of which—the turtledove—was given a distinct name. Doves could be domesticated for food or sending messages, but could also live in the wild, often nesting in inaccessible cliffs and crags.

I would hurry to my place of shelter. Elsewhere psalmists use the verb *ḥwš* in the imperative to call Yahweh to "hurry" to their deliverance.[17] Here, however, the poet is tempted not to wait for divine deliverance but to exercise *self*-deliverance by fleeing to a "place of shelter." In the Hebrew text, the psalmist desires to flee from "the wind of slander, from the windstorm." The word *soᶜah* ("slander") is used only here and is thus uncertain. The NIV, following one of the suggestions in the *BHS* textual notes, emends the earlier phrase to refer to another type of storm. Holladay understands *soᶜah* as from the verb *sᶜh*, meaning "slander."[18] In light of the later description of the verbal attacks of the enemy (55:12), it seems possible that the psalmist is using the image of the storm to describe the destructive potential of slander. Tate, after reviewing all the options, opts for a translation emphasizing the "raging" or "sweeping" nature of the storm.[19]

Plea for Judgment on the Enemy (55:9–11)

INDICATING THAT THE problem faced is hostile speech, the psalmist appeals to God to "confuse" and "confound" (lit., "split") the enemy's tongue.[20] While the language is not precisely the same, our passage recalls the Tower of Babel story in Genesis 11, where Yahweh "confuses" the "lips" of the unified people building the city in the Plain of Shinar, with the result that they stop building the city and are scattered across the face of the earth as the beginnings of all the nations and families of the earth.

Again, while the contexts are not identical, it is interesting to note that reference to "the city" appears for the first time in this psalm in relation to confusing the speech of the wicked (55:9b). The psalmist may be drawing on the Tower of Babel narrative to speak a word of divine condemnation to the contemporary context. Confusion of speech is needed in his view because the city has become a place of "violence and strife" (*ḥamas werib*).[21]

"Violence" (*ḥamas*) is an attack that sheds blood or takes human life.[22] The city in the psalmist's experience is a place where "destructive forces are at work" (lit., "misery/ruin is in her midst") and the wicked "prowl" ceaselessly about, seeking occasion for malicious and abusive action (55:10). The irony

17. Cf. Pss. 22:19; 38:22; 40:13; 70:1, 5; 71:12; 141:1.

18. *CHALOT*, 258.

19. Tate, *Psalms 51–100*, 52.

20. Some commentators provide an object for the first verb ("their plans," RSV; "the wicked," NIV; "their throat," *BHS*), while others coordinate both verbs as referring to the single object "their tongue." See the discussion in Tate, ibid.

21. The word *rib* normally has the meaning of "law case," but it can refer to a more general "dispute" or "feud" (Judg. 12:2).

22. See 25:19 for comments on *ḥamas*.

is that the city walls, built to provide protection from the attack of the enemy, are entirely ineffective when the true enemy is within—a point to which the psalmist will return in the next section. The walls hem in the populace, preventing them from escaping the malicious plans of the wicked, who roam the city wall like watchmen but are on the alert to do evil to their own people. As a result, the city is the scene of constant struggle, with "destruction," "threats" or oppression, and "lies" in her "streets."[23]

The Faithless Friend (55:12–14)

RETURNING TO THE theme of betrayal from within introduced in the preceding section, the psalmist describes in more personal terms the faithless friend who has become the attacker. "Insults"[24] and attacks are to be expected from an external enemy and endured from behind the protection of strong walls. But the psalmist is being attacked by a fellow Israelite, who is of the "same stripe" (NIV "companion").[25] The use of *ʾenoš* ("vulnerable human/man," 55:13) in this context emphasizes the openness and vulnerability of the relationship between these two. The attacker is an intimate associate, whom the psalmist knows well from long experience and as a "close" confidant. The "sweet fellowship" shared is confidential conversation between friends who trust each another.

The psalmist's former relationship with the detractor is lifted beyond close friendship to that of spiritual communion (NIV "sweet fellowship") by the addition of the final phrase in 55:14 ("as we walked with the throng at the house of God"). The location of the "sweet fellowship" is the temple precincts, so that the two have been spiritually connected and compatible. This last comment heightens the travesty represented by the betrayal.

Verse 14 may also reflect on the larger context to which the psalm speaks. We know of similar circumstances in the experience of the exilic community where, embattled by pressures to assimilate with the majority culture, the exiles developed particularly close relationships to preserve their religious and national identity. Thus, it was particularly disturbing when those within this close community became the perpetrators of abuse and injustice on their fellows. The attempt of the two elders to force Susanna to submit to their

---

23. The Heb. *reḥob*, from a root meaning "wide, broad," is often taken as "street," but it can also indicate a "broad place" or "city plaza/square."

24. The verb *ḥrp* is intense in its sense of rejection and ridicule.

25. The noun *ʿerek* ("row, layer") describes a person who stands alongside another in a row and is thus the same "sort" of person. The idea could be one of rank, although the "matched" character of relationship seems more likely. A person who hits it off with the psalmist is the most appropriate match for a "companion."

sexual desires is one example of the way a "friend" could become an "attacker."[26] While it is not necessary that this psalm was written *for* the exilic context, it would certainly have continued to speak *to* that community's circumstance.

Renewed Call for Judgment (55:15)

THE CALUMNY OF betrayal by an intimate associate brings the psalmist to harsh words. "Death"—sudden, unexpected death—seems the only punishment appropriate for the enemy's abandonment of friend and God's covenant.[27] Tricked by death, they should be brought down to Sheol (NIV "grave") while still alive—an indication of the abrupt and unexpected nature of their departure. The picture is reminiscent of "The Descent of Ishtar to the Netherworld,"[28] where the goddess Ishtar, seeking to wrest control of the netherworld from her sister Ereshkigal, descends to the abode of the dead, apparently thinking her deity should shield her from the effects of death. After having passed through the seven gates into the heart of the realm of death, however, she is powerless to return until later freed by the command of the supreme deity, Ea.

The biblical connection to the descent of the psalmist's enemies is the destruction of Dathan and Abiram as a consequence of their rebellion against God and their rejection of Moses' leadership (Num. 16:1–35, esp. vv. 30, 33). To demonstrate that God had judged their insolence and that their death was not the ordinary lot of human beings, the ground opened up and Dathan, Abiram, and their families (lit.) "went down alive to Sheol." Rather than just destruction, the psalmist is calling for a public indication of God's rejection and judgment on his enemies.

The reason for the psalmist's condemnation of the enemies is stated in more general terms: "for evil finds lodging among them." Unlike God, who in 5:4 is described as "you are not a God who takes pleasure in evil; with you the wicked cannot dwell," these people have created an environment where evil can grow unchecked. Their tolerance—even acceptance—of evil is diametrically opposed to the attitude of radical rejection of evil that is at the heart of the Davidic Psalm 101:4, 7–8:

---

26. The story of Susanna is part of the additions to the book of Daniel included in the Apocrypha.

27. The consonantal Heb. text at the beginning of 55:15 would be taken to mean, "Desolations upon them!" The marginal Masoretic note recommends an alternative reading, in which the word for "desolations" (*yašši̮mawet*) is divided into *yšy [=yšyʾ] mawet*, which is taken to mean either "let death beguile them" or "let death devastate them," depending on whether one takes the verbal root to be *šwʾ* ("devastate" [Gunkel]) or *nšʾ* ("beguile" [Briggs]).

28. An English translation of this text is available in *ANETP*, 1:80–85.

I will have nothing to do with evil. . . .
No one who practices deceit
will dwell in my house;
no one who speaks falsely
will stand in my presence.
Every morning I will put to silence
all the wicked in the land;
I will cut off every evildoer
from the city of the LORD.[29]

By contrast, the speaker in Psalm 101 will constantly observe "the faithful in the land, that they may dwell with me" (101:6a).

Statement of Confidence (55:16–19)

IN CONTRAST TO the quick and certain destruction of the wicked, the psalmist is confident of divine deliverance. When he calls in distress, God answers and saves. The psalmist will be "ransomed unharmed"[30] despite the lopsided advantage enjoyed by his foes (55:18). His confidence is founded on the eternal enthronement of Yahweh as king (55:19)—a king who therefore can hear the pleas of the oppressed and who will act to deliver them from their foes. These foes are described as unrelenting in their evil and in their rejection of God ("[they] never change their ways and have no fear of God").

Reprise: The Faithless Friend (55:20–21)

THE PSALMIST RETURNS to the subject of treacherous attack by a close friend. The opening statement sets the context for the two metaphorical images that follow. The attacker is a "close friend" (*šelom*) who "violates" (lit., "curses") his covenant of friendship.[31] In the first image, the psalmist exploits the various nuances of the verbal root *ḥlq*, which can mean "be smooth, slippery"[32] and thus "false" and is related to an identical root with the sense "divide,

29. It is also suggestive that the verbal root (*gwr*) used in both 5:4 and 55:15 is the less common root for "dwell" and places an emphasis on the more temporary nature of the dwelling. See comments on 5:4 and Wilson, "שׁכן," 4:109–11.

30. The verb *pdh* is used primarily in the context of redeeming the firstborn from sacrifice to Yahweh (Ex. 13:15).

31. While it seems most likely in this context that the covenant broken is that assumed in a close relationship of friendship, it is possible that the larger covenant with Yahweh is also intended, since any unwarranted attack on others within that relationship would be considered a violation of the appropriate relation intended by Yahweh.

32. Rather than the smoothness of "butter" (as in the NIV), *ḥemʾah* refers to a type of "curdled milk"—probably something like yogurt.

separate." The slippery language cloaks the real sentiment and motivation of the opponent behind false words. The lack of integrity—incongruence between inner reality and outward profession—makes true intimacy impossible and ultimately destroys any hope of friendship. The enemy's smooth lies conceal the hostile intent that lurks in the heart.[33] The second image is similar to the first: The enemy's words appear "more soothing" than oil used to anoint and soften, while in reality their intent is to cut and maim like "swords."

Confident Trust in God (55:22–23)

THIS LAST SECTION contains the psalmist's call to others to trust God by casting their cares on him (55:22), a statement directed to God expressing confidence of judgment on the wicked (55:23), and a brief profession of his faith and confidence in God (55:23c). In these few verses we see the anguish and fear that dominated the psalmist's troubled thoughts at the beginning of the psalm (55:1–8) have been resolved into confident trust. This resolution is not the result of the absolute removal of suffering and anguish but the consequence of surrendering cares to God and dwelling in the assurance that God's ultimate purposes preclude the flourishing of the wicked.

The psalmist can rest assured in the midst of attack because God remains a God who does not take pleasure in evil, and as a result evil must ultimately experience divine judgment. The lives of the wicked, described as "bloodthirsty and deceitful" (55:23), will be cut short and will end in the "pit of corruption" (i.e., the grave) before their time. To the contrary, God "will never let the righteous fall" (55:22), and it is to this latter group that the psalmist's simple profession of faith makes connection.

FLEEING TO THE DESERT. Judaism and Christianity have had a long history of "fleeing to the desert." A number of years ago I had opportunity to hike from Jerusalem to Jericho along the Wadi Qelt, a deep, twisting, mostly dry streambed that cuts through the barren wilderness area separating the central highlands of Israel from the Jordan River Valley. Along the way I was impressed by the desolation and isolation of the area and understood better the desperation of the man who was left for dead along the road from Jerusalem to Jericho in the New Testament's parable of the good Samaritan (Luke 10:25–37).

---

33. Rather than the usual word for "war" (*milḥamah*), the psalmist speaks both here and in 55:18 of *qerab* ("[hostile] approach; battle")—possibly a reference to grappling in hand-to-hand combat.

Yet as we walked along the ancient aqueduct that carried water from the En Qelt spring to Jericho, we began to encounter evidence of human occupation, both contemporary and ancient. We stopped midway in our journey to replenish our water supply at St. George's monastery, clinging to the side of the Wadi Qelt. Here a small community of monks continue the heritage of withdrawal to remote areas begun centuries earlier. As we continued toward Jericho, we came across ancient worn paths leading down the cliff face to caves where Christian hermits had lived in isolation, going back to the second century A.D. These hermits, the Desert Fathers and Mothers of our own faith, were preceded by centuries by Jewish monastics and militant rebels against the Greeks and Romans. These also withdrew to caves and other desert dwellings that dot the Judean desert from Jericho, to Qumran and En Gedi, and south to the desert fortress of Masada. At this last place, Jewish revolutionaries turned the once grand palace of Herod the Great into a final fortress against the Roman forces, who quelled the First Jewish Revolt in A.D. 66–70.

Even these Jewish recluses were antedated by other, earlier desert dwellers. The first Israelites left Egypt and wandered the desert reaches of the Sinai Desert for forty years (according to the Pentateuch), and the desert wilderness continued to form an important part of the Israelite experience. On two occasions Elijah fled the persecution of Ahab and Jezebel and hid first under a tree in the Wadi Kerith (1 Kings 17) and later in a cave on Mount Horeb (1 Kings 19). During the Maccabean revolt against the Seleucid king Antiochus IV, the rebels under Judas and Simon Maccabeus made use of the wilderness caves to hide from the enemy.

The Qumran sectarians—generally presumed to be Essenes—fled (ca. 175 B.C.) to a remote monastic center on the northwest edge of the Dead Sea and avoided the impurities of a corrupt society and Jerusalem priesthood for well over two centuries. John the Baptist adopted the dress and rustic diet of the early prophets and roamed the Judean wilderness in preparation for the coming of the Messiah (Matt. 3:1; Luke 1:80). Jesus himself withdrew to the wilderness for forty days following his baptism (Matt. 4:1) and apparently returned on occasion for times of self-reflection and renewal (Luke 5:16).

All these examples exhibit two major reasons for withdrawal into the desert. (1) On the one hand, the desert could be a place to seek and find God. Moses took his father-in-law's flock to the far side of the desert to Mount Horeb/Sinai and encountered God there in the burning bush. The Israelites fled Egypt and traveled through the desert to meet Yahweh at the same mountain. Elijah fled the wrath of Jezebel and came to consult God on Horeb. The Qumran sect's withdrawal to the Dead Sea was not only an escape from the corruption of society but also a retreat to the purity of the desert, where God could be found without the distractions of city life. Jesus' own use of the wilderness as a place of prayer follows this age-old pattern and set the foundation for the later Christian desert monastics.

(2) Equally important, however, was the use of the desert wilderness as a place of refuge and protection in times of political danger. Numerous Judean caves explored in recent surveys show evidence of sporadic temporary occupation levels that can be traced by artifacts to periods of unrest and rebellion in Israel. I have cited a number of biblical accounts viewing the desert in this way. This tradition continues from the time of the Conquest up to the use of the caves of Wadi Murabaᶜat by Jewish revolutionaries during the Bar Kokhba rebellion (A.D. 132–134).[34]

It is this latter view of the wilderness—as a place of refuge from attack—that informs the psalmist's words in 55:4–9. The desert is a refuge, a shelter from the storm raging about him. He longs to escape the fray and "fly away and be at rest." Clearly the wilderness is not the threat we sometimes perceive it to be. That is because much of the Judean wilderness is not, strictly speaking, *desert*. Though it can be inhospitable for the novice and dangerous for the unprepared, there are sources of food for the savvy, and springs of water are sufficient for the careful. I remember on my walk along the Wadi Qelt, struggling along the bottom of a dry, desolate canyon and being surprised at first by the sound of trickling water, then turning a corner to see a rushing waterfall splashing into a cool and shady pool at the base of the canyon wall. At such a place David may have watered his troops, or John the Baptist may have satisfied his thirst while marveling at the abundant blessings of God.

When words and looks *can* hurt. Trash talk has become an expected part of some forms of athletics. I remember when I played on the offensive or defensive line of my high school football team, one would engage in a sort of simplified psychological warfare with the player across from you. I still remember being taunted, "Hey, little boy, does your mommy know you are out here?" That was, of course, among the gentler comments tossed across the intervening space. I knew what was going on and was determined not to allow it to affect my play adversely. I usually decided to show the speaker just how unconcerned I was with his words and threats by taking him decisively out of the action on the next play!

34. To add just two more examples, Samson hid out in the "cave in the rock of Etam" (Judg. 15:8, 15). David utilized the caves and wilderness of Judea in his flight from Saul (1 Sam. 23–26).

"Sticks and stones may break my bones, but words will never harm me!" goes the old adage, a helpful encouragement to children faced by insensitive name-callers. But as we mature, we have to admit that words *do* harm us and injure us—sometimes deeply and permanently.

Politics is just one place where words are often used to injure, maim, and even destroy an opponent. The story is told that Senator Lyndon Johnson told an advisor to float the word that an opponent of his had engaged in improper relations with an animal. The advisor protested that the claim was patently untrue. Johnson replied, "I know. I just want to see him deny it!" Johnson knew the hard political truth that just to be associated with certain words is destructive, even if the words are untrue. Our words can affect the way someone is viewed by others. They can even undermine the way one feels about oneself.

Looks have harmful effects as well. Consider the tape on the nightly news of an individual arrested for a crime. Handcuffed and hustled by police escort from car to courtroom, such people invariably hide their faces in their hands or behind a coat in order to avoid eye-contact with the crowds around them. Why? Not just to shield their identity; often that is all too well known already. They hide because they do not want to see the looks of the disapproving crowds around them. The looks and stares hurt. They invade our self-awareness and damage our ability to convince ourselves we are alright. It is only the most brazen, unrepentant criminal who stares his public coldly down without emotion.

For the psalmist, words and looks hurt. Because of the voice and stares of the wicked, his thoughts are troubled and distraught. Anguish of heart and terror dominate with fear and trembling and the desire to flee. This distress drives him to God, the only source of refuge and safety.

We have much to learn from the psalmist here. Often when I am attacked, I want to fight back. I want to shut the mouth of that opposing football player with a well-placed block. I want to set people straight about the true character of that rumor monger who is running me down. I want to give as good as I get, and then some. The psalmist calls out *to God* for refuge (the ability to stand up to the attacks of the enemy), rescue (deliverance from the distress and danger), and redress (setting things right).

Jesus also serves as a model here. Falsely accused and paraded before the eyes of a jeering public to the place of execution, he did not strike back, even though he could have called an angelic army to his defense. Instead, he went willingly to his death, even pausing in the midst of the painful process to forgive his detractors and to usher a penitent criminal into the joys of paradise. Can we follow this model in the face of hurtful words and injuring looks?

It is a hard model for mere humans to realize. To give up the rights of vindication, to forgive the unforgivable, and to seek the restoration of all who are willing at the same time as we are dying, falsely accused and abandoned by our closest friends, seem an impossible task. Yet that is what we by the power of God's grace are called to do—to allow Christ to live in and through us and to change how we relate to our world. To lose life is to find it after all.

Psalm 56

FOR THE DIRECTOR of music. To the tune of "A Dove on Distant Oaks." Of David. A ***miktam.*** When the Philistines had seized him in Gath.

1 Be merciful to me, O God, for men hotly pursue me;
all day long they press their attack.
2 My slanderers pursue me all day long;
many are attacking me in their pride.

3 When I am afraid,
I will trust in you.
4 In God, whose word I praise,
in God I trust; I will not be afraid.
What can mortal man do to me?

5 All day long they twist my words;
they are always plotting to harm me.
6 They conspire, they lurk,
they watch my steps,
eager to take my life.

7 On no account let them escape;
in your anger, O God, bring down the nations.
8 Record my lament;
list my tears on your scroll—
are they not in your record?

9 Then my enemies will turn back
when I call for help.
By this I will know that God is for me.

10 In God, whose word I praise,
in the LORD, whose word I praise—
11 in God I trust; I will not be afraid.
What can man do to me?

12 I am under vows to you, O God;
I will present my thank offerings to you.

[13]For you have delivered me from death
and my feet from stumbling,
that I may walk before God
in the light of life.

LIKE PSALM 55, Psalm 56 is a plea for deliverance from the attack of personal enemies, and it is likewise marked by a strong sense of confidence (cf. 56:4, 10–11). It continues the so-called Elohistic Psalter (Pss. 42–83); that is, except for the unusual intrusion of Yahweh in 56:10b, the operative designation for God is *ʾelohim* (56:1, 4a, 4b, 7, 9, 10, 11, 12, 13). The one occurrence of Yahweh in verse 10b has the appearance of an insertion since it repeats the preceding phrase and expands the refrain that is stated in its simple form in 56:4.

The psalm is composed of two unequal sections, each ending with an almost identical refrain (56:4, 10–11), and is concluded by a third section vowing to present thank offerings. Here is the overall structure of the psalm: opening plea for divine mercy (56:1–4), description of the enemy and desire for their defeat (56:5–11), and vow of thanksgiving (56:12–13).

The Heading (56:0)

PSALM 56 IS the first of five consecutive psalms (Pss. 56–60) described in their headings as a *miktam*.[1] The headings of these psalms share other common elements as well. All are referred to "the director of music" and are attributed to David;[2] four of the five (Pss. 56; 57; 59; 60) have historical notices connecting them with events in the life of David.[3] In addition, the heading of Psalm 56 contains a reference to what appears to be a tune for singing: (lit.) "according to *A Dove on Distant Oaks*."[4] The historical notice relates the psalm to events "when the Philistines had seized [David] in Gath" (a probable reference to 1 Sam. 21:1–10), although nothing in the text of the psalm makes that connection explicit or necessary.

1. See comments on the heading to Ps. 16, where *miktam* first occurs.

2. On "the director of music," see comments on the heading to Ps. 4; on "David," see comments on Ps. 3.

3. The first such historical notice occurs in the heading of Ps. 3 (see comments there).

4. The three central psalms in this grouping (57; 58; 59) share what appears to be a common reference to a tune for singing: *ʾal tašḥet* ("Do Not Destroy)," while the outer two psalms (56; 60) bear tune names that are distinct—from each other as well as this central phrase. The constellation of so many common elements leaves a strong impression that these psalms constitute a purposeful collection and arrangement.

Opening Plea for Mercy (56:1–4)

THE ENEMY IS depicted like a hound in full pursuit, snapping at the fleeing psalmist's heels.[5] The attack is continual, as indicated by the repetition of the phrase "all day long"[6] no less than three times in the first five verses (56:1b, 2a, 5a). The opponents are "slanderers," who attack the psalmist from a position of advantage (*marom* ["elevation of ground; high social position"] rather than the NIV's "in their pride"). The language is that of close military confrontation and struggle: "They press their attack . . . pursue me."

Yet, in the face of such hot pursuit, the psalmist expresses confidence in God that removes fear: "When I am afraid . . . I will not be afraid" (56:3a, 4b). The reason for his lack of fear is trust in God (56:3b, 4b) and the realization of the consequent impotence of the enemy: "What can mortal man [flesh] do to me?" These confident sentiments are expressed in the refrain that makes its first appearance in 56:4 and concludes this first section of the psalm.

Desired Defeat of the Enemy (56:5–11)

THE PSALMIST DESCRIBES the enemy's attack in terms consistent with the "slanderers" of 56:2a. They "twist [his] words," plot harm, and wait for the opportunity to snuff out his life (56:6). The description here reminds me of a boxing match in which one boxer stalks the other, hitting, falling back, dodging, and waiting for the right opening to strike the knockout blow.

The psalmist appeals to God for redress (56:7), pleading that his enemies not escape their just punishment and that God will "bring [them] down." Here, however, an unanticipated twist takes place. To this point, all indicators point to an identification of the enemy as corrupt persons within his society—perhaps those who are using their high social position to make life difficult for him. One would expect the poet to plead that these proud enemies be taken down a peg or two, or even that those who seek his life will themselves be "brought down" to Sheol.

---

5. The Heb. *šʾp* means "pant, gasp (for breath)," suggesting the breathless hunt of the dog for its prey.

6. The enemy is described with singular nouns and verbs in this verse, contrary to the NIV and the plural reference used in the rest of the psalm. *BHS* rearranges the first two verses to achieve two affirmingly parallel verses with plural reference to the enemy. This requires deletion (as duplications) of the phrases "for men hotly pursue me; all day long they press their attack," and the transposition of the root consonants in *yilḥaṣeni* ("he presses me") to *ḥaṣṣileni* ("Deliver me [O God]!)." The emendation seems unnecessary, since it is perfectly possible for the psalmist to individualize the enemy, and the emendation greatly reduces the urgency created by the frequent repetition of the phrase "all day long" (56:1b, 2a, 5a). Later in the psalm the opposition *is* referred to in single terms as "flesh" (56:4c; NIV "mortal man") and "man" (56:11b).

But he makes an unexpected turn here by requesting that God bring down not such social detractors and opponents, but "the peoples" (*ʿammim*),[7] a reference to the many ethnic and tribal communities that make up the nations and the world population. This broadened reference probably reflects a postexilic viewpoint of the Jewish Diaspora, suffering in the midst of a largely non-Jewish pagan population and seeking to live their lives faithfully in a hostile environment. Although here the psalmist seeks redress for wrongs experienced at the hands of "the peoples," by contrast in 57:9 he vows to praise God among the tribal groups (*ʿammim*) and among the ethnic communities (*leʾummim*).

Record my lament. The psalmist desires a permanent record of his complaint. We know that kings often kept a record of significant events that occurred during their reign so that they could refer back to them at a later date. In Esther, a written record of assistance provided to Xerxes by Mordecai, who uncovered a plot to assassinate the king, played an important dramatic role in the narrative. King Xerxes, having reread the portion of the record where Mordecai's service was described, determined to do great honor to him just as Haman entered the throne room to seek permission to kill Mordecai. The psalmist wants God to record his lament so that it will not be forgotten and will lead ultimately to action.

By this I will know that God is for me. The psalmist seems to imply that if God remembers the plea, he will act so that his enemies will be defeated and "turn back" (56:9). That defeat will be sure evidence that God is acting in his behalf. This kind of visible assurance is not always available to the suffering righteous, as the opening verses of this psalm suggest. For even in the midst of continued suffering, the psalmist remains committed to trust in God (56:3).

What can man do to me? The call for redress against the enemy concludes with the second appearance of the refrain, with two significant modifications from the first. (1) A line is added immediately following the first one and almost exactly repeating it, but replacing the general reference to *ʾelohim* with specific reference to *yhwh* (Yahweh; 56:10b).

> In God [*ʾelohim*], whose word I praise.
> In the LORD [*yhwh*], whose word I praise.

This makes it clear, even in the confines of the Elohistic Psalter, that Yahweh is the source of the psalmist's confidence.

---

7. Here, as in Ps. 47, the Hebrew is not the usual term for "[pagan] nations" (*goyim*) but the word that normally describes tribal and ethnic relationships (*ʿammim*), often translated "peoples" (see comments on Ps. 47).

(2) This second refrain also sounds the primary theme of trust in the midst of suffering: "In God I trust; I will not be afraid. What can man do to me?" But note the significant alteration from the first refrain in that "man" (*ʾadam* ["human being"]) replaces "mortal man" (*bāśar* ["flesh"]). Both terms emphasize the transitory or mortal nature of humanity (as well as animals).[8]

Vow of Thanksgiving (56:12–13)

IN ANTICIPATION OF deliverance by God, the psalmist commits to "present" (*šlm*) the vows made to God in the midst of trouble. Usually such vows (which are not specifically recounted here) are promises to give something to God. Fulfillment of a vow normally took place in the context of public worship and was accompanied with a sacrifice of thanksgiving.

You have delivered me. The promise to fulfill the vow and to offer a sacrifice of thanksgiving are in response to divine deliverance, either actualized or anticipated. The final verse offers a chiastic arrangement of statements, in which the two outer lines are related as are the two inner ones. In the outer lines, the psalmist—by the deliverance of God—passes from death (56:13a) to the "light of life" (56:13d). In the inner lines, God keeps the psalmist's "feet from stumbling" (56:13b) so that they may "walk before God" (56:13c).

LIST MY TEARS on your scroll. The NIV translation of this phrase in 56:8b flies in the face of tradition and interpretively renders a Hebrew word that means "wineskin/waterbag" in all its other occurrences.[9] The reason for the NIV rendering seems to be the dominant emphasis in the context of 56:8 on "recording" (*spr* ["you have written"]) and "documentation" ("in your notebook/scroll"). However, the direct meaning of the original Hebrew is "put my tears in your waterskin." The image seems

8. The Heb. *bāśar* can be used to describe "meat" for eating or the "flesh" of the body. In some contexts, however, the term by extension refers to "living beings," including animals and humans (cf. Num. 18:15 and "all flesh" in Gen. 7:21; Job 34:15). On other occasions *bāśar* is used to emphasize the transitory mortality of humans in comparison to God. In Gen. 6:3, God says (lit.): "My spirit [*ruaḥ*] will not contend with man [*ʾadam*] forever, for he is mortal [*bāśar*]; his days will be a hundred and twenty years." In Isa. 31:3, the Egyptians are "men [*ʾadam*] and not God; their horses are flesh [*bāśar*] and not spirit [*ruaḥ*]." Because of its transitory nature, "flesh" (mortal humanity) is not a valid source of security. Cf. Jer. 17:5: "Cursed is the one who trusts in man [*ʾadam*], who depends on flesh [*bāśar*] for his strength and whose heart turns away from the LORD."

9. Cf. Josh. 9:4, 13; Judg. 4:19; 1 Sam. 16:20; Ps. 119:83, where *noʾd* is regularly considered a skin for holding wine, water, or even milk.

to reflect the practice in the arid climate of ancient Israel to preserve precious liquids—like water, wine, milk, etc.—in a leak-proof leather bag. Its small opening allowed the liquid to be dispersed efficiently into cup or mouth in a thin stream but inhibited evaporation. Although there is no clear evidence of a practice of saving tears in ancient Israel, the image is a potent one: The psalmist's tears of lament are so precious to God that he collects and preserves them as he would water or wine.[10]

Regardless of this particular idiom, 56:8 does stress the recording of the psalmist's lament and tears in God's record book. The invention and introduction of writing in the ancient Near East began ca. 3300 B.C. and is most often associated with the Sumerians.[11] The earliest forms of writing were concerned with records of economic transactions and accounts governing the distribution of goods in an increasingly urban society. From these simple beginnings extensive archives of political, historical, and religious documents gradually developed. The medium of communication in Mesopotamia was cuneiform script impressed on clay tablets. In Egypt early pictographic hieroglyphics and later hieratic script came to be written on sheets and scrolls of papyrus paper. For the Israelites and related peoples using the Phoenician Semitic alphabets, the primary means of writing were pen and ink on leather scrolls.

The biblical narratives are full of accounts of items recorded in writing for later reference. The Books of the Annals of the Kings of Israel and Judah were important resources for the writers of Samuel, Kings, and Chronicles. In the narrative of Esther, the record of Mordecai's uncovering of a plot against the king in the Annals of Xerxes played a crucial and dramatic role in the humiliation of the enemy Haman (Est. 5:9–6:12). Jeremiah's prophecies were recorded on a scroll to ensure they would remain available to the reading public even after the prophet was silenced by the king (cf. Jer. 36; 45; 51). Similarly, prophecies could be sealed and preserved for later reading (Isa. 29; 30; cf. also Dan. 12:4, 9).[12]

In Malachi, a list of those who "feared the LORD" is recorded on a scroll in the presence of God (Mal. 3:16). The idea of producing a record in the

---

10. In spite of there being no evidence for preserving tears, this passage has spawned a product in the tourist industry. I have purchased beautiful, thin, blown-glass "tear bottles" as a souvenir of a visit to the Holy Land. This practical interpretation comes from the KJV of Ps. 56:8: "Thou tellest my wanderings: put thou my tears into thy bottle: are they not in thy book?" Related to this idea of collecting the precious tears of suffering is the reference to God's having "made [his people] drink tears by the bowlful" (80:5; cf. 42:3; 102:9).

11. Daniel C. Snell, *Life in the Ancient Near East* (New Haven, Conn.: Yale Univ. Press, 1997), 16, 64.

12. Other accounts of recording information for later retrieval can be found in Ex. 32:32–33; Josh. 18:9; 1 Sam. 10:25; Job 19:23–24; Isa. 34:16; Dan. 12:1; Mal. 3:16.

presence of Yahweh expands to include Yahweh's keeping his own scroll of remembrance (Isa. 34:16). He keeps a record of names and can "blot out" or remove them from the collection (Ex. 32:32–33; Dan. 12:1).[13] In Psalm 69, this idea of a divine account book in which the names of the righteous are recorded and from which the names of the wicked can be expunged is called the "book of life" (69:28).

This idea and phraseology is picked up in the New Testament, especially in Revelation.[14] There the presence of one's name in the "book of life" makes the difference between salvation and damnation: "If anyone's name was not found written in the book of life, he was thrown into the lake of fire" (Rev. 20:15). What in Psalm 56 is an item of particular comfort and encouragement to the psalmist becomes, by the time of Revelation, a sort of defining characteristic by which individuals are evaluated and judged.

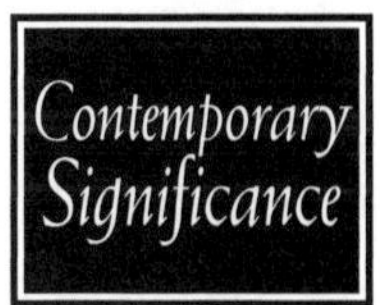

I WILL TRUST IN YOU. Near the beginning of Psalm 56, we find an interesting juxtaposition of verses cast in a sort of chiastic construction (56:3–4):

When I am afraid,
I will trust in you.
In God, whose word I praise,
In God I trust;
I will not be afraid.
What can mortal man do to me?

If you follow the thought process through from beginning to end, you move from *being afraid* (56:3a) to *not being afraid* (56:4c), and the change is set into motion and brought to completion by *trust*: trust in God (56:3b, 4b). At the center of this chiasm is the phrase that carries most weight in this kind of structure. What is the foundation of the psalmist's trust? What is it that enables the psalmist to move from fear to no fear? "In God, whose word I praise" (56:4a). Because of God's praiseworthy word, the psalmist is able to trust, and the real fear that encroaches at the beginning recedes to nonexistence by the

13. This book may contain an account of one's life before it occurs: "Your eyes saw my unformed body. All the days ordained for me were written in your book before one of them came to be" (Ps. 139:16).

14. Cf. Phil. 4:3; Rev. 3:5; 13:8; 20:12, 15; 21:27, where the operative phrase is *to biblion tes zoes*. The LXX of Ps. 69:28 is *biblou zonton*, reflecting the plural of *ḥayyim* ("life") in the underlying Hebrew.

end. Buoyed up by this certainty, the psalmist is assured that there is nothing that human beings can do to undermine his trust in God. "What can mortal man do to me?

Now, obviously, mortal men had been able to make the psalmist's life miserable. They twisted his words, plotted, conspired, and lurked, waiting eagerly to pounce and destroy (56:5–6). He had every reason to be afraid. Yet trust in God's word rendered those fears obsolete.

This is a lesson I would like to learn. How does trusting in God remove fear? Let me mention just three possibilities from the text of this psalm.

(1) First, the obvious. God's Word is a source of confidence to those who are beset by enemies. When we are attacked, we need to be able to draw on the stable assurance of God's Word rather than the wavering perspective of public opinion. In the midst of trouble, even our own words can be twisted and be made to condemn us. Attack by the enemy, fickle public opinion, our own wavering sense of self, guilt, and weakness—all these represent an inadequate measure of reality. Only God sees the true state of our affairs. Only he is able to pronounce a true judgment of righteousness and failure.

That is why a ready familiarity with Scripture is one of the most serious lacks in many contemporary Christians' lives. Too much of our faith is based on emotion and feeling. When the emotions fall—destroyed by the attacks of enemies, the misunderstanding of those around us, or our own failure of self-confidence—our sense of relationship with God can be undermined. At those moments we need to hold our emotions up to the clear testimony of God in Scripture.

(2) The psalmist gains confidence in God when the enemies turn back. I don't mean to suggest that the enemies will just close up shop and go home. Often their attacks continue as before. But in the midst of the attack, the psalmist perceives some divinely given "room" or "breathing space" that was not there before. Perhaps it is something like experiencing his spiritual armor that makes it possible to withstand the attacks of evil (cf. Eph. 6:10–18). This is a kind of armor we put on through study of Scripture, by cultivating a vital relationship with God through prayer and service, and by developing support relationships with fellow Christians. Just when it seems the enemy will overwhelm us, God brings us out into a broad space. "He brought me out into a spacious place; he rescued me because he delighted in me" (18:19). "You have not handed me over to the enemy but have set my feet in a spacious place" (31:8).

(3) Finally, we can be confident in the protective care of God when we "walk before God in the light of life" (56:13). The verb "walk" is the Hithpael infinitive construct of the common verb *hlk*. The Hithpael stem has the force of reiterative action—that is, action that is done over and over and over.

This is a kind of practice that becomes an almost unconscious habit. When we walk consistently and faithfully in the light of life, we learn to trust God in the times of difficulty and challenge. God's light illumines the way that we go. That is because in that regular contact with God, we experience life-giving light that keeps our feet from stumbling and gives us that "abundant life" God wants us to have in Christ (John 10:10). Again, suffering does not disappear, but the experience of God causes the pain of living to recede as we begin to fit within the broader perspective of God's gracious love for us and his purposes for us and his world.

What can mortal man do to me? According to the psalmist and our own experience, mortal humans can do quite a lot to me. They can ruin my reputation with slander. They can fire me from the job I need to support myself and family. They can commit adultery and then abandon me in divorce. Human fathers can even abuse their defenseless daughters. Just the other day two mothers, separated by two thousand miles, were reported on the evening news as having taken the lives of their children when faced with desperate personal circumstances.

The mass graves in the former Yugoslavia (and multiplied many times around the world) are graphic testimony that humans can do much to me. They can exalt me or bring me low. They can love or hate me. We can build up or tear down, value or despise each other. We have the power of life and death in many circumstances. So, what can this psalmist mean by saying twice: "What can mortal man do to me?" Is this just false bravado? Or misguided naiveté?

We have had occasion to ask this question before in considering the psalms, and we will likely face the same question again. In their confident reliance on God's care and deliverance, the psalmists often paint a picture of practical invulnerability, in which they seem to be untouchable by the woes and evils of this life. Yet their psalms continue to give abundant testimony to the vicious realities of life in a fallen world. They are aware in their pleas to God for deliverance and redress that "mortal humans" can do a lot to make their lives miserable, or even very short!

Yet the psalmist's words here bear a truth that returns again and again. If God is for us, who can be against us? When God is on our side, it is possible to find a refuge in the midst of the storm. There is something more precious in a relationship with God than a life free of suffering here and now.

Jesus testifies to this same idea when he sent out his twelve disciples to experience the character of Christian ministry in the world. He warned them they would experience rejection and floggings and be arrested by the authorities. They would be betrayed by siblings and parents; they would be hated and considered in league with Satan. But in spite of all these dangerous and painful realities, Jesus says, "Do not be afraid of those who kill the body but cannot kill the soul. Rather, be afraid of the One who can destroy both soul and body in hell" (Matt. 10:28).[15] Jesus' statement calls us to count the costs of the Christian life as well as its ultimate benefits. As Christians, we are called to experience suffering in this life, even as Jesus did.[16]

Yet, in spite of the suffering caused by human evil, there is a benefit that accrues to those who trust in God or name the name of Christ. That benefit is described as escaping the powers of hell. In Psalm 56, the one who trusts God will walk before God *now* in the light of life.[17]

---

15. Luke's account of this saying is slightly different in context than Matthew and is directed primarily in the context of the Pharisees (see Luke 12:1–5).

16. In Matthew's account, Jesus' statement is preceded by his caution that "a student is not above his teacher, nor a servant above his master," implying that to experience suffering, rejection, and even death is to be "like Jesus."

17. See also the Contemporary Significance section for Ps. 49.

Psalm 57

FOR THE DIRECTOR of music. To the tune of "Do Not Destroy." Of David. A *miktam.* When he had fled from Saul into the cave.

1 Have mercy on me, O God, have mercy on me,
for in you my soul takes refuge.
I will take refuge in the shadow of your wings
until the disaster has passed.

2 I cry out to God Most High,
to God, who fulfills his purpose for me.
3 He sends from heaven and saves me,
rebuking those who hotly pursue me; *Selah*
God sends his love and his faithfulness.

4 I am in the midst of lions;
I lie among ravenous beasts—
men whose teeth are spears and arrows,
whose tongues are sharp swords.

5 Be exalted, O God, above the heavens;
let your glory be over all the earth.

6 They spread a net for my feet—
I was bowed down in distress.
They dug a pit in my path—
but they have fallen into it themselves. *Selah*

7 My heart is steadfast, O God,
my heart is steadfast;
I will sing and make music.
8 Awake, my soul!
Awake, harp and lyre!
I will awaken the dawn.

9 I will praise you, O Lord, among the nations;
I will sing of you among the peoples.
10 For great is your love, reaching to the heavens;
your faithfulness reaches to the skies.

11 Be exalted, O God, above the heavens;
let your glory be over all the earth.

OUR PSALM CONTINUES the Elohistic Psalter with its reduced use of the divine name Yahweh (not used at all in this psalm). Like Psalms 54–56, Psalm 57 is a prayer for deliverance from the slanderous attacks of the enemy (cf. 54:5; 55:3a, 9a, 12a; 56:2a; 57:4). The psalmist seeks refuge in the love and faithfulness of God, who is exalted over the whole earth (57:1, 3, 5, 11), and concludes by confidently singing God's praise among the tribes and ethnic communities of the world (57:7–9).

Structurally, the poem is divided into two relatively balanced sections, each concluding with an identical refrain (57:5, 11). The enigmatic term *selah* appears twice within the psalm (57:3, 6) but does not seem to accord well with the literary structure of the composition. Within this structure, the thematic movement of the psalm can be described as follows: plea for deliverance (57:1–5) and promise of praise (57:6–11).

Other than a few minor differences, Psalm 57:7–11 is almost exactly duplicated in Psalm 108:1–5, where the section *begins* a praise hymn rather than concludes a lament. See comments on 108:1–5 for a treatment of the significant differences between these two psalms.

The Heading (57:0)

NO NEW TERMS appear in the heading of Psalm 57, which is referred to "the director of music" and attributed to David. Psalm 57 is the seventh psalm in the second Davidic collection (Pss. 51–72) and is the second of five consecutive psalms (Pss. 56–60) categorized as *miktam* and sharing numerous similarities in the contents of their headings.[1] Psalm 57 introduces the phrase *ʾal tašḥet* ("Do Not Destroy"), which is apparently a song tune repeated in Psalms 58–59. Outside these psalms, this tune is mentioned only in the heading of the Asaphite Psalm 75.

Psalm 57 also contains a historical note (like Pss. 56; 59; 60 in this grouping) that connects it to an event in the life of David: "When he had fled from Saul into the cave." The reference, while somewhat ambiguous, is generally thought to relate to the episode recorded in 1 Samuel 24:1–3. There is nothing in the text that demands this context, but much of the metaphorical language is appropriate for such a situation of beleaguered attack. The emphasis in verse 9 on testimony among the "peoples" (*ʿammim*) and "ethnic communities" (*leʾummim*) may indicate an adaptation of the psalm to the needs of the postexilic Diaspora community.

1. See the comments on the heading of Ps. 56.

Plea for Deliverance (57:1–5)

THE OPENING WORDS of Psalm 57 are identical with those of Psalm 56 ("Have mercy on me, O God"), but Psalm 57 goes on to emphasize the psalmist's desire for deliverance by repetition of the initial imperative, "have mercy on me." Rather than focusing on the treacherous attack of the wicked as does Psalm 56, the psalmist here brings to the foreground a confident sense of God as the place of "refuge" in time of trouble.

The verb "take refuge" is used twice, the first time in the perfect form indicating past reliance on God (lit., "in you my soul has sought refuge"), and the second in the imperfect, suggesting continued dependence on God as refuge (lit., "in the shadow of your wings I will [continue to] seek refuge").

In the shadow of your wings. The image of hiding under the protective spread of the divine wings is used several times in the Psalter (cf. Pss. 17:8; 36:7; 57:1; 63:7) and may well draw on the image of a protective hen gathering her brood under her wings (cf. Isa. 34:15; Matt. 23:37; Luke 13:34). Some commentators understand this phrase as referring to taking asylum in the Jerusalem temple before the ark of the covenant and under the wings of its overshadowing cherubim.[2] Regardless of which interpretation is followed, the psalmist seeks protection until the "disaster" (*haw-wot*)[3] has passed.

The psalmist's desire to seek refuge is based on an understanding of God that inspires confidence. God is one who "fulfills his purpose" for the psalmist. The precise nature of that purpose is not clarified here, but it is certain that God's divine plans will not be undermined by the plots and attacks of the enemies. In addition, God inspires confidence because he acts in behalf of the psalmist and in opposition to those who "hotly pursue."[4] The psalmist asserts this willingness to protect the faithful in that God "sends his love and his faithfulness" (57:3).

Once again, finding refuge in God does *not* mean the psalmist will escape any vestige of suffering. Rather, as verse 4 makes clear, refuge is *in the midst of trouble* and provides an enduring confidence even in the face of all evidence to the contrary. The psalmist's foes are like ravenous beasts of prey, whose teeth are compared to implements of war—spears, arrows,

---

2. See Kraus, *Psalms 1–59*, 530; Tate, *Psalms 51–100*, 77; see also comments on 17:8 and 36:7.

3. See comments on this term at 52:2.

4. This unusual root translated "hotly pursue" (*šʾp*) occurs twice in 56:1, 2 and otherwise in the Psalter only in 119:131, where it describes the positive desire of the faithful for God's commandments. The presence of such an unusual root in two consecutive psalms suggests a purposeful placement.

and sharp swords.[5] Yet, in such a threatening context, he is able to "lie down" in security (cf. 3:5; 4:8).

Be exalted, O God. The first section of the psalm ends with the first appearance of the refrain that both praises God and marks out the source of the psalmist's hope. In expressing the desire that God be exalted "above the heavens" and that his glory (*kabod*) "be over all the earth" the poet is using a merism[6] to inculcate God's rule over everything that is. Moreover, he calls for God's glorious appearance in *theophany*—an appearance that will vanquish evil and set the world (including the psalmist's circumstances) right.

Promise of Praise (57:6–11)

FOLLOWING THE HOPEFUL refrain, the psalmist returns again to the enemy's attack, but this time with a decided difference. Here the evil of the opponents is seen to return upon themselves (57:6c-d). The placement of the refrain (57:5) in the middle of the discussion of the enemy attack (57:4, 6) demonstrates literarily what the psalmist hopes to experience in reality: God's protective presence in the midst of trouble. The presence of Yahweh turns the table so that the faithful are delivered and the wicked judged.

This result comes somewhat as a surprise. As one reads the four lines that make up verse 6, the tendency is to anticipate affirming parallelism between the two sets of couplets. This is borne out by the initial lines of the two sets of phrases: "They spread a net for my feet. . . . They dug a pit in my path. . . ." Following the answering phrase of the first couplet—"I was bowed down in distress"—one expects the second couplet to respond in some similar way. But the hopeful turn of deliverance comes when the enemy themselves fall into the pit they prepared.

My heart is steadfast. That the psalmist has yet to escape suffering altogether is indicated by his affirmation twice of a steadfast heart (55:7).[7] In spite of oppression his heart remains steadfastly firm in its faith and assurance. So far is his confidence from being undermined that songs of joyous praise well up out of the darkness, heralding the rise of the sun (57:8). Some suggest the

---

5. The alliteration created in this passage by the use of words beginning with the letter *ḥ* (*ḥanit, ḥiṣṣim, ḥereb ḥaddah*) is exceptional. Note also the similar likening of the enemy's slanderous words to swords in 55:21.

6. For a discussion of the poetic technique of merism, see "The Poetry of the Psalms" in the introduction.

7. The Niphal of *kwn* has the sense of "stand firm, fast" and suggests enduring stability and reliability.

mention of the awakening dawn means the psalmist has been participating in an act of "incubation," in which a supplicant spent a whole night in the temple (before the winged cherubim of the ark of the covenant), praying and waiting for a divine promise of deliverance.[8] Elsewhere in the Psalter deliverance comes "in the morning" after a night of suffering and prayer (cf. 5:3; 30:5; 59:16; 88:13; 130:5–6).

Among the nations. Up to this point, Psalm 57 has been an individual lament or plea for deliverance, focused on individual and localized concerns. Now, however, like Psalm 56, this psalm shifts somewhat to include a more international perspective as the psalmist promises to sing God's praises "among the nations [*ʿammim*] . . . among the peoples [*leʾummim*]."[9] Again, this may represent an adaptation of an originally more individually focused psalm to continue to speak to the circumstances of the postexilic Jewish community, who found themselves living among other ethnic communities and often at a disadvantage or actively oppressed. In such adaptations, the identity of the enemies was reinterpreted from oppressive persons within the psalmist's own community to representatives of other opposing groups. The faithful individual would then be understood as representative of the community rather than a faithful individual within the community.

It is an overwhelming sense of God's loyalty and faithfulness that motivates the psalmist's outbreak of praise. God's loyalty to his covenant relationship with the faithful (*ḥesed* denotes "covenant loyalty" rather than the NIV's more ambiguous "love") is inexhaustible, reaching to the limits of the known cosmos ("to the heavens"). His enduring "faithfulness" (*ʾemet*), on which one can rely, extends to the skies.[10]

Be exalted, O God. The psalm concludes with the second appearance of the repeated refrain (cf. 57:5). Again, the effect is to summarize the source of the psalmist's confidence and hope. As God comes in his glory, evil and its effects are vanquished and the faithful affirmed in their enduring loyalty to God.

---

8. See Kraus, *Psalms 1–59*, 531.

9. As noted elsewhere in this commentary, the emphasis here is more on tribal and ethnic communities rather than national entities. See comments on Ps. 47.

10. See comments on *ḥesed* at 17:7 and on *ʾemet* at 15:2; 19:9. Perhaps the poet intends another merism here by juxtaposing *šamayim* and *šeḥaqim*. If the latter is taken as "dust," the expression may represent the opposite end of the continuum from "heavens"—thus meaning something like "God's *ḥesed* and *ʾemet* encompass the whole of the known creation." Note also the assonance in the similar sounding pairs *šamayim/šeḥaqim* and *ḥesed/ʾemet*.

PRAISING YAHWEH AMONG **the nations.** The psalmist promises to "praise you, O Lord, among the nations" (57:9), although the Hebrew behind "nations" downplays a more nationalistic interpretation by replacing the standard political designation *goyim* (non-Jewish "nations") with the sociological term *ʿammim* ("tribes, related people"). A less nationalistic interpretation is confirmed in the next line, where the parallel phrase "among the peoples" uses the designation *leʾummim* ("ethnic group").

The voicing of the praise of Yahweh "among the tribes and ethnic groups of the world" is a repeated reference to Israel's role as witness to the world. In a number of passages where the word *ʿammim* is used, Israel is called to testify primarily in two respects concerning God: his name and his mighty deeds. In 96:3 Israel is exhorted to "declare his glory among the nations [*goyim*], his marvelous deeds among all peoples [*ʿammim*]."[11] Three other verses that are practically identical confirm this encouragement: "Give thanks to the LORD, call on his name; make known among the nations [*ʿammim*] what he has done" (1 Chron. 16:8; Ps. 105:1; Isa. 12:4; cf. Ps. 9:11).

Israel is also to testify to the glory of God's name: "Give thanks to the LORD, call on his name; make known among the nations [*ʿammim*] what he has done, and proclaim that his name is exalted" (Isa. 12:4; cf. 1 Chron. 16:8; Ps. 105:1). The use in the opening phrase of the divine name Yahweh (NIV "LORD") suggests it is this name that is to be proclaimed among the non-Israelite nations. The proclamation of Yahweh's name is tantamount to declaring his universal sovereignty, as Psalm 96:10 confirms: "Say among the nations [*goyim*], 'The LORD reigns.' The world is firmly established, it cannot be moved; he will judge the peoples [*ʿammim*] with equity."[12]

Praising the name and deeds of Yahweh among the peoples of the world was a particularly poignant experience for exilic Israel. Before the Exile, the name and deeds of Yahweh were bound up with the nation Israel/Judah, the

---

11. Ps. 96:10 affirms the emphasis on divine deeds with its statement that "the world is firmly established, it cannot be moved"—an oblique reference to Yahweh's creative and sustaining deeds.

12. Yahweh's name is connected with almost all of the verses in which the phrase "among the nations/peoples" is found. Besides those already mentioned, the name is referenced in 2 Sam. 22:50 = Ps. 18:49 and Ps. 9:11. In two other places the phrase "among the nations/people" is surrounded with multiple repetitions of the actual divine name Yahweh although the Heb. word *šem* ("name") is not found. Cf. 126:2 surrounded by four repetitions of Yahweh; 46:10 with three repetitions of Yahweh in the context. In 57:9, neither *šem* nor Yahweh appear. Instead, God is addressed as "Lord" (*ʾadonay*). But in the duplicate version of this psalm outside the Elohistic Psalter, Yahweh does appear in the place of *ʾadonay* (108:3).

city of Jerusalem, and the Jerusalem temple. Jerusalem was the place Yahweh chose for his name to dwell, the temple was to be built there, and David's eternal kingdom was to be established (Deut. 12:5, 21; 14:24; 2 Sam. 7:5–16; 1 Kings 14:21 = 2 Chron. 12:13; Neh. 1:9; Ezra 6:12; Ps. 132).

But with the collapse of the kingdom and the deportation of most of the populace after the destruction of the temple and city by the Babylonians (ca. 587 B.C.), nation, city, and temple were all far removed from the lives of the Diaspora community. The agony of loss and living "among the nations" is clearly expressed in Psalm 137. The memory of Jerusalem brought tears to the eyes of the exiles and froze their tongues in their mouths: "How can we sing the songs of the LORD while in a foreign land?" (137:4). That is, how is it possible to praise the name and deeds of Yahweh when we have been carried away into the lands of the Babylonian deities?

Surprisingly, the very next psalm (Ps. 138) provides a response in its opening verses.

> I will praise you, O LORD, with all my heart;
> before the "gods" I will sing your praise.
> I will bow down toward your holy temple
> and will praise your name
> for your love and faithfulness,
> for you have exalted above all things
> your name and your word.

Just at the darkest hour, when all seemed lost, the word of praise breaks through even in a foreign land, even "among the nations." Here the singer breaks forth into praise of Yahweh's name "before the gods [*ʾelohim*]"—a probable reference to the gods of the pagan foreigners, those gods who might be thought to have defeated Yahweh and carried his people into captivity. The psalmist is unimpressed by the apparent defeat of Yahweh and orients his prayers to the temple in Jerusalem, to praise Yahweh's name and his "love" [*ḥesed*] and "faithfulness" [*ʾemet*]."[13]

The psalmist's praise fulfills the call to Israel to praise the name and deeds of Yahweh "among the nations," and the result is that the kings of the earth join in the praise of God: "May all the kings of the earth praise you, O LORD, when they hear the words of your mouth. May they sing of the ways of the LORD, for the glory of the LORD is great" (138:4–5). Testifying to the name and deeds of Yahweh in the midst of the nations is one way to fulfill the

13. Note the connection between Ps. 138:2 ("your love and faithfulness") and 57:3 ("God sends his love and his faithfulness"). The reason for praise is the same in both contexts: God's loyalty to his covenant commitment (*ḥesed*) and his enduring faithfulness (*ʾemet*).

calling to be a "light to the nations" so that the whole earth may know the salvation of God.

A PSALM LIKE Psalm 57 shares so much in common with the other laments of the Psalter that it would be easy to get caught up in an endless round of repetition and continue to emphasize the same issues and themes. Those repeated themes are certainly here: God as refuge[14]; the fact that refuge is *within* the experience of attack, pain, suffering; the necessity of trust; and the confidence in divine deliverance. But I would like to focus our attention here on two other aspects of the teaching of Psalm 57—ones that are not, perhaps, as common as those just mentioned, yet stand at the heart of the psalm and our experience of God.

Be exalted, O God. The first aspect is encapsulated in the repeated refrain that structures the psalm in 57:5 and 11. As mentioned in the introductory section on Hebrew poetry, repeated refrains usually drive home the central message of the composition. If so, then Psalm 57 is about the hope expressed in the anticipated exaltation of God over all that he has made. The psalmist desires the exaltation of God "above the heavens" and wants to see his glory spread "over all the earth." In this merism "heaven" and "earth" mark the outer limits of God's creation and represent all he has made. In this phrase, then, the psalmist acknowledges that God is beyond the heavens and unlimited by what he has created, and yet his glory can still fill creation with his presence.

God is not the creation (as in animism), nor is he confined within it (like the pagan gods of Mesopotamia, who feared dissolution along with the earth in the Mesopotamian Flood account). Yahweh is *above* the heavens, outside what he made. Yet he is not *deus absconditus*, a God who created and then withdrew to leave his creation on its own. God's glory can fill his creation when he comes. This God knows and can be known, loves and can be loved in return.

It is important that the first refrain intrudes into the midst of the "disaster" in Psalm 57. The psalmist seeks refuge in the shadow of God's wings "until the disaster has passed" (57:1). There immediately follows a plea for divine deliverance (57:2–3) and then a description of the disaster he experiences (57:4–6). Surrounded by ravenous lions, threatened by destructive beasts, the psalmist is waylaid by enemies and threatened by traps. But right in the middle of this description of threat the first refrain breaks

14. See the discussion of refuge in the comments on 2:12; 5:11; 18:2.

forth. Following the fearsome beasts and just before the treacherous enemies, a song exalting God escapes the tightly clenched lips of the psalmist: "Be exalted, O God, above the heavens; let your glory be over all the earth" (57:5).

This is light breaking forth in the midst of darkness. "The light shines in the darkness, but the darkness has not overcome [NIV text note] it" (John 1:5). Like our own experience of Christ, often God breaks in as light into our own darkness. Darkness may remain before and after, but the light, kindled by the life, death, and work of Jesus, continues to shine in the darkness and not to be overcome. This is a marvelous and encouraging image. Ravening beasts before and an ambush laid behind, but in the middle the hope of the exalted sovereign God over "heaven and earth"!

As the first refrain breaks into the darkness of the psalmist's attack, the second sums up the hope of this psalm. Standing at the end, the final refrain reaffirms the message of the first: God is sovereign over all he has made. He is present with us in and through our experience. He knows and can be known.

God fulfills his purpose for me. The second element to consider almost slides by without notice in the psalm. "I cry out," says the psalmist, "to God Most High, to God *who fulfills his purpose for me*" (57:2). What might this mean, that God fulfills his purpose for me? It ought to be encouraging and comforting. Even in the face of "disaster," God has a purpose that cannot be frustrated or derailed. The curse of God's so-called "perfect plan for our lives," which many of us hear about from an early age, is that we are often left with the impression that unless we attend perfectly to God's leading and discern his will rightly in all instances, we will never be able to fulfill the perfect purpose he has for us. It is as if our lives are a convoluted maze with only one single right path, and every misstep leads us deeper into the tangled maze and further from God's will.

Psalm 57 offers us an alternative understanding of God's wonderful purpose for our lives: *He will fulfill it for me!* Rather than a constantly bifurcating maze with no way of return, the psalmist's view of life is more like an infinite number of pathways, all emanating from the center, which is God. One may choose to move to or away from God on any number of these life paths, but from any point we can make the decision to turn to him and proceed along the path (and others) to ultimate reunion with him. And along the way, as we are seeking our path home, God sends his love (*ḥesed*) and his faithfulness (*ʾemet*) to guide us.[15]

15. For a complete analysis and discussion of God's will and its place in our lives, see Jerry Sittser, *Discovering God's Will* (Grand Rapids: Zondervan, 2000).

What a wonderful source of hope! God will fulfill his purpose for us, and even as we are struggling in the midst of our enemies, he upholds us with his loyalty and enduring faithfulness. No wonder the psalmist breaks forth into praise: "I will praise you, O Lord, among the nations; I will sing of you among the peoples" (57:9).

Psalm 58

FOR THE DIRECTOR of music. To the tune of "Do Not Destroy." Of David. A *miktam.*

1 Do you rulers indeed speak justly?
Do you judge uprightly among men?
2 No, in your heart you devise injustice,
and your hands mete out violence on the earth.
3 Even from birth the wicked go astray;
from the womb they are wayward and speak lies.
4 Their venom is like the venom of a snake,
like that of a cobra that has stopped its ears,
5 that will not heed the tune of the charmer,
however skillful the enchanter may be.

6 Break the teeth in their mouths, O God;
tear out, O LORD, the fangs of the lions!
7 Let them vanish like water that flows away;
when they draw the bow, let their arrows be blunted.
8 Like a slug melting away as it moves along,
like a stillborn child, may they not see the sun.

9 Before your pots can feel the heat of the thorns—
whether they be green or dry—the wicked will be
swept away.
10 The righteous will be glad when they are avenged,
when they bathe their feet in the blood of the wicked.
11 Then men will say,
"Surely the righteous still are rewarded;
surely there is a God who judges the earth."

DESPITE ITS UNUSUAL introductory verse directed to "you rulers" in the second person, Psalm 58 is at its heart a plea to God for deliverance and redress. Acknowledging that the world is dominated by the twisted power of the wicked, the psalmist calls on God to punish them and set everything right so that all humanity will admit that "surely the righteous still are rewarded; surely there is a God who judges the earth" (58:11).

The psalm is divided into three sections: a description of the evil influence of the wicked (58:1–5), a plea for divine judgment (58:6–8), and an expression of confidence (58:9–11).

The Heading (58:0)

NO NEW TERMS are introduced in the heading of Psalm 58. Like all the psalms since Psalm 51, this one is referred to "the director of music" and attributed to David. Additionally, Psalm 58 is the third consecutive psalm categorized as a *miktam*[1] and shares with Psalms 57–59 the suggested tune *ʾal tašḥet* ("Do Not Destroy").[2] Unlike the other psalms in this *miktam* grouping (Pss. 56–60), Psalm 58 does not exhibit in its heading a historical note linking the psalm to an event in the life of David (or any other person).[3]

The Evil Influence of the Wicked (58:1–5)

THE PSALM OPENS with a direct confrontation of the "rulers,"[4] who are responsible to ensure that righteous judgment prevails in the affairs of the community. The psalmist rather sarcastically asks these powerful individuals whether they "indeed" deliver righteous judgments (58:1),[5] and then he provides a negative answer to the question. They "devise injustice" rather than "speak justly/righteously," and they "mete out violence" rather than "judge uprightly."[6] The all-pervasive character of their corruption has persisted from the moment of their birth.[7]

The corrupt judges are likened to dangerous, venomous cobras, who are unwilling to be entranced and controlled even by the most skilled snake

---

1. For these three terms, consult comments on the heading of Pss. 3; 4; 16.

2. For this term, consult comments on the heading of Ps. 57.

3. See comments on the headings of Pss. 56 and 57.

4. The translation "rulers" must be established by an emendation of the text from *ʾelem* ("silence") to a supposed *ʾelîm* ("rams; men of power"). Another possible reading would be *ʾelim* meaning "gods," so that the author's sarcastic comments represent a denigration of the justice and power of the pagan deities. For references to Yahweh's superiority over pagan gods, see Pss. 82; 86:8; 95:3; 96:4–5; 97:7, 9; 135:5. Cf. notes in *BHS*.

5. See comments on the term *ṣedeq* ("rightly") at 4:1–2. The parallel word *mešarim* ("uprightly") has the sense of putting things "in order" as they should be and may have legal connotations of rendering proper judgments.

6. The terms in these two verses are intended to counter one another. Righteousness (*ṣedeq*) is frustrated by perversity/injustice (*ʿawlah*, pl. *ʿolot*), while appropriate order (*mešarim*) is replaced by violent disorder (*ḥamas*). See additional comments on *ḥamas* at 25:16–21.

7. The two words used in 58:3 are synonyms for the human womb or uterus. The first (*reḥem*) is a direct reference to that organ, while the second (*beṭen*) is the more general designation for the "belly" or abdomen. The first verb (*zrr*; NIV "go astray") is graphically descriptive, also having the meaning "be pressed out" as pus from a wound or a child in the birth canal.

charmer. The image draws on the awe that the street-performing snake charmer must have produced in the spectator by his seeming ability to control the deadly and vicious cobra.[8] Here, however, the human vipers are so intent on their evil from birth that they have become completely inured to any persuasion or control, wanting only to lash out and harm.

Plea for Divine Judgment (58:6–8)

THE PSALMIST SWITCHES imagery to call for divine judgment on the corrupt judges. Now they are fierce lions seeking to rend their prey, and he calls on God to render them impotent and toothless. To ask God to "break the teeth" of the enemy sounds like a desire for an incredibly violent and harsh attack, unless the imagery of the beast of prey is kept in mind. The psalmist is not asking for a preemptive strike against those he dislikes. Rather, he is calling on God to break the deadly grip of the ravenous beast on the trapped prey in order to free and deliver it.[9] The context of peril at the mercy of ferocious beasts of prey makes connections with 57:4, where the enemies' teeth are likened to implements of war. The passage also resonates with the thanksgiving offered in 124:6: "Praise be to the LORD, who has not let us be torn by their teeth."

A string of changing images follows, expressing the psalmist's desire that the oppressive wicked may cease to enjoy effective existence. He wants them to evaporate like water poured out on the desert sand (58:7a), their blunted arrows to bounce harmlessly off those whom they attack (58:7b). Although (as anyone who has lived for any period of time in the Pacific Northwest can tell you) slugs do not melt away, the trail of slime they leave behind looks like a cube of ice gradually dissolving away to nothingness. Finally, in the harshest rebuke yet, the psalmist wishes that the wicked had never been born, nipping the long process of their wayward wickedness (cf. 58:3) in the bud.

Expression of Confidence (58:9–11)

PSALM 58 NOW turns to expressions of confidence in deliverance. The fate of the wicked is already sealed—they will be swept away and come to

8. The root of the word for "charmer; enchanter; conjurer" (*lḥš*) seems to imply "whispering" as the means of charming rather than our contemporary image of snake charming with a flute or pipe instrument. The charmer is the "most skillful of all charmers," which uses the common superlative construction "charmer of charmers" (*ḥober ḥabarim*), intensified by the Pual participle of *ḥkm* ("be instructed; expert") as a further modifier.

9. Cf. comments on 3:7, which discusses the similar image of God breaking the teeth of the wicked.

nothing.[10] The righteous are depicted as rejoicing in their vindication[11] in particularly harsh terms. Bathing the feet in the blood of the enemy is a traditional ancient Near Eastern way of expressing the utter defeat of the enemy. The image is not so much of a ritual bathing of the feet as wading through blood left as the result of the carnage of battle. Dahood also suggests that the phrase could be translated "wash from the feet the blood of the enemy" as a final act after a successful campaign.[12]

Vindication comes with the public recognition and acknowledgment that the righteous are "rewarded" by God. The use of the double *ʾak* ("surely") emphasizes the change in public perception that this final acknowledgment affirms. Those willing to accept the perverted judgments of the wicked judges are now forced to accept the truth.

The final line drives home the reality that God is concerned with human justice and that the justice humans mete out is (or at least ought to be) reflective of the kind of justice God himself would (and eventually will) render as judge of the earth.

A GOD OF VENGEANCE. "The righteous will be glad when they are avenged, when they bathe their feet in the blood of the wicked" (58:10). These statements of vengeful glee seem a bit over the top! I have difficulty squaring splashing joyfully about in my enemy's blood with an appropriate Christian response to the world. Yet these are traditional images of victory over one's enemies—especially the national variety that threaten a whole people or the universal defeat of the powers and minions of Satan. Besides our passage, Psalm 68:21–23 offers a similar picture: "Surely God will crush the heads of his enemies ... [he] will bring them

10. Verse 9 is difficult and literally says something like: "Before your cooking pots can perceive the thorn(s), like life or like anger they will be swept away (in a gale)." A variety of translations and emendations are offered by the translators and commentators, but none with any particular persuasiveness. In any case, the main idea that the wicked will be swept away is clear.

11. It is generally accepted that *nqm* has the meaning of "defensive or punitive vindication" rather than vengeance. See G. Mendenhall, *The Tenth Generation: The Origins of the Biblical Tradition* (Baltimore: Johns Hopkins Univ. Press, 1973), 69–104. The utter defeat of the enemy is seen as public confirmation of the cause and claims of the righteous.

12. Dahood, *Psalms*, 2:63; 3:391–93. He also mentions the similar description of Anath cleansing herself after battle. Cf. the Egyptian text in which the goddess Hathor is tricked into thinking beer dyed red and poured out ankle deep on the fields is human blood. When she drinks this liquid, she becomes drunk and is unable to carry out her intentions to destroy humankind. An English translation of this last text is available in *ANETP*, 1:3–5.

from Bashan ... that you may plunge your feet in the blood of your foes, while the tongues of your dogs have their share."

Consider as well the picture of the victorious Yahweh fresh from judgment on the nations: "Why are your garments red," the narrator asks, "like those of one treading the winepress?" Yahweh replies, "I have trodden the winepress alone; from the nations no one was with me. I trampled them in my anger and trod them down in my wrath; their blood spattered my garments, and I stained all my clothing" (Isa. 63:2–3). Compare Isaiah's image with Revelation's description of the judging angels: "The angel swung his sickle on the earth, gathered its grapes and threw them into the great winepress of God's wrath. They were trampled in the winepress outside the city, and blood flowed out of the press, rising as high as the horses' bridles for a distance of 1,600 stadia" (Rev. 14:19–20).[13] Ezekiel similarly pictures God's judgment on Sidon: "I will send a plague upon her and make blood flow within her. The slain will fall within her, with the sword against her on every side. Then they will know that I am the LORD" (Ezek. 28:23).

These are extreme images of the ultimate defeat of God's enemies—enemies whose rampant evil has made the life of the righteous a hell on earth. These incorrigible vipers are removed by God so that the intended order of creation can be restored. Though the images are extreme, the joy in response to the restoration of God's true order is real and ought not to be denigrated. (See also the Bridging Contexts section of Ps. 3.)

Rulers or gods? The opening verse of Psalm 58 introduces what may be an intentional wordplay. The consonantal Hebrew text behind the word translated "rulers" is *ʾlm*, and these three consonants are variously vocalized with vowels: *ʾelem* ("silence"; the traditional but less probable reading); *ʾelîm* ("rulers"; the plural of *ʾayil* ["ram/ruler"]); or *ʾelim* ("gods"; the plural of *ʾel*, the generic term for deity in the ancient Near East). These last two words would have sounded almost identical to a listener, and herein lies the force of the wordplay. Both gods and rulers were expected to oversee the administration of justice on the earth, to limit violence, and maintain social order.

But who could take the gods to task for any failure in these ideals? The gods in common understanding were above human reproach. It is not so much that they were thought to be morally perfect or even superior to humans. In fact, it seems clear especially in Mesopotamia that the gods and goddesses were ruled by the same emotions, passions, and foibles as their human counterparts. They fought among themselves for power. They could

13. Again in Revelation, the figure of Christ is depicted as wearing clothes stained with blood, having tread the enemies of God in the "winepress of the fury of the wrath of God Almighty" (19:13–15).

be deceived and tricked, misled by humans and other gods alike. The only real distinctions separating gods and humans were power and immortality; the gods were immensely powerful and were thought to live forever, so that humans had to deal carefully with the gods.[14]

The rather quick transition from the opening castigation of the *ʾlm* to the chaotic results of their misrule leaves the decision ambiguous whether we are describing human "rulers" or "gods." While either is possible, the general attitude of the opening verses seems to come down on the side of "gods." With the emphasis on "judging uprightly *among men*" and the parallel phrase "your hands mete out violence *on the earth*," divine rulers of all humanity and the whole earth seem more likely.[15] As a confirmation, the concluding verse of the psalm hints at a contrast between the morally defective and ineffective rule of the pagan gods and the upright and powerful God of Israel. The inconsistent rule of the former leads to violence and anarchy among humans, while the sovereignty of the true God leads to the destruction of the wicked and the reward of the righteous (58:11). Along the way, however, the wordplay ensures that venal, human rulers will receive their comeuppance as well.[16]

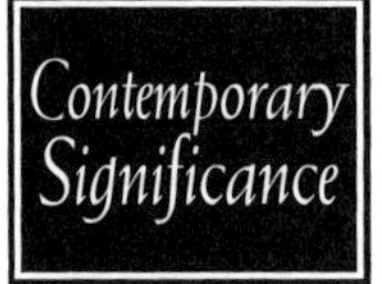

SETTING ALL THINGS RIGHT. As a child growing up in southeast Texas, I learned early on that "the only good snake is a dead snake!" We lived in a rural area where snakes in general and poisonous snakes in particular abounded. We saw ground rattlesnakes, copperheads, coral snakes, and cottonmouth water moccasins with regularity. By the time I could remember, my mother had been bitten by a cottonmouth and my sister by a ground rattler. I remember returning home one Sunday after church and having to wait until my father killed a large black snake that had invaded our screened back porch while we were gone.

We were skittish about snakes, to say the least! They were a fact of life we had to deal with. While playing in the weed and vine-filled patch of "pasture" that served as our playground, I often crawled around a corner in the pathway and confronted a coiled cottonmouth blocking the way. I would then simply back around the corner again and find another way to my objec-

14. Cf. Ps. 82.

15. Lest the reference in 58:3 to "birth" and "from the womb" cause confusion, many (if not all) of the gods in Mesopotamia (in particular) and in Egypt were understood to originate through sexual intercourse, conception, pregnancy, and birth.

16. See the discussion of henotheism and monotheism in the Bridging Contexts section of Ps. 29.

tive. Snakes were not our friends, and often we killed them first and then checked to see if they were poisonous or not.

I must admit I never felt guilty about killing those snakes. They were enemies. They were evil. They were a threat to life and disrupted the blessings of God available in our little two-acre patch of God's creation. As I grew older, I mended my ways and began to try to distinguish between poisonous and nonpoisonous varieties of snakes. King snakes, milk snakes, rat snakes, garden snakes were allowed to ply their way across our small kingdom without hindrance. I could even appreciate the benefit some offered in keeping the rural rodent population in check. But I never quite lost my fear of snakes or my knee-jerk flight-or-fight reaction to a sudden encounter.

The destruction of God's enemies is part of bringing a fallen and distorted creation back under his sovereignty. It is part of transforming the world by removing evil once and for all in order to restore God's original purpose and intention. What can a charmer do with a cobra that refuses to participate harmoniously in the charming game? The cobra that has "stopped its ears" and seeks only to destroy will itself be eliminated from the restored creation of God.

I long for that restoration, when evil will be destroyed and creation harmony reigns at last between human beings, humans and animals, and all of us with the physical world itself. I am just not sure how comfortable I will be with snakes in heaven![17]

Does your god matter? It does matter, it seems, whether your god is a deity of moral consistency, compassionate justice, and equity. Without these characteristics of stability the four hundred plus pagan deities of the ancient Near East made life among humans a painful, uncertain, chancy thing at best. Even if your personal deity was on your side, you could not always rely on his or her power to match that of any opposing deity.

In the Mesopotamian Flood account, Enki, the god of wisdom who conceived the creation of humans and thus continued to have a warm spot in his divine heart for them, three times was able to avert complete destruction of humankind when the chief god, Enlil, determined to destroy them all. Enki was able to teach humans to avert plagues, famines, and droughts sent by Enlil to eliminate them, but only after the human population had been severely depleted. Ultimately, Enlil realized that Enki was undoing his plans and struck back with cunning. He bound Enki (and all the other gods) to an unbreakable oath not to warn any human of the upcoming new destruction. Then Enlil employed the restricted waters of chaos—the domain under Enki's own control—to accomplish the destruction.

---

17. See also comments on Ps. 54:5 and the Bridging Contexts and Contemporary Significance sections of that psalm.

Enki, however (being the god of wisdom after all), was still able to warn his human follower Atrahasis by means of a ruse that also allowed him technically to keep his vow. Enki stood outside the hut where Atrahasis was sleeping at night and spoke (loudly!) to the wall of the hut. His message was something like, "Wall! Wall! If I were you, I would build a boat!" Atrahasis, being no fool, got the message, built the boat, and survived the subsequent flood in which the rest of humanity drowned.

After the flood, Enlil (who was at first enraged to find he had been neutralized once again) was finally persuaded by Enki to accept a resolution of the divine-human problem that allowed humans to continue to live. The solution was to reduce human population (and thus the incessant activity and noise that had caused the conflict with Enlil in the first place) by instituting certain forms of population control: infertility, miscarriage, still birth, high infant mortality. What must have been agonizing experiences for men and women in the ancient world are here reinterpreted as the necessary barrier preventing the total destruction of humans by their gods.

It *does* matter who your god is! Yahweh is the God who takes no pleasure in evil. Wickedness does not dwell with him. Yahweh is at the same time incompatible with evil and relentlessly good. As the preceding Psalm 57 put it, "great is [his] covenant loyalty reaching to the heavens; [his] enduring faithfulness reaches to the skies" (57:10, lit. trans.). Psalm 58 agrees, for in Yahweh "there is a God who judges the earth" with uprightness (58:1, 11).

Psalm 59

FOR THE DIRECTOR of music. To the tune of "Do Not Destroy." Of David. A *miktam*. When Saul had sent men to watch David's house in order to kill him.

1 Deliver me from my enemies, O God;
protect me from those who rise up against me.
2 Deliver me from evildoers
and save me from bloodthirsty men.

3 See how they lie in wait for me!
Fierce men conspire against me
for no offense or sin of mine, O LORD.
4 I have done no wrong, yet they are ready to attack me.
Arise to help me; look on my plight!
5 O LORD God Almighty, the God of Israel,
rouse yourself to punish all the nations;
show no mercy to wicked traitors. *Selah*

6 They return at evening,
snarling like dogs,
and prowl about the city.
7 See what they spew from their mouths—
they spew out swords from their lips,
and they say, "Who can hear us?"
8 But you, O LORD, laugh at them;
you scoff at all those nations.

9 O my Strength, I watch for you;
you, O God, are my fortress, 10 my loving God.

God will go before me
and will let me gloat over those who slander me.
11 But do not kill them, O Lord our shield,
or my people will forget.
In your might make them wander about,
and bring them down.
12 For the sins of their mouths,
for the words of their lips,
let them be caught in their pride.

For the curses and lies they utter,
13 consume them in wrath,
consume them till they are no more.
Then it will be known to the ends of the earth
that God rules over Jacob. *Selah*

14 They return at evening,
snarling like dogs,
and prowl about the city.
15 They wander about for food
and howl if not satisfied.
16 But I will sing of your strength,
in the morning I will sing of your love;
for you are my fortress,
my refuge in times of trouble.

17 O my Strength, I sing praise to you;
you, O God, are my fortress, my loving God.

PSALM 59 CONTINUES the string of laments that goes back to Psalm 54. Once again the primary theme is the verbal attack of the enemy—twice described as a snarling band of dogs (59:6, 14)—through slander and curses. The besieged psalmist remains confident, however, because God is a refuge (*miśgab*) and fortress (*manos*) in times of trouble (59:16).[1] Rather than death for the enemies, the psalmist desires public exposure of their slander and affirmation of his own righteousness.

After an initial invocation of God and plea for deliverance, the psalm is divided into two stanzas, each of which concludes with a similar refrain (59:9, 17). Each refrain is preceded by a section describing the enemy as a roaming pack of dogs (59:6, 14). The first stanza includes descriptions of the enemy attack along with pleas for deliverance, while the second stanza describes hoped-for punishment of the wicked along with expressions of confidence. Thus, this structure can be expressed as an introductory plea for

1. God as "refuge" and "fortress" is a common theme in the psalms. See esp. comments on 18:2, where a number of related terms are used. Within the Psalter, *manos* appears only here and at 142:4. The underlying meaning is "place of fleeing" from the verbal root *nws* ("flee, escape").

deliverance (59:1–2), the enemy attack (59:3–9), and punishment and confidence (59:10–17).[2]

Like Psalms 56 and 57 before, Psalm 59 appears to have been adapted to the needs of the postexilic community by the introduction of an otherwise unexpected concern with divine punishment of the nations (*goyim* in 59:5, 8). The laughter of God at the empty words of the nations (59:8) links this psalm thematically with the similar phrases in 2:4.

Although Psalm 59 stands in the midst of the Elohistic Psalter, the divine name Yahweh appears three times in these few verses (59:3, 5, 8), once in the traditional phrase *yhwh ʾelohim ṣebaʾot ʾelohe yiśraʾel* (lit., "the LORD God of hosts, God of Israel").[3]

The Heading (59:0)

NO NEW TERMS appear in the heading. The psalm is referred to "the director of music" and is attributed to David. It is the fourth of five consecutive psalms (Pss. 56–60) categorized as *miktam*,[4] and it shares with Psalms 57–58 the identical tune title *ʾal tašḥet* ("Do Not Destroy").[5] Like Psalms 56–57 and 60, Psalm 59 also includes a historical note linking the psalm to an event in David's life (this one recorded in 1 Sam. 19:11). There is nothing in the text of this psalm that specifically recalls this event; in fact, the emphasis in the psalm on vicious verbal attacks makes it unlikely in my opinion that the psalm was composed for that purpose.

Introductory Plea (59:1–2)

THE PSALMIST PLEADS for "deliverance" and "protection"[6] from enemies who "rise up" against him. In verse 2 these opponents are further described as "evildoers" (*poʿale ʾawen*)[7] and "bloodthirsty men" (*ʾanše damim*).[8]

---

2. Tate (*Psalms 51–100*, 96) offers a variety of possible structural divisions of this psalm and remarks that the *selah* indicators do seem in this case to reflect points of literary division of the text.

3. The term *ʾelohim* seems to intrude here into the more normal phrase *yhwh ṣebaʾot* ("Yahweh of hosts").

4. On these three terms, see the headings of Pss. 3; 4; 16.

5. See the commentary on the heading of Ps. 57, where this phrase first occurs.

6. The verb *śgb* shares the same root as the noun *miśgab* ("fortress"), which appears later in v. 16. The base meaning is to "make high/inaccessible" so that one cannot be reached or touched by attackers.

7. See comments on 14:4, 6.

8. See comments on 5:5–6 (where the singular form *ʾiš damim* occurs along with *poʿale ʾawen*); also 26:9.

The Enemy Attack (59:3–9)

IT IS NOT immediately clear that the enemy attack is a matter of "slander" (59:10). The enemy "lie in wait/ambush" and "attack" (cf. 56:6) the psalmist for no cause (59:3c, 4a). His protestation of innocence is no protection from their rushing attack.[9]

Arise. The psalmist wants God to stir himself and take note of the psalmist's desperate situation. Contrary to the general tendency in the Elohistic Psalter to avoid the divine name Yahweh, the psalmist addresses God three times in this psalm as Yahweh ("LORD" in 59:3, 5, 8). In 59:5, God is even more effusively identified as (lit.) "Yahweh, God of hosts, God of Israel"—the somewhat awkward appearance of both *yhwh* and *ʾelohim* suggesting that an adaptation has been made of the more usual militant designation of the God of Israel as "Yahweh of hosts."[10]

Punish the nations. As in Psalms 56 and 57, the concerns of the individual psalmist for more personal and localized enemies take on a more communal and national flavor. "LORD Almighty" is called to rout the enemy nations and protect his people (cf. 59:8). Tate suggests an original setting in which a king was beset by both domestic and international attacks, though he admits the possibility that an earlier individual lament may have been adapted to a more communal purpose.[11] Regardless, these concerns would have new meaning for the postexilic community living in situations of foreign domination. The local enemies do not escape unscathed, however, as the psalmist pleads for God to show no favor to "wicked traitors." The verb *bgd*, from which the term "traitors" is derived, has the meaning "deal faithlessly" and implies a breach of agreement, covenant, or other obligation.

---

9. The second of these verbs is particularly difficult. Holladay (*CHALOT*, 153) takes the form as an unusual Hithpolel form, in which the infixed *taw* of the expected form *yitkonanu* has assimilated to the following *kap* and now appears as a doubled *kap* : *yikkonanu*. According to Holladay, the meaning of the Hithpolel of *kwn* is "draw oneself up (in battle array)."

10. By far the more common and widespread appellation of God is *yhwh ṣebaʾot* ("Yahweh of hosts"). This title occurs some 259 times scattered through the historical books and esp. the prophetic literature. The phrase occurs eight times in the psalms (Pss. 24:10; 46:7, 11; 48:8; 69:6; 84:1, 3; 84:12). Alternative forms of this epithet also occur, but much less frequently: e.g., *ʾelohim ṣebaʾot* (2x in Ps. 80:8, 15). Combinations of these forms include *yhwh ʾelohe ṣebaʾot* (15x) and *yhwh ʾelohim ṣebaʾot* (4x in Pss. 59:6; 80:5, 20; 84:9). It is interesting to note that in all its forms, this designation of the God of Israel as the leader of its military host is concentrated in the first three books of the Psalter with *no mention* coming after Ps. 89. See the discussion of "The Shape of the Psalter" in vol. 2 of this commentary.

11. Tate, *Psalms 51–100*, 94–95.

Snarling like dogs. In 59: 6 and again later (59:14), the enemy is characterized as a roving pack of dogs that roam the city looking for vulnerable prey. Comparison of humans to dogs is normally a form of disparagement and contempt; similar negative comparisons are found in the ancient Near Eastern literature outside Israel.[12]

Some suggest that the reference to "evening" in these verses, coupled with the vow to sing of God's love "in the morning" (59:16), point to an underlying context of "incubation," where an individual in distress spent the night before Yahweh in the temple, pleading for deliverance and receiving a priestly proclamation of release in the morning.[13] Tate notes that the phrase "hire of a dog" (Deut. 23:18) is normally taken to mean the wages of a male prostitute, confirming the negative comparison associated with the term "dog."[14]

Who can hear us? As in 55:21 and 57:4, the enemy's verbal attacks are likened to vicious thrusts with a sword. The enemy "spew out swords from their lips" (59:7b), thinking they can speak and act with impunity: "Who can hear us?"[15] But the psalmist is confident that God does hear—both the violent words of the enemy and the psalmist's pleas for deliverance—and that God holds the enemies' pretensions to unbridled power in scorn. In words that recall his contempt for the rebellious plots of the kings in 2:4, God "laughs" and "scoffs" at the blustering enemy nations.[16]

O my Strength. Yahweh is the psalmist's "Strength" and "refuge," although deliverance is still an anticipated future experience. Like the watchman of a besieged city straining to see the expected arrival of the relieving troops, the psalmist "watches" for the appearance of "my loving God" (59:10a).[17] This refrain ends the first major section of the psalm.

Punishment and Confidence (59:10–17)

FOLLOWING THE FIRST refrain, the psalmist shifts to a description of the hoped-for response by God to the empty pride of the enemy. God—who is the

---

12. See comments of P. K. McCarter, *1 Samuel* (AB; New York: Doubleday, 1980), 384–85; idem, *2 Samuel* (AB; New York: Doubleday, 1980), 261.

13. See esp. Kraus, *Psalms 1–59*, 540.

14. Tate, *Psalms 51–100*, 97.

15. Cf. similar examples of bravado of being able to escape detection in 12:4; 64:5; 73:11; 94:7.

16. The verbs used here for "laugh" and "scoff" are the same ones used in 2:4. The latter verb (*lʿg*) means to stammer derisively in another's face.

17. The NIV takes the phrase *ʾelohe ḥasdo* to mean "loving God" and shifts it from the beginning of verse 10 to complete the preceding verse. The phrase is difficult and variously rendered in the versions (see the *BHS* textual apparatus), but it could begin verse 10 with the sense "My loving/faithful God goes before me."

"shield" (*magen*)[18] of his people—will go before them into the conflict with the enemy.[19] As a result, the psalmist will "see [triumph]" (rather than the NIV's "gloat")[20] over "those who slander me."[21] He desires both public vindication and the destruction of the enemy. He does not ask for a complete decimation of the opponents ("do not kill them"), but he does want God to reduce their power and make them wander rootlessly through society as a constant reminder of the consequences of opposing the righteous. The picture may well depict the kind of rootless sense of homelessness that the exiled communities experienced in the Diaspora.

The ultimate consequence is, of course, the final destruction and disappearance of the enemy. The psalmist asks that God "bring them down"—a probable reference to being brought down to Sheol, the abode of the dead[22]—and "consume them till they are no more" (59:13). This object lesson has two purposes: (1) to punish the enemy for their arrogant slander (59:12a, b), and (2) to make it clear that God, not the "nations," is the effective ruler of Israel (59:13b).

Snarling like dogs. Once again the enemy is described as a pack of prowling dogs, scouring the city for food. But whereas the first description (59:6–7) viewed the dogs as vicious and fearsome attackers roaming about seeking to do harm, now they are pathetic hungry beasts, unsatisfied and constantly on the move in search of food. The tables have been turned, and the fearsome beast has become the starving wanderer.

I will sing of your strength. By contrast, the psalmist (and the besieged people of God) are set free within the protective "fortress" (*miśgab*) and "refuge" (*manos*) provided by God to sing praises for the gifts of God's "strength" and "love" (*ḥesed*, "enduring loyalty") rather than to howl in want like the miserable dogs.

---

18. See the discussion of this and other words for "shield" in the comments on 3:3; 5:12. As the NIV note indicates, the term *magen* can sometimes be used metaphorically for "ruler(s)," but here the idea of divine protection seems to be foremost.

19. The verse is difficult because of the uncertainty surrounding the interpretation of the consonantal text of the opening phrase *ʾlhy ḥsdw*. The Kethib suggests "My God, his loyal love goes before me," while the Qere implies "My loyal loving God goes before me." The LXX supports the reading of the Kethib, although this may represent the translators' choice between existing alternatives. Tate (*Psalms 51–100*, 94) also reminds us that the verb *qdm* ("go before") can also have the sense "meet" and understands the context as describing the psalmist's hope for a theophanic appearance of God to "meet" his needs.

20. Cf. the similar use of the verb *rʾh* ("see") in 22:17.

21. For the use of this word, see comments on 54:5.

22. Alternatively this may refer to being "taken down a peg or two," having their prideful stature reduced.

O my Strength! In this new context, this concluding refrain takes on a subtly different meaning. In its first occurrence (59:9), the psalmist responded to the enemy's attack by watching diligently for the coming of God's strength as deliverance. Here God's "strength" has already become a cause for praise, and the psalmist moves to acknowledge that God is the source of his own strength (also using *ʿoz*). God is not only the power that delivers but also provides the psalmist with strength to endure faithfully in the face of the enemy onslaught. That is standing within the protective refuge of God.

THE SNARLING DOGS. The use of dogs as a characterization of the wicked deserves further discussion. Obviously from the number of times they are mentioned in the Old Testament, dogs were a common phenomenon in the ancient Near East. Some dogs were used for work, such as herding sheep (Job 30:1), while others may have been kept to serve as watchdogs (Isa. 56:10). Despite this useful potential, dogs were not particularly well thought of in Israel, and to call another person a "dog" was a serious insult,[23] although self-designation could be a form of humility or self-deflation, usually with an edge of sarcasm.[24]

Packs of ravenous dogs seem to have represented a continuing feature of urban settings (although wild dogs may also have roamed the countryside). "Dogs will eat those belonging to Jeroboam who die in the city, and the birds of the air will feed on those who die in the country. The LORD has spoken!" (1 Kings 14:11). "'I will send four kinds of destroyers against them,' declares the LORD, 'the sword to kill and the dogs to drag away and the birds of the air and the beasts of the earth to devour and destroy'" (Jer. 15:3).[25] Other than in our psalm, dogs are described as a surrounding threat also in Psalm 22:16, 22.

The images employed in Psalm 59, then, are common enough to have struck a chord with city dwellers. The plight of ill-fed dogs scavenging the streets for anything edible—including garbage and the bodies of executed persons left exposed as a last indignity—would have stuck in the minds of urban citizens and provided an apt cautionary warning. Dogs are dangerous, but ultimately they are an unloved and despised creature doomed to starvation and death.

---

23. Cf. 1 Sam. 17:43; 24:14; 2 Sam. 16:9; Eccl. 9:4.
24. Cf. 2 Sam. 9:8; 2 Kings 8:13.
25. See also 1 Kings 16:4; 21:19, 23–24; 22:38; 2 Kings 9:10, 36; Ps. 68:23.

The wandering witnesses. Like the starving dogs wandering the streets seeking any scrap of food, the rejected enemies are not to be killed but forced to live an agonizing public life of rejection and approbation. Whenever they are seen, they will spark a memory of their vicious sin and God's punishment. Their hollow eyes will offer testimony to the abandonment of God and the loss of his blessings. The isolated sinners on the fringe of society will provide a cautionary warning to others not to follow their path. The psalmist does not want these "dogs" to be considered a vicious power to be feared and reckoned with, but crushed and unsatisfied creatures living forgotten on the fringes of society.

Scripture records other people who were allowed to live in order to provide continuing testimony and warning. Cain, after he killed his brother, was marked by God to preserve his life and left to wander restlessly (Gen. 4:1–16). Adoni-Bezek, the Canaanite king of Bezek, boasted of having "seventy kings with their thumbs and big toes cut off," picking up scraps (like dogs!) under his table. These defeated and humiliated kings testified daily to the power of Adoni-Bezek—until he himself suffered the same fate at the hands of the Israelites (Judg. 1:4–7). Similarly Mephibosheth, the crippled son of Saul, was spared by David and sat at David's table as a continuing sign of the king's mercy and largess. (I am sure there might have been a less positive motive of showing David's power and defeat of the family of Saul!) The last true Judahite king, Jehoiachin, was taken into exile by the Babylonians and regularly displayed at the table of the Babylonian king along with the kings of other defeated nations.[26]

Feeding conquered kings at the table of a sovereign monarch is akin to feeding the dogs with table scraps (cf. Matt. 15:27; Luke 16:21), as the Adoni-Bezek episode makes clear. The monarch displays not only his power and wealth but also his gloating to have all these formerly powerful figures surrounding him. They have been reduced from powerful enemies to practically invisible and certainly powerless dogs, dependent on scraps the king gives out. The same change marks the shift in the "dogs" of Psalm 59—from vicious attackers to starving beasts slinking away at the edges of our peripheral vision.

At the center of the change is God, who laughs with scorn at their pretensions of power (59:8). God is unconcerned by their vicious attack, not in the sense that he does not care about the harm they may do but in the sense

---

26. A Babylonian text has survived listing the provisions set aside for the support of Jehoiachin and his retinue. See W. F. Albright, "King Joiachin in Exile," in *The Biblical Archaeologist Reader*, ed. G. Ernest Wright and David Noel Freedman (Garden City, N.Y.: Anchor Books, 1961), 1:106–12.

that their actions in no way hinder or damage his own purposes. Their visible destruction on the world stage is testimony to "the ends of the earth that God rules over Jacob" (59:13).

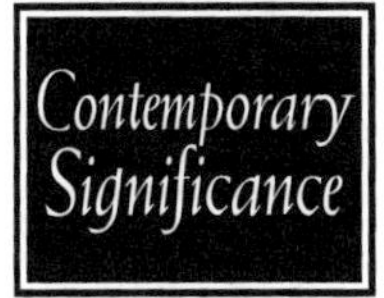

A LAUGHING GOD. The dogs of our lives remain. They still snarl in the background, bare their fangs, and nip at our heels, threatening to undo us. They have not disappeared as we might have hoped. To us their power is still effective and greatly destructive. I am sure that when technology stocks took a huge beating recently, there were many who felt as if they were being torn and devoured by dogs.

There are many ways the "dogs" of our world continue to plague us. Our economic woes seem minor when we begin to think globally and see the immense pressures of inflation and joblessness that confront many in the Third World. While our own context is relatively free of wars and threats of wars, the same is not true of the rest of the world. Israel, Africa, Indonesia, parts of Latin America—all must deal with the reality of death and destruction. And where there is no war, there is bigotry, hatred, oppression, abuse, and exploitation. On the health front we have AIDS and cancer as well as numerous other common threats to our existence. The environment is invaded by global warming, pollution, and species eradication. Yes, the dogs continue to prowl about the city and the countryside.

What keeps us from dissolving into fear and despair? Most of these problems are beyond my ability to solve. What hope do I have? Psalm 59 offers us the picture of a laughing God. The dogs rip and tear at us. The world seems to spin out of control on its way to destruction, and yet God laughs!

I have often imagined that God must have a great sense of humor. Anyone who would set poor Adam looking for a soul mate among the camels and hippopotamuses must like a good joke. But God's laughter here is not just good humor breaking to the surface. Nor is it that kind of nervous laughter I emit when I am uncomfortable or embarrassed. God laughs because he is completely relaxed. Even with the vicious snarling and snapping of all the dogs of our world, God remains unconcerned.

By unconcerned I do not mean that God is uncaring and flippant. He knows the snarling dogs for the wicked threat they are. He does not take pleasure in evil. It doesn't make him laugh because he thinks it is funny. God is unconcerned, but he is not uncaring. He laughs because the dogs' pretension to ultimate power over life is ridiculous! His laughter is an evidence that he is unimpressed. In the Tower of Babel narrative (Gen. 11:1–9), Yahweh is confronted by the tower built by rebellious humankind, yet he remains unconcerned. Now this is a tower that the humans thought lifted its top "into the heavens." But Yahweh has to stoop down—get on his knees in the dust of the Plain of Shinar—maybe even get his magnifying glass out of his pocket just to see this tiny pimple protruding from the skin of the earth.

That's funny! We humans take ourselves so seriously that we think the world revolves around *us*! And God laughs! I am thankful for a laughing God. Have you ever been approached by a fearful child? My mother-in-law recounts the time my son, who was two or three at the time, wanted to "hep you, Gramma!" to do the vacuuming. But every time the vacuum went on my son was terrified by the noise. Finally Gramma allowed him to vacuum with the noise off!

We may chuckle at the fears of our children. And God may break out in gusts of outright laughter at ours—not because the threats aren't real to us but because they hold no ultimate power to destroy. "The One enthroned in heaven laughs" (2:4), because he sees the end from the beginning. Because *he is the end and the beginning*—Alpha and Omega, reigning forever and ever. Amen!

A loving God. It is not enough that God laughs. He also loves! We don't trust God just because the powers of evil do not concern him. That is important, but it is not enough. Not only is God creator and sustainer, sovereign and all-powerful, but he is a loving God as well. Without the last, God would be a powerful deity with whom we had to deal, but we would not likely *trust* him. It would be a little like living under a totalitarian dictatorship. The government would exercise the power of life and death over all aspects of our world, and we would have to deal with it and consider it in all our decisions and actions; but we would not have to trust it.

But God is not just sovereign and in control; he is loving. Of course, we are not talking about a romantic or erotic love-god here. God is not in love with us in a sentimental or sexual way. Sometimes the pagan fertility religions got this kind of sexual, emotional "love" mixed up with worship. But Yahweh is not a fertility deity; he is a God of covenant loyalty. The kind of divine love described in Psalm 59, and elsewhere in the Old Testament, is tied to the Hebrew word *ḥesed* ("covenant loyalty"). The kind of love God expresses toward us is not based on looks, or hormones, or mutual compatibility, or even what I get out of it. Instead, God's love for us is grounded in a commitment to a relationship. This kind of love is actually what marriage is supposed to be all about: "for richer or poorer, for better or worse, in sickness and in health. . . ." It is not about emotion or feeling or even benefit, but about commitment.

We trust God because he has shown and continues to show that he is committed to us absolutely. He loves us in that he is willing to suffer our anger and rejection, our sin and rebellion, and still accomplish his will and purpose for us—to woo us to himself in a restored relationship.[27] Thus, when the world seems chaotic and beyond control, when our lives seem to disintegrate around us, when the dogs bare their fangs and seek to devour us or to carry us away, we need to remember the laughing God, who is "my fortress, my loving God" (59:17).

27. See God's commitment graphically displayed in the prophecy of Hosea, esp. chs. 1–3!

Psalm 60

FOR THE DIRECTOR of music. To the tune of "The Lily of the Covenant." A *miktam* of David. For teaching. When he fought Aram Naharaim and Aram Zobah, and when Joab returned and struck down twelve thousand Edomites in the Valley of Salt.

1 You have rejected us, O God, and burst forth upon us;
you have been angry—now restore us!
2 You have shaken the land and torn it open;
mend its fractures, for it is quaking.
3 You have shown your people desperate times;
you have given us wine that makes us stagger.

4 But for those who fear you, you have raised a banner
to be unfurled against the bow. *Selah*

5 Save us and help us with your right hand,
that those you love may be delivered.
6 God has spoken from his sanctuary:
"In triumph I will parcel out Shechem
and measure off the Valley of Succoth.
7 Gilead is mine, and Manasseh is mine;
Ephraim is my helmet,
Judah my scepter.
8 Moab is my washbasin,
upon Edom I toss my sandal;
over Philistia I shout in triumph."

9 Who will bring me to the fortified city?
Who will lead me to Edom?
10 Is it not you, O God, you who have rejected us
and no longer go out with our armies?
11 Give us aid against the enemy,
for the help of man is worthless.
12 With God we will gain the victory,
and he will trample down our enemies.

PSALM 60 IS a national (communal) lament and plea for deliverance following a painful defeat by a foreign enemy. The defeat is viewed as divine rejection and punishment, and the plea is for restoration of divine love and favor. The middle part of the psalm is an oracle—a divine pronouncement possibly given by a priest "from the sanctuary" (60:6a)—that promises hope in the coming of God as divine warrior to defeat the enemy nations (60:6b–8). In verse 9 the human king anticipates divine empowerment to achieve military victory over Edom—perhaps the major foe in this context.

Verses 5–12 reappear in almost identical form as part of Psalm 108 (vv. 6–13), where they are preceded by five verses that are practically identical with 57:7–11.[1] The comparison of these three psalms (57; 60; 108) demonstrates how psalms or psalmic segments could be recombined and reused to speak to different settings and times. The use in Psalm 108 of 60:5–12 also helps indicate structural divisions within our psalm. It has three sections: the lament proper (60:1–4),[2] an oracle of divine deliverance (60:5–8), and a final plea for divine leadership and deliverance (60:9–12). This structure has the benefit of maintaining three balanced stanzas of four verses each.

The Heading (60:0)

OTHER THAN A distinctive tune title ("According to The Lily of the Testimony"),[3] the heading contains only a single new term. Following an initial reference to "the director of music," attribution to David, categorization as a *miktam* (the fifth and final consecutive psalm so designated in the group stretching from Pss. 55–60),[4] the phrase *lelammed* ("for teaching") is introduced. Since

1. See comments on 57:7–11.

2. Some commentators (including those in the notes of *The NIV Study Bible*, 846) conclude the first section with verse 3. The lament certainly ends there. However, in my opinion, verse 4 provides a questioning foil for the sense of rejection the community was feeling and should be included here rather than with what follows. The appearance of *selah* at the end of v. 4, while not conclusive, is certainly supportive of such a division (see comments on *selah* in Ps. 3). The sense would be: "You have rejected us, *even though* your normal and expected procedure is to provide military leadership and protection for those who fear you."

3. The term that the NIV translates "covenant" is not the traditional word for covenant (*berit*), but the word *ᶜedut* ("testimony, witness"). The idea is of an almost visible reminder/memorial that serves as a "warning sign" (Holladay, *CHALOT*, 266) against breaking a commitment. Cf. references to the tablets of the law as *luḥot haᶜedut* ("the tablets of the Testimony," Ex. 31:18) and the ark of the covenant as *haʾaron laᶜedut* ("the ark of the Testimony," 31:7)—presumably because it contained the tablets of the law (Deut. 10:1–5).

4. See comments on the heading of Ps. 56.

this term occurs only here in the psalm headings, it is difficult to make any conclusions regarding its meaning, and the psalm exhibits no peculiarly didactic characteristics.

Psalm 60 also contains a historical note referring the psalm to an event in David's life.[5] The connection does not appear apt in this case since the narrative passages describe a great military victory while the psalm itself seems to presume a significant defeat for Israel. Together with the similar historical notes in the headings of Psalms 56–57 and 59, this completes the kind of envelope pattern that brackets these five consecutive *miktam* psalms.[6]

Psalm 60 continues the reticence to employ the divine name Yahweh characteristic of the Elohistic Psalter, of which it is a part.[7]

The Lament (60:1–4)

THE PSALM LAMENTS a particularly significant defeat that is interpreted as divine judgment on Israel. God is described as the source of Israel's suffering in a series of verbal expressions that extends through 60:3. The series begins and ends with parallel descriptions of divine rejection and judgment. God has "rejected" and "burst forth"[8] against them (60:1a, b); he has "shown ... desperate times" to his people and given them "wine that makes [them] stagger" (60:3). In between lie two descriptions of divine action countered by the psalmist's plea for reversal:

> You have been angry—now restore us!
> You have shaken the land and torn it open;
> Mend [heal] its fractures, for it is quaking.

You have raised a banner. Verse 4 is particularly difficult and has received a variety of interpretations. The opening phrase is clear: "You have raised a banner." The "banner" is a type of standard or flag used in battle to provide visibility during hand-to-hand combat and to offer a rallying point. The dif-

---

5. The events mentioned may be those recounted in 2 Sam. 8; 1 Chron. 18, although there is some difference in those accounts and the psalm heading over how many Edomites were struck down (2 Sam. 8 and 1 Chron. 18 say 18,000, while the psalm heading mentions 12,000) and who did the deed (2 Sam. 8 says David, 1 Chron. 18 mentions Joab's brother Abishai, while the psalm heading says Joab).

6. See comments on the heading of Ps. 56.

7. See commentary on Ps. 42, at the beginning of the Elohistic Psalter.

8. The verb *prṣ* normally describes the breaching of a city or house wall by attackers or robbers—in which case God is viewed as acting like an enemy laying siege to his own people. On occasion it may also describe water that overflows and breaks out of its bounds (Prov. 3:10; Mic. 2:13).

ficulty is in how to understand God's provision of a "banner" in this context. The preceding string of verbs have all described God in negative relation to Israel. He "rejected" them, "broke" their defenses, was "angry" with them, "shook" the land, and "tore it apart." Now suddenly God raises a banner for "those who fear [him]."

How one understands this latest act of God depends on how the verb *lehitnoses* (NIV "unfurled") is interpreted. It may be from *nws* ("flee, escape"), in which case the rallying banner does not provide safety but exposes Israel to the firepower of the enemy archers.[9] In such an interpretation, verse 4 continues the negative actions of God toward his people begun in 60:1–3 and assumes the Hebrew noun *qošeṭ* ("truth") that appears in the text is a mistake for one of the similar sounding nouns *qošet* ("bowman") or *qešet* ("bow").[10]

Other interpreters and translators (including the NIV and NRSV) understand the verse as describing a change to positive action by God. They take "unfurled" from an otherwise unknown verb that shares the same root as *nws* and assume it means "rally to" or "unfurled." The resulting translation assumes a positive offer of protection from the archers to "those who fear you."[11]

Oracle of Deliverance (60:5–8)

REGARDLESS WHETHER THE preceding section concluded with continued negative response from God or a hopeful sign of divine protection, the psalm now moves into a confident promise of divine power and victory. This section begins with a renewed plea for deliverance (60:5) and continues with a word from God himself—an *oracle* spoken from the "sanctuary" (lit., "in his holiness"). This divine word expresses God's power and authority over all those national enemies who confront his people.

In triumph I will parcel out. The scene is sketched as a moment of divine conquest and victory—perhaps drawn from the early conquest of Canaan by the Israelites under God's leadership. Having subdued the enemies of his people, God now divides the conquered territory among his servant people. "Shechem" is located to the west of the Jordan River while the "Valley of Succoth" lies almost directly east on the other side of the river. The parceling

9. Cf. Tate's translation (*Psalms 51–100*, 100): "You who put up a banner for those who fear you—only to let them flee before the bowmen!"

10. The LXX and other versions (including the Syriac) understand *qošet* as "the bow," indicating they were reading the text as *qešet*.

11. Cf. the NRSV: "You have set up a banner for those who fear you, to rally to it out of bowshot"; and the NIV: "But for those who fear you, you have raised a banner to be unfurled against the bow."

out of these two territories may recall the original division of the lands east and west of the Jordan among the twelve tribes.[12]

Gilead is mine . . . Judah my scepter. The east-west theme is continued with the reference to "Gilead" (a location east of the Jordan occupied by half of the tribe of Manasseh) and "Manasseh," who also settled west of the river. Coupled with "Ephraim" (a northern tribe whose name came to be synonymous with the northern kingdom) and "Judah" (the southern tribe from which the Davidic dynasty came), the passage intends to include *all Israel*. The special relationship of all Israel with God is indicated both by the possessive claim of God that they are his and by their association with symbols of divine power ("my helmet")[13] and authority ("my scepter"). This expression of special relationship with God turns the tables in the psalm to hope of deliverance and victory over Israel's enemies, as becomes apparent in following verses.

Moab is my washbasin. Check a Bible map and you will see that the nations mentioned—Moab, Edom, Philistia—are all ancient enemies who surrounded Israel to the east (Moab, Edom) and the west (Philistia). These nations are associated here with symbols—not of power and authority but of menial service ("my washbasin")[14] and defeat ("I toss my sandal").[15] God is depicted as claiming ownership over the enemy nations, victoriously subduing their pretensions to power and subjecting them to menial servitude. The acknowledgment that God is powerful and in control, even in the face

---

12. It is also suggestive that the towns of Shechem and Succoth figure prominently in the narratives of Judg. 8–9. In Judg. 8, while Gideon is pursuing the fleeing kings of Midian, the citizens of Succoth incur his wrath when they refuse to feed his starving troops because he has yet to capture the kings of Midian. When he is successful in his pursuit, Gideon returns and teaches the men of Succoth a "lesson" with "desert thorns and briers." In Judg. 9, it is Gideon's son Abimelech who destroys the citizens of Shechem after they change from support to opposition for his ill-fated attempt at kingship.

13. "Helmet" is an interpretive translation of the Hebrew *maʿoz roʾši* (lit., "stronghold of my head"). Possibly this refers instead to "my chief [or foremost] stronghold."

14. The job of washing feet was the task of menial servants and slaves. Jesus transported this act of humble servanthood into a voluntary act of love and submission to God when he washed his disciples' feet (John 13:1–17).

15. Discussion continues regarding the precise understanding of this idiom. It may be another sign of menial servitude, as when the master tosses his sandals at a slave to be cared for. Or, following the lead of the story of Ruth (Ruth 4:7–10), it may represent a public claim of ownership. Alternatively, casting the sandal may be related to the acts of a conquering king over the defeated ruler of a conquered people. The triumphant king made the defeated ruler his "footstool," placing his foot on the king's neck as a public display of raw power and subjection. Of course, it may well be that in this passage a combination of all three of these is at work. These enemy nations are God's possession, have been subdued by him, and will be forced to labor as the servants of his people.

of enemy threats, provides the readers with confidence in his ability to deliver and save.

Plea for Divine Leadership and Deliverance (60:9–12)

PSALM 60 CONCLUDES with a plea for God to act as he is capable and to enable his people to defeat their enemies. The enemy is now viewed as a fortified city under siege and is specifically identified as Edom (60:9b). The plea stands in tension between the confidence that God is *able* to defeat all enemies (as the preceding verses have demonstrated) and the continuing awareness that Israel is experiencing divine abandonment and rejection (60:1–3, 10). The psalmist calls on God directly to aid his people against their enemies (60:11a) and acknowledges that human power is ultimately of no avail (60:11b).

We will gain the victory. The confident assurance of the concluding verse 12 must be read as a hopeful profession of faith, standing as it does in such close proximity with the preceding pictures of divine abandonment and human powerlessness. Israel has no hope unless her God is willing to act in her behalf, as he acted in the Conquest to establish his covenant people in the land. The earlier commitment of God (depicted in 60:6–8) to subdue and divide the land for the sake of his people remains the hope that God yet has plans to fulfill and maintain his covenant promises. Thus, the psalm is able to conclude with a triumphant shout: "With God we will gain the victory,[16] and he will trample down our enemies."

DIVINE REJECTION AND ABANDONMENT. The Old Testament is full of descriptions of divine abandonment. From Genesis 3 on, humans living in relationship with Yahweh have known times when God seemed absent or even hostile to them. Cast out of the garden, Adam and Eve no longer experienced those intimate walks and talks in the cool of the evening. Their days were spent in grueling toil to eke out a meager existence from a world grown hostile to them.

(1) Often these experiences of divine withdrawal were seen as the result of a human failure of commitment. Adam and Eve disobeyed the commandment of God. Cain killed his brother Abel. Achan violated the injunction against taking booty before the defeat of Israel at Ai. Israel's failure of

16. The phrase *naʿaśeh ḥayil* probably means something more like "accomplish deeds of military prowess" than an actual claim of victory.

commitment resulted in an incomplete conquest of the Promised Land (Josh. 12–24). Life under the judges became a cycle of sin, judgment, oppression, repentance, deliverance, rest, and back to sin again (Judg. 2). The kings of Israel and Judah were consistently evaluated according to their commitment to Yahweh. Their success and failure against their enemies were often related to the strength of their commitment.

(2) On other occasions, however, God's withdrawal from his people is viewed as simple abandonment on his part. In these cases Israel pleaded with God to explain his distance, to remember his covenant commitments, and to respond in renewed relationship and deliverance. Job questions God in this way because of the undeserved suffering that consumed his life. The psalms are also full of this kind of pleading with God: "Why are you so far off? How long? Will you abandon us forever?"[17]

While some of these accounts may reflect Israel's failure of commitment, most stand as a reminder that true victory is possible only through the power of God. When God delays, as in the case of Job, his absence drives home the necessity of his power in ways no act of deliverance ever could. Confronted by their own human impotence in the face of attack or suffering, the psalmists are forced to approach the only stronghold and hope they have: the absent God. "Save us and help us with your right hand, that those you love[18] may be delivered.... Give us aid against the enemy, for the help of man is worthless" (60:5, 11).

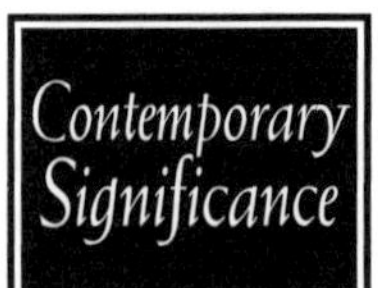

When plans fail. When our campaigns are brought up short in failure, this psalm can help us evaluate the causes and discover the way forward. When our plans fail, we must at least consider whether that is a sign God was not in it. The psalmist articulates this as rejection, even as punishment (60:1), and our experience shows that this can be the case. To act in our own strength or out of our own sinful motives can be to act out of weakness.

Often we can see the devastating consequences of sin as it works itself out in relationships over generations. Addiction to drugs can beget robbery and murder to support a habit and cover one's tracks. Adultery can destroy marriages and warp and distort the lives of children ill-prepared to understand and deal with it. When we look at our own society and its abuses, we can even

17. Cf. Pss. 6:3; 10:1; 13:1; 35:17; 44:23–24; 74:10–11; 79:5; 80:4; 89:46; 90:13; 119:84.

18. Here the term is *yadid* ("beloved"), which indicates that Yahweh's relation is based on more than just loyalty and commitment.

describe the consequences in much the same terms as the psalmist: The land "shaken" and "torn open," "fractured" and "quaking," are all appropriate terms to describe the world around us now. Much of the fragmentation we see and experience is the direct result of our own selfish choices and attempts to control and manipulate the world to our satisfaction.

But we need to be careful in our evaluation. Not all failure is the result of sin or the punishment of God. Some suffering falls on the righteous for no failing of their own. The world is a complex place, and its fallen character means that the blessings and pains of natural circumstance (refreshing rain, destructive hurricane, crop-killing drought, devastating earthquake) can come on rich and poor, righteous and wicked alike. Moreover, being righteous is no guarantee of security from the evil deeds of others and the long-term consequences of such deeds. Similarly, the failure of our hopes and plans need not always be the result of divine punishment for our sin. Only Achan was revealed as the culprit who took booty before the failed campaign at Ai (Josh. 7), but all Israel—including their leader, Joshua—experienced the defeat.

Thus, if the failure of our plans cannot tell us absolutely whether it is the result of our sin or some other circumstance, what *can* it tell us? Here are several ideas taken from Psalm 60, which I think are being driven home to us in a time when our plans fail.

(1) To take the fortified city requires God's power and assistance (60:9–12). We may have certain successes in our lives by our own resources, intelligence, and strength, but the "fortified city"—the final goal of bringing the fortified outposts of entrenched evil under the rule of God—can only be accomplished in God's power. He is the creator and sustainer of all, and he is the one who restores and heals fragmented lives undone by human evil. Relying on human strength alone is worthless (60:11).

(2) Our failures (whatever the cause) do not undermine God's plans and purposes. No matter how broken and fragmented our world becomes because of our own and others' sin, God can mend and heal up its fractures. Our failures do not mean that God has failed. Note that when the psalmist recalls the Conquest in 60:6–8, all the places mentioned remain the possession of God even when his people fail to take them.[19] Interestingly, the account of the incomplete conquest in Judges 2:1–3:6 indicates that the failure of the Israelite conquest

19. Cf. the accounts of complete and incomplete conquests in Joshua and Judges. Josh. 1–11 describes what appears to be a completely successful conquest (10:40–43; 11:10–23). Josh. 12–24 and Judg. 2:1–3:6 make it clear, however, that the campaign was far from complete and that Israel's failure of commitment had prevented their accomplishing a thorough conquest.

of Canaan was both because of Israel's loss of commitment to Yahweh (2:1–3) and because of Yahweh's testing of his people's faithfulness (3:1–4).

(3) *Broken relationships can be restored.* Destruction, no matter how desperate, can be mended (60:2). God offers deliverance from sin. He has established a way to restore broken relationships with him. When we are tempted to label ourselves (or others) unredeemable, God steps firmly into the breach with an offer of salvation. This relentless goodness—God's desire to see all return to him—is the source of the psalmist's great hope. This hope also extends to those of us who have been severely damaged—in body, mind, and spirit—through the destructive, abusive evil of others against us. Rape; long term mental, emotional, physical, or sexual abuse; torture—all these leave deep life-affecting damage. Yet the psalmist offers us hope that such damage can be mended.

Anatoly Sharansky tells in his prison memoir, *Fear No Evil*, how God (mostly through the psalms) enabled him to maintain his sense of worth and human dignity in spite of years of torture, isolation, and attempts to rob him of his humanity in the Russian prison and Gulag system. After his father died while Anatoly was still imprisoned, when he was prevented from even writing in condolence to his mother about the loss, Sharansky embarked on a forty-day program of copying and reading the psalms from the Hebrew book of Psalms given him by his wife. The effect was remarkable. As Sharansky writes: "Day after day I reconciled myself with the past, and my feelings of grief and loss were gradually replaced by sweet sorrow and fond hopes."[20] Sharansky still languished in prison for years. The physical, mental, and psychological toll on his person was great, but his spirit remained intact, buoyed up by the power of God's words in the psalms to mend brokenness and to retake territory occupied by evil.

20. Anatoly Sharansky, *Fear No Evil* (New York: Public Affairs, 1998), 270.

Psalm 61

FOR THE DIRECTOR of music. With stringed instruments. Of David.

1 Hear my cry, O God;
listen to my prayer.

2 From the ends of the earth I call to you,
I call as my heart grows faint;
lead me to the rock that is higher than I.
3 For you have been my refuge,
a strong tower against the foe.

4 I long to dwell in your tent forever
and take refuge in the shelter of your wings. *Selah*
5 For you have heard my vows, O God;
you have given me the heritage of those who fear
your name.

6 Increase the days of the king's life,
his years for many generations.
7 May he be enthroned in God's presence forever;
appoint your love and faithfulness to protect him.

8 Then will I ever sing praise to your name
and fulfill my vows day after day.

WHILE NOT USUALLY included in the accepted list of "royal" psalms, Psalm 61 does have the needs of the king in mind at its core (61:6–7). This psalm follows the two complexes of related psalms—four *maśkil* psalms (52–55) and five *miktam* psalms (56–60)—and a series of related themes stitch together the seven consecutive Psalms 61–67.

Psalm 61 is an individual plea for deliverance and refuge. The circumstances from which the psalmist seeks deliverance are not clarified beyond a single reference to "the foe" (61:3b). Although the reference to the king suggests a preexilic origin for this psalm, the psalmist's call "from the ends of the earth" (61:2a) lends itself to continued resonance with the experience of the exilic and postexilic communities. The psalmist draws on past experience of rescue by God (61:3) as grounds of hope for continued rescue (61:2). As in Psalm 23, his desire is to "dwell in [God's] tent forever" (61:4).

Structurally, the psalm is composed of two stanzas, followed by a concluding vow of praise: opening plea for hearing and refuge (61:1–5), prayer for long life for the king (61:6–7), and concluding vow to praise (61:8).

The Heading (61:0)

THE HEADING IS similar to that of Psalm 4 and offers only variations on terms already encountered there. The psalm is referred to "the director of music" and is to be performed "with stringed instruments."[1] Whereas Psalm 4 is classified as a *mizmor*, Psalm 61 is left without any genre designation. Both psalms are attributed to David.

Opening Plea for Hearing (61:1–5)

HEAR MY CRY. As in so many of the pleas for deliverance, the psalmist begins by calling God to listen to his plight. The cry is urgent because he is speaking from far outside the traditional boundaries of Israel—"from the ends of the earth." The psalmist's sense of isolation and distance from the traditional sources of hope and security (land, family, community, nation) is almost palpable and is heightened by the repeated use in these brief lines of verbs and nouns of calling ("my cry" in 61:1a; "my prayer" in 61:1b; "I call" in 61:2a; "I call" in 61:2b). The phrase "the ends of the earth" is used elsewhere in the Psalter and the rest of the Old Testament to refer to the most removed and isolated areas of the world.

While there is no decisive indication that Psalm 61 is exilic in its composition, the isolation of the psalmist at the "ends of the earth" certainly lends itself to the experience of the exilic and postexilic communities, who found themselves scattered throughout the world in just such a fashion.[2] The phrase also provides a thematic thread that links Psalm 61 back to 59:13

---

1. Cf. comments on the heading of Ps. 4. The Hebrew in Ps. 61 is *ʿal neginat* ("on stringed instrument"), a singular construct phrase that lacks any concluding noun. *BHS* notes a number of manuscripts that use the plural absolute form instead. Ps. 4 has the alternative phrase *binginot* ("with stringed instruments").

2. Deut. 28:63–64 warns the Israelites as they prepare to enter the Promised Land that failure to follow Yahweh's commandments will result in their being "uprooted from the land" and that "the LORD will scatter you among all nations, from one end of the earth to the other."

and ahead to 65:5; 67:7; 72:8.[3] I will return to this point in the Bridging Contexts section.

My heart grows faint. Isolated and distant from the sources of support and hope, the psalmist's heart "grows faint." The concept of growing faint most often describes extreme physical weakness when one is in danger of death from hunger or thirst (cf. 77:3; 102:0; 142:3; Isa. 29:8; 40:31; 44:12; 57:16; Jer. 31:25; Lam. 2:11; Amos 8:13; Jonah 4:8), but it can also take on the nuance "lose heart" or "be discouraged" (cf. Ps. 143:4), as in our passage. The psalmist's sense of distance from God is so extreme that it threatens to erode even confidence in his power to save.

Lead me to the rock. The psalmist is in need of refuge and protection. In this verse, that refuge is envisioned as a remote rocky crag in the wilderness. The word "rock" (*ṣur*) used here normally describes a rocky outcropping that could provide natural defenses to those on the run from their enemies. The psalmist desires to be whisked away by God to a protective crag that is beyond his own reach ("higher than I"). One can almost see the psalmist—hotly pursued by foes—frantically reaching upward along the rock and seeking the downstretched hand of God to pull him to safety.[4]

You have been my refuge. The psalmist continues to hope that God will act on his behalf. Past experiences of deliverance and protection foster new hope that God is still his "strong tower against the foe" (61:3).[5] Proverbs 18:10 describes Yahweh as a "strong tower" that provides safety to the righteous, who run to him for protection. Such towers were often included in city defenses and formed the final secure place, should the city walls be breached. They were not always, however, a guarantee of safety, as the citizens of Shechem discovered when Abimelech burned down their tower and destroyed all with it (Judg. 9:46–49).

I long to dwell in your tent forever. The psalmist switches metaphors to envision an even more secure life dwelling in the "tent" of God "forever." The verb "dwell" (*gwr* ["sojourn, live as a resident alien"]) is a cohortative

---

3. It is interesting that of eleven occurrences of the phrase "ends of the earth" in the Psalter, seven occur within the bounds of the Elohistic Psalter (46:9; 48:10; 59:13; 61:2; 65:5; 67:7; 72:8) and only four outside this collection (2:8; 22:27; 98:3; 135:7); this seems to represent part of the distinctive vocabulary of this section.

4. Cf. esp. 27:4–6, where the themes of dwelling with Yahweh, hiding in his "tent" (*ʾohel*; NIV "tabernacle"), and being set "high upon a rock" come together. In 27:5, the phrase "set me high upon a rock" is the Heb. *beṣur yeromemeni*, which is similar to 61:2 (*beṣur yarum mimmenni*). *BHS* also notes that the Greek text of 61:2 assumes an underlying Hebrew *teromemeni* ("you will set me high [on a rock]").

5. For further discussion of God as "refuge," see comments on 18:2.

form, emphasizing the desire of the speaker (NIV "long to dwell"). The resonance with the similar expression in 23:6 is unmistakable. There, however, the verb is a consecutive perfect form, indicating future completion and stability. The verbal root in Psalm 23 (*yšb*) stresses settled permanence, while in 61:4 *gwr* denotes a more tentative stance. The psalmist desires the absolute security of the divinely exalted "rock" but will settle for the less permanent status of resident alien in the tent of God.[6]

The heritage of those who fear your name. The psalmist recalls to mind (God's mind as well as his own!) the vows he has made to praise God's name (cf. 61:5). This mention of vows is repeated in the final verse (61:8); together these verses form a sort of inclusio around the final stanza of the psalm. The psalmist's vow to praise God's name in the face of such threatening isolation is a measure of his faith—the ability to "fear" God (61:5). Fear of God is no trembling terror. It is instead the appropriate awareness that one is absolutely and completely dependent on God for everything: life, health, protection, and care.

The "heritage" given by God exceeds the gift of land with boundaries described in the division of the land by Joshua and recalled in God's triumphant words of authority in the preceding psalm (cf. 60:6–8). Although described as *yeruššah*—land parceled out after conquest—this heritage is one that sustains those who fear God even when they find themselves calling from the "ends of the earth" (61:2).

Long Life for the King (61:6–7)

IN AN UNEXPECTED shift, the psalmist moves from an individual plea for protection to a prayer for long life and enduring reign for the king. It is clear that during the monarchical period, such prayers must have been commonplace, since communal well-being was closely bound up with the stability provided by a king's enduring just reign. In the postexilic period, however, when the kings were no longer a factor, this section must have taken on eschatological overtones as the desire that the king "be enthroned in God's presence forever" closely parallels the psalmist's own desire to "dwell in [God's] tent forever." While the psalmist is satisfied to hope for the less permanent security of "resident alien" status associated with the verb *gwr* (cf. 61:4a), the king is expected to settle more permanently (Heb. *yšb* ["sit, dwell"]) in the divine

6. For the theme of dwelling with Yahweh, see comments on 23:6. The theme receives expansion in 27:4–6 as well. The *selah* that occurs at the end of 61:4 seems misplaced if it is intended to mark a structural division. The particle *ki* ("for") that begins 61:5 clearly links that verse with 61:4.

presence (61:7a)[7] and to be protected by God's loyal love (*ḥesed*) and enduring faithfulness (*ʾemet*).[8]

Concluding Vow of Praise (61:8)

THE PSALM ENDS with a promise to praise God's name daily as a fulfillment of the vow mentioned earlier in 61:5. The "fulfillment" (from *šlm* ["complete/make perfect"]) of a vow was often a public act of declaration in the course of temple worship accompanied with a sacrifice. The poetic structure of the verse parallels "make music to your name"[9] with "fulfill my vows," making it clear that these two acts are different aspects of the same act of public testimony.

THE ENDS OF THE EARTH. The phrase "the ends of the earth" functions prominently in this group of psalms (Pss. 59–72). A variety of Hebrew expressions are translated in this fashion. In 2:8, God promises to make the "ends of the earth" (*ʾapse ʾereṣ*) the "possession" of his anointed king. The same Hebrew phrase appears in 22:27; 59:13; 67:7; 72:8; 98:3. The phrase used in Psalm 61 is *qeṣe haʾareṣ* ("end of the earth"), an idiom that also appears in 46:9 and 135:7. A variation of the last is the less common *qaṣwe ʾereṣ* ("ends of the earth"), found in 48:10 and 65:5.

The idea of an "end, edge, extremity" of the earth may suggest a cosmology of a flat earth as dry land surrounded by seas. All this is topped by an inverted bowl (the "firmament"; *raqiaʿ*), so that together earth and firmament hold off the chaotic waters "under and over the earth." This provides a stable environment for life. In other contexts, the "ends of the earth" seem

7. The NIV's translation of *yešeb* (Qal imperfect of *yšb*) as the passive "be enthroned" rather than the more common "sit, dwell" obscures the intentional parallel between psalmist and king in these verses.

8. For further discussion of *ḥesed*, see comments on 17:7; for *ʾemet*, see comments on 15:2; 19:9. *Ḥesed* describes loyalty to obligations assumed as part of a covenant relationship, while *ʾemet* stresses enduring reliability, long-term trustworthiness. These terms are paired together throughout in the Psalter: 25:10; 26:3; 40:10–11; 57:3, 10; 61:7; 69:13; 85:10; 86:15; 89:14; 108:4; 115:1; 117:2; 138:2. (Note esp. 40:10–11, where the NIV translates *ʾemet* as "truth," emphasizing the reliability of God and his utterance.) The NIV in 61:7 takes the uncertain Heb. verb *man* as an imperative of *mnh* ("count, apportion, appoint"). *BHS*, by contrast, suggests the word should be omitted as the result of dittography.

9. The Heb. *zmr* more normally describes performing instrumental musical accompaniment than singing.

to denote the farthest reaches of the inhabitable earth,[10] since it is from there that God calls human beings to do his will. In all cases, the "end/s of the earth" are employed metaphorically to emphasize the distance from all that is common or familiar to the poet.

God calls foreign peoples to attack Israel as part of his judgment.[11] He then calls his exiled people to return from "the ends of the earth."[12] The psalmist in Psalm 61 feels far from God—at the ends of the earth. The image can also be used to stress the completeness of creation under consideration. God sees to the ends of the earth, meaning "everything under the heavens" (Job 28:24). God is the creator of the ends of the earth (Isa. 40:28) and can, therefore, give it to whomever he wills (cf. Ps. 2:8).

God judges the ends of the earth (1 Sam. 2:10) and offers salvation to them as well (Isa. 45:22). In the final restoration of all things, even the "ends of the earth" will acknowledge Yahweh's sovereignty and will praise him. "From the ends of the earth we hear singing: 'Glory to the Righteous One'" (Isa. 24:16).[13]

The shelter of your wings. Two phrases compete in the Old Testament to provide this image of birds protected under the wings of their mother. One uses the Hebrew *ṣel* ("shadow") while the second refers to *seter* ("hiding place"; NIV "shelter"). Both terms are used in parallel in 91:1 to describe the confident hope of the psalmist: "He who dwells in the shelter [*seter*] of the Most High will rest in the shadow (*ṣel*) of the Almighty." The image is basically the same in both cases: a mother hen, or eagle, or owl, protectively gathering her chicks under her wing. The extension of the image as a metaphor for divine protection is clearest in Ruth 2:12, where Boaz blesses Ruth for her loyalty to her mother-in-law, Naomi: "May you be richly rewarded by the LORD, the God of Israel, under whose wings you have come to take refuge."

Some commentators have suggested that the image may have been further associated with the wings of the cherubim that overarched the ark of the

---

10. Cf. "Then the LORD will scatter you among all nations, from one end of the earth to the other. There you will worship other gods—gods of wood and stone, which neither you nor your fathers have known" (Deut. 28:64). "At that time those slain by the LORD will be everywhere—from one end of the earth to the other. They will not be mourned or gathered up or buried, but will be like refuse lying on the ground" (Jer. 25:33).

11. "The LORD will bring a nation against you from far away, from the ends of the earth, like an eagle swooping down, a nation whose language you will not understand" (Deut. 28:49).

12. "I will say to the north, 'Give them up!' and to the south, 'Do not hold them back.' Bring my sons from afar and my daughters from the ends of the earth" (Isa. 43:6).

13. "All the ends of the earth will remember and turn to the LORD, and all the families of the nations will bow down before him" (Ps. 22:27; see also Isa. 42:10).

covenant in the Most Holy Place of the tabernacle or temple. In this case the protective wings of Yahweh might become effective when one flees to the temple and seeks asylum there[14] (cf. also 17:8; 36:7; 57:1; 63:7).

CRYING FROM THE **ends of the earth.** What is the functional equivalent of living in exile today? I have had the privilege of knowing a number of displaced folk over the last thirty years, including Palestinians driven out of their homeland by the increasing violence in the region, Vietnamese and Hmong refugees from Southeast Asia, the children of Iranian government workers sent to school abroad during the Khomeini revolution, and Indonesian students sent to the United States by parents to avoid the dangers of the current political situation. I can remember their hunger for news about those left behind during any outbreak of violence and their sense of being torn between wanting to see family, friends, and their country and yet hating the fear and uncertainty that ruled life at home.

Few of us in the Western world have experienced that kind of exile. We may have chosen to leave family and home far behind when we joined the general American migration in search of personal freedom, independence, and well-being. We may regret the distance that separates us from parents and siblings. But we are not in exile—most of us—to the "ends of the earth."

How can these verses speak to us in ways that actually describe our condition? I think we must realize that this phrase was a metaphor for the psalmist who spoke it and those who heard and adopted it as their own. Yes, perhaps the Diaspora community had more experience of exile than we do now. But they too were using this sense of immense distance as a metaphor for their sense of abandonment by a God who seemed removed as far away as the "ends of the earth." In this condition they are no different from us.

Think of just a few of the ways in which God seems removed and distant from us now. On the world scene, we have only to consider the growing evidence of inhumanity to wonder just where God is in the mass graves of Kosovo, or the AIDS epidemic of Africa, or the desperation of those seeking illegally to enter the United States from Mexico, at the risk of their lives. On a more personal level, where is God in the human agony of our lives? As I write, a mother and father in Northern California are losing hope about their young adult daughter, who disappeared two months ago without a trace. A husband just buried his five children—drowned by their mother. An uncle

14. See esp. Kraus, *Psalms 1–59*, 248–49 (on Ps. 17:8). Cf. also comments above on 17:8; 57:1.

is lying in a hospital bed at home, waiting for an end that never seems to come.

I don't think we need to take a trip to visit the "ends of the earth." More often than not, they come to us unbidden and suck us away from God so that our hearts grow faint (61:2). It may be grief or guilt; disease, depression, or death; poverty, perversion, or pain that confront us. But we find God absent, and our voices speak as if from the bottom of a deep well, with little hope of being heard.

Yet cry we do, and cry we should! The psalmist cries out even with a weak heart because God has been a refuge and a strong tower against the foe in the past. Thus, the psalmist and we look with hope for the "rock that is higher than I"—a place to rise above the sweeping flood until the danger is past. You have seen people perching on housetops, car tops, and treetops, staying above the rushing flood waters until rescue comes. One African woman even gave birth to a child in a tree: new life in the face of death, hope in the face of disaster. May we look to the rock and scramble to the refuge it affords. And from that vantage point let us sing praises to the God who appoints his loyalty and faithfulness to protect us (61:7).

Taking refuge in the shelter of God's wings. Like young birds that hide under their mother's wings, we do want to find shelter and divine protection. Like such birds, however, we seem to run for cover only when trouble approaches. That may work for a while, but too many adventuresome chicks have not made it back in time to avoid the coyote. The psalmist of 61:4 gives a few suggestions how to keep our eyes on our refuge and the pathway clear so we will be unhindered in times of trouble.

(1) Note first that there will indeed be times of trouble. That is perhaps the biggest obstacle preventing us from entering the refuge of God. If we assume that the righteous will never experience trouble, we will be unprepared when it comes, and we may be consequently unsure whether a God who allows us to suffer is worthy of our trust.

(2) Another help is to remember the psalmist's strong desire and longing to dwell in the security of God's tent—under his protective wings—forever. When that kind of longing desire characterizes our relationship with God, little can block our way to refuge. We keep track of those persons and things we long for. We know where they are and stick close to them. That should also characterize our longing for God.

(3) Finally, the psalmist is committed in his relationship to God. It is not just a matter of longing and desire. He is bound by vows made openly to God. This is not some secret promise made to himself but a commitment made to God in truth. Nor is the psalmist's vow just a one-time affair; rather, it is a pact or covenant that requires daily renewal and fulfillment (61:8). It is a bit like

a marriage. At the wedding, vows are said by both parties. But those vows are not just a wedding ritual; they are commitments that must be renewed every day, day after day, year after year. To leave commitment at the wedding altar is almost invariably to condemn the relationship to failure from the start.

Thus, if we would truly desire to find protection under the wings of God, we must bind ourselves to him in longing and desire and build a relationship of continuing and lasting commitment. As God is a God of loyal love (*ḥesed*) and enduring faithfulness (*ʾemet*), we must become people shaped by the same characteristics: commitment and love.

Psalm 62

FOR THE DIRECTOR of music. For Jeduthun. A psalm of David.

1 My soul finds rest in God alone;
  my salvation comes from him.
2 He alone is my rock and my salvation;
  he is my fortress, I will never be shaken.

3 How long will you assault a man?
  Would all of you throw him down—
  this leaning wall, this tottering fence?
4 They fully intend to topple him
  from his lofty place;
  they take delight in lies.
With their mouths they bless,
  but in their hearts they curse. *Selah*

5 Find rest, O my soul, in God alone;
  my hope comes from him.
6 He alone is my rock and my salvation;
  he is my fortress, I will not be shaken.
7 My salvation and my honor depend on God;
  he is my mighty rock, my refuge.
8 Trust in him at all times, O people;
  pour out your hearts to him,
  for God is our refuge. *Selah*

9 Lowborn men are but a breath,
  the highborn are but a lie;
if weighed on a balance, they are nothing;
  together they are only a breath.
10 Do not trust in extortion
  or take pride in stolen goods;
though your riches increase,
  do not set your heart on them.

11 One thing God has spoken,
  two things have I heard:

that you, O God, are strong,
12 and that you, O Lord, are loving.
Surely you will reward each person
according to what he has done.

WHILE PSALM 62 seems to reflect a situation of trouble for the psalmist, it does not follow the usual pattern of the laments or pleas for deliverance. Instead, it has more in common with instructive discourses both to the wicked (who are castigated in 62:3–4) and the reader, for whom the psalm is mostly intended as exhortation to faithful endurance. The latter half of the psalm (62:9–12) is a series of aphoristic sayings similar to the wisdom sages.

The psalm contains two major sections, linked by two central verses (62:7–8) that focus on God as refuge and shift the individual concerns of the first section to the communal concerns of the second. The first section is framed by an inclusio, while the second section is a series of aphorisms. Structurally, then, the psalm can be presented as: assault of the wicked (62:1–6), God as rock and refuge (62:7–8), and exhortations to the community (62:9–12).[1]

The Heading (62:0)

NO NEW TERMS appear in the heading of Psalm 62. In fact, the title is a near duplicate of the heading of Psalm 39. The psalm is referred to "the director of music"[2] and attributed to David. Between these two terms stands the more enigmatic *ʿal yedutun* ("upon/concerning Jeduthun").[3] Introduced by the preposition *ʿal*, this term in a psalm heading most often suggests a possible tune or melody for performance,[4] or perhaps a tuning for the harp accompaniment.[5]

1. Alternatively the psalm could be divided into three stanzas of four verses each (vv. 1–4, 5–8, 9–12), with the first two introduced with the near duplicate statement of confidence and the last being a collection of aphorisms. This has the benefit of agreeing with the presence of *selah* at the end of vv. 4 and 8.

2. See comments on the heading to Ps. 4.

3. In Ps. 39, this term is presented as *lidutun* ("to/for/by Jeduthun"), and a few manuscripts of Psalms render the term in Ps. 62 as *lidutun* as well (see the critical apparatus in *BHS*). See also the comments on Jeduthun in the heading of Ps. 39.

4. Cf. (lit.) "According to the Lilies" in the heading of Ps. 45.

5. Cf. "According to *sheminith*" in the heading of Ps. 6, or "According to *gittith* [tuning]" in the heading of Ps. 8.

The Assault of the Wicked (62:1–6)

THE FIRST SECTION of the psalm describes an assault on the psalmist by the wicked. This description itself takes up two central verses (62:3–4) bracketed before and behind by a near inclusio (62:1–2, 5–6), in which the psalmist expresses unshakable trust in God as "my rock," "my salvation," and "my fortress." Particularly distinctive here is the use of the particle *ʾak* ("surely, indeed") to introduce each line of the inclusio.[6] The effect of the inclusio is to "surround" the attacking enemy with the power and protection of God, so that any strength or effectiveness attributed to the enemy is nullified from the start. The intentions of the wicked have no real substance since they are engulfed by the power of God, which renders them void.

Finds rest. The primary point of discussion in regards to the inclusio has to do with the identification and translation of the word *dumiyyah* in 62:1 and its counterpart *dommi* in 62:5. As it stands, the first seems to be a noun meaning "silence." This makes the relationship of the words in the first phrase (lit., "surely to God silence my soul") unclear. The NIV apparently takes the last phrase as "silence [is] my soul" and interpretively renders it as "my soul *finds rest*." The apparatus of *BHS* suggests an emendation of *dumiyyah* to a form of the verb *dmh* ("be silent").

The circumstance is complicated by the variations of this concept in verse 5. The opening phrase reads *ʾak leʾlohim dommi napši* (lit., "surely to God stand still my soul"). In this case, *dommi* is taken as an imperative of *dmm* ("stand still, keep still"[7]); this is the path taken by the NIV.[8] Thus, what is *described* in the first set of lines (the psalmist's soul finding rest in God) is *exhorted* in the second set. The psalmist's soul is undeterred by the threat of the enemy envisioned in the intervening lines, because God remains a rock of salvation and a fortress.

Toward the end of the first verse of the inclusio one encounters a second significant variation. In 62:1b the psalmist affirms: "From him [God] comes *my salvation* [*mimmennu yešuʿati*]," while in its counterpart in 62:5b, the phrase is altered to read: "From him comes *my hope* [*mimmennu tiqwati*]." The change

---

6. Besides these four appearances of *ʾak*, the word appears twice more—at the beginnings of vv. 4 and 9—for a total of six occurrences in this psalm.

7. See Holladay, *CHALOT*, 72.

8. There is another alternative, employing a different verb with the same root *dmm*. This alternative form has the root meaning "wail, lament," which would provide the translation: "Lament to God, O my soul!" While this is a possible rendering, it undermines the apparent purpose of surrounding the threat of the enemy with the strength of divine protection in the inclusio. The apparatus of *BHS* notes that a few manuscripts have made the second appearance of the inclusio conform to the first, so that *dumiyyah* is found in both.

is significant in light of the shift in focus from individual concerns of the narrator to the perspective of the community. The testimony of the psalmist to the reality of divine salvation in 62:1 provides the foundation for the community's hope in 62:5.

This may also explain the final variation between the two parts of the inclusio, involving the last statement in each. The first concludes with the somewhat qualified affirmation, (lit.) "I will not be *greatly* moved" (62:2b).[9] In the second set of lines, this affirmation has become even more confident by the removal of the qualifier "greatly" to leave the unqualified declaration (lit.): "I will not be moved [at all]!" (62:6b).

How long will you assault a man? Within the new context of divine power established by the inclusio, the vicious assault of the wicked (62:3–4) appears practically impotent. The assault is depicted as a rather opportunistic attempt to take advantage of those already weakened and about to fall. Like the schoolyard bully, the wicked practice their evil on those ill-equipped to defend themselves: "this leaning wall, this tottering fence" (62:3). Both phrases describe walls—of houses or cities—in an advanced state of decay or ruin. Especially the last suggests a wall of rough field stones without mortar, which is already *deḥuyah* ("pushed in").

From his lofty place. The beginning of 62:4 has occasioned numerous suggestions and emendations. Some read *miśśe᾿eto* ("from his/its elevation") as *maššiḥ᾿ot* ("deceptions") and read together with the following verb as "Indeed they are planning deceptions."[10] Tate takes *miśśe᾿eto* as a "person of high status" and rather awkwardly translates the phrase: "Yes, despite being a person of high status."[11] If, however, the metaphor of the toppling walls is recalled, the relatively straightforward translation of the MT may be best. In this scenario, *miśśe᾿eto* means "from the *wall's* elevation" (and by analogy, the elevation of the assault victim as well). The wicked, then, "plan to scatter/disperse"[12] the stones of the tottering walls as an enemy army would knock down the walls of a defeated city.

They take delight in lies. For the psalmist, however, the attack is less physical and more verbal—an assault on reputation and honor. The enemies enjoy the game of deception and misinformation. What they say with their mouths and what they truly mean are diametrically opposite: "With their mouths they bless [*brk*], but in their hearts they curse [*qll*]." This type of assault on one's character may be less physical, but it is no less damaging.

---

9. The NIV apparently takes *rabbah* as an emphatic and translates "I will *never* be shaken."

10. Kraus, *Psalms 60–150* (Minneapolis: Augsburg, 1989), 11–12, drawing on Ps. 73:18.

11. Tate, *Psalms 51–100*, 117–18.

12. A Hiphil infinitive construct of *ndḥ* with the preposition *le*-, which in the Hiphil means "scatter, disperse" (Holladay, *CHALOT*, 229).

Having described the attack of the enemy, the first section concludes with the second appearance of the inclusio, by which the power of the enemy attack is again nullified in God's power, and the foundation of hope is laid for an unshakable future for individual and community.

God as Rock and Refuge (62:7–8)

THESE CENTRAL VERSES provide the transition from the more individual reflections in 62:1–6 and the community oriented aphorisms in 62:9–12. The "glue" that holds the two together is the brief reflection in these verses on God who is the "refuge" of both psalmist and community (62:2b, 7b). The section moves from testimony to exhortation, with the former providing the basis of the latter. In 62:7, the psalmist affirms confidence in God. The psalmist's "salvation" and "honor" (*kabod*)[13] are both dependent on the divine power that renders the enemy impotent in the preceding inclusio. God is the "mighty rock" that provides "refuge" in the face of attack.[14] The God who is the psalmist's "refuge" is exhorted as the refuge of the whole community at the end of 62:8: "For God is *our* refuge."

Trust in him. The psalmist's testimony becomes the basis of exhortation to the community. Plural imperatives call the faithful people (*ʿam*) to follow the example of the psalmist in trusting God and pouring out their hearts to him. This call to trust God "at all times" sets the stage for the series of aphorisms that form the final section of the psalm.

Exhortations to the Community (62:9–12)

THE FINAL SECTION of Psalm 62 is a collection of three aphorisms that drive home the preceding exhortation for the community to place their trust in God as refuge. These sayings are similar in structure, content, and vocabulary with comparable aphorisms known from the biblical wisdom literature.

Lowborn . . . highborn. The first aphorism deflates any reliance on social status and position. Neither low nor high status provides any basis for confidence, since the one is "a breath" (*hebel*)[15] and the other "a lie" (*kazab*). In a

---

13. See the comments on *kabod* at 3:3–4.

14. The reference to "rock" (*ṣur*) and "refuge" (*maḥsi*) in 62:7 provides an effective link back to 61:2–3, where the psalmist seeks the "rock that is higher than I" to serve as "refuge" against the enemy.

15. A word commonly employed in Ecclesiastes, where it appears thirty-six times with the meaning "valueless, worthless." The term also appears with basically the same meaning in Job (Job 7:16; 9:29; 21:34; 27:12; 35:16); Isaiah (Isa. 30:7; 49:4; 57:13); and Lamentations (Lam. 4:17). In Deut. 32:21; 1 Kings 16:13, 26; 2 Kings 17:15; and nine times in Jeremiah, *hebel* refers to pagan idols. In Proverbs, the predominant image is of an insubstantial "fleeting vapor" (Prov. 21:6) and extensions by analogy to dishonest gain (13:11) and beauty (31:30).

scale they have no weight. Even if weighed together, they remain "a breath." Human status is a worthless source of human trust.

Extortion . . . riches. Like status, the human ability to control and manipulate life through human power is ultimately worthless. The hearers are cautioned not to adopt the tactics of the wicked (those castigated in vv. 3–4). Oppression of others and extortion is no sound basis for trust. Like "stolen goods"[16] such ill-gotten gains may increase but cannot provide a foundation for pride or security. A similar aphorism in Proverbs 23:4–5 cautions against placing much stock in riches in general: "Do not wear yourself out to get rich; have the wisdom to show restraint. Cast but a glance at riches, and they are gone, for they will surely sprout wings and fly off to the sky like an eagle."[17]

One thing . . . two things. The section concludes with a numerical saying similar to those found in Proverbs 30:7–31. "One thing God has spoken, two things have I heard. . . ." The twofold description of the character of God provided in this saying offers the necessary basis of confidence and trust that was missing in human status and corrupt power. God can be trusted because he is at one and the same time "strong" and "loving."[18] Weiser makes the point well: "It is in the *union* of power and grace that the essential nature of the Old Testament belief in God is truly expressed; for power without grace does not admit of any trust, and grace without power is deprived of its ultimate seriousness."[19]

The psalmist's God is caring, capable, and committed. The power that surrounds and nullifies the attack of the wicked is a continuing source of trust for psalmist and community alike. The power of God is not abusive but committed through his covenant relationship to the protection and benefit of his covenant people.

Because God is strong and committed to his covenant purpose, the preceding aphoristic exhortations assume even more importance. God is able to accomplish his purposes and will judge humans according to how their deeds relate to his will. The psalm concludes with the reminder that each person will be rewarded "according to what he has done" (62:12).

---

16. From a verbal root *gzl* ("strip off/away; take by force"), the term describes "robbery" and is prohibited in Lev. 6:1–7.

17. See also Prov. 11:28; 27:24; Eccl. 7:7.

18. The term is *ḥesed* ("covenant loyalty; loyal love and commitment").

19. A. Weiser, *Psalms: A Commentary*, trans. H. Hartwell (OTL: Philadelphia: Westminster, 1971), 452.

Being still. Psalm 62 begins with the awkward but impressive image of finding a place of stillness in relation to God. In this passage the Hebrew root describes a kind of motionless waiting—a sort of "holy inactivity" in anticipation of divine action and deliverance. The lack of movement—the stillness of the whole being (*nepeš*; NIV "soul")—indicates the psalmist's trust and confidence. There are a variety of Hebrew words and phrases in the Old Testament to capture aspects of this kind of "holy inactivity." In what follows, I will consider what each has to add to this biblical idea.

(1) *Keep still.* In Exodus 14, the Israelites, having fled Egypt following the death of the firstborn, find themselves in a difficult spot. The pursuing army of Pharaoh has caught them up against the sea, with no way to escape. The Israelites, aware of the approaching Egyptians, mob Moses in a panic, expressing their fear in terms of wishing they had never left Egypt in the first place. Moses responds in words most often used to encourage troops just before an attack: "Do not be afraid. Stand firm and you will see the deliverance the LORD will bring you today" (14:13).

I can imagine the Israelites fingering what few weapons they may have possessed in fearful anticipation of a clash with the professional Egyptian charioteers. But Moses goes on: "The LORD will fight for you; you *need only to be still*" (Ex. 14:14). That is a decidedly *un*militaristic exhortation, especially since the word employed (*ḥrš*) means "keep still, be silent; let someone do something without objection."[20] The Israelites were encouraged *not to fight* but to allow God to fight for them. Their inactivity was to be a sign of their trust and reliance on God, that he would do what they could not hope to do alone.[21]

The verb used in Psalm 62:1 (*dmm*) expresses much of the same idea as *ḥrš*. Both have the sense of *remaining* still, not beginning activity, although *dmm* may have a bit more emphasis on motionlessness. Note Psalm 4:4: "In your anger do not sin; when you are on your beds, search your hearts and be silent [*dmm*]."[22] The point is not to get caught up in frantic activity that relies on human strength.

Another related term is the verb *šqṭ* ("have peace, quiet; be at peace, in a tranquil state"). This word often describes political tranquility in the land or a city (Josh. 11:23; 2 Kings 11:20; Isa. 32:17), though it can also speak of divine (Isa. 18:4; 62:1) or human (Ruth 3:18) inactivity.

---

20. Holladay, *CHALOT*, 118.

21. In some occurrences of *ḥrš* is a sense of "keep silent" (e.g., 2 Kings 18:36). See also Gen. 24:21; Num. 30:4.

22. See also Ps. 37:7; Isa. 23:2; Jer. 47:6.

A different nuance is added by the Hebrew verb *rph*, normally in the Hiphil. Here activity is in process and *must be stopped*. "Cease! Desist!" most accurately captures the force of this verb. With this word Yahweh commands the nations of the world to cease their endless struggles for power and domination and to acknowledge God's sovereignty: "Be still, and know that I am God; I will be exalted among the nations, I will be exalted in the earth" (Ps. 46:10).[23]

(2) *Be silent.* Silence is another way to demonstrate "holy inactivity." Often it seems that Israel did not "do" silence well. (They would have had a difficult time being Quakers!) They constantly voiced their complaints and laments to God and his human representatives. (We should probably be grateful for their verbal persistence, since much of their conversation with God has found its way into Scripture for our benefit.) Sometimes their "many words" needed to be stilled in order to allow them to hear God speaking or to see him acting in their behalf.[24]

Several Hebrew verbs capture this sense of silence. The most common verb (*hsh*) is often used as an imperative interjection commanding silence. Something like an emphatic "Shhhh!" *hsh* means "Hush!" or "Be quiet!" In Nehemiah 8:11 the Levites quieted the vocal lamenting of the people by commanding them to "be still, for this is a sacred day. Do not grieve." The prophet Zechariah admonishes humankind at the approach of Yahweh: "Be still before the LORD, all mankind, because he has roused himself from his holy dwelling" (Zech. 2:13).[25]

Two less frequent verbs also offer a similar case of "be silent." One (*skt*) occurs only once in Deuteronomy 27:9, where Moses and the Levitical priests call the gathered Israelites to "be silent ... and listen" to the commands of God. The second (*ʾlm*) appears in Psalm 31:18, where the psalmist appeals to God to let the "lying lips [of his enemies] be silenced, for with pride and contempt they speak arrogantly against the righteous."[26]

Stillness and quietness, then, reflect a strong theme in Israel's understanding of her relationship to Yahweh. When Yahweh comes, silence shows proper respect and attention in order to learn his will and purpose. Cessation of activity mirrors the Sabbath rest, which witnesses to Israel's dependence

23. See also Ex. 4:26; Judg. 8:3; 1 Sam. 15:16.

24. See Eccl. 5:3, 7; Matt. 6:7.

25. See also Judg. 3:19.

26. The verb *ʾlm* is found also in God's warning to Ezekiel that "I will make your tongue stick to the roof of your mouth so that you will be silent"; as a result, Ezekiel was unable to prophesy against his people until released from his divinely imposed muteness (Ezek. 3:26; cf. 24:27; 33:323, where the prophet is at last allowed to speak). The noun of the same root describes those who are mute (cf. Ex. 4:11; Ps. 38:13; Isa. 35:6)

on God rather than on human strength and endeavor. Frantic activity, whether in conflict with the enemy or in pursuit of wealth and personal security, does not acknowledge the strength and power of God as the place of refuge and ultimate security in the midst of trouble. Quiet repose in the face of attack is the ultimate evidence of trust in God and reliance on *his* strength.[27]

Divine temple oracles. It seems apparent from this and other psalms that God "spoke" to his people in the context of temple worship. If Israel is anything like the peoples in her ancient Near Eastern context, this probably means that there were in the service of the temple certain cultic "prophets," whose role was to provide a divine word at particular points in the worship liturgy. Most likely this kind of prophetic utterance was not a regular feature of worship but came in response to sporadic needs and significant events that seemed to call for divine insight and direction. Such an occasion may have been the enthronement of the new king, and the divine pronouncement of authorization recorded in 2:6–7 seems to capture the speech of the cultic prophet in Yahweh's behalf: "I have installed my king on Zion, my holy hill. . . . . You are my son, today I have become your father."[28] This scene may have been replayed as often as a new king took the throne of the kingdom.

In Psalm 50, almost the entire psalm (50:7–23) is given over to a word of Yahweh against the emptiness of sacrifice accompanied with dishonesty, theft, and slander. Similarly 81:6–16 is occupied with an extended divine speech rehearsing Israel's failure to respond faithfully to God's gracious care.[29]

In other psalms the voice of God punctuates in smaller utterances. Take, for example, Psalm 110, where two brief oracles are reported (110:1, 4) in the midst of a more extended discussion of divine support of the king. In 46:10, God breaks into the psalmist's ongoing description of God's mighty deeds to call all nations to acknowledge his sovereignty: "Be still, and know that I am God; I will be exalted among the nations, I will be exalted in the earth."[30]

---

27. This does not, of course, mean that God expected Israel never to act or work to secure her life and well-being. The Sabbath rest did not preclude labor on the other six days. God's action against Israel's enemies did not eliminate the need for an army and fortress cities. The focus is on the source of ultimate security and the elimination of frantic activity as a result of reliance on faulty human power.

28. Though the NIV uses "Son" and "Father," I have made them lowercase (see comments on 2:6–7).

29. Others would include the entrance liturgies (Pss. 12; 15; 24; 36; and others) in this group of extended divine pronouncements given by cult prophets in the context of worship. See esp. the commentary of C. Broyles on these psalms. Cf. also 82:2–7.

30. Other examples of brief divine utterances that may have been delivered by a cult prophet include: 75:3–5; 91:14–16; 95:8–11.

Considerable debate has developed among the scholars regarding the presence and function of prophetic personnel in association with the temple and worship.[31] General consensus seems to support the conclusion that some temple personnel had the responsibility to respond to inquiries with a divine "word" of insight or direction. Such words might be of condemnation and judgment, exhortation and direction, or deliverance and hope. Statements such as those mentioned above in the psalms reflect the public promulgation of these divine utterances within the context of temple worship.

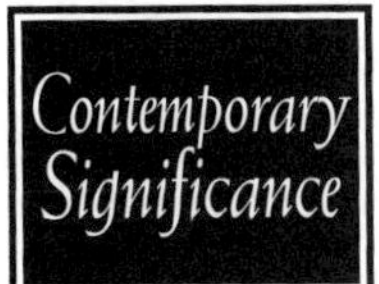

FINDING REST IN GOD ALONE. As a child and young adult growing up in southeast Texas, not far from the Gulf of Mexico, one of my most vivid memories is of enduring the frequent hurricanes that battered the coastal areas between Galveston and New Orleans. On more than one occasion my family took in provisions, boarded up and taped the windows of the old frame house in which we lived, turned on the battery-operated radio, and hunkered down to wait the storm out. As the flood waters rose in the yard outside, invariably the lights went out, and we sat in the dark listening to the radio report of the storm's progress and the damage left in its wake. Outside the winds howled, the trees were whipped in the wind, and often broken limbs, large and small, lay strewn on the yard and occasionally on the roof.

The display of nature unleashed was always powerful and impressive, but for me the eeriest and most unnerving part of the whole experience was the unnatural calm that descended on us as the eye of the storm moved over us. The winds ceased, and an almost smothering quiet ruled the night. Rain, if there was any, fell gently and almost straight down rather than driven horizontally by the wind. This continued, sometimes for an extended period, until the other side of the eye reached us, and the wind resumed its battering attack on our home and anything left standing in its path.

Later, the calm in the eye of the storm came to provide for me an experiential metaphor for the kind of inward calm needed to face the hurricanes life sometimes tosses at us. It is not an entirely accurate metaphor, perhaps, because the dying winds at the storm's center carry a sort of sinister edge insofar as we know it is only a brief respite before the storm returns. But it does provide a helpful image of a moment of calm at the center when all around you is swirling out of control and life is being turned upside down by the destructive power of the storm.

31. For a helpful summary, see the article on "Prophets" in *ISBE*², 3:992–93.

Having personally gone through several hurricanes since those early days in Texas, I know what it is like to long for a place of confident calm in the midst of the chaotic attack of life gone amok. I have hungered for the kind of confident repose that permeates Psalm 62, with its repeated inclusio: "My soul finds rest [stillness] in God alone; my salvation comes from him. He alone is my rock and my salvation; he is my fortress, I will never be shaken" (62:1–2; cf. vv. 5–6). What can this psalm tell us about achieving unshakable calm? How do we find the still point?

Artur Weiser offers a powerful translation of the opening phrase: "My soul is still if focused on God alone."[32] With eyes on the storm, there seems no hope to overcome it. With eyes turned toward self, there is no personal power equal to the task. Only when one is able to focus on God alone does the power of the storm recede in response to his command, "Peace! Be still!" Only then is our lack of power swallowed up in his complete adequacy. Here are three avenues to the calm center we seek, based on God's word in Psalm 62.

(1) In the face of the attack. The kind of calm confidence we seek is not found in the absence of an attack. The narrator of the psalm acknowledges that outside the center of calm, all hell is *still* breaking loose. The winds still howl, the rain still blows horizontally. Yet there is calm at the center. My experience has been that as long as I am intent on escaping or avoiding the trouble that assails me, there is no hope for a quiet still point in my life. The trouble, whatever it might be, assumes impossible proportions beyond any hope. But simply to acknowledge to myself and another that the trouble is real is to begin to rob the situation of its power to attack me.

(2) Acknowledging my dependence on God. Giving up my attempts to escape or avoid attack also forces me to acknowledge just how dependent I am on God alone. As the psalmist puts it: "My salvation and my honor depend on God; he is my mighty rock, my refuge" (62:7). Whenever I accept the lack of power and control I have over any situation, calm begins to descend. It is strange but true. To acknowledge my rightful place in the world—that I am not particularly unique and that I am powerless, out of control, needy, dependent—actually restores a sense of calm. If there is nothing I can do, I don't have to do anything. I am able to "be still and know that [he] is God" (46:10). I am able to allow God to fight for me so that I have only to be still (Ex. 14:14).

(3) Pour out your hearts to him. This kind of confident stillness does carry a price tag. It involves vulnerability and transparency before God. The words the psalmist uses are "pour out your hearts to him" (62:8). The verb "pour out"

32. Weiser, *Psalms*, 448.

describes the complete pouring out of a liquid with no reserve—nothing held back. That might be water on the desert sands;[33] a libation of oil or wine before Yahweh;[34] the lifeblood of a murder victim or sacrifice;[35] or metaphorically anger,[36] God's spirit,[37] one's mind,[38] or the heart.[39] To enter the still point of confidence afforded by God's power means opening ourselves completely to God: our need, our fears, our weakness, our sin. This kind of vulnerable honesty is characteristic of the psalmists as a whole and is the foundation of their trust in God.

33. Ex. 4:9; 1 Sam. 7:6; Ps. 22:14.
34. Judg. 6:20; Isa. 57:6.
35. Cf., e.g., Gen. 9:6; 37:22; Ex. 29:12; Lev. 4:7; 17:13.
36. Isa. 42:25; Ezek. 9:8.
37. Joel 2:28–29.
38. Ps. 42:4.
39. 1 Sam. 1:15; Lam. 2:19.

Psalm 63

A PSALM OF David. When he was in the Desert of Judah.

1 O God, you are my God,
earnestly I seek you;
my soul thirsts for you,
my body longs for you,
in a dry and weary land
where there is no water.

2 I have seen you in the sanctuary
and beheld your power and your glory.
3 Because your love is better than life,
my lips will glorify you.
4 I will praise you as long as I live,
and in your name I will lift up my hands.
5 My soul will be satisfied as with the richest of foods;
with singing lips my mouth will praise you.

6 On my bed I remember you;
I think of you through the watches of the night.
7 Because you are my help,
I sing in the shadow of your wings.
8 My soul clings to you;
your right hand upholds me.

9 They who seek my life will be destroyed;
they will go down to the depths of the earth.
10 They will be given over to the sword
and become food for jackals.

11 But the king will rejoice in God;
all who swear by God's name will praise him,
while the mouths of liars will be silenced.

PSALM 63 IS a plea for God's presence that is most closely related to the psalms of confidence. The psalmist speaks about an experience of isolation from God that is characterized in 63:1 as an earnest search for water in a "dry and weary land." This imagery allows God

to be seen both as the "water of life" that satisfies completely (63:5; cf. John 4:7–15) and as the God who saves from life-threatening circumstances—whether the imagined desert or the enemies surrounding the psalmist (Ps. 63:9–10).

Certain phrases ("in the sanctuary," 63:2a; "on my bed," 63:6a; "watches of the night," 63:6b; "shadow of your wings," 63:7b) suggest an experience of "incubation," in which a supplicant spends a night in the temple seeking a word from God.[1] Alternatively, the psalm may refer to one under attack who seeks asylum in the temple from those "who seek my life" (63:9).

Various connections link Psalm 63 with Psalm 61. These include the "divine name theology" (63:4; cf. 61:5, 8),[2] taking shelter under God's "wings" (63:7; cf. 61:4),[3] a vow to endless praise of God's name (63:4; cf. 61:8), and a shift to third-person reference to the king at the end (63:11; cf. 61:6–7). On this last issue, it is uncertain whether the psalmist is thought to be the narrator of the entire psalm or is expressing his personal concern only in the final verse.

Structurally the psalm falls into three sections: the opening search for God (63:1), the satisfying vision of God in the sanctuary (63:2–8), and a concluding confidence of deliverance (63:9–11).

The Heading (63:0)

THE PSALM IS simply attributed to David and contains the brief and general statement of historical context: "when he [David] was in the Desert of Judah." The phrase most likely pictures the (considerable) period of time in David's early career when he was fleeing Saul and found refuge in the rugged terrain of the Negev region south of Hebron. No specific event is detailed here, but the general setting is provided by 1 Samuel 21–31.

Thirst for God (63:1)

THE PSALMIST BEGINS with an expression of commitment to God. "O God [*ʾelohim*],[4] you are my God, earnestly I seek you." Despite the sense of isolation

---

1. For further discussion of incubation, see comments on 57:6–11.

2. See the discussion of the divine name Yahweh in the comments on Ps. 8.

3. See also the similar reference in 57:1: "I will take refuge in the shadow of your wings."

4. If the phrase, "O God, you are my God" seems a bit awkward and redundant, it is. Ps. 63 is part of what is called the Elohistic Psalter (see comments on Ps. 42), and the more generic term *ʾelohim* (God) often appears where the more specific divine name Yahweh is expected. Cf. Isa. 25:1, which begins with a similar affirmation of Yahweh as God ("O LORD, you are my God"), while in Ps. 140:6 the psalmist speaks of Yahweh using almost the exact phrase: ("O LORD, I say to you, 'You are my God'").

from God that follows, the psalmist remains committed in relationship with God, and it is this commitment that lays the foundation for his confidence of deliverance.

The narrative continues with the effective imagery of a parched traveler searching for life like looking for water in a "dry and weary land."[5] For the psalmist, God is just such a rare and life-giving commodity for which he longs. The verb "seek" has the edge of an "earnest, intent, focused" search. The one who has crossed the desert on foot knows the life-and-death importance of water sources and keeps an intent lookout for any evidences of moisture. In the same way, the psalmist is keeping an intent lookout for any evidence of God's saving presence.

It seems obvious, then, that the psalmist regards his circumstances as life-threatening and senses a distance—even isolation—from God. The distinction between his "soul" (*nepeš*) and "body" (*baśar*) is not the tension between an enduring "spirit" and the transient "body" characteristic of Greek thought. Instead, the *nepeš* emphasizes the divinely animated being that is capable of self-awareness and reflection, while *baśar* encapsulates the psalmist's physical wants and needs. His entire being is intently focused on experiencing the liberating presence of God.

Satisfying Vision of God (63:2–8)

I HAVE SEEN **you in the sanctuary.** In the midst of the psalmist's isolation and an earnest search for God, he experiences a vision of God that sustains him. The verb translated "have seen" is not the usual verb for seeing (*rʾh*) but its more uncommon counterpart, *ḥzh*. This latter verb frequently describes a vision from God. Often a prophetic message is conveyed in such a vision.[6]

The psalmist's vision is of God "in the sanctuary." This is reminiscent of Isaiah's vision of Yahweh in the Jerusalem temple (Isa. 6:1–9) and has the similar effect of reminding the psalmist in an almost overwhelming way of God's "power and ... glory" (63:2). This experience provides him with two sustaining insights: (1) God remains powerful despite the psalmist's sense of distance and abandonment, and (2) God's love (*ḥesed*) is even more satisfying than life itself. The former provides the psalmist with hope that God may yet act in deliverance; the latter offers the courage to remain faithfully committed in the

5. The two terms mean "waterless" (*ṣiyyah*) and "faint, exhausted" (*ʿayep* here probably "with thirst").

6. Cf. the visions of Ezekiel in Ezek. 8. Amos received visions from Yahweh that are recorded in Amos 7–8. Note the reference to "vision" as the mode of prophetic reception in the opening verses of Isaiah, Obadiah, Micah, and Nahum.

face of the possibility of death.[7] The remainder of this section of the psalm follows this division as the psalmist first praises God for his power (63:3b–5) and then commits faithfully to cling to God's sustaining love (63:6–8).

My lips will glorify you. The vision catapults the psalmist into a paean of hopeful praise. Verbs of praise dominate these verses as he promises: "My lips will glorify [*šbḥ*] you"; "I will bless [*brk*; NIV praise] you";[8] "I will lift up [*nś'*] my hands";[9] and "my mouth will praise [*hll*] you." The psalmist's praise is no hidden or silent prayer but a public display that involves spoken testimony, physical gestures ("lift the hands"), and joyous singing ("my singing lips"). The promise to praise God "as long as I live" is reminiscent of the similar promise in 61:8: "Then will I ever sing praise to your name."

My soul will be satisfied. The vision of God's glorious power and committed love provides the thirsting psalmist with life-sustaining satisfaction. Again, it is not some disembodied spiritual part of the psalmist that is being fed but his whole animated being—the self-aware *nepeš*, which includes mind and body together. The earnest search in the opening verses finds its object in the vision of God's sustaining power and love.

On my bed I remember you. Remembering God while "on my bed" or "through the watches of the night" means the psalmist is not calmly sleeping but wakefully worrying! In the midst of this nocturnal tension, however, he recalls the vision of God's enduring, committed love (*ḥesed*) and is sustained by that memory. Because of God's help he is able to "sing in the shadow of [God's] wings" (63:7),[10] and the "self" (*nepeš*) that was satisfied in 63:5 now "clings" to the protective care of God (63:8).

Confidence of Deliverance (63:9–11)

FROM THE PLACE of confidence gained through the vision in the sanctuary of God's glorious power and sustaining concern, the psalmist is also able to

---

7. A similar insight motivated Daniel's three friends Shadrach, Meshach, and Abednego when confronted with the choice between bowing down to the pagan idol or being thrown into the fiery furnace (Dan. 3). Their response to the king exhibits a similar tension between hope and resolution: "If we are thrown into the blazing furnace, the God we serve is able to save us from it, and he will rescue us from your hand, O king. But even if he does not, we want you to know, O king, that we will not serve your gods or worship the image of gold you have set up" (3:17–18).

8. Once again the NIV demonstrates its hesitancy to ascribe to humans the ability to *bless* God, preferring instead to translate *brk* as "praise" (see comments on 16:7).

9. The act of "lifting up the hands" to God is a gesture of worship—primarily denoting prayer or direct communication with God. This can be supplication (cf. Ex. 17:16; Pss. 28:2; 141:2; Lam. 2:19), confession (Lam. 3:41), or (as here) praise (cf. Pss. 119:48; 134:2).

10. A probable reference to the "wings" of the seraphim that overshadow the ark of the covenant in the sanctuary (cf. comments on 57:1).

envision the destruction of the enemy. "They who seek [his] life" will themselves experience destruction[11] and will descend into "the depths of the earth"—a euphemism for Sheol, the abode of the dead.

They will be given over to the sword. Two violent images follow the more general statements of confidence in the enemy's defeat. In the first the life of the enemy (lit.) "pours out" upon the "handles" of a (violently thrusted) "sword." In the second, the body of the slain enemy, left exposed on the battleground, becomes "food for jackals"—not a pleasant picture, but one common enough to those familiar with the carnage left in the aftermath of pitched battle. It is certainly no accident that God satisfies the hunger and thirst of the psalmist while the enemies themselves become "food" for jackals. He is confident that God will defeat the enemy decisively so that there is no doubt of his ability to exercise protective care over the faithful.

The king will rejoice in God. Up to here there has been no mention of the king, so his appearance here at the end is unexpected. Similarly, the king was mentioned toward the end of Psalm 61, where an individual plea for deliverance directed to God in the first person turned unexpectedly to a third-person supplication for the long life and eternal reign of the king, before returning to a final first-person promise to praise.[12] Here at the end of Psalm 63, the king surfaces once again in a third-person reference. As in Psalm 61, this final section adds the voices of "all who swear by [God's?] name" to the plea of the psalmist/king.[13] The confidence of the gathered community is unmistakable. King and people *will* find cause for rejoicing and praise, while those who attack the king "will be silenced"—an indication that their primary offense is verbal assault rather than physical.

---

11. The first half of 63:9 is difficult and reads more literally, "and they to destruction [or 'in vain'] they seek my life." The difference in the consonantal text between "to destruction" (*lšwʾh*) and "in vain" (*lšwʾ*) is the matter of a single final letter *-h*, which is in this case a *mater lectionis* added to mark a long vowel. The normal Hebrew phrase for the NIV's "they who seek my life" is *mebaqše napši* rather than *yebaqšu napši*, as in this verse.

12. See comments on 61:6–7.

13. The NIV translation makes explicit what is left ambiguous in the Heb. text. In the Heb. the phrase reads: "All those who swear by *him* will praise," so that it remains unclear whether the people are swearing by *God* or by the *king*. In addition, it is striking that in the consonantal text the Niphal participle from *šbʿ* ("those who swear") would look identical to the Niphal participle from *śbʿ* (*hanniśbaʿ*, "those who are satisfied")—a reading that would make important connections with the psalmist's earlier phrase, "my soul will be satisfied" (*tiśbaʿ napši*), in 63:5.

THIRSTING FOR GOD. On tours to Israel, one of the first pieces of information a tour guide shares is a warning about the dangers and symptoms of dehydration. Almost everyone carries bottled water with them wherever they go since public drinking water is not commonly available. One quickly learns to distinguish the earliest sign of dehydration not as a desire for water but as a dull headache that sets in behind the eyes.

The idea of thirst is a common figure in biblical literature. The land of the Bible is arid, the sources of water limited, and the consequences of dehydration severe or deadly. Thirst played a prominent role in the travels of the Exodus Israelites,[14] and the memory of this thirst and God's quenching of it continued as an important memory of the community.[15] In the Prophets, thirst is often mentioned as a sign of divine punishment,[16] while abundant water indicates his blessing.[17]

As an image of spiritual longing for God, thirst appears in Psalm 42:2 ("my soul thirsts for God, for the living God") and in 143:6 ("my soul thirsts for you like a parched land"), as well as the beginning of Psalm 63. Those who thirst after God will find satisfaction with him. "Come, all you who are thirsty, come to the waters.... Come, buy wine and milk without money and without cost.... Listen, listen to me, and eat what is good, and your soul will delight in the richest of fare" (Isa. 55:1–2; cf. Ps. 63:5a).

This image is picked up in the New Testament, where the appropriate attitude of desire for God will be satisfied: "Blessed are those who hunger and thirst for righteousness, for they will be filled" (Matt. 5:6). "Everyone who drinks this water will be thirsty again, but whoever drinks the water I give him will never thirst" (John 4:13–14). "If anyone is thirsty, let him come to me and drink" (John 7:37). "'Come!' Whoever is thirsty, let him come; and whoever wishes, let him take the free gift of the water of life" (Rev. 22:17).

The name of God. Reference to the "name" (*šem*) of God in 63:4 opens an important thematic link with the group of psalms extending at least from Psalms 61–72.[18] The significance of the divine name "Yahweh" has been discussed before (cf. esp. Ps. 8), and references to his "name" (Heb. *šem*) are common throughout the Psalter. Such an emphasis on the "name" of God in

---

14. Cf. Ex. 15:22–27; 17:1–6; Num. 20:2–11; 33:14; Deut. 8:15; 23:4.

15. Ps. 78:15–20; Neh. 9:15, 20.

16. Isa. 5:13; 50:2; Jer. 14:3; Hos. 2:3; Amos 8:13.

17. Pss. 65:9; 104:10–11; 105:41; 107:35; Isa. 44:3; 49:10.

18. It might be possible to trace this linkage all the way back to Ps. 44, near the beginning of Book 2.

the Elohistic Psalter is interesting, for this section of the Psalter is characterized by a reduction (or even elimination) of the number of times the Tetragrammaton *yhwh* (Yahweh) appears.[19]

Just by looking at the occurrences of *šem* in Book 2 a sort of ideology of that name can be developed. In Psalm 44, we learn that "the name" provides power to "trample our foes" (44:5) and that to "forget the name" (44:20) is synonymous to worshiping other gods. God's "name" is praiseworthy (44:8; 54:6; 61:8; 63:4; 66:4; 68:4; 69:30), and by his "name" knowledge of God is extended throughout the earth (48:10). The name of God is "good" (52:9; 54:6) and the source of Israel's hope (52:9). "Fear" of God's name is the equivalent of "fear of the LORD" and is the source of divine relationship and benefit (61:5). God's name ensures commitment and honesty as the basis of swearing (63:11). God's name, like his deeds, is glorious (66:2–3), and love of his name is the foundation of dwelling in the land (69:36).

The gift of the divine name to Israel bespeaks a special relationship in which Yahweh's people define themselves in relationship to the character the name signifies. The classic priestly benediction on Israel in Numbers 6:24–26 contains a threefold repetition of the divine name Yahweh and concludes with the explanatory gloss from God: "So they [the priests] will put my name on the Israelites, and I will bless them" (Num. 6:27). To "put" Yahweh's name on Israel is to claim them as his special possession under his sovereign authority and care, and it defines their character henceforth in relation to him alone.

To "praise" or "bless" the name of Yahweh means more than to verbally pronounce blessing or praise. There is a real sense in which for Israel to live in ways that are consistent with the character of Yahweh is to live up to his name and thus to bless and praise it. On the contrary, however, Israel blasphemes God's name, not when she uses the name in crude profanity, but when she takes his name as her defining characteristic and then lives in such ways that violate the very nature of God. Thus, to take Yahweh's name and then to worship other gods is to thumb one's nose at his "jealous," monotheistic character. To rely on the "temple of the LORD, the temple of the LORD, the temple of the LORD" (Jer. 7:4) to protect Yahweh's people and to exploit others in the community through deceit, injustice, abusive power, and so on, is to reject the character of Yahweh, the judge. To rely exclusively on the power of king, military, politics, or economics is to deny the kingship and power of Yahweh and thus to blaspheme his name.

The psalms in this section of the Psalter, especially those mentioning the "name" (*šem*), stress the need to rely on God alone as strength, refuge, and

19. See the discussion of the Elohistic Psalter in the comments on Pss. 42–43.

fortress. Thus they affirm, praise, and commit themselves to the power and character of the "name" and the God who bears it.

YOUR LOVE IS **better than life.** When is God's love better than life? Jewish and Christian martyrs had to make this decision when confronted with the choice of recanting their faith in God or facing torturous forms of death. Such choices were known during the exilic period. Shadrach, Meshach, and Abednego resolved to die in the flames of the fiery furnace set up by Nebuchadnezzar rather than to worship the Babylonian gods (Dan. 3). Daniel himself faced the lions' den when he chose to continue to pray to Yahweh after the worship of non-Babylonian deities had been outlawed. (Dan. 6). The narratives in 2 Maccabees 6–7 describes the savage suppression of Judaism under Antiochus IV and the willingness of faithful Jews to accept death rather than forsake their beliefs. The New Testament also speaks of martyrs (including Stephen) who were more willing to hold on to God's love than their lives (cf. Heb. 11:35–40).

The teaching of both Old and New Testaments agrees that knowing God and his love is more satisfying than life itself. Job refuses to end his suffering by cursing God and declares his enduring faith in the classic profession: "Though he [God] slay me, yet will I hope in him" (Job 13:15).[20] Jesus teaches that only those willing to lose their lives will truly experience the nature of Christian life dependent on God's power and love (Matt. 16:25; Mark 8:35; Luke 9:24).

What would we be willing to die for today? Not too much in our comfortable society. Perhaps we would give up our lives for family—that is, our spouse or children. But our psalm tells us that God's love, his *ḥesed*, is "better than life itself." Kraus puts it well: "Even life, which in the OT is the 'highest good,' pales in the brilliance of *ḥsd*, which alone provides the gifts of satisfaction and fulfillment."[21] Is there some way here and now that the love of God—his fierce loyalty to his covenant relationship—makes that kind of difference in your life? Does it make such a difference that it wouldn't be worth living without it? Is your connection with God so important to you that you would sacrifice all your future hopes and dreams to keep connected with God?

---

20. An alternative reading of this passage raises some question whether Job is expressing such a robust faith: "He will surely slay me; I have no hope—yet I will defend my ways to his face."

21. Kraus, *Psalms 60–150*, 21.

That is what Abraham did in Genesis 22. He had finally won his way through a long process of growing understanding that God intended to carry out the restoration of his whole creation through his descendants. God clarified that regardless of Abraham's advanced age and his wife's infertility, his descendants were to come through his own physical child, not through an adopted slave or the child of a handmaiden. Having seen the miracle of Isaac's impossible birth accomplished beyond all hope, we might wonder how Abraham could possibly then take that special son on a three-day journey to Mount Moriah, specifically for the purpose of sacrificing him there at the command of God (Gen. 22). He did it because his relationship with God was more important than theology, or logic, or human emotion. It was better than life!

Jesus didn't *want* to die on the cross. He asked God if he could pass—if there wasn't some other way (Matt. 26:39). But he went to the cross willingly because God's love (for Jesus, and through Jesus for you and for me) was better than life. This is no "pie in the sky by and by" Christianity. It is a realistic, hard, true, here-and-now faith that endures faithfully because God lives and loves faithfully and enduringly in our lives now and here. May God's committed covenant love so fill you that you will come to know the abundant life that does not depend on our ability to stay alive.

Psalm 64

FOR THE DIRECTOR of music. A psalm of David.

[1] Hear me, O God, as I voice my complaint;
protect my life from the threat of the enemy.
[2] Hide me from the conspiracy of the wicked,
from that noisy crowd of evildoers.

[3] They sharpen their tongues like swords
and aim their words like deadly arrows.
[4] They shoot from ambush at the innocent man;
they shoot at him suddenly, without fear.

[5] They encourage each other in evil plans,
they talk about hiding their snares;
they say, "Who will see them?"
[6] They plot injustice and say,
"We have devised a perfect plan!"
Surely the mind and heart of man are cunning.

[7] But God will shoot them with arrows;
suddenly they will be struck down.
[8] He will turn their own tongues against them
and bring them to ruin;
all who see them will shake their heads in scorn.

[9] All mankind will fear;
they will proclaim the works of God
and ponder what he has done.
[10] Let the righteous rejoice in the LORD
and take refuge in him;
let all the upright in heart praise him!

PSALM 64 CONTINUES the common thread of pleading for deliverance from the vocal assaults of the enemy begun in Psalm 63. At the end of that psalm, the psalmist (identified in the closing verses as the king) anticipated that his detractors would be "silenced" (63:11c). Psalm 64 begins with a description of "that noisy crowd of evildoers," who

use their vocal skills ("tongues . . . words") like weapons ("swords . . . arrows") to ambush the psalmist (64:2–4).

Psalm 64 is also part of the larger complex of Psalms 56–68, in which God's mighty acts demonstrate his power over *all* the earth so that an increasingly expansive group joins in praising him. This increasing crescendo of praise ultimately includes the "whole earth" (66:1, 4, 8; 67:3–5; 68) as the nations are subdued (66:7), acknowledge God's power, and join in praise for his works (67:3–4, 7).[1] Psalm 64, while acknowledging the reality of present suffering and attack, anticipates a future in which all humanity will fear God, proclaim his works, and reflect on what he has done (64:9). Thus, rejoicing is the present and future vocation of the righteous, who find their refuge in God (64:10).

The psalm is divided into four units: an opening plea for deliverance (64:1–2), a description of the arrogance of the wicked (64:3–6), anticipated judgment (64:7–8), and concluding praise and trust (64:9–10).

The Heading (64:0)

NO NEW TERMS appear in the heading of Psalm 64. There is the by now familiar reference to "the director of music,"[2] and the composition is described in most general terms as a "psalm [*mizmor*] of David."[3]

Plea for Deliverance (64:1–2)

THE OPENING PLEA calls "God"[4] to "hear" the complaint that occupies the psalmist's concern. The problem is a terrifying (*paḥad*) and life-threatening

---

1. Note the progression of praise begun esp. in 61:8 (I will "ever sing praise to your name"), continued in 63:11 ("all who swear by God's name will praise him"), escalated in 64:9 ("all mankind will fear . . . proclaim . . . ponder . . . rejoice . . . take refuge . . . praise him"). This praise is anticipated in 65:1 and culminates in the two (non-Davidic) praise hymns, Pss. 66 and 67: "Shout with joy to God all the earth! Sing the glory of his name. . . . All the earth bows down to you" (66:1–4); "May the peoples . . . all the peoples praise you . . . nations of the earth . . . all the ends of the earth will fear him" (67:3–7). In this context Ps. 68, with its description of the triumphant Yahweh, fresh from subduing the nations and entering the sanctuary to the praise of the whole world, forms a fitting conclusion to this series of psalms.

2. See the comments on the heading of Ps. 4.

3. See the comments on the heading of Ps. 3.

4. The operative term for God in this psalm is *ʾelohim*, as is the tendency throughout the Elohistic Psalter (Pss. 42–83). This phenomenon (of using *ʾelohim* rather than the more personal divine name *yhwh* [Yahweh]) is particularly exaggerated in Pss. 60–67, where *yhwh* occurs only once (64:10). Nowhere else in the Elohistic Psalter does such a stretch of psalms with so few appearances of *yhwh* occur. This is particularly striking in this group of

attack by his enemies. The attack is characterized as a "conspiracy" (*sod* ["circle of confidants"]) and the attackers as a "noisy crowd of evildoers." In the following verses, the enemy attack is described primarily in terms of *vocal* attack (cf. 64:3, 5, 6, 8), but—like a shouting lynch mob—one with possibly lethal results. The psalmist seeks divine protection and refuge from the enemy attack.

The Arrogance of the Wicked (64:3–6)

THE DEADLY WORDS of the enemies cut and pierce. They are metaphorically described as "swords," which they "sharpen" for the attack, and "deadly arrows"[5] are unleashed toward the unsuspecting psalmist (64:3–4). He is "innocent" (*tam*)[6] and completely unprepared for the "ambush" that comes without warning. The utter arrogance of the wicked is displayed in their sense of impunity. They feel they can attack without "fear"—either of God or human opponents.

The enemy find courage in numbers and plot their attacks in advance. This is no series of scattered individual attacks but a well-orchestrated attempt to bring the psalmist down.[7] He describes well the mutual encouragement to evil with a resulting false sense of security that arises in such grumbling plots. The enemy embolden one another, assuming that no one (including God) will observe or hinder their attack. They convince themselves their plan has no possible flaw.[8]

The section concludes with the ironic comment of the narrator: "Surely the mind and heart of man are cunning" (64:6c). Perhaps a more apt

---

psalms since at the same time reference is made to the "name" (*šem*) of God—an oblique pointer to *yhwh*—on no fewer than five occasions (61:5, 8; 63:4; 66:2, 4). On either side of this group of eight psalms the reticence about the use of the name *yhwh* disappears. The name occurs three times in Ps. 59, five times in Ps. 68, five times in Ps. 69, and an additional five in the combined Pss. 70–71.

5. The word "deadly" does not actually appear in the Heb. text, either of this verse or the related reference to God's arrows in 64:7a. For related imagery of attack with arrows—both divine and human—cf. Job 6:4; Ps. 7:13; Prov. 26:18; Jer. 9:8; Ezek. 5:16.

6. The same term is used by God of Job in his conversation with Satan (Job 1:8; 2:3) and is coupled there (and elsewhere) with the further descriptor of righteousness: *yašar* ("upright"). The word *tam* has the sense "complete, whole, right" and denotes life lived as God intends.

7. There is much in these verses that resonates with the grumbling conspiracy and association with the wicked that characterizes Pss. 1 and 2.

8. They cry out together: *tamnu ḥepeś meḥupaś* (lit., "We have perfected a well-researched plot"). It is striking that the enemy employ the verb *tmm*, which has the same root meaning ("whole, complete, perfect") as the noun *tam*, used to describe the innocence of the psalmist (64:5a).

translation that captures his negative assessment of the enemies' plotting would be: "The inward deliberations of a man and his heart are impenetrable!" You can almost see the psalmist's head shaking with ironic confusion over how the enemy could come to such a misguided and totally erroneous conclusion.

Judgment Is Coming (64:7–8)

HOW LITTLE UNDERSTANDING the cunning conspirators possess is driven home as the God whom they assume takes no notice of their attack takes unerring aim to strike them down. The weapons he uses in judgment mirror those the enemy deployed in their attack. God shoots them with arrows, and they find themselves cut down just as unexpectedly as they had planned to attack the psalmist (64:7). Even the verbal swords they had honed to razor-sharp edges will be turned to their own destruction (64:8). Far from carrying out their plot in secret, they will be exposed to public ridicule as "all who see them" (cf. 64:5; lit., "Who will see them [our deeds]?" unite in "shaking their heads in scorn" (64:8c).[9]

Concluding Praise and Trust (64:9–10)

THE CONSEQUENCES OF God's rebuke of the enemies far exceeds the local context of the psalmist—the whole of humanity (*ʾadam*) will take note.[10] The shift to "all humanity" is somewhat unexpected in the psalm as a whole, but it is fitting in the context of the group of Psalms 56–68, where the theme of universal recognition of God's authority and power repeatedly surfaces.[11] Because God upholds justice and protects those who are unjustly attacked, all humanity will be drawn to proclaim and consider the works of God.

The righteous, the psalmist affirms, need have no fear of such attackers but should take refuge in Yahweh,[12] assured of his protective care. Their

---

9. This difficult phrase assumes the verbal root *ndd*, with the meaning "wander, flee," and it takes the phrase to describe society avoiding the discredited enemies, who have become pariahs. However, this root does not occur elsewhere in the Hithpael stem as here. More commonly the verb is taken from the root *nwd* with the meaning in the Hithpael of "shake in disapproval/disdain (or lament?)" concerning something.

10. Whether humanity will "fear" (*yrʾ*) as in the text or "see" (*rʾh*) as *BHS* notes many manuscripts read, is a matter of uncertainty—and perhaps not of great significance ultimately.

11. See opening comments, above.

12. The appearance of the divine name "Yahweh" (*yhwh*; NIV "LORD") is almost startling here since we have not encountered it at all since 59:8 and will not see it again until Ps. 68! See comments and notes on vv. 1–2, above.

confidence and trust inspires both the "righteous" (*ṣaddiq*) and the "upright in heart" (*yišre leb*) to praise (64:10c).

COURAGE IN NUMBERS. The plotting of the noisy evildoers against the righteous is similar to the scene described in Psalm 2, where nations and kings conspire against God and his anointed (2:1–2). There is a dangerous courage that may result from crowd psychology. Perhaps it is the illusion of being lost in the crowd and thus without accountability. Or perhaps it is the growing sense of invulnerability in a large group surging forward in a common purpose.

There can be good moments of solidarity, as in moments of mass civil disobedience in protest against racial injustice or against unjust wars. The kind of strength to stand our ground against impossible odds has great moral power—as Gandhi's nonviolent resistance showed in India and the best of the civil-rights protests did in the United States. This kind of solidarity and strength is behind the biblical exhortation for the individual to bind himself or herself to the community of faith. The solidarity of Israel or the church means that individual believers did not stand alone but were empowered by their gathering as the united people of God.

But there is also a negative form of mutual encouragement and solidarity, as when an unruly lynch mob overwhelms the protective authorities and carries its victims to an unjust death. We see the result of such a "conspiracy of the wicked" in our psalm. In such an environment, it is easy to deny responsibility or culpability: "Who will see?" It is possible to be convinced that the only measure of guilt is whether we are discovered or brought to accountability.

In Psalm 64 as well as in Psalm 2, a different standard is applied in the judgment of such human arrogance. God, not human agency, is the judge of right and wrong. The power of the mob fades before the righteous judge of the universe. In Psalm 2, the arrogant confidence of the conspiring nations and kings runs hard against the strong rock of the laughing God enthroned in the heavens. In Psalm 64, the "perfect plan" and "cunning" plot of the evildoers are punctured and dismembered by God, who returns their own implements of destruction upon them.

Yet the psalm ends with a renewed call to solidarity. The destruction of the wicked will bring "all mankind" together in their understanding of the power of God. Then the righteous and upright will *together* rejoice and praise the God of their refuge.

A JUST RETRIBUTION. This psalm envisions another enactment of the principle of retribution: You get what you deserve. In this case there is a slight twist in that the wicked get what they had planned to visit on others. The arrows they shoot off at the righteous boomerang around and attack them unexpectedly from the rear. It is somewhat like the recent tragic event in which a group of military spotters guiding a flight of bombers into a target were, through a series of errors, themselves bombed by the very planes they were guiding, with terrible loss of life.

We do not have much pity when a terrorist bomb-maker blows himself or herself up while creating a bomb. "He got what he deserved," we might say, thinking it a sort of appropriate justice that the bomb intended for others got the terrorist instead. But these kinds of scenarios in the psalms always carry a hidden price tag. When we rejoice in the destruction of the wicked, when we are glad that they "get what they deserve," we might want to be cautious. What if we were to receive what *we deserve*?

That is a scary thought if we are honest. Like the angry mob ready to stone the woman caught in adultery, we can get tripped up by Jesus' deceptively simple solution: "If any one of you is without sin, let him be the first to throw a stone at her" (John 8:7). When we rejoice at the destruction of the wicked, we may be joining the teachers of the law and the Pharisees in stone-throwing. In the incident just noted, even the Jewish leaders knew when they were defeated, for they withdrew without carrying out their judgment.

This kind of hope for justice has a double edge. It is in a sense a reverse variation on the Golden Rule: "Do unto others what you would have them do unto you." We sinners have no complaint when we receive from God the justice we wished on others.

Proclaim and ponder. When God acts to judge the wicked, the whole world is brought up short. The usual assumption that "no one sees or cares," that "no one can call us to account," are put to the lie. Recently an Eastern European leader was taken into custody by his own people and, after considerable delay, was delivered to the war crimes tribunal in the Hague to stand trial for his participation and authorization of atrocities during the earlier civil war in his country. While I know that there are all sorts of political and economic manipulations and pressures going on behind the scenes to bring this circumstance to pass, it was almost a shocking moment to realize that the impossible had happened and that at long last, some response was going to be made to the growing evidence of wrong levied against this man.

God's judgment of the wicked in Psalm 64 is such an event, in which the world watches to see what will happen and "ponders" the significance of what it sees. On a much less universal level, I think we can find the last two verses of this psalm working their way out in the lives of the faithful. We perhaps should spend less time proclaiming God's works on the "wicked" we see out there and trying to convince others that God is bringing punishment for their sins. Those who like to proclaim the AIDS epidemic as God's judgment on gay and promiscuous sexuality have to ignore the many innocents who have contracted the disease from blood transfusions or sex within a marriage relationship. To gloat when abortion clinics are blown up or when abortionists are injured or even killed is not to proclaim the works of God, nor will it bring all humankind to fear God.

A better plan—even more cunning and certainly more honest than the plan of the evildoers—is to proclaim the works of God in judgment and grace poured out *in our own lives*. There we will have far less chance of distorting the unspoken motivations of others. There we will be less likely to be self-serving at the expense of others. When we proclaim what God has done in our own lives, we truly give the world something to ponder.

I am always amazed at how the disciples of Jesus passed on their foibles, their thick-headedness, and even their venality in the biblical record when they could so easily have whitewashed their thoughts and actions after the fact. Their honest vulnerability serves as a challenging example for us. God has done small miraculous things to, with, for, and through us that are far more impressive (and hopeful to common people, who want to believe in the life-changing works of God) than all our dire proclamation against the evil of the world.

When the righteous are able honestly to proclaim the works of God in their own lives, the world can actually see God at work in common lives like their own and to understand why we take refuge in him and sing his praises.

Psalm 65

FOR THE DIRECTOR of music. A psalm of David. A song.

1 Praise awaits you, O God, in Zion;
to you our vows will be fulfilled.
2 O you who hear prayer,
to you all men will come.
3 When we were overwhelmed by sins,
you forgave our transgressions.
4 Blessed are those you choose
and bring near to live in your courts!
We are filled with the good things of your house,
of your holy temple.

5 You answer us with awesome deeds of righteousness,
O God our Savior,
the hope of all the ends of the earth
and of the farthest seas,
6 who formed the mountains by your power,
having armed yourself with strength,
7 who stilled the roaring of the seas,
the roaring of their waves,
and the turmoil of the nations.
8 Those living far away fear your wonders;
where morning dawns and evening fades
you call forth songs of joy.

9 You care for the land and water it;
you enrich it abundantly.
The streams of God are filled with water
to provide the people with grain,
for so you have ordained it.
10 You drench its furrows
and level its ridges;
you soften it with showers
and bless its crops.
11 You crown the year with your bounty,
and your carts overflow with abundance.

[12]The grasslands of the desert overflow;
the hills are clothed with gladness.
[13]The meadows are covered with flocks
and the valleys are mantled with grain;
they shout for joy and sing.

PSALM 65 CONTINUES the growing crescendo of praise begun in Psalm 56. In doing so it exhibits a number of themes and phrases in common with the preceding group of psalms. It begins with a promise to fulfill "our vows," a phrase reminiscent of the concluding promise of 61:8 ("fulfill my vows day after day") and reflected in 56:12 ("I am under vows to you") and 66:13–14 ("I will . . . fulfill my vows to you—vows my lips promised and my mouth spoke when I was in trouble").[1]

The psalm also speaks of the universal recognition and acknowledgment of Israel's God. "All men [*kol baśar*; lit., all flesh] will come" to God, seeking forgiveness (65:2–3) from the one who is the "hope of all the ends of the earth" (65:5—a phrase found also in 59:13; 61:2; 67:7; 72:8); "those living far away fear your wonders."[2] In addition, Psalm 65 shares with this broader group of psalms a concern with the temple of God (cf. 65:4) and its blessings.[3] In particular, we encounter expressions of the psalmist's desire and hope to "dwell" in God's sanctuary and presence (cf. 57:1; 61:4; 63:7).

The psalm is a thanksgiving for forgiveness of sin (65:3), for God's provision of security and stability in the midst of turmoil (65:7), and especially for his abundant provision of the necessities of life for humankind and beasts (65:9–13). It may have originated as a thanksgiving for abundant crops and perhaps even accompanied the offering of firstfruits.[4] The structure exhibits three sections: praise for forgiveness of sin (65:1–4), praise for God's stabilizing power (65:5–8), and praise for the blessings of the land (65:9–13).

1. Outside these psalms, the idea of making vows to God surfaces only six more times, widely scattered through the Psalter (22:25; 50:14; 76:14; 116:14, 18; 132:2). To find *half* of the twelve occurrences of this theme concentrated within a group of just ten psalms seems hardly coincidental.

2. Although this probably refers to distant, non-Israelite humanity drawn to praise God because of the blessings they see poured out on Israel, the phrase certainly must have resonated with the circumstances of the far-flung Diaspora community.

3. Within this group of psalms, references to the temple occur at 60:6; 63:2; 65:4; 66:13; 68:5, 17, 24, 29, 35; 69:9.

4. Legislation governing the giving of the offering of firstfruits is found in Ex. 23:16, 19; 34:22, 26; Lev. 2:12, 14; 23:17, 20; Num. 18:12, 13; 28:26; Deut. 26:2, 10.

The Heading (65:0)

THE HEADING OFFERS no new terms. It is referred to "the director of music" and (like the preceding Pss. 62–64) is described as a "psalm [*mizmor*] of David."[5] The term "song" (*šir*)[6] is also appended at the end, perhaps as a way of binding the following two *non*-Davidic psalms (Pss. 66 and 67)—which also bear the two terms *mizmor* ("psalm") and *šir* ("song") in their headings—more firmly into the Davidic collection.[7]

Forgiveness of Sin (65:1–4)

THE PSALMIST DIRECTS praise to God, who is in Zion.[8] Zion is most often associated with the hill in Jerusalem on which the temple stood and is, therefore, the place at which God in particular is thought to come down to dwell with his people. In 2:6, Zion is Yahweh's "holy hill," where the king is established as God's "son." Zion is thus the place where Israel's religious and political hopes come together. In this particular psalm, however, the political elements are not evident, and it seems to be the temple and its redemptive action in forgiveness of sin that are foremost in the psalmist's mind in these verses.

Our vows will be fulfilled.[9] As noted above, this phrase reflects one of the common concerns of the larger group of Psalms 56–67. The vow that will be fulfilled is apparently one to "praise" God after deliverance from trouble (cf. 61:8; 66:13–14). That "trouble" most often is described as the attacks of the enemy. Here, however, distress is the result of sin (65:3a), and praise is a response to God's forgiveness (65:3b). Since God is the one who hears

---

5. For further comments on these notations, see the headings of Pss. 3 and 4.

6. The term *šir* first appears as a simple notation in the heading of Ps. 30.

7. Note how at the end of a series of four psalm headings (62–65) bearing the common phrase "psalm of David" (*mizmor ledawid*) the additional genre term *šir* is added to the heading of Ps. 65. This links forward to the non-Davidic Pss. 66 and 67, which contain both *mizmor* and *šir* in their headings. The linkage continues on to include the heading of the Davidic Ps. 68, which is also designated *ledawid mizmor šir*. For comments on this technique of binding psalms together employing similar phrases in the psalm headings, see Wilson, *The Editing of the Hebrew Psalter*, 163–64, 190–91.

8. The passage is made difficult by the uncertainty of meaning attached to the word that the NIV translates "awaits" (*dumiyyah*). In Pss. 22:2 and 39:2 the same word is taken as a noun and seems to connote "silence." That meaning makes little sense in our context, however. The note in *BHS* suggest emending on the basis of the Greek and Syriac to a Qal participial form with the meaning "silent one." In that case the verse would mean something like: "To you, O silent one, [is] praise, O God in Zion."

9. The Heb. actually says, "To you *a* vow will be fulfilled." The NIV's rendering is an interpretive expansion, based on the plural voice exhibited in the remainder of the psalm.

prayer, "all flesh" (*kol baśar*; NIV "all men") will come to him seeking forgiveness. The phrase "all flesh" reaches far beyond the confines of Israel to include *all* humanity, and even in many instances the animal world. This phrase first appears in the Flood account (Gen. 6–9) to describe the living creatures—human and animal—that Noah brought by pairs into the ark. Those that remained outside perished: "And *all flesh* died that moved on the earth, birds, domestic animals, wild animals, all swarming creatures that swarm on the earth, and all human beings" (7:21, lit. trans.).

In the prophets, "all flesh" is a particularly inclusive term encompassing *all* humanity—Israelite and Gentile alike. While the animal world is not clearly stressed in these contexts, it is likewise not clear that they are *excluded* in such statements as Jeremiah's wonderful proclamation: "See, I am Yahweh, the God of all flesh; is anything too hard for me?" (Jer. 32:27, lit. trans.).

But it is in Isaiah 66:18–24 that our psalm finds its closest parallel and, perhaps, its foundational vision. At the conclusion of Isaiah, Yahweh proclaims his intention to reunite all humanity—fractured at Babel—so that "they will come and see my glory" (Isa. 66:18). The scattering of exiles throughout the nations is seen as a "sign" and a mission to the nations to "proclaim my glory among the nations" (66:19). As a result, representatives of "all the nations" will be brought to Yahweh's "holy mountain in Jerusalem," where they will become "priests and Levites" (66:20–21). Then "all flesh [lit.] will come and bow down before me" (66:23).

When we were overwhelmed . . . you atoned. The psalmist's prayer seems to champion the cause of all humanity. Coming as it does in the context of "all flesh," the plural reference in "we" seems to seek the restoration of all humanity rather than just Israel. This broader concern is also reflected in the later description of God as "our Savior, the hope of *all the ends of the earth and of the farthest seas*" (65:5, italics added)—another clear reference to far-flung humanity.

Acknowledging an overwhelming sense of guilt for sin (65:3a), the psalmist nevertheless affirms past experience of God's forgiveness and restoration (65:3b–4). Not only are the supplicants forgiven, but they are even chosen to live in the presence of God. The reference in 65:4b to living in the "courts" of God might be taken as an indication of priestly status for the psalmist, but it is more likely a metaphor for experiencing the nearness of God that his association with the "holy temple" (65:4c-d) offers.[10] Those who are forgiven are also chosen to come near to live in God's courts and experience the blessing of that association when they "are filled with the good things of

10. Even the Gentiles will be able to approach God effectively in his sanctuary (see Isa. 56:1–7).

your house" (65:4c). God is a gracious and generous host, providing abundantly for the needs of his guests.

God's Stabilizing Power (65:5–8)

NOT ONLY DOES God forgive sin, but he also provides a stabilizing influence on a world beset with turmoil. God hears the prayer of the sinner and responds "with awesome deeds of righteousness" (65:5a). The Savior God, the "hope of all the ends of the earth," is acknowledged as the powerful creator of the mountains, who was able to provide effective boundaries to the chaotic waters at creation and will similarly provide limits to the power of the "nations" and "the turmoil" that results from their striving (65:7).

It is important to note here that the NIV's "nations" obscures the redemptive thrust of this passage. "Nations" is the normal translation of *goyim*, a word that emphasizes the "otherness" of the non-Israelite nations, who are not part of Yahweh's covenant relationship and who oppose him by their allegiance to other gods. The term that appears here, however, is *leʾummim* ("peoples")—a less exclusive term that describes the ethnic groups that compose the larger geopolitical nation. By using the less exclusive term, the poet paves the way for the inclusion of the "peoples" of the world into the blessings of God.[11]

Where morning dawns and evening fades. The result of God's continuing control of the universe and the human powers within it is that those who dwell at its furthest limits (an attempt to be all-inclusive rather than selective) are amazed by God's wondrous power and righteousness (cf. 65:5, 8) and are inspired to shouts of joy. The divine acts are described (lit.) as "righteous acts that inspire fear" (65:5)[12] and "wonders" or signs—intentional divine acts of communication to the inhabitants of the world. By his acts of concerned power, God confirms his protective care over the whole world and calls everyone—Israelite and Gentile alike—into a relationship of blessing and joy.

The Blessings of the Land (65:9–13)

THE FINAL SEGMENT of the psalm centers around the abundant blessings of the land enriched by God's care (65:9). God so "cares for" or loves the land that he pours out his blessing on it. Everything is described in terms of excess. The streams are "filled with water"—an unusual circumstance in the arid conditions of Israel. The furrows and ridges are "drenched." The grain is so abun-

11. See comments on 56:5–11.

12. Again, this is not "terror" but acknowledgment of one's total dependence on God for all aspects of life.

dant that the gathering carts "overflow" (65:11), and the normally parched steppelands yield copious grass to support the flocks of sheep and goats. As a result, the flocks increase and "cover" the meadows of the land (65:13) while the fertile valleys "are mantled" with grain.

All this excess is clearly attributed to the gracious care and effective power of God, who rules the earth from "where morning dawns and evening fades" (65:8) and to "all the ends of the earth and of the farthest seas" (65:5). It is God who is at work in this miraculous season to top all seasons: "*You* care for the land and water it; *you* enrich it abundantly" (65:9); "*you* drench its furrows ... *you* soften it with showers and bless its crops" (65:10); "*you* crown the year with your bounty" (65:11). As a result, the land throws a party! The awesome deeds of God "call forth songs of joy" from the ends of the earth (65:8); and in these final verses the earth joins its voice in the singing, as the meadows and valleys, covered with flocks and grain like a warm cloak, "shout for joy and sing" (65:13).

The psalm in its original state seems to have been a national thanksgiving for a season of abundant crops and increasing herds. As such the place of the *leʾummim*—the non-Israelite nations—would have been primarily as spectators, driven to awe at the blessings poured out on Israel by their gracious God. The first four verses, however, reshape the meaning of the psalm in different and more inclusive directions. The abundant display of God's care is now an evidence of his gracious mercy and forgiveness of sin. What might have been considered evidence of Israel's special status as the people chosen for divine blessing has now become an example of God's desire to draw "all flesh" (65:2) to himself to experience his salvation. In this light—and in the growing universal context of Psalms 56–68—God's purposes are revealed to be far more than a single season of blessing for Israel. He desires nothing less than the restoration for all humanity of his original creation intention. That is reason for us to join in the party!

BROUGHT NEAR TO **live in your courts.** Psalm 65 brings together a number of themes that are characteristic of the grouping of Psalms 56–72. Most of these themes circle around the temple (60:6; 63:2; 65:4; 66:13) and its role as the dwelling of God (61:4; 65:4), where vows are fulfilled (56:12; 65:1) and humans can find refuge (57:1; 59:9, 17; 61:3; 62:2, 6, 7, 8; 64:10).

Dwelling with God. The temple is the place where Yahweh causes his "name" to dwell (Deut. 12:5–7; Neh. 1:9) and where he is especially *present* with and in the midst of his people (Ps. 26:8). Because of its association with the protective and blessed presence of God, the loss of the temple by its destruction (and the continuing distance separating the Diaspora community even after its reconstruction) was a source of great pain to the exilic community (Pss. 74:1–11; 137). By contrast, the hope of visiting and seeing Jerusalem and the rebuilt temple was for an exiled pilgrim one of life's highest joys (Pss. 84; 122; 126).

Perhaps one of the most beautiful images used in the psalms is the joyous hope of "dwelling" in the house of God. To experience the hospitality of Yahweh as host was the ultimate in luxury and honor (23:5–6; 36:8; 52:8; 65:4; 92:13–14) and provided a sense of security as well (23:4–6; 27:5; 31:20). It is unlikely that all these references suggest the actual possibility of pilgrims "dwelling in the house of God." More likely the metaphor expresses the longing of the passionate worshiper for the nearness of God and the sustaining practices of worship associated with the temple.

Perhaps the longing cry of 84:10 best captures the urgency of this desire: "Better is one day in your courts than a thousand elsewhere; I would rather be a doorkeeper in the house of my God than dwell in the tents of the wicked." The pilgrim, having experienced the glory of the temple, the restoration of its worship, and the nearness of God experienced in its precincts, now faces the long journey home, perhaps never to return. He or she is almost willing to take up the menial status of doorkeeper in order to remain forever in the center of God's sustaining presence.

Taking refuge. God's house is also viewed as a secure place of refuge for the beleaguered faithful. While the enemy lurks outside, the trusting guest enjoys the abundance of God's table as well as his protection (Ps. 23). Yahweh hides the fleeing person deep in the inner recesses of the sanctuary (27:5), a possible reference to the use of the temple as a place of asylum (1 Kings 2:28–35).

The protective character of Yahweh's temple and its promise of God's presence with his people could lead to some dangerous distortions, however. By the time of the later monarchy, for example, the temple was seen as an absolute guarantee of divine protection. As long as it stood and the daily rituals and sacrifices performed, the temple and the nation would stand secure. Jeremiah, however, confronted the nation with the emptiness of this hope in his famous temple sermon (Jer. 7; 26), in which he deflated the deceptive belief that the temple without evidence of covenant loyalty and obedience could protect a perverse people from divine judgment.

If the temple fails to provide an enduring sense of security and hope (and this idea of the inviolability of the temple was surely dashed by the events of the Exile), where do a suffering people turn? Psalms 90 and 91 take the concept of dwelling in the *house* of Yahweh and renew its hopeful expectation by speaking instead of making *Yahweh himself* the place of dwelling: "Lord, you have been our dwelling place throughout all generations" (90:1); "if you make the Most High your dwelling—even the LORD, who is my refuge—then no harm will befall you, no disaster will come near your tent" (91:9–10; cf. also 91:1–2).

This shift of focus from a building to the person of God, from a location to the ever-present Yahweh, paves the way for an understanding of God's presence that breaks out of the national, political, and geographical limitations of ancient Israel. Yahweh is now the God of the whole earth (as the group of Pss. 56–72 increasingly attest) and can be present with those who fear him wherever and whoever they may be. The stage is set, so to speak, for the creator God of "all flesh" to seek the redemption of all humankind and the restoration of his original intention for the cosmos.

A subtle irony is expressed in the blessing of 65:4 on "*those you choose* and bring near to live in your courts!" Clearly the term "choose" has its roots in the theology of Israel's election by Yahweh. In this context, however, immediately preceded by the hopeful proclamation, "O you who hear prayer, to you *all men [kol bāśar] will come*" (65:2), Yahweh's election is quietly expanded to include the whole of humanity who "come." God is indeed "*our* Savior, the hope of *all the ends of the earth and of the farthest seas*" (65:5, italics added).

SEEKING THE RESTORATION **of all flesh.** This psalm celebrates the restoration of God's world and all who dwell within it. The creator God, who has the power to subdue and restrict the chaotic waters at creation (65:7a-b), is also more than capable of stilling the "turmoil" of the "peoples" (65:7c—*leʾummim*, not *goyim*), so that those living at the very edges of the world will fear God (65:8a–b) and will join in the chorus in praise of his wondrous works (65:8c). This psalm calls us to join in the restoration of "all flesh" to the purposes of God. How do we do that?

The contemporary mission movement developed out of a desire to fulfill this calling, especially as laid out in the Great Commission of Matthew 28:19–20: "Therefore go and make disciples of all nations,[13] baptizing them in the name of the Father and of the Son and of the Holy Spirit, and teaching them to obey everything I have commanded you." Christ's commission is as inclusive as Psalm 65 in its intent to bring all peoples into the redemptive purposes of God. Missionaries attempt to reach "every people group" by

13. The Greek word translated "nations" is *ethne*, a term related to the English adjective ethnic.

communicating the words of God's redemption "to the ends of the earth."[14] Since Jesus spoke to the Samaritan woman (John 4), the Syro-Phoenician woman (Mark 7), and the Roman centurion (Matt. 8), and since Philip instructed the Ethiopian eunuch and Paul and Barnabas began their mission to the Gentiles, the church has viewed going to the world as part of their purpose for being in the world.

But in the last fifty years or so, the world has been coming to us. As part of the thrust of contemporary urbanism, more and more persons of diverse ethnic and national origin have been congregating in world cities in order to access the resources available in developed societies like ours.[15] The nations have flooded the developed world. The world has come to the city.

With all the problems it brings—diversity, cultural and religious pluralism, conflicting values and agendas, conflicts of identity—the influx of peoples represents a great opportunity to the church (and each of us individually) to understand how we can work to fulfill the vision of Psalm 65 in our own communities, cities, and nation. Here are just a few general suggestions of how we might begin to do just that.

(1) Gratitude for our own choosing. Praise and thanksgiving communicate a lot. Our own thanksgiving for the work of God in transforming our lives is one of the most attractive and contagious aspects of our churches. When we join the chorus of praise and thanksgiving, we are inviting others to stand alongside us and to experience the joy we share.

(2) Confession and forgiveness. Along with joyous praise, however, we need to include a healthy dose of confession of sin. Unless those who see us know why we are joyous, they may question whether what we experience is real, whether it can have any effect on the trouble and pain of their own lives. Unless we can communicate how those "overwhelming sins" have been forgiven, we may be offering nothing better than those who encourage masking reality with drugs, or booze, or wealth, or sex.

(3) The inclusive nature of God's redemptive love. Despite the insistence of some church-growth specialists that churches grow better and faster when they are more ethnically, culturally, and financially similar, the call of Psalm 65 (and of the Great Commission, for that matter) is to bring "all flesh" to God's redemptive love. However we have to do that, we *must* get the word

14. As I write, I have before me a brochure from CBInternational, in which these last two phrases are used (see www.cbi.org).

15. Read the statistics provided in Ray Bakke, "The Lord Is Shaking Up the City," in *The Urban Christian* (Downers Grove, Ill.: InterVarsity, 1987), 28–44; also the introduction in idem, *A Theology as Big as the City* (Downers Grove, Ill.: InterVarsity, 1997), 11–15. Also consider the excellent introduction to urban theology by Robert Linthicum, *City of God, City of Satan: A Biblical Theology for the Urban Church* (Grand Rapids: Zondervan, 1991).

across by our actions that God's redemption is *inclusive* and not *exclusive.* God wants peoples near and far to fear his wondrous works, not by standing on the outside and looking in longingly but by standing shoulder to shoulder and joining in the chorus of praise:" O God our Savior, the hope of *all the ends of the earth!"*

Psalm 66

FOR THE DIRECTOR of music. A song. A psalm.

1 Shout with joy to God, all the earth!
2 Sing the glory of his name;
make his praise glorious!
3 Say to God, "How awesome are your deeds!
So great is your power
that your enemies cringe before you.
4 All the earth bows down to you;
they sing praise to you,
they sing praise to your name." *Selah*

5 Come and see what God has done,
how awesome his works in man's behalf!
6 He turned the sea into dry land,
they passed through the waters on foot—
come, let us rejoice in him.
7 He rules forever by his power,
his eyes watch the nations—
let not the rebellious rise up against him. *Selah*

8 Praise our God, O peoples,
let the sound of his praise be heard;
9 he has preserved our lives
and kept our feet from slipping.
10 For you, O God, tested us;
you refined us like silver.
11 You brought us into prison
and laid burdens on our backs.
12 You let men ride over our heads;
we went through fire and water,
but you brought us to a place of abundance.

13 I will come to your temple with burnt offerings
and fulfill my vows to you—
14 vows my lips promised and my mouth spoke
when I was in trouble.

[15]I will sacrifice fat animals to you
and an offering of rams;
I will offer bulls and goats. ***Selah***

[16]Come and listen, all you who fear God;
let me tell you what he has done for me.
[17]I cried out to him with my mouth;
his praise was on my tongue.
[18]If I had cherished sin in my heart,
the Lord would not have listened;
[19]but God has surely listened
and heard my voice in prayer.
[20]Praise be to God,
who has not rejected my prayer
or withheld his love from me!

WITHIN THE CONTEXT of the group of Psalms 56–68, Psalm 66 (along with its companion piece, Ps. 67) offers a fitting litany of universal praise of God for his "awesome deeds" (66:3a) and power. The particular fit of Psalms 66 and 67 is heightened by the fact that while neither is explicitly attributed to David, both have been bound together with Psalms 65 and 68 by the use of similar genre terms in the headings of all four psalms (see the comments on "The Heading," below). These efforts are certainly purposeful as these two psalms share a number of the significant themes addressed in the related group of Psalms 56–68, including: (1) universal concern with the whole earth and the nations of the earth (66:1, 4; 67:2, 3, 4, 5, 7); (2) glory and praise to God's "name" (66:1, 4); (3) the offering of sacrifices in the temple and the fulfillment of vows (66:13–15); (4) the acknowledgment of God's power by the nations and their involvement in praising God for his just rule (66:1, 4, 8; 67:3, 4, 5).

Psalm 66 is a song of praise for the "awesome" deeds of God (66:3, 5) that exceed the confines of Israel and break forth to demonstrate his universal rule of all humanity. In it Israel calls on the inhabitants of the earth to "praise *our* God, O peoples" for the evidence of divine power displayed in the preservation of Israel "from slipping" (66:8–9). Defeat and trouble are interpreted as divine *testing* (66:10–12), which does not, however, undermine the blessing that God brings to those who continue to fear him (66:12c). The psalm concludes with an individual testimony of deliverance by God couched in first-person singular language (66:13–20). In the context of the opening verses, however, these individual words seem to take on the testimony of all Israel to the surrounding nations of the faithfulness of their God.

The structure of the poem can be described as follows: an opening call to universal praise of the awesome deeds of God (66:1–15) and a renewed call to praise with personal testimony of forgiveness (66:16–20).

The Heading (66:0)

AS NOTED PREVIOUSLY, this psalm stands out from its immediate context by being the first one since Psalm 50 *not* to be attributed to David. There are no new terms offered in the heading, but the psalm is referred to "the director of music" and is labeled both "a song" (*šir*) and a "psalm" (*mizmor*).[1] The latter two designations are the most general genre designations in the Psalter and would deserve no further comment except that in this particular context, they serve to bind the two non-Davidic Psalms 66 and 67 more firmly into the broader context of Psalms 56–68. Psalms 62–64 have each been designated *mizmor ledawid* ("psalm of David"), while Psalms 69 and 70–71 avoid the terms *mizmor* or *šir* altogether. In Psalms 65–68, however, the two genre terms *mizmor* and *šir* appear in all four headings.

Call to Universal Praise of God (66:1–15)

THIS FIRST MAJOR section is further subdivided into three segments, each marked by an imperative call to participation. The conclusion of each segment is marked with the enigmatic term *selah*.[2] The segments are: a call to praise God (66:1–4), a call to witness God's mighty deeds (66:5–7), and an extended call to praise, coupled with an individual vow (66:8–15). The first and third of these segments both contain an internal shift from a third-person reference to God to a second-person address of God. In this way communal praise also becomes testimony to the deeds for which praise is extended.

(1) Initial call to praise God (66:1–4). *Shout with joy . . . all the earth!* This first subdivision opens with a call to the universal praise of God by "all the earth" (66:1a). This phrase is one of the characteristic expressions in the extended group of Psalms 56–68. Here in 66:1 the mighty works of God exceed the boundaries of Israel and make themselves known to all the inhabitants of the earth, who are exhorted to shout as an army does in victory over its enemy. This is not simply a shout of joy but also one of triumph, which encourages the faithful while striking fear into the heart of the enemy.

---

1. See comments on the headings of Pss. 3; 4; 30; and 65.
2. See comments on the term *selah* at 3:1–2.

Sing the glory of his name. Praising God is synonymous with glorifying his "name." Again we run across the tension characteristic of this portion of the Elohistic Psalter—reference to the "name" of God when that name (clearly Yahweh) is systematically avoided (cf. 66:4c).[3] Rather than vocal singing, the verb *zmr* ("sing") most often describes making instrumental music either alone or as accompaniment to singing. "Glory" (*kabod*) is the very essence of a person—what makes you what you are. It is akin to honor and reputation; it is not just an invisible, internal quality but is bound up with how one is known and accepted in society at large. Here the whole earth is called to acknowledge openly the praiseworthy, honorable glory of Israel's God.

How awesome are your deeds! The basis for this universal recognition of God's glory is his mighty deeds, which leave no doubt about his authority and power. In the next section (66:5–7) we will be introduced in more detail to the kind of awesome deeds of God the psalmist has in mind. The verb *kḥš* (NIV "cringe") is most often translated "feign submission" (cf. Deut. 33:29; 2 Sam. 22:45; Ps. 18:44). The enemies of God are so overwhelmed that they must at the very least put on a submissive face—even if their hearts rebel.

All the earth bows down to you. In contrast to the enemies of God, who are forced to act submissively, "all the earth" (cf. 66:1a) bows willingly and faithfully to worship him. The verb here is *yištaḥawu*—the unusual Hishtaphel form that is regularly employed to describe heartfelt human worship of God. There is no pretense here, no grudging submission by reason of defeat or default. Overwhelmed by the glory of God displayed by his deeds, the world falls to its collective knees in wonder and praise to his name (66:4a-c).

(2) Call to witness God's mighty deeds (66:5–7). This second subsection describes the works of God "in man's behalf" (66:5–7). What God has done has both a specific Israelite component and a more universal edge. The psalmist remembers God's deliverance of Israel at the Red Sea: "He turned the sea into dry land, they passed through the waters on foot" (66:6a-b). This specific national event becomes the basis of his continued call to praise: "Come, let us rejoice in him" (66:6c).

This national celebration is coupled with a more universal recognition of the ruling power and authority of God that keeps the rebellious nations in check (66:7). Within the context of the opening call of "all the earth" to praise God, these last statements become more than Israel's thanksgiving for divine protection. The whole world experiences the benefit of God's effective control of the warring nations. The circumstance is somewhat akin to that in 65:5–7, where God is acknowledged as the "hope of all the ends of the

---

3. See comments on the Elohistic Psalter at Ps. 42; see also comments on the term "God" (*ʾelohim*) at 64:1–2.

earth" (65:5) because he "stilled ... the turmoil of the nations." God's eternal rule (66:7a) and vigilance (66:7b) mean that he is always prepared to quell the rebellious storms of the restless nations (66:7c).

(3) Praise and vow (66:8–15). *Preserved ... and ... tested.* The third subsection begins, as did the first, with a universal call to praise God.[4] Here those invoked are called "O peoples" (*ʿammim*), a plural reference that extends the call beyond the confines of Israel. In light of the immediately preceding allusion to the Exodus (66:6), what follows, although couched in more general terms, constitutes Israel's personal testimony before the nations of God's effective work in his relationship with her. Israel affirms that God "has preserved our lives and kept our feet from slipping"[5] (66:9).

You ... tested ... refined us. Israel's experience of God has been a learning one, characterized by divine testing and refinement. The Hebrew uses two terms to describe the kind of testing God makes: *bḥn* and *ṣrp*. Both have to do with the smelting of precious metals, such as gold and silver. In this process, the heat applied to the mixed ore melts the precious metal and separates it from the nonprecious carrier material. The precious metal is then revealed and proves itself. After the separation, the carrier material is discarded.

The imagery of smelting is frequently used in the Old Testament as a metaphor for divine testing and purification of the faithful.[6] Through the "heat" of stress and suffering, the true nature of the faithful or the unbelieving was revealed. Additional trials could purify the believer of those areas of sin or lack of dependence on God that remained. The stresses experienced by the suffering faithful are described in a series of general metaphors: "prison ... burdens on our backs ... men [riding] over our heads ... [going] through fire and water" (vv. 11–12).

Despite the fierce suffering, God's intentions for his people were good from the beginning (cf. 66:9) and proved to be blessing at the end when the community of faith admitted that God "brought us to a place of abundance" (66:12c). It is possible that the distress described in these verses is intended to recall the imprisonment, slavery, and escape of the Exodus along with the

---

4. As I have noted elsewhere in the commentary (see, e.g., comments on 16:7), the NIV has translated an original Hebrew *brk* ("bless") as "praise," revealing an interpretational reluctance to admit that humans can actually *bless* God in a way that truly affects him. Israel had no such reluctance, as this passage and many others attest.

5. Two idioms are used here for God's preservation: He is (lit.) "the one who establishes our *nepeš* in life [*baḥayyim*]" and the one who "has not given/allowed our foot to slip [*lammoṭ*]." For other uses of *moṭ* ("totter, shake, slip"), see comments on Pss. 15–17.

6. For *bḥn*, see Pss. 7:9; 11:4, 5; 17:3; 81:7; Jer. 6:27; 11:20; 12:3. For *ṣrp*, see 2 Sam. 22:31; Pss. 12:6; 17:3; 18:30; Isa. 1:25; 40:19, among others.

entry into the land of abundant "milk and honey." Far from being specific, however, the metaphors allow renewed and continued reinterpretation in the changing circumstances of the people and may later have been applied to the pains and hopes associated with the Diaspora.

I will come to your temple. This subsection closes with the form of a vow to offer sacrifice in the temple once deliverance has been experienced (66:13–15). The vow was spoken during a time of distress (66:14) as a way of affirming one's confidence in God's good intent and actualizing hope. The ultimate fulfillment of the vow in the communal worship of the temple also provided opportunity for public testimony of God's faithfulness in the presence of fellow worshipers. Thus, the vow included both a sacrifice and an verbal offering of praise and thanksgiving (cf. 61:8; 65:1).[7] While coming to the temple with one's sacrifice was part of the experience of worship during the period of the monarchy, these words would have had special significance for the Diaspora community, for whom the approach to the Jerusalem temple was most often a rare fulfillment of a lifelong dream.

I will sacrifice fat animals ... rams ... bulls and goats. The offer of so many animals is probably hyperbole, indicating the psalmist's extreme joy at being delivered. The psalmist's thanksgiving pours out in the piling up of offering upon offering.[8]

Personal Testimony (66:16–20)

THE FINAL SECTION of the psalm begins again with an invitation to a larger community of participants—presumably those gathered to worship in the temple. In this case it is "all you who fear God" who are invited to witness the psalmist's testimony to God's gracious deliverance (66:16). There follows a brief résumé of the psalmist's entreaty and God's response.

The interchange is structured in a balanced form. Verse 16 invites the attention of the witnesses and offers the psalmist's promise to tell of God's faithfulness; verse 20 supplies the psalmist's promised testimony and praise. Verses 17 and 19 provide the psalmist's entreaty and God's attentive response, respectively. At the center of the section, verse 18 stands alone at the heart of the psalmist's awareness that sin can stand in the way of divine

---

7. Once again, the reference to "temple" links this psalm with Pss. 56–68 (cf. comments on these psalms).

8. It is probably futile to speculate on the nature of the psalmist's sin based on the type and combination of sacrificial animals mentioned in this passage. Nowhere does such a constellation of offerings appear in association with a particular type of sin offering—or thanksgiving offering, for that matter. Also, the abundance of the offerings is probably no indication of the wealth or status of the offerer, since poetic hyperbole is most likely at work.

deliverance. It is not so much the sin that stands in the way; we have already seen in 65:3 that God is able to forgive what appear to be overwhelming transgressions. What blocks God from acting is an attitude of "cherish[ing] sin in my heart" (66:18). This idiom means to "look (with enjoyment) at evil in my heart" and suggests an attitude that resists repentance for wrongdoing and instead gloats[9] over evil deeds. God, says the psalmist, will not respond in grace to such arrogance. The fact that God does in fact act graciously is positive proof that the psalmist has adopted the appropriate stance of repentance and reliance on God's mercy, which is at the core of the "fear [of] God."

At the conclusion of the section (66:20a), the psalmist offers a personal "blessing" (*brk*; NIV "praise") on God, who has not "rejected" (lit., "caused to turn aside") either the psalmist's prayer or God's own answering "loyalty" (*ḥesed*). A single verb governs both halves of the verse: the rejection of the prayers and the withholding of God's "love." The picture is almost as if a wide receiver, instead of grabbing a well-thrown touchdown pass, should intentionally bat it aside. God has not deflected the well-aimed entreaties of the psalmist so that they fail to reach their target in the hearing of God, nor does he allow his gracious deliverance to miss the mark.

In the context of the extended group of Psalms 56–68, Psalm 66 becomes the testimony of Israel among the nations (*goyim*) that God is in decisive control over the world (66:2–7) and delivers those who adopt the proper attitude of repentance of sin (66:17–20). Israel's loss of national identity and independence in the Exile is to be understood not as criticism of God's power, but as divine testing of the faithful, which will ultimately lead to abundant life (66:8–12). The goal of this testimony is to call "all the earth" (66:1) and the "peoples" (66:8) to experience the blessing and to join in the praise of God. This purpose links Psalm 66 clearly with Psalm 67, in which the same theme dominates. Together these two non-Davidic psalms provide the universal perspective needed to shift the national concerns of Diaspora Israel to the universal praise of Psalm 68.

THE RELATIONSHIP OF Psalms 65–68 could use more explanation. The exposition of the individual psalms in the group has revealed a constellation of related themes that bind them together. A few of these themes are: (1) a focus on "all the earth" and "all the peoples of

9. The verb *rʾh* ("look, see") is used similarly in 22:17, where the enemies are described as staring and gloating (*rʾh*) over the narrator's condition.

the earth" (66:1, 3, 8; 65:2, 5, 8; 67:2–5, 7); (2) the growing crescendo of praise to God (66:1–2, 4, 8, 20; 65:1, 8, 13; 67:3–5); (3) the universal fear of God (66:16; 65:8; 67:7); and (4) the salvation of the nations (65:2–3, 5; 66:4; 67:2). In light of this unusual group of related themes, the previously mentioned manipulation of genre terms in the psalm headings of Psalms 65–68 would seem to have more than casual significance. This is further confirmed by the fact that these four psalms represent an unusual group of praise psalms that stand out rather drastically from their immediate context, where pleas for deliverance dominate.[10]

Another less than usual feature of Psalm 66 finds explanation against the background of the combined effect of this group of psalms. The psalm begins with a segment of communal praise expressed in the second-person plural (66:1–12) and then rather abruptly shifts to an individual testimony in the first-person singular (66:13–20). While these two sections may originally have functioned separately,[11] their combination here is particularly apt in light of the continuing development in this group of psalms.

As the psalm now stands, it serves to mediate between the description of divine blessing in 65:9–13 and the communal benediction in 67:1–7. In this context, 65:1–12 sounds a call to testimony and joyous celebration of the divine blessing that so drenches the earth that the valleys and meadows "shout for joy and sing" (65:13). Then in 66:1–12, creature and creation join to praise the great power of God (66:3) that defeats his enemies and brings his people "to a place of abundance," like that just described in the whole of Psalm 65. A similar reflection takes place in 67:6: "Then the land will yield its harvest, and God, our God, will bless us."

At this point (66:13), the individual voice breaks through to offer particular and specific testimony to the general praise of the cosmos. The testimony is directed to "all you who fear God" (66:16a), a possible reflection back to the "those living far away" who "fear your wonders" and respond with "songs of joy" (65:8). This larger invocation prepares the way for the more universal perspective expressed in Psalms 67 and 68, where the hope is that "the people [will] praise you, O God; may all the peoples praise you" (67:3, 5). I will return to this thematic development in the Bridging Contexts sections of the next two psalms.

---

10. Cf. Wilson, *The Editing of the Hebrew Psalter,* 164, 190–91. Pss. 51–64 and 69–71 are consistently pleas for deliverance or confrontation of evil that provide a contrasting backdrop for the brilliant praise profession concentrated in Pss. 65–68.

11. See the comments of Tate, *Psalms 51–100*, 147–48.

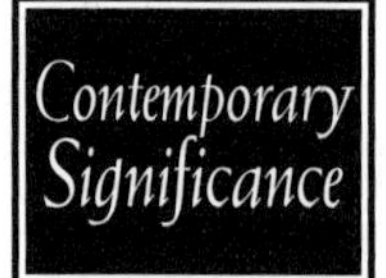

GLORIFYING GOD'S NAME. According to the response to the first question of the Shorter Westminster Catechism, the chief end of man is "to glorify God, and to enjoy him forever." Psalm 66 takes almost the same position when it calls "all the earth" to "sing the glory of his name; make his praise glorious!" (66:2). While I might wish to interpret the Catechism's rather abbreviated exhortation to "glorify God" to make sure that the implications of service to fellow humans and the rest of the creation were brought out firmly, I do think this statement captures in its essence the nature of human responsibility in this life and on this earth. We are in our deeds, words, thoughts, and relationships to "glorify God"—in other words, to make his glory known to the cosmos. That is what being in the image and likeness of God (Gen. 1:26) is all about: being the place where the divine likeness is communicated to his creation.[12]

Thus, how *do* we "glorify" God's name? While the answer provided in Psalm 66 may not be a complete one, focused as it is on testimony and praise, it certainly provides a true beginning. Here are several suggestions, drawn from the text of Psalm 66.

(1) Awesome deeds. One of the first ways to glorify God is to say both *to* and *of* God: "How awesome are your deeds" (66:3). This testimony is not just praise to God, but it also becomes witness to others in 66:5: "Come and see what God has done, how awesome his works in man's behalf." The verses that follow describe the delivering power of God unleashed in the lives of the Exodus Israelites and the continuing sovereignty of God in spite of rebellious humans.

(2) Suffering and abundance. God's power is expressed and his presence is real in our experience of both suffering and abundance. Often critics of the Christian faith and of God point to the continuation of radical suffering in the world as a reason to reject the idea of a sovereign God of love. How can a loving God allow the kind of pain and suffering we all see displayed constantly in the evening news? Our testimony to the "awesome deeds of God" stands in the face of this contrary evidence of human suffering.

The kind of testimony we give is not a sort of rational explanation or proof—although those may sometimes be called for and effective. What we testify to is *our own* experience of God alive and working in our lives *in the midst* of our pain and the graphic evidence of world evil and human suffering.

In the recent movie *Life Is Beautiful*, an Italian Jewish father and his small son are transported to a concentration camp during World War II. The father

12. See comments on the image of God at Ps. 8.

expends massive amounts of energy to shield his son from the desperate reality of their situation. Claiming they are part of a national contest offering as grand prize one's very own military tank, the father mugs, prances, cajoles, and mostly lies to keep the truth from his son. He largely succeeds, and at the end marches off to his death prancing comically before the eyes of his hidden son, carrying out the ruse to the bitter end.

The son was shielded from the truth for a while, but the most powerful message of the film comes in the voice-over narration where the grown son recounts the story of his father's selfless acts against the sure knowledge of the truth. It is here, when the truth is fully known and measured against the father's acts, that the true power is unleashed in the understanding that right and good continue to exist—in fact, refuse to bow to the grossest inhumanities that humans perpetrate against one another.

We sometimes think that God's power can only be displayed when we live charmed, painless lives of abundant goodness. Such a perspective inhibits us from talking honestly and openly about the failures, struggles, hurts, and attacks that characterize our lives. But this is not the path the psalmists take—or most of the biblical witnesses, for that matter. Abraham and Moses, Paul and Peter—all are strongly aware that it is in their weakness that the power of God is made known. Paul says it openly in 2 Corinthians 12:7–10:

> To keep me from becoming conceited because of these surpassingly great revelations, there was given me a thorn in my flesh, a messenger of Satan, to torment me. Three times I pleaded with the Lord to take it away from me. But he said to me, "My grace is sufficient for you, for my power is made perfect in weakness." Therefore I will boast all the more gladly about my weaknesses, so that Christ's power may rest on me. That is why, for Christ's sake, I delight in weaknesses, in insults, in hardships, in persecutions, in difficulties. For when I am weak, then I am strong.[13]

Our tendency to stress the "trouble-free" Christian life can have the unfortunate effect of alienating those whose experience of the world and life is far from trouble-free. On the one hand, our professed view is considered naive, uninformed, or outright deceptive and is discounted for any or all of these reasons. On the other hand, those who are in the midst of suffering may feel themselves excluded from the purpose and care of God.

But our psalm (and the rest of the Bible, I submit) acknowledges human struggle and suffering as real, but they are no barrier to the experience of the power and love of God. "We went through fire and water," the psalmist says,

---

13. See also Paul's statement in Phil. 4:11–13.

"but you brought us to a place of abundance" (66:12). Like the grown son in *Life Is Beautiful*, true abundance is measured against the reality of suffering and want.

(3) *Prayer not rejected, love not withheld.* Finally, our testimony is to a relationship of communication with God in the midst of life. At the conclusion of this psalm, the psalmist calls the reader/listener to "come and listen . . . let me tell you what he has done for me" (66:16). In the testimony that follows this call, we discover one of the interesting aspects of this psalm. Although in many ways it approaches the lament form, nowhere do we find the articulation of a plea for deliverance. As near as we get is 66:17a: "I cried out to him with my mouth." But even here, the latent plea is never consummated but is deflected into praise (66:17b). What the psalmist experiences rather than deliverance, however, is clearly stated and repeated: God has heard, listened, and accepted his prayer (66:18b–20). In the middle of the struggle of life we are assured of continued communication with God.

Besides communication with God—the assurance of being heard—we testify to our experience of communion with God. Not only does God not reject our prayer, but he has not "withheld his love from [us]" as well. The love God gives freely here is his *ḥesed*, his covenant loyalty and commitment that does not fail.

Psalm 67

FOR THE DIRECTOR of music. With stringed instruments.
A psalm. A song.

1 May God be gracious to us and bless us
and make his face shine upon us, *Selah*
2 that your ways may be known on earth,
your salvation among all nations.

3 May the peoples praise you, O God;
may all the peoples praise you.
4 May the nations be glad and sing for joy,
for you rule the peoples justly
and guide the nations of the earth. *Selah*

5 May the peoples praise you, O God;
may all the peoples praise you.

6 Then the land will yield its harvest,
and God, our God, will bless us.
7 God will bless us,
and all the ends of the earth will fear him.

THE SEVEN BRIEF verses of Psalm 67 are almost wholly taken up with the concern that all humanity—Israelite and non-Israelite—should know, acknowledge, and respond in praise for the blessing of God's salvation. The nonadversarial attitude taken toward the pagan nations (*goyim*) is particularly striking here. The underpinnings of the psalmist's thought appear to be the covenant of God with Abraham (Gen. 12:1–3), in which the blessing of Abraham (and Israel through him) is linked with God's ultimate intention to bless "all peoples on the earth." Psalm 66 evidences a similar understanding that blessing on God's people is linked with the extension of his salvation to the whole earth (66:1–4; cf. 67:2) and that the blessings of the land will come when "all the peoples" praise God (66:8–12; cf. 67:5–6).

Psalm 67

Along with Psalm 66,[1] Psalm 67 provides a fitting transition from the group of Psalms 56–65 (with their shared themes of the growing universal recognition and praise of God's power and authority) to the climactic celebration of those same themes in Psalm 68.

Structurally, this psalm is divided into three brief stanzas separated by the repeated refrain: "May the peoples praise you, O God; may all the peoples praise you." The structure provides the following divisions: a communal benediction invoking divine blessing and salvation (67:1–3), a prayer for universal praise for the just rule and guidance of God (67:4–5), and confidence in the universal blessing of God (67:6–7). While the enigmatic term *selah* appears twice in the psalm (at the ends of vv. 1 and 4), its placement does not coincide with the obvious indications of thematic and literary structure.[2]

The Heading (67:0)

NO NEW ELEMENTS appear in the heading of Psalm 67. The psalm is referred to "the director of music,"[3] and, like Psalms 65–68, is described both as a "psalm" (*mizmor*) and a "song" (*šir*). As mentioned in the heading of Psalm 66, this move binds these two non-Davidic compositions tightly into the second Davidic collection (Pss. 51–71).[4] The heading also describes the nature of musical accompaniment for the psalm with the term *binginot* ("with stringed instruments").[5]

Communal Benediction (67:1–3)

THE PSALM BEGINS with a communal blessing that shares certain diction and resonances with the classic benediction on Israel in Numbers 6:24: "The LORD bless you and keep you; the LORD make his face shine upon you and be gracious to you; the LORD turn his face toward you and give you peace." In Numbers the focus is almost entirely on the well-being of Israel. Here, however, the blessing on Israel is extended to include the salvation of "all nations."[6]

---

1. See the Bridging Contexts section of Ps. 66.

2. See comments on Ps. 3, where this term first appears.

3. See comments on the heading of Ps. 4.

4. See comments on the heading of Ps. 66.

5. See comments on the heading of Ps. 4, where this term first appears. The same term appears also in the headings of Pss. 6; 54; 55; 61; and 76.

6. Not only do the nations learn to "fear God" because *Israel* receives blessings from him, but *they all* experience the blessings of divine rule and are glad (67:4). Thus, the final result anticipated is not just awe or fear on the part of the nations (because of his protective care for Israel), but covenant commitment to God.

Make his face shine upon us. While sun imagery is perhaps here being used in reference to God,[7] it seems more likely that the shining of God's face alludes to the numinous splendor attached to his presence in all his "glory" (*kabod*). Throughout the psalms the shining of God's "face" or "light" is regularly coupled with the anticipation of deliverance, redemption, or salvation.[8] There is a quality of judgment reflected in the divine light that distinguishes the wicked from the righteous in order to judge the one and save the other.[9]

May the peoples praise you. This first segment concludes with the first appearance of a refrain that resurfaces in 67:5. Often a repeated refrain drives home the main point of a psalm.[10] In this case the main point is the hope or expectation that all the peoples of the earth will join in the praise of Israel's God. The verb translated "praise" here is *ydh*, which is more often rendered "give thanks." Such verbal thanks as is invoked here is normally a response to God's deliverance of the faithful and would be spoken formally in public worship to accompany the thank offering (the Todah). By joining in singing this refrain, the reader/listener is affirming and accepting the thanksgiving of *all* the "peoples" (*ʿammim*)[11] of the world, including the pagan nations.

The thanksgiving of all peoples comes as the result of their knowing the "ways" of God (67:2) and their experience of his "salvation."[12] While some understand this to mean that the nations will come to realize how God is concerned for and protective of his special people Israel, the continuing and growing emphasis in this psalm and in the whole group of Psalms 56–68 on the universal praise of God suggests that these verses describe the salvation of God as extending to and including those other nations (*goyim*), who learn to "fear him" (67:7).

The Just Rule and Guidance of God (67:4–5)

THIS SECOND SECTION of the psalm continues the note of universal thanksgiving begun in the first refrain. In the first section the nations (*goyim*) of the earth give thanks for God's salvation. Now the world's tribes (*leʾummim*) are "glad" and "sing for joy" because of God's just rulership and guidance of all the peoples and tribes of the earth (67:4). Taken together the two sections imply that God's salvation is expressed and known through his extending his

---

7. Cf. comments on 19:1–6; 50:1–6.

8. See esp. 31:16; 80:1, 3, 7, 19; 118:27.

9. See 50:1–6; 94:1–3.

10. See the discussion of repeated refrains in the introduction.

11. See comments of the various nouns for "people/nations" in Ps. 47.

12. See the discussion of salvation at 44:4–9. On the salvation of the nations, see 1 Chron. 16:23; Pss. 74:12; 98:3; Isa. 26:18; 45:8; 49:6; 52:10.

authority to the whole earth. By his just rule and guidance the nations are held in check (cf. 65:5–7), and by his guidance all are assured of his blessing.

May the peoples praise you. This section concludes, like the first, with the refrain. The repetition emphasizes that those who read, pray, or sing this psalm are aligning themselves with a future in which God's purpose includes the salvation of "all the peoples" who give thanks to him.

The Universal Blessing of God (67:6–7)

THE PSALM CONCLUDES with a description of the earth bringing forth abundant crops, which is a sign of God's blessing (67:6b). The last two verses form a chiasm:

> Then the land will yield its harvest,
>   and God, our God, will bless us.
>   God will bless us,
> and all the ends of the earth will fear him.

The implication of this structure is that the outer elements relate to one another as do the inner elements. In some way the abundant "harvest" of the land is connected to the faithful stance adopted by "all the ends of the earth." There is an apocalyptic expectation in that as the fractured and corrupted earth (Gen. 3:17–19) will be restored to its originally intended productivity, so fractured and divided humanity (11:1–9) will be restored to its originally intended unity and reliance on God.

All the ends of the earth. The final verse reintroduces the theme and universal language that stitches together the group of Psalms 56–68. In 61:2, the voice of the psalmist captures the plight of the faithful exiles, who call out for deliverance "from the ends of the earth." By 65:5 God has become more than Israel's refuge; he is "the hope of all the ends of the earth." Now, just before the great celebration of the universal power and rule of God in Psalm 68, Psalm 67 concludes with the expectation that "all the ends of the earth will fear [God]." The growing theme has reached its climax, and all is ready for the celebration to begin.

AN EVANGELISTIC TRACT **for the peoples.** I have mentioned previously that the major feature of the Elohistic Psalter (Pss. 42–83) is the reduced appearance of the divine name, Yahweh (NIV "LORD"), in these psalms as compared to the rest of the Psalter.[13] This ten-

13. See discussion of the Elohistic Psalter in the comments on Pss. 42–43.

dency is particularly pronounced in the group of psalms extending from 60–67. This group is the longest run of psalms in the Elohistic Psalter, interrupted by a single appearance of Yahweh at 64:10, and it contains the longest run of psalms without any mention of Yahweh (Pss. 60–63). On either side of this group the name Yahweh appears three times in Psalm 59, five times in Psalm 68, five times in Psalm 69, and five times in the combined Psalms 70–71. Indeed, *after* this group of psalms there is only one other psalm before the end of the Elohistic Psalter that does *not* mention Yahweh at least once.[14] References to the "name" (*šem*) of God are not lacking in this same group but appear five times. It is the name Yahweh itself that does not appear.

The almost complete omission of the covenant name Yahweh from this group of psalms is even more perplexing in light of the emphasis on the universal praise of God and the expansion of his salvation to include all the peoples of the world. Might the inclusion of the nations here be one reason behind the almost complete omission of the name? In relation to the pagan nations, the more generic reference to *ʾelohim* might seem more appropriate than the name Yahweh, with its exclusive connections with Israel. Might this section of the Elohistic Psalter (and perhaps the Elohistic Psalter as a whole) be considered an "evangelistic pamphlet" preparing the "peoples of the earth" for their inclusion in the saving purposes of the creator God of the whole earth and its inhabitants?[15]

RULING AND GUIDING. The inclusion of all the peoples and nations of the earth in God's saving plans calls forth a paean of universal praise. This inclusion takes effect in a variety of ways. The key verses are 67:2 and 4. In both, an invocation of joy (66:1, 4a) gives away to the cause of joy (66:2, 4b-c). It is in these causal portions that we see the effective nature of God's saving plan laid out. Verses 2 and 4b-c, despite their separation, occupy a sort of chiastic relationship[16] to one another, so that

14. This one last psalm is Ps. 82, which focuses on interaction within the heavenly council of the many gods. Although the God of Israel is viewed in this psalm as the Most High God, there may have remained some reluctance to insert the name of the one true God, Yahweh, into this rather pagan, polytheistic environment.

15. This group may also have downplayed the negative associations of the name Yahweh with the defeat of the kingdoms of Israel and Judah, which likely undermined the confidence of non-Israelite peoples in Yahweh's power to save.

16. See the discussion of chiasm in the section on "The Poetry of the Psalms" in the introduction.

what appears at first to be four causes for joy actually coalesce into two views from varying aspects. The chiastic relation can be expressed as follows:

> that your ways may be known on earth
> your salvation among all nations (67:2)
> for you rule the peoples justly
> and guide the nations of the earth (67:4b-c)

In this relation, the outer lines relate to guidance of the peoples and nations in the way[17] of God, while the inner lines understand the character of God's salvation in terms of his rule of justice and equity over all peoples.[18]

I am grateful for this image of a divine rulership tempered with guidance. As much as I long for and desire equity and justice, I am terrified by it, because I know I fall short of its excellent standard. But along with his justice, God provides guidance for his people in the earth. The term "guidance" here is the Hebrew verb *nḥh*. Its use in two other Old Testament passages is instructive and links the idea of guidance with God's "way." In the first, Abraham's servant (who has made a long journey to Aram Naharaim in Mesopotamia in order to find a wife for Isaac) praises God for the successful completion of his task by saying: "I praised the LORD, the God of my master Abraham, who had led [*nḥh*] me on the right road" (Gen. 24:48). The right way requires guidance, and God is ready to provide it. The second passage describes how Israel was guided in the desert by the pillars of cloud and of fire. "By day the LORD went ahead of them in a pillar of cloud to guide (*nḥh*) them on their way" (Ex. 13:21).

The kind of guidance Yahweh provides is not just offered through his designated leaders, such as Moses. Nor does he guide simply by pointing us to his written Word. Both the written Word and the assistance of others can be an important source of divine guidance, and I have made use of both at times. But God has also promised to guide us himself, to go before us and to make his way known. As we make our way through the forest of life, the blazes on the trees left behind by our pathfinding God may seem few and far between. But our attention to the details of God's rule among us will sharpen our vision along with our faith to follow him.

Facing God. As noted above, the opening verses of Psalm 67 ("May God be gracious to us and bless us and make his face shine upon us") have close

---

17. Although the apparatus of *BHS* offers several textually supported alternatives, all of which are plural, the word as it stands in the MT is *darkeka* ("your way"), in the singular.

18. It is significant that in the *Yahweh malak* psalms (93, 95–98) the chief characteristic of Yahweh as king is his coming to judge the earth in "truth" and "righteousness" (96:13), in "righteousness" and "equity" (98:9). In both instances Yahweh's judgment of the earth is the cause of universal joy and praise.

resonances with the classic priestly benediction over Israel given in Numbers 6:24–26. By this blessing, Yahweh "put [his] name on the Israelites" (6:27) to establish and confirm his special relationship with them.[19] They were to become his people, known by his name. And he was to become their God, who gave them identity and purpose and through whom their character was to be formed and measured.[20]

It is particularly interesting that while the Numbers benediction concludes the formal covenant relationship between Yahweh and Israel, Psalm 67 turns immediately to speak of God's *universal* purposes for salvation for "all nations [*goyim*]" as a prelude to the universal praise of "all peoples" (both *ᶜammim* and *leʾummim*) that fills the rest of the psalm. Within the context of the growing universal flavor of Psalms 56–68, Psalm 67 lends voice to the chorus of all creation near and far, Israelite and non-Israelite—"all the ends of the earth" who fear Yahweh (67:7).[21]

It is especially poignant for me—a non-Israelite, a non-Jew, a member of the *goyim* from the "ends of the earth"—to hear these words of special relationship pronounced over me and all my brothers and sisters in Christ. We truly have much to be thankful for, that we have been "grafted into"[22] the family of God through the work of Jesus to establish God's salvation "among all the nations," that we can look forward with joy to sharing the glory of God rather than trembling with fear at the consequences our own sin have wrought. Indeed, "may the peoples praise you, O God; may *all the peoples* praise you!"

---

19. It is, of course, remarkable that the formative name Yahweh is *not* used in the benediction of Ps. 67—a further indication of the revisionist character of the Elohistic Psalter, of which it is a part.

20. See comments on the divine name at Ps. 8. See also the discussion of "name theology" in the Bridging Contexts section of Ps. 63.

21. The final clause of the priestly benediction in Num. 6 does not appear in Ps. 67. In Num. 6:26, the benediction concludes: "[May] the LORD turn [lift up] his face toward you and give you peace." Note the tension that underlies this statement: To "lift up" the divine face is to allow the full force of divine glory to be seen and directly experienced—a fearsome prospect for sinful humans, for "no one may see [God's] face and live" (Ex. 33:19–20). Yet the benediction remains confident that when Yahweh "lifts his face" on Israel, he will give, *not* destruction and judgment, but "peace" (wholeness, completeness, communion) to the recipient. While this aspect of the benediction is not emphasized in Ps. 67, it must have formed a part of the background knowledge and understanding of the hearer/reader and would have informed the interpretation of the universal purposes of Yahweh. In this way the salvation of God would be known among all the nations on earth (67:3)—through the blessing of God poured out (67:6–7). The turn from judgment of the nations/peoples (66:7) to salvation may come as a result of confession of sin as described in 65:3 and 66:18. The ability to stand in God's presence and share his "glory" without fear is expressed in the New Testament in Rom. 5:1–11.

22. Rom. 11:17–24.

Psalm 68

FOR THE DIRECTOR of music. Of David. A psalm. A song.

1 May God arise, may his enemies be scattered;
may his foes flee before him.
2 As smoke is blown away by the wind,
may you blow them away;
as wax melts before the fire,
may the wicked perish before God.
3 But may the righteous be glad
and rejoice before God;
may they be happy and joyful.

4 Sing to God, sing praise to his name,
extol him who rides on the clouds—
his name is the LORD—
and rejoice before him.
5 A father to the fatherless, a defender of widows,
is God in his holy dwelling.
6 God sets the lonely in families,
he leads forth the prisoners with singing;
but the rebellious live in a sun-scorched land.

7 When you went out before your people, O God,
when you marched through the wasteland, *Selah*
8 the earth shook,
the heavens poured down rain,
before God, the One of Sinai,
before God, the God of Israel.
9 You gave abundant showers, O God;
you refreshed your weary inheritance.
10 Your people settled in it,
and from your bounty, O God, you provided for
the poor.

11 The Lord announced the word,
and great was the company of those who proclaimed it:
12 "Kings and armies flee in haste;
in the camps men divide the plunder.

13 Even while you sleep among the campfires,
the wings of my dove are sheathed with silver,
its feathers with shining gold."
14 When the Almighty scattered the kings in the land,
it was like snow fallen on Zalmon.

15 The mountains of Bashan are majestic mountains;
rugged are the mountains of Bashan.
16 Why gaze in envy, O rugged mountains,
at the mountain where God chooses to reign,
where the LORD himself will dwell forever?
17 The chariots of God are tens of thousands
and thousands of thousands;
the Lord has come from Sinai into his sanctuary.
18 When you ascended on high,
you led captives in your train;
you received gifts from men,
even from the rebellious—
that you, O LORD God, might dwell there.

19 Praise be to the Lord, to God our Savior,
who daily bears our burdens. *Selah*
20 Our God is a God who saves;
from the Sovereign LORD comes escape from death.

21 Surely God will crush the heads of his enemies,
the hairy crowns of those who go on in their sins.
22 The Lord says, "I will bring them from Bashan;
I will bring them from the depths of the sea,
23 that you may plunge your feet in the blood of your foes,
while the tongues of your dogs have their share."

24 Your procession has come into view, O God,
the procession of my God and King into the sanctuary.
25 In front are the singers, after them the musicians;
with them are the maidens playing tambourines.
26 Praise God in the great congregation;
praise the LORD in the assembly of Israel.
27 There is the little tribe of Benjamin, leading them,
there the great throng of Judah's princes,
and there the princes of Zebulun and of Naphtali.

28 Summon your power, O God;
show us your strength, O God, as you have done before.
29 Because of your temple at Jerusalem
kings will bring you gifts.
30 Rebuke the beast among the reeds,
the herd of bulls among the calves of the nations.
Humbled, may it bring bars of silver.
Scatter the nations who delight in war.
31 Envoys will come from Egypt;
Cush will submit herself to God.

32 Sing to God, O kingdoms of the earth,
sing praise to the Lord, *Selah*
33 to him who rides the ancient skies above,
who thunders with mighty voice.
34 Proclaim the power of God,
whose majesty is over Israel,
whose power is in the skies.
35 You are awesome, O God, in your sanctuary;
the God of Israel gives power and strength to his people.

Praise be to God!

PSALM 68 HAS been variously interpreted as a collection of psalm titles/incipits[1] or a unified poem. Some see it as an adaptation of an original Baal hymn, or at least an adaptation of earlier Canaanite motifs (cf. esp. the concept of riding on the clouds in 68:4, 33).[2] There is no question that the psalm is challenging and that a satisfying structure is difficult to delineate. However, there is a *thematic cohesion* to the piece that appropriately reflects the growing concern expressed in the extended group of Psalms 56–67. Clear within this otherwise difficult poem are Yahweh's demonstration of his universal power and authority, the acknowledgment of that authority by the nations and their submission to it, and joyful praise for Yah-

1. W. F. Albright, "A Catalogue of Early Hebrew Lyric Poems," *HUCA* 23 (1950–1951): 1–39.

2. F. M. Cross, *Canaanite Myth and Hebrew Epic* (Cambridge, Mass.: Harvard Univ. Press, 1973), 147–63.

weh's righteous kingship by the whole earth. As a unified composition, then, Psalm 68 is a praise hymn celebrating the power of Yahweh to save.

The structure of this psalm is made complex by a lack of clarity about unifying principles. The following is an attempt to provide a sense of how the various segments of the psalm contribute to the thematic cohesion mentioned above. The psalm can be shaped around the following outline: desire that God will arise to scatter the enemies of the faithful (68:1–3), call to praise him for his protection of the defenseless (68:4–6), theophanic appearance of God as abundant rain (68:7–10), the divine word scattering the enemy (68:11–14), Yahweh's coming to his sanctuary (68:15–27), the submission of the nations to God's power (68:28–31), and concluding call for all kingdoms of the earth to praise God (68:32–35).

The Heading (68:0)

NO NEW TERMS grace the heading of Psalm 68. The psalm is referred to "the director of music," is attributed to David, and like Psalms 66–67 is described as both "psalm" (*mizmor*) and "song" (*šir*).[3]

Desire for God to Scatter His Enemies (68:1–3)

THE PSALMIST USES the imagery of the dissipation of smoke before a wind and the melting away of wax before a flame[4] to describe the utter defeat of God's enemies, who scatter and flee in total disarray before him (68:2–3). The NIV translates the imperfect verb forms in these verses as jussives even though the initial verb (*yaqum*) does not take the expected form of the jussive (*yaqom*) and the remaining verbs have forms in which jussive and imperfect are indistinguishable. The difference is between expressing the hope or desire that God will come (the jussive) and the prophetic envisioning of the present reality of God's arising (the imperfect), that he is even now acting to exert his power and authority over the world and its nations.

While the wicked will perish when God comes (a natural result of the conflict between their sin and his holiness), the righteous have nothing to fear.

---

3. See comments on the headings of Pss. 3; 4; 30; and 65.

4. We probably envision the wax of a candle shrinking away from the flame of the burning wick, but the early Israelites—to whom candles were unknown—more likely are thinking of the wax figures used to form a clay mold for casting metal. The wax was carved into the finished shape and then coated with the clay of the mold. After the clay was hardened, molten metal was poured into the mold through an opening left for this purpose. The wax model was vaporized as the hot metal replaced it. Alternatively, an Old Aramaic treaty from the mid-eighth century B.C. mentions the burning of a wax figure as part of a ritual of self-imprecation affirming the treaty relationship. See W. Beyerlin, *Near Eastern Religious Texts Relating to the Old Testament* (Philadelphia: Westminster, 1978), 259.

Their response is emphatically positive and described with a series of joyful verbs: "be glad,"[5] "rejoice," "be happy."

Praise for Protection of the Defenseless (68:4–6)

THE COMING OF God is an occasion for great joy, and the gathered worshipers are called to join in singing his praise (68:4). God appears in association with the power of the storm (cf. 68:33–34) and is proclaimed the one "who rides on the clouds"—an epithet also known to be applied to the Canaanite deity Baal.[6] This may be the reason the divine name Yahweh is introduced at this point, so that no mistake can be made.[7] Elsewhere in the psalms God is also associated with powerful storm phenomena (cf. esp. Ps. 29).

Father to the fatherless. The God who comes is not just a powerful judge deciding between the righteous and the wicked. The God whose power is unmistakably displayed in the storm imagery is also the compassionate deity concerned with the welfare of those who have little status or power in the patriarchal society of the ancient Near East.

In ancient male-dominated society, adult males represented the family and provided access to the resources the society offered. Those who had no male representative—especially orphans (NIV "the fatherless") and widows, as here—were at a disadvantage, having no one to secure their rights or basic needs. Such persons were wholly dependent on their own ability to scratch out a meager existence on the margins of society or were dependent on acts of charity by compassionate individuals.[8] Israelite law contained regulations to mitigate the circumstances of such defenseless persons by describing their plight, encouraging compassion toward them, and laying down commandments regarding their care and treatment by society at large.[9]

---

5. The same verb describes the joyous response of the "nations" to the just rule and guidance of God in 67:4.

6. Cf. Beyerlin, *Near Eastern Texts Relating to the Old Testament*, 196, note q; 210, note h.

7. This is the first appearance of the divine name Yahweh since 64:10 and only the third occurrence since 59:3. In light of the tendency of the Elohistic Psalter (Pss. 42–83) to omit reference to Yahweh, Ps. 68 (with five appearances of the name), Ps. 69 (an additional five occurrences), and the combined Pss. 70–71 (five more appearances of the name) mark a radical departure.

8. The story of the two widows Naomi and Ruth makes this point clearly.

9. Cf. Deut. 14:29; 16:11, 14; 24:17–21; 26:12, 13; 27:19. The fact that the preponderance of this legislation is found in Deuteronomy—which came to its final form and position in the Pentateuch in the Exile—suggests this problem of the rights and needs of the "fatherless and widows" is particularly acute in the late monarchical and early exilic period. This is borne out as well by the number of prophetic allusions to injustice and indignity visited on these marginalized people during this same period (cf. Isa. 1:17, 23; 9:17;

During the monarchy, it was the responsibility of the king and leaders of society to ensure justice for these persons and to oversee their welfare.[10]

The compassionate nature of Yahweh is exhibited in his taking on the responsibility that king and leaders have failed to assume: God becomes "father to the fatherless, a defender of widows" (68:5). In addition, God works to provide new families for those left alone and releases prisoners from the dungeons (so they can return to their unprotected families?).[11]

In his holy dwelling. God's compassionate concern emanates from his divine residence. Often the dwelling of Yahweh is assumed to be the temple in Jerusalem. In other instances it is his *heavenly* dwelling that is in view. Which of the two is intended here is uncertain, since allusions to both appear in the remainder of the psalm. In 68:15–16 the mountains of Bashan gaze enviously at the "mountain where God chooses to reign, where the LORD himself will dwell forever"—a probable reference to Mount Zion in Jerusalem. In 68:17, Yahweh is described as having "come from Sinai into his sanctuary"—another reference to the Jerusalem temple (cf. 68:24b, 35). Verse 18 reports how victorious Yahweh "ascended on high ... that you, O LORD God, might dwell there." Here, what might be taken as a reference to the heavenly abode of Yahweh can also be understood as his ascent to the heights of Zion to be enthroned in the temple.

The rebellious. God's compassionate care is poured out on those who acknowledge their need and find their refuge in him alone—an example of the appropriate attitude of "fear of Yahweh." But those who refuse to acknowledge God's power and their dependence on it are called the "rebellious" (Heb. "stubborn ones"), whose life is like a "sun-scorched land" (68:6).[12]

10:2; Jer. 7:6; 22:3; Ezek. 22:7; Zech. 7:10; Mal. 3:5). Any increase in the "fatherless and widows" during this period may well have been the result of the deaths or physical displacement of many males in the military engagements and resulting captivity of the Exile.

10. See esp. the condemnations of Isa. 1:17, 23; 10:2; Jer. 7:6; 22:3; and Ezek. 22:6–7. That even outside Israel kings were expected to protect the rights of widows and orphans is illustrated by the Epilogue to the Law Code of Hammurabi, where that great king takes care to proclaim that one reason for the promulgation of his law code was to ensure justice for orphans and widows (cf. G. R. Driver and J. C. Miles, *The Babylonian Law* [Oxford: Oxford Univ. Press, 1955], 2:95–99).

11. Again the circumstances described fit well with the devastation of the Exile: fathers killed in battle, or carried off to prison outside the homeland, and leaving their defenseless families bereft of protection and representation.

12. The word translated "sun-scorched" may mean instead "bare, barren," indicating a desert or wilderness region devoid of vegetation. While this may be the result of intense sun, the emphasis here in on the barrenness of the landscape and not the heat.

God Appears as Abundant Rain (68:7–10)

IN CONTRAST TO the environs experienced by the "rebellious" (68:6), the faithful experience Yahweh as refreshing showers that provide bounty even in the wasteland. In what appears to be an allusion to the Exodus and subsequent conquest of Canaan, God is described as going before his people and marching with them "through the wasteland" (68:7). This allusion is heightened in the following verses by the phrases "God, the One of Sinai" (68:8c), "inheritance" (68:9), and "settled in it" (68:10). In contrast, the references to the ground shaking (68:8a) and pouring rain (68:8b) are never used in association with the Sinai event but are used elsewhere to describe the theophanic appearance of God (cf. esp. Ps. 29). Here, however, phenomena that most often demonstrate the awesome power of God (e.g., the shaking of the earth and breaking of cedars in Ps. 29) are heralds of God's gifts of abundance and bounty (68:9–10).

The Exodus-Conquest motifs of desert wandering and entry into the land are artfully expanded in these verses by the inclusion of storm imagery, which both displays God's power and affirms his concern to provide for his people. As in the preceding section, Yahweh is concerned to demonstrate his compassion for the defenseless of society ("fatherless" and "widows")—here, his abundance provides ultimately for the "poor" (68:10).

The Divine Word Scatters the Enemy (68:11–14)

NOT ONLY DOES Yahweh provide bountiful crops for his people, turning the "weary inheritance" (68:9) into "a land flowing with milk and honey" (cf. Ex. 3:8, 17; Deut. 26:9, 15), but he also removes the enemies that threaten them. This passage is a difficult one, with several uncertain phrases,[13] but the primary message is clear: Yahweh comes, and "kings and armies flee" (68:12a) and are scattered like snow on the mountaintops (68:14).[14] The "word" that God pronounces at the beginning of this passage (68:11a) is possibly the announcement of his impending visit (cf. 68:17). Even the prospect of God's coming is enough to send the "mighty" kings of the earth into a panic.

---

13. (1) The phrase *newat bayit* (68:12b) lit. means something like "remote pasturage of a house." The NIV's translation as "in the camps" is speculative. (2) The reference to "among the campfires" (68:13a) has adapted the Hebrew text (*ben šepatayim* ["between two lips"]) in response to a similar phrase in Judg. 5:16 (*ben hammišpetayim* ["between the two saddlebags"; NIV "among the campfires"). (3) The meaning here of the reference in 68:13b-c to "the wings of my dove are sheathed with silver, its feathers with shining gold" remains opaque.

14. Zalmon (68:14b) is a mountain located near Shechem (cf. Judg. 9:48), while the mountains of Bashan (68:15) are situated east of the Sea of Galilee, on the eastern side of the Jordan River.

Yahweh Comes to His Sanctuary (68:15–27)

THE MOUNTAINS OF BASHAN. The psalmist contrasts the rugged grandeur of the mountains of Bashan, located to the northeast of the Jordan River, with the relatively insignificant topography of Zion—the rocky ridge on which Jerusalem and the temple stand. Yet the craggy mountains of Bashan[15] gaze down with envy, not because of Zion's great heights or rugged beauty but simply because it is the place "where God chooses to reign, where Yahweh himself will dwell forever" (68:16). The very presence of God gives this simple location stature.

The chariots of God. Yahweh comes like a victorious king supported by an army of massed chariotry. In 2 Kings 6:8–17, when Elisha's servant reports to his master that they are surrounded by an army of horse-drawn chariots sent by the king of Aram intent on capturing Elisha, the prophet reveals a host of invisible flaming chariots sent by God to protect him.

Elsewhere the chariots of God depict judgment, as Isaiah proclaims: "See, the LORD is coming with fire, and his chariots are like a whirlwind; he will bring down his anger with fury, and his rebuke with flames of fire" (Isa. 66:15). Note also Habakkuk 3:8: "Were you angry with the rivers, O LORD? Was your wrath against the streams? Did you rage against the sea when you rode with your horses and your victorious chariots?" God's claim of world authority is no empty posturing but is backed up with the power to bring down the armies of the kings of the earth.

From Sinai. God approaches from the southern deserts, where Mount Sinai is located. Again, this associates Psalm 68 with Exodus and Conquest memories. As Israel approached the land of promise from the experience of covenant-making at Sinai, so God comes to his people and his "sanctuary" from the same geographical direction and in response to the same covenant.

When you ascended on high. As a victorious king entered a city and sanctuary, God ascends the throne, from which he rules his kingdom. The victory procession of a returning king was common in the ancient Near East. Captives were paraded as a visible representation of the king's far-flung conquests. As the victorious army returned home through various subject nations, the parade of captives drove home to any who might entertain notions of rebellion the power of the king and how he had defeated those who had

---

15. The phrase "the mountains of Bashan are *majestic* mountains" is an interesting one since it involves the use of the more generic word for God/god (*ʾelohim*) as a sort of superlative adjective. The passage literally reads: "[the] mountain of God [is] Mount Bashan" (*har ʾelohim har bašan*). The NIV's translation "majestic" is most likely an interpretation taken from the parallel phrase *har gabnunnim har bašan* ("a mountain of high arches [is] Mount Bashan").

resisted his authority. Even the "rebellious" (68:18; cf. 68:6) here will hurry with gifts to prove their loyalty to God.[16]

Our God is a God who saves. God's presence in his sanctuary is a source of hope for his people. Yahweh is not an austere king who is aloof and unconcerned about his people. He "daily bears [their] burdens" (68:19b) and provides "escape from death" (68:20b). Therefore, God is acknowledged as "Savior" (68:19a) and is worthy of daily "blessing" (rather than the NIV's "praise").[17] Yahweh's "salvation" is seen in terms of his defeat of "his enemies"—the enemies of God rather than Israel's opponents, although the two must often have coincided in Israel's thinking. Here God's enemies are those throughout the world who "go on in their sins." The Hithpael participle *mithallek* (from *hlk* ["walk, go"]) describes repeated or habitual action. Those whom God condemns here are no casual sinners but those who make a habit of sin and rebellion.

I will bring them from Bashan . . . from the depths of the sea. The display of the conquered enemy in the victorious capital has been noted above. Yahweh, the king, intends to bring his conquered enemies to Jerusalem so that the people there can see and even share in the defeat of their opponents. The conquered come from Bashan, one of the chief cities of King Og defeated by the Israelites during their approach to the Promised Land (cf. Num. 21:33–35). Bashan and its majestic mountains (68:15a) lie to the northeast of Jerusalem and across the Jordan River. The "sea" mentioned as the source of additional defeated enemies (68:22b) is the Mediterranean, which borders Israel on the west. The effect of using these two geographical references creates a merism,[18] which mentions two extremes as a way of describing all that lies between. Yahweh will bring *all* his enemies from east to west to demonstrate his power.

This is a particularly harsh passage. We know that some ancient peoples made public spectacles of their defeated enemies. The Philistines blinded Samson and put him on public display. The Romans used defeated enemies in gladiatorial contests while others were fed to wild animals or crucified as a public deterrent to rebellion. That Israel practiced this particularly violent form of public humiliation of enemies seems clear from such passages as Gideon's execution of Zebah and Zalmunna (Judg. 8:13–21) and that of Agag king of Amalek by Samuel (1 Sam. 15:30–33). Whether Israel and

16. The gifts are received "from men" (*ʾadam*), a more generic allusion to all humanity as is characteristic of this group of Pss. 56–68.

17. On this issue, see comments on 16:3–8.

18. See the discussion of merism in the section on "The Poetry of the Psalms" in the introduction.

Judah ever paraded their defeated enemies through the streets of Jerusalem before a public execution is not clear. We do know from Egyptian hieroglyphs and Mesopotamian relief carvings that the Judahites themselves had experienced such treatment at the hands of the Babylonians.

That you may plunge your feet. The harsh description reaches its climax with this picture of bloodletting. The scene depicts the execution of captives from the defeated nations in the streets of Jerusalem so that the general populace can participate in the humiliation of their enemies and know personally the great victory Yahweh has accomplished for them. Wading ankle deep in the blood of one's defeated enemies is an image known from other texts both inside and outside the Bible.[19] Dogs lapping the blood of the slain is found in the description of the deaths of King Ahab and his wife Jezebel (1 Kings 21:17–19; 22:34–38; 2 Kings 9:30–37).

Your procession has come into view, O God. The psalmist mixes the image of the victorious king entering his capital city—defeated enemies following in his train—with the cultic procession of celebrants to the Jerusalem temple. Perhaps the image is of the ark of the covenant—the sign of the invisible presence of Yahweh—carried through the streets to the gates of the temple compound. Psalm 24:7–10 contains what may be a liturgical snippet from such a processional moment, when the glorious divine king, fresh from victory over his enemies, demands entrance to his earthly dwelling place.

My God and King. Clearly the victorious king is Yahweh here. Just what part the earthly king played in these festivities—whether he stood in as the representative of Yahweh or took some more subordinate role—is not clear.

The great congregation. The scene takes place in the "great congregation ... in the assembly of Israel"—a reference to God's faithful people gathered for worship at the Jerusalem temple. The victorious king is surrounded by singers and musicians and is accompanied by representatives of all the tribes, although only four are mentioned: Benjamin[20] and Judah (the two tribal members of the Davidic southern kingdom), and Zebulun and Naphtali (representatives of the northern tribes). These tribes at the geographical edges of the united Davidic kingdom form a merism, standing for the whole kingdom between these points.

---

19. Biblical texts include Ps. 58:10; Isa. 63:3, 6; Ezek. 28:23. Cf. the related passages in 2 Kings 21:16; Hos. 6:8; Prov. 1:12; Rev. 14:20. Outside the Bible, cf. Hathor in "The Deliverance of Mankind from Destruction," *ANETP*, 1:3–5.

20. Just why the tribe of Benjamin is called "little" is not immediately clear. Benjamin is described as the youngest son of Jacob/Israel in the Joseph narratives (Gen. 37–50). Perhaps the intent is to enhance the stature of the Davidic homeland, Judah, which is described here as a "great throng."

The Nations Submit to God's Power (68:28–31)

THE VICTORY OF Yahweh brings submission by the nations of the earth to his rule. Because of his "power" and "strength" (68:28), they hasten to bring gifts and tribute, acknowledging their allegiance to him (68:29–30).[21] In imaginative language the humbled nations are described as "the beast among the reeds" (an allusion to Egypt in the southwest, where papyrus reeds grew in abundance in the Delta region) and "the herd of bulls among the calves of the nations" (probably another reference to Bashan—renowned for its cattle—to the northeast; cf. 68:15, 22). "Egypt" (along with "Cush," i.e., Upper Egypt) is explicitly mentioned in 68:31 as sending envoys in order to submit to the authority of God and to entreat peace with him.

The Kingdoms of the Earth Praise God (68:32–35)

IN A REPRISE of earlier praises, the psalmist reissues the call to "sing to God," first heard in 68:4. As there, God is associated with storm phenomena (particularly thunder, 68:33) and is described as the one "who rides [*rkb*] the ancient skies" (cf. 68:4).[22] Here, however, it is the "kingdoms of the earth" (*mamlekot haʾareṣ*) who are called to join in the praise of God—those nations who have just been described as defeated and forced to submit to the rule of Yahweh.

Having been brought captive to Jerusalem, the nations witness the awesome power of Yahweh as he enters his sanctuary. Once having seen his glory, these rebellious nations are unable to resist the praise of God, who is king both in the heavens and on the earth (68:34). Yahweh's power is manifest in his temple, and his presence in Israel imparts "power and strength to his people" (68:35). Thus, at the end—overwhelmed with the power and majesty of God as with the smashing thunder of the storm (68:33)—Israelite and non-Israelite alike can only respond: "Blessed be God! [NIV Praise be to God!]."[23]

---

21. The latter half of verse 30 is particularly difficult. The Hithpael participle *mitrappes* means something like "muddy themselves"; depending on how one takes the following participle *beraṣṣe* (from *rṣh* or *rwṣ*) might suggest prostrating themselves in the dirt/mud or splashing mud on themselves while running in haste to deliver their tribute and entreaties for peace.

22. The latter phrase (*bišme šeme qedem*) is difficult, and *BHS* suggests a possible emendation to *baššamayim qedem*. While the parallel with 68:4 is not exact, it is sufficiently similar to suggest these verses serve as related expansions on the theme of Yahweh revealed in the power of the storm.

23. Once again, see comments on 16:3–8.

COSMIC CONQUEROR. How do we deal with the violent language that stands at the center of this psalm? The psalmist expresses the certainty that "God will crush the heads of his enemies, the hairy crowns of those who go on in their sins" (68:21). He will bring captives to Jerusalem so that local citizens can join in the joyous bloodbath of their execution (68:22–23). We have encountered other psalms, and will again before we reach the end of the Psalter, where we have been challenged and discomfited by the violent language of judgment and vengeance.[24] But in this case, another factor may be at work to help us understand the graphic language of destruction and conquest.

Part of the answer, I think, is involved in recognizing that the poet is adapting what appears to be ancient Canaanite mythological imagery to speak of the sovereignty of Yahweh over all the earth. We have been building up, as you will remember, over the last six or seven psalms an expanding thematic picture of God's sovereignty over all the earth: the ultimate submission of all peoples, Israelite or non-Israelite, to the authority of God; the outbreak of divine blessing on the earth as a result of the restoration of divine sovereignty; the growing crescendo of praise from all flesh in response to God's just rule and effective guidance of all who fear him. I went so far as to suggest the Psalms 60–67 form a sort of "evangelistic pamphlet" to encourage the non-Israelite nations to submit to Yahweh and to avail themselves of the blessings of his reign.

In this light, Psalm 68 is praising Yahweh's defeat of his enemies and describing the submission of the nations to his sovereign rule. In the process the poet employs cosmic mythological imagery familiar to the worshipers of Baal and adapts it to reflect Yahweh's defeat of his cosmic opponents. With language used of Baal in Canaanite myths, Yahweh is described as the "rider of the clouds" and is associated, like Baal, with the storm, thunder, and lightning.

In the Canaanite legend of Baal and Anat,[25] Baal fights with Mot ("Death") and is defeated and taken down to the underworld through Mot's gullet. Baal's sister, Anat, confronts Mot, defeats him in battle, and secures the release of her brother. In an earlier conflict, Baal struggles with the chaotic powers of the waters known as Judge Nahar (river) and defeats him by striking him on the head (*qdqd*), much as Yahweh crushes the heads (*qodqod*; NIV "crown")

24. See the Bridging Contexts section of Ps. 58.

25. An English translation of this text is found in *ANETP*, 1:92–118. For the section about the struggle between Baal, Mot, and Anat, see esp. 106–15.

of his enemies (68:21).[26] The fact that Yahweh's striking the heads of the enemies is immediately preceded by the affirmation that "our God is a God who saves; from the Sovereign LORD comes escape from death [*mawet*]" suggests a link with the mythological struggle of Baal and Mot.

The use of the imagery works in two ways. Mythological struggles have been provided a foothold in the real world of human experience by being connected with the defeat of God's enemies here and now. At the same time, however, the introduction of cosmic struggle language seems to demand a sort of cosmic, eschatological fulfillment on a universal scale.

What this means in terms of our own response is that this violent language has been shifted out of our present context of treatment of our captive enemies into the eschatological conflict between Yahweh and his cosmic opponents. The violence has become a metaphor for the completeness of God's power and the certainty of the defeat of his cosmic foes. On this level the language is no more offensive than the blood that flows from the winepress through the streets of the new Jerusalem in Revelation 14:20.[27]

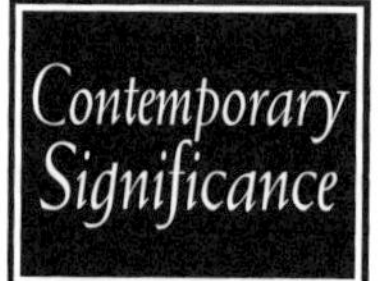

THE LANGUAGE OF THEOPHANY. Like the violent language discussed above, the language of theophany is language in the extreme. Human language is pressed into service to describe what it was never meant to describe: the very holiness of God arriving in the human world of our sinful experience. To describe God is to move firmly into the realm of hyperbole, that is, language stretched to its utmost—even beyond its utmost. You have only to read the tortured—though majestic and fascinating—vision of God in Ezekiel 1 to understand just how ill-suited human language is for describing the ineffable nature of God. It is perhaps understandable that the rabbis came ultimately to prohibit the public reading of Ezekiel 1 or to prohibit anyone who had not reached a mature age to study the passage.

We may think we do better when we use the language of philosophy or theology to talk *about* God. We can maintain our distance, so to speak, and organize our thoughts rationally and logically. But try comparing the passages on God from Aquinas's *Summa Theologica*, Barth's *Kirchliche Dogmatik*, or

---

26. In the legend of Aqhat, Anat is described as slaying Aqhat son of Danʾel by striking him on the head (*roʾš*) and pate (*qdqd*).

27. It is almost impossible to reduce the "offense" of God's violent judgment of those who oppose him—whether in this world or cosmically—without undermining or ignoring altogether the justice of God, who does not wink at evil but must act in condemnation to what stands in adamant opposition to his essential character.

Shedd's *Systematic Theology* and you will realize that something is lost in all the words, no matter how sublime they may be. There is passion in theophanic language—passion to lead the reader into an *experience*, not an *understanding*, of God.

To do this borders on violence, because to experience God in this way is to experience him with all the guards let down and the boundaries removed. It is to know the terrible, awesome, fearsome, threatening being of the one who created us and yet is now unleashed among us to challenge our sinful beings to provide any justification for our continued existence. Isaiah's response to such a theophany (Isa. 6:1–9) shows us just how scary that kind of experience can be! That is why the rabbis wanted to restrict access to Ezekiel's theophanic vision, for they feared that the untutored public or an immature student might be caught up in a partial understanding of God's glory and so act in ways that would bring harm—even destruction—on themselves and their community.

Just to talk about theophany is to lessen its power and impact. Nevertheless, we do talk about it to enable those to whom the language is alien (and therefore suspect) to understand it and hopefully to enter into it as it was intended. But it is really not enough to stand back and look at theophany. This language is intended to draw the reader in—to open the eyes, and ears, and nose, and heart to the very presence of God. Note how Isaiah (Isa. 6:1–9) uses sight, sound, feeling, and smell to envelop the reader into the experience of God. Here are just a few comments about theophanic language intended to provide access rather than to explain it fully.[28]

(1) Excessive. Theophany is excessive. It uses the language of hyperbole. God is, of course, larger than life and requires a vocabulary on the edges of language's capabilities to encapsulate his description. When God comes, big things happen: The earth shakes (68:8); rains pour down in the desert (68:8); tens of thousands of divine chariots light up the sky (68:17); representatives of all the nations of the earth bring gifts to him (68:18); the hometown crowd wade ankle deep in the blood of their executed enemies (68:23). This is language out of the ordinary, but so is the God it seeks to describe.

(2) Violent. As violent as it is excessive, theophany often offends our modern sensibilities. When God comes, the mountains smoke (Ex. 19:18; Ps. 104:32) or melt away (Ps. 97:5; Mic. 1:4; Nah. 1:5); the wicked blow away like smoke or melt like wax before a fire (Ps. 68:2); the bodies of defeated kings lie like snow on the hills (68:14); God drags his defeated enemies from town to town for public display (68:18); he crushes the heads and hairy

28. For fuller explanation of theophany read the helpful articles on the subject in *IDB* and *ISBE*[2].

crowns of those who oppose him (68:21); the people dance in the blood of their enemies (68:23; cf. 58:10).

These images of violence are excessive. They describe actions of God whose powers outstrip and ultimately nullify even the most violent efforts human beings can sum up (and we are pretty good at violence!). Thus, God's theophanic violence is on the one hand a *negating response* to human violence, which it overcomes. God responds in kind; our violence calls forth a response of divine violence.

On the other hand, however, the violence of theophany is the *natural* consequence of a holy God entering an unholy world. It is the necessary result of God's incompatibility with evil that when he encounters wickedness and sin, he judges and destroys it. Theophanic depictions of divine violence, then, are examples of the unsettling "otherness" of God raised to their highest quotient. God is so other that even his coming into our world with saving intent is a threat to our sinful selves. Like Isaiah, we fall prostrate before the glory of holy God, fully expecting the destruction we deserve, only to be mystified by the experience of divine grace and forgiveness.

(3) *Progressive.* Finally, the theophany in Psalm 68 is also progressive. The coming of Yahweh into the world has a beginning and an end. Many have noted the movement in this psalm from Sinai (68:8) to the Jerusalem temple (68:35).[29] In this view, the first half of the psalm (68:1–17) describes the rising of Yahweh to deliver his people from Egypt, the passage through the desert, the struggle with the nations along the way, and the establishment of the temple in Jerusalem as the place where God will continue to dwell among Israel. The second half of the psalm (68:18–35) depicts the continued residency of God in Jerusalem and the consequent submission of the nations to his power.

The purpose of God's coming in the Exodus event was to bring his people to a new place of covenant relationship, a land in which they would dwell as the holy nation of God in whose midst Yahweh himself was pleased to dwell in the temple. The theophanic approach of God in Psalm 68 traces the same steps but raises the experience to the eschatological extreme. This time, when Yahweh establishes his throne in his sanctuary, his kingdom will include the whole earth. The kings of the nations will submit to him and bring him gifts of submission and praise.

The path of God's conquest in our lives ought to follow the same path: From the desert of our sin to the fruitful land of the kingdom of God, from the battles of evil within and without to the destruction of the foes and submission to God's sovereignty, from the isolation of self-concern to the communal gathering of praise in the sanctuary, God is leading his children along.

---

29. See the comments of Tate, *Psalms 51–100*, 185–86; Mays, *Psalms*, 225–29.

Psalm 69

FOR THE DIRECTOR of music. To the tune of "Lilies." Of David.

1 Save me, O God,
for the waters have come up to my neck.
2 I sink in the miry depths,
where there is no foothold.
I have come into the deep waters;
the floods engulf me.
3 I am worn out calling for help;
my throat is parched.
My eyes fail,
looking for my God.
4 Those who hate me without reason
outnumber the hairs of my head;
many are my enemies without cause,
those who seek to destroy me.
I am forced to restore
what I did not steal.

5 You know my folly, O God;
my guilt is not hidden from you.

6 May those who hope in you
not be disgraced because of me,
O Lord, the LORD Almighty;
may those who seek you
not be put to shame because of me,
O God of Israel.
7 For I endure scorn for your sake,
and shame covers my face.
8 I am a stranger to my brothers,
an alien to my own mother's sons;
9 for zeal for your house consumes me,
and the insults of those who insult you fall on me.
10 When I weep and fast,
I must endure scorn;
11 when I put on sackcloth,
people make sport of me.

12 Those who sit at the gate mock me,
  and I am the song of the drunkards.

13 But I pray to you, O LORD,
  in the time of your favor;
in your great love, O God,
  answer me with your sure salvation.
14 Rescue me from the mire,
  do not let me sink;
deliver me from those who hate me,
  from the deep waters.
15 Do not let the floodwaters engulf me
  or the depths swallow me up
  or the pit close its mouth over me.
16 Answer me, O LORD, out of the goodness of your love;
  in your great mercy turn to me.
17 Do not hide your face from your servant;
  answer me quickly, for I am in trouble.
18 Come near and rescue me;
  redeem me because of my foes.

19 You know how I am scorned, disgraced and shamed;
  all my enemies are before you.
20 Scorn has broken my heart
  and has left me helpless;
I looked for sympathy, but there was none,
  for comforters, but I found none.
21 They put gall in my food
  and gave me vinegar for my thirst.

22 May the table set before them become a snare;
  may it become retribution and a trap.
23 May their eyes be darkened so they cannot see,
  and their backs be bent forever.
24 Pour out your wrath on them;
  let your fierce anger overtake them.
25 May their place be deserted;
  let there be no one to dwell in their tents.
26 For they persecute those you wound
  and talk about the pain of those you hurt.
27 Charge them with crime upon crime;
  do not let them share in your salvation.

[28] May they be blotted out of the book of life
and not be listed with the righteous.

[29] I am in pain and distress;
may your salvation, O God, protect me.

[30] I will praise God's name in song
and glorify him with thanksgiving.
[31] This will please the LORD more than an ox,
more than a bull with its horns and hoofs.
[32] The poor will see and be glad—
you who seek God, may your hearts live!
[33] The LORD hears the needy
and does not despise his captive people.

[34] Let heaven and earth praise him,
the seas and all that move in them,
[35] for God will save Zion
and rebuild the cities of Judah.
Then people will settle there and possess it;
[36] the children of his servants will inherit it,
and those who love his name will dwell there.

FOLLOWING THE GROUP of Psalms 56–68 with their striking connected themes of praising God (who is clearly identified as Yahweh in Ps. 68) for his universal creative power and authority acknowledged by all nations, Psalms 69 introduces a new psalm grouping (Pss. 69–71) that returns to earlier themes of lament and pleas for deliverance from mocking and threatening enemies. The hoped-for divine rule over the nations gives way here to the reality of something far less—isolation, oppression, and ridicule by the enemy. The psalmist—who acknowledges sin (69:5) and accepts divine discipline (69:26)—experiences an environment of scorn and rejection that seems out of proportion to his real guilt.

It is clear from the concluding verses (69:33–36) that this individual lament has been reinterpreted to speak to the exilic community. In this later context the rejection the psalmist experiences should perhaps be understood as scorn from those cynical captives who pour out contempt on his expressions of zeal for the Jerusalem temple (69:9) and on his contrition for the communal sins that brought the nation to this pass. At some level the psalmist's suffering is vicarious—both for God (69:9) and for the people (69:26).

Perhaps also the psalmist's enemies can be understood to include the mocking, victorious enemy, although for the most part the textual clues suggest fellow members of the community of faith (69:8, 27–28) who are forfeiting their share in God's coming salvation by persecuting the suffering faithful. Together with Psalms 70–71, Psalm 69 prepares the way for the exalted hopes for the enduring and righteous rule of the king in Psalm 72—a rule that will last as long as the moon and will reach to the ends of the earth (72:5–8).[1]

Structurally, Psalm 69 is divided into seven segments: a plea for deliverance from enemies using the imagery of drowning (69:1–4), the psalmist's admission of guilt coupled with a description of the scorn experienced (69:5–12), a renewed plea for deliverance from enemies again using the imagery of drowning (69:13–18), continued description of the scorn experienced by the psalmist (69:19–21), desire for divine judgment on the enemy (69:22–29), the psalmist's vow to praise and his confidence of deliverance (69:30–33), and a final call to praise Yahweh, reflecting the situation of the exilic community (69:34–36).

The Heading (69:0)

THE PSALM IS referred to "the director of music" and is attributed to David.[2] The heading also includes a reference to a tune for accompaniment: "To the tune of 'Lilies'" (*ʿal šōšannim*), a term that appears also in the heading of Ps. 45.[3]

Plea for Deliverance from Enemies (69:1–4)

SAVE ME, **O God.** The psalmist begins with an urgent plea for deliverance. The difficulties he faces are clearly identified in the rest of the psalm as the mocking attacks of the enemy. The imagery he chooses to dramatize the situation is the desperate struggle of a shipwreck survivor trying to stay afloat in a pounding sea.[4] The waters are up to his "neck"—a play on the double meaning of the Hebrew *nepeš* as "throat/neck" or "self/being." The waters that threaten to overwhelm him also threaten to snuff out his "being" or "self."[5]

1. This reference in 72:8 links this psalm with the whole complex of Pss. 56–71, so that they represent a growing thematic unity.

2. See comments on the headings to Pss. 3 and 4.

3. See comments on the heading of Ps. 45; note also the related term *šušan ʿedut* in the heading to Ps. 60.

4. It is, of course, possible that a flashflood or deep river crossing is in mind, but the bottomless expanse of ocean water seems more expressive here.

5. For comments on the meaning of *nepeš*, see 3:2.

I sink in the miry depths. The series of terms emphasizes the depth of water into which the psalmist has fallen. He "sinks" into the "miry depths" (*yewen meṣulah*),[6] where there is no possibility of finding a footing; he is "engulfed" by "deep waters" and "floods" (perhaps "torrents" or "waves").

I am worn out. The shipwrecked psalmist is tiring from the seemingly endless struggle to stay alive and afloat. The futility of calling for help ("I am worn out ... my throat is parched") and of looking for divine rescue ("my eyes fail, looking for my God") is beginning to sink in. Just as in his despair he is about to slip for the last time beneath the waves, the psalm moves out of the metaphorical imagery of drowning to describe the real circumstances of suffering.

Those who hate me. The real threat is not the pounding waves of the sea but the pounding attack of enemies who seek to destroy. Like the ceaseless waves, the psalmist's enemies are everywhere and seem without number.

Without cause. The psalmist considers the attack of the enemy groundless. Their hatred is "without reason" (*ḥinnam* ["in vain, undeservedly"]) and "without cause" (*šeqer* ["falsely"]). The latter term suggests that the enemy attack is more than a misguided vendetta; it is a purposefully deceitful attempt to "get" the psalmist by distorting the truth—submerging any protestations under the flood of their false accusations. He emphasizes the injustice of the attack by claiming, "I am forced to restore what I did not steal."

Folly and Scorn (69:5–12)

ALTHOUGH THE PSALMIST characterizes the enemy's attacks as groundless and false, the second section begins with an admission—directly to God—of his "folly"[7] and "guilt."[8] The exact nature of his offense is never clarified, so just how the enemy's accusations can be considered groundless or false is a matter of speculation. What remains clear, however, is that the psalmist acknowledges guilt to God and accepts divine "wounding," "hurt," and "pain" without objection (69:26).

Because of me. The psalmist acknowledges that individual failing has corporate consequences. The collapse of an individual reflects on the broader community. This is true in his mind whether or not the accusations and scorn he experiences are deserved or not. He hopes that the unjust scorn poured out on him will not result in "disgrace" and "shame" for the community of the

---

6. See also the discussion of "stuck in the muck" in the Bridging Contexts section of Ps. 40.

7. Heb. *ʾiwwelet*, which has the edge of *impious* folly; folly that is offensive to God.

8. The plural form of the word in Heb. suggests multiple offenses as the basis of the psalmist's guilt.

faithful.[9] The theme of shame and disgrace as a result of the attacks of the enemy stitch together Psalms 69 and 70–71.[10] As noted earlier,[11] for Israelites shame and disgrace were not internal emotions but visible actions of communal rejection and detraction. It is as if the psalmist, having been judged guilty by certain influential members of society, must wear some sign of disgrace, like Hester Prynne in Hawthorne's *The Scarlet Letter*. Or perhaps he experiences some sort of "shunning" by the community at large. Regardless of the method, he is faced with a communal assumption of guilt that takes obvious and visible form.

Those who hope in you. The psalmist feels a sense of solidarity with the faithful contingent within society who still trust in God. The enemies seem to be excluded from this group, and this allows the possibility, at least in the postexilic reinterpretation of Psalm 69, that the enemy can be identified with foreign detractors of the Diaspora Jewish community. In such circumstances of isolation within a dominant culture, the fall of one Israelite could occasion great distress for the whole community. The story in Esther of Haman's great hatred for Mordecai that led to his plan to destroy the whole Jewish race is a case in point. It is this kind of general disgrace to the community of the faithful that the psalmist appeals to God to avoid.

I endure scorn for your sake. Whatever the nature of the guilt the psalmist admits to God in 69:5, the scorn he experiences results from his commitment to God rather than personal failing. He endures both scorn and shame[12] for God's sake and receives "insults"[13] intended for God because of his "zeal" for God's house. What form this "zeal" takes is not clear from the text, although the following verses (69:10–11) suggest a public display of weeping, fasting, and wearing of sackcloth. From an exilic viewpoint, this might represent the psalmist's active mourning for the loss of the Jerusalem temple.[14]

---

9. See the similar sentiments expressed in Pss. 25:2–3; 34:5, and the counter claim for shame against the enemy in 35:4, 26 and 40:14, 15.

10. Cf. 69:6–7, 19 with 70:2; 71:1, 13.

11. See comments on 25:1–3, 16–23.

12. In this case "shame" (*kelimmah*) is said to "cover" the psalmist's face—possibly a reference to the act of hiding his own face from public view, as prisoners in our own society often do to avoid a reporter's camera. Or perhaps more likely, this refers to the act of spitting in the psalmist's face by angry enemies as an indication of public disgrace and rejection (cf. Num. 12:14; Deut. 25:9; Job 20:15; 30:10; cf. the experience of Jesus in Matt. 26:67).

13. Heb. *ḥerpot* is stronger than "insult" and bears the meaning of a public "rebuke" or scathing "reproach."

14. Were this interpretation of these verses correct, it would have the effect of dating this version of Ps. 69 to the period between the destruction of the first temple (587 B.C.) and its reconstruction in the postexilic period.

People make sport of me. The public response to the psalmist's fervent and visible grief is ridicule and mocking (69:11–12). His antics are the object of great fun among the detractors, and zealous grief for the temple becomes fodder for mocking drinking songs. Those who scorn him span the classes of society—from the drunkards to the influential leaders who "sit at the gate" of the city.[15]

Renewed Plea for Deliverance (69:13–18)

HAVING DESCRIBED THE experience of communal shame and ridicule, the psalmist returns again to entreat God for deliverance. The resulting prayer acknowledges the need for a "time" of divine "favor." Such a view realizes that for each of the varied "times" in life there is a proper course of action—whether divine or human—and that humans are to seek to discern and accommodate their actions, hopes, and expectations to this divinely instituted chronology.[16] This is not to say that all events are fixed ahead of time, like some type of "fate" or *kismet*, only that wise individuals capable of "knowing the times" (cf. 1 Chron. 12:32; Eccl. 3:1; 8:5–6) will be able to discern the proper course of action in every circumstance. Here the psalmist entreats Yahweh for a time of divine favor in which the proper human response is trust and God's appropriate action is enduring salvation.[17]

The psalmist's desperation is illumined by the repeated appearance of the imperative call "Answer me" in 69:13, 16, 17. The grounds for his assumption that *now* is the appropriate time for divine favor[18] is the perception of God's "great love" (*rob ḥasdeka*, 69:13; cf. *ṭob ḥasdeka* ["goodness of your love"], 69:16) and "mercy" (*rob raḥameka*, 69:16). The former describes Yahweh's fierce loyalty to his covenant commitments while the latter refers to the

15. Those who "sit in the city gate" are not the homeless or unemployed who loiter because they have nowhere else to go. The city gate was the site for public administration of justice and community affairs (cf. Gen. 23:10; Ruth 4:1; 1 Kings 22:10; Est. 2:19, 21; 5:13; 6:10; Jer. 38:7). Those who "sit in the city gate" are the recognized elders and rulers of the people, who are responsible for governance and guidance.

16. The same sort of thinking lies behind the legal determination of an individual's righteous or sinful character. Once the "time" is properly understood, the appropriate course of action for all participants in an event can be determined and true judgment rendered. Those who have fulfilled the proper course of action are declared *ṣedeq* ("righteous") while those who have not are pronounced *ʾawen* ("wicked"). See also comments on 4:1–2; 7:6–9.

17. Once again the Heb. *ʾemet* ("true, sure, established, firm") has a sense of "enduring" and "trustworthy." Compare the comments on this term in 25:4–7.

18. Cf. Paul's pronouncement that "now is the time of God's favor" (2 Cor. 6:2), which flows out of his study and quotation of Isa. 49:8: "In the time of my favor I will answer you, and in the day of salvation I will help you." Paul's quotation of Isaiah, however, renders "I will answer you" as "I heard you," following the Greek *epekousa* ("I heard," an aorist form).

deep, warm, motherly compassion he has toward those who have bound themselves to him in relationship.[19]

Rescue me from the mire. The psalmist's plea for deliverance recalls in specific terms the description of the threatening circumstances with which the psalm began. His plea is that each image of threat elaborated in the earlier passage be countered with evidence of God's saving grace. He desires to be rescued "from the mire" (69:14, *miṭṭiṭ*; cf. 69:2, *yawen*)[20] and not to "sink" (69:14; cf. 69:2), and he pleads to be delivered from "those who hate me" (69:14; cf. 69:4), who are also identified with the "deep waters" (69:14d; cf. 69:2) as well as the "floodwaters" (69:15a; cf. 69:2d) and "depths" (69:15b; cf. 69:2a) that threaten to "engulf" (69:15a; cf. 69:2d) him. The deadly threat of these attacks is carried one step further by the reference in 69:15c to the "pit"—a metaphor for Sheol, the abode of the dead—that seeks to "close its mouth over" the psalmist.[21]

Do not hide your face. This section concludes with the plea that God end his inactive and hidden state and come quickly to the psalmist's rescue. For God to "hide his face" (69:17) from his covenant people was considered a sign of divine rejection and punishment for sin—most usually the worship of other gods.[22] This the psalmist claims is not true since he remains God's "servant," however much in need of "redemption."[23]

Continued Description of Scorn (69:19–21)

IF GOD MUST be called to action, his seeming absence is not the result of ignorance. God knows the psalmist's circumstance and is aware of the scorn

---

19. The Heb. word for "compassion, mercy" here is *raḥamim*, which is related to the word *reḥem* ("womb") and describes the "tender compassion" a mother experiences toward the child in her womb. This kind of compassion and tender mercy Yahweh expresses toward those who "fear him" or, in the words of *this* psalm, those who "hope in" him (69:6), "seek" him (69:6, 32), or "love his name" (69:36; cf. esp. Ps. 103:8–13; Ex. 34:7; Num. 14:18.)

20. While the two terms are different, the concept is the same; these two distinct words are also united in 40:2, where the psalmist celebrates a similar deliverance when God lifted him "out of the slimy pit, out of the mud and mire [*miṭṭiṭ hayyawen*]."

21. Canaanite mythology includes the graphic depiction of the god of death, Mot, who waits "one lip to earth and one to heaven" to swallow those who go down through his gullet to Sheol (cf. *ANETP*, 1:108).

22. Cf. esp. Deut. 31:17, 18; 32:20; Jer. 33:5; Mic. 3:4, and the related passages Job 13:24; Pss. 13:1; 27:9; 44:24; 88:14; 102:2; 104:29; 143:7.

23. Both terms translated in this verse as "rescue" (*gʾl*) and "redeem" (*pdh*) are used in the sense of "buy back" a person or item (such as a house) that has been sold or fallen in captivity. The verb *gʾl* has the additional association with the levirate marriage, in which the brother-in-law is said to "redeem" (*gʾl*) the right of the deceased brother by creating a son through the deceased man's widow. In this light the term takes on the nuance "deliver."

the enemies pour out on him. "You know," he cries almost as an accusation, "all my enemies are before you"—they are so visible to God as to be impossible for him to overlook. Undeserved scorn has left him heartbroken and "helpless" (lit., "I am sick, weak"), with none to sympathize or comfort (69:20). Instead of comfort, his enemies provide only "gall" and "vinegar" to assuage his raging thirst (69:21). This painful lack of concern—even sadistic toying with the urgent needs of the suffering—is used in the New Testament to describe the scornful treatment of the suffering Christ on the cross.[24]

Desire for Divine Judgment on the Enemy (69:22–29)

THE PSALMIST'S EXPERIENCE of such unjust suffering—or at least suffering beyond all bounds of propriety in relation to his real guilt—wrenches out a rather angry desire for divine retribution on the heartless enemies. He hopes that "the table set before them"—a clear allusion to the honorific and protective table set for the narrator of Ps. 23:5[25]—will become "a snare ... retribution ... and a trap" for the enemy. The implication is that the table that the enemy takes as a sign of God's presence with their cause will "be turned" on them to become the means of their downfall. The "snare" and "trap" are self-springing devices used to trap unsuspecting birds and are frequently used metaphorically for sudden entrapment of humans by their own deeds. Here, for the deeds and accusations of the enemy to return on them would be fitting "retribution."[26]

May their eyes be darkened. The psalmist's pain pours out in hurtful words directed at the enemy but spoken to God. The suffering and anger are real emotions, truly felt, as he is entirely open before God. These honest expressions of anger are placed, however, within the context of anticipated *divine* retribution. It is God who is called to "pour out ... wrath ... [and]

24. The New Testament writers use these verses to emphasize the intense agony of abandonment and betrayal Jesus experienced on the cross. Spectators mock him as he dies and respond to his acknowledgment of thirst with a sponge full of vinegar (cf. Matt. 27:48; Luke 23:36; John 19:29). The context of Ps. 69 sides against those who would understand this gesture in the New Testament passages as a "compassionate" attempt to relieve the final agony of Jesus by offering some sort of deadening drug.

25. With the exception of Pss. 23:5 and 69:22, the other references in the Old Testament to a "table set before *someone*" are consistently allusions to the Table of the Presence set before Yahweh in the temple (cf. Ex. 25:30; Lev. 24:6; Ezek. 23:41; 41:22; 44:16). In Ps. 23:5, the table set in the presence of the psalmist's enemies is a sign of God's protective care and concern that wards off enemy attack (cf. comments on this verse).

26. Following the suggested emendation in the *BHS* apparatus from *šelomim* ("kindnesses") to *šillumim* ("retribution"), based on the Greek.

fierce anger" (69:24). The blindness, constant burdens, decimation of descendants, and striking of the enemy's name from the "book of life" (69:28) are God's actions against those who injure people under his protection.

Interestingly, however, in calling for divine action against the enemy, the psalmist acknowledges that God is already in the process of disciplining him as well. The opponents are to be punished because they are persecuting "those you [God] wound" and are mocking the pain of "those you [God] hurt" (69:26). It seems that the opponents are not so much accusing the psalmist falsely as they are ridiculing his acts of grief and contrition in response to the chastisement of God. In the exilic community, the psalmist may have been taken as representative of those who had accepted responsibility for the sin of the nation that led to the divine punishment of the Exile and who were seeking (like Dan. 9) to repent of that sin.

Charge them with crime upon crime. The enemy offer only mocking disregard of the psalmist's grief and contrition. After the Exile the mocking enemy would mirror the attitudes of those who assumed no responsibility for the Exile and saw no reason to make amends. These, says the psalmist, deserve to be excluded from the saving grace of God's "salvation" (69:27) and should be "blotted out of the book of life," in which only "the righteous" (including the psalmist, who acknowledges sin) are written. He calls to God for retribution against the enemy. Underneath the NIV's "charge them with crime upon crime" lies the Hebrew *tenah* ᶜ*awon* ᶜ*al* ᶜ*awonam*, a phrase that is probably better rendered "give evil for their evil"—an almost exact retribution approaching the New Testament's "reap what you sow" (Gal. 6:7).[27]

The psalmist concludes this section with a plea for God's salvation and protection (69:29). Some commentators take this verse as beginning the next segment, but a decisive shift from second-person direct address to God to third-person reference about God occurs immediately after this verse and indicates that the final verses (69:30–36) represent a connected grouping distinct from what has gone before.

---

27. The NIV seems to reflect a reluctance to attribute "evil" to God, but in avoiding that offense it obscures the retributive content of the psalmist's plea. When God allows someone to receive the due of their evil actions, this is just punishment in his view and not divinely fomented "evil." Both Old and New Testaments assume that such retributive processes are at work in response to human evil. Cf. "those who plow evil and those who sow trouble reap it" (Job 4:8); "he who sows wickedness reaps trouble" (Prov. 22:8); "they sow the wind and reap the whirlwind" (Hos. 8:7); "whoever sows sparingly will also reap sparingly, and whoever sows generously will also reap generously" (2 Cor. 9:6); "do not be deceived: God cannot be mocked. A man reaps what he sows" (Gal. 6:7).

Vow to Praise God's Name (69:30–33)

THE SHIFT MENTIONED above is further indicated by a change of mood and content from distressed plea for deliverance to a vow to "praise God's name in song" (69:30). In addition, it is in these last verses that allusions to the circumstances of the exilic community are more readily apparent. They are Yahweh's "captive people" (69:33), who look forward to the day when God will "rebuild the cities of Judah" so that people "will settle there and possess it . . . inherit it, and . . . dwell there" (69:35–36).

I will praise God's name in song. As noted in the comments on 66:1, it is striking to find this reference to the "name" of God—clearly an allusion to the divine name, Yahweh—in the midst of the so-called Elohistic Psalter, where the use of the name has been diminished in preference for the more generic designation *ʾelohim* ("God"). Following the almost complete omission of the name in the group of related Psalms 60–67—psalms that nevertheless refer to the "name" (*šem*) of God on five occasions—the divine name returns with a vengeance, appearing five times each in Psalms 68 and 69, and another five times in the combined Psalms 70–71.[28]

The psalmist vows to praise God in song and thanksgiving (*todah*). While the latter might refer to the "thank offering" of the same name (*todah*), the following statements make it clear that no physical sacrifice is intended here. His joyous and grateful song is more pleasing to Yahweh than any offering of "ox" or "a bull with its horns and hoofs" (69:31). While this emphasis on the interior attitude of joy as the valued element of sacrifice need not require a setting in the exilic period (when temple sacrifice was no longer possible because of the destruction of the temple), these sentiments clearly lent themselves to affirm the postexilic piety of a community far removed from the temple and unable to participate in its sacrificial rites.[29]

The poor will see. Verses 32–33a contain the core expression of the preexilic form of Psalm 69. The focus is on the "poor" (*ʿanawim*) and the "needy" (*ʾebyonim*),[30] who, although "despised" by the wealthy, are heard by God,

---

28. It is striking that the increased use of the divine name, Yahweh, at the end of Book 2 is paralleled by a similar build-up at the conclusion of Book 3. While the first eleven psalms of the Book 3 (73–83) only sparsely use the name Yahweh (73–77, 79, one occurrence each; 78, 80–81, 83, two occurrences each; and 82, no occurrences), the increased use in the remaining psalms is immediate and obvious (84, seven occurrences; 85, four; 86, four; 87, two; 88, four; and 89, eleven including the doxology). This sudden shift is the reason the Elohistic Psalter is considered to conclude with Ps. 83. The parallel build-up at the ends of these two books does not appear accidental but may represent evidence of an editorial shaping of the older *elohistic* materials.

29. Cf. the similar response to the sacrificial ritual in 40:6; 51:16.

30. See comments on these terms at 10:16–18.

who recognizes their essential piety (they "seek God," 69:32b). In this earlier form of the psalm the enemies are those who despise the poverty of the needy, mock their pretensions of piety, and exploit them abusively. Such exploiters will be blotted out of God's book while the righteous poor will be heard by him and will live.

His captive people. In the final shaping of the psalm as we now have it, the original focus on the poor has been broadened to make room for the concerns of the Diaspora community. This becomes increasingly clear in the concluding verses of the psalm, beginning with the last half of verse 33. While it is the "needy" whom Yahweh hears (69:33a), it is "his captive people" whom he refuses to despise.

Concluding Call to Praise (69:34–36)

IN THE FINAL segment of the psalm, the psalmist calls "heaven and earth," the "seas," and their inhabitants (69:34) to join in the praise of God. The shift begun at the end of verse 33 continues as he envisions God's salvation of Zion (69:35a) and the reconstruction (69:35b) and repopulation (69:35c) of the devastated cities of Judah. This future event is cast in terms reminiscent of the original conquest of Canaan. People will "settle" in the land and "possess" it, "inherit" it, and continue to "dwell" there (69:36).[31] In this way the children of the Exile, who live daily bereft of land and temple, are encouraged to anticipate a future return in which God's promises to the patriarchs are established once again for those who "seek" him (69:32b), who are "children of his servants" (69:36a), and who "love his name" (69:36b).[32]

THE BOOK OF LIFE. The idea of a divine account book in which the names of the righteous were entered (along with evidences of their righteousness) appears in several Old Testament accounts besides our psalm. In Exodus 32, after the Israelites worship the golden calf, Moses entreats an angry God intent on destruction to forbear and seeks to bring pressure on God by demanding that, if he will not forgive their sin, "then blot me [Moses] out of the book [*seper*] you have written" (32:32). Yahweh refuses on the basis that "whoever has sinned against me I will blot out

31. Similar hopes for a postexilic return to Zion and possession of the land are expressed in Isa. 65:9.

32. Note again the similarity of these sentiments with Isa. 65:9, where Yahweh will raise up a "seed" for Jacob and Judah who will "possess" the land so that God's "servants" will "dwell" (*škn*) there.

of my book" (32:33). The divine record book also appears in Psalm 56:8, where the psalmist asks God to "record my lament; list my tears on your scroll—are they not in your record?"[33] In these passages and in Psalm 69:28, "the book of life" appears to contain a listing of names and evidence of righteousness.

In 139:16, we encounter a similar, but slightly different allusion to a divine record book: "Your eyes saw my unformed body. All the days ordained for me were written in your book before one of them came to be." It is not clear whether this denotes a preordained account of the daily events in the life of each human or just a tally of the number of days allotted for each individual to live. The latter understanding seems more probable from a brief survey of passages on the days of human life: "Show me, O LORD, my life's end and the number of my days; let me know how fleeting is my life" (39:4); "teach us to number our days aright" (90:12).[34]

The length of a human life is at best about seventy or eighty years (90:10). God is able to lengthen a person's life: "Increase the days of the king's life, his years for many generations" (61:6); but he can cut life short as well: "You have cut short the days of his youth" (89:45); "in the course of my life he broke my strength; he cut short my days" (102:23). Knowledge of the numbers of days allotted in God's book helps each of us to know how best to maximize our time on earth.[35] The request in 69:28 that the enemies' names "be blotted out of the book of life" is tantamount to cutting their days short in death. Thus, there does not appear to be any clear justification for a book of life containing a list of those who enter eternal life after death.

In the New Testament, however, it is ultimately *eternal* life that seems to be accorded by inscription in the book of life. For Paul, the book of life seems to record the names of the faithful servants of God, including Paul's coworkers in the gospel.[36] In the early chapters of Revelation, the book records the names of the faithful who will be acknowledged by Christ before God and his angels.[37] But, by the end of Revelation, the book of life denotes

---

33. Despite the NIV here, the more probable rendering of the central phrase is "put my tears in your (leather) waterbag." See the comments on 56:8 and the extended discussion in the Bridging Contexts section of this psalm.

34. See also 23:6; 27:4; 37:18, 61:6; 89:45; 102:11, 23–24.

35. See 39:4–5; 90:3–12.

36. Cf. Phil. 4:3: "I ask you, loyal yokefellow, help these women who have contended at my side in the cause of the gospel, along with Clement and the rest of my fellow workers, whose names are in the book of life."

37. "He who overcomes will, like them, be dressed in white. I will never blot out his name from the book of life, but will acknowledge his name before my Father and his angels" (Rev. 3:5).

the means of judging between those who will be thrown into the lake of fire and those who will enter the heavenly Jerusalem to live forever. Since God is the one who keeps the record, entering and expunging names from the pages of his book, he alone knows what the book contains (Rev. 20:1–15).

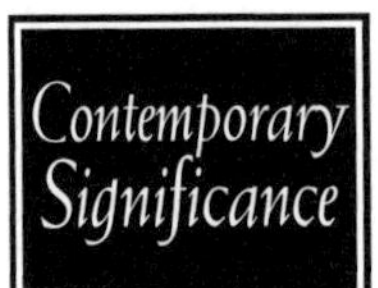

MAY THEIR EYES be darkened . . . their backs be bent forever (69:23). Once again in this psalm, we hear the psalmist lapse into imprecations against his enemies. Again we must remember in brief that these open and honest words of anger challenge us to be as open about our own feelings of anger and hate. These emotional words are spoken to God, who alone can heal the pain and redress the wrongs that motivate them. To deny such feelings does not eliminate them but simply prevents us from releasing them to God. The expression of our pain to God is good "therapy" and good "theology" at the same time. To say what we feel does not justify acting our words out. Jesus' call to forgive and pray for our enemies and abusers is the safer path for fallible humans to follow, leaving vengeance and judgment to God (cf. Rom. 12:17–21).

The other side of these imprecations is once again the recognition that, even if we have no experience with this kind of anger and hate, there are those who do, and they need to know from us that honest expression of their emotions does not keep them from a relationship with a loving God. People who suffer the agony of abuse, torture, and all sorts of other undeserved pain need our sympathy and empathy, not our judgment. God knows their pain and in Jesus has even experienced similar suffering and pain unto death. If God went so far to stand in solidarity with the suffering of the world, how can we do less?

More pleasing than an ox. According to the psalmist, praise and thanksgiving is more pleasing to God "than ox, more than a bull with its horns and hoofs" (69:30–31). As noted above, this passage may indicate that this psalm has been interpreted in an exilic or postexilic context, where the temple and sacrificial system were no longer available for the far-flung exilic community. Even after the temple was rebuilt, individual participation in sacrifice was a once-in-a-lifetime experience for most exiles. How, then, was it possible for Jews living in Babylon, or Spain, or northern Africa to fulfill their obligations to the sacrificial law?

This passage, and similar ones from the Psalms and Prophets,[38] suggest that at least by the seventh and sixth centuries B.C., some within Israel were

38. Cf. Pss. 50:9–13; 51:16; Isa. 1:11–15; Jer. 7:21–23; Hos. 6:6; Amos 4:4–5; 5:21–25; Mic. 6:6–8.

making a clear distinction between the spiritual attitude with which sacrifices were made and the physical sacrifices themselves. Even Deuteronomy emphasizes the need to offer gifts and sacrifices to Yahweh with wholehearted devotion (cf. Deut. 4:29; 8:2; 10:12; 11:13; 26:16; 30:1–18).

The New Testament speaks of offering our whole bodies as "living sacrifices" to God (Rom. 12:1). That certainly realizes that "sacrifice" is more than things we do or things we give to God. Sacrificing has something to do with giving ourselves wholeheartedly to God. I am often driven back to the Sermon on the Mount in this regard. So much of what Jesus says there has to do with the tension between inner relationship and outer action that was at the heart of Old Testament sacrifice. When Jesus begins the sermon with the Beatitudes, he is saying that the kingdom of God will produce visibly distinctive characteristics in its citizens. No one can be a kingdom citizen who has not been transformed as the Beatitudes suggest.

But, at the same time, outer actions are an insufficient measure of one's commitment to the kingdom of God. Like sacrifice, undeniably good actions can be set in motion by undeniably bad motivation. It is like salt and light, Jesus says. What makes salt identifiably salt is not its color, its crystalline structure, or even the way it dissolves in water or melts away on food. Other similar minerals may well mimic those characteristics of salt. What identifies salt, Jesus says, is *invisible* to the eye. But just put a bit on the tip of your tongue and you will know: It *tastes* like salt, or it just isn't salt, no matter what it looks like. If it were possible for salt to lose its savor, then it would cease to be salt altogether and would be useless for any purpose. We are salt, in that it is our invisible heart commitment to God that gives value to our outwardly perceivable actions. It is our relationship that makes us truly citizens of God's kingdom.

Light works the other way around. What makes light identifiably light is its *visible* characteristic of illumination. Without this characteristic, light ceases to be light. We don't have flash*darks*, you know! Therefore, Jesus says, it makes no sense to light a candle (whose purpose is to give illumination) and then hide it under a cover. Similarly, if we are kingdom citizens, spiritually connected to God through his Son, that relationship will work itself out in visible ways; we will be distinctively different from those who have not entered God's kingdom.

I don't believe that praise and thanksgiving are the only distinctives that set us apart from the world. I believe that what Christ unleashed within us changes the ways we understand and relate to ourselves. We can know healing and wholeness that is impossible for those who don't know Christ. We can also learn a new way of looking at others and the world that is not based on self-interest and focus. People stop being objects to fulfill my needs; the environment ceases to be a resource for my pleasure and comfort. I can relate to people as those whom God has chosen to complete my incompleteness so that his image can be displayed in the world.[39] The world can become my place of service as I work for the restoration of God's original intention for the whole cosmos. When we get beyond ourselves in this way, "the poor will see and be glad" (69:32), and the "heaven and earth [will] praise him, the seas and all that move in them" (69:34).

39. See the discussion of the image of God in the comments on Ps. 8.

Psalms 70 and 71

FOR THE DIRECTOR of music. Of David. A petition.

70:1 Hasten, O God, to save me;
O LORD, come quickly to help me.
2 May those who seek my life
be put to shame and confusion;
may all who desire my ruin
be turned back in disgrace.
3 May those who say to me, "Aha! Aha!"
turn back because of their shame.
4 But may all who seek you
rejoice and be glad in you;
may those who love your salvation always say,
"Let God be exalted!"

5 Yet I am poor and needy;
come quickly to me, O God.
You are my help and my deliverer;
O LORD, do not delay.

71:1 In you, O LORD, I have taken refuge;
let me never be put to shame.
2 Rescue me and deliver me in your righteousness;
turn your ear to me and save me.
3 Be my rock of refuge,
to which I can always go;
give the command to save me,
for you are my rock and my fortress.
4 Deliver me, O my God, from the hand of the wicked,
from the grasp of evil and cruel men.

5 For you have been my hope, O Sovereign LORD,
my confidence since my youth.
6 From birth I have relied on you;
you brought me forth from my mother's womb.
I will ever praise you.
7 I have become like a portent to many,
but you are my strong refuge.
8 My mouth is filled with your praise,
declaring your splendor all day long.

9 Do not cast me away when I am old;
do not forsake me when my strength is gone.
10 For my enemies speak against me;
those who wait to kill me conspire together.
11 They say, "God has forsaken him;
pursue him and seize him,
for no one will rescue him."
12 Be not far from me, O God;
come quickly, O my God, to help me.
13 May my accusers perish in shame;
may those who want to harm me
be covered with scorn and disgrace.

14 But as for me, I will always have hope;
I will praise you more and more.
15 My mouth will tell of your righteousness,
of your salvation all day long,
though I know not its measure.
16 I will come and proclaim your mighty acts,
O Sovereign LORD;
I will proclaim your righteousness, yours alone.
17 Since my youth, O God, you have taught me,
and to this day I declare your marvelous deeds.
18 Even when I am old and gray,
do not forsake me, O God,
till I declare your power to the next generation,
your might to all who are to come.

19 Your righteousness reaches to the skies, O God,
you who have done great things.
Who, O God, is like you?
20 Though you have made me see troubles, many and bitter,
you will restore my life again;
from the depths of the earth
you will again bring me up.
21 You will increase my honor
and comfort me once again.

22 I will praise you with the harp
for your faithfulness, O my God;
I will sing praise to you with the lyre,
O Holy One of Israel.

[23] My lips will shout for joy
when I sing praise to you—
I, whom you have redeemed.
[24] My tongue will tell of your righteous acts
all day long,
for those who wanted to harm me
have been put to shame and confusion.

TOWARD THE END of Book 2 of the Psalter, we again discover two consecutive psalms of which the second lacks any heading. Like Psalms 9–10, 32–33, and 42–43 before them, Psalms 70 and 71 are combined in many ancient manuscripts, indicating they were (in some traditions at least) read as a single psalm. A slightly altered form of Psalm 70 occurs earlier as 40:13–17.[1] There these verses provide a concluding plea for deliverance following a long rehearsal of past experience of divine deliverance (40:1–4), an avowal of personal faithfulness and witness (40:5–10), and an initial description of the need for divine aid (40:11–12).

Here, however, Psalm 70 serves to introduce the more extensive plea of Psalm 71, and an extensive number of connecting links bind these two psalms together both thematically and verbally. Below is a brief account of the most significant links.

Both psalms are laments or pleas for delivery from trouble and share specific phrases associated with their pleas. The unusual word *ḥušah* ("hasten, come quickly") appears twice in Psalm 70 (70:1, 5) and once in Psalm 71 (71:12)—twice with a preceding *leʿezrati* (lit., "to my aid/help"; 70:1; 71:12). Elsewhere in the psalms we discover only isolated occurrences of the phrase *ḥušah li* ("Come quickly to me," 141:1) or *leʿezrati ḥušah* ("Come quickly to help me," 22:19; 38:22; 40:13). Outside the psalms *ḥušah* occurs only twice, once as a personal name (1 Chron. 4:4) and once in a narrative context meaning "Hurry!" (1 Sam. 20:38). The presence of so many occurrences in two consecutive psalms and (as we will see) in significant positions within these psalms suggests more than a coincidental relationship.

The two psalms also share terminology expressing the desire for "shame" and "confusion" to be visited on the enemies of the psalmist. Forms of the word *boš* ("shame") referring to the enemies appear in 70:2, 3 and 71:13, 24; "confusion" is found in 70:2 and 71:24. Once again the placement of these shared terms is significant.

1. See comments on Ps. 40.

Words for deliverance and salvation are also shared between Psalms 70 and 71. The Hebrew *nṣl* ("snatch away, deliver") appears in 70:1; 71:2 ("help"), and a negative construction ("no one will rescue him") is used in 71:11. The cognate nouns for deliverance (*yešuʿah* and *tešuʿah*) appear in 70:4 and 71:15 respectively, while synonyms of *plṭ* occur in 70:5 and 71:2, 4.

Other phrases link these psalms as well. The Hebrew word *tamid* ("always, continually") is found in 70:4; 71:3, 6, 14.[2] Similar phrases describing the psalmist's enemies as "those who seek my life" (70:2), "those who want to harm me" (71:13, 24), those "who desire my ruin" (70:2), or "those who accuse my life" (lit., 71:13) are used in significant groupings. All these varied verbal and thematic links strongly suggest these psalms were purposely placed alongside one another and should be read together. In the commentary that follows, I will assume a combined Psalm 70–71, while making a few comments about each viewed separately.

The five verses of Psalm 70 function as an introduction to the combined composition. As brief as it is and considered independently from Psalm 71, these five verses constitute a desperate plea for deliverance from enemies who "seek [the psalmist's] life" and "desire [his] ruin." The desire for speedy relief is emphasized four times at beginning and end (70:1, "Hasten . . . come quickly"; 70:5, "Come quickly . . . do not delay"). Despite the difficulty of the circumstances, the psalmist expresses hope in the form of a wish for the faithful to rejoice and praise God (70:4).

In Psalm 71, the structure continues with renewed petitions (71:1–4), the foundation of hope (71:5–9), the primary complaint (71:10–13), and praise and confidence (71:14–24). At the end of the combined psalm, the trouble has been resolved favorably as the concluding statement in the past tense indicates: "For those who wanted to harm me have been put to shame and confusion." The fact that these concluding statements respond precisely to the opening petitions expressed in Psalm 70 adds further confirmation to the interpretation as a united composition.

The Heading (70:0)

PSALM 70 IS attributed to David while the performance is referred to "the director of music."[3] The term *lehazkir* appears for the second (and last) time, having been used in the heading of Psalm 38. The NIV translates this term "A petition" in both cases, although a more direct interpretation would be "to

---

2. This term occurs in six consecutive psalms beginning with Ps. 69 and continuing through Ps. 74. Elsewhere in the psalms *tamid* appears in only eleven other psalms, never with more than two consecutive psalms involved (34:1 and 35:27; 50:8 and 51:3).

3. See comments on the headings of Pss. 3 and 4.

call to remembrance" or perhaps "for a memorial." Some take this as a reference to the *ʾazkarah* or "incense offering," with the suggestion that the two psalms bearing this term in their headings were appropriate examples of psalms to be recited during the presentation of this offering.[4]

Invocation (70:1–5)

COME QUICKLY. Psalm 70 is framed at the beginning and end by the psalmist's pleas for speedy assistance. While not identical, these phrases form a sort of a thematic inclusio around the psalm. This repetition emphasizes his sense of desperation and immediate need. Without the addition of Psalm 71, the reason for this sense of urgency remains unclear, since the distress described (70:2–3) centers around those seeking to disgrace and ruin the psalmist, who are publicly wagging their heads in knowing disapproval over a shameful situation. Psalm 71 makes clear that it is the psalmist's advancing years (71:9, 18) that heighten the need for immediate action lest his tenuous hold on life slip away altogether.[5]

The opening phrase of verse 1 is somewhat awkward, lacking a verb to entreat God's action in deliverance. The existing phrase can be translated literally as: "O God, to deliver me!" The parallel in 40:13 supplies the lack with the imperative *reṣeh* ("Be pleased"). Some commentators insert the imperative in 70:1, while others resist the emendation and assume that the *ḥušah* ("come quickly") at the end of the second phrase governs the whole verse. The sense is the same regardless of the textual decision made.[6]

Shame and confusion . . . disgrace. Verse 2 introduces the theme of shame, confusion, and disgrace, which returns as a major motif in the combined Psalm 70–71. In the independent Psalm 70, the psalmist offers contrasting hopes for the enemies (70:2–3) and the faithful sufferer (70:4).

---

4. See the discussion in Kraus, *Psalms 1–59*, 29. It is also of note that in the Dead Sea scroll 4QPs[a], fragment g, Pss. 38 and 71 are found written together as a single composition. An investigation of the phraseology of Ps. 38 reveals significant similarities with both Pss. 70 and 71. In particular, the phrase *leʿezrati ḥušah* (mentioned above as linking Pss. 70 and 71) also appears in Ps. 38:23. Another characteristic phrase, *mebaqše napši . . . doreše raʿati* ("those who seek my life . . . those who would harm me"), is used in 38:12.

5. It is interesting to note that even though this psalm stands within the putative Elohistic Psalter, the divine name Yahweh appears twice in these five verses, while Elohim is used but three. In the duplicate version found in 40:13–17, Yahweh appears three times (replacing Elohim in 40:13 = 70:1 and 40:16 = 70:4), and Adonai replaces Elohim once in 40:17 = 70:5. Elohim appears but once in 40:17 ("My God, do not delay"; cf. 70:5).

6. Tate, *Psalms 51–100*, 202–3, allows the text of Ps. 70 to stand unemended, while Kraus, *Psalms 60–150*, 60, and Rogerson and McKay, *Psalms 51–100*, 102–3, modify the verse on the basis of 40:13.

He feels the enemies not only seek his life but also seek public humiliation—as their cry "Aha! Aha!" in verse 3 suggests. In response he desires God to mete out reciprocal punishment on the opponents. He wants those who desire to shame and humiliate him instead to experience their own shame and humiliation. The term translated "confusion" in the NIV is more usually rendered "be ashamed, abashed, dismayed."

Let God be exalted! While the psalmist's enemies respond to his situation with the deprecating expression "Aha! Aha!" (something akin to a rather unsympathetic "Isn't it just *too bad* about. . ."), he points the way to exaltation of God even in difficult circumstances. While those around the psalmist seek to put a humiliating "spin" of shame on the circumstances, he turns to God. There is an intentional contrast developed here between "those who seek" his life and ruin (70:2) and "all who seek" God (70:4). The former say "Aha! Aha!" while the latter cry out, "Let God be exalted!" For the former the psalmist desires shame and disgrace (70:2), while the latter will "rejoice and be glad" in God (70:4).

Poor and needy. The psalmist concludes the psalm with an acknowledgment of his state of neediness before God. In this context, these terms are not directed to material or economic want but affirm his spiritual and emotional dependence on God. The "poor" and "needy"[7] throughout the psalms are those who are vulnerable to the manipulation and control of others. They have no personal independence of their own and are, therefore, subject to the control of others. Consequently, their only recourse in the face of oppression is to trust in God for deliverance and redress. The psalmist acknowledges his weakness and reliance on God and couples this desperate vulnerability with an expression of confidence ("You are my help and my deliverer") to heighten the final appeal for God's immediate response (70:5).

Renewed Petitions (71:1–4)

THE OPENING SECTION of Psalm 71 continues the petitioning of Yahweh begun in Psalm 70 but introduces the new theme of "refuge" that dominates verses 1–8. Concern with Yahweh as refuge begins as early as Psalm 2,[8] and because of its appearance in that introductory psalm, this theme plays an important role in the shaping of the whole collection.[9] The theme of refuge

7. See comments on 10:16–18.

8. See comments on 2:12.

9. See my comments regarding the thematic function of "refuge" in *The Editing of the Hebrew Psalter*, 215–19. Cf. also the thorough study of this topic by Jerome F. D. Creach, in his revised doctoral dissertation, *Yahweh as Refuge and the Editing of the Hebrew Psalter* (Sheffield: JSOT Press, 1996).

and related terms appear five times in 71:1–8 ("take refuge," 71:1; "rock of refuge," 71:3; "rock and . . . fortress," 71:3; "hope," 71:5; "strong refuge," 71:7).

The theme of shame and disgrace introduced in Psalm 70 reappears in Psalm 71 as well. Here, however, the psalmist hopes to avoid, by God's help, what had been wished on the enemies in 70:2, "Let me never be put to shame" (71:1). A concern with shame resurfaces twice more in 71:13, 24. The first resumes the desire for shame on the enemies initiated in 70:2, while the second concludes the combined psalm with the assurance that what the psalmist desired has been accomplished, "for those who wanted to harm me have been put to shame and confusion."

Rescue . . . deliver . . . save. The psalmist uses three different verbs in verse 2 to describe the hoped-for deliverance by God. The first (*nṣl*) depicts the initial act of "snatching" prey out of the claws or mouth of the foe. The second (*pltֽ*) pictures the liberated prey being "brought safely out" of the environment of danger, while the last verb (*yšʿ*) envisions the final product of deliverance: complete salvation. It is interesting that salvation as the psalmist understands and desires it is a function of God's righteousness, not his mercy alone. This is so because righteousness is a juridical term meaning "performing or upholding right conduct." It is God's righteousness that gives the psalmist confidence that his decision will be in the psalmist's behalf. Therefore, he can anticipate deliverance as well as just punishment for the enemies.

Rock of refuge. In this time of trouble, the righteous God offers a place of refuge for the beleaguered psalmist.[10] He uses several terms for this place of safety. The phrase "rock of refuge" is a combination of *ṣur* ("rock") and *maʿoz* ("mountain stronghold").[11] Later in verse 3 we encounter "my rock and my fortress" (*salʿi umeṣudati*). The term *salʿi* describes a massive rock formation or cliff, in contrast to *ṣur*, which refers to a single, large boulder. "Fortress" (*meṣudah*) is a synonym for *maʿoz*. In the final reference to "refuge" (71:7) the noun *maḥaseh* comes from the same root as the verb "take refuge" in 71:1. The variation on this theme involving so many distinct but related terms is not apparent in translation.[12] The refuge God provides is always available to those in need to enter (71:3).

---

10. Kraus assumes a specific context of asylum in the temple precincts. While a plausible interpretation, this approach seems more specific than necessary here, esp. in light of the use elsewhere of other refuge terms (e.g., "my rock and my fortress") that are more appropriate to military contexts.

11. The MT has *maʿon* ("dwelling"), but many other Heb. manuscripts, the LXX, and the Aramaic Targumim reflect *maʿoz*.

12. The variation is certainly artful, but it also creates a broad context for understanding the concept and experience of refuge. The breadth of terminology also opens up multiple connections with the theme of refuge as displayed in the rest of the Psalter.

Give the command. This statement is unusual and somewhat difficult. Usually the psalmists seek direct action from God himself. It is unclear in the NIV translation just who is to be commanded and how delivery is anticipated. It is better, in my opinion, to take this phrase as referring back to the earlier "rock of refuge" and to render the construction as "[which] you have decreed for my deliverance."[13]

From the hand of the wicked. The psalmist piles up negative terms to describe his enemies. They are "wicked," "evil" (from *ᶜwl* ["act wrongly"]), and "cruel" (from *ḥmṣ* ["oppress, be ruthless"]). The request to be delivered "from the hand" of these enemies fits well with the progression from "snatch away" through "take to safety" to "save" mentioned in verse 2.

The Foundation of Hope (71:5–9)

THE PSALMIST TURNS to the foundation of hope on which the preceding plea for deliverance is grounded. For the first time it becomes clear that he is speaking from the experience and vulnerability of old age. His sustaining hope is based on a lifetime ("since my youth"; "from birth") of confident reliance on Yahweh.[14]

The images used for birth are not clearly rendered in translation. Rather than "from birth," the psalmist claims to have "leaned on" God for support "from the belly/womb," so that reliance is perceived as antedating birth. What the NIV renders as "you brought me forth from my mother's womb" (*mimmeᶜe ʾimmi ʾattah gozi*) more literally means "from the inward parts of my mother you were the one cutting me loose." God is depicted acting as the midwife at the psalmist's birth and cutting the umbilical cord. He realizes that dependence on Yahweh predates even birth, to the time when he was being formed in his mother's womb. This realization causes praise to well up in him: "I will ever praise you"—using the same word *tamid* ("continually") as was used in verse 3 to describe God as a refuge who is "always" available.

A portent to many. The psalm explores the tension between public perception and the psalmist's own understanding of suffering. For "many" the

---

13. Kraus, *Psalms 60–150*, 70, considers the phrase "senseless" and emends to *lebet meṣudot* ("a solid fortress"). See also the discussion in Tate, *Psalms 51–100*, 209.

14. The NIV's translation "Sovereign LORD" reflects the appearance side-by-side of the term of respect *ʾadonay* (usually translated "Lord") and the divine Tetragrammaton *yhwh* (usually translated "LORD"). Kraus, *Psalms 60–150*, 69–70, redivides the line to take *ʾadonay* with the first half of the sentence and Yahweh with the second half. This does produce poetic balance. The Masoretic pointing breaks the line after "my hope" and points the Tetragrammaton so that it will be pronounced *ʾelohim* immediately following *ʾadonay* ("Lord God").

psalmist's suffering is a "portent" (*mopet*) or dreadful sign of divine punishment. A similar use of *mopet* occurs in Deuteronomy 28:46, where the curses that fall on disobedient Israel—bad harvests, locusts, worms, captivity, and oppression—will serve as a *mopet* to future generations. To understand the psalmist's suffering this way allows his enemies to assume the worst and justifies their disparaging comments later in verse 11.

Despite negative public opinion and increasing ridicule, the psalmist knows the truth: God has been his "refuge" in the past and will continue to remain an accessible "fortress" in the future (71:3). "But," says the psalmist, indicating opposition to the opinion of the many, "you are my strong refuge" (71:7). God is not merely a refuge, or even an always accessible fortress; rather, he is a *strong* refuge—strong enough to counter the attacks of the opponents. These attacks do not undermine his confidence, and praise still springs forth. "My mouth is filled with your praise, declaring your splendor all day long."

Do not cast me away. Verse 9 does double duty, providing transition to the following complaint section while concluding the preceding segment. A similar structure shapes 71:14–18, where the segment begins with "hope" (71:14; cf. 71:5), includes a promise to praise the Lord Yahweh (71:15–16), mentions the psalmist's youth (71:17; cf. 71:5), and concludes with the plea not to be forsaken "when I am old" (71:18; cf. 71:9).

The Complaint (71:10–13)

IN THESE VERSES of complaint, the psalmist makes it clear that the trouble faced—as so often in the lament psalms—is a well-orchestrated conspiracy of verbal attack and false accusation with murderous intent. The enemies' speech concerning the psalmist (71:10) may refer (as in the NIV) to their general attacks, or it may look ahead to the quotation attributed to them in 71:11: "God has forsaken him ... no one will rescue him." The opponents are pictured watching closely for an opportunity to press their attack home.[15]

This conspiracy is grounded in a perception that the psalmist's suffering is a dreadful sign or "portent" of divine punishment (71:7). Since God seems to have forsaken him, his enemies feel justified in hounding him and in seeking to harm him (71:11–13). The psalmist, knowing that their perceptions

15. The phrase "those who wait to kill me" (lit., "those who carefully watch/guard my life") is somewhat awkward as a description of the enemy, since *šmr* ("watch, guard") almost always implies *protective* care. But it may be that the idea of watching carefully (as in guarding a prisoner) has allowed this extension of the meaning. Another slight possibility is that this may represent an error of textual transmission, in which *šomere* has been substituted for *śoṭene* ("accusers/haters"), as in the phrase *śoṭene napši* in 71:13.

and accusations are false, turns desperately to God for immediate deliverance—"Come quickly, O my God, to help me" (71:12)—and desires the shame and disgrace the enemies seek to pour out on him to return instead on them (71:13).

Praise and Confidence (71:14–24)

DIRECT FROM THE enemies' attack, the psalmist returns to the theme of "hope," introduced earlier in 71:5. His present and future hope is based on the hope that has sustained him since his youth. Despite the difficulty of changing circumstance, he expresses a constancy of hope in the "Sovereign LORD." The psalmist's praise recounts the character and deeds of Yahweh that serve as the basis of his hope and the reason for his praise. Two elements dominate this expression of praise and confidence: the righteousness of Yahweh and his saving deeds. The former is mentioned three times (71:15, 16, 19) while the latter appears four times (71:15, 16, 17, 19).

Tell . . . proclaim. This section emphasizes the psalmist's vow to testify to the mighty acts of God. Beginning in verse 14, a series of verbs and expressions for speaking/proclaiming pile up, illustrating his determination to make God's deeds known; "praise you more and more" (71:14; actually the phrase means something like "I will add to/increase your praise); "tell of your righteousness" (71:15; *spr* ["recount"]); "proclaim your mighty acts" (71:16; perhaps better, "I will begin with . . ."); "proclaim your righteousness" (71:16; perhaps better, "I will cause to remember"); "declare your marvelous deeds" (71:17); and "declare your power" (71:18). The psalmist's proclamation is considered constant (71:15, "all day long") and lifelong (71:17, "since my youth"; 71:18, "even when I am old and gray").

Do not forsake me. In verse 18 the psalmist pleads to God not to be forsaken in old age so that this lifelong testimony to the praiseworthy acts of Yahweh can be transmitted to a new generation, thereby extending the efficacy of praise and testimony beyond his own lifetime.

Who . . . is like you? In the midst of the psalmist's repeated promise to proclaim praise to Yahweh, his confidence breaks through in 71:19–21. Once again the foundation of confidence is the awareness of God's righteousness and mighty acts (71:19). The contemplation of this dual character of Yahweh leads the psalmist to the almost spontaneous ejaculation of praise with which verse 19 ends: "Who, O God, is like you?" The question is, of course, rhetorical—anticipating no answer—as indeed there is no one who can compare to Israel's Yahweh. (But, in a strange way, as we will see in the following Ps. 72, Israel, their king, and humankind in general are called to *be like* their God in significant ways.) This expression of God's incomparability is on the one hand the pinnacle of the psalmist's praise of Yahweh, while on the other hand it provides the foundation for his confidence expressed in 71:20–21.

Because of who Yahweh has been, is, and will continue to be, the psalmist anticipates deliverance and restoration. The "many and bitter" troubles experienced "from my youth" are no barrier to his faith or the saving work of God. The series of comforting verbs of deliverance pile up much as did the verbs of praise in the preceding verses 14–17: "You will restore"; "you will again bring me up"; "you will increase my honor"; "[you will] comfort me once again."[16]

You will restore my life. The picture here is that of the psalmist, on the brink of death, anticipating full restoration to life by the grace of God. While it is unlikely that this represents a full-blown faith in resurrection, this kind of phraseology of hope certainly laid the foundation for the later development of that theology.

From the depths of the earth. Once again this might suggest resurrection from the grave, but it probably indicates the psalmist's confidence of being delivered from a life-threatening circumstance. Ancient Near Eastern religious narratives inform us of several individuals who descended into the depths of the earth to the abode of the dead—known in Hebrew as Sheol and more generally in the ancient Near East as "the land of no return"; some of these people are described as being restored to the land of the living. In the ancient Akkadian text known as *The Descent of Ishtar to the Nether World*,[17] the Akkadian fertility goddess, Ishtar, is depicted as descending to the Land of No Return through a series of seven gates, at each of which she was stripped of some article of clothing or ornamentation, symbolizing identity and power, until she arrived naked and powerless in the abode of the dead.[18]

---

16. The parallel between these phrases is remarkable. With the exception of the third phrase (*tereb gedullati*) where the second word is a noun construction, each phrase consists of two verbs of which the first (*tašub* twice in 71:20 and *tissob* in 71:21) provides the nuance of "do again," which influences the second verb (restore *again*, raise *again*, comfort *again*). In the third phrase, the verb *tereb* carries the meaning "make great, increase," which in this context is comparable to the other three. The repetition of the first common singular pronominal suffix in each phrase completes the parallelism.

17. For an English version see "The Descent of Ishtar to the Nether World," in Pritchard, *ANETP*, 1:80–84.

18. The description of the abode of the dead in this text is instructive: "the Land of No Return ... the dark house ... the house which none leave who have entered it ... the road from which there is no way back ... the house wherein the entrants are bereft of light, where dust is their fare and clay their food, where they see no light, residing in darkness, where they are clothed like birds, with wings for garments, and where over door and bolt is spread dust."

The psalmist may have a similar picture of a subterranean abode of the dead approached through a long descending passageway. A gradual descent with equally gradual loss of power, authority, and identity is an apt parallel to the loss of vital force, energy, and identity through the approach of death. Thus, to be restored to life "from the depths of the earth" probably describes deliverance from a close call rather than a resurrection from an actual death.

I will praise you. The psalmist concludes the psalm with a renewed vow to praise God to the accompaniment of "harp" and "lyre."[19] Once again the reason for praise centers on the dual foundation of God's righteousness and mighty acts—here collapsed into the single phrase, "your righteous acts" (71:24)—which the psalmist promises to declare "all day long" (cf. 71:15).[20]

Whom you have redeemed. The use here of the expression translated "whom you have redeemed" (*ʾašer padita*) is interesting, especially in light of the appearance earlier in this psalm (71:5, 16) of the title "Sovereign LORD." While "Sovereign LORD" (*ʾadonay yhwh*) appears frequently throughout the Old Testament (some 288 times in all), *ʾašer padita* occurs only six times in the whole Old Testament (Deut. 9:26; 21:8; 2 Sam. 7:23 = 1 Chron. 17:21; Ps. 71:23; Neh. 1:10). With one exception,[21] all these occurrences are recollections of the "redemption" of Israel from Egypt by God's "great power" and "mighty hand." It is especially remembered that it was this deliverance that established Israel as the special people of Yahweh.

In the first of these occurrences (Deut. 9:26)—to which the rest are referring—*ʾašer padita* is preceded (as in Ps. 71) by the honorific title of God, "O Sovereign LORD." This may suggest that the psalmist has this Deuteronomy passage in mind. If so, he is taking a largely communal recollection of corporate deliverance and making it serve as a model for *individual* salvation. It is his *nepeš* ("life, soul") that has been redeemed by the righteous acts of God, just as Yahweh redeemed Israel from the hand of Pharaoh. As Israel's deliverance constituted her special status with God, so the psalmist anticipates a similar relationship. This instance of individual salvation serves to remind the

---

19. See the discussion of these and other instruments in the comments on Ps. 150.

20. In 71:22, the psalmist refers to God with the phrase "O Holy One of Israel." This title appears some twenty-five times in Isaiah compared to three appearances in the Psalter (Pss. 71:22; 78:41; 89:18) and only three times elsewhere in the Old Testament (1 Kings 19:22; Jer. 50:29; 51:5). In Isa. 1–39, the title describes Yahweh in his role as judge of Israel/Judah. After Isa. 40, however, the term is unexpectedly coupled with the description of Yahweh as "redeemer," so that the Holy One of Israel (who has judged and punished his people) is now the one who will also redeem his people. It is probably no coincidence that here in Ps. 71:22–23, the title is also connected with God's role in redemption.

21. Deut. 21:8 describes the "redemption" of Israel from bloodguilt when a body is discovered in open country without the murderer being known.

whole community of God's mighty act in her behalf and encourages the people to retain their covenant relationship with God.

Verse 24 returns to the concerns expressed at the beginning of the combined Psalm 70–71. There the psalmist called on Yahweh for speedy deliverance and desired that "those who seek my life be put to shame and confusion" (70:2). In 71:24, he concludes with the answering assurance: "For those who wanted to harm me have been put to shame and confusion." The almost exact correspondence between these verses leaves little doubt (along with the abundant evidence of linkage noted above) that these two psalms are to be read together as a unit.

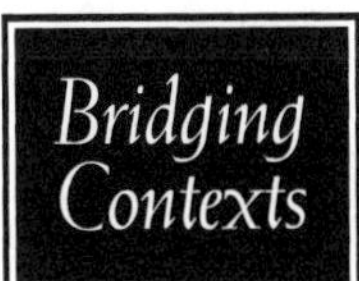

A MESSAGE FOR **the aged.** Like most laments, the combined Psalm 70–71 speaks from a context of suffering and oppression. The unique voice heard in this psalm that sets it apart from the laments in general is the voice of age and diminished capacity expressed by the psalmist. In what I set forth below, I am going to focus on the message of this psalm to those facing the aging process. I do that because I think that is the dominant focus of this psalm and because so little is said on this important issue that when the opportunity arises naturally, it ought not to be missed. Also, I think there is a danger of so generalizing interpretation so that it is applicable to *everyone* that the distinctive message of the passage is lost.

Having said this, however, I hasten to add, as have many other commentators, that there is little in this psalm that is *not* applicable to a reader of any age. Mays has put it well:

> But we must not overlook how plastic the idioms of psalmic language are. The prayers for help use every resource to describe trouble. Old age means declining powers and can be read as a metaphor for neediness. Let the young be reminded that they will be old and in times of weakness are infirm like the old. . . .The psalm has been read corporately by the community of faith aware of its need of regeneration.[22]

So, young person, read on, and, God willing, you will find much to challenge your youthful life in this psalm.

The psalmist speaks of a lifetime of experience of God's acts of grace and deliverance, having relied on God "since my youth . . . from birth" (71:5–6, 17). It is the approach of old age (71:9), when he is "old and gray" (71:18), that raises fear of abandonment by God (71:9, 11, 18).

22. Mays, *Psalms*, 235.

Along with old age comes diminished power and capacity (71:9), with a corresponding sense of vulnerability (70:5; 71:10), shame, and disgrace (71:1). The enemies seize on the psalmist's growing weakness as an opportunity to press their attacks and intimidation. His preoccupation with the desire to have shame, disgrace, and confusion return on their heads indicates that their attacks were attempts to project the same on the psalmist. His hope for the restoration of honor or dignity (71:21) clearly counters the sense of loss of personal worth induced by their devaluing attacks. The central character of his life is undermined by the external misperception that his suffering is the result of divine judgment (71:7).

Confusion is often a characteristic of advancing age—especially in a rapidly changing world, with the death of friends and loved ones and the loss of the familiar routines of home, family, and work. When one is no longer able to participate in activities that gave one respect, value, and identity, many respond with a growing sense of wrongness that can easily deteriorate into shame. This is especially true with the loss of independence and increased necessity to rely on others.

It is generally true that in the Old Testament world, old age was considered a time of wisdom and experience, so that elders were honored and given deference along with positions of authority. Aging was not entirely a positive experience, however. Ecclesiastes 12:1–7 describes graphically the deterioration of faculties that accompanies the aging process and encourages his reader to "remember your Creator in the days of your youth, before the days of trouble come and the years approach when you will say, 'I find no pleasure in them'" (12:1). In other passages, old age leads to disease (1 Kings 15:23), blindness (Gen. 27:1; 1 Sam. 4:15), loss of mobility (Isa. 46:4; Zech. 8:4), and general deterioration of faculties (2 Sam. 19:35; 1 Kings 1:1).

Most likely, even though the aged were respected and honored, they saw a similar diminishment of capacity, independence, and freedom as the elderly do today. Our psalmist himself anticipates such loss, along with the approach of death (71:20). It is in this light that we must understand his fear of shame and his desire to take refuge in God. Lifelong experience has taught the psalmist that youth or advanced age makes no difference in the need for the faithful to rely entirely on God (71:6) and to proclaim his mighty acts boldly (71:17).

Regardless of any diminished capacity, the psalmist remains able to declare the righteous acts of God to all who will listen. Note especially 71:18: "Even when I am old and gray, do not forsake me, O God, till I declare your power to the next generation, your might to all who are to come." This is a significant shift from "preserve my life" to "allow me to leave a legacy of hope and faithfulness." While the psalmist cannot stave off death forever, he desires to live long enough to transmit his faithful message to those who come after. The repeated requests for restoration of life (71:20), to be brought up from the depths of the earth (71:20), and to receive increased honor (71:21) are not simply so that the psalmist may receive pleasure and benefit but so that his message of praise will be heard and received with respect.

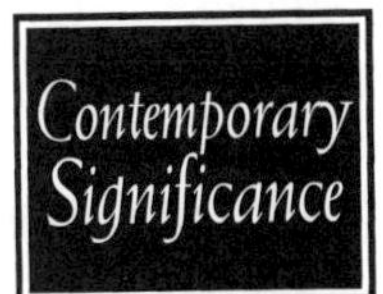

AGING. AGING HAS become a major concern in our day. Especially as the Baby Boomer generation ripens collectively past middle age into the so-called "golden years," by their sheer numbers they are creating a shift in the amount of attention, concern, and money applied to the issues surrounding the aging process. Many companies have been commercially successful in selling products that purport to delay, reduce, mask, or ameliorate the effects of aging.

I wish I could report that all this concern is the result of a deep sense of respect and appreciation for the aged in our society. But I am afraid this is generally not so. The commercial products and processes mentioned are our key here. Most of these products make money by helping to "hide" the realities of aging or delaying its most obvious effects as long as possible. Some—such as diet, exercise, methods of relaxation—do offer positive effects on quality of life. Others—such as plastic surgery, hair implants, impotency remedies, chemical and herbal supplements—have little or nothing to do with improved physical health but respond primarily to a pattern in our society that equates "good" and "valued" with "young" and "beautiful."

As a result, while aging is becoming an increasing concern of society, our concern is not so much to enhance spiritual, emotional, and physical health and satisfaction among the aging population but to delay or eliminate the effects of aging—at all costs. The *Star Trek* vision of practically immortal humans living youthful lives for centuries on end is the product of our collective fear of aging and our determination to find ways to avoid it. In many ways we have difficulty empathizing with Elizabeth Barrett Browning's wondrous and yet mysterious lines:

> Grow old with me, the best is yet to be,
> the end of life for which the first began.

For most of us—and I am speaking from the experience of my mid-fifties—aging is a lamentable inevitability that cannot be avoided but is anticipated with anxiety and a great sense of loss.

How we as a society treat our aging population also indicates the fear and dismay aging holds for us. While we give lip service to respect for the elderly, reality demonstrates a frightening disrespect and disregard for our senior citizens. Forcibly retired at sixty-five or seventy, we offer modest discounts on products and services to substitute for significant roles and important work. Rather than incorporating our elders as respected leaders and counselors in our homes and communities, most are shuffled off to nursing homes and retirement centers to create a new subculture of life, where they associate primarily with their peers and pursue endless entertainment, while staying out of the way of those of us who are doing the work of the world.

The situation is certainly complex, but one cannot visit the average nursing home and encounter the inevitable vacant-eyed elderly person sitting unattended in the hallway without coming away with the deep impression of senior adults abandoned to care facilities, where we allow others to care for their needs. Those of us faced with the prospect of dealing with the issues surrounding aging parents know the dilemma that this circumstance presents. The changing of roles when once independent parents must surrender their driving privileges, give up their private dwelling, and depend on others for mobility, security, provision—these are a substantial challenge in a day that values neither old age nor self-sacrificing service.

Our psalm, however, offers a message of hope into our contemporary context. The psalmist—no stranger to the effects of aging—speaks an encouraging word from a lifetime of experience. First, consider a quick list of the turmoil of aging the psalmist mirrors in this psalm:

- the fear of death (70:2; 71:10–11, 20)
- the loss of honor and dignity (70:3; 71:1, 21)
- the loss of strength (71:9)
- a sense of vulnerability 70:2, 5; 71:4, 11, 18)
- forced dependence (the "refuge" theme throughout, esp. in 71:6, 9, 18)
- the fear that one's life will be misinterpreted and devalued (70:3; 71:7, 11).

While the individual elements of this list may enter human experience at any point of life from cradle to grave, they are particularly prominent and poignant at the end of life, when the shortness of time and the passing of energy leaves little opportunity for change.

The psalmist is no different from any of us. O yes, to be sure he (or she!) lived centuries ago in a less technologically advanced age and in a society that placed a bit more premium on its aged members than we seem to. But his fears, mirrored in this psalm, resonate with ours and reflect fears we face today in spite of the centuries separating us and our different contexts. Consequently, we can be assured that the message of the psalm can offer hopeful instruction to our situation as well. Let's consider four reasons for hope the psalmist affirms.

(1) *Accepting God's evaluation of our life.* It is easy for us to accept the world's evaluation of our life. Much of what we consider valuable is learned from rubbing shoulders with our contemporary society. And our world tells us that youth is good, high energy is in, busy is better. We are supposed to work long, party hard, live fast, and look good while we do it. Ours is a society that pokes fun at getting older. Hippie kids in the 1960s were fond of saying, "Don't trust anyone over thirty!" Our own decade holds funerals for those who turn forty. Novelty stores are full of mournful cards and black balloons and jelly beans to "celebrate" the passing of our aged friends. Along with these comic attacks is the less funny reality of "ageism" in the workplace, as anyone who is forced to look for a job in their mid-fifties can attest.

It is especially difficult for many who have retired and are no longer a daily part of the "productive workforce" to feel valued. I heard one such retired computer engineer speaking with an interviewer on public radio. This man had retired only a year earlier and wanted to put his years of experience and skills to work providing consultation. To his dismay, however, he discovered that technology was moving so quickly that his skills were already out of date and no longer of interest to those he approached. He then tried to market the kind of general understanding of computer processes and organizational utilization of them that had made him successful during his career. No one was buying, so he called the radio host for advice how to put his considerable experience and talent to work. Her response? There is little chance—the field and technology has moved so far beyond where the caller had been when he retired as to render his skills obsolete and virtually useless in the marketplace. As far as the working world of computer engineering was concerned, this former top engineer was out of touch and worthless.

The psalmist experiences a similar external evaluation of his life. Those who look on from the outside and see the suffering he is facing consider his life a "portent"—a sign (or admonition) to others of divine punishment. Most of us probably remember our parents admonishing us by using someone else as a particularly visible and memorable example of undesirable consequences. "Don't drink and drive, or you'll end up like John X!" "If you sleep around, you may find yourself pregnant like Stephanie X!" And you may have trembled under the fear that you yourself might become such an example—a "portent," so to speak—to others. Or else you bridled at the very suggestion that your parents could misunderstand you so badly as to think you might participate in the behavior they condemned.

The psalmist found himself in such a position: Misunderstood, attacked falsely, considered abandoned by God, and vulnerable, his whole life devalued as a portent. The psalmist surely was tempted to capitulate to this negative evaluation. But instead we find him recalling a lifetime of faithful reliance *on* God (71:5–6), faithful teaching *by* God (71:17), and faithful waiting *for* God (71:14). This active recall of a life faithfully spent allows him to accept *God's* evaluation of a faithful life well spent and to proclaim confidently that, despite the present appearance of "many and bitter" troubles (71:20), God's evaluation was: "Well done, good and faithful servant!" God *will* restore the psalmist's life, God *will* bring him up from the depths of the earth, God *will* increase his honor, and God *will* comfort him once again (71:20–21).

External circumstances or the evaluation of others is no reliable measure of the value of a human life spent faithfully in the service of God. Christ on the cross is, of course, the ultimate example of a life that by all external indications and measurements could only be described as a miserable failure. Yet the "scandal of the gospel"—that the anticipated conquering Messiah could die a disgusting criminal's death on the cross—became the power of resurrected life for all who believe (1 Cor. 1:18). At any time in our lives, but especially at its end, we need to allow God's evaluation of our lives to overcome the many voices—both internal or external—that seek to tear us down. "I/you only . . . I/you never . . . Why didn't I/you . . . ? If only I/you had. . . ." These kinds of destructive evaluations need to be caught up and obliterated in the psalmist's confident "*You* will increase my honor and comfort me once again" (71:21).

(2) *Taking refuge in God.* This is a recurring theme throughout the Psalter (see comments on 2:12; 7:1). Apparently life among the ancient Israelites was such that they frequently felt the need for a place of refuge or for a fortress from which to withstand the attacks of the enemy—not so different, I suggest, from our own time.

But a refuge or fortress must be entered to be effective. In the Old Testament are several narratives in which the enemies of Israel were defeated when they were deceived by a ruse into leaving their walled cities to pursue what they thought was a demoralized and fleeing enemy. Our psalmist demonstrates that the ability to enter into God's waiting refuge in time of trouble is sometimes a matter of lifelong practice. "From birth I have relied on you" (71:6). There is a certain truth and comfort in the proverbial statement, "Train a child in the way he should go, and when he is old he will not turn from it" (Prov. 22:6). Patterns engrained in one's mind, heart, and experience from childhood are often enduring patterns.

The college professor I knew who gradually lost his memory of even his teaching field remained a sweet, gentle spirit, even when all else was gone. I remember another woman who, in advanced Alzheimer's disease, could remember little else but was still able to sing the great hymns of her faith from childhood through old age. God does stand ready as refuge and protective fortress for those who in old age (or youth or middle age) have lost their ability for independent living and choice, who are increasingly dependent on and vulnerable to the decisions made for them by others.

Each of us needs to begin building that refuge in God now—raising its walls stone by stone, event by event, experience by experience. We must enter the gate frequently to survey its rising defenses prepared for us in times of trouble, admitting a lack of control over our lives and acknowledging our dependence on a God of grace, who stands ready to be Savior and guide.

(3) *God's power in place of my weakness.* When did you first come to realize and acknowledge the limits of your human strength? When we are young, many of us have a rather unthinking sense of invulnerable "immortality." It often takes some event to shake that confidence and establish a more realistic awareness of our limits. Perhaps it was the first time you wrestled with your son and realized he was just "toying" with you—allowing you to win. Or perhaps it was when your body failed you by not recovering quickly from a more minor injury that previously would not have troubled you. Or it may have been the unexpected loss of a friend or significant loved one through death. Or a serious financial reversal—job loss—that undermined your confidence in your ability to take care of yourself and your family. Loss of a marriage through divorce can have this effect as well.

Regardless of the event, most of us have had or will have an experience that will usher in a new and striking awareness of our own inability to control our lives—a sense of our vulnerability to things, people, and events beyond our control that render our own efforts weak and ineffective. Our psalmist certainly understood this sense of powerlessness: "Do not cast me away when I am old; do not forsake me when my strength is gone" (71:9). Yet his response is instructive. Rather than seek renewed personal strength and control, he acknowledges the need to rely continually on the strength and power of God. This is a potent message for all of us, but particularly for those who in old age see their personal power waning.

Paul subscribes to a powerful understanding of human weakness rightly understood when he speaks in 2 Corinthians about his "thorn in the flesh," which he sought three times to have God remove—without success. Instead, he heard Jesus say to him, "My grace is sufficient for you, for my power is made perfect in weakness" (2 Cor. 12:9). "Therefore," continues Paul, "I will boast all the more gladly about my weaknesses, so that Christ's power may rest on me." Our weakness can become an opportunity through which the power of God can be manifested. As Christ on the cross manifested human weakness vulnerable to the powers of others—even to the power of death—so God was able to demonstrate in that event the power of God to overcome death once and for all. When we are able to meet the increasing powerlessness of our old age with loving grace and acceptance, we become an opportunity for the power of God to speak through us to others and to draw them to himself.

(4) *A continued and valued purpose.* The final hopeful lesson this psalm offers us is that even at the end of a lifetime, when former positions and jobs are ended, when strength and energy are on the wane, God offers the faithful person who takes refuge in him a continued and valued purpose. Our psalmist pleads in verse 18 that God not forsake him in old age, "till I declare your power to the next generation, your might to all who are to come." The golden opportunity of our golden years, according to the psalmist, is to transmit to our children (whether real or spiritual) and our children's children God's power and might.

As age takes its toll on our strength and energy, as we are forced to withdraw from many activities and pursuits that society considers meaningful and valuable, age becomes the natural opportunity to testify to the strength of God. With the obvious evidence of decreasing strength, old age need not decrease our ability to declare the strength and power of God. "Since my youth ... you have taught me, and to this day I declare your marvelous deeds. Even when I am old and gray ..." (71:17–18).

Having followed two children born eight years apart through their rather separate experiences of *Mr. Roger's Neighborhood* on public television, I am now, after a number of years (the youngest of those two children is now in college), left with some enduring impressions of the show and its characters. One of the most memorable is Mr. McFeeley, the Postman, who was always hustling about on his rounds, trying to avoid any delays, and cutting short conversations by calling out "Speedy Delivery! Speedy Delivery!" and dashing on his way.

I am struck today, at the end of this combined Psalm 70–71, with how much we, like the psalmist, want "Speedy Delivery! Speedy Delivery!" We are creatures of instant gratification—wanting pleasure and release *now!* Too often for my own comfort, however, God allows our suffering to continue, calling us to a life of faithful suffering. May we like the psalmist recognize the refuge we have in God in the midst of trouble and allow our times of pain to become opportunities to mirror the power of God made perfect in our weakness, leaving a legacy of enduring faith to those who come after us.

Psalm 72

F SOLOMON.

1 Endow the king with your justice, O God,
the royal son with your righteousness.
2 He will judge your people in righteousness,
your afflicted ones with justice.
3 The mountains will bring prosperity to the people,
the hills the fruit of righteousness.
4 He will defend the afflicted among the people
and save the children of the needy;
he will crush the oppressor.

5 He will endure as long as the sun,
as long as the moon, through all generations.
6 He will be like rain falling on a mown field,
like showers watering the earth.
7 In his days the righteous will flourish;
prosperity will abound till the moon is no more.

8 He will rule from sea to sea
and from the River to the ends of the earth.
9 The desert tribes will bow before him
and his enemies will lick the dust.
10 The kings of Tarshish and of distant shores
will bring tribute to him;
the kings of Sheba and Seba
will present him gifts.
11 All kings will bow down to him
and all nations will serve him.

12 For he will deliver the needy who cry out,
the afflicted who have no one to help.
13 He will take pity on the weak and the needy
and save the needy from death.
14 He will rescue them from oppression and violence,
for precious is their blood in his sight.

15 Long may he live!
May gold from Sheba be given him.

May people ever pray for him
and bless him all day long.
16 Let grain abound throughout the land;
on the tops of the hills may it sway.
Let its fruit flourish like Lebanon;
let it thrive like the grass of the field.

17 May his name endure forever;
may it continue as long as the sun.
All nations will be blessed through him,
and they will call him blessed.

18 Praise be to the LORD God, the God of Israel,
who alone does marvelous deeds.
19 Praise be to his glorious name forever;
may the whole earth be filled with his glory.
Amen and Amen.

20 This concludes the prayers of David son of Jesse.

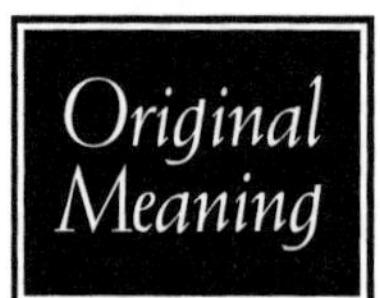

AS ONE OF only two psalms in the Psalter that are attributed to Solomon, the son of David who succeeded him on the throne of the united kingdom of Israel,[1] Psalm 72 stands at the end of Book 2 of Psalms (42–72), marked by the doxology in 72:18–19.[2] The addition of 72:20 ("This concludes the prayers of David son of Jesse"), the only postscript in the Psalter,[3] suggests that the first two books of the Psalter have been combined into a unified "Davidic" collection.

---

1. Solomon was the second son of David and Bathsheba and was called at birth Jedidiah ("beloved of Yahweh"). Most likely Solomon ("man of peace") was a throne name adopted at his accession to the kingship and symbolizing the period of peace into which Israel had entered with his reign (cf. 2 Sam. 12:24–25; 1 Kings 1–2).

2. The doxology of 72:18–19 is by far the most expansive and developed of the doxologies at the ends of the first four books. Brueggemann ("Bounded by Obedience and Praise: The Psalms as Canon," in *The Psalms and the Life of Faith*, ed. Patrick D. Miller (Minneapolis: Augsburg Fortress, 1995), 189–213) suggests this was a late development to set Pss. 72 and 73 apart as the central pivot around which the dual themes of the Psalter—obedience and praise—revolve.

3. See comments in Wilson, *The Editing of the Hebrew Psalter*, 139–41.

Psalm 72 is one of the "royal psalms"[4]—psalms whose content is focused on the life and well-being of the kings of Israel/Judah—and is essentially a series of entreaties that God will establish and extend the righteous rule of the monarch so that all nations will submit to his reign and experience the blessings of God's kingdom through him (72:11, 17). The structure of the psalm, including the final editorial comments, is as follows: opening entreaty (72:1), hope for just rule (72:2–4), desire for enduring reign (72:5–7), plea for worldwide dominion (72:8–11), hope for compassionate justice (72:12–14), desire for prosperous kingdom (72:15–17), doxology concluding Book 2 (72:18–19), and postscript concluding the "prayers of David" (72:20).

The Heading (72:0)

THE PSALM IS simply entitled *lišlomoh* (NIV "Of Solomon"). The simplicity of the heading emphasizes the ambiguity of these kinds of titular attributions to specific persons. Some commentators understand the psalm to represent David's blessing on his successor, in which case the heading means something like "To/For Solomon." Others understand the psalm as the utterance of Solomon himself and take the heading to mean "By Solomon." Those who suspect neither David nor Solomon are behind this psalm interpret the heading as "About Solomon."

There is nothing in the text of the psalm to resolve this issue. Regardless, the clear intent of the heading is to associate Solomon in *some* fashion with the vision of enduring kingship articulated in the psalm. The traditional connection with Solomon is perhaps seen as a response to the reference in 72:1 to "the king [David?]" and the "royal son [Solomon?]." In addition, the petitionary tone of the psalm seeking righteous and enduring rule for the king has some resonance with the tone of Solomon's prayer for wisdom and righteous rule in 1 Kings 3:6–15.

Opening Entreaty (72:1)[5]

THE PSALM OPENS with a direct entreaty for God to empower "the king" with the necessary resources for just and righteous rule. The verb *ntn* ("give"; NIV "endow") is the only imperative form in the psalm and emphasizes God as the

---

4. See comments on the "Royal Psalms" in the section on "Types of Psalms" in the introduction.

5. Whether this opening verse constitutes a separate section of the psalm as suggested here or is a part of the following four verses is a matter for continued discussion. I have chosen to separate it because (1) it is the only *imperative* verb form in the psalm, and (2) it appears to encapsulate the message of the whole poem: the God-given foundation for just and righteous rule over God's people.

ultimate source of the king's ability to rule rightly. It is *God's* "justice" (*mišpaṭ*)[6] and *God's* "righteousness" (*ṣedaqah*) that the psalmist seeks—divine righteousness mediated through the earthly rule of the human king. That this entreaty has in mind the continued blessing of right rule through the Davidic dynasty rather than any one particular monarch is implied by the balanced reference to the "king" and the "royal son."

Just Rule (72:2–4)

IF THE KING takes God's righteous judgments to heart, the result will be continued evidence of just rule over his people by their human monarchs. Most of the verb forms used in the rest of this psalm are of a type that can be understood as either *imperfects* (indicating description of anticipated future events) or as *jussives* (expressing the desire of the speaker). The difference is between statements of almost absolute assurance (as in the NIV's translation of vv. 2–14: "He *will* judge.... All kings *will* bow down to him and ... serve him.... He *will* rescue them") and of hopeful but less certain affirmations of desire (as in the NIV's rendering of vv. 15–17: "Long *may* he live!... *Let* grain abound.... *May* his name endure").

Only a few Hebrew verbs of this type take a distinctive form for the jussive, and only three such distinctive forms occur in Psalm 72, all in verses 15–17 ("may he live," 72:15; "let [grain] be [abundant]," 72:16; and "let [his name] be [forever]," 72:17). Depending on how one takes the remaining forms in the psalm, either the psalmist is anticipating with confidence the fulfillment of the hopes for righteous rule expressed in the psalm (taking the forms as imperfects), or he is pleading with God to make such righteous rule a reality (considering the forms as jussives). Since either interpretation is possible, translations of this psalm vary considerably. The NIV has chosen to take the ambiguous forms as confident affirmations (or prophetic declarations) of an anticipated fulfillment, while noting the alternative in a textual note. This treatment lends itself to a messianic reading of this passage as speaking prophetically to a future descendant of David who will completely fulfill these hopes. I will return to this issue in the Bridging Contexts section.

Regardless of how the verbs are understood, the message is plain: God is the source of right rule, and those monarchs who allow themselves to be so

6. The reference here is in the plural "your judgments" rather than the NIV's abstract idea of "justice." A *mišpaṭ* is a judge's decision regarding what ought to have occurred in a particular case—a decision against which the conduct of the involved parties is measured in order to determine whether they are "righteous" or "guilty." The use of the plural "judgments" here indicates that "justice" is the end result of long-term consistent decisions for the right, not some intangible attitude. For further discussion of these terms see comments on Pss. 4:1–2; 7:6–9.

empowered will rule so that the defenseless[7] are protected, the oppressor crushed, and the whole land experiences *šalom* ("prosperity") and *ṣedaqah* ("righteousness"). While *šalom* can have the sense "prosperity" as the NIV suggests, it usually has the nuance of "wholeness, completeness" and in this context seems to intend the type of restoration of relational wholeness and balance that God intended in creation.

Enduring Reign (72:5–7)

THE PSALMIST NOW describes (or entreats) the enduring reign of the just monarch just introduced. The "sun" and "moon," established by God at creation, antedate humankind and often serve as symbols of longevity and endurance.[8] The moon returns at the end of this section (72:7), once again as an example of endurance.

Longevity of just reign is the foundation of prosperity and blessing. The just king is like "rain falling on a mown field, like showers watering the earth" (72:6). In an arid environment such as Israel had, the rains were essential for crop production and were considered evidence of divine blessing. Because the monarch pours righteous judgment on the land, the "righteous" will "burst forth" (NIV "flourish") and "prosperity" (*šalom*)[9] will "abound." The picture is of abundant crops as a response to the supply of water.

Worldwide Dominion (72:8–11)

THE PSALMIST ENVISIONS the right rule of the monarch as having effects far beyond the borders of Israel. Using a creation image, the psalmist describes the monarch as fulfilling the intended role of humanity: "he will rule" (72:8a). The verb for "rule" (*rdh*) is the same as used in Genesis 1:26 to describe the intended role of all humanity in creation. Rather than autocratic rule, however, the term most often means to bring under the authority of another—in this case, God.[10] The monarch is here envisioned as establishing the

---

7. The passage has particularly in mind the "afflicted" (*ʿaniyye ʿam*) and the "needy" (*ʾebyon*)—here represented by their children; the most defenseless persons within Israelite society. These groups reappear in 72:12–13, where once again the king's responsibility to protect those who are unable to protect themselves is emphasized. For further discussion of these classes of people, see comments on 10:16–18.

8. The Heb. here is a bit difficult and is more literally translated: "They will *fear you* with the sun, and before the moon. . . ." The NIV follows the emendation suggested by *BHS* and reads the verb as "he will endure." The difference is replacing a *waw* by a *yodh*. These two characters are so similar in handwritten Hebrew that confusion is common.

9. See comments on 72:3, above.

10. Cf. Gerald H. Wilson, "Renewing the Image: Perspectives on a Biblical View of Creation," *Quaker Religious Thought* 24/4 (1990): 11–21.

intended creation order—God's kingdom—throughout the whole earth: "from sea to sea and from the River to the ends of the earth."[11]

All nations will serve him. Like a concert organist, the psalmist pulls out all the stops and describes kings of distant nations coming to acknowledge the authority of the Israelite monarch. They come from the desert in the East ("desert tribes"), from the distant reaches of the Mediterranean Sea ("Tarshish and ... distant shores"), and from the Arabian peninsula ("Sheba and Seba"). Ultimately "all kings ... and all nations" (72:11) will submit to his authority.

It is unlikely that such worldwide recognition of and submission to the kings of Israel was ever a real possibility—even during its most golden period. These rather grandiose sentiments most likely were part of the official ideology of the Davidic dynasty in Jerusalem and represent the hopes of that group of monarchs, based on the promises of the Davidic covenant in 2 Samuel 7. While these hopes were clearly never completely fulfilled in any one of the historical kings, the language continued to express the hopes of the exilic community for restoration and fulfillment of God's purposes for Israel. In this later context of exile, this language of hope in *human* kingship is transferred to a future "son of David"—the Messiah—who will usher in the kingdom of God (see the Bridging Contexts and Contemporary Significance sections, below).

A few of the terms and phrases used to describe those nations who will submit to the king need further explanation. The "desert tribes" (72:9) are likely the inhabitants of the desert regions to the east of Israel across the Jordan River in what is today modern Jordan. "Sheba" and "Seba" were kingdoms located in the southern Arabian peninsula and (perhaps) Ethiopia (Gen. 10:7; Isa. 43:3), respectively. From the former kingdom, the Queen of Sheba visited Jerusalem to inspect and test the wisdom of Solomon (1 Kings 10) and brought rich gifts of gold and precious stones. As for "Tarshish," most scholars place this city to the extreme west, perhaps in Spain. It was to this distant port that Jonah was headed when God sent a storm to halt his flight (Jonah 1).

Compassionate Justice (72:12–14)

THE READER IS never allowed to let the extreme hopes and language of the preceding passage divert attention from the primary understanding of the king's responsibility—to rule rightly over God's people. This rule is now brought back to earth by linking the picture of world dominion just elaborated with the necessity of compassionate justice for the defenseless. Not only is the

11. This final phrase, "the ends of the earth," reprises a significant theme that binds together the group of psalms beginning with Ps. 56 and culminating here at the end of Book 2 of the Psalter. This segment presents a growing expectation of the divine rule of God in which all kings and nations will acknowledge his rule and will join in his praise.

king a universal ruler, but he is also defender of the poor and needy. The link is provided in this context by the small Hebrew word *ki* (NIV "for"), with which this section begins. The nations of the world will submit to the king *because* (*ki*) he maintains the practice of delivering "the needy who cry out."

Once again, as in 72:4, the king has the task of defending those who are unable to defend themselves in society. This defense is not the result of some cold, legalistic administration of law but flows from a true sense of compassion that mirrors the compassion of God. The king will "take pity"[12] on "the weak and the needy ... for precious is their blood in his sight" (72:13–14). The king will use his world power to "save" and "rescue" those who are oppressed by violence and on the verge of losing their lives. Two forms of oppression are envisioned: "oppression" and "violence" (*ḥamas*). The former emphasizes the exploitation of the powerless by the powerful, while the latter captures the ruthless disregard for life that characterizes such exploitation. In both cases the defenseless are in danger of losing their *nepeš* ("soul"; NIV "them" in 72:14)—that divinely animated core being that is the source of self-awareness and self-determination.[13]

Prosperous Kingdom (72:15–17)

THE PSALM DRAWS to a conclusion with a renewed expression of the desire for the enduring and prosperous reign of the king. Here the verbal forms leave no doubt of their jussive character as the psalmist leads the entreaty of the wider community in declaring: "Long may he live!" (72:15a); "let grain abound ..." (72:16a); "may his name endure ..." (72:17a).

The fervent hope of the psalmist and people—their confident expectation—is that the enduring reign of right rule will usher in a golden age akin to the opulence of the reign of Solomon, with whom the heading connects this psalm. The connection is supported by the appearance in these last verses of references to "gold from Sheba" (72:15b) and the abundance of Lebanon—both localities linked with the richness of Solomon's reign.[14] Such a king will be loved by his people, who will pray daily for his well-being (72:15c) and bless him (72:15d).[15]

---

12. The verb means "be troubled about; look compassionately on" someone. Here the "weak" (*dal*) and the "needy" (*ʾebyon*) are in view.

13. See comments on 3:1–2.

14. Cf. 1 Kings 6–10.

15. It did not turn out, however, that Solomon was universally loved and praised by his people. His policies of heavy taxation and forced labor, as well as the religious ambiguities introduced in deference to his many foreign wives, led ultimately to disapprobation and the division of the kingdom (cf. 1 Kings 10–12).

All nations will be blessed through him. The psalm concludes on a note of universal benediction *for* and *from* the golden king of Israel. In a sense, this universal praise mirrors that received by the paradigmatic king of opulent glory, Solomon. Indeed, the whole psalm owes much to the description of Solomon's wisdom, opulence, and world influence as described in 1 Kings 9–10. The visit of the admiring Queen of Sheba and her astonishment at Solomon's wisdom, the account of his growing wealth through trade and political alliance, and the international reputation of this young king all provide the background from which Psalm 72 draws its impetus and thrust.

But even Solomon in all his glory fades in comparison to the golden king of Psalm 72. In a subtle interweaving of the covenantal promises to David and Abraham, the nations are said to "be blessed through him" at the same time they "call him blessed" (72:18). This is clearly a reworking of the original statement of the covenant with Abraham in Genesis 12:2–3:

I will make you into a great nation
  and I will bless you;
I will make your name great,
  and you will be a blessing.
I will bless those who bless you,
  and whoever curses you I will curse;
and all peoples on earth
  will be blessed through you.

The expectation begins to move here toward an eschatological restoration of God's original creation intention through the agency of the coming one. We will look at the development of this idea in the Bridging Contexts section.

Doxology (72:18–19)

AS THE FINAL psalm in Book 2 of the Psalter, Psalm 72 concludes with a doxology, blessing Yahweh.[16] Similar doxologies mark the conclusions of the first four books, while the conclusion of Book 5 and the whole Psalter is formed by the combined praise of Psalms 146–150.[17] The doxology here is by far the most expansive of the concluding doxologies. In addition to the more basic elements shared by all the concluding doxologies,[18] verse 20

---

16. Note again the NIV's peculiar avoidance of "blessing" God by translating the normal term for "blessed be" (*baruk*, from *brk*) with the unusual "Praise." See the comments on 16:5–8.

17. See comments on 41:13 and the essay on "The Shape of the Psalter" in vol. 2 of this commentary.

18. The following elements are shared by all four of the doxologies and appear in each in the same order: (1) *baruk yhwh* (lit., "blessed be Yahweh"); (2) a reference to endurance (*mehaᶜolam weᶜad haᶜolam* or *leᶜolam*); (3) a concluding affirmation (*ʾamen weʾamen* or simply

includes phrases blessing Yahweh for his "marvelous deeds" (72:18b)[19] and directs blessing to Yahweh's "glorious name" (72:19a). In this sense the doxology ties in particularly well with the preceding emphasis on the "name" of God/Yahweh observed in the group of psalms from 56–71.[20]

The final word of the doxology is an entreaty that "the whole earth be filled with his glory" (72:19b). This sentiment is another one particularly well suited to bring to a close the developing theme of the preceding group of Psalms 56–72. In those psalms we have observed an increasing emphasis on the universal rule of God, in which the nations acknowledge his authority and submit to it, while joining in an ever-increasing chorus of praise to his "name." In this group also, the phrases "the whole earth" and "the ends of the earth" repeatedly capture the universal bounds of God's dominion. The appearance of these phrases and themes here suggests that the concluding doxology of Book 2 has been well adapted to its function. Thus, Book 2 comes to an end with a fitting pronouncement of blessing on the worldwide dominion of God.

Concluding Postscript (72:20)

THE VERY END of Psalm 72:20 is marked by the only appearance in the Psalter of an instructional *postscript*.[21] This final comment remarks on the conclusion of "the prayers of David son of Jesse." Standing as it does *after* the concluding doxology of Book 2, the postscript suggests a reference to the whole of the combined collection of Books 1 and 2, which are here understood as a collection of Davidic prayers. The reference is not a completely apt one. Although David is by far the dominant author cited in these books, a number of psalms are either unattributed (e.g., Pss. 10; 33; 44; 66; 67) or associated with persons other than David (Asaph in Ps. 50; Solomon in Ps. 72; Sons of Korah in Pss. 42; 44–49). This final comment has the effect of turning these first two books into a Davidic prayer book.

ʾamen). Three of the four also include a reference to *ʾelohe yiśraʾel* ("God of Israel") immediately following the initial blessing. In addition to these regular elements, 72:20 adds (1) to the initial blessing the divine descriptor *ʾelohim*; (2) prior to the statement of endurance the extended expansion *ʿośeh niplaʾot lebaddo ubaruk šem kebodo* ("who alone does great wonders. And bless his glorious name"); (3) before the concluding affirmation, another extended expansion *weyimmaleʾ kebodo ʾet kol haʾareṣ* ("and may his glory fill the whole earth").

19. Deeds that inspire awe and appropriate "fear" of Yahweh (see comments on Ps. 66).

20. See comments on 63:4, 11; 69:30–33.

21. Other phrases stand in final position but seem to participate in the message of the psalm to which they are attached. Most notable of these phrases is the frequently repeated *halleluyah* (lit., "Praise Yahweh!"). Occasionally the enigmatic term *selah* may appear at the end of a psalm (cf. Pss. 3 and 24), although this seems to be more accidental than purposeful. See the comments on postscripts in the introduction.

The term for "prayers" used here is the Hebrew *tepillah/tepillot*, which most commonly reflects petition or entreaty on behalf of the sufferer. As such the term *is* a fitting description of the primary emphasis of the first half of the Psalter, which is dominated by the lament form.[22]

MESSIANIC EXPECTATION. At the end, Psalm 72 passes subtly from a description of hoped-for grandeur of human kingship into what can only be described as a universalizing messianic expectation. The groundwork has already been laid with the hyperbolic description of the universal sovereignty of the monarch (72:8–11) and the exaggerated hopes for the abundance of crops (72:16). But the shift begins most decisively in 72:17a with the jussive entreaty: "May his name endure forever, may it continue as long as the sun."

While this plea is ostensibly directed toward the long life of the righteous king and shares much in common with the similar expression in 72:5—"He will endure as long as the sun, as long as the moon, through all generations"—the introduction of the phrase "his name" links back to the growing theme of the universal authority and dominion of Yahweh that has marked the sequence of Psalms 56–72. Throughout these psalms it has been the name *of God* that has focused the praise of the psalmists.[23] The king has appeared in these psalms as well, but his name—the king's name—is never the object of praise.[24]

Here at the end of Psalm 72, however, at the end of Book 2 of the Psalter (the book that in combination with the first constitutes the collection of "the prayers of David son of Jesse"), the line between this king and God are becoming blurred. This king will so rule that the reign of God will be extended to the earth, and the earth will respond with abundant produce. This king will be the source of blessing, not only for Israel but for all the nations of the earth (72:17). This king, then, will provide the resolution to the age-old division that has separated nation from nation and humanity from God. This king will usher in the blessing of Israel and of all the families of the earth that was promised to Abraham in Genesis 12:1–3.[25]

22. See the section on "The Shape of the Psalter" in vol. 2 of this commentary.

23. References to the *name of God* appear at Pss. 61:5, 8; 63:4, 11; 66:2, 4; 68:4 [2x]; 69:30, 36. In the core group of these psalms (56–67), while the name of God is mentioned five times, the actual name Yahweh is found only at 64:10.

24. See in particular the references to the king in 61:6 and 63:11.

25. It is also possible that the promise to Abraham that God will "make your name great" (Gen. 12:2) has played a significant part in interpreting the enduring name of the king in 72:17.

With this last promise (or entreaty) we have clearly passed over into *messianic* expectation. What is subtly implied by the reference to "his name" in 72:17a-b is now driven home in 72:17c-d. Sandwiched between the hopes for the king's name in 72:17a and the blessing of the "glorious name of Yahweh" forever in the concluding doxology (72:19), the promise of blessing couched in terms so similar to the Abrahamic promise of Genesis 12 has the effect of universalizing the preceding discussion and catapulting it eschatologically to the culmination of God's intention for all humanity.

Much of the expectation of future fulfillment expressed in this psalm rests on the exploitation of the ambiguity allowed by the imperfect verb forms used throughout. The tendency in translation to opt for the imperfect, with its implication of prophetic actualization (this *will* happen!) rather than the less certain jussive (O, how I *want* this to happen!), demonstrates the powerful draw these promises have on the reader for hopeful fulfillment.

In the few instances (72:15, 16, 17) where a distinct jussive form exists, the passage consistently uses the jussive rather than the imperfect. That could be taken to imply that the other indistinguishable forms should also be taken as jussives in this context. In those instances where the jussive is unambiguously used, it is clear that these verbs express the hopeful pleas of the psalmist for the benefits of righteous rule. The ambiguity in the largest portion of the passage, however, allows these unfulfilled hopes for the existing monarch to be powerfully projected into the future to rest on God's *Messiah*, who is to come to usher in God's rule and kingdom. That is an option that few interpreters are able to resist.

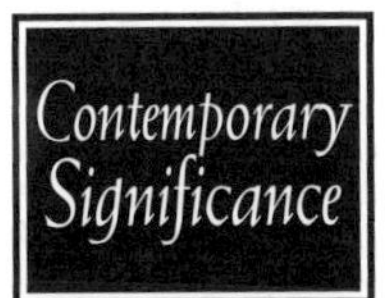

THE KINGDOM OF God on earth. What right do we have to measure our own political leadership against the call to righteous rule that Psalm 72 presents? Our national leadership—regardless to what nation we trace our citizenship—is far different from God's people embodied in the nation of Israel. Ideally Israel was understood as a theocracy—a nation ruled over by God. The kings in this understanding were leaders placed before the people as representatives of God. There is even some evidence in the election of Saul and David that God titled his human leaders *nagid* ("one placed before")[26] rather than the

26. Although this term is traditionally translated "prince," the root meaning is akin to *neged* ("in front of; over against"), the term that describes the woman's relationship to the Adam in Gen. 2:18–25. There is in this term no sense of superiority as might be inferred from the translation "prince."

traditional term "king" (*melek*) used by the people.[27] Kings led Israel with the understanding that they would meet certain expectations set down by God: dependence on Yahweh alone rather than the traditional forms of kingly power,[28] worshiping Yahweh to the exclusion of other pagan gods, and maintaining justice and equity. The right of leadership could be removed from a rebellious or disobedient king, as Solomon's descendants and the later monarchs discovered.

By contrast, our modern nations generally make no claims to being ruled by God.[29] They may appeal to religious values or ideals but work hard to maintain a clear separation between state and religion. When "religion" is acknowledged, it is usually in a pluralistic sense, which includes all religions. How then can we hold secular states and leaders up to the scrutiny of the theocratic state of ancient Israel? Isn't that foolish? Or even wrong?

It would be, if we were simply measuring our contemporary leaders against ancient Israel. But that is not what Psalm 72 is calling us to do. The picture of leadership/rulership given in this psalm is idealized by its subtle shifting to an eschatological hope for the messianic kingdom of God. As such, it actually judges the ancient monarchy of Israel for its many failures to meet the expectations of God for justice, equity, righteousness, mercy, compassion, and so on. As a result, it stands not as a description of Israel's human kingship but as God's standard for leadership that unites the whole world under the kingship of Yahweh himself.

Former President Jimmy Carter understood this in his inaugural address when he adopted Micah's vision of divine expectation as a standard for humane governance that would underlie his own administration: "He has showed you, O man, what is good. And what does the LORD require of you? To act justly and to love mercy and to walk humbly with your God" (Mic. 6:8). How ridiculous, we might say, to hold unbelieving politicians to this

---

27. See the account of the anointing of Saul in private as *nagid* (NIV "leader") in 1 Sam. 9:15–10:1. Later Saul is acclaimed *melek* in a public ceremony (10:9–27). While the term *nagid* is never used in the description of the anointing of David in 1 Sam. 16:1–13 (neither is the term *melek*!), it becomes clear later that David himself understood his anointing to be as *nagid*: "The LORD, who chose me rather than [Saul] or anyone from his house when he appointed me ruler [*nagid*] over the LORD's people Israel" (2 Sam. 6:21). God affirms the same understanding of David's anointing in 2 Sam. 7:8: "I took you from the pasture and from following the flock to be ruler [*nagid*] over my people Israel."

28. Cf. Deut. 17:14–20.

29. That goes even for the modern secular state of Israel, which was founded in 1947 by mostly nonpracticing, unbelieving modernists of Jewish extraction. Some of the greatest struggles in Israeli political circles are between the secularists and the influence wielded by the small but vocal ultra-orthodox communities, who seek to shape modern Israel along the lines of the ancient theocracy.

standard. How impossible to conform pragmatic decision-making to such an idealistic rule!

But that is exactly what God does. He has made us, we are his, and he holds us—all of us, believer or unbeliever alike—to his standard. Paul claimed that all humans can see the nature and purposes of God writ large in the universe and are therefore without excuse when it comes to living up to God's standard: "Although they know God's righteous decree that those who do such things deserve death, they not only continue to do these very things but also approve of those who practice them. You, therefore, have no excuse" (Rom. 1:32–2:1).

While we may need to modify our strident, religiously oriented rhetoric in order to gain a hearing from secular politicians and leaders, we need not sacrifice God's standards of justice, equity, compassion, and truth to the modern "god" of pragmatism. God calls us, Psalms 72 calls us, not only to pray for the well-being of our leaders but for their wisdom to see that all justice is ultimately God's justice and that righteousness is not measured by what works but by the character of God, who empowers leaders and who will ultimately set all things right "from sea to sea and from the River to the ends of the earth."

Scripture Index

Genesis

1–11 ... 352
1 ... 219, 443, 716
1:1–5 ... 594
1:1 ... 595
1–2 ... 374
1:2 ... 344
1:3 ... 717
1:6 ... 802
1:6–13 ... 344
1:6–10 ... 375
1:18 ... 208
1:22 ... 206
1:24–31 ... 206
1:24–25 ... 208
1:26–31 ... 426
1:26–28 ... 109, 109, 213
1:26–27 ... 204, 206, 208, 628
1:26 ... 217, 801, 922, 987
1:27 ... 40–41, 48, 801
1:28 ... 208
2–3 ... 422
2 ... 219, 530, 593, 730
2:1–3 ... 442
2:7 ... 129, 530, 530
2:8–14 ... 593
2:10 ... 717
2:18–25 ... 993
2:18 ... 801
2:19–20 ... 801
2:23 ... 730, 801
2:24–25 ... 801
2:24 ... 690, 730
3 ... 802
3:4–6, 10–13 ... 272
3:12, 14–15 ... 730
3:16 ... 208, 731
3:17–19 ... 731, 928
3:19 ... 422, 690
3:22 ... 801
4–11 ... 730
4:1–16 ... 731, 854
4:9 ... 278
4:13 ... 550
6–9 ... 47, 352, 362, 595, 716, 907
6 ... 34, 559
6:1–13 ... 731
6:5–13 ... 456
6:5–7 ... 288
6:5 ... 292
6:11–13 ... 288, 466
6:11 ... 581
6:12 ... 292
6:13 ... 581
6:17 ... 507
7:6, 7, 10 ... 507
7:11–12 ... 374
7:17 ... 507
7:21 ... 823, 907
9:6 ... 887
9:11 ... 507
9:12–17 ... 362
9:15 ... 507
9:20–27 ... 731
9:28 ... 507
10:1 ... 507
10:7 ... 988
10:32 ... 507
11 ... 252, 276, 320, 422, 725, 727
11:1–9 ... 291, 855, 928
11:1 ... 731
11:7, 10 ... 801
12 ... 993
12:1–3 ... 657, 925, 992
12:2–3 ... 422, 731, 990
12:2 ... 992
12:3 ... 422, 666
13 ... 594
13:7–8 ... 766
14 ... 135
14:18–22 ... 194
15:1–2 ... 653
15:2 ... 278
15:5 ... 204
15:17 ... 405
16 ... 569
17:7 ... 558
18–19 ... 253, 288
18 ... 267
18:21 ... 292
19:24 ... 253, 374
19:28 ... 404
20:5–6 ... 662
20:6 ... 662
22 ... 419, 569, 583, 740, 754, 896
22:2 ... 418, 583
22:8, 14 ... 257
23:10 ... 953
24:21 ... 882
24:48 ... 930
25:27 ... 662
26:15, 18 ... 778
26:19–22 ... 766
27:1 ... 976
27:28 ... 374
28 ... 173
28:10–22 ... 357
28:16–17 ... 703
28:18 ... 702
30:6 ... 477
31:36 ... 766
32 ... 212
32:22–30 ... 210
32:30 ... 327
33:5 ... 152
37–50 ... 941
37:19–28 ... 645
37:22 ... 516, 887
37:28 ... 495
37:33 ... 765
38 ... 653
40:13 ... 131
41:19 ... 658, 659
44:28 ... 765
45:24 ... 156
49:24–25 ... 374
49:27 ... 765
50:20 ... 185

Exodus

2:10 ... 344
2:16–19 ... 594
2:16 ... 19, 515
3 ... 6, 173, 229, 569
3:1–16 ... 392
3:1–6 ... 357
3:6 ... 383, 518
3:8 ... 938
3:14 ... 210, 393
3:15 ... 210, 383
3:17 ... 938
4:5 ... 383
4:9 ... 887
4:11 ... 883
4:26 ... 883
6:7 ... 558, 762
8:3 ... 405
8:22 ... 155
9:4 ... 155
9:10 ... 404
11:7 ... 155
13:2, 12–13 ... 753
13:13 ... 749
13:14–15 ... 753
13:15 ... 813
13:21 ... 930
14 ... 561, 882
14:12 ... 561
14:13–14 ... 561, 882
14:14 ... 721, 886
15 ... 515
15:1–18 ... 323
15:1 ... 323, 515
15:6 ... 323
15:11 ... 504, 508, 586
15:12–13 ... 323
15:18 ... 728
15:22–27 ... 893
16:12 ... 762
16:20 ... 415
17:16 ... 891
18:21 ... 518
19:18 ... 945
20:2 ... 761, 762
20:3 ... 140, 509
20:4–6 ... 213
20:5 ... 522
20:7 ... 199, 433
20:18–21 ... 353

20:20 ....637, 789
20:21 342
20:24 707
21:6 639
21:13–14 ....436, 439, 476
21:14 439
21:18 766
21:19 435
21:30 752
22:25 300
22:29 753
23:1 581
23:2 766
23:3 ....658, 766
23:6 766
23:8 300
23:12 456
23:13 707
23:16 ....19, 905
23:32–33 508
24:17 ....353, 404, 761
25:4 415
25:21–22 752
25:22 367
25:30 955
28:38 550
29:12 887
29:40 309
30:12 752
30:15 658
31:7 859
31:18 ....367, 859
32 958
32:12 180
32:13 728
32:15 367
32:32–33 ..824, 825
32:32 958
33 327
33:11 ....327, 353
33:16 155
33:18–33 533
33:18 173
33:19–20 931
33:20–23 327
33:20 ....173, 353
33:22–33 173
34:7 ....550, 954
34:14 522
34:19–20 753
34:22 ....26, 905
34:29–35 533
34:29 ....367, 568
39:35 367

Leviticus

2:4 405
2:12, 14 905
4:7 887
5:1 550
5:17 550
6:1–7 881
6:10 404
7:9 405
9:24 404
10:2 404
11:35 405
11:45 558
13:45–46 302
14:1–3 302
14:21 ....658, 659
14:40–43 180
17:13 887
17:16 550
19:15 658
19:16 764
20:24 728
21:10 702
22:33 558
23:13 309
23:17 905
23:20 905
24:6 955
25 457
25:35–38 300
25:38 558
25:39 300
25:43, 46 214
25:47–55 630
25:53 214
26:12 558
26:16 153
26:17 214
26:20 153
26:26 405
26:27–30 394
27:6 753

Numbers

3:40–51 753
5:1–4 302
5:31 550
6 931
6:22–26 368
6:24–26 ....533, 894, 931
6:24 926
6:25–26 ....158, 327
6:27 ....894, 931
7:10–11 ....84, 88, 514
8:15–19 753
10:10 762
10:35 ....133, 384
11:1 404
12:8 ....327, 328
12:14 952
14:18 ....550, 954
15:5, 7, 10 309
15:41 ....558, 762
16:1–35 812
16:35 404
18–21 310
18:12–13 905
18:15 823
20:2–11 893
21:18 435
21:28 404
21:33–35 940
22–24 271
22 ....569, 570
23:19 272
24:10 726
26:55 310
28:14 309
28:26 905
30:4 882
30:15 550
32:22 215
33:14 893
34:2 728
35:6–32 439
35:25 440

Deuteronomy

1:31 498
3:8–9 506
3:28 487
4:1 485
4:9 ....684, 765
4:11 342
4:20 ....404, 488
4:21 ....310, 728
4:23 765
4:24 ...353, 404, 522
4:26 761
4:29 ....226, 961
4:31 765
4:35 140
4:37–38 685
4:39 140
4:40 315
5:1 485
5:4–5 353
5:4 327
5:6 ....761, 762
5:7 140
5:9 522
5:11 433
5:14 456
5:22 342
5:25 404
6:3 485
6:4 ....94, 152, 485, 761
6:5 226
6:6–7 684
6:7 94
6:8 152
6:12 765
6:14 508
6:15 522
6:20–23 684
7:7–8 ....280, 685
8:2 961
8:11 ....14, 765
8:15 893
8:19 ....508, 765
9:1 485
9:4–6 685
9:26 974
10:1–5 859
10:12 ....226, 961
11:13 961
11:16–17 374
11:18–21 684
11:18 152
11:19 94
12:5–7 909
12:5 835
12:16 309
12:21 835
12:24 309
14:24 835
14:29 936
15:23 309
16:6 315
16:11 ....14, 936
17:8 766
17:14–20 ....165, 172, 391, 406, 407, 641, 994
17:18–20 646
19:1–13 439
19:16–19 581
19:17 ....766, 767
20:3 485
20:5 514
20:8 395
21:5 766
21:8 974
22:27 321
23:4 893

23:14 302
23:19–20 300
24:17–21 936
25:1 .... 766, 767
25:4 456
25:5–10 653
25:9 952
26:2 905
26:5 442
26:9 938
26:10 905
26:12 .... 13, 936
26:15 938
26:16 .... 226, 961
27:9 883
27:19 936
27:25 300
28 691
28:1–2 537
28:3–14 538
28:12 374
28:14 288
28:15–68 692
28:29 321
28:30 705
28:31 321
28:39 415
28:46 971
28:49 872
28:53 795
28:63–64 868
28:64 872
29:6 762
29:13 558
30:1–18 961
30:2 .... 6, 10, 226
30:15–16 315
30:19 .... 315, 761
31:6 .... 487, 524
31:7 .... 487, 491
31:17–18 .. 327, 518
31:17 954
31:18 954
31:23 .... 487, 491
31:28 761
32 323
32:14 417
32:15 323
32:18–19 765
32:20 .... 518, 954
32:21 880
32:35 477
33:2 341
33:7 485
33:12 314
33:16 449
33:17 421
33:26 .... 342, 509, 586
33:29 ... 93, 586, 917
34:5 335
34:10 .... 327, 353

Joshua

1–11 865
1:1 335
1:5 314
1:6 ..... 487, 491, 536
1:7 .... 487, 491
1:9 .... 487, 491, 536, 686
1:13, 15 335
1:18 .... 487, 491
6 .... 384, 562
7 865
7:1–11 282
8:31, 33 335
9:4, 13 823
10:25 .... 487, 491
11:12 335
11:23 .... 728, 882
12–24 .... 314, 864, 865
12:6 335
13:8 335
13:23 310
14:4 310
14:7 335
15:13 310
17:5 .... 310, 314
18:1 215
18:7 335
18:9 824
20:1–9 439
20:6 440
21:13, 21, 27, 32, 38 439
22:2, 4, 5 335
23:7–8 314
23:7 707
23:9 684
23:15–16 314
24:2–13 684
24:9 335
24:12–13 684
24:14–24 314
24:19 522

Judges

1:4–7 854
2:1–3:6 865
2 864
2:8 335
2:10–3:4 322
2:12 765
3:7 765
3:9, 15 321
3:19 883
4:19 823
5:4–5 341
5:4 341
5:16 938
5:30 416
6:15 .... 658, 659
6:20 887
6:21 435
8–9 862
8:3 883
8:13–21 940
9:15, 20 404
9:46–49 869
9:48 938
11:34 .... 418, 419
12:2 810
13 212
13:19–22 522
14 748
15:1–5 606
15:8, 15 815
16:25 110
18:9 133
19:12 630

Ruth

2:12 .... 322, 872
3:10 .... 658, 658
3:18 882
4:1 953
4:7–10 862

1 Samuel

1:9 340
1:15 887
2:1 .... 226, 339
2:8 ..... 447, 448, 658
2:10 ... 339, 422, 872
3:3 340
4–6 393
4:3 .... 5, 384
4:15 976
7:6 887
8:3 .... 300, 518
8:11–18 165
9:3–10:16 154
9:15–10:1 994
9:26 133
10:9–27 994
10:25 824
12:3 752
12:9 765
12:19–25 391
12:20–25 392
13 562
13:1–15 .... 406, 491
13:5–10 389
13:7–14 121
13:14 395
14:7 395
14:39 321
15:1–34 406
15:16 883
15:22–23 394
15:22 638
15:30–33 940
16:1–13 994
16:7 451
16:11 .... 19, 432
16:20 823
17:1–11 764
17:15 .... 20, 432
17:34–37 432
17:43 853
18:14–15 652
19:11 849
20:38 965
21–31 889
21:1–10 820
21:10–15 567
22:9–10 785
23–26 815
23:19–29 798
24:1–3 830
24:14 853
24:15 .... 477, 767
25 581
25:26 230
26:15 586

2 Samuel

2:8 642
3:1 .... 658, 659
4:15 976
5 122
5:7 740
6 384
6:12–15 121
6:17–19 .... 121, 389
6:21 994
7 988
7:4–16 111
7:5–16 835
7:7–8 432
7:8 994
7:14 .... 107, 111

7:22 ... 586
7:23 ... 974
8 ... 860
8:11 ... 215
9:8 ... 853
11:11 ... 384
12:16 ... 453
12:24–25 ... 984
13:4 ... 658, 659
14:14 ... 197
15–16 ... 128
15:1–6 ... 707
15:1–4 ... 767
15:11 ... 662
15:25–26 ... 258, 393, 562
16:7–8 ... 476
16:7 ... 230
16:9 ... 853
18:18 ... 707
19:35 ... 976
21:1 ... 230, 327, 453, 488
22 ... 337, 349, 350, 351
22:1–51 ... 119, 335
22:1 ... 336
22:2 ... 339
22:9 ... 404
22:17 ... 344
22:19 ... 435
22:31 ... 918
22:43 ... 350, 645
22:44 ... 339
22:45 ... 917
22:50 ... 834
23:1 ... 383, 591
23:2–3 ... 591
24 ... 282, 392, 569
24:18–25 ... 384, 389
24:24–25 ... 121

1 Kings

1–2 ... 147, 984
1:1 ... 976
1:50–53 ... 436, 439, 476
2 ... 122
2:28–35 ... 439, 910
2:28–30 ... 436, 476
2:31–33 ... 439
3 ... 384
3:1 ... 705
3:3–4 ... 389
3:4 ... 121
3:6–15 ... 985
3:15 ... 121, 389
5:6–10 ... 505
5:16 ... 214
6–10 ... 989
7:1–12 ... 505
7:23 ... 24, 33, 702
8:7 ... 170
8:12 ... 342
8:23 ... 586
8:51 ... 404, 488
8:60 ... 140
8:62–63 ... 384, 389
8:62 ... 121
8:63 ... 514
9–10 ... 990
9:4 ... 662
9:16 ... 705
9:23 ... 214
9:26–28 ... 706
10–12 ... 989
10 ... 988
10:3 ... 474
10:8 ... 93
10:18–20 ... 705
10:22 ... 737
11 ... 165
11:4 ... 395
12:31–33 ... 389
14:11 ... 853
14:21 ... 835
15:3 ... 395
15:23 ... 976
16:4 ... 853
16:13 ... 26, 880
16:34 ... 754
17 ... 815
18 ... 282
19 ... 815
19:1–18 ... 500
19:18 ... 282
19:22 ... 974
21 ... 274
21:10 ... 13, 573
21:17–19 ... 941
21:19 ... 853
21:23–24 ... 853
22 ... 559
22:1–40 ... 389
22:10 ... 953
22:19 ... 729
22:24 ... 134
22:34–38 ... 941
22:34 ... 662
22:38 ... 853
22:39 ... 705
22:48 ... 706

2 Kings

1:10 ... 12, 14, 404
3:19 ... 25, 778
3:26–27 ... 389
3:27 ... 754
5 ... 562
6:8–17 ... 939
7:17 ... 190
8:13 ... 853
9:10 ... 853
9:30–37 ... 941
9:36 ... 336, 853
11:20 ... 882
13:5 ... 321
14:14 ... 658
14:25 ... 336
16:12 ... 384
16:15 ... 384
17:15 ... 880
18:12 ... 335
18:36 ... 882
19 ... 569
19:26 ... 604
21:13 ... 773
21:16 ... 941
23:14 ... 795
25:12 ... 658

1 Chronicles

4:4 ... 965
6:14 ... 586
6:16–44 ... 670
6:39 ... 759
8:33 ... 642
9:39 ... 642
12:32 ... 532, 953
15:5–24 ... 670
15:20 ... 150, 715
15:21 ... 150
16:1–4 ... 759
16:4 ... 616, 759
16:8 ... 834
16:11 ... 154, 327
16:19 ... 629
16:23 ... 927
16:25 ... 509
16:30 ... 447, 448
16:31 ... 728
16:41–42 ... 24, 625, 670, 759
17:20 ... 586
17:21 ... 974
18 ... 860
21 ... 282, 569
22:6–10 ... 476, 520
22:7–9 ... 337
22:12 ... 652
22:13 ... 487, 491
22:18 ... 215
25:1–26:1 ... 123
25:1–8 ... 670
25:1 ... 625
25:6 ... 625
28–29 ... 147
28:3 ... 476
28:20 ... 487, 491

2 Chronicles

1:3 ... 335
5:12 ... 24
6:14–42 ... 520
6:14 ... 586
6:16–17 ... 521
6:41 ... 133
7:1–3 ... 475
7:1 ... 404
7:5, 9 ... 514
7:14 ... 327
8:10 ... 214
9:7 ... 93
11:7 ... 487
12:13 ... 835
13:7 ... 487
14:11 ... 586
18:18 ... 729
18:33 ... 662
20 ... 382, 386
20:37 ... 737
24:6 ... 335
29:21–23 ... 384
31:3 ... 384
32:3–4 ... 778
32:7 ... 487, 491
32:30 ... 778
35:15 ... 625
35:16 ... 384

Ezra

9:5–15 ... 692

Nehemiah

1:5–11 ... 692
1:9 ... 835, 909
1:10 ... 974
3:11 ... 405
5:5 ... 300
8:11 ... 721, 883
9:15 ... 893
9:20 ... 893
9:28 ... 214
12:27 ... 514
12:38 ... 405

Esther

1:7–8 314
1:13 532
2:11 473
2:19 .... 21, 953
5 177
5:3 484
5:6 .... 484, 489
5:9–6:12 824
5:13 953
6:10 953
7 214
7:7 489
7:8 215

Job

1:1 662
1:5 573
1:6 508
1:8 .... 662, 899
1:9–11 574
1:11 573
2:1 508
2:3 .... 662, 899
2:5 573
2:8 112
2:9 572
2:11–13 626
3:5 688
4:6 662
4:7–9 610
4:8 956
5:16 658
5:17 93
6:4 .... 616, 899
6:29 180
7:12 375
7:16 880
7:18 473
8:1–7 610
8:12 604
8:20 .... 610, 662
9:3, 14 272
9:14–15 768
9:20–22 662
9:29 880
9:32–35 768
10:2 767
10:21 688
11:2 477
11:11 474
11:13–20 610
12:15 42
12:16 371
13:6 767
13:15 .... 162, 693, 895
13:24 .... 518, 954
14:21 374
15:20–35 610
15:34 404
16:10 134
17:7 368
17:16 422
18:5–21 610
19:23–24 824
20:4–29 610
20:10 658
20:15 952
20:19 .... 658, 659
20:26 404
20:27 761
21:7–16 610
21:33 662
21:34 880
22:2 652
22:14 374
23:1–7 537
23:7 339
24:1–12, 18–24 610
26:12–13 375
27:12 880
27:13–23 610
28:1 270
28:24 872
28:43 487
29:17 .... 134, 137
30:1 853
30:8 433
30:10 952
31:6 537
31:16 658
31:35 767
32:8 530
33:4 530
33:24 752
34:6 616
34:13 .... 447, 448
34:14 530
34:15 .... 422, 690, 823
34:19 .... 658, 658
34:26 726
34:28 658
34:29 .... 327, 518
34:37 726
35:16 880
36:18 752
36:22 586
36:30 375
37:12 447
38:8–11 344
38:36 778
39:16 153
39:25 584
40:2 767
41:25 .... 504, 508
42:1–6 .... 356, 478, 804
42:2 684
42:5 .... 331, 679, 684
42:7–9 478
42:7 694

Psalms

1–89 .... 30, 139, 182
1–41 .... 76, 123, 127, 182, 555, 650
1–8 224
1 .... 74, 78, 108, 113, 168, 223, 555, 610, 625, 650, 651, 657, 670, 788, 899
1:1 .... 37, 473, 474, 495, 592, 651, 657
1:2 .... 164, 376, 618
1:3 788
1:4 788
1:6 .... 48, 278, 367, 384, 441
2–89 .... 108, 114, 115, 709, 710, 711
2–72 114
2 .... 31, 66, 67, 78, 173, 223, 249, 336, 381, 387, 397, 398, 402, 455, 555, 615, 650, 651, 657, 670, 710, 741, 899, 901
2:1–3 .... 203, 866
2:1–2 901
2:1 .... 96, 153, 164, 618, 717
2:2 .... 110, 165, 387, 497, 657, 736
2:3 110
2:4 .... 520, 605, 651, 849, 851, 856
2:6–7 884
2:6 .... 165, 906
2:7 113
2:8 .... 422, 666, 871, 872
2:9 350
2:11 .... 337, 727
2:12 .... 170, 189, 229, 306, 347, 471, 527, 651, 657, 715, 836, 968, 980
3–89 297
3–72 21
3–42 20
3–41 .... 650, 656
3–7 198
3–4 249
3 .... 61, 65, 80, 127, 146, 149, 150, 267, 277, 279, 287, 297, 335, 360, 382, 397, 413, 431, 447, 461, 472, 483, 494, 503, 514, 527, 544, 567, 579, 590, 603, 615, 621, 625, 636, 650, 715, 726, 735, 759, 773, 792, 798, 820, 840, 843, 849, 898, 906, 916, 926, 935, 950, 966, 991
3:1–4 866
3:1–2 .... 321, 366, 451, 483, 579, 585, 618, 916, 989
3:2 .... 154, 189, 253, 950
3:3–4 .... 312, 400, 561, 579, 752, 880
3:3 .... 153, 337, 454, 496, 852
3:4 .... 151, 496
3:5 .... 159, 832
3:7 .... 427, 841
3:8 .... 246, 561, 620
4 .... 116, 177, 267, 277, 287, 335, 360, 374, 382, 397, 413, 527, 590, 625, 636, 650, 701, 715, 726, 747, 773, 792, 798, 820, 840, 849, 868, 877, 898, 906,

916, 926, 935, 950, 966
4:1 319
4:1–2 ....298, 319, 423, 484, 557, 702, 738, 774, 840, 953, 986
4:2.....278, 452, 537
4:4 882
4:6 533
4:7–8..................44
4:8 ....312, 832
5 475
5:1–2.................140
5:2 115
5:3 ....562, 833
5:4–7.................610
5:4–5 ....353, 355
5:4 ....231, 297, 299, 610, 813
5:5–6.................849
5:5 181
5:7–8 ....292, 415
5:7 773
5:9 499
5:11–12 ...289, 293, 306, 439, 483
5:11 ....170, 189, 229, 337, 527, 715, 836
5:12 ....171, 852
6.........79, 146, 267, 544, 772, 798, 877, 926
6:1–5 ....463, 516
6:1 150
6:3 ....278, 864
6:4 189
6:5 ....312, 518
6:7 531
6:9–10...............144
6:10 368
7–10...235–36, 239
7 ....59, 80, 127, 227, 228, 249, 567
7:1.....229, 527, 980
7:2 765
7:3–9.................694
7:5 233
7:6–9 ....319, 478, 557, 705, 738, 774, 953, 986
7:6 133
7:8 662
7:9 ....320, 918
7:10...250, 322, 496
7:11 319
7:12 180
7:13 899
7:14–16.............610
7:16 41
7:17 145
8.........65, 109, 227, 229, 231, 232, 235, 241, 242, 269, 273, 294, 362, 393, 419, 433, 503, 627, 628, 703, 738, 797, 877, 889, 893, 922, 931, 962
8:1 ....52, 383, 392, 464
8:3–8.................131
8:3–4.................463
8:3 375
8:4 702
8:5.....399, 400, 408
8:6............594, 727
8:9 ....52, 383
9–10 ....55, 73, 148, 556, 602, 965
9..........56, 79, 108, 545, 668, 715
9:1–6.................427
9:1–3 ....367, 475
9:3 483
9:4–8.................774
9:4–6.................807
9:7–8 ....251, 320
9:9–14...............383
9:9 527
9:11 ....290, 834
9:14 ....620, 621
9:17 312
9:18 404
9:19 133
10–145..............224
10........56, 78, 108, 146, 545, 668, 670, 991
10:1 864
10:2–6...............517
10:4 130
10:6...279, 318, 809
10:11–18 289
10:11 328
10:12 133
10:16–18..269, 300, 464, 465, 567, 747, 957, 968, 987
10:16 115
11–146.............224
11 ....75, 269, 270, 326
11:1 ....129, 254
11:2–3...............254
11:4–6.............320, 472, 478
11:4–5.............254, 320, 473
11:4 ....472, 918
11:5–6...............254
11:5 ....559, 918
11:6 314
11:7 ....250, 320, 326, 328
12 ....146, 884
12:1–2...............270
12:1 150
12:2 ....271, 298
12:4...267, 270, 851
12:5 272
12:6 ....267, 918
13–16...............326
13 ....146, 794
13:1–2.............384, 518, 794
13:1 ...776, 864, 954
13:2 794
13:3 368
13:4 ....318, 809
13:5–6 ......321, 621
13:5 620
13:6 145
14 ....139, 374, 791–92, 793
14:1–7...............791
14:1–3...............793
14:1–2...............320
14:1 ....130, 157
14:2–3...............478
14:2 ....545, 559
14:4...298, 793, 849
14:5 ....326, 794
14:6 849
14:7 ....238, 290, 384, 794
15–17...............918
15.........69, 75, 318, 473, 884
15:1 ....297, 313, 318, 323, 327
15:2–5...............472
15:2 ....833, 871
15:4 727
15:5..306, 311, 313, 314, 318, 517, 716, 794, 809
16.......58, 318, 820, 840, 849
16:2–4...............314
16:2 316
16:3–8 ......940, 942
16:5–8 ......496, 990
16:5–6...............314
16:5 ....254, 330
16:7 ....891, 918
16:8 ....279, 314, 316, 318, 322, 716, 809
16:9 314
16:10 312
16:11 ....315, 316, 318, 320, 322, 323, 326
17–21................399
17.......59, 102, 152, 318, 399
17:1–5...............472
17:2–5...............478
17:2–3...............330
17:3–5...............473
17:3 ....347, 472–73, 472, 495, 499, 918
17:4–5...............330
17:4 320
17:5 ....318, 323, 348, 477
17:6 307
17:7 ....170, 318, 833, 871
17:8...170, 831, 873
17:10 499
17:12 765
17:13 ....133, 339
17:15 ....318, 330, 331
18–23................431
18...........61, 66, 80, 119, 127, 373, 381, 397, 399, 414, 514, 567, 590, 673
18:0 335
18:1–3...............485
18:1–2 ......347, 373
18:2 ....318, 351, 373, 496, 836, 848, 869
18:4–19............505
18:5 312

18:6 337
18:7–15 401, 448, 505
18:8 362, 404
18:11 354
18:12 354
18:18 435
18:19 826
18:20–29 355
18:20–24 337, 347, 357, 358, 694
18:25–27 347
18:30 358, 373, 496, 918
18:31 318, 351
18:32 358
18:35–36 350
18:35 385, 704
18:42 322, 645
18:43 337, 339
18:44 917
18:46–49 120
18:46 347
18:47 337
18:48 339
18:49 834
18:50 337, 381, 414, 497, 497
19 96, 283, 382, 397, 559, 759
19:1–6 927
19:1 378
19:4–6 364
19:4 447
19:7–11 74, 373
19:9 703, 833, 871
19:12–14 495
19:12–13 378
19:14 399
20–21 67
20 66, 107, 119, 121, 397, 402, 403, 406, 414, 700, 736
20:1–4 382
20:1–3 121
20:1 387, 388
20:2 290, 561
20:3 382
20:4 399
20:5 382, 386, 397
20:6 381, 382, 389, 397, 398, 402, 414, 497
20:7–8 382
20:7 397, 400, 707
20:9 381, 387, 397, 398
21 66, 119, 121, 381, 382, 403, 414
21:1 115, 381, 414
21:2 385
21:5 414, 703
21:6 702
21:7 115, 301, 318, 381, 517, 716, 809
21:8–12 398
21:8–10 121
21:10 702
22 31, 65, 281, 403, 430, 435, 460, 590, 689
22:1 140, 281
22:2 906
22:3 418
22:4,8 339
22:9 418, 463
22:13 765
22:14 887
22:16 853
22:17 515, 852, 920
22:19 810, 965
22:20 465
22:22 853
22:25 905
22:27 871, 872
22:30 737
23–30 438, 470, 475, 476, 482, 486, 488, 498
23–29 507, 514
23–28 494
23 75, 132, 446, 447, 462, 498, 503, 514, 910
23:1 498
23:3 464, 483, 486
23:4–6 910
23:4 483, 688, 809
23:5–6 488, 910
23:5 254, 485, 702, 955
23:6 297, 471, 482, 487, 498, 870, 959
24–30 431
24 69–70, 75, 132, 439, 475, 884, 991
24:1 448
24:3–6 482
24:3 437
24:4 461, 474, 475
24:5 478
24:6 154, 327, 383, 484, 486
24:7–10 25–26, 115, 504, 728, 941
24:10 718, 850
25–28 78, 461, 472
25 55, 73, 139, 451, 470, 471, 473, 514, 566, 602
25:1–3 466, 952
25:1 452
25:2–3 952
25:2 472, 483, 537
25:3 537, 562
25:4–7 465, 953
25:4 483
25:5 473, 562
25:6 473
25:7 465, 473, 487, 774
25:8–10 465
25:8 466, 486, 487
25:9 483
25:10 462, 871
25:11 466, 774
25:12 314, 486
25:16 46, 419
25:16–23 952
25:16–21 840
25:19 486, 810
25:20 537
25:21 562, 662
25:22 238, 477
26 102, 466, 514, 587
26:1–12 694
26:1 483, 662
26:2 495
26:3 871
26:4–5 495
26:4 452
26:6–7 25
26:8 436, 438, 441, 482, 909
26:9–11 471
26:9 495
26:11 662
26:12 476, 486
27 514
27:1 497
27:2 795
27:4–6 870
27:4 297, 436, 438, 440, 959
27:5 515, 910
27:6 497, 515, 516
27:7–10 803
27:7 519
27:8 154, 327
27:9 497, 518, 519, 776, 954
27:12 581
27:13 487
27:14 479, 562
28 139, 504, 507, 514
28:2 431, 451, 482, 494, 496, 891
28:3 499
28:7 516
29 65, 520, 844, 936, 938
29:1–2 46
29:9 431, 475, 482, 504, 519
30 24, 535, 677, 701, 715, 735, 906, 916, 935
30:0 482
30:3 312, 518
30:5 833
30:6–7 516, 522
30:6 279, 318, 535, 716, 809
30:7 158, 776
30:10 485, 561
30:12 497, 516
31 139, 146, 337, 547, 548, 580, 609, 677
31:1–5 580
31:1 339
31:2, 4 497
31:5 272, 540, 541, 786
31:7 452
31:8 826
31:9–11 546
31:11–13 528
31:12 112

31:15 531
31:16 533, 927
31:17–18 580
31:17 312, 529
31:18 883
31:19 487
31:20 910
31:21–24 567
31:22 540
31:23–24 238, 533, 677
31:24 560, 562
31:25 487
32–33 965
32 78, 102, 108, 287, 544, 556, 560, 615, 657, 670, 677, 701, 728, 772, 785, 792, 798
32:1–2 551, 619
32:1 238, 651, 657
32:2 651, 657
32:5 549, 551, 552
32:6 551
32:7 534, 549, 551
32:8–10 551
32:8 314
32:10 560
32:11 238, 250, 555, 561
33 65, 71, 108, 545, 549, 566, 657, 991
33:1 557
33:3 280, 637, 646
33:4–5 564
33:7 375
33:8–9 448
33:8 448
33:12 651, 657
33:16–17 620
33:16 115, 250
33:20 496
34 55, 61, 74, 80, 127, 461, 602, 637, 657, 677
34:1 572, 966
34:3 515
34:5 537, 952
34:6–7 610
34:7 580
34:8 651, 657
34:15–16 610
34:16 328
34:17 569
34:19 569, 689
35 146
35:1–2 140
35:2 133
35:3 129, 620
35:4 537, 585, 618, 952
35:5–6 570
35:5 569
35:6 569
35:7–8 580
35:7 584
35:9–10 621
35:9 620
35:11–12, 15–16 141
35:17 141, 278, 864
35:19 515
35:24 477, 515
35:26 515, 537, 952
35:27 478, 966
35:28 164
36 585, 603, 884
36:0 335
36:1–9 585
36:6 595
36:7–9 438
36:7–8 436
36:7 318, 322, 441, 831, 873
36:8 440, 910
36:9 441
36:10 250, 250, 593
36:11–12 585
37–40 644
37 55, 56, 73, 590, 602, 636, 759
37:2 606
37:3 606
37:4–5 606
37:7 562, 636, 721, 882
37:9 562
37:10 607
37:14 250
37:18 959
37:20 607
37:21–22 42–43
37:21 152
37:24 483
37:26 152
37:31 477
37:34 562, 636
37:37 250, 662
37:39 497, 620
37:40 318, 339
38 24, 79, 102, 544, 615, 636, 772, 966, 967
38:1–2, 4–5 625
38:10 279, 625
38:11 625
38:12 164, 786, 967
38:13–16 625
38:13–14 626
38:13 883
38:15 562, 636
38:16 301, 515
38:17–18 625
38:20 582
38:22 418, 810, 965
38:23 967
39 24, 636, 877, 877
39:1–2 628
39:1 647, 662
39:2 906
39:3 164
39:4–5 959
39:4 959
39:7 142, 644
39:12 297, 319, 485
40 657, 951, 965
40:1–4 643, 965
40:1 636, 636
40:2 954
40:3–4 644
40:3 556, 637
40:4 154, 637, 644, 657
40:5–10 965
40:6 957
40:7 651
40:9–10 621
40:10–11 871
40:11–12 965
40:12 625
40:13–17 965, 967
40:13 418, 810, 965, 967
40:14 537, 952
40:15 537, 584, 952
40:16 967
40:17 339, 967
41–42 108
41 76
41:1 755
41:4–9 651
41:4 625
41:8 702
41:12 662
41:13 89, 990
42–83 644, 669, 758, 759, 792, 820, 898, 928, 936
42–72 91, 719, 760, 984
42–49 701
42–44 708, 709
42–43 556, 682, 683, 685, 689, 701, 715, 758, 785, 792, 894, 928, 965
42 20, 24, 54–55, 78, 108, 545, 650, 701, 726, 728, 735, 747, 797, 860, 889, 991
42:2 673, 893
42:3 824
42:4 887
42:5 562, 685
42:9 674
42:11 562, 685
43 54–55, 108
43:1 339, 477
43:2 497, 708
43:3–4 671
43:5 562, 685
44–49 20, 24, 991
44 545, 701, 728, 758, 785, 893, 894, 991
44:3 385
44:4–9 927
44:4 115, 712, 736
44:5 894
44:6 385
44:7 385, 537
44:8 894
44:9–14 758
44:9 689
44:10 708
44:11 351
44:12 709
44:15 537
44:20–21 758

44:20 ... 894
44:22 ... 609, 690
44:23–24 ... 864
44:24 ... 518, 954
44:26 ... 133
45–49 ... 709
45–47 ... 735
45 ... 66, 67, 119, 397, 514, 545, 715, 728, 758, 785, 877, 950, 950
45:2–7 ... 117
45:3 ... 400
45:6 ... 707, 758
45:9 ... 115
45:11 ... 115, 708
45:13 ... 720
46–53 ... 760
46–49 ... 759
46–48 ... 760
46 ... 55, 514, 701, 725, 726, 738, 741
46:1 ... 717, 718
46:2–3 ... 376, 719
46:2 ... 301, 708, 717
46:4–5 ... 736, 741
46:4 ... 719, 735, 736
46:5 ... 318
46:6 ... 725
46:7 ... 383, 718, 735, 736, 850
46:8–10 ... 746
46:8 ... 708
46:9 ... 869
46:10 ... 724, 725, 726, 728, 729, 834, 883, 884, 886
46:11 ... 383, 716, 735, 736, 850
46:12 ... 708
47 ... 71, 109, 746, 822, 833, 927
47:1 ... 746
47:2 ... 115, 735, 736
47:3 ... 708, 746
47:5–6 ... 728
47:5 ... 729
47:6 ... 115
47:7–9 ... 746
47:7 ... 115, 736
47:8 ... 70, 727
47:9 ... 727, 746, 747
48–53 ... 760
48 ... 514, 701, 741
48:1–2 ... 719
48:1 ... 719
48:2 ... 115, 760, 760, 777
48:3 ... 741
48:4 ... 708
48:7 ... 737
48:8 ... 718, 719, 741, 850
48:10 ... 871, 894
48:11–12 ... 777
48:11 ... 760
48:12–14 ... 737
48:12 ... 760
48:13 ... 737
49 ... 53, 55, 73, 738, 828
49:5 ... 751
49:6–20 ... 785
49:7 ... 752
49:9 ... 751
49:10 ... 893
49:11 ... 751
49:12 ... 748
49:14 ... 250, 312
49:15 ... 312, 749
49:20 ... 748, 750
50 ... 20, 24, 78, 884, 991
50:1–6 ... 927
50:2 ... 290, 777
50:5 ... 781
50:7–23 ... 884
50:7–21 ... 785
50:7–15 ... 800
50:8–14 ... 772, 966
50:9–13 ... 960
50:12 ... 449
50:14–15 ... 766
50:14 ... 772, 905
50:16 ... 759
50:21 ... 761
50:23 ... 772, 800
51–72 ... 830
51–71 ... 792, 926
51–70 ... 772
51–65 ... 76, 785
51–64 ... 921
51 ... 61, 80, 127, 337, 544, 567, 615, 758, 772
51:1 ... 776
51:2 ... 40, 775
51:3 ... 966
51:7–12 ... 785
51:9 ... 518
51:12 ... 794, 795
51:13 ... 794
51:14 ... 620, 621
51:16–17 ... 785, 800, 957
51:16 ... 960
51:18–19 ... 785
51:18 ... 760
51:19 ... 800
52–55 ... 785, 792, 867
52 ... 61, 80, 127, 146, 545, 567, 677, 728, 794, 797, 808
52:2 ... 831
52:5 ... 487
52:7 ... 497, 797
52:8–9 ... 795
52:8 ... 436, 438, 441, 910
52:9 ... 562, 798, 800, 894
53 ... 139, 146, 287, 545, 728, 792, 797
53:1–4 ... 802
53:1 ... 797
53:2 ... 559
53:4 ... 797
53:5 ... 537
53:6 ... 238, 290, 760
54–56 ... 830
54 ... 61, 80, 127, 146, 545, 567, 728, 799, 807, 808, 848, 926
54:1 ... 477
54:2 ... 319, 747, 807, 808
54:4 ... 561
54:5 ... 845, 852
54:6–7 ... 145
54:6 ... 894
55–60 ... 859
55 ... 545, 728, 798, 807, 820, 926
55:1–8 ... 814
55:1 ... 319
55:12 ... 809, 810
55:14 ... 110
55:15 ... 312
55:18 ... 814
55:21 ... 499, 832, 851
55:22 ... 301, 517, 716
55:23 ... 476
56–72 ... 909, 911, 991, 992
56–71 ... 950, 991
56–68 ... 898, 900, 909, 915, 919, 920, 927, 928, 931, 940, 949
56–67 ... 906, 934, 992
56–65 ... 926
56–60 ... 58, 306, 808, 820, 840, 849, 867
56–57 ... 807, 849, 860
56 ... 55, 58, 61, 80, 127, 567, 830, 831, 833, 840, 849, 850, 860, 905, 988
56:1–2 ... 831
56:5–11 ... 908
56:6 ... 850
56:8 ... 959
56:12 . 145, 905, 909
57–59 ... 840
57–58 ... 849
57 ... 55, 58, 61, 80, 127, 567, 840, 846, 849, 850
57:1 .. 873, 873, 889, 891, 905, 909
57:3 ... 871
57:4 ... 841, 851
57:5 ... 373
57:6–11 ... 889
57:7–11 ... 859
57:9 ... 238, 822
57:10 ... 846, 871
57:11 ... 373, 859
58–59 ... 830
58 ... 58, 943
58:2 ... 499
58:3 ... 844
58:6 ... 134, 137, 427
58:10 ... 941, 946
58:12 ... 720
59–72 ... 871
59 ... 55, 58, 61, 80, 127, 567, 807, 860, 899, 929
59:3 ... 936
59:5 ... 718
59:6 ... 850
59:9 ... 853, 909
59:10 ... 850

59:11 496
59:13 .... 868, 871, 905
59:16 .... 718, 833
59:17 909
59:18 496
60–67 .... 898, 929, 943, 957
60–63 929
60 .... 58, 61, 78, 80, 127, 567, 567, 701, 807, 849, 950
60:1–3 863
60:2 279
60:6–8 .... 386, 863, 870
60:6 .... 905, 909
60:9 497
60:10 720
60:11 620
61–72 893
61–67 867
61 .... 807, 889, 892, 926
61:1 319
61:2–3 880
61:2 .... 869, 905, 928
61:3 .... 318, 909
61:4 .... 297, 318, 889, 905, 909
61:5 .... 871, 889, 894, 899, 992
61:6–7 .... 889, 892
61:6 .... 959, 992
61:7 871
61:8 .... 145, 889, 894, 898, 899, 905, 906, 992
62–64 .... 906, 916
62 .... 24, 55, 75, 625, 897
62:2 .... 318, 716, 909
62:3 278
62:4 499
62:6 .... 279, 318, 716, 909
62:7 .... 318, 909
62:8 .... 318, 909
62:9 .... 152, 747
63 .... 61, 79, 80, 127, 567, 931
63:2 .... 905, 909
63:4 .... 451, 494, 894, 899, 991, 992
63:5 893
63:6 164
63:7 .... 322, 831, 873, 905
63:11 .... 897, 898, 991, 992
64 677
64:1–2 917
64:4 662
64:5 .... 851, 900
64:10 .... 250, 909, 929, 936, 992
65–68 .... 514, 916, 921, 921, 926
65 .... 81, 657, 915, 916, 935
65:1–12 921
65:1 .... 760, 921
65:2–3 921
65:2 .... 319, 909, 921
65:3 .... 920, 931
65:4 .... 93, 297, 436, 438, 438, 651, 657, 905
65:5–7 928
65:5 .... 869, 871, 907, 909, 921, 928
65:8 .... 909, 921
65:9–13 921
65:9 893
65:13 921
66–67 .... 772, 906, 935
66 .... 677, 758, 792, 906, 926, 991
66:1–4 .... 898, 925
66:1 .... 898, 929, 957
66:2–7 920
66:2–3 894
66:2 .... 899, 929, 992
66:4 .... 894, 898, 899, 929, 992
66:7 .... 898, 931
66:8–12 .... 920, 925
66:8 898
66:9 .... 301, 716
66:13–15 67
66:13–14 .... 905, 906, 909
66:16 238
66:18 931
66:20 720
67–70 115
67 .... 55, 758, 792, 906, 915, 916, 921, 991
67:1–7 921
67:1 .... 158, 327, 368, 533
67:2–5 921
67:2 .... 915, 921
67:3–7 898
67:3–5 .... 898, 921
67:3–4 898
67:3 .... 915, 921
67:4 .... 915, 936
67:5 .... 915, 921
67:6 921
67:7 .... 422, 869, 871, 898, 905, 915, 921
68–70 .... 76, 785
68 .... 898, 899, 906, 915, 921, 926, 928, 929, 949, 957
68:2 606
68:4–10 509
68:4 .... 342, 894, 942, 992
68:5 905
68:6 .... 938, 940
68:7–18 341
68:15–16 937
68:15 .... 938, 942
68:17 .... 905, 937, 938
68:19 621
68:21–23 842
68:22 942
68:23 853
68:24–27 24–25
68:24 .... 115, 905, 937
68:29 905
68:33–34 936
68:35 .... 905, 937
69–71 .... 921, 949
69 .... 139, 412, 899, 916, 929, 936, 966
69:2 .... 645, 954
69:4 954
69:6–7 952
69:6 .... 537, 718, 850, 954
69:7 537
69:9 905
69:10–11 952
69:13 .... 142, 871
69:14 645
69:16 142
69:17 518
69:18 142–43
69:19 952
69:22–25 143
69:26 951
69:27–28 143
69:28 .... 825, 959
69:30 .... 894, 992
69:30–36 956
69:30–33 991
69:32 954
69:34–36 238
69:35–36 957
69:35 .... 290, 760
69:36 .... 894, 954, 992
70–71 .... 643, 899, 916, 929, 936, 950, 952, 957
70 .... 24, 76, 79, 108, 412, 418, 616, 635, 636, 792, 975
70:1–5 643–44
70:1 .... 418, 810
70:2 .... 537, 952, 969, 975
70:3 .... 537, 584
70:4 620
70:5 .... 339, 418, 561, 810, 968
71 .... 76, 78, 108, 412, 418, 636, 643, 792, 808, 967
71:1–8 969
71:1–3 527
71:1 .... 537, 952
71:2 339
71:3 971
71:4 339
71:5–6 416
71:5 972
71:9 967
71:12 .... 418, 810
71:13 .... 143, 537, 952, 969
71:14–18 971
71:15–16 971
71:15 .... 620, 621
71:18 .... 737, 967
71:19 586
71:20–21 144
71:24 .... 164, 537, 969
72 .... 67, 75, 76–77, 109, 111–12, 114, 119, 121,

123, 124, 397, 657, 709, 758, 950, 972
72:4 ... 989
72:5–8 ... 950
72:8–11 ... 66, 111
72:8 ... 214, 422, 869, 871, 905, 950
72:12–13 ... 987
72:13–14 ... 659
72:13 ... 658
72:15–17 ... 986
72:18–19 ... 76
72:20 ... 91, 126, 319
73–89 ... 229, 666, 759
73–83 ... 20, 24, 759, 957
73–77 ... 957
73 ... 74, 102, 748, 984
73:2–11 ... 611
73:11 ... 851
73:13 ... 153, 475, 475
73:18 ... 879
73:28 ... 114, 477
74 ... 65, 139, 146, 545, 728, 966
74:1–11 ... 910
74:1–8 ... 720
74:2 ... 290
74:9 ... 278
74:10–11 ... 142, 864
74:10 ... 278
74:12–17 ... 716
74:12–14 ... 344
74:12 ... 115, 620, 927
74:13–14 ... 375
74:22 ... 133
75:3–5 ... 884
75:8 ... 254
75:9 ... 383
76 ... 741, 926
76:2 ... 290
76:6 ... 383
76:12 ... 115
76:14 ... 905
77 ... 24, 625
77:3 ... 869
77:12 ... 164
77:13–20 ... 238
77:16–19 ... 505, 506
77:18 ... 448
78 ... 75, 545, 728, 765, 957
78:4 ... 737
78:5 ... 367
78:6 ... 737
78:10–11 ... 765
78:15–20 ... 893
78:19 ... 437
78:41 ... 974
78:52 ... 738
78:55 ... 314
78:63 ... 404
78:66 ... 537
78:68 ... 290
78:70–71 ... 432
78:72 ... 662
79 ... 139, 146, 957
79:5 ... 142, 153, 278, 864
79:9 ... 561
79:13 ... 737
80–81 ... 957
80 ... 55, 146
80:1 ... 498, 927
80:3 ... 142, 327, 533, 620, 927
80:4 ... 278, 718, 864
80:5 ... 824, 850
80:7 ... 327, 533, 718, 927
80:8 ... 850
80:14 ... 718
80:15 ... 850
80:17 ... 702
80:19 ... 327, 533, 718, 927
80:20 ... 850
81:1, 4 ... 383
81:6–16 ... 884
81:6 ... 367
81:7 ... 918
82 ... 146, 840, 844, 929, 957
82:1 ... 508
82:2–7 ... 884
82:2 ... 278
82:3–4 ... 659
82:3 ... 658
82:4 ... 339, 658
82:5 ... 318
82:8 ... 133
83 ... 146, 669, 957
83:16 ... 537
84–85 ... 20, 24
84 ... 438, 657, 741, 910, 957
84:1–10 ... 438
84:1–4 ... 436, 438, 718, 850
84:2 ... 678
84:3 ... 115, 678, 718, 850
84:4 ... 93, 297, 651, 657, 741
84:5 ... 93, 651, 657
84:7 ... 290
84:8 ... 319, 383, 485, 718
84:9 ... 850
84:10–12 ... 436, 438, 440
84:10 ... 297, 678, 910
84:11 ... 496, 759
84:12 ... 651, 657, 718, 850
84:16 ... 93
85 ... 146, 957
85:8–13 ... 386
85:10 ... 871
85:11 ... 559
86 ... 59, 146, 152, 318, 957
86:6 ... 319
86:8 ... 508, 586, 840
86:13 ... 312
86:15 ... 871
86:16 ... 45, 46
86:17 ... 537
87–88 ... 20, 24
87 ... 741, 957
87:2 ... 290, 741
87:3 ... 719
87:5–6 ... 741
87:5 ... 290
88 ... 65, 78, 140, 287, 545, 728, 759, 792, 957
88:1 ... 620
88:3 ... 312
88:5 ... 41
88:10–12 ... 722
88:11 ... 518
88:13 ... 833
88:14 ... 518, 954
89 ... 23, 24, 66, 67, 76, 119, 123, 124, 139, 397, 398, 501, 545, 657, 728, 850
89:1 ... 737
89:6–7 ... 504
89:6 ... 504, 586
89:8 ... 586, 718
89:9–10 ... 344
89:9 ... 375
89:11 ... 448, 449
89:14 ... 871
89:15 ... 93, 651, 657
89:18 ... 115, 974
89:21 ... 41
89:29 ... 374
89:38–45 ... 115
89:45 ... 537, 959
89:46 ... 153, 278, 864
89:48 ... 312
90–150 ... 30, 115–16, 281, 710
90–106 ... 65, 66, 488, 604
90 ... 59, 74, 152, 318–19, 627, 910
90:1–2 ... 51
90:1 ... 911
90:2 ... 448, 604
90:3–12 ... 959
90:3 ... 422
90:10 ... 183
90:12 ... 959
90:13 ... 180, 278, 864
91 ... 75, 78, 910
91:1–2 ... 911
91:1 ... 872
91:2 ... 171
91:4 ... 170, 171
91:5–6 ... 50
91:9–10 ... 911
91:9 ... 171
91:14–16 ... 884
91:14 ... 339
91:16 ... 620
92 ... 24, 79
92:7 ... 604
92:12–14 ... 436
92:13–14 ... 910
93–99 ... 63, 64, 123, 147, 173
93–95 ... 81
93 ... 70, 78, 432, 448, 456, 507, 558, 724, 930
93:1 ... 318, 716, 728
93:3–4 ... 325, 344, 375
93:3 ... 47
94 ... 78, 657

94:1–3 927
94:3 278
94:7 374, 383, 851
94:12 93, 651, 657
94:15 250
94:17 533
95–99 448, 456, 507
95–98 432, 930
95 78
95:1–2 68
95:3 116, 508, 509
95:5 375
95:8–11 884
96–99 724
96 78, 556
96:1 45–46
96:2 620, 621
96:4–5 840
96:4 508, 509
96:10 70, 318, 716, 728, 834, 834
96:11 449
96:13 70, 448, 930
97 70, 78
97:1–6 342
97:1 728
97:2 354
97:4 448
97:5 945
97:7 508, 537, 840
97:9 508, 509, 840
97:11 250
98 78, 556
98:1 45–46
98:2–3 620
98:3 422, 620, 871, 927
98:4 620
98:6 116
98:7–8 70
98:7 449
98:8 726
98:9 71, 448, 930
99 55, 70, 78
99:1 728
99:2 290
99:4 71, 116
99:5 209, 515
99:9 515
101 66, 67, 119, 397, 694
101:2–4 120, 662
101:4 812
101:6 120, 813
101:7–8 812
101:8 120, 719
102 59, 146, 152, 318, 544, 615, 627, 772
102:0 869
102:1 485
102:2 518, 954
102:3 606
102:9 824
102:11 604, 959
102:12–22 238, 319
102:13 290
102:15 116
102:16 290
102:18 737
102:19–20 291
102:23–24 959
102:23 959
102:26–28 563
102:26–27 563
102:28 238, 297
103 53, 102, 468
103:8–13 954
103:11–12 50
103:15 604
104 53, 66, 78, 559, 627
104:1–3 759
104:3–4 509
104:3 342, 342
104:5 318, 716
104:10–16 458
104:10–11 893
104:15 533
104:24–30 458
104:27–30 455
104:29 158, 422, 518, 690, 954
104:32 945
105 75, 78, 78, 684
105:1 834
105:4 154, 327
105:12 629
105:14, 20, 30 116
105:41 893
106 53, 75, 76, 78, 657, 688
106:3 93, 651, 651, 657
106:4 620
106:13 765
106:18 404
106:21 322, 765
106:27 351
106:40–47 693
107–150 760
107–145 602
107 53–54, 55, 66, 68, 74, 78, 139, 684, 720
107:10 688
107:12 561
107:13–16 54
107:14 688
107:19–22 54
107:32 515
107:35 893
107:42 250
108:1–5 830
108:3 834
108:4 871
108:5 373
108:6–13 859
108:9 497
108:12 620
109 146
109:26 561
109:28–29 537
109:30 25, 68, 145
110 31, 44, 66, 67, 119, 121, 281, 390, 397, 884
110:1–2 386
110:1 209, 884
110:2 214, 290
110:4 884
110:5 116
111–117 79
111 44, 55, 56, 73, 78, 602
111:1 250
112 55, 56, 73, 78, 602, 657
112:1 93, 651, 657
112:2 250
112:4 250
112:6 301, 318, 716
112:10 605
113 53, 78, 79
113:4 373
113:5 586
113:7 658, 659
114 78, 79
114:7 383
115 78
115:1 871
115:3–4 43–44
115:7 164
115:9–11 496, 561
115:17 533
116 66, 78, 535
116:3 312
116:9 487
116:11 535
116:12–14 25, 621
116:13 451
116:14 905
116:17–18 25
116:18 905
117:2 871
118 78, 79
118:6–7 524
118:13 561
118:14 620
118:15 385
118:19–20 68
118:27 68, 475, 927
118:28 515
119 34–35, 55, 56, 73, 74, 78, 96, 234, 366, 602, 765
119:1 651, 657
119:2 93, 651, 657
119:6 537
119:25 377
119:31 537
119:35 533
119:37 377, 452
119:38 369, 373
119:41 620
119:46 116, 537
119:48 891
119:50 377
119:58 327
119:70 323, 376
119:77 376
119:78, 80 537
119:83 823
119:84 278, 864
119:86 561
119:88 367
119:89–90 374
119:92–93, 97 376
119:107 377
119:113 376
119:114 496
119:123 620
119:131 831
119:132 46, 93
119:135 327
119:149 376
119:154 377
119:156 377
119:163 376

119:165 483
119:166 .....562, 620
119:173 561
119:174 .....376, 620
120–134 ......20, 28, 58, 720
121:1 561
121:2 561
121:3–4............292
121:3..301, 477, 716
121:4 191
122 ....741, 910
122:4 367
122:5 398
124:4–5............344
124:6 841
125:1..301, 318, 716
125:4 250
126 910
126:1 291
126:2 834
127 657
127:5 ....93, 537, 651, 657
128 657
128:1–2............93, 651, 657
128:5 290
129:5–8............238
129:5 537
129:6 604
130 ....65, 544, 615, 772
130:2 485
130:5–6............833
130:5 ....562, 636
130:7–8............238
130:7 562
130:8 693
131 75
131:2 216
131:3 238
132 ....66, 67, 116, 119, 121, 123, 390, 397, 741, 741, 835
132:1–4............741
132:1 398
132:2 905
132:8 133
132:10–11 398
132:11–18 741
132:13.......290, 741
132:17 398
132:18 537
133:3 290
134:2..451, 494, 891
134:3 290
135 ....53, 78
135:5 ....508, 840
135:6 449
135:14 477
135:21 290
136 ....25, 55, 66, 68–69, 78
136:2 508
137 ....28, 78, 139, 146, 315, 351, 501, 509, 695, 717, 910
137:1–4..............27
137:3 741
137:4 ....673, 835
137:5–6............719
137:7 687
137:8–9.............93, 651, 657
138 ....78, 835
138:1 508
138:2 ....835, 871
138:4–5............835
139 104
139:7–12 673
139:8 312
139:16 ....825, 959
139:19–22 476
139:19 476
139:23–24 663
140 150
140:6 889
140:7 620
140:10 ....116, 318, 809
140:13 ....250, 297
141:1 ....418, 810, 965
141:2 ....494, 891
141:3 658
141:7 312
141:8 318
142 ....59, 61, 80, 127, 152, 318, 545, 567, 728
142:3 869
142:4 848
142:5 ....318, 487
143 ....544, 615, 772
143:1 ....319, 485
143:2 ....294, 357
143:4 869
143:5 164
143:6 893
143:7 ....518, 776, 954
144 ....66, 71, 78, 119, 123, 124, 126, 337, 627
144:1–11 ....66, 397
144:2 ....339, 496
144:9 556
144:10 ....385, 398
144:14–15 238
144:15 ....93, 651, 657
145 ....55, 73, 74, 602, 627, 657
145:1..116, 123, 515
145:4 737
146–150 ......53, 65, 73, 77, 78, 124, 224, 373, 657, 990
146 ....124, 165, 224, 627
146:3–5 ....123, 802
146:3–4............172
146:3 ....621, 702
146:4 530
146:5 ....93, 383, 561, 651, 657
146:6 375
146:9 42
146:10 728
147 224
148:13 373
149 ......71, 556, 724
149:1 45
149:2 ....116, 290
149:4 620
150 974

Proverbs

1–9 ....74, 96, 748
1:12 941
1:22 95
2:7 662
3:10 860
3:13 93
3:14 ....538, 605
3:34 95
5:6 315
5:21 272
6:13 584
6:23 315
6:35 752
8:19 605
8:26 ....447, 448
8:29 375
8:31 ....447, 448
8:32, 34 93
9:7–8............95, 95
10–31 98
10:1 41
10:3 499
10:5 652
10:9 ....99, 662
10:10 584
10:15 658
10:16...99, 499, 610
10:17 315
10:19 652
10:22 ....499, 610
10:24 99
10:27 355
10:29 662
11:4 ....355, 499
11:8 355
11:15 726
11:19–20 355
11:19 ....499, 610
11:21 610
11:28..499, 610, 881
12:9 605
12:21 499
13:1 95
13:6 662
13:8 752
13:11 880
13:21, 25 499
14.................34–35
14:6 95
14:11 499
14:12 272
14:21 93
14:31 658
14:35 652
15:1–2..............271
15:3 355
15:4 271
15:6 ....499, 610
15:12 95
15:16 ....356, 499, 538, 605, 610, 692
15:17 ....538, 605
15:19 99
15:24...99, 315, 652
15:26 ....99, 355
15:28 271
15:29 ....99, 355
15:33 704
16:2 272
16:4, 7 99
16:8 ....356, 499, 538, 605, 610, 692

16:16.......499, 538, 605, 610, 692
16:17..................99
16:19..............499, 605, 692
16:20.........93, 355, 499, 610, 652
16:25..........99, 272
16:30................584
16:32................605
17:1..........538, 605
17:2..................652
17:3..................404
17:8..................300
17:12................605
17:13................582
17:18................726
17:23................300
17:27................271
18:6–8..............271
18:12................704
18:21................271
19:1...499, 605, 662
19:4..................658
19:5..................271
19:16..................42
19:17................658
19:19................538
19:22................605
19:25, 29............95
20:1....................95
20:5..................515
20:7............93, 662
20:20................271
21:2..................272
21:6..........610, 880
21:9..................605
21:11..................95
21:12................652
21:13................658
21:14................300
21:18................752
21:19................605
21:23................271
21:24..................95
21:28................271
22:1.........433, 499, 538, 605
22:4..................704
22:6..........514, 980
22:8..................956
22:9..................658
22:10..................95
22:16........610, 658
22:22................658
22:26................726
23:4–5.....610, 881
23:15–16..........271
24:9....................95
24:12................320
24:19–20..........610
24:19................603
25:7, 24............605
26:18................899
26:22–26..........271
27:5, 10............605
27:21................404
27:24................881
28:3..........658, 659
28:6.........499, 538, 605, 610, 662, 692
28:8..........610, 658
28:11................658
28:14..................93
28:15................658
28:20, 25..........610
29:7..................658
29:8....................95
29:9..................156
29:10........476, 662
29:14........658, 659
29:18..................93
30:4..................422
30:7–31............881
30:20................773
31:10–31......56, 73
31:30................880

Ecclesiastes

1:2–11..............204
1:2....................627
1:3–11..............563
1:4....................204
1:9–11..............563
1:11..........204, 676
3:1....................953
3:18–21............422
3:19–21............722
3:20..................422
5:3................7, 883
5:18–20............587
7:1....................433
7:4......................42
7:7....................881
7:15..................610
7:20..........294, 357
8:5–6................953
8:7–10..............587
8:14..........356, 610
9:1–6................422
9:3–4................722
9:4....................853
9:8....................702
10:17..................93
12:1–7..............976
12:3..................368
12:7..................530
12:8..................627
12:13........331, 356

Song of Songs

5:2....................662
6:9....................662

Isaiah

1–39..173, 195, 974
1:2....................761
1:7....................630
1:11–15....762, 960
1:17..........936, 937
1:23...300, 936, 937
1:25..................918
2:2–4................732
2:3....................383
3:1....................435
3:13..................767
5:7....................593
5:13..................893
5:23..................300
6:1–9......174, 302, 357, 522, 533, 703, 729, 945
6:3....................511
6:5.....173, 241, 327
6:26..................419
9:2....................688
9:6....................216
9:17..................936
10:2....658, 936–37
10:6..................645
10:17................404
11:1..................390
11:4..................658
11:6–7..............732
12:4..........707, 834
13:12................706
13:16................705
14:6..................214
14:21................447
14:30................658
15:2..................515
15:16................604
16:8..................178
17:10................676
18:3..................447
18:4..................882
18:7..................707
19:20................321
20:3..................336
21–23..............595
23:1..................737
23:2..................882
23:7..................707
23:14................737
24:4–5..............448
24:4..................447
24:16................872
24:22................646
24:23................728
25:1..........515, 889
25:4..................658
25:5..................799
25:6...422, 437, 593
26:6..................658
26:9..........447, 448
26:11................404
26:13........388, 707
26:18..447, 448, 927
28:2..................487
29....................824
29:5..................630
29:8..................869
29:20..................95
30....................824
30:7..........153, 880
30:12–14..........112
30:14................112
30:18..................93
30:27................404
30:30................404
31:3..................823
31:9..................405
32:17................882
32:20..................93
33:14........353, 404
33:21................201
33:24................550
34:1–17............448
34:1..........447, 449
34:15........322, 831
34:16........824, 825
35:3..................487
35:6..................883
35:9..................320
37:27................604
37:36................569
38:10................535
38:11................487
40–66................195
40:3..................769
40:6–8..............604
40:18–20..........508
40:19................918
40:22–23..........596

40:28 872
40:31 869
41:14 174
41:21 767
41:21–24 508
41:25 ....190, 645
42:1–9 336
42:1–6 282
42:1–4 ....107, 696
42:6 732
42:10 ..449, 556, 872
42:18–19 336
42:19 335
42:25 887
43–63 322
43:3 ....752, 988
43:6 872
43:9–20 508
43:14 174
43:16–21 488
44:3 893
44:6 174
44:7 586
44:8 140
44:9–18 628
44:12 869
44:24 174
44:26–28 720
45:5–6 140
45:8 927
45:9 767
45:14, 18 140
45:22 ....140, 141, 422, 872
46:1–4 498
46:3–7 508
46:4 976
46:9 140
47:4 174
47:9 662
47:14 606
48:10 ....404, 488
48:17 174
49:1–7 336
49:1–6 ....282, 696
49:1 707
49:4 ....153, 880
49:6 ....732, 927
49:7 174
49:8 953
49:10 738
50:2 893
50:4–11 ....282, 336, 696
50:6 518
50:8 ....478, 766
51:4 732
51:6 ....375, 606
51:9–10 344
51:12 604
51:13 ....676, 765
51:17, 22–23 254
52:7 728
52:10 ....422, 927
52:13–53:12 ....282, 336, 696
53 ....550, 696
53:7 707
53:8 487
53:9 546
53:12 550
54:5 174
54:8 ....174, 518
54:17 478
55:1–2 893
55:2 593
55:11 269
55:12 726
56:1–7 907
56:2 93
56:10 853
57:6 887
57:13 880
57:16 869
57:17 518
58:14 593
60 34–35
60:1–3 354
60:5 568
60:9 737
60:14 719
60:16 174
61:1–9 890
61:3 705
62:1 882
63:2–3 843
63:3 941
63:6 941
63:9 498
63:14 738
63:16 174
65:9 958
65:11 765
65:16 ....272, 540
65:23 153
65:25 732
66:13 216
66:15 939
66:18–24 907

Jeremiah

1:10 496
2:6 688
2:9 767
2:13 ....593, 597
2:20 118
2:27 133
2:32 ....676, 765
3:17 720
3:21 676
4:28 180
5:4 658
5:5 118
5:19 630
5:22 344
6:20 ....638, 768
6:27 918
7 910
7:1–15 521
7:2–15 717
7:4–10 521
7:4 ....719, 894
7:6 937
7:11 320
7:13 ....593, 597
7:21–23 ....762, 960
7:23 558
8:1 795
8:16 449
9:8 899
10:12 ....447, 448
11:4 ...404, 488, 558
11:16 788
11:19 ....487, 788
11:20 918
12:3 918
12:4 604
13:25 676
14:3 893
14:8 321
15:3 853
16:19 ....422, 718
17:5 823
17:6 788
17:7–8 97
17:8 788
17:27 404
18:8, 10 193
18:15 676
18:20 582
19:1–13 112
19:9 795
20:7–10 ....626, 627
21:8 315
21:14 404
22:3 937
23:27 765
24:7 161
25:15, 17, 28 254
25:33 872
25:34 112
26 910
26:1–6 521
26:3, 13, 19 193
30:8 630
30:10 321
30:21 201
30:22 558
30:23 365
31:19 726
31:20 463
31:25 869
31:34 161
32:17 373
32:27 907
32:31–32 365
33:5 ...365, 518, 954
33:7 720
36 ....640, 824
38:7 953
39:10 658
40:7 658
41:4–9 645
45 824
46:16 133
47:2 449
47:6 ....721, 882
48:25 339
49:19 586
49:27 404
50:29 974
50:32 404
50:44 586
51 824
51:5 974
51:10 478
51:15 ....447, 448
51:34 153
51:58 153
52:15–16 658

Lamentations

2:11 869
2:15 726
2:16 605
2:19 ....451, 494, 887, 891
2:20 795
3:30 134
3:41 ...451, 494, 891
3:50 291
4:11 404
4:12 447
4:17 880

4:21 254
5:10 405
5:17 368

Ezekiel

1 .... 342, 944
2–3 640
3:12 475
3:26 883
4:4, 6 550
5:1 795
5:16 899
6:12 835
7:21 630
8 890
9:8 887
10–11 522
10 342
12:19 449
15:7 404
16:43 156
17:22–24 788
18:19 550
19:7 449
19:12 .... 14, 404
20:23 351
20:47 404
22:6–7 937
22:7 937
22:12 676
22:18, 20, 22 404
22:25, 27 765
23:25 404
23:31–33 254
23:35 676
23:41 955
24:27 883
25:3 584
25:6 726
25:14 365
26:2 584
26:20 487
27:25 737
28:3 779
28:7 799
28:18 404
28:23 .... 843, 941
29:15 214
30:12 449
31:12 799
32:15 449
32:23–27, 32 487
33:32 883
34:4 214
34:12 354
36:2 584
36:6 365
36:28 558
37–48 720
37 .... 793, 795
39:18 417
39:24, 29 518
41:22 955
43:4–5 475
44:4 475
44:10,12 550
44:16 955

Daniel

3 .... 438, 452, 891, 895
3:6 .... 11, 15, 405
3:16–18 621
3:17–18 .... 478, 891
3:17 .... 19–23, 26, 405
3:29 .... 140, 141
5:23 508
6 .... 438, 452, 895
6:20 336
8:26 779
9 .... 282, 956
9:4–19 692
9:25 720
11:36–37 509
11:36 504
12:1 .... 824, 825
12:3 652
12:4 .... 9, 779, 824
12:10 652
12:12 93

Hosea

1–3 857
1:4–9 210
2:3 893
2:13 765
2:20 161
4:1–6 768
4:1 .... 161, 676, 766
4:6 161
4:12 508
5:14 .... 765, 766
5:15 .... 327, 453
6:6 .... 762, 768, 960
6:8 941
7:4, 6, 7 405
7:9 630
8:7 956
8:14 404
9:4 309
10:6 707
11:1–8 463
11:3–4 118
12:2 767
12:12 288
13:4 321
13:6 765

Joel

1:6 134
2:1–2 354
2:14 193
2:27 140
2:28–29 887
3:1 720
3:20 720

Amos

1:4, 7, 10, 12, 14 404
2:2 404
2:4 154
2:5 404
2:7 658
2:14 487
3:8 627
3:12 766
4:1 .... 417, 658
4:4–5 .... 762, 960
5:5 453
5:8 688
5:11 .... 658, 659
5:12 752
5:13 652
5:21–25 .... 394, 762, 960
5:21–24 768
5:22 638
6:10 707
7–8 890
8:6 658
8:13 .... 869, 893

Obadiah

18 404

Jonah

1:1–3 .... 809, 988
1:3ff. 737
2:8 452
3:3 .... 434, 592
3:9 .... 180, 192
4:2 193
4:7 .... 415, 415
4:8 869

Micah

1:2 449
1:4 945
2:1 157
2:13 860
3:1–3 795
3:3 289
3:4 .... 518, 954
3:11 300
4:1–4 732
4:2 .... 383, 720
4:7 728
5:1 134
5:4 422
5:8 765
6:1–2 767
6:2 767
6:6–8 .... 762, 960
6:7 754
6:14 339
7:10 645
7:18 .... 550, 586
7:19 215

Nahum

1:5 .... 447, 448, 945
2:1 487
2:12 765
3:13, 15 404
3:19 .... 726, 726

Habakkuk

2:13 153
2:16 254
3 75
3:1 .... 19, 75
3:2–19 341
3:3 341
3:8–10 344
3:8 .... 385, 939

Zephaniah

1:8 630
1:15–17 354
1:18 404
2:3 704
3:8 404
3:10 707
3:12 658

Zechariah

1 569
2 721
2:13 883
3 569
7:10 937
8:3–4 720
8:4 .... 435, 976

8:7 321
8:22 720
9:3 645
9:4 404
9:10 422
9:11 646
9:15 215
10:5 645
11:9 795
12 569
12:1 530
14:11 720

Malachi

2:11 630
3:1 769
3:5 937
3:16 824
4:1 .... 405, 606

Matthew

4:1 815
5–7 ... 101, 451, 495
5:3 573
5:3–12 573
5:3–10 103
5:6 .... 573, 893
5:8–10 573
5:11–12 293
5:17 377
5:20 379
5:39 136
5:44 .... 135, 136
5:45 374
5:48 378
6:7 883
6:8 216
6:25–34 458
6:25 .... 697, 698, 722, 749
7:13–14 102
7:23 278
7:24–27 103
8 912
8:11 593
9:9–13 661
9:11 102
9:12–13 .... 102, 469
10:28 828
13 405
15:27 854
16:24–25 756
16:25 .... 265, 895
16:26 749
18:20 .... 213, 293
20:28 756
22:1–14 593
22:32 383
22:35–40 769
23:37 831
25:1–13 645
25:40 293
26:39 896
26:67 952
27:35 .... 412, 418
27:39 412
27:43 .... 412, 416
27:46 .... 412, 424
27:48 955
28:18–20 246
28:19–20 911

Mark

2:16 102
2:17 469
7 912
8:27, 29 258
8:35 .... 265, 895
8:37 749
10:45 756
11:24 394
12:26 383
14:62 210
15:24 418
15:34 .... 281, 413, 424

Luke

5:4, 8 511
5:16 815
5:30 102
5:31–32 469
6:28 174
6:45 157
7:45 113
7:46 702
9:24 .... 265, 895
10:25–37 814
12:1–5 828
12:28 604
13:29 593
13:34 .... 322, 831
14:15 .... 422, 437
14:16–24 593
16:21 854
20:37 383
23:34 .... 418, 804
23:36 955
23:46 .. 429, 530, 541

John

1:4–5 354
1:5 837
1:9 354
1:12–13 107
1:12 216
1:47–51 546
2 598
3:20–21 480
4 .... 593, 912
4:7–30 597
4:7–15 889
4:15–18 104
7:37 893
8:7 902
9:1–12 575
9:1–2 178
9:2 691
9:3 697
10:10 827
10:30 .... 218, 328
11:4 697
13–17 101
13:1–17 862
13:18 654
14:9 ... 218, 328, 684
19:23–24 .. 412, 418
19:24 424
19:28 412
19:29 955
19:30 429
20:17 216
20:29 684
20:30–31 684

Acts

2:1–21 733
2:25–31 313
2:30–35 390
2:30 591
7:46 383
7:59 530
8–15 377
9:1–19 357
10:34–35 246
13:33 ..... 21, 92, 108
13:35–37 313
13:47 732
15:12–29 377

Romans

1:18–23 363
1:19–20 218
1:20 375
1:32–2:1 995
3:5 480
3:9–12 294
3:10 357
3:21–24 480
3:23 .... 294, 694
4:6–25 358
5:1–11 931
5:1–5 480
5:5 424
6:23 783
8:15 216
8:17 696
8:21 .... 118, 551
8:28 185
8:31 270
8:36 693
11:17–24 931
12:1 961
12:14 174
12:17–21 960
12:17–19 136

1 Corinthians

1:18 980
13:12 .... 211, 278, 441

2 Corinthians

4:4, 6 328
5:17 596
5:21 550
6:2 953
9:6 956
12:7–10 923
12:9–10 408
12:19 981

Galatians

3:28 246
6:7 956

Ephesians

2:11–22 246
5:19 .... 22, 30
6:10–18 .... 348, 826

Philippians

2:3 733
2:4–11 212
2:5–8 744
3:2 424
3:8–14 770
3:10 244
4:3 .... 825, 959
4:11–13 923
4:11–12 523
4:13 523

Colossians

1:15 328

3:16 .... 22, 30

1 Timothy

2:6 756

2 Timothy

4:17 424

Hebrews

1:1–2 218
1:3 450
1:8–9 703
2:5–8 207
2:12 424
3 442
4:3 442
4:7 .... 20, 23
4:10 442
4:12–16 105
7:11–25 390
9:15 756
9:28 550
10:1–10 648
10:26–27 404
11 443
11:35–40 895
11:35–38 696
12:29 .. 353, 404, 405
13:5–6 524
13:8 180

James

1:26 786
2:26 378
3:5–9 786
5:1–3 404
5:3 404

1 Peter

1:24 604
2:22 546
2:24 550
3:10 786
3:12 328
4:12–15 696

2 Peter

3:12 375
3:13 596

1 John

1:5 167
1:8–10 ...... 144, 647
1:9 .... 553, 622, 647, 782

Revelation

1:12–16 341
3:5 .... 825, 959
3:14 656
5:9 556
6:16 .... 328, 518
7:9 246
8:7 604
13:8 825
14:3 556
14:6 246
14:19–20 843
14:20 .... 941, 944
19:13–15 843
20–22 720
20:1–15 960
20:12 825
20:15 825
21:1–5 596
21:1 357
21:10 720
21:23–24 594
21:27 825
22:1–2 593
22:3–4 328
22:17 893

Subject Index

absence of God, 278–79, 280–81, 283–84, 414–17, 426, 673–74, 863–64
abundant life, 432–33
access to God, 211–13, 296–304, 547–48
acrostic psalms, 55–57, 224, 460–61, 566–67, 602
advancing parallelism, 43–46, 47
affirming parallelism, 40–41, 46, 47, 177, 567, 639–40
agape, 443
aging, 678–80, 975–82
Alcoholics Anonymous, 104, 408, 622
aliens, 629–30, 632–33, 870
Amish communities, 263
anapestic rhythm, 33
ancient types of psalms, 58–59, 79
anger: and discipline, 178; of God, 110–11, 178, 516, 517–18; and invocation of God, 177–78, 616–17; and prayer, 803–4; and sin, 156; toward enemies, 136, 138–39, 143–44
anointing with oil, 386–87, 497–98, 705, 709
antithetical parallelism, 41–43
Apostle, The, 329
Aquinas, Thomas, 944
Asaph, 21, 24, 28, 758, 759
attacks on the faithful and helpless, 137–39, 147–48, 168–69, 181, 234, 254–56, 417–19, 426–27, 528–29, 536, 582–83, 617–19, 799, 878–80, 951–53, 971–72; in modern society, 261–62
Auffret, Pierre, 52
authorship of the psalms, 19–23, 78–79

Babylonian empire, 26
ballast lines, 45
Beatitudes, New Testament, 573
benediction, communal, 926–27
betrayal, 654
blessing: deliverance as, 134; eternal, 400; God, 572–73; on kings, 398–400, 870–71, 989–90, 993–95; on the land, 908–9, 938; and the law, 376–77; and lifestyles, 95–97, 436; proclamation of, 545–46, 657; on the righteous, 170–71, 452, 498, 606–8, 788–89; and the universal blessing of God, 928; on the weak, 651–52, 658–59
Blue Max, The, 637
Bonhoeffer, Dietrich, 264–65
book of life, 825, 958–60
Braveheart, 117
breath prayers, 104
bribery, 300
brides, 706–7
Brothers Grimm, 60
Browning, Elizabeth Barrett, 977
Buber, Martin, 304
Burgess, Gelett, 32n3
burnt offerings, 393–94, 772. *See also* sacrifices

cannibalism, 795–96
Canterbury Tales, 19
Carter, Jimmy, 994
Catholic Integrated Community, 328
Chaucer, Geoffrey, 19
chiasm, 50–52, 339–40
children and infants, 202, 573; firstborn, 753–54; and God as the foundation of hope, 970–71; of kings, 705–6; recording history for, 743–44
Christianity; and adoption of the psalms, 30–31; and keeping God's law, 377–80
cleansing, plea for, 775–76
climatic parallelism, 46–47
commitment to God, 310–11, 530–31, 537–38, 541–42, 889–90
compression in poetry, 34

confession: of faith, 307–8, 647–48; of sin, 544, 546–47, 549–53, 774–75, 783
confidence psalms, 75, 305–6, 430–31, 477, 480, 482, 483, 487–88, 530–531, 590, 595, 609, 650–53, 799, 813, 814, 841–42, 851–53, 891–92, 972–75
confrontations, 763–66
conventions, poetic, 31–35
corruption, 287–88, 292, 840–41
covenant of God and His people, 111–12, 116, 155, 160, 280, 393, 688, 694, 763–64, 766–68
Creation, 373
creative power of God, 201–5, 217–18, 361–62, 373–74, 447–50, 455–56, 595–97, 836–37; and empowerment and responsibility of man, 205–9; and human existence, 352–53
cultural assimilation, 264
cultural isolation, 263–64

dactylic rhythm, 33
darkness and dark clouds, 342, 343, 353–54
David: descendants of, 111–12, 114–17, 123–24; flight from Jerusalem of, 128; and hymns, 335–37, 360, 590–91; prayer of, 318–19; as psalms author, 20–23, 28, 625–26, 650; and royal psalms, 107, 115–17, 124–26, 382–83, 391–92
Davidic kings, 111–12, 114–17, 124–26, 172, 389, 395, 432, 520–21, 708–711, 986, 988
Day of Atonement, 302
Dead Sea Scrolls, 31, 56
death: and faith, 895–96; images of impending, 189, 653–54; journey to, 434; life after, 722–23, 755–56; and memory, 676; and mortality of man, 204–5, 749–50; as punishment, 812–13; salvation from, 230, 279, 313, 751–52; and suffering, 689, 873–74
deceit and lies, 267–68, 271–72, 654, 763–64, 786–87, 879–80; in modern society, 273–76
deliberations on faith, 157
deliverance: as blessing, 134, 651–52; communal, 497–98, 685–86; confidence of, 891–92; descriptions of past, 636–38; and distress, 340–41, 808–10; from enemies, 128–30, 138, 176–77, 181–82, 227, 266, 322–24, 339, 350–51, 386–87; hope for, 167–68; oracle of, 861–63; personal testimony of, 568–70; pleading with God for, 133, 140, 151–54, 164–66, 179–80, 188, 231–32, 233–34, 268–69, 325–26, 372–73, 418, 462–63, 485–87, 494, 518–19, 527–530, 579, 619, 629, 635–36, 643–44, 674–75, 689–90, 798–99, 808, 831–32, 849, 868–70, 898–99, 950–51, 953–54; praise for, 496–97; prayer for, 578–79; realization of, 132–34, 344–45, 519; thanksgiving for, 225–27, 823; and trust in god, 532–33; and waiting for God, 561–62; and water, 950–51
delusions, 153–54
De sacra poesi Hebraeorum, 39
Descent of Ishtar to the Nether World, 973
dignity, 131–32, 137–38
disasters: drought, 149, 152–53; and duration of suffering, 153; and false gods, 149–50; water, 343–44, 361–62, 507, 509–10, 731, 845, 885–87
discipline: angry, 178, 616–17; lack of, 288–89
distress, 340–41
divine otherness, 352–53
divine scrutiny, 291–92, 319–20, 472–75, 478, 559
divine sonship, 107, 114
divine transparency, 272–73, 303–4
divorce, 196, 489
Does God Need the Church?, 328–29
Dove on Distant Oaks, A, 820
doxologies, concluding, 76–77, 655–56, 990–91
drought, 152–53
Duvall, Robert, 329

dwelling with God, 297–98, 436–37, 444–45, 471, 484–85, 607–8, 717, 869–70, 909–10

earthquakes, 341, 356–57
effective word, the, 271–72, 275–76
empowerment and responsibility, 205–9, 213–15, 242, 346–49, 406–9
enemies: attacks by, 417–19, 850–51, 878–80, 951–53, 971–72; confrontation of, 181–82; and deceit, 786–87, 879–80; defeat of, 349–50, 386–87, 704, 821–23, 938, 940–41, 942–43; deliverance from, 128–30, 138, 181–82, 227, 230, 266, 322–24, 350–51, 402–3, 418, 485–87, 494, 518–19, 527–30, 568–70, 579, 619, 629, 643–44, 674–75, 689–90, 950–51, 953–54; desire for God to scatter, 935–36; fear of, 133; flight from, 736–37, 809–10, 814–16; of God, 202–3, 801; God as a shield from, 130–32, 171, 496–97, 561; and God's mercy and grace, 168, 321–24, 466; identity of the, 147–48; judgment on, 168–70, 230–32, 401–2, 810–11, 955–56; and legal conflict, 581–83; loving and praying for our, 136, 501, 588; and public vindication, 133–34, 136–37, 319, 452, 477–78, 528–29, 579–80, 584–85, 587–88, 619, 800, 841–42; superiority over defeated, 209, 349, 940–41; training for battle against, 348; and victory from God, 402–3, 685–86, 704
entrance liturgies, 75
eschatological vision of hope, 425, 712–13
Ethan, 24
Evangeline, 33n4
exile: of the Israelites, 26–30, 115, 238, 282, 290–91, 488, 500, 508–9, 683, 689–693, 708–9, 834–36, 882; in modern society, 873–74

fairy tales, 60
faith: and the absence of God, 283–84; and admonition to the faithful, 346, 764–65; attacks on those of, 137–39, 147–48, 168–69, 181, 417–19, 426–27, 528–29, 536, 582–83, 617–19, 695–98, 799, 878–80, 951–53, 971–72; and being grounded in the Word, 329–30; and blessings on the faithful, 606–8; community of, 683–85; confession of, 307–8, 647–48; and confidence in God, 269–70, 285; deliberations on, 157; dying for, 895–96; and the godly, 155–56; and God's law, 379–80, 688–89; God's response to those of, 155, 374; lure of pragmatic, 160–61; and praise for God's faithfulness, 463–64, 557; profession of, 307–8; and righteousness, 98–99, 101–2; and sacrifices, 157–58, 257; of sinners, 467–68; and tree imagery, 97–98; vows of witness and, 638–42; and the way of victory, 347–51
false gods, 149–50, 153–54, 159–61, 342–43, 451–52, 586–587, 637–38, 762, 843–44, 845–46; and henotheism, 507–9; and polytheism, 369; and pragmatism, 160–61; refusal to worship, 308–10; unholiness of, 166–67
fear: and aging, 978; and anguish, 179; of enemies, 133, 136, 289; of evil, 435, 789–90; of God, 357–58, 419–20, 464–65, 569–70, 570, 637, 870, 937
Fear No Evil, 866
fellowship: in modern worship, 303; and race, 243–44
fertility deities, 149–50, 153–54, 159–60. *See also* false gods
fire, judgment by, 403–5
flight from enemies, 736–37, 809–10, 814–16
foreigners, 629–30, 632–33
forgiveness, 463, 545–46, 773–74
fortresses, 338
freedom: and modern society, 117–18; and obedience to God, 117–18; from oppression and repression, 117, 289
fruitful living, 97–98

gloating, 515
glory: God's, 201, 207, 362, 453–55, 567–68, 891, 917, 922–24, 991; human, 131, 153, 399–400
God: absence of, 278–79, 280–81, 283–84, 414–17, 426, 673–74, 863–864; access to, 211–13, 296–304, 547–48; anger of, 110–11, 516, 517–18; bargaining with, 184; blessing, 572–75, 641–42; brightness of, 343; chariots of, 939; city of, 717, 719–20, 739–43; commitment to, 310–11, 530–31, 537–38, 541–42, 733, 889–90; and communal benediction, 926–27; compassion of, 988–89; confidence in, 269–70, 311–13, 477, 480, 483, 487–88, 530–31; as counselor and teacher, 311, 314, 320–21, 435, 486–87, 530, 570–71, 744, 927–28; creative power of, 201–5, 217–18, 361–62, 373–74, 447–50, 455–56, 595–97, 836–37; and divine otherness, 352–53; and divine scrutiny, 291–92, 319–20, 472–75, 478, 559; and divine transparency, 272–73, 303–4; dwelling with, 297–98, 436–37, 444–45, 471, 484–85, 607–8, 717, 869–70, 909–10; enduring love of, 563–64; fear of, 357–58, 419–20, 464–65, 569–70, 570, 637, 870, 937; forgetting, 679–80, 707–8, 764–65; glory of, 201, 207, 362, 453–55, 567–68, 891, 917, 922–24, 991; grace of, 465–66; and his purpose for man, 837–38; holiness of, 166–67, 173–74, 313, 353–54, 511–12; hospitality of, 598–99; incomparability of, 586–87; incompatibility with evil, 166–67, 170, 464, 533–34, 846; as judge, 151–52, 168–70, 178, 190–93, 196–97, 227–29, 251–54, 288–89, 401–2, 403–5, 456, 759–61, 765–66, 810–11, 841, 872, 900; knowledge of the presence, 161, 211, 276; longing to meet, 670–72; love of, 180, 205, 279–80, 321–24, 463, 473, 480, 535–36, 592–94, 673, 738, 856–57, 912–13; and for man, 205, 345, 353–54, 374, 458, 881, 908–9; mercy of, 151–52, 168, 178, 450, 463, 494, 531–32, 642, 655, 821; name of, 199–201, 209–11, 216–18, 229–30, 433, 893–94; obedience to, 103, 226, 246–47; opponents of, 94–95, 101–2, 109–10, 148, 154–58, 232–33, 401–2, 405, 571–72, 598–99, 799, 935–36; perfection of, 347, 348–49, 358, 366; petitioning, 968–70; power of, 341–44, 398, 402, 406–9, 505–6, 510–12, 557–58, 836–37, 852–53, 908, 942, 944–46; presence of, 161–62, 217, 284–85, 303–4, 352–53, 440–41, 450–53, 475–77, 485–86, 523–24, 534, 716–18, 736; promises of, 210, 397, 992–93; as protector, 306–7, 383, 521, 548, 561, 652–53, 716–18, 742–43, 802–3, 826–27, 872–73, 936–37; questioning, 278–79; as refuge, 195–96, 249–50, 256–58, 264–65, 292–93, 321–24, 347–48, 436–37, 476, 490, 527–29, 715–16, 831–32, 869, 874–75, 880, 910–11, 969, 980–981; revelation of, 360–63, 365–71, 373–76; righteousness of, 194, 254, 369–70, 374, 423, 529–30, 537–38, 557, 585, 586, 588, 641–42, 646–47, 774–75, 908, 985–86; as salvation, 91, 386, 619–21, 929–31, 940; security in, 312–13, 314, 517–18, 522, 523–24, 637; seeing, 326–28, 421, 484–86, 488, 890–91; separation from, 632–33; as shepherd, 431–45, 498, 738; as source of strength, 337–38, 496–97, 507, 826; strength from, 337–40, 348, 529, 852–53, 892; submission to, 110–11, 117–18; as supreme ruler and king, 110–11, 116–17, 165–66, 171–73, 228–29, 234–35, 453–55, 506–7, 685, 724–25, 728–29, 732–33, 863, 929–31, 993–95; transgression against, 371–72; trust

in, 158, 248–49, 279–80, 367, 388, 392–93, 400, 416–17, 461–62, 472, 479, 532–33, 547–48, 558–60, 560–61, 594, 603–4, 715–16, 718–19, 750–752, 787–88, 814, 825–27, 880, 886–87, 900–901; universal blessing of, 928; and vengeance, 842–43; waiting for, 490–91, 561–62, 626–27, 636, 644–45, 882; wonders of, 226; wrath of, 110–11, 178, 341
grace of God, 465–66
guilt: by association, 93–97; freedom from, 451; versus shame, 536–37; and sin, 94–95, 536–37, 546–47, 549–51, 621–23, 845, 907–8
Gunkel, Hermann, 60–63

Hasidic Jews, 263, 304
Haydn, Franz Joseph, 373
hazing, college, 426
headings, psalm, 75–81
healing, 515–16, 866
heaven, 180; and the creative authority of God, 447–50, 836–837; God descending from, 341–42, 375–76; and heavenly beings, 206–7; revelation of God in, 360–63, 373–76; stars and planets of, 362–63, 374–75; and the sun, 363–65
Hebrew poetry: and acrostic psalms, 55–57; art of, 35–39; and chiasm, 50–52; conclusions, 39; and inclusio, 52–53; and merism, 50; meter in, 36–37; and parallelism, 39–48; repetition in, 52–55; rhythm in, 36; syllable counting in, 38; techniques of, 39–57; tone stress in, 37; and word pairs, 48–50
Heman, 24
henotheism, 507–9
Henry, Patrick, 117
Herod's temple, 28–30
Highwayman, The, 33
historical use of the psalms, 75; in Christian worship, 30–31; in private prayer, 26–30; in temple worship, 23–26, 63–64, 67–70; holiness, 166–67, 173–74, 313, 353–54, 511–12
Holocaust, the, 264–65, 283, 285, 328–29, 695
hope: eschatological vision of, 425, 712–13; future, 738; God as the foundation of, 970–71; and hopelessness, 539, 869; and trust in God, 462, 561–62; and worship, 427–29
human frailty, 202, 203–5, 215–16, 559–60, 592, 627–28; and security in God, 312–13, 314, 316, 981–82
humility, 240–41, 703–4

iambic rhythm and meter, 32–34
imagery in poetry, 34, 341–44, 363–65, 447–50, 505–6, 548–49
inclusio, 52–53, 345
incubation, 133
influence, undue, 159–60
injustice, 183–84
innocence, protestation of, 189–90, 319–21, 450, 472, 473–74, 477, 478–80, 687–89, 694
integration, 328–29, 661–63, 711–12
international conspiracies, 109–10
interpretive approach to psalms, 239–40
invocations, 140–41, 151–54, 164–66, 177–81, 189, 616–17, 808, 916–19, 967–68
Israelites: aliens among, 629–31; exile of, 26–28, 238, 282, 290–91, 488, 500, 508–9, 683, 689–93, 708–9, 719–20, 834–36, 882; and henotheism, 507–9; and redemption, 752–54; and Roman rule, 28–30; suffering of, 264–65, 282–83, 686–87, 690–93, 918–19

Janneus, Alexander, 55
Jeduthun, 24
Jerusalem, 760–61; as the city of God, 717, 719–20, 739–43; David's flight from, 128; temple, 26–28, 132, 296, 301–2, 323, 383–84, 514, 519–22, 937; and Zion, 290, 383–84, 393, 777–78, 906
Jesus Christ: abandonment experienced by, 281, 413–14; and blessings from God, 575; and the care of God, 458,

542; death of, 895–96; and divine sonship, 107, 114; and enemies of believers, 443–44; and the face of God, 328; falsely accused, 817–18; on God's law, 377–78; holiness of, 313; and life after death, 722–23, 756; and living water, 104–5; message and purpose of, 258; obscuring God the father, 218; personal freedom through, 118; and redemption, 911–12; on sinners, 469, 479, 661; as "son of man," 205, 212; and suffering, 501; on suffering, 697–98; understanding through psalms, 31, 124–26, 390, 424–25; and use of "amen," 656; on wise and foolish house builders, 103

Johnson, Lyndon, 817

journaling, 284

joy: and confidence in God, 311–13; and deliverance, 519, 568–69, 832–33, 919–20; and faith, 158–59; God's law giving, 367, 376–77; and military victory, 385

Judaism: and cultural isolation, 263–64; and the destruction of the first temple, 26–28; and the destruction of the second temple, 28–30; and exile of the Israelites, 26–28, 115, 282, 290–91, 488, 500, 508–9, 683, 689–93, 708–9, 719–20, 834–36, 882; and henotheism, 507–9; and mercy, 168–70; and the Romans, 28–30; and suffering of the Jews, 264–65, 282–83, 686–87, 690–93, 918–19; and the use of the psalms in communal worship, 23–26

judgment: on enemies, 168–70, 319, 401–2, 498, 810–11, 955–56; by fire, 403–5; and forgiveness, 463; God's preparation for, 192–93, 456, 759–61, 900; and justice, 191, 251–54, 546–47, 841; and mercy, 151–52, 168; and punishment, 169–70, 178, 765–66, 812–13; righteous, 190–92, 196–97, 227–29, 499–500, 761, 872; on the wicked, 288–89, 494–96, 793–94, 902–3

justice, 191, 251–54, 326, 546–47, 593, 927–28; church involvement in, 243; compassionate, 988–89; and deception, 274; in modern society, 711–12; and retribution, 136–37, 140–41, 143–44, 495–96

kings. *See* leaders

Kirchliche Dogmatik, 944

knowledge of the presence of God, 161, 211, 217, 276

lament psalms, 65, 128, 139, 182–83, 277, 318–19, 412, 514, 615, 679, 822, 848, 859, 860–61, 949–50; body of, 141–44; conclusions to, 144–46; form of, 140–46; and identity of the enemies, 147–48; introductions to, 140–41; occasion of, 146–47

law, the: and blessed lifestyles, 95–96, 376–77; giving joy, 367, 376–77; Jesus Christ on, 377–78; and legalism in modern society, 379–80; and polytheism, 369; preciousness of, 370–71; rejected by kings and rulers, 109–10; revelation through, 365–71; and trust in God, 367

Lawrence, Brother, 103, 161

leaders: anointed with oil, 386–87, 497–98, 705, 709; blessings on, 398–400, 870–71, 989–90, 993–95; brides of, 706–7; conspiracies among, 109–10; daughters of, 705–6; Davidic, 111–12, 114–17, 172, 389, 395, 432, 520–21, 708–11, 986, 988; and freedom, 117–18; and God as supreme ruler, 110–11, 165–66, 171–73, 228–29, 234–35, 453–55, 506–7, 726–28, 728–29, 732–33, 863, 993–95; as gods, 843–44; and judgment on nations, 227–29, 230–32; just rule by, 986–87; man's place in the world as, 208, 213–15, 390–91; and power, 406–8; praise for, 701–6, 986–87; righteousness of, 703–4; and superiority over a defeated enemy, 209; warnings to,

112–14, 117; worldwide dominion of, 987–88
legal conflict, 581–83, 766–68
Lewis, C. S., 491–92, 741
Life Is Beautiful, 285, 922–23
lifestyles: and abundant life, 432–33; to avoid, 94; and blessed life, 95–97, 436; and fruitful living, 97–98; and life as a pilgrimage, 441–43; righteous, 95–97, 98–99, 101–2, 170–71, 298, 300–301, 357–58; and secure life, 433–35; of sin, 94–95; and ultimate consequences, 98–99
light: God as the source of life and, 441, 961; God's law giving, 367–68; and lightning, 343, 510–11; and the power of God, 510–11, 593–94; of the sun, 363–65; and waiting for God, 491–92, 674–75
limitations on human power, 241–42, 552–53, 559–60, 592, 627–28
liturgical use of the psalms, 23–26, 62–64, 67–74, 447, 450; and royal psalms, 121–23
living water, 104–5
Lohfink, Gerhard, 328–29
Longfellow, W. W., 33
love: agape, 443; God's, 180, 195, 205, 279–80, 321–24, 463, 473, 480, 535–36, 592–94, 673, 738, 856–57, 912–13
Lowth, Robert, 39

man: and access to God, 211–13, 296–304, 547–48; and aging, 678–80, 975–82; and blessing God, 572–75; and cannibalism, 795–96; and character, 215–16; created in God's image, 208, 211–13, 218–20; and divine otherness, 352–53; empowerment and responsibility of, 205–9, 213–15, 242, 346–49, 406–9; and expendable people in modern society, 796; and failure of human relationships, 489–90, 618–19, 811–12, 813–14, 864–66; and futility of human wealth, 749–50, 881; God's care for, 205, 345, 353–54, 374, 458, 881, 908–9; God's purpose for, 837–38, 982; and heavenly beings, 206–7; and human frailty, 202, 203–5, 215–16, 312–13, 314, 316, 559–60, 592, 627–28, 981–82; and human words, 272; limitations on, 241–42, 552–53, 559–60, 592, 627–28; and living a transparent life, 329–30, 778–83; mortality of, 204–5, 749–50, 752, 822–23, 827–28; perceptions of, 523, 539, 548–49; and personal identity, 259–60; place in the universe of, 204, 213–15, 886; and questioning God, 278–79; and relationships between men and women, 801–2; and seeing God, 326–28; self-centeredness of, 162, 457–58; and social status, 880–81; and transferring individual experience to the community, 244–45; and transgression against God, 371–72, 773–74, 794–95, 801–2
Mays, James L., 96
McCann, J. C., 93, 708–9
meditation: on God's love, 738; importance of, 96–97, 103–4, 924; on the psalms, 99–100; silent, 626–27, 882–84; on sin, 157. *See also* prayer
mercy, God's, 151–52, 168, 178, 450, 463, 494, 531–32, 642, 655, 821
merism, 50
Mesopotamia, 171–72, 740, 824, 843–44, 845
Messiah, the, 390, 651, 710, 720, 992–93. *See also* Jesus Christ
meter, poetic, 33–34, 36–37
military settings, 132, 133–34, 135–36, 348, 385, 386–87, 389–90, 569–70, 579–80, 702–3, 718–19, 720–21, 736–37, 741–42, 843
millennialism, 259, 263
morning sacrifices, 166
Mowinckel, Sigmund, 62–64
Murray, Andrew, 490–91
musical nature of the psalms, 21, 23–26, 60–61, 79–80, 150, 188, 199, 244–45, 335–37, 351, 590, 792, 798, 830, 877
muzzling the tongue, 631–32

603–4, 754–55, 786–87, 899–900; and assault of the wicked, 878–80; avoiding, 101–2, 299, 608; and betrayal, 654; and cleansing, 775–76; confession of, 544, 546–47, 549–53, 774–75, 783; consequences of, 98–99, 193–94, 228–29, 405, 476, 499–500, 538, 604, 605–6, 608–9, 645–46, 782, 901–3, 935–36, 956; and corruption, 287–88, 292, 840–41; and the covenant for sinners, 467–68; and deceit and lies, 267–69, 271–72, 763–64, 786–87, 879–80; and delusions, 149–50; and drought, 152–53; and enemies disguised as faithful, 147–48, 811–12, 813–14; and false gods, 149–50, 153–54, 159–61, 369, 451–52, 637–38, 762, 843–44, 845–46; and fear, 435, 789–90; flight from, 250–51, 255–56, 262–65; and folly of evildoers, 287–88, 598–99, 793, 951–53; and the foolish wicked, 287–88; and forgiveness, 463, 545–46, 773–74, 906–8; God's incompatibility with, 166–67, 170, 464, 533–34, 846; and guilt, 94–95, 539–40, 546–47, 549–51, 588, 621–23, 845, 907–8; and hurtful words, 816–18, 899–900; and identifying with the wicked, 293–95; and Jesus Christ, 469, 479, 661; and judgment on the wicked, 288–89, 494–96, 793–94, 902–3; meditation on, 157; in modern society, 174–75, 827–28, 855–56; from within ourselves, 196–97, 781–83, 864–66; and prayer, 803–4; and the presence of God, 162; and public contrition, 776–77; punishment for, 169–70, 178, 253–54, 571–72, 609–12, 765–66, 789–90, 812–13, 841, 850, 851–53, 865, 935–36, 955–56; rejecting, 184–85; and repentance, 197; and retribution, 136–37, 140–41, 143–44, 495–96, 498, 597–98, 610–12, 901–3, 960; and scorn, 953–55; and separation from God, 632–33; and shame, 182, 461–62, 466, 528–29, 533, 536–37, 539, 580, 953, 965–66, 967–68, 968; and slander, 169, 298–99, 821; and spiritual restoration, 776; and transgression against God, 371–72, 730–31; and vindication against the wicked, 134; and the wicked as dogs, 851, 853–55

slander, 169, 298–99, 821

sleep: in the face of difficulty, 158–59; God's protection during, 133

Solomon, 984, 985, 989–90

Solomon, temple of, 26, 393

songs of praise, 226–27, 230, 244–45, 337–40, 351, 549, 556–57, 700, 728, 736, 957–58, 974

sonship, divine, 107, 114

Sons of Korah, 21, 24, 28, 726, 735, 747

speech and language, 363, 851; and hurtful words, 816–18, 899–900, 901

Star Trek, 977

strength from God, 337–40, 348, 529, 826, 852–53, 892

submission: to anointed leaders, 112–14; to God, 110–11, 117–18

suffering, 153, 176, 178, 179, 673–74; and aging, 678–80, 975–77; blaming God for, 686–87; emotional, 808–10; and healing, 515–16, 866; of Jesus Christ, 281, 501; of Jews, 264–65, 282–83, 686–87, 690–93, 918–19; in modern society, 185–86, 695, 754–55, 866, 873–74; physical, 617–18, 678–79, 689; recording, 823–25; relational consequences of, 618–19; and scorn, 953–55; silent, 631–32; and taking refuge in God, 264–65, 866, 922–23; weariness from, 181, 951

Summa Theologica, 944

sun, the, 363–65

superscripts, 78–80

survivalism, 262

syllable counting in poetry, 38

synonymous parallelism, 40–41

Systematic Theology, 945

temple of Solomon, 26
temple worship and the psalms, 23–26, 63–64, 67–74, 150, 301–2, 519–22; and dwelling with God, 438–41; and the end of the first temple, 26–28; and the end of the second temple, 28–30; and oracles, 884–85
Ten Boom, Corrie, 264
Ten Commandments, 763
thanksgiving psalms, 65–66, 146, 225–27, 544, 823, 905, 912, 927, 957–58
theophany, 341–44, 357, 502–3, 504–6, 759–61, 944–46
title of the book of Psalms, 21–23
tone stress in poetry, 37
traditional word pairs, 49–50
transparency, divine, 272–73, 303–4
trees, imagery of, 97–98, 505, 788–90
trochaic rhythm, 33
trust in God, 158, 248–49, 279–80, 367, 388, 392–93, 400, 416–17, 461–62, 472, 479, 532–33, 547–48, 558–60, 560–61, 594, 603–4, 715–16, 718–19, 750–752, 787–88, 814, 825–27, 880, 886–87, 900–901
truth, 267–68, 274–75, 298–99, 462, 479, 540–41, 703–4
types of psalms: ancient, 58–59, 79; confidence, 75; entrance liturgy, 75; and Hermann Gunkel, 60–63; historical, 75; lament, 65; liturgical, 23–26, 63–64, 67–70; minor, 75; modern attempts to categorize, 59–64; praise, 65; royal, 66–67; and Sigmund Mowinckel, 62–64; thanksgiving, 65–66; and three primary categories, 65–75; wisdom and Torah, 71–74, 93; *Yahweh malak*, 70–71

ultimate consequences, 98–99
usury, 300

vengeance. *See* retribution
victory, 402–3, 427
vindication, 133–34, 136–37, 319, 452, 472, 477–78, 528–29, 579–80, 584–85, 587–88, 674–75, 691–92, 841–42

Wailing Wall, 474
Wallace, William, 117
war and violence: and deliverance from one's enemies, 132, 133–34, 135–36, 720–21, 892, 942–43; and hope for divine intervention and victory, 383–85, 941
waters: and authority of God over all creation, 449–50, 507, 716; chaotic and flooding, 343–44, 361–62, 507, 509–10, 731, 845, 885–87; and deliverance, 950–51; God appearance in, 938; and God's river of delights, 593, 596–97, 671; and oppression, 672–73, 778–79
Watson, Wilfred G. E., 52
wedding ceremonies, 706–8
Weiser, Artur, 64, 886
Wesley, Charles, 316
wisdom and Torah psalms, 71–74, 93, 355–56, 746–47, 785
wonders of God, 226
word pairs in poetry, 48–50
World War I, 637
World War II, 264–65, 283, 285, 328, 695, 922–23
worship: call to, 503–4; communal, 677–78, 679–80, 926–27; and dwelling with God, 438–41; and hope, 427–29; and meeting with God, 670–72; modern, 303–4; and oracles, 884–85; of praise, 737–38; right, 769–70; temple, 23–26, 63–64, 67–74, 150, 301–2, 419, 422, 670–71, 884–85
wrath of God, 110–11, 178, 341

Y2K millennium bug, 259, 263
Yahweh. *See* God
Yahweh malak psalms, 70–71, 115–16
Yoḥanan, 29, 780

Zion, 290, 383–84, 393, 739–43, 906, 937; destruction on, 736–37; plea for restoration of, 777–78; presence of God in, 736, 760–61; songs, 735